D0538294

PRENTICE HALL

2002

·MAGRUDER'S·

AMERICAN GOVERNMENT

Revised by

William A. McClenaghan

Department of Political Science
Oregon State University

Prentice
Hall

Needham, Massachusetts
Upper Saddle River, New Jersey
Glenview, Illinois

Magruder's American Government,

first published in 1917 and revised annually, is an enduring symbol of the author's faith in American ideals and American institutions. The life of Frank Abbott Magruder (1882–1949) was an outstanding example of Americanism at its very best. His career as a teacher, author, and tireless worker in civic and religious undertakings remains an inspiring memory to all who knew him.

The Close Up Foundation is the nation's largest civic education organization. Since 1971, Close Up has been a leader in the social studies field, reaching millions of students, educators, and other adults. The Foundation's mission of informed participation in government and democracy drives its experiential civic education programs in Washington, D.C., for students and teachers, as well as its television programs on C-SPAN, and its award-winning publications and videos. Close Up's work represents a multidimensional approach to citizenship education by increasing community involvement and civic literacy—one student, one citizen, at a time.

Program Consultants

Constitution Consultant

Dr. Christine L. Compston
University of Massachusetts
Boston, Massachusetts

Reading Consultant

Dr. Bonnie Armbruster
University of Illinois at
Urbana-Champaign
Champaign, Illinois

Curriculum and Assessment Specialist

Jan Moberley
Dallas, Texas

Internet Consultant

Dr. Larry Elowitz
Professor of Political Science
Georgia College and State
University
Milledgeville, Georgia

Block Scheduling Consultant

Gwen L. Patterson
Marcus High School
Flower Mound, Texas

Copyright © 2002 by Mary Magruder Smith. All rights reserved. Printed in the United States of America. This publication is protected by copyright, and permission should be obtained from the publisher prior to any prohibited reproduction, storage in a retrieval system, or transmission in any form or by any means, electronic, mechanical, photocopying, recording, or likewise. For information regarding permission(s), write to: Rights and Permissions Department, 1 Lake Street, Upper Saddle River, New Jersey, 07458.

ISBN 0-13-063075-6

2 3 4 5 6 7 8 9 10   06 05 04 03 02

Program Reviewers

Teacher Reviewers

Elizabeth Battle
Aldine Independent School District
Houston, Texas

Sam Brewster
Shawnee Mission East High School
Shawnee Mission, Kansas

Judith Cannizzaro
Metro Nashville Public Schools
Nashville, Tennessee

Greg Clevenger
Adams High School
Rochester Hills, Michigan

Mary Ellen Daneels
Community High School
West Chicago, Illinois

Les Fortune
Tallwood High School
Virginia Beach, Virginia

Rita Geiger
Norman Public Schools
Norman, Oklahoma

Taddie Hamilton
Hurst-Euless-Bedford ISD
Euless, Texas

Bruce Hitchcock
Noblesville High School
Noblesville, Indiana

Margaret J. Jamison
Pasadena Independent School District
Pasadena, Texas

Mary Lynn Johnson
Spring Independent School District
Houston, Texas

Richard Kean
Central High School
Cheyenne, Wyoming

David Kenewell
Utica Schools
Sterling Heights, Michigan

Vicki Kuker
Bishop Dwenger High School
Fort Wayne, Indiana

Bridget Loft
Wakefield High School
Arlington, Virginia

Lawrence Moaton
Memphis City Schools
Memphis, Tennessee

Elizabeth Morrison
Parkway South High School
Manchester, Missouri

K. Chaka K. Nantambu
Central High School
Detroit, Michigan

Yoshi Negoro
St. Lucie West Centennial High School
Port St. Lucie, Florida

Carol Schroder
Decatur High School
Federal Way, Washington

Ninfa Sepúlveda
Stephen F. Austin High School
Houston, Texas

Kate Sintros
Concord Public Schools
Concord, New Hampshire

Bill Smiley
Leigh High School
San Jose, California

Barbara Maness Stafford
Central High School
Little Rock, Arkansas

Gerald A. Stupiansky
Lakewood High School
Lakewood, Ohio

Kristena M. Watson
Spring Woods High School
Houston, Texas

Student Reviewers

Brannen Bagley
Tallwood High School
Virginia Beach, Virginia

Rebekah Kaufman
Bishop Dwenger High School
Fort Wayne, Indiana

Andrew Kreamer
Leigh High School
San Jose, California

Chuyen Phan
Stephen F. Austin High School
Houston, Texas

Adam Valadez
Community High School
West Chicago, Illinois

Program Advisors

Pat Easterbrook
Social Studies Consultant
Cary, North Carolina

Michal Howden
Social Studies Consultant
Zionsville, Indiana

Kathy Lewis
Social Studies Consultant
Fort Worth, Texas

Richard Moulden
Social Studies Consultant
Federal Way, Washington

Sharon Pope
Social Studies Consultant
Houston, Texas

Joe Wieczorek
Social Studies Consultant
Baltimore, Maryland

Table of Contents

UNIT 2

Special Features

CLOSE UP Features

Close Up on the Supreme Court

Background information and key arguments on landmark Supreme Court Cases

Close Up on Primary Sources

Excerpted documents highlight key issues

Franklin D.
Roosevelt

Close Up Student Poll

Students' views about government and politics

SKILLS FOR LIFE

Step-by-step lessons to learn and practice important skills

Technology

Citizenship

Critical Thinking

Charts and Graphs

Voices on Government

Opinions, views, and comments on the American political system

Madeleine M. Kunin

The *Living* Constitution

You Can Make a Difference

The *Living* Constitution

Redefining Federalism | 1800 | 1850

The Framers of the Constitution sought to balance the rights of individual States and the powers of the new Federal Government. Their solution was a federal system, which divides powers between the two levels of government. Although the Constitution is the "supreme law of the land," questions about States' rights and national power have arisen throughout American history, as the Supreme Court cases on this time line show.

1819
In *McCulloch* v. *Maryland*, the Court rules that a State cannot tax the Federal Government.

1824
In *Gibbons* v. *Ogden*, the Court affirms the Federal Government's right to regulate interstate trade.

1886
In *Wabash, St. Louis & Pacific Railway Co.* v. *Illinois*, the Court rules that States cannot regulate railroad rates on the parts of interstate journeys that fall within their borders.

Political Cartoons

Maps, Graphs, Charts, Diagrams, Time Lines, and Tables

Maps

Graphs, Charts, Diagrams

Time Lines

Tables

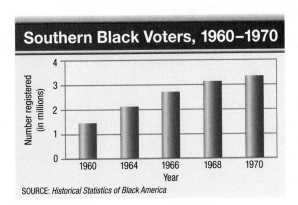

Southern Black Voters, 1960–1970

SOURCE: *Historical Statistics of Black America*

The Six Basic Principles of the Constitution

*T*he Constitution of the United States is built on six basic principles of government. The Framers of the Constitution drew on their knowledge and experience to craft a document that serves as "the supreme law of the land." The descriptions at the beginning of each unit will help you see how these six principles—and the Constitution itself—have proved an enduring yet flexible guide for governing the nation for over 200 years.

Popular Sovereignty

The Preamble to the Constitution begins with this bold phrase: "We the people..." These words announce that in the United States, the people establish government and give it its power. The people are sovereign. Since the government receives its power from the people, it can govern only with their consent.

BALLOT

Limited Government

Because the people are the source of government power, the government has only as much authority as the people give it. Much of the Constitution, in fact, consists of specific limitations on government power. Limited government means that neither the government itself nor any government official is "above the law" and can overstep these constitutional bounds.

Separation of Powers

Government power is not only limited; it is also divided. The Constitution assigns specific powers to each of the three branches: the legislative (Congress), the executive (President), and the judicial (federal courts). This separation of powers is intended to prevent misuse of power by any of the three branches of government.

Checks and Balances

The system of checks and balances extends the restrictions established by the separation of powers. Each branch of government has the authority to restrain the actions of either of the other two branches. This system makes government less efficient but also prevents tyranny by one branch of government.

Judicial Review

Who decides whether an act of government oversteps the limits placed on it by the Constitution? Historically, the federal courts have done so. The principle of judicial review was established early in this nation's history. It means that federal courts have the power to review governmental actions and to nullify (cancel) any that are unconstitutional, any that violate some provision of the Constitution.

Federalism

A federal system divides power between a central government and several regional (local) governments. This sharing of power is intended to ensure that the central government is powerful enough to be effective, yet not so powerful as to threaten the existence of the regional governments or the rights of the people. It also allows individual States to deal with local problems as they choose—so long as their actions are constitutional.

Studying *Magruder's American Government*

The American system of government's fundamental principles and its basic structure have remained constant over time. Many of its other characteristics, however, have changed. A number of the features in this book are designed to help you understand how our government works and to encourage you to be an active, participating citizen.

Chapter 5 in Brief

SECTION 1

Parties and What They Do (pp. 116–118)
★ The primary purpose of the two major American political parties is to control government through winning election to public office.
★ Political parties nominate candidates, rally their supporters, participate in government, act as a "bonding agent" for their own officeholders, and act as a watchdog over the other party.

SECTION 2

The Two-Party System (pp. 119–124)
★ The two-party system is a product of our history and tradition, the electoral system, and the American ideological consensus.
★ Multiparty systems, provide more choice for the electorate but a less stable government. In one-party systems, only the ruling party can participate in elections.
★ While the two major parties are broadly based, each party does tend to attract certain segments of the electorate.

SECTION 3

The Two-Party System in American History (pp. 126–131)
★ The first American parties originated in the battle over ratifying the Constitution.
★ There have been three eras of single party domination in U.S. history from 1800–1968.
★ An era of divided government—not dominated by either political party—began in 1968 and continues to this day.

Preview or Review the Chapter

Every chapter begins with a Chapter in Brief outline that can be used to preview the chapter content or to review for an exam.

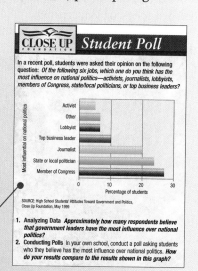

CLOSE UP FOUNDATION · *Student Poll*

In a recent poll, students were asked their opinion on the following question: *Of the following six jobs, which one do you think has the most influence on national politics—activists, journalists, lobbyists, members of Congress, state/local politicians, or top business leaders?*

SOURCE: High School Students' Attitudes Toward Government and Politics, Close Up Foundation, May 1999

1. **Analyzing Data** Approximately how many respondents believe that government leaders have the most influence over national politics?
2. **Conducting Polls** In your own school, conduct a poll asking students who they believe has the most influence over national politics. *How do your results compare to the results shown in this graph?*

Participate in Government

The results of a recent Student Poll appear throughout the book. Use these poll questions to gauge your classmates' opinions on various government-related topics.

SKILLS FOR LIFE

TECHNOLOGY
CITIZENSHIP
CRITICAL THINKING
CHARTS and GRAPHS

Casting Your Vote

Why have people risked their lives to get and keep the right to vote? In the United States, we tend to take this right for granted. Yet if we were ever deprived of it, we would surely come to recognize its great value.

The voting process may vary slightly from place to place, but in general, these steps apply:
1. Determine if you are eligible to vote. To qualify to vote, you must be an American citizen at least 18 years of age and a resident of the State in which you vote.
2. Register to vote. In every State except North Dakota, you must register to vote. You can register locally, usually at city hall or the county courthouse. Registration tables are often set up in shopping malls, supermarkets, libraries, and fire stations before an election. You can register by mail, and in some places, via the Internet. To register you will need proof of your age, such as a birth certificate.
3. Study the candidates and issues. Identify the candidates for each office and the duties of the office. Then research the candidates' views on major issues. Besides voting for candidates for office, voters often have the opportunity to directly approve or reject proposed State and local

BALLOTS

laws. Don't wait until you are in the voting booth to become familiar with these issues.
4. Go to your polling place. In many States, voters receive a voter registration card identifying their precinct and polling place. Newspapers often publish lists of polling places prior to an election. Polls are usually open from 7:00 or 8:00 A.M. to 7:00 or 8:00 P.M. At the polling place, your name will be checked against a list of registered voters to make sure you are eligible to vote. You will be directed to a booth with a voting machine, or you will be given a paper ballot or punch card and directed to a voting booth.
5. Cast your vote. Follow the instructions on the voting machine or ballot, so your vote will be counted properly. Do not feel rushed. If you have a question, ask an attending official. Make sure you've made a selection in every contest in which you wish to vote.

Test for Success

(a) Brainstorm at least three possible sources of voter information for voters in your area. (b) What sources would you consider most reliable?

★ You Can Make a Difference

ONE GOOD WAY to study party politics is to work in a campaign. Early in the 2000 presidential race, some college students learned about politics firsthand in the New Hampshire State's primary. Political science majors from Quinnipiac College spent their winter break as volunteers in the Bush, Bradley, Gore, or McCain campaigns. They canvassed voters, helped with mailings, held up signs, and met candidates. "I like to have the hands-on kind of learning," said Jessica Cieslak about the Bradley campaign. Sally Roden, addressing postcards for Governor Bush, commented, "It seems like we're contributing small pieces to a greater puzzle."

WHY IT MATTERS

Each State has two seats in the Senate, the smaller and more prestigious house of Congress. Senators are generally older and more experienced than representatives, and their long terms protect them from political pressure.

Connect Government to Your Life

Every chapter begins with a You Can Make a Difference story that shows how young people can participate in government and their community. You Can Make a Difference activities at the end of every chapter suggest ways for you to take an active role in your community. The Why It Matters statement in every section preview helps you understand why government is important in your life.

Learn to Be an Active Citizen

The Skills for Life features teach important citizenship, critical thinking, technology, and chart and graph skills.

Learn About Important Supreme Court Cases

Close Up on the Supreme Court features in every chapter outline landmark cases and encourage you to evaluate the arguments of both sides.

CLOSE UP *on the Supreme Court*

Who Decides Who May Vote?

The Constitution gives States authority to set voting qualifications. In the past, some States misused this authority by setting voting qualifications designed to exclude groups of voters, such as African Americans, women, and Asian Americans. Does Congress have the authority to pass laws that set restrictions on State voting qualifications?

Oregon v. Mitchell (1970)

In 1970, the States of Oregon, Texas, and Idaho sued the Federal Government (specifically, Attorney General John Mitchell) to challenge some provisions of the Voting Rights Act Amendments passed by Congress that year. One provision lowered the minimum voting age in State and federal elections from 21 to 18. Another barred the use of literacy tests and other similar tests in State and federal elections for a five-year period. A third provision prevented States from establishing residency requirements, which permit people to vote only if they have lived in the State for a certain period of time. The final provision established national rules for absentee voting in presidential elections. (In absentee voting, people who will not be able to go to their polling place on election day mark their ballots and submit them by mail before election day.) These provisions were intended to allow more people to participate in the electoral process.

The case was heard by the Supreme Court in its original jurisdiction. (In other words, the case was not appealed to the Court from a lower court.) Fifteen States, though not part of the suit, filed briefs (written arguments) with the Court on the case. Also filing briefs were the American Civil Liberties Union, the NAACP, the Democratic National Committee, and various other groups concerned with voting rights.

Arguments for Oregon

1. Only the States have the power to set voting qualifications for State and local elections. Congress has no authority to require the States to allow persons between 18 and 21 to vote in State and local elections.

2. The Constitution does not give Congress the right to require the States to use different qualifications for voting in federal elections than the States adopt for their own elections.

3. States have the authority to set standards for voters, such as a minimum level of literacy or a minimum period of residence in the State.

Arguments for Mitchell

1. Congress may set standards for voter qualifications in federal elections.

2. Congress may prevent the States from excluding certain groups of citizens from the voting rolls for State elections, if the exclusion tends to discriminate against people based on characteristics such as race or national origin. (Such discrimination by States would violate the Fourteenth Amendment's Equal Protection Clause.)

3. Congress may prevent States from imposing a residency requirement that makes it impossible for people who have recently moved to vote in presidential elections.

Decide for Yourself

1. Review the constitutional grounds on which each side based its arguments and the specific arguments each side presented.

2. Debate the opposing viewpoints presented in this case. Which viewpoint do you favor?

3. Predict the impact of the Court's decision on changes in voter eligibility and voter participation in the United States. (To read a summary of the Court's decision, turn to the Supreme Court Glossary on page 799.)

Voters and Voter Behavior **173**

Comparative Government

Use of Capital Punishment Worldwide

- **6%** allow death penalty only for wartime and other exceptional crimes.
- **37%** of countries do not allow death penalty.
- **11%** allow death penalty but have had no executions for 10 or more years.
- **63%** of countries allow death penalty.

SOURCE: Amnesty International

Interpreting Graphs Over half of the world's countries allow the death penalty. *What percentage of these countries allow the death penalty only for "exceptional" crimes or have had no executions for ten years or longer?*

Keep Up-to-Date

Learning about government means learning about change. The Living Constitution time lines show how the interpretation of the Constitution has changed over the years. In addition, you'll find key graphs, charts, and tables marked with the Internet Update logo. Updated versions of these illustrations with the most recent data appear on the *Magruder's American Government* Web site at **www.phschool.com**

The *Living* Constitution

Redefining Federalism

The Framers of the Constitution sought to balance the rights of individual States and the powers of the new federal government. Their solution was a federal system, which divides powers between the two levels of government. Although the Constitution is the "supreme law of the land," questions about States' rights and national power have arisen throughout American history, as the Supreme Court cases on this time line show.

1819 In McCulloch v. Maryland, the Court rules that a State cannot tax the federal government.

In Gibbons Court affir govern regulate int

Take It to the Net

Chapter 5 Self-Test As a final review activity, take the Chapter 5 Self-Test in the Social Studies area at the Web site listed below, and receive immediate feedback on your answers.

www.phschool.com

Prepare for Tests

To practice for standardized tests, answer the questions at the end of every section and chapter. Pay special attention to the critical thinking and analyzing political cartoons questions. Go to the *Magruder's American Government* Web site to take a practice Self-Test for each chapter.

Section 5 Assessment

Key Terms and Main Ideas

1. What are the major causes of the decentralized nature of political parties?
2. What are the four main parts of major party organization at the national level?
3. Describe how **wards** and **precincts** are part of the local party organization.
4. What is **split-ticket voting**, and how has its increase contributed to the weakened state of the two major parties?

Critical Thinking

5. **Drawing Conclusions** Based on what you know about parties, their goals, and the American people, why do you think local party organizations vary so widely?

6. **Formulating Questions** A growing number of voters consider themselves to be independents. Compose three questions that a pollster might ask in an attempt to learn why this is the case.
7. **Predicting Consequences** Do you think parties will survive and emerge from their current period of decline? Why or why not?

Take It to the Net

8. Visit your State's Republican or Democratic Party Web site. Prepare a site map that shows the major elements of the site, and give a brief summary of the contents of each. Use the links provided in the Social Studies area at the following Web site for help in completing this activity. **www.phschool.com**

◆ Conservators preserving the Star Spangled Banner at the National Museum of American History

Foundations of American Government

CONSTITUTIONAL PRINCIPLES

Popular Sovereignty The Declaration of Independence embraced the theory that people form governments to protect their natural rights, and that the powers of government must be based on the consent of the governed. In doing so, the document justified the colonies' split from Great Britain and established precedent for a government that is responsible to its people.

Separation of Powers The Constitution gives certain powers to each branch of government. Distributing government's powers among the executive, legislative, and judicial branches prevents any one branch from exercising too much authority.

Federalism In the United States, powers are divided between the National Government and the State governments. Thus, the Constitution helps to ensure the National Government's strength, while protecting the uniqueness of State governments.

The Impact on You

Government powers, such as the need to meet State graduation requirements, can directly affect your life. However, to limit any negative effects of these powers, the U.S. government derives its power from the consent of the governed and divides power not only between the Federal Government and State governments, but also between the various branches within the Federal Government.

CHAPTER 1

Principles of Government

"The way of democracy is both frustrating and invigorating. It lacks the orderly directives of dictatorship, and instead relies on millions to demonstrate self-discipline and enlightened concern for the common good."
—Nancy Landon Kassebaum (1996)

Governments hold power in every society, but they exercise that power in different ways. Governments have various structures and forms, from dictatorships to democracies. American democracy rests on such basic concepts as individual rights and majority rule.

◆ New Americans celebrate taking the oath of citizenship.

★ You Can Make a Difference

AS SENATOR KASSEBAUM knew, democracy relies on all of its citizens. Activists of any age can work for causes they believe in. Danny Seo, once called the "Green Teen," says, "If all of us start taking action, we can change the world." Danny first took up a cause—animal rights and the environment—on Earth Day 1989, his twelfth birthday. With other kids in Shillington, Pennsylvania, he started Earth 2000. In a few years, the grassroots group became a national movement. Danny has won many awards for his activism. He wrote a guide for young activists and became a popular advocate for an eco-friendly lifestyle.

Keep It Current

Items marked with this logo are periodically updated on the Internet. Keep up-to-date with what's in the news. To get current information on forms of government, go to **www.phschool.com**

SECTION 1

Government and the State (pp. 4–10)

★ Government enables a society to protect the peace and carry out its policies.
★ A state, not to be confused with one of the fifty States of the United States, is a land with people, a defined territory, and a sovereign government.
★ Several theories attempt to explain the origin of the state.
★ Among these theories, the political philosophy of John Locke had the most profound impact on the Declaration of Independence and the United States Constitution.
★ The goals of the Federal Government are described in the Preamble to the Constitution.

SECTION 2

Forms of Government (pp. 12–16)

★ Each government is unique, but governments can be grouped into categories according to three sets of characteristics.
★ Democratic governments rely on the participation of the people, while dictatorships concentrate power in the hands of a few.
★ The distribution of power between local governments and a central government determines whether a government is unitary, federal, or confederate.
★ Presidential governments divide power among several branches of government, while parliamentary governments focus power in one dominant branch.

SECTION 3

Basic Concepts of Democracy (pp. 18–22)

★ Democracy is built upon five principles: respect for the individual, equality of all persons, acceptance of majority rule and minority rights, compromise, and protection of individual freedoms.
★ The free enterprise system of the United States, like democracy, relies on individual freedoms.
★ In a mixed economy, the government plays a role in the economy.
★ The Internet has opened up new opportunities for democracy, but users must carefully evaluate the information that they find.

1 Government and the State

Section Preview

OBJECTIVES

1. **Define** government and the basic powers every government holds.
2. **Describe** the four defining characteristics of the state.
3. **Identify** four theories that attempt to explain the origin of the state.
4. **Understand** the purpose of government in the United States and other countries.

WHY IT MATTERS

Government is essential to the existence of human beings in a civilized society. What any particular government is like and what that government does have an extraordinary impact on the lives of all people who live within its reach.

POLITICAL DICTIONARY

★ government
★ public policy
★ legislative power
★ executive power
★ judicial power
★ constitution
★ dictatorship
★ democracy
★ state
★ sovereign

Today, the United States is at war. That war—the war against terrorism—is a new and a different kind of war, against a new and a different kind of enemy. The conflict began with sudden and shocking violence on September 11, 2001, when terrorists hijacked four airliners. They crashed two of them into the twin towers of the World Trade Center in New York City and another into the Pentagon. The heroic actions of the passengers on the fourth plane forced it to crash in western Pennsylvania, short of its intended target, which was probably in Washington, D.C. The government, acting with the full support of the American people, began to respond to that monstrous assault immediately. President Bush vowed that the nation will "answer these attacks and rid the world of [the] evil" of terrorism. Congress quickly authorized the President to use "all necessary and appropriate force" against those who brought on this war.

Government in this country is now focused on the fight against terrorism, both at home and abroad. Still, government has many other and important tasks to perform. It must provide for education, guard the public's health, and protect the environment. It must also pave the streets, punish criminals, protect civil rights, care for the elderly, and do much, much more.

What Is Government?

Government is the institution through which a society makes and enforces its public policies. Government is made up of those people who exercise its powers, those who have authority and control over people.

The **public policies** of a government are, in short, all of those things a government decides to do. Public policies cover matters ranging from taxation, defense, education, crime, and health care to transportation, the environment, civil rights, and working conditions. The list of public policy issues is nearly endless.

Governments must have power in order to make and carry out public policies. Power is the ability to command or prevent action, the ability to achieve a desired end.

Every government has and exercises three basic kinds of power: (1) **legislative power**—the power to make law and to frame public policies; (2) **executive power**—the power to execute, enforce, and administer law; and (3) **judicial power**—the power to interpret laws, to determine their meaning, and to settle disputes that arise within the society. These powers of government are often outlined in a country's constitution. A **constitution** is the body of fundamental laws setting out the principles, structures, and processes of a government.

The ultimate responsibility for the exercise of these powers may be held by a single person or by a small group, as in a **dictatorship.** In this form of government, those who rule cannot be held responsible to the will of the people. When the responsibility for the exercise of these powers rests with a majority of the people, that form of government is known as a **democracy.** In a democracy, supreme authority rests with the people.

Government is among the oldest of all human inventions. Its origins are lost in the mists of time. But, clearly, government first appeared when human beings realized that they could not survive without some way to regulate both their own and their neighbors' behavior.

The earliest known evidences of government date from ancient Egypt. More than 2,300 years ago, the Greek philosopher Aristotle observed that "man is by nature a political animal."[1] As he wrote those words, Aristotle was only recording a fact that, even then, had been obvious for thousands of years.

What did Aristotle mean by "political"? That is to say, what is "politics"? Although people often equate the two, politics and government are very different things. Politics is a process, while government is an institution.

More specifically, politics is the process by which a society decides how power and resources will be distributed within that society. Politics enables a society to decide who will reap the benefits, and who will pay the costs, of its public policies.

The word *politics* is sometimes used in a way that suggests that it is immoral or something to be avoided. But, again, politics is a *process*, the means by which government is conducted. It is neither "good" nor "bad," but it is necessary. Indeed, it is impossible to conceive of government without politics.

The State

Over the course of human history, the state has emerged as the dominant political unit in the world. The **state** can be defined as a body of people, living in a defined territory, organized politically (that is, with a government), and with the power to make and enforce law without the consent of any higher authority.

▲ *Patriotism in a Time of Crisis* Americans showed their pride in their country and support for their government in the wake of the terrorist attacks on the World Trade Center and the Pentagon.

There are more than 190 states in the world today. They vary greatly in size, military power, natural resources, and economic importance. Still, each of them possesses all four characteristics of a state: population, territory, sovereignty, and government.

Note that the state is a legal entity. In popular usage, a state is often called a "nation" or a "country." In a strict sense, however, the word *nation* is an ethnic term, referring to races or other large groups of people. The word *country* is a geographic term, referring to a particular place, region, or area of land.

Population

Clearly, a state must have people—a population. The size of that population, however, has nothing directly to do with the existence of a state. One of the world's smallest states, in population terms, is San Marino. Bounded on all sides by Italy, it has only some 25,000

---

[1]In most of the world's written political record, the words *man* and *men* have been widely used to refer to all of humankind. This text follows that form when presenting excerpts from historical writings or documents and in references to them.

The Four Characteristics of the State

 Population

 Territory

 Sovereignty

 Government

Interpreting Charts To be considered a state, a group of people must have a defined body of land and an independent, sovereign government. ***Does your school qualify as a state? If not, which requirements does it lack?***

people. The People's Republic of China is the world's most populous state with more than 1.25 *billion* people—just about one fifth of the world's population. The more than 285 million who live in the United States make it the world's third most populous, after China and India.

The people who make up a state may or may not be *homogeneous*. The adjective homogeneous describes members of a group who share customs, a common language, and ethnic background. Today, the population of the United States includes people from a wide variety of backgrounds. Still, most Americans think of themselves as exactly that: Americans.

Territory

Just as a state cannot exist without people, so it must have land—territory, with known and recognized boundaries. The states in today's world vary as widely in terms of territory as they do in population. Here, too, San Marino ranks as one of the world's smallest states. It covers less than 24 square miles—smaller than thousands of cities and towns in the United States.[2]

Russia, the world's largest state, stretches across some 6.6 million square miles. The total area of the United States is 3,787,425 square miles.

Sovereignty

Every state is **sovereign**—it has supreme and absolute power within its own territory and can decide its own foreign and domestic policies. It is neither subordinate nor responsible to any other authority.

Thus, as a sovereign state, the United States can determine its form of government. Like any other state in the world, it can frame its economic system and shape its own foreign policies. Sovereignty is the one characteristic that distinguishes the state from all other, lesser political units.

The States within the United States are not sovereign and so are not states in the international, legal sense. Each State is subordinate to the Constitution of the United States.[3]

Government

Every state is politically organized. That is, every state has a government. Recall, a government is the institution through which society makes and

---

[2]The United States also recognizes the State of Vatican City, with a permanent population of some 850 persons and a roughly triangular area of only 109 acres. The Vatican is wholly surrounded by the City of Rome. American recognition of the Vatican, which had been withdrawn in 1867, was renewed in 1984.

[3]In this book, state printed with a small "s" denotes a state in the family of nations, such as the United States, Great Britain, and Mexico. State printed with a capital "S" refers to a State in the American union.

enforces its public policies. A government is the agency through which the state exerts its will and works to accomplish its goals. Government includes the machinery and the personnel by which the state is ruled.

Government is necessary to avoid what the English philosopher Thomas Hobbes (1588–1679) called "the war of every man against every man." Without government, said Hobbes, there would be "continual fear and danger of violent death and life [would be] solitary, poor, nasty, brutish, and short." The world has seen a number of examples over recent years of what happens when a government disappears: In Lebanon, Bosnia, Somalia, and many other places, life became "nasty, brutish, and short."

Origins of the State — STOP

For centuries, historians, philosophers, and others have pondered the question of the origin of the state. What factor or set of circumstances first brought it into being?

Over time, many different answers have been offered, but history provides no conclusive evidence to support any of them. However, four theories have emerged as the most widely accepted explanations for the origin of the state.

The Force Theory Many scholars have long believed that the state was born of force. They hold that one person or a small group claimed control over an area and forced all within it to submit to that person's or group's rule. When that rule was established, all the basic elements of the state—population, territory, sovereignty, and government—were present.

The Evolutionary Theory Others claim that the state developed naturally out of the early family. They hold that the primitive family, of which one person was the head and thus the "government," was the first stage in political development. Over countless years the original family became a network of related families, a clan. In time the clan became a tribe. When the tribe first turned to agriculture and gave up its nomadic ways, when it first tied itself to the land, the state was born.

The Divine Right Theory The theory of divine right was widely accepted in much of the Western world from the fifteenth through the eighteenth centuries. It held that God created the state and that God had given those of royal birth a "divine right" to rule. The people were bound to obey their ruler as they would God; opposition to "the divine right of kings" was both treason and mortal sin.

During the seventeenth century, philosophers began to question this theory. Much of the thought upon which present-day democratic government rests began as a challenge to the theory of divine right.

Force

Evolutionary

Divine Right

Social Contract

◄ Different explanations have been offered for the origin of the state. Pharoah Akenhaton of Egypt (middle) believed that power flowed from Aton, the god of the sun disk. *Critical Thinking Can more than one of these theories accurately explain the origin of the state? Explain why or why not.*

The notion of divine right was not unique to European history. The rulers of many ancient civilizations, including the Chinese, Egyptian, Aztec, and Mayan civilizations, were held to be gods or to have been chosen by the gods. The Japanese emperor, the *mikado,* governed by divine right until 1945.

The Social Contract Theory In terms of the American political system, the most significant of the theories of the origin of the state is that of the "social contract." Philosophers such as Thomas Hobbes, James Harrington (1611–1677), and John Locke (1632–1704) in England and Jean Jacques Rousseau (1712–1778) in France developed this theory in the seventeenth and eighteenth centuries.

Hobbes wrote that in earliest history humans lived in unbridled freedom, in a "state of nature," in which no government existed and no person was subject to any superior power. That which people could take by force belonged to them. However, all people were similarly free in this state of nature. No authority existed to protect one person from the aggressive actions of another. Thus, individuals were only as safe as their own physical strength and intelligence could make them.

Human beings overcame their unpleasant condition, says the social contract theory, by agreeing with one another to create a state. By contract, people within a given area agreed to give up to the state as much power as was needed to promote the safety and well-being of all. In the contract (that is, through a constitution), the members of the state created a government to exercise the powers they had voluntarily given to the state.

In short, the social contract theory argues that the state arose out of a voluntary act of free people. It holds that the state exists only to serve the will of the people, that they are the sole source of political power, and that they are free to give or to withhold that power as they choose. The theory may seem far-fetched today. The great concepts that this theory promoted, however—popular sovereignty, limited government, and individual rights—were immensely important to the shaping of the American governmental system.

The Declaration of Independence (see pages 40–43) justified its revolution through the social contract theory, arguing that King George III and his ministers had violated the contract. Thomas Jefferson called the document "pure Locke."

The Purpose of Government

What does government do? You can find a very meaningful answer to that question in the Constitution of the United States. The American system of government was created to serve the purposes set out there.

FROM THE **Constitution** *"We the People of the United States, in Order to form a more perfect Union, establish Justice, insure domestic Tranquility, provide for the common defence, promote the general Welfare, and secure the Blessings of Liberty to ourselves and our Posterity, do ordain and establish this Constitution for the United States of America."*
—Preamble to the Constitution

CAN YOU STAND THE THOUGHT OF FUTURE GENERATIONS HAVING IT AS GOOD AS THIS?

NO.

GOOD! -- LET'S FORM A GOVERNMENT.

Reproduced by permission of Johnny Hart and Field Enterprises

Interpreting Political Cartoons American government was influenced strongly by the social contract theory. *How does this cartoon poke fun at that theory?*

Form a More Perfect Union

The United States, which had just won its independence from Great Britain, faced an altogether uncertain future in the postwar 1780s. In 1781, the Articles of Confederation, the nation's first constitution, created "a firm league of friendship" among the 13 States. That league soon proved to be neither firm nor friendly. The government that the Articles established was powerless to overcome the intense rivalries and jealousies among the States that marked the time.

The Constitution of today was written in 1787. The original States adopted it in order to link them, and the American people, more closely together. That Constitution was built in the belief that in union there is strength.

Establish Justice

To provide justice, said Thomas Jefferson, is "the most sacred of the duties of government." No purpose, no goal of public policy, can be of greater importance in a democracy.

But what, precisely, is justice? The term is difficult to define, for justice is a concept—an idea, an invention of the human mind. Like other concepts such as truth, liberty, and fairness, justice means what people make it mean.

As the concept of justice has developed over time in American thought and practice, it has come to mean this: The law, in both its content and its administration, must be reasonable, fair, and impartial. Those standards of justice have not always been met in this country. We have not attained our professed goal of "equal justice for all." However, this, too, must be said: The history of this country can be told largely in terms of our continuing attempts to reach that goal.

"Injustice anywhere," said Martin Luther King, Jr., "is a threat to justice everywhere." You will encounter this idea again and again in this book.

Insure Domestic Tranquility

Order is essential to the well-being of any society, and keeping the peace at home has always been a prime function of government. Most people can only imagine what it would be like to live in a state of anarchy—without government, law, or order. In fact, people do live that way in some parts of the world today. For

Voices on Government

Barbara Jordan was the first African American woman ever elected to the Texas legislature. She went on to represent her State in the U.S. House of Representatives (1973–1979). Famous for her eloquent speeches, Barbara Jordan often seemed to serve as the conscience of the government. In her keynote speech at the 1976 Democratic National Convention, she noted:

❝ *A nation is formed by the willingness of each of us to share in the responsibility for upholding the common good.*
A government is invigorated when each of us is willing to participate in shaping the future of this nation. . . .
Let each person do his or her part. If one citizen is unwilling to participate, all of us are going to suffer. For the American idea, though it is shared by all of us, is realized in each one of us. ❞

Evaluating the Quotation

How do Jordan's expectations for Americans relate to the basic ideas that underlie our democracy?

years now, Somalia, which is located on the eastern tip of Africa, has not had a functioning government; rival warlords control different parts of the country.

In *The Federalist* No. 51, James Madison observed: "If men were angels, no government would be necessary." Madison, who was perhaps the most thoughtful of the Framers of the Constitution, knew that most human beings fall far short of this standard.

Provide for the Common Defense

Defending the nation against foreign enemies has always been one of government's major responsibilities. You can see its importance in the fact that defense is mentioned far more often in the Constitution than any of the other functions of the government. The nation's defense and its foreign policies are but two sides of the same coin: the security of the United States.

Principles of Government   9 ★★★★

The United States has become the world's most powerful nation, but the world remains a dangerous place. The United States must maintain its vigilance and its armed strength. Just a glance at today's newspaper or at one of this evening's television news programs will furnish abundant proof of that fact.

Promote the General Welfare

Few people realize the extent to which government acts as the servant of its citizens, yet you can see examples everywhere. Public schools are one illustration of government's work to promote the general welfare. So, too, are government's efforts to protect the quality of the air you breathe, the water you drink, and the food you eat. The list of tasks government performs for your benefit goes on and on.

Some governmental functions that are common in other countries—operating steel mills, airlines, and coal mines, for example—are not carried out by government in this country. In general, the services that government provides in the United States are those that benefit all or most people. These are the services that are not very likely to be provided by the voluntary acts of private individuals or groups.

Secure the Blessings of Liberty

This nation was founded by those who loved liberty and prized it above all earthly possessions. They believed with Thomas Jefferson that "the God who gave us life gave us liberty at the same time." They subscribed to Benjamin Franklin's maxim: "They that can give up essential liberty to obtain a little temporary safety deserve neither liberty nor safety."

The American dedication to freedom for the individual recognizes that liberty cannot be absolute. It is, instead, a relative matter. No one can be free to do whatever he or she pleases, for that behavior would interfere with the freedoms of others. As Clarence Darrow, the great defense lawyer, once said: "You can only be free if I am free."

Both the Federal Constitution and the State constitutions set out many guarantees of rights and liberties for the individual in this country. That does not mean that those guarantees are so firmly established that they exist forever, however. To preserve and protect them, each generation must learn and understand them anew, and be willing to stand up for them when necessary.

For many people, the inspiration to protect our rights and liberties arises from deep feelings of patriotism. Patriotism is the love of one's country; the passion which aims to serve one's country, either in defending it from invasion, or by protecting its rights and maintaining its laws and institutions in vigor and purity. Patriotism is the characteristic of a good citizen, the noblest passion that animates a man or woman in the character of a citizen. As a citizen, you, too, must agree with Jefferson: "Eternal vigilance is the price of liberty."

STOP

Section 1 Assessment

Key Terms and Main Ideas

1. What is the difference between a **government** and a **state**?
2. Who holds power in a **dictatorship**?
3. What is the purpose of a **constitution**?
4. Give an example of a use of **judicial power**.

Critical Thinking

5. **Making Comparisons** The United States is sovereign, but cities and towns within the United States are not sovereign. What powers of a sovereign state do cities lack?
6. **Understanding Point of View** In the past, most European kings and queens were strong believers in the divine right theory. What are two possible explanations for why they held this belief?
7. **Drawing Conclusions** Explain how the language of the Preamble reflects the idea of the social contract.

 Take It to the Net

8. Read about Hobbes, Locke, and Rousseau and create a chart that compares and contrasts these three philosophers on three different topics. Be sure to explain their similarities and differences. Use the links provided in the Social Studies area at the following Web site for help in completing this activity. **www.phschool.com**

Second Treatise of Government

In 1690, English philosopher John Locke produced two treatises (essays) on government. In his second treatise, he discussed the responsibilities of a government and claimed that the people have the right to overthrow an unjust government. Locke's ideas greatly influenced Thomas Jefferson and other supporters of the American Revolution. In this selection, Locke explains why people form governments.

John Locke
1632–1704

To understand political power aright . . . we must consider what estate all men are naturally in, and that is, a state of perfect freedom to order their actions, and dispose of their possessions and persons as they think fit, within the bounds of the law of nature, without asking leave or depending upon the will of any other man. . . .

Men being . . . by nature, all free, equal and independent, no one can be put out of this estate and subjected to the political power of another without his own consent, which is done by agreeing with other men, to join and unite into a community for their comfortable, safe and peaceable living, one amongst another, in a secure enjoyment of their properties, and a greater security against any that are not of it. . . .

When any number of men have, by the consent of every individual, made a community, they have thereby made that community one body, with a power to act as one body, which is only by the will and determination of the majority. . . . And thus every man, by consenting with others to make one body politic under one government, puts himself under an obligation to every one in that society to submit to the determination [decision] of the majority, and to be concluded by it. . . .

If man in the state of nature . . . be absolute lord of his own person and possessions, equal to the greatest and subject to nobody, why will he part with his freedom, this empire, and subject himself to the dominion [authority] and control of any other power? . . . It is obvious to answer that though in the state of nature he hath such a right, yet the enjoyment of it is very uncertain and constantly exposed to the invasion of others; for all being kings as much as he, every man his equal, . . . the enjoyment of the property he has in this state is very unsafe, very insecure. This makes him willing to quit this condition which, however free, is full of fears and continual dangers; and it is not without reason that he seeks out and is willing to join in society with others . . . for the mutual preservation of their lives, liberties and estates, which I call by the general name—property.

The great and chief end, therefore, of men uniting into commonwealths, and putting themselves under government, is the preservation of their property. . . .

Analyzing Primary Sources

1. According to Locke, what freedoms did people have before the founding of governments?
2. What are the potential dangers of a person living in what Locke called "perfect freedom"?
3. According to Locke, how are governments formed?
4. What trade-off does Locke say occurs when people live under governments?

2 Forms of Government

Section Preview

OBJECTIVES

1. **Classify** governments according to three sets of characteristics.
2. **Define** systems of government based on who can participate.
3. **Identify** different ways that power can be distributed, geographically, within a state.
4. **Describe** a government by how power is distributed between the executive branch and legislative branch.

WHY IT MATTERS

Governments come in many different forms—democratic or dictatorial, unitary or federal or confederate, presidential or parliamentary. But, whatever its form, government has an impact on nearly every moment and nearly every aspect of your life.

POLITICAL DICTIONARY

★ autocracy
★ oligarchy
★ unitary government
★ federal government
★ division of powers
★ confederation
★ presidential government
★ parliamentary government

Does the form a government takes, the way in which it is structured, have any importance? Political scientists, historians, and other social commentators have long argued that question. The English poet Alexander Pope weighed in with this couplet in 1733:

> *"For Forms of Government let fools contest; Whate'er is best adminster'd is best. . . . "*
>
> —*Essay on Man*

Was Pope right? Does it matter what form a government takes? Pope thought not, but you can form your own opinion as you read this section.

Classifying Governments

No two governments are, or ever have been, exactly alike, for governments are the products of human needs and experiences. All governments can be classified according to one or more of their basic features, however. Over time, political scientists have developed many bases upon which to classify (and so to describe, compare, and analyze) governments.

Three of those classifications are especially important and useful. These are classifications according to (1) who can participate in the governing process, (2) the geographic distribution of governmental power within the state, and (3) the relationship between the legislative (lawmaking) and the executive (law-executing) branches of the government.[4]

Who Can Participate

To many people, the most meaningful of these classifications is the one that depends on the number of persons who can take part in the governing process. Here there are two basic forms to consider: democracies and dictatorships.

Democracy

In a democracy, supreme political authority rests with the people. The people hold the sovereign power, and government is conducted only by and with the consent of the people.[5]

Abraham Lincoln gave immortality to this definition of democracy in his Gettysburg Address in 1863: "government of the people, by the people, for the people." Nowhere is there a better, more concise statement of the American understanding of democracy.

A democracy can be either direct or indirect in form. A direct democracy, also called a pure democracy, exists where the will of the people

---

[4]Note that these classifications are not mutually exclusive. A government can be defined using two or three of these classifications.

[5]The word *democracy* is derived from the Greek words *dēmos* meaning "the people" and *kratia* meaning "rule" or "authority." The Greek word *dēmokratia* means "rule by the people."

is translated into public policy (law) directly by the people themselves, in mass meetings. This can work only in very small communities, where it is possible for the citizenry to meet in a central place, and where the problems of government are few and relatively simple.

Direct democracy does not exist at the national level anywhere in the world today. However, the New England town meeting, which you will read about in Chapter 25, and the *Landsgemeinde* in a few of the smaller Swiss cantons are excellent examples of direct democracy in action.[6]

Americans are more familiar with the indirect form of democracy—that is, with representative democracy. In a representative democracy, a small group of persons, chosen by the people to act as their representatives, expresses the popular will. These agents of the people are responsible for carrying out the day-to-day conduct of government—the making and executing of laws and so on. They are held accountable to the people for that conduct, especially at periodic elections.

At these elections, the people have an opportunity to express their approval or disapproval of their representatives by casting ballots for or against them. To put it another way, representative democracy is government by popular consent—government with the consent of the governed.

Some people insist that the United States is more properly called a republic rather than a democracy. They hold that in a republic the sovereign power is held by those eligible to vote, while the political power is exercised by representatives chosen by and held responsible to those citizens. For them, democracy can be defined only in terms of direct democracy.

Many Americans use the terms *democracy, republic, representative democracy,* and *republican* form of government interchangeably, although they are not the same things. Whatever the terms used, remember that in a democracy the people are sovereign. They are the only source for any and all of government's power. In other words, the people rule.

STOP

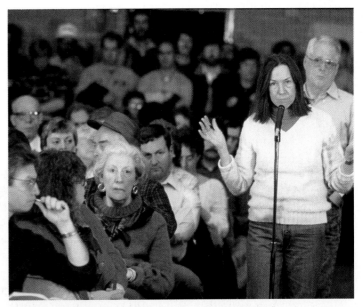

▲ *Direct Democracy Today* At this town meeting in New Hampshire, every citizen in the town enjoys the right to speak out and vote on issues. *Critical Thinking Why are town meetings impractical in large cities?*

Dictatorship

A dictatorship exists where those who rule cannot be held responsible to the will of the people. The government is not accountable for its policies, nor for how they are carried out. Dictatorship is probably the oldest, and it is certainly the most common, form of government known to history.[7]

Dictatorships are sometimes identified as either autocracies or oligarchies. An **autocracy** is a government in which a single person holds unlimited political power. An **oligarchy** is a government in which the power to rule is held by a small, usually self-appointed elite.

All dictatorships are authoritarian—those in power hold absolute and unchallengeable authority over the people. Modern dictatorships have tended to be totalitarian, as well. That is, they exercise complete power over nearly every aspect of human affairs. Their power embraces all matters of human concern.

The leading examples of dictatorship in the modern era have been those in Fascist Italy (from 1922 to 1943), in Nazi Germany (from 1933 to 1945), in the Soviet Union (from 1917

---

[6]The *Landsgemeinde,* like the original New England town meeting, is an assembly open to all local citizens qualified to vote. In a more limited sense, lawmaking by initiative petition is also an example of direct democracy; see Chapter 24.

[7]The word *dictatorship* comes from the Latin *dictare,* meaning to dictate, issue orders, give authoritative commands. *Dictator* was the ancient Roman republic's title for the leader who was given extraordinary powers in times of crisis. Julius Caesar (100–44 B.C.) became the first of the Roman dictators, in 49 B.C.

until the late 1980s), and one that still exists in the People's Republic of China (where the present regime came to power in 1949).

Although they do exist, one-person dictatorships are not at all common today. A few close approaches to such a regime can now be found in Libya, which has been dominated by Muammar al-Qaddafi since 1969, and in some other Arab and African states.

Most present-day dictatorships are not nearly so absolutely controlled by a single person or by a small group as may appear to be the case. Outward appearances may hide the fact that several groups—the army, religious leaders, industrialists, and others—compete for power in the political system.

Dictatorships often present the outward appearance of control by the people. The people often vote in popular elections; but the vote is closely controlled, and ballots usually contain the candidates of but one political party. An elected legislative body often exists, but only to rubber-stamp the policies of the dictatorship.

Typically, dictatorial regimes are militaristic in character. They usually gain power by force. The military holds many of the major posts in the government. After crushing all effective opposition at home, these regimes may turn to foreign aggression to enhance the country's military power and prestige.

STOP

▲ **Dictatorship and Democracy in Germany** Today, the Federal Republic of Germany is a vigorous democracy. It was born out of the defeat of Adolf Hitler's Nazi dictatorship in World War II.

Geographic Distribution of Power

In every system of government the power to govern is located in one or more places, geographically. From this standpoint, three basic forms of government exist: unitary, federal, and confederate governments.

Unitary Government

A **unitary government** is often described as a centralized government. All powers held by the government belong to a single, central agency. The central (national) government creates local units of government for its own convenience. Those local governments have only those powers that the central government chooses to give them.

Most governments in the world are unitary in form. Great Britain is a classic illustration. A single central organization, the Parliament, holds all of the government's power. Local governments exist solely to relieve Parliament of burdens it could perform only with difficulty and inconvenience. Though unlikely, Parliament could do away with these and other agencies of local government at any time.

Be careful not to confuse the unitary form of government with a dictatorship. In the unitary form, all of the powers held by the government are concentrated in the central government. That government might not have *all* power, however. In Great Britain, for example, the powers held by the government are limited. British government is unitary and, at the same time, democratic.

Federal Government

A **federal government** is one in which the powers of government are divided between a central government and several local governments. An authority superior to both the central and local governments makes this **division of powers** on a geographic basis; and that division cannot be changed by either the local or national level acting alone. Both levels of government act directly on the people through their own sets of laws, officials, and agencies.

In the United States, for example, the National Government has certain powers and the 50 States have others. This division of powers is set out in the Constitution of the United States. The Constitution stands above both levels of government; and it cannot be changed unless the people, acting through both the National Government and the States, agree to that change.

Australia, Canada, Mexico, Switzerland, Germany, India, and some 20 other states also have federal forms of government today. In the United States, the phrase "the Federal Government" is often used to identify the National Government, the government headquartered in Washington, D.C. Note, however, that each of the 50 State governments in this country is unitary, not federal, in form.

Confederate Government

A **confederation** is an alliance of independent states. A central organization, the confederate government, only handles those matters that member states assign to it. Typically, confederate governments hold limited powers in such fields as defense and foreign commerce.

Most often, they have not had the power to make laws that apply directly to individuals, at least not without some further action by the member states. A confederate structure makes it possible for the several states to cooperate in matters of common concern and also retain their separate identities.

Confederations are very rare in today's world. The European Union (EU) is the closest approach to a confederation today. Through its institutions, the EU has established free trade among its 15 members, launched a common currency, and is moving toward the close coordination of its members' foreign and defense policies. In our own history, the United States under the Articles of Confederation (1781 to 1789) and the Confederate States of America (1861 to 1865) are also examples of this form of government.

STOP

Relationship Between Legislative and Executive Branches

Political scientists also classify governments based on the relationship between their legislative and executive agencies. This view yields

Comparative Government

Forms of Government

Country	Where is the power?		What is the relationship between the legislative and executive branches?		Who can participate?	
	Unitary	Federal	Parliamentary	Presidential	Democracy	Dictatorship
Botswana	✓		✓		✓	
Brazil		✓		✓	✓	
Costa Rica	✓		✓		✓	
Cuba	✓		✓			✓
France	✓			✓	✓	
India		✓	✓		✓	
Syria	✓			✓		✓
United States		✓		✓	✓	

Interpreting Tables Some combinations of governmental forms, such as parliamentary democracy and unitary dictatorship, are more common than others. *Why is a state unlikely to be both a confederation and a dictatorship?*

two basic forms of government: presidential and parliamentary.

Presidential Government

In a **presidential government,** the executive and legislative branches of the government are separate, independent of one another, and coequal. The chief executive (president) is chosen independently of the legislature, holds office for a fixed term, and has broad powers not subject to the direct control of the legislative branch.

The two branches regularly have several powers with which each can block actions by the other branch. Usually, as in the United States, a written constitution provides for the separation of powers between the branches.

The United States is the world's leading example of presidential government. In fact, the United States invented the form. Most of the other presidential systems in the world are also found in the Western Hemisphere.

Presidential and Parliamentary Governments

The Presidential Relationship Voters elect the Legislature and the Chief Executive who is part of the Executive Branch. The legislature and executive are independent and coequal.

Voters

Legislative Branch

Executive Branch

Chief Executive

The Parliamentary Relationship Voters elect the Legislature. The Chief Executive is drawn from the Legislature.

Voters

Legislative Branch

Chief Executive

Interpreting Diagrams Compare presidential and parliamentary forms of government. **In which form of government is the chief executive both elected from and part of the legislature?**

Parliamentary Government

In **parliamentary government,** the executive is made up of the prime minister or premier, and that official's cabinet. The prime minister and cabinet themselves are members of the legislative branch, the parliament. The prime minister is the leader of the majority party or of a likeminded group of parties in parliament and is chosen by that body. With parliament's approval, the prime minister selects the members of the cabinet from among the members of parliament. The executive is thus chosen by the legislature, is a part of it, and is subject to its direct control.

The prime minister and the cabinet (often called "the government") remain in office only as long as their policies and administration have the confidence of a majority in parliament. If the parliament defeats the prime minister and cabinet on an important matter, the government may receive a "vote of no confidence," and the prime minister and his cabinet must resign from office. Then a new government must be formed. Either parliament chooses a new prime minister or, as often happens, all the seats of parliament go before the voters in a general election.

A parliamentary government avoids one of the major problems of the presidential form: prolonged conflict and sometimes deadlock between the executive and legislative branches. On the other hand, it should be noted that the checks and balances of presidential government are not a part of the parliamentary system. Nevertheless, the British, Canadian, Japanese, and a majority of all of the other governments in today's world have a parliamentary government.

STOP —

Section 2 Assessment

Key Terms and Main Ideas

1. What defines a **unitary government?**
2. How is power distributed in a **federal government?**
3. Who holds power in an **oligarchy?**
4. What specific trait gives the United States a **presidential system** of government?

Critical Thinking

5. **Making Decisions** Reread the Preamble to the Constitution on page 8. In your opinion, which combination of governmental forms would be best able to establish justice? Which combination would be best able to provide for the common defense? Explain your answers.

6. **Drawing Conclusions** Many people have suggested using the Internet to create a direct democracy in the United States where every citizen could vote. List one benefit and one drawback of this proposal.

 Take It to the Net

7. Create your own chart comparing governments according to several categories. Create at least five categories, including type of leader, economy, and governing body. Use the links provided in the Social Studies area at the following Web site for help in completing this activity. **www.phschool.com**

SKILLS FOR LIFE

TECHNOLOGY
CITIZENSHIP
CRITICAL THINKING
CHARTS and GRAPHS

Recognizing Propaganda

The term *propaganda* is highly charged. People tend to think of it as deceptive information, but in fact the term has a broader meaning. Propaganda is information—either true or false—intended to persuade people to think or act in a certain way. True or not, propaganda is usually a one-sided explanation or opinion. Some typical propaganda techniques are shown at right.

Propaganda can be a powerful tool for promoting or destroying attitudes, beliefs, and values. In the 1930s, Adolf Hitler rose to power in part through his skillful use of propaganda to whip up hatred toward various minority groups. To counter Nazi propaganda, in 1942 the United States created a radio network called the Voice of America (VOA) to broadcast propaganda about American ideals, values, and democracy.

For much of the twentieth century, the United States engaged in a propaganda war with its chief rival for power, the Soviet Union. One of the chief targets of American propaganda was Soviet leader Josef Stalin, who boldly predicted that communism would ultimately spread throughout the world. Stalin is depicted in the pamphlet at right. Use these steps to evaluate the content on the cover:

1. Determine whether the item constitutes propaganda. Which of the propaganda techniques listed here are used in the pamphlet? Explain.

2. Analyze the purpose of the propaganda. This pamphlet was published in the United States in 1938. (a) Who is it intended to influence? (b) What beliefs or behavior are people being urged to follow?

3. Draw conclusions. How and why might this propaganda have been effective in influencing Americans' beliefs about communism?

Propaganda Techniques

Most Americans encounter propaganda during political campaigns, when candidates try to sway voters.

Celebrity Testimonials Using endorsements from famous people—from actors to sports figures—to try to persuade you: *Mr. Action Hero says, "Vote for X. He's my choice."*

Multiple Identities Claiming to be just like you, no matter who you are: *"I'm one of you. I share your beliefs and concerns."*

The Bandwagon Argument Urging you to follow the crowd, the majority: *"A is voting for me. So are B, C, and D. Why not you, too?"*

Name Calling Attacking and labeling the opposition instead of discussing issues: *"My opponent is un-American."*

Scare Tactics Using words or pictures to persuade people to act out of fear of consequences, real or perceived: *"A vote for my opponent will destroy our children's future."*

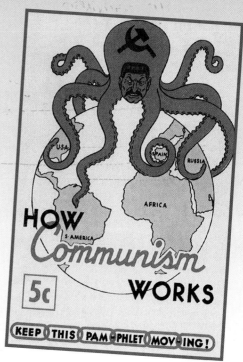

HOW *Communism* WORKS
5c
KEEP THIS PAMPHLET MOVING!

Test for Success

Complete one of the following activities: (a) Find a political cartoon in this book that uses propaganda techniques. List the techniques and explain how they are used. (b) Create a fictitious political poster that uses at least two propaganda techniques.

Section Preview

OBJECTIVES

1. **Understand** the foundations of democracy.
2. **Analyze** the connections between democracy and the free enterprise system.
3. **Identify** the role of the Internet in a democracy.

WHY IT MATTERS

Democracy insists on the fundamental importance of each and every individual. The free enterprise system is a natural counterpart to democracy–for it, too, is built on the concept of individualism.

POLITICAL DICTIONARY

★ compromise
★ free enterprise system
★ law of supply and demand
★ mixed economy

What do you make of James Bryce's assessment of democracy? "No government demands so much from the citizen as Democracy, and none gives so much back." What does democratic government demand from you? What does it give you in return?

Foundations

Democracy is not inevitable. It does not exist in the United States simply because Americans regard it as the best of all possible political systems. Rather, democracy exists in this country because the American people believe in its basic

concepts. It will continue to exist only for as long as we, the people, continue to subscribe to and practice those concepts.

Winston Churchill (1874–1965) once argued for democracy this way: "No one pretends that democracy is perfect or all-wise. Indeed, it has been said that democracy is the worst form of government except all those other forms that have been tried from time to time."

The American concept of democracy rests on these basic notions:

(1) A recognition of the fundamental worth and dignity of every person;

(2) A respect for the equality of all persons;

(3) A faith in majority rule and an insistence upon minority rights;

(4) An acceptance of the necessity of compromise; and

(5) An insistence upon the widest possible degree of individual freedom.

Of course, these ideas can be worded in other ways. No matter what the wording, however, they form the very minimum that anyone who professes to believe in democracy must agree to.

Worth of the Individual

Democracy is firmly based upon a belief in the fundamental importance of the individual. Each individual, no matter what his or her station in life, is a separate and distinct being.

This concept of the dignity and worth of the individual is of overriding importance in democratic thought. At various times, of course, the welfare of one or a few individuals

▲ At Gettysburg, Pennsylvania, Abraham Lincoln declared that the United States was "conceived in liberty, and dedicated to the proposition that all men are created equal." *Critical Thinking Which of the five foundations of democracy are best described by this quote?*

is subordinated to the interests of the many in a democracy. People can be forced to do certain things whether they want to or not. Examples range from paying taxes to registering for the draft to stopping at a stop sign.

When a democratic society forces people to pay a tax or obey traffic signals, it is serving the interests of the many. However, it is *not* simply serving the interests of a mass of people who happen to outnumber the few. Rather, it is serving the many who, as individuals, together make up that society.

Equality of All Persons

Hand-in-hand with the belief in the worth of the individual, democracy stresses the equality of all individuals. It holds, with Jefferson, that "all men are created equal."

Certainly, democracy does *not* insist on an equality of condition for all persons. Thus, it does not claim that all are born with the same mental or physical abilities. Nor does it argue that all persons have a right to an equal share of worldly goods.

Rather, the democratic concept of equality insists that all are entitled to (1) equality of opportunity and (2) equality before the law. That is, the democratic concept of equality holds that no person should be held back for any such arbitrary reasons as those based on race, color, religion, or gender. The concept holds that each person must be free to develop himself or herself as fully as he or she can (or cares to), and that each person should be treated as the equal of all other persons by the law.

We have come a great distance toward the goal of equality for all in this country. It is clear, however, that the journey is far from over.

Majority Rule, Minority Rights

In a democracy, the will of the people and not the dictate of the ruling few determines public policy. But what is the popular will, and how is it determined? Some device must exist by which these crucial questions can be answered. The only satisfactory device democracy knows is that of majority rule. Democracy argues that a majority of the people will be right more often than they will be wrong, and that the majority will also be right more often than will any one person or small group.

▲ *Equality of Opportunity* The democratic ideal states that people should have equal opportunity to reach their fullest potential as individuals.

Democracy can be described as an experiment or a trial-and-error process designed to find satisfactory ways to order human relations. Democracy does *not* say that the majority will always arrive at the best decisions on public matters. In fact, the democratic process does not intend to come up with "right" or "best" answers. Rather, the democratic process searches for *satisfactory* solutions to public problems.

Of course, democracy insists that the majority's decisions will usually be more, rather than less, satisfactory. Democracy does admit the possibility of mistakes; it acknowledges the possibility that "wrong" or less satisfactory answers will sometimes be found. Democracy also recognizes that seldom is any solution to a public problem so satisfactory that it cannot be improved upon, and that circumstances can change over time. So, the process of experimentation, of seeking answers to public questions, is never-ending.

Certainly, a democracy cannot work without the principle of majority rule. Unchecked, however, a majority could destroy its opposition and, in the process, destroy democracy as well. Thus, democracy insists upon majority rule restrained by minority rights. The majority must always recognize the right of any minority to become, by fair and lawful means, the majority. The majority must always be willing to listen to a minority's argument, to hear its objections, to bear its criticisms, and to welcome its suggestions.

Necessity of Compromise

In a democracy, public decision making must be largely a matter of give-and-take among the various competing interests. It is a matter of **compromise** in order to find the position most acceptable to the largest number. Compromise is the process of blending and adjusting competing views and interests.

Compromise is an essential part of the democratic concept for two major reasons. First, remember that democracy puts the individual first and, at the same time, insists that each individual is the equal of all others. In a democratic society made up of many individuals and groups with many different opinions and interests, how can the people make public decisions except by compromise?

Second, few public questions have only two sides. Most can be answered in several ways. Take the apparently simple question of how a city should pay for the paving of a public street. Should it charge those who own property along the street? Or should the costs be paid from the city's general treasury? Or should the city and the adjacent property owners share the costs? What about those who will use the street but do not live in the city? Should they have to pay a toll?

Remember, compromise is a process, a way of achieving majority agreement. It is never an end in itself. Not all compromises are good, and not all are necessary.

Interpreting Political Cartoons If the two chefs represent lawmakers in a democracy, what might the stew represent?

Individual Freedom

It should be clear by this point that democracy can thrive only in an atmosphere of individual freedom. However, democracy does not and cannot insist on *complete* freedom for the individual. Absolute freedom can exist only in a state of anarchy—the total absence of government. Anarchy can only lead, inevitably and quickly, to rule by the strong and ruthless.

Democracy does insist, however, that each individual must be as free to do as he or she pleases as far as the freedom of all will allow. Justice Oliver Wendell Holmes once had this to say about the relative nature of each individual's rights: "The right to swing my fist ends where the other man's nose begins."

Drawing the line between the rights of one individual and those of another is far from easy. Still, the drawing of that line is a continuous and vitally important function of democratic government. As John F. Kennedy put it: "The rights of every man are diminished when the rights of one man are threatened."

Striking the proper balance between freedom for the individual and the rights of society as a whole is similarly difficult—and vital. Abraham Lincoln once stated democracy's problem in these words:

PRIMARY Sources "*Must a government of necessity be too strong for the liberties of its own people, or too weak to maintain its own existence?*"
—*Response to a Serenade,* November 10, 1864

Human beings desire both liberty and authority. Democratic government must work constantly to strike the proper balance between the two. The authority of government must be adequate to the needs of society. At the same time, that authority must never be allowed to become so great that it restricts the individual beyond necessity.

Democracy and the Free Enterprise System

The American commitment to freedom for the individual is deep-rooted, and it is as evident in the nation's economic system as it is in the political system. The American economic system is often called the **free enterprise system.**

It is an economic system characterized by the private ownership of capital goods, investments made by private decision, not by government directive, and success or failure determined by competition in the marketplace. The free enterprise system is based on four fundamental factors: private ownership, individual initiative, profit, and competition.

How the System Works

The free enterprise system is often called capitalism, and it is also known as the private enterprise system and as a market-based system. It does not rely on government to decide what items are to be produced, how much of any particular item should be produced, or how much any item is to sell for. Rather, those decisions are to be made by the market, through the **law of supply and demand.** That law states that when supplies of goods and services become plentiful, prices tend to drop. When supplies become scarcer, prices tend to rise.

Democracy and the free enterprise system are not the same thing. One is a political system, and the other is an economic system. However, both are firmly based on the concept of individual freedom. America's experience with both systems clearly suggests that the two reinforce one another in practice.

Government and the Free Enterprise System

The basis of the American economic system is the free market. However, government plays a role in the American economy, and always has. An economy in which private enterprise exists in combination with a considerable amount of government regulation and promotion is called a **mixed economy.** Government's participation in the economy serves a two-fold purpose: to protect the public and to preserve private enterprise.

Government's participation in the economy can be seen at every level in this country: national, State, and local. Here are but a few examples: Economic activities are *regulated* by government through antitrust laws, pure food and drug laws, anti-pollution standards, and city and county zoning ordinances and building codes.

The nation's economic life is *promoted* in a great number of public ways. The government

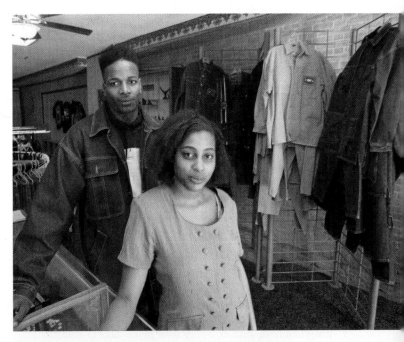

▲ Entrepreneurs are the foundation of the American system of free enterprise. Businesses like this clothing store in Los Angeles help consumers find the clothes they need at market prices. *Critical Thinking What qualities define an entrepreneur?*

grants money for transportation systems, scientific research, and the growing of particular food crops; builds roads and operates public schools; provides services such as the postal system, weather reports, and a national currency; and much more.

Thus some activities that might be carried out privately are in fact conducted by government. Public education, the postal system, local fire departments, city bus systems, and road building are examples of long standing.

How much should government participate, regulate and promote, police and serve? Many of the most heated debates in American politics center on that question, and we are often reminded of Abraham Lincoln's advice:

PRIMARY **Sources** ❝*The legitimate object of government, is to do for a community of people, whatever they need to have done, but can not do, at all, or can not, so well do, for themselves—in their separate, and individual capacities.*❞

—Abraham Lincoln, July 1, 1854

Most Americans believe that a well-regulated free enterprise system—one of free choice, individual initiative, private enterprise—is the best guarantee of a better life for everyone.

CLOSE UP
FOUNDATION

Student Poll

In a recent poll, students were asked their opinion of the following question: *How closely do you follow national politics and govern-ment—very closely, fairly closely, just somewhat closely, or not closely at all?*

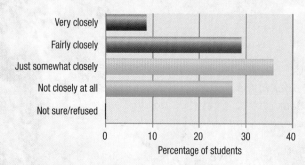

Very closely

Fairly closely

Just somewhat closely

Not closely at all

Not sure/refused

Percentage of students

SOURCE: High School Students' Attitudes Toward Government and Politics, Close Up Foundation, May 1999

1. **Analyzing Data** *Approximately what percentage of students follow national politics just somewhat closely? Not closely at all?*
2. **Conducting Polls** In your own school, conduct a poll asking students how closely they follow national politics and government. *How do your results compare to the results shown in this graph?*

Democracy and the Internet

More than 50 million Americans can now log on to the Internet to send and receive e-mail, to buy or sell practically anything, to entertain themselves, to inform themselves, and to do any number of other things. Clearly, cyberspace has become a major marketplace and an important channel of communication.

Democracy demands that the people be widely informed about their government. Thus, democracy and the Internet would seem to be made for one another. Once online, anyone can access a huge amount of information about pub-lic affairs. Internet users can check out the Web sites of political candidates, find out what's hap-pening on the floor of Congress, and read about recent Supreme Court decisions. Theoretically, this makes knowledgeable participation in the democratic process easier than ever before.

However, the speed with which and the quan-tity in which information can be found on the World Wide Web does *not* guarantee the reliabil-ity of that data. Experience shows that there is a vast amount of unverified, often unverifiable, and frequently false information in cyberspace. Citizens must take responsibility for checking the reliability of the sources they use. Every fact or quote found online should be checked against a second, independent source whenever possible.

What effect is this easy access to information likely to have on democracy? Many people believe that voters will soon be able to cast their ballots online, or even to vote directly on issues. Arizona first experimented with online voting in the 2000 Democratic presidential primary, and other States are exploring the possibilities. A leap to online elections appears unlikely to us today, particularly since it would entail moving from representative to direct democracy. It seems clear, however, that those who choose to can now be better informed on the issues they care about.

Section 3 Assessment

Key Terms and Main Ideas
1. Why is **compromise** an important part of democracy?
2. List three characteristics of the **free enterprise system.**
3. How does the **law of supply and demand** help determine the price of an item?
4. What is the role of government in a **mixed economy?**

Critical Thinking
5. **Recognizing Cause and Effect** List three examples of gov-ernment actions that promote the free market and three examples of government actions that might conflict with the free market.
6. **Drawing Inferences** Describe, in your own words, the responsibilities of the majority in a system of "majority rules, minority rights."

7. **Predicting Consequences** How might the growth of the Internet affect the relationship between government and the people?

 Take It to the Net

8. Read about the origins of the American economy. Then review the different types of economic systems. Select a few aspects of the American economic system that you have seen first-hand and explain how they affect your life. Use the links provided in the Social Studies area at the following Web site for help in completing this activity. **www.phschool.com**

Must Voting Districts Be Equal in Population?

If two voting districts have the same number of representatives in the State legislature but contain unequal numbers of voters, each voter in the more populous district has less influence than each voter in the less populous district. Does the Constitution require States to ensure that all voting districts are roughly equal in population?

Baker v. Carr (1962)

Tennessee's constitution required that the seats in that State's legislature be distributed among the State's 95 counties on the basis of the number of qualified voters in each county. A 1901 law directed that those seats be redistributed, in line with new census figures, every ten years. No reapportionments were made over the next sixty years, however.

Charles W. Baker, the mayor of Nashville, and several others went to the federal courts with a suit against Tennessee's chief election officer, Secretary of State Joe C. Carr. They claimed that the apportionment made in 1901 had been faulty, and they insisted that population changes over the years since had made it even more unfair. They argued that the inequalities produced by that unfair distribution of seats amounted to a violation of the equal protection of the laws guaranteed by the 14th Amendment to the federal Constitution.

The federal district court dismissed the suit, ruling that State apportionment was an issue for the elected branches and could not be reviewed by the courts. The plaintiffs appealed to the Supreme Court.

Arguments for Baker

1. The federal courts have the authority to consider this case because they have the power to prevent States from depriving people of their constitutional rights (in this case, the right to equal protection of the laws).
2. Although the States are responsible for electing their own officials and structuring their own governments, they must do so in ways that do not deprive their citizens of their constitutional rights.
3. The Tennessee apportionment harms voters in more-populous districts and thus violates the Equal Protection Clause of the 14th Amendment.

Arguments for Carr

1. The Constitution does not authorize the Federal Government to interfere in the States' election of their own officials.
2. The States have great flexibility to structure their own governments, and the Federal Government may not override the States' choices in this matter.
3. The Tennessee apportionment was created by the Tennessee legislature. The manner of electing officials is a political question, one not subject to review by the federal courts.

Decide for Yourself

1. Review the constitutional grounds on which each side based its arguments and the specific arguments each side presented.
2. Debate the opposing viewpoints presented in this case. Which viewpoint do you favor?
3. Predict the impact of the Court's decision on State elections and on the composition of State legislatures. (To read a summary of the Court's decision, turn to the Supreme Court Glossary on page 799.)

Political Dictionary

government (p. 4)

public policy (p. 4)

legislative power (p. 4)

executive power (p. 4)

judicial power (p. 4)

constitution (p. 5)

dictatorship (p. 5)

democracy (p. 5)

state (p. 5)

sovereign (p. 6)

autocracy (p. 13)

oligarchy (p. 13)

unitary government (p. 14)

federal government (p. 14)

division of powers (p. 14)

confederation (p. 15)

presidential government (p. 15)

parliamentary government (p. 16)

compromise (p. 20)

free enterprise system (p. 20)

law of supply and demand (p. 21)

mixed economy (p. 21)

Practicing the Vocabulary

Matching *Choose a term from the list above that best matches each description.*

1. Describes a state that has supreme power within its territory
2. The institution through which society makes and enforces its policies
3. That which a government decides to do
4. An alliance of independent states that expressly delegates limited powers to a central government
5. A form of government that is often totalitarian and authoritarian; can be led by one person or many people

Fill in the Blank *Choose a term from the list above that best completes the sentence.*

6. In a _____, the executive branch of government is led by members of the legislative branch.
7. A _____ is also known as a centralized government.
8. The basic structure and principles of a government may be found in its _____.
9. _____ is the power to write new laws.
10. Government regulates and promotes businesses in a _____.

Reviewing Main Ideas

Section 1

11. What characteristics define a state?
12. Briefly describe the four most widely held theories that attempt to explain the origin of the state.
13. What theory on the origin of the state was most influential in the founding of the United States?
14. For what reasons do people form governments?
15. Describe briefly the purposes of government set out in the Preamble to the Constitution.

Section 2

16. List the three questions that can be used to classify governments.
17. (a) In a democracy, to whom is the government responsible? (b) In a dictatorship, to whom is the government responsible?
18. What is the difference between an autocracy and an oligarchy?

19. Name and briefly describe the three forms of government that can result depending on how governmental power is distributed geographically.
20. Explain how power is distributed in a presidential government.

Section 3

21. Briefly describe the five basic concepts of democracy.
22. What is the difference between equality of opportunity and equality of condition?
23. Describe the relationship between the rights of the individual and the rights of the overall society.
24. (a) What is the free enterprise system? (b) How does it differ from a mixed economy?
25. List one benefit and one drawback of using the Internet for research.

Critical Thinking Skills

26. *Applying the Chapter Skill* Using a library or the Internet, find an American propaganda poster from World War I or World War II. **(a)** Who was this poster attempting to influence? **(b)** What was the poster encouraging the reader to do? **(c)** Do you believe students today would react positively to this poster? Explain your answer.

27. *Recognizing Point of View* Consider Martin Luther King, Jr.'s statement that "injustice anywhere is a threat to justice everywhere." **(a)** What is your understanding of that statement? **(b)** Why is such a belief necessary to maintain a democratic society?

28. *Drawing Inferences* Review the ideas of Thomas Hobbes regarding the social contract theory and the origin of the state. **(a)** What is Hobbes's view about the nature of human beings? Explain why you agree or disagree with this view. **(b)** Given Hobbes's view, do you think it makes sense for human beings' mutual protection?

29. *Making Comparisons* One of the five basic concepts of democracy is equality of all persons. **(a)** Which do you feel is more important to a democracy, equality of opportunity, described in the chapter, or equality of income, housing, and property? **(b)** Can these two forms of equality co-exist in pure form? Explain your answer.

Analyzing Political Cartoons

Using your knowledge of government and this cartoon, answer the questions below.

"The Athenians are here, Sire, with an offer to back us with ships, money, arms, and men—and of course, their usual lectures about democracy."

30. What form of government is represented by the King in this cartoon?

31. What does this cartoon imply about the origins of democracy?

★ You Can Make a Difference

Do certain issues—pollution, poverty, recycling—excite and energize you? Do you like a challenge? Perhaps you're not ready to start your own grassroots organization. You can still make a difference by joining an existing group working on that issue. First, take time to examine and define the causes you care about. Watch the news. Read newspapers and news magazines. Take notes of the issues that you feel strongly about. What do you want to do about them? Your answer can help you define your role as an activist.

Participation Activities

32. *Current Events Watch* In several countries around the world, groups are working to form new states. Examples include Quebec, in Canada, and the Basque region of Spain. Read through news reports to learn more about an independence movement active today. **(a)** Describe how the proposed country would meet the four criteria of a state. **(b)** What steps would be necessary to win independence? **(c)** In your opinion, how likely is it that this independence movement will succeed?

33. *Time Line Activity* Scan world news reports for an example of a country that is currently moving toward, or away from, democracy. Research political events there over the last fifty years, including revolutions, new constitutions, and free elections. Assemble at least five events into a time line. How long did the transition from one form of government to the other take?

34. *It's Your Turn* Write your own "social contract" in which you express your feelings about what should be required of members of a political society, and what government should provide the people. Start by creating a chart with two columns. In one column, list the responsibilities of the citizens in your proposed social contract. In the other column, list what you feel government should provide its citizens. Then detail your ideas for the contract. Proofread and revise for corrections. Then, prepare a final copy. **(Creating a Chart)**

 Take It to the Net

Chapter 1 Self-Test As a final review activity, take the Chapter 1 Self-Test in the Social Studies area at the Web site listed below, and receive immediate feedback on your answers.

www.phschool.com

CHAPTER 2

Origins of American Government

"*It is, Sir, the people's Constitution, the people's government, made for the people, made by the people, and answerable to the people.*"

—Daniel Webster (1830)

The Constitution grew out of a long heritage of law and politics. Before Americans could create their new government, they endured years of turmoil and revolution. In writing the Constitution, the Framers had to consider the rights and interests of many factions. Two hundred years later, Americans still seek and debate their rights.

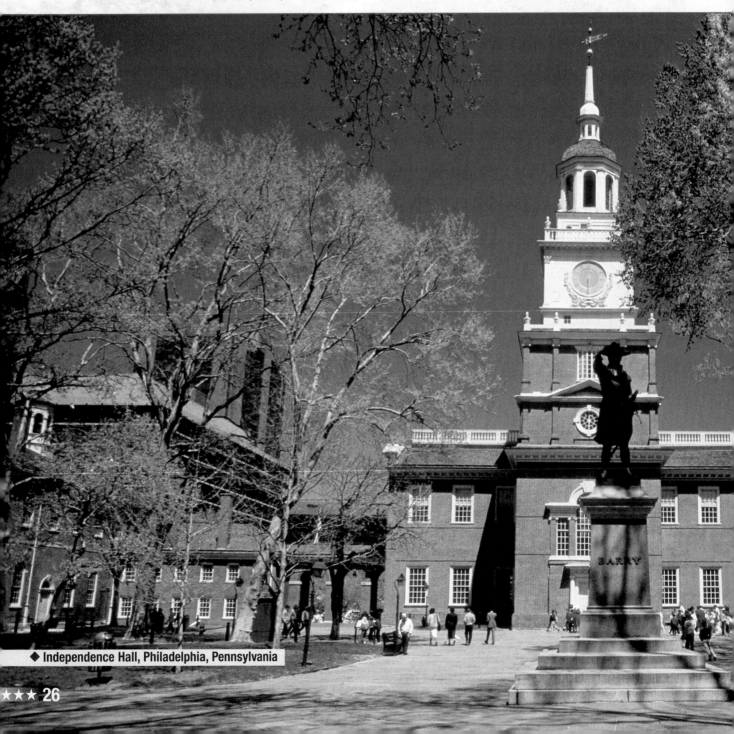

◆ Independence Hall, Philadelphia, Pennsylvania

★ You Can Make a Difference

WHO IS ENTITLED to the basic rights promised in the Constitution? Everyone? Or just adults who can vote? In 1996, Ben Smilowitz decided that high school students needed an organization to stand up for their constitutional rights. "You can't just sit back and watch," he said. The 17-year-old from West Hartford, Connecticut, became a co-founder of the International Student Activism Alliance. Members throughout the country alert each other about issues of students' rights, such as censorship and privacy. Ben also worked to get two student representatives appointed to the Connecticut State board of education. By staying informed, you can protect your constitutional rights.

Keep It Current

Items marked with this logo are periodically updated on the Internet. Keep up-to-date with what's in the news. To get current information on issues related to the Constitution, go to **www.phschool.com**

SECTION 1

Our Political Beginnings (pp. 28–32)
★ American colonists benefited from a developing English tradition of ordered, limited, and representative government.
★ This tradition was based on landmark documents, including the Magna Carta, the Petition of Right, and the English Bill of Rights.
★ The English established three types of colonial governments, all of which provided training for the colonists in the art of government.

SECTION 2

The Coming of Independence (pp. 34–39)
★ Great Britain became more involved with the colonies in the 1760s.
★ The colonists reacted to the changes in British policies by taking small steps toward unity.
★ Twelve of the 13 colonies joined in the First Continental Congress to plan opposition to the British policies.
★ In May of 1775, the Second Continental Congress began. It became the government of the new United States and produced the Declaration of Independence.
★ The newly formed States wrote constitutions that would later influence the U.S. Constitution.

SECTION 3

The Critical Period (pp. 44–47)
★ To provide a more lasting plan of government, the Second Continental Congress created the Articles of Confederation.
★ The Articles contained many weaknesses and led to bickering among the States.
★ The chaos of this critical period led to a movement for change toward a more powerful central government at the Constitutional Convention in May 1787.

SECTION 4

Creating the Constitution (pp. 48–54)
★ The Constitutional Convention in Philadelphia involved delegates from every State but Rhode Island.
★ The Virginia and New Jersey Plans each offered ways to organize the new government.
★ The delegates agreed to compromises that allowed them to agree on the configuration of Congress and other issues.

SECTION 5

Ratifying the Constitution (pp. 56–58)
★ The Federalists promoted the Constitution.
★ The Anti-Federalists attacked the document out of fear of the plan's strong central government and because it lacked a bill of rights.
★ The new Congress convened in March 1789 in what was then the capital, New York City. On April 30, 1789, George Washington was inaugurated as the nation's first President.

Section Preview

OBJECTIVES

1. **Identify** the three basic concepts of government that influenced government in the English colonies.
2. **Explain** the significance of the following landmark English documents: the Magna Carta, the Petition of Right, the English Bill of Rights.
3. **Describe** the three types of colonies that the English established in North America.

WHY IT MATTERS

Our system of government has its origins in the concepts and political ideas that English colonists brought with them when they settled North America. The colonies served as a school for learning about government.

POLITICAL DICTIONARY

★ **limited government**
★ **representative government**
★ **Magna Carta**
★ **Petition of Right**
★ **English Bill of Rights**
★ **charter**
★ **bicameral**
★ **proprietary**
★ **unicameral**

The American system of government did not suddenly spring into being with the signing of the Declaration of Independence in 1776. Nor was it suddenly created by the Framers of the Constitution in 1787.

The beginnings of what was to become the United States can be found in the mid-sixteenth century when explorers, traders, and settlers first made their way to North America. The French, Dutch, Spanish, Swedes, and others contributed to the European domination of this continent—and to the domination of those Native Americans who were here for centuries before the first Europeans arrived. It was the English, however, who came in the largest numbers. And it was the English who soon controlled the 13 colonies that stretched for some 1,300 miles along the Atlantic coast.

◄ English settlers brought to North America a political system as well as the skills needed to create household items, such as this carved Hadley chest.

Basic Concepts of Government

The earliest English settlers brought with them knowledge of a political system—established laws, customs, practices, and institutions—that had been developing for centuries.

The political system they knew was that of England, of course. But some aspects of that structure had come to England from other times and places. For example, the concept of the rule of law that influenced English political ideas had roots in the early river civilizations of Africa and Asia.[1] More directly, the ancient Romans who occupied much of England from A.D. 43 to 410 left behind a legacy of law, religion, and custom to the people. From this rich political history, the English colonists brought to North America three ideas that were to loom large in the shaping of government in the United States.

---

[1]For example, King Hammurabi of Babylonia developed a codified system of laws known as Hammurabi's Code around 1750 B.C. Its 282 laws covered real estate, trade, and business transactions, as well as criminal law. The code distinguished between major and minor offenses, established the state as the authority that would enforce the law, and tried to guarantee social justice. Because of the Babylonians' close contact with the Hebrews, many of their laws became part of the Hebrew law and thus later a part of the Old Testament of the Bible—for example, "An eye for an eye." The English and the English colonists were familiar with and devoutly attracted to this Biblical concept of the rule of law.

Foundations of American Rights

1215 Magna Carta	1689 English Bill of Rights	1776 Virginia Bill of Rights
❶❷❸	❶❷❹❺❻❼	❺❽❾❿⓫

| 1200 | 1400 | 1600 | 1800 |

1791 Bill of Rights
❶❷❸❹❺❻❼
❽❾❿⓫

RIGHTS

❶ Trial by jury
❷ Due process
❸ Private property
❹ No cruel punishment
❺ No excessive bail or fines
❻ Right to bear arms
❼ Right to petition
❽ No unreasonable searches and seizures
❾ Freedom of speech
❿ Freedom of the press
⓫ Freedom of religion

Interpreting Charts The rights established in these landmark documents were revolutionary in their day. They did not, however, extend to all people when first granted. Over the years, these rights have influenced systems of government in many countries. *How might the right to petition, first granted in the English Bill of Rights, prevent abuse of power by a monarch?*

Ordered Government

Those first English colonists saw the need for an orderly regulation of their relationships with one another—that is, for government. They created local governments, based on those they had known in England. Many of the offices and units of government they established are still with us today: the offices of sheriff, coroner, assessor, and justice of the peace, the grand jury, counties, townships, and several others.

Limited Government

The colonists also brought with them the idea that government is not all-powerful. That is, government is restricted in what it may do, and each individual has certain rights that government cannot take away.

This concept is called **limited government,** and it was deeply rooted in English belief and practice by the time the first English ships reached the Americas. It had been planted in England centuries earlier, and it had been developing there for nearly 400 years before Jamestown was settled in 1607.

Representative Government

The early English settlers also carried another important concept to America: **representative government.** This idea that government should serve the will of the people had also been developing in England for centuries. With it had come a growing insistence that the people should have a voice in deciding what government should and should not do. As with the concept of limited government, this notion of "government of, by, and for the people" found fertile soil in America, and it flourished here.

Landmark English Documents

These basic notions of ordered government, of limited government, and of representative government can be traced to several landmark documents in English history.

The Magna Carta

A group of determined barons forced King John to sign the **Magna Carta—** the Great Charter—at Runnymede in 1215. Weary of John's military campaigns and heavy taxes, the

▶ King John's conflicts with English nobles led to the signing of the Magna Carta. *Critical Thinking Could the basic notions of ordered, limited, and representative government have developed without the signing of the Magna Carta? Explain your answer.*

barons who developed the Magna Carta were seeking protection against heavy-handed and arbitrary acts by the king.

The Magna Carta included such fundamental rights as trial by jury and due process of law—protection against the arbitrary taking of life, liberty, or property. These protections against the absolute power of the king were originally intended only for the privileged classes. Over time, they became the rights of all English people and were incorporated into other documents. The Magna Carta established the principle that the power of the monarchy was not absolute.

The Petition of Right

The Magna Carta was respected by some monarchs and ignored by others for 400 years. During this time, England's Parliament, a representative body with the power to make laws, slowly grew in influence. In 1628, when Charles I asked Parliament for more money in taxes, Parliament refused until he signed the **Petition of Right.**

The Petition of Right limited the king's power in several ways. Most importantly, the document demanded that the king no longer imprison or otherwise punish any person but by the lawful judgment of his peers, or by the law of the land. It also insisted that the king not impose martial law (rule by the military) in time of peace, or require homeowners to shelter the king's troops without their consent. In addition, the Petition stated that no man should be:

> **PRIMARY Sources** ❝compelled to make or yield any gift, loan, benevolence, tax, or such like charge, without common consent by act of parliament. ❞
> —X, Petition of Right

The Petition challenged the idea of the divine right of kings, declaring that even a monarch must obey the law of the land.

The Bill of Rights

In 1688, after years of revolt and turmoil, Parliament offered the crown to William and Mary of Orange. The events surrounding their ascent to the throne are known in English history as the Glorious Revolution. To prevent abuse of power by William and Mary and all future monarchs, Parliament, in 1689, drew up a list of provisions to which William and Mary had to agree.

This document, the **English Bill of Rights,** prohibited a standing army in peacetime, except with the consent of Parliament, and required that all parliamentary elections be free. In addition, the document declared

> **PRIMARY Sources** ❝that the pretended power of suspending the laws, or the execution of laws, by regal authority, without consent of Parliament is illegal . . . .
>
> that levying money for or to the use of the Crown . . . without grant of Parliament . . . is illegal . . .
>
> that it is the right of the subjects to petition the king . . . and that prosecutions for such petitioning are illegal . . . ❞
> —English Bill of Rights

The English Bill of Rights also included such guarantees as the right to a fair trial, and freedom from excessive bail and from cruel and unusual punishment.

Our nation has built on, changed, and added to those ideas and institutions that settlers brought here from England. Still, much in American government and politics today is based on these early English ideas.

The English Colonies

England's colonies in North America have been described as "13 schools of government." The colonies were the settings in which Americans first began to learn the difficult art of government.[2]

The 13 colonies were established separately, over a span of some 125 years. During that long period, outlying trading posts and isolated farm settlements developed into organized

---

[2]The Europeans who came to the Americas brought with them their own views of government, but this does not mean that they brought the idea of government to the Americas. Native Americans had governments. They had political institutions that worked to accomplish the goals of the state; they had political leaders; and they had policies toward other states.

Some Native American political organizations were very complex. For example, five Native American tribes in present-day New York State—the Seneca, Cayuga, Oneida, Onondaga, and Mohawk—formed a confederation known as the Iroquois League. The League was set up to end conflicts among the tribes, but it was so successful as a form of government that it lasted for over 200 years.

communities. The first colony, Virginia, was founded with the first permanent English settlement in North America at Jamestown in 1607.[3] Georgia was the last to be formed, with the settlement of Savannah in 1733.

Each of the colonies was born out of a particular set of circumstances, and so each had its own character. Virginia was originally organized as a commercial venture. Its first colonists were employees of the Virginia Company, a private trading corporation. Massachusetts was first settled by people who came to North America in search of greater personal and religious freedom. Georgia was founded largely as a haven for debtors, a refuge for the victims of England's harsh poor laws.

But the differences between and among the colonies are really of little importance. Of much greater significance is the fact that all of them were shaped by their English origins. The many similarities among all 13 colonies far outweighed the differences.

Each colony was established on the basis of a **charter,** a written grant of authority from the king. Over time, these instruments of government led to the development of three different kinds of colonies: royal, proprietary, and charter.

The Thirteen Colonies, 1775

Royal colonies
Proprietary colonies
Charter colonies

miles
0 100 200 300

Interpreting Maps Despite the different circumstances surrounding the settlement of each colony, they all shared a common English background. *How were royal colonies governed?*

Royal Colonies

The royal colonies were subject to the direct control of the Crown. On the eve of the American Revolution in 1775, there were eight: New Hampshire, Massachusetts, New York, New Jersey, Virginia, North Carolina, South Carolina, and Georgia.

The Virginia colony did not enjoy the quick success its sponsors had promised. So, in 1624, the king revoked the London Company's charter, and Virginia became the first royal colony. Later, as the original charters of other colonies were canceled or withdrawn for a variety of reasons, they became royal colonies.

A pattern of government gradually emerged for each of the royal colonies. The king named a governor to serve as the colony's chief executive. A council, also named by the king, served as an advisory body to the royal governor. In time, the governor's council became the upper house of the colonial legislature. It also became the highest court in the colony. The lower house of a **bicameral** (two-house) legislature was elected by those property owners qualified to vote.[4] It

---

[3]St. Augustine, Florida, is the oldest continuously populated European settlement in what is now the United States. St. Augustine was founded by Pedro Menéndez in 1565 to establish Spanish authority in the region.

[4]The Virginia legislature held its first meeting in the church at Jamestown on July 30, 1619, and was the first representative body to meet in the North American English colonies. It was made up of burgesses—that is, representatives—elected from each settlement in the colony. Virginia called the lower house of its colonial legislature the House of Burgesses; South Carolina, the House of Commons; Massachusetts, the House of Representatives.

owed much of its influence to the fact that it shared with the governor and his council the power of the purse—that is, the power to tax and spend. The governor, advised by the council, appointed the judges for the colony's courts.

The laws passed by the legislature had to be approved by the governor and the Crown. Royal governors often ruled with a stern hand, following instructions from London. Much of the resentment that finally flared into revolution was fanned by their actions.

The Proprietary Colonies

By 1775, there were three **proprietary** colonies: Maryland, Pennsylvania, and Delaware.[5] These colonies were organized by a proprietor, a person to whom the king had made a grant of land. By charter, that land could be settled and governed much as the proprietor (owner) chose. In 1632 the king had granted Maryland to Lord Baltimore and in 1681, Pennsylvania to William Penn. In 1682 Penn also acquired Delaware.

The governments of these three colonies were much like those in the royal colonies. The governor, however, was appointed by the proprietor. In Maryland and Delaware, the legislatures were bicameral. In Pennsylvania, the legislature was a **unicameral** (one-house) body. There, the governor's council did not act as one house of the

---

[5]New York, New Jersey, North Carolina, South Carolina, and Georgia also began as proprietary colonies. Each later became a royal colony.

legislature. As in the royal colonies, appeals from the decisions of the proprietary colonies could be carried to the king in London.

The Charter Colonies

Connecticut and Rhode Island were charter colonies. They were based on charters granted in 1662 and 1663, respectively, to the colonists themselves.[6] They were largely self-governing.

The governors of Connecticut and Rhode Island were elected each year by the white, male property owners in each colony. Although the king's approval was required before the governor could take office, it was not often asked. Laws made by their bicameral legislatures were not subject to the governor's veto nor was the Crown's approval needed. Judges in charter colonies were appointed by the legislature, but appeals could be taken from the colonial courts to the king.

The Connecticut and the Rhode Island charters were so liberal for their time that, with independence, they were kept with only minor changes as State constitutions—until 1818 and 1843, respectively. In fact, many historians say that had Britain allowed the other colonies the same freedoms and self-government, the Revolution might never have occurred.

---

[6]The Massachusetts Bay Colony was established as the first charter colony in 1629. Its charter was later revoked and Massachusetts became a royal colony in 1691. Religious dissidents from Massachusetts founded Connecticut in 1633 and Rhode Island in 1636.

Section 1 Assessment

Key Terms and Main Ideas

1. Explain the concepts of ordered government, **limited government,** and **representative government.**
2. What were some of the fundamental rights and principles established in the **Magna Carta,** the **Petition of Right,** and the **English Bill of Rights?**
3. Identify and describe the three types of government in the English colonies.
4. Explain the difference between a **bicameral** and a **unicameral** legislative body.

Critical Thinking

5. **Testing Conclusions** The concept of limited government would not have developed in England without the signing of

the Magna Carta and the Petition of Right. To what degree is this an accurate statement?
6. **Making Comparisons** In what ways were the colonial governments similar? How did they differ?

 Take It to the Net

7. Find out more about colonial charters. What rights and privileges did charters grant to colonists? Pick one charter and write a paragraph explaining why it was important for the development of that colony. Use the links provided in the Social Studies area at the following Web site for help in completing this activity. **www.phschool.com**

The Magna Carta

Signed by England's King John in 1215, the Magna Carta (Great Charter) was the first document to limit the power of England's monarchs. The result of tough negotiations between the king and rebellious nobles, the Magna Carta established the principle that rulers are subject to law—a major step toward constitutional government.

King John signs the Magna Carta.

We . . . by this our present Charter, have confirmed, for us and our heirs forever: —

1. That the English Church shall be free and shall have her whole rights and her liberties inviolable [secure from harm]. . . .

9. Neither we nor our bailiffs shall seize any land or rent for any debt while the chattels [possessions] of the debtor are sufficient for the payment of the debt. . . .

12. No scutage [tax] or aid [subsidy] shall be imposed in our kingdom, unless by the common counsel of our kingdom. . . .

14. And also to have the common council of the kingdom to assess and aid, . . . and for the assessing of scutages, we will cause to be summoned the archbishops, bishops, abbots, earls, and great barons, . . . And besides, we will cause to be summoned . . . all those who hold of us in chief, at a certain day . . . and to a certain place; and in all the letters of summons, we will express the cause of the summons; and the summons being thus made, the business shall proceed on the day appointed, according to the counsel of those who shall be present, although all who have been summoned have not come. . . .

39. No free-man shall be seized, or imprisoned, or dispossessed, or outlawed, or in any way destroyed; nor will we condemn him, nor will we commit him to prison, excepting by the legal judgment of his peers, or by the laws of the land.

40. To none will we sell, to none will we deny, to none will we delay right or justice.

41. All merchants shall have safety and security in coming into England, and going out of England, and in staying and in traveling through England . . . to buy and sell, . . . excepting in the time of war, and if they be of a country at war against us. . . .

42. It shall be lawful to any person . . . to go out of our kingdom, and to return safely and securely, by land or by water, saving his allegiance to us, unless it be in time of war, for some short space, for the common good of the kingdom. . . .

52. If any have been disseised [deprived] or dispossessed by us, without a legal verdict of their peers, of their lands, castles, liberties, or rights, we will immediately restore these things to them. . . .

63. Wherefore our will is . . . that the men in our kingdom have and hold the aforesaid liberties, rights, and concessions . . . fully and entirely, to them and their heirs, . . . in all things and places forever.

Analyzing Primary Sources

1. What basic American right has its origins in Article 39 of the Magna Carta?
2. Which article provides the basis for the Fifth Amendment to the Constitution, which states that no person can "be deprived of life, liberty, or property, without due process of law"?
3. What limits does Article 12 place on the king's power to tax?

2 The Coming of Independence

Section Preview

OBJECTIVES

1. **Explain** how Britain's colonial policies contributed to the growth of self-government in the colonies.
2. **Identify** some of the steps that led to growing feelings of colonial unity.
3. **Compare** the outcomes of the First and Second Continental Congresses.
4. **Analyze** the ideas in the Declaration of Independence.
5. **Describe** the drafting of the first State constitutions and summarize the constitutions' common features.

WHY IT MATTERS

Changes in British colonial policies led to resentment in the colonies and eventually to the American Revolution. Ideas expressed in the early State constitutions influenced the development of the governmental system under which we live today.

POLITICAL DICTIONARY

★ confederation
★ Albany Plan of Union
★ delegate
★ boycott
★ repeal
★ popular sovereignty

"**W**e must all hang together, or assuredly we shall all hang separately." Benjamin Franklin is said to have spoken these words on July 4, 1776, as he and the other members of the Second Continental Congress approved the Declaration of Independence. Those who heard him may have chuckled. But they also may have felt a shiver, for Franklin's humor carried a deadly serious message.

In this section, you will follow the events that led to the momentous decision to break with Great Britain.[7] You will also consider the new State governments that were established with the coming of Independence.

▲ Colonists who made their tea in this pot voiced their opposition to the Stamp Act.

Britain's Colonial Policies

The 13 colonies, which had been separately established, were separately controlled under the king, largely through the Privy Council and the Board of Trade in London. Parliament took little part in the management of the colonies. Although it did become more and more interested in matters of trade, it left matters of colonial administration almost entirely to the Crown.[8]

Over the century and a half that followed the first settlement at Jamestown, the colonies developed within that framework of royal control. In theory, they were governed in all important matters from London. But London was more than 3,000 miles away, and it took nearly two months to sail that distance across a peril-filled Atlantic. So, in practice, the colonists became used to a large measure of self-government.

Each colonial legislature began to assume broad lawmaking powers. Many found the power of the purse to be very effective. They often bent a royal governor to their will by not voting the money for his salary until he came to terms with them. As one member of New Jersey's Assembly put it: "Let us keep the dogges poore, and we'll make them do as we please."

---

[7]England became Great Britain by the Act of Union with Scotland in 1707.

[8]Much of English political history can be told in terms of the centuries-long struggle for supremacy between monarch and Parliament. That conflict was largely settled by England's Glorious Revolution of 1688, but it did continue through the American colonial period and into the nineteenth century. However, Parliament paid little attention to the American colonies until very late in the colonial period.

By the mid-1700s, the relationship between Britain and the colonies had become, in fact if not in form, federal. This meant that the central government in London was responsible for colonial defense and for foreign affairs. It also provided a uniform system of money and credit and a common market for colonial trade. Beyond that, the colonies were allowed a fairly wide amount of self-rule. Little was taken from them in direct taxes to pay for the central government. The few regulations set by Parliament, mostly about trade, were largely ignored.

This was soon to change. Shortly after George III came to the throne in 1760, Britain began to deal more firmly with the colonies. Restrictive trading acts were expanded and enforced. New taxes were imposed, mostly to support British troops in North America.

Many colonists took strong exception to these moves. They objected to taxes imposed on them from afar. This arrangement, they claimed, was "taxation without representation." They saw little need for the costly presence of British troops on North American soil, since the French had been defeated and their power broken in the French and Indian War (1754–1763).

The colonists considered themselves British subjects loyal to the Crown. They refused, however, to accept Parliament's claim that it had a right to control their local affairs.

The king's ministers were poorly informed and stubborn. They pushed ahead with their policies, despite the resentments they stirred in America. Within a few years, the colonists faced a fateful choice: to submit or to revolt.

Growing Colonial Unity

A decision to revolt was not one to be taken lightly—or alone. The colonies would need to learn to work together if they wanted to succeed. Indeed long before the 1770s, several attempts had been made to promote cooperation among the colonies.

Early Attempts
In 1643 the Massachusetts Bay, Plymouth, New Haven, and Connecticut settlements formed the New England Confederation. A **confederation** is a joining of several groups for a common purpose. In the New England Confederation, the

Voices on Government

Benjamin Franklin dedicated years to public service, including time as a delegate to the Second Continental Congress, a commissioner to France during the War for Independence, and a member of the Constitutional Convention. Franklin proposed the Albany Plan of Union to provide for the defense of the American colonies. In his autobiography, he spoke of its defeat and defended his plan:

❝ *The different and contrary Reasons of dislike to my Plan, makes me suspect that it was really the true Medium; and I am still of Opinion it would have been happy for both Sides the Water if it had been adopted. The Colonies so united would have been sufficiently strong to have defended themselves; there would then have been no need of Troops from England; of course the subsequent Pretence for Taxing America, and the bloody Contest it occasioned, would have been avoided.* ❞

Evaluating the Quotation
What did Franklin see as the ultimate result of the failure to adopt the Albany Plan of Union? Do you think this was a reasonable conclusion?

settlements formed a "league of friendship" for defense against the Native Americans. As the danger from Native Americans passed and friction among the settlements grew, the confederation lost importance and finally dissolved in 1684.

In 1696 William Penn offered an elaborate plan for intercolonial cooperation, largely in trade, defense, and criminal matters. It received little attention and was soon forgotten.

The Albany Plan
In 1754 the British Board of Trade called a meeting of seven of the northern colonies at Albany: Connecticut, Maryland, Massachusetts, New Hampshire, New York, Pennsylvania, and Rhode Island. The main purpose of the meeting was to discuss the problems of colonial trade and the danger of attacks by the French and their Native American allies. Here, Benjamin Franklin offered what came to be known as the **Albany Plan of Union.**

In his plan, Franklin proposed the formation of an annual congress of **delegates** (representatives) from each of the 13 colonies. That body would have the power to raise military and naval forces, make war and peace with the Native Americans, regulate trade with them, tax, and collect customs duties.

Franklin's plan was ahead of its time. It was agreed to by the representatives attending the Albany meeting, but it was turned down by the colonies and by the Crown. Franklin's plan was to be remembered later.

The Stamp Act Congress

Britain's harsh tax and trade policies of the 1760s fanned resentment in the colonies. Parliament had passed a number of new laws, among them the Stamp Act of 1765. That law required the use of tax stamps on all legal documents, on certain business agreements, and on newspapers.

The new taxes were widely denounced, in part because the rates were perceived as severe, but largely because they amounted to "taxation without representation." In October of 1765, nine colonies—all except Georgia, New Hampshire, North Carolina, and Virginia—sent delegates to the Stamp Act Congress in New York. They prepared a strong protest, called the Declaration of Rights and Grievances, against the new British policies and sent it to the king. These actions marked the first time a significant number of the colonies had joined to oppose the British government.

▲ This colored engraving, printed in 1793, is the earliest known American depiction of the Boston Tea Party. *Critical Thinking* **What did the colonists hope to accomplish by destroying the cargo of tea?**

Parliament repealed the Stamp Act, but frictions mounted. New laws were passed and new policies were made to tie the colonies more closely to London. Colonists showed their resentment and anger in wholesale evasion of the laws. Mob violence erupted at several ports, and many colonists supported a **boycott** of English goods. A boycott is a refusal to buy or sell certain products or services. On March 5, 1770, British troops in Boston fired on a jeering crowd, killing five, in what came to be known as the Boston Massacre.

Organized resistance was carried on through Committees of Correspondence, which had grown out of a group formed by Samuel Adams in Boston in 1772. These committees soon spread throughout the colonies, providing a network for cooperation and the exchange of information among the patriots.

Protests multiplied. The famous Boston Tea Party took place on December 16, 1773. A group of men, disguised as Native Americans, boarded three tea ships in Boston harbor and dumped the cargo into the sea to protest British control of the tea trade.

The First Continental Congress

In the spring of 1774, Parliament passed yet another set of laws, this time to punish the colonists for the troubles in Boston and elsewhere. These new laws, denounced in America as the Intolerable Acts, prompted widespread calls for a meeting of all the colonies.

Delegates from every colony except Georgia met in Philadelphia on September 5, 1774. Many of the ablest men of the day were there: Samuel Adams and John Adams of Massachusetts; Roger Sherman of Connecticut; Stephen Hopkins of Rhode Island; John Dickinson and Joseph Galloway of Pennsylvania; John Jay and Philip Livingston of New York; George Washington, Richard Henry Lee, and Patrick Henry of Virginia; and John Rutledge of South Carolina.

For nearly two months the members of that First Continental

▲ Washington once complained that his soldiers were forced to "eat every kind of horse food but hay." He won the respect of the men who served under his command when he demanded that Congress provide better treatment for the army. *Critical Thinking How does this nineteenth-century engraving of Washington and his troops welcoming a train of supplies reinforce Washington's image as a strong leader?*

Congress discussed the worsening situation and debated plans for action. They sent a Declaration of Rights, protesting Britain's colonial policies, to King George III. The delegates urged each of the colonies to refuse all trade with England until the hated taxes and trade regulations were **repealed**, or revoked. The delegates also called for the creation of local committees to enforce that boycott.

The meeting adjourned on October 26, with a call for a second congress to be convened the following May. Over the next several months, all the colonial legislatures, including Georgia's, gave their support to the actions of the First Continental Congress.

The Second Continental Congress

During the fall and winter of 1774–1775, the British government continued to refuse to compromise, let alone reverse, its colonial policies. It reacted to the Declaration of Rights as it had to other expressions of colonial discontent—with even stricter and more repressive measures.

The Second Continental Congress met in Philadelphia on May 10, 1775. By then, the Revolution had begun. The "shot heard 'round the world" had been fired. The battles of Lexington and Concord had been fought three weeks earlier, on April 19.

Representatives

Each of the 13 colonies sent representatives to the Congress. Most of those who had attended the First Continental Congress were again present. Most notable among the newcomers were Benjamin Franklin of Pennsylvania and John Hancock of Massachusetts.

Hancock was chosen president of the Congress.[9] Almost at once, a continental army was created, and George Washington was appointed its commander in chief. Thomas Jefferson then took Washington's place in the Virginia delegation.

Our First National Government

The Second Continental Congress became, by force of circumstance, the nation's first national government. However, it rested on no constitutional base. It was condemned by the British as an unlawful assembly and a den of traitors. But it was supported by the force of public opinion and practical necessity.

The Second Continental Congress served as the first government of the United States for five fateful years, from the formal adoption of the

---

[9]Peyton Randolph, who had also served as president of the First Continental Congress, was originally chosen for the office. He resigned on May 24, however, because the Virginia House of Burgesses, of which he was the speaker, had been called into session. Hancock was then elected to succeed him.

Declaration of Independence in July 1776 until the Articles of Confederation went into effect on March 1, 1781. During that time the Second Continental Congress fought a war, raised armies and a navy, borrowed funds, bought supplies, created a money system, made treaties with foreign powers, and did those other things that any government would have had to do in the circumstances.

The unicameral Congress exercised both legislative and executive powers. In legislative matters, each colony—later, State—had one vote. Executive functions were handled by committees of delegates.

The Declaration of Independence

Slightly more than a year after the Revolution began, Richard Henry Lee of Virginia proposed to the Congress:

PRIMARY Sources *"Resolved, That these United Colonies are, and of right ought to be, free and independent States, that they are absolved from all allegiance to the British Crown, and that all political connection between them and the State of Great Britain is, and ought to be, totally dissolved."*

—Resolution of June 7, 1776

Congress named a committee of five— Benjamin Franklin, John Adams, Roger Sherman, Robert Livingston, and Thomas Jefferson—to prepare a proclamation of independence. Their momentous product, the Declaration of Independence, was almost wholly the work of Jefferson.

On July 2, the final break came. The delegates agreed to Lee's resolution—but only after spirited debate, for many of the delegates had serious doubts about the wisdom of a complete separation from England. Two days later, on July 4, 1776, they adopted the Declaration of Independence, proclaiming the existence of the new nation.

The Declaration announces the independence of the United States in its first paragraph. Much of the balance of the document—nearly two thirds of it—speaks of "the repeated injuries and usurpations" that led the colonists to revolt. At its heart, the Declaration proclaims:

PRIMARY Sources *"We hold these truths to be self-evident, that all men are created equal, that they are endowed by their Creator with certain unalienable Rights, that among these are Life, Liberty and the pursuit of Happiness. That to secure these rights, Governments are instituted among Men, deriving their just powers from the consent of the governed; That whenever any Form of Government becomes destructive of these ends it is the Right of the People to alter or to abolish it, and to institute new Government, laying its foundations on such principles and organizing its powers in such form, as to them shall seem most likely to effect their Safety and Happiness."*

—The Unanimous Declaration of the Thirteen United States of America

With these brave words, the United States of America was born. The 13 colonies became free and independent States. The 56 men who signed the Declaration sealed it with this final sentence:

"And for the support of this Declaration, with a firm reliance on the protection of Divine Providence, we mutually pledge to each other, our lives, our Fortunes, and our sacred Honor."

The First State Constitutions

In January 1776, New Hampshire adopted a constitution to replace its royal charter. Less than three months later, South Carolina followed suit. Then, on May 10, nearly two months before the adoption of the Declaration of Independence, the Congress urged each of the colonies to adopt: "such governments as shall, in the opinion of the representatives of the people, best conduce to the happiness and safety of their constituents."

Drafting State Constitutions

In 1776 and 1777, most of the States adopted written constitutions—bodies of fundamental laws setting out the principles, structures, and processes of their governments. Assemblies or conventions were commonly used to draft and then adopt these new documents.

Massachusetts set a lasting example in the constitution-making process. There, a convention submitted its work to the voters for ratification. The Massachusetts constitution of 1780 is the oldest of the present-day State constitutions. In fact, it is the oldest written constitution in force anywhere in the world today.[10]

Common Features

The first State constitutions differed, sometimes widely, in detail. Yet they shared many similar features. The most common features were the principles of **popular sovereignty** (government can exist only with the consent of the governed), limited government, civil rights and liberties, and separation of powers and checks and balances. These principles are outlined in detail in the table at right.

The new State constitutions were rather brief documents. For the most part, they were declarations of principle and statements of limitation on governmental power. Memories of the royal governors were fresh, and the new State governors were given little real power. Most of the authority that was granted to State government was placed in the legislature. Elective terms of office were made purposely short, seldom more than one or two years. The right to vote was limited to those adult males who could meet rigid qualifications, including property ownership.

---

[10]From independence until that constitution became effective in 1780, Massachusetts relied on its colonial charter, in force prior to 1691, as its fundamental law.

Common Features of State Constitutions

POPULAR SOVEREIGNTY	The principle of popular sovereignty was the basis for every new State constitution. That principle says that government can exist and function only with the consent of the governed. The people hold power and the people are sovereign.
LIMITED GOVERNMENT	The concept of limited government was a major feature of each State constitution. The powers delegated to government were granted reluctantly and hedged with many restrictions.
CIVIL RIGHTS AND LIBERTIES	In every State it was made clear that the sovereign people held certain rights that the government must respect at all times. Seven of the new constitutions contained a bill of rights, setting out the "unalienable rights" held by the people.
SEPARATION OF POWERS AND CHECKS AND BALANCES	The powers granted to the new State governments were purposely divided among three branches: executive, legislative, and judicial. Each branch was given powers with which to check (restrain the actions of) the other branches of the government.

Interpreting Tables Most of the newly created States adopted written constitutions in the two years following the Declaration of Independence. *Why did the first State constitutions share several common features?*

We shall return to the subject of State constitutions later, in Chapter 24. For now, note this very important point: The earliest of these documents were, within a very few years, to have a marked impact on the drafting of the Constitution of the United States.

Section 2 Assessment

Key Terms and Main Ideas

1. Why did some colonists support a **boycott** of English goods?
2. What was the **Albany Plan of Union** and how was it received by the colonies and by the Crown?
3. Explain the concept of **popular sovereignty.**
4. What was the outcome of the First Continental Congress?
5. In what ways did the Second Continental Congress serve as the first national government?

Critical Thinking

6. **Distinguishing Fact from Opinion** The Declaration of Independence states that all men are endowed "with certain unalienable Rights, that among these are Life, Liberty and the pursuit of Happiness." Is this statement a fact or opinion? Explain your answer.
7. **Expressing Problems Clearly** What problems arose from changes in British policy toward the colonies in the 1760s?

Take It to the Net

8. Read the Albany Plan as proposed by Benjamin Franklin. Create a list of three ways that this plan could help the colonies. Next, create a list of three ways the Albany Plan could hurt the colonies. Use the links provided in the Social Studies area at the following Web site for help in completing this activity. www.phschool.com

The Declaration *of* Independence

In Congress, July 4, 1776

The Unanimous Declaration of the Thirteen United States of America

▲ The Declaration of Independence was largely the work of Thomas Jefferson, who chaired the five-person committee assigned to the task.

When in the Course of human events, it becomes necessary for one people to dissolve the political bands which have connected them with another, and to assume among the powers of the earth, the separate and equal station to which the Laws of nature and of Nature's God entitle them, a decent respect to the opinions of mankind requires that they should declare the causes which impel them to the separation.

We hold these truths to be self-evident, that all men are created equal, that they are endowed by their Creator with certain unalienable Rights, that among these are Life, Liberty and the pursuit of Happiness. That to secure these rights, Governments are instituted among Men, deriving their just powers from the consent of the governed; That whenever any Form of Government becomes destructive of these ends it is the Right of the People to alter or to abolish it, and to institute new Government, laying its foundation on such principles and organizing its powers in such form, as to them shall seem most likely to effect their Safety and Happiness. Prudence, indeed, will dictate that Governments long established should not be changed for light and transient causes; and accordingly all experience hath shown, that mankind are more disposed to suffer, while evils are sufferable, than to right themselves by abolishing the forms to which they are accustomed. But when a long train of abuses and usurpations, pursuing invariably the same Object evinces a design to reduce them under absolute Despotism, it is their right, it is their duty, to throw off such Government, and to provide new Guards for their future security.

Such has been the patient sufferance of these Colonies; and such is now the necessity which constrains them to alter their former Systems of Government. The history of the present King of Great Britain is a history of repeated injuries and usurpations, all having in direct object the establishment of an absolute Tyranny over these States. To prove this, let Facts be submitted to a candid world.

He has refused his Assent to Laws, the most wholesome and necessary for the public good.

He has forbidden his Governors to pass Laws of immediate and pressing importance, unless suspended in their operation till his Assent should be obtained; and when so suspended, he has utterly neglected to attend to them.

He has refused to pass other Laws for the accommodation of large districts of people, unless those people would relinquish the right of Representation in the Legislature, a right inestimable to them and formidable to tyrants only.

He has called together legislative bodies at places unusual, uncomfortable, and distant from the depository of their Public Records, for the sole purpose of fatiguing them into compliance with his measures.

He has dissolved Representative Houses repeatedly, for opposing with manly firmness his invasions on the rights of the people.

He has refused for a long time, after such dissolutions, to cause others to be elected; whereby the Legislative powers, incapable of Annihilation, have returned to the People at large for their exercise; the State remaining in the mean time exposed to all the dangers of invasions from without, and convulsions within.

He has endeavored to prevent the population of these States; for that purpose obstructing the Laws for Naturalization of Foreigners; refusing to pass others to encourage their migration hither, and raising the conditions of new Appropriations of Lands.

He has obstructed the Administration of Justice, by refusing his Assent to Laws for establishing Judiciary powers.

He has made Judges dependent on his Will alone for the tenure of their offices, and the amount and payment of their salaries.

He has erected a multitude of New Offices, and sent hither swarms of Officers to harass our people and eat out their substance.

He has kept among us in time of peace, Standing Armies, without the Consent of our legislatures.

He has affected to render the Military independent of, and superior to, the Civil Power.

He has combined with others to subject us to a jurisdiction foreign to our constitutions, and unacknowledged by our laws; giving his Assent to their Acts of pretended Legislation:

For quartering large bodies of armed troops among us;

For protecting them, by a mock Trial, from punishment for any Murders which they should commit on the Inhabitants of these States;

For cutting off our Trade with all parts of the world;

For imposing Taxes on us without our Consent;

For depriving us, in many cases, of the benefits of Trial by Jury;

For transporting us beyond Seas to be tried for pretended offenses;

For abolishing the free System of English Laws in a neighboring Province, establishing therein an Arbitrary government, and enlarging

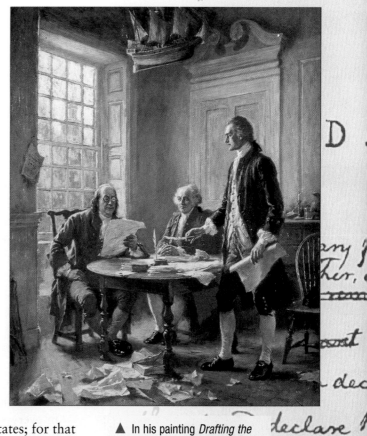

▲ In his painting *Drafting the Declaration of Independence,* artist Jean Leon Gerome Ferris (1888–1930) shows members of the committee reviewing Jefferson's proposed Declaration.

Declaration

▲ This hand-colored woodcut shows the scene at the signing of the Declaration of Independence.

▼ John Hancock was the first to sign the Declaration of Independence.

its Boundaries so as to render it at once an example and fit instrument for introducing the same absolute rule into these Colonies;

For taking away our Charters, abolishing our most valuable Laws, and altering fundamentally the Forms of our Governments;

For suspending our own Legislatures, and declaring themselves invested with Power to legislate for us in all cases whatsoever.

He has abdicated Government here, by declaring us out of his Protection, and waging War against us.

He has plundered our seas, ravaged our Coasts, burned our towns, and destroyed the lives of our people.

He is at this time transporting large Armies of foreign mercenaries to complete the works of death, desolation and tyranny, already begun with circumstances of Cruelty and perfidy scarcely paralleled in the most barbarous ages, and totally unworthy the Head of a civilized nation.

He has constrained our fellow Citizens taken Captive on the high Seas to bear Arms against their Country, to become the executioners of their friends and Brethren, or to fall themselves by their Hands.

He has excited domestic insurrections amongst us, and has endeavored to bring on the inhabitants of our frontiers the merciless Indian Savages whose known rule of warfare, is an undistinguished destruction of all ages, sexes, and conditions.

In every stage of these Oppressions We have Petitioned for Redress in the most humble terms. Our repeated Petitions have been answered only by repeated injury. A Prince, whose character is thus marked by every act which may define a Tyrant, is unfit to be the ruler of a free People.

Nor have We been wanting in attentions to our British brethren. We have warned them from time to time of attempts by their legislature to extend an unwarrantable jurisdiction over us. We have reminded them of the circumstances of our emigration and settlement here. We have appealed to their native justice and magnanimity, and we have conjured them by the ties of our common kindred to disavow these usurpations, which, would inevitably interrupt our connections and correspondence. They too have been deaf to the voice of justice and of consanguinity. We must, therefore, acquiesce in the necessity, which denounces our Separation, and hold them, as we hold the rest of mankind, Enemies in War, in Peace Friends.

We, therefore, the Representatives of the United States of America, in General Congress, Assembled, appealing to the Supreme Judge of the world for the rectitude of our intentions, do, in the Name, and by the Authority of the good People of these Colonies, solemnly publish and declare, That these United Colonies are, and of right ought to be Free and Independent States; that they are Absolved from all Allegiance to the British Crown, and that all political connection between them and the State of Great Britain, is and ought to be totally dissolved, and that as Free and Independent States, they have full Power to levy

War, conclude Peace, contract Alliances, establish Commerce, and to do all other Acts and Things which Independent States may of right do. And for the support of this Declaration, with a firm reliance on the protection of Divine Providence, we mutually pledge to each other our Lives, our Fortunes and our sacred Honor.

John Hancock
President of the Continental Congress 1775–1777

New Hampshire
Josiah Bartlett
William Whipple
Mathew Thornton

Massachusetts Bay
Samuel Adams
John Adams
Robert Treat Paine
Elbridge Gerry

Rhode Island
Stephan Hopkins
William Ellery

Connecticut
Roger Sherman
Samuel Huntington
William Williams
Oliver Wolcott

New York
William Floyd
Philip Livingston
Francis Lewis
Lewis Morris

New Jersey
Richard Stockton
John Witherspoon
Francis Hopkinson
John Hart
Abraham Clark

Delaware
Caesar Rodney
George Read
Thomas M'Kean

Maryland
Samuel Chase
William Paca
Thomas Stone
Charles Carroll of
   Carrollton

Virginia
George Wythe
Richard Henry Lee
Thomas Jefferson
Benjamin Harrison
Thomas Nelson, Jr.
Francis Lightfoot Lee
Carter Braxton

Pennsylvania
Robert Morris
Benjamin Rush
Benjamin Franklin
John Morton
George Clymer
James Smith
George Taylor
James Wilson
George Ross

North Carolina
William Hooper
Joseph Hewes
John Penn

South Carolina
Edward Rutledge
Thomas Heyward, Jr.
Thomas Lynch, Jr.
Arthur Middleton

Georgia
Button Gwinnett
Lyman Hall
George Walton

Reviewing the Declaration

Vocabulary
Choose ten words in the Declaration with which you are unfamiliar. Look them up in the dictionary. Then, on a piece of paper, copy the sentence in the Declaration in which each unfamiliar word is used. After the sentence, write the definition of the unfamiliar word.

Comprehension
1. Which truths in the second paragraph are "self-evident"?
2. Name the three unalienable rights listed in the Declaration.
3. From what source do governments derive their "just powers"?
4. In the series of paragraphs beginning, "He has refused his Assent," to whom does the word "He" refer?

5. According to the Declaration, what powers does the United States have "as Free and Independent States"?

Critical Thinking
6. **Recognizing Cause and Effect** Why do you think the colonists were unhappy with the fact that their judges' salaries were paid by the king?
7. **Identifying Assumptions** Do you think that the statement "All men are created equal" was intended to apply to all human beings? Explain your reasoning.
8. **Drawing Conclusions** What evidence is there that the colonists had already unsuccessfully voiced concerns to the king?

Section Preview

OBJECTIVES

1. **Describe** the structure of the government set up under the Articles of Confederation.
2. **Explain** why the weaknesses of the Articles led to a critical period for the government in the 1780s.
3. **Describe** how a growing need for a stronger national government led to plans for a Constitutional Convention.

WHY IT MATTERS

The Articles of Confederation established a fairly weak central government, which led to conflicts among the States. The turmoil of the Critical Period of the 1780s led to the creation of a stronger National Government.

POLITICAL DICTIONARY

★ **Articles of Confederation**
★ **ratification**
★ **presiding officer**

The First and Second Continental Congresses rested on no legal base. They were called in haste to meet an emergency, and they were intended to be temporary. Something more regular and permanent was clearly needed. In this section, you will look at the first attempt to establish a lasting government for the new nation.

The Articles of Confederation

Richard Henry Lee's resolution leading to the Declaration of Independence also had called on the Second Continental Congress to propose "a plan of confederation." Off and on, for 17 months, they considered the problem of uniting the former colonies. Finally, on November 15, 1777, the delegates approved a plan of government called the **Articles of Confederation.**

The Articles of Confederation established "a firm league of friendship" among the States. Under this plan, each State kept "its sovereignty, freedom, and independence, and every Power, Jurisdiction, and right . . . not . . . expressly delegated to the United States, in Congress assembled." The States came together "for their common defense, the security of their Liberties, and their mutual and general welfare. . . ."

The Articles did not go into effect immediately, however. The **ratification,** or formal approval, of each of the 13 States was needed first. Eleven States agreed to the document within a year. Delaware added its approval in February 1779. But Maryland did not ratify until March 1, 1781, and the Second Continental Congress declared the Articles effective on that date.

Governmental Structure

The government set up by the Articles was simple indeed. A Congress was the sole body created. It was unicameral, made up of delegates chosen yearly by the States in whatever way their legislatures might direct. Each State had one vote in the Congress, whatever its population or wealth.

The Articles established no executive or judicial branch. These functions were to be handled by committees of the Congress. Each year the

▶ Articles of Confederation

Congress would choose one of its members as its president. That person would be its **presiding officer** (chair), but not the president of the United States. Civil officers such as postmasters were to be appointed by the Congress.

Powers of Congress

Several important powers were given to the Congress. It could make war and peace; send and receive ambassadors; make treaties; borrow money; set up a money system; establish post offices; build a navy; raise an army by asking the States for troops; fix uniform standards of weights and measures; and settle disputes among the States.

State Obligations

By agreeing to the Articles, the States pledged to obey the Articles and acts of the Congress. They would provide the funds and troops requested by the Congress; treat citizens of other States fairly and equally with their own; and give full faith and credit to the public acts, records, and judicial proceedings of every other State. In addition, the States agreed to surrender fugitives from justice to one another; submit their disputes to Congress for settlement; and allow open travel and trade between and among the States.

Beyond these few obligations, the States retained those powers not explicitly given to the Congress. They, not the Congress, were primarily responsible for protecting life and property. States were also accountable for promoting the general welfare of the people.

Weaknesses

The powers of the Congress appear, at first glance, to have been considerable. Several important powers were missing, however. Their omission, together with other weaknesses, soon proved the Articles inadequate to the needs of the time.

The Congress did not have the power to tax. It could raise money only by borrowing and by asking the States for funds. Borrowing was, at best, a poor source. The Second Continental Congress had borrowed heavily to support the costs of fighting the Revolution, and many of those debts had not been paid. And, while the Articles remained in force, not one State came close to meeting the financial requests made by the Congress.

Weaknesses of the Articles of Confederation

- One vote for each State, regardless of size.
- Congress powerless to lay and collect taxes or duties.
- Congress powerless to regulate foreign and interstate commerce.
- No executive to enforce acts of Congress.
- No national court system.
- Amendment only with consent of all States.
- A 9/13 majority required to pass laws.
- Articles only a "firm league of friendship."

Interpreting Tables The thirst for independence made the new States wary of strong central government. *How is this caution reflected in the weaknesses built into the Articles of Confederation?*

Nor did the Congress have the power to regulate trade between the States. This lack of a central mechanism to regulate the young nation's commerce was one of the major factors that led to the adoption of the Constitution.

The Congress was further limited by a lack of power to make the States obey the Articles of Confederation or the laws it made. Congress could exercise the powers it did have only with the consent of 9 of the 13 State delegations. Finally, the Articles themselves could be changed only with the consent of all 13 of the State legislatures. This procedure proved an impossible task; not one amendment was ever added to the Articles of Confederation.

The Critical Period, the 1780s

The long Revolutionary War finally ended on October 19, 1781. America's victory was confirmed by the signing of the Treaty of Paris in 1783. Peace, however, brought the new nation's economic and political problems into sharp focus. Problems, caused by the weaknesses of the Articles of Confederation, soon surfaced.

With a central government unable to act, the States bickered among themselves and grew increasingly jealous and suspicious of one another. They often refused to support the new central government, financially and in almost every other way. Several of them made agreements with foreign governments without the approval of the

National Government, even though that was forbidden by the Articles. Most even organized their own military forces. George Washington complained, "We are one nation today and 13 tomorrow. Who will treat with us on such terms?"

The States taxed one another's goods and even banned some trade. They printed their own money, often with little backing. Economic chaos spread throughout the colonies as prices soared and sound credit vanished. Debts, public and private, went unpaid. Violence broke out in a number of places as a result of the economic chaos.

The most spectacular of these events played out in western Massachusetts in a series of incidents that came to be known as Shays' Rebellion. As economic conditions worsened, property holders, many of them small farmers, began to lose their land and possessions for lack of payment on taxes and other debts. In the fall of 1786, Daniel Shays, a former American officer in the War for Independence, and other local leaders led an uprising that forced the Supreme Court in Springfield, Massachusetts, to close. Early

▲ *Shays' Rebellion* Following the series of incidents known as Shays' Rebellion, the Supreme Court of Massachusetts condemned to death Daniel Shays and about a dozen others. Shays petitioned for and received a pardon in 1788.

the next year they unsuccessfully attacked a federal arsenal. State forces moved in to quiet the rebellion and Shays fled to Vermont. In response to the rebellion, the Massachusetts legislature eventually passed laws to ease the burden of debtors.

A Need for Stronger Government

The Articles had created a government unable to deal with the nation's troubles. Inevitably, demand grew for a stronger, more effective national government. Those who were most threatened by economic and political instability —large property owners, merchants, traders, and other creditors—soon took the lead in efforts to that end. The movement for change began to take concrete form in 1785.

Mount Vernon

Maryland and Virginia, plagued by bitter trade disputes, took the first step in the movement for change. Ignoring the Congress, the two States agreed to a conference on their trade problems. Representatives from the two States met at Alexandria, Virginia, in March 1785. At George Washington's invitation, they moved their sessions to his home at nearby Mount Vernon.

Their negotiations proved so successful that on January 21, 1786, the Virginia General Assembly called for "a joint meeting of [all of] the States to recommend a federal plan for regulating commerce."

Annapolis

That joint meeting opened at Annapolis, Maryland, on September 11, 1786. Turnout was poor, with representatives from only 5 of the 13 States attending.[11] Disappointed, but still hopeful, the convention called for yet another meeting of the States

PRIMARY *Sources* "*at Philadelphia on the second Monday in May next, to take into consideration the situation of the United States, to devise such further provisions as*

---

[11]New York, New Jersey, Pennsylvania, Delaware, and Virginia. Although New Hampshire, Massachusetts, Rhode Island, and North Carolina had appointed delegates, none attended the Annapolis meeting.

▲ **Mount Vernon** George Washington's graceful home overlooking the Potomac River served as the location for trade talks between Maryland and Virginia. The success of this meeting caused some to move for further steps toward a stronger federal government.

shall appear to them necessary to render the constitution of the Federal Government adequate to the exigencies of the Union. **"**

—Call of the Annapolis Convention

By mid-February of 1787, seven of the States had named delegates to the Philadelphia meeting. These were Delaware, Georgia, New Hampshire, New Jersey, North Carolina, Pennsylvania, and Virginia. Then on February 21, the Congress, which had been hesitating, also called upon the States to send delegates to Philadelphia

PRIMARY Sources **"** *for the sole and express purpose of revising the Articles of Confederation and reporting to Congress and the several legislatures such alterations and provisions therein as shall when agreed to in Congress and confirmed by the States render the [Articles] adequate to the exigencies of Government and the preservation of the Union.* **"**

—The United States in Congress Assembled, February 21, 1787

That Philadelphia meeting became the Constitutional Convention.

Section 3 Assessment

Key Terms and Main Ideas

1. What were the **Articles of Confederation** and what powers did they grant to Congress?
2. Before the Articles of Confederation could go into effect, how many States were needed for **ratification?**
3. Identify at least three weaknesses of the government under the Articles of Confederation.
4. What was the result of the meetings at Mount Vernon and Annapolis in 1785 and 1786?

Critical Thinking

5. **Identifying Central Issues** The Articles of Confederation contained several weaknesses. Why would the States purposefully create a weak government under the Articles?

6. **Drawing Conclusions** For what reasons is the period during which the Articles were in force called the Critical Period in American history?

 Take It to the Net

7. Review the early plans for the U.S. government and write a paragraph explaining four major differences between the Articles of Confederation and the Constitution. Explain the significance of these differences and how they affected the young nation. Use the links provided in the Social Studies area at the following Web site for help in completing this activity. **www.phschool.com**

Section Preview

OBJECTIVES

1. **Identify** the Framers of the Constitution and discuss how the delegates organized the proceedings at the Philadelphia Convention.
2. **Compare** and contrast the Virginia Plan and the New Jersey Plan for a new constitution.
3. **Summarize** the major compromises that the delegates agreed to make and the effects of those compromises.
4. **Identify** some of the sources from which the Framers of the Constitution drew inspiration.
5. **Describe** the delegates' reactions to the Constitution as they completed their work.

WHY IT MATTERS

The Framers of the Constitution created a document that addressed the major concerns of the States attending the Philadelphia Convention. By reaching compromise on items about which they disagreed, the Framers created a new National Government capable of handling the nation's problems.

POLITICAL DICTIONARY

★ **Framers**
★ **Virginia Plan**
★ **New Jersey Plan**
★ **Connecticut Compromise**
★ **Three-Fifths Compromise**
★ **Commerce and Slave Trade Compromise**

Picture this scene. It's hot—sweltering, in fact. Yet the windows are all closed to discourage eavesdroppers. Outside, soldiers keep interested onlookers at a distance. Inside, the atmosphere is tense as men exchange their views. Indeed, some become so angry that they threaten to leave the hall. A few carry out their threats.

This was the scene throughout much of the Philadelphia meeting that began on Friday, May 25, 1787.[12] Over the long summer months, the participants labored to build a new government that would best meet the needs of the nation. In this section, you will consider that meeting and its work.

▶ Delegates to the Constitutional Convention gathered in Independence Hall.

The Framers

Twelve of the 13 States, all but Rhode Island, sent delegates to Philadelphia.[13] In total, 74 delegates were chosen by the legislatures in those 12 states. For a number of reasons, however, only 55 of them actually attended the convention.

Of that 55, this much can be said: Never, before or since, has so remarkable a group been brought together in this country. Thomas Jefferson, who was not among them, called the delegates "an assembly of demi-gods."

The group of delegates who attended the Philadelphia Convention, known as the **Framers** of the Constitution, included many outstanding individuals. These were men of wide knowledge and public experience, of wealth and prestige. Their collective record of public service was truly impressive. Many of them had fought in the Revolution; 39 had been members of the Continental Congress or the Congress of the

---

[12]Not enough States were represented on the date Congress had set, Monday, May 14, to begin the meeting. The delegates who were present met and adjourned each day until Friday the 25th, when a quorum (in this case, a majority) of the States was on hand.

[13]The Rhode Island legislature was controlled by the soft-money forces, mostly debtors and small farmers who were helped by inflation and so were against a stronger central government. The New Hampshire delegation, delayed mostly by lack of funds, did not reach Philadelphia until late July.

Selected Framers of the Constitution

Name	State	Background
George Washington	Virginia	Planter, commander of the Continental Army
James Madison	Virginia	Legislator, major figure in movement to replace Articles
Edmund Randolph	Virginia	Lawyer, governor of Virginia
George Mason	Virginia	Planter, author of Virginia's Declaration of Rights
Benjamin Franklin	Pennsylvania	Writer, printer, inventor, legislator, diplomat
Gouverneur Morris	Pennsylvania	Lawyer, merchant, legislator
Robert Morris	Pennsylvania	Merchant, major financier of the Revolution
James Wilson	Pennsylvania	Lawyer, legislator, close student of politics, history
Alexander Hamilton	New York	Lawyer, legislator, champion of stronger central government
William Paterson	New Jersey	Lawyer, legislator, attorney general of New Jersey
Elbridge Gerry	Massachusetts	Merchant, legislator, major investor in land, government securities
Rufus King	Massachusetts	Legislator, opponent of extensive changes to Articles
Luther Martin	Maryland	Lawyer, legislator, attorney general of Maryland
Oliver Ellsworth	Connecticut	Lawyer, legislator, judge, theologian
Roger Sherman	Connecticut	Merchant, mayor of New Haven, legislator, judge
John Dickinson	Delaware	Lawyer, historian, major advocate of independence
John Rutledge	South Carolina	Lawyer, legislator, principal author of South Carolina's constitution
Charles Pinckney	South Carolina	Lawyer, legislator, leader in move to replace Articles

Interpreting Tables In reference to creating the Constitution, James Madison noted that considering "the natural diversity of human opinions on all new and complicated subjects, it is impossible to consider the degree of concord which ultimately prevailed as less than a miracle." *What similarities and differences can you see in the Framers' backgrounds? Do you think their personal experiences helped or hurt their ability to draft the Constitution?*

Confederation, or both. Eight had served in constitutional conventions in their own States, and seven had been State governors. Eight had signed the Declaration of Independence. Thirty-one of the delegates had attended college in a day when there were but a few colleges in the land, and their number also included two college presidents and three professors. Two were to become Presidents of the United States, and one a Vice President. Seventeen later served in the Senate and eleven in the House of Representatives.

Is it any wonder that the product of such a gathering was described by the English statesman William E. Gladstone, nearly a century later, as "the most wonderful work ever struck off at a given time by the brain and purpose of man"?

Remarkably, the average age of the delegates was only 42, and nearly half were only in their 30s. Indeed, most of the real leaders were in that age group—James Madison was 36, Gouverneur Morris 35, Edmund Randolph 34, and Alexander Hamilton 32. At 81, Benjamin Franklin was the oldest. His health was failing, however, and he was not able to attend many of the meetings. George Washington, at 55, was one of the few older members who played a key role in the making of the Constitution.

By and large, the Framers of the Constitution were of a new generation in American politics. Several of the better-known leaders of the Revolutionary period were not in Philadelphia. Patrick Henry said he "smelt a rat" and refused to attend. Samuel Adams, John Hancock, and Richard Henry Lee were not selected as delegates by their States. Thomas Paine was in Paris. So, too, was Thomas Jefferson, as American minister to France. John Adams was our envoy to England and Holland at the time.

Organization and Procedure

The Framers met that summer in Philadelphia's Independence Hall, probably in the same room in which the Declaration of Independence had been signed 11 years earlier.

► This nineteenth-century engraving shows George Washington presiding over the Constitutional Convention in 1787. *Critical Thinking What impressions did the artist try to convey about this historic gathering?*

They organized immediately on May 25, unanimously electing George Washington president of the convention.[14] Then, and at the second session on Monday, May 28, they adopted several rules of procedure. A majority of the States would be needed to conduct business. Each State delegation was to have one vote on all matters, and a majority of the votes cast would carry any proposal.

Working in Secrecy

The delegates also decided to keep their deliberations secret. The convention had drawn much public attention and speculation. So, to protect themselves from outside pressures, the delegates adopted a rule of secrecy. On the whole, the rule was well kept.

A secretary, William Jackson, and other minor, nonmember officials were appointed. Jackson kept the convention's *Journal*. That official record, however, was quite sketchy. It was mostly a listing of members present, motions put forth, and votes taken; and it was not always accurate at that.

Fortunately, several delegates kept their own accounts of the proceedings. Most of what is known of the work of the convention comes from James Madison's voluminous *Notes*. His brilliance and depth of knowledge led his

---

[14]Twenty-nine delegates from seven States were present on that first day. The full number of 55 was not reached until August 6, when John Francis Mercer of Maryland arrived. In the meantime, some delegates had departed, and others were absent from time to time. Some 40 members attended most of the daily sessions of the convention.

colleagues to hold him in great respect. Quickly, he became the convention's floor leader. Madison contributed more to the Constitution than did any of the others, and still he was able to keep a close record of its work. Certainly, he deserves the title "Father of the Constitution."

The Framers met on 89 of the 116 days from May 25 through their final meeting on September 17. They did most of their work on the floor of the convention. They handled some matters in committees, but the full body ultimately settled all questions.

A Momentous Decision

The Philadelphia Convention was called to recommend revisions in the Articles of Confederation. However, almost at once the delegates agreed that they were, in fact, meeting to create a *new* government for the United States. On May 30 they adopted this proposal:

 PRIMARY Sources *"Resolved, . . . that a national Government ought to be established consisting of a supreme Legislative, Executive and Judiciary."*
–Edmund Randolph, Delegate from Virginia

With this momentous decision, the Framers redefined the purpose of the convention. From that point on, they set about the writing of a new constitution. This new constitution was intended to replace the Articles of Confederation. Their debates were spirited, even bitter. At times the convention seemed near collapse. Once they had passed Randolph's resolution, however, the goal of a majority of the convention never changed.

The Virginia Plan

No State had more to do with the calling of the convention than Virginia did. It was not surprising, then, that its delegates should offer the first plan for a new constitution. On May 29 the **Virginia Plan,** largely the work of Madison, was presented by Randolph.

The Virginia Plan called for a new government with three separate branches: legislative, executive, and judicial. The legislature—Congress—would be bicameral. Representation in each house was to be based either upon each State's population or upon the amount of money it gave for the support of the central government. The members of the lower house, the House of Representatives, were to be popularly elected in each State. Those of the upper house, the Senate, were to be chosen by the House from lists of persons nominated by the State legislatures.

Congress was to be given all of the powers it held under the Articles. In addition, it was to have the power "to legislate in all cases to which the separate States are incompetent" to act, to veto any State law in conflict with national law, and to use force if necessary to make a State obey national law.

Under the proposed Virginia Plan, Congress would choose a "National Executive" and a "National Judiciary." Together, these two branches would form a "Council of revision." They could veto acts passed by Congress, but a veto could be overridden by the two houses. The executive would have "a general authority to execute the National laws." The judiciary would "consist of one or more supreme tribunals [courts], and of inferior tribunals."

The Virginia Plan also provided that all State officers should take an oath to support the Union, and that each State be guaranteed a republican form of government. Under the plan, Congress would have the exclusive power to admit new States to the Union.

The Virginia Plan, then, would create a new constitution by thoroughly revising the Articles. Its goal was the creation of a truly national government with greatly expanded powers and, importantly, the power to enforce its decisions.

The Virginia Plan set the agenda for much of the convention's work. But some delegates—especially those from the smaller States of Delaware, Maryland, and New Jersey, and from New York—found it too radical.[15] Soon they developed their counterproposals. On June 15 William Paterson of New Jersey presented the position of the small States.

The New Jersey Plan

Paterson and his colleagues offered several amendments to the Articles, but not nearly so thorough a revision as that proposed by the Virginia Plan. The **New Jersey Plan** retained the unicameral Congress of the Confederation, with each of the States equally represented. To those powers Congress already had, would be added closely limited powers to tax and to regulate trade between the States.

The New Jersey Plan also called for a "federal executive" of more than one person. This plural executive would be chosen by Congress and could be removed by it at the request of a majority of the States' governors. The "federal judiciary" would be composed of a single "supreme Tribunal," appointed by the executive.

Among their several differences, the major point of disagreement between the two plans centered on this question: How should the States be represented in Congress? Would it be on the basis of their populations or financial contributions, as in the Virginia Plan? Or would it be on the basis of State equality, as in the Articles and the New Jersey Plan?

For weeks the delegates returned to this conflict, debating the matter again and again. The lines were sharply drawn. Several delegates, on both sides of the issue, threatened to withdraw. Finally, the dispute was settled by one of the key compromises the Framers were to make as they built the Constitution.

Compromises

The disagreement over representation in Congress was critical. The large States expected to dominate the new government. The small

---

[15]The Virginia Plan's major support came from the three largest States: Virginia, Pennsylvania, and Massachusetts. New York was then only the fifth largest State. Alexander Hamilton, the convention's most outspoken champion of a stronger central government, was regularly outvoted by his fellow delegates from New York.

Slavery in the United States, 1790			
State	**Total Population**	**Slave Population**	**Percent Slave Population**
Connecticut	238,000	2,648	1.11
Delaware	59,000	8,887	15.06
Georgia	83,000	29,264	35.26
Maryland	320,000	103,036	32.20
Massachusetts	476,000	0	0.0
New Hampshire	142,000	157	0.11
New Jersey	184,000	11,423	6.21
New York	340,000	21,193	6.23
North Carolina	394,000	100,783	25.58
Pennsylvania	434,000	3,707	0.85
Rhode Island	69,000	958	1.39
South Carolina	249,000	107,094	43.01
Virginia	692,000	292,627	42.29

SOURCES: *Historical Statistics of Black America;*
Historical Statistics of the United States, Colonial Times to 1970

Interpreting Tables The agricultural economy of the southern States relied on slave labor to produce cotton and other crops. ***Why did the southern States want slaves counted in their States' total population?***

States feared that they would not be able to protect their interests. Tempers flared on both sides. The debate became so intense that Benjamin Franklin suggested that "henceforth prayers imploring the assistance of Heaven . . . be held in this Assembly every morning before we proceed to business."

The Connecticut Compromise

The conflict was finally settled by a compromise suggested by the Connecticut delegation. Under the **Connecticut Compromise,** it was agreed that Congress should be composed of two houses. In the smaller Senate, the States would be represented equally. In the House, the representation of each State would be based upon its population.

Thus, by combining basic features of the rival Virginia and New Jersey Plans, the convention's most serious dispute was resolved. The agreement satisfied the smaller States in particular, and it made it possible for them to support the creation of a strong central government.

The Connecticut Compromise was so pivotal to the writing of the Constitution that it has often been called the Great Compromise.

The Three-Fifths Compromise

Once it had been agreed to base the seats in the House on each State's population, this question arose: Should slaves be counted in the populations of the southern States?

Again debate was fierce. Most delegates from the slave-holding States argued that slaves should be counted. Most of the northerners took the opposing view. The table above shows the significant percentage of slaves among the populations of the southern States.

Finally, the Framers agreed to the **Three-Fifths Compromise.** It provided that all "free persons" should be counted, and so, too, should "three-fifths of all other persons." (Article I, Section 2, Clause 3. For "all other persons" read "slaves.") For the three-fifths won by the southerners, the northerners exacted a price. That formula was also to be used in fixing the amount of money to be raised in each State by any direct tax levied by Congress. In short, the southerners could count their slaves, but they would have to pay for them.

This odd compromise disappeared from the Constitution with the adoption of the 13th Amendment, which abolished slavery, in 1865. For nearly 140 years now, there have been no "all other persons" in this country.

The Commerce and Slave Trade Compromise

The convention agreed that Congress had to have the power to regulate foreign and interstate trade. To many southerners that power carried a real danger, however. They worried that Congress, likely to be controlled by northern commercial interests, would act against the interests of the agricultural South.

They were particularly fearful that Congress would try to pay for the new government out of export duties, and southern tobacco was the major American export of the time. They also feared that Congress would interfere with the slave trade.

Before they would agree to the commerce power, the southerners insisted on certain protections. So, according to the **Commerce and Slave Trade Compromise,** Congress was forbidden the power to tax the export of goods from any State. It was also forbidden the power to act on the slave trade for a period of at least 20 years. It could not interfere with "the migration or importation of such persons as any State now existing shall think proper to admit," except for a small head tax, at least until the year 1808.[16]

A "Bundle of Compromises"

The convention spent much of its time, said Franklin, "sawing boards to make them fit." The Constitution drafted at Philadelphia has often been called a "bundle of compromises." These descriptions are apt, if they are properly understood.

There were differences of opinion among the delegates, certainly. After all, the delegates came from 12 different States that were widely separated in geographic and economic terms. The delegates often reflected the interests of their States. Bringing these interests together did require compromise. Indeed, final decisions on issues such as selection of the President, the treaty-making process, the structure of the national court system, and the amendment process were reached as a result of compromise.

But by no means did all, or even most, of what shaped the document come from compromises. The Framers agreed on many of the basic issues they faced. Thus, nearly all the delegates were convinced that a new *national* government, a federal government, had to be created, and had to

---

[16]Article I, Section 9, Clause 1. Congress promptly banned the importation of slaves in 1808, and in 1820 it declared the slave trade to be piracy. The smuggling of the enslaved into this country continued until the outbreak of the Civil War, however.

have the powers necessary to deal with the nation's grave social and economic problems. The Framers were also dedicated to the concepts of popular sovereignty and of limited government. None questioned for a moment the wisdom of representative government. The principles of separation of powers and of checks and balances were accepted almost as a matter of course.

Many disputes did occur, and the compromises by which they were resolved came only after hours and days and even weeks of heated debate. The point here, however, is that the differences were not over the most fundamental of questions. They involved, instead, such vital but lesser points as these: the details of the structure of Congress, the method by which the President was to be chosen, and the practical limits that should be put on the several powers to be given to the new central government.

Sources of the Constitution

The Framers were well educated and widely read. They were familiar with the governments of ancient Greece and Rome and those of contemporary Great Britain and Europe. They knew the political writings of their time, of such works as William Blackstone's *Commentaries on the Laws of England,* the Baron de Montesquieu's *The Spirit of the Laws,* Jean Jacques Rousseau's *Social Contract,* John Locke's *Two Treatises of Government,* and many others.

More immediately, the Framers drew on their own experiences. Remember, they were familiar with the Second Continental Congress, the Articles of Confederation, and their own State governments. Much that went into the Constitution came directly, sometimes word for word, from the Articles. A number of provisions were drawn from the several State constitutions, as well.

The Convention Completes Its Work

For several weeks, through the hot Philadelphia summer, the delegates took up resolution after resolution. Finally, on September 8, a committee was named "to revise the stile of and arrange the articles which had been agreed to" by the

▲ Detail from Washington's chair at the Constitutional Convention.

convention. That group, the Committee of Stile and Arrangement headed by Gouverneur Morris, put the Constitution in its final form.

Then, on September 17, the convention approved its work and 39 names were placed on the finished document.[17] Perhaps none of the Framers were completely satisfied with their work. Nevertheless, wise old Benjamin Franklin put into words what many of the Framers must have thought on that final day:

PRIMARY Sources *"Sir, I agree with this Constitution to all its faults, if they are such; because I think a general Government necessary for us . . . I doubt . . . whether any other Convention we can obtain, may be able to make a better Constitution. For when you assemble a number of men to have the advantage of their joint wisdom, you inevitably assemble with those men, all their prejudices, their passions, their errors of opinion, their local interests, and their selfish views. From such an assembly can a perfect production be*

expected? It therefore astonishes me, Sir, to find this system approaching so near to perfection as it does . . . "
—Notes of Debates in the Federal Convention of 1787, James Madison

On Franklin's motion, the Constitution was signed. Madison tells us that

PRIMARY Sources *". . . Doctor Franklin, looking toward the President's chair, at the back of which a rising sun happened to be painted, observed to a few members near him, that Painters had found it difficult to distinguish in their art a rising from a setting sun. I have, said he, often and often in the course of the Session . . . looked at that behind the President without being able to tell whether it was rising or setting. But now at length I have the happiness to know that it is a rising and not a setting sun. "*
—Notes of Debates in the Federal Convention of 1787, James Madison

---

[17]Three of the 41 delegates present on that last day refused to sign the proposed Constitution: Edmund Randolph of Virginia, who later did support ratification and served as Attorney General and then Secretary of State under President Washington; Elbridge Gerry of Massachusetts, who later became Vice President under Madison; and George Mason of Virginia, who continued to oppose the Constitution until his death in 1792. George Read of Delaware signed both for himself and for his absent colleague John Dickinson.

Section 4 Assessment

Key Terms and Main Ideas

1. Identify the **Framers** of the Constitution and describe, in general, their backgrounds and experiences.
2. What momentous decision did the Framers make at the beginning of the Philadelphia Convention?
3. Why did the delegates from the smaller States object to the **Virginia Plan?**
4. What was agreed to under the **Connecticut Compromise?**
5. What sources influenced the Framers in writing the Constitution?

Critical Thinking

6. **Making Comparisons** Compare and contrast the Virginia Plan and the New Jersey Plan.
7. **Determining Relevance** The Three-Fifths Compromise and the Commerce and Slave Trade Compromise were included in the Constitution at the insistence of the southern States. Why did States in the South think these items were important and what price, if any, did southern States pay for their inclusion?
8. **Drawing Conclusions** The Constitution has been called a "bundle of compromises." Is this an accurate description of the document? Explain your answer.

 Take It to the Net

9. Select two of the delegates to the Constitutional Convention and learn more about their backgrounds. Summarize your findings and explain why your selected delegates were important to the creation of a new government. Use the links provided in the Social Studies area at the following Web site for help in completing this activity. **www.phschool.com**

SKILLS FOR LIFE

Making Comparisons

You've probably been making comparisons ever since you first tasted food. Making comparisons means examining two or more ideas, objects, events, or people to find out how they are either similar or different. In the study of government, you will often use this skill to evaluate differing proposals on public issues. To make valid comparisons, use these steps:

1. Identify the basis of comparison. Comparing two or more items works only when the items have some attribute in common. Consider the Virginia Plan and the New Jersey Plan, discussed on page 51. Both plans put forth models for creating a new government. What else did they have in common?

2. Identify the attributes of each item to be compared. An easy way to compare complex items is to create a list or chart of their key attributes. The charts at right summarize the main features of the Virginia and New Jersey Plans.

3. Find ways in which the items are similar. Once you put the attributes in a chart, it becomes easy to identify similarities. Study the charts. Then list the similarities of the Virginia Plan and the New Jersey Plan.

4. Find ways in which the items are different. The two Constitution plans differ not only in what they offer, but also in what they do not offer. List the differences.

5. Summarize and evaluate your comparison. Decide whether the two items you are comparing are mostly similar or mostly different, and analyze why. Write a sentence or two summarizing the main differences between the Virginia Plan and the New Jersey Plan.

Test for Success

Controversy over the size and powers of the Federal Government is as lively today as ever. Find two sources of opinion on this issue and write a brief comparison of them.

Virginia Plan

- Branches of government: legislative, executive, judicial
- Structure of legislative branch: bicameral, with a lower house, the House of Representatives, and an upper house, the Senate
- How representation is apportioned: by population or by amount of money contributed to the National Government
- Congress retains powers given to it under the Articles of Confederation: Yes.
- National powers vs. State powers: strong
- Structure of executive branch: single executive who executes national laws
- How executive is chosen: by Congress
- Structure of judicial branch: one or more supreme courts with lower courts
- How judiciary is chosen: by Congress

New Jersey Plan

- Branches of government: legislative, executive, judicial
- Structure of legislative branch: unicameral Congress of the Confederation
- How representation is apportioned: equal number of votes for every State
- Congress retains powers given to it under the Articles of Confederation: Yes.
- National powers vs. State powers: weak
- Structure of executive branch: plural executive (more than one person)
- How executive is chosen: by Congress
- Structure of judicial branch: single supreme court
- How judiciary is chosen: by the executive

5 *Ratifying the Constitution*

Section Preview

OBJECTIVES

1. **Identify** the opposing sides in the fight for ratification and describe the major arguments for and against the Constitution.
2. **Describe** the inauguration of the new government of the United States of America.

WHY IT MATTERS

The Constitution could not take effect until it had been ratified by nine States. The battle between those who supported and those who opposed the Constitution was hard fought in all the States.

POLITICAL DICTIONARY

★ **Federalists**
★ **Anti-Federalists**
★ **quorum**

Today, the Constitution of the United States is the object of extraordinary respect and admiration, both here and abroad. But in 1787 and 1788, it was widely criticized, and in every State there were many who opposed its adoption. The battle over the ratification of the Constitution was not easily decided.

The Fight for Ratification

Remember, the Articles of Confederation provided that changes could be made to them only if all of the State legislatures agreed. But the new Constitution was intended to replace, not amend, the Articles. The Framers had seen how crippling the unanimity requirement could be. So, the new Constitution provided that

FROM THE Constitution *" The ratification of the conventions of nine States shall be sufficient for the establishment of this Constitution between the States so ratifying the same. "*

—Article VII

The Congress of the Confederation agreed to this irregular procedure. After a short debate, it sent copies of the new document to the States on September 28, 1787.

Federalists and Anti-Federalists

The Constitution was printed, circulated, and debated vigorously. Two groups emerged in each of the States: the **Federalists**, who favored ratification, and the **Anti-Federalists**, who opposed it.

The Federalists were led by many of those who had attended the Philadelphia Convention. Among them, the most active and the most effective were James Madison and Alexander Hamilton. Their opposition was headed by such well-known Revolutionary War figures as Patrick Henry, Richard Henry Lee, John Hancock, and Samuel Adams.

The Federalists stressed the weaknesses of the Articles. They argued that the difficulties facing the Republic could be overcome only by a new government based on the proposed Constitution.

The Anti-Federalists attacked nearly every part of the new document. Many objected to the ratification process, to the absence of any mention of God, to the denial to the States of

▲ *Interpreting Political Cartoons* This cartoon, printed in the New Hampshire *Gazette* on June 26, 1788, shows the States as pillars, with nine upright and a tenth being raised. *What is the message of the words in the cartoon?*

a power to print money, and to many other features of the Framers' proposals.

Two major features of the proposed Constitution drew the heaviest fire: (1) the greatly increased powers of the central government and (2) the lack of a bill of rights. The proposed document did not provide for such basic liberties as freedom of speech, press, and religion, nor for the rights of fair trial. At Virginia's ratifying convention, Patrick Henry said of the proposed Constitution, "I look upon that paper as the most fatal plan that could possibly be conceived to enslave a free people."

Nine States Ratify

The contest for ratification was close in several States, but the Federalists finally won in all of them. Delaware was the first State to ratify. On June 21, 1788, New Hampshire brought the number of ratifying States to nine.

Under Article VII, New Hampshire's ratification should have brought the Constitution into effect, but it did not. Neither Virginia nor New York had yet ratified, and without either of these key States the new government could not hope to succeed.

Virginia's Ratification

Virginia's vote for ratification followed New Hampshire's by just four days. The brilliant debates in its convention were followed closely throughout the State. The Federalists were led by Madison, the young John Marshall, and Governor Edmund Randolph (even though he had refused to sign the Constitution at Philadelphia). Patrick Henry, leading the opposition, was joined by such outstanding Virginians as James Monroe, Richard Henry Lee, and George Mason (another of the non-signers).

Although George Washington was not one of the delegates to Virginia's convention, his strong support for ratification proved vital. With Madison, he was able to get a reluctant Jefferson to support the document. Had Jefferson fought as did other Anti-Federalists, Virginia might never have ratified the Constitution.

An Era of Revolutions

1789 French Revolution begins

1775 American Revolution begins

1821 Mexico gains independence from Spain

1791 Haitian revolt against France begins

1819 Colombia achieves independence from Spain

1821 Peru declares independence from Spain

1822 Brazil proclaims independence from Portugal

1825 Bolivia achieves independence from Spain

1811 Paraguay proclaims independence from Spain

1818 Chile declares independence from Spain

Interpreting Maps The American Revolution was one of many struggles for independence that took place around the world between 1775 and 1825. ***Do you think this global turmoil was coincidence, or were the events in various countries somehow connected?***

Ratification of the Constitution

State	Date	Vote
Delaware	December 7, 1787	30–0
Pennsylvania	December 12, 1787	46–23
New Jersey	December 18, 1787	38–0
Georgia	January 2, 1788	26–0
Connecticut	January 9, 1788	128–40
Massachusetts	February 6, 1788	187–168
Maryland	April 28, 1788	63–11
South Carolina	May 23, 1788	149–73
New Hampshire	June 21, 1788	57–46
Virginia	June 25, 1788	89–79
New York	July 26, 1788	30–27
North Carolina	November 21, 1789*	195–77
Rhode Island	May 29, 1790	34–32

*Second vote; ratification was originally defeated on August 4, 1788, by a vote of 184–84.

Interpreting Tables Virginia's ratification came only after a long struggle. ***In what other States was ratification won by only a narrow margin?***

▲ **Defending the Constitution** All the essays in *The Federalist* were signed with the pen name Publius. Modern scholars attribute fifty-one to Hamilton (right), five to Jay (left), and twenty-nine to Madison.

New York, The Last Key State

A narrow vote in the New York convention brought the number of States to 11. New York ratified only after a long battle. The Anti-Federalists were led by Governor George Clinton and by two of the State's three delegates to the Philadelphia Convention.[18]

The contest in New York gave rise to a remarkable campaign document: *The Federalist*. It was a collection of 85 essays supporting the Constitution written by Alexander Hamilton, James Madison, and John Jay. Those essays were first published as letters to the people in various newspapers of the State and soon were collected in book form. Though written in haste, they remain an excellent commentary on the Constitution, and are among the best political writings in the English language.

Inaugurating the Government

On September 13, 1788, with 11 of the 13 States "under the federal roof," the Congress of the Confederation paved the way for its successor.[19] It chose New York as the temporary capital.[20] It set the first Wednesday in January as the date on which the States would choose presidential electors. The first Wednesday in February was set as the date on which those electors would vote, and the first Wednesday in March as the date for the inauguration of the new government.

The new Congress convened on March 4, 1789. It met in Federal Hall, on Wall Street in New York City. But because it lacked a **quorum** (majority), it could not count the electoral votes until April 6. Finally, on that day, it found that George Washington had been elected President by a unanimous vote. John Adams was elected Vice President with a substantial majority.

On April 30, after his historic trip from Mount Vernon to New York, Washington took the oath of office as the first President of the United States.

---

[18]Robert Yates and John Lansing had quit Philadelphia in July, arguing that the convention had gone beyond its authority. Like many other Anti-Federalist leaders, Governor Clinton later supported the Constitution.

[19]Neither North Carolina nor Rhode Island had ratified the new Constitution before it became effective. As you can see in the table on p. 57, the Constitution failed in a first convention in North Carolina and was finally approved by a second one in late November of 1789. Rhode Island did not hold a ratifying convention until May of 1790, more than a year after Washington's inauguration.

[20]The District of Columbia did not become the nation's capital until 1800. Congress moved its sessions from New York to Philadelphia in December 1790. It held its first meeting in the new "federal city," Washington, D.C., on November 17, 1800.

Section 5 Assessment

Key Terms and Main Ideas

1. What was the **Federalist** position on the adoption of the Constitution? Why did they feel that way?
2. Who were the **Anti-Federalists**?
3. What was "irregular" about the ratification of the Constitution?

Critical Thinking

4. **Expressing Problems Clearly** Why might the failure of New York and Virginia to ratify have doomed the Constitution?
5. **Understanding Point of View** The Anti-Federalists were greatly concerned that the proposed Constitution increased the powers of the central government and lacked a bill of rights. Why would these specific issues have been important to them?

Take It to the Net

6. Read the analysis of *The Federalist Papers*. Then create a graphic organizer showing how these articles exemplified the Federalists' beliefs. Include at least four beliefs and cite examples. Use the links provided in the Social Studies area at the following Web site for help in completing this activity. **www.phschool.com**

Is Flag-Burning "Free Speech"?

Free speech, one of Americans' most cherished freedoms, is commonly thought of in terms of spoken or printed words. Yet speech also can take the form of a symbolic action, like the burning of an American flag. Does the reverence with which most Americans regard the flag override our commitment to free speech? In other words, can the government restrict the ways in which national symbols such as the flag can be used in protests?

United States v. Eichman (1990)

In the 1989 case *Texas* v. *Johnson*, the Supreme Court struck down a State law that forbade the destruction of the United States flag. That law, ruled the Court, violated the 1st Amendment guarantee of free expression. Congress reacted to the decision by passing the Flag Protection Act of 1989, which stated that anyone who "knowingly mutilates, defaces, physically defiles, burns, maintains on the floor or ground, or tramples upon" a United States flag can be prosecuted. (Disposing of worn or soiled flags was permitted under the law.) Violators could be fined or imprisoned for up to one year.

The United States prosecuted Eichman and others for knowingly setting fire to several American flags. These flag-burnings took place both on the steps of the Capitol (to protest certain government policies) and in Seattle (to protest the passage of the Flag Protection Act itself).

The defendants asked the courts to dismiss the charges on the grounds that the Act violated the First Amendment. They cited *Texas* v. *Johnson* as giving First Amendment protection to flag-burning as a means of expression. Federal courts in Washington State and the District of Columbia both ruled that the Act was unconstitutional. The Federal Government then appealed these decisions to the Supreme Court.

Arguments for the United States

1. The Flag Protection Act does not outlaw flag-burning in order to prevent the expression of a particular point of view. Rather, it prohibits mistreatment of the flag for any reason in order to protect the flag's identity as a national symbol.

2. Desecration (abuse) of the flag is deeply offensive to many Americans. The government should have the right to protect its national symbols against mistreatment.

3. Protection of the flag would not interfere with protesters' ability to express their opinions by other means.

Arguments for Eichman

1. The government's effort to protect the flag limits the free expression of opposition to government policies.

2. The destruction of a flag does not diminish the flag's importance as a symbol of this country.

3. Although many people are offended by flag desecration, the government cannot prohibit expression of ideas simply because the ideas may be offensive or disagreeable to many people.

Decide for Yourself

1. Review the constitutional grounds on which each side based its arguments and the specific arguments each side presented.

2. Debate the opposing viewpoints presented in this case. Which viewpoint do you favor?

3. Predict the impact of the Court's decision on ways in which people may choose to protest government policies. (To read a summary of the Court's decision, turn to the Supreme Court Glossary on page 799.)

CHAPTER 2 · Assessment

Political Dictionary

limited government (p. 29)
representative government (p. 29)
Magna Carta (p. 29)
Petition of Right (p. 30)
English Bill of Rights (p. 30)
charter (p. 31)
bicameral (p. 31)
proprietary (p. 32)
unicameral (p. 32)
confederation (p. 35)

Albany Plan of Union (p. 35)
delegate (p. 36)
boycott (p. 36)
repeal (p. 37)
popular sovereignty (p. 39)
Articles of Confederation (p. 44)
ratification (p. 44)
presiding officer (p. 45)
Framers (p. 48)

Virginia Plan (p. 51)
New Jersey Plan (p. 51)
Connecticut Compromise (p. 52)
Three-Fifths Compromise (p. 52)
Commerce and Slave Trade
    Compromise (p. 53)
Federalists (p. 56)
Anti-Federalists (p. 56)
quorum (p. 58)

Practicing the Vocabulary

Using Words in Context *For each of the terms below, write a sentence that shows how it relates to this chapter.*

1. Articles of Confederation
2. Three-Fifths Compromise
3. charter
4. boycott
5. bicameral
6. ratification
7. quorum
8. proprietary
9. Commerce and Slave Trade Compromise
10. delegate

Word Relationships *Three of the terms in each of the following sets of terms are related. Choose the term that does not belong and explain why it does not belong.*

11. **(a)** Magna Carta **(b)** Albany Plan of Union **(c)** English Bill of Rights **(d)** Petition of Right
12. **(a)** Articles of Confederation **(b)** Virginia Plan **(c)** New Jersey Plan **(d)** Connecticut Compromise
13. **(a)** limited government **(b)** popular sovereignty **(c)** ratification **(d)** representative government
14. **(a)** Framers **(b)** Federalists **(c)** Anti-Federalists **(d)** boycott

---

Reviewing Main Ideas

Section 1

15. What three ideas about government did the colonists bring with them from England?
16. How was the development of English government affected by **(a)** the Magna Carta? **(b)** The Petition of Right? **(c)** The English Bill of Rights?
17. Explain the development of colonial government.

Section 2

18. Describe how the British governed the colonies **(a)** before the 1760s. **(b)** After the 1760s.
19. What was the colonists' response to the change in British policies in the 1760s?
20. **(a)** Who wrote the Declaration of Independence? **(b)** What rights are outlined in the document? **(c)** How do they signify the colonists' relationship to Britain?
21. Describe the common features of the first State constitutions.

Section 3

22. What were the major characteristics of the Articles of Confederation?
23. How did the States respond to the weaknesses of the Articles of Confederation?

Section 4

24. Who were the Framers of the Constitution?
25. Explain the New Jersey Plan. Why was it introduced at the Constitutional Convention?
26. What major issues did the Framers disagree upon and what, if any, compromises did they reach?

Section 5

27. Why did the Federalists want to replace the Articles?
28. What were the main arguments used by the Anti-Federalists?
29. Why was ratification by Virginia and New York essential for the success of the Constitution?

Critical Thinking

30. *Applying the Chapter Skill* The proposed Constitution sent to the States in 1787 drew heated reactions. Review the discussion of the fight for ratification on pages 56–58. Then create a table summarizing the positions of the Federalists and Anti-Federalists. Compare the arguments of the two groups and write a sentence or two explaining how their views on the Constitution differed.

31. *Recognizing Ideologies* The Second Continental Congress met in violation of British law. **(a)** Why did the colonists feel justified to rebel? **(b)** How would you respond to such a gathering today? **(c)** Give an example.

32. *Formulating Questions* Weaknesses in the Articles of Confederation surfaced during the Critical Period in American history. Write three questions that will help you understand why many leaders of the day urged a stronger national government, and how they could achieve this.

33. *Checking Consistency* How does the history of America from the 1600s to 1789 demonstrate that "questions of politics and economics are, in fact, inseparable"?

Analyzing Political Cartoons

Using your knowledge of American government and this cartoon, answer the questions below.

34. This cartoon, originally published by Benjamin Franklin in 1754, appeared in several versions during the American Revolution. **(a)** What do the segments of the snake represent? **(b)** How do you know?

35. (a) What is the message of the cartoon? **(b)** In your opinion, is this cartoon an effective means of persuasion? Why or why not?

★ You Can Make a Difference

What issues and rights are important to students in your school? Are there questions about censorship or privacy rights? What about disputes between different student groups? Is there a council that mediates when the interests of different students come into conflict? Write an editorial for your school newspaper in which you point out some issues in your school. Suggest methods that could be used to find compromises for these conflicts.

Participation Activities

36. *Current Events Watch* The Framers drew on their skills, knowledge, and experience in creating the Constitution. What kinds of experience and training do political leaders draw on today? Select a current political leader—a member of Congress or the governor of your State, for example—and write a brief biography of this person. Your biographical sketch should identify the skills, knowledge, and experience that person draws upon in his or her current position.

37. *Time Line Activity* Using information from the chapter, create a time line showing the steps that led to the ratification of the Constitution. Include at least eight entries in your time line. You might begin with the First Continental Congress of 1774. What, in your opinion, was the most important step in the process? Why?

38. *It's Your Turn* It is 1788. Write a letter to the editor of your local paper in which you express your opinion on whether or not the Constitution should be ratified. First, create a list of what you see as the positive aspects of the document. Then, list the negative features. Note any suggestions you have for improvements. Next, write a draft of the letter in which you politely offer your ideas. Revise your letter, making certain that each idea is clearly explained. Proofread your letter and draft a final copy. **(Writing a Letter)**

Take It to the Net

Chapter 2 Self-Test As a final review activity, take the Chapter 2 Self-Test in the Social Studies area at the Web site listed below, and receive immediate feedback on your answers.

www.phschool.com

CHAPTER 3

The Constitution

"These principles form the bright constellation which has gone before us and guided our steps through an age of revolution and reformation."
—Thomas Jefferson (1801)

The Constitution rests on basic principles that have made the United States government unique in world history. Those principles have not gone out of date, yet the Constitution has been changed in various ways to adapt to a growing nation. Some provisions have been modified by laws and custom, while formal amendments have revised the original words.

◆ George Washington presiding over the Constitutional Convention

You Can Make a Difference

WHEN THE 26TH AMENDMENT was ratified in 1971, it created 11 million new voters from 18 to 20 years old. Campaigns urged teenagers to register to vote and get involved. Young people's votes made the difference in many recent elections. Some teenagers even ran for local offices and won. In Detroit, students at Cass Technical High School got first-hand experience working as interns in government and community agencies. Robyn Ray's time with the Equal Justice Council changed her attitude about voting. "When certain judges are up for election, I'll know how to vote. And if there is a chance to work and vote for judicial reform, I'll be there."

Keep It Current

Items marked with this logo are periodically updated on the Internet. Keep up-to-date with what's in the news. To get current information on the Constitution, go to **www.phschool.com**

The Six Basic Principles

Section Preview

OBJECTIVES

1. **Outline** the important elements of the Constitution.
2. **List** the six basic principles of the Constitution.

WHY IT MATTERS

The Constitution is a brief, straightforward document that has guided American government for over 200 years. Its authors wrote the Constitution based on the principles that political power resides with the people, and that the National Government should be limited and divided into three branches to limit the power of any one group.

POLITICAL DICTIONARY

★ **Preamble**
★ **articles**
★ **constitutionalism**
★ **rule of law**
★ **separation of powers**
★ **checks and balances**
★ **veto**
★ **judicial review**
★ **unconstitutional**
★ **federalism**

The Constitution of the United States dates from the latter part of the eighteenth century. It was written in 1787, and took effect in 1789. The fact that the Constitution is more than 200 years old does *not* mean, however, that now, in the twenty-first century, it is only an interesting historical artifact, fit for museums and dusty shelves. It is, instead, a vitally important and vibrant document.

The Constitution is this nation's fundamental law. It is, by its own terms, "the supreme Law of the Land"—the highest form of law in the United States.

An Outline of the Constitution

The Constitution sets out the basic principles upon which government in the United States was built and operates today. The document lays out the basic framework and procedures of our government, and sets out the limits within which that government must conduct itself.

The Constitution is a fairly brief document. Its little more than 7,000 words can be read in half an hour. You will find the text of the Constitution beginning on page 758. As you read it, think about the surprising fact that this brief document has successfully guided this nation through two centuries of tremendous growth and change. One of the Constitution's greatest strengths is that its words deal largely with matters of basic principle. Unlike most other constitutions—those of the 50 States and those of most other nations—the document is not weighted down with detailed and cumbersome provisions.

As you read the Constitution, you will also see that it is organized in a simple and straightforward way. It begins with a short, noteworthy

▶ Although the members of the Federal Government are continually changing, from leaders of the past like Senator Henry Cabot Lodge (R., Massachusetts) to new lawmakers such as first-term Senator Michael Crapo (R., Idaho), the Constitution provides a lasting link between the past and present.

introduction, the **Preamble,** and the balance of the original document is divided into seven numbered sections called **articles.** The first three articles deal with the three branches of the National Government: Congress, the presidency, and the federal court system. These articles outline the basic organization and powers of each branch and the methods by which the members of Congress, the President and Vice President, and federal judges are chosen. Article IV deals mostly with the place of the States in the American Union and with their relationship with the National Government and with one another. Article V explains how formal amendments may be added to the document. Article VI declares that the Constitution is the nation's supreme law. Finally, Article VII states the requirements for ratification.

The seven articles of the original document are followed by 27 amendments, printed in the order in which they were adopted.

The Basic Principles

The Constitution is built around six basic principles: popular sovereignty, limited government, separation of powers, checks and balances, judicial review, and federalism.

Popular Sovereignty

In the United States, all political power resides in the people. The people are sovereign. They are the *only* source for any and all governmental power. Government can govern only with the consent of the governed.

The principle of popular sovereignty, so boldly proclaimed by the Declaration of Independence, is

Articles of the Constitution	
Section	**Subject**
Preamble	States the purpose of the Constitution
Article I	Legislative branch
Article II	Executive branch
Article III	Judicial branch
Article IV	Relations among the States
Article V	Amending the Constitution
Article VI	National debts, supremacy of national law, and oaths of office
Article VII	Ratifying the Constitution

Interpreting Tables The Constitution sets up the basic structure of our Federal Government. ***How do the first three articles differ from those that follow?***

woven throughout the Constitution. In its very opening words, in the Preamble, the Constitution declares: "We the People of the United States . . . do ordain and establish this Constitution for the United States of America."

In essence, the National Government draws its power from the people of the United States, and the people have given their government the power that it has through the Constitution. Similarly, each one of the State governments draws its authority from the people of that State, through that State's constitution.

Limited Government

The principle of limited government holds that no government is all-powerful, that a government may do *only* those things that the people have given it the power to do.

In effect, the principle of limited government is the other side of the coin of popular sovereignty. It is that principle stated the other way around: The people are the only source of any and all of government's authority; and government has only that authority the people have given to it.

The concept of limited government can be expressed another way: Government must obey the law. Stated this way, the principle is often called **constitutionalism**—that is, that government must be conducted according to constitutional

▲ **The Rule of Law** During the Watergate scandal prosecutors accused many of President Richard Nixon's closest advisers of breaking the law. This poster implies that Nixon shared their guilt and would soon be exposed.

principles. The concept of limited government is also described as the **rule of law,** which holds that government and its officers are always subject to—never above—the law.

In large part, the Constitution is a statement of limited government. Much of it reads as clear prohibitions of power to government.[1] For example, notice the Constitution's guarantees of freedom of expression. Those great guarantees—of freedom of religion, of speech, of press, of assembly, and of petition—are vital to democratic government. They are set out in the First Amendment, which begins with the words: "Congress shall make no law. . . ."

Separation of Powers

Recall the brief discussion of the parliamentary and the presidential forms of government in

---

[1]See, especially, Article I, Sections 9 and 10; the 1st through the 10th amendments; and the 13th, 14th, 15th, 19th, 24th, and 26th amendments.

Section 2 of Chapter 1. In a parliamentary system the legislative, executive, and judicial powers of government are all gathered in the hands of a single agency. British government is a leading example. In a presidential system, these basic powers are distributed—separated—among three distinct and independent branches of the government.

This concept is known as **separation of powers.** The idea had been written into each of the State constitutions adopted during the Revolution. A classic expression of the doctrine can be found in the Massachusetts constitution of 1780:

PRIMARY Sources *❝In the government of this commonwealth, the legislative department shall never exercise the executive and judicial powers, or either of them: The executive shall never exercise the legislative and judicial powers, or either of them: The judicial shall never exercise the legislative and executive powers, or either of them: to the end it may be a government of laws and not of men. ❞*

—Part the First, Article XXX

The Constitution of the United States distributes the powers of the National Government among the Congress (the legislative branch), the President (the executive branch), and the courts (the judicial branch). This separation of powers is clearly set forth in the opening words of each of the first three Articles of the Constitution.

Article I, Section 1 declares: "All legislative Powers herein granted shall be vested in a Congress of the United States. . . ." Thus, Congress is the lawmaking branch of the National Government.

Article II, Section 1 declares: "The executive Power shall be vested in a President of the United States of America." Thus, the President is given the law-executing, law-enforcing, law-administering powers of the National Government.

Article III, Section 1 declares: "The judicial Power of the United States shall be vested in one supreme Court, and in such inferior Courts as the Congress may from time to time ordain and establish." Thus, the federal courts, and most importantly the Supreme Court, interpret and apply the laws of the United States in cases brought before them.

Remember, the Framers of the Constitution intended to create a stronger government for the United States. Yet they also intended to limit the powers of that government. The doctrine of separation of powers was designed to that end.

Defending this arrangement, James Madison wrote:

PRIMARY Sources *"The accumulation of all powers, legislative, executive, and judiciary, in the same hands, whether of one, a few, or many . . . may justly be pronounced the very definition of tyranny."*
—*The Federalist* No. 47

Checks and Balances

The National Government is organized around three separate branches. As you have just seen, the Constitution gives to each branch its own field of governmental authority: legislative, executive, and judicial.

These three branches are not entirely separated nor completely independent of one another. Rather, they are tied together by a complex system of **checks and balances.** This means that each branch is subject to a number of constitutional checks (restraints) by the other branches. In other words, each branch has certain powers with which it can check the operations of the other two.

The chart on the next page describes the major features of the check-and-balance arrangement. As you can see, the Congress has the power to make law, but the President may **veto** (reject) any act of Congress. In its turn, Congress can override a presidential veto by a two-thirds vote in each house. Congress can refuse to provide funds requested by the President, or the Senate may refuse to approve a treaty or an appointment made by the President. The President is the commander in chief of the armed forces, but Congress provides that military force; and so on.

The chart also shows how the system of checks and balances links the judicial branch to the legislative and the executive branches. The President has the power to name all federal judges. Each appointment, however, must be approved by a majority vote in the Senate. At the same time, the courts have the power to determine the constitutionality of acts of Congress and of presidential actions, and to strike down those they find unconstitutional.

Head-on clashes between the branches do not often happen. The checks-and-balances system operates all the time, however, and in routine fashion. The very fact that it exists—that each branch has its several checks—affects much of what happens in Washington, D.C.

For example, when the President picks someone to serve in some important office in the executive branch—as, say, secretary of state or director of the Central Intelligence Agency (CIA)—the President is quite aware that the Senate must confirm that appointment. So, the President is apt to pick someone who very likely will be approved by the Senate. In a similar sense, when Congress makes law, it does so with a careful eye on both the President's veto power and the power of the courts to review its actions.

Spectacular clashes—direct applications of the check-and-balance system—do sometimes occur, of course. The President does veto some acts of Congress. On rare occasion, Congress does override one of those vetoes. Similarly,

"Hey, the Constitution isn't engraved in stone."

Interpreting Political Cartoons *What does the speaker in this cartoon mean when he says "the Constitution isn't engraved in stone"?*

The Constitution 67

Checks and Balances

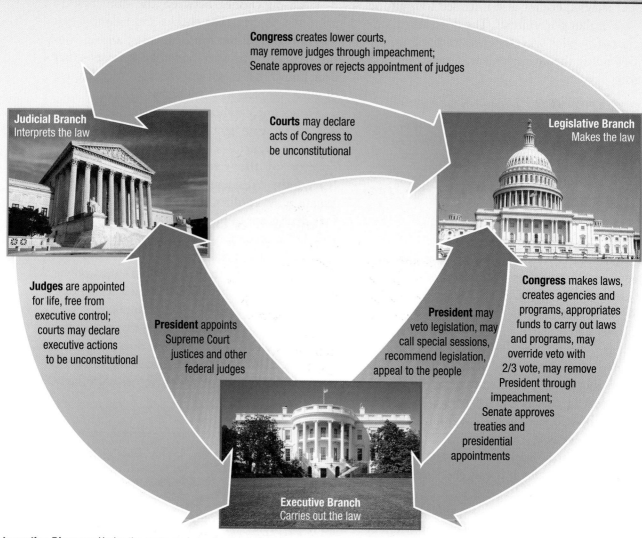

Congress creates lower courts, may remove judges through impeachment; Senate approves or rejects appointment of judges

Courts may declare acts of Congress to be unconstitutional

Judicial Branch
Interprets the law

Legislative Branch
Makes the law

Judges are appointed for life, free from executive control; courts may declare executive actions to be unconstitutional

President appoints Supreme Court justices and other federal judges

President may veto legislation, may call special sessions, recommend legislation, appeal to the people

Congress makes laws, creates agencies and programs, appropriates funds to carry out laws and programs, may override veto with 2/3 vote, may remove President through impeachment; Senate approves treaties and presidential appointments

Executive Branch
Carries out the law

Interpreting Diagrams Under the system of checks and balances, each branch of government can check the actions of the others. *In what way can the power of the judiciary be checked by the other branches?*

the Senate can reject one of the President's appointees. And twice in our history, the House of Representatives has impeached, or brought charges against, a President—Andrew Johnson in 1868 and Bill Clinton in 1998—although on both occasions the President was acquitted by the Senate.

But, again, these and other direct confrontations are not common. Congress, the President, and even the courts try to avoid them. The check-and-balance system makes compromise necessary—and compromise is a vital part of democratic government.

Over time, the check-and-balance system has worked quite well. It has done what the Framers intended it to do. It has prevented "an unjust combination of the majority." At the same time, it has not very often forestalled a close working relationship between the executive and legislative branches.

Note, however, that that working relationship runs more smoothly when the President and a majority in both houses of Congress have been of the same political party. When the other party controls one or both houses, conflicts play a larger than usual part in that relationship.

In fact, the American people have lately become accustomed to divided government, to a political environment in which one of the major parties holds the presidency and the other party controls Congress. Since the Eisenhower era in the 1950s, one of the two major parties (most often the Republican party) has usually occupied the White House, while the other party (regularly the Democratic party) has had a firm grip on Capitol Hill.

That now-familiar pattern of divided government has had a marked effect on the conduct of business between the President and Congress. Much of the executive-legislative relationship has been rooted in partisanship in recent years. It has been much more difficult and much more confrontational over those years than it has been through most of the nation's history.

Judicial Review

One aspect of the principle of checks and balances is of such overriding importance in the American constitutional system that it stands, by itself, as one of that system's basic principles: judicial review.

The power of **judicial review** is the power of courts to determine whether what government does is in accord with what the Constitution provides. More precisely, judicial review may be defined this way: It is the power of a court to determine the constitutionality of a governmental action.

In part, then, judicial review is the power to declare **unconstitutional**—to declare illegal, null and void, of no force and effect—a governmental action found to violate some provision in the Constitution. The power of judicial review is held by all federal courts and by most State courts, as well.[2]

The Constitution does not provide for judicial review in so many words. Yet it seems clear that the Framers intended that the federal courts, and in particular the Supreme Court, should have that power. In *The Federalist* No. 78 Alexander Hamilton wrote that "independent judges" would prove to be "an essential safeguard against the effects of occasional ill humors in society." In *The Federalist* No. 51 James Madison called the judicial power one of the "auxiliary precautions" against the possible dominance of one branch of government over another.

In practice, the Supreme Court established the power of judicial review in the landmark case of *Marbury* v. *Madison* in 1803. (We shall take a close look at that case and the doctrine of judicial review in Chapter 18.) Since *Marbury,* the Supreme Court and other federal and State courts have used the power in thousands of cases. For the most part, the courts have

---

[2]Generally, the power is held by all courts of record. These are courts that keep a record of their proceedings and have the power to punish for contempt. Usually, only the lowest courts in a State—justice of the peace courts, for example—are not courts of record.

▲ The Supreme Court has struck down federal laws that regulated child labor and outlawed the burning of the United States flag. *Critical Thinking What characteristic of a law can lead the Supreme Court to overturn it?*

upheld challenged governmental actions. That is, in most cases in which the power of judicial review is exercised, the actions of government are found to be constitutional.

That is not always the case. To date, the Supreme Court has decided some 150 cases in which it has found an act or some part of an act of Congress to be unconstitutional. It has struck down several presidential and other executive branch actions as well. The Court has also voided hundreds of actions of the States and their local governments, including more than 1,000 State laws.

Federalism

As you know, the American governmental system is federal in form. The powers held by government are distributed on a territorial basis. The National Government holds some of those powers, and others belong to the 50 States.

The principle of **federalism**—the division of power among a central government and several regional governments—came to the Constitution out of both experience and

▲ This statue in Concord, Massachusetts, pays tribute to the Minutemen who fought British troops to protect self-government.

necessity. In Philadelphia, the Framers faced a number of difficult problems, not the least of them: How to build a new, stronger, more effective National Government while preserving the existing States and the concept of local self-government.

The colonists had rebelled against the harsh rule of a powerful and distant central government. They had fought for the right to manage their local affairs without the meddling and dictation of the king and his ministers in far-off London. Surely, they would not now agree to another such government.

The Framers found their solution in federalism. In short, they constructed the federal arrangement, with its division of powers, as a compromise. It was an alternative to the system of nearly independent States, loosely tied to one another in the weak Articles of Confederation, and a much feared, too powerful central government. We shall explore the federal system at length in the next chapter.

Section 1 Assessment

Key Terms and Main Ideas

1. What is the purpose of the **Preamble** to the Constitution?
2. List two examples of how **checks and balances** work in the Federal Government.
3. What is the immediate effect if a law is declared **unconstitutional**?
4. Explain **federalism** in your own words.

Critical Thinking

5. **Making Comparisons** What are the different roles of the executive branch, legislative branch, and judicial branch?
6. **Understanding Point of View** Why were the Framers of the Constitution careful to limit the powers of the Federal Government?

7. **Drawing Conclusions** Some people consider the judicial branch the least democratic of the three branches of the government because federal judges are not elected and cannot be easily removed. How can voters and their elected representatives check the power of the judicial branch?

 Take It to the Net

8. Read about the division of power in the United States, Britain, and France and write a paragraph explaining how this element of the Constitution differentiates our Federal Government from the French and British systems. Use the links provided in the Social Studies area at the following Web site for help in completing this activity.
www.phschool.com

SKILLS FOR LIFE

Using the Internet for Research

The Internet is a network of computers that links governments, organizations, and individuals around the world. The World Wide Web is one part of the Internet. Since the Internet has no central organization, finding the information you need can be difficult. To focus your search you can use search engines, the databases that track thousands of Web pages by subject.

Congress uses the Internet to communicate with the public. Congressional Web sites provide general information about legislators, committees, and hearings. These sites also provide information on proposed legislation. Use the steps below to locate and track the progress of a bill in Congress.

1. Plan the scope of your search. Choose a research topic that is not too vague. Searching for a broad subject can yield thousands of results that would be impossible to sift through. Try to state your research topic as a specific question. Then think of search terms that might return answers to your question. For example, rather than searching for broad terms such as *Congress* or *legislation,* identify a public issue that Congress is working on, such as *funding for disaster relief.* Then do a search on that topic.

2. Refine your search. Your first set of results usually includes Web sites that do not contain the information you need. Many search engines offer an advanced search option that allows you to narrow your search. You might decide to make your search terms more specific; for instance, *disaster relief AND earthquakes.* Or you might exclude unwanted information, as in *disaster relief NOT hurricanes.*

3. Navigate the sites. Once you find a site that meets your needs, explore its home page to determine how to find the information you need. Does the information in the site fully answer your question? Does the site have its own search tool to explore information contained in the site? Does it provide links to other Web sites that might better aid your research? To whom does the site belong, and is it a reliable source? (The Social Studies area at the following Web site has many useful research links: **www.phschool.com**)

For example, if your search led you to the Web site of the Federal Emergency Management Agency (FEMA), you might search within the site for *budget AND earthquakes* to find out how much funding FEMA has requested to cover damage from a particular earthquake. Then you might go to a congressional site to find out the status of the budget request for FEMA.

Test for Success

Conduct Internet research on an important public issue that is currently being debated in Congress. Find out what legislation is being proposed on this topic. Check the status of the legislation. Has it been proposed in both houses of Congress? At what stage is the bill in each house?

▶ Aftermath of the October 1989 earthquake in Oakland, California

Section Preview

OBJECTIVES

1. **Describe** four different ways to formally amend, or change the wording of, the Constitution.
2. **Explain** the limits of the formal amendment process.
3. **Understand** the history of the 27 amendments to the Constitution, including the Bill of Rights.

WHY IT MATTERS

The Constitution has grown and changed with the United States through the addition of 27 amendments. The first ten amendments guarantee many of our basic freedoms and are known as the Bill of Rights.

POLITICAL DICTIONARY

★ **amendment**
★ **formal amendment**
★ **Bill of Rights**

The Constitution of the United States has now been in force for more than 200 years—longer, by far, than the written constitution of any other nation in the world.[3]

When the Constitution became effective in 1789, the United States was a small agricultural nation of fewer than four million people. That population was scattered for some 1,300 miles along the eastern edge of the continent. Travel and communications among the 13 States were limited to horseback and sailing ships. The new States struggled to stay alive in a generally hostile world.

Today, more than 285 million people live in the United States. The now 50 States stretch across the continent and beyond, and the country also has many far-flung commitments. The United States is today the most powerful nation on Earth, and its modern, highly industrialized and technological society has produced a standard of living that has long been the envy of the rest of the world.

How has the Constitution, written in 1787, endured and kept up with that astounding change and growth? The answer lies in this highly important fact: The United States Constitution of today *is*, and at the same time *is not*, the document of 1787. Many of its words are the same, and much of their meaning remains the same. But some of its words have been changed, some have been eliminated, and some have been added. And, very importantly, the meanings of many of its provisions have been modified as well.

This process of constitutional change, of modification and growth, has come about in two basic ways: (1) by formal amendment and (2) by informal amendment. In this section, you will look at the first of them: the addition of formal amendments to the Constitution.

Formal Amendment Process

The Framers knew that even the wisest of constitution makers cannot build for all time. Thus, the Constitution provides for its own **amendment**—that is, for changes in its written words.

Article V sets out two methods for the proposal and two methods for the ratification of constitutional amendments. So, there are four

Population Growth

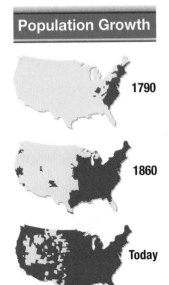

1790

1860

Today

More than 2 persons per square mile
SOURCE: MapQuest.com, Inc.

◀ The United States population has grown and expanded across the continent since the Constitution was adopted. The Constitution has been amended to meet the changing needs of the country.

---

[3]The British constitution dates from well before the Norman Conquest of 1066, but it is not a single, written document. Rather, it is an "unwritten constitution," a collection of principles, customs, traditions, and significant parliamentary acts that guide British government and practice. Israel, which has existed only since 1948, is the only other state in the world without a written constitution.

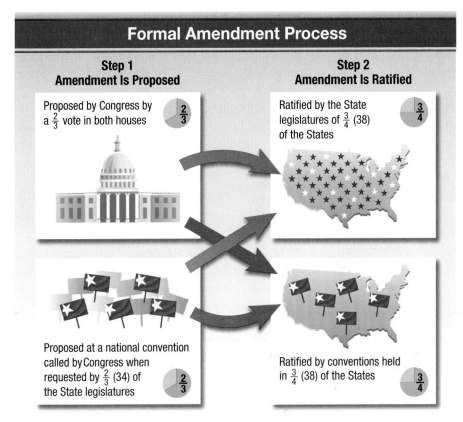

Formal Amendment Process

Step 1
Amendment Is Proposed

Proposed by Congress by a $\frac{2}{3}$ vote in both houses — $\frac{2}{3}$

Proposed at a national convention called by Congress when requested by $\frac{2}{3}$ (34) of the State legislatures — $\frac{2}{3}$

Step 2
Amendment Is Ratified

Ratified by the State legislatures of $\frac{3}{4}$ (38) of the States — $\frac{3}{4}$

Ratified by conventions held in $\frac{3}{4}$ (38) of the States — $\frac{3}{4}$

Interpreting Diagrams The four different ways in which amendments may be added to the Constitution are shown here. Conventions are rarely used. All but one of the 27 amendments were proposed in Congress and then ratified by the State legislatures. *How does the formal amendment process illustrate federalism?*

possible methods of **formal amendment**—changes or additions that become part of the written language of the Constitution itself. The diagram above sets out these four methods.

First Method An amendment may be proposed by a two-thirds vote in each house of Congress and be ratified by three fourths of the State legislatures. Today, 38 State legislatures must approve an amendment for it to become a part of the Constitution. Twenty-six of the Constitution's 27 amendments were adopted in this manner.

Second Method An amendment may be proposed by Congress and then ratified by conventions, called for that purpose, in three fourths of the States. Only the 21st Amendment, added in 1933, was adopted in this way. Conventions were used to ratify the 21st Amendment largely because Congress felt that the conventions' popularly elected delegates would be more likely to reflect public opinion on the question of repeal than would State legislators.

Third Method An amendment may be proposed by a national convention, called by Congress at the request of two thirds of the State legislatures—today, 34. As you can see in the diagram, it must then be ratified by three fourths

of the State legislatures. To this point, Congress has not called such a convention.[4]

Fourth Method An amendment may be proposed by a national convention and ratified by conventions in three fourths of the States. Remember that the Constitution itself was adopted in much this same way.

Federalism and Popular Sovereignty

Note that the formal amendment process emphasizes the federal character of the governmental system. Proposal takes place at the national level and ratification is a State-by-State matter. Also note that when the Constitution is amended, that action represents the expression of the people's sovereign will. The people have spoken.

Some criticize the practice of sending proposed amendments to the State legislatures rather than to ratifying conventions, especially

---

[4]The calling of a convention has been a near thing twice in recent years. Between 1963 and 1969, 33 State legislatures, one short of the necessary two thirds, sought an amendment to erase the Supreme Court's "one-person, one-vote" decisions; see Chapter 24. Also, between 1975 and 1983, 32 States asked for a convention to propose an amendment that would require that the federal budget be balanced each year, except in time of war or other national emergency.

because it permits a constitutional change without a clear-cut expression by the people. The critics point out that State legislators, who do the ratifying, are elected to office for a mix of reasons: party membership; name familiarity; their stands on such matters as taxes, schools, welfare programs; and a host of other things. They are almost never chosen because of their stand on a proposed amendment to the federal Constitution. On the other hand, the delegates to a ratifying convention would be chosen by the people on the basis of only one factor: a yes-or-no stand on the proposed amendment.

The Supreme Court has held that a State cannot require an amendment proposed by Congress to be approved by a vote of the people of the State before it can be ratified by the State legislature. It made that ruling in *Hawke* v. *Smith* in 1920. However, a state legislature can call for an advisory vote by the people before it acts, as the Court most recently held in *Kimble* v. *Swackhamer* in 1978.

Proposed Amendments

The Constitution places only one restriction on the subjects with which a proposed amendment may deal. Article V declares that "no State, without its Consent, shall be deprived of its equal Suffrage in the Senate."

When both houses of Congress pass a resolution proposing an amendment, Congress does not send it to the President to be signed or vetoed, though the Constitution would seem to require it.[5] This is because when Congress proposes an amendment, it is not making law (not legislating).

If a State rejects a proposed amendment, it is not forever bound by that action. It may later reconsider and ratify the proposal. Most constitutional scholars agree that the reverse is not true,

---

[5]See Article I, Section 7, Clause 3. This practice of not submitting proposed amendments to the President is an example of the many "informal amendments" to the Constitution, a matter we shall turn to shortly.

The *Living* Constitution

| Changing Views of Free Speech | 1800 | 1925 |

Many Americans, including many who supported the new Constitution, criticized the document because it lacked a bill of rights—a listing of the basic rights held by the people against the new National Government. That criticism was soon met: ten amendments, the Bill of Rights, were added to the Constitution in 1791. The guarantees of freedom of speech and press, set out in the 1st Amendment, have produced controversy for more than 200 years now.

1798 Sedition Act makes it a crime to criticize the government in speech or writing. The law is not renewed after the election of 1800.

1919 Supreme Court rules that sending written material to draftees urging them to resist the draft is unlawful because it creates a "clear and present danger" to national security. (*Schenck* v. *United States*)

however. Once a State has approved an amendment, that action is final and unchangeable.

More than 10,000 joint resolutions calling for amendments to the Constitution have been proposed in Congress since 1789. Only 33 of them have been sent on to the States. Of those, only 27 have been finally ratified. One of the unratified amendments had been offered by Congress in 1789—along with 10 other proposals that became the Bill of Rights in 1791, and another that became the 27th Amendment in 1992. The unratified amendment of 1789 dealt with the distribution of seats in the House of Representatives. A second amendment, proposed in 1810, would have voided the citizenship of anyone accepting any foreign title or other honor. Another, in 1861, would have prohibited forever any amendment relating to slavery. A fourth, in 1924, was intended to empower Congress to regulate child labor. A fifth one, proclaiming the equal rights of women (ERA), was proposed by Congress in 1972; it fell three States short of ratification and died in 1982. An amendment to give the District of Columbia seats in Congress was proposed in 1978; it died in 1985. Congress can place "a reasonable time limit" on the ratification process, *Dillon* v. *Gloss*, 1921. When Congress proposed the 18th Amendment (in 1917), it set a seven-year deadline for its ratification. It has set a similar deadline for the ratification of each of the amendments (except the 19th) it has proposed since, although Congress granted the ERA a three-year extension in 1979.

The 27 Amendments

The Constitution's 27 amendments are described in the table on the next page. As you review the amendments, note this important fact: As significant as they are, these 27 amendments have not in fact been responsible for the extraordinary vitality of the Constitution. That is to say, they

1969 Supreme Court decides that the 1st Amendment protects students who wear armbands in school to protest the Vietnam War. (*Tinker* v. *Des Moines School District*)

1989 Supreme Court rules that burning an American flag as a political protest is "symbolic speech," protected by the 1st Amendment. (*Texas* v. *Johnson*)

1950　　1975　　2000

1951 Eleven American Communists are convicted of sedition for advocating the overthrow of the government. Supreme Court decides that the 1st Amendment does not protect them. (*Dennis* v. *United States*)

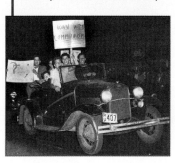

1971 Government tries to stop the *New York Times* publication of the "Pentagon Papers" about the Vietnam War. The Supreme Court upholds the paper's right to do so. (*New York Times* v. *United States*)

2002 Supreme Court strikes down ban on "virtual" child pornography and similar computer-generated images. (*Ashcroft* v. *Free Speech Coalition*)

Analyzing Time Lines

1. What was the Court's reason for protecting a protester who burned an American flag?
2. Both the *Schenck* case (1919) and the *Tinker* case (1969) involved antiwar protests. How would you explain the difference between the Supreme Court decisions?

have *not* been a major part of the process by which the Constitution has kept pace with more than two centuries of far-reaching change.

The Bill of Rights

The first ten amendments were added to the Constitution less than three years after it became effective. They were proposed by the first session of the First Congress in 1789 and were ratified by the States in late 1791. Each of these amendments arose out of the controversy surrounding the ratification of the Constitution itself. Many people, including Thomas Jefferson, had agreed to support the Constitution only if a listing of the basic rights held by the people were added to it immediately.

Collectively, the first ten amendments are known as the **Bill of Rights.** They set out the great constitutional guarantees of freedom of belief and expression, of freedom and security of the person, and of fair and equal treatment before the law. We shall consider these guarantees at some length in Chapters 19 and 20. The 10th Amendment does not deal with civil rights as such. Rather, it spells out the concept of reserved powers in the federal system.

The Later Amendments

Each of the other amendments that have been added to the Constitution over the past 200 years also grew out of some particular, and often interesting, set of circumstances. For example, the 11th Amendment declares that no State may be sued in the federal courts by a citizen of another State or by a citizen of any foreign state. It was proposed by Congress in 1794 and ratified in 1795, after the State of Georgia had lost its case in the United States Supreme Court. The case (*Chisholm* v. *Georgia*, decided by the Court in 1793) had been brought to the brand new federal court system by a man who lived in South Carolina.

Amendments to the Constitution

Amendment	Subject	Year	Time Required for Ratification
1st–10th	Bill of Rights	1791	2 years, 2 months, 20 days
11th	Immunity of States from certain lawsuits	1795	11 months, 3 days
12th	Changes in electoral college procedures	1804	6 months, 6 days
13th	Abolition of slavery	1865	10 months, 6 days
14th	Citizenship, due process, equal protection	1868	2 years, 26 days
15th	No denial of vote because of race, color, or previous enslavement	1870	11 months, 8 days
16th	Power of Congress to tax incomes	1913	3 years, 6 months, 22 days
17th	Popular election of U.S. Senators	1913	10 months, 26 days
18th	Prohibition of alcohol	1919	1 year, 29 days
19th	Woman suffrage	1920	1 year, 2 months, 14 days
20th	Change of dates for start of presidential and Congressional terms	1933	10 months, 21 days
21st	Repeal of Prohibition (18th Amendment)	1933	9 months, 15 days
22nd	Limit on presidential terms	1951	3 years, 11 months, 6 days
23rd	District of Columbia vote in presidential elections	1961	9 months, 13 days
24th	Ban of tax payment as voter qualification	1964	1 year, 4 months, 27 days
25th	Presidential succession, vice presidential vacancy, and presidential disability	1967	1 year, 7 months, 4 days
26th	Voting age of 18	1971	3 months, 8 days
27th	Congressional pay	1992	202 years, 7 months, 12 days

Interpreting Tables These 27 amendments have been added to the Constitution since it became effective in 1789. ***Which amendment was adopted in the shortest time? Which one took the most time to ratify?***

The 12th Amendment was added to the Constitution in 1804 after the electoral college had failed to produce a winner in the presidential election of 1800. Thomas Jefferson became the third President of the United States in 1801, but only after a long, bitter fight in the House of Representatives.

The 13th Amendment, added in 1865, provides another example. It abolished slavery in the United States and was a direct result of the Civil War. So, too, were the 14th Amendment on citizenship (in 1868) and the 15th Amendment on the right to vote (in 1870).

As you can see in the table on page 76, the 18th Amendment, establishing a nationwide prohibition of alcohol, was ratified in 1919. What came to be known as "the noble experiment" lasted fewer than 14 years. The 18th Amendment was repealed by the 21st in 1933.

The 22nd Amendment (1951) was proposed in 1947, soon after the Republican Party had gained control of Congress for the first time in 16 years. Over that period, Franklin D. Roosevelt, a Democrat, had won the presidency four times.

The 26th Amendment was added in 1971. It lowered the voting age to 18 in all elections in the United States. Many of those who backed the amendment began to work for its passage during World War II, with the argument "Old enough to fight, old enough to vote." Its ratification was spurred by the war in Vietnam.

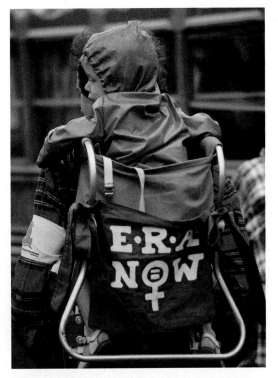

▲ *Two ERA Supporters* People fought unsuccessfully in the 1970s and 1980s to add the Equal Rights Amendment to the Constitution.

The most recent amendment, the 27th, was among the first to be offered by Congress. This amendment forbids members of Congress from raising their own pay during that term. It was proposed in 1789 and ratified nearly 203 years later, in 1992.

Section 2 Assessment

Key Terms and Main Ideas

1. How many **amendments** were added to the Constitution in the twentieth century?
2. Describe the four possible methods of **formal amendment.**
3. In your own words, describe three freedoms protected by the **Bill of Rights.**

Critical Thinking

4. **Drawing Conclusions** Why does the Constitution provide that *both* houses of Congress must agree to the proposal of an amendment?

5. **Determining Cause and Effect** Cite three events or controversies that led to amendments to the Constitution, and explain how each of these amendments settled a particular question.
6. **Drawing Inferences** Why does the Constitution require an extraordinary majority for the ratification of amendments to the Constitution?

Take It to the Net

7. Read a recent debate on a proposed amendment to the Constitution and write a letter to one member of Congress to explain why you support or oppose this amendment. Use the links provided in the Social Studies area at the following Web site for help in completing this activity. **www.phschool.com**

Letters of Liberty

Thomas Jefferson and James Madison enjoyed a lifelong friendship. While Jefferson served in Paris as United States Minister to France (1785 to 1789), he and Madison exchanged several letters. Their correspondence included the letters below, in which they discuss the addition of a bill of rights to the recently drafted Constitution.

James Madison
1751–1836

JEFFERSON TO MADISON
December 20, 1787

I will now add what I do not like [about the Constitution]. First the omission of a bill of rights providing clearly . . . for freedom of religion, freedom of the press, protection against standing armies, restriction against monopolies, . . . and trials by jury in all matters of fact triable by the laws of the land. . . . Let me add that a bill of rights is what the people are entitled to against every government on earth, general or particular, and what no just government should refuse, or rest on inference. . . .

MADISON TO JEFFERSON
October 17, 1788

. . . My own opinion has always been in favor of a bill of rights, provided it be so framed as to not imply powers not meant to be included. . . . At the same time, I have never thought the omission a material defect. . . . I have favored it because I supposed it might be of use, and if properly executed could not be of disservice. . . .

Experience proves the [ineffectiveness] of a bill of rights on those occasions when its control is most needed. Repeated violations of these parchment barriers have been committed by overbearing majorities in every state. In Virginia I have seen the [state constitution's] bill of rights violated in every instance where it has been opposed to a popular current. . . . Wherever the real power in a government lies, there is the danger of oppression. In our government, the real power lies in the majority of the community, and the invasion of privacy rights is chiefly to be [feared], not from acts of government contrary to the sense of its constituents, but from acts in which the government is the mere instrument of the major number of constituents. . . .

JEFFERSON TO MADISON
March 15, 1789

. . . In the arguments in favor of a declaration of rights, you omit one which has great weight with me, the legal check which it puts into the hands of the judiciary. This is a body, which if rendered independent, and kept strictly to their own department merits great confidence for their learning and integrity. . . .

. . . Experience proves the [ineffectiveness] of a bill of rights. True. But [though] it is not absolutely [effective] under all circumstances, it is of great potency always. . . .

Analyzing Primary Sources

1. Why did Jefferson want a bill of rights added to the Constitution?
2. According to Madison, from where did the greatest danger to individual rights come?
3. What did Madison mean when he referred to a bill of rights as a "parchment barrier"?
4. Why, as Jefferson states, would a bill of rights strengthen the judicial branch of government?

·3· Informal Amendment

Section Preview

OBJECTIVES

1. **Identify** how basic legislation has changed the Constitution over time.
2. **Explain** the powers of the executive branch and the courts to amend the Constitution.
3. **Analyze** the role of party practices and custom in shaping the Federal Government.

WHY IT MATTERS

In addition to the 27 formal amendments, Americans have made many more informal changes to the Constitution. As the Federal Government expanded, all three branches introduced new ways to govern that do not conflict with the original Constitution.

POLITICAL DICTIONARY

★ **informal amendment**
★ **executive agreement**
★ **treaty**
★ **electoral college**
★ **Cabinet**
★ **senatorial courtesy**

The Constitution is a comparatively short document. Much of it is devoted to matters of principle and of basic organization, structure, and process. Most of its sections are brief, even skeletal in nature. For this reason, the real key to constitutional change and development lies in the process of **informal amendment.** Informal amendment is the process by which over time many changes have been made in the Constitution which have not involved any changes in its written words.

To understand the Constitution and the process of constitutional change, you must understand a key point: there is much in the Constitution that cannot be seen with the naked eye. The informal amendments are the result of the day-to-day, year-to-year experiences of government under the Constitution.

This highly important process of informal amendment has taken place—and continues to occur—in five basic ways: through (1) the passage of basic legislation by Congress; (2) actions taken by the President; (3) key decisions of the Supreme Court; (4) the activities of political parties; and (5) custom.

Basic Legislation

Congress has been a major agent of informal amendment in two important ways. First, it has passed a number of laws to spell out several of the Constitution's brief provisions. That is,

Congress has added flesh to the bones of those sections of the Constitution that the Framers left purposely skeletal for Congress to add details and meaning as circumstances have required.

Take the structure of the federal court system as an example. In Article III, Section 1, the Constitution provides for "one supreme Court, and . . . such inferior Courts as the Congress may from time to time ordain and establish." Beginning with the Judiciary Act of 1789, all of the federal courts, except the Supreme Court, have been set up by acts of Congress. Or, similarly, Article II creates only the offices of President and Vice President. The many departments, agencies,

▲ *Campaign Artifacts*
Political parties are a basic feature of the American governmental system, but they are not mentioned in the Constitution.

▲ **Across the Border** Congress can pass laws under its constitutional power to regulate interstate commerce, or trade that crosses State boundaries.

and offices in the now huge executive branch have been created by acts of Congress.

As another example, the Constitution deals with the matter of presidential succession, but only up to a point. The 25th Amendment says that if the presidency becomes vacant, the Vice President automatically succeeds to the office. Who becomes President if both the presidency and the vice presidency are vacant? The Constitution leaves the answer to that question to Congress and its lawmaking power.

Second, Congress has added to the Constitution by the way in which it has used many of its powers. The Constitution gives to Congress the expressed power to regulate

foreign and interstate commerce.[6] But what is "foreign commerce"? What is "interstate commerce"? What, exactly, does Congress have the power to regulate? The Constitution does not say. Congress has done much to define those words, however, by exercising its commerce power with the passage of literally thousands of laws. As it has done so, Congress has informally amended—added much to—the Constitution.

Executive Action

The manner in which various Presidents have used their powers has also produced a number of important informal amendments. For example, the Constitution states that only Congress can declare war.[7] But the Constitution also makes the President the commander in chief of the nation's armed forces.[8] Acting under that authority, several Presidents have made war without a declaration of war by Congress. In fact, Presidents have used the armed forces abroad in combat without such a declaration on several hundred occasions in our history.

Take the use of executive agreements in the conduct of foreign affairs as another example here. An **executive agreement** is a pact made by the President directly with the head of a foreign state. A **treaty**, on the other hand, is a formal agreement between two or more sovereign states. The principal difference between these agreements and treaties is that executive agreements need not be approved by the Senate. They are as legally binding as treaties, however. Recent Presidents have often used them in our dealings with other countries, instead of the much more cumbersome treaty-making process outlined in Article II, Section 2 of the Constitution.

Court Decisions

The nation's courts, most tellingly the United States Supreme Court, interpret and apply the Constitution in many

▲ President Bush used his power as commander in chief to commit armed forces to Afghanistan in 2001. *Critical Thinking **Should the President be able to make war without a declaration of war by Congress?***

[6]Article I, Section 8, Clause 3.
[7]Article I, Section 8, Clause 11.
[8]Article II, Section 2, Clause 1.

cases they hear. You have already read about several of these instances of constitutional interpretation—that is, informal amendment—by the Court, such as in *Marbury* v. *Madison,* 1803. You will encounter more of these landmark cases throughout this book, for the Supreme Court is, as Woodrow Wilson once put it, "a constitutional convention in continuous session."

Party Practices

The nation's political parties have also been a major source of informal amendment over the course of American political history, despite the fact that the Constitution makes no mention of political parties. In fact, most of the Framers were opposed to their growth. In his Farewell Address in 1796, George Washington warned the people against what he called "the baneful effects of the spirit of party." Washington feared the divisive effect of party politics. Yet, even as he spoke, parties were developing in this country. They have played a major role in the shaping of government and its processes ever since. There are numerous examples of that point.

Neither the Constitution nor any law provides for the nomination of candidates for the presidency. From the 1830s on, however, the major parties have held national conventions to do just that. The parties have converted the **electoral college,** the group that makes the formal selection of the nation's President, from what the Framers intended into a "rubber stamp" for each State's popular vote in presidential elections. Both houses of Congress are organized and conduct much of their business on the basis of party. The President makes appointments to office with an eye to party politics. In short, government in the United States is in many ways government through party.

Custom

Unwritten customs may be as strong as written laws, and many customs have developed in our governmental system. Again, there are many examples. By custom, not because the Constitution says so, the heads of the 14 executive departments make up the **Cabinet,** an advisory body to the President traditionally made up of the heads of the executive departments and other officers.

Voices on Government

John Marshall (Chief Justice of the United States) set precedents that established important powers of the federal courts. Marshall served as Chief Justice of the United States from 1801 until 1835. As a Federalist, he established the independence of the judicial branch. In *Marbury* v. *Madison,* Marshall claimed for the Supreme Court the power to declare a law unconstitutional, and he affirmed the superiority of federal authority under the Constitution in *McCulloch* v. *Maryland* and *Gibbons* v. *Ogden.* In *McCulloch* v. *Maryland,* he wrote:

❝ *This provision is made in a constitution, intended to endure for ages to come, and consequently, to be adapted to the various crises of human affairs.* ❞

Evaluating the Quotation

Write a paragraph showing how Marshall's quote exemplifies the concept of a living Constitution. Use information from your reading of the text to support your answer.

On each of the eight occasions when a President died in office, the Vice President succeeded to that office—most recently in 1963. Yet, the written words of the Constitution did not provide for this practice until the adoption of the 25th Amendment in 1967. Until then, the Constitution said only that the powers and duties of the presidency—but *not* the office itself—should be transferred to the Vice President.[9]

It is a long-established custom that the Senate will only approve those presidential appointees that are acceptable to the senator or senators of the President's party from the State involved, for example, a federal judge or a United States marshal. This practice is known as **senatorial courtesy,** and it is closely followed in the Senate. Notice that its practical effect is to shift a portion of the appointing power from the

[9]Read, carefully, Article II, Section 1, Clause 6, and then Section 1 of the 25th Amendment.

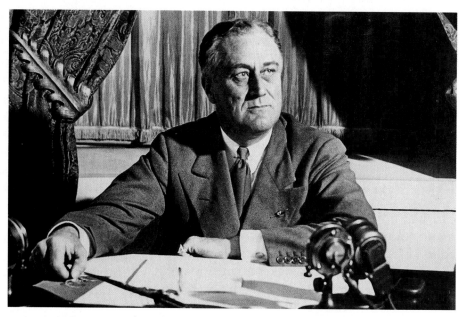

▲ The tradition of limiting Presidents to two terms became a major issue in the presidential campaign of 1940 and again in 1944. *Critical Thinking Why did Roosevelt's reelection lead supporters of the "no-third-term" tradition to push for a constitutional amendment?*

President, where the formal wording of the Constitution puts it, to certain members of the Senate.

Both the strength and the importance of unwritten customs can be seen in the reaction to the rare circumstances in which one of them has not been observed. For nearly 150 years, the "no-third-term tradition" was a closely followed rule in presidential politics. The tradition began in 1796, when George Washington refused to seek a third term as President, and several later Presidents followed that lead. In 1940, and again in 1944, however, Franklin Roosevelt broke the no-third-term custom. He sought and won a third and then a fourth term in the White House. As a direct result, the 22nd Amendment was added to the Constitution in 1951. What had been an unwritten custom, an informal amendment, became a written part of the Constitution itself.

Section 3 Assessment

Key Terms and Main Ideas

1. How does **informal amendment** differ from formal amendment?
2. What role does the **Cabinet** play in government?
3. What is the current role of the **electoral college**?
4. What is an **executive agreement**?

Critical Thinking

5. **Drawing Conclusions** Explain, in your own words, why informal amendment is such an important part of constitutional change.

6. **Determining Cause and Effect** What do you think would happen if the President appointed federal officials without concern for senatorial courtesy? How does the Constitution provide for a solution?

 Take It to the Net

7. The Constitution continually adapts as American society changes. Read about why it is often referred to as "The Living Constitution." Then create a chart that shows the various ways in which the Constitution can be modified. Use the links provided in the Social Studies area at the following Web site for help in completing this activity. **www.phschool.com**

May Schools Use Corporal Punishment?

The 8th Amendment declares, in part, that "cruel and unusual punishment" may not be inflicted. It does not, however, state on whom such punishment may not be inflicted. The amendment is commonly applied to convicted criminals. Does it also protect others, such as students, from physical punishments?

Ingraham v. Wright (1977)

James Ingraham and Roosevelt Andrews, students in the eighth and ninth grades in a Dade County, Florida, junior high school, were paddled in 1970 for violating school rules. Florida law allowed corporal punishment of students as a means of maintaining discipline, so long as it was not "degrading or unduly severe" and was administered only after the principal or teacher in charge of the school had been consulted.

Ingraham and Andrews filed suit in federal court against Willie J. Wright (their school's principal) and other school officials. They said that the paddlings had violated their 8th Amendment protection against cruel and unusual punishment. They presented evidence showing the seriousness of the discipline they had received, which caused both students physical injuries. The trial court ruled against them, finding that the punishment was not sufficiently arbitrary, severe, or unacceptable under contemporary standards to violate the 8th Amendment.

The students then appealed to the court of appeals. A panel of the court concluded that the punishment was too severe, and that the students should have been given an opportunity to be heard before being punished. The entire court of appeals then heard the case. It concluded that the punishment did *not* violate the Constitution and that students did *not* have a right to a hearing before being punished. The students then appealed to the Supreme Court.

Arguments for Ingraham

1. The 5th Amendment gives students the right to receive proper notice and to have an opportunity to be heard before the government can punish them. These rights help ensure that the government does not punish people improperly.
2. Severe paddlings are unacceptable in a civilized society and should not be permitted under the 8th Amendment.
3. Convicted criminals cannot be paddled. Criminals should not have greater constitutional protection against cruel and unusual punishment than school children do.

Arguments for Wright

1. Corporal punishment has long been accepted as a means of maintaining discipline in public schools. When this case arose, only two States prohibited corporal punishment in schools.
2. Because teachers may be sued for damages if they use excessive or unreasonable force, there is no need to create a special constitutional rule governing the use of corporal punishment in school.
3. The 8th Amendment protects criminals, and should not be applied to schoolchildren.

Decide for Yourself

1. Review the constitutional grounds on which each side based its arguments and the specific arguments each side presented.
2. Debate the opposing viewpoints presented in this case. Which viewpoint do you favor?
3. Predict the impact of the Court's decision on the rights of public school students. (To read a summary of the Court's decision, turn to the Supreme Court Glossary on page 799.)

Political Dictionary

Preamble (p. 65)

articles (p. 65)

constitutionalism (p. 65)

rule of law (p. 66)

separation of powers (p. 66)

checks and balances (p. 67)

veto (p. 67)

judicial review (p. 69)

unconstitutional (p. 69)

federalism (p. 70)

amendment (p. 72)

formal amendment (p. 73)

Bill of Rights (p. 76)

informal amendment (p. 79)

executive agreement (p. 80)

treaty (p. 80)

electoral college (p. 81)

Cabinet (p. 81)

senatorial courtesy (p. 81)

Practicing the Vocabulary

Matching *Choose a term from the list above that best matches each description.*

1. Changing the Constitution without changing its written words
2. A group that makes the formal selection of the nation's President
3. The idea that government must work in accordance with the principles of the Constitution
4. The power of courts to determine if a law or government action is constitutional
5. A system by which any one branch of government can be restrained by one or both of the other branches

Fill in the Blank *Choose a term from the list above that best completes each sentence below.*

6. Under the principle of _____ , the Federal Government has three equal branches.
7. _____ is the process by which the Constitution has been changed and added to during the course of United States history.
8. The first ten amendments to the United States Constitution are known as the _____.
9. _____ results in changes to the written words of the Constitution.
10. The principle of _____ states that government must be bound by a fundamental law.

Reviewing Main Ideas

Section 1

11. How is the text of the Constitution organized?
12. What are the six basic principles of the Constitution?
13. (a) How are popular sovereignty and limited government related? (b) Why were these principles important to the Framers of the Constitution?
14. What is the purpose of checks and balances?
15. (a) How can the judicial branch check the legislative branch? (b) How can the executive branch check the legislative branch?

Section 2

16. How many amendments have been formally added to the Constitution?
17. (a) What has been the most common method for adding an amendment to the Constitution? (b) Which method has been used only once?
18. How does the formal amendment process reflect federalism?

19. (a) Which amendment required the longest amount of time to ratify? (b) How long did it take?
20. What event led to the 13th, 14th, and 15th amendments?

Section 3

21. What are the five ways that the Constitution can be informally amended?
22. How can Congress informally amend the Constitution?
23. Identify two examples of presidential powers that illustrate the informal amendment process.
24. What is the role of custom in government?

Critical Thinking Skills

25. *Applying the Chapter Skill* Use the Internet to find three recent proposed amendments to the Constitution. Who is promoting these amendments, and why?

26. *Drawing Conclusions* The Preamble to the Constitution begins with the words "We the People." **(a)** Was every person living in the United States in 1789 included in that collective "We"? **(b)** Which, if any, of the 27 amendments to the Constitution corrected that situation?

27. *Demonstrating Reasoned Judgment* James Madison defended the concepts of separation of powers and checks and balances in *The Federalist* No. 51. What did he mean when he wrote that, to guard against a concentration of power in one of the branches of government, "ambition must be made to counteract ambition"?

28. *Testing Conclusions* The text says that the United States Constitution is a flexible document. Find evidence from the text that you believe supports the validity of that conclusion.

Analyzing Political Cartoons

Using your knowledge of American government and this cartoon, answer the questions below.

29. What point is the cartoonist trying to make about the ease or difficulty of proposing constitutional amendments?

30. Based on your reading, do you agree or disagree with the cartoonist's opinion? Explain your answer.

 You Can Make a Difference

The passage of the 26th Amendment brought a spurt of interest in voting and political action by young people. Do you think many teenagers today are still as interested in politics and voting? Prepare a 10-question survey of student attitudes. Ask, for instance, whether the person is registered to vote, knows where to vote, and plans to vote in an upcoming election. Does he or she think that giving 18-year-olds the vote was a good idea? Then use your survey to interview people between the ages of 16 and 21. Record your answers in a table.

Participation Activities

31. *Current Events Watch* The Constitution gives the President the power to appoint all federal judges. However, it also gives the Senate the power to confirm or reject those appointments by majority vote. Research the recent appointment of a federal judge and write a brief report on his or her background and how senators from the opposing party responded to the President's nomination.

32. *Time Line Activity* Create a time line of the Equal Rights Amendment, beginning with its proposal in 1972 and ending with its failure to be ratified ten years later. List the number of States that voted to ratify it each year and include the three-year extension to the time limit passed in 1979. Compare this time line to the table on page 76. What does your time line tell you about the ratification process? Do you think the ten-year time limit was fair? Explain your answer.

33. *It's Your Turn* You are a newspaper editor in the late 1700s. Alexander Hamilton has just referred to democracy as "mobocracy." Write an editorial in response to Hamilton's view. Define the position that you want to take in the editorial. Next, list your arguments. As you revise your editorial, make certain that your arguments are persuasive. Finally, proofread and make a final copy.

 Take It to the Net

Chapter 3 Self-Test As a final review activity, take the Chapter 3 Self-Test in the Social Studies area at the Web site listed below, and receive immediate feedback on your answers.

www.phschool.com

CHAPTER 4

Federalism

"The true 'essence' of federalism is that the States as States have legitimate interests which the National Government is bound to respect even though its laws are supreme."

—Justice Sandra Day O'Connor (1985)

The federal system divides power between the National Government and the States. In this way, federalism ensures that the National Government is strong enough to meet the nation's needs. At the same time, federalism preserves the strength and uniqueness of the individual States.

◆ **National and State flags**

★ You Can Make a Difference

UNDER FEDERALISM, National and State government agencies cooperate in a variety of ways. One way is by sponsoring programs for high school and college students. In Colorado, for example, young men and women in the Youth in Natural Resources (YNR) program help protect parks and natural resources by building trails and mapping the State's resources. At the same time, they study environmental science, earn money, and develop career skills. One team leader, college student Brian Roman, said, "When I think of the YNR program, I think of hope—hope for the wildlife in Colorado . . . hope in tomorrow's leaders."

Keep It Current

Items marked with this logo are periodically updated on the Internet. Keep up-to-date with what's in the news. To get current information on issues involving federalism, go to **www.phschool.com**

SECTION 1

Federalism: The Division of Power (pp. 88–95)

★ The Framers sought to create a central government strong enough to meet the nation's needs and still preserve the strength of the States.

★ The National Government has only those powers delegated to it by the Constitution.

★ The States are governments of reserved powers, or powers that the Constitution does not grant to the National Government or deny to the States.

★ Most of the powers of the National Government are exercised by the National Government alone.

★ The concurrent powers are possessed by both the National Government and the States.

★ Local governments exist only as part of their parent State.

★ The Constitution stands above all other forms of law in the United States.

SECTION 2

The National Government and the 50 States (pp. 97–103)

★ The National Government guarantees the States a representative government, protection against invasion and internal disorder, and respect for territorial integrity.

★ Congress has the power to admit new States.

★ The American federal system involves a broad range of shared powers between the National Government and the States.

SECTION 3

Interstate Relations (pp. 105–108)

★ The States can make interstate compacts that enable them to cooperate on matters of mutual concern.

★ The Constitution requires each State to respect the laws, official records, and court actions of other States.

★ The Constitution requires each State to return fugitives to the State from which they fled.

★ No State can draw unreasonable distinctions between its own residents and residents of other States.

Federalism: The Division of Power

1

Section Preview

OBJECTIVES

1. **Define** federalism and explain why the Framers chose this system of government.
2. **Identify** powers delegated to and denied to the National Government, and powers reserved for and denied to the States.
3. **Understand** that the National Government holds exclusive powers; it also holds concurrent powers with the States.
4. **Explain** the place of local governments in the federal system.
5. **Examine** how the Constitution functions as "the supreme Law of the Land."

WHY IT MATTERS

The federal system divides government power in order to prevent its abuse. There are two basic levels of government in the federal system—National and State. The Supreme Court settles disputes between the two.

POLITICAL DICTIONARY

★ **federalism**
★ **division of powers**
★ **delegated powers**
★ **expressed powers**
★ **implied powers**
★ **inherent powers**
★ **reserved powers**
★ **exclusive powers**
★ **concurrent powers**

You know that federal law requires young men to register for military service at age 18; that most employers must pay their workers at least $5.15 an hour and time-and-a-half for overtime; and that no person can be denied a job on the basis of his or her race or ethnicity.

You also know that State law says that you must have a driver's license in order to drive a car; that it is illegal for anyone under 21 to buy alcoholic beverages, or for anyone under 18 to buy cigarettes or other tobacco products; and that only those persons who can satisfy certain requirements can buy or own firearms.

These examples illustrate a very complex system: the division of governmental power in the United States between National and State governments. This section will help you better understand that complicated arrangement.

▲ State laws forbid the sale of cigarettes to minors.

Why Federalism?

When the Framers of the Constitution met at Philadelphia in 1787, they faced a number of difficult issues. Not the least of them: How

could they possibly create a new central government that would be strong enough to meet the nation's needs and, at the same time, preserve the strength of the existing States?

Few of the Framers favored a strong central government based on the British model; and all of them knew that the Revolution had been fought in the name of self-government. Yet they also knew that the government under the Articles of Confederation had proved too weak to deal with the nation's many problems.

Remember, most of the Framers were dedicated to the concept of limited government. They were convinced (1) that governmental power poses a threat to individual liberty, (2) that therefore the exercise of governmental power must be restrained, and (3) that to divide governmental power, as federalism does, is to curb it and so prevent its abuse.

Federalism Defined

Federalism is a system of government in which a written constitution divides the powers of government on a territorial basis between a central, or national, government and several regional governments, usually called states or provinces. Each of these levels of government has its own substantial set of powers. Neither level, acting alone, can change the basic division of powers the constitution has created. In addition, each level of government operates through its own agencies and acts directly through its own officials and laws.

The American system of government stands as a prime example of federalism. The basic design of this system is set out in the Constitution. This document provides for a **division of powers** between the National Government and the States. That is, it assigns certain powers to the National Government and certain powers to the States. This division of powers was implied in the original Constitution and then spelled out in the Bill of Rights:

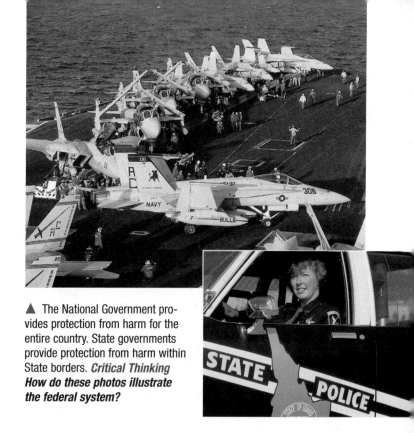

▲ The National Government provides protection from harm for the entire country. State governments provide protection from harm within State borders. *Critical Thinking How do these photos illustrate the federal system?*

> **FROM THE Constitution** ❝*The powers not delegated to the United States by the Constitution, nor prohibited by it to the States, are reserved to the States respectively, or to the people.*❞
>
> —10th Amendment

In effect, federalism produces a dual system of government. That is, it provides for two basic levels of government, each with its own area of authority. Each operates over the same people and the same territory at the same time.

Federalism's major strength is that it allows local action in matters of local concern, and national action in matters of wider concern. Local traditions, needs, and desires vary from one State to another, and federalism allows for this very significant fact.

Illustrations of this point are nearly endless. For example, a third of the States are directly involved in the liquor business, operating it as a public monopoly; elsewhere private enterprise is the rule. In 48 States many gas stations are self-service; in New Jersey and Oregon, the law forbids motorists to pump their own gas. Only one State—North Dakota—does not require voters to register in order to cast their ballots. Only Nebraska has a unicameral (one-house) legislature. Oregon is the only State that has legalized physician-assisted suicide. Only five States—Alaska, Delaware, New Hampshire, Montana, and Oregon—do not impose a general sales tax.

While federalism allows individual States to handle State and local matters, it also provides for the strength that comes from union.

National defense and foreign affairs offer useful illustrations of this point. So, too, do domestic affairs. Take, for example, a natural disaster. When a flood, drought, winter storm, or other catastrophe hits a particular State, the resources of the National Government and all of the other States may be mobilized to aid the stricken area.

Powers of the National Government

The National Government is a government of **delegated powers.** That is, it has only those powers delegated (granted) to it in the Constitution. There are three distinct types of delegated powers: expressed, implied, and inherent.

The Expressed Powers

The **expressed powers** are delegated to the National Government in so many words—spelled out, expressly, in the Constitution. These powers are also sometimes called the "enumerated powers."

You can find most of the expressed powers in Article I, Section 8. There, in 18 clauses, the Constitution expressly gives 27 powers to Congress. They include the power to lay and collect taxes, to coin money, to regulate foreign

Expressed Power

Implied Power

Inherent Power

▲ The powers delegated to the National Government include the power to coin money, to pro-hibit race-based discrimination, and to conduct foreign relations. In 1971, Richard Nixon (right) became the first American President to visit China; his historic trip led to United States recognition of the government of the People's Republic of China. *Critical Thinking Why is establishing diplomatic relations considered an inherent power?*

and interstate commerce, to raise and maintain armed forces, to declare war, to fix standards of weights and measures, to grant patents and copyrights, and to do many other things.

Several other expressed powers are set out elsewhere in the Constitution. Article II, Section 2 gives several powers to the President. They include the power to act as commander in chief of the armed forces, to grant reprieves and pardons, to make treaties, and to appoint major federal officials. Article III grants "the judicial Power of the United States" to the Supreme Court and other courts in the federal judiciary. Finally, several expressed powers are found in various amendments to the Constitution; thus, the 16th Amendment gives Congress the power to levy an income tax.

The Implied Powers

The **implied powers** are not expressly stated in the Constitution but are reasonably suggested— implied—by the expressed powers. The constitutional basis for the implied powers is found in one of the expressed powers. Article I, Section 8, Clause 18 gives Congress the "necessary and proper power." The Necessary and Proper Clause says that

FROM THE Constitution *"to make all Laws which shall be necessary and proper for carrying into Execution the foregoing Powers and all other Powers vested by this Constitution in the Government of the United States, or in any Department or Officer thereof."*

—Article I, Section 8, Clause 18

Through congressional and court interpretation, the words *necessary and proper* have come to mean, in effect, "convenient and useful." Indeed, the Necessary and Proper Clause is sometimes called the Elastic Clause, because, over time, it has been stretched to cover so many situations.

Here are but a few of the thousands of examples of the exercise of implied powers. Congress has provided for the regulation of labor-management relations, the building of hydro-electric power dams, and the building of the 42,000-mile interstate highway system. It has made federal crimes of such acts as moving stolen goods, gambling devices, and kidnapped persons across State lines. It has prohibited racial discrimination in granting access to such places as restaurants, theaters, hotels, and motels.

Congress has taken these actions, and many more, because the power to do so is reasonably implied by just one of the expressed powers: the power to regulate interstate commerce.[1]

The Inherent Powers

The **inherent powers** belong to the National Government because it is the government of a sovereign state within the world community. Although the Constitution does not expressly provide for them, they are powers that national governments have historically possessed. It stands to reason that the Framers intended that the National Government they created would hold these powers.

The inherent powers are few in number. The major ones include the power to regulate immigration, to deport undocumented aliens, to acquire territory, to grant diplomatic recognition to other states, and to protect the nation against rebellion or other attempts to overthrow the government.

One can argue that most of the inherent powers are implied by one or more of the expressed powers. For example, the power to regulate immigration is suggested by the expressed power to regulate foreign trade. The power to acquire territory can be drawn from the treaty-making power and the several war powers. But the doctrine of inherent powers holds that it is not necessary to go to these lengths to find these powers in the Constitution. In short, these powers exist because the United States exists.

Powers Denied to the National Government

Although the Constitution delegates certain powers to the National Government, it also denies the National Government certain powers. It does so in three distinct ways.

First, the Constitution denies some powers to the National Government in so many words—expressly.[2] Among them are the powers to levy duties on exports; prohibit freedom of religion,

---

[1]Article I, Section 8, Clause 3. The doctrine of implied powers is treated in greater detail in Chapter 11.

[2]Most of the expressed denials of power are found in Article I, Section 9 and in the 1st through the 8th amendments.

Voices on Government

Senator Fred Thompson (R., Tennessee) was first elected to the United States Senate in 1994 and won a second term in 2000. Senator Thompson ardently supports the protection of State and local governments from unnecessary Federal intrusion. He has this to say on the subject of federalism:

"The Founding Fathers divided power between the federal government and the states. The constitutional principle of federalism—embodied in the Tenth Amendment—raises two fundamental questions that policy makers should answer: What should government be doing? And what level of government should do it? Everything flows from them. That's why federalism is at the heart of our democracy."

Evaluating the Quotation

Based on your reading of the selection, how do you think Senator Thompson would respond to the following statement: "State and local governments are often in a better position than the Federal Government to respond to the people's concerns"?

speech, press, or assembly; conduct illegal searches or seizures; nor deny to any person accused of a crime a speedy and public trial or a trial by jury.

Second, several powers are denied to the National Government because of the silence of the Constitution. Recall that the National Government is a government of delegated powers; it has only those powers the Constitution gives to it expressly, implicitly, or inherently.

Among the many powers not granted to the National Government are the powers to create a public school system for the nation, to enact uniform marriage and divorce laws, and to set up units of local government. The Constitution says nothing that would give the National Government the power to do any of these things—expressly, implicitly, or inherently.

Third, some powers are denied to the National Government because of the federal system itself.

Clearly the Constitution does not intend that the National Government should have any power to take action that would threaten the existence of that system. For example, in the exercise of its power to tax, Congress cannot tax any of the States or their local units in the carrying out of their governmental functions. If it could, it would have the power to destroy—tax out of existence—one or more, or all, of the States.[3]

The States

The 50 States are the other half of the very complicated equation we call federalism. Their role in the American federal system is no less important than the role of the National Government.

Powers Reserved to the States

As you recall, the 10th Amendment declares that the States are governments of reserved powers. (See page 89.) The **reserved powers** are those powers that the Constitution does not grant to the National Government and does not, at the same time, deny to the States.

Thus, any State can forbid persons under 18 to marry without parental consent, or those under 21 to buy liquor. It can ban the sale of pornography, outlaw prostitution, and permit some forms of gambling and prohibit others. A State can require that doctors, lawyers, hairdressers, and plumbers be licensed in order to practice in the State. It can confiscate automobiles and other property used in connection with such illicit activities as illegal drug trafficking or prostitution. It can establish public schools, enact land use laws, regulate the services and restrict the profits of such public utilities as natural gas, oil, electric power, and telephone companies, and do much, much more.

In short, the sphere of powers held by each State—the scope of the reserved powers—is huge. The States can do all of those things just mentioned, and much more, because (1) the Constitution does not give the National Government the power to take these actions and (2) it does not deny the States the power to take them.

How broad the reserved powers really are can be understood from this fact: Most of what government does in this country today is done by the States (and their local governments), not by the National Government. The point can also be seen from this fact: The reserved powers include the vitally important police power—the power of a State to protect and promote the public health, the public morals, the public safety, and the general welfare.

The Constitution does not grant expressed powers to the States, with one exception. Section 2 of the 21st Amendment gives the States a virtually unlimited power to regulate the manufacture, sale, and consumption of alcoholic beverages.

Powers Denied to the States

Just as the Constitution denies many powers to the National Government, it also denies many powers to the States. Some of these powers are denied to the States in so many words.[4] For example, no State can enter into any treaty, alliance, or confederation. Nor can a State print or coin money or deprive any person of life, liberty, or property without due process of law.

Some powers are denied to the States inherently—that is, by the existence of the federal system. Thus, no State (and no local government)

▲ *Land Use* Enacting land use laws in order to preserve open spaces is one of many powers reserved to the States.

---

[3]But note that when a State, or one of its local units, performs a so-called nongovernmental function—for example, maintains liquor stores, runs a bus system, or operates a farmers market—it is liable to federal taxation. We shall come back to this point later, in Chapter 25.

[4]Most of these expressed prohibitions of power to the States (and so, too, to their local governments) are found in Article I, Section 10 and in the 13th, 14th, 15th, 19th, 24th, and 26th Amendments.

can tax any of the agencies or functions of the National Government. Remember, too, each State has its own constitution. That document also denies many powers to the State.[5]

The Exclusive and the Concurrent Powers

Most of the powers that the Constitution delegates to the National Government are **exclusive powers.** These powers can be exercised by the National Government alone. They cannot be exercised by the States under any circumstances.

Some of these powers are expressly denied to the States. Examples include the power to coin money, to make treaties with foreign states, and to lay duties (taxes) on imports. Some powers are not expressly denied to the States but are, nonetheless, among the exclusive powers of the Federal Government because of the nature of the particular power involved. The power to regulate interstate commerce is a leading example of this point. If the States could exercise that power, trade between and among the States would be at best chaotic and at worst impossible.[6]

Some of the powers delegated to the National Government are **concurrent powers.** The concurrent powers are those powers that both the National Government and the States possess and exercise. They include, for example, the power to levy and collect taxes, to define crimes and set punishments for them, and to condemn (take) private property for public use.

The concurrent powers are held and exercised separately and simultaneously by the two basic levels of government. That is, the concurrent powers are those powers that the Constitution does not grant exclusively to the National Government and that, at the same

The Division of Powers

National Powers	Concurrent Powers	State Powers
• Coin money	• Levy and collect taxes	• Regulate trade and business within the State
• Regulate interstate and foreign trade	• Borrow money	• Establish public schools
• Raise and maintain armed forces	• Establish courts	• Pass license requirements for professionals
• Declare war	• Define crimes and set punishments	• Regulate alcoholic beverages
• Govern U.S. territories and admit new States	• Claim private property for public use	• Conduct elections
• Conduct foreign relations		• Establish local governments

Examples of . . .

Interpreting Tables The federal system determines the way that powers are divided and shared between the National and the State governments. *Name one national, one State, and one concurrent power.*

time, does not deny to the States. The concurrent powers, in short, are those powers that make it possible for a federal system of government to function.

The Federal System and Local Governments

Government in the United States is often discussed in terms of three levels: national, State, and local. However convenient this view may be, it is at best misleading. Recall that there are only two basic levels in the federal system: the National Government and the State governments.

Governments do exist at the local level all across the country, of course. In fact, there are more than 87,000 units of local government in the United States today. You will take a look at them later in this book. For now, keep this important point in mind: All of these thousands of local governments are parts—subunits—of the various State governments.

Each of these local units is located within one of the 50 States. In its constitution and in its laws,

---

[5]Study your own State's constitution on the powers denied to the States. As you do, note the significance of the words "or to the people" in the 10th Amendment in the Federal Constitution. We shall look at State constitutions later, and in more detail, in Chapter 24.

[6]The States cannot regulate interstate commerce as such, but they can and do affect it. For example, in regulating highway speeds, the States regulate vehicles not only operating wholly within the State, but also those operating from State to State. Generally, the States can affect interstate commerce, but they may not impose an unreasonable burden on it.

City and County Charters and Ordinances

State Statutes

Washington State passes statutes to help ensure oil tanker safety (1994).

State Constitutions

Acts of Congress and Treaties

Congress also enacts laws governing oil tanker safety (1936, 1972, 1978, 1990).

United States Constitution

In *U.S.* v. *Locke,* 2000, the Supreme Court rules that Federal law supersedes Washington State law.

Interpreting Charts The Supremacy Clause creates a hierarchy of laws. Local law (city and county charters and ordinances) must yield to State law. State law must yield to federal law. At the top of the hierarchy is the United States Constitution, which stands above all other forms of law in the United States. *How does the case of* **United States** *v.* **Locke** *illustrate this hierarchy of laws?*

each State has created these units. None exists apart from its parent State. Local government can provide services, regulate activities, collect taxes, and do many other things. It can do these things, however, only because the State has established and given it the power to do so. In short, when local governments exercise their powers, they are actually exercising State powers.

Another way of putting all of this is to remind you of a point that was first made in Chapter 1. Each of the 50 States has a unitary form of government—a central government that creates local units of government for its own convenience.

The Supreme Law of the Land

As you have just seen, the division of powers in the American federal system produces a dual system of government, one in which two basic levels of government operate over the same territory and the same people at the same time.

Such an arrangement is bound to result in conflicts between national law and State law.

The Supremacy Clause

The Framers anticipated these conflicts—and so they wrote the Supremacy Clause into the Constitution. That provision declares that

FROM THE
Constitution

" This Constitution, and the Laws of the United States which shall be made in Pursuance thereof; and all Treaties made, or which shall be made, under the Authority of the United States, shall be the supreme Law of the Land; and the Judges in every State shall be bound thereby, any Thing in the Constitution or Laws of any state to the Contrary notwithstanding. "

—Article VI, Section 2

As you can see from the chart above, the Constitution and the laws and treaties of the United States are "the supreme Law of the Land." This means that the Constitution stands above all other forms of law in the United States. Acts of Congress and treaties stand immediately beneath the Constitution.[7]

The Supremacy Clause has been called the "linchpin of the Constitution" because it joins the National Government and the States into a

---

[7]Acts of Congress and treaties stand on equal planes with one another. Neither can conflict with any provision in the Constitution. In the rare case of conflict between the provisions of an act and those of a treaty, the one more recently adopted takes precedence—as the latest expression of the sovereign people's will. The Supreme Court has regularly held to that position from the first cases it decided on the point, *The Head Money Cases,* 1884.

single governmental unit, a federal government. In other words, the Supremacy Clause holds together the complex structure that is the American federal system.

The Supreme Court and Federalism

The Supreme Court is the umpire in the federal system. One of its chief duties is to apply the Supremacy Clause to the conflicts that the dual system of government inevitably produces.

The Court was first called to settle a clash between a national and a State law in 1819. The case, *McCulloch* v. *Maryland*, involved the controversial Second Bank of the United States. The bank had been chartered by Congress in 1816. In 1818, the Maryland legislature, hoping to cripple the bank, placed a tax on all notes issued by its Baltimore branch. James McCulloch, the branch cashier, refused to pay the tax, and the Maryland courts convicted him for that refusal.

The Supreme Court unanimously reversed the Maryland courts. Speaking for the Court, Chief Justice John Marshall based the decision squarely on the Constitution's Supremacy Clause:

PRIMARY Sources *" [If] any one proposition could command the universal assent of mankind, we might expect it would be this—that the government of the Union, though limited in its powers, is supreme within its sphere of action . . . . [T]he states have no power . . . to retard, impede,*

burden, or in any manner control, the operations of the constitutional laws enacted by Congress. . . . " [8]

—*McCulloch* v. *Maryland*, Opinion of the Court

Since this landmark case, it has been impossible to overstate the significance of the Court's function as the umpire of the federal system. Had the Court not taken this role, the federal system and probably the United States itself could not have survived its early years. Justice Oliver Wendell Holmes once made the point in these words:

PRIMARY Sources *" I do not think the United States would come to an end if we [the Court] lost our power to declare an Act of Congress void. I do think the Union would be imperiled if we could not make that declaration as to the laws of the several States. "*

—Collected Legal Papers[9]

[8] The case is also critically important in the development of the constitutional system because in deciding it, the Court for the first time upheld the doctrine of implied powers. It also held the National Government to be immune from any form of State taxation.

[9] The Supreme Court first held a State law unconstitutional in a case from Georgia, *Fletcher* v. *Peck*, 1810. The Court found that a Georgia law of 1795 making a grant of land to John Peck amounted to a contract between the State and Peck. It ruled that the legislature's later repeal of that law violated the Constitution's Contract Clause (Article I, Section 10, Clause 1). Since then, the Court has found more than 1,000 State laws unconstitutional (and has upheld the constitutionality of thousands of others).

Section 1 Assessment

Key Terms and Main Ideas

1. Why did the Framers settle on **federalism** as the system of government for the new nation?
2. Explain each of the following: **expressed powers, implied powers,** and **inherent powers.**
3. Do local governments have powers other than those granted to them by their State? Explain your answer.
4. What is the significance of *McCulloch* v. *Maryland* in the development of the federal system?

Critical Thinking

5. **Making Decisions** Suppose you are creating a student government. Would that government be federal in form? Why or why not?

6. **Drawing Conclusions** The Framers could not foresee all of the specific issues that would arise once the federal system was implemented. How did they nevertheless make provisions for addressing these issues?
7. **Determining Relevance** Name several issues in your community that are best addressed locally rather than by the Federal Government.

 Take It to the Net

8. There are many different perspectives on the ways federalism works in the United States. Read several of these perspectives. Then choose one, and outline it in detail. Use the links provided in the Social Studies area at the following Web site for help in this activity. www.phschool.com

More Power to the States

Linda Chavez is the president of the Center for Equal Opportunity in Washington, D.C. She served as White House Director of Public Liaison in the Reagan administration. Here, Ms. Chavez argues that shifting responsibility for many social programs back to the States keeps power closer to the people.

The United States flag and the Wisconsin State flag fly at Wisconsin's State capitol in Madison.

One of the things the Founders of our nation most feared was centralized government power. Indeed, our Constitution and our Bill of Rights were written explicitly to ensure that power rested with the people and that no single branch of government—whether the executive, legislative, or judicial—gains a monopoly of power.

The Tenth Amendment to the Constitution also guaranteed that powers not specifically delegated to the federal government or prohibited to the states by the Constitution be retained by the states or the people.

Despite the intent of the founders, the history of our government, particularly in the last half of the twentieth century, has been one of growing federal power. Some of this has been accomplished directly by the government taking over certain functions; some has come indirectly, especially by the "power of the purse strings."

Whenever the federal government gives money to the states or to local governments or agencies, certain obligations or rules follow. . . . [T]he federal government gives billions of dollars a year to support public elementary and secondary schools, and along with the money comes federal dictates about exactly how the money can be spent. . . .

For a limited number of functions—national defense being the most obvious—the federal government is clearly the only institution that can properly manage and fund the necessary programs. . . . But many other functions that the federal government performs, and taxes citizens to pay for, would be better decided on and funded at the local or state level, where people can keep track of what is being done and how much it costs. . . .

Efficiency and accountability are two reasons why state and local governments are better equipped to undertake certain tasks, but another . . . is flexibility. Some social problems are particularly difficult to solve, and what may work in one community may not be appropriate for another. . . .

Unfortunately, the federal government's involvement sometimes makes matters worse. It takes the decision making out of the hands of elected officials closest to the people and puts it in the hands of unelected bureaucrats in Washington. The founders of our nation anticipated the problems of centralized power and established constitutional guarantees to safeguard against it, but the people must make sure those guarantees are enforced.

Analyzing Primary Sources

1. According to Chavez, how has the Federal Government extended its power over the States?
2. Why is Chavez concerned about the growing power of the Federal Government?
3. Why does Chavez believe States are better able to handle local problems?

2 The National Government and the 50 States

Section Preview

OBJECTIVES

1. **Summarize** the obligations that the Constitution places on the nation for the benefit of the States.
2. **Explain** the process for admitting new States to the Union.
3. **Examine** the many and growing areas of cooperative federalism.

WHY IT MATTERS

In this country, the power to govern is shared by the National Government and each of the 50 States (including their thousands of local governments). Given this fact, conflicts are inevitable—and cooperation is absolutely necessary.

POLITICAL DICTIONARY

★ enabling act
★ act of admission
★ grants-in-aid program
★ revenue sharing
★ categorical grant
★ block grant
★ project grant

Have you ever really focused on the words *United States?* The United States is a union of States, the several States joined together, the States united.

The Constitution created and is intended to preserve that union. To that end, the Constitution (1) requires the National Government to guarantee certain things to the States and (2) makes it possible for the National Government to do certain things for the States.

The Nation's Obligations to the States

The Constitution places several obligations on the National Government for the benefit of the States. Most of them are found in Article IV.

Republican Form of Government

The Constitution requires the National Government to "guarantee to every State in this Union a Republican Form of Government."[10] The Constitution does not define "Republican Form of Government," and the Supreme Court has regularly refused to do so. The term is generally understood to mean a "representative government."

The Supreme Court has held that the question of whether a State has a republican form of government is a political question. That is, it is one to be decided by the political branches of the government—the President and Congress—and not by the courts.[11]

---

[10]Article IV, Section 4.

[11]The leading case here is *Luther* v. *Borden,* 1849. This case grew out of Dorr's Rebellion, a revolt led by Thomas W. Dorr against the State of Rhode Island in 1841–1842. Dorr and his followers had written and proclaimed a new constitution for the State. When they tried to put the new document into operation, however, the governor in office under the original constitution declared martial law, or temporary rule by military authorities. The governor also called on the Federal Government for help. President John Tyler took steps to put down the revolt, and it quickly collapsed. Although the question of which of the competing governments was the legitimate one was a major issue in *Luther* v. *Borden,* the Supreme Court refused to decide the matter.

▲ After the Civil War, the "Republican Form of Government" figured prominently as laws were broadened to help recognize African American voting rights.

The Major Disaster Process	
STEP 1	**Local Government Responds.** If overwhelmed, turns to the State for assistance.
STEP 2	**The State Responds** with State resources, such as the National Guard and State agencies.
STEP 3	**Damage Assessment** by local, State, Federal, and volunteer organizations.
STEP 4	**A Major Disaster Declaration** is requested by the governor, based on damage assessment.
STEP 5	**FEMA Evaluates** the request and recommends action to the White House.
STEP 6	**The President Approves** the request or FEMA informs the governor it has been denied.

SOURCE: Federal Emergency Management Agency

Interpreting Tables The Federal Emergency Management Agency (FEMA) helps State and local governments in the case of a natural disaster such as a hurricane. **Explain the steps that lead to a community receiving federal disaster aid. How does this process illustrate federalism?**

The only extensive use ever made of the republican-form guarantee came in the years immediately following the Civil War. Congress declared that several southern States did not have governments of a republican form. It refused to admit senators and representatives from those States until the States had ratified the 13th, 14th, and 15th amendments and broadened their laws to recognize the voting and other rights of African Americans.

Invasion and Internal Disorder

The Constitution states that the National Government must also

FROM THE Constitution *"protect each of them [States] against Invasion; and on Application of the Legislature, or of the Executive (when the Legislature cannot be convened) against domestic Violence."*
—Article IV, Section 4

Today it is clear that an invasion of any one of the 50 States would be met as an attack on the United States itself. This constitutional guarantee is therefore now of little, if any, significance.

That was not the case in the late 1780s. During that time, it was not at all certain that all 13 States would stand together if a foreign power attacked one of them. So, before the 13 States agreed to give up their war-making powers, each demanded an ironclad pledge that an attack on any single State would be met as an attack on all States.

The federal system assumes that each of the 50 States will keep the peace within its own borders. Thus, the primary responsibility for curbing insurrection, riot, or other internal disorder rests with the individual States. However, the Constitution does accept that a State might not be able to control some situations. It therefore guarantees protection against internal disorder, or what the Constitution calls "domestic Violence," in each of them.

The use of federal force to restore order within a State has historically been a rare event. Several instances did occur in the 1960s, however. When racial unrest exploded into violence in Detroit during the "long, hot summer" of 1967, President Lyndon Johnson ordered units of the United States Army into the city. He acted at the request of the governor of Michigan, George Romney, and only after Detroit's police and firefighters, supported by State Police and National Guard units, could not control riots, arson, and looting in the city. In 1968, again at the request of the governors involved, federal troops were sent into Chicago and Baltimore to help put down the violence that erupted following the assassination of Martin Luther King, Jr.

Normally, a President has sent troops into a State only in answer to a request from its governor or legislature. If national laws are being broken, national functions interfered with, or national property endangered, however, a President does not need to wait for such a plea.[12]

The ravages of nature—storms, floods, drought, forest fires, and such—can be more destructive than human violence. Here, too, acting to protect the States against "domestic Violence," the Federal Government stands ready to aid stricken areas.

Respect for Territorial Integrity

The National Government is constitutionally bound to respect the territorial integrity of each of the States. That is, the National Government must recognize the legal existence and the physical boundaries of each State.

The basic scheme of the Constitution imposes this obligation. Several of its provisions do so, as well. For example, Congress must include, in both of its houses, members chosen in each one of the States.[13] Recall, too, that Article V of the Constitution declares that no State can be deprived of its equal representation in the United States Senate without its own consent.

Admitting New States

Only Congress has the power to admit new States to the Union. As part of the National Government's guarantee of respect for each State's territorial integrity, the Constitution places only

*PUERTO RICO: "TO BE, OR NOT TO BE"

Interpreting Political Cartoons Whether or not Puerto Rico should become the 51st State has been the subject of continuing debate. **What does the cartoon suggest about the issue?**

one restriction on that power. A new State cannot be created by taking territory from one or more of the existing States without the consent of the legislature(s) of the State(s) involved.[14]

Congress has admitted 37 States since the original 13 formed the Union, as the map on the next page shows. Five States (Vermont, Kentucky, Tennessee, Maine, and West Virginia) were created from parts of already existing States. Texas was an independent republic before admission. California was admitted shortly after being ceded to the United States by Mexico. Each of the other 30 States entered the Union only after a longer period of time, frequently more than 15 years, as an organized territory.

Admission Procedure

The process of admission to the Union is usually fairly simple. The area desiring Statehood first asks Congress for admission. If and when Congress chooses, it passes an **enabling act,** an act directing the people of the territory to frame a proposed State constitution. A convention prepares the constitution, which is then put to a popular vote in the proposed State. If the voters

---

[12]President Grover Cleveland ordered federal troops to put an end to rioting in the Chicago rail yard during the Pullman Strike in 1894 despite the objections of Governor William Altgeld of Illinois. The Supreme Court upheld his actions in *In re Debs,* 1895. The Court found that rioters had threatened federal property and impeded the flow of the mails and interstate commerce. Thus, more than a single State was involved. Since then, several Presidents have acted without a request from the State involved. More recently, President Dwight Eisenhower did so at Little Rock, Arkansas, in 1957, and President John Kennedy did so at the University of Mississippi in 1962 and at the University of Alabama in 1963. In each of those instances, the President acted to halt the unlawful obstruction of school integration orders issued by the federal courts.

[13]In the House, Article I, Section 2, Clause 1; in the Senate, Article I, Section 3, Clause 1 and the 17th Amendment.

[14]Article IV, Section 3, Clause 1. Some argue that this provision was violated with West Virginia's admission in 1863. That State was formed from the 40 western counties that had broken away from Virginia over the issue of secession from the Union. The consent required by the Constitution was given by a minority of the members of the Virginia legislature—those who represented the 40 western counties. Congress accepted their action, holding that they were the only group legally capable of acting as the Virginia legislature at the time.

approve the constitution, it is submitted to Congress for its consideration. If Congress still agrees to Statehood after reviewing the document, it passes an **act of admission,** an act creating the new State. If the President signs the act, the new State enters the Union.

The two newest States, Alaska and Hawaii, shortened the usual process of gaining admission to the Union. Each adopted a proposed constitution without waiting for an enabling act, Hawaii in 1950 and Alaska in 1956. Both became States in 1959.

Conditions for Admission

Before finally admitting a new State, Congress has often set certain conditions. For example, in 1896, Utah was admitted on condition that its constitution outlaw polygamy, the practice of having more than one spouse at a time. In the act admitting Alaska to the Union as the 49th State, Congress forever prohibited that State from claiming title to any lands legally held by any Native American.

Each State enters the Union on an equal footing with each of the other States. Thus,

although Congress can set certain conditions like those just described, it cannot impose conditions of a political nature on the States. For example, when Oklahoma was admitted to the Union in 1907, Congress said the State could not remove its capital from Guthrie to any other place before 1913. In 1910, however, the Oklahoma legislature moved the State's capital to Oklahoma City. When this step was challenged, the United States Supreme Court held, in *Coyle* v. *Smith,* 1911, that Congress can set conditions for a prospective State's admission. But the Court also held that the conditions cannot be enforced when they compromise the independence of a State to manage its own internal affairs.

Consider one more example: President William Howard Taft vetoed a resolution to admit Arizona to the Union in 1911. He did so because Arizona's proposed constitution provided that members of the State's judiciary could be recalled (removed from office) by popular vote. This provision meant, said Taft, that a judge would have to keep one eye on the law and the other on public opinion. In

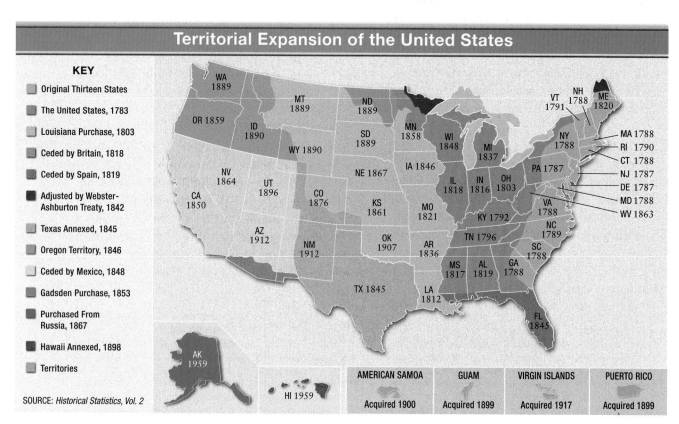

Territorial Expansion of the United States

KEY
- Original Thirteen States
- The United States, 1783
- Louisiana Purchase, 1803
- Ceded by Britain, 1818
- Ceded by Spain, 1819
- Adjusted by Webster-Ashburton Treaty, 1842
- Texas Annexed, 1845
- Oregon Territory, 1846
- Ceded by Mexico, 1848
- Gadsden Purchase, 1853
- Purchased From Russia, 1867
- Hawaii Annexed, 1898
- Territories

SOURCE: *Historical Statistics, Vol. 2*

WA 1889 · OR 1859 · MT 1889 · ID 1890 · WY 1890 · ND 1889 · SD 1889 · MN 1858 · WI 1848 · MI 1837 · VT 1791 · NH 1788 · ME 1820 · NY 1788 · MA 1788 · RI 1790 · CT 1788 · NJ 1787 · DE 1787 · MD 1788 · WV 1863 · PA 1787 · NV 1864 · UT 1896 · CO 1876 · NE 1867 · IA 1846 · IL 1818 · IN 1816 · OH 1803 · VA 1788 · CA 1850 · KS 1861 · MO 1821 · KY 1792 · NC 1789 · AZ 1912 · NM 1912 · OK 1907 · AR 1836 · TN 1796 · SC 1788 · MS 1817 · AL 1819 · GA 1788 · TX 1845 · LA 1812 · FL 1845 · AK 1959 · HI 1959

AMERICAN SAMOA	GUAM	VIRGIN ISLANDS	PUERTO RICO
Acquired 1900	Acquired 1899	Acquired 1917	Acquired 1899

Interpreting Maps Thirty-seven States have joined the original 13. ***When did your State join the Union? How much of the nation's present area did the United States cover at that time?***

response to Taft's concern, Arizona removed the recall section from the document. In 1912 Congress passed, and the President signed, another act of admission for Arizona. Almost immediately after admission, however, the new State amended its new constitution to provide for the recall of judges. That provision remains a valid part of Arizona's constitution today.

Cooperative Federalism

As you know, federalism produces a dual system of government in which powers are divided between the States and the Federal Government. You have also read that as a result of this complex arrangement, competition, tensions, and conflicts are a regular part of American federalism. In short, the American governmental system is like a tug-of-war, a continuing power struggle between the National Government and the States, with the Supreme Court acting as referee, or umpire.

On the other hand, the American federal system also involves a broad area of shared powers. That is, in addition to the two separate spheres of power held and exercised by the two basic levels of government, there are large and growing areas of cooperation between them. These areas include the funds that the Federal Government grants to the States as well as the various services that the States perform for the Federal Government.

Federal Grants-in-Aid

Perhaps the best-known examples of this intergovernmental cooperation are the many federal **grants-in-aid programs**—grants of federal money or other resources to the States and/or their cities, counties, and other local units. Many of these governments are regularly strapped for funds; these grants often help them perform a large share of their everyday functions.

The history of grants-in-aid programs goes back more than 200 years, to the period before the Constitution. In the Northwest Ordinance of 1787, the Congress under the Articles of Confederation provided for the government of the territory beyond the Ohio River. Looking forward to the existence of new States on that frontier, the Congress set aside sections of land for the support of public education in those

The Massachusetts Central Artery project, known as the "Big Dig," is the largest, most complex, and technologically challenging public works project to date in American history. *Critical Thinking* *How does this project illustrate cooperative federalism?*

Federal funding 54%

State and local funding 46%

future States. On through the nineteenth century, States received grants of federal lands for a number of purposes: schools and colleges, roads and canals, flood control work, and several others. A large number of the major State universities, for example, were founded as land-grant colleges. These schools were built with money obtained from the sale of public lands given to the States by the Morrill Act of 1862.

Congress began to make grants of federal money quite early, too. In 1808, it gave the States $200,000 to support the militia. Cash grants did not come to play a large role, however, until the Depression years of the 1930s. Many of the New Deal programs aimed at bringing the nation out of its economic crisis were built around grants of money.

Since then, Congress has set up hundreds of grants-in-aid programs. In fact, more than 500 are now in operation. Dozens of programs function in a variety of areas: in education, mass transit, highway construction, health care, on-the-job training, and many others.

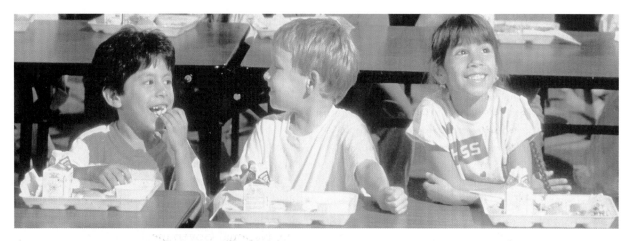

▲ Federal monies help fund school lunch programs in schools across the country.
Critical Thinking **What examples of cooperative federalism affect your own life?**

Grants-in-aid are based on the National Government's taxing power. The Constitution gives Congress that power in order

FROM THE Constitution *"to pay the Debts and provide for the common Defense and general Welfare of the United States. . . . "*

—Article I, Section 8, Clause 1

Today, these grants total more than $250 billion, and account for some 25 percent of all State and local government spending each year.

These grants make it possible for the Federal Government to operate in many policy areas in which it would otherwise have no constitutional authority—for example, in such fields as education, low-income housing, local law enforcement, and mental health. In this way, grants-in-aid blur the line of division of powers in the federal system.

Critics of grants-in-aid have long made this point. They also argue that the grants often give Washington a major—and they say an unwarranted—voice in making public policy at the State and local levels.

Revenue Sharing

One form of federal monetary aid, known as **revenue sharing,** was in place from 1972 to 1987. Under this program, Congress gave an annual share of the huge federal tax revenue to the States and their cities, counties, and townships. Altogether, those "shared revenues" amounted to more than $83 billion over the years the program was in force.

Virtually no strings were attached to this money. In fact, Congress placed only one major restriction on the use of the funds. The money could not be spent for any program in which discrimination on the basis of race, sex, national origin, age, religious belief, or physical disability was evident. Otherwise, the "shared revenues" could be used very largely as the States and their local units chose to spend them.

Needless to say, revenue sharing was quite popular with and strongly supported by many governors, mayors, and other State and local officials. It was opposed by the Reagan Administration, however, and fell victim to the financial needs of the deficit-ridden National Government. Various efforts to revive revenue sharing in today's more prosperous climate have not won significant support in Congress, at least to this point in time.

Types of Federal Grants

Today, Congress appropriates money for three types of grants-in-aid. These include categorical grants, block grants, and project grants.

Over time, most grants have been categorical. **Categorical grants** are made for some specific, closely defined purpose: for school lunches or for the construction of airports or wastewater treatment plants, for example. Categorical grants are usually made with conditions attached. These "strings" require the State to (1) use the federal monies only for the specific purpose involved, (2) make its own monetary contribution, often a matching amount but sometimes much less, (3) provide an agency to administer the grant, and (4) obey a set of guidelines tailored to the particular purpose for which the monies are given.

Block grants have come into wide use over the last several years. They are made for much more broadly defined purposes than are categorical grants, such as health care, social services, or welfare. They are also made with fewer strings attached, so State and local governments have much greater freedom in deciding just how and on what to spend block grant dollars. Beginning in the Reagan years, from the 1980s on, many programs once supported by separate and fragmented categorical grants have been merged into broader block grants.

Congress also provides money for **project grants.** These are grants made to States, localities, and sometimes private agencies that apply for them. The Department of Health and Human Services makes many project grants—through its National Institutes of Health, for example, to support scientists engaged in research on cancer, diabetes, neurological disease, and other medical issues. Many State and local governments also apply for these grants to fund their job training and employment programs.

Other Forms of Federal Aid

The National Government aids the States in several other important ways. For example, the FBI gives extensive help to State and local police. The army and the air force equip and train each State's National Guard units. The Census Bureau's data are essential to State and local school, housing, and transportation officials as they plan for the future.

Many other forms of aid are not nearly so visible. "Lulu payments," for example, are federal monies that go to local governments in those areas in which there are large federal landholdings. These direct payments are made in lieu of—to take the place of—the property taxes that those local governments cannot collect from the National Government.

State Aid to the National Government

Intergovernmental cooperation is a two-way street. That is, the States and their local units of government also aid the National Government in many ways.

Thus, State and local election officials conduct national elections in each State. These elections are financed with State and local funds, and they are regulated largely by State laws. The legal process by which aliens can become citizens, called naturalization, takes place most often in State, not federal, courts. Those who commit federal crimes and are sought by the FBI and other federal law enforcement agencies are often picked up by State and local police officers and then held in local jails. And the examples go on and on.

Section 2 Assessment

Key Terms and Main Ideas

1. What are three obligations that the Constitution places on the National Government for the benefit of the States?
2. Explain the difference between an **enabling act** and an **act of admission.**
3. **(a)** What is a **block grant?**
   (b) How do block grants reflect cooperative federalism?
4. In what ways do the States aid the National Government?

Critical Thinking

5. **Recognizing Ideologies** If the Framers had been alive, how do you think they might have reacted when, only a few years ago, several States had to raise the legal drinking age to avoid losing a substantial portion of their federal grants for highway construction? Explain your answer.

6. **Making Comparisons** Suppose your State is to receive increased federal funding for a program to provide day care for some working parents. Is this funding likely to come as a categorical grant, a block grant, or a project grant? Why?
7. **Expressing Problems Clearly** In what type of situation would your State be most likely to need federal protection against "domestic Violence?" Explain your answer.

 Take It to the Net

8. Should Puerto Rico become the 51st State? Find out about the island's history, its status as a Commonwealth, and the arguments for and against Statehood. Then plan a debate on the following question: Should Puerto Rico become a State? Use the links provided in the Social Studies area at the following Web site for help in completing this activity. **www.phschool.com**

Expressing Problems Clearly

To express a problem clearly means to describe the nature of an issue that is difficult, puzzling, or open to debate. Expressing a problem clearly is the first step in solving it.

1. Gather information. When you are confronted with a problem, gather information on the topic. For example, in *McCulloch* v. *Maryland* (1819), Chief Justice John Marshall addressed questions about the relationship between the Federal Government and the States. Reread the passage about *McCulloch* v. *Maryland* on page 95. Then read the excerpt below.

2. Identify the basic concepts involved. Specific problems often relate to a general principle. For example, the Supreme Court often chooses to rule on a specific case that illustrates a broad principle that

can be applied to similar cases. To identify the problem in *McCulloch* v. *Maryland*, state what each side wants to achieve.

3. Identify supporting details or arguments. In the *McCulloch* excerpt, find the arguments that support the plaintiffs' view and the defendants' view.

4. Express the problem clearly. Now that you have identified the main area of dispute and stripped away details, you're ready to express the problem clearly. In your own words, state the nature of the problem that the Supreme Court addressed in 1819.

Test for Success

Find a newspaper editorial in print or on the Internet. Analyze the editorial using the steps listed above to express the problem or controversy in a clear and concise way.

How does each side make its case?

What are the arguments for and against the bank?

What's the main issue in this case?

How can I summarize the case?

"In the case now to be determined, the defendant, a sovereign State [Maryland], denies the obligation of a law enacted by [Congress], and the plaintiff [the National Bank] contests the validity of an act which has been passed by the legislature of that State. . . .

In discussing this question, the counsel for the State of Maryland have deemed it of some importance . . . to consider [the U.S. Constitution] not as emanating from the people, but as the act of sovereign and independent States. The powers of the [national] government, it has been said, are delegated by the States . . . and must be exercised in subordination to the States, who alone possess supreme dominion. . . .

It being the opinion of the Court, that the act incorporating the bank is constitutional . . . we proceed

to inquire . . . [w]hether the State of Maryland may, without violating the constitution, tax that branch [the branch in Maryland]?

That the power of taxation is . . . retained by the States; that it is not [reduced] by the grant of a similar power to the government of the Union . . . are truths which have never been denied. But . . . States are expressly forbidden to lay any duties on imports or exports . . . . If [this limitation on States' power to tax] must be conceded, the same [principle] would seem to restrain . . . a State from such other exercise of this power. . . . On this ground the counsel for the bank place its claim to be exempted from the power of a State to tax its operations."

—*Chief Justice John Marshall*, McCulloch v. Maryland, *1819*

Section Preview

OBJECTIVES

1. **Explain** why States make interstate compacts.
2. **Understand** the purpose of the Full Faith and Credit Clause.
3. **Define** *extradition* and explain its purpose.
4. **Discuss** the purpose of the Privileges and Immunities Clause.

WHY IT MATTERS

What if Texas citizens were not allowed to travel into Oklahoma, or needed a special passport to do so? What if your North Carolina driver's license were not valid when you drove through Ohio? Fortunately, several key provisions in the Constitution promote cooperation between and among the States.

POLITICAL DICTIONARY

★ **interstate compact**
★ **Full Faith and Credit Clause**
★ **extradition**
★ **Privileges and Immunities Clause**

As you know, conflict among the States was a major reason for the adoption of the Constitution in 1789. The fact that the new document strengthened the hand of the National Government, especially regarding commerce, lessened many of those frictions. So, too, did several of the Constitution's provisions that deal directly with the States' relationships with one another. This section is concerned with those provisions.

Interstate Compacts

No State can enter into any treaty, alliance, or confederation. However, the States may, with the consent of Congress, enter into **interstate compacts**—agreements among themselves and with foreign states.[15]

By 1920, the States had made only 26 compacts. Since then, the number of interstate compacts has been growing. New York and New Jersey led the way in 1921 with a compact creating the Port of New York Authority to manage and develop the harbor facilities bordering both States. More than 200 compacts are now in force, and many involve several States. In fact,

all 50 States have joined in two of them: the Compact for the Supervision of Parolees and Probationers and the Compact on Juveniles. These two compacts enable States to share important law-enforcement data. Other agreements cover a widening range of subjects. They include, for example, compacts designed to coordinate the development and conservation of such resources as water, oil, wildlife, and fish; prevent forest fires; combat stream and harbor pollution; provide for tax collections; promote motor vehicle safety; facilitate the licensing of drivers; and encourage the cooperative use of public universities.

▲ Seven western States belong to the Colorado River Compact, which apportions the waters of the Colorado River Basin.

---

[15] Article I, Section 10, Clause 3. The Supreme Court has held that Congressional consent is not needed for compacts that do not tend to increase the political power of the States, *Virginia* v. *Tennessee,* 1893. But it is often difficult to decide whether an agreement is political or nonpolitical. So, most interstate agreements are submitted to Congress as a matter of course.

Full Faith and Credit

The Constitution commands that

FROM THE *Constitution* *"Full Faith and Credit shall be given in each State to the public Acts, Records, and judicial Proceedings of every other State."*
—Article IV, Section 1

The term *public acts* refers to the laws of a State. *Records* refers to such documents as birth certificates, marriage licenses, deeds to property, car registrations, and the like. The words *judicial proceedings* relate to the outcome of court actions: damage awards, the probating (proving) of wills, divorce decrees, and so forth.

The **Full Faith and Credit Clause** most often comes into play in court matters. Take this example: Allen sues Bill in Florida, and the Florida court awards Allen $50,000 in damages. Bill cannot escape payment of the damages by moving to Georgia, because Allen could simply ask the Georgia courts to enforce the damage award. Neither would the case have to be retried in Georgia. Instead, the Georgia courts would have to give full faith and credit to—recognize and respect the validity of—the judgment made by the Florida court.

▲ *Full Faith and Credit* The Full Faith and Credit Clause ensures that records such as birth certificates and marriage licenses are recognized in all 50 States.

In a similar vein, a person can prove age, place of birth, marital status, title to property, and similar facts by securing the necessary documents from the State where the record was made. The validity of these documents will be recognized in each of the 50 States.

Exceptions

The Full Faith and Credit Clause is regularly observed and usually operates routinely between and among the States. This rule has two exceptions, however. First, it applies only to civil, not criminal, matters. One State cannot enforce another State's criminal law. Second, full faith and credit need not be given to certain divorces granted by one State to residents of another State.

On the second exception, the key question is always this: Was the person who obtained the divorce in fact a resident of the State that granted it? If so, the divorce will be accorded full faith and credit in other States. If not, then the State granting the divorce did not have the authority to do so, and another State can refuse to recognize it.

Williams v. North Carolina

The matter of interstate "quickie" divorces has been troublesome for years, especially since the Supreme Court's decision in a 1945 case, *Williams* v. *North Carolina*. In that case, a man and a woman had traveled to Nevada, where each wanted to obtain a divorce so they could marry each other. They lived in Las Vegas for six weeks, the minimum period of State residence required by Nevada's divorce law. The couple received their divorces, were married, and soon after returned to North Carolina. Problems arose when that State's authorities refused to recognize their Nevada divorces. North Carolina brought the couple to trial and a jury convicted each of them of the crime of bigamous cohabitation (marrying and living together while a previous marriage is still legally in effect).

On appeal, the Supreme Court upheld North Carolina's denial of full faith and credit to the Nevada divorces. It ruled that the couple had not in fact established bona fide—good faith, valid—residence in Nevada. Rather, the Court held that

▲ Each State requires new residents to obtain a State-issued license. **Critical Thinking Why are nonresident drivers allowed to drive from State to State without obtaining a new license?**

the couple had remained legal residents of North Carolina. The Court thus found that Nevada lacked the authority to grant their divorces.

A divorce granted by a State court to a bona fide resident of that State must be given full faith and credit in all other States. To become a legal resident of a State, a person must intend to reside there permanently, or at least indefinitely. Clearly, the Williamses had not intended to do so.

The *Williams* case, and later ones like it, cast dark clouds of doubt over the validity of thousands of other interstate divorces. The later marriages of people involved in these divorces, and the frequently tangled estate problems produced by their deaths, suggest the confused and serious nature of the matter.

Extradition

According to the Constitution

FROM THE *Constitution* **❝** *A Person charged in any State with Treason, Felony, or other Crime, who shall flee from Justice, and be found in another State, shall on Demand of the executive Authority of the State from which he fled, be delivered up, to be removed to the State having Jurisdiction of the Crime.* **❞**

— Article IV, Section 2, Clause 2

This clause refers to **extradition,** the legal process by which a fugitive from justice in one State is returned to that State. Extradition is designed to prevent a person from escaping justice by fleeing a State.

The return of a fugitive from justice is usually a routine matter; governors regularly approve the extradition requests they receive from other States' chief executives. Some of those requests, however, are contested. This is especially true in cases with strong racial or political overtones, and in those increasingly frequent instances of parental kidnapping of children involved in custody disputes as a result of a divorce.

Until the 1980s, governors could, and on occasion did, refuse to return fugitives. In *Kentucky* v. *Dennison*, 1861, the Supreme Court held that the Constitution did not give the Federal Government any power with which to compel a governor to act in an extradition case. So, for more than a century, the Constitution's word *shall* in the Extradition Clause had to be read as "may."

The Supreme Court overturned this ruling in 1987. In *Puerto Rico* v. *Branstad*, a unanimous Court held that the federal courts can indeed order an unwilling governor to extradite a fugitive.

Privileges and Immunities

The Constitution also provides that

FROM THE *Constitution* **❝** *The Citizens of each State shall be entitled to all Privileges and Immunities of Citizens in the several States.* **❞**

—Article IV, Section 2, Clause 1[16]

This clause, known as the **Privileges and Immunities Clause,** means that no State can draw unreasonable distinctions between its own residents and those persons who happen to live in other States.

Each State must recognize the right of any American to travel in or become a resident of that State. It must also allow any citizen, no matter where he or she lives, to use its courts and make contracts; buy, own, rent, or sell property; or marry within its borders.

---

[16]The provision is reinforced in the 14th Amendment.

Tuition at State Universities

University	In-State	Out-of-State
Oklahoma State University	$2,412	$6,492
Tennessee State University	$2,308	$7,132
Indiana State University	$3,426	$8,554
University of North Carolina	$2,364	$11,530
University of Virginia	$4,130	$16,603
Idaho State University	$2,398	$8,638
Arkansas State University	$2,972	$6,644
University of Texas	$3,128	$9,608
Michigan State University	$5,079	$11,820
Florida State University	$2,195	$9,184
University of Massachusetts	$5,212	$13,365

SOURCE: *Barron's Profiles of American Colleges,* 24th Edition, 2001

Interpreting Tables Under the Privileges and Immunities Clause, colleges and universities may charge different tuition rates for in-state and out-of-state residents. ***Do you think that this practice is justified? Explain your answer.***

At the same time, a State cannot do such things as try to relieve its unemployment problems by requiring employers to give a hiring preference to in-State residents, *Hicklin* v. *Orbeck*, 1978. Nor can it set the welfare benefits it pays to newly arrived residents at a level below the benefits it provides to its long-term residents, *Saens* v. *Roe*, 1999.

However, the Privileges and Immunities Clause does allow States to draw *reasonable* distinctions between its own residents and those of other States. Thus, any State can require that a person live within the State for some time before he or she can vote or hold public office. It also can require some period of residence before one can be licensed to practice law, medicine, dentistry, and so on.

In another example, the wild fish and game in a State are considered to be the common property of the people of that State. So, a State can require nonresidents to pay higher fees for fishing or hunting licenses than those paid by residents—who pay taxes to provide fish hatcheries, enforce game laws, and so on. By the same token, a State university often charges higher tuition to students from other States than it does to residents.

Section 3 Assessment

Key Terms and Main Ideas

1. What agreements does the Constitution prohibit the States from making?
2. What is the meaning of the **Full Faith and Credit Clause?**
3. What is the purpose of **extradition?**
4. **(a)** Give at least two examples of actions protected under the **Privileges and Immunities Clause. (b)** What types of actions are not protected by this clause?

Critical Thinking

5. **Predicting Consequences** What difficulties might result if each State were not required to give full faith and credit to the public acts, records, and judicial proceedings of other States? Provide at least two examples to support your conclusion.
6. **Drawing Inferences** Provide at least two examples of how the Privileges and Immunities Clause has affected your life or might do so in the future.

 Take It to the Net

7. Every State is a part of the Interstate Compact for the Placement of Children. Read this document and write a brief essay explaining its importance. Use the links provided in the Social Studies area at the following Web site for help in this activity. **www.phschool.com**

Should States Be Required to Enforce Federal Laws?

States are required to obey the federal Constitution and federal laws and treaties. Can Congress require State officials to help enforce federal laws and regulations?

Printz v. United States (1997)

The Gun Control Act of 1968 outlined rules for the distribution of firearms. Dealers were prohibited from selling guns to persons under 21, out-of-state residents, and convicted felons and fugitives. The Brady Act, a 1993 amendment to that law, required the attorney general to establish by 1998 a national system for conducting instant background checks on prospective handgun buyers.

The Brady Act also created a temporary background check system. Before selling a handgun, a firearms dealer was required to obtain identification from the purchaser, and to forward that information to the "chief law enforcement officer" (CLEO) of the purchaser's residence. The Brady Act required CLEOs to make a reasonable effort to determine within the five business days whether the purchaser may lawfully possess a gun.

Jay Printz and Richard Mack, sheriffs serving as CLEOs in counties in Montana and Arizona, respectively, challenged the Brady Act in federal district court. They argued that the provisions requiring them to perform federal functions and execute federal laws were unconstitutional. The district court agreed with their argument, but the court of appeals found the entire Act constitutional, and the case went to the Supreme Court for review.

Arguments for Printz

1. The balance of power between Federal and State governments would be disrupted if the Federal Government could force the States to implement federal laws, especially if the States had to pay the implementation costs.
2. Under the Constitution, executing the laws of the United States is the function of the President.

The Brady Act would transfer part of this function to State and local officials, over whom the President has no meaningful control.
3. The Framers of the Constitution rejected the idea of having the central government act through the States in favor of a federal system of government.

Arguments for the United States

1. Congress has the expressed power to regulate commerce among the States. The Brady Act provisions are "necessary and proper" to carry out this power and thus are a lawful exercise of the power.
2. The burden imposed by the Brady Act on State or local officials is small, and therefore does not threaten the balance of power between States and the Federal Government.
3. Congress found that there is an "epidemic" of gun violence, and it can lawfully require State and local officials to help deal with emergency situations on a temporary basis.

Decide for Yourself

1. Review the constitutional grounds on which each side based its arguments and the specific arguments each side presented.
2. Debate the opposing viewpoints presented in this case. Which viewpoint do you favor?
3. Predict the impact of the Court's decision on federal programs that require local enforcement. (To read a summary of the Court's decision, turn to the Supreme Court Glossary on page 799.)

Political Dictionary

federalism (p. 88)

division of powers (p. 89)

delegated powers (p. 89)

expressed powers (p. 89)

implied powers (p. 90)

inherent powers (p. 91)

reserved powers (p. 92)

exclusive powers (p. 93)

concurrent powers (p. 93)

enabling act (p. 99)

act of admission (p. 100)

grants-in-aid program (p. 101)

revenue sharing (p. 102)

categorical grant (p. 102)

block grant (p. 103)

project grant (p. 103)

interstate compact (p. 105)

Full Faith and Credit Clause (p. 106)

extradition (p. 107)

Privileges and Immunities Clause (p. 107)

Practicing the Vocabulary

Matching *Choose a term from the list above that best matches each description.*

1. The powers that the Constitution grants to the National Government in so many words
2. Congressional measure admitting a United States territory into the Union as a State
3. A type of federal grant-in-aid that is used for a specific, narrowly defined purpose
4. A system of government in which a constitution divides the powers of government between a National Government and several regional governments
5. Agreements made by the States among themselves and with foreign powers

Fill in the Blank *Choose a term from the list above that best completes the sentence.*

6. _____ are those powers held by the States in the federal system.
7. _____ are those powers granted to the National Government in the Constitution.
8. Some people have questioned whether the _____ gives the National Government too much say in matters of State and local concern.
9. Congress directs a territory desiring Statehood to frame a proposed State constitution in a(n) _____ .
10. Those powers that can only be exercised by the National Government are called _____ .

Reviewing Main Ideas

Section 1

11. How did the principle of federalism enable the Framers to solve the problems they faced in 1787?
12. Briefly describe the powers the Constitution provides to the National Government.
13. (a) In what three ways does the Constitution deny powers to the National Government? (b) Give at least one example of each.
14. Briefly describe the powers of the States as stated in the Constitution.
15. What is the role of the Supreme Court in the federal system?

Section 2

16. According to the Constitution, what are the National Government's obligations to the States?
17. Outline the steps Congress takes in admitting new States to the Union.

18. What is cooperative federalism?
19. Give at least three examples of cooperative federalism at work.
20. (a) What is a block grant? (b) Give an example of a program that a State might fund using block grant money.

Section 3

21. List at least three examples of the kinds of interstate compacts that exist today.
22. Under what circumstances can a State deny full faith and credit to a law, a public record, or the outcome of a court case in another State?
23. Explain the purpose of the Privileges and Immunities Clause.
24. What is the significance of the Supreme Court's decision in *Williams* v. *North Carolina?*
25. Can governors refuse to return fugitives from justice to the State from which they fled? Explain your answer.

Critical Thinking Skills

26. *Applying the Chapter Skill* What problems might arise if the Federal Government did not have the power to regulate interstate commerce?

27. *Drawing Conclusions* Why might a governor be reluctant to call for federal troops in the event that violence breaks out in a city in his or her State?

28. *Expressing Problems Clearly* What are the advantages and disadvantages of the federal system? Support your answer with examples from the text.

29. *Drawing Conclusions* Teachers must obtain State certification in order to teach within a given State. Not all States recognize certification from other States, however. Explain how this can be so.

Analyzing Political Cartoons

Using your knowledge of American government and this cartoon, answer the questions below.

30. What does the cartoon suggest about the relative importance of local government?

31. The cartoon portrays three levels of government—Federal, State, and local. From what you have read about the federal system, is this portrayal entirely accurate? Explain your answer.

★ You Can Make a Difference

Telephone or e-mail the offices of your representatives in Congress to find out the answers to the following questions: What local projects are supported by government block grants or by joint State/Federal funding in your community? How important are federal funds in your community or school? Is the money used for highways and parks? For school computers? For housing projects? Write a short report summarizing your findings. Include your opinion as to whether or not these funds are being used wisely.

Participation Activities

32. *Current Events Watch* Find three to five examples in the news that illustrate a power of the National Government, such as sending troops abroad or regulating immigration. Do the same for powers reserved to the States, such as establishing and regulating public schools. Prepare an oral presentation explaining how the State and national powers that you have chosen affect you and your community.

33. *Time Line Activity* Research how your State (or another State of your choosing) became a State. Then create a time line in which you explain your findings. Illustrate main events in your time line with drawings or copies of photos. Be sure to point out anything unique about the process by which your selected State entered the Union.

34. *It's Your Turn* When a person moves from one State to another, he or she must do such things as obtain a new driver's license and change his or her automobile and voter registrations. Create a newsletter to advise persons moving to your State how they can accomplish these tasks. **(Writing a Newsletter)**

 Take It to the Net

Chapter 4 Self-Test As a final review activity, take the Chapter 4 Self-Test in the Social Studies area at the Web site listed below, and receive immediate feedback on your answers.

www.phschool.com

IN THIS UNIT

◆ Americans expressing their patriotism

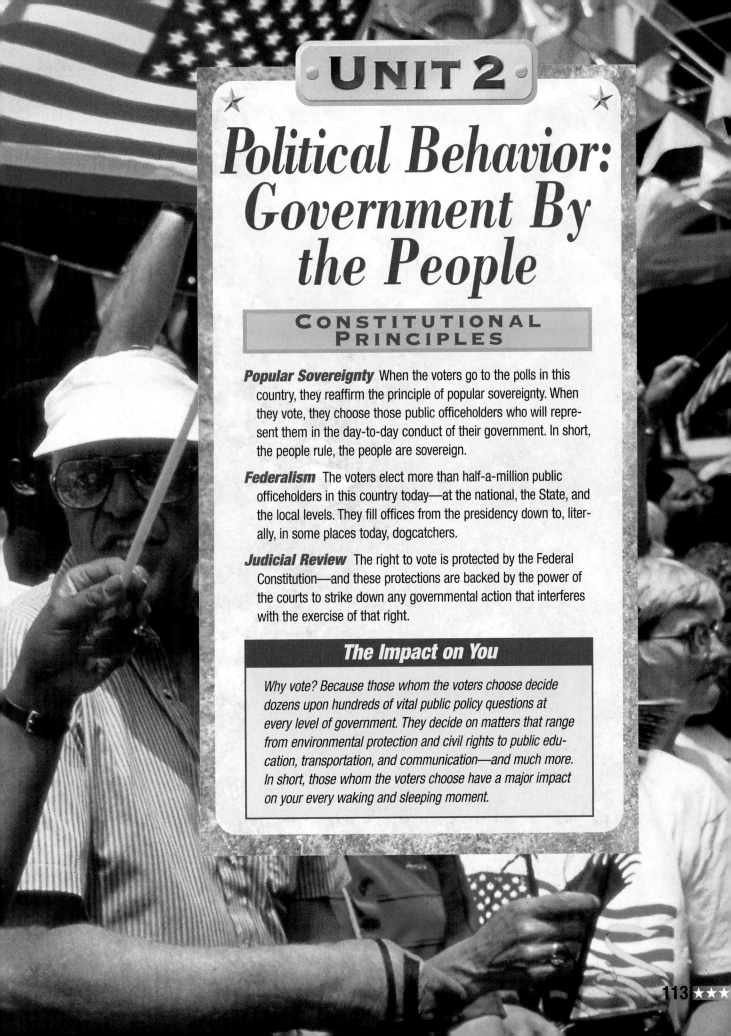

UNIT 2

Political Behavior: Government By the People

CONSTITUTIONAL PRINCIPLES

Popular Sovereignty When the voters go to the polls in this country, they reaffirm the principle of popular sovereignty. When they vote, they choose those public officeholders who will represent them in the day-to-day conduct of their government. In short, the people rule, the people are sovereign.

Federalism The voters elect more than half-a-million public officeholders in this country today—at the national, the State, and the local levels. They fill offices from the presidency down to, literally, in some places today, dogcatchers.

Judicial Review The right to vote is protected by the Federal Constitution—and these protections are backed by the power of the courts to strike down any governmental action that interferes with the exercise of that right.

The Impact on You

Why vote? Because those whom the voters choose decide dozens upon hundreds of vital public policy questions at every level of government. They decide on matters that range from environmental protection and civil rights to public education, transportation, and communication—and much more. In short, those whom the voters choose have a major impact on your every waking and sleeping moment.

Political Parties

"A party of order or stability, and a party of progress or reform, are both necessary elements of a healthy state of political life."

—John Stuart Mill (1859)

John Stuart Mill, a British philosopher, noted the benefits of two competing political parties. In this country, the balance of power has historically switched between two broad-based parties. Our major parties choose candidates and play important roles in government. Minor parties have challenged, but never really changed, this two-party system.

◆ A political party holds its national convention.

You Can Make a Difference

ONE GOOD WAY to study party politics is to work in a campaign. Early in the 2000 presidential race, some college students learned about politics first hand in the New Hampshire primary. Political science majors from Quinnipiac College spent their winter break as volunteers in the Bush, Bradley, Gore, or McCain campaigns. They canvassed voters, helped with mailings, held up signs, and met candidates. "I like to have the hands-on kind of learning," said Jessica Cieslak about the Bradley campaign. Sally Roden, addressing postcards for Governor Bush, commented, "It seems like we're contributing small pieces to a greater puzzle."

Keep It Current

Items marked with this logo are periodically updated on the Internet. Keep up-to-date with what's in the news. To get current information about the political parties, go to **www.phschool.com**

SECTION 1

Parties and What They Do (pp. 116–118)

★ The primary purpose of the two major American political parties is to control government through winning election to public office.

★ Political parties nominate candidates, rally their supporters, participate in government, act as a "bonding agent" for their own officeholders, and act as a watchdog over the other party.

SECTION 2

The Two-Party System (pp. 119–124)

★ The two-party system is a product of our history and tradition, the electoral system, and the American ideological consensus.

★ Multiparty systems provide more choice for the electorate but a less stable government. In one-party systems only the ruling party can participate in elections.

★ While the two major parties are broadly based, each party does tend to attract certain segments of the electorate.

SECTION 3

The Two-Party System in American History (pp. 126–131)

★ The first American parties originated in the battle over ratifying the Constitution.

★ There have been three eras of single-party domination in U.S. history from 1800–1968.

★ An era of divided government—not dominated by either political party—began in 1968 and continues to this day.

SECTION 4

The Minor Parties (pp. 132–135)

★ Minor parties in the United States include ideological parties, single-issue parties, economic protest parties, and splinter parties.

★ Even though they do not win national elections, minor parties play an important role as critics and innovators.

★ Strong third-party candidacies can influence elections.

SECTION 5

Party Organization (pp. 137–142)

★ The major parties have a decentralized structure because of federalism and the sometimes divisive nominating process.

★ At the national level, the four basic elements of both major parties are the national convention, the national committee, the national chairperson, and the congressional campaign committee.

★ At the State level, the party is organized around a State central committee headed by a State chairperson, while local organizations vary widely.

★ Party structure can also be viewed as made up of the party organization, or machinery; the people who usually vote the party ticket; and the party's officeholders.

★ Parties are currently in decline: fewer people identify themselves as major party members, and many people vote a split ticket.

① *Parties and What They Do*

Section Preview

OBJECTIVES

1. **Define** a political party.
2. **Describe** the major functions of political parties.

WHY IT MATTERS

Political parties are essential to democratic government. In the United States, political parties have shaped the way the government works. Today, the major parties perform several important functions without which our government could not function.

POLITICAL DICTIONARY

★ **political party**
★ **major parties**
★ **partisanship**
★ **party in power**

"Winning isn't everything; it's the only thing." So said legendary football coach Vince Lombardi. Lombardi was talking about teams in the National Football League. His words, however, could also be used to describe the Republican and Democratic parties. They, too, are in the business of competing and winning.

What Is a Party?

A **political party** is a group of persons who seek to control government through the winning of elections and the holding of public office. This definition of a political party is broad enough to fit any political party. It certainly describes the two **major parties** in American politics, the Republican and the Democratic parties.

Another, more specific definition can be used to describe most political parties, both here and abroad. That is, a political party is a group of persons, joined together on the basis of common principles, who seek to control government in order to affect certain public policies and programs.

▲ Bumper stickers reveal party loyalty.

This definition, with its emphasis on principles and public policy positions, will not fit the two major American parties, however. The Republican and Democratic parties are not primarily principle- or issue-oriented. They are, instead, election-oriented.

What Do Parties Do?

It is clear from American history, as well as from the histories of other peoples, that political parties are essential to democratic government. Parties are the major mechanisms behind the development of broad policy and leadership choices; they are the medium through which those options are presented to the people.

Political parties are a vital link between the people and their government; that is, between the governed and those who govern. Many observers argue that political parties are the principal means by which the will of the people is made known to government and by which government is held accountable to the people.

Parties serve the democratic ideal in another important way. They work to blunt conflict; they are "power brokers." Political parties bring conflicting groups together. They modify and encourage compromise among the contending views of different interests and groups, and so help to unify, rather than divide, the American people. They soften the impact of extremists at both ends of the political spectrum.

Again, political parties are indispensable to American government. This fact is underscored by the major functions they perform.

Nominating Candidates

The major function of a political party is to nominate, or name, candidates for public office. That is, the parties select candidates and then present them to the voters. Then the parties work to help their candidates win elections.

To have a functioning democracy, there must be a procedure for finding (recruiting and choosing) candidates for office. There must also be a mechanism for gathering support (votes) for these candidates. Parties are the best device yet found to do those jobs.

The nominating function is almost exclusively a party function in the United States.[1] It is the one activity that most clearly sets political parties apart from all of the other groups in politics.

Informing and Activating Supporters

Parties inform the people, and inspire and activate their interest and participation in public affairs. Other groups also perform this function—in particular, the news media and interest groups.

Parties try to inform and inspire voters in several ways. Primarily, they campaign for their candidates, take stands on issues, and criticize the candidates and the positions of their opponents.

Each party tries to inform the people as it thinks they should be informed—to its own advantage. For example, a party selects information in order to present its own positions and candidates in the best possible light. It conducts this "educational" process through pamphlets, signs, buttons, and stickers; with advertisements in newspapers and magazines and on radio, television, and the Internet; in speeches, rallies, and conventions; and in many other ways.

Remember, both parties want to win elections, and that consideration has much to do with the stands they take on most issues. Both parties try to shape positions that will attract as many voters as possible—and that will, at the same time, offend as few voters as possible.

The Bonding Agent Function

A bond is an insurance agreement protecting a person or a business against loss caused by a third party. In a sense, a political party acts as

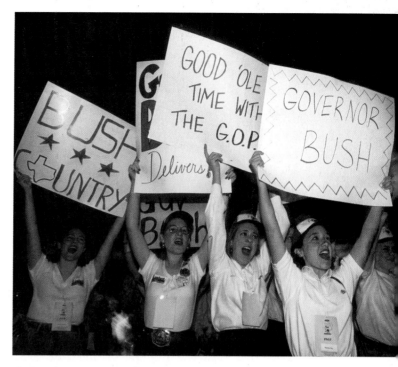

▲ *Campaign Fever* Without the support of thousands of enthusiastic campaign workers, political parties would fade away. Young volunteers represent the future of their parties.

a "bonding agent," to ensure the good performance of its candidates and officeholders. In choosing its candidates, the party tries to make sure that they are men and women who are both qualified and of good character, or, at least, that their candidates are not unqualified and have no serious blemishes on their records.

The party also prompts its successful candidates to perform well in office. The democratic process imposes this bonding agent function on a party, whether the party really wants to perform it or not. If it fails to assume this responsibility, both the party and its candidates may suffer the consequences in future elections.

Governing

In several respects, government in the United States is government by party. For example, public officeholders—those who govern—are regularly chosen on the basis of party. Congress and the State legislatures are organized on party lines, and they conduct much of their business based on **partisanship**. This means that firm allegiance to a political party is the basis for government action. In addition, most appointments to executive offices, at both the federal and State levels, are made with an eye to party considerations.

[1]The exceptions are in nonpartisan elections and in those rare instances in which an independent candidate enters a partisan contest. Nominations are covered at length in Chapter 7.

▲ From left to right: Al Gore accepts the Democratic nomination for President; Rick Lazio, Republican candidate for the Senate, discusses the issues with New York voters; the powerful House Ways and Means Committee holds a hearing. *Critical Thinking What party functions are represented by these three photos?*

In yet another sense, parties provide a basis for the conduct of government. In the complicated separation of powers arrangement, the executive and legislative branches must cooperate with one another if government is to accomplish anything. It is political parties that regularly provide the channels through which these two branches are able to work together.

Political parties have played a significant role in the process of constitutional change by informal amendment. Consider this important example: The Constitution's cumbersome system for electing the President works principally because political parties reshaped it in its early years and have made it work ever since.

Acting as Watchdog

Parties act as watchdogs over the conduct of the public's business. This is particularly true of the party out of power. It plays this role as it criticizes the policies and behavior of the **party in power.**

In American politics the party in power is the party that controls the executive branch of government—the presidency at the national level or the governorship at the State level.

In effect, the party out of power attempts to convince the voters that they should "throw the rascals out," that the "outs" should become the "ins" and the "ins" the "outs." The scrutiny and criticism by the "out" party tends to make the "rascals" more careful of their public charge and more responsive to the wishes and concerns of the people. In short, the party out of power plays the important role of "the loyal opposition"—opposed to the party in power but loyal to the people and the nation.

Section 1 Assessment

Key Terms and Main Ideas

1. What is a **political party?**
2. Explain two functions of political parties.
3. In what ways is American government conducted on the basis of **partisanship?**
4. (a) At this time, which is the **party in power** in your State? (b) In the nation?

Critical Thinking

5. **Analyzing Information** In what ways do political parties tend to unify, rather than divide, the American people?

6. **Drawing Conclusions** The party out of power serves an important function in American government. Explain that function.

 Take It to the Net

7. Locate both the Republican and Democratic party Web sites. Write a summary showing how the sites reflect the two parties' similarities and differences. Use the links provided in the Social Studies area at the following Web site for help in completing this activity. **www.phschool.com**

2 The Two-Party System

Section Preview

OBJECTIVES

1. **Identify** the reasons why the United States has a two-party system.
2. **Understand** multiparty and one-party systems and how they affect the functioning of government.
3. **Describe** party membership patterns in the United States.

WHY IT MATTERS

The two-party system in the United States is a product of historical forces, our electoral system, and the ideological consensus of the American people. It provides more political stability than a multiparty system and more choice than a one-party system.

POLITICAL DICTIONARY

★ minor party
★ two-party system
★ single-member district
★ plurality
★ bipartisan
★ pluralistic society
★ consensus
★ multiparty
★ coalition
★ one-party system

Does the name Earl Dodge mean anything to you? Probably not. Yet Mr. Dodge has run for President of the United States five times. He was the presidential candidate of the Prohibition Party in 1984, 1988, 1992, 1996, and again in 2000.

One of the reasons Mr. Dodge is not very well known is that he belongs to a **minor party,** one of the political parties without wide support. The two major parties dominate American politics. That is to say, this country has a **two-party system.** In a typical election, only the Republican or the Democratic Party's candidates have a reasonable chance of winning public office.

Why a Two-Party System?

On the whole and through most of its history, the United States has been a two-party nation. Still, it is true that in some States, and in many local communities, one of the two major parties may be overwhelmingly dominant. And it is also true that this may remain the case for a long period of time; for example, the Democrats controlled politics in the South for decades. Nevertheless, for the most part, our government has been characterized by two strong major parties.

A number of factors help to explain why America has had and continues to have a two-party system. No one reason, taken alone, offers a wholly satisfactory explanation for the phenomenon. Taken together, however, several reasons do make quite a persuasive answer.

The Historical Basis

The two-party system is rooted in the beginnings of the nation itself. The Framers of the Constitution were opposed to political parties. As you saw in Chapter 2, the ratification of the Constitution saw the birth of America's first two parties: the Federalists, led by Alexander Hamilton, and the Anti-Federalists, who followed Thomas Jefferson. In short, the American party system *began* as a two-party system.

The Framers hoped to create a unified country; they sought to bring order out of

▶ The symbols of the political parties turn up in many forms—especially in an election year.

Voices on Government

Mary Matalin was a campaign advisor to George W. Bush and Dick Cheney in 2000. After the Bush administration took office, she was made assistant to the President and counselor on matters of politics and communication to Vice President Cheney. Here she comments on how political campaigns look from the inside:

❝ *Politics is about winning. . . . Participating in a presidential campaign full-time, as a professional, is very emotional and very draining. You don't want to put that much effort into a race unless you have a real chance. . . . In the culture of campaigns it's not ideological. Most of us have a philosophical grounding—we're working for Republicans only—but in terms of issues the differences between candidates are often pretty small.* ❞

Evaluating the Quotation

How does Matalin's view of political campaigns fit in with what you have read about the two major parties?

the chaos of the Critical Period of the 1780s. To most of the Framers, parties were "factions," and therefore agents of divisiveness and disunity. George Washington reflected this view when, in his Farewell Address in 1796, he warned the new nation against "the baneful effects of the spirit of party."

In this light, it is hardly surprising that the Constitution made no provision for political parties. The Framers could not foresee the ways in which the governmental system they set up would develop. Thus, they could not possibly know that two major parties would emerge as prime instruments of government in the United States. Nor could they know that those two major parties would tend to be moderate, to choose middle-of-the-road positions, and so help to unify rather than divide the nation.

The Force of Tradition

Once established, human institutions are likely to become self-perpetuating. So it has been with the two-party system. The very fact that the

nation began with a two-party system has been a leading reason for the retention of a two-party system. Over time, it has become an increasingly important, self-reinforcing reason.

The point can be made this way: Most Americans accept the idea of a two-party system simply because there has always been one. This inbred support for the arrangement is a principal reason why challenges to the system—by minor parties, for example—have made so little headway. In other words, America has a two-party system *because* America has a two-party system.

The Electoral System

Several features of the American electoral system tend to promote the existence of but two major parties. That is to say, the basic shape, and many of the details, of the election process work in that direction.

The prevalence of **single-member districts** is one of the most important of these features. Nearly all of the elections held in this country—from the presidential contest on down to those at the local levels—are single-member district elections. That is, they are contests in which only one candidate is elected to each office on the ballot. In these winner-take-all elections, the winning candidate is the one who receives a **plurality,** or the largest number of votes cast for the office. Note that a plurality need not be a majority, which is more than half of all votes cast.

The single-member district pattern works to discourage minor parties. Because only one winner can come out of each contest, voters usually face only two viable choices: They can vote for the candidate of the party holding the office, or they can vote for the candidate of the party with the best chance of replacing the current office-holder. In short, most voters think of a vote for a minor party candidate as a "wasted vote."

Another important aspect of the electoral system works to the same end. Much of American election law is purposely written to discourage non-major party candidates.[2] Republicans and Democrats regularly act in a **bipartisan** way in

---

[2]Nearly all election law in this country is State, not federal, law—a point discussed at length in the next two chapters. But, here, note this very important point: Nearly all of the more than 7,600 State legislators—nearly all of those persons who make State law—are either Democrats or Republicans. Only a handful of minor party members or independents now sit, or have ever sat, in State legislatures.

this matter. That is, the two major parties find common ground and work together here.

They deliberately shape election laws to preserve, protect, and defend the two major parties and the two-party system, and thus to frustrate the minor parties. In most States it is far more difficult for minor parties and independent groups to get their candidates listed on the ballot than for the major parties to do so.

The 2000 presidential election offered a striking illustration of the point. Both George W. Bush and Al Gore were on the ballots of all 50 States and the District of Columbia. None of the several other serious presidential hopefuls made the ballot everywhere in 2000.

To this point, non-major party candidates have made it to the ballot everywhere in only seven presidential elections. The Socialist Party's Eugene V. Debs was the first to do so, in 1912. The Socialist candidate in 1916, Allan L. Benson, also appeared on the ballots of all of the then 48 States. In 1980 Ed Clark, the Libertarian nominee, and independent John Anderson, and in 1988 Lenora Fulani of the New Alliance Party made the ballots of all 50 States and the District of Columbia. So, too, did Libertarian Andre Marrou and independent Ross Perot in 1992. Every ballot contained the names of Libertarian Harry Browne and the Reform Party's Ross Perot in 1996.

In 2000 Harry Browne of the Libertarian Party was on the ballot in 49 States and the District of Columbia. The Reform Party's Pat Buchanan made it in 49 States, Ralph Nader of the Green Party in 43 States and the District of Columbia, and the Constitution Party's Howard Phillips in 41 States. But most minor party candidates suffered their usual fate: they managed to gain the ballot in only a handful of States.

The American Ideological Consensus

Americans are, on the whole, an ideologically homogeneous people. That is, over time, the American people have shared many of the same ideals, the same basic principles, and the same patterns of belief.

This is not to say that Americans are all alike. Clearly, this is not the case. The United States is a **pluralistic society**—one consisting of several distinct cultures and groups. Increasingly, the members of various ethnic, racial, religious, and other

"And I promise to always be loyal to my party, even if I have to change parties to do it!"

Interpreting Political Cartoons *What does the cartoon imply about what parties—and candidates—stand for?*

social groups compete for and share in the exercise of political power in this country. Still, there is a broad **consensus**—a general agreement among various groups—on fundamental matters.

Even given this overall consensus, it is certainly not true that Americans always agree with one another in all matters. Far from it. The nation has been deeply divided at times: during the Civil War and in the years of the Great Depression, for example, and over such critical issues as racial discrimination, the war in Vietnam, and abortion.

On the other hand, the nation has not been regularly plagued by sharp political divisions.

▲ Colorado Senator Ben Nighthorse Campbell was elected as a Democrat in 1992. He became a Republican in 1995, and was easily reelected in 1998. *Critical Thinking What might cause a politician to switch parties?*

▲ *Multiparty Government* German Chancellor Gerhard Schroeder (front row, center) was elected in 1998. With only 40.9 percent of the seats in the Assembly, Schroeder's Social Democratic Party (SPD) formed a coalition government with a smaller party, Alliance 90/The Greens.

The United States has been free of long-standing, bitter disputes based on such factors as economic class, social status, religious beliefs, or national origin.

Those conditions that could produce several strong rival parties simply do not exist in this country. In this way, the United States differs from most other democracies. In short, the realities of American society and politics simply do not permit more than two major parties.

This ideological consensus has had another very important impact on American parties. It has given the nation two major parties that look very much alike. Both tend to be moderate. Both are built on compromise and regularly try to occupy "the middle of the road." Both parties seek the same prize: the votes of a majority of the electorate. To do so, they must win over essentially the same people. Inevitably, each party takes policy positions that do not differ a great deal from those of the other major party.

This is not to say that there are no significant differences between the two major parties today. There are. For example, the Democratic Party, and those who usually vote for its candidates, are more likely to support such things as social welfare programs, government regulation of business practices, and efforts to improve the status of minorities. On the other hand, the Republican Party and its adherents are much more likely to favor the play of private market forces in the economy and to argue that the Federal Government should be less extensively involved in social welfare programs.

Multiparty Systems

Some critics argue that the American two-party system should be scrapped. They would replace it with a **multiparty** arrangement, a system in which several major and many lesser parties exist, seriously compete for, and actually win, public offices. Multiparty systems have long been a feature of most European democracies, and they are now found in many other democratic societies elsewhere in the world.

In the typical multiparty system, the various parties are each based on a particular interest, such as economic class, religious belief, sectional attachment, or political ideology. Those who favor such an arrangement for this country say that it would provide for a broader representation of the electorate and be more responsive to the will of the people. They claim that a multiparty system would give voters a much more meaningful choice among candidates and policy alternatives than the present two-party system does.

Clearly, multiparty systems do tend to produce a broader, more diverse representation of the electorate. At the same time, that strength is also a major weakness of a multiparty system. It often leads to instability in government. One party is often unable to win the support of a majority of the voters. As a result, the power to govern must be shared by a number of parties, in a **coalition.** A coalition is a temporary alliance of several groups who come together to form a working majority and so to control a government.

Several of the multiparty nations of Western Europe have long been plagued by governmental crises. They have experienced frequent changes in party control as coalitions shift and dissolve. Italy furnishes an almost nightmarish example: It has had a new government on the average of once every nine months ever since the end of World War II.

Historically, the American people have shunned a multiparty approach to politics. They have refused to give substantial support to any but the two major parties and their candidates. Two of the factors mentioned above—single-member districts and the American ideological consensus—seem to make the multiparty approach impossible in the United States.

One-Party Systems

In nearly all dictatorships today, only one political party is allowed. That party is the party of the ruling clique. For all practical purposes, it is quite accurate to say that in those circumstances the resulting **one-party system** is really a "no-party" system.

In quite another sense, this country has had several States and many local areas that can be described in one-party terms. Until the late 1950s, the Democrats dominated the politics of the South. The Republican Party was almost always the winner in New England and in the upper Midwest.

Effective two-party competition has spread fairly rapidly in the past 30 years or so. Democrats have won many offices in every northern State. Republican candidates have become more and more successful throughout the once "Solid South." Nevertheless, about a third of the States can still be said to have a modified one-party system. That is, one of the major parties regularly wins most elections in those States. Also, while most States may have vigorous two-party competition at the Statewide level, within most of them are many areas dominated by a single party.

Party Membership Patterns

Membership in a party is purely voluntary. A person is a Republican or a Democrat, or belongs to a minor party, or is an independent—belonging to no organized party—because that is what he or she chooses to be.[3]

Remember, the two major parties are broadly based. In order to gain more votes than their opponents, they must attract as much support as they possibly can. Each party has always been composed, in greater or lesser degree, of a cross section of the nation's population. Each is made up of Protestants, Catholics, and Jews; whites, African Americans, Latinos, and other minorities; professionals, farmers, and union members. Each party includes the young, the middle-aged,

▲ Dictator Joseph Stalin, who was both leader of the Communist Party and premier of the Soviet Union, ruthlessly crushed all political opposition. *Critical Thinking Why might silencing other political points of view be a disadvantage to a government?*

and the elderly; city-dwellers, suburbanites, and rural residents among its members.

It is true that the members of certain segments of the electorate tend to be aligned more solidly with one or the other of the major parties, at least for a time. Thus, in recent decades, African Americans, Catholics and Jews, and union members have voted more often for Democrats. In the same way, white males, Protestants, and the business community have been inclined to back the GOP.[4] Yet, never have all members of any group tied themselves permanently to either party.

Individuals identify themselves with a party for many reasons. Family is almost certainly the most important among them. Studies show that nearly two out of every three Americans follow the party allegiance of their parents.

---

[3]In most States a person must declare a preference for a particular party in order to vote in that party's primary election. That declaration is usually made as a part of the voter registration process, and it is often said to make one "a registered Republican (or Democrat)." The requirement is only a procedural one, however, and wholly a matter of individual choice.

[4]GOP is common shorthand for the Republican Party. The initials stand for Grand Old Party, a nickname acquired in the latter part of the 19th century. The nickname may owe its origins to British politics. Prime Minister William Gladstone was dubbed "the Grand Old Man," often abbreviated "GOM," by the English press in 1882. Soon after, "GOP" appeared in headlines in the *New York Tribune,* the *Boston Post,* and other American papers.

Political Party Resources

MAJOR POLITICAL PARTIES

 Republican Party
310 First St. SE, Washington, DC 20003
http://www.rnc.org

 Democratic Party
430 So. Capitol St. SE, Washington, DC 20003
http://www.democrats.org

OTHER MAJOR POLITICAL ORGANIZATIONS

The Libertarian Party (Founded 1971)
2600 Virginia Ave., N.W., Washington, DC 20037 http://www.lp.org
Stresses individual liberty; opposes taxes, foreign involvements, government intrusion into private lives.

The Communist Party USA (Founded 1919)
235 West 23rd St., New York, NY 10011 http://www.cpusa.org
Terms itself "the Party of the American Working class." Looks forward to the restructuring of American political and economic systems.

Prohibition National Committee (Founded 1869)
P.O. Box 2635, Denver, Colorado 80201 http://www.prohibitionists.org
Advocates a nationwide prohibition of the manufacture, distribution, and sale of alcoholic beverages.

Green Party USA (Founded 1972)
P.O. Box 1134, Lawrence, MA 01842 http://www.greens.org
Promotes environmental concerns with the slogan: "We do not inherit the Earth from our parents, we borrow it from our children."

The Reform Party (Founded 1995)
9129 E. Shonto Ln., Tucson, AZ 85749 http://www.reformparty.org
Founded by Ross Perot but now conservative party; promotes Christian beliefs, opposes immigration, free trade.

The Socialist Labor Party (Founded 1891)
(In Minnesota: Industrial Government Party)
P.O. Box 218, Mountain View, CA 94042 http://www.slp.org
Seeks the peaceful abolition of capitalism, and the social ownership of the means of production and distribution.

The Constitution Party (Founded 1992)
23 North Lime St., Lancaster, PA 17602 http://www.constitutionparty.org
Advocates "free pursuance of happiness, not the regulation of it."

The Natural Law Party (Founded 1992)
P.O. Box 1900, Fairfield, IA 52556 http://www.natural-law.org
Hopes "to bring national life into harmony with natural law."

Interpreting Tables **Which of the minor parties shown in the table has the most specific platform?**

Major events can also have a decided influence on the party affiliation of voters. Of these, the Civil War and the Depression of the 1930s have been the most significant in American political history.

Economic status also influences party choice, although generalizations are quite risky. Historically though, those in higher income groups are more likely to be Republicans, while those with lower incomes tend to be Democrats.

Several other factors also affect both party choice and voting behavior, including age, place of residence, level of education, and work environment. Some of those factors may conflict with one another in the case of a particular individual—and they often do. Therefore, predicting how a person or group will vote in any given election is a risky business, which keeps the pollsters and the analysts busy until the votes are counted.

Section 2 Assessment

Key Terms and Main Ideas

1. Briefly explain four reasons why the United States has a **two-party system.**
2. How do the terms **pluralistic** and **consensus** both apply to American society?
3. **(a)** What is a **multiparty system? (b)** Why do some people favor it for the United States?
4. Many factors tend to influence party choice. Name four.

Critical Thinking

5. **Synthesizing Information** What does the fact that the major parties cooperate to discourage minor parties and yet compete vigorously against each other during elections tell you about party politics in the United States?

6. **Recognizing Ideologies** You are campaigning for one of the two major parties. Create a short political advertisement to appeal to large numbers of voters and to distinguish your party from the other major party.

 Take It to the Net

7. Survey the polling data on the Gallup Organization's Web site. Which issues do Americans seem to agree on? Which issues divide Americans? Graph the results of one poll that reflects a range of opinions. Then tell where you stand on that issue. Use the links provided in the Social Studies area at the following Web site for help in completing this activity. **www.phschool.com**

Identifying Political Roots and Attitudes

A s a voter, how will you evaluate political parties and candidates and make voting decisions? Will you vote the way your friends are voting? The better way of making voting decisions is to analyze the political traditions that have shaped the candidates' views, and then make a decision based on your own values.

Identifying political traditions will help you understand the shorthand that politicians often use. For instance, if a candidate says she's a "pro-labor Democrat" or a "religious conservative," these labels imply a whole set of beliefs with deep roots in American politics and culture. With no historical frame of reference, you would have difficulty interpreting what these labels really mean and what policies a candidate or party supports.

Whether you're examining your own political roots or someone else's, try these steps:

1. Learn about political traditions. You read in this section that American politics has long been dominated by two political parties, Republican and Democrat. A basic knowledge of the origins and history of these parties is necessary in order to understand most political dialogue in this country. (a) What specific policies or goals do many Republicans favor? (b) What do many Democrats favor?

2. Identify major cultural influences. Our beliefs can be influenced by several factors: education, occupation, location, ethnic and religious ties, and the types of activities we pursue.

While being careful not to stereotype people, we can often predict the political views of many people based on such cultural factors. For example, in areas where Christian groups are politically active, you might find strong support for prayer in public schools. What political views might you expect to be held by people who (a) like to hunt; (b) have a college degree; (c) are Native American; (d) work in a factory?

3. Analyze the effects of personal experience. People and events in our lives can have a powerful effect,

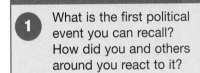

Finding Your Political Roots

1	What is the first political event you can recall? How did you and others around you react to it?
2	If you have politically active family members or friends, to what political party do they belong?
3	If you discuss politics with family or friends, how have they influenced your thinking, if at all?
4	Where do you get information about politics— newspapers, television, the Internet? Are you influenced most by what you read or see or hear?
5	How would you describe your political attitudes? Do you lean toward a particular political party? Are your views mostly liberal, mostly conservative, or a mixture of both? Explain.

positive or negative, on our political views. During the 2000 presidential campaign, both Texas Governor George W. Bush and Vice President Albert Gore, Jr., said their political careers were inspired by their famous fathers. Arizona Senator John McCain, a former prisoner of war in Vietnam, favored a strong military. Some candidates base their political ideals on their religious beliefs. Have your political views been influenced by your personal experiences? Explain.

Test for Success

(a) Use the questionnaire above and the steps outlined above to describe how political traditions influenced your political attitudes.
(b) Interview a friend or family member. Write a paragraph summarizing his or her political roots and attitudes.

The Two-Party System in American History

Section Preview

OBJECTIVES

1. **Understand** the origins of political parties in the United States.
2. **Identify** and describe the three major periods of single-party domination and describe the current era of divided government.

WHY IT MATTERS

The origins and history of political parties in the United States help explain how the two major parties work today and how they affect American government.

POLITICAL DICTIONARY

★ **incumbent**
★ **faction**
★ **electorate**
★ **sectionalism**

Henry Ford, the great auto maker, once said that all history is "bunk." Ford knew a great deal about automobiles and mass production, but he did not know much about history or its importance.

Listen, instead, to Shakespeare: "The past is prologue." Today is the product of yesterday. You are what you are today because of your history. Therefore, the more you know about your past, the better prepared you are for today, and for tomorrow.

Much the same can be said about the two-party system in American politics. The more you know about its past, the better you will understand its workings today.

The Nation's First Parties

The beginnings of the American two-party system can be traced to the battle over the ratification of the Constitution. The conflicts of the time, centering on the proper form and role of government in the United States, were not stilled by the adoption of the Constitution. Rather, those conflicts were carried over into the early years of the Republic. They led directly to the formation of the nation's first full-blown political parties.

The Federalist Party was the first to appear. It formed around Alexander Hamilton, who served as secretary of the treasury in the new government organized by George Washington. The Federalists were, by and large, the party of "the rich and the well-born." Most of them had supported the Constitution.

Led by Hamilton, the Federalists worked to create a stronger national government. They favored vigorous executive leadership and a set of policies designed to correct the nation's economic ills. The Federalists' program appealed to financial, manufacturing, and commercial interests. To reach their goals, they urged a liberal interpretation of the Constitution.

Thomas Jefferson, the nation's first secretary of state, led the opposition to the Federalists.[5] Jefferson and his followers were more sympathetic to the "common man" than were the Federalists. They favored a very limited role for the new government created by the Constitution. In their view, Congress should dominate that new government, and its policies should help the nation's small shopkeepers, laborers, farmers, and planters. The Jeffersonians insisted on a strict construction of the provisions of the Constitution.

▲ This ticket provided admission to the convention that nominated President Roosevelt for a second term.

[5]As you recall, George Washington was opposed to political parties. As President, he named arch foes Hamilton and Jefferson to his new Cabinet to get them to work together—in an unsuccessful attempt to avoid the creation of formally organized and opposing groups.

Jefferson resigned from Washington's Cabinet in 1793 to concentrate on organizing his party. Originally, the new party took the name Anti-Federalist. Later it became known as the Jeffersonian Republicans or the Democratic-Republicans. Finally, by 1828, it became the Democratic Party.

These two parties first clashed in the election of 1796. John Adams, the Federalists' candidate to succeed Washington as President, defeated Jefferson by just three votes in the electoral college. Over the next four years, Jefferson and James Madison worked tirelessly to build the Democratic-Republican Party. Their efforts paid off in the election of 1800. Jefferson defeated the **incumbent,** or current officeholder, President Adams; Jefferson's party also won control of Congress. The Federalists never returned to power.

American Parties: Four Major Eras

The history of the American party system since 1800 can be divided into four major periods. Through the first three of these periods, one or the other of the two major parties was dominant, regularly holding the presidency and usually both houses of Congress. The nation is now in a fourth period, much of it marked by divided government.

In the first of these periods, from 1800 to 1860, the Democrats won 13 of 15 presidential elections. They lost the office only in the elections of 1840 and 1848. In the second era, from 1860 to 1932, the Republicans won 14 of 18 elections, losing only in 1884, 1892, 1912, and 1916.

The third period, from 1932 to 1968, began with the Democrats' return to power and Franklin Roosevelt's first election to the presidency. The Democrats won seven of the nine presidential elections, losing only in 1952 and 1956. Through the fourth and current period, which began in 1968, the Republicans have won six of nine presidential elections, and they hold the White House today. But the Democrats have controlled both houses of Congress over much of the current period—although they do not do so today.

The Era of the Democrats, 1800–1860

Thomas Jefferson's election in 1800 marked the beginning of a period of Democratic domination that was to last until the Civil War. As the time line on pages 128–129 shows, the Federalists, soundly defeated in 1800, had disappeared altogether by 1816.

For a time, through the Era of Good Feeling, the Democratic-Republicans were unopposed in national politics. However, by the mid-1820s, they had split into **factions,** or conflicting groups.

Interpreting Political Cartoons Political cartoonist Thomas Nast is credited with popularizing the party symbols in his 1874 cartoons for *Harper's Weekly.* At left, the Republican elephant trumpets Democratic Party defeats. At right, the Democratic donkey kicks Lincoln's Secretary of War. *What characteristics of the elephant and the donkey do you think Nast wanted to associate with each party?*

Four Eras of Political Parties

1800 Thomas Jefferson is elected President in 1800, ushering in an era of Democratic domination lasting until the Civil War.

1860 The 1860 election of Abraham Lincoln and the start of the Civil War mark the beginning of 75 years of Republican Party control.

Era of Democrats 1800–1860

Era of Republicans 1860–1932

ELECTION YEAR	1800	1804	1808	1812	1816	1820	1824	1828	1832	1836	1840	1844	1848	1852	1856	1860	1864	1868	1872	1876	1880	1884	1888
PARTY WINNING THE PRESIDENCY	●	●	●	●	●	●	●	●	●	●	●	●	●	●	●	●	●	●	●	●	●	●	●

1828 The Democratic-Republican Party is by now generally known as the Democratic Party.

1854 The Republican Party is formed in 1854, attracting many former Whigs and antislavery Democrats. They elect their first President in 1860.

Interpreting Time Lines This time line shows the parties that have won each presidential election. *Since 1860, which party has controlled the presidency for the longest period of time?*

By the time of Andrew Jackson's administration (1829–1837), a potent National Republican (Whig) Party had arisen to challenge the Democrats. The major issues of the day—conflicts over public lands, the Second Bank of the United States, high tariffs, and slavery—all had made new party alignments inevitable.

The Democrats, led by Jackson, were a coalition of small farmers, debtors, frontier pioneers, and slaveholders. They drew much of their support from the South and West. The years of Jacksonian democracy produced three fundamental changes in the nation's political landscape: (1) voting rights for all white males, (2) a huge increase in the number of elected offices around the country, and (3) the practice of awarding public offices, contracts, and other governmental favors to those who supported the party in power.

The Whig Party was led by the widely popular Henry Clay and the great orator, Daniel Webster. The party consisted of a loose coalition of eastern bankers, merchants and industrialists, and many owners of large southern plantations. The Whigs were opposed to the tenets of Jacksonian democracy and strongly supported a high tariff. However, the Whigs' victories were few. Although they were the other major party from the mid-1830s to the 1850s, the Whigs were able to elect only two Presidents, both of

them war heroes: William Henry Harrison in 1840 and Zachary Taylor in 1848.

By the 1850s, the growing crisis over slavery split both major parties. Left leaderless by the deaths of Clay and Webster, the Whigs fell apart. Meanwhile, the Democrats split into two sharply divided camps, North and South. During this decade, the nation drifted toward civil war.

Of the several groupings that arose to compete for supporters among the former Whigs and the fragmented Democrats, the Republican Party was the most successful. Founded in 1854, it drew many Whigs and antislavery Democrats. The Republicans nominated their first presidential candidate, John C. Frémont, in 1856; they elected their first President, Abraham Lincoln, in 1860.

With Lincoln's election, the Republican Party became the only party in the history of American politics to make the jump from third-party to major-party status. As you will see, even greater things were in store for the Republicans.

The Era of the Republicans, 1860–1932

The Civil War signaled the beginning of the second era of one-party domination. For nearly 75 years, the Republicans dominated the national scene. They were supported by business and financial interests, and by farmers, laborers, and newly freed African Americans.

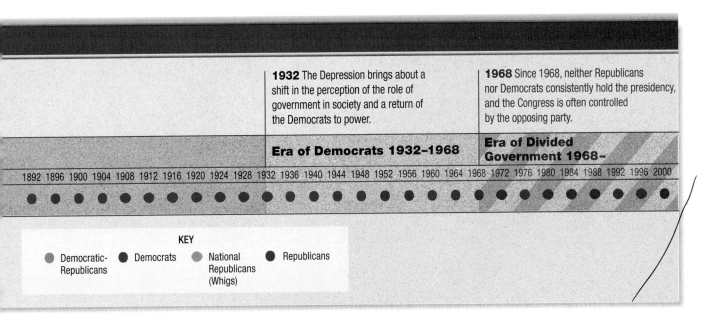

1932 The Depression brings about a shift in the perception of the role of government in society and a return of the Democrats to power.

1968 Since 1968, neither Republicans nor Democrats consistently hold the presidency, and the Congress is often controlled by the opposing party.

Era of Democrats 1932–1968

Era of Divided Government 1968–

1892 1896 1900 1904 1908 1912 1916 1920 1924 1928 1932 1936 1940 1944 1948 1952 1956 1960 1964 1968 1972 1976 1980 1984 1988 1992 1996 2000

KEY

● Democratic-Republicans ● Democrats ● National Republicans (Whigs) ● Republicans

The Democrats, crippled by the war, were able to survive mainly through their hold on the "Solid South," after the era of Reconstruction came to a close in the mid-1870s. For the balance of the century, they slowly rebuilt their electoral base. In all that time, they were able to place only one candidate in the White House: Grover Cleveland in 1884 and again in 1892. Those elections marked only short breaks in Republican supremacy. Riding the crest of popular acceptance and unprecedented prosperity, the GOP remained the dominant party well into the twentieth century.

The election of 1896 was especially critical in the development of the two-party system. It climaxed years of protest by small business owners, farmers, and the emerging labor unions against big business, financial monopolies, and the railroads. The Republican Party nominated William McKinley and supported the gold standard. The Democratic candidate was William Jennings Bryan, a supporter of free silver, who was also endorsed by the Populist Party.

With McKinley's victory in 1896, the Republicans regained the presidency. In doing so, they drew a response from a broader range of the **electorate**—the people eligible to vote. This new strength allowed the Republicans to maintain their role as the dominant party in national politics for another three decades.

The Democratic Party lost the election of 1896, but it won on another score. Bryan, its young, dynamic presidential nominee, campaigned throughout the country as the champion of the "little man." He helped to push the nation's party politics back toward the economic arena, and away from the divisions of **sectionalism** that had plagued the nation for so many years. Sectionalism emphasizes a devotion to the interests of a particular region.

The Republicans suffered their worst setback of the era in 1912, when they renominated incumbent President William Howard Taft. Former President Theodore Roosevelt, denied the nomination of his party, left the Republicans to become the candidate of his "Bull Moose" Progressive Party. Traditional Republican support was divided between Taft and Roosevelt. As a result, the Democratic nominee, Woodrow Wilson, was able to capture the presidency. Four years later, Wilson was reelected by a narrow margin.

Again, however, the Democratic successes of 1912 and 1916 proved only a brief interlude. The GOP reasserted its control of the nation's politics by winning each of the next three presidential elections: Warren Harding won in 1920, Calvin Coolidge in 1924, and Herbert Hoover in 1928.

The Return of the Democrats, 1932–1968

The Great Depression, which began in 1929, had a massive impact on nearly all aspects of American life. Its effect on the American political landscape was considerable indeed. The landmark election of 1932 brought Franklin Roosevelt to the presidency and the Democrats back to power at the

▲ This 1900 campaign poster uses powerful imagery to win Republican votes. *Critical Thinking How does the poster contrast Republican achievements since 1896 with earlier conditions when the Democrats were in power?*

national level. Also, and of fundamental importance, that election marked a basic shift in the public's attitude toward the proper role of government in the nation's social and economic life.

Franklin Roosevelt and the Democrats engineered their victory in 1932 with a new electoral base. It was built largely of southerners, small farmers, organized labor, and big-city political organizations. Roosevelt's revolutionary economic and social welfare programs, which formed the heart of the New Deal of the 1930s, further strengthened that coalition. It also brought increasing support from African Americans and other minorities to the Democrats.

President Roosevelt won reelection in 1936. He secured an unprecedented third term in 1940 and yet another term in 1944, each time by heavy majorities. Roosevelt's Vice President, Harry S Truman, completed the fourth term following FDR's death in 1945. Truman was elected to a full term of his own in 1948, when he turned back the GOP challenge led by Governor Thomas E. Dewey of New York.

The Republicans did manage to regain the White House in 1952, and they kept it in 1956. World War II hero Dwight Eisenhower led the Republicans to victory in these elections. Both times, Eisenhower defeated the Democratic nominee, Governor Adlai Stevenson of Illinois.

The Republicans' return to power was short-lived, however. Senator John F. Kennedy of

Massachusetts recaptured the White House for the Democrats in 1960. He did so with a razor-thin win over the Republican standard bearer, then Vice President Richard M. Nixon. Lyndon B. Johnson succeeded to the presidency when Kennedy was assassinated in late 1963. Johnson won a full presidential term in 1964, by overwhelming his Republican opponent, Senator Barry Goldwater of Arizona.

The Start of a New Era

Richard Nixon made a successful return to presidential politics in 1968. In that year's election, he defeated Vice President Hubert Humphrey. Humphrey was the candidate of a Democratic Party torn apart by conflicts over the war in Vietnam, civil rights, and a variety of social welfare issues. Nixon also faced a strong third-party effort by the American Independent Party nominee, Governor George Wallace of Alabama. The Republicans won with only a bare plurality over Humphrey and Wallace.

In 1972, President Nixon retained the White House when he routed the choice of the still-divided Democrats, Senator George McGovern of South Dakota. However, Nixon's role in the Watergate scandal forced him from office in 1974.

Vice President Gerald Ford then became President and filled out the balance of Nixon's second term. Beset by problems in the economy, by the continuing effects of Watergate, and by his pardon of former President Nixon, Ford lost the presidency in 1976. The former governor of Georgia, Jimmy Carter, and the resurgent Democrats gained the White House that year.

A steadily worsening economy, political fallout from the Iranian hostage crisis, and his own inability to establish himself as an effective President spelled defeat for Jimmy Carter in 1980. Led by Ronald Reagan, the former governor of California, the Republicans scored an impressive victory that year. Reagan won a second term by a landslide in 1984, overwhelming a Democratic ticket headed by former Vice President Walter Mondale.

The GOP kept the White House with a third straight win in 1988. Their candidate, George Bush, had served as Vice President throughout the Reagan years. Bush led a successful campaign against the Democrats and their nominee, Governor Michael Dukakis of Massachusetts.

The Reagan and Bush victories of the 1980s triggered wide-ranging efforts to alter many of the nation's foreign and domestic policies. These Republican successes also led many observers to conclude that most Americans now favored more conservative, rather than liberal, responses to most public-policy questions.

Republican successes did not continue, however. President Bush lost his bid for another term in 1992. Democrat Bill Clinton, then the governor of Arkansas, defeated Bush and turned back an independent challenge by Texas billionaire Ross Perot. Clinton won again in 1996, defeating the Republican candidate Bob Dole and, at the same time, thwarting a Perot third-party effort.

The GOP regained the presidency in a very close contest in 2000. Their candidate, George W. Bush, was then the governor of Texas and is the son of the former Republican President. Mr. Bush failed to win the popular vote but did capture a bare majority of the electoral votes—and so won the White House. His Democratic opponent, Vice President Al Gore, became the first presidential candidate since 1888 to win the popular vote and yet fail to win the presidency.

The years since 1968 have been marked by divided government. Through most of the period, the Republicans have held the White House while the Democrats have controlled Congress.[6] That situation was reversed in President Clinton's first term, however. In 1994, the

Interpreting Political Cartoons **What does the cartoon suggest about voter preference? Do you agree?**

Republicans captured control of both houses of Congress and maintained that hold through the elections of 2000.

In earlier periods, a newly elected President almost always swept many of his party's candidates into office with him. The victories of several recent Presidents—most recently George W. Bush's win in 2000—did not include that kind of coattail effect. The GOP lost seats in both houses of Congress in that election.

[6]The Democrats held almost uninterrupted control of Congress from 1933 to 1995. Over those years, the Republicans controlled both houses of Congress for only two two-year periods—first, after the congressional elections of 1946 and then after those of 1952. The GOP did win control of the Senate (but not the House) in 1980; the Democrats recaptured the upper chamber in 1986.

Section 3 Assessment

Key Terms and Main Ideas

1. Since political parties are not mentioned in the Constitution, why did they develop so quickly in the new nation?
2. Why would the development of **factions** within a political party hurt that party's chances for success?
3. Explain how **sectionalism** played an important role in party politics during at least one period of American history.
4. Describe one period of single-party domination.

Critical Thinking

5. **Determining Relevance (a)** Does the present era of divided government mean that most voters favor split control of the White House and Congress? **(b)** Why might they favor this? **(c)** Why might they oppose it? **(d)** What else might it indicate?

6. **Checking Consistency** The first parties, led by Alexander Hamilton and Thomas Jefferson, had opposing positions on how much power the National Government should have. How are these beliefs reflected in the two major parties today?

 Take It to the Net

7. Read more about either the Republican or the Democratic Party and one of the historical parties, the Whigs or the Federalists. Make a chart comparing the two parties on at least five topics, such as why they were formed, who tended to support them, and their stands on important issues. Use the links provided in the Social Studies area at the following Web site for help in completing this activity. **www.phschool.com**

The Minor Parties

Section Preview

OBJECTIVES

1. **Identify** the types of minor parties that have been active in American politics.
2. **Understand** why minor parties are important despite the fact that none has ever won the presidency.

WHY IT MATTERS

Many minor parties have been active in American politics. They provide alternatives to the positions of the major parties, and sometimes have affected particular elections and shaped public policies.

POLITICAL DICTIONARY

★ **ideological parties**
★ **single-issue parties**
★ **economic protest parties**
★ **splinter parties**

Libertarian, Reform, Socialist, Prohibition, Natural Law, Communist, American Independent, Green, Socialist Labor, Constitution—these are only some of the many parties that fielded presidential candidates for 2000. You know that none of these parties or their candidates had any real chance of winning. But this is not to say that minor parties are unimportant. The bright light created by the two major parties too often blinds us to the vital role several minor parties have played in American politics.

Minor Parties in the United States

Their number and variety make minor parties difficult to describe and classify. Some have limited their efforts to a particular locale, others to

a single State, and some to one region of the country. Still others have tried to woo the entire nation. Most have been short-lived, but a few have existed for decades. And, while most have lived mothlike around the flame of a single idea, some have had a broader, more practical base.

Still, four distinct types of minor parties can be identified:

1. The **ideological parties** are those based on a particular set of beliefs—a comprehensive view of social, economic, and political matters. Most of these minor parties have been built on some shade of Marxist thought; examples include the Socialist, Socialist Labor, Socialist Worker, and Communist parties.

Some ideological parties have had a quite different approach, however. One example is the Libertarian Party of today, which emphasizes individualism and calls for doing away with most of government's present functions and programs.

The ideological parties have seldom been able to win many votes. As a rule, however, they have been long-lived.

2. The **single-issue parties** concentrate on only one public-policy matter. Their names have usually indicated their primary concern. For example, the Free Soil Party opposed the spread of slavery in the 1840s and 1850s; the American Party, also called the "Know Nothings," opposed Irish-Catholic immigration in the 1850s; and the Right to Life Party opposes abortion today.

Most of the single-issue parties have faded into history. They died away as events have

Ralph Nader 2000

Green Party

NATURAL LAW PARTY

Leadership for the New Millennium

▲ These are just two of the active minor parties in the United States.

Four Types of Minor Parties

Ideological Party

Our Party Believes...

Vote

VOTE

Single Issue Party

VOTE GREEN

VOTE GREEN

VOTE GREEN

Economic Protest Party

BANK

Better Times

Vote

NO Foreign Imports!

Splinter Party

MAJOR PARTY

Vote

Vote

VOTE

Interpreting Charts (a) According to the chart, which type of minor party is the most closely related to a major party? (b) Which type is likely to be the most cohesive and united?

passed them by, as their themes have failed to attract voters, or as one or both of the major parties have taken their key issues as their own.

3. The **economic protest parties** have been rooted in periods of economic discontent. Unlike the socialist parties, these groups have not had any clear-cut ideological base. Rather, they have proclaimed their disgust with the major parties and demanded better times, and have focused their anger on such real or imagined enemies as the monetary system, "Wall Street bankers," the railroads, or foreign imports.

Most often, they have been sectional parties, drawing their strength from the agricultural South and West. The Greenback Party, for example, tried to take advantage of agrarian discontent from 1876 through 1884. It appealed to struggling farmers by calling for the free coinage of silver, federal regulation of the railroads, an income tax, and labor legislation. A descendant of the Greenbacks, the Populist Party of the 1890s also demanded public ownership of railroads, telephone and telegraph

companies, lower tariffs, and the adoption of the initiative and referendum.

Each of these economic protest parties has disappeared as the nation has climbed out of the difficult economic period in which that party arose.

4. **Splinter parties** are those that have split away from one of the major parties. Most of the more important minor parties in our politics have been splinter parties. Among the leading groups that have split away from the Republicans are Theodore Roosevelt's "Bull Moose" Progressive Party of 1912, and Robert La Follette's Progressive Party of 1924. From the Democrats have come Henry Wallace's Progressive Party and the States' Rights (Dixiecrat) Party, both of 1948, and George Wallace's American Independent Party of 1968.

Most splinter parties have formed around a strong personality—most often someone who has failed to win his major party's presidential nomination. These parties have faded or collapsed when that leader has stepped aside. Thus, the Bull Moose Progressive Party passed away when Theodore Roosevelt returned to the Republican fold after the election of 1912. Similarly, the American Independent Party lost nearly all of its brief strength when Governor George Wallace rejoined the Democrats after his strong showing in the 1968 election.

The Green Party USA, founded in 1984, points up the difficulties of classifying minor parties in American politics. The Greens began as a classic single-issue party but, as the party has evolved, it simply will not fit into any of the categories set out here. The Green Party came to prominence in 2000, when it picked Ralph Nader as its presidential nominee. Nader's campaign was built around a smorgasbord of issues—environmental protection, of course, but also universal health care, gay and lesbian rights, restraints on corporate power, campaign finance reform, opposition to global free trade, and much more.

Why Minor Parties Are Important

Even though most Americans do not support them, minor parties have still had an impact on American politics and on the major parties.

For example, it was a minor party, the Anti-Masons, that first used a national convention to nominate a presidential candidate in 1831. The Whigs and then the Democrats followed suit in 1832. Ever since, national conventions have been used by both the Democrats and the Republicans to pick their presidential tickets.

Minor parties can have an impact in another way. A strong third-party candidacy can play a decisive role—often a "spoiler role"—in an election. Even if a minor party does not win any electoral votes, it can pull votes from one of the major parties, as the Green Party did in 2000. This spoiler effect can be felt in national, State, or local contests, especially where the two major parties compete on roughly equal terms.

The 1912 election dramatically illustrated this point. A split in the Republican Party and Roosevelt's resulting third-party candidacy produced the results shown below. Almost certainly, had Roosevelt not quit the Republican Party, Taft would have enjoyed a better showing, and Wilson would not have become President.

Historically, however, the minor parties have been most important in their roles of critic and innovator. Unlike the major parties, the minor

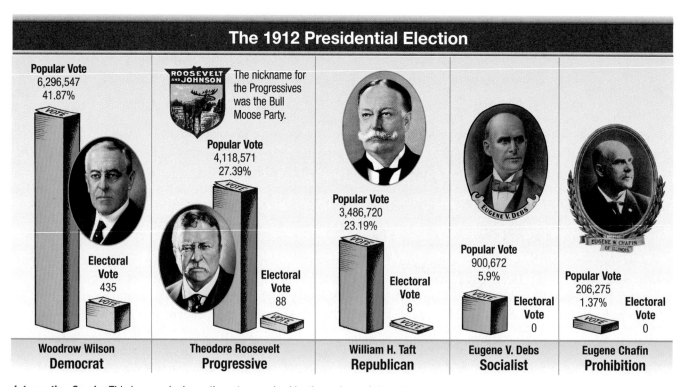

The 1912 Presidential Election

Woodrow Wilson — Democrat
Popular Vote 6,296,547 41.87%
Electoral Vote 435

Theodore Roosevelt — Progressive
ROOSEVELT AND JOHNSON
The nickname for the Progressives was the Bull Moose Party.
Popular Vote 4,118,571 27.39%
Electoral Vote 88

William H. Taft — Republican
Popular Vote 3,486,720 23.19%
Electoral Vote 8

Eugene V. Debs — Socialist
Popular Vote 900,672 5.9%
Electoral Vote 0

Eugene Chafin — Prohibition
EUGENE W. CHAFIN OF ILLINOIS
Popular Vote 206,275 1.37%
Electoral Vote 0

Interpreting Graphs This bar graph shows the votes received by the major and the minor parties in 1912. *(a) Which party "came in second"? (b) Even though the Bull Moose Progressives were a minor party, how did they help determine which major party won the election?*

parties have been ready, willing, and able to take quite clear-cut stands on controversial issues. Minor-party stands have often drawn attention to some issue that the major parties have preferred to ignore or straddle.

Over the years, many of the more important issues of American politics were first brought to the public's attention by a minor party. Examples include the progressive income tax, woman suffrage, railroad and banking regulation, and old-age pensions.

Oddly enough, this very important innovator role of the minor parties has also been a major source of their frustration. When their proposals have gained any real degree of popular support, one and sometimes both of the major parties have taken over these ideas and then presented the policies as their own. The late Norman Thomas, who was the Socialist Party's candidate for President six times, complained that "the major parties are stealing from my platform."

Minor parties continue to be active today. The presidential nominees of more than 20 minor parties made it to the ballots of at least one State in 2000. At least that many will likely do so in the year 2004. In 2000 the most visible minor-party presidential campaigns were those of the Reform, Libertarian, Natural Law, Constitution, Socialist, Prohibition, and Green parties. More than a thousand candidates from a wide variety of minor parties also sought seats in Congress or ran for various State and local offices.

Significant Minor Parties in Presidential Elections, 1880–2000*

Year	Party	Candidate	% Popular Vote	Electoral Vote
1880	Greenback	James B. Weaver	3.36	—
1888	Prohibition	Clinton B. Fisk	2.19	—
1892	Populist	James B. Weaver	8.54	22
	Prohibition	John Bidwell	2.19	—
1904	Socialist	Eugene V. Debs	2.98	—
1908	Socialist	Eugene V. Debs	2.82	—
1912	Progressive (Bull Moose)	Theodore Roosevelt	27.39	88
	Socialist	Eugene V. Debs	5.99	—
1916	Socialist	Allan L. Benson	3.17	—
1920	Socialist	Eugene V. Debs	3.45	—
1924	Progressive	Robert M. La Follette	16.61	13
1932	Socialist	Norman M. Thomas	2.22	—
1948	States' Rights (Dixiecrat)	Strom Thurmond	2.41	39
	Progressive	Henry A. Wallace	2.37	—
1968	American Independent	George C. Wallace	13.53	46
1996	Reform	Ross Perot	8.5	—
2000	Green	Ralph Nader	3.0	—

*Includes all minor parties that polled at least 2% of the popular vote
Source: *Historical Statistics of the United States, Colonial Times to 1970;* the Gallup Organization

Interpreting Tables (a) Which minor party received the most electoral votes in an election? (b) Which other parties received enough support to influence an election? Explain.

Section 4 Assessment

Key Terms and Main Ideas

1. Why do **single-issue parties** tend to be short-lived?
2. (a) What are **economic protest parties?** (b) Why are they formed in times of economic distress?
3. Most of the more important minor parties in our history have been of which type? Explain the effect of one such party.
4. Why is the innovator role a source of frustration to minor parties?

Critical Thinking

5. **Expressing Problems Clearly** Suppose you are considering voting for a presidential candidate from a minor party. Explain the benefits and drawbacks of casting your vote that way.

6. **Predicting Consequences** Minor parties usually are willing to take definite stands on controversial issues. How might voters react to this tendency?

Take It to the Net

7. Locate the Web site for one of the following minor parties: Reform, Libertarian, Natural Law, Constitution, Socialist, Prohibition, Green. Make an outline of the major issues on which the party ran in the most recent presidential election or in a previous election. Use the links provided in the Social Studies area at the following Web site for help in completing this activity. **www.phschool.com**

Green Party Goals

Ralph Nader accepted the presidential nomination of the Green Party on June 25, 2000. In his speech that day he laid out the goals of his party and encouraged all citizens who desire change to support his campaign.

Ralph Nader

On behalf of all Americans who seek a new direction, who yearn for a new birth of freedom to build the just society, who see justice as the great work of human beings on Earth, who understand that community and human fulfillment are mutually reinforcing, who respect the urgent necessity to wage peace, to protect the environment, to end poverty and to preserve values of the spirit for future generations, who wish to build a deep democracy by working hard for a regenerative progressive politics, as if people mattered—to all these citizens and the Green vanguard, I welcome and am honored to accept the Green Party nomination for President of the United States.

The Green Party stands for a nation and a world that consciously advances the practice of deep democracy. A deep democracy facilitates people's best efforts to achieve social justice, a sustainable and bountiful environment and an end to systemic bigotry and discrimination against law-abiding people merely because they are different. Green goals place community and self-reliance over dependency on ever larger absentee corporations and their media, their technology, their capital, and their politicians. Green goals aim at preserving the commonwealth of assets that the people of the United States already own so that the people, not big business, control what they own, and using these vast resources of the public lands, the public airwaves, and trillions of worker pension dollars to achieve healthier environments, healthier communities, and healthier people. . . .

To the youth of America, I say, beware of being trivialized by the commercial culture that tempts you daily. I hear you saying often that you're not turned on to politics. The lessons of history are clear and portentous. If you do not turn on to politics, politics will turn on you. The fact that we have so many inequalities demonstrates this point. Democracy responds to hands-on participation. And to energized imagination. That's its essence. We need the young people of America to move into leadership positions to shape their future as part of this campaign for a just society. Let's prepare to take the politicians and the lobbyists on a tour of the People's America. . . .

With a new progressive movement, we the people have the ability to vastly improve our lives and to help shape the world's course to one of justice and peace for years to come.

Analyzing Primary Sources

1. What are the goals of the Green Party?
2. Do you think that a third party like the Green Party could win the presidency? Why or why not?
3. Would you label this speech propaganda? Why or why not?

⑤ Party Organization

Section Preview

OBJECTIVES

1. **Understand** why the major parties have a decentralized structure.
2. **Describe** the national party machinery and how parties are organized at the State and local levels.
3. **Identify** the three components of the parties.
4. **Examine** the future of the major parties.

WHY IT MATTERS

The major parties of the United States have a decentralized structure, and the different parts and elements work together primarily during national elections. The parties themselves have been in decline, or losing influence, since the 1960s.

POLITICAL DICTIONARY

★ **ward**
★ **precinct**
★ **split-ticket voting**

How strong, how active, and how well organized are the Republican and Democratic parties in your community? Contact the county chairperson or another official in one or both of the major parties. They are usually not very difficult to find. For starters, try the telephone directory.

The Decentralized Nature of the Parties

The two major parties are often described as though they were highly organized, close-knit, well-disciplined groups. However, neither party is anything of the kind. Rather, both are highly decentralized, fragmented, disjointed, and often beset by factions and internal squabbling.

Neither party has a chain of command running from the national through the State to the local level. Each of the State party organizations is only loosely tied to the party's national structure. By the same token, local party organizations are often quite independent of their parent State organizations. These various party units usually cooperate with one another, of course—but that is not always the case.

The Role of the Presidency

The President's party is usually more solidly united and more cohesively organized than the opposing party. The President is automatically the party leader. He asserts that leadership with such tools as his access to the media, his popularity, and his power to make appointments to federal office and to dispense other favors.

The other party has no one in an even faintly comparable position. Indeed, in the American party system, there is seldom any one person in the opposition party who can truly be called its leader. Rather, a number of personalities, frequently in competition with one another, form a loosely identifiable leadership group in the party out of power.[7]

---

[7] The party does have a temporary leader for a brief time every fourth year: its presidential candidate, from nomination to election day. A defeated presidential candidate is often called the party's "titular leader"—a leader in title, by custom, but not in fact. What's more, if he lost by a wide margin, the defeated candidate's leadership may be largely discredited.

▲ The parties have many local headquarters, such as this one in Bennington, Vermont.

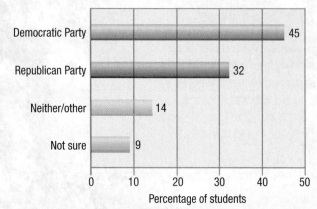

CLOSE UP Student Poll

In a recent poll, students were asked their opinion on the following question: *From what you know about the political parties, do you think that the Democratic Party or the Republican Party better represents your views?*

Democratic Party — 45
Republican Party — 32
Neither/other — 14
Not sure — 9

Percentage of students

SOURCE: High school students' attitudes toward government and politics, Close Up Foundation, May 1999

1. **Analyzing Data** *Approximately what percentage of students polled identified with the major parties?*
2. **Conducting Polls** In your own school, conduct a poll asking students which party they feel most closely represents their views. *How do your results compare to the results shown in this graph?*

The Impact of Federalism

Federalism is one major reason for the decentralized nature of the two major political parties. Remember, the basic goal of the major parties is to gain control of government; they try to do this by winning elective offices.

Today there are more than half a million elective offices in the United States. In the American federal system, those offices are widely distributed at the national, the State, and the local levels. In short, because the governmental system is decentralized—giving many powers to States and localities—so, too, are the major parties that serve it.

The Role of the Nominating Process

The nominating process is also a major cause of party decentralization. Recall, from page 117, that the nominating process has a central role in the life of political parties. You will consider the selection of candidates at some length in Chapter 7, but, for now, look at two related aspects of that process.

First, candidate selection is an intraparty process. That is, nominations are made within the party. Second, the nominating process can be, and often is, a divisive one. Where there is a fight over a nomination, that contest pits members of the same party against one another: Republicans fight Republicans; Democrats battle Democrats. In short, the prime function of the major parties—the making of nominations—is also a prime cause of their highly fragmented character.

National Party Machinery

The structure of both major parties at the national level has four basic elements. These elements are the national convention, the national committee, the national chairperson, and the congressional campaign committees.

The National Convention

The national convention is often described as the party's national voice. The convention meets in the summer of every presidential election year to nominate the party's presidential and vice-presidential candidates. It also performs some other functions, including the adoption of the party's rules and the writing of its platform.

Beyond that, the convention has little authority. It has no control over the selection of the party's candidates for other offices nor over the policy stands those nominees take. You will take a longer look at both parties' national nominating conventions in Chapter 13.

The National Committee

Between conventions, the party's affairs are handled, at least in theory, by the national committee and by the national chairperson. For years, each party's national committee was composed of a committeeman and a committeewoman from each State and several of the territories. They were chosen by the State's party organization. However, in recent years, both parties have expanded the committee's membership.

Today, the Republican National Committee (RNC) also seats several of the party's chairpersons in each State, the District of Columbia, Guam, American Samoa, Puerto Rico, and the Virgin Islands. Representatives of such GOP-related groups as the National Federation of Republican Women also serve on the RNC.

▲ **Step Right Up** Volunteers of all ages help their parties in national, State, and local races.

▲ **Madam Chairperson** Mary Louise Smith was national chairperson of the Republican Party in the 1970s.

The Democratic National Committee (DNC) is an even larger body. In addition to the committeeman and -woman from each State, it now includes the party's chairperson and vice-chairperson from every State and the several territories. It also includes additional members from the party organizations of the larger States, and up to 75 at-large members chosen by the DNC itself. Several members of Congress, as well as governors, mayors, and Young Democrats, also have seats.

On paper, the national committee appears to be a powerful organization loaded with many of the party's leading figures. In fact, it does not have a great deal of clout. Most of its work centers on staging the party's national convention every four years.

The National Chairperson

In each party, the national chairperson is the leader of the national committee. In form, he or she is chosen to a four-year term by the national committee, at a meeting held right after the national convention. In fact, the choice is made by the just-nominated presidential candidate and is then ratified by the national committee.

Only two women have ever held that top party post. Jean Westwood of Utah chaired the DNC from her party's 1972 convention until early 1973; and Mary Louise Smith of Iowa headed the RNC from 1974 until early 1977. Each lost her post soon after her party lost a presidential election. Ron Brown, the Democrats' National Chairman from 1989 to 1993, is the only African American ever to have held the office of national chairperson in either major party.

The national chairperson directs the work of the party's headquarters and its small staff in Washington. In presidential election years, the committee's attention is focused on the national convention and then the campaign. In between presidential elections, the chairperson and the committee work to strengthen the party and its fortunes. They do so by promoting party unity, raising money, recruiting new voters, and otherwise preparing for the next presidential season.

The Congressional Campaign Committees

Each party also has a campaign committee in each house of Congress.[8] These committees work to reelect incumbents and to make sure that seats given up by retiring party members remain in the party. The committees also take a hand in selected campaigns to unseat incumbents in the other party, at least in those House or Senate races where the chances for success seem to justify such efforts.

In both parties and in both houses, the members of these campaign committees are chosen by their colleagues. They serve for two years—that is, for a term of Congress.

State and Local Party Machinery

National party organization is largely the product of custom and of the rules adopted by the national conventions. At the State and

---

[8]They are the National Republican Campaign Committee and the Democratic Congressional Campaign Committee in the House; in the Senate, they are the National Republican Senatorial Campaign Committee and the Democratic Senatorial Campaign Committee.

States are divided into **congressional districts.**

In cities, districts are divided into **wards.**

Wards are divided into **precincts.**

In large cities, the smallest unit of party organization may be a single apartment building.

Interpreting Diagrams (a) According to the diagram, which unit of local party organization is the largest in a State? (b) Which is the smallest?

local levels, however, party structure is largely set by State law.

The State Organization

At the State level, party machinery is built around a State central committee, headed by a State chairperson.

The chairperson may be an important political figure in his or her own right. More often than not, however, the chairperson fronts for the governor, a U.S. senator, or some other powerful leader or group in the politics of the State.

Together, the chairperson and the central committee work to further the party's interests in the State. Most of the time, they attempt to do this by building an effective organization and party unity, finding candidates and campaign funds, and so on. Remember, however, both major parties are highly decentralized, fragmented, and sometimes torn by struggles for power. This can complicate the chairperson's and the committee's job.

Local Organization

Local party structures vary so widely that they nearly defy even a brief description. Generally, they follow the electoral map of the State, with a party unit for each district in which elective

offices are to be filled: congressional and legislative districts, counties, cities and towns, wards, and precincts. A **ward** is a unit into which cities are often divided for the election of city council members. A **precinct** is the smallest unit of election administration; the voters in each precinct report to one polling place.

In most larger cities, a party's organization is further broken down by residential blocks and sometimes even by apartment buildings. In some places, local party organizations are active year-round, but most often they are inactive except for those few hectic months before an election.

The Three Components of the Party

There is another way to look at the structure of the two major parties: the roles of their members. From this perspective, the parties are made up of three basic and closely interrelated components:

1. *The party organization.* These are the leaders, the activists, and the hangers-on who control and run the party machinery.

2. *The party in the electorate.* This consists of the party's loyalists who vote the straight party ticket or usually vote for its candidates.

3. *The party in government.* These are the party's officeholders at all levels of government.

The Future of the Major Parties

Political parties have never been very popular in this country. Rather, over time, most Americans have had very mixed feelings about them. Most of us have accepted parties as necessary institutions, but, at the same time, people feel that they should be closely watched and controlled. To many, political parties have seemed little better than necessary evils.

Political parties have been in a period of decline since at least the late 1960s. Their decline has led some analysts to conclude that the parties are not only in serious trouble, but that the party system itself may be on the point of collapse.

The present, weakened state of the parties can be traced to several factors. They include:

1. A sharp drop in the number of voters willing to identify themselves as Republicans or Democrats, and a growing number who regard themselves as independents.

▲ *Direct Access* Voters can see and hear the candidates for themselves by watching televised events such as this Republican debate during the 2000 presidential primary campaign. From left to right: Gary Bauer, Texas Governor George W. Bush, Alan Keyes, Arizona Senator John McCain, and Steve Forbes.

2. A big increase in **split-ticket voting**—voting for candidates of different parties for different offices at the same election.

3. Various structural changes and reforms that have made the parties more "open," but have also led to greater internal conflict and disorganization. These changes range from the introduction of the direct primary in the early 1900s to recent and far-reaching changes in campaign finance laws.

4. Changes in the technology of campaigning, especially the heavy use of television and of

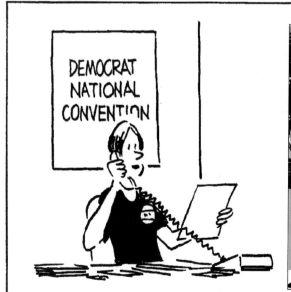

"YES, MR. VICE PRESIDENT, YOU GO ON RIGHT AFTER 'BUDDY'."

Interpreting Political Cartoons Both major parties use national conventions to adopt the party's platform, nominate the presidential ticket, and build party unity. *What do these cartoons suggest about the way in which the 2000 conventions were organized? (Buddy was President Clinton's dog.)*

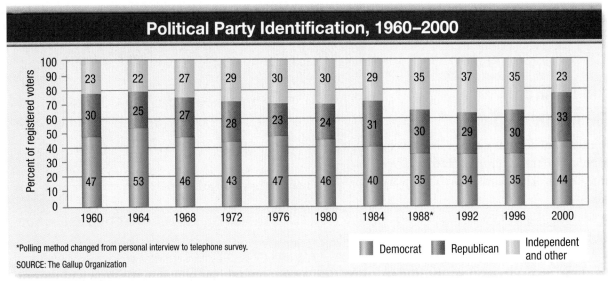

Political Party Identification, 1960–2000

Percent of registered voters

	1960	1964	1968	1972	1976	1980	1984	1988*	1992	1996	2000
Independent and other	23	22	27	29	30	30	29	35	37	35	23
Republican	30	25	27	28	23	24	31	30	29	30	33
Democrat	47	53	46	43	47	46	40	35	34	35	44

*Polling method changed from personal interview to telephone survey.

SOURCE: The Gallup Organization

■ Democrat ■ Republican ■ Independent and other

Interpreting Graphs This graph shows the percentage of voters who identify with the two major parties and the percentage of independents. **(a) Which group shows the biggest gain in support between 1960 and 2000? (b) Which group lost the most support during that time?**

the Internet, professional campaign managers, and direct-mail advertising. These changes have made candidates much less dependent on party organizations since, in many cases, they can now "speak" directly to the electorate.

5. The growth of single-issue organizations. These interest groups take sides for or against candidates based on the group's views in some specific area of public policy. One way such groups are making their presence felt is through political action committees (PACs). PACs raise and distribute money to candidates who will further their goals. In

that way, PACs have lessened candidates' reliance on party organizations for financial support.

You will look at the matters affecting the condition of the parties in later chapters. As you do so, remember that political parties are indispensable to democratic government. The major American parties have existed longer than has any other party anywhere in the world. And, as you have seen, the major parties perform a number of necessary functions. In short, reports of their passing may be premature, and may even be farfetched.

Section 5 Assessment

Key Terms and Main Ideas

1. What are the major causes of the decentralized nature of political parties?
2. What are the four main elements of major party organization at the national level?
3. Describe how **wards** and **precincts** are part of the local party organization.
4. **(a)** What is **split-ticket voting? (b)** How has its increase contributed to the weakened state of the two major parties?

Critical Thinking

5. **Drawing Conclusions** Based on what you know about parties, their goals, and the American people, why do you think local party organizations vary so widely?
6. **Formulating Questions** A growing number of voters consider themselves to be independents. Compose three

questions that a pollster might ask in an attempt to learn why this is the case.
7. **Predicting Consequences** Do you think the major parties will survive and emerge from their current period of decline? Why or why not?

 Take It to the Net

8. Visit your State's Republican or Democratic Party Web site. What are its major elements and their contents? How easy is the site to navigate? How appealing is its design? Based on your evaluation of the existing site, design a State party site specifically for young voters. Use the links provided in the Social Studies area at the following Web site for help in completing this activity. **www.phschool.com**

Can Candidates Be Forced to Sign Oaths?

Candidates must meet certain requirements in order to have their name placed on the ballot. For example, they must file a written application by a certain date. Can they be forced to meet requirements regarding their personal beliefs as well?

Communist Party of Indiana v. Whitcomb (1974)

In 1972, the Communist Party of Indiana applied to place on the Indiana ballot candidates for President and Vice President of the United States. The Indiana State Election Board rejected that application because the Party did not submit a written statement, made under oath, that the Party did not "advocate the overthrow of local, State or National Government by violence." Indiana law required this statement from any political party that wanted to have the names of its candidates printed on the ballot.

The Party filed suit against Indiana's Governor Edgar Whitcomb, arguing that the oath violated its 1st Amendment right of free speech. The court ruled that the oath did not violate the Constitution. The court ordered the State Election Board to list the Communist Party candidates if the Party submitted the required statement. The Party then submitted the statement, but added a sentence explaining that the word *advocate*, as the Party understood it, did not include the teaching of "principles divorced from action." The Election Board rejected this statement, and the parties returned to court. When the district court refused to change its order, the Communist Party of Indiana appealed to the Supreme Court.

Arguments for the Communist Party

1. The constitutional right of free speech applies to a candidate's political beliefs, and a candidate or political party may not be prevented from running for elected office because of those beliefs.
2. Arguing that force is necessary in certain situations is not the same as actually preparing for violent action, and is protected speech under the 1st Amendment.
3. Even if the loyalty oath itself is constitutional, the Election Board discriminated against the Communist Party by requiring an oath from the Communists but not from the Democratic and Republican parties.

Arguments for Whitcomb

1. Since States may lawfully ban acts of violence aimed at overthrowing the government, they may exclude from the ballot any candidates who do not renounce the use of violence.
2. States have broad power to administer the electoral process, set qualifications for voters, and supervise the conduct of elections. This broad power gives States the authority to regulate speech in the context of deciding which candidates will be on election ballots.
3. A group that seeks the violent overthrow of our democratic form of government should not be allowed to use the democratic process to gain public support for its destructive plans.

Decide for Yourself

1. Review the constitutional grounds on which each side based its arguments and the specific arguments each side presented.
2. Debate the opposing viewpoints presented in this case. Which viewpoint do you favor?
3. Predict the impact of the Court's decision on States' ability to establish qualifications for public offices. (To read a summary of the Court's decision, turn to the Supreme Court Glossary on page 799.)

Political Dictionary

political party (p. 116)

major parties (p. 116)

partisanship (p. 117)

party in power (p. 118)

minor party (p. 119)

two-party system (p. 119)

single-member district (p. 120)

plurality (p. 120)

bipartisan (p. 120)

pluralistic society (p. 121)

consensus (p. 121)

multiparty (p. 122)

coalition (p. 122)

one-party system (p. 123)

incumbent (p. 127)

faction (p. 127)

electorate (p. 129)

sectionalism (p. 129)

ideological parties (p. 132)

single-issue parties (p. 132)

economic protest parties (p. 133)

splinter parties (p. 133)

ward (p. 140)

precinct (p. 140)

split-ticket voting (p. 141)

Practicing the Vocabulary

Using Words in Context *For each of the terms below, write a sentence that shows how it relates to this chapter.*

1. multiparty
2. pluralistic society
3. party in power
4. minor party
5. split-ticket voting
6. one-party system
7. consensus
8. splinter parties
9. single-member district
10. two-party system

True/False *Determine whether each of the following statements is true or false. If it is true, write "true." If it is false, rewrite the sentence to make it true.*

11. A plurality is more than half the votes cast.
12. A ward is a unit into which cities are often divided for the election of city council members.
13. An ideological party arises over a particular issue or crisis and soon fades away.
14. Partisanship means membership in one of the major parties.

Reviewing Main Ideas

Section 1

15. What is the major function of a political party?
16. Which term better describes political parties in American politics: *divisive* or *unifying?* Why?
17. Cite two examples that show why American government may be described as government by party.

Section 2

18. In what two ways does the American electoral system tend to promote a two-party system?
19. How can the diversity of views represented in a multiparty system be seen as both a strength and a weakness?
20. How is the ideological consensus of the American electorate reflected in the membership of the major parties?

Section 3

21. **(a)** Which political party was the first to appear in the new United States? **(b)** Who was its leader and what type of government did it favor?

22. **(a)** How did the Republican Party begin? **(b)** How was its development unique in American politics?
23. What effect did the Great Depression have on American political parties?
24. What unusual feature characterizes the present era of American two-party history?

Section 4

25. Briefly describe the four types of minor parties.
26. Historically, what have been the most important roles of minor parties? Briefly explain one of these roles.

Section 5

27. Why is the party in power more cohesive than the opposition party?
28. Describe the role of the national chairperson.
29. List and explain four factors that have contributed to the present weakened state of the major parties.

Critical Thinking

30. *Applying the Chapter Skill* Choose an issue in the news. It might be a national issue such as gun control or a local issue such as allowing development of park land or mandatory school uniforms. State your position, and then tell where you got information about the issue, and who or what influenced your opinion. If you have not taken a stand on the issue, explain why you have no opinion.

31. *Determining Relevance* If there had not been a group opposed to the adoption of the Constitution in the 1780s, do you think a strong two-party system would have developed in the United States? Why or why not?

32. *Distinguishing Fact from Opinion* Explain why you agree or disagree with this statement: "A vote for a minor party candidate is a vote wasted."

33. *Recognizing Cause and Effect* How has television affected the state of the two-party system?

Analyzing Political Cartoons

Using your knowledge of American government and this cartoon, answer the questions below.

34. What does the cartoonist imply about the relationship between the two major parties? Explain how he conveys this idea.
35. Does the cartoonist regard the minor parties as a serious threat to the status quo? How do the major parties react to this threat?

 You Can Make a Difference

Even if you are not yet eligible to vote, you can still find a place in party politics. Local party organizations welcome volunteer help during a campaign. You may find yourself answering phones, tacking up posters, or stuffing envelopes—all part of grassroots politics. To begin, look up the local headquarters of the two major parties and any minor parties that are currently active in your area. Choose a candidate whose positions on issues are similar to your own. Then offer your help.

Participation Activities

36. *Current Events Watch* Look in newspapers or news magazines for a local or national issue on which there is public disagreement. See if the two major parties have taken stands on the issue. If not, look for the positions taken by elected officials and other representatives of the major parties. Using the information you have found, prepare a report telling whether each party is united or divided in its response to the issue and whether the two major parties oppose each other on this issue. Support your conclusions with examples.

37. *Time Line Activity* Using information from the chapter, create a time line showing the major political events of the current era of divided government. Include at least ten entries in your time line. You might begin with Richard Nixon's election to the presidency in 1968. So far, which party has held the White House more frequently during this era?

38. *It's Your Turn* Election law in this country is often written to discourage minor party candidates. Draw a political cartoon in which you comment on this situation. Take either the pro or the con position in your cartoon. **(Drawing a Cartoon)**

 Take It to the Net

Chapter 5 Self-Test As a final review activity, take the Chapter 5 Self-Test in the Social Studies area at the Web site listed below, and receive immediate feedback on your answers.

www.phschool.com

CHAPTER 6

Voters and Voter Behavior

> *"It is not enough that people have the right to vote. . . . People must have the reason to vote as well."*
>
> —Jesse Jackson (1988)

People who have struggled to win the right to vote know how important it is. Although, since 1789, suffrage has expanded to include many more people—notably African Americans and women—many Americans do not exercise this important right. A variety of factors influence whether and how people vote.

◆ *Stump Speaking*, a hand-colored engraving by Louis-Adolphe Gautier, 1856, shows a candidate addressing voters.

You Can Make a Difference

IN MOST STATES an important first step in exercising your right to vote is registration. In Roswell, Georgia, high school senior Tyler Mann discovered that less than half of 18- to 20-year-olds had registered for the 1996 presidential election. "I knew that people my age were concerned about public issues and the future of this country. . . . I thought about what I could do to increase participation in the voting process." Tyler started a project to encourage students to register as soon as they turned 18. With school approval, he made up a list of students' 18th birthdays. He sent them personal reminder letters and organized regular voter registration drives.

Keep It Current

Items marked with this logo are periodically updated on the Internet. Keep up-to-date with what's in the news. To get current information on voters and voting trends, go to **www.phschool.com**

SECTION 1

The Right to Vote (pp. 148–150)

★ The history of the United States has been marked by five stages in a steady expansion of suffrage, or the right to vote.
★ The Constitution places five restrictions on the States' power to set voting qualifications.

SECTION 2

Voter Qualifications (pp.152–157)

★ All of the States have citizenship, residence, and age requirements for voting.
★ Other voting qualifications have been required by different States over time. Literacy tests and tax payment have been eliminated, but registration is still required by all but one State.

SECTION 3

Suffrage and Civil Rights (pp. 159–163)

★ The 15th Amendment, ratified in 1870, declared that the right to vote cannot be denied to a citizen because of race.
★ Southern States used a variety of devices to circumvent the 15th Amendment and deny African Americans the vote. These tactics included literacy tests, white primaries, and gerrymandering.
★ Congress finally took action to protect minority voting rights in the Civil Rights Acts of 1957, 1960, and 1964.
★ The Voting Rights Act of 1965 and its later amendments finally ensured African American suffrage.

SECTION 4

Voter Behavior (pp. 164–172)

★ Millions of Americans who are qualified to vote do not vote.
★ Those who choose not to vote often lack a feeling of political efficacy. Age, education, income, and geography also affect whether a person is likely to vote or not.
★ Sociological factors—such as occupation, gender, and ethnic background—influence a person's voting choices.
★ Psychological factors—including party identification and perception of the candidates and issues—also contribute to voter behavior.

1 *The Right to Vote*

Section Preview

OBJECTIVES

1. **Summarize** the history of voting rights in the United States.
2. **Identify and explain** constitutional restrictions on the States' power to set voting qualifications.

WHY IT MATTERS

Successful democratic government depends on the participation of its citizens through voting. The history of the United States has been marked by a steady expansion of the electorate through the elimination of restrictions on voting qualifications.

POLITICAL DICTIONARY

★ **suffrage**
★ **franchise**
★ **electorate**

Soon, you will be eligible to vote—but will you exercise that right? The record suggests that while *you* may do so, many of your friends will not, at least not for some time. The record also suggests that some of your friends will never vote. Yet, clearly, the success of democratic government depends on popular participation, and, in particular, on the regular and informed exercise of the right to vote.

The History of Voting Rights

The Framers of the Constitution purposely left the power to set suffrage qualifications to each State. **Suffrage** means the right to vote. **Franchise** is another term with the same meaning.[1]

▲ These historical flags (left to right: pre-1777, c. 1820, c. 1865) illustrate the expansion of the nation and growth of the electorate.

Expansion of the Electorate

When the Constitution went into effect in 1789, the right to vote in the United States was restricted to white male property owners. In fact, probably not one in fifteen adult white males could vote in elections in the different States. Benjamin Franklin often lampooned this situation. He told of a man whose only property was a jackass and noted that the man would lose the right to vote if his jackass died. "Now," asked Franklin, "in whom is the right of suffrage? In the man or the jackass?"

Today, the size of the American **electorate**—the potential voting population—is truly impressive. More than 205 million people, nearly all citizens who are at least 18 years of age, can qualify to vote. That huge number is a direct result of the legal definition of suffrage. In other words, it is the result of those laws that determine who can and cannot vote. It is also the result of some 200 years of continuing, often bitter, and sometimes violent struggle.

The history of American suffrage since 1789 has been marked by two long-term trends. First, the nation has experienced the gradual elimination of several restrictions on the right to vote. These restrictions were based on such factors as

---

[1]Originally, the Constitution had only two suffrage provisions. Article I, Section 2, Clause 1 requires each State to allow anyone qualified to vote for members of "the most numerous Branch" of its own legislature to vote as well for members of the national House of Representatives. Article II, Section 1, Clause 2 provides that presidential electors be chosen in each State "in such Manner as the Legislature thereof may direct."

religious belief, property ownership, tax payment, race, and sex. Second, a significant share of what was originally the States' power over the right to vote has gradually been assumed by the Federal Government.

Extending Suffrage: The Five Stages

The growth of the American electorate to its present size and shape has come in five fairly distinct stages. The two trends described above—elimination of voting restrictions and growing federal control over voting—are woven through those stages. You will see several illustrations of both of these trends over the course of this chapter.

1. The first stage of the struggle to extend voting rights came in the early 1800s. Religious qualifications, instituted in colonial days, quickly disappeared. No State has had a religious test for voting since 1810. Then, one by one, States began to eliminate property ownership and tax payment qualifications. By mid-century, almost all white adult males could vote in every State.

2. The second major effort to broaden the electorate followed the Civil War. The 15th Amendment, ratified in 1870, was intended to protect any citizen from being denied the right to vote because of race or color. Still, for nearly another century, African Americans were systematically prevented from voting, and they remained the largest group of disenfranchised citizens in the nation's population.

3. The 19th Amendment prohibited the denial of the right to vote because of sex. Its ratification in 1920 completed the third expansion

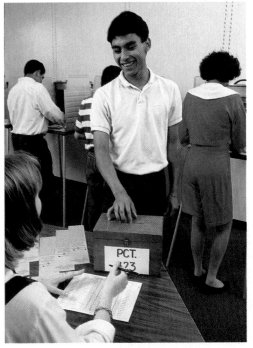

◀ This 18-year-old is casting a vote for the first time. *Critical Thinking Do you think 18 is the right minimum age for voting? Why or why not?*

of suffrage. Wyoming, while still a territory, had given women the vote in 1869. By 1920 more than half of the States had followed that lead.

4. A fourth major extension took place during the 1960s. During that time, federal legislation and court decisions focused on securing African Americans a full role in the electoral process in all States. With the passage and vigorous enforcement of a number of civil rights acts, especially the Voting Rights Act of 1965 and its later extensions, racial equality finally became fact in polling booths throughout the country.

The 23rd Amendment, passed in 1961, added the voters of the District of Columbia to the presidential electorate. The 24th Amendment, ratified in 1964, eliminated the poll tax

◀ *Suffragist Struggle* American suffragists first demanded the right to vote in 1848 at a meeting in Seneca Falls, New York. It took until 1920 to achieve ratification of the 19th Amendment.

(as well as any other tax) as a condition for voting in any federal election.

5. The fifth and latest expansion of the electorate came with the adoption of the 26th Amendment in 1971. It provides that no State can set the minimum age for voting at more than 18 years of age. In other words, those 18 and over were given the right to vote by this amendment.

The Power to Set Voting Qualifications

The Constitution does not give the Federal Government the power to set suffrage qualifications. Rather, that matter is reserved to the States. The Constitution does, however, place five restrictions on how the States use that power.

1. Any person whom a State allows to vote for members of the "most numerous branch" of its own legislature must also be allowed to vote for representatives and senators in Congress.[2] This restriction is of little real meaning today. With only minor exceptions, each of the States allows the same voters to vote in all elections within the State.

2. No State can deprive any person of the right to vote "on account of race, color, or previous condition of servitude" (15th Amendment).[3]

3. No State can deprive any person of the right to vote on account of sex (19th Amendment).[4]

4. No State can require payment of any tax as a condition for taking part in the nomination or election of any federal officeholder. That is, no State can levy any tax in connection with the selection of the President, the Vice President, or members of Congress (24th Amendment).

5. No State can deprive any person who is at least 18 years of age of the right to vote because of age (26th Amendment).[5]

Beyond these five restrictions, remember that no State can violate any other provision in the Constitution in the setting of suffrage qualifications—or in anything else that it does. A case decided by the Supreme Court in 1975, *Hill* v. *Stone*, illustrates this point.

The Court struck down a section of the Texas constitution that declared that only those persons who owned taxable property could vote in city bond elections. The Court found the drawing of such a distinction for voting purposes—between those who do and those who do not own taxable property—to be an unreasonable classification, prohibited by the 14th Amendment's Equal Protection Clause.

---

[2]Article I, Section 2, Clause 1; the 17th Amendment extended the "most numerous branch" provision to the election of senators.

[3]The phrase "previous condition of servitude" refers to slavery. This amendment does not guarantee the right to vote to African Americans, or to anyone else. Instead, it forbids discrimination on these grounds when the States set suffrage qualifications.

[4]This amendment does not guarantee the right to vote to women as such. Technically, it forbids States the power to discriminate against males or females in establishing suffrage qualifications.

[5]This amendment does not prevent any State from allowing persons younger than age 18 to vote. It does prohibit a State from setting a maximum age for voting.

Section 1 Assessment

Key Terms and Main Ideas

1. Describe two long-term trends that have characterized the history of **suffrage** in the United States.
2. Describe five distinct stages in the growth of the American **electorate**.
3. Who exercises the **franchise**?
4. What restrictions does the Constitution place on the States in setting suffrage qualifications?

Critical Thinking

5. **Demonstrating Reasoned Judgment** It is the year 1970. Suppose that you are a young adult testifying before Congress in favor of granting the vote to 18-year-olds. What arguments would you present in order to make your case?

6. **Drawing Inferences** Why do you think the Federal Government took more and more control over the setting of voter qualifications? Why could the States not have accomplished the same ends?

 Take It to the Net

7. Read about the history of voting rights in the District of Columbia. In a paragraph, (a) explore why residents of the capital city have not had the same voting rights as the rest of the nation, and (b) describe the efforts to correct this problem. Use the links provided at the Social Studies area of the following Web site for help in completing this activity. **www.phschool.com**

SKILLS FOR LIFE

TECHNOLOGY

CITIZENSHIP

CRITICAL THINKING

Predicting Consequences

CHARTS and GRAPHS

The Motor Voter Law requires States to allow people to register to vote when they apply for a driver's license. Several other of its provisions also make voter registration a more convenient process (see page 155).

The law became effective in 1995, and many predicted that it would reverse the downward trend in voter turnout. They were wrong. Voter registrations did reach record levels for the presidential elections of 1996 and 2000. But voter turnout in both elections fell well short of what it had been in 1992.

Consider another example. Many who fail to vote say that they are too busy—at work, at school, and so on—to take the time to go to the polls. Some suggest that this problem can be met by allowing both registration and voting via the Internet. To predict the consequences of Internet voting, follow these steps:

1. Identify the problem, cause, or decision. Begin by writing a question that summarizes and clarifies what you're trying to predict. What question might summarize issues involved in voting on the Internet?

1. Registration and voter turnout rise for all ages, sexes.

2. Voting increases, but only among younger voters.

Online Voting Becomes Legal

3. Turnout remains low.

4. Voting increases, but mainly among male voters.

5. Voting increases, but mainly among wealthier computer owners.

2. Brainstorm and chart possible outcomes. Jot down all the possible consequences, good and bad, that you think could occur. At first, don't rule out any possibilities. Create a web diagram like the one above to display all the possibilities.

3. Apply prior knowledge or new information. To rule out some of the possible consequences, you probably need to apply existing or new knowledge about voting behavior. Policymakers often look for a historical *precedent*—a similar situation in the past. They also rely on their own intuition and experience. There is no precedent for Internet voting. But which prediction might you favor if you read about (a) a new study showing that most computer users are women, or (b) a new poll showing overwhelming voter disinterest in the election?

4. Make a prediction. State your prediction about the results of Internet voting in a way that makes your reasoning clear.

Voting Booth
Information Voting Booth (IVB)

Photo	Candidate	Click To Vote	Attendence At Last Post	% Money From Companies & Organizations	Largest Single Contribution From A Company	% Money From Individuals	Largest Single Contribution From An Individual	Educational Qualifications	Stand On Issues	Champaign Web Site
	Wilson Henry		50%	70%	40,000	30%	$100			
	Silvia Jones		75%	65%	25,000	35%	5000			
	Henry Oscar		98%	20%	400	80%	150			
	Fritz Hertz		20%	79%	5,000,000	21%	50			

◀ Back   ▲ Up   ▶ Next

Efforts are underway in several States to allow voting on the Internet. Here is one mock-up of what an online ballot might look like.

Test for Success

Use the steps above and the following facts to make a prediction about voting patterns: (1) Voter participation tends to be highest among older Americans. (2) The "baby boom" population is entering into its 50s and beyond.

Voters and Voter Behavior 151 ★★★

Section Preview

OBJECTIVES

1. **Identify** the universal requirements for voting in the United States.
2. **Explain** the other requirements that States have used or still use as voting qualifications.

WHY IT MATTERS

All States have citizenship, residence, and age requirements for voting. Other voting qualifications differ from State to State. Some requirements—especially those that were used to disenfranchise certain groups—have been eliminated over time.

POLITICAL DICTIONARY

★ transient
★ registration
★ purge
★ poll books
★ literacy
★ poll tax

Are you qualified to vote? Probably not—at least not yet. Do you know why? In this section, you will see how the States, including yours, determine who is qualified to vote. You will also see that the various qualifications they set are not very difficult to meet.

Universal Requirements

Today, every State requires that any person who wants to vote must be able to satisfy qualifications based on three factors: (1) citizenship, (2) residence, and (3) age. The States have some leeway in shaping the details of the first two of these factors; they have almost no discretion with regard to the third one.

Citizenship

Aliens—foreign-born residents who have not become citizens—are generally denied the right to vote in the United States. Still, nothing in the Constitution says that aliens cannot vote, and any State could allow them to do so if it chose. At one time about a fourth of the States permitted those aliens who had applied for naturalization to vote. Typically, the western States did so to help attract settlers.[6]

Only one State now draws any distinction between native-born and naturalized citizens with regard to suffrage. The Minnesota constitution requires a person to have been an American citizen for at least three months before he or she can vote in elections there.

In practice, a few aliens do vote, though in what number no one knows. They either wrongly believe that they are citizens or unlawfully claim to be citizens at their polling places.

Residence

In order to vote in this country today, one must be a legal resident of the State in which he or she wishes to cast a ballot. In most States a person must have lived in the State for at least a certain period of time before he or she can vote.

The States adopted residence requirements for two reasons: (1) to keep a political machine from importing (bribing) enough outsiders to affect the outcome of local elections (a once common practice), and (2) to ensure that every

▲ These people are participating in a ceremony making them American citizens—one qualification for voting.

---

[6]Arkansas, the last State in which aliens could vote, adopted a citizenship requirement in 1926. In a few States, local governments can permit noncitizens to vote in local contests—e.g., city council elections—and a handful do.

voter has at least some time in which to become familiar with the candidates and issues in an election. For decades, all States imposed a comparatively lengthy residence requirement. They typically mandated at least a year in the State, 60 or 90 days in the county, and 30 days in the local ward or precinct.[7] Residence requirements for voting are not nearly so long today. The details vary, but only slightly, among the 50 States.

Nearly half of the States now require voters to have lived in the State for at least 30 days. In several States, the period is even shorter. For example, the requirement is only 20 days in Delaware and Oregon, 15 days in South Dakota, 14 days in Kansas, and 10 days in Alabama and Iowa. Arizona does have a 50-day rule, but it is the only State in which a new resident must wait for more than 30 days to become an eligible voter.[8] A growing number of States now require a voter to be a legal resident of the State but attach no time period to that requirement.

Today's much shorter requirements are a direct result of a 1970 law and a 1972 Supreme Court decision. In the Voting Rights Act Amendments of 1970, Congress banned any requirement of longer than 30 days for voting in presidential elections.[9] In *Dunn* v. *Blumstein,* 1972, the Supreme Court found Tennessee's requirement—at the time, a year in the State and 90 days in the county—unconstitutional. The Court held such a lengthy requirement to be an unsupportable discrimination against new residents and so in conflict with the 14th Amendment's Equal Protection Clause. The Supreme Court said that "30 days appears to be an ample period of time." Election law and practice among the States quickly accepted that standard.

Nearly every State does prohibit **transients,** or persons living in the State for only a short time, from gaining a legal residence there. Thus, a traveling sales agent, a member of the armed services, or a college student usually cannot vote in a State where he or she has only a temporary physical

"THAT'S WHAT'S THE MATTER."
BOSS TWEED. "As long as I count the votes, what are you going to do about it? say?"

Interpreting Political Cartoons This 1870 cartoon depicts the "boss" of a corrupt New York City political "machine." *How do you think a dishonest city government might arrange to "count the votes" to its own advantage?*

residence. In several States, however, the courts have held that college students who claim the campus community as their legal residence can vote there.

Age

The 26th Amendment, added to the Constitution in 1971, declares:

FROM THE Constitution **"** *The right of citizens of the United States, who are eighteen years of age or older, to vote shall not be denied or abridged by the United States or by any State on account of age.* **"**
—26th Amendment

Thus, no State may set the minimum age for voting in any election at more than 18. In other words, the amendment extends suffrage to citizens who are at least 18 years of age. Notice, however, that any State could set the age at less than 18, if it chose to do so.

Until the 26th Amendment was adopted, the generally accepted age requirement for voting was 21. In fact, up to 1970, only four States had put the age under 21. Georgia was the first State to allow 18-year-olds to vote; it did so in 1943, in the midst of World War II. Kentucky followed suit in 1955. Alaska entered the Union in 1959 with the

---

[7]Recall, the precinct is the smallest unit of election administration; see page 140. The ward is a unit into which cities are often divided for the election of members of the city council.

[8]The Arizona requirement is 50 days for voting in State and local elections and 30 days for presidential elections. The Supreme Court upheld Arizona's residence law in *Marston* v. *Lewis* in 1973, but it also declared that that law "approaches the outer constitutional limits."

[9]The Supreme Court upheld this in *Oregon* v. *Mitchell* in 1970.

Interpreting Political Cartoons **(a) What attitudes make this cartoon character a nonvoter? (b) What is the cartoonist's opinion of these attitudes?**

Those States allow anyone whose 18th birthday falls after the primary but before the general election to vote in the primary election.

One State, Nebraska, has come very close to effectively lowering the voting age to 17 for all elections. There, any person who will be 18 by the Tuesday following the first Monday in November can qualify to vote in any election held during that calendar year.

Other Qualifications

The States have imposed a number of other qualifications over time—notably, requirements based on literacy, tax payment, and registration. Only registration has survived as a significant requirement.

Registration

Forty-nine States—all except North Dakota—require that most or all voters be registered to vote. **Registration** is a procedure of voter identification intended to prevent fraudulent voting. It gives election officials a list of those persons who are qualified to vote in an election. Several States also use voter registration to identify voters in terms of their party preference and, thus, their eligibility to take part in closed primaries.

Voter registration became a common feature of State election law in the early 1900s. Today, most States require all voters to register in order to vote in any election held within the State. A few do not impose the requirement for all elections, however. In Wisconsin, for example, only those in urban areas must register to vote.[10]

Typically, a prospective voter must register his or her name, age, place of birth, present address, length of residence, and similar facts. The information is logged by a local official, usually a registrar of elections or the county clerk. A voter typically remains registered unless or until he or she moves, dies, is convicted of a serious crime, or is committed to a mental institution.

State law directs local election officials to review the lists of registered voters and to remove the names of those who are no longer eligible to

voting age set at 19, and Hawaii became a State later that same year with a voting age of 20.

Both Alaska and Hawaii set the age above 18 but below 21 to avoid potential problems caused by high school students voting in local school-district elections. Whatever the fears at the time, there have been no such problems in any State since the passage of the 26th Amendment.

Efforts to lower the voting age to 18 nationwide began in the 1940s, during World War II. These efforts were capped by the adoption of the 26th Amendment in 1971, during the war in Vietnam. That amendment was ratified more quickly than any other amendment to the Constitution. This fact is testament to the emotional weight of the principal argument in its favor: "Old enough to fight, old enough to vote."

How have 18-to-20-year-olds responded to the 26th Amendment? In 1972, 58 percent of that age group registered to vote, and 48.4 percent of them reported that they did vote that year. By 1996, however, the registration figure had dropped to 45.6 percent, and only 31.2 percent said they actually went to the polls. Contrast the turnout of these young people with that of Americans 65 and older: In 1996, 77 percent of them were registered, and 67 percent voted. Indications are that the low-turnout behavior of 18-to-20-year-olds continued in 2000.

In a growing number of States, some 17-year-olds can now cast ballots in primary elections.

---

[10]Wisconsin does not require registration by voters who live in rural areas or in cities with populations of less than 10,000.

vote. This process is known as **purging,** and it is usually supposed to be done every two or four years. Unfortunately, the requirement is often ignored. The **poll books** in those places are cluttered with a large number of persons who no longer meet voting requirements. Poll books are the lists of all registered voters in each precinct.

The registration requirement for voting has become controversial in recent years. Some people argue that it should be done away with. They view registration as a bar to voter turnout, especially among the poor and the less-educated.

Those critics buttress their case by noting that voter turnout began to decline in the early 1900s, just after most States adopted a registration requirement. They also point to the fact that voter turnout is much higher in most European democracies than in the United States. In those countries voter registration is not a matter of individual choice; by law, public officials must enter the names of all eligible citizens on registration lists. The United States is the only democratic country

in which each person decides whether or not he or she will register to vote.

Most people who have studied the problem favor keeping the registration requirement as a necessary defense against fraud. However, they also favor making the process a more convenient one. In short, they see the problem in these terms: Where is the line between making it so easy to vote that fraud is encouraged, and making it so difficult that legitimate voting is discouraged?

Most States have eased the registration process over the last several years, and in 1993 Congress passed a law that required every State (but North Dakota) to do so. That law, dubbed the "Motor Voter Law," became effective in 1995. It directs every State to (1) allow all eligible citizens to register to vote when they apply for or renew a driver's license; (2) provide for voter registration by mail; and (3) make registration forms available at the local offices of State employment, welfare, and other social service agencies. The Federal Election Commission reports that by 2000 some

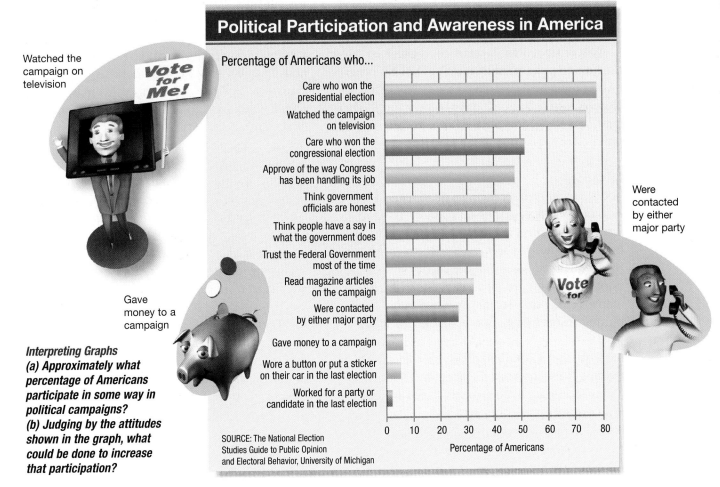

Political Participation and Awareness in America

Watched the campaign on television

Were contacted by either major party

Gave money to a campaign

Percentage of Americans who...

- Care who won the presidential election
- Watched the campaign on television
- Care who won the congressional election
- Approve of the way Congress has been handling its job
- Think government officials are honest
- Think people have a say in what the government does
- Trust the Federal Government most of the time
- Read magazine articles on the campaign
- Were contacted by either major party
- Gave money to a campaign
- Wore a button or put a sticker on their car in the last election
- Worked for a party or candidate in the last election

Percentage of Americans

0   10   20   30   40   50   60   70   80

SOURCE: The National Election Studies Guide to Public Opinion and Electoral Behavior, University of Michigan

Interpreting Graphs
(a) Approximately what percentage of Americans participate in some way in political campaigns?
(b) Judging by the attitudes shown in the graph, what could be done to increase that participation?

Interpreting Political Cartoons Voter literacy tests were often used to discourage African American voters. ***According to the cartoonist, what unexpected results did these tests sometimes have?***

"By th' way, what's that big word?"

8 million persons had registered to vote as a direct result of the Motor Voter Law.

The law also requires every State to mail a questionnaire to each of its registered voters every four years, so that the poll books can be purged for deaths and changes of residence. It also forbids the States to purge for any other reason, including failure to vote.

Wisconsin allows voters to register at any time, up to and including election day. Elsewhere a voter must be registered by some date before an election, often 20 or 30 days beforehand.[11] That cutoff gives election officials time to prepare the poll books for an upcoming election.

Literacy

Today, no State has a suffrage qualification based on voter **literacy**—a person's ability to read or write. At one time, the literacy requirement could be, and in many places was, used to make sure that a qualified voter had the capacity to cast an informed ballot. It also was used unfairly in many places to prevent or discourage certain groups from voting. For many years, it was a device to keep African Americans from voting in parts of the South, and Native Americans and Latinos from voting in the West and Southwest.

Some literacy requirements called for potential voters to prove they had the ability to read; other States required proof of the ability to both read and write. Still others required the ability to read, write, and "understand" some printed

material, usually a passage taken from the State or Federal Constitution. Often, whites were asked simple questions; African Americans were asked questions so complex that they would stump even a judge who was familiar with the passage.

Connecticut adopted the first literacy qualifications in 1855. Massachusetts followed in 1857. Both of these States were trying to limit voting by Irish Catholic immigrants. Mississippi adopted a literacy requirement in 1890, and shortly, most of the other southern States followed suit. Southern literacy qualifications usually included an "understanding clause"—again, requiring potential voters to demonstrate comprehension of some printed material.

While those qualifications had been aimed at disenfranchising African Americans, they sometimes had unintended effects. Several States soon found that they needed to adjust their voting requirements by adding so-called "grandfather clauses" to their constitutions. These grandfather clauses were designed to enfranchise those white males who were unintentionally disqualified by their failure to meet the literacy or taxpaying requirements.

A grandfather clause was added to the Louisiana constitution in 1895; Alabama, Georgia, Maryland, North Carolina, Oklahoma, and Virginia soon added them as well. These clauses stated that any man, or his male descendants, who had voted in the State before the adoption of the 15th Amendment (1870) could become a legal voter without regard to any literacy or taxpaying qualifications. The Supreme Court found the Oklahoma provision, the last to be adopted (in 1910), in conflict with the 15th Amendment in *Guinn* v. *United States* in 1915.

A number of States outside the South also adopted literacy qualifications of various sorts. Wyoming did so in 1889, California in 1894, Washington in 1896, New Hampshire in 1902, Arizona in 1913, New York in 1921, Oregon in 1924, and Alaska in 1949.

Its unfair use finally led Congress to eliminate literacy as a suffrage qualification in the Voting Rights Act Amendments of 1970. The Supreme Court agreed in *Oregon* v. *Mitchell*, 1970:

---

[11]In Idaho, Maine, Minnesota, New Hampshire, and Wyoming, a person who is qualified to vote but misses the deadline can register (and then vote) on election day.

PRIMARY Sources

" In enacting the literacy test ban . . . Congress had before it a long history of the discriminatory use of literacy tests to disfranchise voters on account of their race. "
—Justice Hugo Black, Opinion of the Court

At the time Congress banned literacy tests, 18 States had some form of a literacy requirement for voting.

Tax Payment

Property ownership, proved by the payment of property taxes, was once a very common suffrage qualification. For decades several States also demanded the payment of a special tax, called the **poll tax**, as a condition for voting. Those requirements and others that called for the payment of a tax in order to vote have disappeared.

The poll tax was once found throughout the South. Beginning with Florida in 1889, each of the 11 southern States adopted the poll tax as part of their effort to discourage voting by African Americans. The device proved to be of only limited effectiveness, however. That fact, and opposition to the use of the poll tax from within the South as well as elsewhere, led most of those States to abandon it. By 1966, the poll tax was still in use only in Alabama, Mississippi, Texas, and Virginia.[12]

The 24th Amendment, ratified in 1964, outlawed the poll tax, or any other tax, as a condition for voting in any federal election. The Supreme Court finally eliminated the poll tax as a qualification for voting in all elections in 1966. In *Harper* v. *Virginia Board of Elections*, the Court held the Virginia poll tax to be in conflict

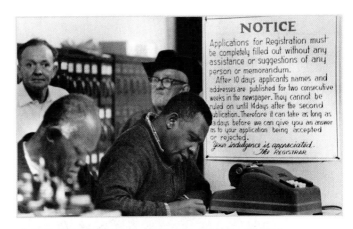

▲ This photo was taken in Mississippi, in 1978, when African American suffrage was supposed to be assured. *Critical Thinking What tactics does the sign use to intimidate African Americans who want to register to vote?*

with the 14th Amendment's Equal Protection Clause. The Court could find no reasonable relationship between the act of voting on the one hand and the payment of a tax on the other.

Persons Denied the Vote

Clearly, democratic government can exist only where the right to vote is very widely held. Still, every State does purposely deny the vote to certain persons. For example, none of the 50 States allows people in mental institutions, or any other persons who have been legally found to be mentally incompetent, to vote. Nearly all States also disqualify those who have been convicted of serious crimes. A few States also do not allow anyone dishonorably discharged from the armed forces to vote.

---

[12]By that time, the poll tax had been abolished in North Carolina (1924), Louisiana (1934), Florida (1937), Georgia (1945), South Carolina (1950), Tennessee (1951), and Arkansas (1964).

Section 2 Assessment

Key Terms and Main Ideas

1. For what reasons do most States require voter **registration?**
2. What is the Motor Voter Law? What is its purpose?
3. **(a)** Why do election officials keep **poll books?** **(b)** Why is it a good idea to **purge** them every few years?
4. How was the **poll tax** used as a voting qualification?

Critical Thinking

5. **Drawing Conclusions (a)** Do you think that being able to read is necessary for being a well-informed voter? Why or why not? **(b)** Do you think literacy is more or less important now than it was 100 years ago?

6. **Recognizing Bias** What were grandfather clauses? How did they demonstrate a "double bias" against African Americans?

Take It to the Net

7. Find your State's voting requirements. Do you qualify to vote? What if you move to another State? Make a chart comparing the voting requirements of your State with those of three other States. Use the links provided in the Social Studies area of the following Web site for help in completing this activity. www.phschool.com

CLOSE UP
FOUNDATION

on Primary Sources

The Dangers of Voter Apathy

Curtis Gans directs the Committee for the Study of the American Electorate, a non-partisan research organization that studies the causes of declining voter participation and looks for solutions. Here, Gans discusses low voter turnout and what can be done to reverse the trend.

Over [recent decades], the percentage of eligible Americans who vote has declined by 20 percent in both presidential and off-year elections. More than 20 million Americans who used to vote frequently have ceased participating altogether. The United States—with voter turnouts of around 50 percent in presidential elections and 35 percent in off-year elections—now has the lowest rate of voter participation of any democracy in the world.

More than half of America's nonparticipants are chronic nonvoters: people who have never voted or hardly ever vote, whose families have never voted, and who are poorer, less-educated, and less-involved participants in American society. But a growing number of Americans are simply dropping out of the political process—many of whom are educated, white-collar professionals. In addition, a growing number of younger Americans are failing to enter the political process. Both of these trends constitute a major national concern, for there is a very real danger that the habits of good citizenship will die and that government of the people, for the people, and by the people will become government of, for, and by the few. . . .

The scars of the Vietnam War and the Watergate scandal run deep. To many Americans, politics seem to be characterized by poor public leadership, increasingly complex issues, and ever-growing and inflexible government with few successes in meeting public needs. . . .

"Never mind what the voters are saying. What are the pollsters saying?"

What does the cartoon suggest about voter apathy?

Sadly, for the average citizen, nonparticipation is becoming an increasingly rational act. Reversing this trend and instilling both hope and vigor among American voters will not be an easy task. But I think a few steps will improve participation in America. For example, we need to increase the amount and sophistication of civic education in our homes and schools. We must also develop policies that address the central concerns of the electorate, while realigning and strengthening the two-party system. . . . It is important for us to instill in our young people a sense of values that emphasizes something larger than the self.

In the end, voting is a religious act. Each citizen must come to believe that—despite the thousands of elections that are not decided by one vote—his or her vote *does* make a difference. It is that faith that needs to be restored.

Analyzing Primary Sources

1. How much has voter participation declined in recent decades?
2. What reasons does Gans give to explain the decline in voter participation?
3. What suggestions does Gans give for increasing voter participation?
4. Why should we be concerned about the declining rate of voter participation in the United States?

-3- Suffrage and Civil Rights

Section Preview

OBJECTIVES

1. **Describe** the 15th Amendment and the tactics used to circumvent it in an effort to deny African Americans the vote.
2. **Explain** the significance of the early civil rights legislation passed in 1957, 1960, and 1964.
3. **Analyze** the provisions and effects of the Voting Rights Act of 1965.

WHY IT MATTERS

The 15th Amendment declared that the right to vote cannot be denied on account of race. Nevertheless, a variety of tactics were used in southern States to disenfranchise African Americans. The Supreme Court struck down a number of these efforts, and, beginning in the 1950s, Congress passed laws to protect minority voting rights.

POLITICAL DICTIONARY

★ **gerrymandering**
★ **injunction**
★ **preclearance**

How important is the right to vote? For those who do not have it, that right can seem as important as life itself. Indeed, in the Deep South of the 1960s, civil rights workers suffered arrest, beatings, shocks with electric cattle prods, even death—all in the name of the right to vote. Their efforts inspired the nation and led to large-scale federal efforts to secure suffrage for African Americans and other minority groups in the United States.

The Fifteenth Amendment

The effort to extend the franchise to African Americans began with the 15th Amendment, which was ratified in 1870. It declares that the right to vote cannot be denied to any citizen of the United States because of race, color, or previous condition of servitude. The amendment was plainly intended to ensure that African American men, nearly all of them former slaves and nearly all of them living in the South, could vote.

The 15th Amendment is not self-executing, however. In other words, simply stating a general principle without providing for a means to enforce implementation was not enough to carry out the intention of the amendment. To make it effective, Congress had to act. Yet for almost 90 years the Federal Government paid little attention to voting rights for African Americans.

During that period, African Americans were generally and systematically kept from the polls in much of the South. White supremacists employed a number of tactics to that end. Their major weapon was violence. Other tactics included more subtle threats and social pressures, such as firing an African American man who tried to register or vote, or denying his family credit at local stores.

More formal "legal" devices were used, as well. The most effective were literacy tests. White officials regularly manipulated these tests to disenfranchise African American citizens.

Registration laws served the same end. As written, they applied to all potential voters. In practice, however, they were often administered to keep African Americans from qualifying to vote. Poll taxes, "white primaries," gerrymandering, and several other devices were also regularly used to disenfranchise African Americans. **Gerrymandering** is the practice of drawing electoral district lines (the boundaries of the geographic area from which a candidate is elected to a public office) in order to limit the voting strength of a particular group or party.

The white primary arose out of the decades-long Democratic domination of politics in the South. It was almost a given that the Democratic candidate for an

▶ An African American woman registers to vote.

office would be elected. Therefore, almost always, it was only the Democrats who nominated candidates, generally in primaries. In several southern States, political parties were defined by law as "private associations." As such, they could exclude whomever they chose, and the Democrats regularly refused to admit African Americans. Because only party members could vote in the party's primary, African Americans were then excluded from a critical step in the public election process.

The Supreme Court finally outlawed the white primary in a case from Texas, *Smith* v. *Allwright*, 1944. The Court held that nominations are an integral part of the election process. Consequently, when a political party holds a primary it is performing a public function and it is, therefore, bound by the terms of the 15th Amendment.

The Supreme Court outlawed gerrymandering when used for purposes of racial discrimination in a case from Alabama, *Gomillion* v. *Lightfoot*, in 1960. In this case, the Alabama legislature had redrawn the electoral district boundaries of Tuskegee, effectively excluding all blacks from the city limits. The Court ruled that the legislature's act violated the 15th Amendment because the irregularly shaped district clearly was created to deprive blacks of political power.

Led by these decisions of the Supreme Court, the lower federal courts struck down many of the practices designed to disenfranchise African Americans in the 1940s and 1950s. Still, the courts could act only when those who claimed to be victims of discrimination sued. That case-by-case method was, at best, agonizingly slow.

Finally, and largely in response to the civil rights movement led by Dr. Martin Luther King, Jr., Congress was moved to act. It has passed several civil rights laws since the late 1950s. Those statutes contain a number of sections specifically intended to implement the 15th Amendment.

Early Civil Rights Legislation

The first law passed by Congress to implement the 15th Amendment was the Civil Rights Act of 1957, which set up the United States Civil Rights Commission. One of the Commission's major duties is to inquire into claims of voter discrimination. The Commission reports its findings to Congress and the President and, through the media, to the public. The Act also gave the attorney general the power to seek federal court orders to prevent interference with any person's right to vote in any federal election.

The *Living* Constitution

Government by the People

1900

When the Constitution was written, only white male property owners (about 10 to 16 percent of the nation's population) had the right to vote. Over the past two centuries, though, the term "government by the people" has become a reality. During the first half of the 1800s, States gradually dropped property requirements for voting. Later, groups such as African Americans, women, and young adults gained the right to vote. Other reforms made the voting process fairer and easier. The time line lists some historic developments in the growing power of the people.

1870
Fifteenth Amendment—designed mainly to give former slaves the right to vote—protects the voting right of adult male citizens of every race.

1913
Seventeenth Amendment calls for members of the U.S. Senate to be elected directly by the people instead of by State legislatures.

The Civil Rights Act of 1960 added an additional safeguard. It provided for the appointment of federal voting referees. These officers were to serve anywhere a federal court found voter discrimination. They were given the power to help qualified persons to register and vote in federal elections.

The Civil Rights Act of 1964

The Civil Rights Act of 1964 is much broader and much more effective than either of the two earlier measures. It outlaws discrimination in several areas, especially in job-related matters. With regard to voting rights, its most important section forbids the use of any voter registration or literacy requirement in an unfair or discriminatory manner.

The 1964 law continued a pattern set in the earlier laws. In major part, it relied on judicial action to overcome racial barriers and emphasized the use of federal court orders called injunctions. An **injunction** is a court order that either compels (forces) or restrains (limits) the performance of some act by a private individual or by a public official. The violation of an injunction amounts to contempt of court, a crime punishable by fine and/or imprisonment.

Dramatic events in Selma, Alabama, soon pointed up the shortcomings of this approach. Dr. King mounted a voter registration drive in that city in early 1965. He and his supporters hoped that they could focus national attention on the issue of African American voting rights— and they most certainly did.

Their registration efforts were met with insults and violence by local white civilians, by city and county police, and then by State troopers. Two civil rights workers were murdered, and many were beaten when they attempted a peaceful march to the State capitol. The nation saw much of the drama on television and was shocked. An outraged President Lyndon Johnson urged Congress to pass new and stronger legislation to ensure the voting rights of African Americans. Congress responded quickly.

The Voting Rights Act of 1965

The Voting Rights Act of 1965 made the 15th Amendment, at long last, a truly effective part of the Constitution. Unlike its predecessors, this act applied to *all* elections held anywhere in this country—State and local, as well as federal.

Originally, the Voting Rights Act was to be in effect for a period of five years. Congress has

1924
General Citizenship Act grants all Native Americans the rights of citizenship, including the right to vote in federal elections.

1995
Federal "Motor Voter Law" takes effect, making it quicker and easier to register to vote.

| 1925 | 1950 | 1975 | 2000 |

1920
Nineteenth Amendment guarantees American women the right to vote in federal and State elections.

1965
Voting Rights Act protects the rights of minority voters and eliminates voting barriers such as the literacy test.

1971
Twenty-sixth Amendment sets the minimum voting age at 18.

Analyzing Time Lines

1. Which amendments have granted voting rights to specific groups of people?
2. What has been the general trend of constitutional changes related to voting?

Southern Black Voters, 1960–1970

SOURCE: *Historical Statistics of Black America*

Interpreting Graphs In the photo at left, civil rights demonstrators risk injury and even death in the 1965 Selma march for voting rights. *How many new African American voters registered in the South between 1960 and 1970?*

extended its life three times, in the Voting Rights Act Amendments of 1970, 1975, and most recently 1982. The present version of the law was made effective for 25 years; its provisions are scheduled to expire in 2007.

The 1965 law directed the attorney general to challenge the constitutionality of the remaining State poll-tax laws in the federal courts. That provision led directly to *Harper* v. *Virginia Board of Elections*, in 1966 (see page 157).

The law also suspended the use of any literacy test or similar device in any State or county where less than half of the electorate had been registered or had voted in the 1964 presidential election. The law authorized the attorney general to appoint voting examiners to serve in any of those States or counties. It also gave these federal officers the power to register voters and otherwise oversee the conduct of elections in those areas.

Preclearance

The Voting Rights Act of 1965 created a further restriction on those States where a majority of the electorate had not voted in 1964. The act declared that no new election laws, and no changes in existing election laws, could go into effect in any of those States unless first approved —given **preclearance**—by the Department of Justice. Only those new or revised laws that do not "dilute" (weaken) the voting rights of minority groups can survive the preclearance process.

The preclearance hurdle has produced a large number of court cases since the passage of the law. Those cases show that the laws most likely to run afoul of the preclearance requirement are those that make these kinds of changes:

(1) the location of polling places;

(2) the boundaries of election districts;

(3) deadlines in the election process;

(4) from ward or district election to at-large elections;

(5) the qualifications candidates must meet in order to run for office.

Any State or county subject to the voter-examiner and preclearance provisions can be removed from the law's coverage through a "bail-out" process. That relief can come if the State can show the United States District Court in the District of Columbia that it has not applied any voting procedures in a discriminatory way for at least 10 years.

The voter-examiner and preclearance provisions of the 1965 Voting Rights Act originally applied to six entire States: Alabama, Georgia, Louisiana, Mississippi, South Carolina, and Virginia. The act also applied to 40 North Carolina counties.

The Supreme Court upheld the Voting Rights Act in 1966. In *South Carolina* v. *Katzenbach*, a unanimous Court declared:

PRIMARY *Sources* "*The Voting Rights Act was designed by Congress to banish the blight of racial discrimination in voting, which has infected the electoral process in parts of our country for nearly a century. . . . Congress assumed the power to prescribe these remedies from Section 2 of the 15th Amendment, which authorizes the National Legislature to effectuate by "appropriate" measures the constitutional prohibition against racial discrimination in voting. We* *hold that the sections of the Act which are properly before us are an appropriate means for carrying out Congress' constitutional responsibilities and are consonant with all other provisions of the Constitution.* **"**

—Chief Justice Earl Warren, Opinion of the Court

Amendments to the Act

The 1970 amendments extended the law for another five years. The 1968 elections were added to the law's triggering formula; the result was that a number of counties in six more States (Alaska, Arizona, California, Idaho, New Mexico, and Oregon) were added to the law's coverage.

The 1970 law also provided that, for five years, no State could use literacy as the basis for any voting requirement. That temporary ban as well as residence provisions outlined in the law were upheld by the Supreme Court in *Oregon* v. *Mitchell* in 1970.

In 1975, the law was extended again, this time for seven years, and the five-year ban on literacy tests was made permanent. Since 1975, no State has been able to apply any sort of literacy qualification to any aspect of the election process.

The law's voter-examiner and preclearance provisions were also broadened in 1975. Since then they have also covered any State or county where more than 5 percent of the voting-age population belongs to certain "language minorities." These groups are defined to include all

▲ *I Have a Dream* This famous speech, delivered by civil rights leader Martin Luther King, Jr., was a highlight of the 1963 March on Washington, which drew more than 200,000 people.

persons of Spanish heritage, Native Americans, Asian Americans, and Alaskan Natives.

This addition expanded the law's coverage to all of Alaska and Texas and to several counties in 24 other States, as well. In these areas, all ballots and other official election materials must be printed both in English and in the language of the minority, or minorities, involved.

The 1982 amendments extended the basic features of the act for another 25 years. In 1992 the law's language-minority provisions were revised: they now apply to any community that has a minority-language population of 10,000 or more persons.

Section 3 Assessment

Key Terms and Main Ideas

1. What is **gerrymandering?** What other devices were used to disenfranchise African Americans?
2. What part do **injunctions** play in the Civil Rights Act of 1964?
3. What is **preclearance?** How can a State "bail out" of the preclearance provisions of the Voting Rights Act of 1965?
4. (a) Identify the major civil rights laws enacted since 1950. (b) Describe voting rights provisions in these laws.

Critical Thinking

5. **Drawing Conclusions** Even after the ratification of the 15th Amendment, African Americans in the South were denied the right to vote because the amendment was not implemented. (a) What does that tell you about American attitudes from 1870 until the 1950s? (b) Why did those attitudes change?

6. **Recognizing Cause and Effect (a)** How do you think the historical denial of voting rights to African Americans affected the makeup of Congress and many State legislatures? **(b)** How did that result, in turn, affect the likelihood that these legislatures would pass civil rights laws?

 Take It to the Net

7. Read about Dr. Martin Luther King, Jr.'s march from Selma to Montgomery, Alabama. Write a paragraph explaining how this march was instrumental in changing American opinion and spurring government action on voting rights. Use the links provided in the Social Studies area at the following Web site for help in completing this activity. **www.phschool.com**

4 Voter Behavior

Section Preview

OBJECTIVES

1. **Examine** the problem of nonvoting in this country, and describe the size of the problem.
2. **Identify** why people do not vote.
3. **Examine** voting behavior of voters and nonvoters.
4. **Understand** the sociological and psychological factors that affect voting and how they work together to influence voter behavior.

WHY IT MATTERS

Low voter turnout is a serious problem in this country. Among those who do vote, sociological and psychological factors work together to influence voter behavior over time and in particular elections.

POLITICAL DICTIONARY

★ off-year election
★ political efficacy
★ political socialization
★ gender gap
★ party identification
★ straight-ticket voting
★ split-ticket voting
★ independent

"Your vote is your voice. Use it." That's the advice of Rock the Vote, an organization that encourages young voters ages 18–25 to participate in the election process. In the United States, and in other democratic countries, we believe in all voices being heard. That is, we believe in voting.

Over the next several pages you will look at voter behavior in this country—at who votes and who does not, and at why those people who do vote, vote as they do.

Nonvoters

The word *idiot* came to our language from the Greek. In ancient Athens, idiots (*idiotes*) were those citizens who did not vote or otherwise take part in public life.

Tens of millions of Americans vote in presidential and congressional elections; in State elections; and in city, county, and other public elections. Still, there are many millions of other Americans who, for one reason or another, do not vote. There are some quite legitimate reasons for not voting, as you will see. But this troubling fact remains: Most of the millions of Americans who could—but do not—go to the polls cannot claim any of those justifications. Indeed, they would have been called idiots in the Greece of 2000 years ago.

The Size of the Problem

The table on page 165 lays out the major facts of the nonvoter problem in American elections. Notice that on election day in 2000 there were an estimated 205.8 million persons of voting age in the United States. Yet only some 105.4 million of them—only 51.2 percent—actually voted in the presidential election. More than 100 million persons who might have voted did not.

In 2000 some 99 million votes were cast in the elections held across the country to fill the 435 seats in the House of Representatives. That means that only some 48 percent of the electorate voted in those congressional elections. (Notice the even lower rates of turnout in the **off-year elections**—that is, in the congressional elections held in the even-numbered years between presidential elections.)

Several facets of the nonvoter problem are not very widely known. Take, for example, this striking fact: There are millions of nonvoters *among those who vote*. Look again at the 2000 figures on page 165. More than six million persons who voted in the last presidential election could also have voted for a congressional candidate, but they did not choose to do so.

"Nonvoting voters" are not limited to federal elections. In fact, they are much more common in State and local elections. As a general rule, the farther down the ballot an office is, the fewer the

Interpreting Political Cartoons **What reasons for nonvoting does this cartoon suggest?**

OUR LATEST EXIT POLL SHOWS "HEADS" LEADING "TAILS" 51% TO 49%...

VOTE

Voter Turnout, 1956–2000

Year	Population of Voting Age[1] (in millions)	Votes Cast for President (in millions)	Votes Cast for President (percent)	Votes Cast for U.S. Representatives (in millions)	Votes Cast for U.S. Representatives (percent)
1956	104.515	62.027	59.3	58.426	55.9
1958	106.447	—	—	45.818	43.0
1960	109.672	68.838	62.8	64.133	58.5
1962	112.952	—	—	51.267	45.4
1964	114.090	70.645	61.9	65.895	57.8
1966	116.638	—	—	52.908	45.4
1968	120.285	73.212	60.9	66.288	55.1
1970	124.498	—	—	54.173	43.5
1972	140.777	77.719	55.2	71.430	50.7
1974	146.388	—	—	52.495	35.9
1976	152.308	81.556	53.5	74.422	48.9
1978	158.369	—	—	55.332	34.9
1980	163.945	86.515	52.8	77.995	47.6
1982	169.643	—	—	64.514	38.0
1984	173.995	92.653	53.3	83.231	47.8
1986	177.922	—	—	59.619	33.5
1988	181.956	91.595	50.3	81.786	44.9
1990	185.812	—	—	61.513	33.1
1992	189.524	104.425	55.1	96.239	50.8
1994	193.650	—	—	70.781	36.6
1996	196.507	96.278	49.0	89.863	45.8
1998	200.929	—	—	66.033	33.9
2000	205.813	105.397	51.2	99.457	48.4

[1]As estimated by Census Bureau. Population 18 years of age and over since ratification of 26th Amendment in 1971; prior to 1971, 21 years and over in all States, except: 18 years and over in Georgia since 1943 and Kentucky since 1955, 19 years and over in Alaska and 20 and over in Hawaii since 1959.

SOURCE: *Statistical Abstract of the United States;* Federal Election Commission

Interpreting Tables This table shows voter turnout two ways: total numbers and percent of eligible voters. **(a) In what year shown did voting percentage peak for presidential races? (b) In what year did voting peak for congressional races?**

number of votes that will be cast for it. This phenomenon is sometimes called "ballot fatigue." The expression suggests that many voters exhaust their patience and/or their knowledge as they work their way down the ballot.

Some quick examples illustrate the phenomenon of ballot fatigue: In every State, more votes are regularly cast in the presidential election than in the gubernatorial election. More votes are generally cast for the governorship than for other Statewide offices, such as lieutenant governor or secretary of state. More voters in a county usually vote in the races for Statewide offices than vote in the contests for such county offices as sheriff, county clerk, or district attorney, and so on.

There are other little-recognized facets of the nonvoter problem, too. For example, the table on this page shows that turnout in congressional elections is consistently higher in presidential years than it is in off-year elections. That same pattern holds among the States in terms of the types of elections; more people vote in general elections than in either primary or special elections.

Why People Do Not Vote

Why do we have so many nonvoters? Why, even in a presidential election, do as many as half of those who could vote stay away from the polls?

Clearly, the time that it takes to vote should not be a significant part of the answer. For most people, it takes more time to go to a video store and pick out a movie than it does to go to their neighborhood polling place and cast a ballot. So we must look elsewhere for answers.

"Cannot-Voters"

To begin with, look at another of those little-recognized aspects of the nonvoter problem. Several million persons who are regularly identified as nonvoters can be more accurately described as "cannot-voters." That is, although it is true that they do not vote, the fact is that they cannot do so.

The 2000 data support the point. Included in that figure of more than 100 million who did not vote in the last presidential election are some 10 million who are resident aliens. Remember, they are barred from the polls in every State.

Interpreting Political Cartoons What does the "weight" of the nonvoters tell you about the kind of difference they are making?

Another 5 to 6 million citizens were so ill or otherwise physically disabled that they simply could not vote in an election. An additional 2 or 3 million persons were traveling suddenly and unexpectedly, and so could not vote.

Other groups of cannot-voters can be discovered in the nonvoting group. They include some 500,000 persons in mental health care facilities or under some other form of legal restraint because of their mental condition; nearly two million adults in jails and prisons; and perhaps as many as 100,000 who do not (cannot) vote because of their religious beliefs (for example, those who believe that acts such as voting amount to idolatry).

Actual Nonvoters

Even so, there are millions of actual nonvoters in the United States. Thus, in 2000 more than 80 million Americans who could have voted in the presidential election did not.

There are any number of reasons for that behavior. For example, many people deliberately choose not go to the polls. They do not vote because they are convinced that it makes no real difference who wins a certain election. Others are satisfied with the political world as they see it. They believe that, no matter who wins elections, things will continue to go well.

However, a large number of those who deliberately stay away from the polls do so because they distrust politics and politicians.

They have no sense of **political efficacy.** That is, they lack any sense of their own influence or effectiveness in politics. Many of them believe that they have been squeezed out of the political process. They are convinced that "government by the people" has been taken over by entrenched politicians, powerful special interests, and the media.

Factors Affecting Turnout

Other factors also affect whether voters show up at the polls. Cumbersome election procedures—for example, inconvenient registration requirements, long ballots, and long lines at polling places—discourage voters from turning out on election day. Bad weather also tends to discourage turnout.

Another possible, though hotly debated, factor is the so-called "time-zone fallout" problem. This refers to the fact that, in presidential elections, polls in States in the eastern and central time zones close before polls in States in the Mountain and Pacific time zones. Based on early returns from the East and Midwest, the news media often project the outcome of the presidential contest before all the voters in the West have gone to the polls. Some people fear that such reports have discouraged western voters from casting their ballots.

Of all the reasons that may be cited, however, the chief cause for nonvoting is, purely and simply, a lack of interest. Those who lack sufficient interest, who are indifferent and apathetic, and who just cannot be bothered are usually woefully uninformed. Most often, they do not know even the simplest facts about the candidates and issues involved in an election.

Comparing Voters and Nonvoters

One useful way to get a handle on the problem of nonvoting is to contrast those persons who tend to go to the polls regularly with those who do not. There are many differences between them.

The people most likely to vote display such characteristics as higher levels of income, education, and occupational status. They are usually well integrated into community life. They tend to be long-time residents who are active in or at least comfortable with their surroundings. They are likely to have a strong sense of party identification and to believe

Voting by Groups in Presidential Elections, 1968–2000 (By Percentage of Votes Reported Cast)

	1968 D	1968 R	1968 AIP	1972 D	1972 R	1976 D	1976 R	1980 D	1980 R	1980 I	1984 D	1984 R	1988 D	1988 R	1992 D	1992 R	1992 I	1996 D	1996 R	1996 P	2000 D	2000 R	2000 G
National Vote	43.0	43.4	13.6	37.5	60.7	50	48	41	50.7	6.6	41	59	46	54	43.2	37.8	19	49.2	40.7	8.4	48.7	48.6	2.7
Sex																							
Men	41	43	16	37	63	53	45	38	53	7	36	64	44	56	41	37	22	45	44	11	43	52	3
Women	45	43	12	38	62	48	51	44	49	6	45	55	48	52	46	38	16	54	39	7	53	45	2
Race																							
White	38	47	15	32	68	46	52	36	56	7	34	66	41	59	39	41	20	46	45	9	43	55	3
Nonwhite	85	12	3	87	13	85	15	86	10	2	87	13	82	18	77	11	12	82	12	6	87	9	4
Education																							
College	37	54	9	37	63	42	55	35	53	10	39	61	42	58	43	40	17	47	45	8	46	51	3
High school	42	43	15	34	66	54	46	43	51	5	43	57	46	54	40	38	22	52	34	14	52	46	2
Grade school	52	33	15	49	51	58	41	54	42	3	51	49	55	45	56	28	16	58	27	15	55	42	3
Age																							
Under 30	47	38	15	48	52	53	45	47	41	11	40	60	37	63	40	37	23	54	30	16	47	47	6
30–49	44	41	15	33	67	48	49	38	52	8	40	60	45	55	42	37	21	49	41	10	45	53	2
50 and older	41	47	12	36	64	52	48	41	54	4	41	59	49	51	46	39	15	50	45	5	53	45	2
Religion																							
Protestant	35	49	16	30	70	46	53	39	54	6	39	61	42	58	41	41	18	44	50	6	42	55	3
Catholic	59	33	8	48	52	57	41	46	47	6	39	61	51	49	47	35	18	55	35	10	52	46	2
Politics																							
Republican	9	86	5	5	95	9	91	8	86	5	4	96	7	93	7	77	16	10	85	5	7	92	1
Democrat	74	12	14	67	33	82	18	69	26	4	79	21	85	15	82	8	10	90	6	4	89	10	2
Independent	31	44	25	31	69	38	57	29	55	14	33	67	43	57	39	30	31	48	33	19	44	49	7
Region																							
East	50	43	7	42	58	51	47	43	47	9	46	54	51	49	47	35	18	60	31	9	55	42	3
Midwest	44	47	9	40	60	48	50	41	51	7	42	58	47	53	44	34	22	46	45	9	48	49	3
South	31	36	33	29	71	54	45	44	52	3	37	63	40	60	38	45	17	44	46	10	45	54	1
West	44	49	7	41	59	46	51	35	54	9	40	60	46	54	45	35	20	51	43	6	48	47	5

D = Democratic candidate; R = Republican candidate; AIP = American Independent Party candidate (George Wallace, 1968); I = Independent candidate (John B. Anderson, 1980; Ross Perot, 1992); P = Reform Party candidate (Ross Perot, 1996); G = Green Party candidate (Ralph Nader, 2000). Figures do not add to 100% in some groups because of rounding and/or minor party votes.   SOURCE: The Gallup Organization.

Interpreting Tables Some groups of voters have favored one or the other major party over time. *In this table, which group most clearly demonstrates that point?*

that voting is an important act. They also are likely to live in those areas where laws, customs, and competition between the parties all promote turnout.

The opposite characteristics produce a profile of those less likely to vote. Nonvoters are likely to be younger than age 35, unmarried, and unskilled. More nonvoters live in the South and in rural, rather than urban or suburban, locales. Today, women are more likely to vote than men. This fact of political life has been apparent since the presidential election of 1988 and was reaffirmed in 2000.

A few of the factors that help determine whether or not a person will vote are so important that they influence turnout even when they are not supported by, or are in conflict with, other factors. Thus, those persons with a high sense of political efficacy are likely to vote—no matter what their income, education, age, race, and so on.

The degree of two-party competition has much the same kind of general, across-the-board effect. It, too, has an extraordinary impact on participation. Thus, the greater the competition between candidates, the more likely people will be to go to the polls, regardless of other factors.

Despite the greater weight of some factors, however, note this point: It is the combined presence of several factors, not the influence of one of them alone, that usually determines whether a person will be a voter or a nonvoter.

Voters and Voting Behavior

As you have just seen, tens of millions of potential voters do not go to the polls in this country. But many millions more do. How do those who do vote behave? What prompts many to vote most often for Republicans and many others to support the Democratic Party?

Answers to these questions are not as hard to find as you might think. Voting has been studied more closely than any other form of political participation in the United States. This is due partly to the importance of the topic and partly to the almost unlimited amount of data available. (There have been innumerable elections in which millions of voters have cast billions of votes over time.)[13] That research has produced a huge amount of information about why people tend to vote as they do.

Studying Voting Behavior

Most of what is known about voter behavior comes from three sources.

1. The results of particular elections. Of course, how individuals vote in a given election is secret in the United States. However, careful study of the returns from areas populated largely by African Americans or Catholics or high-income families will indicate how those groups voted in a given election.

2. The field of survey research. The polling of scientifically determined cross sections of the population is the method by which public opinion is most often identified and measured. The Gallup Organization conducts perhaps the best known of these polls today.

3. Studies of **political socialization.** This is the process by which people gain their political attitudes and opinions. That complex process begins in early childhood and continues through each person's life. Political socialization involves all of the experiences and relationships that lead people to see the political process, and to act in it, as they do.

In the rest of this chapter, you will consider voter behavior—how and why people vote as they do. In Chapter 8, you will look at public opinion, at the techniques of survey research, and the process of political socialization.

Factors That Influence Voters

Observers still have much to learn about voter behavior, but many sociological and psychological factors clearly influence the way people vote. Sociology is the study of groups and how people behave within groups. The sociological factors affecting voter behavior are really the many pieces of a voter's social and economic life. Those pieces are of two broad kinds: (1) a voter's personal characteristics—age, race, income, occupation, education, religion, and so

Comparative Government

Voter Turnout* in Selected Democracies

	Percentage of voters
Austria	
Belize	
Canada	
Denmark	
India	
Malta	
Mexico	
South Africa	
United States	
Venezuela	

(Scale: 0, 25, 50, 75, 100)

*Percentage of registered voters participating in the last national election

SOURCES: International Foundation for Election Systems; Election Commission of India; Instituto Federal Electoral

Interpreting Graphs The right to vote does not ensure that people will vote. Study the graph. ***In which of these nations did more than three-quarters of eligible voters actually vote?***

---

[13]Much of the most useful research on voter behavior is done at academic institutions—most notably the Center for Political Studies at the University of Michigan.

on; and (2) a voter's group affiliations—family, co-workers, friends, and the like.

Psychology is the study of the mind and of individual behavior. The psychological factors that influence voter behavior are a voter's perceptions of politics, that is, how the voter sees the parties, the candidates, and the issues in an election.

The differences between these two kinds of influences are not so great as they might seem. In fact, they are closely related and constantly interact with one another. How voters look at parties, candidates, or issues is often shaped by their own social and economic backgrounds.

Sociological Factors

From the table on page 167, you can draw a composite picture of the American voter in terms of a number of sociological factors. A word of caution here: Do not make too much of any one of these factors. As you examine the data, keep this point in mind: The table reports how voters, identified by a *single* characteristic, voted in each presidential election from 1968 through 2000. Remember, however, that each voter possesses *several* of the characteristics shown in the table.

The point can be illustrated this way: College graduates are more likely to vote Republican. So are persons over 50 years of age. Catholics are more likely to vote for Democrats. So are members of labor unions. How, then, would a 55-year-old, college-educated Catholic who belongs to the AFL-CIO vote?

Income, Occupation

Voters in lower income brackets are more likely to be Democrats. Voters with higher incomes tend to be Republicans. This pattern has held up over time; in fact, it can be seen even in the exceedingly close presidential election of 2000. Voters with incomes below $15,000 a year backed Democrat Al Gore by a 3 to 2 margin; those making between $15,000 and $29,999 gave him a 4 to 3 edge. Those with incomes in the $30,000 to $49,999 range also supported Mr. Gore, but by only a very slight margin.

Voters with higher incomes backed Republican George W. Bush by telling margins. Thus, among voters making more than $100,000 a year, he held a 5 to 4 edge over his opponent.

▲ *Worth the Wait* Blacks in South Africa fought for many years to gain the right to vote. In the first multiracial elections, held in 1994, many people stood in long lines for hours in order to exercise this hard-won right.

Most often, how much one earns and what one does for a living are closely related. Professional and business people, and others with higher incomes, tend to vote for Republican candidates. Manual workers, and others in lower income groups, usually vote for Democrats. Thus, with the single exception of 1964, professional and business people have voted heavily Republican in every presidential election in the modern era, including 2000.

Education

Studies on voter behavior reveal that there is also a close relationship between the level of a voter's education and how he or she votes. College graduates vote for Republicans in higher percentages than do high-school graduates; and high-school graduates vote Republican more often than do those who have only gone through grade school.

Gender, Age

There are measurable differences between the partisan choices of men and women today. This phenomenon is known as the **gender gap,** and it first appeared in the presidential election of 1980. Women generally tend to favor the Democrats by a margin of five to ten percent, and men often give the GOP a similar edge.

A number of studies show that men and women are most likely to vote differently when such issues as abortion, health care or other social welfare matters, or military involvements abroad are prominent in an election. In 2000, 53 percent of all female voters cast their ballots for Democrat Al Gore for President.

Traditionally, younger voters have been more likely to be Democrats than Republicans. Older voters are likely to find the GOP and its candidates more attractive. Thus, in every presidential election from 1960 through 1980, the Democrats won a larger percentage of the votes of the under-30 age group than of the 50-and-over age bracket. That long-standing pattern was broken by Ronald Reagan's appeal to younger voters in 1984, and by George Bush in 1988. However, Bill Clinton restored the Democrats' claim to those voters in 1992 and 1996. In 2000, Al Gore won 47 percent of the under-30 vote, George W. Bush received 47 percent, and most of the balance (6 percent) went to the Green Party's Ralph Nader.

Religious, Ethnic Background

In the North, a majority of Protestants prefer the GOP. Catholics and Jews are much more likely to be Democrats.

Historical factors account for much of this pattern. Most of those who first came from Europe to settle this country were of English stock and Protestant. The later tides of immigration, from southern and eastern Europe, brought many Catholics and Jews to the United States.

Those later immigrants were often greeted with hostility by the largely Protestant establishment. These minority groups settled most often in the larger cities, where local Democratic Party organizations helped them to become citizens and voters. From the New Deal period of the 1930s on, social welfare programs have strengthened the ties of most minority groups to the Democratic Party.[14]

In recent times, nonwhites have supported the Democratic Party consistently and massively. They form the only group that has given the Democratic candidate a clear majority in every presidential election since 1952. There are now more than 34 million African Americans, and they make up the second most important racial minority in the country.

In the North, African Americans generally voted Republican until the 1930s, but then moved away from the party of Abraham Lincoln with the coming of the New Deal. The civil rights movement of the 1960s led to greater African American participation in the South. Today, African Americans vote overwhelmingly Democratic in that region, too.

The United States is now home to more than 35 million Latinos, people with Spanish-speaking backgrounds. Until now, Latinos have tended to favor Democratic candidates. Note, however, that the label "Latino" conceals differences among Cuban Americans, who most often vote Republican, and Mexican Americans and Puerto Ricans, who are strongly Democratic. The rate of turnout among Latinos is comparatively low—33 percent in 2000.

Geography

Geography—the part of the country, the State, and/or the locale in which a person lives—also has an impact on voter behavior. After the Civil War, the States of the old Confederacy voted so consistently Democratic that the southeast quarter of the nation became known as the Solid South. For more than a century, most Southerners, regardless of any other factor, identified with the Democratic Party.

The Solid South is now a thing of the past. Republican candidates have been increasingly successful throughout the region over the past 30 years or so. This has been true in presidential elections and at the State and the local levels, as well. Historically, the States that have supported the Republicans most consistently are Maine and Vermont in the Northeast and Kansas, Nebraska, and the Dakotas in the Midwest.

Voters' attitudes also vary in terms of the size of the communities in which they live. Generally, the Democrats draw strength from the big cities of the North and East. Many white Democrats have moved from the central cities and taken their political preferences with them, but Republican voters still dominate much of suburban America. Voters in smaller cities and rural areas are also likely to be Republicans.

---

[14]In 1960, John F. Kennedy became the first Roman Catholic President. His election marked a sharper split between Catholic and Protestant voters than that found in any of the elections covered by the table on page 167.

Family and Other Groups

To this point, you have seen the American voter sketched in terms of several broad social and economic characteristics. The picture can also be drawn on the basis of much smaller and more personal groupings, especially family, friends, and co-workers.

Typically, the members of a family vote in strikingly similar ways. Nine out of ten married couples share the same partisan leanings. As many as two out of every three voters follow the political attachments of their parents. Those who work together and circles of friends also tend to vote very much alike.

This like-mindedness is hardly surprising. People of similar social and economic backgrounds tend to associate with one another. In short, a person's group associations usually reinforce the opinions he or she already holds.

Psychological Factors

Although they are certainly important, it would be wrong to give too much weight to the sociological factors in the voting mix. For one thing, these factors are fairly static. That is, they tend to change only gradually and over time. To understand voter behavior, you must look beyond such factors as occupation, education, ethnic background, and place of residence. You must also take into account a number of psychological factors. That is, you must look at the voters' *perceptions* of politics: how they see and react to the parties, the candidates, and the issues in an election.

Party Identification

A majority of Americans identify themselves with one or the other of the major parties early in life. Many never change. They support that party, election after election, with little or no regard for either the candidates or the issues.

The hefty impact of **party identification,** or the loyalty of people to a particular political party, is the single most significant and lasting predictor of how a person will vote. A person who is a Democrat or a Republican will, for that reason, very likely vote for all or most of that party's candidates in any given

Voices on Government

Ray Suarez has been a news reporter and correspondent for about 25 years, most recently for *The News Hour with Jim Lehrer.* He has won numerous awards for his stories. In this excerpt, Suarez discusses how city populations and voting patterns are changing.

❝One million Latinos in Chicago and its suburbs, and more than two million each in Los Angeles and New York, force you away from a binary black-white view of the struggles over the city. The new math means that standing between white and black is a new brown interest group waiting to be courted, often holding the balance of power in municipal elections. In Miami, San Antonio, and, increasingly, Dallas, you can't win without Latino support. ❞

Evaluating the Quotation

According to Suarez, how has the ethnic balance in cities been changing? How does this change affect politics?

election. The practice of voting for candidates of only one party in an election is called **straight-ticket voting.**

Party identification is, therefore, a key factor in American politics. Among many other things, it means that each of the major parties can regularly count on the votes of millions of faithful supporters in every election.

Several signs suggest that, while it remains a major factor, party identification has lost some of its impact in recent years. One of those signs is the weakened condition of the parties themselves. Another is the marked increase in **split-ticket voting**—the practice of voting for the candidates of more than one party in an election. That behavior, which began to increase in the 1960s, is fairly common today.

Another telling sign is the large number of voters who now call themselves **independents.** This term is regularly used to identify those people who have no party affiliation. It includes voters who are independent of both the Republicans and the Democrats (and of any minor party, as well). "Independent" is a tricky term, however.[15] Many who claim to be independents actually support one or the other of the major parties quite regularly.

The loose nature of party membership makes it difficult to determine just what proportion of the electorate is independent. The best guesses put the number of independents at somewhere between a fourth and a third of all voters today. The role that these independent voters play is especially critical in those elections where the opposing major party candidates are more or less evenly matched.

Until recently, the typical independent was less concerned, less well informed, and less active in politics than those voters who identified themselves as Republicans or Democrats. That description still fits many independents.

However, a new breed of independent voter appeared in the 1960s and 1970s, and their ranks have grown over the years. Largely because of the political events and personalities of that period, these "new" independents preferred not to join either major party. These independents are often young and above average in education, income, and job status.

---

[15]Note that the term "independent" is sometimes mistakenly used to suggest that independents form a more or less cohesive group that can be readily compared with Republicans and Democrats. (Although the Gallup Poll data on page 142 do not intend such comparisons, they can be misread to that effect.) In short, independents in American politics are not only independent of Republicans and Democrats; each of them is also independent of all other independents.

Candidates and Issues

Party identification is a long-term factor. While most voters identify with one or the other of the major parties and most often support its candidates, they do not always vote that way. One or more short-term factors can cause them to switch sides in a particular election, or at least vote a split ticket. Thus, in 2000, exit polls indicate that 8 percent of those persons who usually vote Republican voted for Al Gore for President, and 11 percent of those who normally support Democratic candidates marked their ballots for George W. Bush.

The most important of these short-term factors are the candidates and the issues in an election. Clearly, the impression a candidate makes on the voters can have an impact on how they vote. What image does a candidate project? How is he or she seen in terms of personality, character, style, appearance, past record, abilities, and so on?

Just as clearly, issues can also have a large impact on voter behavior. The role of issues varies, however, depending on such things as the emotional content of the issues themselves, the voters' awareness of them, and the ways in which they are presented to the electorate.

Issues have become increasingly important to voters over the past 40 years or so. The tumultuous nature of politics over the period—highlighted by the civil rights movement, the Vietnam War, the feminist movement, the Watergate scandal, and economic problems—is likely responsible for this heightened concern.

Section 4 Assessment

Key Terms and Main Ideas

1. How does a person's sense of **political efficacy** affect his or her voting behavior?
2. What is the **gender gap**?
3. How are **party identification** and **straight-ticket voting** related?
4. List three sociological factors that affect voting behavior.

Critical Thinking

5. **Predicting Consequences** What might be the results for the nation if all eligible voters were required to cast ballots? Why?

6. **Formulating Questions** Suppose you are a pollster. List three questions you would ask to determine if someone will vote in the next election, and three questions to find out what party he or she would be likely to support.

Take It to the Net

7. Rock the Vote promotes participation in the political process among 18- to 24-year-olds. Visit their Web site, and make a chart showing which suggestions you think would be effective, which would not, and why. Add suggestions of your own, if you have any. Use the links provided in the Social Studies area at the following Web site for help in completing this activity. **www.phschool.com**

CLOSE UP
FOUNDATION

on the Supreme Court

Who Decides Who May Vote?

The Constitution gives States authority to set voting qualifications. In the past, some States purposely used that power to exclude certain groups—most notably African Americans—from the electoral process. Does Congress have the authority to limit the power of States to set voter qualifications?

Oregon v. *Mitchell* (1970)

In 1970, the States of Oregon, Texas, and Idaho sued the Federal Government (specifically, Attorney General John Mitchell) to challenge four provisions of the Voting Rights Act Amendments passed by Congress that year. One provision lowered the minimum voting age to 18 in all elections in the United States—federal, State, and local. Another barred the use of any literacy test in any election in this country for a five-year period. A third provision prohibits the States from setting residence requirements for voting in presidential elections at more than 30 days. The final provision established national rules for absentee voting in presidential elections. (Absentee voting allows people unable to go to their polling places on election day to receive and mark their ballots, and return them—usually by mail—before or no later than election day.) These provisions were clearly intended to allow more people to participate in the electoral process.

The case was heard by the Supreme Court in its original jurisdiction. (In other words, the case was not appealed to the Court from a lower court.) Fifteen States, though not part of the suit, filed briefs (written arguments) with the Court in the case. The American Civil Liberties Union, the NAACP, the Democratic National Committee, and various other groups also filed briefs.

Arguments for Oregon

1. Only the States have the power to set voting qualifications for State and local elections. Congress has no authority to require the States to allow persons between 18 and 21 to vote in State and local elections.

2. The Constitution does not give Congress the right to require the States to use different qualifications for voting in federal elections than those States adopt for their own elections.

3. States have the authority to set standards for voters, such as a minimum level of literacy or a minimum period of residence in the State.

Arguments for Mitchell

1. Congress may set standards for voter qualifications in federal elections.

2. Congress may prevent the States from excluding certain groups of citizens from the voting rolls for State elections, if the exclusion tends to discriminate against people based on characteristics such as race or national origin. (Such discrimination by States violates the 14th Amendment's Equal Protection Clause.)

3. Congress may prevent States from imposing a residency requirement that makes it impossible for people who have recently moved to vote in presidential elections.

Decide for Yourself

1. Review the constitutional grounds on which each side based its arguments and the specific arguments each side presented.

2. Debate the opposing viewpoints presented in this case. Which viewpoint do you favor?

3. Predict the impact of the Court's decision on changes in voter eligibility and voter participation in the United States. (To read a summary of the Court's decision, turn to the Supreme Court Glossary on page 799.)

Political Dictionary

suffrage (p. 148)

franchise (p. 148)

electorate (p. 148)

transient (p. 153)

registration (p. 154)

purge (p. 155)

poll books (p. 155)

literacy (p. 156)

poll tax (p. 157)

gerrymandering (p. 159)

injunction (p. 161)

preclearance (p. 162)

off-year election (p. 164)

political efficacy (p. 166)

political socialization (p. 168)

gender gap (p. 169)

party identification (p. 171)

straight-ticket voting (p. 171)

split-ticket voting (p. 171)

independent (p. 171)

Practicing the Vocabulary

Using Words in Context *For each of the terms below, write a sentence that shows how it relates to this chapter.*

1. suffrage
2. electorate
3. registration
4. poll tax
5. injunction
6. off-year election
7. political efficacy
8. political socialization
9. straight-ticket voting
10. independents

Fill in the Blank *Choose a term from the list above that best completes the sentence.*

11. Suffrage and _____ mean approximately the same thing.
12. A(n) _____ is a court order that can be used to compel a public official to carry out a law.
13. Some people do not have a sense of _____ and therefore do not bother to vote.
14. Voters with a strong allegiance to a party often engage in _____ when they go to the polls.

Reviewing Main Ideas

Section 1

15. What two long-term trends mark the expansion of the American electorate?
16. What are the five stages of the extension of suffrage?
17. What are the constitutional restrictions on the power of the States to set voting qualifications?

Section 2

18. What are the universal requirements for voting in the United States?
19. For what two reasons did States adopt residence requirements for voting?
20. What is a literacy requirement for voting, and how was it used to deny suffrage to certain groups?
21. What is a grandfather clause, and what was its purpose in literacy tests?
22. How did Congress require States to ease their registration requirements in 1993?

Section 3

23. (a) What was the purpose of the 15th Amendment? (b) List three ways that some southern States tried to circumvent the 15th Amendment.
24. To whom does the Civil Rights Commission report its findings?
25. How did Dr. Martin Luther King, Jr.'s voter registration drive affect the passage of national civil rights legislation?
26. Explain two key provisions of the Voting Rights Act of 1965.

Section 4

27. (a) What is a nonvoting voter? (b) How is this phenomenon related to so-called "ballot fatigue"?
28. Describe three differences between voters and nonvoters.
29. Explain how income, education, and age usually affect party affiliation.
30. Explain how party identification develops, and how it affects the way individuals vote.

Critical Thinking

31. ***Applying the Chapter Skill*** What do you think the consequences would be if voting requirements were eliminated and anyone who wished to could vote in federal, State, and local elections?

32. ***Identifying Central Issues*** What does the record of the expansion of suffrage tell you about trends in the United States from 1789 to the present?

33. ***Demonstrating Reasoned Judgment*** Do you think that resident aliens, those who have summer homes in a town, and other tax-paying transients should be allowed to vote in elections that determine how their taxes will be spent? Explain the reasons for your answer.

34. ***Testing Conclusions*** Some people suggest that we should not try to increase voter turnout in this country because that would only encourage uninformed voting and result in bad choices made for the wrong reasons. Do you agree or disagree? Why?

Analyzing Political Cartoons

Use your knowledge of American history and government and this cartoon to answer the questions below.

35. Many factors affect voter behavior. At which factor is the cartoonist poking fun?

36. What do you think the cartoonist thinks of the way the American electorate chooses its leaders today versus 150 years ago?

★ You Can Make a Difference

Chances are that many of your 18-year-old friends and classmates have not registered to vote. You and your classmates can help other teens make a difference in the political process. Since laws vary from State to State, start by asking your local election officials how and where one registers to vote in your community. Take a poll of students to see how many have already registered. Then, working with school administrators, plan a voter registration drive, using posters and press releases to publicize your campaign.

Participation Activities

37. ***Current Events Watch*** There are still places in the world where people are struggling to achieve the right to choose the leaders who govern them. Select one such country, and read about recent efforts to gain or expand suffrage there. Write a brief report on the struggle. Conclude by predicting whether and/or when the struggle for suffrage will succeed.

38. ***Time Line Activity*** Using information from the chapter, make a time line of the federal laws (including constitutional amendments) that were designed to ensure the suffrage of African Americans. Which, in your opinion, was the most important law? Why?

39. ***It's Your Turn*** You have been hired to increase voter turnout in local elections in your community. Review the causes for low voter turnout and determine how they might apply to various groups in your community. Prepare a proposal to the election committee. Describe three tactics you would use to increase local voter turnout and explain why they might work. **(Writing a Proposal)**

Take It to the Net

Chapter 6 Self-Test As a final review activity, take the Chapter 6 Self-Test in the Social Studies area at the Web site listed below, and receive immediate feedback on your answers.

www.phschool.com

CHAPTER 7

The Electoral Process

"*Any American who cannot bother to vote and who thinks that a single vote does not matter is letting America down.*"
—Marian Wright Edelman (1992)

Democracy relies on the willingness of the people to participate—and to participate intelligently—in every aspect of the electoral process.

◆ **Presidential national convention delegates**

★ *You Can Make a Difference*

ELECTION CAMPAIGNS TODAY spend millions of dollars on advertising designed to sway voters. Groups such as Project Vote Smart try to offset this advertising by distributing unbiased, non-partisan information. Students in the National Internship Program of Project Vote Smart learn to research candidates and issues, write press releases, track legislation, and maintain the group's Web site. Interns also do the day-to-day work of political organizing, from answering phones to stuffing envelopes. They work at the project's headquarters in Montana or its office at Northeastern University in Boston, Massachusetts.

SECTION 1

The Nominating Process (pp.178–186)

★ The nominating process is critically important to democratic government.
★ Five major nominating methods are used in American politics.
★ The most widely used nominating method today is the direct primary.

SECTION 2

Elections (pp.188–194)

★ The election process is regulated mostly by State law.
★ Voting takes place in local precincts and polling places, although early voting is becoming increasingly common.
★ Every State now uses the Australian ballot, which is of either the party-column or the office-group type.
★ Voting machines and electronic vote-counting systems are in wide use throughout the United States.

SECTION 3

Money and Elections (pp.196–202)

★ Money plays a key role in politics but presents serious problems to democratic governments.
★ Most campaign money comes from private sources, including political action committees (PACs).
★ Federal campaign laws are administered by the Federal Election Commission (FEC).
★ Loopholes in campaign finance laws allow candidates and contributors to avoid some regulations.

Keep It Current

Items marked with this logo are periodically updated on the Internet. Keep up-to-date with what's in the news. To get current information on the electoral process, go to **www.phschool.com**

The Nominating Process

Section Preview

OBJECTIVES

1. **Explain** why the nominating process is a critical first step in the election process.
2. **Describe** self-announcement, the caucus, and the convention as nominating methods.
3. **Discuss** the direct primary as the principal nominating method used in the United States today.
4. **Understand** why some candidates use the petition as a nominating device.

WHY IT MATTERS

The nominating process narrows the field of possible candidates for office. It is thus an essential part of an election. The caucus and convention were important nominating methods in the past. The direct primary has largely replaced them. Self-announcement and petitions are also used today as nominating devices.

POLITICAL DICTIONARY

★ **nomination**
★ **general election**
★ **caucus**
★ **direct primary**
★ **closed primary**
★ **open primary**
★ **blanket primary**
★ **runoff primary**
★ **nonpartisan election**

Suppose your teacher stood in front of the class and said: "Here's a $1,000 bill. Who'd like to have it?" You, and everyone else in the room, would promptly say, or at least think: "Me!" Suppose the teacher then said: "Okay, we'll hold an election. The person who wins the most votes gets the money."

What would happen? If the election were held immediately, it is likely that each member of the class would vote for himself or herself. A few might vote for a friend. Almost certainly, however, the election would end in a tie. No one would win the money.

But suppose the teacher said: "We'll hold the election tomorrow." What do you think would happen then? As you think about the answer to that question, you begin to get a sense of the practical importance of the nominating process—the first step in the process of electing candidates to office.

A Critical First Step

The nominating process is the process of candidate selection. **Nomination**—the naming of those who will seek office—is a critically important step in the election process.

You have already seen two major illustrations of the significance of the nomination process. In Chapter 5, you read about the making of nominations (1) as a prime function of political parties in the United States, and (2) as a leading reason for the decentralized character of the two major parties.

The nominating process also has a very real impact on the exercise of the right to vote. In the typical election in this country, voters can make only one of two choices for each office on the ballot. They can vote for the Republican or they can vote for the Democratic candidate.[1]

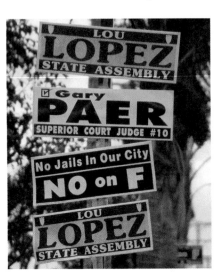

► Campaign signs urging voters to support particular candidates appear in towns and cities across the country before elections.

---

[1]Other choices are sometimes listed, of course—minor party or independent nominees. These are not often meaningful alternatives, however; most voters choose not to "waste" their votes on candidates who cannot win. Also, nonpartisan elections are an exception to this statement since candidates are not identified by party labels.

George Wallace
Four-time Democratic governor of Alabama, Wallace won 13% of the popular vote in 1968 as the populist candidate of the newly formed American Independent Party.

Eugene McCarthy
A representative and senator from Minnesota (1949–1971), McCarthy sought the Democratic nomination for President in 1968 as a critic of the Vietnam War. He ran in 1976 as an independent, winning 0.9% of the popular vote.

John Anderson
A Republican representative from Illinois (1961–1981), Anderson ran for President as an independent in 1980, winning 6.7% of the popular vote.

Ross Perot
Business executive and billionaire Ross Perot ran as an independent for President in 1992, winning 19% of the popular vote. (In 1996, Perot received 8% of the popular vote as the Reform Party nominee.)

Interpreting Charts These presidential candidates made use of self-announcement as a nominating device. *(a) Why do some candidates choose self-announcement as a method for getting on the ballot? (b) How might a self-announced candidate affect the ultimate outcome of an election?*

This is another way of saying that we have a two-party system in the United States. It is also another way to say that the nominating stage is a critically important part of the electoral process. Those who make nominations place real, very practical limits on the choices that voters can make in an election.

In one-party constituencies (those areas where one party regularly wins elections), the nominating process is usually the only point at which there is any real contest for a public office. Once the dominant party has made its nomination, the general election is little more than a formality.

Dictatorial regimes point up the importance of the nominating process. Many of them hold **general elections**—regularly scheduled elections at which voters make the final selection of officeholders—much as democracies do. But typically, the ballots used in those elections list only one candiate for each office—the candidate of the ruling clique; and those candidates regularly win with majorities approaching 100 percent.

There are five ways in which nominations are made in the United States. They include (1) self-announcement, (2) caucus, (3) convention, (4) direct primary, and (5) petition.

Self-Announcement

Self-announcement is the oldest form of the nominating process in American politics. First used in colonial times, it is still often found at the small-town and rural levels in many parts of the country.

The method is quite simple. A person who wants to run for office simply announces that fact. Modesty or local custom may dictate that someone else make the candidate's announcement, but, still, the process amounts to the same thing.

Self-announcement is sometimes used by someone who failed to win a regular party nomination or by someone unhappy with the party's choice. Note that whenever a write-in candidate appears in an election, the self-announcement process has been used. In recent history, four prominent presidential contenders have made

Nominating and Electing a Candidate

Ways to Nominate a Candidate

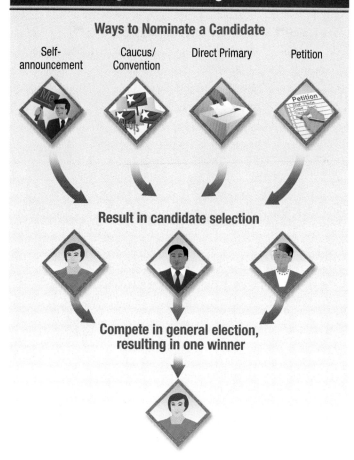

Self-announcement | Caucus/Convention | Direct Primary | Petition

Result in candidate selection

Compete in general election, resulting in one winner

Interpreting Diagrams Nomination is a critical step in the election process because it narrows the field of candidates. In the general election, voters chose from this small field of candidates to select a single winner. **Why is it important for voters to participate in the nominating process?**

use of the process: George Wallace, who declared himself to be the American Independent Party's nominee in 1968; and independent candidates Eugene McCarthy in 1976; John Anderson in 1980; and Ross Perot in 1992.

The Caucus

As a nominating device, a **caucus** is a group of like-minded people who meet to select the candidates they will support in an upcoming election. The first caucus nominations were made toward the end of the colonial period, probably in Boston in the mid-1720s.[2] One of the earliest descriptions of a caucus can be found in John Adams's diary, in an entry he made in February 1763:

 PRIMARY Sources

"This day learned that the Caucus Club meets at certain Times in the Garret of Tom Dawes, the Adjutant of the Boston Regiment. He has a large House, and he has a moveable Partition in his Garret, which he takes down, and the whole Club meets in one Room. There they smoke tobacco till you cannot see from one End of the Garret to the other. There they drink flip I suppose, and they choose a Moderator, who puts Questions to the Vote regularly, and select Men, Assessors, Collectors, Wardens, Fire Wards, and Representatives are Regularly chosen before they are chosen in the Town."

—Charles Francis Adams (ed.), *The Works of John Adams* (1856)

Originally the caucus was a private meeting consisting of a few influential figures in the community. As political parties appeared in the late 1700s, they soon took over the device and began to broaden the membership of the caucus.

The coming of independence brought the need to nominate candidates for State offices: governor, lieutenant governor, and others above the local level. The legislative caucus—a meeting of a party's members in the State legislature—took on the job. At the national level, both the Federalists and the Democratic-Republicans in Congress were, by 1800, choosing their presidential and vice-presidential candidates through the congressional caucus.

The legislative and congressional caucuses were quite practical in their day. Transportation and communication were difficult at best. Since legislators already gathered regularly in a central place, it made sense for them to take on the nominating responsibility. The spread of democracy, especially in the newer States on the frontier, spurred opposition to caucuses, however. More and more, people condemned them for their closed, unrepresentative character.

Criticism of the caucus reached its peak in the early 1820s. The supporters of three of the

[2]The origin of the term *caucus* is not clear. Most authorities suggest that it comes from the word *caulkers,* because the Boston Caucus Club met at times in a room formerly used as a meeting place by caulkers in Boston's shipyards. (Caulkers made ships watertight by filling seams or cracks in the hulls of sailing vessels with tar or oakum.)

leading contenders for the presidency in 1824—Andrew Jackson, Henry Clay, and John Quincy Adams—boycotted the DemocraticRepublicans' congressional caucus that year. In fact, Jackson and his supporters made "King Caucus" a leading campaign issue. The other major aspirant, William H. Crawford of Georgia, became the caucus nominee at a meeting attended by fewer than one third of the Democratic-Republican Party's members in Congress.

Crawford ran a poor third in the electoral college balloting in 1824, and the reign of King Caucus at the national level was ended. With its death in presidential politics, the caucus system soon withered at the State and local levels, as well.

The caucus is still used to make local nominations in some places, especially in New England. There, a caucus is open to all members of a party, and it only faintly resembles the original closed and private process.

The Convention

As the caucus method collapsed, the convention system took its place. The first national convention to nominate a presidential candidate was held by a minor party, the Anti-Masons, in Baltimore in 1831. The newly formed National Republican (soon to become Whig) Party also held a convention later that same year. The Democrats picked up the practice in 1832. All major-party presidential nominees have been chosen by conventions ever since. By the 1840s, conventions had become the principal means for making nominations at every level in American politics.

On paper, the convention process seems perfectly suited to representative government. A party's members meet in a local caucus to pick candidates for local offices and, at the same time, to select delegates to represent them at a county convention.[3]

At the county convention, the delegates nominate candidates for county offices and select delegates to the next rung on the convention ladder, usually the State convention. There, the delegates from the county conventions pick the party's nominees for governor and other State-wide offices. State conventions also send delegates to the party's national convention, where the party selects its presidential and vice-presidential candidates.

In theory, the will of the party's rank and file membership is passed up through each of its representative levels. Practice soon pointed up the weaknesses of the theory, however, as party bosses found ways to manipulate the process. By playing with the selection of delegates, usually at the local levels, they soon dominated the entire system.

As a result, the caliber of most conventions declined at all levels, especially during the late 1800s. How low some of them fell can be seen in this description of a Cook County, Illinois, convention in 1896:

PRIMARY Sources *"Of [723] delegates, those who had been on trial for murder numbered 17; sentenced to the penitentiary for murder or manslaughter and served sentence, 7; served terms in the penitentiary for burglary, 36; served terms in the penitentiary for picking pockets, 2; served*

◄ *Campaign Ribbons* These precursors of today's political buttons were widely used in the 1840s to 1890s.

---

[3]The meetings at which delegates to local conventions are chosen are still often called *caucuses*. Earlier, they were also known as primaries—that is, first meetings. The use of that name gave rise to the term *direct primary*, to distinguish that newer nominating method from the convention process.

terms in the penitentiary for arson, 1; . . . jailbirds identified by detectives, 84; keepers of gambling houses, 7; keepers of houses of ill-fame, 2; convicted of mayhem, 3; ex-prize fighters, 11; poolroom proprietors, 2; saloon keepers, 265; . . . political employees, 148; no occupation, 71; . . . **"**

—R.M. Easley, "The Sine qua Non of Caucus Reform," *Review of Reviews* (Sept. 1897)

Many people had hailed the change from caucus to convention as a major change for the better in American politics. The abuses of the new device soon dashed their hopes. By the 1870s, the convention system was itself under attack as a major source of evil in American politics. By the 1910s, the direct primary had replaced the convention in most States as the principal nominating method in American politics.[4]

The Direct Primary

A **direct primary** is an intra-party election. It is held within a party to pick that party's candidates for the general election. Wisconsin adopted the first State-wide direct primary law in 1903; several other States soon followed its lead. Every State now makes at least some provision for its use.

---

[4]The few States that still use the convention include Connecticut, Michigan, Utah, and Virginia. In those States the convention system is closely regulated by State law. No adequate substitute has yet been found at the presidential level, however.

In most States, State law requires that the major parties use the primary to choose their candidates for the United States Senate and House of Representatives, for the governorship and all other State offices, and for most local offices as well. In a few States, however, different combinations of convention and primary are used to pick candidates for the top offices.

In Michigan, for example, the major parties choose their candidates for the U.S. Senate and House, the governorship, and the State legislature in primaries. Nominees for lieutenant governor, secretary of state, and attorney general are picked by conventions.[5]

Although the primaries are party-nominating elections, they are closely regulated by law in most States. The State usually sets the dates on which primaries are held, and it regularly conducts them, too. The State, not the parties, provides polling places and election officials, registration lists and ballots, and otherwise polices the process.

Two basic forms of the direct primary are in use today: (1) the closed primary and (2) the open primary. The major difference between the two lies in the answer to this question: Who can vote in a party's primary—only qualified voters who are party members, or *any* qualified voter?

The Closed Primary

Twenty-six States and the District of Columbia use the **closed primary.** A closed primary is a party nominating election in which only declared party members can vote.[6]

In most of the closed primary States, party membership is established by registration. (See Chapter 6.) When voters appear at the polling places on primary election day, their names are

Interpreting Political Cartoons What aspect of primary campaigning does this cartoon suggest?

"MY FORMER OPPONENT IS SUPPORTING ME IN THE GENERAL ELECTION. PLEASE DISREGARD ALL THE THINGS I HAVE SAID ABOUT HIM IN THE PRIMARY."

---

[5]In most States, minor parties are required to make their nominations by other, more difficult processes, usually in conventions or by petition. For the significance of this point, see Chapter 5.

[6]The Supreme Court has held that a State's closed primary law cannot forbid a party to allow independent voters to participate in its primary if the party itself chooses to do so. In *Tashjian* v. *Republican Party of Connecticut*, 1986, the Court struck down such a State law. Note that the Court did not outlaw the closed primary in this case, nor did it hold that a political party *must* allow Independents to vote in its primary. The Court found that the Connecticut law violated the 1st and 14th amendment guarantees of the right of association—here the right of Connecticut Republicans to associate with Independents (invite Independents to join them) in making GOP nominations.

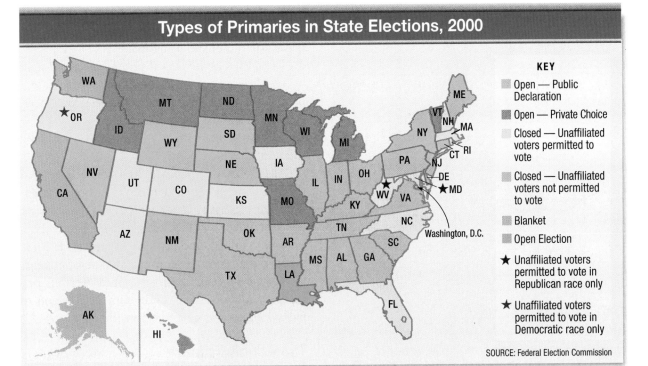

Types of Primaries in State Elections, 2000

KEY
- Open — Public Declaration
- Open — Private Choice
- Closed — Unaffiliated voters permitted to vote
- Closed — Unaffiliated voters not permitted to vote
- Blanket
- Open Election
- ★ Unaffiliated voters permitted to vote in Republican race only
- ★ Unaffiliated voters permitted to vote in Democratic race only

SOURCE: Federal Election Commission

Interpreting Maps This map shows the types of primaries held in each State for State elections. In 2000, California, Alaska, and Washington used a blanket primary. As a result of the Court's decision in *California* v. *Jones,* these States will likely use a different form of the primary in future elections, however. ***What type of primary is used in your State?***

checked against the poll books—the lists of registered voters for each precinct. Each voter is then handed the ballot of the party in which he or she is registered. That voter may mark *only* that party's ballot—that is, he or she may vote only in that party's primary.

The Open Primary

The **open primary** is a party nominating election in which *any* qualified voter can take part. Although it is the form in which the direct primary first appeared, the open primary is now found in only 24 States, as you can see on the map above.

When voters go to their polling places in some open primary States, they are handed the ballots of each of the parties holding a primary election. Voters then pick the party primary in which they wish to participate in the privacy of the voting booth. In other open primary States, voters must ask for the ballot of the party in whose primary they want to participate. That is, voters must make a *public*, not a private, choice of party before they enter the voting booth.

Through 2000, three States used a different version of the open primary—the **blanket primary,** sometimes called the "wide-open primary." Washington adopted the first blanket primary law in 1935. Alaska followed suit in 1970, and California did so in 1996. In those three States, every voter received the same primary ballot—a long one containing the names of all contenders, regardless of party, for each nomination to be made at the primary election. Voters could participate in the primary however they chose. They could confine themselves to one party's primary by voting to nominate only Democratic candidates or, instead, only Republican candidates. Or they could switch back and forth between the parties' primaries, voting to nominate a Democrat for one office, a Republican for another, and so on down the ballot.

The Supreme Court ruled against the blanket primary in 2000, however. In *Democratic Party of California* v. *Jones,* it found that the blanket primary process violated the 1st Amendment's guarantee of the right of association. The Court held that a State cannot force a political party to associate with outsiders—that is, with members of other parties or with independent voters—when it picks its candidates for public office. "In no area is the party's right to exclude

Voter Turnout in Statewide Primaries

Percentage of eligible voters (y-axis: 0 to 100)
Year (x-axis: 1964, 1968, 1972, 1976, 1980, 1984, 1988, 1992, 1996, 2000)

SOURCE: Committee for the Study of the American Electorate

Interpreting Graphs This graph shows the percentage of eligible voters who cast ballots in Statewide primaries from 1964 to 2000. **(a) What does this chart suggest about voter interest in these elections? (b) Why do you think primary turnout is greater in presidential years than it is in off-years?**

more important," said the Court, "than in the process of selecting its nominees."

Louisiana has yet another form of the open primary, which was not affected by the Court's decision in *Jones*. Its unique "open-election law" provides for what amounts to a combination primary and election. The names of all the people who seek nominations are listed by office on a single primary ballot. A contender who wins more than 50 percent of the primary votes wins the office. In these cases, the primary becomes the election. In contests where there is no majority winner, the two top vote-getters, regardless of party, face off in the general election.

Closed vs. Open Primary
The two basic forms of the primary have caused arguments for decades. Those who favor the closed primary regularly make three arguments in support of it:

1. It prevents one party from "raiding" the other's primary in the hope of nominating weaker candidates in the other party.

2. It helps make candidates more responsive to the party, its platform, and its members.

3. It helps make voters more thoughtful, because they must choose between the parties in order to vote in the primaries.

The critics of the closed primary contend that:

1. It compromises the secrecy of the ballot, because it forces voters to make their party preferences known in public, and

2. It tends to exclude independent voters from the nomination process. [7]

Advocates of the open primary believe that their system of nominating addresses both of these criticisms. In many open primaries, (1) voters are not forced to make their party preferences known in public, and (2) the tendency to exclude independent voters is eliminated. The opponents of the open primary insist that it (1) permits primary "raiding" and (2) undercuts the concepts of party loyalty and party responsibility.

The Runoff Primary
In most States, candidates need to win only a plurality of the votes cast in the primary to win their party's nomination.[8] (A plurality is the greatest number of votes won by any candidate, whether a majority or not.) In ten States,[9] however, an absolute majority is needed to carry a primary. If no one wins a majority in a race, a **runoff primary** is held a few weeks later. In the runoff primary, the two top vote-getters in the first party primary face one another, and the winner of that vote becomes the nominee.

The Nonpartisan Primary
In most States all or nearly all of the elected school and municipal offices are filled in **nonpartisan elections.** These are elections in which candidates are not identified by party labels. About half of all State judges are chosen on nonpartisan

---

[7]See the discussion of *Tashjian* v. *Republican Party of Connecticut*, 1986, in footnote 6. The closed primary States have now amended their primary laws to comply with that decision.

[8]In Iowa, if no candidate wins at least 35 percent of the votes in a primary, the party must then nominate its candidate for that office by convention. In South Dakota, if no one who seeks a party's nomination for governor, U.S. senator, or U.S. representative wins at least 35 percent, the party's candidate for that office must be picked in a runoff primary two weeks later. In North Carolina a runoff is held when no candidate wins 40 percent of the primary vote.

[9]Alabama, Arizona, Arkansas, Florida, Georgia, Mississippi, Oklahoma, South Carolina, Texas—and Louisiana under its unique "open election" law.

ballots, as well. The nomination of candidates for these offices takes place on a nonpartisan basis, too, often in nonpartisan primaries.

Typically, a contender who wins a clear majority in a nonpartisan primary then runs unopposed in the general election, subject only to write-in opposition. In many States, however, a candidate who wins a majority in the primary is declared elected at that point. If there is no majority winner, the names of the two top contenders are placed on the general election ballot.

The direct primary first appeared as a partisan nominating device. Many people have long argued that it is not well suited for use in nonpartisan elections. Instead, they favor the petition method, which you will read about later in this section.

Evaluation of the Primary

A number of criticisms have been leveled at the primary process. For example, in States that have a closed primary, many voters resent having to declare their party preferences. In those States where the typical open primary is used, many people are upset because they cannot express their choices for nominations in more than one party.[10] Many voters are also annoyed by the "bedsheet" ballot—that is, the long list of candidates that typically appears on the primary ballot. They fail to understand that the use of the primary almost automatically means a long ballot. These factors, combined with a lack of appreciation for the importance of primaries, results in this fact: Voter turnout in the primary elections in most States is usually less than half of that in general elections.

As a further criticism, when two or more candidates seek the same nomination, primary campaigns can be quite expensive. The fact that successful contenders for the nomination must mount—and find the money for—yet another campaign for the general election adds to the money problems that so many

candidates face. It is unfortunately true that the financial facts of political life in the United States mean that some well-qualified people do not seek public office simply because they cannot muster the necessary funds.

The nominating process, whatever its form, can also have a very divisive effect on a party. Remember, the process takes place *within* a party. Because primaries are so public in nature, the direct primary magnifies the potential for division within the party. A bitter contest in the primaries can so wound and divide a party that it cannot recover in time to present a united front for the general election. Many a primary fight has cost a party an election.

Finally, because many voters are uninformed, the primary places a premium on name familiarity. That is, it often gives an edge to a contender who has a well-known name or a name that sounds like that of a well-known person. This occurs even though name familiarity in and of itself has little or nothing to do with a candidate's qualifications.

Obviously, the primary is not without its problems, nor is any other nominating device. Still, it does give a party's members the opportunity to participate at the very core of the political process.

---

[10]Remember that the direct primary came to American politics in the early 1900s as a reaction to the boss-dominated and often corrupt convention system of nominating candidates. The direct primary was intended to take the nominating function away from the party organization and put it in the hands of the party's membership. These conflicts and how they developed make it easier to understand the importance of how the nominating function is managed today.

Interpreting Political Cartoons *What aspect of the primary process does this cartoon critique?*

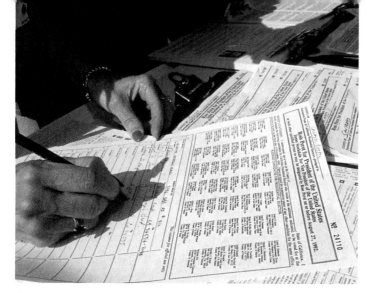

▲ *Getting on the Ballot* Petitions are widely used as nominating devices, particularly in nonpartisan elections at the local level.

The Presidential Primary

The presidential primary developed as an offshoot of the direct primary. It is not a nominating device, however. Rather, the presidential primary is an election that is held as one part of the process by which presidential candidates are chosen.

The presidential primary is a very complex process. It is one or both of two things, depending on the State involved. It is a process in which a party's voters elect some or all of a State party organization's delegates to that party's national convention; and/or it is a preference election in which voters can choose (vote their preference) among various contenders for a party's presidential nomination. Much of what happens in presidential politics in the early months of every fourth year centers on this very complicated process. (See Chapter 13 for an extended discussion of the presidential primary.)

Petition

One other nominating method is used fairly widely at the local level in American politics today—nomination by petition. Where this process is used, candidates for public office are nominated by means of petitions signed by a certain required number of qualified voters in the election district.[11]

Nomination by petition is found most widely at the local level, chiefly for nonpartisan school posts and municipal offices in medium-sized and smaller communities. It is also the process usually required by State law for nominating minor party and independent candidates. (Remember, the States often purposely make the process of getting on the ballot difficult for those candidates.)

The details of the petition process vary widely from State to State, and even from one city to the next. Usually, however, the higher the office and/or the larger the constituency represented by the office, the greater the number of signatures needed for nomination.

---

[11]The petition device is also an important part of the recall and the initiative and referendum processes; see Chapter 24.

Section 1 Assessment

Key Terms and Main Ideas

1. For what reasons is the making of **nominations** so important in the electoral process?
2. Explain the difference between a **closed primary** and an **open primary.**
3. What is a **nonpartisan election**?
4. What is a **caucus,** and what events led to its demise as a method for nominating candidates?

Critical Thinking

5. **Making Decisions** You read in this section that voter turnout in primaries is usually less than half of what it is in general elections. What steps could you take in your community to increase voter turnout in primary elections?
6. **Identifying Central Issues** Explain why the nominating process is a vital first step in the electoral process.

 Take It to the Net

7. Read about the history of primaries and how they function. Then suppose you are a campaign manager, and create a list of the five most important considerations your candidate should keep in mind during the primaries. Use the links provided in the Social Studies area at the following Web site for help in completing this activity. **www.phschool.com**

Establishing Primary Elections

In a 1901 speech to the Wisconsin legislature, Governor Robert La Follette called for an end to caucus and convention nominations and for the nomination of each party's candidates directly by the voters. Shortly thereafter, Wisconsin became the first State to establish Statewide primary elections.

Governor Robert La Follette
1855–1925

It is a fundamental principle of this republic that each citizen should have equal voice in government. This is recognized and guaranteed to him through the ballot. . . . Since government, with us, is conducted by the representatives of some political party, the citizen's voice in making and administering the laws is expressed through his party ballot. This privilege is vital. . . . It is here government begins. . . . Control lost at this point is never regained. . . .

For many years the evils of the caucus and convention system have multiplied. . . . The system in all its details is inherently bad. It not only favors, but . . . produces manipulation, scheming, trickery, fraud and corruption. The delegate elected in caucus is nominally [supposedly] the agent of the voter to act for him in convention. Too frequently . . . he acts not for the voter, but serves his own purpose instead. This fact in itself taints the trust from the outset, and poisons the system at its very source. No legitimate business could survive under a system where authority to transact its vital matters were delegated and re-delegated to agents and sub-agents, who controlled their own selection . . . and were responsible to nobody. . . .

The officials nominated by the [party] machine become its faithful servants and surrender judgment to its will. This they must do in self-preservation or they are retired to public life. Wielding a power substantially independent of the voter, it is quite unnecessary to regard him as an important factor in government . . . .

It is of primary importance that the public official should hold himself directly accountable to the citizen. This he will do only when he owes his nomination directly to the citizen. If between the citizen and the official there is a complicated system of caucuses and conventions, by the easy manipulation of which the selection of candidates is controlled by some other agency or power, then the official will so render his services as to have the approval of such agency or power. The overwhelming demand of the people of this state, whom you represent, is that such intervening power and authority, and the complicated system which sustains it, shall be torn down and cast aside. . . .

Analyzing Primary Sources

1. Why did La Follette think that an elected official selected by convention will be more loyal to party bosses than to the voters?
2. According to La Follette, how would primaries make officials more accountable to the people?
3. What argument did La Follette use to show that primary elections are the foundation of government in a republic?

Elections

Section Preview

OBJECTIVES

1. **Analyze** how the administration of elections in the United States helps make democracy work.
2. **Define** the role of precincts and polling places in the election process.
3. **Describe** the various ways in which voters can cast their ballots.
4. **Outline** the role that voting machines and other innovations play in the election process.

WHY IT MATTERS

The election process lies at the very heart of the democratic concept. Indeed, it is impossible to picture a democratic government in which popular elections are not held.

POLITICAL DICTIONARY

★ absentee voting
★ coattail effect
★ precinct
★ polling place
★ ballot

Many high school students are not old enough to vote. In some parts of the country, however, high school students can serve on local election boards. First in Hawaii and Oregon and now in several States, 16- and 17-year-olds can become full-fledged members of the panels that administer elections.

Americans hold more elections and vote more often than most people realize. Indeed, Sundays and holidays are about the only days of the year on which people do not go to the polls somewhere in the United States. Americans also elect far more officeholders than most people realize—in fact, more than 500,000 of them.

▲ **Election Observers** In many parts of the world, election observers are needed to ensure that elections are free and fair. Here former President Jimmy Carter observes an election in Haiti.

Obviously, the election of public officials is very serious business. In this section, you will read about the federal and State laws that seek to ensure the integrity of this vital process.

The Administration of Elections

English novelist H. G. Wells once called elections democracy's "feast, its great function." Democratic government cannot succeed, however, unless elections are free, honest, and accurate. Many people look at the details of the election process as too complicated, too legalistic, too dry and boring to worry about. Those people miss the vital part such details play in making democracy work. Recall, you saw how important the details of election law can be when you looked at voter qualifications and voter registration in the last chapter and again just a few pages ago when you considered the complexities of the direct primary.

Extent of Federal Control

Nearly all elections in the United States are held to choose people to fill offices at the State and local levels. Given this fact, it is quite understandable that most election law in the United States is State law.

Despite this fact, a body of federal election law does exist. The Constitution gives Congress the power to fix "[t]he Times, Places, and Manner of holding Elections" of members of

Congress.[12] Congress also has the power to set the time for choosing presidential electors, to set the date for casting electoral votes, and to regulate other aspects of the presidential election process.[13]

Congress has set the date for holding congressional elections as the first Tuesday following the first Monday in November of every even-numbered year. It has set the same date every fourth year for the presidential election.[14] Thus, the next (off-year) congressional elections will be held on November 5, 2002. The next presidential election will fall on November 2, 2004.

Congress has required the use of secret ballots and allowed the use of voting machines in federal elections. It has passed several laws to protect the right to vote in all elections. Congress has also prohibited various corrupt practices and regulated the financing of campaigns for federal office.

State law deals with all other matters relating to national elections. State law also covers all of the details involved in choosing the thousands of State and local officials.

When Elections Are Held

Most States hold their elections to fill State offices on the same date Congress has set for national elections: in November of every even-numbered year. The "Tuesday-after-the-first-Monday" formula prevents election day from falling on Sundays (to maintain the principle of separation of church and state). This formula also prevents election day from falling on the first day of the month, which is often payday and therefore potentially subject to campaign pressures.

Some States do fix other dates for some offices, however. Louisiana, Mississippi, New Jersey, and Virginia elect the governor, other executive officers, and State legislators in November of the odd-numbered year. City, county, and other local election dates vary from State to State. When those elections are not held in November, they generally take place in the spring.

---

[12]Article I, Section 4, Clause 1; 17th Amendment; see pages 276 and 277.

[13]Article II, Section 1, Clause 4; 12th Amendment; see pages 378 and 379.

[14]Congress has made an exception for Alaska. Because of the possibility of severe weather in much of Alaska in early November, that State may, if it chooses, elect its congressional delegation and cast its presidential vote in October. So far, however, Alaska has used the November date.

Voices on Government

Senator Maria Cantwell (D., Washington) was elected to the United States Senate in 2000 after a campaign in which she pledged to travel to every State in the Union and to forego money from special interests. During Senate debate over the McCain-Feingold campaign finance reform legislation, Cantwell had this to say about the election process.

❝ *The only way we have to truly level the playing field, both between candidates and parties of opposing ideologies, and more importantly, between new candidates and incumbents, is to commit the resources to the process of getting people elected. Not until we create a campaign system with a shorter and more intensive campaign period—something I think the public would truly applaud—funded with finite and equal resources available to all candidates, will we be able to really listen carefully to what the people want.* ❞

Evaluating the Quotation

What advantages and disadvantages are there—for both voters and candidates—of "a shorter and more intensive campaign period . . . funded with finite and equal resources available to all candidates"?

Early Voting

Most States make provision for **absentee voting,** or voting by those unable to get to their regular polling places on election day. Absentee voting laws usually cover three groups of potential voters: (1) those too ill or disabled to make it to their polling places; (2) those who expect to be away from home on election day (on a business trip, away at college, or on vacation, for example); and (3) those serving in the armed forces. Voters can apply for an absentee ballot within a specified period before an election. They then mark that ballot, seal it, and return it to the proper local election official.

Another form of early voting has spread among the States in recent years. In an effort to make voting more convenient and increase voter turnout, a third of the States now allow voters to cast ballots over a period of several days before an election—not as absentee ballots, but as though they were voting on election day itself. Texas has the most liberal of these early voting laws. There, any registered voter can cast his or her ballot up to 17 days before any primary or general election.

The Coattail Effect

The **coattail effect** occurs when a strong candidate running for an office at the top of the ballot helps attract voters to other candidates on the party's ticket. In effect, the lesser-known office seekers "ride the coattails" of the more prestigious personalities. In 1980 and 1984, for example, Ronald Reagan's coattails helped many Republican candidates win office. The coattail effect is usually most apparent in presidential elections. However, a popular candidate for senator or governor can have the same kind of pulling power.

A reverse coattail effect can occur, too. This happens when a candidate for high office is less than popular with many voters—for example, Barry Goldwater as the Republican presidential nominee in 1964, and George McGovern for the Democrats in 1972. President Carter's coattails were also of the reverse variety in 1980.

Some people argue that all State and local elections should be held on dates other than those set for federal elections. This, they say, would help voters pay more attention to State and local candidates and issues. At the same time, it would lessen the coattail effects of presidential contests.

Precincts and Polling Places

A **precinct** is a voting district. Precincts are the smallest geographic units for conducting elections. State law regularly restricts their size, generally to an area with no more than 500 to 1,000 or so qualified voters. A **polling place**—the place where the voters who live in a precinct actually vote—is located somewhere in or near each precinct.

A precinct election board supervises the polling place and the voting process in each precinct. Typically, the county clerk or county board of elections draws precinct lines, fixes the location of each polling place, and picks the members of the precinct boards.

The precinct board opens and closes the polls at the times set by State law. In most States, the polls are open from 7:00 or 8:00 A.M. to 7:00 or 8:00 P.M. The precinct election board must also see that the ballots and the ballot boxes or voting machines are available. It must make certain that only qualified voters cast ballots in the precinct. Often the board also counts the votes cast in the precinct and then sends the results to the proper place, usually to the county clerk or county board of elections.

Poll watchers, one from each party, are allowed at each polling place. They may challenge any person they believe is not qualified to vote, check to be sure that their own party's supporters do vote, and monitor the whole process, including the counting of the ballots.

Casting the Ballot

A **ballot** is the device by which a voter registers a choice in an election.[15] It can take a number of different forms. Whatever its form, however, it is clearly an important and sensitive part of the election process.

Each State now provides for a secret ballot. That is, State law requires that ballots be cast in such manner that others cannot know how a person has voted.

Voting was a public process through much of the nation's earlier history, however. Paper ballots were used in some colonial elections, but voting was more commonly *viva voce*—by voice. Voters simply stated their choices to an election board. With suffrage limited to the privileged few, many people defended oral voting as the only "manly" way in which to participate. Whatever the merits of that view, the expansion of the electorate brought with it a marked increase in intimidation, vote buying, and other corruptions of the voting process.

Paper ballots were in general use by the mid-1800s. The first ones were unofficial—slips of paper that voters prepared themselves and dropped in the ballot box. Soon candidates and parties began to prepare ballots and hand them to voters to cast, sometimes paying them to do so. Those party ballots were often printed on distinctively colored paper, and

---

[15]The word comes from the Italian *ballotta,* "little ball," and reflects the practice of dropping black or white balls into a box to indicate a choice. The term *blackball* comes from the same practice.

Office-Group and Party-Column Ballots

OFFICE-GROUP BALLOT

Voters select each candidate by marking an X in the square

OFFICIAL BALLOT, GENERAL ELECTION

Candidates are grouped by office

Names are listed in random order

President and Vice President of the United States ☒

Four year term. Vote for one only.

BUCHANAN, Pat/FOSTER, Ezola ☐
Reform

GORE, Al/LIEBERMAN, Joe ☐
Democratic

BUSH, George W./CHENEY, Dick ☐
Republican

NADER, Ralph/LA DUKE, Winona ☐
Green

Office of the United States Senate

Six year term. Vote for one only.

HOLDEN, Bob ☐
Democrat

MACY, Elgar ☐
Republican

KLINE, Richard ☐
Reform

PARTY-COLUMN BALLOT

Party symbol and name at the top of the column that lists all of the party's candidates running for office

OFFICIAL BALLOT, GENERAL ELECTION

To vote for all the candidates of a party, voters mark an X in the circle

REPUBLICAN	DEMOCRATIC	REFORM	GREEN
○	○	○	○
For President of the United States GEORGE W. BUSH	For President of the United States AL GORE	For President of the United States PAT BUCHANAN	For President of the United States RALPH NADER
For Vice President of the United States DICK CHENEY	For Vice President of the United States JOE LIEBERMAN	For Vice President of the United States EZOLA FOSTER	For Vice President of the United States WINONA LA DUKE
For United States Senator ELGAR MACY	For United States Senator BOB HOLDEN	For United States Senator RICHARD KLINE	

To vote for candidates of different parties, voters mark an X in the square next to the chosen candidate or candidates

Interpreting Diagrams By highlighting the office, rather than the party, an office-group ballot encourages split-ticket voting. *How does a party-column ballot encourage voters to vote along party lines?*

---

anyone watching could tell for whom voters were voting.

By the end of the 1800s, political machines—local political party organizations capable of mobilizing or "manufacturing" large numbers of votes on behalf of candidates for political office—were dominant in many places. They fought all attempts to make voting a more dependably fair and honest process. The political corruption of the post-Civil War years brought widespread demand for ballot reforms.

The Australian Ballot

A new voting arrangement was devised in Australia, where it was first used in an election in Victoria in 1856. Its successes there led to its use in other countries. By 1900 nearly all of the States were using it. It remains the basic form of the ballot throughout the United States today.

The Australian Ballot has four essential features:

1. It is printed at public expense;
2. It lists the names of all candidates in an election;
3. It is given out only at the polls, one to each qualified voter;
4. It is marked in secret.

Two basic varieties of the Australian ballot have developed over the years. Most States now use the office-group ballot. Only a handful of States use the party-column ballot.

The Office-Group Ballot

The office-group ballot is the original form of the Australian ballot. It is also sometimes called the Massachusetts ballot because of its early (1888) use there. On the office-group ballot, the candidates for an office are grouped together under the title of that office. Because the names of the candidates thus appear as a block, the form is also sometimes called the office-block ballot.

At first, the names of the candidates were listed in alphabetical order. Most States using the form now rotate the names. This is so that each candidate will have whatever psychological advantage there may be in having his or her name at the top of the list of candidates.

The Party-Column Ballot

The party-column ballot is also known as the Indiana ballot, from its early (1889) use in that State. It lists each party's candidates in a column under the party's name. Often there is a place at the top of each column where, with a single X, the voter can vote for all of that party's candidates.

Professional politicians tend to favor the party-column ballot. It encourages straight-ticket voting, especially if the party has a strong candidate at the head of the ticket. Most students of the political process favor the office-group form because it encourages voter judgment and split-ticket voting.

Sample Ballots

Sample ballots, clearly marked as such, are available in most States before an election. In some States they are mailed to all voters, and they appear in most newspapers. They cannot be cast, but they can help voters prepare for an election.

First in Oregon (1907), and now in several States, an official voter's pamphlet is mailed to voters before every election. It lists all candidates and measures that will appear on the ballot. In Oregon, each candidate is allowed space to present his or her qualifications and position on the issues. Supporters and opponents of ballot measures are allowed space to present their arguments as well.

Bedsheet Ballots

The ballot in a typical American election is lengthy, often and aptly called a "bedsheet" ballot. It frequently lists so many offices, candidates, and ballot measures that even the most well-informed voters have a difficult time marking it intelligently.

The long ballot came to American politics in the era of Jacksonian Democracy in the 1830s. Many held the view at the time that the greater the number of elective offices, the more democratic

▲ **Campaign Ticket, 1864**
Sometimes tickets such as these were cast as ballots.

the governmental system. The idea remains widely accepted today.

Generally, the longest ballots are found at the local level, especially among the nation's 3,000-odd counties. The list of elected offices may include several commissioners, a clerk, a sheriff, one or more judges, a prosecutor, coroner, treasurer, assessor, surveyor, school superintendent, engineer, sanitarian, and even the proverbial dogcatcher.

Critics of the long ballot do not accept the argument that the more people you elect, the more democratic you are. They believe that quite the reverse is true: With a smaller number of elected offices to fill, the voter can better know the candidates and their qualifications. Critics also point to "ballot fatigue." This refers to the drop-off in voting that can run as high as 20 to 30 percent at or near the bottom of the typical bedsheet ballot.

There seems little, if any, good reason to elect such local officials as clerks, coroners, surveyors, and engineers. Their jobs do not carry policy-making responsibilities. Rather, they carry out policies made by others. Many people believe that in order to shorten the ballot, the rule should be: Elect those who make public policies, but appoint those whose job it is to administer those policies.

Voting Machines and Innovations

Thomas Edison took out the first American patent for a voting machine. The community of Lockport, New York, first used his invention in 1892. The use of similar devices has long since spread to the polling places of every State.

Only a few States make the use of voting machines mandatory. Most often the machines are used only in some areas of a State, usually the more populous. All told, however, over half of all the votes in national elections today are cast on some form of voting machine.

The typical voting machine serves as its own booth. By pulling a lever, the voter encloses himself or herself within a three-sided curtain, and the machine itself becomes the fourth side of the voting booth. Pulling the lever also unlocks the voting machine. The ballot appears on the face of the machine, and the voter makes choices by pulling down the small levers over the names of the candidates he or she favors. The machine also has space for ballot measures, with *yes* and *no* levers for each of them.

In most States that use the party-column ballot, the voter can pull a master lever to vote a straight ticket. The machine is programmed so that a voter can cast only one vote per contest. Once all levers are in the desired positions, the voter opens the curtain. That action records the votes and, at the same time, clears the machine for the next voter.

Voting machines do away with the need for manual vote counting, reduce the number of people needed to administer elections, and speed the voting process. They also increase the number of voters who can be handled per precinct, make ballot mutilation impossible, and minimize fraud and counting errors.

Electronic Vote Counting

Electronic data processing (EDP) techniques were first applied to the voting process in the 1960s. California and Oregon began the trend and since then, more than two thirds of the States have followed suit to some degree.

The most widely used adaptation of EDP in elections involves punch-card ballots, which are counted by computers. Many States and locales are now turning to two other EDP-based voting processes. One involves paper ballots that are counted by optical scanners. The other is a touch-screen system; see the illustration on this page for one version of this process.

Vote-by-Mail Elections

A number of States conduct some elections by mail. Voters receive a ballot in the mail, make their choices, then mail the ballot back to election officials.

The first vote-by-mail election was held in Monterey County, California, in 1977; and the first large-scale use of mail-in ballots took place in San Diego in 1981. Vote-by-mail elections are now held in several other places.

Usually, vote-by-mail elections have been confined to the local level and to voting on city or county measures, not on candidates for local offices. A few States do choose local officials by mail-in ballots, however.

In fact, Oregon now holds all of its elections by mail and has done so since 1998. The State

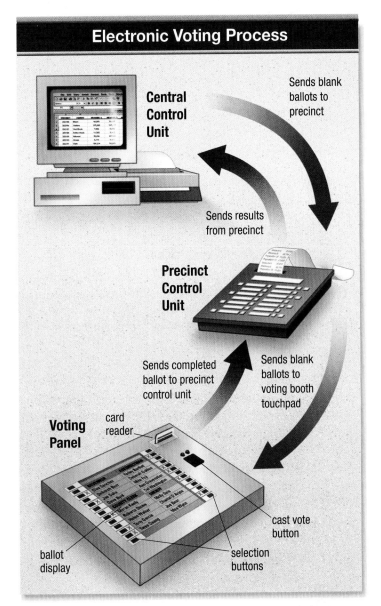

Electronic Voting Process

Central Control Unit

Sends blank ballots to precinct

Sends results from precinct

Precinct Control Unit

Sends completed ballot to precinct control unit

Sends blank ballots to voting booth touchpad

Voting Panel

card reader

cast vote button

ballot display

selection buttons

Interpreting Diagrams Electronic voting is becoming increasingly common, gradually replacing mechanical voting machines. Voters make their choices on a touchpad similar to that on an automated teller machine. *How are votes counted in an electronic voting system?*

held the first-ever all-mail primary election (including the presidential election) and the first-ever all-mail general election in 2000.

Vote-by-mail elections have stirred growing controversy. Critics fear that the process threatens the principle of the secret ballot. They worry about fraud, especially the possibility that some voters may be subjected to undue pressures when they mark their ballots at home or any place other than within the security of a voting booth.

Supporters, on the other hand, say that vote-by-mail elections can be as fraud-proof as any other method of voting. They also cite this fact:

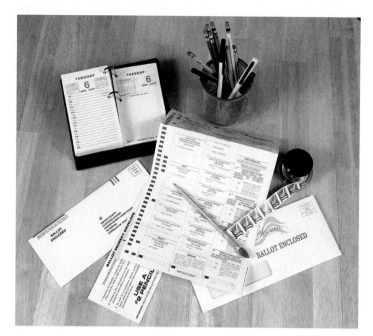

▲ This photo shows the mail-in ballot used by Oregon voters, who now vote by mail in all elections. *Critical Thinking How can voting by mail help increase the number of votes cast in an election?*

The mail-in process increases voter turnout in elections and, at the same time, reduces the costs of conducting them.

Online Voting

Online voting—e-voting, or casting ballots on the Internet—will likely become widespread, perhaps even commonplace, in the next few years or so. Several States are now moving in that direction. Online voting has many of the same advantages and disadvantages as voting by mail.

Online voting is not an entirely new phenomenon. The first e-vote was cast in November 1997. In that year, election officials in Harris County, Texas, permitted astronaut David Wolf to vote in Houston's city election by e-mail from the space station *Mir*.

The nation's first public election in which voters cast their ballots online was held in Arizona in March 2000. The Arizona Democratic Party allowed voters to participate in the party's presidential primary by voting (1) in person at their precinct polling places, (2) by mail, or (3) via the Internet. The Defense Department also conducted a limited online voting project in November 2000. In that test program, some 250 members of the military who were stationed abroad cast votes in their home States by computer.

A number of public officials in several States and a number of dot.com companies promote online voting. These supporters claim that it will make participation much more convenient, increase voter turnout, and reduce the costs of conducting elections.

Many skeptics believe that the electronic infrastructure is not ready for e-voting. Some fear digital disaster: jammed phone lines, blocked access, hackers, viruses, denials of service attacks, fraudulent vote counts, and violations of voter secrecy. Critics also point out that because not everyone can afford home computers, online voting could undermine basic American principles of equality.

Section 2 Assessment

Key Terms and Main Ideas

1. What is the purpose of **absentee voting** laws?
2. How can the **coattail effect** influence election results?
3. What factor determines the location of each voter's **polling place**?
4. (a) What is a **ballot**? (b) What different forms does it take in the United States?

Critical Thinking

5. **Predicting Consequences** Consider elections held in your school for class president and student council. How might the absence of secret ballots affect these elections?

6. **Expressing Problems Clearly (a)** What are the advantages and disadvantages of voting by mail and voting online? **(b)** Do you support these voting methods? Explain your answer.

 Take It to the Net

7. Find out more about voting in your State. Then create a brochure for newcomers to your State explaining registration requirements, State voting patterns, and any interesting information you discover about voting in your State. Use the links provided in the Social Studies area at the following Web site for help in completing this activity. **www.phschool.com**

Casting Your Vote

Why have people risked their lives to get and keep the right to vote? In the United States, we tend to take this right for granted. Yet if we were ever deprived of it, we would surely come to recognize its great value.

The voting process may vary slightly from place to place, but in general, these steps apply:

1. Determine if you are eligible to vote. To qualify to vote, you must be an American citizen at least 18 years of age and a resident of the State in which you vote.

2. Register to vote. In every State except North Dakota, you must register to vote. You can register locally, usually at city hall or the county courthouse. Registration tables are often set up in shopping malls, supermarkets, libraries, and fire stations before an election. You can register by mail, and in some places, via the Internet. To register you will need proof of your age, such as a birth certificate.

3. Study the candidates and issues. Identify the candidates for each office and the duties of the office. Then research the candidates' views on major issues. Besides voting for candidates for office, voters often have the opportunity to directly approve or reject proposed State and local

laws. Don't wait until you are in the voting booth to become familiar with these issues.

4. Go to your polling place. In many States, voters receive a voter registration card identifying their precinct and polling place. Newspapers often publish lists of polling places prior to an election. Polls are usually open from 7:00 or 8:00 A.M. to 7:00 or 8:00 P.M. At the polling place, your name will be checked against a list of registered voters to make sure you are eligible to vote. You will be directed to a booth with a voting machine, or you will be given a paper ballot or punch card and directed to a voting booth.

5. Cast your vote. Follow the instructions on the voting machine or ballot, so your vote will be counted properly. Do not feel rushed. If you have a question, ask an attending official. Make sure you've made a selection in every contest in which you wish to vote.

Test for Success

(a) Brainstorm at least three possible sources of voter information for voters in your area. (b) What sources would you consider most reliable?

3 *Money and Elections*

Section Preview

OBJECTIVES

1. **Explain** the issues raised by campaign spending.
2. **Describe** the various sources of funding for campaign spending.
3. **Examine** federal laws that regulate campaign finance.
4. **Outline** the role of the Federal Election Commission in enforcing campaign finance laws.
5. **Describe** loopholes in today's campaign finance laws.

WHY IT MATTERS

Money is an indispensable campaign resource. Yet money also poses a variety of problems in the election process. That's why the use of money is regulated in today's elections.

POLITICAL DICTIONARY

★ **political action committee (PAC)**
★ **subsidy**
★ **soft money**
★ **hard money**

▲ Seal of the Federal Election Commission, which administers federal law dealing with campaign finance.

Running for public office costs money, and often a lot of it. That fact creates some difficult problems in American politics. It leaves open the possibility that candidates will try to buy their way into public office. It also makes it possible for special interests to try to buy favors from those who are in office.

Clearly, government by the people must be protected from these dangers. But how? Parties and candidates must have money. Without it, they cannot campaign or do any of the things they must do to win elections.

In short, money is an absolutely necessary campaign resource. Yet, the getting and spending of campaign funds can corrupt the entire political process.

Campaign Spending

No one really knows how much money is spent on elections in the United States. Reliable estimates of total spending in recent presidential elections are shown in the table on page 197. These figures include nominations and general elections for offices at all levels.

The presidential election eats up by far the largest share of campaign dollars. For 2000, total spending for the major and minor parties—including primaries, conventions, and presidential campaigns—came to at least $1.5 billion.

The vast sums spent on congressional campaigns also continue to climb, election after election. Spending in all the Senate and House races in 1998 came to nearly $750 million. That figure passed the $1 billion mark in 2000.

Radio and television time, professional campaign managers and consultants, newspaper advertisements, pamphlets, buttons, posters and bumper stickers, office rent, polls, data processing, mass mailings, Web sites, travel—these and a host of other items make up the huge sums spent in campaigns. Television is by far the largest item in a typical campaign budget. A single half-hour of network TV time can run as much as $500,000, and a 30-second spot in prime time runs to at least $150,000. As Will Rogers put it years ago, "You have to be loaded just to get beat."

Of course the total amount spent in particular races varies widely. How much depends on the office involved, the opposition, the candidate, whether he or she is the incumbent, and the availability of campaign funds.

Sources of Funding

Parties and their candidates draw their money from two basic sources—private contributors and the public treasury.

Private and Public Sources

Private givers have always been the major source of campaign funds in American politics. Those givers include the following:

1. Small contributors—those who give $5 or $10 or so, and only occasionally. In fact only about 10 percent of people of voting age ever make campaign contributions; parties and candidates must thus look to other places for much of their funding.

2. Wealthy individuals and families—the so-called "fat cats," who can afford large donations and find it in their best interest to make them.

3. Candidates—both incumbents and challengers, their families, and, importantly, people who hold and want to keep appointive public offices. Ross Perot holds the all-time record in this category. He spent some $65 million of his own money on his independent bid for the presidency in 1992.

4. Various nonparty groups—especially **political action committees (PACs).** Political action committees are the political arms of special-interest groups, which have a major stake in public policy.

5. Temporary organizations—groups formed for the immediate purposes of a campaign, including fund-raising. Hundreds of these short-lived units spring up every two years, and at every level in American politics.

Then, too, parties and their candidates often hold fund-raisers of various sorts. The most common are $100-, $500-, and $1,000-a-plate luncheons, dinners, picnics, receptions, and similar gatherings. Some of these events reached the $100,000-or-more level during the 2000 presidential campaign. Direct mail requests, telethons, and Internet solicitations are also among the oft-used tools of those who raise campaign money.

Another source of funds has recently emerged: public subsidies from federal and/or State treasuries. A **subsidy** is a grant of money, usually from a government. Subsidies have so far been most important at the presidential level, as you will see shortly.[16]

Why People Give

Campaign donations are a form of political participation. Those who make them do so for a number of reasons. Many contributors give

Total Campaign Spending, 1960–2000

Year	Estimated spending	Voter turnout*	Spending per voter
1960	$175 million	68.8 million	$2.54
1964	$200 million	70.6 million	$2.83
1968	$300 million	73.2 million	$4.10
1972	$425 million	77.7 million	$5.47
1976	$540 million	81.6 million	$6.62
1980	$1.2 billion	86.6 million	$13.87
1984	$1.8 billion	92.7 million	$19.42
1988	$2.7 billion	91.6 million	$29.48
1992	$3.2 billion	104.4 million	$30.65
1996	$4.0 billion	96.5 million	$41.45
2000	$5.1 billion	105.4 million	$48.39

*Federal elections

SOURCES: Federal Election Commission; Herbert E. Alexander, *Financing Politics*

Interpreting Tables Total campaign spending has risen dramatically in recent elections. *What factors may account for this rise?*

simply because they believe in a party or a candidate. Many of those who give, however, want access to government, and they hope to get it by helping their "friends" win elections. Hence some contributors give to both sides in a contest: Heads they win and tails they still win.

Some big donors want appointments to public office, and others want to keep the ones they have. Some long for social recognition. For them, dinner at the White House, meeting with a Cabinet official, or knowing the governor on a first-name basis may be enough. Organized labor, business, professional, and various other groups have particular policy aims. They want certain laws passed, changed, or repealed, or certain administrative actions taken.

Regulating Campaign Finance

Congress first began to regulate the use of money in federal elections in 1907. In that year, it became unlawful for any corporation or national bank to make "a money contribution in

---

[16]Public funds for presidential campaigns come from the federal treasury. Several States now also have some form of public financing for parties and/or candidates at the State and even the local level.

any election" to candidates for federal office. Since then, Congress has passed several laws to regulate the use of money in presidential and congressional campaigns. Today, these regulations are found in three detailed laws: the Federal Election Campaign Act (FECA) of 1971, the FECA Amendments of 1974, and the FECA Amendments of 1976.

The earliest federal laws were loosely drawn, not often obeyed, and almost never enforced. The 1971 law replaced them. The 1974 law was the major legislative response to the Watergate scandal of the Nixon years. The 1976 law was passed in response to a landmark Supreme Court decision, *Buckley* v. *Valeo,* in 1976. A few minor changes were made to these laws in 1979.

Congress does not have the power to regulate the use of money in State and local elections. Every State now regulates at least some aspects of campaign finance, however—some of them more effectively than others.[17]

The Federal Election Commission

The Federal Election Commission (FEC) administers all federal law dealing with campaign finance. Set up by Congress in 1974, the FEC is

---

[17]A useful summary of State campaign finance laws can be found in *The Book of the States,* a biennial publication of the Council of State Governments.

an independent agency in the executive branch. Its six members are appointed by the President, with Senate confirmation.

The laws that the FEC enforces cover four broad areas. They (1) require the timely disclosure of campaign finance data, (2) place limits on campaign contributions, (3) place limits on campaign expenditures, and (4) provide public funding (subsidies) for several parts of the presidential election process.

Disclosure Requirements

Congress first required the reporting of certain campaign finance information in 1910. Today, the disclosure requirements, which are intended to spotlight the place of money in federal campaigns, are very detailed. In fact, the reports that candidates must file with the FEC are so comprehensive that nearly all candidates for federal office find that their campaign organizations must include at least one and often several certified public accountants.

No individual or group can make a contribution in the name of another. Cash gifts of more than $100 are prohibited. So, too, are contributions from any foreign source.

All contributions to a candidate for federal office must be made through a single campaign committee. Only that committee can spend that candidate's campaign money. All contributions and spending must be closely accounted

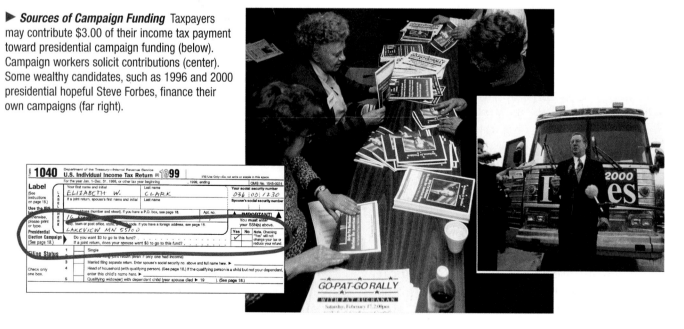

▶ *Sources of Campaign Funding* Taxpayers may contribute $3.00 of their income tax payment toward presidential campaign funding (below). Campaign workers solicit contributions (center). Some wealthy candidates, such as 1996 and 2000 presidential hopeful Steve Forbes, finance their own campaigns (far right).

for by that one committee. Any contribution or loan of more than $200 must be identified by source and by date. Any spending over $200 must also be identified by the name of the person or firm to whom payment was made, by date, and by purpose.

Any contribution of more than $5,000 must be reported to the FEC no later than 48 hours after it is received. So, too, must any sum of $1,000 or more that is received in the last 20 days of a campaign.

Limits on Contributions

Congress first began to regulate campaign contributions in 1907, when it outlawed donations by corporations and national banks. A similar ban was first applied to labor unions in 1943. Individual contributions became subject to regulation in 1939.

Today, no person can give more than $1,000 to any federal candidate in a primary election. In addition, no person can give more than $1,000 to any federal candidate's general election campaign. Also, no person can give more than $5,000 in any year to a political action committee, or $20,000 to a national party committee. The total of any person's contributions to federal candidates and committees must be limited to no more than $25,000 in any one year.

Those limits may seem generous; in fact, they are very tight. Before those limits were imposed in 1974, many wealthy individuals gave far larger amounts. In 1972, for example, W. Clement Stone, a Chicago insurance executive, contributed more than $2 million to President Richard Nixon's reelection campaign. Richard Mellon Scaife, heir to oil, aluminum, and banking fortunes, gave more than $1 million to that campaign.

PAC Contributions

Neither corporations nor labor unions can contribute to any candidate running for a federal office. Their political action committees, however, can and do.

Recall that PACs are the political arms of special-interest groups—business, labor, professional, cause, and other organizations that try to influence government policies. You will look at

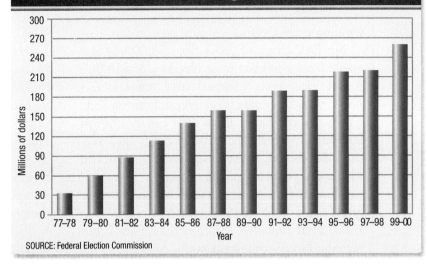

PAC Contributions to Congressional Candidates

SOURCE: Federal Election Commission

 Interpreting Graphs Political action committees (PACs) have become a major source of campaign money. *How do you think the growth of PACs has affected political campaigns since the 1970s?*

interest groups at length in Chapter 9, but their PACs deserve special attention here. While PACs operate in every part of the political scene, their clout comes mostly from their ability to raise campaign money and their willingness to give it to their "friends" who run for public office.

Some 4,000 PACs are registered with the Federal Election Commission today. Leading examples include: BIPAC (the Business-Industry Political Action Committee), COPE (the AFL-CIO's Committee on Political Education), AMPAC (the American Medical Association's Political Action Committee), and the National Education Association's NEAPAC.

Any list of the most powerful of these groups must also include the American Bankers Association's BANKPAC, the American Trial Lawyers PAC, and EMILY's List, which seeks to increase the number of women among the Democratic members of Congress. (EMILY's List takes its name from this political maxim: Early Money Is Like Yeast—it makes the dough rise.)

PACs fill their campaign war chests with contributions from their members. Members are found among the executives, employees, and stockholders of corporations, labor union members, doctors, dentists, teachers, and lawyers, those who favor or oppose gun control or abortion, and so on. These groups bundle all of their members' gifts of money, pooling them together. Then they distribute money to those candidates who (1) are sympathetic to the PAC's policy goals, and (2) have a reasonable chance of winning their races.

No PAC can give more than $5,000 to any one federal candidate in an election, or $10,000 per election cycle (primary and general election). However, there is no overall limit on PAC giving to candidates. Each PAC can give up to $5,000 per election to as many candidates as it chooses. A PAC may also contribute up to $15,000 a year to a political party.

PACs put an estimated $400 million into the presidential and congressional campaigns in 2000. They funneled untold other millions into State and local contests as well.

Limits on Expenditures

Congress first began to limit federal campaign spending in 1925. Most of the limits now on the books apply only to presidential (not congressional) elections. This fact is due mostly to the Supreme Court's decision in *Buckley* v. *Valeo*, 1976.

In *Buckley*, the High Court struck down several spending limits set by the FECA Amendments of 1974. It held each of those restrictions to be contrary to the First Amendment's guarantees of freedom of expression. In effect, said the Court, in politics "money is speech."

The most important of the provisions the Court threw out (1) limited campaign expenditures by candidates running for seats in the House or Senate, (2) limited how much of their own money candidates could put into their own campaigns, and (3) said that no person or group could spend more than $1,000 on behalf of any federal candidate without that candidate's permission.

The Court also held that several limits that the FEC law of 1974 placed on spending apply only to candidates who accept campaign subsidies from the FEC. Candidates who do not take FEC money are not bound by those limits.[18]

---

[18]As of the presidential election in 2000, only three major party aspirants have refused to accept federal funds—all three in the pre-convention period, all three Republicans, and one of them twice: John Connally, who tried for the Republican nomination in 1980; Steve Forbes, who sought the GOP nod in 1996 and again in 2000; and George W. Bush in 2000. Mr. Bush did accept FEC funds for his general election campaign in 2000.

For 2000, major party contenders who used FEC money could spend no more than $40.5 million in the preconvention period. (George W. Bush, who did not accept FEC money until his general election campaign, spent approximately twice that much before the Republicans held their convention in Philadelphia in July.)

After the conventions, in the general election campaign, the two major party nominees (Al Gore and George W. Bush) could not spend more than $67.6 million. In addition, neither the Democratic nor the Republican national committee could lay out more than $13.7 million for the presidential campaign.

It is also possible for a minor party's presidential candidate to qualify for an FEC subsidy. In 2000, the Reform Party's Pat Buchanan received $12.7 million for his campaign.

Public Funding of Presidential Campaigns

Congress first began to provide for the public funding of presidential campaigns in the Revenue Act of 1971. It broadened sections of that law in 1974 and again in 1976.

The 1971 law set up the Presidential Election Campaign Fund. Every person who files a federal income tax return can "check off" (assign) three dollars of his or her tax payment (six dollars on a joint return) to the fund. The monies in the fund are used every four years to finance (1) preconvention campaigns, (2) national conventions, and (3) presidential election campaigns. The FEC administers the public subsidy process.

1. *Preconvention Campaigns.* Presidential primary and caucus campaigns are supported by the private contributions a candidate raises plus the public money he or she receives from the FEC. To be eligible for public funds, a contender must raise at least $100,000 in contributions from individuals (not organizations). That amount must be gathered in $5,000 lots in each of at least 20 States, with each of those lots built from individual donations of not more than $250. This requirement is meant to discourage frivolous candidates.

For each presidential hopeful who passes this test, the FEC will match the first $250 of each individual's donation to that candidate, up to a total of half of the overall limit on primary spending. Thus, in 2000 the FEC could give some contenders nearly $20 million because the ceiling was close to $40 million for each candidate. The FEC does not match contributions from PACs or other political organizations.

For 2000, all the major party presidential hopefuls combined spent nearly $200 million on their preconvention campaigns. This figure included some $80 million in matching funds from the FEC.

2. *National Conventions.* If a major party applies for the money, it automatically receives a grant to pay for its national convention. The two parties each received $13.5 million from the FEC for that purpose in 2000. The Reform Party received $2.5 million for its convention, as well.

3. *Presidential Election Campaigns.* Every major party nominee automatically qualifies for a public subsidy to cover the costs of the general election campaign. For the 2000 election, that subsidy amounted to $67.6 million. A candidate can refuse that money, of course. Should that ever happen, the candidate would be free to raise however much he or she could from private sources.

So far (from 1976 through 2000), the nominees of both major parties have taken the public money each time. Because they did so, each automatically (1) could spend no more than the amount of the subsidy, and (2) could not accept campaign funds from any other source.

A minor party candidate can also qualify for public funding, but not automatically. To be eligible, the minor party must either (1) have won at least five percent of the popular vote in the last presidential election, or (2) win at least that much of the total vote in the current election.

In the latter case, the public money is received *after* the election and so could not possibly help the candidate in that election. (Remember, many provisions of both federal and State election law are purposely drawn to discourage minor party and independent efforts and thus help strengthen the two-party system.)

Except for Ross Perot in 1996, few minor party candidates have come even remotely close to winning five percent of the popular vote in any election since the subsidy arrangement was put in place. Over that period (1976 through 2000), however, two independent candidates did exceed the five-percent threshold.

John Anderson received 6.7 percent of the popular vote in 1980. He therefore received

Interpreting Political Cartoons *(a) Explain the difference between "hard" and "soft" money. (b) How does the cartoon help make that difference clear?*

$4.2 million from the FEC after that election. Ross Perot won 19 percent of the vote in 1992. Thus, the FEC ruled that he was eligible to receive $29.2 million from the Presidential Election Campaign Fund to finance his Reform Party candidacy in 1996. Perot won 8 percent of the popular vote in 1996, and so the Reform Party's candidate, Pat Buchanan, qualified for the federal subsidy in 2000.

Loopholes in the Law

Nearly 40 years ago, President Lyndon Johnson described the then-current body of federal campaign finance law as "more loophole than law." We have come very close to the point at which that comment could be applied to today's federal election-money statutes. Three immense loopholes have appeared in those laws over the past 25 years, and huge torrents of cash have gushed through them. Those loopholes involve (1) soft money, (2) independent campaign spending, and (3) issue ads.

1. *Soft money.* Federal law neither limits nor requires the reporting of **soft money.** Soft money includes those contributions made to State and local party organizations for such "party-building activities" as voter registration and get-out-the-vote drives, party mailings and advertisements, and similar efforts.

"I may be awhile. I'm soliciting funds for my reëlection campaign."

Interpreting Political Cartoons From what sources might this candidate solicit funds?

Soft money contributions come from wealthy individuals, many PACs, and elements of both major parties' national organizations. Those funds bypass the reporting requirements and the amount limits that apply to **hard money,** or campaign money that is subject to regulation by the FEC.

State and local organizations in both major parties have found it easy to filter this unregulated money into the parties' presidential and congressional campaigns. The soft money loophole ballooned from an estimated $19 million in 1980 to some $500 million in 2000.

2. *Independent campaign spending.* According to federal election law, an "independent person or group" is one that participates in a campaign entirely on its own, with no connection to a candidate or party involved in that election. Such a person or group can spend—not contribute to a candidate or a party, but *spend* as it chooses—an unlimited amount of money in that campaign. That spending can be made to help a candidate, of course; but it has much more often been directed *against* a candidate.

Congress tried to minimize such independent activity in 1974 by limiting that spending to no more than $1,000 per candidate in an election. In 1976, however, the Supreme Court struck down that limit in *Buckley* v. *Valeo,* again on the money-is-speech ground. Independent campaign spending has played an increasingly important part in both presidential and congressional elections ever since.

3. *Issue ads.* The congressional campaigns of 1998 and the presidential and congressional contests in 2000 saw a surge in a new form of political advertising: the so-called "issue ads." These pitches, found mostly on radio and television, deal with such controversial areas of public policy as social security, health care, and foreign trade.

Issue ads do not mention the names of those candidates the ads' sponsors support or hope to defeat. Since they do not say, in so many words, "Vote for Joe Smith" or "Vote Against Sue Sprat," they are not covered by the disclosure requirements or spending limits of federal law. Most voters have little trouble making the connections these ads intend, however.

Section 3 Assessment

Key Terms and Main Ideas

1. What are **political action committees (PACs)?**
2. **(a)** What is a **subsidy? (b)** At what level in the election process are campaign subsidies most important?
3. How has **soft money** created a loophole in federal election-finance law?
4. How do soft money and **hard money** differ?

Critical Thinking

5. **Distinguishing Fact From Opinion** Explain why you agree or disagree with this statement: "Democracy would be best served if campaigns were entirely supported by the small contributions of millions of American voters."

6. **Drawing Conclusions** How might the electoral process change if campaign spending were more limited and current loopholes closed?

 Take It to the Net

7. Find the campaign finance information disclosed to the FEC by your representative and his or her opponent(s) during the last election. Make a chart showing how much money each candidate raised from various sources. How do the candidates' sources and amounts of funding compare? Use the links provided in the Social Studies area at the following Web site for help in completing this activity. **www.phschool.com**

Can States Limit Campaign Contributions?

Campaign finance laws attempt to prevent wealthy individuals and organizations from exercising undue influence in elections and on public officeholders. However, in Buckley v. Valeo, 1976, the Supreme Court struck down several limits on campaign contributions as violations of the 1st Amendment's guarantee of freedom of speech. Does that decision mean that States cannot limit campaign contributions?

Nixon v. Shrink Missouri Government PAC (2000)

In 1994, Missouri passed a law limiting the amount of money that individuals and organizations could give to political candidates. The specific limits depended on the particular office and were changed periodically to reflect changes in the cost of living. The Shrink Missouri Government Political Action Committee and Zev David Fredman, a candidate for State office, filed suit against Jeremiah J. Nixon, the Missouri attorney general, charging that the contribution limits violated their 1st Amendment rights. Shrink Missouri stated that it would have given more money to Fredman if the law had not prevented it, and Fredman argued that he could not campaign effectively without larger contributions.

The federal district court upheld the law. It held that the law supported the government's aim of increasing citizens' trust in government by reducing public fears that wealthy campaign donors had too much influence over government. The court of appeals reversed that decision, finding in part that the State legislature had not proven that large campaign contributions had caused actual corruption. Nixon then sought review by the Supreme Court.

Arguments for Nixon

1. The State has a legitimate interest in preventing corruption and the appearance of corruption that large campaign contributions can create.
2. The contribution limits imposed by Missouri were not unreasonably low. They did not prevent candidates from raising enough money to run effective campaigns.

3. Money is property; it is not speech. The "right" to contribute money is not entitled to the same high level of protection as is freedom of speech.

Arguments for Shrink Missouri

1. Missouri did not present actual evidence showing that large campaign contributions were creating corruption or even the appearance of corruption. Without such evidence, the abstract concern about the effect of large contributions does not justify restricting citizens' right to contribute.
2. Limits on campaign contributions make it more difficult for outside candidates who do not have the support of the media and of established political interests to conduct effective campaigns.
3. Campaign contributions are entitled to strong 1st Amendment protection, not because they themselves are speech but because they enable donors to promote the speech of candidates who share their views.

Decide for Yourself

1. Review the constitutional grounds on which each side based its arguments and the specific arguments each side presented.
2. Debate the opposing viewpoints presented in this case. Which viewpoint do you favor?
3. Predict the impact of the Court's decision on ways in which States may seek to regulate campaign financing in the future. (To read a summary of the Court's decision, turn to the Supreme Court Glossary on page 799.)

Political Dictionary

nomination (p. 178)

general election (p. 179)

caucus (p. 180)

direct primary (p. 182)

closed primary (p. 182)

open primary (p. 183)

blanket primary (p. 183)

runoff primary (p. 184)

nonpartisan election (p. 184)

absentee voting (p. 189)

coattail effect (p. 190)

precinct (p. 190)

polling place (p. 190)

ballot (p. 190)

political action committee (PAC) (p. 197)

subsidy (p. 197)

soft money (p. 201)

hard money (p. 202)

Practicing the Vocabulary

Matching *Choose a term from the list above that best matches each description.*

1. A group of like-minded people who meet to choose candidates for office
2. The political arm of a special-interest group
3. An election held within a political party at which the voters choose candidates who will appear on the ballot in an upcoming general election
4. The place where voters go to cast their ballots
5. The device by which voters register their choices in an election

Fill in the Blank *Choose a term from the list above that best completes the sentence.*

6. In a _____, voters must choose between the two top finishers in an earlier primary election.
7. Because of the _____, candidates can benefit from the popularity of another candidate on the ballot from their party.
8. _____ is given to State and local party organizations for "party-building activities."
9. One commonly heard criticism of the _____ is that it encourages "raiding."
10. Each _____ has one polling place.

Reviewing Main Ideas

Section 1

11. You have read that the nominating process has "a very real impact on the exercise of the right to vote." Explain this statement in your own words.
12. What are the five broad categories that describe the way most nominations are made?
13. How has the nominating process in American politics changed over the course of American history?
14. Describe the different types of direct primaries that have been used in American politics.
15. Explain the arguments for and against the closed primary.

Section 2

16. What is the overall purpose and importance of election law in the American political process?
17. To what extent are the States involved in governing elections?
18. (a) To what extent is the Federal Government involved in governing elections? (b) Give at least three examples of federal laws governing elections.

19. (a) Describe the basic difference between the office-group ballot and the party-column ballot. (b) What are the advantages of each?
20. Describe recent technological advances and changes that make it easier for Americans to vote.

Section 3

21. Briefly describe the role and importance of money in the election process.
22. (a) Identify five types of private donors to political campaigns. (b) Why might these individuals and groups wish to contribute money to political candidates?
23. Outline the limitations placed on individual and PAC contributions to federal candidates and political parties.
24. (a) How does a candidate for President qualify for public funding? (b) What rules must candidates follow if they accept public funds?
25. Identify and explain the three major loopholes in today's federal election-money statutes.

Critical Thinking Skills

26. *Applying the Chapter Skill* What criteria would you use in deciding for whom to vote in a local, State, or national election?

27. *Drawing Conclusions* Use what you have read in this chapter to make an argument for or against the following statement: *In the American political system, the nomination of candidates is more important than the general election.*

28. *Expressing Problems Clearly* Explain the effects of the Supreme Court's decision in *Buckley* v. *Valeo* (1976) on federal campaign finance law. How does this decision pose a problem for those who wish to close the loopholes in federal election-money statutes?

29. *Identifying Alternatives* What are the different types of primaries that a State may decide to use? What are the advantages and disadvantages of each type?

Analyzing Political Cartoons

Using your knowledge of American government and this cartoon, answer the questions below.

30. **(a)** Who are the characters in the cartoon? **(b)** Why are two of them covered in mud?
31. What can be the effect of a divisive primary on a political party?

★ **You Can Make a Difference**

Create an unbiased information sheet on political candidates. Obtain a list of candidates in a forthcoming local or State election—for example, people running for the State legislature. Start with a brief biography of each candidate. Include the person's personal and political history, stands he or she has taken on issues, and other relevant information. Use the back files of local newspapers as well as the Internet, the library, and other sources. Write your findings as a voters' guide.

Participation Activities

32. *Current Events Watch* Keep track of stories in the news about money spent on election campaigns and about campaign finance reform. Then use what you have learned to write an essay explaining why you would favor or oppose legislation that limits the amount of money candidates can spend on campaigns.

33. *Chart Activity* Create a chart or calendar for the current election cycle in your State. The calendar should list the date of the next primary and general election, candidate filing deadlines, voter registration deadlines, and any other important dates. (Since in most States the secretary of state oversees election laws, that office is a good source for election information.)

34. *It's Your Turn* Write a letter to the governor of your State in which you express your opinion about public financing for the election of State and local officials. Begin your letter by stating your purpose. Then, write one paragraph for each of the reasons for your opinion. Conclude the letter by thanking the governor for considering your ideas. Proofread and correct errors. Then prepare a final copy. **(Writing a Letter)**

 Take It to the Net

Chapter 7 Self-Test As a final review activity, take the Chapter 7 Self-Test in the Social Studies area at the Web site listed below, and receive immediate feedback on your answers.

www.phschool.com

Mass Media and Public Opinion

"The hand that rules the press, the radio, the screen, and the far-spread magazine rules the country."

—Judge Learned Hand (1942)

Since Judge Hand made this observation, new types of media have emerged, but the power of the media remains strong. The media, along with influences such as family and education, help shape our opinions about politics and many other aspects of our lives.

◆ Computer image of U.S. telecommunications network

You Can Make a Difference

ONE TEENAGER WHO has already made a place for herself in the media world is Jessica Johnson. In 1997, she began to host a weekly radio show on station WFKX in Jackson, Tennessee. The show gave local young people a chance to talk about issues and to highlight community activists. In late 1999, Jessica became one of the "Point of View Journalists" (POV-J), a network of young writers working as reporters for the new Oxygen cable network and Web site. After graduating, Jessica plans to attend Howard University.

SECTION 1

The Formation of Public Opinion (pp. 208–213)

★ Public opinion refers to the attitudes of a significant number of people on matters of government and politics.
★ Family and education are two of the most important factors in shaping public opinion.
★ Additional factors that shape public opinion include peer groups, opinion leaders, historic events, and mass media.

SECTION 2

Measuring Public Opinion
(pp. 215–221)

★ Public opinion can be determined to some extent through elections, interest groups, the media, and personal contacts.
★ The best way to measure public opinion is through opinion polls.
★ The complex process of scientific polling results in the most reliable poll data.
★ Although it is important to measure public opinion, public opinion is only one of many factors that shape public policy.

SECTION 3

The Mass Media (pp. 223–230)

★ The American public gets information on public issues through several forms of mass media, especially through television.
★ The media influence American politics by helping to set the public agenda and by playing a central role in electoral politics.
★ The influence of the media is limited, in part because many people use mass media as sources of entertainment rather than information.

Keep It Current

Items marked with this logo are periodically updated on the Internet. Keep up-to-date with what's in the news. To get current information on mass media and public opinion, go to **www.phschool.com**

The Formation of Public Opinion

Section Preview

OBJECTIVES

1. **Examine** the term *public opinion* and understand why it is difficult to define.
2. **Analyze** how family and education shape public opinion.
3. **Describe** four additional factors that shape public opinion.

WHY IT MATTERS

You no doubt have opinions on a variety of issues, from school prayer to which political party should be in power. Several factors help shape your opinions. The two most important factors are family and education.

POLITICAL DICTIONARY

★ **public affairs**
★ **public opinion**
★ **mass media**
★ **peer group**
★ **opinion leader**

Do you like broccoli? Blue fingernail polish? Hard rock? What about sports? Old cars? Country music?

You almost certainly have an opinion on each of those things. On some of them, you may hold strong opinions, and those opinions may be very important to you. Still, each of those opinions is your own view, your *private* opinion. None of them qualifies as *public* opinion.

What Is Public Opinion?

Few terms in American politics are more widely used, and less well understood, than the term *public opinion*. It appears regularly in newspapers and magazines, and you hear it frequently on radio and television.

Quite often, the phrase is used to suggest that all or most of the American people hold the same view on some public issue, such as arms control or environmental protection. Thus, time and again, politicians say that "the people" want such and such, television commentators tell us that "the public" favors this or opposes that, and so on.

In fact, there are very few matters about which all or nearly all of "the people" think alike. "The public" holds many different and often conflicting views on nearly every public issue.

To understand what public opinion is, you must recognize this important point: Public opinion is a complex collection of the opinions of many different people. It is the sum of all of their views. It is *not* the single and undivided view of some mass mind.

Different Publics

Many publics exist in the United States—in fact, too many to be counted. Each public is made up of all those individuals who hold the same view on some particular public issue. Each group of people with a differing point of view is a separate public with regard to that issue.

For example, the people who think that Congress should establish a national health insurance program belong to the public that holds that view. People who believe that the President is doing an excellent job as chief executive, or that capital punishment should be abolished, or that prayers should be permitted in the public schools are members of separate publics with those particular opinions. Clearly, many people belong to more than one of those publics; but almost certainly only a very few belong to all four of them.

Notice this important point: Not many issues capture the attention of all—or even nearly all—Americans. In fact, those that do are few and far between. Instead, most public issues attract the interest of *some* people (and sometimes millions of them), but those same issues are of little or no interest to many (and sometimes millions of) other people.

This point is crucial, too: In its proper sense, public opinion includes only those views that relate to **public affairs.** Public affairs include politics, public issues, and the making of public policies—those events and issues that concern the people at large. To be a public opinion, a view must involve something of general concern

The Political Spectrum

LEFT ←		CENTER		→ RIGHT
Radical	**Liberal**	**Moderate**	**Conservative**	**Reactionary**
Favors extreme change to create an altered or entirely new social system.	Believes that government must take action to change economic, political, and ideological policies thought to be unfair.	Holds beliefs that fall between liberal and conservative views, usually including some of both.	Seeks to keep in place the economic, political, and social structures of society.	Favors extreme change to restore society to an earlier, more conservative state.

Interpreting Diagrams People who have similar opinions on political issues are generally grouped according to whether they are "left," "right," or "center" on the political spectrum. The general range, or spectrum, of political opinions is shown here. *(a) How might a liberal and a conservative differ on an issue such as raising taxes? (b) Where do your views fall on the political spectrum?*

and of interest to a significant portion of the people as a whole.

Of course, the American people as a whole are interested in many things—rock groups and symphony orchestras, the New York Yankees and the Dallas Cowboys, candy bars and green vegetables, and a great deal more. Many people have opinions on each of these things, views that are sometimes loosely called "public opinion." But, again, in its proper sense, public opinion involves only those views that people hold on such things as parties and candidates, taxes, unemployment, welfare programs, national defense, foreign policy, and so on.

Definition

Clearly, public opinion is so complex that it cannot be readily defined. From what has been said about it to this point, however, **public opinion** can be described this way: those attitudes held by a significant number of people on matters of government and politics.

As we have suggested, you can better understand the term in the plural—that is, as public opinions, the opinions of different publics. In addition, a view must be expressed in order to be a public opinion. Otherwise, it cannot be identified with any public. Public opinion is thus also made up of expressed group attitudes.

The expression of an opinion need not be oral (spoken). The expression can be written, of course—on paper or in an e-mail, for example. It can also take any number of other forms, as well: a protest demonstration, a film, a billboard, a vote for or against a candidate, and so on. The essential point is that a person's private thoughts on an issue enter the stream of public opinion only when those thoughts are expressed publicly.

Family and Education

No one is born with a set of attitudes about government and politics. Instead, each of us learns our political opinions, and we do so in a lifelong "classroom" and from many different "teachers." In other words, public opinion is formed out of a very complex process. The factors involved in it are almost infinite.

You have already considered much of this in Chapter 6 with regard to voting behavior. In effect, that detailed look at why people vote as they do amounted to an extensive look at how public opinion is formed.

"Harold, would you say you are left of center, right of center, center, left of left, right of left, left of right, or right of right, or what?"

Interpreting Political Cartoons **What does the cartoon suggest about the political spectrum?**

In Chapter 6, remember, we described the process by which each person acquires political opinions—the process of political socialization. That complex process begins in early childhood and continues through a person's lifetime. It involves all of the experiences and relationships that lead us to see the political world and to act in it as we do.[1]

There are many different agents of political socialization at work in the opinion-shaping process. Again, you looked at these agents in Chapter 6: age, race, income, occupation, residence, group affiliations, and many others. Here, look again at two of them, the family and education. These have such a vital impact that they deserve another and slightly different discussion here.

The Family

Most parents do not think of themselves as agents of political socialization, nor do the other members of most families. Parents and other family members are, nonetheless, very important factors in this process.

Children first see the political world from within the family and through the family's eyes. They begin to learn about politics much as they begin to learn about most other things. Children learn from what their parents have to say, from the stories that their older brothers and sisters bring home from school, from watching television with the family, and so on.

Most of what smaller children learn in the family setting are not really political opinions. Clearly, toddlers are not concerned with the wisdom of spending billions of dollars on an anti-missile defense system or the pros and cons of the monetary policies of the Federal Reserve Board.

Young children do pick up some fundamental attitudes, however. With those attitudes, they acquire a basic slant toward such things as authority and rules of behavior, property, neighbors, people of other racial or religious groups, and the like. In short, children lay some important foundations on which they will later build their political opinions.

---

[1]The concept of socialization comes from the fields of sociology and psychology. There, it is used to describe all of the ways in which a society transforms individuals into members of that society. To put this another way: Socialization is the multi-sided, lifelong process in which people come to know, accept, and follow the beliefs and practices of their society. *Political socialization* is a part of that much broader process.

▲ Family and education are the primary factors that shape one's values and opinions. These photos show a preschooler, whose opinions are largely shaped by family (left); school-age children practicing American values by reciting the Pledge of Allegiance (center); and a young adult putting her values to work through community service (right). *Critical Thinking How have your family and education shaped your own opinions and values?*

A large number of scholarly studies report what common sense also suggests. The strong influence the family has on the development of political opinions is largely a result of the near monopoly the family has on the child in his or her earliest, most impressionable years. Those studies also show that

PRIMARY Sources *"Children tend to absorb the political views of parents and other caregivers, perhaps without realizing it. . . . Children raised in households in which the primary caregivers are Democrats tend to become Democrats themselves, whereas children raised in homes where their caregivers are Republican tend to favor the GOP."*

—Benjamin Ginsberg, Theodore Lowi, and Margaret Weir, *We the People*

The Schools

The start of formal schooling marks the initial break in the influence of the family. For the first time, children become regularly involved in activities outside the home.

From the first day, schools teach children the values of the American political system. They work to indoctrinate the young, to instill in them loyalty to a particular cause or idea. In fact, training students to become good citizens is an important part of our educational system.

Schoolchildren salute the flag, recite the Pledge of Allegiance, and sing patriotic songs. They learn about George Washington, Abraham Lincoln, Susan B. Anthony, Martin Luther King, Jr., and other great Americans. From the early grades on, they pick up growing amounts of specific political knowledge, and they begin to form political opinions. In high school, they are often required to take a course in American government and even to read books such as this one.

School involves much more than books and classes, of course. It is a complex bundle of experiences and a place where a good deal of informal learning occurs—about the similarities and differences among individuals and groups, about the various ways in which decisions can be made, and about the process of compromise that must often occur in order for ideas to move forward.

Once again, the family and education are *not* the only forces at work in the process by which opinions are formed. A number of other influences are part of the mix. These two factors are singled out here to underscore their leading roles in that process.

Other Factors

No factor, by itself, shapes a person's opinion on any single issue. Some factors do play a larger role than others, however. Thus, in addition to family and education, occupation and race are usually much more significant than, say, gender or place of residence.

For example, on the question of national health insurance, the particular job a person has—how well-paying it is, whether its benefits include coverage by a private health-insurance plan, and so on—will almost certainly have a greater impact on that person's views than his or her gender or place of residence. On the other hand, the relative weight of each factor that influences public opinion also depends on the issue in question. If the issue involves, say, equal pay for women or the restoration of Lake Michigan, then gender or where one lives will almost certainly loom larger in the opinion-making mix.

Besides family, education, and such factors as occupation and race, four other factors have a major place in the opinion-making process. They are the mass media, peer groups, opinion leaders, and historic events.

Mass Media

The **mass media** include those means of communication that reach large, widely dispersed audiences (masses of people) simultaneously. No one needs to be told that the mass media, including newspapers, magazines, radio, the Internet, and in particular television, have a huge effect on the formation of public opinion.

Take this as but one indication of that fact: The Census Bureau reports that there is at least one television set in 98 percent of the nation's 120 million households. There are two or more sets in more than 91 million homes and millions more in many other places. Most of those sets are turned on for at least seven hours a day, for a mind-boggling total of more than a billion hours a day.

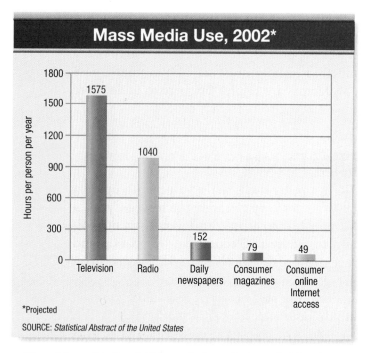

Mass Media Use, 2002*

Hours per person per year

- Television: 1575
- Radio: 1040
- Daily newspapers: 152
- Consumer magazines: 79
- Consumer online Internet access: 49

*Projected

SOURCE: Statistical Abstract of the United States

Interpreting Graphs This graph shows the hours that Americans spend each year on various forms of media. **Why do Americans spend more time watching television than on other forms of media?**

The chart above shows how much time Americans spend on various types of mass media. You will take a longer look at the influence of the mass media later in this chapter.

Peer Groups

Peer groups are made up of the people with whom one regularly associates, including friends, classmates, neighbors, and co-workers. When a child enters school, friends and classmates become an important factor in shaping his or her attitudes and behavior. The influence of peer groups continues throughout adulthood.

Belonging to a peer group usually reinforces what a person has already come to believe. One obvious reason for this is that most people trust the views of their friends. Another is that the members of a peer group have shared many of the same socializing experiences, and so tend to think along the same lines.

To put this observation another way, contradictory or other unsettling opinions are not often heard within a peer group. Most people want to be liked by their friends and associates. As a result, they are usually reluctant to stray too far from what their peers think and how their peers behave.

Opinion Leaders

The views expressed by **opinion leaders** also bear heavily on public opinion. An opinion leader is any person who, for any reason, has an unusually strong influence on the views of others. These opinion shapers are a distinct minority in the total population, of course, but they are found everywhere.

Many opinion leaders hold public office. Some write for newspapers or magazines, or broadcast their opinions on radio or television. Others are prominent in business, labor, agriculture, and civic organizations. Many are professionals—doctors, lawyers, teachers, ministers, and rabbis—and have contact with large numbers of people on a regular basis. Many others are active members of their neighborhood or church, or have leadership roles in their local communities.

Whoever they may be—the President of the United States, a network television commentator, the governor, the head of a local citizens committee, or even a local talk-show host—these opinion leaders are people to whom others listen and from whom others draw ideas and convictions. Whatever their political, economic, or social standing or outlook may be, opinion leaders play a significant role in the formation of public opinion.

Historic Events

Historic events can have a major impact on the views of large numbers of people—and so have a major impact on the content and direction of public policy. Our history affords many examples of this point, not the least of them the Great Depression. This period began in 1929 and lasted for the better part of a decade.

The Depression was a shattering national experience. Almost overnight, need and poverty became massive national problems. Millions of Americans—one out of every four in the labor force—lost their jobs. Millions more were impoverished. Hunger and despair stalked the land. In 1929, some two million people were unemployed in the United States. Just four years later, that number climbed to 13.5 million. In 1935, some 18 million men, women, and children were wholly dependent on public emergency relief programs. Some 10 million workers had no employment other than that provided by temporary public projects.

All of this changed the way millions of people viewed the proper place of government in the United States. The Depression persuaded a large majority of Americans to support a much larger role for government—and, in particular, for the National Government—in the nation's economic and social life.

As a result, the Great Depression also prompted a majority of Americans to shift their political loyalties from the Republican to the Democratic Party. The Republicans had dominated politics from Abraham Lincoln's election in 1860 to the onset of the Depression. Franklin D. Roosevelt's landslide victory in 1932, however, began nearly 40 years of Democratic domination.

The turbulent politics of the 1960s and early 1970s furnish another example of the way in which significant occurrences can impact and shape opinions. The American people had emerged from World War II and the prosperity of the 1950s with a largely optimistic view of the future and of the United States' place in the world. That rose-colored

▲ During the Great Depression, millions of Americans were out of work.

outlook was reflected in a generally favorable, even respectful, attitude toward government in this country.

The 1960s and early 1970s changed all that. Those years were highlighted by a number of traumatic events. Of special note were the assassinations of President John Kennedy in 1963 and of the Reverend Martin Luther King, Jr., and Senator Robert Kennedy in 1968. This period also included the civil rights movement and the Vietnam War, with all of the protests, violence, and strong emotions that accompanied both of those chapters in this nation's life. The era ended with the Watergate Scandal and the near-impeachment and subsequent resignation of President Richard Nixon in 1974.

Those years of turmoil and divisiveness produced a dramatic decline in the American people's estimate of their government—and most especially their evaluation of its trustworthiness. More recently, however, the September 11, 2001, terrorist attacks resulted in increased support for the President and for a strong United States foreign policy.

Section 1 Assessment

Key Terms and Main Ideas

1. What is **public opinion,** and what factors shape it?
2. Give three examples of an **opinion leader.**
3. Describe the political socialization of a young child.
4. **(a)** What are the **mass media? (b)** What evidence can you give that the mass media influence public opinion?

Critical Thinking

5. **Drawing Conclusions** Is it likely that interaction with one's peer group would prompt one to switch his or her allegiance from one major party to the other? Why or why not?
6. **Synthesizing Information** Why is it so difficult to define public opinion?

Take It to the Net

7. Look at data for at least three issues on which Americans have expressed their opinions. Then take a poll of your class to find out whether your classmates agree with public opinion on these issues. Use the links provided in the Social Studies area at the following Web site for help in completing this activity. **www.phschool.com**

The Latino Media Story

With the rise in the Latino population of the United States, the demand for Spanish-language newspapers, radio, and other media has grown. In this article from **The Christian Science Monitor,** *staff writer Kim Campbell reports on how Latino media are scrambling to meet the new demand.*

Rural Georgia is not the place you'd expect to find a boom in Spanish-language media. But Dalton, a small town in the north, is now home to three Spanish-language newspapers and a Spanish-language pop radio station.

Hispanic media have grown in the past decade—newspapers alone have increased 55 percent—and with the news . . . from the [2000] census that Hispanics are the largest U.S. minority, more attention is being paid to how to reach this group that has a purchasing power of more than $490 billion a year. . . .

With the demand for more media has come a need for bilingual journalists. Some are being wooed away from mainstream media by Spanish-language publications and networks. Those who do the hiring say it can be tough to find staff who can speak and write well in both languages. Some Latinos, for example, don't speak Spanish; others have strong Spanish skills but can't do interviews in English or translate written reports.

Those who do cross over say there are advantages to working in Spanish-language media, including the opportunity to advance into management, to work with colleagues who understand the needs of the Hispanic community, and to practice advocacy-based journalism in which the target audience is clear. "There is this sense that you are really doing something to help the community," says Angelo Figueroa, editor of the monthly *People*

Martin Berlanga, of Spanish-language network Univisión, prepares for a live shot in Austin, Texas.

en Español. . . .

Spanish-language media often take a different approach from mainstream outlets—focusing, not surprisingly, on issues of importance to their audience. . . . In Miami, *The Miami Herald* and its Spanish-language sister paper, *El Nuevo Herald,* often take different approaches to the same issue. . . . "People pick up *El Nuevo Herald* not only because it's in Spanish, but because it speaks to them," says Barbara Gutiérrez, a reader representative for both papers, who points out that *El Nuevo Herald* has shorter articles and is more opinionated. "It's just a different kind of style, and closer, I think, to what many Hispanics are used to."

The census took some people by surprise, but Ms. Gutiérrez says she and her colleagues could see what was coming. She looks forward to what happens next: "The next 10 years are going to be very exciting."

Analyzing Primary Sources

1. Why is the growth of the U.S. Latino population an important consideration to the media?
2. How might the rise in the Latino population affect the formation of public opinion?
3. If you were planning on a career in the media, how might the information in this article affect you?

2 *Measuring Public Opinion*

Section Preview

OBJECTIVES

1. **Describe** the challenges involved in measuring public opinion.
2. **Explain** why scientific opinion polls are the best measure of public opinion.
3. **Identify** five steps in the polling process.
4. **Understand** the challenges of evaluating polls.
5. **Recognize** the limits on the impact of public opinion in a democracy.

WHY IT MATTERS

Have you ever responded to a poll? Taken a poll yourself? Scientific polls are the most effective means for measuring public opinion. Other measures include election returns, the activities of interest groups, and direct personal contact.

POLITICAL DICTIONARY

- **mandate**
- **interest group**
- **public opinion poll**
- **straw vote**
- **sample**
- **random sample**
- **quota sample**

How many times have you heard this phrase: "According to a recent poll . . ."? Probably more than you can count, especially in the months leading up to an important election. Polls are one of the most common means of gauging public opinion.

If public policy is to reflect public opinion, one needs to be able to find the answers to these questions: What are people's opinions on a particular issue? How many people share a given view on that issues? How firmly do they hold that view? In other words there must be a way to "measure" public opinion.

measure public opinion. Elections, interest groups, the media, and personal contacts with the public all—at least to some degree—provide the means of measurement.

Elections

In a democracy, the voice of the people is supposed to express itself through the ballot box. Election results are thus very often said to be indicators of public opinion. The votes cast for the various candidates are regularly taken as evidence of the people's approval or rejection of the stands taken by those candidates and their parties.

Measuring Public Opinion

The general shape of public opinion on an issue can be found through a variety of means. These include voting; lobbying; books; pamphlets; magazine and newspaper articles; editorial comments in the press and on radio and television; paid advertisements; and letters to editors and public officials.

These and other means of expression are the devices through which the general direction of public opinion becomes known. Usually though, the means by which a view is expressed tells little—and often nothing reliable—about the size of the group that holds that opinion or how strongly it is held. In the American political system, this information is vital. To find this information, some effort must be made to

▲ The AIDS Memorial Quilt is a unique expression of public opinion. Here the quilt is laid out in front of the Washington Monument.

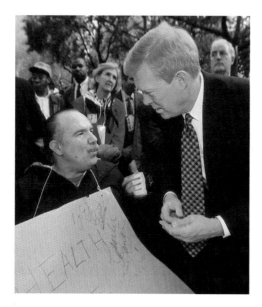

► Richard Gephardt (D., Missouri) meets a constituent. *Critical Thinking* **What kinds of information can officials learn from meeting directly with the public?**

As a result, a party and its victorious candidates regularly claim to have received a **mandate** to carry out their campaign promises. In American politics a mandate refers to the instructions or commands a constituency gives to its elected officials.[2]

In reality, however, election results are seldom an accurate measure of public opinion. Voters make choices in elections for any of several reasons, as you have seen. Very often, those choices have little or nothing to do with the candidates' stands on public questions. Then, too, candidates often disagree with some of the planks of their party's platform. In addition, candidates and parties often express their positions in broad, vague terms.

In short, much of what you have read about voting behavior, and about the nature of parties, adds up to this: Elections are, at best, only useful indicators of public opinion. To call the typical election a mandate for much of anything other than a general direction in public policy is to be on very shaky ground.

Interest Groups

Interest groups are private organizations whose members share certain views and work to shape public policy. These organizations are also very aptly known as pressure groups and special-interest groups.

---

[2]The term *mandate* comes from the Latin *mandatum*, meaning a command.

Interest groups are a chief means by which public opinion is made known. They present their views (exert their pressures) through their lobbyists, by letters and telephone calls, in political campaigns, and by a number of other methods. In dealing with them, however, public officials often have difficulty determining two things: How many people does an interest group really represent? And just how strongly do those people hold the views that an organization says they hold?

The Media

Earlier you read some very impressive numbers about television. Those huge numbers help describe the place of the media in the opinion process; you will read more of those numbers later. Here, recognize this point: The media are also a gauge for assessing public opinion.

The media are frequently described as "mirrors" as well as "molders" of opinion. It is often said that the views expressed in newspaper editorials, syndicated columns, news magazines, television commentaries, and so on, are fairly good indicators of public opinion. In fact, however, the media are not very accurate mirrors of public opinion, often reflecting only the views of a vocal minority.

Personal Contacts

Most public officials have frequent and wide-ranging contacts in many different forms with large numbers of people. In each of these contacts, they try to read the public's mind. Indeed, their jobs demand that they do so.

Members of Congress receive bags of mail and hundreds of phone calls and e-mails everyday. Many of them make frequent trips "to keep in touch with the folks back home." Top administration figures are often on the road, too, selling the President's programs and gauging the people's reactions. Even the President does some of this, with speaking trips to different parts of the country.

Governors, State legislators, mayors, and other officials also have any number of contacts with the public. These officials encounter the public in their offices, in public meetings, at social gatherings, and even at ball games.

Can public officials find "the voice of the people" in all of those contacts? Many can and do, and often with surprising accuracy. But some public officials cannot. They fall into an ever-present trap: They find only what they want to find, only those views that support and agree with their own.

Polls—The Best Measure

Public opinion is best measured by **public opinion polls,** devices that attempt to collect information by asking people questions.[3] The more accurate polls are based on scientific polling techniques.

Straw Votes

Public opinion polls have existed in this country for more than a century. Until the 1930s, however, they were far from scientific. Most earlier polling efforts were of the **straw vote** variety. That is, they were polls that sought to read the public's mind simply by asking the same question of a large number of people. Straw votes are still fairly common. Newspapers often run "clip-out and mail-in" ballots, radio talk shows ask listeners to respond to questions with phone calls, and so on.

The straw-vote technique is highly unreliable, however. It rests on the false assumption that a relatively large number of responses will provide a fairly accurate picture of the public's views on a given question. The problem is this: Nothing in the process ensures that those who respond will represent a reasonably accurate cross section of the total population. The straw vote emphasizes the quantity rather than the quality of the sample to which its question is posed.

The most famous of all straw-polling mishaps took place in 1936. A periodical called the *Literary Digest* mailed postcard ballots to more than 10 million people and received answers from more than 2,376,000 of them. Based on that huge return, the magazine confidently predicted the outcome of the presidential election that year. It said that Governor Alfred Landon, the Republican nominee, would easily defeat incumbent Franklin Roosevelt. Instead, Roosevelt won in a landslide. He captured more than 60 percent of the popular vote and carried every State but Maine and Vermont.

The *Digest* had drawn its sample on an altogether faulty basis: from automobile registration lists and telephone directories. The *Digest* had failed to consider that in the mid-Depression year of 1936, millions of people could not afford to own cars or have private telephones.

The *Digest* poll failed to reach most of the vast pool of the poor and unemployed, millions of blue-collar workers, and most of the ethnic minorities in the country. Those were the very segments of the population from which Roosevelt and the Democrats drew their greatest support. The magazine had predicted the winner of each of the three previous presidential elections, but its failure to do so in 1936 was so colossal that it ceased publication not long thereafter.

Scientific Polling

Serious efforts to take the public's pulse on a scientific basis date from the mid-1930s. Attempts began with the work of such early pollsters as George Gallup and Elmo Roper. The techniques that they and others have developed since then have reached a highly sophisticated level.

▲ **Polls Then and Now** The 1936 *Literary Digest* survey (right) drew a faulty conclusion about the winner of that year's presidential race because its sample was flawed. Today's scientific polls, such as the Harris Survey (above) are designed to avoid such errors.

---

[3]*Poll* comes from the old Teutonic word *polle,* meaning the top or crown of the head, the part that shows when heads are counted.

Interpreting Political Cartoons (a) According to the cartoon, how seriously should we view the answers to opinion polls? (b) Does the text agree or disagree with this assessment?

There are now more than 1,000 national and regional polling organizations in this country. Many of them do mostly commercial work. That is, they tap the public's preferences on everything from toothpastes and headache remedies to television shows and thousands of other things. However, at least 200 of these polling organizations also poll the political preferences of the American people. Among the best known of the national pollsters today are the Gallup Organization (the Gallup Poll) and Louis Harris and Associates (the Harris Survey).

The Polling Process

Scientific poll-taking is an extremely complex process that can best be described in five basic steps. In their efforts to discover and report public opinion, pollsters must (1) define the universe to be surveyed; (2) construct a sample; (3) prepare valid questions; (4) select and control how the poll will be taken; and (5) analyze and report their findings to the public.

Defining the Universe

The *universe* is a term that means the whole population that the poll aims to measure. It is the group whose opinions the poll will seek to discover. That universe can be all voters in Chicago, or every high school student in Texas, or all Republicans in New England, or all Democrats in Georgia, or all Catholic women over age 35 in the United States, and so on.

Constructing a Sample

If a poll's universe is very small—say, the 25 members of a high school class—the best way to find out what that universe thinks about some issue would be to poll every one of them. In most cases, however, it is not possible to interview a complete universe. This is certainly true in matters of public policy that affect all the people in the nation. There are simply too many people in that universe to talk to. So the pollster must select a **sample,** a representative slice of the total universe.

Most professional pollsters draw a **random sample,** also called a probability sample. In a random sample, the pollster interviews a certain number of randomly selected people who live in a certain number of randomly selected places. A random sample is thus a sample in

Effect of Poll Wording on Reliability

1

The Federal Government should see to it that all people have adequate housing.

| Agree 55.1% | Disagree 44.9% |

2

Some people feel the Federal Government should see to it that all people have adequate housing, while others feel each person should provide his or her own housing. Which comes closest to how you feel about this?

| Government responsible 44.6% | Government not responsible 55.4% |

3

Some people feel each person should provide his or her own housing, while others feel the Federal Government should see to it that all people have adequate housing. Which comes closest to how you feel about this?

| Government responsible 29.5% | Government not responsible 70.5% |

SOURCE: *Questions and Answers in Attitude Surveys,* 1981

Interpreting Charts This chart demonstrates the importance of carefully wording each question in a poll. *(a) Which question is worded in the least biased manner? (b) How do you know?*

which each member of the universe and each geographic area within it have a mathematically equal chance of being included.

Each major national poll usually interviews just over 1,500 people to represent the universe of the nation's entire adult population (just over 200 million people today). How can the views of so few people represent the opinions of so many?

The answer to that question lies in the mathematical law of probability. Flip a coin 1,000 times. The law of probability says that, given an honest coin and an honest flip, heads will come up 500 times. Furthermore, the law states that the results of this test will be the same no matter how often you perform it, and no matter what kind of coin you use.

The law of probability is regularly applied in a great many situations. It is used by insurance companies to compute life expectancies, by food inspectors to check the quality of a farmer's truckload of beans, and by others who "play the odds," including pollsters who draw random samples.

In short, if the sample is of sufficient size and is properly selected at random from the entire universe, the law of probability says that the result will be accurate to within a small and predictable margin of error. Mathematicians tell us that a properly drawn random sample of some 1,500 people will reflect the opinions of the nation's entire adult population and will be accurate to within a margin of plus or minus (±) 3 percent.

Pollsters acknowledge that it is impossible to construct a sample that would be an absolutely accurate reflection of a large universe. Hence, the allowance for error. A margin of ±3 percent means a spread of 6 percentage points, of course. To reduce the sampling error from ±3 percent to ±1 percent, the size of the sample would have to be 9,500 people. The time and money needed to interview so big a sample make that a practical impossibility.

Some pollsters use a less complicated, but less reliable, sampling method. They draw a **quota sample,** a sample deliberately constructed to reflect several of the major characteristics of a given universe.

For example, if 51.3 percent of a universe is female, 17.5 percent of it is African American, and so on, then the quota sample will be made up of 51.3 percent females, 17.5 percent African Americans, and so on. Of course, most of the people in the sample will belong to more than one category. This fact is a major reason why such a sample is less reliable than random samples.

Preparing Valid Questions

The way in which questions are worded is very important. Wording can affect the reliability of any poll. For example, most people will probably say "yes" to this question put this way: "Should local taxes be reduced?" Many of those same people will also answer "yes" to this question: "Should the city's police force be increased to

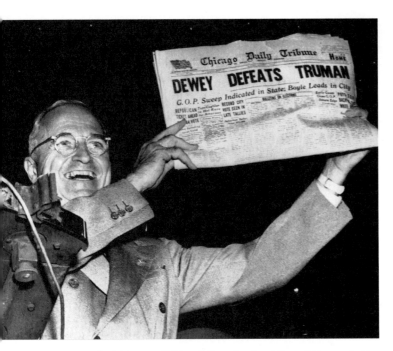

▲ **A Famous Polling Failure** An elated Harry S Truman holds up a newspaper headline wrongly announcing his defeat in 1948. Pollsters and others had predicted an easy victory for Thomas E. Dewey in that election.

can influence the replies he or she receives, and thus alter the validity of the poll's results.

If the questions are not carefully worded, some of the respondent's replies may be snap judgments or emotional reactions. Others may be answers that the person being interviewed thinks "ought" to be given; or they may be replies that the respondent thinks will please—or offend—the interviewer. Thus, polling organizations try to hire and train their interviewing staffs very carefully.

Analyze and Report Findings

Polls, whether scientific or not, try to measure people's attitudes. To be of any real value, however, someone must analyze and report the results. Scientific polling organizations today collect huge amounts of raw data. In order to handle these data, computers and other electronic hardware have become routine parts of the process. Pollsters use these technologies to tabulate and interpret their data, draw their conclusions, and then publish their findings.

Evaluating Polls

How good are polls? On balance, the major national polls are fairly reliable. So, too, are most of the regional surveys around the country. Still, they are far from perfect. Fortunately, most responsible pollsters themselves are quite aware of that fact and readily acknowledge the limits of their polls. Many of them are involved in continuing efforts to refine every aspect of the polling process.

Pollsters know that they have difficulty measuring the intensity, stability, and relevance of the opinions they report. *Intensity* is the strength of feeling with which an opinion is held. *Stability* (or fluidity) is the relative permanence or changeableness of an opinion. *Relevance* (or salience) is how important a particular opinion is to the person who holds it.

Another potential problem is that polls and pollsters are sometimes said to shape the opinions they are supposed to measure. Some critics of polls say that in an election, for example, pollsters often create a "bandwagon effect." That is, some voters, wanting to be with the winner, jump on the bandwagon of the candidate who is ahead in the polls. This charge is most often leveled against those polls that appear as syndicated columns in many newspapers.

fight the rising tide of crime in our community?" Yet, expanding the police force almost certainly would require more local tax dollars.

Responsible pollsters acknowledge these issues and thus phrase their questions very carefully. They purposely try not to use "loaded," emotionally charged words, or terms that are difficult to understand. They also try to avoid questions that are worded in a way that will tend to shape the answers that are given to them.

Interviewing

How the pollsters communicate with the sample respondents can also affect accuracy. Most polls are taken face-to-face. That is, the interviewers question the respondents in person. However, pollsters conduct an increasing number of surveys by telephone and by mail.

Professional pollsters see both advantages and drawbacks to each of these approaches. They all agree, however, that whichever technique they use to gather information, they must employ the same technique in questioning all the respondents in a sample.

The interview itself is a very sensitive point in the process. The pollster's appearance, dress, attitude, and tone of voice in asking questions

In spite of these criticisms, it is clear that scientific polls are the most useful tools there are for the difficult task of measuring public opinion. Although they may not be always or precisely accurate, they do offer reasonably reliable guides to public thought. Moreover, they help to focus attention on public questions and to stimulate discussion of them.

Limits on the Impact of Public Opinion

More than a century ago, the Englishman Lord Bryce described government in the United States as "government by public opinion." Clearly, the energy devoted to measuring public opinion in this country suggests something of its powerful role in American politics. However, Lord Bryce's observation is true only if it is understood to mean that public opinion is the major, but by no means the only, influence on public policy in this country. Its force is tempered by a number of other factors—for example, by interest groups.

Most importantly, however, remember that our system of constitutional government is not designed to give free, unrestricted play to public opinion—and especially not to majority opinion. In particular, the doctrines of separation of powers and of checks and balances, and the constitutional guarantees of civil rights and liberties are intended to protect minority interests against the excesses of majority views and actions.

Interpreting Political Cartoons **(a) What is the cartoon's message? (b) Does the text support this message?**

Finally, polls are not elections, nor are they substitutes for elections. It is when faced with a ballot that voters must decide what is important and what is not. Voters must be able to tell the difference between opinions and concrete information, and should know the difference between personalities and platforms.

Democracy is more than a simple measurement of opinion. Democracy is about making careful choices among leaders and their positions on issues, and among the governmental actions that may follow. Ideally, democracy is the thoughtful participation of citizens in the political process.

Section 2 Assessment

Key Terms and Main Ideas

1. Why are **interest groups** uncertain gauges for measuring public opinion?
2. What is the major problem with the **straw vote** polling technique?
3. How is it that a **random sample** gives a fairly accurate representation of public opinion?
4. For what reasons is public opinion measured?

Critical Thinking

5. **Determining Relevance** List two good reasons for following polls during a presidential campaign.
6. **Understanding Point of View** How might the Framers of the Constitution have viewed public opinion polls?

7. **Predicting Consequences** What positive and/or negative effects might there be if polls were taken among student voters before a student government election?

 Take It to the Net

8. Read through some of the recent polls taken by the Harris Survey and analyze how the poll data are explained and presented. Then, using the Harris Surveys as a model, conduct and present your own poll on a public issue of your choice. Use the links provided in the Social Studies area at the following Web site for help in completing this activity. **www.phschool.com**

Taking a Poll

Politicians have a love/hate relationship with public opinion polls. When a poll shows them gaining public approval, they hail the results as an endorsement of their views. When it shows their popularity slipping, they claim that they never pay attention to polls!

Indeed, a poorly constructed survey can deliver invalid information that can mislead decision makers or can be used to make false claims. Whether a poll is nationwide or within your classroom, certain standards of poll-taking apply. For instance:

1. Define the population to be polled. Decide what group you need to poll in order to find the answer to your question. For example, if you want to learn what percentage of registered voters in Tyler, Texas, voted in the last election, then it would not make sense to poll people who had not registered to vote.

2. Construct a sample. Within the group that you're polling, you can take a random sample—people chosen purely by chance. Or you can take a quota sample—a representative number of people from each subgroup in your survey.

3. Prepare valid questions. Ask objective questions rather than ones that lead the subject toward a particular answer. Try to ask questions that can be answered in one word, so your results will be easy to tally. Avoid wording that is difficult to understand, especially if your subjects are young or not fluent in English.

4. Select and control the means by which the poll will be taken. Decide whether you will conduct an in-person interview, a telephone interview, a mail interview, or an online interview. Be sure to interview all members of a group in the same manner. Choose interviewers who are careful not to influence the responses by their dress, attitude, or tone of voice.

5. Report your findings. Make a table of the results of your poll. Analyze the data to determine the answer to your original question.

Test for Success

Work individually or in small groups to design, conduct, and present the findings from a poll of your class. Create a topic, or choose from one of the following: (a) television viewing habits; (b) career plans; (c) consumption of genetically engineered foods.

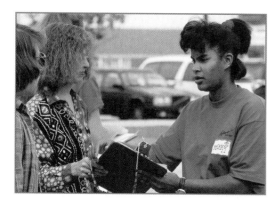

▲ Above, a student conducts a survey. At right is the Web site of a major national polling service, the Gallup Organization.

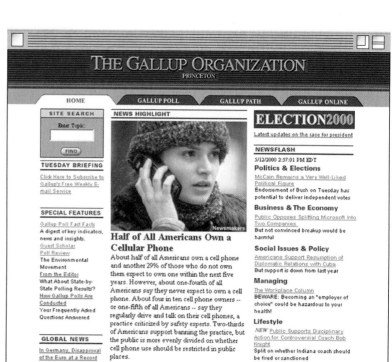

3 The Mass Media

Section Preview

OBJECTIVES

1. **Examine** the role of the mass media in providing the public with political information.
2. **Explain** how the mass media influence politics.
3. **Understand** the factors that limit the influence of the media.

WHY IT MATTERS

How often do you watch television, read a newspaper or magazine, listen to the radio? While these media provide entertainment, they are also our most important sources of political information.

POLITICAL DICTIONARY

★ **medium**
★ **public agenda**
★ **sound bite**

How much television do you watch each day? Little or none? Two hours a day? Three hours? More? However much you watch, you no doubt know that your peers spend a great deal of time in front of the TV. Studies show that by the time the average person graduates from high school today, he or she has spent nearly 11,000 hours in classrooms and nearly 14,000 hours watching television.

Television has an extraordinary impact on the lives of everyone in this country. As you will see in this section, so do the other elements of the mass media.

The Role of Mass Media

A **medium** is a means of communication; it transmits some kind of information. *Media* is the plural of medium. As you have read, the mass media include those means of communication that can reach large, widely dispersed audiences simultaneously.

Four major mass media are particularly important in American politics. Ranked in terms of impact, they are television, newspapers, radio, and magazines. Other media—books, films, and audio- and videocassettes, for example—play a lesser role. So, too, does the Internet, though its communicating capabilities are becoming increasingly important.

The mass media are not a part of government. Unlike political parties and interest groups, they do not exist primarily to influence government. They are, nonetheless, an important force in politics.

Besides providing entertainment, the media present people with political information. They do so directly when they report the news, in a newscast or in the news columns of a newspaper, for example. The media also provide a large amount of political information less directly—for example, in radio and television programs, newspaper stories, and magazine articles. These venues often deal with such public topics as crime, health care, or some aspect of American foreign policy. Either way, people acquire most of the information they know about government and politics from the various forms of media.

Television

Politics and television have gone hand in hand since the technology first appeared. The first public demonstration of television occurred at the New York World's Fair in 1939. President Franklin Roosevelt opened the fair on camera,

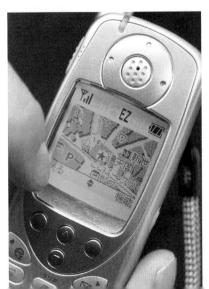

◀ **The "Wireless Web"**
Some mobile phones provide access to the Internet, an increasingly important form of mass media.

and viewers watched him on tiny five- and seven-inch screens.

World War II interrupted the development of the new medium, but it began to become generally available in the late 1940s. Television boomed in the 1950s. The first transcontinental broadcast came in 1951, when President Harry Truman, speaking in Washington, addressed the delegates attending the Japanese Peace Treaty Conference in San Francisco.

Today, television is all-pervasive. As you read earlier, there is at least one television set in 98 percent of the nation's 120 million households. In fact, there are more homes in this country today with a television set than with indoor plumbing facilities!

Television replaced newspapers as the principal source of political information for a majority of Americans in the early 1960s. Today, television is the principal source of news for an estimated 80 percent of the population.

The more than 1,400 television stations in this country include more than 1,000 commercial outlets and over 300 public broadcasters. Three major national networks have dominated television from its infancy: the Columbia Broadcasting System (CBS), the American Broadcasting Company (ABC), and the National Broadcasting Company (NBC). Those three giants furnish about 90 percent of the programming for some 700 local stations. That programming accounts for about 45 percent of all television viewing time today.

The major networks' audience share has been declining in recent years, however. The main challenges to their domination have come from three sources: (1) several independent broadcasting groups—for example, the Fox Network; (2) cable broadcasters[4]—for example, Turner Broadcasting, and especially its Cable News Network (CNN); and (3) the Public Broadcasting System (PBS) and its more than 350 local stations.

Some of the most highly touted presentations on television—a Super Bowl game, for example, or a debate between the major presidential candidates—are seen by as many as 100 million people. From 15 to 40 million watch the more popular sitcoms. Each of the three major network's nightly news programs draws 7 to 10 million viewers. In addition, more than 75 million places, including nearly two thirds of the nation's households, are now hooked up to cable systems.

---

[4]C-SPAN, the Cable-Satellite Public Affairs Network, is sponsored by the cable industry. C-SPAN and C-SPAN II present both live and taped coverage of a broad range of public events—including major floor debates and committee hearings in Congress, presidential and other press conferences, and speeches by notable public figures.

▲ Television viewing boomed during the 1950s. Today 98 percent of American households have at least one set. *Critical Thinking* **How does television provide political information both directly and indirectly?**

Newspapers

The first regularly published newspaper in America, the *Boston News-Letter*, appeared in 1704.[5] Other papers soon followed, in Boston and then in Philadelphia, New York, Annapolis, and elsewhere. By 1775, 37 newspapers were being published in the colonies. All of them were weekly papers, and they were printed on one sheet that was usually folded to make four pages. The nation's first daily newspaper, the *Pennsylvania Evening Post and Daily Advertiser*, began publication in 1783.

Those first papers regularly carried political news. Several spurred the colonists to revolution, carrying the news of independence and the text of the Declaration to people throughout the colonies. Thomas Jefferson marked the vital role of the press in the earliest years of the nation when, in 1787, he wrote to a friend:

 " *. . . were it left to me to decide whether we should have a government without newspapers or newspapers without a government, I should not hesitate a moment to prefer the latter.* **"**
—Letter to Colonel Edward Carrington,
January 16, 1787

The 1st Amendment, added to the Constitution in 1791, made the same point regarding the importance of newspapers with its guarantee of the freedom of the press.

Today, more than 10,000 newspapers are published in the United States, including almost 1,500 dailies, more than 7,200 weeklies, some 550 semi-weeklies, and several hundred foreign-language papers. Those publications have a combined circulation of about 150 million copies per issue. About 45 percent of the nation's adult population read a newspaper every day.

The number of daily newspapers has been declining for decades, however, from more than 2,000 in 1920 to 1,745 in 1980 and to not quite 1,500 today. Radio and television, and more

---

[5] The world's first newspaper was almost certainly the *Acta Diurna*, a daily gazette in Rome dating from 59 B.C. Another very early forerunner of today's newspapers was *Tsing Pao*, a court journal in Beijing. Press historians believe that its first issues, printed from stone blocks, were published beginning in A.D. 618; its last issue appeared in 1911.

Trends in News Consumption

SOURCE: The Pew Research Center

 Interpreting Graphs While television and newspapers have declined as sources for news, use of the Internet as a news source is rising. ***Briefly explain what you see as the reasons behind these trends.***

recently the Internet, have been major factors in that downward trend.

So, too, have been the battles over readers and advertisers that competing papers have fought in many places nationwide. Often, those struggles have left only one survivor. Competing daily papers exist in fewer than 50 cities today. This represents a major change from only a few decades ago, when at least two and sometimes three, four, or five newspapers existed in most major cities.

Nevertheless, newspapers rank second only to television as the public's primary source of information about government and politics. Most newspapers cover stories in greater depth than television does, and many try to present various points of view in their editorial sections. Those newspapers that have the most substantial reputations and national influence today include the *New York Times*, the *Washington Post*, the *Chicago Tribune*, the *Los Angeles Times*, the *Wall Street Journal*, *USA Today*, and the *Christian Science Monitor*.

Most newspapers are local papers. That is, most of their readers live in or near the communities in which they are published. While local papers do carry some national and international news, most focus on their own locales.

Advances in telecommunications and computerized operations are changing that basic fact, however. Today, each day's editions of the *New York Times*, the *Wall Street Journal*, and the *Christian Science Monitor* are generally available on the day of publication around the country, *USA Today*, which began publication in the early 1980s, has become a popular national newspaper.

Radio

Radio as it exists today began in 1920. On November 2nd of that year, station KDKA in Pittsburgh went on the air with presidential election returns. Radio soon became immensely popular.

By 1927, 733 commercial stations were on the air, Americans owned more than seven million radio sets, and two national networks were in operation. NBC was established in 1926 and CBS in 1927. The Mutual Broadcasting System was formed in 1934, and ABC was formed in 1943. The advent of networks made it possible for broadcasters to present their programs and advertising messages to millions of people all over the country.

By the 1930s, radio had assumed much of the role in American society that television has today. It was a major entertainment medium, and millions of people planned their daily schedules around their favorite programs. The networks also provided the nation with dramatic coverage of important events, and radio exposed the American people to national and international politics as never before.

President Franklin Roosevelt was the first major public figure to use radio effectively. Author David Halberstam has described the impact of FDR's famous fireside chats:

 PRIMARY Sources *"He was the first great American radio voice. For most Americans of [that] generation, their first memory of politics would be of sitting by a radio and hearing that voice, strong, confident, totally at ease. . . . Most Americans in the previous 160 years had never even seen a President; now almost all of them were hearing him, in their own homes. It was literally and figuratively electrifying."*
—David Halberstam, *The Powers That Be*

Many people thought that the arrival of television would bring the end of radio as a major medium. Radio has survived, however, in large part because it is so conveniently available. People can hear music, news, sports, and other radio programs in many places where they cannot watch television—in their cars, at work, in the country, and in a number of other places and situations.

Radio remains a major source of news and other political information. The average person hears 20 hours of radio each week. No one knows how many radios there are in this country—in homes, offices, cars, backpacks, and a great many other places. Those radios can pick up more than 12,000 stations on the AM and FM dials.

Many AM stations are affiliated with one or another of the national networks.

U.S. Radio Stations and Sales

Year	Radio stations on air	Unit sales
1946	961	N.A.
1950	2,773	N.A.
1955	3,211	7,327
1960	4,133	18,031
1965	5,249	31,689
1970	6,760	34,049
1975	7,744	25,276
1980	8,566	27,104
1985	10,359	21,575
1990	10,788	21,585
1991	10,989	18,530
1992	11,118	21,553
1993	11,371	19,697
1994	11,565	18,323
1995	11,834	17,051
1996	12,295	17,581
1997	12,482	17,664
1998	12,641	18,734
1999	12,641	19,178*

*Estimate

SOURCE: *The New York Times Almanac*

 Interpreting Tables The number of radio stations on the air has risen steadily since the 1940s. *(a) Describe trends in radio sales as shown on the table. (b) How can you explain the reasons behind these trends?*

Unlike television, however, most radio programming is local. There are also some 700 public radio stations, most of them on the FM dial. These noncommercial outlets are part of National Public Radio (NPR), which is radio's counterpart of television's PBS.

In most large cities there is at least one station that broadcasts nothing but news and public affairs programs. In addition, many stations serve the preferences of African American, Latino, or other minority audiences.

Magazines

Several magazines were published in colonial America. Benjamin Franklin began one of the very first, his *General Magazine,* in Philadelphia in 1741. On into the early 1900s, most magazines published in the United States were generally devoted to literature and the social graces. The first political magazines—among them, *Harper's Weekly* and the *Atlantic Monthly*—appeared in the mid-1800s.

The progressive reform period in the early 1900s spawned several journals of opinion, including a number that featured articles by the day's leading muckrakers.[6] For decades before radio and television, magazines constituted the only national medium.

Some 12,000 magazines are published in the United States today. Most are trade publications, such as *Veterinary Forum* and the *Automotive Executive,* or periodicals that target some special personal interest, such as *Golf Digest, Teen,* and *American Rifleman.* Magazines with the highest circulation today are *Modern Maturity, TV Guide,* and *Reader's Digest.* They each sell some 10 to 20 million or more copies per issue.

Three news magazines, *Time, Newsweek,* and *U.S. News & World Report,* rank in the top

---

[6]The muckrakers were journalists who exposed wrongdoing in politics, business, and industry. The term was coined by Theodore Roosevelt in 1906 and is derived from the raking of muck—that is, manure and other barnyard debris. The muckrakers set the pattern for what is now called investigative reporting.

Comparative Government

Access to Media in Selected Countries

Country	Population in millions	Television sets per 1,000 persons	Radios per 1,000 persons	Daily newspaper circulation per 1,000 persons
United States	281.0	847	2,115	215
Japan	126.5	708	957	578
Bangladesh	129.2	5	63	9
Nigeria	123.3	61	197	24
Mexico	100.3	257	329	97
Italy	57.6	483	874	104
India	1,014.0	68	117	21
Chile	15.1	280	305	101
Canada	31.3	708	1,078	157
Nicaragua	4.8	48	206	31

SOURCE: *The World Almanac,* 2001

Interpreting Tables Access to media varies considerably from country to country. *(a) In which countries shown in the table do people have the least access to the media? (b) How might people in these countries become informed about public affairs?*

25 periodicals in terms of circulation. They have a combined circulation of nearly 10 million copies a week, and they are important sources of political news and comment. There are several other magazines devoted to public affairs, most of them vehicles of opinion, including the *Nation,* the *New Republic,* the *National Review,* and the *Weekly Standard.*

The Media and Politics

Clearly, the media play a significant role in American politics. Just how significant that role is, and just how much influence the media have, is the subject of a long, still unsettled debate.

Whatever its weight, the media's influence can be seen in any number of situations. It is most visible in two areas: (1) the public agenda and (2) electoral politics.

The Public Agenda

The media play a very large role in shaping the **public agenda,** the societal problems that political leaders and citizens agree need government attention. As they report and comment on events, the media determine to a very large extent what public issues the people will think and talk about—and, so, those matters that public-policy makers will be concerned about. As a result, the media ultimately influence those matters of concern to public-policy makers.

To put the point another way, the media have the power to focus the public's attention on a particular issue. They do so by emphasizing some things and ignoring or downplaying others. For example, they feature certain items on the front page or at the top of the newscast and bury others.

It is not correct to say that the media tell the people *what* to think; but it is clear that they tell the people what to think *about.* A look at any issue of a daily newspaper or a quick review of the content of any television news program will demonstrate that point. Remember, people rely on the media for most of the information they receive on public issues.

The mass media also has a direct impact on the nation's leaders. Some years ago, Stephen Hess, a widely respected authority on the media, identified several news organizations that form the "inner ring" of influence in Washington, D.C. He cited the three major television networks, CBS, ABC, and NBC; three newspapers, the *New York Times,* the *Washington Post,* and the *Wall Street Journal;* the leading news wire service, the Associated Press (AP); and the three major news weeklies, *Time, Newsweek,* and *U.S. News & World Report.* CNN, MSNBC, Fox News, Reuters and *USA Today* have since joined that select group.

Top political figures in and out of government pay close attention to these sources. In fact, the President receives a daily digest of the news reports, analyses, and editorial comments that these and other sources broadcast and publish.

Electoral Politics

You have seen several illustrations of the media's importance in electoral politics as you have read in this book. Recall, for example, the fact that the media, and in particular television, have contributed to a decline in the place of parties in American politics.

Television has made candidates far less dependent on party organizations than they once were. Before television, the major parties generally dominated the election process. They recruited most candidates who ran for office, and they ran those

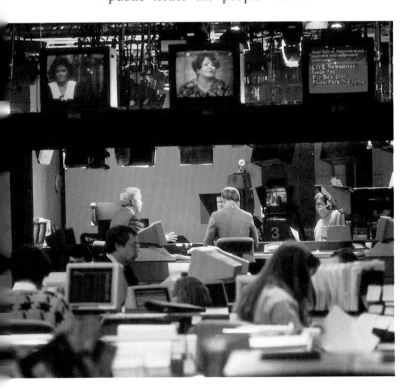

▲ *Power of the Press* The media transmit information across the country and around the world instantly. They thus help to shape the public agenda and affect the outcome of elections. Shown here is a CNN newsroom.

candidates' campaigns. The candidates depended on party organizations in order to reach the voters.

Now, television allows candidates to appeal directly to the people, without the help of a party organization. Candidates for major office need not be experienced politicians who have worked their way up a party's political ladder over the course of several elections. Today it is not at all unusual for candidates to assemble their own campaign organizations and operate with only loose connections to their political parties.

Remember, too, that how voters see a candidate—the impressions they have of that candidate's personality, character, abilities, and so on—is one of the major factors that influence voting behavior. Candidates and professional campaign managers are quite aware of this fact. They know that the kind of "image" a candidate projects in the media can have a telling effect on the outcome of an election.

Candidates regularly try to manipulate media coverage to their advantage. Campaign strategists understand that most people learn almost everything they know about a candidate from television. They therefore plan campaigns that emphasize television exposure. Such technical considerations as timing, location, lighting, and camera angles loom large, often at the expense of such substantive matters as the issues involved in an election or a candidate's qualifications for public office.

Good campaign managers also know that most television news programs are built out of stories that (1) take no more than a minute or two of air time, and (2) show people doing something interesting or exciting. Newscasts seldom feature "talking heads," speakers who drone on and on about some complex issue.

Instead, newscasts featuring candidates are usually short, sharply focused **sound bites**— snappy reports that can be aired in 30 or 45 seconds or so. Staged and carefully orchestrated visits to historic sites, factory gates, toxic-waste dumps, football games, and the like have become a standard part of the electoral scene.

Limits on Media Influence

Having said all this, it is all too easy to overstate the media's role in American politics. A number of built-in factors work to limit the media's impact on the behavior of the American voting public.

Voices on Government

Joseph Turow, a professor at the Annenberg School of Communications, studies the ways in which the media influence our political perspectives. Turow examines the mass media—from radio to the Internet—and their impact on people.

❝ *We have to make people a little more sophisticated about video images. . . . News and entertainment are, essentially, a battle over the definition of the world. You've got various sources in public relations, and interest groups and political organizations are always maneuvering to have a reporter write this or that, and we don't know, for example, why this person is on this television show. One of the things I tell my students is to interrogate the newspaper, interrogate the television show.* ❞

Evaluating the Quotation

What do you think Turow means by "interrogating" a newspaper or a television news program? How would following his advice change you as a "consumer" of the news?

For one thing, few people follow international, national, or even local political events very closely. Many studies of voting behavior show that in the typical election, only about 10 percent of those who can vote and only about 15 percent of those who do vote are well informed on the many candidates and issues under consideration in that election. In short, only a small part of the public actually takes in and understands much of what the media have to say about public affairs.

Moreover, most people who do pay some attention to politics are likely to be selective about it. That is, they most often watch, listen to, and read those sources that generally agree with their own viewpoints. They regularly ignore those sources with which they disagree. Thus, for example, many Democrats do not watch the televised campaign appearances of Republican candidates. Nor do many Republicans read newspaper stories about the campaign efforts of Democratic candidates.

Another important limit on the media's impact is the content the media carries. This is especially true of radio and television. Most television programs, for example, have little or nothing to do with public affairs, at least not directly. (A number of popular programs do relate to public affairs in an indirect way, however. Thus, many are "crime shows," and crime is certainly a matter of public concern. Many also carry a political message—for example, that the police are hard-working public servants.)

Advertisers who pay the high costs of television air time want to reach the largest possible audiences. Because most people are more interested in being entertained than in being informed about public issues, few public-affairs programs air in prime time. There are exceptions, however, such as *60 Minutes*, *20/20*, *Dateline*, and *Inside Politics*.

Radio and television mostly "skim" the news. They report only what their news editors judge to be the most important and/or the most interesting stories of the day. Even on widely watched evening news programs, most reports are presented in 60- to 90-second time slots. In short, the broadcast media seldom give the kind of in-depth coverage that a good newspaper can supply.

Newspapers are not as hampered as many other media in their ability to cover public affairs. Still, much of the content of most newspapers is nonpolitical. Like nearly all of television and radio, newspapers depend on their advertising revenues, which in turn depend on producing a product with the widest possible appeal. Newspaper readers are often more interested in the sports pages and the social, travel, advertising, and entertainment sections of a newspaper than they are in its news and editorial pages.

In-depth coverage of public affairs is available in the media to those who want it and will seek it out. There are a number of good newspapers around the country. In-depth coverage can also be found in several magazines and on a number of radio and television stations, including public broadcast outlets. Remember, however, that there is nothing about democracy that guarantees an alert and informed public. Like voting and other forms of political participation, being an informed citizen requires effort.

▲ **News or Entertainment?** Newspapers offer a variety of information, much of it not about politics, in order to appeal to the widest possible audience.

Section 3 Assessment

Key Terms and Main Ideas

1. Why is the Internet considered a **medium**?
2. How do the media influence the **public agenda**?
3. What limits are there on media influence?
4. Why has radio survived despite television's enormous appeal?

Critical Thinking

5. **Drawing Inferences** How might campaign managers use a presidential debate among the candidates to their client's advantage?
6. **Demonstrating Reasoned Judgment** You are a candidate for the presidency. Draw up an advertising plan that shows the percentages of your advertising budget that you will allocate to each type of media. Then write a rationale to back up your plan.

Take It to the Net

7. Select an issue on the public agenda and follow links to read more about it. Then prepare an oral report in which you explain the issue to the rest of your class. What role have the media played in bringing this issue to the public's attention? Use the links provided in the Social Studies area at the following Web site for help in completing this activity. **www.phschool.com**

Do Candidates Deserve "Equal Time"?

A free press plays an essential role in political campaigns. It not only informs voters of candidates' views on key issues but also provides analysis and commentary on those views and issues. Often, of course, candidates strongly disagree with the press's opinions. In such cases, does the press have an obligation to give candidates an equal opportunity to respond?

Miami Herald Publishing Co. v. *Tornillo* (1974)

In 1972, while Pat Tornillo was running for a seat in the Florida House of Representatives, the *Miami Herald* published a series of editorials that were critical of his candidacy. Tornillo demanded that the newspaper print his responses to the editorials. He based his demand on a Florida "right of reply" law, which provided that if a newspaper attacked a political candidate's personal character or political record, the candidate could require the paper to print his or her reply. Under the law, the reply had to appear in as prominent a place and in the same kind of type as the criticisms themselves, so long as the reply was no longer than the original criticisms. The newspaper could not charge the candidate for publishing the reply.

The *Herald* refused to print Tornillo's reply, and instead sought a court ruling that the right of reply law was unconstitutional. The State circuit court ruled that the law unconstitutionally limited freedom of the press. The Florida Supreme Court then reversed that opinion, and the paper appealed the Florida decision to the Supreme Court.

Arguments for Miami Herald Publishing Co.

1. The right of reply law is unconstitutional. It violates the First Amendment by regulating the content of a newspaper.
2. The law is so broadly worded that it cannot be enforced. A newspaper editor would not be able to determine which words in an editorial might create an obligation for the paper to print the candidate's reply.
3. The law unconstitutionally restricts the right of a newspaper to make critical comments on matters of public importance.

Arguments for Tornillo

1. Since many local newspapers are owned by a small number of national news organizations, those few organizations have great power to select and shape the news that is distributed to the public. Furthermore, it is economically difficult for opponents of those newspapers to create competing papers. Measures like the right of reply law are therefore necessary to ensure that the public receives a full range of views.
2. The right of reply law does not restrict the *Herald's* right of free speech because it does not prevent the paper from saying anything it wants to. The law merely provides a balancing mechanism for presenting opposing points of view.
3. The right of reply is an appropriate way to protect an individual's interest in his or her reputation, and presents an acceptable method of correcting harm to a person's reputation when it occurs.

Decide for Yourself

1. Review the constitutional grounds on which each side based its arguments and the specific arguments each side presented.
2. Debate the opposing viewpoints presented in this case. Which viewpoint do you favor?
3. Predict the impact of the Court's decision on press coverage of campaign issues and on the extent to which Americans will be adequately informed on political matters. (To read a summary of the Court's decision, turn to the Supreme Court Glossary on page 799.)

Political Dictionary

public affairs (p. 208)

public opinion (p. 209)

mass media (p. 211)

peer group (p. 212)

opinion leader (p. 212)

mandate (p. 216)

interest group (p. 216)

public opinion poll (p. 217)

straw vote (p. 217)

sample (p. 218)

random sample (p. 218)

quota sample (p. 219)

medium (p. 223)

public agenda (p. 228)

sound bite (p. 229)

Practicing the Vocabulary

Matching *Choose a term from the list above that best matches each description.*

1. The people with whom one usually associates
2. A means of communication
3. The attitudes held by a significant number of people on matters of government and politics
4. A person who has an unusual amount of influence on the views held by other people
5. News reports that are brief and sharply focused
6. An organization that tries to influence public policy

Fill in the Blank *Choose a term from the list above that best completes each sentence.*

7. A type of sample that is carefully constructed to reflect the major characteristics of a particular universe is called a _____.
8. Winners of elections often claim that their victories at the polls represent a _____ to carry out their proposed programs.
9. A _____ is a type of sample in which each member of the sample universe has a mathematically equal chance of being included.
10. _____ are those means of communication that can reach large numbers of people.

Reviewing Main Ideas

Section 1

11. Why is it incorrect to say that public opinion represents the single, undivided view of the American people?
12. Why are the influences of education and family so powerful in the development of political attitudes?
13. Besides education and family, what other forces help influence public opinion in American society?
14. Name at least three ways in which public opinion can be expressed.
15. **(a)** Why is your opinion about a rock group not a public opinion? **(b)** Give at least three examples of topics on which a group of people may have a public opinion.

Section 2

16. Elections, interest groups, the media, and personal contacts all are means of measuring public opinion. **(a)** Describe how each is used to measure public opinion. **(b)** What are the limitations of each?

17. What is the most reliable means of measuring public opinion? Explain your answer.
18. Why it is only partly correct to say that government in the United States is "government by public opinion"?
19. How does a straw vote differ from a scientific poll?
20. What factors can make a public opinion poll less than completely accurate?

Section 3

21. **(a)** What are the four major sources of political information in the United States? **(b)** List at least one advantage of each source.
22. Name two reasons for the decline in the number of daily newspapers in the United States.
23. Explain the impact of the mass media on the public agenda.
24. What is the impact of the mass media on electoral politics?
25. What factors limit the impact of the mass media on American politics?

Critical Thinking Skills

26. *Applying the Chapter Skill* Write five questions that you would ask if you were conducting a poll on the significance of mass media in the lives of American voters.

27. *Drawing Inferences* Political scientist V. O. Key, Jr., once described public opinion as those expressions that governments "find it prudent to heed." Do you agree with Key's definition? Explain your answer.

28. *Expressing Problems Clearly* You have read that schools are key agents of political socialization. What are the most important elements of citizenship in American society that you think students ought to learn in school?

29. *Distinguishing False From Accurate Images* In spite of its powerful and important role in American society, television is often criticized for its lack of content on important issues. **(a)** Considering what you have read in this chapter, do you feel that it is accurate to characterize television as lacking in real content? **(b)** If so, what do you think is to blame for the quality of television programming?

Analyzing Political Cartoons

Using your knowledge of American government and this cartoon, answer the questions below.

30. Who are the characters in the cartoon intended to represent?
31. What does the cartoon suggest about television coverage of candidate debates?

★ You Can Make a Difference

In what ways could your school be improved—increased recycling, a "say no to graffiti" campaign, more interest in student government? Choose an area that would benefit your school, and then decide on a medium—print, radio, or television—for getting your ideas across to the rest of the student body. Write a story or script for your chosen medium, including interviews if appropriate. If you have chosen radio or television, and equipment is available, record your piece for broadcast.

Participation Activities

32. *Current Events Watch* Choose a current topic, such as the death penalty or prayer in public schools, and find two newspaper reports about it. One should be a factual report, and one should be an editorial. Summarize the main points of each report. Then contrast the language, selection of details, and point of view of the two reports to explain how an editorial differs from a news story.

33. *Time Line Activity* Create a time line showing events in the development of television, newspaper, radio, magazine, and Internet news and information reporting. Include a summary of the trends in the roles of the various media that your time line illustrates.

34. *It's Your Turn* Create a poster that urges students to spend more time educating themselves about public issues. As you plan your poster, remember that the purpose of your poster is to encourage good citizenship. Show reasons why you think students should become more involved and suggest ways in which they might do so. Display your class's posters throughout the school. **(Creating a Poster)**

Take It to the Net

Chapter 8 Self-Test As a final review activity, take the Chapter 8 Self-Test in the Social Studies area at the Web site listed below, and receive immediate feedback on your answers.

www.phschool.com

Interest Groups

"We are a nation of communities, of tens and tens of thousands of ethnic, religious, social, business, labor union, neighborhood, regional and other organizations, all of them varied, voluntary, and unique. . . ."

—George H.W. Bush (1988)

Do you think that interest groups represent only people with money, power, and influence? On the contrary, many interest groups serve as the voice of ordinary people who care passionately about a cause or policy. They represent the diversity of Americans and their opinions about issues.

◆ Minnesota farmers' protest

★ You Can Make a Difference

IN THE LATE 1990s, gun violence became a serious issue for schools. In response, Ben Gelt and David Winkler, recent Denver high school graduates, postponed their college plans to start SAFE Students, a national youth movement. In July 1999, they led a group of 95 Colorado students to Washington to lobby Congress for gun control laws. The group's goal is to teach members "how to become involved in the political process, and that their voices do matter." SAFE Students works to educate students about the gun debate, organize local groups across the country, and lobby at the national party conventions.

SECTION 1

The Nature of Interest Groups (pp. 236–240)

★ Interest groups are private organizations that try to persuade public officials to respond to the shared attitudes of their members.

★ Unlike political parties, interest groups do not nominate candidates, focus on winning elections, or concern themselves with a broad range of issues.

★ Among their positive benefits, interest groups stimulate interest in public affairs and serve as a vehicle for participation in the political process.

★ Interest groups have been criticized for having influence disproportionate to their size and occasionally using unethical tactics.

SECTION 2

Types of Interest Groups (pp. 242–247)

★ Most people belong to several organizations that meet the definition of an interest group.

★ Most interest groups represent economic interests such as business, labor, agriculture, and certain professions.

★ Some interest groups are devoted to specific political and social causes, religious interests, or the welfare of a certain segment of the population.

★ Public-interest groups work for some aspect of the public good.

SECTION 3

Interest Groups at Work (pp. 249–254)

★ Interest groups supply the public with information favorable to the group's cause, work to build a positive image for the group, and promote the group's policies.

★ Interest groups frequently use propaganda to achieve their goals.

★ While most interest groups take a balanced approach to affecting public policy, single-interest groups focus on an individual issue and fight for this issue aggressively.

★ Lobbyists use a variety of techniques to try to persuade policy makers to share an interest group's point of view.

Keep It Current

Items marked with this logo are periodically updated on the Internet. Keep up-to-date with what's happening in the news. To get current information on interest groups, go to **www.phschool.com**

The Nature of Interest Groups

Section Preview

OBJECTIVES

1. **Describe** the role of interest groups in influencing public policy.
2. **Compare and Contrast** political parties and interest groups.
3. **Explain** why people see interest groups as both good and bad for American politics.

WHY IT MATTERS

Aware of it or not, you almost certainly belong to at least one interest group today. And, knowingly or not, you will join several more of these groups over coming years.

POLITICAL DICTIONARY

★ **public policy**
★ **public affairs**

An interest group is a private organization that tries to persuade public officials to respond to the shared attitudes of its members. You may not think that you belong to any interest groups, but as you read this section, you may well discover that you do. In fact, you might even belong to several of them. You will probably also realize that you will become a part of many more of these organizations in the years to come. This is because interest groups provide one of the most effective means by which Americans try to get government to respond to their wants and needs.

The Role of Interest Groups

Where do you stand on the question of gun control? What about prayer in public schools? Abortion? An increase in the minimum wage? What can you do to lend support to your views on these and other issues? How can you increase the chance that your position on these issues will carry the day?

Joining with others who share your views is both practical and democratic. Organized efforts to protect group interests are a fundamental part of the democratic process. Moreover, the right to do so is protected by the Constitution. Remember that the 1st Amendment guarantees "the right of the people peaceably to assemble, and to petition the Government for a redress of grievances."

Interest groups are sometimes called pressure groups. They are also known as special interests, organized interests, and lobbies. They give themselves a variety of additional names, too, such as committees, clubs, associations, leagues, and federations.

However they label themselves, interest groups seek to influence public policy. Used in this general sense, **public policy** includes all of the goals a government sets and the various courses of action it pursues as it attempts to realize these goals. Laws governing speed limits and seat-belt

▲ Interest groups often send members items such as buttons and bumper stickers to help publicize their causes.

▲ Americans participate in a wide variety of interest groups. Families USA advocates for family health care (left). The Gray Panthers call attention to the special concerns of senior citizens (center). Students from the Texas School for the Deaf acted as members of an interest group when they marched on their State capital to protest funding cuts that affected their school (right). *Critical Thinking What do these groups have in common?*

use are examples of public policy. So is a President's decision to send military aid to a foreign country.

Because interest groups exist to shape public policy, they operate wherever those policies are made or can be influenced. They also function at every level of government. They therefore can be found on Capitol Hill and elsewhere in Washington, D.C., in every one of the 50 State capitals, in thousands of city halls and county courthouses, and in many other places at the local level all across the country. In short, as diplomat and historian Lord Bryce put it somewhat indelicately more than a century ago: "Where the body is, there will the vultures be gathered."

Remember, our society is a pluralistic one. It is not dominated by any single elite. It is, instead, composed of a number of distinct cultures and groups. Increasingly, the members of various ethnic, racial, religious, and other groups compete for and share in the exercise of political power in this country.

Political Parties and Interest Groups

Interest groups are made up of people who unite for some political purpose. So, too, are political parties. These two types of political organizations

necessarily overlap in a number of ways. However, they differ from one another in three striking respects: (1) in the making of nominations, (2) in their primary focus, and (3) in the scope of their interests.

First, parties nominate candidates for public office; interest groups do not. Remember, making nominations is a major function of political parties. If an interest group were to nominate candidates, it would, in effect, become a political party.

Interest groups do, of course, try to affect the outcomes of primaries and other nominating contests. However, interest groups do not themselves pick candidates who then run under their labels. It may be widely known that a particular interest group actively supports a candidate, but that candidate seeks votes as a Republican or Democrat.[1]

Second, political parties are chiefly interested in winning elections and controlling government. Interest groups are chiefly concerned with controlling or influencing the *policies* of government. Unlike parties, interest groups do not face the problems involved in trying to appeal to the largest possible number of people. In short, political parties are mostly interested in the *who,*

[1]Note that this discussion centers on the differences between interest groups and major parties. There are some striking parallels between interest groups and most minor parties—for example, in terms of their scope of interest.

and interest groups are mostly concerned with the *what*, of government. To put it another way, political parties focus mostly on the candidate, while interest groups focus mostly on an issue such as environmental protection or gun control.

Third, political parties are necessarily concerned with the whole range of public affairs, with everything of concern to voters. Interest groups almost always concentrate only on those issues that most directly affect the interests of their members.

In addition, interest groups are private organizations. Unlike political parties, they are not accountable to the public. Their members, not the voters, pass judgment on their performance.

Interest Groups: Good or Bad?

Do interest groups pose a threat to the well-being of the American political system? Or, on the contrary, are they a valuable part of that system? The argument over the merit of interest groups goes back to the beginnings of the Republic.

Two Early Views

Many people have long viewed interest groups with deep suspicion. In 1787, James Madison warned the new nation against the dangers of what he called "factions." He made his view of those groups clear when he defined a faction as

PRIMARY Sources *"a number of citizens, whether amounting to a majority or minority of the whole, who are united and actuated by some common impulse of passion, or of interest, adverse to the rights of other citizens, or to the permanent and aggregate interests of the community."*
— *The Federalist* No. 10[2]

Despite his mistrust, Madison thought that factions were inevitable in human society, and he was opposed to any attempt to abolish them. A society could only eliminate factions, he said, by eliminating freedom. Instead, wrote Madison, it was necessary to moderate the potential extremism of factions with a balance of powers; that is, with the governmental system set out in the proposed Constitution. The separations of power in that system would mean, said Madison, that factions would tend to counteract and balance each others' power. Thus, none could become a dominating influence.

Nearly fifty years later, Alexis de Tocqueville was deeply impressed by the vast number of organizations he found in the United States. Tocqueville was a Frenchman who toured much

---

[2] The text of *The Federalist* No. 10 appears in the historic documents section that begins on page 780.

▶ These photos show a vacant lot in Berkeley, California, being turned into a park by community activists. Many such activists belong to interest groups that work to persuade local governments to clean up and improve unused land in towns and cities throughout the United States. *Critical Thinking What are the advantages to an individual citizen of joining an interest group?*

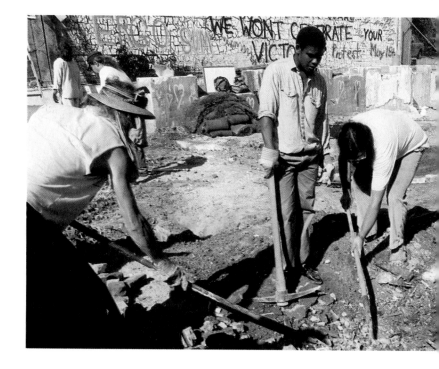

of this country in the early 1830s. In *Democracy in America* he wrote that

PRIMARY Sources

"In no country in the world has the principle of association been more successfully used, or more unsparingly applied to a multitude of different objects, than in America. **"**
— *Alexis de Tocqueville*

In a similar vein, he also observed that

"Americans of all ages, all conditions, and all dispositions, constantly form associations . . . not only commercial and manufacturing . . . but . . . of a thousand other kinds—religious, moral, serious, futile, extensive or restricted, enormous or diminutive. **"**

Are interest groups "good" or "bad"? To determine the answer, you must weigh, on the one hand, the functions those groups perform in American politics and, on the other, the various criticisms that are often leveled at them.

Valuable Functions of Interest Groups

First, among their several valuable functions, interest groups help to stimulate interest in **public affairs.** Public affairs are those issues and events that concern the people at large. Interest groups raise awareness of public affairs mostly by developing and promoting those policies they

favor and by opposing those policies they see as threats to their interests.

Second, interest groups represent their members on the basis of shared attitudes rather than on the basis of geography—by what their members think as opposed to where they happen to live. Public officials are elected from districts drawn on maps. But many of the issues that concern and unite people today have less to do with *where* they live than with, say, *how* they make a living. A labor union member who lives in Chicago may have much more in common with someone who does the same kind of work in Seattle than he or she does with someone who owns a business in Chicago or runs a farm in another part of Illinois.

Third, organized interests often provide useful, specialized, and detailed information to government—for example, on employment, price levels, or the sales of new and existing homes. These data are important to the making of public policy, and government officials often cannot obtain them from any other source. This flow of information works both ways, as well. Interest groups frequently get information from public agencies and pass it along to their members.

Fourth, interest groups are vehicles for political participation. They are a means through which like-minded citizens can pool their resources and channel their energies into collective political action. One mother concerned about drunk driving cannot accomplish very much acting alone. Thousands of people joined in an organization like MADD (Mothers Against Drunk Driving) certainly can.

Fifth, interest groups add another element to the checks-and-balances feature of the political process. Many of them keep close tabs on the work of various public agencies and officials and thus help to make sure that they perform their tasks in responsible and effective ways.

Finally, interest groups regularly compete with one another in the public arena. That competition places a very real limit on the lengths to which some groups might otherwise go as they seek to advance their own interests. For example, the automotive industry may work to weaken or postpone auto emission standards imposed under the Clean Air Act. Their efforts may be opposed—and to some

Interpreting Political Cartoons *What does the cartoon suggest about the relationship between interest groups and Congress?*

extent counterbalanced—by environmental and health-related organizations.

Criticisms

All of what has just been said is not meant to suggest that interest groups are above reproach. On the contrary, they can be, and often are, criticized on several counts.

The potential "bad" side of interest groups is sometimes all too apparent. Many of them push

their own special interests which, despite their claims to the contrary, are not always in the best interests of other Americans. Their critics often make these more specific charges:

1. Some interest groups have an influence far out of proportion to their size, or, for that matter, to their importance or contribution to the public good. Thus, the contest over "who gets what, when, and how" is not always a fair fight. The more highly organized and better-financed groups often have a decided advantage in that struggle.

2. It is sometimes hard to tell just who or how many people a group really represents. Many groups have titles that suggest that they have thousands—even millions—of dedicated members. Some organizations that call themselves such things as "The American Citizens Committee for . . ." or "People United Against . . ." are, in fact, only "fronts" for a very few people with very narrow interests.

3. Many groups do not in fact represent the views of all of the people for whom they claim to speak. Very often, both in and out of politics, an organization is dominated by an active minority who conduct the group's affairs and make its policy decisions.

4. Finally, some groups use tactics that, if they were to become widespread, would undermine the whole political system. These practices include bribery and other heavy-handed uses of money, overt threats of revenge, and so on. They are not altogether common, but the danger is certainly there.

Section 1 Assessment

Key Terms and Main Ideas

1. What is **public policy**?
2. List and describe the three main areas in which political parties and interest groups differ.
3. **(a)** How do interest groups stimulate interest in **public affairs**? **(b)** Name at least three additional functions of interest groups.
4. On what bases are interest groups often criticized?

Critical Thinking

5. **Demonstrating Reasoned Judgment** Suppose that you want to form a group in your school to combat racial discrimination. Which of the functions of interest groups described in this section would your group most likely fulfill? Explain your answer.

6. **Making Decisions** Suppose that you are asked to contribute money to an interest group that calls itself "Citizens for Better Schools." What information would you want to find out about this group before making a contribution?

 Take It to the Net

7. Select some groups that interest you and follow links to their Web sites. If you were to support one of these groups, which would it be? Write a paragraph explaining your choice. Use the links provided in the Social Studies area at the following Web site for help in completing this activity. **www.phschool.com**

Recognizing Bias

When you're doing research—for instance, trying to become informed on a ballot issue—you need to know whether the information you find is biased or unbiased. Why? Information that is biased reflects a particular point of view. It might exclude, intentionally or not, other legitimate views, or present them in an unfavorable way.

Recognizing bias is especially important now that so much information is available on anonymous Web sites across the Internet. The following steps will help you to identify biased information when you encounter it:

1. Identify the source. Who provided the information? Some interest groups choose names that do not truly disclose who they represent. They may use names that are designed to appeal to your beliefs or values. Be on the lookout for names that sound vague, often patriotic. Read the fictitious press release at right. (a) Identify the source of the "facts." (b) Who might this group represent?

2. Identify the purpose. Determine whether the information is intended to inform or to persuade. An item designed to persuade might leave out information that does not support the author's viewpoint. What is the purpose of this press release?

3. Read carefully for evidence of bias. Use the checklist (at upper right) to evaluate the item.

4. Decide if the item is biased. Remember, a biased account is not necessarily deceptive or bad. It might in fact reflect a worthy yet one-sided account. If you are looking for a balanced account of an issue, you should find one that avoids the pitfalls explained here. Is the press release shown here biased? If so, note the language that indicates the bias.

A BIAS TEST

■ Does it present a single viewpoint, or more than one view?

■ Is the conclusion supported by verifiable, relevant facts?

■ Does the item contain opinion disguised as fact?

■ Is it based on valid assumptions?

■ Does it include stereotypes or generalizations?

■ Does it exclude important information?

Study Says
Pastries Are Health Food

NEW YORK: The Society for Better Living today released a new study showing conclusively that certain types of pastries actually help reduce heart attacks. The study tracked the incidence of heart attacks in consumers of Creampuff Healthy Pastries and found that most consumers felt "completely healthy."

"We're pleased with the results," a Creampuff spokesman said today. "We think our customers are smart enough to assess the state of their own health. In the interest of free enterprise and free choice, we demand that the government stop forcing pastry manufacturers to list the amount of calories and fat in their products."

Test for Success

Find a report or a quotation in the news that reflects bias. What items in the Bias Test (upper right) does it violate?

Section Preview

OBJECTIVES

1. **Explain** how the American tradition of joining organizations has resulted in a wide range of interest groups.
2. **Describe** four categories of groups based on economic interests.
3. **Outline** the reasons why other interest groups have been created.
4. **Identify** the purpose of public-interest groups.

WHY IT MATTERS

America is "a nation of joiners"— including joiners of interest groups. Some of these groups are based on economic interests, some on other issues. Some are public-interest groups, which seek to benefit all Americans.

POLITICAL DICTIONARY

★ trade association
★ labor union
★ public-interest group

"Everything from A to Z." That expression can be aptly applied to the many interest groups in this country. These organizations include, among thousands of others, the American Association of Advertising Agencies, the American Association of Retired Persons, the Association on American Indian Affairs, the Amateur Athletic Union of the United States, the Zionist Organization of America, and the American Zoo and Aquarium Association. All of these thousands of organizations can be more or less readily classified and, so, usefully described, as interest groups.

▲ *Habitat for Humanity* This interest group combats homelessness by using volunteer labor to build affordable housing.

An American Tradition

The United States has often been called "a nation of joiners." Recall Alexis de Tocqueville's observations cited in the previous section. Tocqueville's comments, true when he made them, have become even more accurate over time.

No one really knows how many associations exist in the United States today. There are thousands upon thousands of them, however, and at every level in society. Each one is an interest group whenever it tries to influence the actions of government in order to promote its own goals and special interests.

Interest groups come in all shapes and sizes. They may have thousands or even millions of members, or only a handful. They may be well- or little-known, long-established or new and even temporary, highly structured or quite loose and informal, wealthy or with few resources. No matter what their characteristics, they are found in every field of human activity in this country.

The largest number of interest groups have been founded on the basis of an economic interest, especially on the bases of business, labor, agricultural, and professional interests. Some groups are grounded in a geographic area, such as the South, the Columbia River Basin, or the State of Indiana.

Other groups have been born out of a cause or an idea, such as prohibition of alcohol, environmental protection, or gun control. Still other interest groups exist to promote the welfare of certain groups of people—veterans, senior citizens, a racial minority, the homeless, women, people with disabilities and so on.

Many people belong to a number of interest groups. A car dealer, for example, may belong to the local Chamber of Commerce, a car dealers' association, the American Legion, a local taxpayers' league, a garden club, a church, the PTA, the American Cancer Society, the National Wildlife Federation, and several other local, regional, or national groups. All of these are, to one degree or another, interest groups—including the church and the garden club, even though the car dealer may never think of these groups in that light.[3]

Many people may belong to groups that take conflicting stands on political issues. For example, a program to improve the city's streets may be supported by the local Chamber of Commerce and the car dealers' association but opposed by the taxpayers' league. The taxpayers' league may endorse a plan to eliminate plantings in traffic islands while the garden club wants to keep the plantings.

Groups Based on Economic Interests

Most interest groups are formed on the basis of economic interests. That is, they are based on the manner in which people make their living. Among these groups, the most active—and certainly the most effective—are those representing business, labor, agriculture, and certain professions.

Business Groups

Business has long looked to government to promote and protect its interests. Recall that merchants, creditors, and property owners were the people most responsible for calling the Constitutional Convention in 1787. In the early years of the Republic, business interests fought

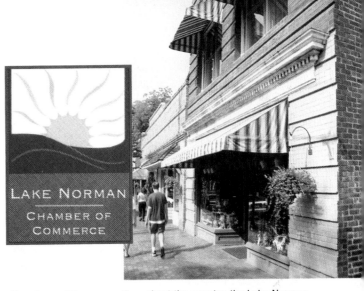

▲ Like Chambers of Commerce throughout the country, the Lake Norman, North Carolina, Chamber of Commerce supports local businesses. *Critical Thinking What might be the advantages for small businesses of joining an interest group?*

for and won the protective tariff. Along with organized labor, many of them continue to work to maintain it, even now.

The United States Brewers' Association, the oldest organized interest group at work in national politics today, was born in 1862 when Congress first levied a tax on beer. The association's purpose was to assure the brewing trade that its interests would be "vigorously prosecuted before the legislative and executive departments."

Hundreds of business groups now operate in Washington, D.C., in the 50 State capitals, and at the local level across the country. The two best-known business organizations are the National Association of Manufacturers (NAM) and the Chamber of Commerce of the United States.

Formed in 1895, NAM now represents some 14,000 firms. It generally speaks for "big business" in public affairs. The Chamber of Commerce was founded in 1912. Over the years, it has become a major voice for the nation's thousands of smaller businesses. It has more than 4,000 local chambers and now counts more than 200,000 business and professional firms and some 5 million individuals among its members.

Another major group, the Business Roundtable, has also taken a large role in promoting and defending the business community in recent years. Begun in 1972, the Roundtable is composed of the chief executive officers of 200 of the nation's largest, most prestigious, and most influential corporations.

---

[3]Churches often take stands on such public issues as drinking, curfew ordinances, and legalized gambling, and they often try to influence public policy in those matters. Garden clubs often try to persuade cities to do such things as improve public parks and beautify downtown areas. Not every group to which people belong can properly be called an interest group, of course. But the point is that many groups that are not often thought to be interest groups in fact are.

Membership in Labor Unions

Note: Statistics are for nonfarm employees.

SOURCE: AFL-CIO

 Interpreting Graphs Although membership in labor unions has declined, organized labor remains a powerful force. Here pro-labor and other protestors express their views at the 1999 World Trade Organization negotiations in Seattle, Washington. **(a) In what years did union membership peak? (b) What factors might account for this peak and subsequent decline?**

Most segments of the business community also have their own interest groups, often called **trade associations.** They number in the hundreds and include the American Trucking Association, the Association of American Railroads, the American Bankers Association, the National Restaurant Association, and many more.

Despite their common goal of promoting business interests, business groups do not always present a solid front. In fact, they often disagree, and sometimes fight, among themselves. The trucking industry, for example, does its best to get as much federal aid as possible for highway construction. The railroads, however, are unhappy with what they see as "special favors" for their competition. At the same time, the railroads see federal taxes on gasoline, oil, tires, and other "highway users fees" as legitimate and necessary sources of federal income. The truckers take quite another view.

Labor Groups

A **labor union** is an organization of workers who share the same type of job or who work in the same industry. Labor unions press for government policies that will benefit their members.

The strength and clout of organized labor have ebbed over the past several years. Some 16 million Americans, less than 13.5 percent of the nation's labor force, belong to labor unions today. In the 1940s and 1950s, as many as a

third of all working Americans were union members; and as recently as 1975, union membership accounted for fully a fourth of the labor force. In spite of recent declines in union membership, however, labor unions remain a powerful force in American politics.

A host of groups represent the interests of organized labor. The largest, in both size and political power, is the AFL-CIO (the American Federation of Labor-Congress of Industrial Organizations). It is now made up of some 100 separate unions, such as the Retail Clerks International Union, the International Association of Machinists and Aerospace Workers, and the American Federation of State, County, and Municipal Employees. With all its unions, the AFL-CIO has about 13 million members. Each union, like the AFL-CIO itself, is organized on a national, State, and local basis.[4]

There are also a number of independent unions, that is, unions not affiliated with the AFL-CIO. The largest and most powerful of them include such groups as the Fraternal Order of Police, the National Treasury Employees Union, and the International Longshore and Warehouse Union.

Organized labor generally speaks with one voice on such social welfare and job-related matters as Social Security programs, minimum wages, and unemployment. Labor sometimes opposes labor, however. White-collar and blue-collar workers, for example, do not always share the same economic interests. Then, too, such factors as sectional interests (East-West, North-South, urban-rural, and so on) sometimes divide labor's forces. Production and transportation

---

[4]The AFL was formed in 1886 as a federation of craft unions. A craft union is made up of those workers who have the same craft or skill—for example, carpenters, plumbers, or electricians. The growth of mass-production industries created a large class of workers not skilled in any particular craft, however. The AFL found it difficult to organize these workers. Many of its craft unions opposed the admission of unions of unskilled workers to the AFL. In 1935, after years of bitter fighting, a group led by John L. Lewis of the United Mine Workers was expelled from the AFL. That group formed the CIO in 1938. The rivalries between these two major national unions eased to the point where a merger took place in 1955, creating the AFL-CIO.

interests (trucks versus railroads versus airplanes, for example) may create divisions as well.

Agricultural Groups

For much of our history, most Americans lived in the country, and most of them lived on farms. The First Census, taken in 1790, set the nation's population at 3,929,214 persons. It found that nearly all the Americans of that day—94.9 percent of them—lived outside any city or town.

The nation's population has increased dramatically since 1790, of course—to more than 285 million today. Over that period the nation's farm population has plummeted. Fewer than five million people—less than two percent of the population—live on farms in this country today. Still, farmers' influence on the government's agricultural policies is and has been enormous. Several powerful associations serve the interests of agriculture. They include several broad-based farm groups and a larger number of groups that represent farmers who raise particular commodities.

The most prominent farm groups are the National Grange, the American Farm Bureau Federation, and the National Farmers Union. The Grange, established in 1867, is the oldest and generally the most conservative of these groups. Over the years, it has been as much a social as a political organization, concerned about the welfare of farm families. Some 400,000 farm families are now members, and much of the Grange's strength is centered in the Northeast and the Mid-Atlantic States.

The Farm Bureau is the largest and generally most effective of the three agricultural groups. Formed in 1919, it now claims some four million farm-family members and is especially strong in the Midwest. The Farm Bureau generally supports federal programs to promote agriculture. However, it opposes most government regulation and favors the free market economy.

The National Farmers Union draws its strength from smaller and less prosperous farmers. It now has some 300,000 farm-family members, most of them in the upper Midwest and West. The National Farmers Union often calls itself the champion of the dirt farmer, and frequently disagrees with the other two major organizations. It regularly argues for increased federal aid to the nation's family-sized farms.

Many other groups speak for the producers of specific farm commodities, such as dairy products, grain, fruit, peanuts, livestock, cotton, wool, corn, and soybeans. For example, there are the National Association of Wheat Growers, the American Meat Institute, the National Cattlemen's Beef Association, the National Cotton Council, and many others.

Like business and labor groups, farm organizations sometimes find themselves at odds with one another. Thus, dairy, corn, soybean, and cotton groups compete as each of them tries to influence State laws regulating the production and sale of such products as margarine and yogurt. California and Florida citrus growers, each with their own groups, are sometimes pitted against one another, and so on.

Professional Groups

The professions are generally defined as those occupations that require extensive and specialized training, such as medicine, law, and teaching. These groups also maintain organizations to protect and promote their interests. Most professional groups are not nearly as large, well-organized, well-financed, or effective as most business, labor, and farm groups.

Three major professional groups are exceptions to the rule, however: the American

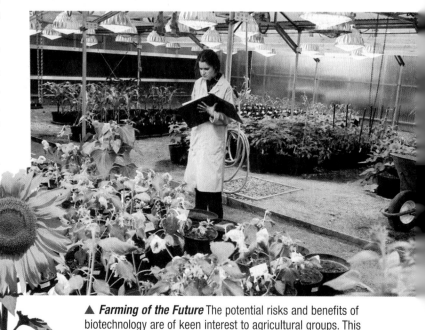

▲ *Farming of the Future* The potential risks and benefits of biotechnology are of keen interest to agricultural groups. This scientist is studying bioengineered sunflowers.

Voices on Government

General Colin Powell retired from the Army in 1993 after 35 years of service. The son of Jamaican immigrants, he rose through the military ranks, and headed the Joint Chiefs of Staff during the Gulf War. Today, he is the Secretary of State. Before that, he led America's Promise—The Alliance for Youth, a national organization whose mission is to build the character and competence of our nation's youth. Of the group's mission, he stated:

" *Reclaiming the next generation of Americans is a national challenge that requires a national response. That response is America's Promise. It calls on all Americans to scale up their investment in our youth; to challenge young people by having high expectations of them; and to engage youth with opportunities to realize those expectations through constructive, character-building activities.* "

Evaluating the Quotation

Based on what you have read in this chapter, how do the ideals of a group like America's Promise compare with the goals of other types of interest groups?

Medical Association (the AMA, to which some 300,000 physicians belong), the American Bar Association (the ABA, with more than 400,000 lawyers as members), and the National Education Association (the NEA, with more than 2.4 million teachers on its membership rolls). Each of these organizations has a very real impact on public policies, and at every level of government.

There are hundreds of less well-known and less politically active professional organizations: the American Society of Civil Engineers, the American Library Association, the American Political Science Association, and many more. Much of their effort centers on such matters as the standards of the profession, the holding of professional meetings, and the publication of scholarly journals. Still, each acts in some ways as an interest group, bent on influencing government policies for the welfare of the profession and its members.

Other Interest Groups

Most interest groups are based on economic concerns, but hundreds have been formed for other reasons. Many of these other groups have a good deal of political clout.

Groups That Promote Causes

A large number of groups exist to promote a cause or an idea. It would take several pages just to list them here, and so what follows is only a sampling of the more important ones.

The American Civil Liberties Union was born in 1920. The ACLU now has some 250,000 members. It fights in and out of court to protect civil and political rights. Common Cause dates from 1970, and its membership now exceeds 270,000. It calls itself "the citizen's lobby" and works for major reforms in the political process. The League of Women Voters of the United States and its many local leagues have been dedicated to stimulating participation in and greater knowledge about public affairs since 1920. The League now has more than 100,000 members.

The list of groups devoted to causes goes on and on. Many groups—such as the National Women's Political Caucus and several others—carry the women's rights banner. Many other groups, including the National Wildlife Federation, the Sierra Club, the Wilderness Society, and Friends of the Earth, are pledged to conservation and environmental protection.

Some interest groups are devoted to opposing certain causes. Other groups support those same causes. The National Right-to-Life Committee, Women Exploited by Abortion, and other groups oppose abortion. They are countered by the National Abortion Rights Action League, Planned Parenthood, and their allies. Similarly, the National Rifle Association fights most forms of gun control; Handgun Control, Inc. works for it.

Organizations That Promote the Welfare of Certain Groups

A number of interest groups seek to promote the welfare of certain segments of the population. Among the best known and most powerful are the American Legion and the Veterans of Foreign Wars, which work to advance the interests of the country's veterans. Groups like Older Americans, Inc. and the American Association of Retired

Persons (AARP) are very active in such areas as pensions and medical care for senior citizens.

Several organizations—notably the National Association for the Advancement of Colored People (NAACP), the National Urban League, and People United to Save Humanity (PUSH)—are concerned with public policies affecting African Americans. Other organizations, such as the Japanese American Citizens League, the Mexican American Legal Defense Fund, and the National Association of Arab Americans, support the country's many ethnic groups.

Religious Organizations

Religious organizations also try to influence public policy in several important areas. Many Protestants and their local and national churches do so through the National Council of Churches. Other Protestants belong to such groups as Christian Voice and the Christian Coalition.

The National Catholic Welfare Council represents the interests of Roman Catholics. The American Jewish Congress and B'nai B'rith's Anti-Defamation League represent the interests of the Jewish community.

Public-Interest Groups

Recall that interest groups seek public policies of special benefit to their members—business, labor, agriculture, veterans, teachers, environmentalists

and so on—and they work against policies that threaten their members' interests. Some groups, often called public-interest groups, have a broader goal. They work for the "public good." That is, a **public-interest group** is an interest group that seeks to institute certain public policies of benefit to all or most people in this country, whether or not they belong to or support that organization.[5]

Unlike most interest groups, public-interest groups focus on the roles that all Americans share. That is, they represent people as citizens, as consumers, as breathers of air, as drinkers of water, and so on.

Public-interest groups have become quite visible over the past 30 years or so. Among the best known and most active are Common Cause and the several organizations that make up Ralph Nader's Public Citizen, Inc. Some have existed for a much longer time—for example, the League of Women Voters, which has roots that reach deep into the history of woman suffrage.

---

[5]Of course, nearly all interest groups claim that they work for the "public good." Thus, the National Association of Manufacturers (NAM) says that lower taxes on business will stimulate the economy and so help everyone. The AFL-CIO says the same thing about spending more public dollars for more public works programs. But, as a general rule, most interest groups support or oppose public policies on a much narrower basis: on what they see to be the best interests of their own members.

Section 2 Assessment

Key Terms and Main Ideas

1. At what point does an organization become an interest group?
2. **(a)** What are the four major types of economically based interest groups? **(b)** List an example of each major type. **(c)** How does a **trade association** differ from a **labor union?**
3. For what reasons, other than economic ones, are interest groups created?
4. **(a)** What is a **public-interest group?** **(b)** How does it differ from other interest groups?

Critical Thinking

5. **Predicting Consequences** You have read that interest groups can disagree over certain issues, such as land use or taxes. Choose two groups mentioned in this section and create a scenario in which these groups conflict.

6. **Understanding Point of View** To which of the interest groups mentioned in this section might these persons belong: **(a)** Maria, an attorney in a city with a large minority population; **(b)** Bill, a retired midwestern soybean farmer? **(c)** To which groups might they both belong?

 Take It to the Net

7. Read about some specific labor unions. Then choose one union and prepare a brief oral report outlining that union's main concerns and its methods for effecting change. If applicable, include the role that women and minorities play in the union. Use the links provided in the Social Studies area at the following Web site for help in completing this activity. **www.phschool.com**

Destination: The American Dream

The National Urban League was founded in 1910 to help African Americans arriving in northern cities from the southeast. Today, the National Urban League continues to represent African Americans with branches in 34 States and the District of Columbia. At a recent national convention, President Hugh B. Price offered a plan to bridge the economic gap between poor Americans of color and the rest of the nation.

Hugh B. Price

There are regions of America where all that folks know of the economic boom is what they see on the evening news.

Everyone says we should depend less on government largesse and start our own businesses like everybody else. That sounds fine.

But the truth is that even to this day, according to a study just published by the Federal Reserve Board, black entrepreneurs seeking small business loans are rejected twice as much as whites with the same credit rating. . . .

There won't be One America until the gulf that divides minorities from mainstream America disappears once and for all. . . .

The National Urban League is proposing Ten Opportunity Commandments for the 21st Century. . . . I'm not talking about dead-end expenditures that don't pay off. These investments are proven winners. They'll pay handsome dividends to society for generations to come. . . .

1. Offer quality pre-school education to every child whose parents cannot afford it.

2. Provide affordable health care for the 41 million Americans who are uninsured.

3. Ensure that every public school serving poor children equips them for self-reliance.

4. Vastly increase support for proven programs that get the estimated 15 million high school dropouts back on track.

5. Guarantee universal access to affordable higher education.

6. Maintain national economic policies that promote high employment and economic growth in communities that have missed out on the good times.

7. Eliminate the digital divide by making the acquisition of computers and use of the Internet affordable for everyone.

8. Assure full participation of minorities in higher education, employment and contracting. There must be no retreat to tokenism.

9. Eradicate the homeownership gap along ethnic lines by providing 100 percent mortgage guarantees for credit-worthy, working class minority families.

10. Equalize access to capital by totally eliminating discriminatory business loan practices, so that minority entrepreneurs can join the chorus in proclaiming that the business of America is business.

Analyzing Primary Sources

1. What problem is Price seeking to solve in this speech?
2. (a) How many of Price's proposals are directly related to education? (b) Why might the National Urban League place such a great emphasis on education?
3. Name three institutions that could help solve the problems described by Price, and explain what specific steps they should take.

3 Interest Groups at Work

Section Preview

OBJECTIVES

1. **Explain** interest groups' three major goals in influencing public opinion.
2. **Describe** how interest groups use propaganda to persuade people to their point of view.
3. **Analyze** how interest groups try to influence political parties and elections.
4. **Examine** how lobbying brings group pressures to bear on the process of making public policy.

WHY IT MATTERS

Flip through a newspaper or magazine and you will no doubt see examples of interest groups at work—that is, using propaganda aimed at influencing public attitudes. Interest groups also work through political action committees and lobbyists to influence political parties and public policy.

POLITICAL DICTIONARY

★ propaganda
★ single-interest group
★ lobbying
★ grass roots

Interest groups exist to influence public policies. That is why they are good illustrations of the saying that politics is all about "who gets what, when, and how." Today, most interest groups use a wide variety of techniques as they try to influence public opinion, work to affect the outcome of elections, and lobby those who make public policy.

Influencing Public Opinion

Public opinion is the most significant long-term force in American politics. It is abundantly clear that, over the long run, no public policy can be followed successfully without the support of a sizeable portion of the population—and interest groups know this.

Interest groups regularly reach out to the public to accomplish one or all of three major goals:

1. To supply the public with information an organization thinks the people should have. This information is presented to support that group's interests. Thus, Handgun Control, Inc. often runs full-page magazine ads keyed to one fact: the number of Americans who are killed by handguns each year.

2. To build a positive image for a group. Thus, the National Rifle Association frequently runs ads

that feature the NRA's gun-safety programs and the many shooting tournaments it sponsors.

3. To promote a particular public policy. This, of course, is the purpose of most interest groups' efforts.

Propaganda

Interest groups try to create the public attitudes they want by using **propaganda.**[6] Propaganda is a technique of persuasion aimed at influencing individual or group behaviors. Its goal is to create a particular belief. That belief may be completely true or false, or it may lie somewhere

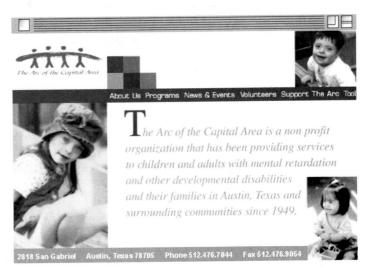

▲ Like Austin Arc, an advocacy group for people with developmental disabilities, many interest groups reach out to supporters on the Internet.

---

[6]The term comes from the Latin *propagare*—to propagate, to spread, to disseminate. It has been a part of the American political vocabulary since the 1930s.

between those extremes. Today, people tend to think of propaganda as a form of lying and deception. As a technique, however, propaganda is neither moral nor immoral; it is amoral.

Propaganda does not use objective logic. Rather, it begins with a conclusion. Then it brings together any evidence that will support that conclusion and disregards information that will not. Propagandists are advertisers, persuaders—and occasionally even brainwashers—who are interested in influencing others to agree with their point of view.

The development of the mass media in this country encouraged the use of propaganda, first in the field of commercial advertising, and then in politics. To be successful, propaganda must be presented in simple, interesting, and credible terms. Talented propagandists almost never attack the logic of a policy they oppose. Instead, they often attack it with name-calling. That is, they attach such labels as "communist" or "fascist." Other labels include "ultraliberal," "ultraconservative," "pie-in-the-sky," or "greedy." Or, they try to discredit a policy or person by card-stacking; that is, presenting only one side of the issue.

Policies that propagandists support receive labels that will produce favorable reactions. They use such glittering generalities as "American," "sound," "fair," and "just." Symbols are often used to elicit those reactions, too: Uncle Sam and the flag are favorites. So, too, are testimonials—endorsements, or supporting statements, from well-known television stars or professional athletes. The bandwagon approach, which urges people to follow the crowd, is another favorite technique. The plain-folks approach, in which the propagandist pretends to be one of the common people, gets heavy use, too. (For more information on propaganda techniques, see Skills for Life on page 17.)

Propaganda is spread through newspapers, radio, television, the Internet, movies, billboards, books, magazines, pamphlets, posters, speeches—in fact, through every form of mass communication. The more controversial or less popular a group's position, the more necessary the propaganda campaign becomes. Competing groups will likely be conducting campaigns of their own.

Influencing Parties and Elections

As you know, interest groups and political parties are very different creatures. They exist in the same environment, however, and their paths often cross.

For their part, leaders of interest groups know that political parties play a central role in selecting those people who make public-policy decisions. They are quite aware, too, that much of the government's policy-making machinery is organized by and through political parties.

Interest groups thus try to influence the behavior of political parties, and they do so in a number of ways. Some groups keep close ties with one or the other of the major parties. Most hope to secure the support of both of them. Several urge their members to become active in party affairs and try to win posts in party organizations.

An interest group's election tactics often have to involve some very finely tuned decisions. The group must consider how its actions on behalf of or against a candidate might affect its overall goal of influencing policy.

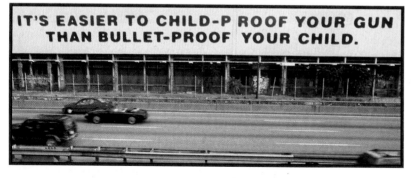

▲ Pro- and anti-gun control groups use billboards as one way to get their messages across to the public. *Critical Thinking Which forms of mass communication do you think are the most effective in helping interest groups spread their messages? Explain your answer.*

Growth of PACs

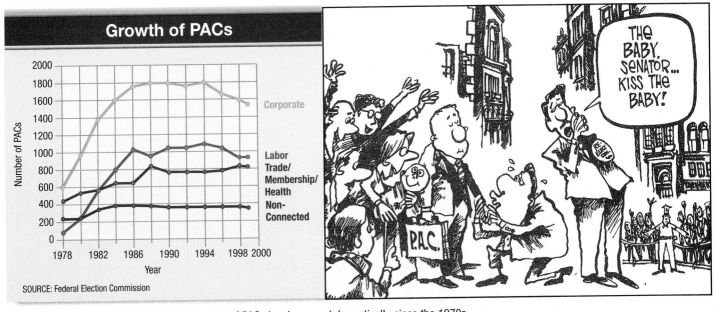

The Baby Senator... Kiss the Baby!

SOURCE: Federal Election Commission

Interpreting Graphs The total number of PACs has increased dramatically since the 1970s. *(a) How would you describe the growth of PACs during the 1990s? (b) What does the growth of PACs suggest about the way political campaigns are financed?*

If, for example, a group supports the Democratic candidate for a seat in the U.S. Senate, it may not want to help that candidate by attacking the Republican nominee in the race, especially if the Republican has some chance of winning. If the Republican does win the race, the group will not only have failed to advance its cause, but likely will have created an enemy. The interest group might also be concerned that another Republican candidate who wins some other office might be offended by attacks on a party colleague, even if he or she agrees with the group's policy aims.

Campaigns for public office cost a great deal of money. Interest groups are quite aware of this fact, and they are a major source of campaign funds today. Much of their financial help now goes to parties and their candidates through political action committees (PACs). As you know, PACs raise and distribute money to candidates who will further their goals. (See Chapter 7, Section 3.)

The number of PACs has grown dramatically over the past 20 years or so. One particular variety, often called **single-interest groups,** has grown most rapidly. These organizations are PACs that concentrate their efforts on one issue, such as abortion, gun control, or health care. They work for or, more often, against a candidate solely on the basis of that candidate's stand on that one

issue. For them, all other considerations—the candidate's record on other questions, his or her party identification or political experience, and so on—are of little or no importance.

Most interest groups focus on the public policy-making process. Any part they play in the electoral process is an offshoot of that primary concern. The efforts of single-interest groups stand as a notable exception to that rule.

Lobbying

Lobbying is usually defined as those activities by which group pressures are brought to bear on legislators and the legislative process. Certainly, it is that, but it is also much more. Realistically, lobbying includes all of the methods by which group pressures are brought to bear on all aspects of the public policy-making process.

What happens in a legislative body is often of deep concern to several different, and competing, interests. A bill to regulate the sale of firearms, for example, excites the interest of many individuals and groups. Those companies that make guns, those that sell them, and those that produce or sell ammunition, targets, scopes, hunting jackets, sleeping bags, and related products have a clear stake in that bill's contents and its fate. So, too, do law-enforcement agencies, hunters, wildlife conservationists, such groups

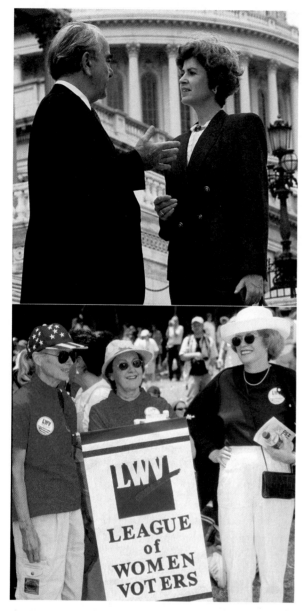

▲ **Making Their Views Known** Lobbyists make their interests known in a variety of ways, including direct contact with legislators (top). The League of Women Voters, which often works at the grassroots level, promotes active participation in government (bottom).

interest groups often have to carry their lobbying efforts beyond the legislative arena. Lobbying is thus also often brought into one and sometimes several agencies in the executive branch and sometimes into the courts, as well.

Nearly all of the more important organized interests in the country—business groups, labor unions, farm organizations, the professions, veterans, churches, and many more—maintain lobbyists in Washington. Most estimates put the number of people who earn at least part of their living by lobbying Congress at no fewer than 20,000. Lobbyists are also stationed in the 50 State capitals, and their number grows whenever the State's legislature is in session.[7]

Lobbyists at Work

Lobbyists themselves often prefer to be known by some other title—"legislative counsel" or "public representative," for example. Whatever they call themselves, their major task is to work for those matters that benefit their clients and against those that may harm them.

A lobbyist's effectiveness depends in large part on his or her knowledge of the political system. The competent lobbyist is thoroughly familiar with government and its procedures, with the facts of current political life, and with the techniques of "polite" persuasion. Some have been members of Congress or the State legislature. They know the "legislative ropes" and have many close contacts among present-day members. Many others are lawyers, former journalists, or men and women who have come into lobbying from the closely related field of public relations.

Lobbyists at work use a number of techniques as they try to persuade legislators and other policy makers to share their points of view. They see that articles, reports, and all sorts of other information favorable to their causes reach those officeholders. Many testify before legislative committees. If the House Committee on the Judiciary is considering a

as the National Rifle Association and the American Civil Liberties Union, and many others. These groups all seek to influence legislators as they consider the passage of that bill.

Public policy is made by much more than the words in a statute, however. What happens after a law has been passed is often of real concern to organized interests, too. How is the law interpreted? How vigorously is it applied by the agency that enforces it? What position will the courts take if the law is challenged on some legal ground? These questions point to the fact that

[7]The "lobby" is actually an outer room or main corridor or some other part of a capitol building to which the general public is admitted. The term *lobby-agent* was being used to identify favor-seekers at sessions of the New York State legislature in Albany by the late 1820s. By the 1830s the term had been shortened to lobbyist and was in wide use in Washington and elsewhere.

gun control bill, for example, representatives of all those groups with an interest in firearms mentioned earlier are certain to be invited, or to ask for the opportunity, to present their views. The testimony that lobbyists give is usually "expert," but, of course, it is also couched in terms favorable to the interests they represent.

Most lobbyists also know how to bring "grass-roots" pressures to bear. **Grass roots** means of or from the people, the average voters. The groups that the lobbyists speak for can mount campaigns by e-mail, letter, postcard, and phone from "the folks back home"—and often on short notice. Favorable news stories, magazine articles, advertisements, radio and television appeals, endorsements by noted personalities: These and the many other weapons of publicity are in the arsenal of the good lobbyist.

Several interest groups now publish ratings of members of Congress. These rankings are based on the votes cast on measures that those groups regard as crucial to their interests. Among the most prominent of the many organizations that now compile and publish such ratings are the Americans for Democratic Action (ADA), the American Civil Liberties Union (ACLU), the various State Public Interest Research Groups (PIRG), the American Conservative Union (ACU), the National Tax Limitation Committee (NTLC), and the Chamber of Commerce of the United States.

Each of these groups selects a number of key measures and then rates each member on the basis of his or her votes on those bills. In the usual rating scheme, each senator or representative is given a score that reflects how often he or she voted in accordance with the views of the interest group.

Interest groups see to it that the mass media publicize these ratings. They also distribute the ratings to the group's membership. Their ultimate objective is twofold: either to persuade unfriendly legislators to change their voting behavior or to help bring about their defeat in future elections.

The typical lobbyist of today is a far cry from those of an earlier day, and from many of the fictitious ones still found on television and in novels and the movies. The once fairly common practice of bribery and the widespread use of unethical practices are almost unknown. Most present-day lobbyists work openly, and their major techniques come under the headings of friendliness, persuasion, and helpfulness.

▲ Some interest groups rate members of Congress on issues of concern to their members. *Critical Thinking* **Why is using the Internet an effective way for interest groups to publish this kind of information?**

Lobbyists are ready to make campaign contributions, provide information, write speeches, and even draft legislation. The contributions are welcome, the information usually quite accurate, the speeches forceful, and the bills well-drawn. Most lobbyists know that if they behaved otherwise (gave false information, for example) they would damage, if not destroy, their credibility and thus their overall effectiveness.

Lobbyists work hard to influence committee action, floor debate, and the final vote in a legislative body. If they fail in one house, they carry their fight to the other. If they lose there too, they may turn to the executive branch and perhaps to the courts, as well.[8]

Lobby Regulation

Lobbying abuses do occur now and then, of course. False or misleading testimony, bribery, and other unethical pressures are not common, but they do happen. The first major attempt to corral lobbying came in 1946 when Congress passed the Federal Regulation of Lobbying Act. This law required lobbyists to register with the clerk of the House and the secretary of the Senate. More specifically, it required the registration

---

[8]Notice that various government agencies often act much like interest groups in their relations with Congress or with a State's legislature—for example, when they seek funds or when they offer testimony for or against a bill in committee.

of those individuals and groups who collected or spent money for the "principal purpose" of influencing legislation.

That vague phrase "principal purpose" proved to be a huge loophole through which many very active groups avoided registration. The 1946 law was also ineffective because its provisions applied only to lobbying efforts aimed at members of Congress, not at congressional staff members or at officials in the executive branch.

Congress finally responded to years of criticism of the 1946 law with a much tighter statute, the Lobbying Disclosure Act of 1995. That law eliminates the "principal purpose" standard. It requires registration by all individual lobbyists and organizations that seek to influence members of Congress, their staffers, or any policymaking official in the executive branch, from the President on down. Those who must register are required to supply such basic information as name, address, and principal place of business, plus a general description of their activities. They must also furnish similar information about their clients and describe in detail their lobbying activities in semiannual reports.

Each State also has its own law or laws regulating lobbying activities. The variations among them are extreme, however. Although most States have laws that are weaker than the federal statute, a few States have fairly rigorous laws. On the other hand, a few States condone virtually anything a lobbyist chooses to do.

Section 3 Assessment

Key Terms and Main Ideas

1. For what three reasons do interest groups reach out to the public?
2. (a) Why do interest groups use **propaganda?** (b) Identify at least three major propaganda techniques.
3. (a) Why do interest groups try to influence political parties? (b) What is a **single-interest group?**
4. How is **lobbying** used to influence public policy?

Critical Thinking

5. **Expressing Problems Clearly** Create a "Help Wanted" ad for a lobbyist. Include a job description as well as the preferred professional experience and abilities that a candidate should bring to the position.

6. **Recognizing Propaganda** Choose an issue of interest to students, such as year-round schooling or censorship of school publications. Then write a paragraph in which you use at least two of the propaganda techniques described in this section to persuade your audience to support your point of view.

Take It to the Net

7. Compare the contributions of various PACs to Republicans and Democrats. Which PACs primarily support Republicans? Which primarily support Democrats? Create a table to show your conclusions. Use the links provided in the Social Studies area at the following Web site for help in completing this activity. **www.phschool.com**

May Taxpayers Challenge Federal Spending Laws?

The federal courts possess the power of judicial review, but they can exercise that power only in those cases properly brought to them. May anyone who questions the constitutionality of a federal law challenge that law in court?

Flast v. Cohen (1968)

Flast was one of a group of seven taxpayers who objected to the use of federal funds to help support religious schools under the Elementary and Secondary Education Act of 1965. The group believed that public funding of these schools violated the First Amendment in two ways. First, such aid constituted an "establishment of religion." Second, by forcing the group to pay taxes to support religious activities, such aid interfered with the free exercise of their own religion. The group sued Secretary of Health, Education and Welfare Wilbur J. Cohen and other federal officials whose job it was to implement the Act.

The majority of a special three-judge federal court ruled that the Flast group did not have "standing" to proceed with the suit. "Standing" is a legal requirement under which a person can file a suit only if he or she has a personal stake in the outcome of the case. The court ruled that the plaintiffs' only stake in the outcome of the case was in their capacity as taxpayers, and this was not enough to give them standing. (In 1923, in the case of *Frothingham* v. *Mellon,* the Supreme Court had ruled that an individual could not challenge an act of Congress simply because that act affected the individual's tax bill.) The plaintiffs appealed to the Supreme Court, which considered whether its decision in *Frothingham* barred their suit.

Arguments for Flast

1. The *Frothingham* decision does not mean that a taxpayer may never challenge the constitutionality of an act of Congress. It merely means that a person's status as a taxpayer does not, by itself, give him or her standing to pose such a challenge. The plaintiffs in this case have a personal stake in the outcome of the case and should be allowed to proceed.
2. There is a connection between the plaintiffs' status as taxpayers and their claims in this case. The 1st Amendment's Establishment Clause limits Congress's power to collect taxes in support of religion. Thus the plaintiffs' role as taxpayers gives them a direct and concrete interest in the outcome of the case.

Arguments for Cohen

1. Federal courts already have a high caseload. The requirement that plaintiffs have sufficient standing helps prevent unnecessary lawsuits by ensuring that only those with a serious stake in the outcome bring cases.
2. People with no special interest in a controversy besides the tiny amount of their taxes that may be involved should not be allowed to sue in federal court.

Decide for Yourself

1. Review the constitutional grounds on which each side based its arguments and the specific arguments each side presented.
2. Debate the opposing viewpoints presented in this case. Which viewpoint do you favor?
3. Predict the impact of the Court's decision on other potential taxpayer suits challenging federal laws. (To read a summary of the Court's decision, turn to the Supreme Court Glossary on page 799.)

Political Dictionary

public policy (p. 236)

public affairs (p. 239)

trade association (p. 244)

labor union (p. 244)

public-interest group (p. 247)

propaganda (p. 249)

single-interest group (p. 251)

lobbying (p. 251)

grass roots (p. 253)

Practicing the Vocabulary

Matching *Choose a term from the list above that best matches each description.*

1. A type of interest group that represents business interests
2. The events and issues of concern to all the people in a society
3. Political action committee devoted to one issue
4. A type of interest group that works for the public good
5. The means by which group pressures are brought to bear on all aspects of the policy-making process
6. Of or from the common people, the average voters

Word Recognition *Replace the underlined definition with the correct term from the list above.*

7. Interest groups exist for the purpose of influencing all the things that a government endeavors to do in order to achieve certain goals.
8. In many industries workers have formed organizations of those who share the type of job or who work in the same industry.
9. One type of interest group is a(n) organization devoted to the interests of all the people.
10. The development of mass media encouraged the use of the technique of persuasion aimed at influencing individual or group behaviors.
11. Interest groups help to stimulate interest in the events and issues that concern people at large.

Reviewing Main Ideas

Section 1

12. Why are interest groups sometimes called "pressure groups" or "special interests"?
13. At what levels of government can you find interest groups operating?
14. In what ways are interest groups both similar to and different from political parties?
15. Summarize the debate over the role of interest groups in the American political system.
16. How do interest groups add an element to the checks-and-balances feature of the political process?

Section 2

17. For what reason has the United States often been called "a nation of joiners"?
18. Into what category do most interest groups fall?
19. What is the difference between private and public-interest groups?

20. **(a)** On what kinds of issues do labor groups generally agree? **(b)** On what kinds of issues might labor interests have different points of view?
21. **(a)** Describe three types of interest groups that are not based on economic interests. **(b)** List at least one example of each type of group.

Section 3

22. **(a)** For what reason must interest groups be concerned with public opinion? **(b)** For what purposes do interest groups appeal to public opinion?
23. What are the goals of a propagandist?
24. **(a)** To what extent are most interest groups concerned about elections? **(b)** What group provides an exception to this rule?
25. At what stages of policymaking must lobbyists be involved? Explain your answer.
26. The Lobbying Disclosure Act requires registration by all those individuals and organizations that do what?

Critical Thinking Skills

27. *Applying the Chapter Skill* In which of the following would you expect to find bias: **(a)** a newspaper account explaining the issues raised in a city council meeting **(b)** an editorial on the need for more computers in schools **(c)** an Internet article sponsored by an environmental group on the need to preserve open spaces? Explain your answer.

28. *Demonstrating Reasoned Judgment* You have read that forming interest groups is "both practical and democratic." **(a)** Explain your understanding of this statement. **(b)** What issues in your school or community might usefully be addressed by forming interest groups?

29. *Drawing Conclusions* Consider the discussion of the functions and criticisms of interest groups in Section 1. Based on this information, discuss your opinion about whether or not interest groups are positive or negative influences on the American political process.

Analyzing Political Cartoons

Using your knowledge of American government and this cartoon, answer the questions below.

30. (a) What does the building in the cartoon represent?
(b) What is the source of the words on the building?
31. What is the cartoon saying about the influence of special-interest groups on the political process?

You Can Make a Difference

With a group of friends, think of a policy issue on which you have a definite opinion. Then outline a plan for a group that would lobby for your side of that issue. Use the following suggestions for starting a local interest group.
  (1) Find a faculty sponsor.
  (2) Have a kickoff meeting.
  (3) Gain attention and publicity in a variety of ways—tell your friends, announce your group on the PA system, write an editorial, put up fliers, speak to existing school clubs.

Participation Activities

32. *Current Events Watch* Scan recent newspapers and magazines to find a reference to an interest group at work. Then answer the following questions: What is the interest group? What appears to be its goal? How is it attempting to reach that goal? Share your findings with those of your classmates. Of the interest groups you and your classmates have found, which seem to be the most powerful? Why?

33. *Chart Activity* Create a chart that summarizes the types of interest groups mentioned in Section 2. Use the headings in blue as your categories, and list up to five examples in each category. Then choose one of these groups and find out more about it: the issues it follows, how it attempts to influence public policy, its history, the groups from which it draws its membership, and its success rate in reaching its goals.

34. *It's Your Turn* Take a poll to find out what interest groups people in your community belong to and why. Before you begin your interviews, write down the questions you wish to ask. Be sure that groups not commonly thought of as interest groups, such as church clubs, are included in your poll. Plan to interview at least ten people. What conclusions can you reach based on your interviews? **(Conducting a Poll)**

 Take It to the Net

Chapter 9 Self-Test As a final review activity, take the Chapter 9 Self-Test in the Social Studies area at the Web site listed below, and receive immediate feedback on your answers.

www.phschool.com

◆ The Capitol, Washington, D.C.

The Legislative Branch

CONSTITUTIONAL PRINCIPLES

Separation of Powers The Constitution gives Congress the power to make laws. Separating the power to make laws from the power to enforce and the power to review them prevents the misuse of governmental authority.

Checks and Balances The Constitution gives Congress a number of powers with which it can check the actions of the executive and the judicial branches.

Limited Government Congress can exercise only those powers given to it by the Constitution—and, in doing so, it cannot violate any provision in the Constitution.

The Impact on You

What Congress does has an effect on you, quite directly—when it sets the minimum wage, for example, and when it decides how much tax you will pay on your wages. Among many other examples: Congress has decreed that all public high schools must allow student religious groups to meet in the school, on the same terms that other student groups may do so.

CHAPTER 10

Congress

"Any one who is unfamiliar with what Congress actually does and how it does it, with all its duties and all its occupations, . . . is very far from a knowledge of the constitutional system under which we live."

—Woodrow Wilson (1885)

Wilson saw Congress, the legislative branch, as the most basic part of a democratic, constitutional government. The men and women elected to the House and Senate give the people a voice in setting public policy and making laws.

◆ Representatives and aides outside the Capitol

⭐ You Can Make a Difference

PROBABLY THE BEST way to learn about the day-to-day work of Congress is to be part of it. High school students who serve as congressional pages do just that—they carry messages between members of Congress and help staff members with office tasks. In 1971, Paulette Desell, a 16-year-old from Alexandria, Virginia, became the first female page. She was chosen by New York Senator Jacob Javits. In applying to be a page, Paulette wrote: "To have a thorough understanding of how the government operates is the best aid in encouraging young minds to want to learn."

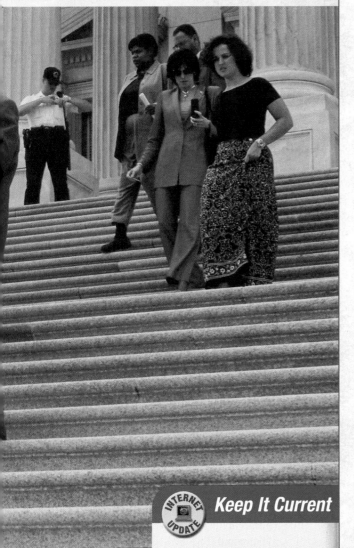

Keep It Current

Items marked with this logo are periodically updated on the Internet. Keep up-to-date with what's in the news. To get current information on Congress, go to
www.phschool.com

SECTION 1

The National Legislature (pp. 262–265)

★ Congress is bicameral, or divided into two houses.
★ Each State has two members in the Senate.
★ In the House of Representatives, States are represented according to population.
★ Congress meets for two-year terms, divided into two one-year sessions.

SECTION 2

The House of Representatives (pp. 267–273)

★ Each member of the House of Representatives represents a district of roughly equal population and is up for reelection every two years.
★ After each census, seats in the House are redistributed among the States, and districts are redrawn to reflect changes in population.
★ Politicians frequently "gerrymander" districts into odd shapes to gain a political advantage.

SECTION 3

The Senate (pp. 275–278)

★ The Senate includes 100 members, two from each State, who are elected to six-year terms.
★ Senators usually have more experience, power, and prestige than their colleagues in the House.
★ Senators are protected from some political pressures because they serve for a long period between elections.

SECTION 4

The Members of Congress (pp. 279–284)

★ Members of Congress are likely to be older and wealthier than the average American, and most members are men.
★ Members bring a variety of viewpoints and career backgrounds to Congress.
★ Members of Congress juggle a number of roles by working as lawmakers, party members, and servants of the voters.
★ Congress sets its own pay and other compensations—and that fact poses peculiar problems for its members.

Section Preview

OBJECTIVES

1. **Explain** why the Constitution provides for a bicameral Congress.
2. **Describe** a term of Congress.
3. **Summarize** how sessions of Congress have changed over time.

WHY IT MATTERS

The Framers of the Constitution created a Congress with two bodies: a small Senate and a much larger House of Representatives. Each Congress since 1789 has met for a term of two years; those terms are now divided into two one-year sessions.

POLITICAL DICTIONARY

★ **term**
★ **session**
★ **adjourn**
★ **prorogue**
★ **special session**

You know that you live in a democracy, and in a democracy, the people rule. But what does that really mean? You are one of "the people," but you do not rule, at least not in the hands-on sense. You do not make laws, collect taxes, arrest criminals, or decide court cases.

You do not do those or all of the other things that government does because you live in a *representative* democracy. Here, it is the representatives of the people who are responsible for the day-to-day work of government.

Congress stands as a leading example of that fact. It is the legislative branch of the National Government. Congress, then, is charged with the most basic governmental function in a democratic society—that of translating the public will into public policy in the form of law.

James Madison called Congress "the first branch" of the National Government. Just how profoundly important he and the other Framers thought Congress to be can be seen in this fact: the very first and longest of the articles of the Constitution is devoted to it.

> **FROM THE Constitution** *❝All legislative Powers herein granted shall be vested in a Congress of the United States, which shall consist of a Senate and House of Representatives. ❞*
>
> —Article I, Section 1, Clause 1

A Bicameral Congress

As you have just read, the Constitution immediately establishes a bicameral legislature—that is, one made up of two houses. It does so for historical, practical, and theoretical reasons.

1. **Historical** The British Parliament had consisted of two houses since the 1300s. The Framers and most other Americans knew the British system of bicameralism quite well. Most of the colonial assemblies and, in 1787, all but two of the new State legislatures were also bicameral. Among the original thirteen colonies, only

▲ *Party Leaders* In the Senate, the two parties are led by Senator Tom Daschle (D., South Dakota) (left) and Senator Trent Lott (R., Mississippi) (right).

Georgia and Pennsylvania had unicameral colonial and then State legislatures. Georgia's legislature became bicameral in 1789 and Pennsylvania's in 1790.[1]

2. **Practical** The Framers had to create a two-chambered body to settle the conflict between the Virginia and the New Jersey Plans at Philadelphia in 1787. As you have read in Chapter 2, the most populous States wanted to distribute seats in Congress in proportion to the population of each State, while smaller States demanded an equal voice in Congress. Bicameralism is a reflection of federalism. Each of the States is equally represented in the Senate and represented proportional to its population in the House.

3. **Theoretical** The Framers favored a bicameral Congress in order that one house might act as a check on the other.

A leading constitutional historian recounts a breakfast-table conversation between Thomas Jefferson and George Washington. Jefferson, who had just returned from France, told Washington that he was opposed to a two-chambered legislature. As he made his point, he poured his coffee into his saucer, and Washington asked him why he did so. "To cool it," replied Jefferson. "Even so," said Washington, "we pour legislation into the senatorial saucer to cool it."

The Framers were generally convinced that Congress would dominate the new National Government. As Madison wrote,

PRIMARY Sources *In a republican government, the legislative authority necessarily predominates. The remedy for this inconveniency is to divide the legislature into different branches.*
—*The Federalist* No. 51

The Framers saw bicameralism as a way to diffuse the power of Congress and so prevent it from overwhelming the other two branches of government.

For more than 200 years now, some people have argued that the Senate should be abolished.[2] They say that because the States, not the

---

[1] Today, only Nebraska (since 1937) has a unicameral legislative body.
[2] There is not the remotest chance that that would ever be done. Recall, the Constitution provides in Article V that "no State, without its Consent, shall be deprived of its equal Suffrage in the Senate."

Representation in Congress

State	Population*	Senators	House Members
Wyoming	493,782	2	1
California	33,871,648	2	53

*as of April 1, 2000 SOURCE: U.S. Census Bureau

Interpreting Maps California and Wyoming each elect two senators, despite a huge difference in their populations. *How does the distribution of Senate seats among the States illustrate the principle of federalism?*

people, are equally represented in the Senate, that body is undemocratic. Those critics often point to the two extremes to make their case. The State with the least population, Wyoming, has only some 500,000 residents. The largest State, California, now has more than 34 million. Yet each of these States has two senators.

Those who argue against State equality in the Senate ignore a vital fact. The Senate was purposely created as a body in which the States would be represented as coequal members and partners in the Union. Remember, had the States not been equally represented in the Senate, there might never have been a Constitution.

Terms and Sessions

Some years ago, a woman, incensed at something her senator had just done, said to him: "You know, 535 of you people in Congress meet every two years. There are some of us who think that it would be much better if just two of you met every 535 years."

Legislative Bodies

Country	Legislative Body	Houses if Bicameral	Number of Members	How Elected	Term of Office
United States	Congress	House of Representatives	435	Direct popular vote	2 years
		Senate	100	Direct popular vote	6 years
Costa Rica	Legislative Assembly		57	Direct popular vote	4 years
France	Parlement	National Assembly	577	Direct popular vote	5 years
		Senate	321	Local electoral colleges	9 years
Israel	Knesset		120	Direct popular vote	4 years
Japan	Diet	House of Councillors	252	Direct popular vote	6 years
		House of Representatives	500	Direct popular vote	4 years
Saudi Arabia	Consultative Council		90	Appointed by the king	4 years

Interpreting Tables The size and makeup of legislative bodies vary widely among countries. ***Why might the legislatures of Israel and Costa Rica have fewer members than the House of Representatives in the United States?***

While that story may or may not be true, the government has never followed this woman's advice. Ever since 1789, Congress has met for two-year terms.

Terms of Congress

Each **term** of Congress lasts for two years, and each term is numbered consecutively.[3] Congress began its first term on March 4, 1789, and that term ended two years later, on March 4, 1791.

The date for the start of each new term was changed by the 20th Amendment in 1933. In the 1790s, the four-month gap between elections in November and the start of a new term in March allowed for delays in communicating election results around the country. It also allowed for the arrival of new lawmakers to Washington, D.C. However, the March starting date restricted the amount of work Congress could accomplish, and by the 1930s communications and travel were no longer an issue. The start of a new term is now "noon of the 3d day

of January" of every odd-numbered year. So the term of the 107th Congress began on January 3, 2001, and it will end at noon on January 3, 2003.

Sessions

A **session** of Congress is that period of time during which, each year, Congress assembles and conducts business. There are two sessions to each term of Congress—one session each year. The Constitution provides

> **"** *The Congress shall assemble at least once in every year, and such meeting shall begin at noon on the 3d day of January, unless they shall by law appoint a different day.* **"**
> —20th Amendment, Section 2

In fact, Congress often does "appoint a different day." The second session of each two-year term frequently begins a few days or even two or three weeks after the third of January.

Congress **adjourns,** or suspends until the next session, each regular session as it sees fit. Until World War II, a typical session lasted four or five months. Today, however, the many pressing issues facing Congress force it to remain in

---

[3]Article I, Section 2, Clause 1 dictates a two-year term for Congress by providing that members of the House "shall be . . . chosen every second Year."

session through most of each year. Both houses recess for several short periods during a session.

Neither house may adjourn *sine die* (finally, ending a session) without the consent of the other. The Constitution provides that

> **FROM THE Constitution** *"Neither House . . . shall, without the Consent of the other, adjourn for more than three days, nor to any other Place than that in which the two Houses shall be sitting."*
>
> —Article I, Section 5, Clause 4

Article II, Section 3 of the Constitution does give the President the power to **prorogue,** or adjourn, a session, but only when the two houses cannot agree on a date for adjournment. No President has ever had to use that power.

Special Sessions

Only the President may call Congress into **special session**—a meeting to deal with some emergency situation.[4] Only 26 special sessions of Congress have ever been held. President Harry Truman called the most recent one in 1948, to consider anti-inflation and welfare measures in the aftermath of World War II.

Note that the President can call Congress *or* either of its houses into a special session. The Senate has been called into special session alone

---

[4]Article II, Section 3 says that the President "may, on extraordinary Occasions, convene both Houses, or either of them. . . ."

▲ *Outside Washington* Members of Congress have many responsibilities outside the regular legislative session in Washington. Senator John Edwards (D., North Carolina) meets with constituents after devastating floods hit his State.

on 46 occasions, to consider treaties or presidential appointments, but not since 1933. The House has never been called alone.

Of course, the fact that Congress now meets nearly year-round reduces the likelihood of special sessions. That fact also lessens the importance of the President's power to call one. Still, as Congress nears the end of a session, the President sometimes finds it useful to *threaten* a special session if the two chambers do not act on some measure high on his legislative agenda.

Section 1 Assessment

Key Terms and Main Ideas

1. How long does a **term** of Congress last?
2. How does a **special session** differ from a regular session of Congress?
3. When does Congress **adjourn**?
4. Who has the power to **prorogue** a session of Congress?

Critical Thinking

5. **Determining Cause and Effect** What are the historical, practical, and theoretical reasons for bicameralism in Congress?
6. **Expressing Problems Clearly** Why do some people believe the Senate is undemocratic?

7. **Making Comparisons** Use the chart on page 264 to compare the length of an elected term in the House of Representatives to the terms in the other legislative bodies. What does the difference you find suggest about the American system of government?

Take It to the Net

8. A one-house system of government works very differently from a bicameral system of representation. Select five differences and summarize them in a paragraph. Use the links provided in the Social Studies area at the following Web site for help in completing this activity.
www.phschool.com

SKILLS FOR LIFE

TECHNOLOGY

CITIZENSHIP

CRITICAL THINKING

CHARTS and GRAPHS

Analyzing Maps

Maps bring information to life in a way that words alone cannot. Maps are particularly useful to people who grasp concepts better when they are illustrated. To analyze a map and draw information from it, try these steps:

1. Identify the purpose of the map. The map shown here is a cartogram. It is a special-purpose map used to present statistics geographically. Here, the original 13 States are shown not in proportion to their land area, but according to the relative sizes of their populations in 1770. The cartogram intentionally distorts the sizes and shapes of territories in order to compare them visually. Compare this map with the one on page 31. (a) Which States had a large population for their small physical size? (b) Which States had a rather small population for their large size?

2. Apply prior knowledge to draw conclusions from the map. You read on page 263 about the debate, ongoing since the nation's founding, over whether to have equal representation in the Senate for every State, regardless of its size or population. Knowing this, study the cartogram again. (a) At the nation's founding, which States stood to gain from having equal representation? (b) Which would gain from proportional representation tied to population? (c) How did the Constitution reconcile this problem?

Test for Success

In the library or on the Internet, find a present-day population map of the United States. (a) List three States that would be awarded a large number of senators if they were apportioned according to population size, as in the House of Representatives. (b) List at least three States that would fare poorly with proportional representation in the Senate.

Cartogram: Population of the Thirteen Colonies, 1770

NEW HAMPSHIRE
62,396

NEW YORK
162,920

MASSACHUSETTS
235,308

PENNSYLVANIA
240,057

CONNECTICUT
183,881

RHODE ISLAND
58,196

NEW JERSEY
117,431

DELAWARE
35,496

MARYLAND
202,599

VIRGINIA
447,016

NORTH CAROLINA
197,200

SOUTH CAROLINA
124,244

GEORGIA
23,375

▲ Above, engraving of a map of the United States; at right, cartogram of the colonies

2 The House of Representatives

Section Preview

OBJECTIVES

1. **Describe** the size and the elective terms of the members of the House.
2. **Explain** how House seats are reapportioned among the States after each census.
3. **Describe** a typical congressional election and congressional district.
4. **Analyze** the formal and informal qualifications for election to the House.

WHY IT MATTERS

The 435 members of the House of Representatives represent districts of roughly equal populations but very different characteristics. House members can serve an unlimited number of two-year terms.

POLITICAL DICTIONARY

★ apportion
★ reapportion
★ off-year election
★ single-member district
★ at-large
★ gerrymander

Every other autumn, all across the country, hundreds of men and women seek election to the House of Representatives. Most of them try to attract supporters and win votes with banners and posters, yard signs, billboards, flyers, buttons, and other eye-catching campaign materials. Nearly all of them make their "pitches" with radio and television spots, newspaper ads, and now in cyberspace. In this section, you will discover the general shape of the office that all of those candidates so eagerly pursue.

Size and Terms

The exact size of the House of Representatives—today, 435 members—is not fixed by the Constitution. Rather, it is set by Congress. The Constitution provides that the total number of seats in the House of Representatives shall be **apportioned** (distributed) among the States on the basis of their respective populations.[5]

Each State is guaranteed at least one seat in the House, no matter what its population. Today, seven States—Alaska, Delaware, Montana, North Dakota, South Dakota, Vermont, and Wyoming—have only one representative apiece.

The District of Columbia, Guam, the Virgin Islands, and American Samoa each elect a delegate to represent them in the House and Puerto Rico chooses a resident commissioner. Those officials are not, however, full-fledged members of the House of Representatives.

Article I, Section 2, Clause 1 of the Constitution provides that "Representatives shall be . . . chosen every second Year"—that is, for two-year terms. This rather short term means that, for House members, the next election is always just around the corner. That fact tends to make them pay close attention to "the folks back home."

There is no constitutional limit on the number of terms any member of Congress may serve. In the 1990s, people tried to persuade Congress to offer a constitutional amendment to limit congressional terms. Most versions of such an amendment would put a three- or four-term limit (six or eight years) on service in the House and a two-term limit (twelve years) for the Senate.[6]

Reapportionment

Article I of the Constitution directs Congress to **reapportion**—redistribute—the seats in the House after each decennial census.[7] Until a first census could be taken, the Constitution set the size of the House at 65 seats. That many members served in the First and Second Congresses (1789–1793). The census of 1790 showed a national population of 3,929,214 persons;

---

[5]Article I, Section 2, Clause 3.

[6]The States do not have the power to limit the number of terms their members of Congress may serve, *United States* v. *Thornton,* 1995.

[7]Article I, Section 2, Clause 3. A decennial census is one taken every ten years.

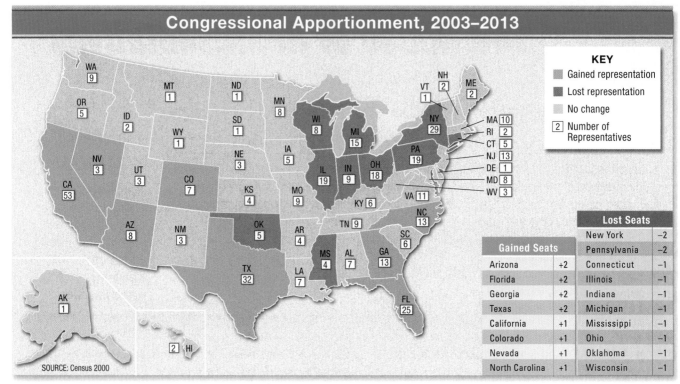

Congressional Apportionment, 2003–2013

KEY
- Gained representation
- Lost representation
- No change
- [2] Number of Representatives

SOURCE: Census 2000

Gained Seats	
Arizona	+2
Florida	+2
Georgia	+2
Texas	+2
California	+1
Colorado	+1
Nevada	+1
North Carolina	+1

Lost Seats	
New York	−2
Pennsylvania	−2
Connecticut	−1
Illinois	−1
Indiana	−1
Michigan	−1
Mississippi	−1
Ohio	−1
Oklahoma	−1
Wisconsin	−1

Interpreting Maps This map shows the changes in State representation due to the reapportionment of the House after the 2000 Census, and in effect from January 3, 2003 to January 3, 2013. The next reapportionment will be based on the census to be taken in 2010. *What general trend in population growth around the country does this map show?*

thus, in 1792 Congress increased the number of House seats by 41, to 106.

A Growing Nation

As the nation's population grew, and as the number of States increased, so did the size of the House. It went to 142 seats after the census of 1800, to 186 seats 10 years later, and so on.[8] By 1912, following the census of 1910 and the admission of Arizona and New Mexico, the House had grown to 435 seats.

With the census of 1920, Congress found itself in a painfully difficult political position. The House had long since grown too large for effective floor action. To reapportion without adding more seats to the House, however, would mean that some States would have to lose seats if every State were to be represented according to its population.

Congress met the problem by doing nothing. So, despite the Constitution's command, there

was no reapportionment on the basis of the 1920 census.

The Reapportionment Act of 1929

Faced with the 1930 census, Congress avoided repeating its earlier lapse by passing the Reapportionment Act of 1929. That law, still on the books, sets up what is often called an "automatic reapportionment." It provides:

(1) The "permanent" size of the House is 435 members. Of course, that figure is permanent only so long as Congress does not decide to change it. Congress did enlarge the House temporarily in 1959 when Alaska and then Hawaii became States. Today each of the 435 seats in the House represents an average of some 650,000 persons.

(2) Following each census, the Census Bureau is to determine the number of seats each State should have.

(3) When the Bureau's plan is ready, the President must send it to Congress.

(4) If, within 60 days of receiving it, neither house rejects the Census Bureau's plan, it becomes effective.

---

[8]Once, following the census of 1840, the size of the House was reduced from 242 to 232 seats.

The plan set out in the 1929 law has worked quite well throughout eight reapportionments. The law leaves to Congress its constitutional responsibility to reapportion the House, but it gives to the Census Bureau the mechanical chores (and political "heat") that go with that task.

Congressional Elections

According to the Constitution, any person whom a State allows to vote for members of "the most numerous Branch" of its own legislature is qualified to vote in congressional elections.[9] The Constitution also provides that

> **FROM THE Constitution** *"The Times, Places and Manner of holding [Congressional] Elections . . . shall be prescribed in each State by the Legislature thereof; but the Congress may at any time by Law make or alter such Regulations. . . ."*[10]
>
> —Article I, Section 4, Clause 1

Date

Congressional elections are held on the same day in every State. Since 1872 Congress has required that those elections be held on the Tuesday following the first Monday in November of each even-numbered year. Congress has made an exception for Alaska, which may hold its election in October. To date, however, Alaskans have chosen to use the November date.

In that same 1872 law, Congress directed that representatives be chosen by written or printed ballots. The use of voting machines was approved in 1899. Today, well over half of all the votes cast in congressional elections are cast on some type of voting machine.

Off-Year Elections

Those congressional elections that occur in the nonpresidential years—that is, between presidential elections—are called **off-year elections.** The most recent ones were held in 2002, and the next ones are due in 2006.

Far more often than not, the party in power—the party that holds the presidency—loses seats in the off-year elections. The time line below illustrates that point. It sets out the House and Senate seats gained (+) or lost (–) by the President's party in the off-year elections from 1970 through 1998. The President's party did particularly poorly in 1974, after President Nixon resigned due to the Watergate Scandal, and in 1994, during President Clinton's first term. The 1998 off-year elections were an exception to the rule. That summer and fall, the Republican Congress held hearings to prepare to impeach President Clinton. Public opinion polls showed weak support for the impeachment, and many believe the hearings prompted significant support for Democratic candidates for Congress.

---

[9]Article I, Section 2, Clause 1.
[10]The Constitution allows only one method for filling a vacancy in the House—by a special election, which may be called only by the governor of the State involved; Article I, Section 2, Clause 4.

Gains and Losses in Off-Year Elections

Congressional Elections	1970 seats: −12 House +2 Senate	1974 seats: −48 House −5 Senate	1978 seats: −15 House −3 Senate	1982 seats: −26 House +1 Senate	1986 seats: −5 House −8 Senate	1990 seats: −8 House −1 Senate	1994 seats: −53 House −8 Senate	1998 seats: +5 House 0 Senate
Presidential Elections	1968 Richard Nixon elected	1972* Richard Nixon reelected	1976 Jimmy Carter elected	1980 Ronald Reagan elected	1984 Ronald Reagan reelected	1988 George Bush elected	1992 Bill Clinton elected	1996 Bill Clinton reelected

*Nixon resigned in August 1974 and was replaced by Gerald Ford.   KEY: Republican   Democrat

Interpreting Time Lines The President's party frequently loses seats in the House and Senate in an off-year election. *In which two election years above did the President's party lose the most seats in the House?*

Districts

The 435 members of the House are chosen by the voters in 435 separate congressional districts across the country. Recall that seven States now each have only one seat in the House of Representatives. There are, then, 428 congressional districts within the other 43 States.

The Constitution makes no mention of congressional districts. For more than half a century, Congress allowed each State to decide whether to elect its members by a general ticket system or on a single-member district basis. Under the **single-member district** arrangement, the voters in each district elect one of the State's representatives from among a field of candidates running for a seat in the House from that district.

Most States quickly set up single-member districts. Several States used the general ticket system, however. Under that arrangement, all of the State's seats were filled **at-large**—that is, elected from the State as a whole, rather than from a particular district. Every voter could vote for a candidate for each one of the State's seats in the House.

At-large elections proved grossly unfair. A party with even a very small plurality of voters Statewide could win all of a State's seats in the House. Congress finally did away with the general ticket system in 1842. Thereafter, all of the seats in the House were to be filled from single-member districts in each State. Since the seven States with the fewest residents each have only one representative in the House, these representatives are said to be elected "at-large." Although each representative represents a single-member district, that district covers the entire State.

The 1842 law made each State legislature responsible for drawing any congressional districts within its own State. It also required that each congressional district be made up of "contiguous territory," meaning that it must be all one piece. In 1872 Congress added the command that the districts within each State have "as nearly as practicable an equal number of inhabitants." In 1901 it further directed that all the districts be of "compact territory"—in other words, a comparatively small area.

These requirements of contiguity, population equality, and compactness were often disregarded by State legislatures, and Congress made no real effort to enforce them. The requirements were left out of the Reapportionment Act of 1929. In 1932 the Supreme Court held (in *Wood* v. *Broom*) that they had therefore been repealed. Over time, then, and most notably since 1929, the State legislatures have drawn many districts

 Interpreting Maps The Texas Legislature was responsible for redrawing district lines following the 2000 Census. ***Does it make any real difference which party controls a State legislature and governorship during the redistricting process?***

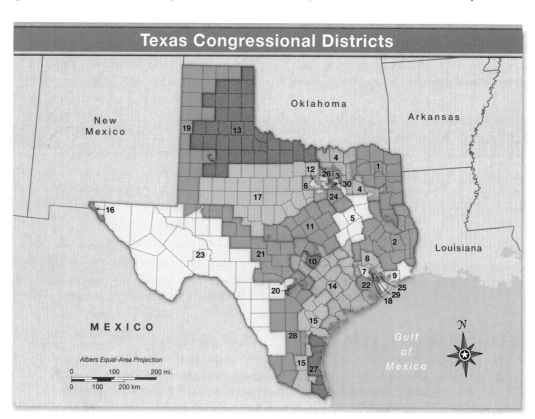

Texas Congressional Districts

with very peculiar geographic shapes. Moreover, until fairly recently, many districts were also of widely varying populations.

Gerrymandering

Congressional district maps in several States show one and sometimes several districts of very odd shapes. Some look like the letters S or Y, some bear a resemblance to a dumbbell or a squiggly piece of spaghetti, and some defy description. Those districts have usually been **gerrymandered.** That is, they have been drawn to the advantage of the political party that controls the State's legislature.

Gerrymandering is widespread today—and not just at the congressional district level. Districts for the election of State legislators are regularly drawn for partisan advantage. In fact, gerrymandering can be found in most places where lines are drawn for the election of public officeholders—in cities, counties, school districts, and elsewhere.

Most often gerrymandering takes one of two forms. The lines are drawn either (1) to concentrate the opposition's voters in one or a few districts, thus leaving the other districts comfortably safe for the dominant party; or (2) to spread the opposition as thinly as possible among several districts, limiting the opposition's ability to win anywhere in the region. Gerrymandering's main goal is to create as many "safe" districts as possible—districts almost certain to be won by the party in control of the line-drawing process. And the computer-driven map-making techniques of today make the practice more effective than ever in its storied past.

For decades, gerrymandering produced congressional districts that differed widely in the number of people they included. State legislatures were responsible for this situation. A number of them regularly drew district lines on a partisan basis—with the Republicans gouging the Democrats in those States where the GOP controls the legislature, and the

▲ **The original Gerrymander** Gerrymandering takes its name from Governor Elbridge Gerry of Massachusetts, who in 1812 drew the State's legislative districts to favor the Democratic-Republicans. It is said that the painter Gilbert Stuart added a head, wings, and claws on a district map hanging over the desk of a Federalist newspaper editor. "That," he said, "will do for a salamander." "Better say Gerrymander," growled the editor.

Democrats doing the same thing to the Republicans where they hold sway. In fact, that circumstance exists in several States today. Historically, most State legislatures were carved up on a rural versus urban as well as a partisan basis—because, through much of history, the typical State legislature was dominated by the less-populated (and over-represented) rural areas of the State.[11]

Wesberry v. *Sanders*, 1964

Suddenly, and quite dramatically, these long-standing patterns of wide population variations among House districts and of rural over-representation in the chamber came to an end in the mid- to late 1960s. These abrupt changes were the direct result of a historic decision by the Supreme Court in 1964. In *Wesberry* v. *Sanders*, the Court held that the population differences among Georgia's congressional districts were so great as to violate the Constitution.

In reaching its landmark decision, the Supreme Court noted that Article I, Section 2 declares that

---

[11] The pattern of rural over-representation in the State legislatures has now all but disappeared as a consequence of the Supreme Court's several "one-person, one-vote" decisions of the 1960s and 1970s. In the leading case, *Reynolds* v. *Sims,* 1964, the Court held that the 14th Amendment's Equal Protection Clause commands that the seats in both houses of a State's legislature must be apportioned on the basis of population equality.

representatives shall be chosen "by the People of the several States" and shall be "apportioned among the several States . . . according to their respective Numbers. . . ." These words, the Court held, mean that "as nearly as practicable one man's vote in a congressional election is to be worth as much as another's."

The Court added that

PRIMARY Sources *While it may not be possible to draw congressional districts with mathematical precision, that is no excuse for ignoring our Constitution's plain objective of making equal representation for equal numbers of people the fundamental goal of the House of Representatives. That is the high standard of justice and common sense which the Founders set for us.*

—Justice Black, *Opinion of the Court*

The importance of *Wesberry* and the Court's later "one person, one vote" decisions cannot be overstated. They had an extraordinary impact on the makeup of the House, on the content of public policy, and on electoral politics in general. The nation's cities and suburbs now speak with a much larger voice in Congress than ever before. Notice, however, that it is quite possible to draw congressional (or any other) district lines in accord with the "one person, one vote" rule and, at the same time, to gerrymander them.

Gerrymandering based solely on race, however, is a violation of the 15th Amendment, *Gomillion* v. *Lightfoot,* 1960. So-called "majority-minority districts" were drawn in some States following the census in 1990 and again in 2000—districts crafted to include a majority of African Americans and/or Latinos and so likely to send African Americans and Latinos to Congress. The Supreme Court struck down those race-based districts in several cases—most notably, in a case from Texas, *Bush* v. *Vera,* 1996. But, most recently, the Court has held this: while race cannot be the controlling factor in drawing district lines, race can be one of the mix of factors that shape that process. It did so in a case from North Carolina, *Hunt* v. *Cromartie,* in 2001.

Qualifications for House Members

You know that there are 435 members of the House of Representatives, and that each one of them had to win an election to get there. Each one of them also had to meet two quite different sets of qualifications to win office: the formal qualifications for membership in the House set out in the Constitution and a number of informal qualifications imposed by the realities of politics.

Formal Qualifications

The Constitution says that a member of the House

(1) must be at least 25 years of age,

(2) must have been a citizen of the United States for at least seven years, and

(3) must be an inhabitant of the State from which he or she is elected.[12]

Longstanding custom, not the Constitution, also requires that a representative must live in the district he or she represents. The custom is based on the belief that the legislator should be closely familiar with the locale he or she represents, its people, and its problems. Rarely, then, does a district choose an outsider to represent it.

Major Differences Between the House and Senate	
HOUSE	**SENATE**
Larger body (435 members)	Smaller body (100 members)
Shorter term (2 years)	Longer term (6 years)
Smaller constituencies (elected from districts within States)	Larger constituencies (elected from entire State)
Younger membership	Older membership
Less prestige	More prestige
Lower visibility in the news media	Higher visibility in the news media
Strict rules, limited debate	Flexible rules, nearly unlimited debate
Most work is done in committees, not on the floor	Work is split more evenly between committees and the floor
No power over treaties and presidential appointments	Approves or rejects treaties and presidential appointments

Interpreting Tables Members of the House and Senate work under very different rules and conditions. ***Why do House members debate most bills in committees before bringing them to the House floor?***

[12]Article I, Section 2, Clause 2; see also Article I, Section 6, Clause 2.

[13]Article I, Section 5, Clause 1.

[14]Article I, Section 5, Clause 2.

The Constitution makes the House "the Judge of the Elections, Returns and Qualifications of its own Members."[13] Thus, when the right of a member-elect to be seated is challenged, the House has the power to decide the matter. Challenges are rarely successful.

The House may refuse to seat a member-elect by majority vote. It may also "punish its Members for disorderly Behavior" by majority vote, and "with the Concurrence of two thirds, expel a Member."[14]

Historically, the House viewed its power to judge the qualifications of members-elect as the power to impose additional standards. It did so several times. In 1900 it refused to seat Brigham H. Roberts of Utah because he was a polygamist—that is, he had more than one wife. In *Powell* v. *McCormack,* 1969, however, the Supreme Court held that the House could not exclude a member-elect who meets the Constitution's standards of age, citizenship, and residence. The House has not excluded anyone since that decision.

Over more than 200 years, the House has expelled only four members. Three were ousted in 1861 for their "support of rebellion." More recently, Michael Myers (D., Pennsylvania) was expelled in 1980 for corruption. Myers had been caught up in the Abscam probe, an undercover FBI investigation of corruption. Over time, a few members have resigned to avoid almost certain expulsion.

The House has not often punished a member for "disorderly Behavior," but such actions are not nearly so rare as expulsions. Most recently, the House voted to "reprimand" Barney Frank (D., Massachusetts) in 1990 for conduct stemming from his relationship with a male prostitute. Mr. Frank, an avowed homosexual, has been easily reelected by the voters in his congressional district every two years since then.

The Speaker of the House left Congress under a cloud in 1989. Jim Wright (D., Texas) resigned his seat after the House Ethics Committee charged him with a number of violations of House rules. Most of those allegations centered around Mr. Wright's financial dealings with individuals and companies with an interest in legislation before the House.

Informal Qualifications

The realities of politics produce a number of informal qualifications for membership in the House—beyond those qualifications set out in the Constitution. These additional qualifications vary somewhat from time to time and from State to State, and sometimes from one congressional district to another within the same State.

Informal qualifications have to do with a candidate's vote-getting abilities. They include such factors as party identification, name familiarity, gender, ethnic characteristics, and political experience. The "right" combination of these factors will help a candidate win nomination and then election to the House. The "wrong" ones, however, will almost certainly spell defeat.

Section 2 Assessment

Key Terms and Main Ideas

1. How are the seats in the House of Representatives **apportioned**?
2. When will the next two **off-year elections** occur?
3. Explain the difference between a **single-member district** seat and an **at-large** seat.
4. Why do politicians **gerrymander** districts?

Critical Thinking

5. **Drawing Inferences** How did *Wesberry* v. *Sanders* change the makeup of Congress?
6. **Predicting Consequences** Since 1910, the average number of people in a congressional district has tripled from 210,000 to well over 650,000. How might this have affected the ability of members of Congress to represent their constituents?
7. **Understanding Point of View** List four informal qualifications that you would look for in a candidate for Congress. Do you think most Americans would choose the same qualifications? Explain why or why not.

Take It to the Net

8. Politicians have used gerrymandering for nearly 200 years to control the outcome of elections. Read about this practice and write a paragraph explaining at least two methods of gerrymandering. Use the links provided in the Social Studies area at the following Web site for help in completing this activity. www.phschool.com

Redistricting and Race

African Americans and Latinos have historically been under-represented in the House of Representatives. After the 1990 Census, several States designed "majority-minority" congressional districts to elect more minority members to Congress. The Supreme Court rejected one such district, North Carolina's 12th, in Shaw v. Reno *in 1993. Writing for the majority, Justice Sandra Day O'Connor outlined the problems with the redistricting plan.*

The second majority black district, District 12, is . . . unusually shaped. It is approximately 160 miles long and, for much of its length, no wider than the I-85 corridor. It winds in snake-like fashion through tobacco country, financial centers, and manufacturing areas "until it gobbles in enough enclaves [culturally distinct units] of black neighborhoods."

What does the cartoon suggest about the process of redistricting?

. . . One state legislator has remarked that "[i]f you drove down the interstate with both car doors open, you'd kill most of the people in the district.". . .

In some exceptional cases, a reapportionment plan may be so highly irregular that, on its face, it rationally cannot be understood as anything other than an effort to "segregat[e] . . . voters" on the basis of race. . . .

We believe that reapportionment is one area in which appearances do matter. A reapportionment plan that includes in one district individuals who belong to the same race, but who are otherwise widely separated by geographical and political boundaries, and who may have little in common with one another but the color of their skin, bears an uncomfortable resemblance to political apartheid [racial segregation]. It reinforces the perception that members of the same racial group—regardless of their age, education, economic status, or the community in which they live—think alike, share the same political interests, and will prefer the same candidates at the polls. We have rejected such

perceptions elsewhere as impermissible racial stereotypes. . . .

By perpetuating such notions, a racial gerrymander may exacerbate [make more severe] the very patterns of racial bloc voting that majority-minority districting is sometimes said to counteract. . . .

The message that such districting sends to elected representatives is equally pernicious [destructive]. When a district obviously is created solely to effectuate the perceived common interests of one racial group, elected officials are more likely to believe that their primary obligation is to represent only the members of that group, rather than their constituency as a whole. This is altogether antithetical [in oppositon to] our system of representative democracy.

Analyzing Primary Sources

1. Why was the 12th Congressional District drawn in such an unusual shape?
2. Why did the Supreme Court order North Carolina to redraw the 12th district?
3. According to this opinion, what are the dangers of dividing congressional districts by race?
4. The Supreme Court has ruled that States can group voters into districts by party, but not by race. Do you agree or disagree with this decision? Give reasons for your position.

3 The Senate

Section Preview

OBJECTIVES

1. **Compare** the size of the Senate to the size of the House of Representatives.
2. **Describe** how States have elected senators in the past and present.
3. **Explain** how and why a senator's term differs from a representative's term.
4. **Identify** the qualifications for serving in the Senate.

WHY IT MATTERS

Each State has two seats in the Senate, the smaller and more prestigious house of Congress. Senators are generally older and more experienced than representatives, and their long terms protect them from political pressure.

POLITICAL DICTIONARY

★ continuous body
★ constituency
★ colleague

You should not be very much surprised by these facts: Nearly a third of the present members of the Senate once served in the House of Representatives; none of the current members of the House has ever served in the Senate. Indeed, many of the men and women who now serve in the House look forward to the day when, they hope, they will sit in the Senate. As you read this section, you will come to see why the Senate is often called the "upper house."

Size, Election, and Terms

Why are there 100 members of the United States Senate? Have the members of the Senate always been elected by the voters of their States? Why do senators serve six-year terms? The organization of the Senate has changed some over time, but it remains a vital part of our government.

Size

The Constitution says that the Senate "shall be composed of two Senators from each State," and so the Senate is a much smaller body than the House of Representatives.[15] The Senate had only 22 members when it held its first session in March of 1789, and 26 members by the end of the First Congress in 1791. Like the House, the size of the upper chamber has grown with the country. Today 100 senators represent the 50 States.

The Framers hoped that the smaller Senate would be a more enlightened and responsible body than the House. Many of them thought that the House would be too often swayed by the immediate impact of events and by the passions of the moment. The Framers reinforced that hope by giving senators a longer term and by setting the qualifications for membership in the Senate a cut above those they set for the House.

▲ Senator Blanche K. Bruce (R., Mississippi) was one of the first two African Americans to serve in the Senate. He served one term from 1875 to 1881.

James Madison saw those provisions as "a necessary fence" against the "fickleness and passion" of the House of Representatives. Nearly a century later, Woodrow Wilson agreed with Madison:

PRIMARY Sources *It is indispensable that besides the House of Representatives which runs on all fours with popular sentiment, we should have a body like the Senate which may refuse to run with it at all when it seems to be wrong—a body which has time and security enough to keep its head, if only now and then and but for a little while, till other people have had time to think.*

—Woodrow Wilson, *Congressional Government*

---

[15]Article I, Section 3, Clause 1 and the 17th Amendment.

How to Write to Your Lawmakers

Choose a method. You can write to your representative's local address or to their Washington address. Check your telephone directory's blue pages to find local addresses. Letters can be sent to representatives in Washington at the following addresses:

Representative _____
House Office Building
Washington, D.C. 20515

Senator _____
Senate Office Building
Washington, D.C. 20510

Write while your issue is still current. Don't wait until a bill is out of the committee or has passed the House (or Senate).

Be specific. Identify the issue that prompted you to write, preferably in your first paragraph. Give the bill number or mention its popular title - e.g. the Minimum Wage Bill, the Child Care Bill.

Be brief, but give the reasons for your position. Avoid these don'ts:
- Don't make threats or promises.
- Don't berate your lawmaker.
- Don't pretend to wield vast political power.
- Don't try to instruct your lawmaker on every issue.

> 9 Robin Court
> New Carrollton, MD 20784
> September 17, 2001
>
> Rep. Albert Wynn
> House Office Building
> Washington, D.C. 20515
>
> Dear Mr. Wynn:
>
> I am writing to express my support for H.R. 113, which would provide $14.2 billion to public high schools for repairs and construction. Since H.R. 113 will be debated next month, I would like to explain why I believe this bill is important to my school and others in the 4th district.
>
> I am a junior at Stevens High School, a public high school in New Carrollton. Like many schools in the United States, Stevens High School was built more than forty years ago and needs major repairs. This year the entire heating system had to be replaced, the roof is in poor condition, and the science laboratories are outdated. Our district simply does not have the money to make all of the repairs that are needed. As you can understand, students find it difficult to learn in this environment.
>
> I understand that lawmakers must make difficult decisions about the federal budget. However, I believe that school funding is crucial and I encourage you to vote "Yes" on H.R. 113.
>
> Sincerely,
> Ethan Locker
> Ethan Locker

SOURCE: *Congressional Quarterly*

Interpreting Diagrams These guidelines were suggested by former Representative Morris Udall (D., Arizona).
Why is it important to write while a bill is still in committee?

Members of the Senate represent entire States. So nearly all of them represent a larger, more diverse population and a broader range of interests than do the representatives from their State. If you look at your own State—at the size, diversity, and major characteristics of its population and at its history, geography, and economy—you will see the point.

Election

Originally, the Constitution provided that the members of the Senate were to be chosen by the State legislatures. Since the ratification of the 17th Amendment in 1913, however, senators have been picked by the voters in each State at the regular November elections. Only one senator is elected from a State in any given election, except when the other seat has been vacated by death, resignation, or expulsion.[16]

Before the coming of popular election, the State legislatures often picked popular and qualified senators. On other occasions, however, their choice was the result of maneuvering and in-fighting among the leaders of various factions in the State. These leaders all spent a great deal of energy trying to gain (and sometimes buy) enough legislators' votes to win a seat in the United States Senate. By the late 1800s, the Senate was often called the "Millionaires' Club," because so many wealthy party and business leaders sat in that chamber.

The Senate twice defeated House-passed amendments to provide for popular election. In 1912, it finally bowed to public opinion and agreed to what became the Seventeenth Amendment. The Senate was also persuaded by the fact that several States had already devised ways to ensure that their legislatures would choose senators who were supported by the people of the State.

---

[16] The 17th Amendment gives each State a choice of methods for filling a Senate vacancy. A State may (1) fill the seat at a special election called by the governor, or (2) allow the governor to appoint someone to serve until the voters fill the vacancy at such a special election or at the next regular (November) election. Most States use the appointment-special election method.

Each senator is elected from the State at-large. The Seventeenth Amendment declares that all persons whom the State allows to vote for members of "the most numerous Branch" of its legislature are qualified to vote for candidates for the United States Senate.

Term

Senators serve for six-year terms, three times the length of those for which members of the House are chosen.[17] Senators may be elected to any number of terms. Strom Thurmond (R., South Carolina) holds the all-time record. Senator Thurmond has been elected to the Senate nine times, and he has served there for nearly 50 years. He was first elected to fill a vacancy in 1954 and won a full term in 1956. He has been reelected every six years since then, and his current term expires in January of 2003.

Senators' terms are staggered. Only a third of them—33 or 34 terms—expire every two years. The Senate is, then, a **continuous body.** That is, all of its seats are never up for election at the same time.

The six-year term gives senators a somewhat greater degree of job security than members of the lower house have. Those six years give senators some insulation from the rough-and-tumble of day-to-day politics. The six-year term is also intended to make senators less subject to the pressures of public opinion and less susceptible to the pleas of special interests than are members of the House.

The larger size and the geographic scope of their **constituencies**—the people and interests the senators represent—are designed to have much the same effect. In other words, senators are supposed to be less concerned with the interests of a specific small locality and more focused on the "big picture" of the national interest. Indeed, senators are in general more likely to be regarded as national political leaders than most House members.

The large size of the House generally prevents representatives from gaining as much notice and public exposure as members of the Senate attract. Senators, and especially those who have presidential ambitions, are better able to capture national media attention. Over the past several elections, the Senate has emerged as a prime source of candidates for the presidential nomination in both parties. Senators also find

it easier to establish themselves as the champions of public policies that appeal to large segments of the American people—areas such as social security or national health care.

Senators are also more likely to be covered by the media in their States. They tend to have more clout in their State's politics than their **colleagues,** or coworkers, in the House.

Qualifications for Senators

A senator must meet a higher level of qualifications than those the Constitution sets for a member of the House. A senator must be at least 30 years of age, must have been a citizen of the United States for at least nine years, and must be an inhabitant of the State from which he or she is elected.[18]

---

[18]Article I, Section 3, Clause 3. Under the inhabitant qualification, a senator need not have lived in the State for any particular period of time. Most often, of course, senators have been longtime residents of their States.

Student Poll

In a recent poll, students were asked their opinion on the following question: *Of the following six jobs, which one do you think has the most influence on national politics—activists, journalists, lobbyists, members of Congress, state/local politicians, or top business leaders?*

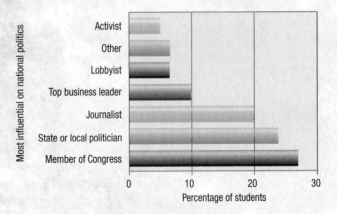

SOURCE: High School Students' Attitudes Toward Government and Politics, Close Up Foundation, May 1999

1. **Analyzing Data** *Approximately how many respondents believe that government leaders have the most influence over national politics?*
2. **Conducting Polls** In your own school, conduct a poll asking students who they believe has the most influence over national politics. *How do your results compare to the results shown in this graph?*

---

[17]Article I, Section 3, Clause 1.

Interpreting Political Cartoons This 1890 cartoon depicts a candidate for the Senate. *Why does the candidate deposit his money in a box labeled "State Legislature"?*

"THE WAY WE BECOME SENATORS NOWADAYS"

The Senate, like the House, judges the qualifications of its members, and it may exclude a member by a majority vote.[19] As has the House, the Senate has at times refused to seat a member-elect. The Senate may also "punish its Members for disorderly Behavior" by majority vote and "with the Concurrence of two thirds, expel a Member."[20]

Fifteen members of the Senate have been expelled by that body, one in 1797 and 14 during the Civil War. Senator William Blount of Tennessee was expelled in 1797 for conspiring to lead two Native American tribes, supported by British warships, in attacks on Spanish Florida and Louisiana. The 14 senators ousted in 1861 and 1862 were all from States of the Confederacy and were expelled for supporting secession.

Since the country was founded, a few senators have resigned in the face of almost certain expulsion. Most recently, the Senate's Ethics Committee had recommended that Senator Bob Packwood (R., Oregon) be expelled from the Senate because of several episodes of sexual harassment and other personal misconduct. Packwood, in his fifth term in the upper house, had fought the charges for years. But the Ethics Committee's chairman, Senator Mitch McConnell (R., Kentucky), noted that lengthy committee investigations had shown "a habitual pattern of aggressive, blatantly sexual advances." Such behavior, McConnell declared, "cannot be tolerated in the United States Senate." Senator Packwood resigned effective October 1, 1995.

The punishing of a senator for "disorderly Behavior" has also been rare. In the most recent case, in 1990, the Senate formally "denounced" Senator David Durenberger (R., Minnesota). The Ethics Committee had found him guilty on several counts of financial misconduct. The Senate called Durenberger's conduct "reprehensible" and declared that he had "brought the Senate into dishonor and disrepute." Senator Durenberger chose not to seek reelection to a third term in 1994.

---

[19]Article I, Section 5, Clause 1.
[20]Article I, Section 5, Clause 2.

Section 3 Assessment

Key Terms and Main Ideas

1. Why is the Senate called a **continuous body**?
2. How does a typical senator's **constituency** differ from that of a typical representative in the House?
3. Why do most senators receive more public attention than their **colleagues** in the House of Representatives?

Critical Thinking

4. **Determining Cause and Effect** Why did the 17th Amendment change the way that senators are chosen?
5. **Making Comparisons** Why did the Framers set each senator's term at six years instead of two years?

6. **Drawing Inferences** In order to expel a senator from the Senate, two thirds of the Senate must agree. Why do you think the Constitution sets such a high requirement?

 Take It to the Net

7. In 1955, the Senate selected five former members who had been significant contributors to the nation. Choose one of the five senators and write a paragraph that explains why the senator you chose is included in the famous five. Use the links provided in the Social Studies area at the following Web site for help in completing this activity. **www.phschool.com**

Section Preview

OBJECTIVES

1. **Identify** the personal and political backgrounds of the current members of Congress.
2. **Compare and contrast** the duties of the job of serving in Congress.
3. **Describe** the compensation and privileges given to members of Congress.

WHY IT MATTERS

Members of Congress must fill several roles as lawmakers, politicians, and servants of the voters. For their work, they receive fairly generous pay and benefits.

POLITICAL DICTIONARY

★ **trustee**
★ **partisan**
★ **politico**
★ **oversight function**
★ **franking privilege**

You have seen help wanted ads in the newspaper—ads that describe jobs to be filled, listing their pay and so on. But you have never seen one that reads: "Wanted: Members of Congress. . . ." How would such an ad describe the duties, the pay, and other aspects of the position? This section will help you answer that question.

Personal and Political Backgrounds

Whatever else they may be, the 535 members of Congress are *not* a representative cross section of the American people. Rather, the "average" member is a white male in his mid-50s. The median age of the members of the House is just over 54 and of the Senate, 60.

The composition of both chambers of Congress has been changing fairly rapidly over recent years. More women now sit in Congress than ever before: 59 of them are members of the House and 13 serve in the Senate. There are 39 African American members of Congress today—only one of them is a Republican, Representative J. C. Watts of Oklahoma. There are also 21 Hispanics and 6 Asian Americans and Pacific Islanders in the lower house. The House also now includes its first-ever Chinese American member, David Wu (D., Oregon), first elected in 1998, and reelected in 2000. The Senate's first full-blooded Native American, Ben Nighthorse Campbell (R., Colorado), was elected in 1992 and reelected in 1998.

Nearly all members are married, a few are divorced, and they have, on the average, two children. Only a few members say they have no religious affiliation. Just about 60 percent are Protestants, 25 percent are Roman Catholics, and some 8 percent are Jewish.

Well over a third of the members of the House and well over half the senators are lawyers. Nearly all went to college. More than four out of five have a college degree and a number have advanced degrees.

Most senators and representatives were born in the States they represent. Only a handful were born outside the United States. Sprinkled among the members of Congress are several millionaires. A surprisingly large number of representatives, however, depend on their congressional salaries as their major source of income.

Most members of Congress have had considerable political experience. The average senator is serving a second term, and the typical representative has served four terms. Nearly a third of the senators once sat in the House. Several senators are former governors. A few senators have held Cabinet seats or other high posts in the executive branch of the Federal Government. The House has a

▲ Representative J. C. Watts (R., Oklahoma) played professional football in Canada years before joining the House in 1995.

large number of former State legislators and prosecuting attorneys among its members.

Again, Congress is not an accurate cross section of the nation's population. Rather, it is made up of upper-middle-class Americans, who are, on the whole, quite able and hard-working people.

The Job

One leading commentary on American politics describes Congress and the job of a member of Congress this way:

PRIMARY Sources *" Congress has a split personality. On the one hand, it is a lawmaking institution and makes policy for the entire nation. In this capacity, all the members are expected to set aside their personal ambitions and perhaps even the concerns of*

their constituencies. Yet Congress is also a representative assembly, made up of 535 elected officials who serve as links between their constituents and the National Government. The dual roles of making laws and responding to constituents' demands forces members to balance national concerns against the specific interests of their States or districts. "
—Burns, et al., *Government by the People*

Members of Congress play five major roles. They are most importantly (1) legislators and (2) representatives of their constituents. Beyond these roles, they are also (3) committee members, (4) servants of their constituents, and (5) politicians. You will take a close look at their lawmaking function in the next two chapters. Here, we consider their representative, committee member, and servant functions.

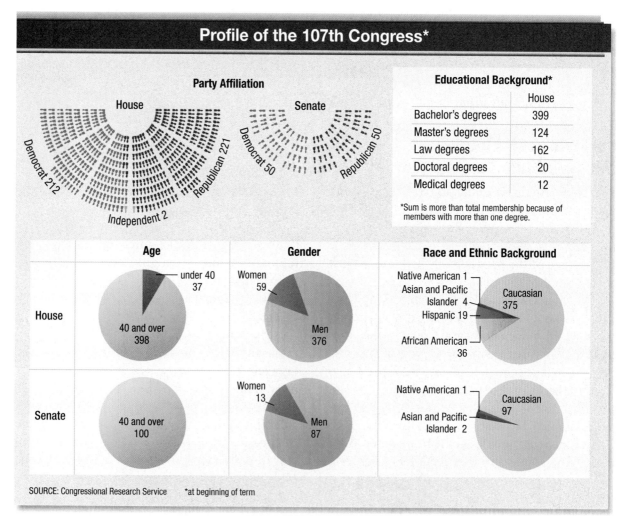

Profile of the 107th Congress*

Party Affiliation

House — Democrat 212, Republican 221, Independent 2

Senate — Democrat 50, Republican 50

Educational Background*

	House
Bachelor's degrees	399
Master's degrees	124
Law degrees	162
Doctoral degrees	20
Medical degrees	12

*Sum is more than total membership because of members with more than one degree.

Age

House — under 40: 37; 40 and over: 398

Senate — 40 and over: 100

Gender

House — Women 59; Men 376

Senate — Women 13; Men 87

Race and Ethnic Background

House — Native American 1; Asian and Pacific Islander 4; Hispanic 19; African American 36; Caucasian 375

Senate — Native American 1; Asian and Pacific Islander 2; Caucasian 97

SOURCE: Congressional Research Service   *at beginning of term

Interpreting Graphs Members of Congress come to Washington, D.C., with a wide variety of backgrounds. ***How does racial and ethnic diversity differ between the House and the Senate?***

Representatives of the People

Senators and representatives are elected to represent people. But what does that really mean? They cast hundreds of votes during each session of Congress. Many of those votes involve quite routine, relatively unimportant matters; for example, a bill to designate a week in May as National Wild Flower Week. But many of those votes, including some on matters of organization and procedure, are cast on matters of far-reaching import.

So, no questions about the lawmaking branch can be more vital than these: How do the people's representatives represent the people? On what basis do they cast their votes?

In broad terms, each lawmaker has four voting options. He or she can vote as a trustee, as a delegate, as a partisan, or as a politico.

Trustees believe that each question they face must be decided on its merits. Conscience and independent judgment are their guides. Trustees call issues as they see them, regardless of the views held by their constituents or by any of the other groups that seek to influence their decisions.

Delegates see themselves as the agents of those who elected them. They believe that they should vote the way they think "the folks back home" would want. They are willing to suppress their own views, ignore those of their party's leaders, and turn a deaf ear to the arguments of colleagues and of special interests from outside their constituencies.

Those lawmakers who owe their first allegiance to their political party are **partisans**. They feel duty-bound to vote in line with the party platform and the wishes of their party's leaders. Most studies of legislators' voting behavior show that partisanship is the leading factor influencing their votes on most important measures.

Politicos attempt to combine the basic elements of the trustee, delegate, and partisan roles. They try to balance these often conflicting factors: their own views of what is best for their constituents and/or the nation as a whole, the political facts of life, and the peculiar pressures of the moment.

Committee Members

In every session of Congress, proposed laws (bills) are referred to committees in each chamber. As committee members, senators and representatives must screen those proposals. They decide which will go on to floor consideration—that is, be considered and acted upon by the full membership of the House or Senate.

Another vital part of their committee work involves the **oversight function**. Oversight is the process by which Congress, through its committees, checks to see that the various agencies in the executive branch are working effectively and acting in line with the policies that Congress has set by law.

Servants

Members of the House and Senate also act as servants of their constituents. Most often, they do this as they (and, more particularly, their staff aides) try to help people who have various problems with the federal bureaucracy. Those problems may involve a Social Security benefit, a passport application, a small business loan, or any one of a thousand other issues.

Some of "the folks back home" believe that members of Congress are in Washington

Voices on Government

For **Alan Simpson**, politics is a family business. His father was governor of Wyoming and a U.S. senator. Simpson began his political career at the State level, and was later elected to the U.S. Senate. His 18 years as a Republican senator gave him this perspective:

❝*I am a legislator. I never wanted to be governor or president or vice president. If you're thinking of politics, make up your mind. You're going to legislate or you want to be governor, president, emperor or king—what is it you're interested in? And make that choice. For me it was to take an idea and personally draft the bill. Which I would do. . . . I did my own amendments, would work the bill myself, manage it on the floor. And so I legislated.*❞

Evaluating the Quotation

Simpson sees a big difference between legislative and executive jobs. How does his description compare with what you have read about Congress in this chapter?

▲ Representative Ileana Ros-Lehtinen (R., Florida) must balance several different roles. Her jobs include publicizing important issues, meeting with constituents, and working with her fellow lawmakers in Washington. ***Critical Thinking Why is it important for a representative to speak often with constituents?***

primarily to do favors for them. Most members are swamped with constituent requests from the moment they take office. The range of these requests is almost without limit—everything from help in securing a government contract or an appointment to a military academy, to asking for a free sightseeing tour of Washington or even a personal loan. Consider this job description offered only half-jokingly by a former representative:

PRIMARY Sources *❝ A Congressman has become an expanded messenger boy, an employment agency, getter-outer of the Navy, Army, Marines, ward heeler, wound healer, trouble shooter, law explainer, bill finder, issue translator, resolution interpreter, controversy oil pourer, gladhand extender, business promoter, convention goer, civil ills skirmisher, veterans' affairs adjuster, ex-serviceman's champion, watchdog for the underdog, sympathizer with the upper dog, namer and kisser of babies, recoverer of lost luggage, soberer of delegates, adjuster for traffic violators, voters straying into Washington and into toils of the law, binder up of broken hearts, financial wet nurse, Good Samaritan, contributor to good causes—there are so many good causes—cornerstone layer, public building and bridge dedicator, ship christener—to be sure he does get in a little flag waving—and a little constitutional hoisting and*

spread-eagle work, but it is getting harder every day to find time to properly study legislation—the very business we are primarily here to discharge, and that must be done above all things. ❞
—Rep. Luther Patrick (D., Alabama)

Most members of Congress know that to deny or fail to respond to these requests would mean to lose votes in the next election. This is a key fact, for all of the roles a member of Congress plays—legislator, representative, committee member, constituent servant, and politician—are related, at least in part, to their efforts to win reelection.

Compensation

The Constitution says that members of Congress "shall receive a Compensation for their Services, to be ascertained by Law. . . ."[21] That is, the Constitution says that Congress fixes that "Compensation."

Salary

Today, senators and representatives are paid a salary of $150,000 a year. A few members are paid somewhat more. The Speaker of the

---

[21] Article I, Section 6, Clause 1. The 27th Amendment modified this pay-setting authority. It provides that no increase in members' pay can take effect until after the next congressional election—that is, not until the voters have had an opportunity to react to the pay raise.

House makes $187,500 a year, the same salary that Congress has set for the Vice President. The Senate's president *pro tem* and the majority and minority floor leaders in both houses receive $162,000 a year.

Nonsalary Compensation

Each member receives a number of "fringe benefits," some of which are quite substantial. For example, each member has a special tax deduction, not available to any other federal income tax payer. That deduction is designed to help members who must maintain two residences, one in his or her home State and another in Washington.

Generous travel allowances offset the costs of several round trips each year between home and Washington. Members pay relatively small amounts for life and health insurance and for outpatient care by a medical staff on Capitol Hill; they can get full medical care, at very low rates, at any military hospital. They also have a generous retirement plan, to which they contribute. The plan pays a pension based on years of service in Congress, and longtime members can retire with an income of $150,000 or more a year. Members of Congress are also covered by Social Security's retirement and medicare programs.

Members are also provided with offices in one of the several Senate and House office buildings near the Capitol and allowances for offices in their home State or district. Each member is given funds for hiring staff and for operation costs related to running those offices. The **franking privilege** is a well-known benefit that allows them to mail letters and other materials postage-free by substituting their facsimile signature (frank) for the postage.

Congress has also provided its members with the free printing—and through franking, the free distribution—of speeches, newsletters, and the like. Radio and television tapes can be produced at very low cost. Each member can choose among several fine restaurants in the Capitol. There are also two first-rate gymnasiums, with swimming pools, exercise rooms, and saunas. Members receive still more privileges, including such things as the help of the excellent services of the Library of Congress and free parking in spaces reserved for them at the Capitol and also at Washington's major airports.[22]

The Politics of Pay

There are only two real limits on the level of congressional pay. One is the President's veto power. The other and more potent limit is the fear of voter backlash, an angry reaction by constituents at the ballot box. That fear of election-day fallout has always made most members reluctant to vote to raise their own salaries.

Congress has often tried to skirt the troublesome and politically sensitive pay question. It has done so by providing for such fringe benefits as a special tax break, a liberal pension plan, more office and travel funds, and other perquisites, or "perks"—items of value that are much less apparent to "the folks back home."

The debate over congressional pay is not likely to end soon—at least not as long as the current method of establishing salaries remains in effect. All sides of the issue present reasonable arguments.

---

[22]For decades, many members of Congress supplemented their salaries with honoraria—speaking fees and similar payments from private sources, mainly special interest groups. Critics long attacked that widespread practice as at least unseemly and, at its worst, a form of legalized bribery. The House finally prohibited its members from accepting honoraria in 1989, and the Senate did so in 1991.

"Congratulations on your raise, sir."

Interpreting Political Cartoons The salaries and benefits enjoyed by members of Congress have long been a sensitive political issue. *Why are voters reluctant to see members of Congress increase their benefits and pay?*

Clearly, decent salaries—pay in line with the responsibilities of the job—will not automatically bring the most able men and women to Congress, or to any other public office. But certainly, decent salaries can make public service much more appealing to qualified people.

Membership Privileges

Beyond the matter of their salaries and other compensation, members of Congress enjoy several privileges. The Constitution commands that senators and representatives

> **FROM THE Constitution** ❝shall in all Cases, except Treason, Felony and Breach of the Peace, be privileged from Arrest during their Attendance at the Session of their respective Houses, and in going to and returning from the same. . . . ❞
>
> —Article I, Section 6, Clause 1

The provision dates from English and colonial practice, when the king's officers often harassed legislators on petty grounds. It has been of little importance in our national history, however.[23]

Another much more important privilege is set out in the same place in the Constitution. The Speech or Debate Clause of Article I, Section 6, Clause 1 declares ". . . for any Speech or Debate in either House, they shall not be questioned in any other Place." The words "any other Place" refer particularly to the courts.

The privilege is intended to "throw a cloak of legislative immunity" around members of Congress. The clause protects representatives and senators from suits for libel or slander arising out of their official conduct. The Supreme Court has held that the immunity applies "to things generally done in a session of the House [or Senate] by one of its members in relation to the business before it."[24] The protection goes, then, beyond floor debate, to include work in committees and all other things generally done by members of Congress in relation to congressional business.

The important and necessary goal of this provision of the Constitution is to protect freedom of legislative debate. Clearly, members must not feel restrained in their vigorous discussion of the sometimes contentious issues of the day. However, this provision is not designed to give members unbridled freedom to attack others verbally or in writing. Thus, a member is not free to defame another person in a public speech, an article, a conversation, or otherwise.

---

[23]The courts have regularly held that the words "Breach of the Peace" cover all criminal offenses. So the protection covers only arrest for civil (noncriminal) offenses while engaged in congressional business.

[24]The leading case is *Kilbourn* v. *Thompson*, 1881. The holding has been affirmed many times since. In *Hutchinson* v. *Proxmire*, 1979, however, the Court held that members of Congress may be sued for libel for statements they make in news releases or in newsletters.

Section 4 Assessment

Key Terms and Main Ideas

1. What does a **delegate** value most when deciding how to vote on a bill?
2. What does a **partisan** value most when deciding how to vote on a bill?
3. How does the **franking privilege** help members of Congress?
4. What is the **oversight function**?

Critical Thinking

5. **Drawing Conclusions** What are the different roles that a member of Congress plays?
6. **Determining Cause and Effect** Why are members of Congress reluctant to pass laws that give them new benefits or higher pay?

7. **Drawing Inferences** Look again at the diagram on page 276. Why might it not be a good idea for a letter writer to berate his or her lawmaker?

 Take It to the Net

8. The Senate's oversight function is an important part of the system of checks and balances. Read about the oversight function and write a paragraph explaining why this is an essential power of the Senate. Use the links provided in the Social Studies area at the following Web site for help in completing this activity. **www.phschool.com**

May Congresspersons Be Sued for Their Statements?

The "Speech or Debate Clause" in Article I, Section 6 of the Constitution provides that senators and representatives "shall not be questioned in any other place" over "any speech or debate in either House." This has been interpreted to mean that they cannot be sued for anything they say in their legislative chambers. How far does this protection extend?

Hutchinson v. Proxmire (1979)

Senator William Proxmire of Wisconsin invented the "Golden Fleece of the Month Award" to publicize what he saw as examples of wasteful government spending. In 1975 he gave awards to various federal agencies for spending almost half a million dollars to fund Professor Ronald Hutchinson's research on emotional behavior. Hutchinson was trying to develop an objective measure of aggression, and his research focused on certain behavior patterns, such as clenching of the jaw.

In an "awards speech" to the Senate, Proxmire stated: "In view of the transparent worthlessness of Hutchinson's study of jaw-grinding and biting by angry . . . monkeys, it is time we put a stop to the bite [that] Hutchinson and the bureaucrats who fund him have been taking of the taxpayer." His remarks were published in the *Congressional Record* and in a press release and in various newsletters.

Hutchinson sued Proxmire, saying his professional reputation had been damaged. Proxmire responded that his remarks were protected by the Speech or Debate Clause and by the First Amendment. The district court and court of appeals ruled in favor of Proxmire, and the case went to the Supreme Court for review.

Arguments for Hutchinson

1. The Speech or Debate Clause should not extend protection to comments that are made outside of the Senate chamber or are not part of the legislative function of the Senate.
2. The newsletters and press release about the Golden Fleece Award were aimed at persons outside Congress and thus are not part of the senator's official duties.
3. Since Professor Hutchinson is not a public figure, he does not have to prove as part of his lawsuit that the senator's remarks were made with actual malice (desire to harm).

Arguments for Proxmire

1. The senator's comments in the Senate about matters of national importance were protected by the Speech or Debate Clause; the use of these comments in a press release and newsletters describing the Senate speech were part of the senator's official duty to inform the public about his activities.
2. The senator's criticisms of wasteful spending of public funds were also privileged under the Free Speech Clause of the First Amendment.
3. Professor Hutchinson is a public figure; therefore, he must prove as part of his suit that Proxmire acted with actual malice.

Decide for Yourself

1. Review the constitutional grounds on which each side based its arguments and the specific arguments each side presented.
2. Debate the opposing viewpoints presented in this case. Which viewpoint do you favor?
3. Predict the impact of the Court's decision on activities and statements by members of Congress outside the House and Senate chambers. (To read a summary of the Court's decision, turn to the Supreme Court Glossary on page 799.)

Political Dictionary

term (p. 264)
session (p. 264)
adjourn (p. 264)
prorogue (p. 265)
special session (p. 265)
apportion (p. 267)
reapportion (p. 267)

off-year election (p. 269)
single-member district (p. 270)
at-large (p. 270)
gerrymander (p. 271)
continuous body (p. 277)
constituency (p. 277)
colleague (p. 277)

trustee (p. 281)
partisan (p. 281)
politico (p. 281)
oversight function (p. 281)
franking privilege (p. 283)

Practicing the Vocabulary

Matching *Choose a term from the list above that best matches each description.*

1. What happens to the seats in the House of Representatives every decade
2. What the President can do if the two houses of Congress cannot agree on a date to adjourn
3. The right of members of Congress to send mail postage-free by using a signature in place of a stamp
4. The function Congress is performing when it checks on the programs of the executive branch
5. How you might describe a congressional district that has been drawn by a legislature in a very odd shape

Fill in the Blank *Choose a term from the list above that best completes the sentence.*

6. Congress can _____, or suspend its meeting, whenever it chooses.
7. Each member of the House represents a _____ of about 630,000 people.
8. A member of the House of Representatives is elected for a two-year _____.
9. In States with a low population, members of the House of Representatives are chosen in _____ districts.
10. A _____ is a member of Congress who votes primarily according to the wishes of his or her party.

Reviewing Main Ideas

Section 1

11. How does bicameralism in Congress reflect the principle of federalism?
12. (a) How are States represented in the House of Representatives? (b) How are States represented in the Senate?
13. (a) What is a special session? (b) Why have special sessions lost their importance?

Section 2

14. For what reasons must seats in Congress be reapportioned every 10 years?
15. In what ways has the redistricting of House seats been used for the political gain of certain groups and parties in the various States?
16. (a) What are the constitutional qualifications that all members of the House must meet? (b) What are the informal qualifications that members of the House should meet?

Section 3

17. How do senators differ from their colleagues in the House of Representatives?
18. (a) How do constituencies vary within the Senate? (b) Which State's senators have the largest constituency?
19. (a) In what ways does the long six-year term affect how senators vote? (b) How does this confirm the Framers' intentions for the Senate?
20. The Constitution sets up what formal qualifications for membership in the Senate?

Section 4

21. (a) Do the members of Congress represent a cross section of the American people? (b) Why or why not?
22. (a) When deciding how to vote, what does a trustee consider? (b) When deciding how to vote, what does a politico consider?
23. How are members of Congress compensated for their work? List several examples.

Critical Thinking Skills

24. *Applying the Chapter Skill* Study the map on page 263. **(a)** What does this map depict? **(b)** Write a summary explaining the information shown on the map. Which is the more effective way of conveying the information shown, the map or the written summary? Why?

25. *Predicting Consequences* Reread the conversation between Thomas Jefferson and George Washington on page 263. According to Washington, how would a unicameral (one-house) legislature produce different results than a bicameral Congress?

26. *Understanding Point of View* Congress is a frequent target of criticism in the media and elsewhere. Yet the text says that the members of Congress are on the whole hard-working and able people. How can you explain the existence of these two opposing viewpoints?

27. *Expressing Problems Clearly* Recall what you have read about the differences between the House and Senate. **(a)** Cite two benefits that flow from senators' six-year terms. **(b)** What are two drawbacks that arise out of those six-year terms?

Analyzing Political Cartoons

Using your knowledge of American government and this cartoon, answer the questions below.

MEASURING POLITICAL CANDIDATES

28. According to this cartoonist, what factor plays an important role in determining who runs for office?

29. Based on your reading in this chapter, is the cartoonist correct? Explain your answer.

★ You Can Make a Difference

Most congressional pages are nominated by the senator or representative from their home State. They are usually high school juniors with good grades and outstanding records in school and community service. Suppose that you want to spend a year in Washington, D.C., as a page in the House or Senate. Find out how to apply for this job. Then draft a letter to your senator or representative in which you explain why you want to be a page, what you think you would learn from the experience, and why you think your record and activities qualify you for the job.

Participation Activities

30. *Current Events Watch* Choose one member of Congress named in a current news report and find out about a political action or decision made by the person while serving in Congress. Analyze the consequences of that action on American society.

31. *Graphing Activity* Turn to the map on page 268 and find the eight States with the greatest number of representatives in the House. Create a circle graph showing each State's representatives as a percentage of the 435 members of the House of Representatives. Remember to label the part of the circle graph that represents the other 42 States. What does this graph tell you about the influence of these States in the House of Representatives?

32. *It's Your Turn* Write a newspaper editorial expressing your views on the qualifications for membership in Congress. List the formal qualifications and those informal ones that you think members should satisfy. Suggest changes (if any) that you would make in those qualifications. Indicate why you think each of the informal qualifications you cite is important. Read your draft for clarity and revise it. Then proofread and draft a final copy. **(Writing an Editorial)**

Take It to the Net

Chapter 10 Self-Test As a final review activity, take the Chapter 10 Self-Test in the Social Studies area at the Web site listed below, and receive immediate feedback on your answers.

www.phschool.com

CHAPTER 11

Powers of Congress

"The range of issues that come before the United States Senate is infinite: from ratifying treaties, to confirming federal judges, . . . to appropriating the federal dollars that fund the programs upon which we all rely."

— Senator Susan Collins (R.) of Maine (2000)

As Senator Collins points out, members of Congress must discuss an amazing array of issues as part of their lawmaking duties. How far the powers of Congress should extend has been a source of debate and controversy throughout the history of the nation.

◆ **Floor of the United States House**

★ You Can Make a Difference

EACH YEAR, SENATORS choose delegates for the U.S. Senate Youth Program, a week-long study of the Federal Government that focuses on the Senate. In 1999, Hawaii Senators Daniel Inouye and Daniel Akaka chose two outstanding students from their State to come to Washington, D.C., to participate. Gavin Maeda of Konawaena High School has worked on political campaigns, served as an election precinct official, and was his school's Senate president. His goal is to have his own criminal defense law firm. The other delegate, Daniel Evans, has participated in the debate club and other groups at Kahuku High School and served as a delegate to the Mock United Nations. He plans to work in government service.

⟳ Keep It Current

Items marked with this logo are periodically updated on the Internet. Keep up-to-date with what's in the news. To get current information on issues related to the powers of Congress go to **www.phschool.com**

SECTION 1

The Scope of Congressional Powers
(pp. 290–292)

★ Congress has only those powers delegated (granted) to it by the Constitution.

★ How those powers should be interpreted and applied—whether strictly or liberally—has been sharply debated throughout our history.

SECTION 2

The Expressed Powers of Money and Commerce *(pp. 294–300)*

★ The Framers gave Congress the taxing power and the commerce power—two hugely important powers that it did not have under the Articles of Confederation.

★ Congress has the vital power to borrow money and to create a monetary system for the country.

SECTION 3

Other Expressed Powers *(pp. 301–304)*

★ Congress shares power with the President in both defense and foreign affairs.

★ Congress regulates several matters that affect everyday life—including such things as mail, weights and measures, and copyrights and patents.

SECTION 4

The Implied Powers *(pp. 305–308)*

★ Congress has a number of important powers not set out in so many words in the Constitution.

★ What Congress can and cannot do in the exercise of its implied powers has been and remains a subject of intense debate.

SECTION 5

The Nonlegislative Powers *(pp. 310–314)*

★ Congress may propose amendments to the Constitution with a two-thirds vote in each house.

★ The House of Representatives decides a presidential election if no candidate wins a majority of electoral votes.

★ The House has the power to impeach (accuse) the President and the Senate may convict (remove) an impeached President. The House has impeached two Presidents—Andrew Johnson and Bill Clinton; neither was convicted by the Senate.

★ The Senate has the power to confirm or reject major presidential appointments and to approve or reject treaties.

★ Congress may investigate any matter that falls within the scope of its legislative powers.

The Scope of Congressional Powers

Section Preview

OBJECTIVES

1. **Identify** the three types of congressional power.
2. **Compare** strict construction of the U.S. Constitution on the subject of congressional power to liberal construction.

WHY IT MATTERS

The Constitution makes Congress the lawmaking branch—the basic policymaking branch of the National Government. The powers of Congress are limited, yes—but those powers are many, and they are also far-reaching.

POLITICAL DICTIONARY

★ **expressed powers**
★ **implied powers**
★ **inherent powers**
★ **strict constructionist**
★ **liberal constructionist**
★ **consensus**

A typical day in either chamber of Congress might suggest that there is no limit to what Congress can do. On any given day, the House might consider bills dealing with such varying matters as inheritance and gift tax rates, the space shuttle program, and grazing on public lands. The Senate might be debating aid to a famine-stricken country in Africa, veterans' benefits, and dairy price supports. Senators might also be considering the President's nomination of a new Supreme Court justice.

At the same time, however, Congress operates under very real limits. Remember that (1) the government of the United States is limited government, and (2) the American system of government is federal in form. These two fundamental facts work both to shape and to limit the powers of Congress.

Congressional Power

Remember, Congress has only those powers delegated (granted, given) to it by the Constitution. Large areas of power are denied to Congress in so many words in the Constitution, by the Constitution's silence on many matters, and because the Constitution creates a federal system.

There is much that Congress cannot do. It cannot create a national public school system, require people to vote or attend church, or set a minimum age for marriage or drivers' licenses. It cannot abolish jury trials, confiscate all handguns, or censor the content of newspaper columns or radio or television broadcasts. Congress cannot do these and a great many other things because the Constitution does not allow it to do so.

Still, Congress *does* have the power to do many things. The Constitution grants it a number of specific powers—and, recall, it does so in three different ways: (1) explicitly, in its specific wording—the **expressed powers;** (2) by reasonable deduction from the expressed powers—the **implied powers;** and (3) by creating a national government for the United States—the **inherent powers.**

HISTORY

OF

THE PROCEEDINGS AND DEBATES

OF

THE HOUSE OF REPRESENTATIVES

OF THE

UNITED STATES.

AT THE FIRST SESSION OF THE FIRST CONGRESS, BEGUN AT THE CITY OF NEW YORK, MARCH 4, 1789.

WEDNESDAY, March 4, 1789.
This being the day fixed for the meeting of the new Congress, the following members of the House of Representatives appeared and took their seats, viz:
From Massachusetts, GEORGE THATCHER, FISHER AMES, GEORGE LEONARD, and ELDRIDGE GERRY.
From Connecticut, BENJAMIN HUNTINGTON, JONATHAN TRUMBULL, and JEREMIAH WADSWORTH.
From Pennsylvania, FREDERICK AUGUSTUS MUHLENBERG, THOMAS HARTLEY, PETER MUHLENBERG, and DANIEL HEISTER.
From Virginia, ALEXANDER WHITE.
From South Carolina, THOMAS TUDOR TUCK-

WEDNESDAY, March 18.
ANDREW MOORE, from Virginia, took his seat. No other member appearing, the House adjourned, from day to day, until the 23d instant.

MONDAY, March 23.
The following members appeared, to wit:— From New Jersey, ELIAS BOUDINOT; and from Maryland, WILLIAM SMITH.
No additional member appeared on the 24th.

WEDNESDAY, March 25.
JONATHAN PARKER, from Virginia, appeared and took his seat.
No additional member arrived until the 30th instant.

▲ *Notes from the First Congress* The gavel came down on the first session of the House of Representatives on March 4, 1789, but the body lacked a quorum and had to adjourn every day until April 1, when enough members finally made it to New York City. The first order of business was to elect a Speaker.

Strict Versus Liberal Construction

The Framers of the Constitution intended to create a new and stronger National Government. The ratification of their plan was opposed by many, and that opposition was not stilled by the adoption of the Constitution. Rather, the conflict between the Federalists and the Anti-Federalists continued into the early years of the Republic. Much of that conflict centered on the powers of Congress. Just how broad, in fact, were those powers?

The **strict constructionists,** led by Thomas Jefferson, continued to argue the Anti-Federalist position from the ratification period. They insisted that Congress should be able to exercise only (1) its expressed powers and (2) those implied powers absolutely necessary to carry out those expressed powers. They wanted the States to keep as much power as possible. They agreed with Jefferson that "that government is best which governs least."

Most of the Anti-Federalists did acknowledge a need to protect interstate trade, and they recognized the need for a strong national defense. At the same time, they feared the consequences of a strong National Government. They believed, for instance, that the interests of the people of Connecticut were not the same as those of South Carolinians or Marylanders or Pennsylvanians. They argued that only the States—not the far-off National Government—could protect and preserve those differing interests.

Voices on Government

Xavier Becerra (D., California), who represents part of Los Angeles in the House, is an active member of the Congressional Hispanic Caucus. Improving education, especially for Hispanic students, is a major focus of his efforts in Congress.

❝ *Talk is not enough when the future of our children is at stake. We must end politics at the schoolhouse door. I urge Congress to work on [an] education . . . plan [that] would reduce class size to a national average of 18, modernize 5,000 schools nationwide, and make the needed investments to provide schools and students with after-school programs, technology and other tools to bring our schools into the 21st century.* ❞

Evaluating the Quotation

What does Becerra mean when he says "We must end politics at the schoolhouse door"?

The **liberal constructionists,** led by Alexander Hamilton, had led the fight to adopt the Constitution. Now they favored a liberal interpretation of the Constitution, a broad construction of the powers given to Congress.

Interpreting Illustrations The debate over the scope of the powers of the Federal Government is as heated today as it was in early America. *What techniques does this illustration use to depict the conflict?*

Liberal Constructionists from Hamilton's time to today have favored a strong Federal Government...

while Strict Constructionists in the tradition of Jefferson have sought to limit the powers of the Federal Government.

How much pruning can we do and still get apples?

Interpreting Political Cartoons What point is the cartoonist making about the big government/small government debate? What details in the drawing help to make the point?

They believed that the country needed, as Hamilton put it, "an energetic government."

The liberal constructionists won that conflict in the early years of the Republic, as you will see. Their victory set a pattern that, in general, has been followed ever since. Over the years, the powers wielded by the National Government have grown to a point that even the most

ardent supporters of liberal construction could not have imagined.

Several factors, working together with the liberal construction of the Constitution, have been responsible for that marked growth in national power. They have included wars, economic crises, and other national emergencies. Spectacular advances, especially in transportation and communication, have also had a real impact on the size and the scope of government. Equally important have been the demands of the people for more and more services from government.

Congress has been led by these and other factors to view its powers in broader and broader terms. Most Presidents have regarded their powers in like fashion. The Supreme Court has generally taken a similar position in its decisions in cases involving the powers of the National Government.

Moreover, the American people have generally agreed with a liberal interpretation of the Constitution. This **consensus,** this general agreement, has prevailed even though United States political history has been marked, and still is, by controversies over the proper limits of national power.

Section 1 Assessment

Key Terms and Main Ideas

1. Explain the differences among Congress's **expressed powers, implied powers,** and **inherent powers.**
2. Compare the views of a **strict constructionist** and a **liberal constructionist.**
3. Give three examples of laws that Congress can enact under the Constitution and three examples of laws that Congress cannot enact.
4. Explain this sentence: *Historically, there has been a con-sensus in this country with regard to a liberal construction of the Constitution.*

Critical Thinking

5. **Understanding Point of View** Why might Alexander Hamilton, a supporter of a strong National Government, be surprised at the scope of the powers of the National Government today?

6. **Making Comparisons** Explain why these two seemingly contradictory statements are both true: **(a)** Most Americans agree with a liberal interpretation of the Constitution. **(b)** The issue of the extent of the Federal Government's power is hotly debated today.

 Take It to the Net

7. Recently, scholars have debated "originalism"—that is, the role the Framers' original intentions should play in determining how much power the Federal Government should have. Check this debate on the Internet and write a brief comment in support of one of the views you find there. Use the links provided in the Social Studies area at the following Web site for help in completing this activity. **www.phschool.com**

Evaluating Leadership

When you participate in representative government, you choose people to make decisions for you. What kind of person do you want representing you? Do you want someone who is full of new ideas? Who knows how to get things done? Who has experience? Which qualities are most important to you?

In an election, candidates compete to convince you that they have the stuff of leadership. Examine their claims carefully. Otherwise you'll be basing your decisions on criteria such as "She's really cool" or "He looks like my cousin."

Whether you're evaluating a candidate for President of the United States or for student council president, consider these steps:

1. Establish your criteria for evaluating a leader. Most people would agree on certain qualities that make a good leader, such as honesty and commitment to duty. Other characteristics may vary widely. Some jobs demand a person with a great deal of experience. Other positions are less dependent on experience, but require creative ideas. Are you looking for a "hands-on" leader (who personally gets things done) or a skilled manager who inspires others to work productively? Make a list of criteria *you* look for in a leader. The table below lists some possible characteristics.

2. Rate your subject. Using the leadership criteria you've established, rate the person you are evaluating on a scale of 0 to 5 (with 5 being the highest), as shown in the table.

3. Compare or contrast your subject with other leaders. Use your checklist to compare candidates' leadership attributes. That might mean doing a little homework, such as calling campaign offices or doing other research on the candidates' views.

4. Summarize your opinion. When you finish, you should be able to say, "So-and-so would make a good leader <u>because</u> . . . ." If you *still* can't think of a reason, perhaps you should vote for somebody else.

Test for Success

Choose someone in a leadership position or someone you think might make a good leader. Evaluate that person, and summarize your findings in a paragraph.

Rating Sheet: Qualities of a Leader

Qualities	Rating
Has fresh ideas	4
Has experience	2
Is honest	5
Takes charge	5
Encourages team building, cooperation	3
Is dynamic	5
Has strong sense of duty	4
Inspires others to excel	3
Is good decision maker	4
Shows political courage	4
Has steady personality, is dependable	2
Keeps promises	4

The Expressed Powers of Money and Commerce

Section Preview

OBJECTIVES

1. **Summarize** key points relating to Congress's power to tax.
2. **Describe** how Congress uses its power to borrow money.
3. **Analyze** the importance of Congress's commerce power.
4. **Identify** the reasons that the Framers gave Congress the power to issue currency.
5. **Explain** how the bankruptcy power works.

WHY IT MATTERS

Its powers to tax and to regulate both interstate and foreign trade give Congress a critical role in the nation's economy. Neither its taxing power nor its commerce power are unlimited, however.

POLITICAL DICTIONARY

★ **tax**
★ **direct tax**
★ **indirect tax**
★ **deficit financing**
★ **public debt**
★ **commerce power**
★ **legal tender**
★ **bankruptcy**

Most, but not all, of the expressed powers of Congress are found in Article I, Section 8 of the Constitution. There, in 18 separate clauses, 27 different powers are explicitly given to Congress.[1]

These grants of power are brief. What they do and do not allow Congress to do often cannot be discovered by merely reading the few words involved. Rather, their meaning is found in the ways in which Congress has exercised its powers since 1789, and in scores of Supreme Court cases arising out of the actions taken by Congress.

As a case in point, take the Commerce Clause, which gives to Congress the power

FROM THE Constitution *"To regulate Commerce with foreign Nations, and among the several States, and with the Indian Tribes."*
—Article I, Section 8, Clause 3

What do these words mean? Congress and the Court have had to answer hundreds of questions about the scope of the Commerce Clause. Here are few examples: Does "commerce" include people crossing State lines or entering or leaving the country? What about business practices?

▲ When they wrote the Commerce Clause, the Framers could not have envisioned this: a warehouse worker in Massachusetts filling orders for an online grocery service.

Working conditions? Radio and television broadcasts? Does the Commerce Clause give Congress the power to ban the shipment of certain goods from one State to another? To prohibit discrimination? To regulate the Internet? What trade is "foreign" and what is "interstate"? What trade is neither?

In answering these and dozens upon dozens of questions arising out of this one provision, Congress and the Court have defined—and are still defining—the meaning of the Commerce Clause. So it is with most of the other constitutional grants of power to Congress.

The Power to Tax

The Constitution gives Congress the power

FROM THE Constitution *"To lay and collect Taxes, Duties, Imposts and Excises, to pay the Debts and provide for the common Defense and general Welfare of the United States. . . ."*
—Article I, Section 8, Clause 1

---

[1]Several of the expressed powers of Congress are set out elsewhere in the Constitution. Thus, Article IV, Section 3 grants Congress the power to admit new States to the Union (Clause 1) and to manage and dispose of federal territory and other property (Clause 2). The 16th Amendment gives Congress the power to levy an income tax. The 13th, 14th, 15th, 19th, 24th, and 26th amendments grant Congress the "power to enforce" the provisions of the amendments "by appropriate legislation."

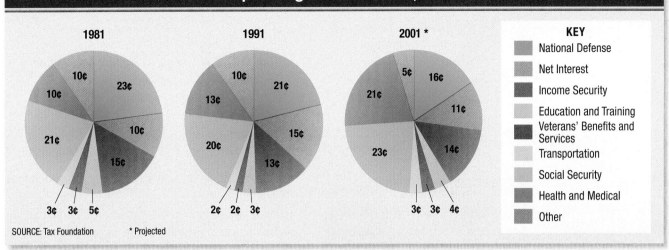

Federal Spending of Tax Dollars, 1981–2001

1981
10¢ 23¢ 10¢ 10¢ 21¢ 15¢ 3¢ 3¢ 5¢

1991
10¢ 21¢ 13¢ 15¢ 20¢ 13¢ 2¢ 2¢ 3¢

2001 *
5¢ 16¢ 21¢ 11¢ 23¢ 14¢ 3¢ 3¢ 4¢

KEY
- National Defense
- Net Interest
- Income Security
- Education and Training
- Veterans' Benefits and Services
- Transportation
- Social Security
- Health and Medical
- Other

SOURCE: Tax Foundation   * Projected

Interpreting Graphs Congress's priorities can be seen in the way it spends tax revenues. These graphs show what proportions of a tax dollar were spent on what federal programs. **What major shifts in federal spending occurred (a) between 1981 and 1991 and (b) between 1991 and 2001?**

Recall that the Articles of Confederation had not given Congress the power to tax. Congress did have the power to requisition (request) funds from the States; that is, Congress could ask (in reality, beg) each of the thirteen States for money. But, through the 1780s, not a single State came even remotely close to meeting the requisitions Congress made, and some States paid nothing at all. The government was powerless, and the lack of a power to tax was a leading cause for the creation of the Constitution.

The Purpose of Taxes

We shall take another and longer look at the taxing power in Chapter 16. But, here, a number of important points: The Federal Government will take in some $2 trillion in fiscal year 2002, and almost certainly an even larger sum in 2003. Most of that money—well over 90 percent of it—will come from the various taxes levied by Congress.

A **tax** is a charge levied by government on persons or property to meet public needs. Notice, however, that Congress sometimes imposes taxes for other purposes. The protective tariff is perhaps the oldest example of this point. Although it does bring in some revenue every year, its real goal is to "protect" domestic industry against foreign competition by increasing the cost of foreign goods.

Taxes are also sometimes levied to protect the public health and safety. The Federal Government's regulation of narcotics is a case in point. Only those who have a proper federal license can legally manufacture, sell, or deal in those drugs—and licensing is a form of taxation.

Limits on the Taxing Power

Congress's power to tax is not unlimited, of course. As with all other powers, it must be used in accord with all other provisions of the Constitution. Thus, Congress cannot lay a tax on church services, for example—because such a tax would violate the 1st Amendment protection of the free exercise of religion. Nor could it lay a poll tax as a condition for voting in federal elections—because that tax would violate the 24th Amendment.

More specifically, the Constitution places four explicit limitations on the taxing power:

(1) Congress may tax only for public purposes, not for private benefit. Article I, Section 8, Clause 1 says that taxes may be levied only "to pay the Debts and provide for the common Defense and general Welfare of the United States. . . ."

(2) Congress may not tax exports. Article I, Section 9, Clause 5 declares "[n]o Tax or Duty shall be laid on Articles exported from any State." Thus, customs duties (tariffs), which are taxes, can be levied only on goods brought into the country (imports), not on those sent abroad (exports).

(3) Direct taxes must be apportioned among the States, according to their populations:

FROM THE Constitution *"No Capitation, or other direct, Tax shall be laid, unless in Proportion to the Census of Enumeration herein before directed to be taken."*
—Article I, Section 9, Clause 4

A **direct tax** is paid by the person on whom it is imposed; for example, a tax on the ownership of land or buildings, or a capitation (head or poll) tax. An income tax is a direct tax, but it may be laid without regard to population:

FROM THE Constitution *"The Congress shall have power to lay and collect taxes on incomes, from whatever source derived, without apportionment among the several States, and without regard to any census or enumeration."*
—16th Amendment

(4) Article I, Section 8, Clause 1 provides that "all Duties, Imposts and Excises, shall be uniform throughout the United States." That is, all indirect taxes must be levied at the same rate in all parts of the country.

In practical terms, the question of whether a tax is direct or indirect is decided by Congress and the Supreme Court. As a general rule, however, an **indirect tax** is one first paid by one person but then passed on to another. It is indirectly paid by that second person. Take, for example, the federal tax on cigarettes. It is paid to the Treasury by the tobacco company that makes the cigarettes. But that company then passes the tax on through the wholesaler and retailer to the person who finally buys the cigarettes.

The Borrowing Power

Article I, Section 8, Clause 2 gives Congress the power "[t]o borrow Money on the credit of the United States." There are no constitutional limits on the amount of money that Congress may borrow, or for what purposes.

Until recently, the Federal Government practiced **deficit financing.** That is, it spent more than it took in each year and borrowed to make up the difference. The government relied on deficit financing to deal with the Depression of the 1930s, to raise money for World War II, and to fund wars and social programs over the next several decades.

In fact, the government's books did not show a surplus (more income than spending) in any year from 1969 to 1998. As a result, the public debt rose year to year—to more than $5.5 trillion at the beginning of fiscal year 1999. The **public debt** is all of the money borrowed by the government over the

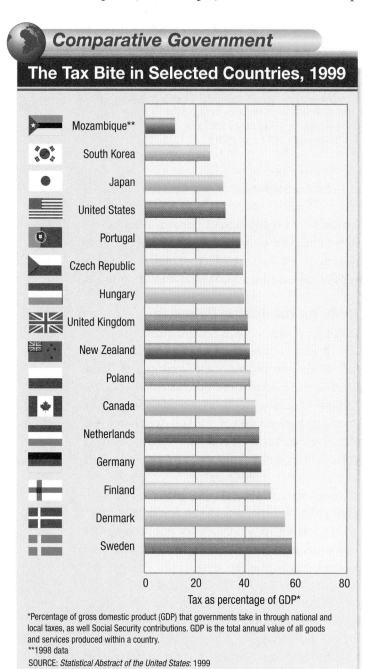

Comparative Government

The Tax Bite in Selected Countries, 1999

Tax as percentage of GDP*

- Mozambique**
- South Korea
- Japan
- United States
- Portugal
- Czech Republic
- Hungary
- United Kingdom
- New Zealand
- Poland
- Canada
- Netherlands
- Germany
- Finland
- Denmark
- Sweden

(scale: 0, 20, 40, 60, 80)

*Percentage of gross domestic product (GDP) that governments take in through national and local taxes, as well Social Security contributions. GDP is the total annual value of all goods and services produced within a country.
**1998 data
SOURCE: *Statistical Abstract of the United States: 1999*

Interpreting Graphs As this bar graph shows, some nations tax their citizens much more heavily than do other nations. Often, countries with higher taxes also provide more government services. *How does the U.S. tax rate compare with that of other countries?*

years and not yet repaid, plus the accumulated interest on that money.

With the passage of the Balanced Budget Act of 1997, Congress and President Clinton agreed to abandon deficit financing and to aim for a balanced budget by the year 2002. However, that goal was realized much more quickly than anyone anticipated. The nation's economy was so robust that the Federal Government's income rose dramatically, to the point where the Treasury Department reported a modest surplus at the end of fiscal year 1998, and larger ones for 1999, 2000, and 2001. The war on terrorism very likely means that red ink will once again be the order of the day, however.

The fact that the Constitution gives Congress the power to borrow makes borrowing a national function. So, the interest the Federal Government pays to those who loan it money cannot be taxed by the States; that makes the Federal Government's notes and bonds quite attractive to investors. We shall return to this whole matter in Chapter 16, but for now remember this: Congress continues to borrow—in the form of bonds and securities issued by the Treasury Department—to service the public debt.

The Commerce Power 🖑

The **commerce power**—the power of Congress to regulate interstate and foreign trade—is as vital to the welfare of the nation as is the taxing power. As you know, the commerce power played a major role in the formation of the Union. The weak Congress created under the Articles of Confederation had no power to regulate interstate trade and little authority over foreign commerce. The Critical Period of the 1780s was marked by intense commercial rivalries and bickering among the States. High trade barriers and spiteful State laws created chaos and confusion in much of the country.

Consequently, the Framers wrote the Commerce Clause. It gives Congress the power:

FROM THE *Constitution*
❝ *To regulate Commerce with foreign Nations, and among the several States, and with the Indian Tribes.* **❞**

—Article I, Section 8, Clause 3

▲ This engraving from the 1830s shows Robert Fulton's steamboat, the *Clermont*. **Critical Thinking** *If Fulton had held on to his riverboat monopoly in New York, what might have been the effects on interstate commerce?*

The Commerce Clause proved to be more responsible for the building of a strong and *United* States out of a weak confederation than any other provision in the Constitution. Its few words have prompted the growth in this country of the greatest open market in the world.

Gibbons v. Ogden, 1824

The first case involving the Commerce Clause to reach the Supreme Court was *Gibbons v. Ogden*, decided in 1824. The case arose out of a clash over the regulation of steamboats by the State of New York, on the one hand, and the Federal Government, on the other. In 1807 Robert Fulton's steamboat, the *Clermont*, had made its first successful run up the Hudson River, from New York City to Albany. The State legislature then gave Fulton an exclusive, long-term grant to navigate the waters of the State by steamboat. Fulton's monopoly then gave Aaron Ogden a permit for steamboat navigation between New York City and New Jersey.

Thomas Gibbons, operating with a coasting license from the Federal Government, began to carry passengers on a line that competed with Ogden. Ogden sued him, and the New York courts held that Gibbons could not sail by steam in New York waters.

Gibbons appealed that ruling to the Supreme Court. He claimed that the New York grant conflicted with the congressional power to regulate commerce. The Court agreed. It rejected Ogden's argument that "commerce" should be defined narrowly, as simply "traffic" or the mere buying and selling of goods. Instead, it read the Commerce Clause in broad terms:

▲ Congress's commerce power affects the daily lives of all Americans—including this worker in a fast-food sushi restaurant in New York City and this student on a school bus wheelchair lift in Berlin, Maryland. **Critical Thinking** *How might the Commerce Clause affect these people?*

PRIMARY Sources *"Commerce undoubtedly is traffic, but it is something more—it is intercourse. It describes the commercial intercourse between nations, and parts of nations, in all its branches, and is regulated by prescribing rules for carrying on that intercourse."*

—Chief Justice John Marshall

The Court's ruling was widely popular at the time because it dealt a death blow to steamboat monopolies. Freed from restrictive State regulation, many new steamboat companies came into existence. As a result, steam navigation developed rapidly. Within a few years, the railroads, similarly freed, revolutionized transportation within the United States.

Over the decades, the Court's sweeping definition of commerce has brought an extension of federal authority into many areas of American life—a reach of federal power beyond anything the Framers could have imagined. As another of the many examples of the point, note this: It is on the basis of the commerce power that the Civil Rights Act of 1964 prohibits discrimination in access to or service in hotels, motels, theaters, restaurants, and in other public accommodations on grounds of race, color, religion, or national origin.[2]

Based on the expressed powers to regulate commerce and to tax, Congress and the courts have built nearly all of the implied powers.

Most of what the Federal Government does, day to day and year to year, it does as the result of legislation passed by Congress in the exercise of these two powers.

Limits on the Commerce Power

Like Congress's taxing power, its commerce power is not unlimited. It, too, must be exercised in accord with all other provisions in the Constitution. Thus, the Supreme Court struck down the Gun-Free School Zone Act of 1990 in *United States* v. *Lopez,* 1995. That act had made it a federal crime for anyone other than a police officer to possess a firearm in or around a school. The Court could find no useful connection between interstate commerce and guns at school, and it held that Congress in this case had invaded the reserved powers of the States.

In more specific terms, the Constitution places four explicit limits on the use of the commerce power. Congress

(1) cannot tax exports, Article I, Section 9, Clause 5;

(2) cannot favor the ports of one State over those of any other in the regulation of trade, Article I, Section 9, Clause 6;

---

[2]The Supreme Court upheld this use of the commerce power in *Heart of Atlanta Motel* v. *United States* in 1964. The unanimous Court noted that there was "overwhelming evidence of the disruptive effect of racial discrimination on commercial intercourse." You will look at this case again in Chapter 21.

(3) cannot require that "Vessels bound to, or from, one State, be obliged to enter, clear or pay Duties in another," Article I, Section 9, Clause 6; and, finally,

(4) could not interfere with the slave trade, at least not until the year 1808, Article I, Section 9, Clause 1. This last limitation, part of the curious slave-trade compromise at the Constitutional Convention, has been a dead letter for nearly two centuries now.

The Currency Power

Article I, Section 8, Clause 5 gives Congress the power "[t]o coin Money [and] regulate the Value thereof." The States are denied that power.[3]

Until the Revolution, the English money system, built on the shilling and the pound, was in general use in the colonies. With independence, that stable currency system collapsed. The Second Continental Congress and then the Congress under the Articles issued paper money. Without sound backing, and with no taxing power behind it, however, the money was practically worthless.

---

[3]Article I, Section 10, Clause 1 forbids the States the power to coin money, issue bills of credit (paper money), or make anything but gold and silver legal tender.

Each of the 13 States also issued its own currency. In several States, this amounted to little more than the State's printing its name on paper and calling it money. Adding to the confusion, people still used English coins, and Spanish money circulated freely in the southern States.

Nearly all the Framers agreed on the need for a single, national system of "hard" money. So the Constitution gave the currency power to Congress, and it all but excluded the States from that field. From 1789 on, among the most important of all of the many tasks performed by the Federal Government has been that of providing the nation with a uniform, stable monetary system.

From the beginning, the United States has issued coins—in gold, silver, and other metals. Congress chartered the first Bank of the United States in 1791 and gave it the power to issue bank notes—that is, paper money. Those notes were not legal tender, however. **Legal tender** is any kind of money that a creditor must by law accept in payment for debts. Congress did not create a national paper currency, and make it legal tender, until 1861.

At first, the new national notes, known as Greenbacks, could not be redeemed for gold or silver coin at the Treasury. Their worth fell to less than half of their face value. Then, in 1870,

---

The Development of a National Currency

CONTINENTAL CURRENCY

One third dollar, 1776
This "Continental" note, engraved by Benjamin Franklin, was issued to finance the American Revolution.

U.S. COINAGE

United States half cent, 1834 On the face of this early American coin is a woman representing Liberty; on the reverse is a laurel wreath.

DEMAND CURRENCY

$10 demand note, 1861
With metal badly needed for the Civil War, Congress issued this "Greenback," the first paper currency since the Continental.

STATE CURRENCY

$5 Louisiana state bank note, 1862 From 1837 to 1863, just about anyone could issue currency—from States to stores to individuals—creating economic chaos.

SILVER CERTIFICATE

$1 silver certificates, 1896
George Washington was not the only member of his family to have his face on a bill; this note, redeemable for silver, features his wife, Martha.

SOURCE: Federal Reserve Bank of San Francisco

Interpreting Charts The colonies, the States, and the young United States experimented with a variety of coins and paper notes in the effort to build a stable currency. For a long time, people trusted coins more than paper. **Why do you think some forms of currency succeeded while others failed?**

the Supreme Court held their issuance to be unconstitutional. In *Hepburn* v. *Griswold* it said "to coin" meant to stamp metal and so the Constitution did not authorize paper money.

The Court soon changed its mind, however, in the *Legal Tender Cases* in 1871 and again in *Juliard* v. *Greenman* in 1884. In both cases it held the issuing of paper money as legal tender to be a proper use of the currency power. The Court also declared this a power properly implied from the borrowing and the war powers.

The Bankruptcy Power

Article I, Section 8, Clause 4 gives Congress the power "[t]o establish . . . uniform Laws on the subject of Bankruptcies throughout the United States." A bankrupt individual or company or other organization is one a court has found to be insolvent—that is, unable to pay debts in full. **Bankruptcy** is the legal proceeding in which the bankrupt's assets—however much or little they may be—are distributed among those to whom a debt is owed. That proceeding frees the bankrupt from legal responsibility for debts acquired before bankruptcy.

The States and the National Government have concurrent power to regulate bankruptcy. Today federal bankruptcy law is so broad that it all but excludes the States. Most bankruptcy cases are heard now in federal district courts.

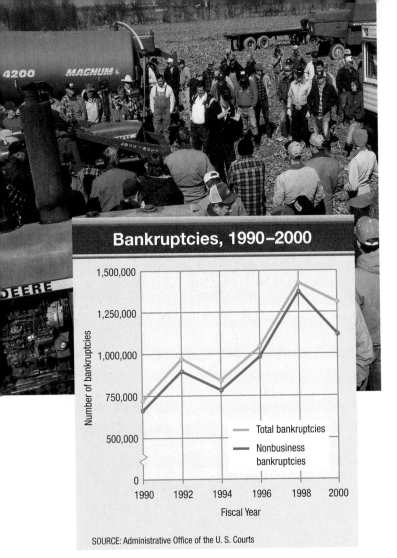

Bankruptcies, 1990–2000

Number of bankruptcies

- Total bankruptcies
- Nonbusiness bankruptcies

Fiscal Year: 1990, 1992, 1994, 1996, 1998, 2000

SOURCE: Administrative Office of the U. S. Courts

Interpreting Graphs Farmers—shown above auctioning off equipment in Manchester, Michigan—contributed to a sharp rise in U.S. bankruptcies during the 1990s. As a result, in 2000 Congress passed legislation making it more difficult for certain people to file for personal bankruptcy. *Describe the change in nonbusiness bankruptcies from 1990 to 2000 as shown in the graph.*

Section 2 Assessment

Key Terms and Main Ideas

1. Explain the difference between a **direct tax** and an **indirect tax,** and give examples of each.
2. Why did the Federal Government finally eliminate **deficit financing?**
3. Give three examples of how Congress uses its **commerce power.**
4. What problems led the Framers to give Congress the power to coin money and make it **legal tender?**

Critical Thinking

5. **Making Inferences** Reread the four ways that the Constitution limits Congress's power to tax (pages 295–296). What can you infer about the Framers' reasons for limiting this power?

6. **Expressing Problems Clearly** This issue is hotly debated today: Should Congress regulate the Internet—for example, to ban false advertising? Do you think the Commerce Clause gives Congress the power to regulate Internet activity? Explain your reasoning.

 Take It to the Net

7. Read Chief Justice John Marshall's opinion for the Court in *McCulloch* v. *Maryland* and write a paragraph explaining how the decision defined Article 1, Section 8, Clause 18 of the Constitution. Use the links provided in the Social Studies area at the following Web site for help in completing this activity. **www.phschool.com**

3 Other Expressed Powers

Section Preview

OBJECTIVES

1. **Identify** the key sources of Congress's foreign relations powers.
2. **Describe** the power-sharing arrangement between Congress and the President on the issues of war and national defense.
3. **List** other key powers exercised by Congress.

WHY IT MATTERS

The Constitution gives Congress several other expressed powers—powers that cover matters that range from foreign affairs and national security to the mail you send and receive and the copyrights on your CDs and DVDs.

POLITICAL DICTIONARY

★ **naturalization**
★ **copyright**
★ **patent**
★ **eminent domain**

We have just reviewed the several expressed powers that Congress has with regard to money and to foreign and interstate commerce. The Constitution grants a number of other very important powers to Congress, and they are the focus of this section.

Foreign Relations Powers

The National Government has greater powers in the field of foreign affairs than in any other area. Congress shares power in this field with the President, who is primarily responsible for the conduct of our relations with other nations. Because the States in the Union are not sovereign, they have no standing in international law. The Constitution does not allow them to take part in foreign relations.[4]

The foreign relations powers of Congress come from two sources: (1) from various expressed powers, especially the war powers and the power to regulate foreign commerce, and (2) from the fact that the United States is a sovereign state in the world community. As the nation's lawmaking body, Congress has the inherent power to act on matters affecting the security of the nation—for example, the regulation of immigration and measures to combat terrorism here and abroad. You will explore this vitally important subject at much greater length in Chapter 17.

War Powers

Eight of the expressed powers given to Congress in Article I, Section 8 deal with war and national defense.[5] Here, too, Congress shares power with the chief executive. The Constitution makes the President the commander in chief of the nation's armed forces,[6] and, as such, the President dominates the field.

The congressional war powers, however, are extensive and substantial. Only Congress may declare war. It has the power to raise and support armies, to provide and maintain a navy, and to make rules pertaining to the governing of land and naval forces. Congress also has the power to provide for "calling forth the Militia" and for the organizing, arming, and disciplining of it. Congress has the power to grant letters of marque and reprisal[7] and to make rules concerning captures on land and water.

With the passage of the War Powers Resolution of 1973, Congress claimed the power to restrict the use of American forces in

---

[4]See Article I, Section 10, Clauses 1 and 3.

[5]The war powers of Congress are set out in Clauses 11 through 16.

[6]Article II, Section 2, Clause 1.

[7]A few of the expressed powers are of little importance today. Thus, Congress has the power to grant letters of marque and reprisal, Article I, Section 8, Clause 11, and the States are denied the power to issue them, Article I, Section 10, Clause 1. Letters of marque and reprisal are written grants of power authorizing private persons to outfit vessels to capture and destroy enemy vessels in time of war. In effect, they authorize a form of legalized piracy. Letters of marque and reprisal are forbidden by international law by the Declaration of Paris, 1856, and the United States honors the rule.

combat in areas where a state of war does not exist; see Chapters 14 and 17.

Other Expressed Powers

The Constitution sets out a number of other expressed powers. Many of these powers have a direct influence on the daily lives of Americans.

Naturalization

The process by which citizens of one country become citizens of another is called **naturalization.** Article I, Section 8, Clause 4 gives Congress the exclusive power "[t]o establish an uniform Rule of Naturalization." Today, our population includes more than nine million naturalized citizens; we shall return to this matter in Chapter 21.

The Postal Power

Article I, Section 8, Clause 7 says that Congress has the power "[t]o establish Post Offices and post Roads." Post roads are all postal routes, including railroads, airways, and waters within the United States, during the time that mail is being carried on them.

The United States Postal Service traces its history back to the early colonial period. Benjamin Franklin is generally credited as the founder of the present-day postal system. Today some 39,000 post offices, branches, stations, and community post offices serve the nation. The Postal Service and its some 750,000 employees handle more than 180 billion pieces of mail a year.

Congress has established a number of crimes based on the postal power. Thus, it is a federal crime for anyone to obstruct the mails, to use the mails to commit any fraud, or to use the mails in the committing of any other crime.

Congress has also prohibited the mailing of many items. Any articles prohibited by a State's laws—for example, firecrackers or switchblade knives—cannot be sent into that State by mail. A great many other items, including chain letters and obscene materials, cannot be sent through the mails.

The States and their local governments cannot interfere with the mails unreasonably. Nor can they require licenses for Postal Service vehicles or tax the gas they use, or tax post offices or any other property of the United States Postal Service.

Copyrights and Patents

The Constitution gives Congress the power

FROM THE *Constitution*

"To promote the Progress of Science and useful Arts, by securing for limited Times to Authors and Inventors the exclusive Right to their respective Writings and Discoveries."

—Article I, Section 8, Clause 8

A **copyright** is the exclusive right of an author to reproduce, publish, and sell his or her creative work. That right may be assigned —transferred by contract—to

Congressional Powers Expressed in Article 1, Section 8

PEACETIME POWERS		WAR POWERS	
Clause	Provision	Clause	Provision
1	To impose and collect taxes, duties, and excises	11	To declare war; to make laws regarding captures on land and water
2	To borrow money		
3	To regulate foreign and interstate commerce	12	To raise and support armies
4	To provide for naturalization; to create bankruptcy laws	13	To provide and maintain a navy
5	To coin money and regulate its value; to regulate weights and measures	14	To make laws governing land and naval forces
6	To punish counterfeiters of federal money and securities	15	To provide for summoning the militia to execute federal laws, suppress uprisings, and repel invasions
7	To establish post offices and post roads		
8	To grant patents and copyrights		
9	To create courts inferior to the Supreme Court		
10	To define and punish crimes at sea and violations of international law	16	To provide for organizing, arming, and disciplining the militia and governing it when in the service of the Union
17	To exercise exclusive jurisdiction over the District of Columbia and other federal properties		
18	To make all laws necessary and proper to the execution of any of the other expressed powers		

Interpreting Tables This table sets out the expressed powers of Congress. *Choose two war powers and two peacetime powers and explain why you think the Framers felt it important to give these powers to Congress.*

Types of Intellectual Property

Utility patents protect useful processes, machines, articles of manufacture, and compositions of matter. Examples: fiber optics, computer hardware, medications.

Design patents prohibit the unauthorized use of new, original, and ornamental designs for manufactured articles. Examples: the look of an athletic shoe, a bicycle helmet, Star Wars characters.

Plant patents protect certain invented or discovered plant varieties. Examples: hybrid tea roses, Silver Queen corn, Better Boy tomatoes.

Copyrights protect works of authorship, such as writings, music, and works of art that have been "tangibly expressed"—that is, in some way published, written, recorded, or made. Examples: *Gone With the Wind* (book and film), Beatles recordings, video games.

Trademarks protect words, names, symbols, sounds, or colors that distinguish goods and services. Trademarks, unlike patents, can be renewed forever, as long as they are being used in business. Examples: the roar of the lion in MGM movies, the pink of the Owens-Corning Pink Panther, the word "three-peat"—coined by former Los Angeles Lakers basketball coach Pat Riley in 1989 in reference to record-setting three-in-a-row NBA championship victories.

Trade secrets are information that companies keep secret to give them an advantage over their competitors. Examples: the recipe for Coca-Cola, the recipe for Kentucky Fried Chicken.

SOURCE: United States Patent and Trademark Museum

Interpreting Charts In 2000, the government created a stir by granting an Internet store, Amazon.com, a patent on the structure of its Web page, which links to other merchants. *(a) Which type of patent listed above might have been given to Amazon.com? (b) Why do you think the granting of this patent was controversial?*

another, as to a publishing firm by mutual agreement between the author and the other party.

Copyrights are registered by the Copyright Office in the Library of Congress. Under present law they are good for the life of the author plus 70 years. They cover a wide range of creative efforts: books, magazines, newspapers, musical compositions and lyrics, dramatic works, paintings, sculptures, cartoons, maps, photographs, motion pictures, sound recordings, and much more.[8]

The Copyright Office does not enforce the protections of a copyright. If a copyright is infringed or violated, the owner of the right may sue for damages in the federal courts.

A **patent** grants a person the sole right to manufacture, use, or sell "any new and useful art, machine, manufacture, or composition of matter, or any new and useful improvement thereof." A patent is good for up to 20 years. The term of a patent may be extended only by a special act of Congress. The Patent and Trademark Office in the Department of Commerce administers patent laws.[9]

Weights and Measures

Article I, Section 8, Clause 5 gives Congress the power to "fix the Standard of Weights and Measures" throughout the United States. The power reflects the absolute need for accurate, uniform gauges of time, distance, area, weight, volume, and the like.

In 1838 Congress set the English system of pound, ounce, mile, foot, gallon, quart, and so on, as the legal standards of weights and measures in this country. In 1866 Congress also legalized the use of the metric system of gram, meter, kilometer, liter, and so on.

In 1901, Congress created the National Bureau of Standards in the Commerce Department. Now known as the National Institute of Standards and Technology, the agency keeps the original standards for the United States. It is these standards by which all other measures in the United States are tested and corrected.

---

[8]Not all publications can be protected by copyright. Thus, the Supreme Court has held that such "factual compilations" as telephone directories "lack the requisite originality" for copyright protection, *Feist Publications, Inc., v. Rural Telephone Service Co.*, 1991.

---

[9]The power to protect trademarks is an implied power, drawn from the commerce power. A trademark is some distinctive word, name, symbol, or device used by a manufacturer or merchant to identify his goods or services and distinguish them from those made or sold by others. A trademark need not be original, merely distinctive. The registration of a trademark carries the right to its exclusive use in interstate commerce for 10 years. The right may be renewed an unlimited number of times.

Federal Land in the Western United States, 1998

KEY
- Bureau of Land Management
- United States Department of Agriculture
- National Parks Service
- Indian Reservation
- Other Federal Lands

Washington 38%
Oregon 57%
Montana 35%
Idaho 66%
Wyoming 53%
Nevada 89%
Utah 72%
California 50%
Colorado 40%
Arizona 73%
New Mexico 46%

SOURCE: National Wilderness Institute

Interpreting Maps The Federal Government owns vast areas of the West. *(a) In which States is most of the land owned by the Federal Government? (b) Why do certain agencies own so much land?*

Power Over Territories and Other Areas

Article I, Section 8, Clause 17 and Article IV, Section 3, Clause 2 give Congress the power to acquire, manage, and dispose of various federal areas. That power relates to the District of Columbia and to the several federal territories, including Puerto Rico, Guam, and the Virgin Islands. It also covers hundreds of military and naval installations, arsenals, dockyards, post offices, prisons, parks and forest preserves, and many other federal holdings.

The Federal Government may acquire property by purchase or gift. It may also do so through the exercise of **eminent domain,** the inherent power to take private property for public use.[10] Territory may also be acquired from a foreign state based on the power to admit new States, on the war powers, and on the President's treaty-making power.

Judicial Powers

As a part of the system of checks and balances, Congress has several judicial powers. These include the expressed power to create all of the federal courts below the Supreme Court and to structure the federal judiciary.

Congress also has the power to define federal crimes and set punishment for violators of federal law. The Constitution mentions only four. Three are found in Article I, Section 8: counterfeiting, piracies and felonies on the high seas, and offenses against international law. Treason is listed in Article III, Section 3. Congress has used its implied powers to establish more than one hundred other federal crimes.

---

[10]The 5th Amendment restricts the government's use of the power with these words: "nor shall private property be taken for public use, without just compensation."

Section 3 Assessment

Key Terms and Main Ideas

1. Explain how Congress and the President share power in the fields of foreign relations and defense.
2. Where does Congress get its power to regulate **naturalization?**
3. How does a **copyright** differ from a **patent?**

Critical Thinking

4. **Drawing Inferences** Choose three congressional powers discussed in this section and indicate why the Framers gave these powers to Congress rather than to the States.
5. **Making Decisions** Some people suggest that the U.S. Postal Service be abolished because they say today's for-profit mail companies could operate more efficiently, effectively, and economically. Do you agree? Explain.

Take It to the Net

6. At the U. S. Postal Service historical page, choose a specific innovation in mail service, and write a short essay explaining how it changed American life. Use the links provided in the Social Studies area at the following Web site for help in completing this activity.
www.phschool.com

4 The Implied Powers

Section Preview

OBJECTIVES

1. **Explain** how the Necessary and Proper Clause gives Congress flexibility in lawmaking.
2. **Summarize** the key developments in the battle over the implied powers of Congress.

WHY IT MATTERS

One clause in the Constitution was an early battleground over congressional power and led to the massive expansion of Congress's power today.

POLITICAL DICTIONARY

★ **appropriate**
★ **Necessary and Proper Clause**
★ **doctrine**

What does the Constitution say about education? Nothing, not a word. Still, Congress **appropriates**—assigns to a particular use—more than $30 billion a year for the U.S. Department of Education to spend in various ways throughout the country. Look around you. What evidence of these federal dollars can you find in your school? If you attend a public school anywhere in the United States, those indications should not be hard to find.

How can this be? You know that Congress has only those powers delegated to it by the Constitution, and the Constitution says nothing about education. The answer lies in the implied powers of Congress.

The Necessary and Proper Clause

Remember that the implied powers are those powers that are not set out in so many words in the Constitution but are implied by those that are. The constitutional basis for the implied powers is found in one of the expressed powers. The **Necessary and Proper Clause** gives to Congress the power:

> **FROM THE** *Constitution* **❝***To make all Laws which shall be necessary and proper for carrying into Execution the foregoing Powers and all other Powers vested by this Constitution in the Government of the United States, or in any Department or Officer thereof.* **❞**

—Article I, Section 8, Clause 18

Much of the vitality and adaptability of the United States Constitution can be traced directly to this provision—and even more so to the ways both Congress and the Supreme Court have interpreted and applied it over the years. For good reason, the Necessary and Proper Clause has often been called the "Elastic Clause," because it has been stretched so far and made to cover so much over the years.

The Battle Over Implied Powers

The Constitution had barely come into force when the meaning of the Necessary and Proper Clause was called into question. In 1790

Interpreting Political Cartoons This cartoon depicts New York State's ratification of the Constitution in 1788. *(a) What does the ship represent? (b) What does the cartoon imply about the Federal Government? (c) Was the cartoonist a Federalist or an Anti-Federalist?*

Alexander Hamilton, as Secretary of the Treasury, urged Congress to set up a national bank. That proposal touched off one of the most important disputes in all of American political history.

The opponents of Hamilton's plan insisted that nowhere did the Constitution give to Congress the power to establish such a bank. Remember, those strict constructionists, led by Thomas Jefferson, believed that the new government had only (1) those powers expressly granted to it by the Constitution, and (2) those powers *absolutely* necessary to carrying out the expressed powers.

Hamilton and other liberal constructionists looked to the Necessary and Proper Clause. They said that it gave Congress the power to do anything that was reasonably related to the exercise of the expressed powers. As for the national bank, they argued that its creation was related to the execution of the taxing, borrowing, commerce, and currency powers.

The strict constructionists were sorely troubled by that broad view of the powers of Congress. They were sure that it would give the new government almost unlimited authority and all but destroy the reserved powers of the States.[11]

Reason and practical necessity carried the day for Hamilton and his side. Congress established the Bank of the United States in 1791. Its charter (the act creating it) was to expire in 1811. During those 20 years, the constitutionality of both the bank and the concept of implied powers went unchallenged in the courts.

McCulloch v. *Maryland,* 1819

In 1816 Congress created the Second Bank of the United States. Its charter came only after

---

[11]In 1801 a bill was introduced in Congress to incorporate a company to mine copper. As Vice President, Jefferson ridiculed that measure with this comment: "Congress is authorized to defend the nation. Ships are necessary for defense; copper is necessary for ships; mines necessary for copper; a company necessary to work the mines; and who can doubt this reasoning who has ever played at 'This Is the House that Jack Built'?" While Jefferson himself was President (1801–1809), he and his party were many times forced to reverse their earlier stand. Thus, for example, it was only on the basis of the implied powers doctrine that the Louisiana Purchase in 1803 and the embargo on foreign trade in 1807 could be justified.

The *Living* Constitution

Expansion of Congressional Power | 1875 | 1925

The powers and duties of the Federal Government have increased greatly over our nation's history. Congress's expressed powers are listed in the Constitution. Congress also has implied powers, which are based on Congress's right to make any laws that are "necessary and proper" to carry out those expressed powers. As the time line shows, the doctrine of implied powers has allowed Congress to pass laws that affect many areas of society, but there are limits to these implied powers.

1890 Sherman Antitrust Act regulates monopolies and other practices that limit competition. (Expressed power: to regulate interstate commerce)

1935 Wagner Act protects the right of labor unions and workers to engage in collective bargaining. (Expressed power: to regulate interstate commerce)

another hard-fought battle over the extent of the powers of Congress.

Having lost in Congress, opponents of the new bank now tried to persuade several State legislatures to cripple its operations. In 1818 Maryland placed a tax on all notes issued by any bank doing business in the State but not chartered by the State legislature. The tax was aimed directly at the Second Bank's branch in Baltimore. James McCulloch, the bank's cashier, purposely issued notes on which no tax had been paid. The State won a judgment against him in its own courts. Acting for McCulloch, the United States then appealed to the Supreme Court.

Maryland took the strict-construction position before the Court. It argued that the creation of the bank had been unconstitutional. The United States defended the concept of implied powers, and also argued that no State could lawfully tax any agency of the Federal Government.

In one of its most important decisions, the Court unanimously reversed the Maryland courts. It held that the Constitution need not expressly empower Congress to create a bank.

The creation of the Second Bank, said the Court, was "necessary and proper" to the execution of four of the expressed powers of Congress: the taxing, borrowing, currency, and commerce powers. In short, the Court gave sweeping approval to the concept of implied powers.[12]

Chief Justice John Marshall wrote the Court's opinion in the case. For the Court, he said:

PRIMARY Sources *"We admit, as all must admit, that the powers of the government are limited, and that its limits are not to be transcended. But we think the sound construction of the Constitution must allow to the national legislature that discretion, with respect to the means by which the powers it confers are to be carried into execution, which will enable that body to perform the high duties assigned to it, in the manner most beneficial to the people."*
—*McCulloch* v. *Maryland,* Opinion of the Court

[12]The Court also invalidated the Maryland tax. Because, said the Court, "the power to tax involves the power to destroy," no State may tax the United States or any of its agencies or functions.

1947 U.S. Air Force is established as a separate branch of the military. (Expressed powers: to raise armies and provide a navy)

1987 Supreme Court upholds law that cuts federal highway funds to States that fail to set 21 as minimum drinking age, *South Dakota* v. *Dole.* (Expressed power: to spend money for the general welfare)

1950   1975   2000

1956 Interstate Highway Act provides federal funds to build a national highway system. (Expressed power: to regulate interstate commerce)

1995 Federal law establishing gun-free zones near schools, defended under the expressed power to regulate interstate commerce, is rejected by the Supreme Court, *United States* v. *Lopez.*

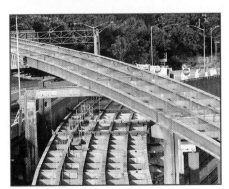

Analyzing Time Lines

1. Which expressed power has been the basis for most of the expansion of Congress's powers? Why do you think this is so?
2. Why do you think the Supreme Court ruled against the federal law regarding gun-free zones?

The Implied Powers of Congress

The expressed power
to lay and collect taxes

↓

implies the power
- to punish tax evaders
- to regulate (license) the sale of some commodities (such as alcohol) and outlaw the use of others (such as narcotics)
- to require States to meet certain conditions to qualify for federal funding

The expressed power
to borrow money

↓

implies the power
to establish the Federal Reserve System of banks

The expressed power
to establish naturalization law

↓

implies the power
to regulate and limit immigration

The expressed power
to raise armies and a navy

↓

implies the power
to draft Americans into the military

The expressed power
to regulate commerce

↓

implies the power
- to establish a minimum wage
- to ban discrimination in workplaces and public facilities
- to pass laws protecting the disabled
- to regulate banking

The expressed power
to establish post offices

↓

implies the power
- to prohibit mail fraud and obstruction of the mails
- to bar the shipping of certain items through the mails

Interpreting Charts This chart indicates the sources of several implied powers, those that are not specifically spelled out in the Constitution but can be reasonably assumed. ***Choose three of the implied powers listed above and explain specifically why we can assume that these powers belong to Congress.***

Then he penned these deathless words:

 PRIMARY Sources **"**Let the end be legitimate, let it be within the scope of the Constitution, and all means which are appropriate, which are plainly adapted to that end, which are not prohibited, but consist with the letter and spirit of the Constitution, are constitutional.**"**
—McCulloch v. Maryland, Opinion of the Court

This broad interpretation of the powers granted to Congress has become firmly fixed in our constitutional system. Indeed, it is impossible to see how the United States could have developed as it has under the Constitution without the principle established by *McCulloch*.

The Doctrine in Practice

A **doctrine** is a principle or fundamental policy. The doctrine of implied powers has been applied in instances almost too numerous to count. The way Congress has looked at and used its powers, along with the supporting decisions of the Supreme Court, have made Article I, Section 8, Clause 18 truly the Elastic Clause. Today the words "necessary and proper" really read "convenient and useful."

This is most especially true when applied to the power to regulate interstate commerce and the power to tax. Yet, recall, Congress cannot do something merely because it seems to promote the "general welfare" or be in the "public interest."

Section 4 Assessment

Key Terms and Main Ideas

1. Explain what it means to **appropriate** funds.
2. (a) What is the **Necessary and Proper Clause** commonly called? (b) How did it get that name?
3. What is the **doctrine** of implied powers?

Critical Thinking

4. **Expressing Problems Clearly (a)** Write a one-sentence summary of the central dispute in the case of *McCulloch* v. *Maryland*. **(b)** Identify the key individuals and institutions involved in the case. **(c)** Summarize the outcome of the case. **(d)** Explain the long-term consequences of the decision.
5. **Evaluating the Quotation** Restate the first quotation from the *McCulloch* v. *Maryland* decision on page 307 in your own words.
6. **Drawing Conclusions** If the strict constructionists had won their battle to limit Congress's implied powers, how might our government be different today?

 Take It to the Net

7. Using examples from your text and from the Internet, write a paragraph explaining this statement: *The Commerce Clause has been used to greatly expand the powers of Congress.* Use the links provided in the Social Studies area at the following Web site for help in completing this activity. **www.phschool.com**

on Primary Sources

Reining in Congress

Over recent years, the Supreme Court has appeared more willing to overturn federal laws when it felt that Congress had exceeded its authority. In this selection, Court observer Dan Carney discusses this trend and how it may impact the way in which Congress exercises its powers in the future.

James Brady (right) and his allies speak in favor of gun control before the Supreme Court building.

In early December [1996], Acting Solicitor General Walter E. Dellinger III argued before the U.S. Supreme Court on the merits of the Brady Act, which allows a police background check on people seeking to buy handguns. Almost in passing, he mentioned that the vast majority of sheriffs and police chiefs support the legislation.

This struck a raw nerve with Chief Justice William H. Rehnquist, who curtly informed Dellinger that the Supreme Court of the United States did not base its rulings on straw polls. If a person's constitutional rights are being violated by a popular statute, Rehnquist reasoned, the Court is not going to say: "Gee, plenty of other people obey this law and here you are complaining about it."

Under normal circumstances, this kind of statement might be dismissed as offhand. But in light of the Court's recent decisions—and cases it is now hearing—the remark illustrates the Court's growing willingness to strike down federal statutes on the grounds that Congress has overstepped its power.

The Supreme Court has undertaken a re-evaluation of Congress's legislative authority. . . .

The chief question in these cases is if Congress has ventured into areas where it has no right to be. . . . All of these cases involve limits to federal power, and most are likely to turn on interpretation of the 10th Amendment, which restricts the Federal Government to those powers specifically enumerated in the Constitution. For Congress, this is not some arcane legal debate taking place at the

Court. It could have a dramatic effect on the type of legislation Congress can enact, and the way that it does it. "There are enough cases now where I think Congress ought to think of it as a wake-up call," says A. E. Dick Howard, a law professor at the University of Virginia. "Surely all this adds up to changing the way Congress does its business." . . . Orrin G. Hatch (R., Utah), chairman of the Senate Judiciary Committee, said he is "very happy with these decisions" because they indicate that "we have a Congress that operates under limited and enumerated powers."

At the very least, the Supreme Court's renewed interest in the 10th Amendment will likely mean more legislation based on the interstate commerce clause in Article I of the Constitution. Congress's authority to regulate such commerce is arguably its broadest and hardest-to-define power.

Analyzing Primary Sources

1. On what basis has the Supreme Court challenged Congress?
2. How does the author suggest that Congress could respond to the Court?
3. What did Chief Justice Rehnquist mean when he said that the Supreme Court did not base its rulings on straw polls?
4. What change in federalism does this analysis suggest will occur?

Section Preview

OBJECTIVES

1. **Describe** Congress's role in amending the Constitution and in deciding elections.
2. **Describe** Congress's power to impeach, and summarize presidential impeachment cases.
3. **Identify** Congress's executive powers.
4. **Describe** Congress's investigatory power.

WHY IT MATTERS

Impeachment trials, close elections, far-reaching constitutional change, congressional committee investigations, presidential appointments—Congress has often captured the undivided attention of the American people as it has exercised one of its several non-legislative powers.

POLITICAL DICTIONARY

★ **successor**
★ **impeach**
★ **acquit**
★ **perjury**
★ **censure**
★ **subpoena**

The Constitution gives Congress a number of other chores besides making laws. This section explores those other chores, the non-legislative powers.

Constitutional Amendments

Article V gives Congress the power to propose amendments by a two-thirds vote in each house. It has done so 33 times so far. Article V also provides that Congress may call a national convention of delegates from each of the States to propose an amendment if requested to do so by at least two thirds of the State legislatures. No such convention has ever been called.

In recent years several State legislatures have petitioned Congress in behalf of amendments that would require that Congress balance the federal budget each year, prohibit flag burning, permit prayer in the public schools, and outlaw abortions. Today, the most vigorous efforts for a convention are being pushed by those who favor an amendment on congressional term limits.

Electoral Duties

The Constitution gives certain electoral duties to Congress. But they are to be exercised only in very unusual circumstances.

The House of Representatives may be called on to elect a President. The 12th Amendment says that if no candidate receives a majority of the electoral votes for President, the House of Representatives, voting by States, must decide the issue. It must choose from among the three highest contenders in the electoral college balloting. Each State has but one vote to cast, and a majority of the States is necessary for election.

The Senate must also choose a Vice President when no candidate wins a majority of the electoral votes. The vote is not by States but by individual senators, with a majority of the full Senate necessary for election.[13]

▲ Suffragettes celebrate passage of the Nineteenth Amendment, giving women the right to vote. In 1972, Congress proposed an Equal Rights Amendment (ERA), but after a long, divisive battle, the effort to win ratification failed. *Critical Thinking Why did the Framers make the amendment process difficult, requiring State ratification in addition to congressional approval?*

---

[13]Notice that the 12th Amendment makes it possible for the President to be of one party and the Vice President another.

The House has twice chosen a President: Thomas Jefferson in 1801 and John Quincy Adams in 1825. The Senate has had to pick a Vice President only once: Richard M. Johnson in 1837.

Remember, too, that the 25th Amendment provides for the filling of a vacancy in the vice presidency. When one occurs, the President nominates a **successor**—a replacement, someone to fill the vacancy, subject to a majority vote in both houses of Congress. That process has been used twice: Gerald Ford was confirmed as Vice President in 1973 and Nelson Rockefeller in 1974.

Impeachment

The Constitution provides that the President, Vice President, and all civil officers of the United States may "be removed from Office on Impeachment for and Conviction of, Treason, Bribery, or other high Crimes and Misdemeanors."[14] The House has the sole power to **impeach**—to accuse, bring charges. The Senate has the sole power to try—to judge, sit as a court—in impeachment cases.[15]

Impeachment requires only a majority vote in the House; conviction requires a two-thirds vote in the Senate. The Chief Justice presides over the Senate when a President is to be tried. The penalty for conviction is removal from office. The Senate may also prohibit a convicted person from ever holding federal office again; and he or she can be tried in the regular courts for any crime involved in the events that led to the impeachment. To date, there have been 17 impeachments and seven convictions; all seven persons removed by the Senate were federal judges.[16]

Two Presidents have been impeached by the House: Andrew Johnson in 1868 and Bill Clinton in 1998. The Senate voted to **acquit** both men—that is, it found them not guilty.

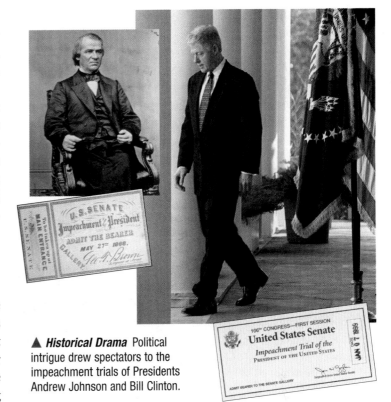

▲ **Historical Drama** Political intrigue drew spectators to the impeachment trials of Presidents Andrew Johnson and Bill Clinton.

Andrew Johnson

Andrew Johnson became the nation's 17th President when Abraham Lincoln was assassinated in 1865. Johnson soon became enmeshed in disputes with the Radical Republicans who controlled Congress. Many of those disagreements centered on the treatment of the defeated Southern States in the immediate post–Civil War period.

Matters came to a head when Congress passed the Tenure of Office Act, over the President's veto, in 1867. President Johnson's deliberate violation of that law triggered his impeachment by a House bent on political revenge. The table on the next page summarizes the episode.

Bill Clinton

Bill Clinton was impeached by the House in 1998. In proceedings steeped in partisanship, the House voted two articles of impeachment against him on December 19. Both articles arose out of the President's admitted "inappropriate relationship" with a White House intern. As you can see in the table on the next page, the first article charged the President with **perjury,** or lying under oath. The second article accused him of obstruction of justice because he withheld information about his affair with the intern.

---

[14]Article II, Section 4. Military officers are not considered "civil officers," nor are members of Congress.

[15]Article I, Section 2, Clause 5; Section 3, Clause 6.

[16]Four other federal judges were impeached by the House but later acquitted by the Senate. Two federal judges impeached by the House resigned before the Senate could act in their cases. One of the seven judges removed from office was later elected to Congress. The only other federal officer ever impeached was William W. Belknap, President Grant's Secretary of War. Belknap had been accused of accepting bribes and, although he had resigned from office, was impeached by the House in 1876. He was then tried by the Senate and found not guilty.

Members of the House who supported the articles of impeachment contended that lying under oath and withholding evidence were within the meaning of the Constitution's phrase "Other High Crimes and Misdemeanors," and justified the President's immediate removal from office.

Their opponents argued that the facts involved in the case did not justify either charge. They insisted that, while the President's conduct was deplorable and should be condemned, that conduct did not rise to the level of an impeachable offense. Many of them pressed for a resolution to **censure** the President—that is, for a formal condemnation of his behavior.

The Senate received the articles of impeachment when the new Congress convened in 1999, and it began to sit in judgment of the President on January 7. The Senate trial and its outcome are summarized in the table below.

Richard Nixon

A few officeholders have resigned in the face of almost certain impeachment—most notably, Richard Nixon, who resigned the presidency in 1974. Nixon's second term in office was cut short by the Watergate scandal.

The Impeachment Process

THE PROCESS	PRESIDENT ANDREW JOHNSON IMPEACHMENT 1868	PRESIDENT BILL CLINTON IMPEACHMENT 1998–1999
Step One The House Judiciary Committee debates charges against the accused and votes on whether to send articles of impeachment to the full House. A simple majority vote is needed to start the process.	**Feb. 22, 1868** House committee votes to send to the full House articles of impeachment against Johnson for having violated the Tenure of Office Act, by firing Secretary of War Edwin Stanton.	**Dec. 11–12, 1998** After three months of hearings, the House Judiciary Committee approves four articles of impeachment against Clinton: two counts of perjury, obstruction of justice, and making false statements relating to his relations with a White House intern.
Step Two Acting much like a grand jury, the House considers the charge(s) brought by the Judiciary Committee. It can subpoena witnesses and evidence. It hears and debates arguments.	**Feb. 22–24, 1868** The House, led by the Radical Republicans, holds a raucous debate on charges against Johnson, a Democrat. The outcome is never in doubt.	**Dec. 18–19, 1998** The House holds 13 hours of bitter, partisan debate, in which more than 200 House members speak. Democrats briefly walk out to protest Republican leaders' refusal to consider the lesser punishment of censure.
Step Three The House votes on each article. If any article is approved by a majority vote, the official is impeached, which is similar to being indicted. The House sends the article(s) of impeachment to the Senate.	**Feb. 24, 1868** The House votes 126 to 47 to impeach. It drafts 11 articles of impeachment, including violation of the Tenure of Office Act and attempting to bring disgrace upon Congress.	**Dec. 19, 1998** The House votes to impeach Clinton on two counts. The votes are 228–206 on one count of perjury and 221–212 on obstruction of justice. Voting is mostly along party lines.
Step Four The Senate tries the case. If the President is to be tried, the Chief Justice of the United States presides. Selected members of the House act as managers (prosecutors).	**March 30, 1868** Opening statements begin in the Senate trial with Chief Justice Salmon P. Chase presiding. Johnson does not attend, but the gallery is packed with observers.	**January 7, 1999** Chief Justice William Rehnquist opens a televised trial. Rep. Henry Hyde of Illinois leads a team of 13 House managers. White House Counsel Charles Ruff leads Clinton defense.
Step Five Senators hear testimony and evidence. House prosecutors and lawyers for both sides present their cases. Additional witnesses may be called. Senators may also vote to curb testimony.	**March 30–May 15, 1868** The trial yields little new evidence. Votes are known from the start. The outcome rests on one swing vote, an undecided Republican, who is offered bribes by both sides.	**Jan. 7–Feb. 11, 1999** With public distaste for impeachment growing, the Senate limits testimony to four witnesses, the intern not among them. Closing arguments follow. For three days, the Senate deliberates in secret (despite Democrats' objections).
Step Six The Senate debates the articles, publicly or privately. It need not render a verdict. It could, for example, vote to drop the case or censure the official. A two-thirds vote is required for conviction.	**May 16, May 26, 1868** In voting on two days, 35 Republicans vote to convict, one vote short of two thirds. Twelve Democrats and seven Republicans, including the swing vote, support acquittal.	**Feb. 12, 1999** In a televised session, the Senate acquits Clinton on both charges, falling well short of the two-thirds vote needed for conviction. On perjury, 45 Democrats and 10 Republicans vote not guilty. On obstruction, the vote splits 50–50.

Interpreting Tables This table details the complex process of impeaching a President.
(a) What measures did the Framers build into the impeachment process to try to make it fair?
(b) Why do you think both attempts to remove U.S. Presidents resulted in failure?

The term *Watergate* comes from a June 1972 attempt by Republican operatives to break into the Democratic Party's national headquarters in the Watergate office complex in Washington, D.C. The investigation of that incident, by the *Washington Post* and then by other media, led to official investigations by the Department of Justice and by the Senate's Select Committee on Presidential Campaign Activities, popularly known as the Senate Watergate Committee.

The probes unearthed a long list of illegal acts, including bribery, perjury, income tax fraud, and illegal campaign contributions. They also revealed the use of the Federal Bureau of Investigation, the Internal Revenue Service, and other government agencies for personal and partisan purposes.

The House Judiciary Committee voted three articles of impeachment against President Nixon in late July 1974. He was charged with obstruction of justice, abuse of power, and failure to respond to the committee's subpoenas. A **subpoena** is a legal order directing one to appear in court and/or to produce certain evidence. Mr. Nixon had ignored the committee's subpoena of several tape recordings of Watergate-related conversations in the Oval Office.

It was quite apparent that the full House would impeach the President and that the Senate would convict him. Those facts prompted Mr. Nixon to resign the presidency on August 9, 1974.

Beyond doubt, the Watergate scandal involved the most extensive and the most serious violations of public trust in the nation's history. Among its other consequences, several Cabinet officers, presidential assistants, and others were convicted of various felonies and misdemeanors—and many of them served jail time.

Executive Powers

The Constitution gives two executive powers to the Senate. One of those powers has to do with appointments to office, and the other with treaties made by the President.[17]

Appointments

All major appointments made by the President must be confirmed by the Senate by majority vote.

◀ *A Final Farewell* It was not impeachment but the threat of impeachment that forced a President from office. Richard Nixon resigned on August 9, 1974, giving a final wave from his helicopter as he left the White House for the last time.

Each nomination is referred to the appropriate standing committee of the Senate. That committee may then hold hearings to decide whether or not to make a favorable recommendation to the full Senate for that appointment. When the committee's recommendation is brought to the floor of the Senate, it may be, but seldom is, considered in executive (secret) session.

The appointment of a Cabinet officer or of some other top member of the President's "official family" is rarely turned down by the Senate. To this point, only 12 of now more than 600 Cabinet appointments have been rejected.[18]

It is with the President's appointment of federal officers who serve in the various States (for example, U.S. attorneys and federal marshals) that the unwritten rule of "senatorial courtesy" comes into play. The Senate will turn down such a presidential appointment if it is opposed by a senator of the President's party from the State involved. The Senate's observance of this unwritten rule has a significant impact on the President's exercise of the power of appointment; in effect, this rule means that some senators virtually dictate certain presidential appointments.

---

[17]Article II, Section 2, Clause 2.

[18]The first was Roger B. Taney, Andrew Jackson's choice for secretary of the treasury. Two years later Jackson named Taney to succeed John Marshall as Chief Justice. The Senate confirmed him, and he served until his death in 1864.

▲ Teenagers testify in Congress about the December 1997 fatal shootings at West Paducah High School in Kentucky. Congress launched an investigation of school gun violence after a series of mass murders in public schools around the country. *Critical Thinking What purpose do congressional investigations serve?*

Treaties

The President makes treaties "by and with the Advice and Consent of the Senate, . . . provided two thirds of the Senators present concur."[19] For a time after the adoption of the Constitution, the President asked the advice of the Senate when a treaty was being negotiated and prepared. Now the President most often consults the members of the Senate Foreign Relations Committee and other influential senators of both parties.

The Senate may accept or reject a treaty as it stands, or it may decide to offer amendments, reservations, or understandings to it. Treaties are sometimes considered in executive session. Because the House has a hold on the public purse strings, influential members of that body are often consulted in the treaty-making process, too.

Investigatory Power

Congress has the power to investigate any matter that falls within the scope of its legislative powers. Congress exercises this authority through its standing committees, and their subcommittees, and often through special committees, as well.

Congress may choose to conduct investigations for several reasons. Most often, those inquiries are held to (1) gather information useful to Congress in the making of some legislation; (2) oversee the operations of various executive branch agencies; (3) focus public attention on a particular subject, from the drug war to movie violence; (4) expose the questionable activities of public officials or private persons; and/or (5) promote the particular interests of some members of Congress.

---

[19]Article II, Section 2, Clause 2. It is often said that the Senate "ratifies" a treaty. It does not. The Senate may give or withhold its "advice and consent" to a treaty made by the President. Once the Senate has consented to a treaty, the President ratifies it by exchanging "instruments of ratification" with other parties to the agreement.

Section 5 Assessment

Key Terms and Main Ideas

1. If the vice presidency becomes vacant, how is a **successor** chosen?
2. (a) What public officers can the House **impeach?** (b) Which two Presidents were impeached by the House? (c) Describe the outcomes of their trials.
3. Why did some Clinton supporters want to **censure** him during his impeachment?
4. What did the House Judiciary Committee seek in the **subpoenas** it served on President Nixon?

Critical Thinking

5. **Making Inferences** Why does the Chief Justice—not the President of the Senate—preside over the impeachment trial of a President?

6. **Recognizing Bias** During the Clinton impeachment hearings and trial, members of Congress from both parties were accused of excessive partisanship. **(a)** Explain this accusation. **(b)** What evidence might support this claim?

Take It to the Net

7. Learn more about the impeachments of Presidents Andrew Johnson and Bill Clinton. Compare and contrast the impeachment charges, the trials, and the outcomes of the two cases. Use the links provided in the Social Studies area at the following Web site for help in completing this activity. **www.phschool.com**

Can Congress Prohibit Discrimination by Private Businesses?

The Fourteenth Amendment guarantees each individual the equal protection of the laws. It has been interpreted to prohibit various forms of discrimination by the government, but it does not deal with discrimination by private firms. Do other parts of the Constitution give Congress the authority to prohibit such forms of discrimination?

Heart of Atlanta Motel, Inc. v. United States (1964)

A provision of the Civil Rights Act of 1964 made it unlawful for hotels, motels, restaurants, or any other place of "public accommodation" to discriminate in granting access or providing service because of a customer's race, sex, color, religion, or national origin. Congress passed the law after hearing testimony on the growing number of people of all races who were traveling from State to State and on African Americans' difficulties in finding accommodations in many parts of the country.

The Heart of Atlanta Motel was one facility that had regularly refused to rent rooms to African Americans. The motel was located in downtown Atlanta, Georgia, close to two State highways and two interstate freeways. It advertised in national media, and about 75 percent of its registered guests came from out of State.

The motel's owner filed suit in federal district court, claiming that the public accommodation provisions were unconstitutional. The court decided that the law was an acceptable use of Congress's power to regulate interstate commerce. The owner then appealed to the Supreme Court.

Arguments for the Heart of Atlanta Motel, Inc.

1. The operation of privately-owned hotels, motels, and restaurants is essentially local. Therefore, Congress may not regulate these firms on the basis of its authority to regulate interstate commerce.
2. The Civil Rights Act prevents the motel owner from operating his business as he wishes. Thus

it deprives him of his liberty and property without due process, and takes his property without just compensation.
3. By requiring the motel owner to rent rooms to anyone against his will, Congress is subjecting him to involuntary servitude in violation of the Thirteenth Amendment.

Arguments for the United States

1. The lack of adequate accommodations for African American travelers interferes significantly with interstate travel. Congress has the authority under the Commerce Clause to pass laws that correct that problem.
2. The Fifth Amendment prohibits the "taking" of property without just compensation, but does not prohibit reasonable regulations that affect the ways in which an owner may use his or her property.
3. The regulations do not constitute involuntary servitude under the Thirteenth Amendment.

Decide for Yourself

1. Review the constitutional grounds on which each side based its arguments and the specific arguments each side presented.
2. Debate the opposing viewpoints presented in this case. Which viewpoint do you favor?
3. Predict the impact of the Court's decision on efforts to reduce discrimination in the United States. (To read a summary of the Court's decision, turn to the Supreme Court Glossary on page 799.)

Political Dictionary

expressed powers (p. 290)

implied powers (p. 290)

inherent powers (p. 290)

strict constructionist (p. 291)

liberal constructionist (p. 291)

consensus (p. 292)

tax (p. 295)

direct tax (p. 296)

indirect tax (p. 296)

deficit financing (p. 296)

public debt (p. 296)

commerce power (p. 297)

legal tender (p. 299)

bankruptcy (p. 300)

naturalization (p. 302)

copyright (p. 302)

patent (p. 303)

eminent domain (p. 304)

appropriate (p. 305)

Necessary and Proper Clause (p. 305)

doctrine (p. 308)

successor (p. 311)

impeach (p. 311)

acquit (p. 311)

perjury (p. 311)

censure (p. 312)

subpoena (p. 313)

Practicing the Vocabulary

Matching *Choose a term from the list above that best matches each description.*

1. To assign money to a particular purpose
2. The money owed by the Federal Government to its creditors
3. A principle
4. Powers of Congress that are specifically spelled out in the Constitution
5. A general agreement
6. Any kind of money that a creditor must, by law, accept in payment of debts
7. The sole right to sell an invention for a certain period of time
8. A charge levied by government on persons or property to meet public needs

Using Words in Context *For each of the terms below, write a sentence that shows how it relates to this chapter.*

9. direct tax
10. naturalization
11. Necessary and Proper Clause
12. implied powers
13. impeach
14. liberal constructionist
15. eminent domain

Reviewing Main Ideas

Section 1

16. Give an example of Congress's (a) expressed powers; (b) implied powers.
17. Was Thomas Jefferson a strict constructionist or a liberal constructionist? Explain.
18. In what ways does the Constitution limit Congress's power?

Section 2

19. Give three examples of Congress's expressed powers relating to money and commerce.
20. The Articles of Confederation did not give Congress the power to tax. Why did the Framers of the Constitution decide to grant Congress this power?
21. Explain the difference between a direct tax and an indirect tax.
22. How does deficit financing lead to public debt?

Section 3

23. What powers does Congress have in the areas of foreign policy and defense?

24. What articles cannot be sent into a State through the U.S. mail?
25. Give three examples of Congress's territorial powers.

Section 4

26. Has the Necessary and Proper Clause been used to expand Congress's power, or to limit it? Explain.
27. What were the long-term consequences of the ruling in *McCulloch* v. *Maryland?*
28. Why is Congress's power to appropriate funds so important?

Section 5

29. What kind of officials have most often been impeached by Congress?
30. (a) What body votes on impeachment? (b) What body conducts an impeachment trial? (c) Who presides at the trial of a President?
31. Under what circumstances may Congress choose a President or Vice President?
32. Why did Richard Nixon resign the presidency?

Critical Thinking Skills

33. ***Applying the Chapter Skill*** Brainstorm a list of the most important leadership qualities you think a member of Congress should have. Then choose any member of Congress, past or present from any State. Rate him or her on a scale of 0 to 5 for each of the qualities you listed, with 0 meaning "does not possess this quality" and 5 meaning "strongly possesses this quality."

34. ***Expressing Problems Clearly*** Why do you think it is difficult for Congress to reach consensus on many issues?

35. ***Evaluating the Quotation*** Reread the quotation from Article I, Section 9, Clause 4 on page 296 and the quotation from the 16th Amendment on page 296. Restate each passage in your own words and explain the difference between them.

Analyzing Political Cartoons

Using your knowledge of American government and this cartoon, answer the questions below.

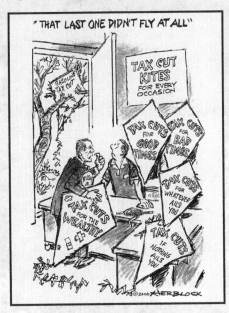

36. **(a)** In the cartoon above, why did the cartoonist choose to represent tax cuts as kites? **(b)** What does the caption at the top of the cartoon mean?
37. What is the central message of the cartoon?

★ You Can Make a Difference

Who are your senators and representatives in Congress? What activities did they pursue in high school and college that might have prepared them for these important and responsible positions? Did they get involved in politics while still in school? Use the Internet and other biographical sources to research the background and experience of one of the members of Congress who represents you. Put your findings into a short biographical sketch.

Participation Activities

38. ***Current Events Watch*** Scan news reports to find at least three stories about legislation that Congress is considering or has recently passed. **(a)** Summarize the key facts about each bill or law. **(b)** Explain what type of power Congress is exercising in writing each piece of legislation. **(c)** Show whether or not each is an example of Congress's expressed powers.

39. ***It's Your Turn*** The year is 1790. Alexander Hamilton has just made his proposal that Congress set up a national bank. Write an address to your colleagues in Congress, arguing for or against the proposal. Begin by summarizing the debate, explaining its importance to the country. Put forth your views on strict construction vs. liberal construction. Then make your specific arguments about the bank plan. Write a conclusion that you hope will rally support to your side.

40. ***Creating a Chart*** Write down all the powers of Congress that are mentioned in this chapter—from commerce powers to territorial powers. Use the information to create a chart that lists those powers, gives one or two examples of each, and tells whether it is an expressed, implied, or inherent power.

Take It to the Net

Chapter 11 Self-Test As a final review activity, take the Chapter 11 Self-Test in the Social Studies area at the Web site listed, and receive immediate feedback on your answers.

www.phschool.com

Congress in Action

"It is very easy to defeat a bill in Congress. It is much more difficult to pass one."
—John F. Kennedy (1962)

Making the nation's laws is the main job of Congress. Yet, as President Kennedy recognized, that is not an easy task. In trying to reach consensus, members of Congress draw on their own knowledge and experience. They also listen to other points of view, from both experts and ordinary citizens.

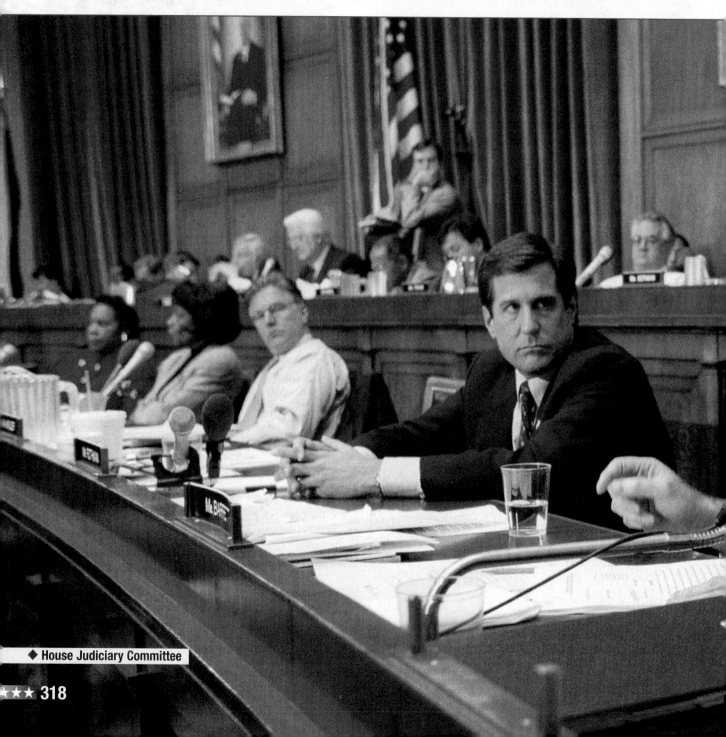

◆ House Judiciary Committee

★ You Can Make a Difference

IF YOU BELIEVE strongly in a cause, you can make your voice heard in Congress. Jennifer Sussal carried her fight against drunk driving all the way to Washington, D.C. Her idea was simple—print warning labels on alcohol containers. Jennifer began her campaign in her hometown of Rockville Centre, New York. She worked with several groups that supported a bill proposing the idea. In 1988, Jennifer testified at a Senate hearing. She told senators about a 17-year-old who had been killed by a drunk driver. The thousands of teens killed each year "cannot speak for themselves," Jennifer said. A few months later, the Senate approved a bill requiring warning labels for alcohol.

Keep It Current

Items marked with this logo are periodically updated on the Internet. Keep up-to-date with what's in the news. To get current information on issues involving Congress, go to **www.phschool.com**

SECTION 1

Congress Organizes (pp. 320–327)

★ Congress begins each new term on January 3 of every odd-numbered year; each new term follows the general election in November.

★ The Speaker of the House, usually the leader of the majority party, controls the agenda in the House of Representatives, while the Vice President and an experienced senator serve as largely ceremonial presidents in the Senate.

★ After the Speaker, the floor leaders and their whips in both houses are the most powerful members of Congress.

★ Committee chairmen, potent in their own domain, are chosen according to the seniority rule.

SECTION 2

Committees in Congress (pp. 329–333)

★ Most work in Congress is divided among committees that focus on special areas like national defense, the budget, agriculture, and the like.

★ The powerful House Rules Committee can speed, delay, or even prevent House action on a bill.

★ Both houses may create select committees, which are special, often temporary, bodies.

★ Joint committees are composed of members of both houses.

SECTION 3

How a Bill Becomes a Law: The House (pp. 334–340)

★ Only a member can introduce a bill in either house.

★ Bills are referred to standing committees, and are usually considered in subcommittees.

★ Bills approved by the appropriate committee and the Rules Committee are given floor consideration by the House.

★ Measures that win House approval are sent to the Senate.

SECTION 4

The Bill in the Senate (pp. 342–346)

★ Debate in the Senate is largely unrestricted.

★ The Senate's dedication to free debate gives rise to the filibuster—the tactic of "talking a bill to death."

★ After both houses approve a bill, it is sent to the President.

★ The President can sign the bill, allow it to become law without his signature, veto it, or apply a pocket veto.

1 Congress Organizes

Section Preview

OBJECTIVES

1. **Describe** how and when Congress convenes.
2. **Compare** the roles of the presiding officers in the Senate and the House.
3. **Identify** the duties of the party officers in Congress.
4. **Describe** how committee chairmen are chosen and explain their role in the legislative process.

WHY IT MATTERS

How Congress is organized, and how its leaders are chosen and who they are, plays a large part in determining what the nation's lawmakers can and will do.

POLITICAL DICTIONARY

★ Speaker of the House
★ president of the Senate
★ president *pro tempore*
★ party caucus
★ floor leader
★ whip
★ committee chairman
★ seniority rule

What comes to mind when you hear the word *Congress?* The Capitol? Some particular bill? Those senators and representatives you often see on the evening news? Of course, you know that Congress is much more than that. It is in fact a very complex enterprise, and much larger than most people realize.

Some 30,000 men and women work for the legislative branch; and Congress has appropriated more than $3 billion to finance its operations this year.[1] Given the large size and complexity of Congress, it must be well organized to conduct its business.

▲ Seal of Congress

Congress Convenes

Congress convenes—begins a new term— every two years, on January 3 of every odd-numbered year. Each new term follows the general elections in November.

_____

[1]More than 15,000 of those who work in the legislative branch have jobs in the House or Senate—in members' offices, as committee staff, or in some part of the congressional administrative organization. The other 15,000 or so work in the various agencies Congress has, over time, established within the legislative branch— especially the Library of Congress, the Government Printing Office, the Congressional Budget Office, and the General Accounting Office.

Opening Day in the House

Every other January, the 435 men and women who have been elected to the House come together at the Capitol to begin a new term. At that point, they are, in effect, just so many representatives-elect. Because all 435 of its seats are up for election every two years, the House technically has no sworn members, no rules, and no organization until its opening-day ceremonies are held.

Representative Sherrod Brown (D., Ohio) remembers his first opening day, in 1993, this way:

> **PRIMARY Sources** *"My first day on the House floor was thrilling—and a little scary. . . . Walking around the chamber . . . I was awed and nervous. . . . Questions gnawed at me when I walked into that august [majestic] room, when I met several members about whom I had read and whom I had seen on television. And then I thought about the President of the United States coming in to address us—'Do I deserve to be here with all these people? How did I get here? Will I measure up? How was I chosen for this privilege?'"*
>
> —Sherrod Brown, *Congress From the Inside*

The clerk of the House in the preceding term presides, or chairs, at the beginning of the first

▲ Opening day in the House of Representatives follows a traditional routine of votes and speeches. The House chooses its Speaker and other officers for the coming term. *Critical Thinking Why are most of the votes on opening day only formalities?*

day's session.[2] The clerk calls the chamber to order and checks the roll of representatives-elect. Those members-to-be then choose a Speaker as their permanent presiding officer. By custom, the Speaker is a long-standing member of the majority party, and election on the floor is only a formality. The majority party's members in the House have settled the matter beforehand.

The Speaker then takes the oath of office. It is administered by the Dean of the House, the member-elect with the longest record of service in the House of Representatives.[3] With that accomplished, the Speaker swears in the rest of the members as a body. The Democrats take their seats to the right of the center aisle; the Republicans, to the left.

Next, the House elects its clerk, sergeant at arms, chief administrative officer, and chaplain. None of these people are members of the House, and the elections are also a formality. The majority party has already decided who these nonmember officers will be.

---

[2]The clerk, a nonmember officer of the House, is picked by the majority party and usually keeps the post until that party loses control of the chamber.

[3]Today, John D. Dingell (D., Michigan), who became a member of the House on December 13, 1955.

Then, the House adopts the rules that will govern its proceedings through the term. The rules of the House have been developing for over 200 years, and they are contained in a volume of about 400 pages. They are readopted, most often with little or no change, at the beginning of each term.

Finally, members of the 19 permanent committees of the House are appointed by a floor vote. With that, the House is organized.

Opening Day in the Senate

The Senate is a continuous body. It has been organized without interruption since its first session in 1789. Recall that only one third of the seats are up for election every two years. From one term to the next, two thirds of the Senate's membership is carried over. As a result, the Senate does not face large organizational problems at the beginning of a term. Its first-day session is nearly always short and routine, even when the elections have brought a change in the majority party. Newly elected and reelected members must be sworn in, vacancies in Senate organization and on committees must be filled, and a few other details attended to.

Interpreting Political Cartoons **What is the cartoonist suggesting about the annual State of the Union address?**

State of the Union Checklist

✔	Raise income tax rate on people earning over $180,000 a year
✘	Complete reform of the health care system
✔	Pass free trade pact with Canada and Mexico
✔	Free child immunizations to prevent disease
✘	$30 billion to build roads and repair buildings
✔	Create 700,000 summer jobs for young people
✔	Put 100,000 more police officers on the street
✘	New tax on energy from non-renewable sources

KEY: ✔ Succeeded   ✘ Failed

Interpreting Charts The President presents his plans for the year in the State of the Union address. President Clinton offered the proposals above in his first State of the Union address, given on February 17, 1993, but not all became law. **How does party control of Congress determine whether the President's proposals become law?**

State of the Union Message

When the Senate is notified that the House is organized, a joint committee of the two is appointed and instructed "to wait upon the President of the United States and inform him that a quorum of each House is assembled and that the Congress is ready to receive any communication he may be pleased to make."

Within a few weeks, the President delivers the annual State of the Union message to a joint session of Congress. The President's speech is a major political event based on this constitutional command:

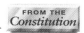 **FROM THE Constitution** **❝**He shall from time to time give to the Congress Information on the State of the Union, and recommend to their Consideration such Measures as he shall judge necessary and expedient . . . **❞**

—Article II, Section 3

The members of both houses, together with the members of the Cabinet, the justices of the Supreme Court, the foreign diplomatic corps, and other dignitaries, assemble in the House chamber to listen.

In his address, the President reports on the state of the nation as he sees it, in both domestic and foreign policy terms. The message is televised live, and it is followed very closely, both here and abroad. In fact, the President's speech is as much a message to the American people, and to the world, as it is an address to Congress. In it, the President lays out the broad shape of the policies his administration will follow and the course he has charted for the nation. His message regularly includes a number of specific legislative recommendations.

With the conclusion of the President's speech, the joint session is adjourned. Each house turns to the legislative business before it.

The Presiding Officers

The Constitution provides for the presiding officers of each house—the Speaker of the House and the president of the Senate. Article I, Section 2, Clause 5 says "The House of Representatives shall choose their Speaker and other Officers. . . ." And Article I, Section 3, Clause 4 declares: "The Vice President of the United States shall be President of the Senate. . . ."

The Speaker of the House

Of the two positions, the **Speaker of the House** is by far the more important and more powerful within the halls of Congress. This is largely because the Speaker is both the elected presiding officer of the House and the acknowledged leader of its majority party.

Although neither the Constitution nor its own rules require it, the House has always chosen the Speaker from among its own members. Today, the post is held by Dennis Hastert (R., Illinois). He was first elected to the House in 1986, and he became Speaker in 1999.[4]

The Speaker is expected to preside in a fair and judicious manner, and he regularly does. He is also expected to aid the fortunes of his party and its legislative goals, and he regularly does that too.

Nearly all of the Speaker's specific powers revolve around two duties: to preside and to keep order. The Speaker presides over every session of the House, or occasionally appoints a member as the temporary presiding officer. No member may speak until he or she is recognized by the Speaker. He also interprets and applies the rules, refers bills to the standing committees, rules on points of order (questions of procedure raised by members), puts motions to a vote, and decides the outcome of most votes taken in the House. (The Speaker can be overridden by a vote of the House, but that almost never happens.) He also names the members of all select and conference committees and signs all bills and resolutions passed by the House.

As a member, the Speaker may debate and vote on any matter before the House. If he chooses to do so, however, he must appoint a temporary presiding officer and that member then occupies the Speaker's chair. The Speaker does not often vote, and the House rules say only that he must vote to break a tie. Notice then, that because a tie vote defeats a question, the Speaker occasionally votes to cause a tie and so defeat a proposal.

The Speaker of the House follows the Vice President in the line of succession to the presidency. This status is a considerable testimony to the power and importance of both the office and the person who holds it.

The President of the Senate

The **president of the Senate,** the Senate's presiding officer, is not a member of the body over which

▲ Dennis Hastert (R., Illinois), who became Speaker of the House in 1999, has maintained a relatively low profile in public. *Critical Thinking How does the role of the Speaker differ from the role of the president of the Senate?*

he presides. Instead, the Constitution assigns the office to the Vice President of the United States. Because he is not a member of the chamber, the president of the Senate occupies a much less powerful chair than the Speaker's in the House.

The Vice President's route to his post is much different from the one the Speaker has traveled. In fact, the Senate's president is sometimes not even a member of the party with a majority of the seats in the upper chamber.

The president of the Senate does have the usual powers of a presiding officer: to recognize members, put questions to a vote, and so on. However, the Vice President cannot take the floor to speak or debate and may vote *only* to break a tie.

Any influence a Vice President may have in the Senate is largely the result of personal abilities and relationships. Several of the more recent Vice Presidents came to that office from the Senate: Harry Truman, Alben Barkley, Richard Nixon, Lyndon Johnson, Hubert Humphrey, Walter Mondale, Dan Quayle, and Al Gore. Each of them was able to build at least some power into the position out of that earlier experience.

The Senate does have another presiding officer, the **president *pro tempore,*** who serves in the Vice President's absence. The president *pro tempore,* or president *pro tem* for short, is elected by the Senate itself and is always a leading member of the majority party—usually its longest serving member. Today, Senator Robert C. Byrd (D.,

---

[4]Speaker Hastert is the 51st person to hold the post. The first Speaker, elected by the House in 1789, was Frederick A. C. Muhlenburg, a Federalist from Pennsylvania. Sam Rayburn (D., Texas) held the office for a record 17 years, 62 days in the period from 1940 to 1961. Mr. Hastert succeeded Newt Gingrich (R., Georgia) whose tenure (1995–1999) marked the first time a Republican had held the post in more than forty years.

Leadership in the 107th Congress

HOUSE

PRESIDING OFFICER AND PARTY LEADER

Speaker of the House
Dennis Hastert
(R., Illinois)
Year Elected 1986

PARTY OFFICERS

Majority Floor Leader
Richard Armey
(R., Texas)
Year Elected 1984

Minority Floor Leader
Dick Gephardt
(D., Missouri)
Year Elected 1976

Majority Whip
Tom DeLay
(R., Texas)
Year Elected 1984

Minority Whip
Nancy Pelosi
(D., California)
Year Elected 1986

SENATE

PRESIDING OFFICERS

President of the Senate
Dick Cheney
(Vice President)
Year Elected 2000

President Pro Tempore
Robert C. Byrd
(D., West Virginia)
Year Elected 1958

PARTY OFFICERS

Majority Floor Leader
Tom Daschle
(D., South Dakota)
Year Elected 1986

Minority Floor Leader
Trent Lott
(R., Mississippi)
Year Elected 1988

Majority Whip
Harry Reid
(D., Nevada)
Year Elected 1986

Minority Whip
Don Nickles
(R., Oklahoma)
Year Elected 1980

Interpreting Charts This chart shows the major leadership posts, both official and party, in both houses of Congress and the people who hold these positions today. **How can you tell which party holds power in the Senate?**

West Virginia) holds the post. Senator Byrd was first elected to the upper house in 1958. He served as president *pro tem* from 1989 to 1995 and was returned to the office when the Democrats regained control of the Senate in 2001.

The president *pro tem* follows the Speaker in the line of presidential succession. Other members of the Senate occasionally preside over the chamber, on a temporary basis.

Party Officers

Congress is a political body. This is so for two leading reasons: (1) because Congress is the nation's central policy-making body, and (2) because of its partisan makeup. Reflecting its political complexion, both houses of Congress are organized along party lines. This organization creates some very powerful positions.

The Party Caucus

The **party caucus** is a closed meeting of the members of each party in each house. It meets just before Congress convenes in January and occasionally during a session. In recent years the Republicans have called their caucus in each

house the party conference, and the Democrats now use this term in the Senate, too.

The caucus deals mostly with matters of party organization, such as the selection of the party's floor leaders and questions of committee membership. It sometimes takes stands on particular bills, but neither party tries to force its members to follow its caucus decisions, nor can it.[5]

The policy committee, composed of the party's top leadership, acts as an executive committee for the caucus. Strictly speaking, that body is known as the policy committee in each party's structure in the Senate and in the Republicans' organization in the House. However, it is called the steering and policy committee by the Democrats in the lower chamber.

The Floor Leaders

Next to the Speaker, the majority and minority **floor leaders** in the House and Senate are the most important officers in Congress. They do

---

[5]A number of informal groupings of members of Congress meet to discuss matters of mutual interest. Some are partisan, others are bipartisan, and several use the word *caucus* in their titles. Some of these informal groups include, for example, the Congressional Black Caucus, the House Republican Study Committee, the Pro-Life Caucus, and the Congressional Hispanic Caucus.

not hold official positions in either chamber. Rather, they are party officers, picked for their posts by their party colleagues.

The floor leaders are legislative strategists. They try to carry out the decisions of their parties' caucuses and steer floor action to their parties' benefit. Each of them is also the chief spokesman for his party in his chamber. All of that calls for political skills of a high order.

The majority leader's post is the more powerful in each house—for the obvious reason that the majority party has more seats (more votes) than the other party has. And, the majority leader very largely controls the order of business on the floor in his chamber.

The two floor leaders in each house are assisted by party **whips.** The majority whip and the minority whip are, in effect, assistant floor leaders. Each of them is chosen by the party caucus, almost always at the floor leader's recommendation. A number of assistant whips serve in the House, and the floor leaders in both houses have a paid staff.

Whips serve as a liaison—a two-way link—between the party's leadership and its rank-and-file members.[6] The whips check with party members and tell the floor leader which members,

and how many votes, can be counted on in any particular matter. The whips also see that all members of the party are present for important votes and that they vote with the party leadership. If a member must be absent for some reason, a whip sees that that member is paired with a member of the other party who will also be absent that day or who agrees not to vote on certain measures. In this way, one nonvote cancels out another.

Committee Chairmen

The bulk of the work of Congress, especially in the House, is really done in committee. Thus, **committee chairmen**—those members who head the standing committees in each chamber—also hold strategic posts. The chairman[7] of each of

---

[6]The term was borrowed from British politics. There, it came from the "whipper-in" in a fox hunt, the rider who is supposed to keep the hounds bunched in a pack.

[7]The title *chairman*, rather than *chairperson*, is used here because this is the form used in both houses of Congress, both officially and informally. Only six women have ever chaired a standing committee. None does so today. The most recent: Nancy Johnson (R., Connecticut), who chaired the House Ethics Committee (1995 to 1997), and Nancy Landon Kassebaum (R., Kansas), the only woman ever to chair a Senate committee, who headed the Senate's Labor and Human Resources Committee (1995–1997).

Party Strength (at beginning of term)

HOUSE 435 MEMBERS			Years	SENATE 100 MEMBERS		
242	192	1	1973 – 1975	56	42	2
291	144		1975 – 1977	61	37	2
292	143		1977 – 1979	61	38	1
277	158		1979 – 1981	58	41	1
242	192	1	1981 – 1983	46	53	1
269	166		1983 – 1985	46	54	
253	182		1985 – 1987	47	53	
258	177		1987 – 1989	55	45	
260	175		1989 – 1991	55	45	
267	167	1	1991 – 1993	56	44	
258	176	1	1993 – 1995	57	43	
204	230	1	1995 – 1997	48	52	
207	227	1	1997 – 1999	45	55	
211	223	1	1999 – 2001	45	55	
212	221	2	2001– 2003*	50	50	

SOURCE: Clerk of the House

*Democrats gained control of the Senate (50 Democrats, 49 Republicans, 1 Independent) in July 2001.

KEY ■ Democrat ■ Republican ■ Other

Interpreting Graphs This graph indicates party strength in Congress over recent years. **Which party controlled the House of Representatives for most of the 1980s? Which party controlled the House of Representatives for the second half of the 1990s?**

these permanent committees is chosen from the majority party by the majority party caucus. Committee chairmen decide when their committees will meet, which bills they will take up, whether they will hold public hearings, and what witnesses the committee should call. When a committee's bill has been reported to the floor, the chairman usually manages the debate and tries to steer it to final passage.

You will take a closer look at committees and their chairs in a moment. But, first, consider the fabled seniority rule.

Seniority Rule

The **seniority rule** is, in fact, an unwritten custom. It dates from the late 1800s, and is still closely followed in both houses today. The seniority rule provides that the most important posts, in both the formal and the party organization, will be held by those party members with the longest records of service in Congress.

The rule is applied most strictly to the choice of committee chairmen. The head of each committee is almost always the longest-serving majority party member of that committee.

Representation by State, 107th Congress

	House D	House R	Senate D	Senate R		House D	House R	Senate D	Senate R		House D	House R	Senate D	Senate R
Alabama	2	5	0	2	Louisiana	2	5	2	0	Ohio	8	11	0	2
Alaska	0	1	0	2	Maine	2	0	0	2	Oklahoma	1	5	0	2
Arizona	1	5	0	2	Maryland	4	4	2	0	Oregon	4	1	1	1
Arkansas	3	1	1	1	Massachusetts	10	0	2	0	Pennsylvania	10	11	0	2
California	32	20	2	0	Michigan	9	7	2	0	Rhode Island	2	0	1	1
Colorado	2	4	0	2	Minnesota	5	3	2	0	South Carolina	2	4	1	1
Connecticut	3	3	2	0	Mississippi	3	2	0	2	South Dakota	0	1	2	0
Delaware	0	1	2	0	Missouri	4	5	1	1	Tennessee	4	5	0	2
Florida	8	15	2	0	Montana	0	1	1	1	Texas	17	13	0	2
Georgia	3	8	2	0	Nebraska	0	3	1	1	Utah	1	2	0	2
Hawaii	2	0	2	0	Nevada	1	1	1	1	Vermont	0	* 0	1	* 0
Idaho	0	2	0	2	New Hampshire	0	2	0	2	Virginia	3	* 7	0	2
Illinois	10	10	1	1	New Jersey	7	6	2	0	Washington	6	3	2	0
Indiana	4	6	1	1	New Mexico	1	2	1	1	West Virginia	2	1	2	0
Iowa	1	4	1	1	New York	19	12	2	0	Wisconsin	5	4	2	0
Kansas	1	3	0	2	North Carolina	5	7	1	1	Wyoming	0	1	1	1
Kentucky	1	5	0	2	North Dakota	1	0	2	0					

* 1 Independent

House

WA, MT, ND, MN, OR, ID, WY, SD, WI, MI, NE, IA, IL, IN, OH, PA, NV, UT, CO, KS, MO, KY, WV, VA, NJ, DE, MD, CA, AZ, NM, OK, AR, TN, NC, MS, AL, GA, SC, TX, LA, FL, VT, ME, NH, NY, RI, CT, HI, AK

Legend: ■ Democratic majority ■ Republican majority ■ Equally divided □ Independent

Senate

WA, MT, ND, MN, OR, ID, WY, SD, WI, MI, NE, IA, IL, IN, OH, PA, NV, UT, CO, KS, MO, KY, WV, VA, NJ, DE, MD, CA, AZ, NM, OK, AR, TN, NC, MS, AL, GA, SC, TX, LA, FL, VT, ME, NH, MA, RI, CT, NY, HI, AK

Legend: ■ Democratic ■ Republican ■ Equally divided □ 1 Democrat, 1 Independent

SOURCE: Clerk of the House and Secretary of the Senate

Interpreting Maps The map and the chart show State-by-State representation in the House and Senate. *Name five States that primarily send Republicans to both houses of Congress, and five States that primarily send Democrats to both houses of Congress.*

◀ John Conyers, Jr. (D., Michigan) is the second-most senior member of the House and the ranking Democratic member of the House Judiciary Committee. He served on that committee during both the 1974 hearings on the Watergate scandal and the 1999 impeachment of President Clinton. *Critical Thinking What are the benefits and drawbacks of the seniority rule?*

Criticism of the Seniority Rule

Critics of the seniority rule are many, and they do make a strong case. They insist that the seniority system ignores ability and discourages younger members. Critics also note that the rule means that a committee head often comes from a "safe" constituency—a State or district in which, election after election, one party regularly wins. With no play of fresh and conflicting forces in those places, critics claim, the chairman of a committee is often out of touch with current public opinion.

Defenders of the seniority rule argue that it ensures that a powerful and experienced member will head each committee. They maintain that the rule is easy to apply, and that it very nearly eliminates the possibility of fights within the party.

Opponents of the rule have gained some ground in recent years. Thus, the House Republican Conference (caucus) now picks several GOP members of House committees by secret ballot. House Democrats use secret ballots to choose a committee chairman whenever 20 percent of their caucus requests that procedure.

House Republicans forged a major change in the seniority rule when they took control of the lower chamber in 1995. They adopted a party rule that limits the tenure of their committee chairmen. Now, no GOP chairman can serve more than six years (three terms of Congress) in his or her post. The rule produced a much larger than usual turnover in chairmanships at the beginning of the 107th Congress in 2001. It was also a factor in the decision of some senior Republicans to retire from the House in 2001, following their sixth (and final) year as chairmen.

Whatever the arguments against the seniority rule, it is unlikely to be eliminated. Those members with the real power to abolish it also reap the largest benefits from it.

Section 1 Assessment

Key Terms and Main Ideas

1. What role does the **Speaker of the House** play?
2. What is the function of the **president of the Senate**?
3. Explain the importance of the party **whips**.
4. Identify the purpose of a **party caucus**.

Critical Thinking

5. **Making Comparisons** Compare the organizational structures of both houses of Congress. Create a Venn diagram showing similarities and differences between the two houses.
6. **Synthesizing Information** What powers make committee chairmen influential?

7. **Predicting Consequences** What might happen if the president of the Senate were given the same powers as the Speaker of the House? What problems could arise?

 Take It to the Net

8. Read an article about the seniority rule and write five questions about its origins and effects. Then pick three of these questions and answer them as fully as possible. Use the links provided in the Social Studies area at the following Web site for help in completing this activity. **www.phschool.com**

CLOSE UP FOUNDATION

on Primary Sources

Organizing Congressional Committees

Pat Schroeder retired from public office in 1996, after 12 terms in Congress. In her memoir, 24 Years of House Work . . . and the Place Is Still a Mess, *she relates her experiences in the House of Representatives. In this excerpt, Schroeder recalls her appointment, as a newly elected representative and a woman, to the powerful House Armed Services Committee.*

Pat Schroeder, former Democratic representative of Colorado

In a setup typical of Congress, where everything is done by committee, there is a committee to decide committee assignments for incoming freshmen. In 1973 it was headed by Representative Wilbur Mills of Arkansas. . . .

Considering that no senior member was going to fall on his sword for me, I expected to be assigned to something like Merchant Marine and Fisheries. Since my Denver district is landlocked . . . it would have meant sudden death for a new congressional career. I wanted to be on the Armed Services Committee. I wanted to be part of the committee that controlled approximately sixty-five cents out of every dollar allocated to Congress. . . .

The Armed Services chairman, F. Edward Hébert, was a seventy-two-year-old Louisiana Democrat who was dead set against my appointment. . . . Even though Mills chaired the [assignments] committee, I couldn't understand why he would override Hébert's veto. There was an unspoken rule that old congressional barons never cross each other. . . . Unbeknownst to me, Mills' wife had taken an interest in my career and apparently kept telling her husband that he should do whatever he could to help me. . . . Mills . . . performed the necessary arm-twisting.

Although I was [put] on the committee, I did not get a seat. Hébert was patronizingly contemptuous [lacking respect] of women in politics. . . . He also objected to the appointment of Congressman Ron Dellums (Democrat from California). Ron had been in the House only one term when it was decided that it was time for an African-American to be on the Armed Services Committee. Hébert didn't appreciate the idea of a girl and a black forced on him. He was outraged that for the first time a chairman's veto of potential members was ignored. He announced that while he might not be able to control the makeup of the committee, he could . . . control the number of chairs in his hearing room, where he was enthroned on a carpet of stars, surrounded by military flags. He said that women and blacks were worth only half of one "regular" member, so he added only one seat to the committee room and made me and Ron share it. Nobody else objected, and nobody offered to scrounge up another chair. . . .

Ron and I had two choices: to go ballistic or to hang in. We decided to hang [in].

Analyzing Primary Sources

1. Why did Schroeder want to serve on the Armed Services Committee?
2. What difficulties did Schroeder face and why?
3. How and why did Hébert embarrass Schroeder?
4. Aside from her gender, why is it surprising that Schroeder was assigned to the Armed Services Committee?

·2· *Committees in Congress*

Section Preview

OBJECTIVES

1. **Explain** how the standing committees function.
2. **Describe** the duties and responsibilities of the House Rules Committee.
3. **Compare** the functions of joint and conference committees.

WHY IT MATTERS

The lawmaking process in both houses is built around committees, and these bodies play a major role in shaping the public policies of the United States.

POLITICAL DICTIONARY

★ **standing committee**
★ **select committee**
★ **joint committee**
★ **conference committee**

Do you know the phrase "a division of labor"? Roughly explained, it means dividing the work to be done, assigning the several parts of the overall task to various members of the group.

The House and the Senate are both so large, and the business they each face is so great, that both chambers must rely on a division of labor. That is to say, much of the work that Congress does is in fact done by committees. Indeed, Representative Clem Miller (D., Calif.) once described Congress as "a collection of committees that comes together periodically to approve one another's actions."

Standing Committees

In 1789 the House and Senate each adopted the practice of naming a special committee to consider each bill as it was introduced. By 1794 there were more than 300 committees in each chamber. Each house then began to set up permanent panels, known as **standing committees,** to which all similar bills could be sent.

Committee Assignments

The number of these committees has varied over the years. The graphic on page 330 lists the current 19 standing committees in the House and the 17 in the Senate today. Each House committee has from 9 to as many as 75 members, and each Senate committee has from 12 to 28. Representatives are normally assigned to one or two standing committees and senators to three

or four. The pivotal role these committees play in the lawmaking process cannot be overstated. Most bills receive their most thorough consideration in these bodies. Members of both houses regularly respect the decisions and follow the recommendations they make. Thus, the fate of most bills is decided in the various standing committees, not on the floor of either house. More than a century ago, Woodrow Wilson described "Congress in its committee rooms" as "Congress at work," and that remains the fact of the matter today.

Some panels are more prominent and more influential than others. As you would expect, most members try to win assignments to these important panels. The leading committees in the House include the Rules, Ways and Means, Appropriations, Armed Services, Judiciary, International Relations, and Agriculture committees. In the Senate, senators compete for places on the Foreign Relations, Appropriations, Finance, Judiciary, Armed Services, and Banking, Housing, and Urban Affairs committees. Of course, some of the other committees are particularly attractive to some members. Thus, a representative whose district lies wholly within a major city might want to sit

▶ The House Committee on Banking and Financial Services considers bills that affect finance, including the proposal that led to the golden dollar coin.

Permanent Committees of Congress

HOUSE STANDING COMMITTEES	JOINT COMMITTEES OF CONGRESS	SENATE STANDING COMMITTEES
Agriculture	Economic	Agriculture, Nutrition, and Forestry
Appropriations	The Library	Appropriations
Armed Services	Printing	Armed Services
Budget	Taxation	Banking, Housing, and Urban Affairs
Education and the Workforce		Budget
Energy and Commerce		Commerce, Science, and Transportation
Financial Services		Energy and Natural Resouces
Government Reform		Environment and Public Works
House Administration		Finance
International Relations		Foreign Relations
Judiciary		Governmental Affairs
Resources		Indian Affairs
Rules		Judiciary
Science		Health, Education, Labor, and Pensions
Small Business		Rules and Administration
Standards of Official Conduct		Small Business and Entrepreneurship
Transportation and Infrastructure		Veterans Affairs
Veterans Affairs		
Ways and Means		

Interpreting Tables Most legislation is considered in standing committees, and party politics can shape those panels. ***What considerations might lead a member of Congress to want to serve on a particular committee?***

on the House Committee on Education and the Workforce. A senator from one of the western States might angle for assignment to the Senate's Committee on Energy and Natural Resources.

Most of the standing committees handle bills dealing with particular policy matters, such as veterans' affairs or foreign relations. There are three standing committees that do not operate as subject-matter bodies, however: in the House the Rules Committee and the Committee on Standards of Official Conduct, and in the Senate the Committee on Rules and Administration.

When a bill is introduced in either house, the Speaker or the president of the Senate refers the measure to the appropriate standing committee. Thus, the Speaker sends all tax measures to the House Ways and Means Committee; in the Senate tax measures go to the Finance Committee. A bill dealing with, say, enlistments in the armed forces goes to the Armed Services Committee in the House *and* to the Armed Services Committee in the Senate.

Recall that the chairman of each of the standing committees is chosen according to the seniority rule. To see the point, look at the tables on pages 331 and 332. Notice that most committee chairmen have served in Congress for at least 15 years and some much longer. The seniority rule is also applied closely in each house when it elects the other members of each of its committees.

The members of each standing committee are formally elected by a floor vote at the beginning of each term of Congress. In fact, each party has already drawn up its own committee roster before the vote, and the floor vote merely ratifies those party choices.

The majority party always holds a majority of the seats on each standing committee.[8] The other party is well represented, however.

---

[8]The only exception is the House Committee on Standards of Official Conduct, with five Democrats and five Republicans. Often called the House Ethics Committee, it investigates allegations of misconduct by House members. In the Senate, a six-member bipartisan Select Committee on Ethics plays a similar role.

Most standing committees are divided into subcommittees, and each subcommittee is responsible for a particular slice of the committee's overall workload. There are now some 150 subcommittees in the two houses; nearly 70 in the Senate and 80 in the House.

To illustrate, the Senate's 25-member Committee on Armed Services does much of its work in six subcommittees. Each member serves on at least two of them, and the subcommittee titles generally describe their focus: the Subcommittee on Emerging Threats and Capabilities; the Subcommittee on Airland Forces; the Subcommittee on Personnel; the Subcommittee on Readiness and Management Support; the Subcommittee on Seapower; and the Subcommittee on Strategic Forces.

The House Rules Committee

The House Committee on Rules is sometimes called the "traffic cop" in the lower house. So many measures are introduced in the House each term that some sort of screening is necessary.

Most bills die in the committees to which they are referred. Still, several hundred are reported out every year. So, before most of these bills can reach the floor of the House, they must also clear the Rules Committee.

Normally, a bill gets to the floor only if it has been granted a rule—been scheduled for floor consideration—by the Rules Committee. The committee decides whether and under what conditions the full House will consider a measure. This means that the powerful 13-member Rules Committee can speed, delay, or even prevent House action on a measure.

In the Senate, where the process is not so closely regulated, the majority floor leader controls the appearance of bills on the floor.

Select Committees

At times, each house finds need for a **select committee.** These groups are sometimes called special committees; they are panels set up for some specific purpose and, most often, for a

House Committee Chairs, 2002

Committee	Name	Age*	Year Elected to House	Party Affiliation and State
Agriculture	Larry Combest	57	1984	R., Texas
Appropriations	C.W. "Bill" Young	72	1970	R., Florida
Armed Services	Bob Stump	75	1976	R., Arizona
Budget	Jim Nussle	42	1990	R., Iowa
Education and the Workforce	John Boehner	53	1990	R., Ohio
Energy and Commerce	W.J. "Billy" Tauzin	59	1980	R., Louisiana
Financial Services	Michael G. Oxley	58	1981	R., Ohio
Government Reform	Dan Burton	64	1982	R., Indiana
House Administration	Robert W. Ney	48	1994	R., Ohio
International Relations	Henry J. Hyde	78	1974	R., Illinois
Judiciary	F. James Sensenbrenner, Jr.	59	1978	R., Wisconsin
Resources	James V. Hansen	70	1980	R., Utah
Rules	David Dreier	50	1980	R., California
Science	Sherwood L. Boehlert	66	1982	R., New York
Small Business	David A. Manzullo	58	1992	R., Illinois
Standards of Official Conduct	Joel Hefley	67	1986	R., Colorado
Transportation and Infrastructure	Don Young	69	1973	R., Alaska
Veterans Affairs	Christopher H. Smith	49	1980	R., New Jersey
Ways and Means	Bill Thomas	61	1978	R., California

SOURCE: *Congressional Directory* and the Clerk of the House   *As of birth date in 2002.

Interpreting Tables Committee chairmen have the power to schedule meetings, decide which bills to address, arrange public hearings, and decide which witnesses are to be called. ***What do their ages, years in the House, and party affiliation tell you about the post each of these members holds?***

limited time. The Speaker of the House or the president of the Senate appoints the members of these special committees, with the advice of the majority and minority leaders.

Most select committees are formed to investigate a current matter. The congressional power to investigate is an essential part of the lawmaking function. Congress must decide on the need for new laws and gauge the adequacy of those already on the books. It also must exercise its vital oversight function, to ensure that federal agencies are following the laws it has already passed. At times, too, a committee may conduct an investigation of an issue—for example, the threat of domestic terrorism—in order to focus public attention on that matter.

Most investigations are conducted by standing committees or by their subcommittees. Select committees occasionally do that work, however. Thus, the Senate's Select Committee on Aging conducts an ongoing study of the elderly. It holds hearings in Washington and around the country, issues reports and press releases, and otherwise tries to bring greater public and governmental attention to the problems facing older Americans.

At times, a select committee becomes a spectacularly important body. This happened, for example, with the Senate's Select Committee on Presidential Campaign Activities, popularly known as the Senate Watergate Committee. As the Watergate scandal began to unfold in 1973, the Senate created that committee. Chaired by Senator Sam Ervin (D., North Carolina), its job was to investigate "the extent, if any, to which illegal, improper, or unethical activities were engaged in by any persons . . . in the presidential election of 1972." Its sensational hearings riveted the nation for months. Eventually, they formed a key link in the chain of events that led to President Richard Nixon's resignation from office in 1974.

Since then, the most notable instance came in 1987, with the work of two panels: the Senate's Select Committee on Secret Military Assistance to Iran and the Nicaraguan Opposition, and the House Select Committee to Investigate Covert Arms Transactions with Iran. These twin committees, often referred to as the Iran-Contra Committee, probed the Reagan administration's conduct of two highly secret projects abroad:

Senate Committee Chairs, 2002

Committee	Name	Age*	Year Elected to Senate	Party Affiliation and State
Agriculture, Nutrition, and Forestry	Tom Harkin	63	1984 (5)	D., Iowa
Appropriations	Robert C. Byrd	85	1958 (4)	D, West Virginia
Armed Services	Carl Levin	68	1978	D., Michigan
Banking, Housing, and Urban Affairs	Paul S. Sarbanes	69	1976 (3)	D., Maryland
Budget	Kent Conrad	54	1986	D., North Dakota
Commerce, Science, and Transportation	Ernest F. Hollings	80	1966	D., South Carolina
Energy and Natural Resources	Jeff Bingaman	59	1982	D., New Mexico
Environment and Public Works	James M. Jeffords	68	1988 (7)	I., Vermont
Finance	Max S. Baucus	61	1978 (2)	D, Montana
Foreign Relations	Joseph R. Biden	60	1972	D., Delaware
Governmental Affairs	Joseph I. Lieberman	60	1988	D., Connecticut
Health, Education, Labor, and Pensions	Edward M. Kennedy	70	1962	D., Massachusetts
Indian Affairs	Daniel K. Inouye	78	1962 (2)	D., Hawaii
Judiciary	Patrick Leahy	62	1974	D., Vermont
Rules and Administration	Christopher J. Dodd	58	1980 (3)	D., Connecticut
Small Business and Entrepreneurship	John F. Kerry	59	1984	D., Massachusetts
Veterans Affairs	John D. Rockefeller, IV	65	1984	D., West Virginia

SOURCES: *Congressional Directory* and Secretary of the Senate

* As of birth date in 2002

Number in parentheses indicates terms served in House.

Interpreting Tables Critics complain that the seniority system discourages younger members of Congress. *How does this table demonstrate the importance of seniority in the United States Senate?*

the covert sale of arms to Iran and clandestine efforts to give military aid to the Contra rebels in Nicaragua. The operation in Iran was intended, at least in part, as an arms-for-hostages deal, and it failed. The aid to the Contras was funded in part with money from the Iranian arms sales, despite an act of Congress that expressly prohibited such aid by the United States.

Most congressional investigations are not nearly so visible, nor so historic. Their more usual shape can be seen when, for example, the House Committee on Agriculture looks at the spruce budworm problem, an infestation affecting trees in the Pacific Northwest.

Joint and Conference Committees

A **joint committee** is one composed of members of both houses. You may recall them from the chart on page 330. Some are select committees set up to serve some temporary purpose. Most are permanent groups that serve on a regular basis. Because the standing committees of the two houses often duplicate one another's work, many have long urged that Congress make much greater use of the joint committee device.

Some joint committees are investigative in nature and issue periodic reports to the House and Senate—for example, the Joint Economic Committee. Most joint committees have routine duties, however—for example, the Joint Committee on Printing and the Joint Committee on the Library of Congress.

Before a bill may be sent to the President, each house must pass it in identical form. Sometimes, the two houses pass differing versions, and the first house will not agree to the changes the other has made. When this happens, a **conference committee**—a temporary, joint body—is created to iron out the differences in the bill. Its job is to produce a compromise bill that both houses will accept.

Student Poll

In a recent poll, students were asked their opinion on the following question: *When a member of Congress casts votes on legislation, should that person try to represent the views of the people in his or her district, or should that person use his or her best judgment about what is right?*

- 29% Use best judgment about what is right
- 61% Represent the views of the people in the district
- 8% Some of both
- Not sure 2%

SOURCE: High School Students' Attitudes Toward Government and Politics, Close Up Foundation, May 1999

1. **Analyzing Data** *According to this poll, what do students believe should be the most important factor to consider when casting a vote?*
2. **Conducting Polls** In your own school, conduct a poll asking students which factor politicians should consider above all when voting on legislation. *How do your results compare with the results shown in this chart?*

Section 2 Assessment

Key Terms and Main Ideas

1. What is a **standing committee** and why are such committees called "subject-matter" committees?
2. What is the role of **select committees** in the lawmaking process?
3. How do **joint committees** differ from **conference committees**?

Critical Thinking

4. **Testing Conclusions** Explain why you agree or disagree with the following statement: The Committee on Rules is the most powerful committee in the House.

5. **Drawing Conclusions** Woodrow Wilson once noted that Congress in its committee rooms is Congress at work. Explain the meaning of this statement in your own words.
6. **Recognizing Cause and Effect** How does the majority party manage to control all the committees in its house, and why does it do so?

 Take It to the Net

7. The committees in Congress do much of the important work. Visit the Web page of one committee from the House of Representatives and make a list of five things that committee does. Use the links provided in the Social Studies area at the following Web site for help in completing this activity. **www.phschool.com**

How a Bill Becomes a Law: The House

Section Preview

OBJECTIVES

1. **List** the first steps in the introduction of a bill to the House.
2. **Describe** what happens to a bill once it is referred to a committee.
3. **Explain** how House leaders schedule debate on a bill.
4. **Explain** what happens to a bill on the House floor, and identify the final step in the passage of a bill in the House.

WHY IT MATTERS

The lawmaking process is quite complicated—indeed, it may be likened to a very difficult obstacle course. Only a small fraction of the bills introduced in either House survive that course.

POLITICAL DICTIONARY

★ bill
★ joint resolution
★ concurrent resolution
★ resolution
★ rider
★ discharge petition
★ subcommittee
★ Committee of the Whole
★ quorum
★ engrossed

These numbers may surprise you: As many as 10,000 proposed laws are introduced in the House and Senate during a term of Congress. Fewer than 10 percent ever become law. Where do all those measures come from? Why are so few of them passed? By what process does Congress make law?

The First Steps

A **bill** is a proposed law presented to the House or Senate for consideration. Most bills introduced in either house do not originate with members of Congress themselves. Instead, most bills—the important as well as the routine—are born somewhere in the executive branch. Business, labor, agriculture, and other special interest groups often draft measures as well. Some bills, or at least the ideas for them, come from private citizens who think "there ought to be a law . . . ." Many others are born in the standing committees of Congress.

◄ A bill introduced in the House must be placed in the hopper.

According to the Constitution:

> **FROM THE Constitution** *All Bills for raising Revenue shall originate in the House of Representatives; but the Senate may propose or concur with amendments as on other Bills.*
>
> —Article I, Section 7, Clause 1

Measures dealing with any other matter may be introduced in either chamber. Only members can introduce bills in the House, and they do so by dropping them into the "hopper," a box hanging on the edge of the clerk's desk. [9]

Types of Bills and Resolutions

The thousands of measures—bills and resolutions—Congress considers at each session take several forms. To begin with, there are two types of bills: public bills and private bills.

Public bills are measures applying to the nation as a whole—for example, a tax measure or an amendment to the copyright laws. Private bills are measures that apply to certain persons or places

---

[9]Puerto Rico's resident commissioner and the delegates from the District of Columbia, Guam, the Virgin Islands, and American Samoa also may introduce measures in the House. Only a senator may introduce a measure in the upper house. He or she does so by addressing the chair.

rather than to the entire nation. As an example, Congress recently passed an act to give an Idaho sheep rancher $85,000 for his losses resulting from attacks by grizzly bears, which had been moved from Yellowstone National Park onto nearby public lands on which he grazed his flock.

Joint resolutions are similar to bills, and when passed have the force of law. Joint resolutions most often deal with unusual or temporary matters. For example, they may be used to appropriate money for the presidential inauguration ceremonies or to correct an error in a statute already passed. Joint resolutions also are used to propose constitutional amendments and they have been used to annex territories.

Concurrent resolutions deal with matters in which the House and Senate must act jointly. However, they do not have the force of law and do not require the President's signature. Concurrent resolutions are used most often by Congress to state a position on some matter—for example, in foreign affairs.

Resolutions deal with matters concerning either house alone and are taken up only by that house. They are regularly used for such things as the adoption of a new rule of procedure or the amendment of some existing rule. Like concurrent resolutions, a resolution does not have the force of law and is not sent to the President for approval.

A bill or resolution usually deals with a single subject, but sometimes a **rider** dealing with an unrelated matter is included. A rider is a provision not likely to pass on its own merit that is attached to an important measure certain to pass. Its sponsors hope that it will "ride" through the legislative process on the strength of the main measure.

Most riders are tacked onto appropriations measures, those in which Congress provides the money to pay for something. In fact, some money bills are hung with so many riders that they are called "Christmas trees." The opponents of those "decorations" and the President are almost always forced to accept them if they want the bill's major provisions to become law.

The First Reading

The clerk of the House numbers each bill as it is introduced. Thus, H.R. 3410 would be the 3,410th measure introduced in the House during the congressional term. Bills originating in the Senate receive the prefix S.—such as S. 210.

Types of Bills and Resolutions	
BILL	A proposed law; a public bill applies to the entire nation; a private bill applies only to certain people or places
JOINT RESOLUTION	A proposal for some action that has the force of law when passed; usually deals with special circumstances or temporary matters
CONCURRENT RESOLUTION	A statement of position on an issue, adopted by the House and Senate acting jointly; does not have the force of law; does not require the President's signature
RESOLUTION	A measure dealing with some matter in one house; does not have the force of law; does not require the President's signature

Interpreting Charts To be considered by Congress, a measure must be introduced in either the House or the Senate in one of the above formats. *In what ways do joint resolutions and concurrent resolutions differ?*

Resolutions are similarly identified in each house in the order of their introduction.[10]

The clerk also gives each bill a short title—a brief summary of its principal contents. Having received its number and title, the bill is then entered in the House *Journal* and in the *Congressional Record* for the day.

The *Journal* contains the minutes, the official record, of the daily proceedings in the House or Senate. The *Congressional Record* is a voluminous account of the daily proceedings (speeches, debates, other comments, votes, motions, etc.) in each house. The *Record* is not quite a word-for-word account, however. Members have five days in which to make changes in each temporary edition. They often insert speeches that were in fact never made, reconstruct "debates," and revise thoughtless or inaccurate remarks.

With these actions the bill has received its first reading. All bills are printed immediately after introduction and distributed to the members.

---

[10] Thus, H.J. Res. 12 would be the 12th joint resolution introduced in the House during the term, and similarly in the Senate, S.J. Res. 19. Concurrent resolutions are identified as H. or S. Con. Res. 4, and other resolutions as H. or S. Res. 166.

▲ **Testifying Before Congress** Committees often call upon citizens to give testimony at public hearings. Actor Michael J. Fox appeared before the Senate Appropriations Committee to discuss Parkinson's disease, a progressive disease with which he has been diagnosed.

Each bill that is finally passed in either house is given three readings along the legislative route. In the House, second reading comes during floor consideration, if the measure gets that far. Third reading takes place just before the final vote on the measure. Each reading is usually by number and title only: "H.R. 3410, A bill to provide. . . ." However, the more important or controversial bills are read in full and taken up line by line, section by section, at second reading.

The three readings, an ancient parliamentary practice, are intended to ensure careful consideration of bills. Today, the readings are little more than way stations along the legislative route. They were quite important in the early history of Congress, however, when some members could not read.

After the first reading, the Speaker refers the bill to the appropriate standing committee. That is, the proposal is sent to the committee that has jurisdiction over its subject matter.

The Bill in Committee

The Constitution makes no mention of standing committees. These bodies play an absolutely essential role in the lawmaking process, however—and in both houses of Congress. Indeed, their place is so pivotal that they are sometimes called "little legislatures."

The standing committees act as sieves. They sift through all of the many bills referred to them—rejecting most, considering and reporting only those they find to be worthy of floor consideration. In short, the fate of most bills is decided in these committees rather than on the floor of either house of Congress.

Most of the thousands of bills introduced in each session of Congress are pigeonholed.[11] That is, they die in committee. They are simply put away, never to be acted upon.

Most pigeonholed bills deserve their fate. On occasion, however, a committee buries a measure that a majority of the House wants to consider. When that happens, the bill can be blasted out of the committee with a discharge petition.

A **discharge petition** enables members to force a bill that has remained in committee 30 days (7 in the Rules Committee) onto the floor for consideration. Any member may file a discharge motion. If that motion is signed by a majority (218) of House members, the committee has seven days to report the bill. If it does not, any member who signed the motion may, on the second and fourth Mondays of each month, move that the committee be discharged, or relieved, of the bill. If the motion carries, the House considers the bill at once. This maneuver is not often tried, and it seldom succeeds.

Gathering Information

Those bills that a committee, or at least its chairman, does wish to consider are discussed at times chosen by the chairman. Today, most committees do most of their work through their several **subcommittees**—divisions of existing committees formed to address specific issues. There are now

---

[11]The term comes from the old-fashioned rolltop desks with pigeonholes—slots into which papers were put and often soon forgotten. Most "by request" bills are routinely pigeonholed; they are the measures that members introduce but only because some constituent or some interest group has asked them to do so.

some 80 of these committees within committees in the House, and nearly 70 in the Senate.

Where an important or controversial bill is involved, a committee, or more often one of its subcommittees, holds public hearings on the measure. Interested persons, special interest groups, and government officials are invited to testify at these information-gathering sessions.[12] If necessary, a committee can force a witness to testify under threat of imprisonment.

Occasionally, a subcommittee will make a junket (trip) to locations affected by a measure. Thus, members of the National Parks and Public Lands Subcommittee of the House Committee on Resources may take a firsthand look at a number of national parks. Or, the Water and Power Subcommittee of the Senate Energy and Natural Resources Committee may visit the Pacific Northwest to gather information on a public power bill.

These junkets are made at public expense, and members of Congress are sometimes criticized for taking them. Some junkets deserve criticism. But an on-the-spot investigation often proves to be the best way a committee can inform itself.

Committee Actions

When a subcommittee has completed its work on a bill, the measure goes to the full committee. That body may do one of several things. It may:
1. Report the bill favorably, with a "do pass" recommendation. It is then the chairman's job to steer the bill through debate on the floor.
2. Refuse to report the bill—that is, pigeonhole it. Again, this is the fate suffered by most measures in both houses.
3. Report the bill in amended form. Many bills are changed in committee, and several bills on the same subject may be combined into a single measure.
4. Report the bill with an unfavorable recommendation. This does not often happen. Occasionally, however, a committee feels that the full House should have a chance to consider a bill or does not want to take the responsibility for killing it.

5. Report a committee bill. This is an entirely new bill that the committee has substituted for one or several bills referred to it.

Scheduling Floor Debate

Before it goes to the floor for consideration, a bill reported by a standing committee is placed on one of several calendars. A calendar is a schedule of the order in which bills will be taken up on the floor.

Calendars

There are five calendars in the House:
(1) The Calendar of the Committee of the Whole House on the State of the Union, commonly known as the Union Calendar,

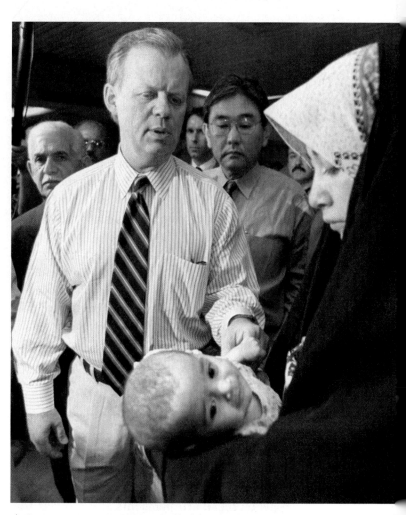

▲ Representative Tony Hall (D., Ohio) visited Iraq to study the effects of economic sanctions that were imposed to discourage that country from developing weapons. *Critical Thinking* ***Which House committee would have been most likely to hear Representative Hall's testimony?***

---

[12]If necessary, a committee may subpoena witnesses. A subpoena is an order compelling one to appear. Failure to obey a subpoena may lead the House or Senate to pass a resolution citing the offender for contempt of Congress—a federal crime punishable by fine and/or imprisonment.

Interpreting Political Cartoons **What does this cartoon imply about political debate?**

for all bills having to do with revenues, appropriations, or government property.

(2) The House Calendar, for all other public bills.

(3) The Calendar of the Committee of the Whole House, commonly called the Private Calendar, for all private bills.

(4) The Corrections Calendar, for all bills from the Union or House Calendar taken out of order by unanimous consent of the House of Representatives. These are most often minor bills to which there is no opposition.

(5) The Discharge Calendar, for petitions to discharge bills from committee.

Under the rules of the House, bills are taken from each of these calendars for consideration on a regularly scheduled basis. For example, bills from the Corrections Calendar are considered on the first and third Mondays of each month. Measures relating to the District of Columbia are to be taken up on the second and fourth Mondays, and private bills every Friday. On "Calendar Wednesdays," the various committee chairmen may each call up one bill from the House or Union calendars that has cleared their committees.

Rules

None of these arrangements is followed too closely, however. What often happens is even more complicated. First, remember that the Rules Committee plays a critical role in the legislative process of the House. It must grant a rule before most bills can in fact reach the floor. That is, before most measures can be taken from a calendar, the Rules Committee must approve that step and set a time for its appearance on the floor.

By not granting a rule for a bill, the Rules Committee can effectively kill it. Or, when the Rules Committee does grant a rule, it may be a special rule—one setting conditions under which the members of the House will consider the measure. A special rule regularly sets a time limit on floor debate. It may even prohibit amendments to certain, or even to any, of the bill's provisions.

Then, too, certain bills are privileged. They may be called up at almost any time, ahead of any other business before the House. The most highly privileged measures include major appropriations (spending) and general revenue (tax) bills, conference committee reports, and special rules from the Rules Committee.

On certain days, usually the first and third Mondays and Tuesdays, the House may suspend its rules. A motion to that effect must be approved by a two-thirds vote of the members present. When that happens, as it sometimes does, the House moves so far away from its established operating procedures that a measure can go through all the many steps necessary to enactment in a single day.

All of these—the calendars, the role of the Rules Committee, and the other complex procedures—have developed over time and for several reasons. In major part, they have developed because of the large size of the House and the sheer number and variety of bills its members introduce. In their own ways, the calendars, rules, and other complex procedures have developed to help members of the House manage their heavy workload. Without such help, no one member could possibly know the contents, let alone the merits, of every bill on which he or she has to vote.

The Bill on the Floor

If a bill finally reaches the floor, it receives its second reading in the House. Many bills the House passes are minor ones, with little or no opposition. Most minor bills are called from the

Corrections Calendar, get their second reading by title only, and are quickly disposed of.

Nearly all the more important measures are dealt with in a much different manner, however. They are considered in the **Committee of the Whole,** an old parliamentary device for speeding business on the floor.

The Committee of the Whole includes all the members of the House. However, they sit as one large committee of the House, not as the House itself. The rules of the Committee of the Whole are much less strict than the rules of the House, and floor action moves along at a faster pace. For example, a **quorum,** or majority of the full membership (218), must be present in order for the House to do business. However, only 100 members need be present in the Committee of the Whole.

When the House resolves itself into the Committee of the Whole, the Speaker steps down because the full House of Representatives is no longer in session. Another member presides. General debate begins, and the bill receives its second reading, section by section. As each section is read, amendments may be offered. Under the five-minute rule, supporters and opponents of each amendment have just that many minutes to make their cases. Votes are taken on each section and its amendment as the reading proceeds.

When the bill has been gone through—and many run to dozens and sometimes hundreds of pages—the Committee of the Whole has completed its work. It then rises, that is, dissolves itself. The House is now back in session. The Speaker resumes the chair, and the House formally adopts the committee's work.

Debate

Its large size has long since forced the House to impose severe limits on floor debate. A rule first adopted in 1841 forbids any member from holding the floor for more than one hour without unanimous consent to speak for a longer time. Since 1880 the Speaker has had the power to force any member who strays from the subject at hand to give up the floor.

The majority and minority floor leaders generally decide in advance how they will split the time to be spent on a bill. But at any time, any member may "move the previous question."

Voices on Government

Lynn Rivers (D., Michigan) was first elected to the House of Representatives in 1994. She arrived in Washington, D.C., wanting to work for "everyday people with everyday problems." She soon discovered the challenges of getting reform legislation through Congress.

" *In the 104th Congress, I spent a lot of time looking for a 'perfect' campaign finance reform plan. Unfortunately, I learned that perfection rarely appears in bills of these types. Inevitably, one must make tradeoffs within particular proposals—gaining in one area while giving up in another. . . . I intend to approach [future] bills looking not for 'perfection' but rather for balance, fairness, and progress toward a better system.* "

Evaluating the Quotation

How does Representative Rivers's experience with the realities of passing a law compare with what you have learned about Congress in this chapter?

That is, any member may demand a vote on the issue before the House. If that motion passes, only 40 minutes of further debate are allowed before a vote is taken. This device is the only motion that can be used in the House to close (end) debate, but it can be a very effective one.

Voting

A bill may be the subject of several votes on the floor. If amendments are offered, as they frequently are, members must vote on each of them. Then, too, a number of procedural motions may be offered, for example, one to table the bill (lay it aside), another for the previous question, and so on. The members must vote on each of these motions. These several other votes can be a better guide to a bill's friends and foes than is the final vote itself. Sometimes, a member votes for a bill that is now certain to pass, even though he or she supported amendments to it that would have scuttled the measure.

The House uses four different methods for taking floor votes:

1. Voice votes are the most common. The Speaker calls for the "ayes" and then the "noes," the members answer in chorus, and the Speaker announces the result.

2. If any member thinks the Speaker has erred in judging a voice vote, he or she may demand a standing vote, also known as a division of the House. All in favor, and then all opposed, stand and are counted by the clerk.

3. One fifth of a quorum (44 members in the House or 20 in the Committee of the Whole) can demand a teller vote. When this happens, the Speaker names two tellers, one from each party. The members pass between the tellers and are counted, for and against. Teller votes are rare today. The practice has been replaced by electronic voting, as you will see below.

4. A roll-call vote, also known as a record vote, may be demanded by one fifth of the members present.[13]

In 1973, the House installed a computerized voting system for all quorum calls and record votes to replace the roll call by the clerk. Members now vote at any of the 48 stations on the floor by inserting a personalized plastic card in a box and then pushing one of three buttons: "Yea," "Nay," or "Present." The "Present" button is most often used for a quorum call—a check to make sure that a quorum of the members is in fact present. Otherwise, it is used when a member does not wish to vote on a question but still wants to be recorded as present.[14]

A large master board above the Speaker's chair shows instantly how each member has voted. The House rules allow the members 15 minutes to answer quorum calls or cast record votes. Voting ends when the Speaker pushes a button to lock the electronic system, producing a permanent record of the vote at the same time. Under the former roll-call process, it took the clerk up to 45 minutes to call each member's name and record his or her vote. Before 1973, roll calls took up about three months of House floor time each session.

Voting procedures are much the same in the Senate. The upper house uses voice, standing, and roll-call votes, but does not take teller votes or use an electronic voting process. Only six or seven minutes are needed for a roll-call vote in the upper chamber.

Final Steps

Once a bill has been approved at second reading, it is **engrossed.** This means the bill is printed in its final form. Then it is read a third time, by title, and a final vote is taken. If the bill is approved at third reading, the Speaker signs it. A page—a legislative aide—then carries it to the Senate and places it on the Senate president's desk.

---

[13]The Constitution (Article I, Section 7, Clause 2) requires a record vote on the question of overriding a presidential veto. No record votes are taken in the Committee of the Whole.

[14]A "present" vote is not allowed on some questions—for example, a vote to override a veto.

Section 3 Assessment

Key Terms and Main Ideas

1. Explain the difference between the two types of **bills.**
2. Why do members of Congress attach **riders** to bills that are almost certain to pass?
3. Why does the House often use the **Committee of the Whole** to consider important measures?
4. What is the purpose of a **discharge petition?**

Critical Thinking

5. **Predicting Consequences** What might happen if all proposed bills were sent directly to the full House for a vote? Cite the pros and cons of such an arrangement.

6. **Understanding Point of View** Why might members of a House committee choose to report a bill with an unfavorable recommendation rather than pigeonhole it?

 Take It to the Net

7. How many separate steps are there in the lawmaking process in the House? At which of these steps can opponents effectively defeat a bill? Why do so many bills fail to become law? Use the links provided in the Social Studies area at the following Web site for help in completing this activity. **www.phschool.com**

Understanding Point of View

An old saying advises you to "walk a mile in your neighbor's shoes." That is, when you're evaluating or contradicting someone's opinion, think about how the issue looks from that person's perspective, or point of view. It might make you more tolerant of the other opinion, or it might help you strengthen your own argument.

Many factors can shape someone's perspective. Here are some guidelines for understanding point of view:

1. Identify the source. Find out whatever you can about the person whose views you are evaluating. Who are the sources of the excerpts below?

2. Identify the view being presented. In the excerpts below, the senators discuss different ways of dealing with the hostility between the North and the South over slavery. To preserve the Union, Senator John C. Calhoun favored nullification, giving Southern States

the right to refuse to carry out federal laws that they opposed. Senator Jefferson Davis spoke nearly a decade later, advocating secession, withdrawal from the Union. (a) Summarize the main idea of each quotation. (b) Identify the intended audience for each speech. (c) Identify the purpose of each.

3. List attributes that might influence the source's point of view. Consider factors such as the person's origins, age, sex, ethnic group, education, socio-economic group, personal experiences, lifestyle, values, and priorities.

Test for Success

Find background information on Calhoun and Davis. Compare and contrast the two points of view on the topic of *nullification* vs. *secession*.

> " . . . [W]hen the Constitution was ratified and the Government put in action, there was nearly a perfect equilibrium between the [North and South], which afforded ample means to each to protect itself against the aggression of the other; but, as it now stands, [the North] has the exclusive power of controlling the Government, which leaves [the South] without any adequate means of protecting itself against its encroachment and oppression. . . . How can the Union be saved? . . . [B]y adopting such measures as will satisfy the [southern states] that they can remain in the Union consistently with their honor and their safety. "
>
> —*South Carolina Senator John C. Calhoun, "Proposal to Preserve the Union," Senate speech, 1850*

> " It was because of his deep-seated attachment to the Union . . . that Mr. Calhoun advocated the doctrine of nullification, which he proclaimed to be peaceful, to be within the limits of State power, not to disturb the Union. . . . Secession belongs to a different class of remedies. It is to be justified upon the basis that the states are sovereign. There was a time when none denied it. I hope the time may come again when a better comprehension of the theory of our Government, and the inalienable rights of the people of the States, will prevent any one from denying that each State is a sovereign, and thus may reclaim the [agreements] which it has made to any [other government] whomsoever. "
>
> —*Mississippi Senator Jefferson Davis, Farewell speech to the Senate, 1861*

4 The Bill in the Senate

Section Preview

OBJECTIVES

1. **Explain** how a bill is introduced in the Senate.
2. **Compare** the Senate's rules for debate with those in the House.
3. **Describe** the role of conference committees in the legislative process.
4. **Evaluate** the actions the President can take after both houses have passed a bill.

WHY IT MATTERS

A bill that survives the legislative obstacle course in one house must still be passed in the other chamber—and face yet more hurdles before it can become law.

POLITICAL DICTIONARY

★ **filibuster**
★ **cloture**
★ **veto**
★ **pocket veto**

The basic steps in the lawmaking process are much the same in the House and the Senate. There are a few critical differences, as you can see in the chart on page 345. Given the many similarities, there is no need here to trace a bill step-by-step through the Senate. However, it is important to look at those differences, and then at what happens to bills once they have passed in each house.

Introducing the Bill

Bills are introduced by senators, who are formally recognized for that purpose. A measure is then given a number and short title, read twice, and referred to committee, where bills are dealt with much as they are in the House.

All in all, the Senate's proceedings are less formal and its rules less strict than those of the much larger House. For example, the Senate has only one calendar for all bills reported out by its committees. Bills are called to the floor at the discretion of the majority floor leader.[15]

Calendar No. 12

105TH CONGRESS
1ST SESSION
S. J. RES. 1

[Report No. 105–3]

Proposing an amendment to the Constitution of the United States to require a balanced budget.

IN THE SENATE OF THE UNITED STATES

JANUARY 21, 1997

Mr. HATCH (for himself, Mr. LOTT, Mr. THURMOND, Mr. CRAIG, Mr. NICK-LES, Mr. DOMENICI, Mr. STEVENS, Mr. ROTH, Mr. BRYAN, Mr. KOHL, Mr. GRASSLEY, Mr. GRAMM, Mr. BOB SMITH, Mr. BAUCUS, Mr. THOMP-SON, Mr. BREAUX, Mr. KYL, Ms. MOSELEY-BRAUN, Mr. DEWINE, Mr. GREGG, Mr. INHOFE, Mr. KEMPTHORNE, Mr. McCONNELL, Mr. MUR-KOWSKI, Mr. SANTORUM, Mr. SHELBY, Mr. SMITH of New Hampshire, and Mr. THOMAS introduced the following joint resolution; which was read twice and referred to the Committee on the Judiciary.

FEBRUARY 3, 1997

Reported under the authority of January 30, 1997 by Mr. Hatch, without amendment

JOINT RESOLUTION

Proposing an amendment to the Constitution of the United States to require a balanced budget.

▲ Senate bill

[15]The Senate does have another, non-legislative calendar, the Executive Calendar, for treaties and appointments made by the President and awaiting Senate approval or, rarely, rejection. The majority leader controls that schedule, too.

Rules for Debate

The major differences between House and Senate procedures involve debate. Floor debate is strictly limited in the House, but almost unrestrained in the Senate. In fact, most senators are intensely proud of belonging to what has often been called "the greatest deliberative body in the world."

As a general matter, senators may speak on the floor for as long as they please. Unlike the House, the Senate has no rule that requires a senator to speak only to the measure before the chamber; and the Senate's rules do not allow any member to move the previous question.

The Senate's consideration of most bills is brought to a close by unanimous consent agreements. That is, discussion ends and the chamber votes at a time previously agreed to by the majority and minority floor leaders. But if any senator objects—and so prevents unanimous consent—the procedure fails.

The Senate does have a "two-speech rule." Under this rule, no senator may speak more than twice on a given question on the same legislative day. By recessing—temporarily interrupting—rather than adjourning a day's session, the Senate can prolong a "legislative day" indefinitely. Thus, the two-speech rule can successfully limit the amount of time the Senate spends on some matters on its agenda.

The Senate's dedication to freedom of debate is almost unique among modern legislative bodies. That freedom is intended to encourage the fullest possible discussion of matters on the floor. The great latitude it allows, however, can be abused by the filibuster.

The Filibuster

Essentially, a **filibuster** is an attempt to "talk a bill to death." It is a stalling tactic, a process in which a minority of senators seeks to delay or prevent Senate action on a measure. The filibusterers try to so monopolize the Senate floor and its time that the Senate must either drop the bill or change it in some manner acceptable to the minority.

Talk—and more talk—is the filibusterers' major weapon. In addition, senators may use time-killing motions, quorum calls, and other parliamentary maneuvers. Indeed, anything to delay or obstruct is grist for the minority's mill as it works to block a bill that would very likely pass if brought to a vote.

Among the many better known filibusterers, Senator Huey Long (D., Louisiana) spoke for more than 15 hours in 1935. He stalled by reading from the Washington telephone directory and giving his colleagues his recipes for "potlikker," corn bread, and turnip greens. In 1947, Glen Taylor (D., Idaho) used more than eight hours of floor time talking of his children, Wall Street, baptism, and fishing. Senator Strom Thurmond (R., South Carolina) set the current filibuster record. He held the floor for 24 hours and 18 minutes in an unsuccessful, one-person effort against what later became the Civil Rights Act of 1957.

No later efforts have come close to matching that one. Still, the practice is often used and to great effect in the Senate. Over the past century and more, well over 200 measures have been killed by filibusters. Just the *threat* of a filibuster alone has resulted in the Senate's failure to consider a number of bills and the amending of many more.

The Senate often tries to beat off a filibuster with lengthy, even day-and-night, sessions to wear down the participants. At times, some little-observed rules are quite strictly enforced. Among them are the requirements that senators stand—not sit, lean on their desks, or walk about—as they speak and that they not use "unparliamentary language." These countermeasures seldom work, however.

▲ Senators rest on cots set up in the old Supreme Court Chamber during the filibuster that attempted to prevent passage of the Civil Rights Act of 1957. *Critical Thinking Why is a filibuster an effective way to kill legislation?*

The Cloture Rule

The Senate's real check on the filibuster is its Cloture Rule, Rule XXII in the Standing Rules of the Senate. It was first adopted in 1917, after one of the most notable of all filibusters in Senate history. That filibuster lasted for three weeks, and took place less than two months before the United States entered World War I on April 6, 1917.

German submarines had renewed their attacks on shipping in the North Atlantic, so President Wilson asked Congress for legislation to permit the arming of American merchant vessels. The bill, widely supported in the country, was quickly passed by the House by a vote of 403–12. The measure died in the Senate, however, because twelve senators filibustered it until the end of the congressional term on March 4th.

The public was outraged. President Wilson declared: "A little group of willful men, representing no opinion but their own, has rendered the great Government of the United States helpless

The Number of Bills that Become Laws*

10,238	Bills introduced
10,178	Referred to or originated in committee
1,205	Reported or discharged by committee
1,201	Floor consideration
1,184	Passed one chamber
667	Passed both chambers
590	**Public laws**

*Statistics represent only measures that can become public laws (bills and joint resolutions) and exclude simple and concurrent resolutions and private bills.

SOURCE: Ilona B. Nickels, Congressional Research Service, Library of Congress, Washington, D.C. Figures are for the 102nd Congress.

Interpreting Charts This chart illustrates the many stages through which a bill must pass before it becomes a law. ***After which step do most bills "die"?***

and contemptible." The Senate passed the Cloture Rule at its next session, later that same year.

Rule XXII provides for **cloture,** or limiting debate. The rule is not in regular, continuing force; it can be brought into play only by a special procedure. A vote to invoke the rule must be taken two days after a petition calling for that action has been submitted by at least 16 members of the Senate. If at least 60 senators—three fifths of the full Senate—then vote for the motion, the rule becomes effective. From that point, no more than another 30 hours of floor time may be spent on the measure. Then it *must* be brought to a final vote.

Invoking the rule is no easy matter. So far, more than 400 attempts have been made to invoke the rule, and only about one third have succeeded. Many senators hesitate to support cloture motions for two reasons: (1) their

dedication to the Senate's tradition of free debate, and (2) their practical worry that the frequent use of cloture will undercut the value of the filibuster that they may some day want to use.

Conference Committees

If you have ever watched a marathon, you know that no matter how well a runner covers the first 25 miles or so, he or she still has some distance to go in order to finish the race. So it is for bills in the legislative process. Even those that survive the long route through committees and rules and the floor in both houses still face some important steps before they can finally become law. Some of those final steps can be very difficult.

Any measure enacted by Congress *must* have been passed by both houses in identical form. Most often, a bill passed by one house and then approved by the other is not amended in the second chamber. When the House and Senate do pass different versions of the same bill, the first house usually concurs in the other's amendments, and congressional action is completed.

There are times when the House or the Senate will not accept the other's version of a bill. When this happens, the measure is turned over to a conference committee, a temporary joint committee of the two houses. It seeks to iron out the differences and come up with a compromise bill.

The conferees, or managers, are named by the respective presiding officers. Mostly, they are leading members of the standing committee that first handled the measure in each house.

Both the House and Senate rules restrict a conference committee to the consideration of those points in a bill on which the two houses disagree. The committee cannot include any new material in its compromise version. In practice, however, the conferees often make changes that were not even considered in either house.

Once the conferees agree, their report, the compromise bill, is submitted to both houses. It must be accepted or rejected without amendment. Only rarely does either house turn down a conference committee's work. This is not surprising, for two major reasons: (1) the powerful membership of the typical conference committee, and (2) the fact that its report usually comes in

How a Bill Becomes a Law

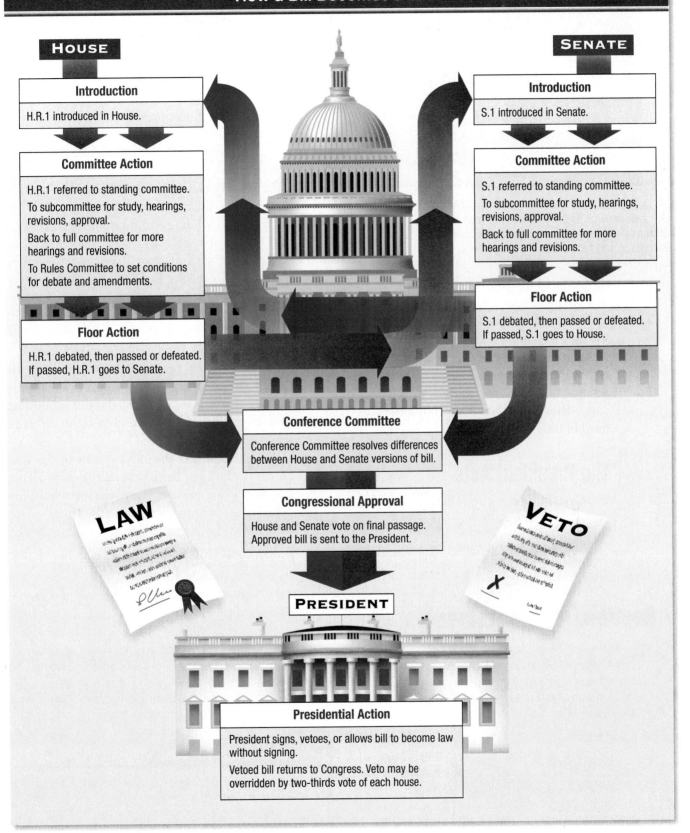

HOUSE

Introduction
H.R.1 introduced in House.

Committee Action
H.R.1 referred to standing committee.

To subcommittee for study, hearings, revisions, approval.

Back to full committee for more hearings and revisions.

To Rules Committee to set conditions for debate and amendments.

Floor Action
H.R.1 debated, then passed or defeated. If passed, H.R.1 goes to Senate.

SENATE

Introduction
S.1 introduced in Senate.

Committee Action
S.1 referred to standing committee.

To subcommittee for study, hearings, revisions, approval.

Back to full committee for more hearings and revisions.

Floor Action
S.1 debated, then passed or defeated. If passed, S.1 goes to House.

Conference Committee
Conference Committee resolves differences between House and Senate versions of bill.

Congressional Approval
House and Senate vote on final passage. Approved bill is sent to the President.

LAW

VETO

PRESIDENT

Presidential Action
President signs, vetoes, or allows bill to become law without signing.

Vetoed bill returns to Congress. Veto may be overridden by two-thirds vote of each house.

Interpreting Charts A typical bill may be introduced in either house. It must be passed by each house before going to the President. ***In what way does the process of moving a bill through the House differ from the process in the Senate?***

▲ **Tax Cut Proposal** President Bush transmitted his tax cut proposal to Congress during a Rose Garden ceremony on February 8, 2001. The President is flanked by Hispanic businesspersons Maria Taxman, Hector Barreto, Jr., and Anna Cablik.

the midst of the rush to adjournment at the end of a congressional session.

The conference committee stage is a most strategic step in the legislative process. A number of major legislative decisions and compromises are often made at that point. Indeed, the late Senator George Norris (R., Nebraska) once quite aptly described conference committees as "the third house of Congress."

The President Acts

The Constitution requires that

 FROM THE *Constitution* ❝*Every Bill which shall have passed the House of Representatives and the Senate, . . . [and] Every Order,*

Resolution, or Vote to which the Concurrence of the Senate and House of Representatives may be necessary (except on a question of Adjournment) shall be presented to the President. . . . ❞

—Article I, Section 7, Clauses 2 and 3

The Constitution presents the President with four options at this point:

1. The President may sign the bill, and it then becomes law.

2. The President may **veto**—refuse to sign the bill. The measure must then be returned to the house in which it originated, together with the President's objections (a veto message). Although it seldom does, Congress may then pass the bill over the President's veto, by a two-thirds vote of the full membership of each house.

3. The President may allow the bill to become law without signing it—by not acting on it within 10 days, not counting Sundays, of receiving it.

4. The fourth option is a variation of the third, called the **pocket veto.** If Congress adjourns its session within 10 days of submitting a bill to the President, and the President does not act, the measure dies.

Congress added another element to the veto power in the Line Item Veto Act of 1996. That law gave the President the power to reject individual items in appropriations bills. The Supreme Court held the law unconstitutional, in *Clinton* v. *New York City,* 1998. You will take a closer look at the veto power in Chapter 14.

Section 4 Assessment

Key Terms and Main Ideas

1. Explain how a **filibuster** is designed to work.
2. What is **cloture,** and why is it hard to achieve?
3. What is the effect of a President's **veto,** and how can Congress respond?

Critical Thinking

4. **Making Comparisons** Why do the Senate's rules allow individual senators much greater freedom to affect the law-making process than can members of the House?
5. **Predicting Consequences** Suppose that there is a bill up for debate on the Senate floor, but a small number of determined members oppose it. Would it be easier or harder for a

majority of senators to pass such a bill than it would be for a majority of House members in a similar situation? Why?

6. **Drawing Conclusions** If you were the President, under what circumstances might you use a pocket veto? Why might you let a bill become law without signing it?

 Take It to the Net

7. Read about different procedures in the two houses of Congress and create a chart that compares the House and Senate on at least three different issues. Use the links provided in the Social Studies area at the following Web site for help in completing this activity.
www.phschool.com

How Broad Is Congress's Power to Investigate?

Congress has broad authority to conduct investigations as part of the legislative process. Through investigations, Congress can evaluate existing laws and determine whether new laws are needed. How far can Congress go in these investigations?

Watkins v. United States (1957)

During the 1950s, the House Un-American Activities Committee (HUAC) investigated possible communist activities and influence in various areas of American life. John Watkins, a leader in the labor movement, was called to testify before a subcommittee of HUAC. In response to questions, he described his background in union activities and his connections with the Communist Party.

A lawyer for the committee then read a list of names to Watkins and asked him to identify the ones he knew to have been members of the Communist Party. Watkins stated that he was willing to answer questions about people who he believed were currently party members, but that he would not identify or answer questions about those who he believed had withdrawn from party membership.

The House requested that the United States attorney prosecute Watkins for his refusal to answer these questions. He was tried, found guilty, and fined $100. His prison sentence (one year) was suspended and he was placed on probation. A three-judge panel of the court of appeals reversed the conviction, but the full court of appeals later approved the conviction. The case then went to the Supreme Court.

Arguments for Watkins

1. Congressional investigations must relate to legitimate subjects of legislative concern. Congress may not force witnesses to testify merely to embarrass or punish people whose beliefs may be unpopular.
2. The questions to Watkins interfered with his First Amendment rights of speech, political belief, and association.

3. The subject matter of a congressional investigation must be stated so that witnesses can decide whether the questions posed to them are relevant to the investigation.

Arguments for the United States

1. Congress has broad authority to investigate matters of national concern, and may require citizens to provide information that may be relevant to these investigations. The Court may not dictate the manner in which Congress conducts its investigations.
2. The questions Watkins refused to answer were sufficiently related to the subject of communist influence in labor organizations. Witnesses should not be permitted to pick and choose which questions they will answer.
3. Although some individuals may be "exposed" as a result of witness testimony, there is no violation of First Amendment rights when Congress has a legitimate reason to ask its questions.

Decide for Yourself

1. Review the constitutional grounds on which each side based its arguments and the specific arguments each side presented.
2. Debate the opposing viewpoints presented in this case. Which viewpoint do you favor?
3. Predict the impact of the Court's decision on other types of congressional investigations. (To read a summary of the Court's decision, turn to the Supreme Court Glossary on page 799.)

Political Dictionary

Speaker of the House (p. 322)

president of the Senate (p. 323)

president *pro tempore* (p. 323)

party caucus (p. 324)

floor leader (p. 324)

whip (p. 325)

committee chairman (p. 325)

seniority rule (p. 326)

standing committee (p. 329)

select committee (p. 331)

joint committee (p. 333)

conference committee (p. 333)

bill (p. 334)

joint resolution (p. 335)

concurrent resolution (p. 335)

resolution (p. 335)

rider (p. 335)

discharge petition (p. 336)

subcommittee (p. 336)

Committee of the Whole (p. 339)

quorum (p. 339)

engrossed (p. 340)

filibuster (p. 343)

cloture (p. 344)

veto (p. 346)

pocket veto (p. 346)

Practicing the Vocabulary

Matching Choose a term from the list above that best matches each description.

1. Selects the party's leaders in each house of Congress
2. Can force a committee to bring a bill to the floor of the House or Senate
3. The minimum number of legislators needed to conduct official business
4. A provision added to a popular bill because it is unlikely to succeed on its own
5. A legislative committee created for a limited time and specific purpose

Word Relationships Three of the terms in each of the following sets are related. Choose the term that does not belong and explain why it does not.

6. (a) committee chairman (b) seniority rule (c) party caucus (d) resolution
7. (a) filibuster (b) whip (c) cloture (d) discharge petition
8. (a) Speaker of the House (b) president of the Senate (c) president *pro tempore* (d) committee chairman
9. (a) discharge petition (b) resolution (c) bill (d) concurrent resolution
10. (a) rider (b) bill (c) quorum (d) resolution

Reviewing Main Ideas

Section 1

11. (a) What happens at the opening sessions in the House and the Senate? (b) What makes those events different in the two houses?
12. What are the duties of the presiding officers in the House and Senate?
13. (a) How does the seniority rule function? (b) What are two criticisms of the seniority rule?

Section 2

14. What role do committees play in turning bills into laws?
15. (a) What are the different types of committees? (b) What are the duties of each type of committee?
16. What are the sources of the bills introduced into Congress?

Section 3

17. What happens to a bill immediately after its introduction in the House?
18. (a) How is a resolution different from a bill? (b) Describe the different types of resolutions.
19. What options does a committee have when reviewing a bill?
20. (a) How have debate and voting rules in the House changed in the past two centuries? (b) What are the benefits of these changes?

Section 4

21. (a) What is the usual purpose of a filibuster? (b) How can the Senate defeat a filibuster?
22. What is the purpose of a conference committee?
23. What are the President's options when he receives a bill from Congress?

Critical Thinking Skills

24. *Applying the Chapter Skill* Find a recent newspaper editorial dealing with a bill or debate in Congress. After reading the editorial, do your own research to learn more about the writer. What is the writer's point of view? Who is the intended audience?

25. *Drawing Inferences* Why does the President's State of the Union address play an important part in each congressional session? What are some possible ways that Congress can react to the speech?

26. *Expressing Problems Clearly* In your opinion, should the steps needed for a bill to become law be simplified? Support your argument with examples of bills that have been defeated and/or passed into law.

27. *Identifying Assumptions* Consider what you have read about the seniority rule. What does the seniority rule imply about qualifications for leadership?

Analyzing Political Cartoons

Using your knowledge of American government and this cartoon, answer the questions below.

28. **(a)** If the flowers and gift represent new legislation, what might the pigs represent? **(b)** What legislative practice is represented by tying the pigs to the flowers and the gift?

29. How might a representative respond to the cartoonist to defend this legislative practice?

★ **You Can Make a Difference**

What would you say to a roomful of senators and news reporters? First identify a cause or issue about which you feel strongly. Then write a proposed bill that presents a way to address that problem. Your bill would be sent to Congress in hopes of becoming a law. Finally, prepare a statement that you would make at a Senate hearing, introducing and defending your proposal. Practice reading your statement aloud as you get ready to "testify" before your class.

Participation Activities

30. *Current Events Watch* Scan news reports for examples of two of the following: a bill that dies in Congress, a bill that passes Congress but is vetoed by the President, and a bill that passes Congress and is signed by the President. Clip two articles and create a wall chart with each class member's contributions.

31. *Graphing Activity* Create a circle graph showing the percentage of bills introduced in Congress that actually became laws during the current session. Then create a second graph showing the same information from the 106th Congress, when a Democratic President governed with a Republican Congress, and the 103rd Congress, when a Democratic President governed with a Democratic Congress. Who controls these branches today, and how do the rates of passage compare?

32. *It's Your Turn* You have recently been elected to the House of Representatives from your home district. Write a letter to your local newspaper in which you talk about the bills you would like to see Congress pass and what steps you will take to make that happen. Also, describe the committees on which you would like to serve, and how these committees will meet the needs of your district and your own interests. Conclude your letter by listing three challenges you expect to encounter in the House. Proofread and revise to correct errors. Then draft a final copy. **(Writing a Letter)**

Take It to the Net

Chapter 12 Self-Test As a final review activity, take the Chapter 12 Self-Test in the Social Studies area at the Web site listed below, and receive immediate feedback on your answers.

www.phschool.com

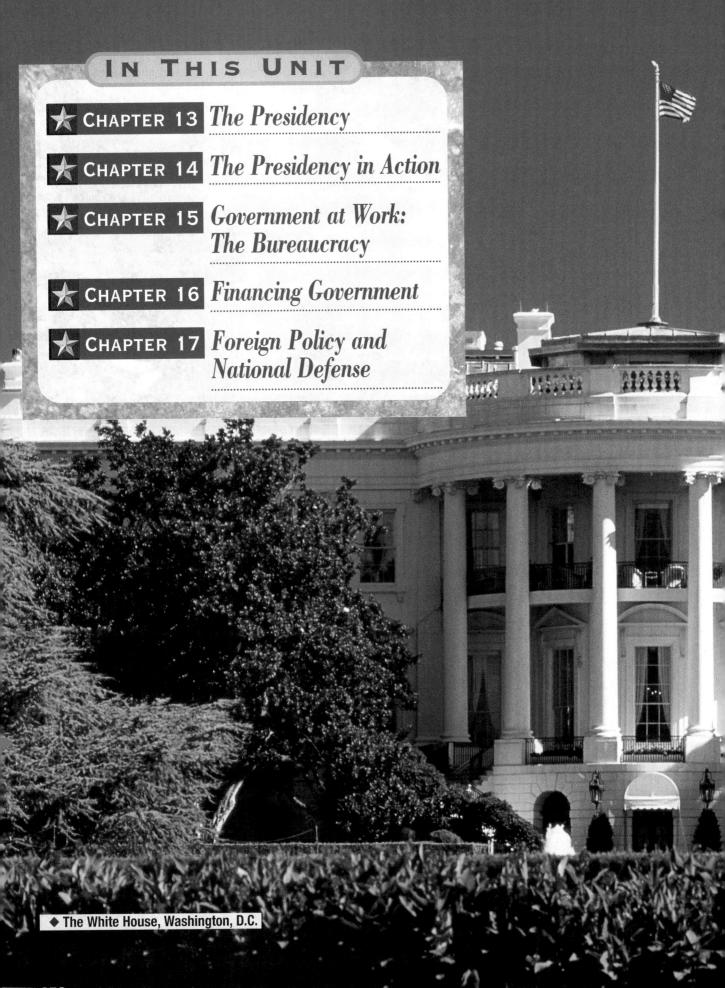

IN THIS UNIT

◆ The White House, Washington, D.C.

UNIT 4

The Executive Branch

CONSTITUTIONAL PRINCIPLES

Limited Government The presidency is often called "the most powerful office in the world." The President is not all-powerful, however. The Constitution puts a number of restrictions on his ability to act.

Separation of Powers The system of separation of powers means that the President must share the power to govern with both the legislative and the judicial branches of the National Government.

Checks and Balances Congress has several powers with which it can limit the President's ability to act. The courts, with the power of judicial review, can also curb the exercise of presidential power.

The Impact on You

While the President is not all-powerful, his powers are nonetheless many and extraordinary. What he says and what he does very largely set the nation's agenda—shape what government, the media, and the people are most concerned about. And it is to the President that the media and the people regularly turn when anything significant occurs, at home or abroad.

The Presidency

Mission Accomplished!?!?

> "The presidency has made every man who occupied it, no matter how small, bigger than he was, and no matter how big, not big enough for its demands."
>
> —Lyndon B. Johnson (1972)

As President Johnson knew, the responsibilities of the President can be overwhelming. The President not only leads the government and the nation, but also heads a political party. Even before he or she reaches the White House, the long and arduous campaign process tests the President's mettle.

◆ President Bush in his role as commander in chief

You Can Make a Difference

AS "CHIEF CITIZEN" of the United States, the President recognizes other citizens for their volunteer service. In 1999, the winners of the President's Service Award included one teenager—Emily Douglas, 17, of Powell, Ohio. Eight years earlier, Emily started "Grandma's Gifts," inspired by her grandmother's stories of growing up poor in Appalachia. Emily's organization began small, with holiday presents for poor families. Soon it was giving food, clothing, books, and toys to children in Ohio, Kentucky, and West Virginia. With support from corporations and others, "Grandma's Gifts" has helped more than 18,500 children.

Keep It Current

Items marked with this logo are periodically updated on the Internet. Keep up-to-date with what's in the news. To get current information on the presidency and the election process, go to **www.phschool.com**

SECTION 1

The President's Job Description (pp. 354–358)

★ The President has eight major roles, which are exercised simultaneously.
★ The Constitution outlines the formal qualifications for the presidency.
★ Presidents are limited to two four-year terms.
★ Congress determines the President's salary.

SECTION 2

Presidential Succession and the Vice Presidency (pp. 359–363)

★ The Constitution provides for an orderly succession of power if the President dies or leaves office.
★ The Constitution provides for the transfer of power should the President become disabled.
★ Although the vice presidency is often belittled, the Vice President is "a heartbeat away" from becoming President.

SECTION 3

Presidential Selection: The Framers' Plan (pp. 365–367)

★ The Framers created the electoral college for choosing the President and Vice President.
★ With the election of 1800, political parties began to control the nominating process.

SECTION 4

Presidential Nominations (pp. 368–375)

★ National conventions play a key role in the presidential nominating process.
★ Most States hold presidential primaries to determine convention delegates.
★ A few States select delegates through the caucus-convention process.
★ National conventions follow a schedule, culminating in the candidate's acceptance speech.
★ The candidate who is considered most electable usually wins the nomination.

SECTION 5

The Election (pp. 377–384)

★ Presidential electors today mainly "rubber-stamp" their party's candidate.
★ The electoral college is plagued by three major flaws.
★ Critics of the electoral college have proposed a variety of reforms.

The President's Job Description

Section Preview

OBJECTIVES

1. **Identify** the President's many roles.
2. **Understand** the formal qualifications necessary to become President.
3. **Discuss** issues involving the length of the President's term.
4. **Describe** the President's pay and benefits.

WHY IT MATTERS

The American people elect a President every four years. Soon, you and your friends will be able to participate in that process—if, in fact, you have not already done so. Before your first vote, you will want to know as much as you can about the office and all it involves.

POLITICAL DICTIONARY

★ chief of state
★ chief executive
★ chief administrator
★ chief diplomat
★ commander in chief
★ chief legislator
★ chief of party
★ chief citizen

Do you know who was the youngest person ever to be President? The oldest? Who held the presidency for the longest time? How long a person must live in the United States in order to run for President? You will find the answers to these questions and many more in this section, which provides a basic overview of the presidential office.

The President's Roles

At any given time, of course, only one person is President of the United States. The office, with all of its powers and duties, belongs to that one individual. Whoever that person may be, he—and

▶ These cowboy boots, a gift to President Eisenhower, are an example of the many gifts that a President receives.

most likely someday she[1]—must fill a number of different roles, and all of them at the same time. The President is simultaneously (1) chief of state, (2) chief executive, (3) chief administrator, (4) chief diplomat, (5) commander in chief, (6) chief legislator, (7) party chief, and (8) chief citizen.

1. To begin with, the President is **chief of state.** This means he is the ceremonial head of the government of the United States, the symbol of all the people of the nation. He is, in President William Howard Taft's words, "the personal embodiment and representative of their dignity and majesty."

In many countries, the chief of state reigns but does not rule. That is certainly true of the queens of England and Denmark, the emperor of Japan, the kings of Norway and Sweden, and the presidents of Italy and Germany. It is most certainly not true of the President of the United States, who both reigns and rules.

2. The President is the nation's **chief executive;** he is vested by the Constitution with "the executive Power" of the United States. That power is immensely broad in both domestic and foreign affairs. Indeed, the American presidency is often described as "the most powerful office in the world."

---

[1]To this point all of the Presidents have been men, but nothing in the Constitution prevents the election of a woman to that office.

3. The President is also the **chief administrator,** or director, of the Federal Government, heading one of the largest governmental machines the world has known. Today, the President directs an administration that employs more than 2.7 million civilians and spends nearly $2 trillion a year.

4. The President is also the nation's **chief diplomat,** the main architect of American foreign policy and the nation's chief spokesperson to the rest of the world. "I make foreign policy," President Harry Truman once said—and he did. What the President says and does is carefully followed in this country and abroad.

5. In close concert with the President's role in foreign affairs, the Constitution also makes the President the **commander in chief** of the nation's armed forces. The 1.4 million men and women in uniform and the nation's entire military arsenal are subject to the President's direct and immediate control.

6. The President is also the nation's **chief legislator,** the main architect of its public policies. Most often it is the President who sets the overall shape of the congressional agenda. As chief legislator, the President initiates, suggests, requests, insists, and demands that Congress enact much of its major legislation.

These six presidential roles all come directly from the Constitution. Yet they do not complete the list. The President must fill still other vital roles.

7. The President acts as the **chief of party,** the acknowledged leader of the political party that controls the executive branch. As you know, parties are not mentioned in the Constitution, yet they play a vital role in the workings of the American governmental system. Thus, much of the real power and influence wielded by the President depends on the manner in which he or she plays this critical role.

8. The office also automatically makes its occupant the nation's **chief citizen.** The President is expected to be "the representative of all the people." As chief citizen, the President is expected to work for and represent the public interest against the many private interests.

"The presidency," said Franklin Roosevelt, "is not merely an administrative office. That is the least of it. It is preeminently a place of moral leadership."

Voices on Government

Robert Reich was a professor at Harvard's John F. Kennedy School of Government before he became President Clinton's Secretary of Labor in 1993. As a member of the Cabinet for four years, Reich was in a good position to observe the presidency:

❝ Unlike Britain and other democratic monarchies, we ask our country's leader to do two jobs simultaneously, to act both as head of government and as the symbol of the nation. It's a hard act. Governing involves tough compromises and gritty reality. Symbolism requires nobility and grandeur. We demand a street-smart wheeler-dealer, but we also want a king and a royal family. ❞

Evaluating the Quotation

What other jobs do Americans expect the President to do? Use Reich's observation and what you read in this chapter to compile a full "job description."

Listing the President's several roles is a very useful way to describe the President's job. But, remember, the President must play all of these roles simultaneously. None of them can be performed in isolation. The manner in which a President plays any one role can have a powerful effect on his ability to play the others.

As two illustrations, take the experiences of Presidents Lyndon Johnson and Richard Nixon. Each was a strong and relatively effective President during his first years in office. Johnson's actions as commander in chief during the agonizing and increasingly unpopular war in Vietnam seriously damaged his effectiveness in the White House, however. In fact the damage was so great that it persuaded the President not to run for reelection in 1968.

The many-sided, sordid Watergate scandal proved to be President Nixon's downfall. The manner in which he filled the roles of party leader and chief citizen so destroyed Mr. Nixon's presidency that he was forced to leave office in disgrace in 1974.

► John F. Kennedy was the youngest person elected President. He is shown here with his son, John F. Kennedy, Jr. *Critical Thinking* **Why do you think that the Framers required that a President be at least 35 years old?**

Formal Qualifications

The Constitution says that the President must:[2]

1. Be "a natural born Citizen." Under the doctrine of *jus sanguinis* it is apparently possible for a person born abroad as an American citizen to become President. Some dispute that view, and the real meaning of this requirement cannot be known until someone born a citizen, but born abroad, does in fact become President.[3]

2. Be at least 35 years of age. John F. Kennedy, at 43, was the youngest person ever to be elected President. Theodore Roosevelt reached the presidency by succession at age 42. Ronald Reagan, who was 69 when he was first elected in 1980, was the oldest man ever elected to the office; and, when he completed his second term eight years later, he was the oldest person ever to hold the office. Most Presidents, though,

have been in their 50s when they reached the White House. George W. Bush was 54 when he became President in 2001.

3. Have lived in the United States for at least 14 years.[4]

While these formal qualifications do have some importance, they are really not very difficult to meet. In fact, more than 100 million people in this country today do so. Clearly, there are other and much more telling *informal* qualifications for the presidency—as you will see shortly.

The President's Term

The Framers considered a number of different limits on the length of the presidential term. Most of their debate centered on a four-year term, with the President eligible for reelection, versus a single six-year or seven-year term. They finally settled on a four-year term.[5] They agreed, as Alexander Hamilton wrote in *The Federalist* No. 71, that four years was a long enough period for a President to have gained experience, demonstrated his abilities, and established stable policies.

Until 1951, the Constitution placed no limit on the number of terms a President might

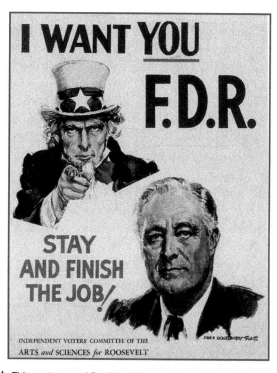

▲ This poster urged President Roosevelt to run for his third term. F.D.R. was the only President to serve more than two terms in office. *Critical Thinking* **Do you agree that a President should serve for no more than two terms? Explain your answer.**

---

[2]Article II, Section 1, Clause 5.

[3]Martin Van Buren, who was born December 5, 1782, was the first President actually born in the United States. His seven predecessors (and his immediate successor) were each born in the colonies, before the Revolution—that is, before there was a United States. But notice that the Constitution anticipated that situation with these words: "or a citizen of the United States at the time of the adoption of this Constitution."

[4]Given Herbert Hoover's election in 1928 and Dwight Eisenhower's in 1952, the 14-year requirement means any 14 years in a person's life. Both Hoover and Eisenhower spent several years before election outside the United States.

[5]Article II, Section 1, Clause 1.

serve. Several Presidents, beginning with George Washington, refused to seek more than two terms, however. Soon, the "no-third-term tradition" became an unwritten rule in presidential politics.

Franklin D. Roosevelt broke this tradition by seeking and winning a third term in 1940, and then a fourth in 1944. To prevent future Presidents from following this precedent, the 22nd Amendment made the unwritten custom limiting presidential terms a part of the written Constitution. This amendment, adopted in 1951, reads in part:

FROM THE
Constitution ❝ *No person shall be elected to the office of the President more than twice, and no person who has held the office of President, or acted as President, for more than two years of a term to which*

some other person was elected President shall be elected to the office of the President more than once. ❞

—22nd Amendment

As a general rule, then, each President may now serve a maximum of two full terms—eight years—in office. A President who succeeds to the office after the midpoint in a term could possibly serve for more than eight years. In that circumstance, the President may finish out the predecessor's term and then seek two full terms of his or her own. However, no President may serve more than 10 years in the office.

Many people, including Presidents Truman, Eisenhower, and Reagan, have called for the repeal of the 22nd Amendment and its limit on presidential service. They argue that the two-term rule

Comparative Government

Heads of State in Selected Countries

Country	Title	Name	Date Acquired Office	Previous Profession/Title
Poland	President	Aleksander Kwasniewski	December 23, 1995	Former communist offical
China	State President	Jiang Zemin	March 27, 1993	General Secretary, Communist Party
Panama	President	Mireya Moscoso	September 1, 1999	Businesswoman, civil servant
South Africa	President	Thabo Mbeki	June 16, 1999	Deputy President
Canada	Governor-General	Adrienne Clarkson	October 7, 1999	Writer and producer
Spain	King	Juan Carlos I	November 22, 1975	Crown Prince
Mexico	President	Vicente Fox	December 1, 2000	Governor, businessman
Jordan	King	Abdullah II	August 20, 1998	Crown Prince
Japan	Emperor	Akihito	January 7, 1989	Crown Prince
Philippines	President	Gloria Macapagal-Arroyo	January 20, 2001	Vice President
United States	President	George W. Bush	January 20, 2001	Governor

SOURCE: CIA Publications

Interpreting Tables The position or occupation from which a head of state came to his or her current office often suggests something about the political system in that country. **What does the table suggest about the governments of Jordan, China, and South Africa?**

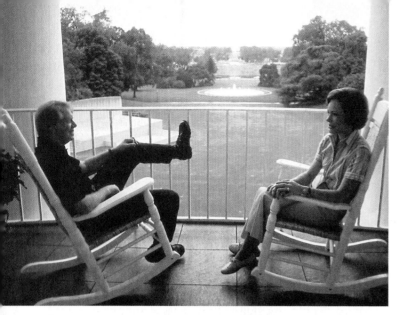

▲ **Benefits of the Presidency** President Jimmy Carter and his wife, Rosalynn, enjoying the White House and its grounds.

is undemocratic because it places an arbitrary limit on the right of the people to decide who should be President. Some critics also say that the amendment undercuts the authority of a two-term President, especially in the latter part of his second term. Supporters of the amendment defend it as a reasonable safeguard against "executive tyranny."

Several Presidents, most recently Lyndon Johnson and Jimmy Carter, have urged a single six-year term. They and others have argued that a single, nonrenewable term would free a President from the pressures of a campaign for a second term. This freedom would allow the chief executive to focus on the pressing demands of the office.

Pay and Benefits

Congress determines the President's salary. It can neither be increased nor decreased during a presidential term.[6] The President's pay was first set at $25,000 a year, in 1789. It is now $400,000 a year. Congress set that figure in 1999, and it became effective on January 20, 2001.

Congress has also provided the President with a $50,000-a-year expense allowance. That money may be spent however the President chooses; it is, in effect, a part of his pay, and it is taxed as part of his income.

The Constitution forbids the President "any other emolument from the United States, or any of them." This clause does not prevent the President from being provided with a great many benefits, however. These include the White House, a magnificent 132-room mansion set on an 18.3-acre estate in the heart of the nation's capital; a sizable suite of offices and a large staff; a fleet of automobiles, the lavishly fitted *Air Force One* and several other planes and helicopters; Camp David, the resort hideaway in the Catoctin Mountains in Maryland; the finest medical, dental, and other health care available; generous travel and entertainment funds; and many other fringe benefits.

---

[6]Article II, Section 1, Clause 7. At Philadelphia, Benjamin Franklin argued that, as money and power might corrupt a man, the President ought to receive nothing beyond his expenses; his suggestion was not put to a vote at the Convention.

Section 1 Assessment

Key Terms and Main Ideas

1. Explain the President's role as **chief of state.**
2. How does the President function as **chief of party** and **chief citizen?**
3. What are the three formal qualifications necessary to become President?
4. What is the purpose of the 22nd Amendment?

Critical Thinking

5. **Synthesizing Information** Admiral George Dewey once said, "the office of President is not such a very difficult one to fill, his duties being mainly to execute the laws of Congress." Do you agree or disagree with this statement? Explain why.
6. **Demonstrating Reasoned Judgment** Create a list of five informal qualifications that you believe are necessary for a

candidate to have in order to become President. Explain your choices.
7. **Making Decisions** At $400,000 a year, the President's salary is far more than that of the average American, yet less than the yearly income of the wealthiest Americans. Do you think that this is fair compensation? Explain your reasoning.

 Take It to the Net

8. Select one President and follow links to specific information regarding his term of office. Write an evaluation of how well he fulfilled at least three of the roles listed on page 354. Use the links provided in the Social Studies area at the following Web site for help in completing this activity. **www.phschool.com**

Presidential Succession and the Vice Presidency

Section Preview

OBJECTIVES

1. **Explain** how the Constitution provides for presidential succession.
2. **Understand** the constitutional provisions for presidential disability.
3. **Describe** the role of the Vice President.

WHY IT MATTERS

Should the President die, be removed from office, or resign, the Vice President will succeed to the presidency. The Vice President is, indeed, just a heartbeat away from the President.

POLITICAL DICTIONARY

★ presidential succession
★ Presidential Succession Act of 1947
★ balance the ticket

Consider these facts. Forty-six men have served as Vice President.[7] Fourteen of them later reached the White House—most recently, George Bush in 1989. Indeed, five of our last eleven Presidents were once Vice President.

The Constitution and Succession

Presidential succession is the scheme by which a presidential vacancy is filled. If a President dies, resigns, or is removed from office by impeachment, the Vice President succeeds to the office.

Originally, the Constitution did not provide for the succession of the Vice President. Rather, it declared that "the powers and duties" of the office—not the office itself—were to "devolve on [transfer to] the Vice President."[8]

In practice the Vice President did succeed to the office when it became vacant. Vice President John Tyler set this precedent in 1841 when he succeeded President William Henry Harrison, who died of pneumonia just one month after taking office. This practice became a part of the Constitution with the adoption of the 25th Amendment in 1967. The amendment provides:

FROM THE Constitution *"In case of the removal of the President from office or of his death or resignation, the Vice President shall become President."*

—25th Amendment, Section 1

Presidential Succession	
1	Vice President
2	Speaker of the House
3	President *pro tempore* of the Senate
4	Secretary of State
5	Secretary of the Treasury
6	Secretary of Defense
7	Attorney General
8	Secretary of the Interior
9	Secretary of Agriculture
10	Secretary of Commerce
11	Secretary of Labor
12	Secretary of Health and Human Services
13	Secretary of Housing and Urban Development
14	Secretary of Transportation
15	Secretary of Energy
16	Secretary of Education
17	Secretary of Veterans Affairs

Interpreting Charts The Vice President is first in line to succeed to the presidency should the office become vacant. Such was the case when Lyndon Johnson took the oath of office aboard *Air Force One* after the assassination of President Kennedy in 1963. ***How does the chart demonstrate the importance of the positions of the Vice President and the Speaker of the House?***

---

[7]No woman has yet held the office, but nothing in the Constitution bars that possibility.
[8]Article II, Section 1, Clause 6.

Congress fixes the order of succession following the Vice President.[9] The present law on the matter is the **Presidential Succession Act of 1947.** By its terms, the Speaker of the House and then the President *pro tem* of the Senate are next in line. They are followed, in turn, by the secretary of state and then by each of the other 13 heads of the Cabinet departments, in order of precedence—the order in which the offices were created by Congress.[10]

Presidential Disability

Before the passage of the 25th Amendment, there were serious gaps in the arrangement for presidential succession. Neither the Constitution nor Congress had made any provision for deciding when a President was disabled. Nor was there anything to indicate by whom such a decision was to be made.

For nearly 180 years, then, the nation played with fate. President Eisenhower suffered three serious but temporary illnesses while in office: a heart attack in 1955, ileitis in 1956,

and a mild stroke in 1957. Two other Presidents were disabled for much longer periods. James Garfield lingered for 80 days before he died from an assassin's bullet in 1881. Woodrow Wilson suffered a paralytic stroke in 1919 and was an invalid for the rest of his second term. He was so ill that he could not meet with his Cabinet for seven months after his stroke.

Sections 3 and 4 of the 25th Amendment fill the disability gap, and in detail. The Vice President is to become Acting President if (1) the President informs Congress, in writing, "that he is unable to discharge the powers and duties of his office," or (2) the Vice President and a majority of the members of the Cabinet inform

---

[9]Article II, Section 1, Clause 6. On removal of the President by impeachment, see Chapter 11.

[10]A Cabinet member is to serve only until a Speaker or a president *pro tem* is available and qualified. Notice that the 25th Amendment also provides for the filling of any vacancy in the vice presidency. In effect, that provision makes the Presidential Succession Act a law with little real significance—except in the highly unlikely event of simultaneous vacancies in the presidency and vice presidency.

The *Living* Constitution

Changes in the Presidency

1800

While historians have often noted the changes in the *power* of the presidency, other important aspects of the office have changed as well. These include how the President is selected, when the President takes office, how many terms the President may serve, and how the office of the President is to be filled when vacant. The time line lists some of the most important amendments, laws, and other developments concerning these areas of the nation's highest office.

1796
George Washington does not run for a third term, setting the precedent of a two-term limit.

1804
12th Amendment requires separate ballots for President and Vice President.

Congress, in writing, that the President is so incapacitated.[11]

In either case, the President may resume the powers and duties of the office by informing Congress that no inability exists. However, the Vice President and a majority of the Cabinet may challenge the President on this score. Congress then has 21 days in which to decide the matter.

To this point, the disability provisions of the 25th Amendment have come into play only once, and then only for a few hours. On July 13, 1985, surgeons removed a malignant tumor from President Reagan's large intestine. Just before surgery, Mr. Reagan transferred the powers of the presidency to Vice President Bush. President Reagan reclaimed those powers immediately after he awoke, seven hours and 54 minutes later. For that very brief period, George Herbert Walker Bush was the Acting President of the United States.

___

[11]The 25th Amendment gives this authority to the Vice President and the Cabinet or to "such other body as Congress may by law provide." To date, no "such other body" has been established.

The Vice Presidency

"I am Vice President. In this I am nothing, but I may be everything." So said John Adams, the nation's first Vice President. Those words could have been repeated, very appropriately, by each of the 45 Vice Presidents who have followed him in that office.

Importance of the Office

The Constitution pays little attention to the office of the Vice President. It assigns the position only two formal duties: (1) to preside over the Senate[12] and (2) to help decide the question of presidential disability.[13] Beyond those duties, the Constitution makes the Vice President a "President-in-waiting."

Through much of the nation's history, in fact, the vice presidency has been treated as an office of little real consequence and, often, as the butt of jokes. Many Vice Presidents themselves have

___

[12]Article I, Section 3, Clause 4; see Chapter 12, Section 1.
[13]25th Amendment, Sections 3 and 4.

1944
FDR wins a fourth term; and Congress later acts (1947) to limit a President to two terms in office (22nd Amendment, ratified in 1951)

1947
Presidential Succession Act lists officials who would succeed to the presidency after the Vice President.

1967
25th Amendment sets up procedures to follow when a President is disabled or vice presidency is vacant.

1985
Disability provision of the 25th Amendment first used when Vice President Bush becomes acting President while President Reagan is in surgery.

1925 | **1950** | **1975** | **2000**

1933
20th Amendment moves President's inauguration from March to January.

The Inaugural Ball 1957

1973
President Nixon, following the 25th Amendment, nominates Gerald Ford to replace Vice President Agnew, who had resigned.

Analyzing Time Lines

1. Which amendment deals with a vacancy in the office of Vice President? When and why was this provision first used?
2. For what reason do you think the 20th Amendment was passed?

It worries me that he just wants to be vice president when he grows up.

Interpreting Political Cartoons *What does the cartoon suggest about the common perception of the vice presidency?*

Vice Presidents Who Succeeded to the Presidency	
Successor	**Reason for Succession**
John Tyler	Death (pneumonia) of William Henry Harrison, April 4, 1841
Millard Fillmore	Death (gastroenteritis) of Zachary Taylor, July 9, 1850
Andrew Johnson	Death (assassination) of Abraham Lincoln, April 15, 1865
Chester A. Arthur	Death (assassination) of James A. Garfield, September 19, 1881
Theodore Roosevelt	Death (assassination) of William McKinley, September 14, 1901
Calvin Coolidge	Death (undisclosed illness) of Warren G. Harding, August 2, 1923
Harry S Truman	Death (cerebral hemorrhage) of Franklin D. Roosevelt, April 12, 1945
Lyndon B. Johnson	Death (assassination) of John F. Kennedy, November 22, 1963
Gerald R. Ford	Resignation of Richard M. Nixon, August 9, 1974

Interpreting Tables Eight Presidents have died in office, and one was forced to resign. In each case, the Vice President succeeded to the office. *What circumstances, other than the death or resignation of the President, may lead to the Vice President succeeding to the presidency?*

had a hand in this. John Adams described his post as "the most insignificant office that ever the invention of man contrived or his imagination conceived." Thomas Jefferson, who followed him, found the office "honorable and easy" and "tranquil and unoffending."

Theodore Roosevelt, who had come to the White House from the vice presidency, was annoyed by the tinkling of the prisms of a chandelier in the presidential study. He ordered it removed, saying: "Take it to the office of the Vice President. He doesn't have anything to do. It will keep him awake." The fixture has been in the Vice President's office ever since.

John Nance Garner, who served for two terms as Franklin D. Roosevelt's Vice President, once said: "The vice presidency isn't worth a warm pitcher of spit." Alben Barkley, who served during Harry Truman's second term, often told the story of a woman who had two sons. One of them, Barkley said, went away to sea and the other one became Vice President, "and neither of them was ever heard from again."

Despite these and a great many other unkind comments, the office is clearly an important one. Its occupant is literally "only a heartbeat away from the presidency." Remember, eight Presidents have died in office, and one, Richard M. Nixon, was forced to resign.

Much of the blame for the low status of the vice presidency can be laid on the two major parties and the way they choose their candidates for the office. Traditionally, each national convention names the hand-picked choice of its presidential candidate. Usually, the presidential candidate picks someone who will **"balance the ticket."** That is, the presidential candidate chooses a running mate who can strengthen his chance of being elected by virtue of certain ideological, geographic, racial, ethnic, gender, or other characteristics.

Vice Presidential Vacancy

The vice presidency has been vacant 18 times thus far: nine times by succession to the presidency, twice by resignation, and seven times by death.[14]

---

[14]John C. Calhoun resigned to become a senator from South Carolina in 1832. Spiro T. Agnew resigned in 1973, after a conviction for income tax evasion and in the face of other charges. The seven who died in office were: George Clinton (1812), Elbridge Gerry (1814), William R. King (1853), Henry Wilson (1875), Thomas A. Hendricks (1885), Garret A. Hobart (1899), and James S. Sherman (1912).

Yet, not until 1967 and the 25th Amendment did the Constitution deal with the matter. The amendment provides, in part:

FROM THE
Constitution **"** *Whenever there is a vacancy in the office of the Vice President, the President shall nominate a Vice President who shall take office upon confirmation by a majority vote of both Houses of Congress.* **"**
—25th Amendment, Section 2

This provision was first implemented in 1973. In that year, President Nixon selected and Congress confirmed Gerald R. Ford to succeed Spiro Agnew as Vice President. It came into play again in 1974, when President Ford named and Congress approved Nelson Rockefeller.

The Vice President Today

Many people have long urged that the Vice President be given a larger role in the executive branch. The more recent Presidents, from Eisenhower on, have in fact made greater use of their Vice Presidents. Vice President Dick Cheney is widely regarded as the most influential Vice President ever. He was President Ford's White House Chief of Staff (1975–1977), a member of the House (from Wyoming, 1979–1989), and later Secretary of Defense in the first Bush Administration (1989–1993).

▲ *An Active Vice President* Vice President Dick Cheney (right) meets with Mexican President Vicente Fox (left).

So far, however, no President has upgraded the Vice President to the role of a true "assistant president." The major reason: Of all the President's official family, only the Vice President—who is elected by the people, rather than appointed by the President—is not subject to the ultimate discipline of removal from office by the President. No matter what the circumstances, the President cannot fire the Vice President.

Section 2 Assessment

Key Terms and Main Ideas

1. What was the purpose of the **Presidential Succession Act of 1947?**
2. How is presidential disability to be determined?
3. Why are vice presidential candidates often chosen to **balance the ticket?**
4. **(a)** What official duties does the Constitution assign to the Vice President? **(b)** How has the role of the Vice President changed in recent years?

Critical Thinking

5. **Formulating Questions** Suppose you have just been offered the vice-presidential nomination. Make a list of questions that will help you decide whether to accept or reject the offer.

6. **Predicting Consequences** You have read that no matter what the circumstances, the President cannot fire the Vice President. **(a)** What might be the reasons for this provision? **(b)** What might be the consequences if this were not the case?

 Take It to the Net

7. Choose an instance when a Vice President succeeded to the presidency and read more about it. Then write a news story from the point of view of a reporter living at the time. Use the links provided in the Social Studies area at the following Web site for help in completing this activity. **www.phschool.com**

Choosing the Vice President

How many of the nation's Vice Presidents can you name? For many political figures, the vice presidency has been a forgettable final stop in their careers. Eminent historian John A. Garraty argues that the method for selecting the Vice President is illogical and undemocratic, and has led to the office's unimpressive history.

Californian Ronald Reagan chose Texan George Bush as his running mate in 1980, thus geographically "balancing the ticket."

When the Founding Fathers created the office of president . . . they had little to say about the vice presidency. . . . They saw the vice president as a kind of understudy . . . in case the star should, as the Constitution explains, die, become incapacitated, resign, or be found guilty of treason, bribery, or "other high Crimes and Misdemeanors." . . .

Yet time after time, both parties [have] selected their vice-presidential candidates with little or no thought of how effective they would be should the single heart between them and the White House cease to beat. Preserving party unity and adding strength to the ticket in a particular state or region . . . , not the ability of the person selected, continued to be the determining factors in nearly every case. Still more disturbing, since television and the increase in the number of presidential primaries have diminished the role of national conventions in the selection of candidates, the choice of a running mate has become a prerogative of the person who wins the presidential nomination.

Presidential candidates have nearly always had a hand in choosing their running mates. But until the decline of the conventions' importance, they had to give some thought to how the delegates would react to their selection. . . .

Leaving the choice to the head of the ticket has not changed the reasons particular candidates are chosen. But despite all their hoopla and sordid

dealing, the old-fashioned nominating conventions gave substance to the idea that the people, through their chosen delegates, were deciding who the party standard-bearers should be.

The primary system is undoubtedly a more effective way of discovering which candidates for president the voters prefer. The primaries practically compel candidates to describe what they intend to do if nominated, but they studiously avoid committing themselves as to whom they want as running mates. And there are no vice-presidential primaries.

Given the frequency with which fate has turned vice presidents into instant presidents, this is disturbing. That presidents should be able to pick their successors is undemocratic. It is also illogical. Since they must be dead, incompetent, or disgraced before the occasion can arise, they are the last persons who should have that power.

Analyzing Primary Sources

1. According to Garraty, for what reasons are most Vice Presidents selected?
2. Why, according to Garraty, has the growth of presidential primaries made the selection of the Vice President less democratic?
3. What two alternatives does Garraty suggest to make the selection of vice-presidential candidates more democratic?

Presidential Selection: The Framers' Plan

3

Section Preview

OBJECTIVES

1. **Explain** the Framers' original provisions for choosing the President.
2. **Outline** how the rise of political parties changed the original provisions set out in the Constitution.

WHY IT MATTERS

Selecting the President is a complex process that many Americans do not fully grasp. Understanding the Framers' plan for choosing the President will help you understand this complicated process.

POLITICAL DICTIONARY

★ **presidential electors**
★ **electoral votes**
★ **electoral college**

In formal terms, the President is chosen according to the provisions of the Constitution.[15] In practice, however, the President is elected through an altogether extraordinary process that is not very well understood by most Americans. That process is a combination of constitutional provisions, State and federal laws, and, in largest measure, a number of practices born of the nation's political parties. To make sense of this very complex system, you must first understand what the Framers had in mind when they designed the presidential election process.

Original Provisions

The Framers gave more time to the method for choosing the President than to any other matter. It was, said James Wilson of Pennsylvania, "the most difficult of all on which we have had to decide." The difficulty arose largely because most of the Framers were against selecting the President by either of the obvious ways: by Congress or by a direct vote of the people.

Early in the Convention, most of the delegates favored selection by Congress. Later, nearly all delegates came to believe that congressional selection would, as Alexander Hamilton said, put the President "too much under the legislative thumb."

Only a few of the Framers favored choosing the President by popular vote. Nearly all agreed

that such a process would lead to "tumult and disorder." Most delegates felt, too, that the people, scattered over so wide an area, could not possibly know enough about the available candidates to make wise, informed choices. George Mason of Virginia spoke for most of his colleagues at the convention: "The extent of the Country renders it impossible that the people can have the requisite capacity to judge of the respective pretensions of the Candidates."

After weeks of debate, the Framers finally agreed on a plan first put forward by Hamilton. Under it, the President and Vice President were to be chosen by a special body of **presidential electors.** These electors would each cast two **electoral votes,** each for a different candidate. The candidate with the most votes would become President. The person with the second

▲ George Washington's inauguration was commemorated by objects such as these. The brass buttons are precursors of today's campaign buttons.

---

[15]The Constitution deals with the process of presidential selection in several places: Article II, Section 1, Clauses 2, 3, and 4, and the 12th, 20th, and 23rd Amendments.

The Presidency   **365** ★★★

The Framers' Plan for the Electoral College

1. Each State would have as many presidential electors as it has senators and representatives in Congress.

2. These electors would be chosen in each State in a manner the State legislature directed.

3. The electors, meeting in their own States, would each cast two votes—each for a different person for President.

4. These electoral votes from the States would be opened and counted before a joint session of Congress.

5. The person receiving the largest number of electoral votes, provided that total was a majority of all the electors, would become President.

6. The person with the second highest number of electoral votes would become Vice President.

7. If a tie occurred, or if no one received the votes of a majority of the electors, the President would be chosen by the House of Representatives, voting by States.

8. If a tie occurred for the second spot, the Vice President would be chosen by the Senate.

Interpreting Charts The Framers' Plan for the electoral college provided for a group of presidential electors to choose the President. *How was the Vice President to be chosen?*

most votes would become Vice President. The chart above details the Framers' plan.[16]

The Framers intended the electors to be "the most enlightened and respectable citizens" from each State. They were to be "free agents" in choosing the people best qualified to fill the nation's two highest offices.

The Rise of Parties

The **electoral college,** then, is the group of people (electors) chosen from each State and the District of Columbia to formally select the President and Vice President. The original version of the electoral college worked as the Framers intended only as long as George Washington was willing to seek and hold the presidency. He did so twice, and was unanimously elected President, in 1789 and again in 1792.

Flaws began to appear in the system in 1796, however, with the rise of political parties. John Adams, the Federalist candidate, was elected to the presidency. Thomas Jefferson, an arch-rival and Democratic-Republican, lost to Adams by just three votes in the electoral balloting. Jefferson then became Adams' Vice President.

The Election of 1800

The system broke down in the election of 1800. By then there were two well-defined parties: the Federalists, led by Adams and Hamilton, and the Democratic-Republicans, headed by Jefferson. Each of these parties nominated presidential and vice-presidential candidates. They also nominated candidates to serve as presidential electors in the several States. Those elector-candidates were picked with the clear understanding that, if elected, they would vote for their party's presidential and vice-presidential nominees.

---

[16]Remember, these were the original provisions, in Article II, Sections 2, 3, and 4; they were modified by the 12th Amendment.

Elections Leading to the 12th Amendment

1789 and 1792 George Washington is unanimously elected President.

1796 John Adams (Federalist) is elected President. Thomas Jefferson (Democratic-Republican), losing to Adams by three electoral votes, becomes Vice President.

1800 After 36 ballots, the House finally breaks the tie between Jefferson and Aaron Burr in 1801. Jefferson becomes President, Burr Vice President.

1804 The 12th Amendment separates the presidential and vice presidential choices in the electoral college and almost certainly guarantees that the President and Vice President will be of the same party.

Interpreting Charts After the elections of 1789 and 1792, the Framers' plan for the electoral college broke down. *How did the election of 1800 show the need for the 12th Amendment?*

Each of the 73 Democratic-Republicans who won posts as electors voted for his party's nominees: Jefferson and Aaron Burr. In doing so, they produced a tie for the presidency. Remember that the Constitution gave each elector two votes, each to be cast for a different person, but each to be cast for someone as President. Popular opinion clearly favored Jefferson for the presidency, and the party had intended Burr for the vice presidency. Still, the House of Representatives had to take 36 separate ballots before it finally chose Jefferson.

The spectacular election of 1800 marked the introduction of three new elements into the process of selecting a President: (1) party nominations for the presidency and vice presidency, (2) the nomination of candidates for presidential electors pledged to vote for their party's presidential ticket, and (3) the automatic casting of the electoral votes in line with those pledges. Gone forever was the notion that the electors would act as "free agents" in the process.

The 12th Amendment

The election of 1800 produced another notable result: the 12th Amendment. This amendment was added to the Constitution in 1804 to make certain there would never be another such fiasco. The amendment is lengthy, but it made only one major change in the electoral college system. It separated the presidential and vice-presidential elections: "The Electors . . . shall name in their ballots the person voted for as President, and in distinct ballots the person voted for as Vice-President."[17]

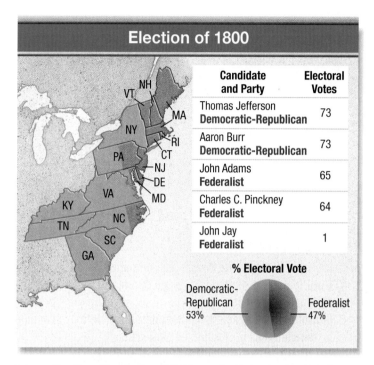

Election of 1800

Candidate and Party	Electoral Votes
Thomas Jefferson **Democratic-Republican**	73
Aaron Burr **Democratic-Republican**	73
John Adams **Federalist**	65
Charles C. Pinckney **Federalist**	64
John Jay **Federalist**	1

% Electoral Vote

Democratic-Republican 53%   Federalist 47%

Interpreting Maps The election of 1800 was decided only after 36 ballots in the House of Representatives. *How does the map show the political divisions in the country in 1800?*

With the appearance of parties, the election of 1800, and the 12th Amendment, the constitutional framework was laid for the presidential selection system as it exists today. That system is, indeed, a far cry from what was agreed to in 1787, as you will see in the sections ahead.

---

[17]Not only does the amendment mean there cannot be a repeat of the circumstances that produced a tie in 1800, it almost certainly guarantees that the President and Vice President will be of the same party.

Section 3 Assessment

Key Terms and Main Ideas

1. Why were most of the Framers opposed to choosing the President by popular vote? By Congress?
2. (a) Outline the original provisions for the **electoral college.** (b) How did the Framers expect the **presidential electors** to vote?
3. In what three ways did the presidential election process change as a result of the election of 1800?

Critical Thinking

4. **Recognizing Ideologies** The Framers intended the presidential electors to be "the most enlightened and respectable citizens" in each State. What does this statement suggest about their definition of good citizenship?
5. **Recognizing Cause and Effect** How did the rise of political parties change the way the electoral college functions?

Take It to the Net

6. Study the data presented on the electoral college home page. Do the data suggest that presidential elections always accurately reflect the will of the people? Write a paragraph explaining your answer. Use the links provided in the Social Studies area at the following Web site for help in completing this activity. **www.phschool.com**

Presidential Nominations

Section Preview

OBJECTIVES

1. **Describe** the role of conventions in the presidential nominating process.
2. **Evaluate** the importance of presidential primaries.
3. **Understand** the role of the caucus-convention process in States that do not hold primaries.
4. **Outline** the events that take place during a national convention.
5. **Examine** the characteristics that determine who is nominated as a presidential candidate.

WHY IT MATTERS

Presidential primaries and party caucuses lead up to the Democratic and Republican national conventions. At these conventions, which take place every four years during the summer before the fall election, each party officially selects its presidential and vice presidential candidates.

POLITICAL DICTIONARY

★ **presidential primary**
★ **winner-take-all**
★ **proportional representation**
★ **national convention**
★ **platform**
★ **keynote address**

The Constitution makes no provision for the nomination of candidates for the presidency. Rather, as you have just seen, the Framers designed a system in which presidential electors would, out of their own knowledge, select the "wisest and best man" to be President. Later, the rise of parties altered that system dramatically.

The Role of Conventions

The first method the parties developed to nominate their presidential candidates was the congressional caucus. As you may recall from Chapter 7, that method was regularly used in the elections of 1800 to 1824. However, the closed, nonrepresentative character of this system led to its downfall in the mid-1820s. For the election of 1832, both major parties turned to the national convention as their nominating device, and it has continued to serve them ever since.

Convention Arrangements

Not only does the Constitution say nothing about presidential nominations; there is, as well, almost no federal or State statutory law on the matter. The convention system has been built almost entirely by the two major parties in American politics.

In both parties, the national committee makes the arrangements for the party's convention. The committee sets the date and picks the place

for that meeting. In recent years, the party out of power has held its convention first, usually in July, and the President's party has met some three weeks later, in the early part of August.

Many of the nation's largest cities bid for the honor—and the financial return to local business—of hosting a convention. The map on the next page shows where the Democratic and Republican national conventions have been held over time. In 2000, the Republican convention was held in Philadelphia and the Democratic convention in Los Angeles.

The Apportionment of Delegates

With the date and the location set, the national committee issues its "call" for the convention. That formal announcement names the time and place. It also tells the party's organization in each State how many delegates it may send to the national gathering.

By tradition, both parties give each State party a certain number of delegates based on that State's electoral vote. Over the past several conventions, both parties have developed complicated formulas that also award bonus delegates to those States that have supported the party's candidates in recent elections.

For 2000, the Republicans' formula produced a convention of 2,067 delegates. The Democrats' more complex plan called for 4,337.[18] Given

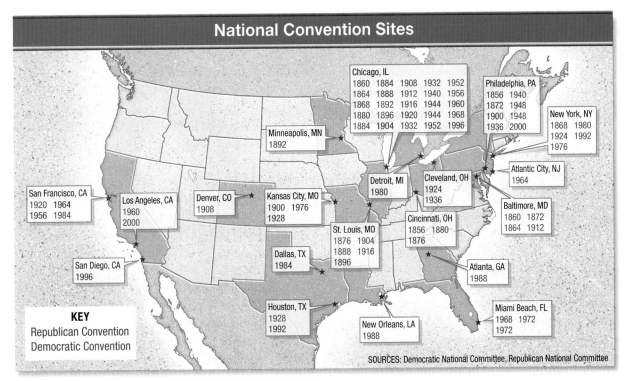

National Convention Sites

Chicago, IL
1860	1884	1908	1932	1952
1864	1888	1912	1940	1956
1868	1892	1916	1944	1960
1880	1896	1920	1944	1968
1884	1904	1932	1952	1996

Philadelphia, PA
1856	1940
1872	1948
1900	1948
1936	2000

New York, NY
1868	1980
1924	1992
1976	

Minneapolis, MN
1892

San Francisco, CA
| 1920 | 1964 |
| 1956 | 1984 |

Los Angeles, CA
| 1960 |
| 2000 |

Denver, CO
1908

Kansas City, MO
| 1900 | 1976 |
| 1928 | |

Detroit, MI
1980

Cleveland, OH
| 1924 |
| 1936 |

Atlantic City, NJ
1964

Baltimore, MD
| 1860 | 1872 |
| 1864 | 1912 |

San Diego, CA
1996

St. Louis, MO
1876	1904
1888	1916
1896	

Cincinnati, OH
| 1856 | 1880 |
| 1876 | |

Dallas, TX
1984

Atlanta, GA
1988

KEY
Republican Convention
Democratic Convention

Houston, TX
| 1928 |
| 1992 |

New Orleans, LA
1988

Miami Beach, FL
| 1968 | 1972 |
| 1972 | |

SOURCES: Democratic National Committee, Republican National Committee

Interpreting Maps Democrats held their first convention in Baltimore in 1832, and met there through 1852. The Republicans held their convention in Philadelphia in 1856. *How can you explain the popularity of such cities as Chicago, New York, and Philadelphia as convention sites?*

those large numbers, it should be fairly clear that neither party's national convention can be called "a deliberative body" able to give each of its decisions thoughtful consideration.

Selection of Delegates

There are really *two* campaigns for the presidency. One is the contest between the Republican and Democratic candidates in the fall. The other is earlier and quite different. It takes place *within* each party: the struggle for convention delegates.

State laws and/or party rules fix the procedures for picking delegates in each State. That fact is a reflection of federalism, and it has produced a jigsaw puzzle of presidential primaries, conventions, and caucuses among the 50 States.

To a large extent, the Republican Party leaves the matter of delegate selection to its State organizations and to State law. The Democrats, on the other hand, have adopted several national rules to govern the process. Most of those rules reflect attempts to broaden participation in the delegate selection process, especially by the young, African Americans, other minorities, and women.

Presidential Primaries

More than three fourths of all the delegates to both parties' conventions come from States that hold presidential primaries. Many of those primaries are major media events. Serious contenders in both parties must make the best possible showing in at least most of them.

Depending on the State, a **presidential primary** is an election in which a party's voters (1) choose some or all of a State party organization's delegates to their party's national convention, and/or (2) express a preference among various contenders for their party's presidential nomination.

---

[18]Both parties allot delegates to the District of Columbia, Puerto Rico, the Virgin Islands, Guam, and American Samoa; the Democrats also provide for delegates who represent Democrats Abroad. The Democratic convention also includes a large number of "superdelegates"—mostly party officers and Democrats who hold major elective offices. They are automatically members of their respective State delegations. More than 750 superdelegates were seated at the 2000 Democratic convention; their number included all of the members of the Democratic National Committee, all Democratic State governors (19), and nearly all of the Democratic members of the House and Senate.

History of the Presidential Primary

The presidential primary first appeared in the early 1900s as part of the reform movement aimed at the boss-dominated convention system. Wisconsin passed the first presidential primary law in 1905, providing for the popular election of national convention delegates. Several States soon followed that lead, and Oregon added a preference primary in 1910. By 1916 nearly half the States had adopted presidential primary laws.

For a time, the primary system fell into disfavor so that by 1968, primaries were found in only 16 States and the District of Columbia. Efforts to reform the national convention process, especially in the Democratic Party, reversed that downward trend in the 1970s, however. The number of presidential primary States is now at an all-time high. For 2000, some form of presidential primary was in place in 44 States, and in the District of Columbia and Puerto Rico, as well.[19]

---

[19]In every State except Alaska, Hawaii, Iowa, Minnesota, Nevada, and North Dakota. In some States, the law permits but does not require a major party to hold a primary. In South Carolina the presidential primary is a product of party rules, not State law.

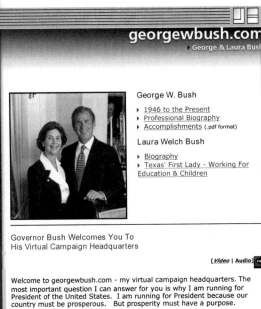

◀ **Campaigning Then and Now**
Campaigning for the presidency has changed dramatically since Harry S Truman's 1948 whistle-stop train tours were one of the best ways to reach voters. Today's candidates can use the Internet to reach potential voters.

Primaries Today

Again, a presidential primary is either or both of two things: a delegate-selection process and/or a candidate preference election. Once that much has been said, however, the system becomes very hard to describe, except on a State-by-State basis.

The difficulty comes largely from two sources: (1) the fact that in each State the details of the delegate-selection process are determined by that State's own law—and those details vary from one State to the next, and (2) the ongoing reform efforts in the Democratic Party. Since 1968, when the Democrats were shattered by disputes over Vietnam and civil rights policies, the Democratic National Committee has written and rewritten the party's rules to promote greater grassroots participation in the delegate-selection process. Those new rules have prompted many changes in most States' election laws.

Even a matter that seems as simple as the date for the primary illustrates the crazy-quilt pattern of State laws. New Hampshire holds the first of the presidential primaries every four years, and it has done so since 1940. New Hampshire guards its first-in-the-nation title with a law that sets the date for its primary as the Tuesday of the week before the date on which any other State schedules its contest. For the 2000 presidential election, the New Hampshire primary was held on February 1, 2000, and all of the others were held at various times over the next four months.

Most States prefer an early date, and so the primary schedule has become heavily "front-loaded." More than half of the primaries, including the contests in most of the larger States, now come in March and early April.

Name recognition and money have always been important factors in the presidential primary process, and front-loading has multiplied their significance. Until lately, a candidate who was not very well known nationally could hope to build a following from primary to primary—as, for example, Bill Clinton did in 1992. The process leaves little or no time for that strategy today, however. Candidates now have to mount (and pay for) campaigns in a number of widely separated States that hold their primaries on the same day or within only a few days of one another.

Proportional Representation

Until fairly recently, most primaries were both delegate-selection and preference exercises. Several primaries were also **winner-take-all** contests. That is, the candidate who won the preference vote automatically won the support of all delegates chosen at the primary.

Winner-take-all primaries have now all but disappeared. The Democratic Party rules now prohibit them. Instead, the Democrats have a complex **proportional representation** rule. Any candidate who wins at least 15 percent of the votes cast in a primary gets the number of State Democratic convention delegates that corresponds to his or her share of that primary vote. Take, for example, a State that has 40 convention delegates. If a candidate wins 45 percent of the primary vote, he automatically gains the support of at least 18 of the delegates.

Most States had to change their primary laws to account for the Democrats' proportional representation rule. So in many States, Republican delegates are also chosen on a proportional representation basis. Still, a few States do permit winner-take-all primaries, and the Republicans hold them where they can.

The Democrats' proportional representation rule had yet another major impact on the shape of presidential primaries. It led several States—among them Oregon and Wisconsin, the States that had pioneered the presidential primary idea—to give up the popular selection of delegates.

More than half of the presidential primary States now hold only a preference primary. The delegates themselves are chosen later, at party conventions. In most of these States, the delegates must be picked to line up with the results of the preference primary—for example, for the Republicans in 2000, so many delegates for John McCain, so many for Steve Forbes, so many for George W. Bush, and so on. In some States, however, the preference vote does not govern the choice of the delegates. In

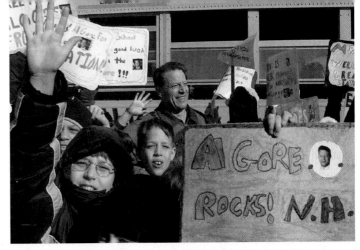

▲ *New Hampshire Primary* Because New Hampshire holds the first-in-the-nation primary, most presidential candidates target the State as essential to their campaigns. Here Al Gore meets a group of future voters during the 2000 primary season.

those States, the preference primary is often called simply a "beauty contest."

Most of the preference contests are also "all-candidate" primaries. These are contests in which all generally recognized contenders for a party's presidential nomination must be listed on that party's preference ballot.

Evaluation of the Primary

No one who surveys the presidential primary system needs to be told that it is complicated, nor that it is filled with confusing variations. Still, these primaries are vital. Over recent years they have played the major part in deciding the presidential nominating contests in both parties—especially the party out of power.

Presidential primaries tend to democratize the delegate-selection process. And, importantly, they force would-be nominees to test their candidacies in actual political combat. For the party out of power, especially, the primaries are often "knock-down, drag-out" battles. Without the unifying force of the President as party leader, the leaders and factions in the party vie with one another, vigorously, for the presidential nomination. In this way, the screening out of the lesser possibilities takes places until only a few contenders for the presidential nomination remain.

Such hard-fought contests occur but are not common in the party in power. This tends to be true either because the President (1) is himself seeking reelection, or (2) has given his backing to someone he favors for the nomination. In either case the President almost always gets his way.

Interpreting Political Cartoons *What does the cartoon suggest about the significance of the Iowa caucus and the New Hampshire primary?*

There are exceptions, of course. Ronald Reagan made a stiff run at President Ford in the Republican Party in 1976; and Senator Edward Kennedy gave President Carter a real fight in the Democratic Party in 1980. The 2000 election provided another exception: Former Senator Bill Bradley's heated battle with President Clinton's choice for the Democratic nod, Vice President Al Gore.

Reform Proposals

The fact that so many States now hold presidential primaries places great demands on candidates in terms of time, effort, money, scheduling, and fatigue. Primary season also tests the public's endurance.

For these and other reasons, many critics of the current system think that each of the major parties should hold a single, nationwide presidential primary. Some of those critics would have both parties nominate their presidential candidates in those contests. They would therefore do away with conventions, except perhaps to pick vice-presidential nominees or to write platforms.

Other critics favor a series of regional primaries, held at two- or three-week intervals in groups of States across the country. Hope for these plans is dim at best, as each plan would require joint action by Congress, the States, and both major parties.

The Caucus-Convention Process

In those States that do not hold presidential primaries, delegates to the national conventions are chosen in a system of caucuses and conventions.[20] The process works basically as described here, although the details differ from State to State.

The party's voters meet in local caucuses, generally at the precinct level. There they choose delegates to a local or district convention, where delegates to the State convention are picked. At the State level, and sometimes in the district conventions, delegates to the national convention are chosen.

The caucus-convention process is the oldest method for picking national convention delegates. Its use has declined significantly over the years, however. In 2000, less than one fifth of all delegates to either party's convention came from those States that still use the caucus-convention process.

The Iowa caucuses generally get the most attention, largely because they are now the first delegate-selection event held in every presidential election season. Iowa purposely schedules the start of its caucus process early. In 2000 the event took place on January 24, eight days before New Hampshire held its first-in-the-nation presidential primary.

The National Convention

Once all of the primaries and caucuses have been held and all of the delegates have been chosen, another event looms large. The two major parties hold their **national conventions,** the meetings at which the delegates vote to pick their presidential and vice-presidential candidates.

For a century and more, those party gatherings were highly dramatic, often chaotic and even stormy affairs at which, after days of heated bargaining, the party finally nominated its presidential candidate. Both parties' conventions have become much tamer in recent years. In large part, this is because there is now little doubt about who will win the convention's grand prize. Regularly, the leading contender has won enough delegates

[20]In 2000, national convention delegates were chosen by the caucus-convention method by both major parties in Alaska, Hawaii, Iowa, Minnesota, Nevada, and North Dakota. In a few other States, one party picked delegates through the caucus process while the other held a presidential primary.

in the primaries and caucuses to lock up the nomination before the convention meets.

Each party's convention remains a major event, nonetheless. Party conventions accomplish three main goals: they (1) name the party's presidential and vice-presidential candidates, (2) bring the various factions and the leading personalities in the party together in one place for a common purpose, and (3) adopt the party's **platform**—its formal statement of basic principles, stands on major policy matters, and objectives for the campaign and beyond.

If the meeting is successful, the convention also does several other things. It promotes party unity, mobilizes support for the party ticket, and captures the interest and attention of the country.

The First Two Days

Both parties' conventions usually meet in one or two daily sessions over a four-day period, and they follow a fairly standard pattern. The first day is devoted to organizing the convention and to rousing speeches. The **keynote address** is almost always the high point of the first session. Traditionally, that speech is delivered by one of the party's most accomplished orators. The keynoter's remarks, and nearly all of the many other speeches made during the convention, follow a predictable form. They glorify the party, its history, its leaders, and its programs; condemn the opposition; underscore the virtues of party harmony; and predict a smashing victory in November.

The presentation and adoption of committee reports take up the better part of the second day's sessions. These sessions can be quite spirited. The convention's committee on rules proposes whatever changes it thinks should be made in the rules that guide the convention itself and in the rules that govern the national party's operations. The committee on platform and resolutions also makes its report. The platform emerges from a draft drawn up by the party's leadership before the convention.

Platform-writing is a fine art. Not only is a platform a statement of party principles and stands on policy matters, it is also a campaign document. Its more controversial planks often prompt arguments in the committee, and that debate may spill over to the convention floor.

However, a platform aims to appeal to as many people and as many groups as possible. So, both parties tend to produce somewhat generalized comments on some of the hard questions of the day. Platforms are regularly criticized for blandness. Listen to this comment, made by the Republican presidential nominee in 1964:

> **PRIMARY Sources** *"Platforms are written to be ignored and forgotten. . . . Like Jell-O shimmering on a dessert plate, there is usually little substance and nothing you can get your teeth into."*
>
> —Barry Goldwater

Still, the platforms are important. They *do* set out a number of hard and fast stands in many policy areas. They also reflect the compromise nature of American politics and of the two major parties.

The Last Two Days

The convention turns to its chief task on the third day: the nomination of the party's candidate for the presidency. The names of any number of contenders may be offered to the delegates.[21] Once their nominating (and several seconding) speeches have been made, the convention begins to vote. The secretary calls the States in alphabetical order. The chair of each delegation announces how that delegation's

---

[21]Most of them have no real chance of becoming the party's nominee, but they are put forward for some other reason. Thus a "favorite son" may be touted because a State delegation wants to honor one of its own.

◀ **Keynote Speaker**
Representative Harold Ford, Jr.'s (D., Tennessee) image is projected on a large-screen monitor as he speaks at the 2000 Democratic National Convention in Los Angeles.

CLOSE UP Student Poll

In a recent poll, students were asked their opinion on the following question: *Of the following six backgrounds or characteristics that a candidate for President might have, which would be the more likely or less likely to influence your vote?*

	More Likely	Less Likely	Little Difference	Not Sure
An experienced politician	65	11	21	3
A military leader	47	18	33	2
A business person	36	19	43	2
A religious leader	34	27	35	4
A third-party candidate who is not from the Republican or Democratic Party	23	26	47	4
A sports figure or entertainer who is active in public affairs	19	36	42	3

SOURCE: High School Students' Attitudes Toward Government and Politics, Close Up Foundation, May 1999

1. **Analyzing Data** *Which of the six backgrounds or characteristics is the most likely to influence the votes of those polled? Which is the least likely to influence voters?*
2. **Conducting Polls** In your own school, conduct a poll asking students which backgrounds or characteristics are the most likely to influence their vote for President. *How do your results compare to the results shown here?*

votes are cast. Occasionally, a delegation passes and its votes are reported after the rest of the States have been called.

Most often, the first ballot produces a candidate. In the 26 conventions held by each party from 1900 through 2000, the Republicans have made a first ballot nomination 22 times and the Democrats 21 times. Indeed, the GOP has not had to take a second ballot since its 1948 convention, and the Democrats not since 1952.[22]

The fourth day brings the nomination of the party's vice-presidential candidate. Whomever the presidential nominee's running mate turns out to be, he or she is almost invariably the hand-picked choice of the party's newly nominated presidential candidate.

With its candidates named, the convention comes to the final major item on its agenda: the presidential candidate's acceptance speech. As that speech ends, the delegates erupt in wild, elated celebration.

Who Is Nominated?

If an incumbent President wants another term, the convention's choice of a nominee is easy. The President is almost certain to get the nomination, and usually with no real opposition from within the party. The President's advantages are immense: the majesty and publicity of the office and the close control of the party's machinery.[23]

When the President is not in the field, up to a dozen or so contenders may surface in the pre-convention period. At most, two or three of them may survive to contest the prize at the convention.

Political Experience

Who among the contenders will win the nomination? The historical record argues this answer: the one who is, in the jargon of politics, the most available—that is, the most electable. Conventions want to pick candidates who can win, those with the broadest possible appeal within the party and to the electorate.

Most presidential candidates come to their nominations with substantial and well-known records in public office. But those records have to be free of controversies that could have antagonized important elements within the party or among the voting public. Generally, presidential candidates have served in elective office, where they have shown vote-getting ability. Seldom does a candidate step from the business world or from the military directly into the role of candidate, as did Wendell Willkie in 1940 or Dwight Eisenhower in 1952.

Historically, the governorships of larger States have produced the largest number of presidential candidacies. Of the 20 men nominated by the two

---

[22]A convention can become deadlocked, unable to make a choice between the top contenders. In that case, a "dark horse"—that is someone who did not seem a likely choice before the convention—may finally emerge as the nominee. The most spectacular deadlock in convention history occurred at the Democratic convention in New York in 1924. That convention took 103 ballots before John W. Davis of West Virginia won the nomination.

[23]In fact, only four sitting Presidents have ever been denied nomination: John Tyler by the Whigs in 1844; Millard Fillmore by the Whigs in 1852; Franklin Pierce by the Democrats in 1856; and Chester Arthur by the Republicans in 1884.

major parties between 1900 and 1956, eleven were either then serving or had once served as a governor.

For a time the Senate became the prime source of major party presidential candidates. In the four elections from 1960 through 1972, each major party nominee had been a senator. None had ever been a governor.

More recently, however, the old pattern has been restored. Jimmy Carter, the former governor of Georgia, was nominated by the Democrats in 1976 and 1980. Ronald Reagan, former governor of California, was the GOP choice in 1980 and again in 1984. The Democrats nominated the governor of Massachusetts, Michael Dukakis, in 1988, and they picked Governor Bill Clinton of Arkansas in 1992 and renominated him in 1996. The Republicans nominated Governor George W. Bush of Texas in 2000.

Other Characteristics

Most leading contenders for presidential nominations have been Protestants. The most notable exceptions, all Democrats and all Catholics, are Alfred E. Smith in 1928, John F. Kennedy in 1960, Eugene McCarthy and Robert F. Kennedy in 1968, and Michael Dukakis (Eastern Orthodox) in 1988.

Most presidential candidates have come from the larger States. Thus, hopefuls from such pivotal States as New York, Ohio, Illinois, Texas, and California have usually been seen as more electable than candidates from smaller States.

Television has reshaped this matter over the past several elections, however. The Republicans picked Barry Goldwater of Arizona in 1964 and Bob Dole of Kansas in 1996. And the Democrats nominated George McGovern of South Dakota in 1972, Jimmy Carter of Georgia in 1976, and Bill Clinton of Arkansas in 1992 and 1996.

Both parties' nominees usually have a pleasant and healthy appearance, seem to be happily married, and have an attractive (and exploitable) family. To this point, only three nominees have been divorced: Adlai Stevenson, the Democratic nominee in 1952 and 1956; Ronald Reagan, the Republican candidate in 1980 and 1984; and Bob Dole, the Republicans' choice in 1996.

A well-developed speaking ability has always been a major factor of availability (electability) in American politics. Of course, being able to project well over television has become a must, as well.

Neither party has, to this point, seriously considered a woman as its candidate for the presidency—or, until 1984 with the Democratic Party's nomination of Geraldine Ferraro, for the vice presidency. Nor has either party yet nominated a member of any minority group for President, although the Democrats nominated an Orthodox Jew, Senator Joseph Lieberman of Connecticut, for Vice President in 2000.

Section 4 Assessment

Key Terms and Main Ideas

1. What are the two major processes used to select delegates to **national conventions?**
2. How does **proportional representation** differ from the **winner-take-all** system?
3. Why are hard-fought **presidential primaries** fairly common in the party out of power and rare for the President's party?

Critical Thinking

4. **Expressing Problems Clearly** As you have read, some critics of the current primary system favor a series of regional primaries held at two- or three-week intervals. What might be the advantages and disadvantages of such a system?

5. **Demonstrating Reasoned Judgment** Presidential contender Adlai Stevenson once said "The hardest thing about any political campaign is how to win without proving that you are unworthy of winning." What do you think he meant?

Take It to the Net

6. Read about the history of presidential campaign advertising and the ads that ran during a recent primary season. Based on this information and campaign ads you have seen, write a letter to an advertising agency describing the types of ads you think should be made for future campaigns. Use the links provided in the Social Studies area at the following Web site for help in completing this activity. **www.phschool.com**

★ ★ ★ ★ ★ ★ ★ ★ ★ ★ ★ ★ ★ ★ ★ ★ ★ ★ ★ ★

SKILLS FOR LIFE

TECHNOLOGY

CITIZENSHIP

CRITICAL THINKING

CHARTS and GRAPHS

Making Decisions

In 1962, U.S. intelligence reports revealed that the Soviet Union was building missile bases in Cuba. An infuriated President John F. Kennedy had to decide how to respond to this new nuclear threat in America's backyard.

President Kennedy summoned his top national security and military advisors to discuss the crisis. What followed is an example of the decision-making process:

1. Identify the issue to be decided. The first step in good decision making is to figure out *whether* a decision is needed and to clarify *what* ultimately needs to be decided. Reports of the Soviet activity in Cuba immediately raised two questions:

(a) Should the United States respond?

(b) If so, how can the Soviet Union be made to withdraw its arsenal without triggering a catastrophic nuclear war?

The two superpowers already had scores of long-range nuclear weapons aimed at each other's cities. Yet Kennedy felt that the Cuba buildup required a swift response. Why do you think he felt that strong action was needed?

2. Gather information. In a memo, National Security Advisor McGeorge Bundy outlined President Kennedy's orders on how to proceed. Read the excerpts from the memo, above right. What part instructs the staff to collect more information on the situation?

3. Identify options. A decision requires choosing among two or more options. What part of the memo concerns identifying options?

4. Predict consequences. What part of the memo concerns predicting consequences of various courses of action?

5. Make a decision. On October 22, President Kennedy announced his decision to launch a naval blockade of Cuba to prevent more missiles from reaching the island. Tense days followed, as the

THE WHITE HOUSE

WASHINGTON

TOP SECRET AND SENSITIVE

August 23, 1962

NATIONAL SECURITY ACTION MEMORANDUM NO. 181

To: Secretary of State / Secretary of Defense / Attorney General / Acting Director, CIA / General Taylor

The President has directed that the following actions and studies be undertaken in the light of the new . . . activity in Cuba. . . .

5. An analysis should be prepared of the probable military, political, and psychological impact of the establishment in Cuba of either surface-to-air missiles or surface-to-surface missiles which could reach the U.S.

6. A study should be made of the advantages and disadvantages of making a statement that the U.S. would not tolerate the establishment of military forces . . . which might launch a nuclear attack from Cuba against the U.S.

7. A study should be made of the various military alternatives which might be adopted in executing a decision to eliminate any installations in Cuba. . . . What would be the pros and cons, for example of pinpoint attack, general counter-force attack, and outright invasion.

8. A study should be made of the advantages and disadvantages of action to liberate Cuba by blockade or invasion or other action . . . .

—Memo from National Security Advisor McGeorge Bundy

superpowers came to the brink of nuclear war. In the end, the Soviets backed down, called back their ships, and dismantled the Cuban bases. Why do you think the President chose the option of blockading Cuba?

Test for Success

Make a decision-making chart on the Cuban Missile Crisis. Identify two or more courses of action that President Kennedy could have taken, and describe the possible consequences (pro and con) of each course of action.

5 The Election

Section Preview

OBJECTIVES

1. **Understand** the function of the electoral college today.
2. **Describe** the flaws in the electoral college.
3. **Outline** the advantages and disadvantages of proposed reforms of the electoral college.

WHY IT MATTERS

Most people do not understand the workings of the electoral college system. They do not understand that, no matter what the popular vote results may be, the electoral votes determine the outcome of a presidential election.

POLITICAL DICTIONARY

★ **district plan**
★ **proportional plan**
★ **direct popular election**
★ **electorate**
★ **national bonus plan**

The presidential campaign—the all-out effort to win the votes of the people—begins soon after the conventions. Each candidate's campaign organization works to present its candidate in the best possible light. Voters are bombarded by radio and television speeches; "whistle-stop" tours; press conferences and press releases; public rallies; party dinners; newspaper, radio, and television advertisements; stickers and buttons; placards and pamphlets; billboards and matchcovers; Web sites and e-mail. The candidates pose for hundreds of photographs and shake thousands of hands as each of them tries to convince the people that he is best for the country.

The presidential campaign ends on election day. Millions of voters go to the polls in all 50 States and the District of Columbia. But the President, whoever that is to be, is not formally elected until the presidential electors cast their votes, several weeks later.

The Electoral College Today

You have arrived at one of the least understood parts of the American political process. As the people vote in the presidential election, they do not cast a vote directly for one of the contenders for the presidency. Instead, they vote to elect presidential electors.

Remember, the Constitution provides for the election of the President by the electoral college, in which each State has as many electors as it has members of Congress. The Framers expected the electors to use their own judgment in selecting a President. But today the electors, once chosen, are really just "rubber stamps." They are expected to vote automatically for their party's candidates for President and Vice President. In short, the electors go through the form set out in the Constitution in order to meet the letter of the Constitution, but their behavior is a far cry from its original intent.

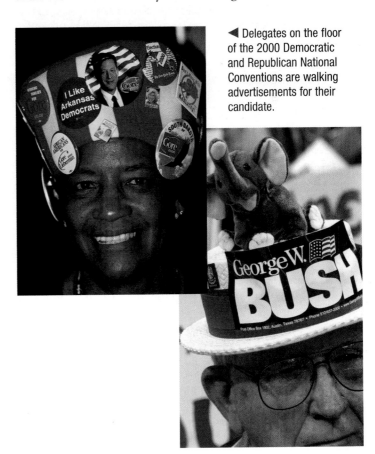

◀ Delegates on the floor of the 2000 Democratic and Republican National Conventions are walking advertisements for their candidate.

Choosing Electors

The electors are chosen by popular vote in every State[24] and on the same day everywhere: the Tuesday after the first Monday in November every fourth year. So the next presidential election will be held on November 2, 2004. In every State except Maine and Nebraska, the electors are chosen at-large.[25] That is, they are chosen on a winner-take-all basis. The presidential candidate—technically, the slate of elector-candidates nominated by his party—receiving the largest popular vote in a State regularly wins all of that State's electoral votes.

Today, the names of the individual elector-candidates appear on the ballot in only a handful of States. In most States, only the names of the presidential and vice-presidential candidates are listed. They stand as "shorthand" for the elector slates.

[24]The Constitution (Article II, Section 1, Clause 2) says that the electors are to be chosen in each State "in such Manner as the Legislature thereof may direct." In several States the legislatures themselves chose the electors in the first several elections. By 1832, however, every State except South Carolina had provided for popular election. The electors were picked by the legislature in South Carolina through the elections of 1860. Since then, all presidential electors have been chosen by popular vote in every State, with two exceptions. The State legislatures chose the electors in Florida in 1868 and in Colorado in 1876.

Counting Electoral Votes

The Constitution provides that the date Congress sets for the electors to meet "shall be the same throughout the United States."[26] The 12th Amendment provides that "the electors shall meet in their respective states." The electors thus meet at their State capitol on the date set by Congress, now the Monday after the second Wednesday in December. There they each cast their electoral votes, one for President and one for Vice President. The electors' ballots, signed and sealed, are sent by registered mail to the president of the Senate in Washington.

Which party has won a majority of the electoral votes, and who then will be the next President of the United States, is usually known by midnight of election day, more than a month before the electors cast their ballots. But the

[25]Maine (beginning in 1972) and Nebraska (1992) use the "district plan." In those States, two electors are chosen from the State at-large and the others are picked in each of the State's congressional districts. The district plan was used by several States in the first few presidential elections, but every State except South Carolina had provided for the choice of the electors from the State at large by 1832. Since then, the district plan has been used only by Michigan in 1892 and by Maine and Nebraska.

[26]Article II, Section 1, Clause 4

The Presidential Election Process

January–June
Primaries In States with presidential primaries, voters select their party's national convention delegates and/or express a preference among the candidates.

Caucuses In States with caucuses, voters in local meetings choose delegates to conventions at the congressional district or State levels—where national convention delegates are picked.

| January | February | March | April | May | June | July | August |

July–August
National Conventions Delegates choose the presidential and vice presidential nominees for each major party.

Interpreting Charts The Framers of the Constitution established the electoral college to allow the most capable citizens in each State to select the President. *Is that how that electoral process works today? Why or why not?*

formal election of the President and Vice President finally takes place on January 6.[27]

On that date, the president of the Senate opens the electoral votes from each State and counts them before a joint session of Congress. The candidate who receives a majority of the electors' votes for President is declared elected, as is the candidate with a majority of the votes for Vice President.

If no candidate has won a majority—at least 270 of the 538 electoral votes today—the election is thrown into the House of Representatives. This happened in 1800 and again in 1824. The House chooses a President from among the top three candidates in the electoral college. Each State delegation has one vote, and it takes a majority of 26 to elect. If the House fails to choose a President by January 20, the 20th Amendment provides that the newly elected Vice President shall act as President until a choice is made.[28]

If no person receives a majority of votes for Vice President, the Senate decides between the top two candidates. It takes a majority of the whole Senate to elect. The Senate has had to choose a Vice President only once, when it elected Richard M. Johnson in 1837.

Flaws in the Electoral College

The electoral college system is plagued by three major defects: (1) the winner of the popular vote is not guaranteed the presidency; (2) electors are not required to vote in accord with the popular vote; and (3) any election might have to be decided in the House of Representatives.

The First Major Defect

There is the ever-present threat that the winner of the popular vote will not win the presidency. This continuing danger is largely the result of two factors. The most important is the winner-take-all feature of the electoral college system. That is, the winning candidate customarily receives all of a State's electoral votes. Thus in 2000 George W.

---

[27]If that day falls on a Sunday, as it did most recently in 1985 (but will not again until 2013), then the ballot-counting is held the following day.

[28]The 20th Amendment further provides that "the Congress may by law provide for the case wherein neither a President-elect nor a Vice President-elect shall have qualified" by inauguration day. Congress has done so in the Succession Act of 1947; see Section 2. The Speaker of the House would "act as President ... until a President or Vice President shall have qualified."

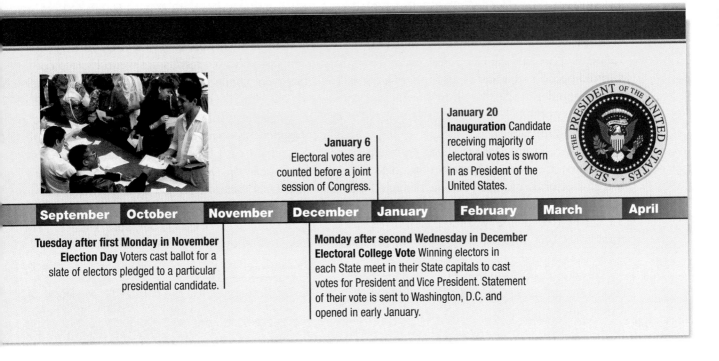

| | | | | **January 6** Electoral votes are counted before a joint session of Congress. | | **January 20** **Inauguration** Candidate receiving majority of electoral votes is sworn in as President of the United States. | | | |
| **September** | **October** | **November** | **December** | **January** | **February** | **March** | **April** |

Tuesday after first Monday in November Election Day Voters cast ballot for a slate of electors pledged to a particular presidential candidate.

Monday after second Wednesday in December Electoral College Vote Winning electors in each State meet in their State capitals to cast votes for President and Vice President. Statement of their vote is sent to Washington, D.C. and opened in early January.

Electoral Votes of Each State, 2004

SOURCE: *U.S. Census Bureau*

Interpreting Maps This pictogram shows the number of electoral votes each State will have in the 2004 election. *Why are those states in which the election outcome is doubtful called "pivotal" States?*

Bush won 49.99 percent of the popular vote in Ohio. Still, he won all of that State's 13 electoral votes—even though some 2.3 million Ohioans voted for Democrat Al Gore and another 118,000 voted for the Green Party's Ralph Nader.

The other major culprit here is the way the electoral votes are distributed among the States. Remember, two of the electors in each State are allotted because of a State's Senate seats, regardless of population. So the allotment of electoral votes does not match the facts of population and voter distribution.

Take the extreme case to illustrate this point: California, the country's most populous State, has 55 electoral votes, one for each 615,848 persons in the State, based on its 2000 population of 33,871,698 residents. Wyoming has three electoral votes, one for each 164,594 persons, based on its 2000 population of 493,782 residents.

The popular vote winner has, in fact, failed to win the presidency four times: in 1824, 1876, 1888, and most recently in 2000. In 1824, Andrew Jackson won the largest share (a plurality, but not a majority) of the popular votes: 151,271, or 41.3 percent of the total. Jackson's nearest rival, John Quincy Adams, received

113,122 votes, or 30.9 percent. Ninety-nine of the 261 electors then voted for Jackson, again more than any other candidate but far short of a majority. The election thus went to the House and, early in 1825, it elected Adams to the presidency.

In the election of 1876, Republican candidate Rutherford B. Hayes received 4,034,311 popular votes and his Democratic opponent, Samuel J. Tilden, won 4,288,546. Tilden received 184 electoral votes. Hayes won 185 electoral votes and so became President.[29]

In 1888 President Grover Cleveland won 5,534,488 popular votes, 90,596 more than his Republican opponent, Benjamin Harrison. Harrison, however, received 233 electoral votes to Cleveland's 168, and so became the 23rd President.

In the most recent presidential election, the Democratic candidate, Vice President Al Gore, won 50,992,335 popular votes—537,179 more votes than his Republican opponent, then-Governor of Texas, George W. Bush. However, Mr. Bush received 271 electoral votes—one more than the bare majority in the electoral college, and so he became the nation's 43rd President.

Florida's 25 electoral votes proved to be decisive in the extraordinarily close 2000 election. The popular vote results in several Florida counties were challenged immediately after the polls closed there. The next five weeks were filled with partisan infighting, several recounts, and a number of court disputes. The United States Supreme Court finally brought an end to the bitter contest on December 12. It ruled, in *Bush* v. *Gore*, that the differing ways in which various counties were recounting votes violated the 14th Amendment's Equal Protection Clause. The Court's 5–4 decision ended those recounts. It also

---

[29]The election of 1876 is often called the "Stolen Election." Two conflicting sets of electoral votes were received from Florida (4 votes), Louisiana (8 votes), and South Carolina (7 votes), and the validity of one vote from Oregon was disputed. Congress set up an Electoral Commission with five senators, five representatives, and five Supreme Court justices to decide the matter. The Commissioners, eight Republicans and seven Democrats, voted on strict party lines, awarding all of the disputed votes, and so the presidency, to Hayes.

preserved George W. Bush's 537-vote lead in the Statewide count and, in effect, gave him Florida's 25 electoral votes. The Court's split decision in *Bush* v. *Gore* remains highly controversial.

Altogether, 15 Presidents have been elected who did not receive a majority of the popular vote. As you have just seen, four won despite the fact that their opponents received more popular votes than they did. Eleven others have won office with a *plurality*, but not a majority, of the popular vote. These "minority Presidents" were James K. Polk (1844), Zachary Taylor (1848), James Buchanan (1856), Abraham Lincoln (1860), James A. Garfield (1880), Grover Cleveland (1884, 1892), Woodrow Wilson (1912, 1916), Harry S Truman (1948), John F. Kennedy (1960), Richard Nixon (1968), Bill Clinton (1992, 1996), and George W. Bush (2000).

By now, you see the point: The "winner-take-all" factor produces an electoral vote that is, at best, only a distorted reflection of the popular vote.

The Second Major Defect

Nothing in the Constitution, nor in any federal statute, requires the electors to vote for the candidate favored by the popular vote in their States. Several States do have such laws, but they are of doubtful constitutionality, and none has ever been enforced.

The electors are expected to vote for the candidate who carries their State and, as loyal members of their parties, they almost always do. Thus far, electors have "broken their pledges"—voted for someone other than their party's presidential nominee—on only nine occasions: in 1796, 1820, 1948, 1956, 1960, 1968, 1972, 1976, and 1988. In 2000, one elector from the District of Columbia refused to cast her vote for someone for President. Had that vote been cast, it would have gone to Al Gore. The elector said she acted as she did to protest the fact that the District of Columbia is not represented in Congress.

In no case has the vote of a "faithless elector" had a bearing on the outcome of a presidential election. But potential is certainly there.

The Third Major Defect

In any presidential election, it is possible that the contest will be decided in the House. This has happened only twice, and not since 1824. In several other elections, however—especially in 1912, 1924, 1948, and 1968—a strong third-party bid has threatened to make it impossible for either major party candidate to win a majority in the electoral college.

In 1968, George Wallace, the American Independent Party candidate, won five States and 46 electoral votes. If Democrat Hubert Humphrey had carried Alaska, Delaware, Missouri, Nevada, and Wisconsin—States where Richard Nixon's margin was thin and in which Wallace had a substantial vote—Nixon's electoral vote would have been 268, Humphrey's 224. Neither would have had a majority. The House would then have had to decide the election.

Three serious objections can be raised regarding election by the House. First, the voting in such cases is by States, not by individual members. A State with a small population, such as Alaska or Nevada, would have as much weight as the most populous State. Second, if the representatives from a State were so divided that no candidate was favored by a majority, the State would lose its vote. Third, the

Popular Vote vs. Electoral Vote				
States	**Popular Vote**	**% Popular Vote**	**Electoral Vote**	**% of Total National Electoral Vote**
Florida				
Bush	2,912,790	48.85	25	4.6
Gore	2,912,253	48.84		
Nader	97,488	1.63		
Iowa				
Bush	634,373	48.22		
Gore	638,517	48.54	7	1.3
Nader	29,374	2.23		
New Mexico				
Bush	286,417	47.85		
Gore	286,783	47.91	5	.09
Nader	21,251	3.55		
Oregon				
Bush	713,577	46.52		
Gore	720,342	46.96	7	1.3
Nader	77,357	5.04		

SOURCE: Federal Election Commision

Interpreting Tables This table shows the election results in the four States where the 2000 presidential race was the closest. *(a) How do these results illustrate the significance of the "winner-take-all" factor? (b) How did Ralph Nader's third-party candidacy affect these results?*

Constitution requires a majority of the States for election in the House—today, 26 States. If a strong third-party candidate were involved, there is a real possibility that the House could not make a decision by Inauguration Day.[30]

Proposed Reforms

Observers have long recognized the defects in the electoral college system. In fact, constitutional amendments to change the process have been introduced in every term of Congress since 1789. Most of the reforms people have offered fall under three headings: the district plan, the proportional plan, and direct popular election.

The District Plan

Over time, many people have proposed the **district plan,** in which the electors would be chosen in each State in the same way as members of Congress. That is, two electors would be chosen from the State at large, and they would cast their electoral votes in line with the result of the Statewide popular vote. The other electors would be elected, separately, in each of the State's congressional districts. Their votes would be cast in accord with the result of the popular vote in their district.[31]

The district plan would do away with the winner-take-all problem in the present system. Its supporters have argued that it would make the electoral vote a more accurate reflection of the popular returns.

The strongest argument against the plan is that it would not eliminate the possibility that the loser of the popular vote could still win the electoral vote. In fact, had it been in effect in 1960, Richard Nixon would have received 278 electoral votes, and he, not John Kennedy, would have won the presidency. Had the plan been in place in 2000, George W. Bush would have won 288 electoral votes.

Further, the results under the district plan would depend very much on how the congressional districts were drawn in each State. Its use would be yet another motive for gerrymandering.

The Proportional Plan

Under the **proportional plan,** each presidential candidate would receive the same share of a State's electoral vote as he or she received in the State's popular vote. Thus, if a candidate won 40 percent of the votes cast in a State with 20 electoral votes, he or she would get 8 of that State's electoral votes.

This plan would cure the winner-take-all problem and eliminate faithless electors. It also would yield an electoral vote more in line with the popular vote, at least for each State.

The proportional plan would not necessarily produce the same result nationally. Because each of the smaller States is overweighted by its two Senate-based electors, the proportional plan would still make it possible for the loser of the popular vote to win the presidency in the electoral vote. In fact, this would have happened in 1896. William Jennings Bryan would have defeated William McKinley, although McKinley had a comfortable popular vote margin of 596,985 (4.3 percent).[32]

Many critics of the proportional plan worry about its effect on the two-party system. Certainly, its adoption would bring an increase in the number and vigor of minor parties. They would no longer need to win entire States in order to get electoral votes. In addition, their candidates would regularly win at least some share of the electoral vote. Then the odds that a presidential election would have to go to the House would be increased.

Most of the plan's backers agree that an increase in minor party clout would mean that the winner of the popular vote would often fail to gain a clear majority of the electoral vote. Hence, advocates of this plan would lower the

---

[30]In such a case, Section 3 of the 20th Amendment states that "the Vice President-elect shall act as President until a President shall have qualified." If no Vice President-elect is available, the Presidential Succession Act would come into play. Note that it is even mathematically possible for the minority party in the House to have control of a majority of the individual State delegations. That party could then elect its candidate, even though he or she may have run second or even third in both the popular and the electoral vote contests.

[31]Maine and Nebraska now use the district plan, as noted earlier. Any other State could do so, but it would take a constitutional amendment to make its use mandatory in all States.

---

[32]In the closest of all the presidential elections, Winfield S. Hancock would have defeated James A. Garfield in 1880, even though Garfield had a popular plurality of only 1,898 votes, 0.0213 percent. On the other hand, there would have been no "Stolen Election" in 1876, and Cleveland would have defeated Harrison in 1888.

present requirement of a majority of the electoral votes to a plurality of at least 40 percent. If no candidate won 40 percent of the electoral votes, the two frontrunners would face one another in a runoff election.

Direct Popular Election

The most common and widely supported proposal is the most obvious one: Do away with the electoral college system altogether and allow **direct popular election** of the President. The arguments for direct election seem overpowering. The strongest one is that it would support the democratic ideal: Each vote would count equally in the national result. The winner would always be the majority or plurality choice. The dangers and confusions of the present system would be eliminated, replaced by a simple and easily understood process.

The fact that the loser of the popular vote nevertheless won the presidency in the most recent election has given added weight to the case of direct election. Several obstacles stand in the way of the reform, however.[33]

The constitutional amendment process itself is a major stumbling block. It is time-consuming, difficult, and cumbersome. Second, the smaller States are greatly overrepresented in the electoral college. They would lose that advantage in a direct election. It is likely that enough senators or representatives of small States would oppose a direct election amendment to kill it.

Some opponents argue that direct election would weaken the federal system because the States, as States, would lose their role in the choice of a President. Others believe that direct election would put too great a load on the election process. They say that because every vote cast in each State would count in the national result, the candidates would have to campaign strenuously in every State. The impact that

Interpreting Political Cartoons *What details in the cartoon suggest that the electoral college is one of the most complex parts of the political process?*

would have on campaign time, effort, and finances would be huge and, opponents argue, probably unmanageable.[34]

Some say that direct election would spur ballot-box stuffing and other forms of voting fraud. That, they predict, would lead to lengthy, bitter, highly explosive post-election challenges.

In many States, a State-wide election often hangs on the behavior of a specific group in the **electorate**—the mass of people who can cast votes in an election. The result depends on how those voters cast their ballots or, even more importantly, on how heavily they do or do not turn out to vote. Thus, for example, the African American vote in Chicago is often decisive in the presidential election in Illinois. In a direct election, these groups would not hold the balance of power they now have, so many of them oppose the direct election plan.

Given all this and despite the current efforts on behalf of direct election, there seems little real chance that that reform will become fact any time soon.

[33]The House of Representatives did approve a direct election amendment by the necessary two-thirds vote in 1969. A Senate filibuster killed the measure in 1970. President Carter championed a similar proposal, but it was rejected by a Senate floor vote in 1979.

[34]In fact, it is possible for a candidate to win the presidency by carrying only the 11 largest States, because they now have a total of 271 electoral votes, one more than the minimum number needed to win the presidency.

The National Bonus Plan

Another and very different plan, called the **national bonus plan,** has recently surfaced. At first glance, the plan seems quite complicated and "off the wall." In fact, it is neither.

The national bonus plan would keep much of the electoral college system intact, especially its winner-take-all feature. It would weight that feature in favor of the winner of the popular vote, however.

Under this plan, a national pool of 102 electoral votes would be awarded, automatically, to the winner of the popular vote. This bloc of electoral votes would be added to the electoral votes that the candidate won in the election. If all those votes added up to a majority of the electoral college—at least 321—the candidate would win the presidency. In the unlikely event that they did not add up to a majority, a runoff election between the two front runners in the popular vote would then be held.

The advocates of this plan see the electors themselves as unnecessary, and so would do away with them. They say that their plan meets all of the major objections to the present system and all of those raised against the other proposals for its reform. They also claim that their plan would almost guarantee that the winner of the popular vote would always be the winner of the electoral vote.

To date, the national bonus plan has not attracted much public attention. Nor has it attracted much understanding, interest, or support.

Electoral College Supporters

Their case is not often heard, but the present electoral college system does have its defenders. They react to the several proposed reforms by raising the various objections you have just read. Beyond that they argue that critics exaggerate the "dangers" in the present system. Only two elections have ever gone to the House of Representatives and none in more than 175 years. They grant the point that the loser of the popular vote has in fact won the presidency four times. But, they note, that has happened *only* four times over the course of now 54 presidential elections; and they add, it has happened only once in the last 120 years.

Supporters also say that the present arrangement, whatever its warts, has two major strengths:

1. It is a known process. Each of the proposed, but untried, reforms may very well have defects that could not be known until they appeared in practice.

2. In most cases, it identifies the winner quickly and certainly. With the exception of the 2000 election, the nation does not have to wait for very long to know the outcome.

Section 5 Assessment

Key Terms and Main Ideas

1. How does the way the electoral college functions today differ from the Framers' intentions?
2. What are the three main weaknesses of the electoral college system?
3. Explain the **district plan,** the **proportional plan,** the **direct popular election plan,** and the **national bonus plan** for reforming the electoral college.
4. What are the arguments for and against **direct popular election?**

Critical Thinking

5. **Identifying Alternatives** Suppose you have been asked to draft a plan for reforming the electoral college. Choose one of the methods discussed in this section, or write one of

your own. Explain how your plan will work and why it is superior to other proposed plans.
6. **Expressing Problems Clearly (a)** How it is possible for the winner of the popular vote to fail to win the presidency? **(b)** How do you think the Framers might reply to this defect in the electoral college system?

 Take It to the Net

7. Read more about the electoral college today. Then plan a debate in which you argue for or against keeping the present system. Include at least three arguments in defense of your position. Use the links provided in the Social Studies area at the following Web site for help in completing this activity. www.phschool.com

May the President Be Sued?

The Constitution contains no specific protection of the President against lawsuits. What kind of protection is appropriate for the President? Are all his actions protected, or only those that are taken in good faith and fall within the scope of his official duties?

Nixon v. Fitzgerald (1982)

In November 1968, A. Ernest Fitzgerald, a management analyst with the Department of the Air Force, revealed in testimony before Congress that development of the Air Force's C-5A transport plane would cost about $2 billion more than had been predicted. He also disclosed unexpected technical problems that had developed with the plane.

Just over a year later, in January of 1970, Fitzgerald's department was reorganized and he was laid off, along with some other employees. Fitzgerald complained to the Civil Service Commission, which found that he had been terminated for "purely personal" reasons but not in retaliation for his testimony. Fitzgerald then sued various Defense Department officials and White House aides who, he said, were responsible for his firing.

Fitzgerald later named President Richard M. Nixon as a defendant in his suit because Fitzgerald believed that the President had played a direct role in his firing. Nixon argued that as President, he had absolute immunity—complete protection—against lawsuits over actions he took while in office. The trial court and then the court of appeals both rejected this immunity defense. Nixon then appealed to the Supreme Court, which had never before ruled on the question of how far a President's immunity against lawsuits extended.

Arguments for Nixon

1. The President occupies a unique position under our Constitution, because he serves as chief executive, policymaker, and law enforcement official. For the President to have to deal with private lawsuits as well would harm the effective operation of our government.

2. Judges and prosecutors have received absolute immunity in order to allow them to deal "fearlessly and impartially" with their official duties. The President should receive similar protection.

3. The President's immunity should cover all of his official functions. Otherwise, courts would have to review his motives in each case in order to determine whether particular actions were covered by the immunity.

Arguments for Fitzgerald

1. Past Supreme Court cases have granted governors and Cabinet officials only partial immunity from lawsuits, which protects them only for actions taken in good faith.

2. If the President did in fact order the firing of an employee who was lawfully entitled to retain his job, then he acted outside the boundary of his proper duties and should be subject to a lawsuit for his actions.

3. Absolute immunity would place the President above the law.

Decide for Yourself

1. Review the constitutional grounds on which each side based its arguments and the specific arguments each side presented.

2. Debate the opposing viewpoints presented in this case. Which viewpoint do you favor?

3. Predict the impact of the Court's decision on other situations in which a President might be sued. (To read a summary of the Court's decision, turn to the Supreme Court Glossary on page 799.)

Political Dictionary

chief of state (p. 354)	Presidential Succession Act	national convention (p. 372)
chief executive (p. 354)	of 1947 (p. 360)	platform (p. 373)
chief administrator (p. 355)	balance the ticket (p. 362)	keynote address (p. 373)
chief diplomat (p. 355)	presidential electors (p. 365)	district plan (p. 382)
commander in chief (p. 355)	electoral votes (p. 365)	proportional plan (p. 382)
chief legislator (p. 355)	electoral college (p. 366)	direct popular election (p. 383)
chief of party (p. 355)	presidential primary (p. 369)	electorate (p. 383)
chief citizen (p. 355)	winner-take-all (p. 371)	national bonus plan (p. 384)
presidential succession (p. 359)	proportional representation (p. 371)	

Practicing the Vocabulary

Matching *Choose a term from the list above that best matches each description.*

1. The group chosen every four years to make the formal selection of the President and Vice President
2. The role in which the President exercises leadership over his or her political party
3. The role in which the President acts as the main architect of the nation's public policies
4. An election at which a party's voters choose delegates to the party's national convention and/or express a preference for candidates for the party's nomination
5. All the people entitled to vote in a given election

Word Recognition *Replace the underlined definition with the correct term from the list above.*

6. In the past, some presidential primaries were <u>contests in which the winner of the preference vote won the support of all the delegates</u>.
7. As <u>the representative of all the people</u>, the President speaks for the people of the nation and offers important moral leadership.
8. As <u>the head of a large organization that employs nearly three million people</u>, the President leads one of the world's largest governmental machines.
9. The <u>written declaration of principles and policy decisions</u> of a party is an important product of each national convention.
10. The <u>speech given at a party convention to set the tone for the convention and the campaign to come</u> is usually delivered by one of the party's best orators.

Reviewing Main Ideas

Section 1

11. Explain the significance of each of the following presidential roles: chief executive, chief diplomat, commander in chief.
12. **(a)** What is the origin of the no-third-term tradition? **(b)** Which President broke with this tradition? **(c)** What is the maximum number of terms that today's Presidents may serve?
13. Why have some critics called for a repeal of the 22nd Amendment?

Section 2

14. How does the Constitution ensure a smooth transition of power in the event of a presidential disability?
15. Explain how the Constitution and the Presidential Succession Act of 1947 address the issue of presidential succession.
16. **(a)** How does the Constitution describe the role of the Vice President? **(b)** How does this description relate to the office's reputation?

Section 3

17. Describe the Framers' plan for the selection of the nation's President.
18. Why did the electoral college cease to function as the Framers had intended?
19. What was the purpose of the 12th Amendment?

Section 4

20. How do presidential primaries differ from the caucus-convention process?
21. For what major purposes do parties hold national conventions?
22. What have been the effects of the Democrats' proportional representation rule?

Section 5

23. **(a)** How are electors chosen for the electoral college? **(b)** How are electoral votes counted?
24. On what grounds is the electoral college system criticized?

Critical Thinking Skills

25. *Applying the Chapter Skill* Suppose the next presidential election is a week away, and you have not yet made up your mind for whom to vote. Describe the steps you should take to help you make your decision.

26. *Distinguishing False from Accurate Images* The following quotation from John Adams appeared earlier in this chapter: "I am Vice President. In this I am nothing, but I may be everything." **(a)** Explain what Adams meant. **(b)** Do you think that a modern Vice President would agree with Adams?

27. *Identifying Alternatives* Review the formal qualifications for President in Section 1. **(a)** Why do you think the Framers chose these particular qualifications? **(b)** Do you think that any of these qualifications should be changed?

28. *Understanding Point of View* Should the major parties make a special effort to recruit a presidential nominee who is a woman or a member of a minority group? Explain your answer.

Analyzing Political Cartoons

Using your knowledge of American government and this cartoon, answer the questions below.

"Hi there. I'm governor of a large State somewhere out West, and I'm running for President."

29. Why is it significant that the candidate in the cartoon is a governor of a large western state?

30. How accurate is the cartoon in portraying the qualifications necessary for a presidential candidate?

★ You Can Make a Difference

What organizations in your community provide help for children and their families who lack books, food, or clothing? Are these groups privately run or sponsored by government agencies? With your classmates, prepare a guidebook of the resources available in your community, what services they provide, and how they are funded. Organize the guide by services and location. Then look into the volunteer opportunities available for you and your friends.

Participation Activities

31. *Current Events Watch* Follow news reports of the President's activities and find examples of the President filling any four of the eight roles outlined on pages 354–355. For each of the four roles, hand in a newspaper or magazine clipping or an Internet printout of the report, along with your explanation of which roles the President is filling.

32. *Chart Activity* Create a chart showing the advantages and disadvantages of the various plans for reforming the electoral college. Include the advantages and disadvantages of keeping the current system. Which, in your opinion, are the weakest and the strongest plans?

33. *It's Your Turn* Draw a political cartoon on one of the following topics: the plight of the Vice President, the flaws of the electoral college, the many roles of the President, the Framers' view of today's election process, or a topic of your own choosing. After you have made a rough sketch, be sure that the point you want to make will be clear to your viewers. Then create a final drawing to display in your classroom. **(Drawing a Cartoon)**

 ## Take It to the Net

Chapter 13 Self-Test As a final review activity, take the Chapter 13 Self-Test in the Social Studies area at the Web site listed below, and receive immediate feedback on your answers.

www.phschool.com

CHAPTER 14

The Presidency in Action

"The President hears a hundred voices telling him that he is the greatest man in the world. He must listen carefully indeed to hear the one voice that tells him he is not."

—Harry S Truman (1964)

Presidents today do have great power—to carry out laws, make policies, choose officials, command the military, and conduct foreign affairs. The Framers gave the President certain "executive powers," which have grown greatly over time. How much power a President actually exercises depends on the person and on the times.

◆ **Vice President Dick Cheney, President George W. Bush, and Secretary of State Colin Powell**

★ You Can Make a Difference

At age 20, Dawn Smalls, a Boston University honor student, became part of the busy "nerve center" of the United States government, as assistant to the White House chief of staff. She handled complaints, answered phone calls to the President, and dealt with senators and Cabinet members. Government service was not new to Dawn, who had interned in the West Wing of the White House. She also has worked with community groups in Washington and Boston, trying to show other young African Americans that "The divide that they see between them and their government . . . is not as great as they think it is."

Keep It Current

Items marked with this logo are periodically updated on the Internet. Keep up-to-date with what's in the news. To get current information on the power of the President, go to **www.phschool.com**

SECTION 1

The Growth of Presidential Power
(pp. 390–392)

★ Article II of the Constitution created the presidency and gives the President certain expressed powers.
★ Yet Article II is remarkably brief, leaving Americans to debate whether the Framers intended the presidency to be relatively strong or weak.
★ Since the nation's founding, the power of the presidency has grown significantly.
★ The power a President exercises depends on his views about the office and how he interprets Article II.

SECTION 2

The President's Executive Powers
(pp. 393–397)

★ Article II gives the President the power and responsibility to "execute the laws."
★ This executive power gives the President a great deal of flexibility in deciding how laws are carried out.
★ Among the President's key powers are those to appoint and remove top federal officials.

SECTION 3

Diplomatic and Military Powers *(pp. 399–403)*

★ The President shares treaty-making and other powers with Congress.
★ Certain diplomatic powers may be carried out without the approval of Congress; increasingly, Presidents have made use of these powers.
★ As commander in chief of the armed forces, the President possesses almost unlimited military power.

SECTION 4

Legislative and Judicial Powers *(pp. 405–408)*

★ The Constitution gives the President important legislative and judicial powers as part of the system of checks and balances in the Federal Government.
★ The President's key legislative powers are to submit legislation for Congress to consider and to reject legislation that he opposes.
★ The Constitution gives the President several powers of clemency—powers with which he can show mercy to those convicted of federal crimes.

The Growth of Presidential Power

Section Preview

OBJECTIVES

1. **Explain** why Article II of the Constitution can be described as "an outline."
2. **List** several reasons for the growth of presidential power.
3. **Explain** how Presidents' own views have affected the power of the office.

WHY IT MATTERS

The Constitution establishes the office of the President in Article II. The interpretation of that article continues to be a battleground for people who want a powerful President and those who want to curb presidential powers.

POLITICAL DICTIONARY

★ **Executive Article**
★ **mass media**
★ **imperial presidency**

The presidency is often called "the most powerful office in the world." Is this what the Framers had in mind when they created the post in 1787? At Philadelphia, they purposely created a single executive with broad powers. They also agreed with Thomas Jefferson, who wrote in the Declaration of Independence that "a Tyrant is unfit to be the ruler of a free people." So, just as purposely, they constructed a "checked," or limited, presidency.

Article II

Article II, the Constitution's **Executive Article,** begins this way:

 "The executive Power shall be vested in a President of the United States of America. **"**

With those few words, the Framers established the presidency. The Constitution sets out other, somewhat more specific grants of presidential power as well. Thus, the President is given the power to command the armed forces, to make treaties, to approve or veto acts of Congress, to send and receive diplomatic representatives, to grant

▲ President Reagan met with Soviet leader Mikhail Gorbachev in Geneva, Switzerland, in 1985.

pardons and reprieves, and "to take Care that the Laws be faithfully executed."[1]

Still, the Constitution deals with the powers of the presidency in a very sketchy fashion. Article II reads almost as an outline. It has been called "the most loosely drawn chapter" in the nation's fundamental law. It does not define "the executive power." The other grants of presidential authority are stated in equally broad terms.

A large part of America's political history has revolved around the struggle over the meaning of the constitutional phrase "executive power." That struggle has pitted those who have argued for a weaker presidency, subordinate to Congress, against those who have pressed for a stronger, independent, co-equal chief executive.

That never-ending contest began at the Philadelphia Convention in 1787. At that time, several Framers agreed with Roger Sherman of Connecticut, who, according to James Madison,

PRIMARY Sources *"considered the executive magistracy as nothing more than an institution for carrying the will of the legislature into effect, that the person or persons [occupying the presidency] ought to be appointed by and accountable to the legislature only, which was the depository of the supreme will of the Society.* **"**

—*Notes of Debates in the Federal Convention of 1787, James Madison*

---

[1]Most of the specific grants of presidential power are found in Article II, Sections 2 and 3. A few are elsewhere in the Constitution, such as the veto power, in Article I, Section 7, Clause 2.

As you know, those who argued for a stronger executive—led by Alexander Hamilton, James Wilson, and James Madison—carried the day. They persuaded the convention to establish a single executive, chosen independently of Congress and with its own distinct powers.

Why Presidential Power Has Grown

Over the course of American history, the champions of a stronger presidency have almost always prevailed. One of the leading reasons they have is the unity of the presidency. The President is the single, commanding head of the executive branch. On the other hand, Congress consists of *two* houses. Both of them must agree on a matter before Congress can do anything. Moreover, one of those two houses is made up of 100 separately elected members, and the other has 435 of them.

Several other factors have strengthened the presidency—not least the Presidents themselves. The nation's increasingly complex social and economic life also has influenced the growth of presidential power. As the United States has become more industrialized and technologically advanced, the people have demanded that the Federal Government play a larger role in transportation, labor, civil rights, health, welfare, communication, education, the environment, and a host of other fields. Americans have looked especially to the President for leadership in these matters.

Another of these closely related factors has been the frequent need for extraordinary and decisive action in times of national emergency, most notably in times of war. The ability of the President—the single, commanding chief executive—to act in such situations has done much to strengthen the executive power.

Congress has also strengthened the presidential hand, as it has passed thousands of laws that have been an essential part of the historic growth of the Federal Government. Congress lacks the time and technical knowledge to provide more than the basic outlines of public policy. It has been forced to delegate authority to the executive branch to carry out its laws.

The President has a unique ability to attract public attention and build support for policies and actions. Every President since Franklin Roosevelt has purposely used the **mass media**—

Presidents on the Presidency

THOMAS JEFFERSON

1801–1809

"[The presidency] is a place of splendid misery."

JOHN QUINCY ADAMS

1825–1829

"The four most miserable years of my life were my four years in the presidency."

RUTHERFORD B. HAYES

1877–1881

"Nobody ever left the presidency with less regret."

JAMES A. GARFIELD

1881

"What is there in this place that a man should ever want to get into it!"

WILLIAM McKINLEY

1897–1901

"I have had all the honor there is in this place and have had responsibilities enough to kill any man."

WILLIAM H. TAFT

1909–1913

"I'm glad to be going—this is the loneliest place in the world."

WARREN G. HARDING

1921–1923

"[The presidency is] a prison."

HARRY S TRUMAN

1945–1953

"There is no exaltation in the office of the President of the United States— sorrow is the proper word."

DWIGHT D. EISENHOWER

1953–1961

"Oh, that lovely title, ex-president."

LYNDON B. JOHNSON

1963–1969

"No one can experience with the President of the United States the glory and agony of his office."

Interpreting Charts Not everyone who occupied the Oval Office has always enjoyed the job. *(a) In the quotations above, what is the common message? (b) What do you think are some of the good and bad aspects of serving as President?*

forms of communication, including printed publications, radio, television, and, most recently, the Internet—for that purpose.

The Presidential View

The nature of the presidency depends on how each President views the office and exercises its powers. Historically, Presidents have held one of two contrasting views. The stronger and more effective of them have taken a broad view of their powers—a view that Theodore Roosevelt called "the stewardship theory":

> **PRIMARY Sources** *"I declined to adopt the view that what was imperatively necessary for the Nation could not be done by the President unless he could find some specific authorization to do it. My belief was that it was not only [a President's] right but his duty to do anything that the needs of the Nation demanded unless such action was forbidden by the Constitution or by the laws. . . . I did not usurp power, but I did greatly broaden the use of executive power. In other words, I acted for the public welfare . . . unless prevented by direct constitutional or legislative prohibition."*
>
> —Theodore Roosevelt,
> *Theodore Roosevelt: An Autobiography,* 1913

Ironically, the strongest presidential statement of the opposing view came from Roosevelt's handpicked successor in the office, William Howard Taft.

> **PRIMARY Sources** *" The true view of the Executive function is, as I conceive it, that the President can exercise no power which cannot be fairly and reasonably traced to some specific grant of power or justly implied and included within such express grant. . . . Such specific grant must be either in the Federal Constitution or in an act of Congress passed in pursuance thereof. There is no undefined residuum of power which he can exercise because it seems to him to be in the public interest."*
>
> —William Howard Taft,
> *Our Chief Magistrate and His Powers,* 1916

In recent decades, critics of strong presidential power have condemned what is called the **imperial presidency.** The term paints a picture of the President as emperor, taking strong actions without consulting Congress or seeking its approval—sometimes acting in secrecy to evade or even to deceive Congress. Critics of the imperial presidency worry that Presidents have become isolated policymakers who are unaccountable to the American people through their representatives in Congress. The term *imperial presidency* has been used frequently in reference to President Richard Nixon and the political tactics that brought about his downfall.

Assertive Presidents, frustrated with the often slow pace and divided membership in Congress, have indeed taken policy matters into their own hands many times in recent history, as you will see in the sections that follow. It is a trend that has supporters as well as critics.

Section 1 Assessment

Key Terms and Main Ideas

1. Why is Article II often called the **Executive Article**?
2. Give three reasons for the growth of presidential power.
3. Summarize the two competing views of the constitutional phrase "executive power."
4. Why do some people worry about an **imperial presidency?**

Critical Thinking

5. **Understanding Point of View** Give two examples of how a President might use the mass media to influence public opinion. Do you think there are legitimate reasons for a President to do so? Explain.

6. **Making Comparisons** Compare and contrast the quotations from Presidents Roosevelt and Taft on this page. **(a)** Whose view do you favor? Why? **(b)** Which view do you think most modern Presidents have favored? Explain.

 Take It to the Net

7. Read about the President's various roles as chief executive. Then write an opinion column on how the President's power has increased or decreased over time. Use the links provided in the Social Studies area at the following Web site for help in completing this activity. **www.phschool.com**

The President's Executive Powers

Section Preview

OBJECTIVES

1. **Identify** the source of the President's power.
2. **Define** the *ordinance power,* and explain where it comes from.
3. **Explain** how the appointing power works.
4. **Summarize** the historical debate over the removal power.

WHY IT MATTERS

Much of the power of the presidency rests on the discretion the President has in the use of his powers to issue executive orders, to execute the laws, and to appoint key federal officials.

POLITICAL DICTIONARY

★ **oath of office**
★ **executive order**
★ **ordinance power**

Thomas Jefferson wrote this to a friend in 1789: "The execution of the laws is more important than the making of them." Whether Jefferson was altogether right about that or not, in this section you will see that the President's power to execute the law endows him with an enormous amount of authority.

Executing the Law

As chief executive, the President executes (enforces, administers, carries out) the provisions of federal law. The power to do so rests on two brief constitutional provisions. The first of them is the **oath of office** sworn by the President on the day he takes office:

> **FROM THE** *Constitution* **"**I do solemnly swear (or affirm) that I will faithfully execute the Office of President of the United States, and will to the best of my Ability, preserve, protect and defend the Constitution of the United States. **"**
>
> —Article II, Section 1, Clause 8

The other provision is the Constitution's command that "he shall take care that the laws be faithfully executed."[2]

The President's power to execute the law covers all federal laws. Their number, and the different subject matters they cover, nearly boggle the mind. The armed forces, social security, the minimum wage law, gun control, affirmative action, environmental protection, air traffic safety, immigration, housing, taxes—these only begin the list. There are scores of others.

The President and the President's subordinates have much to say about the meaning of the law, just as do Congress and the courts. In executing and enforcing law, the executive branch also interprets it. The Constitution requires the President to execute *all* federal laws no matter what the chief executive's own views of any of them may be. Still, the President may, and does, use some discretion as to how vigorously and in what particular way any given law will be applied in practice.

To look at the point more closely: Many laws that Congress passes are written in fairly broad

▲ President George Washington took the oath of office on this borrowed Bible on April 30, 1789.

---

[2]Article II, Section 3; this provision gives the President what is often called the "take care" power.

terms. Congress sets out the basic policies and standards. The specific details—much of the fine print necessary to the actual, day-to-day administration of the law—are usually left to be worked out by the executive branch.

For example, immigration laws require that all immigrants seeking permanent admission to this country must be able to "read and understand some dialect or language." That seems very straightforward, but what does this literacy requirement mean in everyday practice? How well must an alien be able to read and write? What words in some language must he or she know, and how many of them? The law does not say. Rather, such answers come from within the executive branch—in this case, from the Immigration and Naturalization Service in the Department of Justice.

The Ordinance Power

From what has just been said, the President clearly deserves the title of chief administrator as well as chief executive. The job of administering and applying most federal law is the day-to-day work of all of the many departments, bureaus, offices, boards, commissions, councils, and other agencies that make up the huge executive branch of the Federal Government. All of the some 2.7 million

▲ During World War II, President Franklin D. Roosevelt issued executive orders requiring gasoline and other strategic war supplies to be rationed—sold in limited quantities. *Critical Thinking Why is it important that the President have such a power, instead of Congress?*

men and women who staff those agencies are subject to the President's control and direction.

The President has the power to issue executive orders. An **executive order** is a directive, rule, or regulation that has the effect of law. The power to issue these orders, the **ordinance power,** arises from two sources: the Constitution and acts of Congress.

The Constitution does not mention the ordinance power in so many words, but that power is clearly intended. In granting certain powers to the President, the Constitution obviously anticipates their use. In order to exercise those powers, the President must have the power to issue the necessary orders, as well as the power to implement them. The President must also have the power to authorize his subordinates to issue such orders.[3]

The number, the scope, and the complexity of governmental problems has grown over the years. As a result, Congress has found it necessary to delegate more and more discretion to the President

▲ The day-to-day tasks of governing include the management of herds of wild ponies on Assateague Island, off the Virginia coast. To keep their numbers at levels the island can support, the National Park Service rounds up and sells off many of the animals each year. *Critical Thinking Why does this task fall to the executive branch?*

[3]All executive orders are published in the *Federal Register,* which appears five times a week. At least once a year, all orders currently in force are published in the *Code of Federal Regulations.* Both of these publications are issued by the National Archives and Records Administration.

and to presidential subordinates to spell out the policies and programs it has passed. Members of Congress are not, and cannot be expected to be, experts in all of the fields in which they must legislate.

The Appointment Power

A President cannot hope to succeed without loyal subordinates who support the policies of the President's administration. The Constitution provides that the President

> **FROM THE Constitution** **"**by and with the Advice and Consent of the Senate . . . shall appoint Ambassadors, other public Ministers and Consuls, Judges of the Supreme Court, and all other Officers of the United States, whose Appointments are not herein otherwise provided for[4] . . . but the Congress may by Law vest the Appointment of such inferior Officers, as they think proper, in the President alone, in the Courts of Law, or in the Heads of Departments. **"**
> —Article II, Section 2, Clause 2

Acting alone, the President names only a handful of the 2.7 million federal civilian employees. Many of that handful fill the top spots in the White House Office.

With Senate consent, the President names most of the top-ranking officers of the Federal Government. Among them are:

(1) ambassadors and other diplomats;

(2) Cabinet members and their top aides;

(3) the heads of such independent agencies as the Environmental Protection Agency and the National Aeronautics and Space Administration;

(4) all federal judges, U.S. marshals, and attorneys;

(5) all officers in the armed forces.

When the President makes one of these appointments, the nomination is sent to the Senate. There, the support of a majority of the senators present and voting is needed for confirmation.

The unwritten rule of senatorial courtesy plays an important part in this process. That rule applies to the choice of those federal officers who serve within a State—a federal district

judge or a federal marshal, for example. The rule holds that the Senate will approve only those federal appointees acceptable to the senator or senators of the President's party from the State involved. The practical effect of this custom, which is closely followed in the Senate, is to place

The Confirmation Process

For nominees who must be approved by the Senate, a multi-step process leads to their acceptance or rejection. Here are the steps involved in the confirmation of a high-level official nominated by the President, such as a Supreme Court justice.

Nomination
President's staff conducts a thorough search for a competent and acceptable candidate, getting input from key experts inside and outside of government. The President submits his choice to the Senate.

> In 1993, President Clinton nominated Ruth Bader Ginsburg (shown below), a federal Court of Appeals judge for the District of Columbia Circuit, to serve on the Supreme Court.

Senate Committee Hearings
The nomination goes to the appropriate Senate committee. The nominee testifies before the committee—a sometimes grueling process if there is strong opposition to the candidate. The committee calls other experts to testify for and against the nominee. A majority vote is needed to recommend the nominee to the Senate.

> Ginsburg's past doubts about the *Roe* v. *Wade* abortion ruling stirred initial resistance. She had favored a gradual legalization of abortion. But in the hearings she affirmed her support for abortion rights.

Senate Debate
The full Senate considers the nomination. Senators express their views before a floor vote is taken.

> The White House had consulted key senators of both parties before submitting Ginsburg's nomination. Thus, debate was minimal.

Confirmation
If a simple majority votes to approve the nominee, he or she is confirmed.

> On August 3, 1993, by a vote of 97 to 3, the Senate confirmed Ginsburg's nomination. She became the second woman ever to serve on the Supreme Court.

Rejection
If the nominee is rejected, another nomination is made. If strong opposition arises during the process, the President may withdraw the nomination or the nominee bows out to avoid the embarrassment of rejection.

Interpreting Diagrams In recent years, some nominees for top-level jobs have been subjected to bitter, hostile questioning at Senate hearings. Critics worry that the grueling process causes some talented people to shun public service. **Why, do you think, did the Framers create this multi-step process?**

---

[4]Those whose appointments are "otherwise provided for" are the Vice President, senators, representatives, and presidential electors.

a meaningful part of the President's appointing power in the hands of particular senators.

Of course, not all executive branch employees are chosen by the President and Senate. Well over half of all the federal civilian work force is selected on the basis of competitive civil service examinations. Today, the Office of Personnel Management examines applicants for some 1.7 million positions.

The Removal Power

The power to remove is the other side of the appointment coin, and it is as critically important to presidential success as the power to appoint. Yet except for mention of the little-used impeachment process,[5] the Constitution does not say how or by whom appointed officers may be dismissed, whether for incompetence, for opposition to presidential policies, or for any other cause.

The Historical Debate

The question was hotly debated in the first session of Congress in 1789. Several members argued that for those offices for which appointment required Senate approval, Senate

---

[5]Article II, Section 4.

▶ The only removal power outlined in the Constitution is presidential impeachment, the threat of which caused Richard Nixon to step down and transfer power to Gerald Ford in 1974.

consent should also be required for removal. They insisted that this restriction on presidential authority was essential to congressional supervision (oversight) of the executive branch. Others argued that the President could not "take care that the laws be faithfully executed" without a free hand to dismiss those who were incompetent or otherwise undesirable.

The latter view prevailed. The First Congress gave to the President the power to remove any officer he appointed, except federal judges. Over the years since then, Congress has sometimes tried, with little success, to restrict the President's freedom to dismiss.

One notable instance came in 1867. Locked with Andrew Johnson in the fight over Reconstruction, Congress passed the Tenure of Office Act. The law's plain purpose was to prevent President Johnson from removing several top officers in his administration, especially the secretary of war, Edwin M. Stanton. The law provided that any person holding an office by presidential appointment with Senate consent should remain in that office until a successor had been confirmed by the Senate.

The President vetoed the bill, charging that it was an unconstitutional invasion of executive authority. Johnson's veto was overridden, but he ignored Congress and fired Stanton anyway. The veto and Stanton's removal sparked the move for Johnson's impeachment. Ultimately, the President was acquitted, and the law was ignored in practice. It was finally repealed in 1887.

Removal and the Court

The question of the President's removal power did not reach the Supreme Court until *Myers* v. *United States,* 1926. In 1876, Congress had passed a law requiring Senate consent before the President could dismiss any first-class, second-class, or third-class postmaster.

In 1920, without consulting the Senate, President Woodrow Wilson removed Frank Myers as the postmaster at Portland, Oregon. Myers then sued for the salary for the rest of his four-year term. He based his claim on the point that he had been removed in violation of the 1876 law.

The Court found the law unconstitutional. The majority opinion was written by Chief Justice William Howard Taft, himself a former

President. The Court held that the power of removal was an essential part of the executive power, clearly necessary to the faithful execution of the laws.

The Supreme Court did place some limits on the President's removal power in 1935, in *Humphrey's Executor* v. *United States*. President Herbert Hoover had appointed William Humphrey to a seven-year term on the Federal Trade Commission (FTC) in 1931. When Franklin D. Roosevelt entered office in 1933, he found Humphrey to be in sharp disagreement with many of his policies. He asked Humphrey to resign, saying that his administration would be better served with someone else on the FTC. When Humphrey refused, Roosevelt removed him. Humphrey soon died, but his heirs filed a suit for back salary.

The Supreme Court upheld the heirs' claim. It based its decision on the act creating the FTC. That law provides that a member of the commission may be removed only for "inefficiency, neglect of duty, or malfeasance in office."[6] The President had given none of these reasons when he removed Humphrey.

The Court further held that Congress does have the power to set the conditions under which

---

[6]*Malfeasance* is wrongful conduct, especially by someone holding a public office.

DWANE POWELL
Courtesy News & Observer (N.C.)

Interpreting Political Cartoons Reagan's young budget director, David Stockman, cleverly and swiftly pushed through Congress severe budget cuts based on uncertain budget figures. When Stockman admitted as much in a famous magazine interview, Reagan fired him. ***How does this cartoon reflect this newsmaking episode?***

a member of the FTC and other such agencies might be removed by the President. It did so because those agencies, the independent regulatory commissions, are not purely executive agencies—a rather complicated point covered in the next chapter.

As a general rule, the President may remove those whom the President appoints. Occasionally, the President does have to remove someone. Most often, however, what was in fact a dismissal is called a "resignation."

Section 2 Assessment

Key Terms and Main Ideas

1. In taking the **oath of office,** what does the President promise to do?
2. How does the President affect the application of a law passed by Congress?
3. What is an **executive order,** and in what ways does it give the President great power?
4. What is the **ordinance power,** and where does the President get this power?
5. **(a)** Which officials does the President appoint? **(b)** What is the Senate's role in the appointment process?

Critical Thinking

6. **Making Decisions** Should the President have the sole power to remove all officials he appoints? Or should the Senate have a role in deciding whether to remove officials that it confirmed? Summarize the arguments on both sides of this debate. Then decide which side you favor, and explain why.
7. **Making Comparisons** Compare and contrast the Supreme Court rulings in *Myers* v. *United States* and *Humphrey's Executor* v. *United States*.

 Take It to the Net

8. Do Presidents make too many appointments with an eye to politics? Read an Internet article on the topic and write a brief pro or con response. Use the links provided in the Social Studies area of the following Web site for help in completing this activity. **www.phschool.com**

SKILLS FOR LIFE

CITIZENSHIP

CRITICAL THINKING

CHARTS and GRAPHS

Using Time Lines

Even if you have a fantastic memory, it's difficult to keep a lot of dates in your head in the right order. A time line lets you visualize a sequence of events so that you can see relationships among dates and events. Often a time line reveals causes and effects as well as events that recur in time.

The time line below presents key events in the presidency of Richard Nixon. Use the steps below to analyze the time line:

1. Identify the time period covered by the time line. The upper time line shown here spans the years of Richard Nixon's presidency, from his first election in 1968 to his resignation in 1974. (a) How many years does the upper time line cover? A secondary time line appears to pop out from the upper line. This lower time line magnifies in detail the events on a certain segment of the upper time line. (b) How many years does the lower time line cover?

2. Determine how the time line is divided. Most time lines are divided into equal periods, or increments, of time: years, decades, or centuries. (a) What increments of time are used in the upper line? (b) What increments are used in the lower line?
3. Study the time line to see how events are related. (a) State what content is shown in the upper time line. (b) State the content of the lower time line.
4. Use the time line to help you draw conclusions about the period you are studying. What do you think happened to Nixon's popularity between his landslide reelection and his resignation? Explain.

Test for Success

Construct a time line of your life or the life of someone you know. Make a secondary time line of a particular year or grade in school that shows some details from that period.

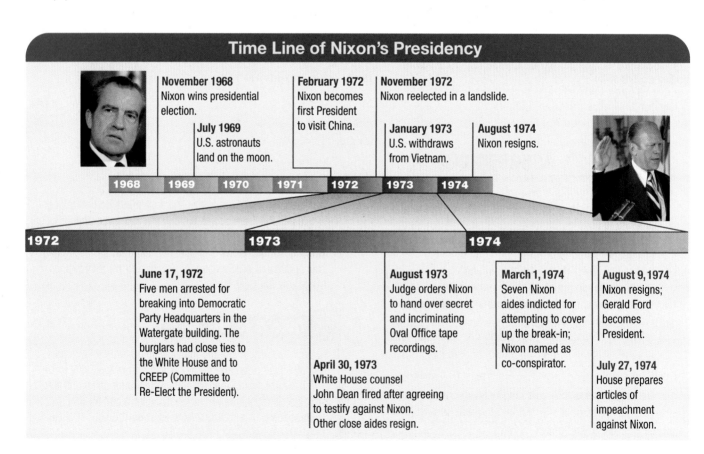

Time Line of Nixon's Presidency

November 1968
Nixon wins presidential election.

July 1969
U.S. astronauts land on the moon.

February 1972
Nixon becomes first President to visit China.

November 1972
Nixon reelected in a landslide.

January 1973
U.S. withdraws from Vietnam.

August 1974
Nixon resigns.

1968 · 1969 · 1970 · 1971 · 1972 · 1973 · 1974

1972 · 1973 · 1974

June 17, 1972
Five men arrested for breaking into Democratic Party Headquarters in the Watergate building. The burglars had close ties to the White House and to CREEP (Committee to Re-Elect the President).

April 30, 1973
White House counsel John Dean fired after agreeing to testify against Nixon. Other close aides resign.

August 1973
Judge orders Nixon to hand over secret and incriminating Oval Office tape recordings.

March 1, 1974
Seven Nixon aides indicted for attempting to cover up the break-in; Nixon named as co-conspirator.

August 9, 1974
Nixon resigns; Gerald Ford becomes President.

July 27, 1974
House prepares articles of impeachment against Nixon.

Diplomatic and Military Powers

3

OBJECTIVES

1. **Explain** how treaties are made and approved.
2. **Explain** why and how executive agreements are made.
3. **Summarize** for what purposes the power of recognition is used, and give historic examples.
4. **Describe** the powers that the President has in the role of commander in chief.

WHY IT MATTERS

The President shares various diplomatic and military powers with Congress, but in some areas the President's power is almost unlimited.

POLITICAL DICTIONARY

★ **treaty**
★ **executive agreement**
★ **recognition**
★ ***persona non grata***

John F. Kennedy once described the pressures of the presidency in these words:

PRIMARY Sources ❝ *When I ran for the presidency . . . I knew the country faced serious challenges, but I could not realize— nor could any man who does not bear the burdens of this office—how heavy and constant would be those burdens.* ❞

—President John F. Kennedy, radio and TV broadcast on the Berlin crisis, July 25, 1961

When President Kennedy made that comment, he had in mind the subject of this section: the President's awesome responsibilities as chief diplomat and as commander in chief.

The Power to Make Treaties

A **treaty** is a formal agreement between two or more sovereign states. The President, usually acting through the secretary of state, negotiates these international agreements. The Senate must give its approval, by a two-thirds vote of the members present, before a treaty made by the President can become effective. Recall, the Constitution makes treaties a part of the "supreme Law of the Land."

Contrary to popular belief, the Senate does not ratify treaties. The Constitution requires the Senate's "Advice and Consent" to a treaty made by the President. Once the Senate has approved a treaty, the President ratifies it by the exchange of formal notifications with the other party or parties to the agreement.

Treaties have the same legal standing as do acts passed by Congress. Congress may abrogate (repeal) a treaty by passing a law contrary to its provisions, and an existing law may be repealed by the terms of a treaty. When a treaty and a federal law conflict, the courts consider the latest enacted to be the law (*The Head Money Cases*, 1884). The terms of a treaty cannot conflict with the higher law of the Constitution (*Missouri* v. *Holland*, 1920), but the Supreme Court has never found a treaty provision to be unconstitutional.

▲ In 1945, the ailing President Franklin D. Roosevelt (right) undertook an ambitious trip to meet at sea with Saudi Arabia's King Ibn Saud, a key ally in the Middle East. *Critical Thinking In what way are the President's diplomatic powers among his strongest?*

Executive Agreements

Many international agreements, especially routine ones, are made as executive agreements. An **executive agreement** is a pact between the President and the head of a foreign state, or between their subordinates. Unlike treaties, executive agreements do not require Senate consent.

Most executive agreements flow out of legislation already passed by Congress or out of treaties to which the Senate has agreed. However, the President can make these executive agreements without any congressional action.[7]

A few executive agreements have been extraordinary—most notably, the destroyers-for-bases deal of 1940. That pact was struck in the first year of World War II, more than a year before the United States became directly involved in the conflict. Under its terms, the United States gave Great Britain 50 "over-age" U.S. destroyers, naval vessels that the British desperately needed to combat German submarine attacks in the North Atlantic. In return, the United States received 99-year leases to a string of air and naval bases extending from Newfoundland to the Caribbean.

The Power of Recognition

When the President receives the diplomatic representatives of another sovereign state, the President exercises the power of **recognition.** That is, the President, acting for the United States, acknowledges the legal existence of that country and its government. The President indicates that the United States accepts that country as an equal in the family of nations. Sovereign states generally recognize one another through the exchange of diplomatic representatives.[8]

Recognition does not mean that one government approves of the character and conduct of another. The United States recognizes several governments about which it has serious misgivings. Among the most notable examples today is the People's Republic of China. The facts of

▲ **The Panama Canal** Former President Jimmy Carter attended the ceremony transferring control of the Panama Canal to Panama on December 14, 1999.

The Framers considered the Senate—with, originally, only 26 members—a suitable council to advise the President in foreign affairs. Secrecy was thought to be necessary and was seen as an impossibility in a body as large as the House.

The two-thirds rule creates the possibility that a relatively small minority in the Senate can kill a treaty. Take one of the most dramatic examples: In 1920 the Senate rejected the Treaty of Versailles, the general peace agreement to end World War I. The treaty included provisions for the League of Nations. Forty-nine senators voted for the pact and 35 against, but the vote was 7 short of the necessary two thirds. More than once a President has been forced to bow to the views of a few senators in order to get a treaty approved, even when this has meant making concessions opposed by the majority.

At times, a President has had to turn to roundabout methods in order to achieve his goals. When a Senate minority defeated a treaty to annex Texas, President Tyler was able to bring about annexation in 1845 by encouraging passage of a joint resolution—a move that required only a majority vote in each house. In 1898 President McKinley used the same tactic to annex Hawaii, again after a treaty his administration had negotiated had failed in the Senate.

---

[7]The Supreme Court has held executive agreements to be as binding as treaties and to be a part of the supreme law of the land, *United States* v. *Belmont,* 1937; *United States* v. *Pink,* 1942.

[8]Recognition may be carried out by other means, such as proposing to negotiate a treaty, since under international law only sovereign states can make such agreements.

life in world politics make relations with these governments necessary.

Recognition is often used as a weapon in foreign relations, too. Prompt recognition of a new country or government may do much to guarantee its life—and withholding of recognition may seriously affect its continued existence.

President Theodore Roosevelt's quick recognition of the Republic of Panama in 1903 is a classic example of the use of the power as a diplomatic weapon. He recognized the new state less than three days after the Panamanians had begun a revolt against Colombia, of which Panama had been a part. Roosevelt's quick action guaranteed their success. Similarly, President Truman's recognition of Israel, within 24 hours of its creation in 1948, helped that new state to survive among its hostile Arab neighbors.

The President may show American displeasure with the conduct of another country by asking for the recall of that nation's ambassador or other diplomatic representatives in this country. The official recalled is declared to be *persona non grata,* an unwelcome person. The same point can be made by the recalling of an American diplomat from a post in another country. The withdrawal of recognition is the sharpest diplomatic rebuke one government may give to another and has often been a step on the way to war.

Commander in Chief

The Constitution makes the President the commander in chief of the nation's armed forces.[9] Although Congress shares the war powers,[10] the President's position in military affairs is as dominant as it is in the field of foreign affairs. In fact, it does not stretch the matter too far to say that the President's powers as commander in chief are almost without limit.

Consider this illustration of the point: In 1907 Theodore Roosevelt sent the Great White Fleet around the world. He did so partly as a training exercise for the Navy, but mostly to impress other nations with America's naval might. Several members of Congress objected to the cost and threatened to block funds for the

President's project. To this Roosevelt replied: "Very well, the existing appropriation will carry the Navy halfway around the world and if Congress chooses to leave it on the other side, all right." Congress was forced to give in.

Presidents delegate much of their command authority to military subordinates. They are not required to do so, however. George Washington actually took command of federal troops and led them into Pennsylvania during the Whiskey Rebellion of 1794. Abraham Lincoln often visited the Army of the Potomac and instructed his generals in the field during the Civil War.

Most Presidents have not become so directly involved in military operations. Still, the President always has the final authority over and responsibility for all military matters.

Making Undeclared War

Presidents have used the armed forces abroad, in combat, without a declaration of war by Congress. In fact, most Presidents have done so, and on several hundred occasions.

John Adams was the first to do so, in 1798. At his command, the Navy fought and won a number of battles with French warships that were harassing American merchantmen in the Atlantic and the Caribbean. Thomas Jefferson and then James Madison followed that precedent in the war against the Barbary Coast pirates of North Africa in the early 1800s. There have been a great many other foreign adventures over the past two centuries. The long military conflicts in Korea (from 1950 to 1953) and in Vietnam

Lincoln, Civil War, 1862

Truman, post-World War II, 1946

Johnson, Vietnam War, 1967

G.H.W. Bush, pre-Gulf War, 1990

G.W. Bush, War on Terrorism, 2001

▲ Presidents have sent the nation's armed forces into combat on hundreds of occasions. *Critical Thinking Why did the Framers choose the President, rather than a military officer, to be commander in chief?*

---

[9]Article II, Section 2, Clause 1; see also Chapter 17.
[10]Article I, Section 8, Clauses 11–17; see also Chapter 11.

Voices on Government

One of the most important roles of an American President is that of world leader and diplomat. **George W. Bush** spoke about the importance of a strong United States military during a speech at the Reagan Presidential Library in 1999, while he was still Governor of Texas.

❝*American defense . . . must be the first focus of a president, because it is his first duty to the Constitution. Even in this time of pride and promise, America has determined enemies, who hate our values and resent our success—terrorists and crime syndicates and drug cartels and unbalanced dictators. The Empire has passed, but evil remains. We must protect our homeland and our allies against missiles and terror and blackmail. We must restore the morale of our military. . . .*❞

Evaluating the Quotation

How have events during the George W. Bush presidency affected the sentiments expressed in the quotation?

(from 1965 to 1973) were until now the largest of those "undeclared wars."

The most recent presidential uses of military forces have come with the war on terrorism. They began on October 7, 2001, when President George W. Bush ordered air strikes against Afghanistan. Those attacks were aimed at destroying (1) the training camps of Osama bin Laden's al Qaida terrorist network and (2) the Taliban regime, which had harbored bin Laden and his cohorts in Afghanistan. The devastating air strikes marked the beginning of what the President has called "a sustained, comprehensive, and relentless campaign" against terrorists and every government that sponsors them.

George H. W. Bush sent the armed forces into battle twice, first in Panama in late 1989 and then into Kuwait and Iraq in early 1991. He ordered the invasion of Panama to oust dictator Manuel Noriega and to safeguard American interests there, notably the Panama Canal.

President Bush also dispatched the armed forces to the Persian Gulf region in mid-1990—as the major part of an international response to Iraq's invasion of oil-rich Kuwait. The Persian Gulf War began in January 1991, with allied air attacks on Iraqi targets in Kuwait and within Iraq itself. In late February an American-led ground attack destroyed the Iraqi army. More than 500,000 Americans saw duty in the Gulf War, and the Air Force continues to patrol the skies above Iraq today.

In 1994, President Bill Clinton used the threat of military force to restore at least the beginnings of democratic government to Haiti. In 1991 a military coup had deposed President Jean-Baptiste Aristide, the first popularly elected leader in Haiti's history. Faced with invasion by the United States, the military dictatorship collapsed.

Mr. Clinton committed military forces to the Balkans—to what was once Yugoslavia—in 1995 and again in 1999. Yugoslavia had collapsed in 1992, shattered by bitter nationalistic rivalries and by longstanding ethnic conflicts in its six individual republics. Bosnia-Herzegovina, Croatia, Macedonia, and Slovenia became independent countries. The other two pieces of the old Yugoslavia, Serbia and Montenegro, formed a new Yugoslav state dominated by Serbia.

For four years, the ethnic Serb, Muslim, and Croat factions of the Bosnian population waged vicious war against one another. That conflict was fueled by Serbia and its president, Slobodan Milosevic. Finally, American-led efforts by the North Atlantic Treaty Organization (NATO) and the UN brought a cease-fire in 1995. Serbian-backed forces in Bosnia agreed to stop fighting only in the face of threatened air strikes by the NATO countries. At that point, President Clinton ordered 20,000 American troops to Bosnia, as part of a NATO peacekeeping force. They remain on duty there today.

A long-smoldering ethnic conflict in Kosovo, a province of Serbia, erupted into full-scale civil war in late 1997. Most Kosovars are ethnic Albanians, and they had resisted Serbian control for decades. In 1998 Serbia began an "ethnic cleansing" campaign—a deliberate effort to eliminate the ethnic Albanians by expulsion and slaughter.

The Milosevic government rebuffed repeated protests by the United States and its NATO allies. Finally, in March 1999, NATO launched an air war against Serbia. A 78-day bombing campaign, by mostly American and British aircraft, and Russian influence forced the Serbs to withdraw from Kosovo. Some 10,000 U.S. troops are now part of yet another NATO peacekeeping force in what was once Yugoslavia.

Wartime Powers

The President's powers as commander in chief are far greater during a war than they are in more normal times. In fact, presidential wartime authority goes far beyond the traditional military field. During World War II, for example, Congress gave the President the power to ration food and gasoline, control wages and prices, and seize and operate private industries vital to the nation's war effort.

The President may use the armed forces to keep the domestic peace.[11] When necessary, the President also has the power to call any State's militia, or all of them, into federal service.[12]

The War Powers Resolution

In today's world, no one can doubt that the President must be able to respond rapidly and effectively to threats to this nation's security. Still,

---

[11]Article IV, Section 4.
[12]Article I, Section 8, Clause 15; Article II, Section 2, Clause 1.

many people have long warned of the dangers inherent in the President's power to involve the nation in undeclared wars. They insist that the Constitution never intended the President to have such power.

The nation's frustrations and growing anguish over the war in Vietnam finally moved Congress to pass the War Powers Resolution of 1973. The act is designed to place close limits on the President's war-making powers. President Nixon vetoed the measure, calling it "both unconstitutional and dangerous to the best interest of our nation." Congress overrode the veto.

The resolution's central provisions require that:

(1) Within 48 hours after committing American forces to combat abroad, the President must report to Congress, detailing the circumstances and the scope of his actions.

(2) Combat commitment must end within 60 days, unless Congress agrees to a longer period. That 60-day deadline may be extended for up to 30 days, however, to allow for the safe withdrawal of the American forces involved.

(3) Congress may end the combat commitment at any time, by passing a concurrent resolution to that effect.

The constitutionality of the War Powers Resolution remains in dispute. A determination of the question must await a situation in which Congress demands that its provisions be obeyed but the President refuses to do so.

Section 3 Assessment

Key Terms and Main Ideas

1. Summarize the process by which treaties are negotiated and approved.
2. What is the difference between a **treaty** and an **executive agreement**?
3. Explain this statement: *The President's power of recognition can be used positively or negatively.*
4. Under what circumstances might the President declare a country's diplomat to be **persona non grata?**
5. Which of the President's powers is almost unlimited? Why?

Critical Thinking

6. **Making Inferences** Why might a new country eagerly seek diplomatic recognition from the United States?

7. **Drawing Conclusions** Framer George Mason said, "The purse and the sword must never be in the same hands." How is this idea reflected in the War Powers Resolution?

 Take It to the Net

8. Read an online discussion of the use of executive agreements and treaties. Create bar charts showing the number of executive agreements made and treaties made in three time periods: (1) the first 50 years after independence (1776–1826); (2) from that early period, up to World War II (1827–1940); and (3) recent decades (1941 to date). **a)** What trend do the graphs show? **(b)** What are some reasons for the trend? Use the links provided in the Social Studies area at the following Web site for help in completing this activity. **www.phschool.com**

The Monroe Doctrine

In the early 1800s, Spain's Central and South American colonies rebelled and gained their independence. U.S. leaders applauded these successful revolutions, but worried that Spain and its allies would reconquer the region. In 1823, President James Monroe discussed these concerns in a message to Congress. That part of his address, known as the Monroe Doctrine, became a cornerstone of American foreign policy.

The occasion has been judged proper for asserting, as a principle in which the rights and interests of the United States are involved, that the American continents, by the free and independent condition which they have assumed and maintain, are henceforth not to be considered as subjects for future colonization by any European powers. . . .

United States military might upholds the Monroe Doctrine against European powers in this early twentieth-century cartoon.

In the wars of the European powers, in matters relating to themselves, we have never taken any part, nor does it comport with our policy so to do. It is only when our rights are invaded or seriously menaced that we resent injuries or make preparation for our defense.

With the movements in this hemisphere we are of necessity more immediately connected. . . . The political system of the [European] powers is essentially different . . . from . . . our own, which has been achieved by the loss of so much blood and treasure. . . . We owe it, therefore, to candor and to the amicable [friendly] relations existing between the United States and those powers to declare that we should consider any attempt on their part to extend their system to any portion of this hemisphere as dangerous to our peace and safety.

With the existing colonies or dependencies of any European power we have not interfered and shall not interfere. But with the governments who have declared their independence and maintained it, . . . we could not view any interposition [intervention]

for the purpose of oppressing them . . . in any other light than as the manifestation of an unfriendly disposition [attitude] toward the United States. . . .

Our policy in regard to Europe . . . remains the same, which is, not to interfere in the internal concerns of any of its powers; . . . to cultivate friendly relations with it, and to preserve those relations by a frank, firm, and manly policy. . . . But, in regard to [the American] continents, circumstances are eminently and conspicuously different. It is impossible that the allied powers should extend their political system to any portion of either continent without endangering our peace and happiness; nor can anyone believe that our southern brethren, if left to themselves, would adopt it of their own accord. . . . It is still the true policy of the United States to leave the parties to themselves in the hope that other powers will pursue the same course.

Analyzing Primary Sources

1. According to Monroe, what is the foreign policy of the United States toward the nations of Europe?
2. Why is Monroe concerned about European expansion in Central and South America?
3. Monroe's statement suggests he is most concerned about whose independence, the South American nations or the United States? Explain.

Legislative and Judicial Powers

4

Section Preview

OBJECTIVES

1. **Describe** the President's two major legislative powers, and explain how these powers are an important part of the system of checks and balances.
2. **Describe** the President's major judicial powers.

WHY IT MATTERS

The Constitution gives the President strong legislative and judicial powers as a part of the system of checks and balances.

POLITICAL DICTIONARY

★ line-item veto
★ reprieve
★ pardon
★ clemency
★ commutation
★ amnesty

As you know, the Federal Government is built on the principles of separation of powers and checks and balances. The Constitution gives to each of the three branches its own powers. It also gives to each of them powers with which to check—to delay or block—actions by the other two branches. As James Madison put it in *The Federalist* No. 51, each branch of the Federal Government has "the necessary constitutional means and personal motives to resist encroachments of the others."

Legislative Powers

With his legislative powers, and the skillful playing of his roles as chief of party and chief citizen, the President can (and often does) have a considerable influence on the actions of Congress. The President is, in effect, the nation's chief legislator.

Recommending Legislation

The Constitution says that the President

FROM THE Constitution

ff *shall from time to time give to the Congress Information on the State of the Union, and recommend to their Consideration such Measures as he shall judge necessary and expedient. . . .* **ff**
—Article II, Section 3

---

[13]Article I, Section 7, Clauses 2 and 3. Recall that, despite these words, joint resolutions proposing constitutional amendments and concurrent resolutions, which do not have the force of law, are not sent to the President.

This provision gives the President what is often called the *message power*.

The Chief Executive regularly sends three major messages to Capitol Hill each year. The first is the State of the Union message, a speech he almost always delivers in person to a joint session of Congress. The President's budget message and the annual Economic Report follow that speech soon after. The President often sends the lawmakers a number of other messages on a wide range of topics. In each of them, he calls on Congress to enact those laws he thinks to be necessary to the welfare of the country.

The Veto Power

The Constitution says that "Every Bill" and "Every Order, Resolution, or Vote to which the Concurrence of the Senate and House of Representatives may be necessary (except on a question of Adjournment) shall be presented to the President."[13]

▲ Every year, huge bound volumes of the President's budget plan arrive at the Capitol, where they are distributed for Congress's consideration.

Remember, the Constitution presents the President with four options when he receives a measure passed by Congress. First, he may sign the bill, making it law. Or he can veto it, and the measure must then be returned to Congress. Of course, Congress can override a presidential veto by a two-thirds vote in each of its two chambers—but it seldom does.

As a third option, the President may allow the bill to become law by not acting on it, neither signing nor vetoing it, within 10 days (not counting Sundays). This rarely happens.

The fourth option, the pocket veto, can be used only at the end of a congressional session. If Congress adjourns within 10 days of sending a bill to the President and the chief executive does not act on it, the measure dies. Most Presidents have used the pocket veto with some frequency, because Congress regularly passes a large number of measures in the closing days of its annual sessions.

The fact that Congress is seldom able to muster the two-thirds majority needed to overturn a presidential veto makes the veto a significant weapon in the Chief Executive's dealings with the legislative branch. The weight that this power has in the executive–legislative relationship is underscored by this important point: The mere threat of a veto is often enough to defeat a bill or to prompt changes in its provisions as it moves through the legislative process. The record of presidential vetoes over the years, and the fact that they are not often overturned, can be seen in the table below.

The Line-Item Veto

If the President decides to veto a bill, he must reject the *entire* measure. He cannot veto only a portion of it.

Since Ulysses S. Grant's day, most Presidents have favored the expansion of the veto power to include a **line-item veto.** That is, they have urged that the President be given the power to cancel specific dollar amounts (line items) in spending bills enacted by Congress. Those Presidents, and the many who have supported their position, have argued over the years that the line-item veto would be a potent weapon against wasteful and unnecessary federal spending.

Over time, opponents of the line-item veto—and there have been many of them—have said that to grant the President such authority would bring a massive and dangerous shift of power to

▶ Presidential signings of legislation are commemorated with special pens, like this one from a Reagan signing.

Presidential Vetoes 1933–2001				
	Regular Vetoes	Pocket Vetoes	Total Vetoes	Vetoes Overridden
Franklin Roosevelt (1933–1945)	372	263	635	9
Harry Truman (1945–1953)	180	70	250	12
Dwight Eisenhower (1953–1961)	73	108	181	2
John Kennedy (1961–1963)	12	9	21	—
Lyndon Johnson (1963–1969)	16	14	30	—
Richard Nixon (1969–1974)	26	14	43	7
Gerald Ford (1974–1977)	48	18	66	12
Jimmy Carter (1977–1981)	13	18	31	2
Ronald Reagan (1981–1989)	39	39	78	9
George H. W. Bush (1989–1993)	29	15	44	1
Bill Clinton (1993–2001)	36	1	37	2

SOURCE: Congressional Research Service, Library of Congress

Interpreting Tables Some Presidents have used their veto power more often than others. **(a) What might explain the huge variations in numbers of total vetoes? (b) Why, do you think, did some Presidents have fewer vetoes overridden?**

the executive branch. To this point, efforts to persuade Congress to propose a line-item veto amendment to the Constitution have failed.

In 1996, however, Congress did pass the Line Item Veto Act. That law gave the President the power to reject individual items in spending bills, and to eliminate any provision of a tax bill that benefited fewer than 100 people. President Clinton hailed the statute as a major step against "special interest boondoggles, tax loopholes, and pure pork."

Opponents of the measure challenged it in the courts, and they won their case in *Clinton* v. *New York City,* 1998. There, the Supreme Court struck down the law. By a 6–3 vote, it held that Congress lacked the authority to give the President a line-item veto by statute. If the President is to have such power, said the Court, it must come via an amendment to the Constitution.

Other Legislative Powers

According to Article II, Section 3 of the Constitution, only the President can call Congress into special session. Most recently, President Truman did so in 1948, to have Congress consider post-World War II economic measures. The same constitutional provision also gives the President the power to prorogue (adjourn) Congress whenever the two houses cannot agree on a date for their adjournment—something that has never happened.

Judicial Powers

The Constitution gives the President the power to

FROM THE Constitution *" . . . Grant Reprieves and Pardons for Offenses against the United States, except in Cases of Impeachment. "*

—Article II, Section 2, Clause 1

A **reprieve** is the postponement of the execution of a sentence. A **pardon** is legal forgiveness of a crime.

The President's power to grant reprieves and pardons is absolute, except in cases of impeachment, where they may never be granted. These powers of **clemency** (mercy or leniency) may be used only in cases involving federal offenses. The President has no such authority with regard to those who violate State law.

Interpreting Cartoons This cartoon comments on the increasing power of the President—in this case, Harry Truman, who was President from 1945–1953. ***According to the cartoonist, who is responsible for this growth in power?***

Presidential pardons are usually granted after a person has been convicted in court. Yet the President may pardon a federal offender before that person is tried, or even before that person has been formally charged.

Pardons in advance of a trial or charge are rare. The most noteworthy pardon, by far, was granted in 1974. In that year, President Gerald Ford gave "a full, free and absolute pardon unto Richard Nixon for all offenses against the United States which he . . . has committed or may have committed or taken part in during the period from January 20, 1969, through August 9, 1974." Of course, that pardon referred to the Watergate scandal—the many and sordid events that ultimately forced Nixon to resign the presidency.

To be effective, a pardon must be accepted by the person to whom it is granted. When one is granted before charge or conviction, as in Nixon's case, its acceptance is regularly seen as an admission of guilt by the person to whom it is given.

Nearly all pardons are accepted, of course, and usually gratefully. A few have been rejected, however. One of the most dramatic refusals led to a Supreme Court case, *Burdick* v. *United States,* 1915. George Burdick, a New York newspaper editor, had refused to testify before a federal grand jury regarding the sources for certain news stories his paper had printed. Those stories

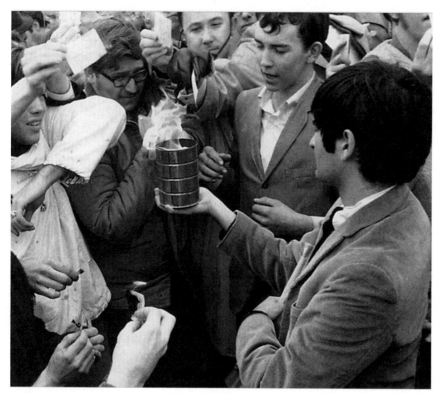

▲ Some men called to serve in the Vietnam War burned their draft cards in protest. Others went into hiding, many fleeing to Canada. In 1977 President Carter pardoned them. *Critical Thinking What might have been Carter's motive for using his presidential power to pardon the draft evaders?*

reported fraud in the collection of customs duties. He invoked the 5th Amendment, claiming that his testimony could incriminate him. President Woodrow Wilson then granted Burdick "a full and unconditional pardon for all offenses against the United States" that he might have committed in obtaining material for the news stories.

Interestingly, Burdick refused to accept the pardon, and he continued to refuse to testify. With that, the federal judge in that district fined and jailed him for contempt. The judge ruled that (1) the President's pardon was fully effective, with or without Burdick's acceptance and (2) there was, therefore, no basis for Burdick's continued claim of protection against self-incrimination.

The Supreme Court overturned the lower court's action. It unanimously upheld the rule that a pardon must be accepted in order to be effective, and it ordered Burdick's release from jail.

The pardoning power includes the power to grant conditional pardons, provided the conditions are reasonable. It also includes the power of **commutation**—that is, the power to commute (reduce) the length of a sentence or a fine imposed by a court.

The pardoning power also includes the power of **amnesty,** in effect a blanket pardon offered to a group of law violators. Thus, in 1893 President Benjamin Harrison issued a proclamation of amnesty forgiving all Mormons who had violated the antipolygamy (multiple marriage) laws in the federal territories. In 1977 President Jimmy Carter granted amnesty to Vietnam War draft evaders.

Section 4 Assessment

Key Terms and Main Ideas

1. What are the President's two major legislative powers?
2. What happened to the **line-item veto** law passed by Congress?
3. Explain how these judicial powers of the President differ: **reprieve, pardon, clemency, commutation, amnesty.**

Critical Thinking

4. **Expressing Problems Clearly** Write two paragraphs summarizing the arguments for and against the line-item veto.
5. **Predicting Consequences** Why, do you think, has no President had to use the power to prorogue Congress?

6. **Making Inferences** In giving the President several important judicial powers, what kinds of situations might the Framers have been anticipating?

 Take It to the Net

7. Read about the types of presidential vetoes and what actions Congress can take once the President vetoes a bill. Create a flowchart that shows the steps in the process and the possible outcomes. Use the links provided in the Social Studies area at the following Web site for help in completing this activity. **www.phschool.com**

Can Groups' Liberties Be Limited During Wartime?

Many difficult questions concerning personal freedoms arise during national emergencies. When the survival of the nation is threatened, strong government action may be necessary to confront the threat. Such action might harm individuals or groups. May government impose limits on civil rights in case of emergencies?

Korematsu v. United States (1944)

Japan's attack on Pearl Harbor, Hawaii, on December 7, 1941, prompted widespread fear that Japan might try to invade the West Coast, and that persons of Japanese ancestry living there might aid the invasion. At that time, about 120,000 persons of Japanese descent lived in the West Coast States; some 70,000 of these were *Nisei* (Japanese Americans whose parents were born in Japan).

On February 19, 1942, President Franklin Roosevelt issued Executive Order No. 9066 authorizing the military to designate military areas and to exclude "any or all persons" from them. This order was intended to help protect the country from espionage or sabotage. Congress then passed a law requiring that all persons excluded from those military areas be sent to "war relocation camps" outside the sensitive military areas.

On March 2, 1942, the general in charge of the West Coast Defense Command issued the first of a series of orders that identified the entire Pacific Coast as Military Area No. 1. Soon, all persons of Japanese descent were ordered out of that area.

Fred Korematsu, a native-born American citizen, refused to leave his home in San Leandro, across the bay from San Francisco. He was arrested, charged with failure to report for relocation, and convicted in federal district court. After losing in the court of appeals, he appealed to the Supreme Court.

Arguments for Korematsu

1. Executive Order 9066 denied Korematsu his liberty without due process of law, in violation of the Fifth Amendment.

2. The military does not have the authority to regulate civilian conduct, and the President cannot delegate that power to the military when martial law has not been declared.

3. The order of exclusion created a classification based on race, in violation of the Constitution.

Arguments for the United States

1. Although the relocation would not be proper in peacetime, the danger of espionage and sabotage justified this denial of liberty to American citizens under wartime circumstances.

2. Because war had been declared, the President had the authority as commander in chief to issue such orders to the military.

3. The United States had been attacked by Japan, so it was logical that people of Japanese ancestry were suspect. The decision to relocate people from sensitive military areas was based on security concerns and not on racial prejudice.

Decide for Yourself

1. Review the constitutional grounds on which each side based its arguments and the specific arguments each side presented.

2. Debate the opposing viewpoints presented in this case. Which viewpoint do you favor?

3. Predict the impact of the Court's decision on discrimination based on race and national ancestry in the United States. (To read a summary of the Court's decision, turn to the Supreme Court Glossary on page 799.)

Political Dictionary

Executive Article (p. 390)

mass media (p. 391)

imperial presidency (p. 392)

oath of office (p. 393)

executive order (p. 394)

ordinance power (p. 394)

treaty (p. 399)

executive agreement (p. 400)

recognition (p. 400)

persona non grata (p. 401)

line-item veto (p. 406)

reprieve (p. 407)

pardon (p. 407)

clemency (p. 407)

commutation (p. 408)

amnesty (p. 408)

Practicing the Vocabulary

Matching *Choose a term from the list above that best matches each description.*

1. Forms of communication, including printed publications, radio, television, and, most recently, the Internet
2. A formal agreement between two or more nations that requires the approval of two thirds of the Senate
3. The President's power to grant reprieves and pardons in cases involving federal offenses
4. A directive, rule, or regulation from the President that has the effect of law
5. The President's constitutional power to issue executive orders
6. Critics' term for the strong use of presidential power in ways that enable the President to evade the will of Congress

Fill in the Blanks *Choose a term from the list above that best completes the sentence.*

7. The _____ had been sought by many Presidents, but it was struck down by the Supreme Court as unconstitutional.
8. Unlike a treaty, a _____ does not need congressional approval.
9. The part of the Constitution that establishes the presidency is called the _____.
10. To show displeasure with another country, the President can declare its diplomatic representative to be _____.
11. A _____ is the legal forgiveness of a crime, whereas _____ is a general pardon of a group of lawbreakers.
12. _____ can be used as a weapon in foreign relations.

Reviewing Main Ideas

Section 1

13. **(a)** Why has the wording of Article II, Section I caused problems? **(b)** What differing views did the Framers hold about the power of the presidency?
14. How has the growing complexity of the nation's social and economic life affected presidential power?
15. What opposing views have Presidents had regarding their proper role in the job?

Section 2

16. How does the responsibility for executing the law give the President great power?
17. Why do we know that the Framers intended the President to have ordinance power?
18. Why is it important that the President have the power to appoint officials?
19. What role does senatorial courtesy have in the appointment process?
20. How did the issue of the removal power result in the impeachment of President Andrew Johnson?

Section 3

21. What types of agreements can the President make with foreign countries?
22. Why did the Framers include the Senate, but not the House, in the treaty-making process?
23. What is the power of recognition, and how can the President use it as a diplomatic tool?
24. **(a)** Describe the President's role in military affairs. **(b)** Give examples of presidential use of the power of commander in chief.

Section 4

25. How do the President's legislative and judicial powers support the system of checks and balances?
26. What are the President's primary legislative powers?
27. How could the line-item veto be added to the President's legislative powers?
28. What are the President's primary judicial powers?
29. What kind of clemency did President Gerald Ford give to former President Richard Nixon?

Critical Thinking Skills

30. **Applying the Chapter Skill** Using the information in the diagram on page 312, create a time line of either the Johnson or Clinton impeachment. How do the time line and the diagram differ in the way they present information?

31. **Drawing Conclusions** Why, do you think, have so many Presidents decided to make undeclared war?

32. **Predicting Consequences** **(a)** If the Supreme Court someday were to declare the War Powers Act unconstitutional, on what grounds might the law be struck down? **(b)** What might be the effect of such a ruling on presidential power?

33. **Drawing Inferences** Article II of the Constitution, which covers the powers of the executive, has been called the most loosely drawn chapter in the Constitution. Why might the Framers have created Article II in this way?

Analyzing Political Cartoons

Using your knowledge of American government and this cartoon, answer the questions below.

34. In the cartoon above, what point is being suggested about how the President and Congress carry out foreign relations? (Note: NATO is the North Atlantic Treaty Organization, which coordinates military defense in Europe.)

★ You Can Make a Difference

Do you and your friends feel cut off from your government? Or do you feel that you have a chance to participate—perhaps as a staffer in the White House or Congress, or as a campaign worker? Prepare a 10- to 15-question opinion poll on attitudes toward government among young people in your area. Try to get at issues such as distrust and to identify the causes. Find out if people over 18 are registered to vote or plan to do so. If not, why not?

Participation Activities

35. **Current Events Watch** Presidents regularly meet with officials from other countries. Find a recent news report of such a meeting and become familiar with the main topic of their discussions. Summarize the main topic and goal of the meeting. Analyze the President's role in the discussions, and describe the outcome. What powers of the presidency did the President use during this event?

36. **Chart Activity** Create a chart that lists the various powers of the President and the sources of each power. Then write a summary statement contrasting the power of the President today with the power that the Framers intended the President to have when they created the position in 1787.

37. **It's Your Turn** You have completed your first year as President. Write the opening paragraphs of a State of the Union address. Explain how you intend to lead the nation in the year ahead. Open with a statement in which you summarize your beliefs about the role of the President. Explain what you predict will be your greatest upcoming challenge and how you will attempt to address it, using your constitutional powers. **(Writing a Speech)**

Take It to the Net

Chapter 14 Self-Test As a final review activity, take the Chapter 14 Self-Test in the Social Studies area at the Web site listed below, and receive immediate feedback on your answers.

www.phschool.com

Government at Work: The Bureaucracy

>"Bureaucracy is not an obstacle to democracy but an inevitable complement to it."
>
>—Joseph A. Schumpeter (1942)

People often criticize and poke fun at the federal bureaucracy. Schumpeter, an economist, knew that it takes millions of bureaucrats to make democratic government work. Americans depend on the civil servants—from accountants to Webmasters—who work in federal agencies throughout the country.

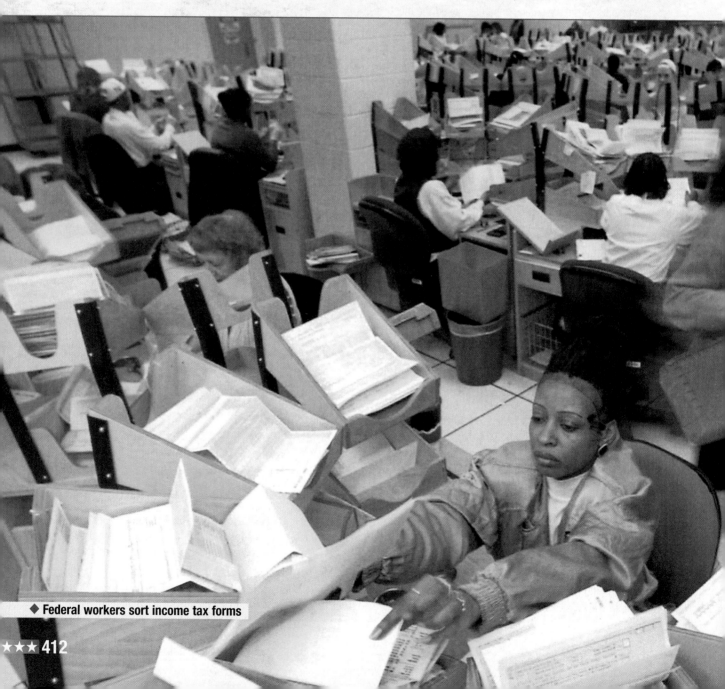

◆ Federal workers sort income tax forms

Chapter 15 in Brief

You Can Make a Difference

"SOMETHING THAT'S IMPORTANT to you—just fight for it."
With that attitude, Andrew Holleman became the youngest winner of a Regional Merit Award from the Environmental Protection Agency, the federal agency that guards the nation's air, land, and water. At age 12, Andrew began a campaign to save a local wetland in Chelmsford, Massachusetts, from a developer's bulldozer. He studied geology, collected neighbors' signatures on a petition, spoke at meetings, and wrote to State and local officials. At last, the Zoning Board turned down the development. Andrew carried his activism on into high school, with plans to study environmental science in college.

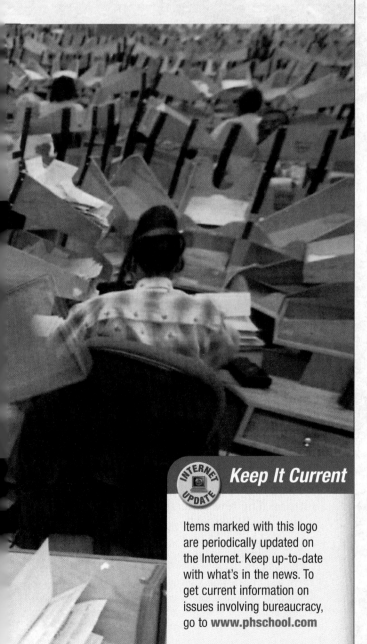

Keep It Current

Items marked with this logo are periodically updated on the Internet. Keep up-to-date with what's in the news. To get current information on issues involving bureaucracy, go to **www.phschool.com**

SECTION 1

The Federal Bureaucracy (pp. 414–418)

★ The federal bureaucracy is a large, highly organized group that carries out the work of the Federal Government.
★ The names given to agencies, including *commission, administration,* and *corporation,* may indicate an agency's nature.
★ Agencies include line agencies, which operate programs, and staff agencies, which support the line agencies.

SECTION 2

The Executive Office of the President
(pp. 419–422)

★ The Executive Office of the President includes several important agencies staffed by the President's closest advisors.
★ The White House Office is the "nerve center" of the Executive Office of the President.
★ Other units of the Executive Office advise the President on domestic affairs and foreign policy.

SECTION 3

The Executive Departments (pp. 424–429)

★ Each of the 14 executive departments manages federal policy in a broad field of activity, such as education, labor, or defense.
★ The heads of the departments meet with the President and other advisors in a group called the Cabinet.
★ The President chooses his nominees to lead executive departments, but the Senate can reject any nominee.
★ The President decides how often to call Cabinet meetings.

SECTION 4

Independent Agencies (pp. 430–435)

★ Independent agencies are not part of the executive departments.
★ The three types of independent agencies are independent executive agencies, independent regulatory commissions, and government corporations.
★ Independence gives these agencies some freedom from political pressure.

SECTION 5

The Civil Service (pp. 437–440)

★ The people who work in the federal bureaucracy make up the civil service.
★ Early on, the spoils system infected the civil service.
★ Corruption was a serious problem until reformers began to reshape the civil service in the 1880s.
★ Today, the vast majority of civil servants are hired and promoted on the basis of merit, not party membership.

The Federal Bureaucracy

OBJECTIVES

1. **Define** a bureaucracy.
2. **Identify** the major elements of the federal bureaucracy.
3. **Explain** how groups within the federal bureaucracy are named.
4. **Describe** the difference between a staff agency and a line agency.

WHY IT MATTERS

The Federal Government is the nation's largest employer. Nearly 2.7 million men and women work in the federal bureaucracy, and they do nearly all of the day-to-day work of the government.

POLITICAL DICTIONARY

★ **bureaucracy**
★ **bureaucrat**
★ **administration**
★ **staff agency**
★ **line agency**

Think about this for a moment: It is impossible for you to live through a single day without somehow encountering the federal bureaucracy. A **bureaucracy** is a large, complex administrative structure that handles the everyday business of an organization.[1] The Federal Government is the largest organization in the country. Federal employees deliver the mail, regulate business practices, collect taxes, manage the national forests, conduct American foreign policy, administer Social Security programs—the list goes on and on.

▲ Bureaucrats once used red ribbon, called "red tape" in Britain, to hold their files together. Today, people use the phrase "red tape" to describe the delays and paperwork they face when working with a bureaucracy.

What Is a Bureaucracy?

To many Americans, the word *bureaucracy* suggests such things as waste, red tape, and delay. While that image is not altogether unfounded, it is quite lopsided. Basically, bureaucracy is an efficient and an effective way to organize people to do work.

Bureaucracies are found wherever there are large organizations. They are found in both the public sector and the private sector in this country. Thus, the United States Air Force, McDonald's, the Social Security Administration, MTV, your town or city government, and the Roman Catholic Church are all bureaucracies. Even your school is a bureaucracy.

Three Features of a Bureaucracy

In dictionary terms, a bureaucracy is a system of organization built on these three principles: hierarchical authority, job specialization, and formalized rules.

1. *Hierarchical authority.* The word *hierarchical* describes any organization that is built as a pyramid, with a chain of command running from the top of the pyramid to the bottom. The few officials and units at the top of the organization have authority over those

---

[1]The term *bureaucracy* is a combination of the French word *bureau,* which originally referred to a desk of a government official and later to the place where an official works, and the suffix *–cracy,* signifying a type of governmental structure.

officials and units at the larger middle level, who in turn direct the activities of the many at the bottom level.

2. *Job specialization.* Each **bureaucrat,** or person who works for the organization, has certain defined duties and responsibilities. There is a precise division of labor within the organization.

3. *Formalized rules.* The bureaucracy does its work according to a set of established regulations and procedures.

The Benefits of a Bureaucracy

These three features—hierarchical authority, job specialization, and formalized rules—make bureaucracy the most effective way for people to work together on large and complex tasks. The hierarchy can speed action by reducing conflicts over who has the power to make decisions. The higher a person's rank in the organization, the greater the decision-making power he or she has.

Job specialization promotes efficiency because each person in the organization is required to focus on one particular job. Each worker thus gains a set of specialized skills and knowledge. Formalized rules mean that workers can act with some speed and precision because decisions are based on a set of known standards, not on someone's likes, dislikes, or inclinations. These rules also enable work to continue even as some workers leave an organization and new workers are hired to replace them.

Recognize this very important point about public bureaucracies: their bureaucrats hold appointive offices. Bureaucrats are *unelected* public-policy makers. This is not to say that bureaucracies are undemocratic. However, in a democracy much depends on how effectively the bureaucracy is controlled by those whom the people *do* elect. Listen to James Madison on the point:

PRIMARY Sources ❝*In framing a government which is to be administered by men over men, the great difficulty lies in this: you must first enable the government to control the governed; and in the next place oblige it to control itself.*❞

—*The Federalist* No. 51

▲ *The Reagan Building* Second only to the Pentagon in size, the Ronald Reagan Building and International Trade Center houses government offices in downtown Washington, D.C.

Major Elements of the Federal Bureaucracy

The federal bureaucracy is all of the agencies, people, and procedures through which the Federal Government operates. It is the means by which the government makes and administers public policy—the sum of its decisions and actions. As the chart on page 417 shows, nearly all of the federal bureaucracy is located in the executive branch.

The Constitution makes the President the chief administrator of the Federal Government. Article II, Section 3 declares that "he shall take Care that the Laws be faithfully executed." But the Constitution makes only the barest mention of the administrative machinery through which the President is to exercise that power.

Article II does suggest executive departments by giving to the President the power to "require

▲ A federal agency can be called a *commission, bureau, administration,* or one of several other names. ***Critical Thinking Why is*** **commission** *an appropriate name for the SEC, which oversees stock markets?*

the Opinion, in writing, of the principal Officer in each of the executive Departments."[2]

Article II anticipates two departments in particular, one for military and one for foreign affairs. It does so by making the President the "Commander in Chief of the Army and Navy," and by giving him the power to make treaties and to appoint "Ambassadors, other public Ministers, and Consuls."[3]

Beyond those references, the Constitution is silent on the organization of the executive branch. The Framers certainly intended for administrative agencies to be created, however. They understood that no matter how wise the President and the Congress, their decisions still had to be acted upon to be effective. Without an **administration**— the government's many administrators and agencies—even the best policies would amount to just so many words and phrases. The President and Congress need millions of men and women to put policies into action in Washington, D.C., and in offices all around the country.

The chief organizational feature of the federal bureaucracy is its division into areas of specialization. As you can see on page 417, the executive branch is composed of three broad groups of agencies: (1) the Executive Office of the President, (2) the 14 Cabinet departments, and (3) a large number of independent agencies.[4]

The Name Game

The titles given to the many units that make up the executive branch vary a great deal. The name *department* is reserved for agencies of Cabinet rank. Beyond the title of *department,* however, there is little standardized use of titles.

Common titles used in the executive branch include *agency, administration, commission, corporation,* and *authority.*

The term *agency* is often used to refer to any governmental body. It is sometimes used to identify a major unit headed by a single administrator of near-cabinet status, such as the Environmental Protection Agency. But so, too, is the title *administration;* for example, the National Aeronautics and Space Administration and the General Services Administration.

The name *commission* is usually given to agencies charged with the regulation of business activities, such as the Federal Communications Commission and the Securities and Exchange Commission. Top-ranking officers called commissioners head these units. The same title, however, is given to some investigative, advisory, and reporting bodies, including the Civil Rights Commission and the Federal Election Commission.

Either *corporation* or *authority* is the title most often given to those agencies that conduct business-like activities. Corporations and authorities are headed by a board and a manager. Examples include the Federal Deposit Insurance Corporation and the Tennessee Valley Authority.

---

[2]Article II, Section 2, Clause 1. There is also a reference to "Heads of Departments" in Clause 2, and to "any Department or Officer" of the government in Article I, Section 8, Clause 18.

[3]Article II, Section 2, Clauses 1 and 2.

[4]The chart is adapted from the current edition of the *United States Government Manual,* published each year by the Office of the Federal Register in the National Archives and Records Administration. The *Manual* includes a brief description of every agency in each of the three branches of the Federal Government. More than 750 of its now nearly 900 pages are devoted to the executive branch.

The Government of the United States

The Constitution
creates three branches
of government

THE LEGISLATIVE BRANCH

CONGRESS

Houses of Congress
Senate and House of Representatives

Legislative Offices and Departments
Architect of the Capitol
General Accounting Office
Government Printing Office
Library of Congress
United States Botanic Garden
Office of Technology Assessment
Congressional Budget Office
Copyright Royalty Tribunal
United States Tax Court

THE EXECUTIVE BRANCH

THE PRESIDENT

The Administration

1 Executive Office of the President

2 Executive Departments

3 Independent Agencies

THE JUDICIAL BRANCH

THE SUPREME COURT OF THE UNITED STATES

Other Courts
Courts of Appeals
District Courts
Federal Claims Court
Court of Appeals for the Federal Circuit
Court of International Trade
Territorial Courts
Court of Appeals for the Armed Forces
Court of Appeals for Veterans
Administrative Office of the United States
Federal Judicial Center

---

1 Executive Office of the President

White House Office
Office of Management and Budget
Council of Economic Advisers
National Security Council
Office of National Drug Control Policy
Office of the United States Trade Representative
Council on Environmental Quality
Office of Science and Technology Policy
Office of Administration
Office of the Vice President
Office of Faith-Based and Community Initiatives
Office of Homeland Security

2 Executive Departments

Department of State
Department of the Treasury
Department of Defense
Department of Justice
Department of the Interior
Department of Agriculture
Department of Commerce
Department of Labor
Department of Health and Human Services
Department of Housing and Urban Development
Department of Transportation
Department of Energy
Department of Education
Department of Veterans Affairs

3 Independent Agencies*

Central Intelligence Agency
Commission on Civil Rights
Commodity Futures Trading Commission
Consumer Product Safety Commission
Corporation for National and Community Service
Defense Nuclear Facilities Safety Board
Environmental Protection Agency
Equal Employment Opportunity Commission
Export-Import Bank of the U.S.
Farm Credit Administration
Federal Communications Commission
Federal Deposit Insurance Corporation
Federal Election Commission
Federal Emergency Management Agency

Federal Housing Finance Board
Federal Maritime Commission
Federal Mediation and Conciliation Service
Federal Reserve System
Federal Trade Commission
General Services Administration
National Aeronautics and Space Administration
National Archives and Records Administration
National Labor Relations Board
National Transportation Safety Board
Nuclear Regulatory Commission
Office of Personnel Management
Peace Corps
Securities and Exchange Commission
Selective Service System
Small Business Administration
Social Security Administration
Tennessee Valley Authority
U.S. Postal Service

*Altogether, there are some 150 independent agencies in the executive branch.

Interpreting Charts The daily workings of government depend on these departments and agencies.
According to this chart, which branch makes up the largest share of the federal bureaucracy?

Within each major agency, the same confusing lack of uniformity in the use of names is common. *Bureau* is the name often given to the major elements in a department, but *service, administration, office, branch,* and *division* are often used for the same purpose. For example, the major units within the Department of Justice include the Federal Bureau of Investigation, the Immigration and Naturalization Service, the Drug Enforcement Administration, the Office of the Pardon Attorney, and the Criminal Division.

Many federal agencies are often referred to by their initials. The EPA, IRS, FBI, CIA, FCC, and TVA are but a few of the dozens of familiar examples.[5] A few are also known by nicknames. For example, the Government National Mortgage Association is often called "Ginnie Mae," and the National Railroad Passenger Corporation is better known as Amtrak.

Staff and Line Agencies

The several units that make up any administrative organization can be classified as either staff or line agencies. **Staff agencies** serve in a support capacity. They aid the chief executive and other administrators by offering advice and other assistance in the management of the organization. **Line agencies,** on the other hand, actually

---

[5]The use of acronyms can sometimes cause problems. When the old Bureau of the Budget was reorganized in 1970, it was also renamed. It is now the Office of Management and Budget (OMB). However, it was for a time slated to be known as the Bureau of Management and Budget (BOMB).

perform the tasks for which the organization exists. Congress and the President give the line agencies goals to meet, and the staff agencies help the line agencies meet these goals as effectively as possible through advising, budgeting, purchasing, management, and planning.

Two illustrations of this distinction are the several agencies that make up the Executive Office of the President and, in contrast, the Environmental Protection Agency. The agencies that make up the Executive Office of the President (the White House Office, the National Security Council, the Office of Management and Budget, and others, as you will read in the next section) each exist as staff support to the President. Their primary mission is to assist the President in the exercise of the executive power and in the overall management of the executive branch. They are not operating agencies. That is, they do not actually operate, or administer, public programs.

The Environmental Protection Agency (EPA), on the other hand, has a different mission. It is responsible for the day-to-day enforcement of the many federal antipollution laws. The EPA operates "on the line," where "the action" is.

This difference between staff agencies and line agencies can help you find your way through the complex federal bureaucracy. The distinction between the two can be oversimplified, however. For example, most line agencies do have staff units to aid them in their line operations. Thus, the EPA's Office of Civil Rights is a staff unit. It was established to ensure that the agency's personnel practices do not violate the Federal Government's antidiscrimination policies.

Section 1 Assessment

Key Terms and Main Ideas

1. Describe the three defining features of a **bureaucracy** in your own words.
2. Why does a government need an **administration?**
3. What is the role of a **staff agency?** A **line agency?**

Critical Thinking

4. **Drawing Conclusions** How would you describe the system of naming federal agencies in one word? Explain your answer.
5. **Drawing Inferences** Explain how the three defining characteristics of a bureaucracy can lead to an effective government.

6. **Predicting Consequences** How might a strong, independent bureaucracy weaken the power of elected representatives?

 Take It to the Net

7. Read how different parts of the federal bureaucracy deal with environmental issues. Then choose two agencies and create a diagram or graphic organizer comparing the different roles that they play in United States environmental policy. Use the links provided in the Social Studies area at the following Web site for help in completing this activity. **www.phschool.com**

The Executive Office of the President

Section Preview

OBJECTIVES

1. **Describe** the Executive Office of the President.
2. **Explain** the duties of the White House Office, the National Security Council, and the Office of Homeland Security.
3. **Identify** additional agencies in the Executive Office of the President.

WHY IT MATTERS

The Executive Office of the President is composed of the President's closest advisors and several support agencies. They aid the chief executive in the formation and execution of the nation's public policies.

POLITICAL DICTIONARY

★ **Executive Office of the President**
★ **federal budget**
★ **fiscal year**
★ **domestic affairs**

Thomas Jefferson performed his presidential duties with the help of two aides, one a messenger and the other his secretary. Like other early Presidents, he paid their salaries out of his own pocket. Indeed, Congress did not provide any money for presidential staff until 1857, when it gave President James Buchanan $2,500 for one clerk.

The situation is remarkably different today. President Jefferson presided over an executive branch that employed only some 2,100 people. Now, some 2.7 million men and women work in the Bush administration. Two institutions—the Executive Office of the President and the President's Cabinet—are at the center of today's huge executive branch.

The Executive Office of the President

Every officer, every employee, and every agency in the executive branch of the Federal Government is legally subordinate to the President. They all exist to help the President—the chief executive—in the exercise of the executive power.

The President's right arm, however, is the **Executive Office of the President** (the EOP). The Executive Office of the President is, in fact, an umbrella agency. It is a complex organization of several separate agencies staffed by most of the President's closest advisors and assistants.

The EOP was established by Congress in 1939. It has been reorganized in every administration since then.

The White House Office

The "nerve center" of the Executive Office—in fact, of the entire executive branch—is the White House Office. It houses the President's key personal and political staff.

The two wings on either side of the White House hold the offices of most of the President's staff. These employees occupy most of the crowded West Wing, which the public seldom sees and where the legendary Oval Office and the Cabinet Room are located. Some staff members work in the East Wing, where public tours of the White House

▲ Federal workers in the West Wing

The West Wing of the White House

MAIN FLOOR

KEY
1. West Wing
2. Mansion
3. East Wing
4. Press Briefing Room
5. Cabinet Room
6. Oval Office
7. Rose Garden
8. Presidential Press Secretary
9. National Security Advisor
10. Vice President's Office
11. Chief of Staff

Interpreting Diagrams The President's closest advisors work in the West Wing of the White House, near the Oval Office. *Why do you think the Cabinet Room is so close to the Oval Office?*

begin. Still others are housed in the historic Old Executive Office Building, across the street from the West Wing.

The chief of staff to the President directs all of the operations of the White House Office and is among the most influential of all the presidential aides. The counselor to the President and a number of senior advisors are also key members of the President's inner circle.

Several other top officials work in the White House Office. Assistants and deputy assistants to the President aid the chief executive in such vital areas as foreign policy, defense, the economy, political affairs, congressional relations, and contacts with the news media and the public.

The staff of the White House Office also includes such other major presidential aides as the press secretary, the counsel (legal advisor) to the President, and the President's physician. The first lady's very visible place in public life today is reflected by the fact that one of the assistants to the President serves as her chief of staff and one of the several deputy assistants is her press secretary. Altogether, the staff of the White House Office now numbers some 400 men and women who, in a very real sense, work for the President.

The National Security Council

Most of the President's major steps in foreign affairs are taken in close consultation with the National Security Council (NSC). It meets at the President's call, often on short notice, to advise him in all domestic, foreign, and military matters that relate to the nation's security.

The President chairs the Council. Its other members are the Vice President and the secretaries of state and defense. The director of the Central Intelligence Agency (CIA) and the chairman of the Joint Chiefs of Staff also attend its meetings.

The NSC has a small staff of foreign and military policy experts. They work under the direction of the President's assistant for national security affairs, who is often called the President's national security advisor. The super-secret Central Intelligence Agency does much of its work at the direction of the NSC.

The National Security Council is a staff agency. That is, its job is to advise the President in all matters affecting the nation's security. However, during the Reagan administration in the 1980s, the NSC's staff actually conducted a number of secret operations. The most spectacular of these involved the sale of arms to Iran, and the use of some of the proceeds (money) from those sales to aid the Contra rebels in

Nicaragua. Congress had prohibited military aid to the Contras, and the disclosure of the NSC's role produced the Iran-Contra scandal of the mid-1980s.

Office of Homeland Security

The Office of Homeland Security is the newest major agency in the EOP. It was created by President Bush immediately after terrorists struck the World Trade Center and the Pentagon on September 11, 2001.

The Office is headed by a director who has Cabinet rank. The President has ordered the Office to "lead, oversee, and coordinate a comprehensive national strategy to safeguard our country from terrorism." That means that the director and his 100-member staff must coordinate the anti-terrorist activities of more than forty federal agencies—the CIA, the FBI, the Coast Guard, the Federal Aviation Administration, and many others.

Other EOP Agencies

The EOP's umbrella covers several other—and important—agencies. Each of them provides essential staff help to the Chief Executive.

Office of Management and Budget

The Office of Management and Budget (OMB) is the largest and, after the White House Office, the most influential unit in the Executive Office. The OMB is headed by a director who is appointed by the President and confirmed by the Senate. The OMB's major task is the preparation of the federal budget, which the President must submit to Congress in January or February each year.

The **federal budget** is a detailed estimate of receipts and expenditures for the coming **fiscal year.** A fiscal year is the 12-month period used by government and business for record keeping, budgeting, and other financial management purposes. The Federal Government's fiscal year runs from October 1 through September 30.

The budget is more than just a financial document. It is a plan—a carefully drawn work plan for the conduct of government. It is an annual statement of the public policies of the United States, expressed in dollar terms.

The creation of each fiscal year's budget is a lengthy process that begins more than a year before the start of the fiscal year for which the budget is intended. In the first stages, each federal agency prepares detailed estimates of its spending needs for that 12-month period. The OMB reviews those proposals, usually in a series of budget hearings that give agency officials the opportunity to defend their dollar requests. Following that review, the revised (and usually lowered) spending estimates are fitted into the President's overall program.

The OMB also monitors the spending of the funds Congress appropriates. That is, it oversees the execution of the budget. The President's close control over the preparation and execution of the budget is a major factor in his ability to command the huge executive branch.

Beyond its budget chores, the OMB is a presidential odd-job agency. It studies the organization and management of the executive branch and keeps the President up-to-date on the work of all its agencies. The OMB checks agency stands on all legislative matters to make certain they agree with the President's positions. It also helps the President prepare the hundreds of executive orders he must issue and the veto messages he occasionally sends to Congress. In short, the OMB earns the word *management* in its title.

Office of Faith-Based and Community Initiatives

The Office of Community and Faith-Based Initiatives was created by President Bush in 2001. Much of the best work being done today to combat drug abuse, homelessness, poverty, and similar problems is being done by private groups—by churches and church-related groups and other not-for-profit organizations. The Office of Faith-Based and Community Initiatives is charged with encouraging and expanding these private efforts.

Office of National Drug Control Policy

The Office of National Drug Control Policy was established in 1989. Its existence dramatizes the nation's concern over drugs. The office is headed by a director who is appointed by the President, subject to the Senate's approval.

The news media regularly identify the director as "the nation's drug czar." To this point, the office has operated mostly as an advisory and planning agency, however.

Council of Economic Advisers

Three of the country's leading economists, chosen by the President with the consent of the Senate, make up the Council of Economic Advisers. It is the chief executive's major source of information and advice on the nation's economy. The Council also helps the President prepare his annual Economic Report to Congress, which, together with a presidential message, goes to Capitol Hill in late January or early February each year.

Other Units in the EOP

A number of other agencies in the Executive Office house key presidential aides. These men and women make it possible for the President to meet his many-sided responsibilities.

The Office of Policy Development advises the Chief Executive on all matters relating to the nation's **domestic affairs**—that is, all matters not directly connected to the realm of foreign affairs.

The Council on Environmental Quality aids the President in environmental policy matters and in the writing of the annual "state of the environment" report to Congress. It sees that federal agencies comply with the nation's many environmental laws and with the President's environmental policies.

The council's three members are appointed by the President, with the Senate's consent. They sometimes act as referees in disputes between or among executive branch agencies, such as a conflict between the Environmental Protection Agency and one or more agencies in the Departments of the Agriculture, Interior, or Energy.

The Office of the Vice President houses the Vice President's staff. It now includes more than 50 men and women who make it possible for the Vice President to perform the duties of his office.

The Office of United States Trade Representative advises the chief executive in all matters of foreign trade. The trade representative, appointed by the President and confirmed by the Senate, carries the rank of ambassador and represents the President in foreign trade negotiations.

The Office of Science and Technology Policy is the President's major advisor in all scientific, engineering, and other technological matters relating to national policies and programs. Its director is drawn from the nation's scientific community.

The Office of Administration is the general housekeeping agency for all the other units in the Executive Office. It provides them with the many support services they must have in order to do their jobs, including clerical help, data processing, library services, transportation, and much more.

Section 2 Assessment

Key Terms and Main Ideas

1. List and explain three duties of the agencies that make up the **Executive Office of the President.**
2. Describe an EOP agency that directly relates to **domestic affairs.**
3. Outline the preparation of the **federal budget.**

Critical Thinking

4. **Testing Conclusions** Cite evidence to show that the Executive Office of the President is an essential part of the executive branch.
5. **Determining Cause and Effect** What are the advantages of having an agency, such as the OMB, write the federal budget and monitor spending?

6. **Understanding Point of View** If you could choose one executive agency for which to work, which would you select? What would you like to accomplish in that agency?

 Take It to the Net

7. Look over statistics, graphs, and charts from the most recent federal budget. List five conclusions you can draw from looking at this data. Who will benefit from this budget? Use the links provided in the Social Studies area at the following Web site for help in completing this activity. **www.phschool.com**

The Making of the Modern Presidency

As he began his second term in 1937, President Franklin D. Roosevelt asked Congress to authorize a major reorganization of the executive branch. Congress responded by creating the Executive Office of the President (EOP), in 1939.

President Franklin D. Roosevelt 1882–1945

The time has come to set our house in order. . . . The executive structure of the Government is sadly out of date. I am not the first President to report to the Congress that antiquated machinery stands in the way of effective administration and of adequate control by the Congress. . . .

Over a year ago. . . . I appointed a Committee on Administrative Management to examine the whole problem . . . .

They say what has been common knowledge for 20 years, that the President cannot adequately handle his responsibilities; that he is overworked; that it is humanly impossible under the system which we have, for him to carry out his constitutional duty as Chief Executive, because he is overwhelmed with minor details and needless contacts arising directly from the bad organization and equipment of the Government. I can testify to this. . . .

The Committee includes these major recommendations:

1. Expand the White House staff so that the President may have a sufficient group of able assistants to keep him in closer and easier touch with the widespread affairs of administration. . . .

2. Strengthen and develop the managerial agencies of the Government, particularly those dealing with the budget and efficiency research, with personnel and with planning, as management-arms of the Chief Executive. . . .

In placing this program before you I realize that it will be said that I am recommending the increase of the powers of the Presidency. This is not true. . . . What I am placing before you is not the request for more power, but for the tools of management and authority to distribute the work so that the President can effectively discharge those powers which the Constitution now places upon him. Unless we are prepared to abandon this important part of the Constitution, we must equip the Presidency with authority commensurate with his responsibilities under the Constitution.

Analyzing Primary Sources

1. Why has the executive structure of government become out-of-date, according to Roosevelt?
2. According to Roosevelt, what problem does the existing executive structure create for the President?
3. What does it imply about the Federal Government that Roosevelt had to speak to Congress to reorganize his office?
4. Roosevelt claimed his request would not increase presidential power. Do you agree or disagree? Explain.

Section Preview

OBJECTIVES

1. **Describe** the origin and work of the executive departments.
2. **Explain** how the members of the Cabinet are chosen.
3. **Identify** the role of the Cabinet in the President's decisions.

WHY IT MATTERS

Fourteen executive departments carry out much of the Federal Government's work. The heads of these departments frequently meet with the President and other officials as the Cabinet.

POLITICAL DICTIONARY

★ executive departments
★ secretary
★ attorney general

In *The Federalist* No. 76, Alexander Hamilton declared that "the true test of a good government is its aptitude and tendency to produce a good administration." Given that comment, it seems strange that Hamilton and the other Framers of the Constitution spent so little time on the organization of the executive branch of the government they were creating. Instead, the machinery of federal administration has been built over time to meet the changing needs of the country.

Executive Departments

Much of the work of the Federal Government is done by the 14 **executive departments**. Often called the Cabinet departments, they are the traditional units of federal administration, and each of them is built around some broad field of activity.

The First Congress created three of these departments in 1789: the Departments of State, Treasury, and War. As the size and the workload of the Federal Government grew, Congress added new departments. Some of the newer ones took over various duties originally assigned to older departments, and they gradually assumed new functions, as well. Over time, Congress has also created and later combined or abolished some departments.

Chief Officers and Staff

Each department is headed by a **secretary,** except for the Department of Justice, whose work is directed by the **attorney general.** As you will see, these department heads serve in the President's Cabinet. However, the duties as the chief officer of their own department take up most of their time.

Each department head is the primary link between presidential policy and his or her own department. Just as importantly, each of them also strives to promote and protect his or her department with the White House, with Congress and its committees, with the rest of the federal bureaucracy, and with the media and the public.

An under secretary or deputy secretary and several assistant secretaries aid the secretary in his or her multidimensional role. These officials are also named by the President and confirmed by the Senate. Staff support for the secretary comes

► President George Washington's (right) first Cabinet included Secretary of State Thomas Jefferson (second left); and Secretary of the Treasury Alexander Hamilton (second right).

Federal Workers Around the Country

Iowa
A scientist with the Department of Agriculture conducts soil tests in Iowa.

California
A physical therapist helps a patient at a Veterans Health Administration hospital.

Maryland
A researcher reviews data at the National Institutes of Health.

Interpreting Diagrams Federal employees can be found wherever the Federal Government has work to do, including a Veterans Health Administration hospital in California, a farm in Iowa, or a federal office in Maryland. *Why do only ten percent of federal employees work in the Washington, D.C., area?*

from assistants and aides with a wide range of titles in such areas as personnel, planning, legal advice, budgeting, and public relations.

Subunits

Each department is made up of a number of subunits, both staff and line. Each of these subunits, or agencies, is usually further divided into smaller working units. Thus, the Criminal Division in the Department of Justice is composed of many sections, including, for example, the Terrorism and Violent Crime Section and the Narcotics and Dangerous Drugs Section. Approximately 80 percent of the men and women who head the bureaus, divisions, and other major units within each of the executive departments are career people, not political appointees.

Many of the agencies in executive departments are structured geographically. Much of the work is done through regional and/or district offices, which, in turn, direct the activities of the agency's employees in the field. In fact, nearly 90 percent of all of the men and women who work as civilian employees of the Federal

Government are stationed somewhere outside the nation's capital.

Take the Veterans Health Administration, part of the Department of Veterans Affairs, to illustrate the point. It does nearly all of its work providing medical care to eligible veterans at 173 medical centers, 376 outpatient clinics, and a large number of other facilities located throughout the country.

The Departments Today

Today, the executive departments vary a great deal in terms of visibility, size, and importance. The Department of State is the oldest and the most prestigious department; but it is also among the smallest, with only about 25,000 employees. The Department of Defense is the largest, with nearly 670,000 civilian workers, and another 1.4 million men and women in uniform.

The Department of Health and Human Services has the largest budget; it accounts for approximately a third of all federal spending each year. The Department of Veterans Affairs became the newest of the departments when Congress created it in 1988.

The Fourteen Executive Departments

DEPARTMENT (YEAR ESTABLISHED)	PRINCIPAL FUNCTIONS	IMPORTANT AGENCIES
State (1789)	• Advises President on foreign policy • Negotiates agreements with foreign countries • Represents the United States abroad and in international organizations	• Foreign Service • Regional Bureaus • Bureau of International Organization Affairs • Bureau of Consular Affairs (Passport Office)
Treasury (1789)	• Produces coins and bills • Collects taxes • Borrows money and manages public debt • Enforces alcohol, tobacco, and firearms laws	• Internal Revenue Service • United States Mint • Bureau of the Public Debt • Customs Service • Bureau of Alcohol, Tobacco, and Firearms • Secret Service
Defense [a] (1789)	• Provides military forces to deter war and protect the nation's security	• Joint Chiefs of Staff • Departments of the Army, the Navy, and the Air Force
Justice [b] (1870)	• Provides legal advice to President • Enforces federal laws • Represents United States in court • Operates federal prisons • Oversees immigration and naturalization	• Federal Bureau of Investigation • Criminal Division • Drug Enforcement Administration • Civil Rights Division • Immigration and Naturalization Service
Interior (1849)	• Manages public lands, wildlife refuges, and national parks • Operates hydroelectric power plants • Helps Native Americans manage their affairs	• U.S. Fish and Wildlife Service • National Park Service • Bureau of Land Management • U.S. Geological Survey • Bureau of Indian Affairs • Bureau of Reclamation
Agriculture (1889)	• Manages national forests • Inspects food • Assists farmers and ranchers • Administers food stamp and school lunch programs	• Agricultural Research Service • Farm Service Agency • Food and Nutrition Service • Forest Service • Food Safety and Inspection Service
Commerce [c] (1903)	• Conducts census • Grants patents and registers trademarks • Promotes international trade, economic growth, and technological development	• Bureau of the Census • National Oceanic and • Patent and Trademark Office Atmospheric Administration • International Trade Administration • Economic Development Administration
Labor (1913)	• Enforces federal laws on minimum wages, maximum hours, and safe working conditions • Operates job training programs • Administers unemployment insurance and workers' compensation programs	• Employment Standards Administration • Occupational Safety and Health Administration • Employment and Training Administration • Bureau of Labor Statistics

Interpreting Tables Over the years, Congress created the 14 Executive Departments to handle the responsibilities of the Federal Government. *Which three Cabinet departments are the most important? Why?*

The 14 departments are profiled in the table on these two pages. The principal functions they perform and the titles of their major agencies provide a useful description of each of them.

The Cabinet

The Cabinet is an informal advisory body brought together by the President to serve his needs. The Constitution makes no mention of it, nor did Congress create it. Instead, the Cabinet is the product of custom and usage.[6]

At its first session in 1789, Congress established four executive posts: secretary of state, secretary of the treasury, secretary of war, and attorney general. By his second term, Washington was regularly seeking the advice of the four outstanding people he had named to those offices: Thomas Jefferson in the Department of State, Alexander Hamilton at the Treasury, Henry Knox in the War Department, and Edmund Randolph, the attorney general. So the Cabinet was born.

---

[6]The closest approach to it is in Article II, Section 2, Clause 1, where the President is given the power to "require the opinion, in writing, of the principal officer in each of the executive departments, upon any subject relating to the duties of their respective offices." The Cabinet was first mentioned in an act of Congress in 1907, well over a century after its birth.

DEPARTMENT (YEAR ESTABLISHED)	PRINCIPAL FUNCTIONS	IMPORTANT AGENCIES
Health and Human Services [d] (1953)	• Funds health care research programs • Conducts programs to prevent and control disease • Enforces pure food and drug laws • Administers Medicare and Medicaid	• Administration for Children and Families • Administration on Aging • Centers for Disease Control and Prevention • Food and Drug Administration • National Institutes of Health
Housing and Urban Development (1965)	• Operates home-financing and public housing programs • Enforces fair housing laws	• Office of Housing • Office of Fair Housing and Equal Opportunity • Government National Mortgage Association
Transportation (1967)	• Administers programs to promote and regulate highways, mass transit, railroads, waterways, air travel, and oil and gas pipelines • Enforces maritime (sea) law	• Federal Highway Administration • Federal Aviation Administration • Maritime Administration • United States Coast Guard
Energy (1977)	• Promotes production of renewable energy, fossil fuels, and nuclear energy • Transmits and sells hydroelectric power • Conducts nuclear weapons research and production	• Office of Energy Efficiency and Renewable Energy • Office of Nuclear Energy, Science and Technology • Regional Power Administration • Office of Defense Programs
Education (1979)	• Administers federal aid to schools • Conducts educational research	• Office of Elementary and Secondary Education • Office of Educational Research and Improvement
Veterans Affairs (1988)	• Administers benefits, pensions, and medical programs for veterans of the armed forces • Oversees military cemeteries	• Veterans Benefits Administration • Veterans Health Administration • National Cemetery System

[a] Congress created the National Military Establishment as an executive department, headed by the Secretary of Defense, in 1947. It was renamed the Department of Defense, in 1949. Since 1947 the department has included the former cabinet-level Departments of War (1789) and the Navy (1798), and the Department of the Air Force. The Secretaries of the Army, the Navy and the Air Force do not hold Cabinet rank.

[b] Congress created the office of Attorney General in 1789 but did not establish the Department of Justice until 1870.

[c] Congress created the Department of Commerce and Labor in 1903; it was replaced by the separate Departments of Commerce and of Labor in 1913.

[d] Congress created the Department of Health, Education, and Welfare in 1953. HEW's education functions were transferred to a new Department of Education in 1979, and HEW was renamed at that time.

By tradition, the heads of the now 14 executive departments form the Cabinet. Each of the last several Presidents has regularly added a number of other top officials to the group, including the director of the OMB, the director of the Office of Homeland Security, and the President's chief domestic policy advisor. Every Vice President since Alben Barkley, who served under President Truman (1949–1953), has also been a regular participant at Cabinet meetings. Several other major figures regularly attend Cabinet meetings in the Bush Administration—in particular the White House chief of staff, the United States trade representative, and the administrator of the Environmental Protection Agency.

Choosing Cabinet Members

The President appoints the head of each of the 14 executive departments. Each of these appointments is subject to confirmation by the Senate, but rejections have been exceedingly rare. The Senate generally respects the personal choice of the President. Of the more than 600 presidential appointments made since 1789, only 12 have been rejected by the Senate. The most recent rejection occurred in 1989, when the Senate refused to confirm President George H.W. Bush's selection of John Tower as secretary of defense.

President George W. Bush's nomination of John Ashcroft as Attorney General generated significant opposition in 2001; the Senate confirmed the President's choice by a narrow vote, however.

Government at Work: The Bureaucracy   **427** ★★★

▲ **The Bush Cabinet** The Cabinet includes the heads of 14 executive departments. Cabinet-rank members also include the Vice President and the heads of several additional agencies.

Many factors influence these presidential choices. Party is almost always important. Republican Presidents do not often pick Democrats, and vice versa. One or more of a new President's appointees usually come from among those who played a major role in the recent presidential campaign.

Of course, professional qualifications and practical experience are also taken into account in the selection of Cabinet secretaries. Geography also plays a part. In broad terms, each President tries to give some regional balance to the Cabinet. Thus, the secretary of the interior often comes from the West, where most of the department's work is carried out.

Many interest groups care about Cabinet secretary appointments, and they do influence some of the choices. Thus, the secretary of agriculture almost always has a background closely related to agriculture. The secretary of the treasury usually comes from the financial community, the secretary of commerce from the ranks of business, and so on.

Other considerations also guide the President's choices. Gender and race, an appointee's stand on the "hot" issues of the day, management abilities and experience, and other personal characteristics—these and a host of other factors play a part in selecting Cabinet members.

Women and Minorities

Women and minorities have only gradually become represented in the Cabinet. Franklin Roosevelt appointed the first woman, Frances T. Perkins, secretary of labor from 1933 to 1945. Lyndon Johnson named the first African American, Robert C. Weaver, as the first secretary of housing and urban development (HUD) in 1966.

The Ford Cabinet was the first to include both a woman (Carla Hills, secretary of HUD) and an African American (William T. Coleman, secretary of transportation); both were appointed in 1975. Jimmy Carter appointed the first African American woman to the Cabinet when he named Patricia Roberts Harris secretary of HUD in 1977 and then secretary of health and human services (HHS) in 1979. Ronald Reagan appointed the first Hispanic Cabinet member; Lauro F. Cavazos became secretary of education in 1988.

President Clinton picked more women, more African Americans, and more Hispanics than any of his predecessors. Over his eight years in office (1993–2001), the Cabinet included five women, six African Americans, four Hispanics, and its first Asian American, Norman Mineta, the Secretary of Commerce in the last year of the Clinton administration. Janet Reno became the first woman to serve as Attorney General and Madeleine Albright the first to be Secretary of State.

President George W. Bush's first Cabinet appointments included two African Americans: Secretary of State Colin Powell and Secretary of Education Rod Paige; three women: Secretary of Labor Elaine Chao, Secretary of the Interior Gale Norton, and Secretary of Agriculture Ann Veneman; and one Hispanic, Secretary of Housing and Urban Development Melvin Martinez. Secretary Chao was born in China and is the first Chinese American to hold a Cabinet office. Norman Mineta, a Democrat, named Secretary of Transportation, also served in the Clinton Cabinet.

The Cabinet's Role

Cabinet members have two major jobs. Individually, each is the administrative head of one of the executive departments. Together, they are advisors to the President.

A number of Presidents have given great weight to the Cabinet and to its advice; others have given it only a secondary role. George H. W. Bush's Cabinet (1989–1993) had more influence with the President than any Cabinet since the Eisenhower presidency in the 1950s. The Cabinet also played a prominent role in the Clinton administration (1993– 2001). On the other hand, John Kennedy described his Cabinet meetings as "a waste of time."

Kennedy's view notwithstanding, most Presidents have held regular Cabinet meetings—where reports are made and discussed, and advice is offered to the chief executive. That advice need not be taken, of course. Abraham Lincoln once laid a proposition he favored before his Cabinet. Each member opposed it, whereupon Lincoln declared: "Seven nays, one aye: the ayes have it."

William Howard Taft put the role of the Cabinet in its proper light years ago:

PRIMARY Sources *"The Constitution . . . contains no suggestion of a meeting of all the department heads, in consultation over general governmental matters. The Cabinet is a mere creation of the President's will. . . . It exists only by custom. If the President desired to dispense with it, he could do so.* **"**
—*Our Chief Magistrate and His Powers*

Interpreting Political Cartoons Madeleine Albright was President Clinton's second secretary of state. *According to this cartoon, why did President Clinton need a secretary of state?*

No President has ever suggested eliminating the Cabinet. However, several Presidents have leaned on other, unofficial advisory groups, and sometimes more heavily than on the Cabinet. Andrew Jackson began the practice when he became President in 1829. Several of his close friends often met with him in the kitchen at the White House and, inevitably, came to be known as the Kitchen Cabinet. Franklin Roosevelt's Brain Trust of the 1930s and Harry Truman's Cronies in the late 1940s were in the same mold.

Section 3 Assessment

Key Terms and Main Ideas
1. How were the **executive departments** created?
2. What is the role of the **secretary** of an executive department?
3. Which department does the **attorney general** lead?
4. Who decides how often the **Cabinet** meets?

Critical Thinking
5. **Drawing Inferences** What are the two most important jobs of the head of an executive department?
6. **Drawing Conclusions** What can the President do to determine who serves in the Cabinet? How does a President shape the importance of the Cabinet?

7. **Determining Cause and Effect** How has the Cabinet changed over time? What factors have driven these changes?

 Take It to the Net

8. Select an executive department and follow a link to that department's Web site. Explore the Web site and write an essay explaining what the department is currently working on. Be sure to give examples of recent events. Use the links provided in the Social Studies area at the following Web site for help in completing this activity. **www.phschool.com**

Independent Agencies

OBJECTIVES

1. **Explain** why Congress has created independent agencies.
2. **Identify** the characteristics of independent executive agencies and independent regulatory commissions.
3. **Describe** the structure of government corporations.

WHY IT MATTERS

Some 150 executive branch agencies are not located within any of the 14 executive departments. Some of them rival Cabinet departments in size of their budgets, their functions, and the number of their employees.

POLITICAL DICTIONARY

★ **independent agencies**
★ **independent executive agencies**
★ **independent regulatory commissions**
★ **quasi-legislative**
★ **quasi-judicial**
★ **government corporation**

Until the 1880s, nearly all that the Federal Government did was done through its Cabinet departments. Since then, however, Congress has created a large number of additional agencies—the **independent agencies**—located outside the departments. Today, they number nearly 150. Most of the more important ones are included in the chart on page 417.

Several independent agencies administer programs similar to those of the Cabinet departments. The work of the National Aeronautics and Space Administration (NASA), for example, is similar to that of a number of agencies in the Department of Defense. NASA's responsibilities are also not very far removed from those of the Department of Transportation.

Neither the size of an independent agency's budget nor the number of its employees provides a good way to distinguish between many of these agencies and the executive departments. The newest and largest of them, the Social Security Administration, became an independent agency in 1994. Since that time, its budget has been larger than that of any Cabinet department. The Administration now employs more than 64,000 people, and so by itself has more workers and a larger payroll than several Cabinet departments.

Why Independent Agencies?

The reasons these agencies exist outside the Cabinet departments are nearly as numerous as the agencies themselves. A few major reasons stand out, however. Some have been set up outside the regular departmental structure because they do not fit well within any department. The General Services Administration (GSA) is a leading example.

The GSA is the Federal Government's major housekeeping agency. Its main chores include the construction and operation of public buildings, purchase and distribution of supplies and equipment, management of real property, and a host of similar services to most other federal agencies. The Office of Personnel Management (OPM) is another example. It is the hiring agency for nearly all other federal agencies.

Congress has given some of these agencies an independent status to protect them from the influence of both partisan and pressure politics. Major examples include the OPM, the Social Security Administration, and the Federal Election Commission. The point can be turned on its head, too; some agencies are located outside any Cabinet department because that is exactly where certain pressure groups want them.

▲ *NASA* This special envelope celebrates NASA's *Apollo* missions to the moon.

Other federal agencies were born as independents largely by accident. No thought was given to future problems of administrative confusion when they were created. Finally, some agencies are independent because of the peculiar and sensitive nature of their functions. This is especially true of the independent regulatory commissions.

The label *independent agency* is a catchall. Most of these agencies are independent only in the sense that they are not located within any of the 14 Cabinet departments. They are not independent of the President and the executive branch. Some are independent in a much more concrete way, however. For most purposes, they do lie outside the executive branch and are largely free of presidential control.

Perhaps the best way to understand all of these independent agencies is to divide them into three main groups: (1) the independent executive agencies, (2) the independent regulatory commissions, and (3) the government corporations.

The Independent Executive Agencies

The **independent executive agencies** include most of the independent agencies. Some are large, with thousands of employees, multimillion-dollar or even billion-dollar budgets, and extremely important public tasks to perform.

The GSA, NASA, and the EPA are three examples of larger independent executive agencies. They are organized much like the Cabinet departments; that is, they are headed by a single administrator with subunits operating on a regional basis, and so on. The most important difference between the independent executive agencies and the 14 executive departments is simply that they do not have Cabinet status.

Some of the agencies in this group are not administrative and policy giants. They do important work, however, and sometimes attract public notice. The Civil Rights Commission, the Peace Corps, the Federal Election Commission, and the National Transportation Safety Board all fall into this category.

Most independent executive agencies operate far from the limelight. They have few employees, small budgets, and rarely attract any attention. The American Battle Monuments Commission,

Voices on Government

Donna Shalala served as secretary of health and human services from 1993 to 2001. Before that, she was president of the University of Wisconsin, the first woman to head a Big Ten university. She is now president of the University of Miami (Florida). Shalala found an earlier experience an important step in her career:

❝ *The Peace Corps is a voice for democracy and American values. . . . I know this from my own service as a Peace Corps volunteer in Iran in the 1960s, and from a trip I took to Thailand just last month where I met with Peace Corps volunteers doing AIDS prevention work. My Peace Corps service not only helped prepare me for my job as Secretary of Health and Human Services, it helped prepare me for life.* ❞

Evaluating the Quotation

What aspects of serving in the Peace Corps would provide useful background for a Cabinet post or other federal job?

the Citizens' Stamp Advisory Committee, and the Migratory Bird Conservation Commission are typical of the dozens of these seldom seen or heard public bodies.

Independent Regulatory Commissions

The **independent regulatory commissions** stand out among the independent agencies because they are largely beyond the reach of presidential direction and control. There are ten of these agencies today, each created to regulate, or police, important aspects of the nation's economy. Their vital statistics appear in the table on the next page.

Structured for Independence

The independent regulatory commissions' large measure of independence from the White House comes mainly from the way in which Congress has structured them. Each is headed by a board or commission made up of five to

The Independent Regulatory Commissions

Agency	Date Established	Number of Members	Term of Members	Major Functions
Board of Governors, Federal Reserve System (the Fed)	1913	7	14 years	Supervises banking system, practices; regulates money supply, use of credit in economy.
Federal Trade Commission (FTC)	1914	5	7 years	Enforces antitrust, other laws prohibiting unfair competition, price-fixing, false advertising, other unfair business practices.
Securities and Exchange Commission (SEC)	1934	5	5 years	Regulates securities, other financial markets, investment companies, brokers; enforces laws prohibiting fraud, other dishonest investment practices.
Federal Communications Commission (FCC)	1934	5	5 years	Regulates interstate and foreign communications by radio, television, wire, satellite, and cable.
National Labor Relations Board (NLRB)	1935	5	5 years	Administers federal labor-management relations laws; holds collective bargaining elections; prevents, remedies unfair labor practices.
Federal Maritime Commission (FMC)	1936	5	5 years	Regulates waterborne foreign, domestic off-shore commerce of the United States; supervises rates, services.
Consumer Product Safety Commission (CPSC)	1972	5	5 years	Sets, enforces safety standards for consumer products; directs recall of unsafe products; conducts safety research, information programs.
Nuclear Regulatory Commission (NRC)	1974	5	5 years	Licenses, regulates all civilian nuclear facilities and civilian uses of nuclear materials.[a]
Commodity Futures Trading Commission (CFTC)	1974	5	5 years	Regulates commodity exchanges, brokers, futures trading in agricultural, metal, other commodities.
Federal Energy Regulatory Commission (FERC)	1977	5	4 years	Regulates, sets rates for transmission, sale of natural gas, electricity, oil by pipeline; licenses hydroelectric power projects.[b]

[a]These functions performed by the Atomic Energy Commission from 1946 to 1974 (when the AEC was abolished); other AEC functions now performed by agencies in the Energy Department.

[b]These functions performed by the Federal Power Commission (created in 1930) until the FPC was abolished in 1977. The FERC is within the Energy Department, but only for administrative purposes; otherwise it is independent (except the Secretary of Energy may set reasonable deadlines for the FERC action in any matter before it). Under terms of National Energy Act of 1978, the FERC's authority to regulate natural gas prices ended in 1985.

Interpreting Tables Independent regulatory commissions are independent of all three branches of government, and are exceptions to the separation of powers rule. *How do the functions listed above show that these commissions have legislative and judicial powers?*

seven members appointed by the President with Senate consent. However, those officials have terms of such length that it is unlikely a President will gain control over any of these agencies through the appointment process, at least not in a single presidential term.

Several other features of these boards and commissions put them beyond the reach of presidential control. No more than a bare majority of the members of each board or commission may belong to the same political party. Thus, several of those officers must belong to the party out of power.

Moreover, the appointed terms of the members are staggered so that the term of only one member on each board or commission expires in any one year. Finally, most of these officers can be removed by the President only for those causes Congress has specified.[7]

As with the other independent agencies, the regulatory commissions are executive bodies. That is, Congress has given them the power to

---

[7]Recall this point from Chapter 14, on page 397. The members of five of these bodies (the SEC, FCC, CPSC, NRC, and CFTC) are exceptions. Congress has provided that any of them may be removed at the President's discretion.

administer the programs for which they were created. However, unlike those other independent agencies, the regulatory commissions are also **quasi-legislative** and **quasi-judicial** bodies.[8] That is, Congress has given them certain legislative-like and judicial-like powers.

These agencies exercise their quasi-legislative powers when they make rules and regulations. Those rules and regulations have the force of law. They implement, spell out the details of, the laws that Congress has directed these regulatory bodies to enforce.

To illustrate the point: Congress has said that those who want to borrow money by issuing stocks, bonds, or other securities must provide a "full and fair disclosure" of all pertinent information to prospective investors. The Securities and Exchange Commission (SEC) makes that requirement effective and indicates how those who offer securities are to meet it by issuing rules and regulations.

The regulatory commissions exercise their quasi-judicial powers when they decide disputes in those fields in which Congress has given them policing authority. For example, if an investor in Iowa thinks a local stockbroker has defrauded (cheated) him, he may file a complaint with the SEC's regional office in Chicago. SEC agents will investigate and report their findings, and the agency will judge the merits of the complaint much as a court would do. Decisions made by the SEC, and by the other independent regulatory bodies, can be appealed to the United States courts of appeals.

In a sense, Congress has created these agencies to act in its place. Congress could hold hearings and set interest rates, license radio and TV stations and nuclear reactors, check on business practices, and do the many other things it has directed the regulatory commissions to do. These activities are complex and time-consuming, however, and they demand constant and expert attention. If Congress did all of this work, it would have no time for its other and important legislative work.

Note that these regulatory bodies possess all three of the basic governmental powers: executive, legislative, and judicial. They are

---

[8]The prefix *quasi* is from the Latin, meaning "in a certain sense, resembling, seemingly."

exceptions to the principle of separation of powers. Technically, they should not be grouped with the other independent agencies. Instead, they should somehow be located somewhere between the executive and legislative branches, and between the executive and judicial branches, too.

Rethinking Regulation

Several authorities, and most recent Presidents, have urged that at least the administrative functions of the independent regulatory commissions be given to executive department agencies. Critics have raised other serious questions about these agencies and proposed to abolish or redesign them.

The most troubling questions are these: Have some of the independent regulatory commissions been captured by the special interests they are expected to regulate? Are all of the many and detailed rules created by these agencies really needed? Do some of these rules have the effect of stifling legitimate competition in the free enterprise system? Do some of them add unreasonably to the costs of doing business and therefore to the prices that consumers must pay?

Congress sets the basic policies of the regulatory agencies, and so it has a major responsibility to answer these questions. It has responded to some questions in recent years, particularly by deregulating much of the nation's transportation

▲ A 1945 map (top) shows one airline's regulated routes in red, while a contemporary map (bottom) lists the routes freely chosen by a different airline. *Critical Thinking* **Why might the government have decided, under regulation, to require airlines to serve certain cities?**

▲ The government created Amtrak as a corporation to provide passenger train service. After years of losing money and relying on federal subsidies to stay afloat, Amtrak was told that Congress would not cover its losses after 2002. *Critical Thinking* **What advantages might Amtrak enjoy as a government corporation?**

industry. Airlines, bus companies, truckers, and railroads have greater freedom to operate today than they did only a few years ago. The same trend can be seen in the field of communications, notably with regard to cable television.

Two major regulatory bodies have actually disappeared in recent years. The Civil Aeronautics Board was created in 1938 to oversee commercial air traffic in the United States. For decades it assigned the routes to be flown and the rates charged by airlines and other commercial air carriers, until it was abolished by Congress in 1985.

The Interstate Commerce Commission was the very first of the regulatory commissions to be established by Congress, in 1887. For a century it issued licenses and regulated the rates and routes and most other aspects of commercial transportation by rail, highway, and water. It, too, was abolished by Congress, in 1996.

The Government Corporations

Several of the independent agencies are **government corporations.** Like most of the other independent agencies, government corporations are within the executive branch and subject to the President's direction and control. Unlike the other agencies, however, they were set up by Congress to carry out certain business-like activities.

Congress established the first government corporation when it chartered the Bank of the United States in 1791. Yet government corporations were little used until World War I and the Depression. In both periods Congress set up dozens of corporations to carry out emergency programs. Several still exist—among them, the Federal Deposit Insurance Corporation (FDIC), which insures bank deposits, and the Export-Import Bank of the United States (Eximbank), which makes loans to help the export and sale of American goods abroad.

There are now more than 50 of these corporations. They deliver the mail (the U.S. Postal Service); insure bank deposits (the FDIC); provide intercity rail passenger service (the National Railroad Passenger Corporation, Amtrak); protect pension benefits (the Pension Benefit Guaranty Corporation); and generate, sell, and distribute electric power (the Tennessee Valley Authority).[9]

---

[9]State and local governments maintain their own government corporations, most often called authorities, to operate airports, turnpikes, seaports, power plants, liquor stores, and housing developments, and to conduct many other corporate activities. The Port Authority of New York and New Jersey is one of the best known.

Government v. Private Corporations

The typical government corporation is set up much like a corporation in the private sector. It is run by a board of directors, with a general manager who directs the corporation's operations according to the policies established by that board. Most government corporations produce income that is plowed back into the business.

There are several striking differences between government and private corporations, however. Congress decides the purpose for which the public agencies exist and the functions they can perform. Their officers are public officers; in fact, all who work for these corporations are public employees. The President selects most of the top officers of government corporations with Senate confirmation.

In addition, these public agencies are financed by public funds appropriated by Congress, not private investors. The Federal Government, representing the American people, owns the stock.

The advantage most often claimed for these agencies is their flexibility. It is said that the government corporation, freed from the controls of regular departmental organization, can carry on its activities with the incentive, efficiency, and ability to experiment that make many private concerns successful. Whether that claim is valid is open to question. At the very least, it raises this complex issue: Is a public corporation's need for flexibility compatible with the democratic requirement that all public agencies be held responsible and accountable to the people?

Degrees of Independence

The degree of independence and flexibility government corporations have varies considerably. In fact, some corporations are not independent at all. They are attached to an executive department.

The Commodity Credit Corporation, for example, is the government's major crop-loan and farm-subsidy agency. It is located within the Department of Agriculture, and the secretary of agriculture chairs its seven-member board. The Commodity Credit Corporation carries out most of its functions through a line agency in the Department of Agriculture—the Farm Service Agency—which is also subject to the direct control of the secretary.

Some corporations do have considerable independence, however. The Tennessee Valley Authority (TVA) is a case in point. It operates under a statute that gives it considerable discretion over its own programs. Although its budget is subject to review by the OMB, the President, and Congress, the TVA has a large say in the uses of the income its several operations produce.[10]

---

[10]The TVA is a major example of government in business. Congress established the TVA in the Tennessee Valley Authority Act of 1933. The act called for the coordinated development and use of the natural resources of parts of seven southern States. The TVA has had an extraordinary impact on the Tennessee River Valley and its approximately eight million residents. Its operations include electric power, flood control, reforestation, soil conservation, agricultural research, recreational facilities, and the promotion of industrial growth. The TVA's power program is self-supporting. Much of its other activities are supported by Congress. Still, it generates considerable revenues from sales of electricity and fertilizer and from its ability to issue bonds.

Section 4 Assessment

Key Terms and Main Ideas

1. How do **independent agencies** differ from the other agencies in the executive branch?
2. What is the main purpose of the **independent regulatory commissions**?
3. What is the difference between a legislative body and a **quasi-legislative** body?

Critical Thinking

4. **Drawing Inferences** Name three reasons why independent agencies operate outside the executive departments.
5. **Making Decisions** Economist Milton Friedman called bureaucracy "both a vehicle whereby special interests can achieve their objectives and an important special interest in its own right." What can the government do to minimize the situation Friedman describes?

 Take It to the Net

6. Read an article about bureaucracy and compose a list of ten facts you learned from the article. Using these facts, write a short essay in which you explore both the positive and negative aspects of a bureaucracy. Use the links provided in the Social Studies area at the following Web site for help in completing this activity. **www.phschool.com**

Gathering Information from Government Sources

You might not know it, but if you're a U.S. citizen, you're a co-owner of a treasure-trove of information. The government uses a portion of the tax dollars it collects from its citizens to generate massive amounts of transcripts, research papers, legal records, maps, statistics, studies, videos, facsimiles, manuscripts, and music.

By far the best way to access federal information today is on the Internet. The growth of public and private Web sites containing government information has revolutionized the research process. If you don't have Internet access, however, many of the sources listed at right are available in print at large libraries. To seek out government information, try these steps:

1. Define what information you're seeking. Knowing what you need will help narrow your search. Do you need federal, regional, State, or local information? Are you looking for records, statistics, primary sources, or other media? Decide on a research objective, and write a question that summarizes it.

2. Determine where to search. What agency of the government is responsible for the topic you're researching? Information on water pollution, for example, might come from the Environmental Protection Agency, the Interior Department, the *Congressional Record*, and State and local sites. Using your question from Step 1, identify agencies that might provide relevant information.

3. Gather information. As you collect material, make note of the source: Is it public or private? Is it reliable? Steer clear of anonymous Web sites.

Test for Success

Choose a government-related topic that interests you. Compile a list of at least five good places to search for the information.

Searching Uncle Sam

First Gov is a government Web site that provides the public with easily accessible online U.S. government resources. http://www.firstgov.gov

The National Archives and Records Administration (NARA) manages and provides access to all federal records dating back to the Declaration of Independence —more than 4 billion pieces of paper and 6 million photographs. http://www.nara.gov

The World Factbook is the authoritative source for country-by-country information from the U.S. Central Intelligence Agency (CIA), published annually. http://www.odci.gov/cia/publications/factbook

The Census Bureau tracks where we live, where we work, what we earn, what we eat—you name it. http://www.census.gov

The FedWorld Information Network is a searchable database with links to government agencies. http://www.fedworld.gov

FedStats is a searchable database created by the Federal Interagency Council on Statistical Policy. Get federal, regional, State, and county statistics presented in tables, graphs, and maps. Contains the indispensable Statistical Abstracts. http://www.fedstats.gov

The Library of Congress (LOC), created in 1800, is the world's largest library, the government's official storehouse of more than 115 million multimedia items. Any item ever copyrighted is here. http://www.loc.gov

Thomas, named after President Thomas Jefferson, is the official record of everything that happens in Congress. Thomas contains the *Congressional Record* as well as information on committee hearings and schedules. http://thomas.loc.gov

FindLaw is an online, private source of legal information: Supreme Court decisions, legal issues, news, and other resources. http://www.findlaw.com

5 The Civil Service

Section Preview

OBJECTIVES

1. **Describe** the development of the civil service.
2. **Identify** characteristics of the civil service as it exists today.
3. **Analyze** the restrictions on the political activities of members of the civil service.

WHY IT MATTERS

Most people who work for the Federal Government are members of the civil service. Over time, civil service reformers have worked to reduce corruption and political influence.

POLITICAL DICTIONARY

★ **civil service**
★ **spoils system**
★ **patronage**
★ **register**
★ **bipartisan**

The **civil service** is composed of those civilian employees who perform the administrative work of government. Some 2.7 million men and women work for the Federal Government today.[11] Only about 300,000 of those work in the Washington area. The rest have jobs in regional, field, and local offices scattered throughout the country and around the world.

The President appoints the people who hold the highest ranking jobs in the executive branch. There are only about 2,500 of those positions—at the top levels of the Executive Office, the Cabinet departments, the independent agencies, and in American embassies and other diplomatic stations. All of the other jobs in the federal bureaucracy are covered by some aspect of the civil service system.

Development of the Civil Service

The Constitution says very little about the staffing of the federal bureaucracy. The only direct reference is in Article II, which says that the President

FROM THE Constitution *"shall nominate, and by and with the Advice and Consent of the Senate, shall appoint Ambassadors, other public Ministers and Consuls, Judges of the supreme Court, and all other Officers of the United States, whose appointments are not herein otherwise provided for, and which shall be established by law: but the Congress may by law vest the appointment of such inferior officers, as they think proper, in the President alone, in the Courts of Law, or in the Heads of Departments. "*

—Article II, Section 2, Clause 2

◀ The civil service includes people like this ranger who works at Grand Canyon National Park in Arizona.

---

[11]Another 1.5 million men and women serve in the armed forces; see Chapter 17. Altogether, there are now some 17.5 million civilian public employees in this country. More than 4 million work for the States, and another 11 million work for local governments (including 6.5 million persons employed by school districts). About 2.5 million of those who work for State and local governments are employed on a part-time basis.

A NICE FAMILY PARTY.

Interpreting Political Cartoons This cartoon comments on the spoils system expanded under Andrew Jackson. ***What metaphor does this cartoon use for the spoils system?***

The Beginnings

When he became President in 1789, George Washington knew that the success of the new government would depend in large part on those whom he appointed to office. Those to be chosen, he said, would be "such persons alone . . . as shall be the best qualified." Still, he favored members of his own party, the Federalists. So did his successor, John Adams.

In 1801 Thomas Jefferson found most federal posts filled by men politically and personally opposed to him. He agreed with Washington's standard of fitness for office, but he combined it with another: political acceptability. Jefferson dismissed several hundred Federalists and replaced them with members of his own party, the Democratic-Republicans.

The Spoils System

By the late 1820s, the number of federal employees had risen above 10,000. When Andrew Jackson became President in 1829, he dismissed over 200 presidential appointees and nearly 2,000 other officeholders. Jacksonian Democrats replaced them.

Ever since, Andrew Jackson has been called the "father" of the **spoils system**—the practice of giving offices and other favors of government to political supporters and friends. The phrase comes from a statement made on the floor of the Senate in 1832. Senator William Learned Marcy of New York, defending Jackson's appointment of an ambassador, declared: "To the victor belongs the spoils of the enemy."

To call Jackson the father of the spoils system is not altogether fair. Jefferson had laid its foundations at the federal level in 1801. The practice of giving jobs to supporters and friends—also known as **patronage**—was in wide use at the State and local levels long before Jackson's presidency.

Jackson saw his appointing policy as democratic. In his first message to Congress, he explained and defended it on four grounds: (1) Since the duties of public office are simple, any normally intelligent person can fill such office. (2) There should be a "rotation in office" so that a large number of people can have the privilege of serving in government. (3) Long service in office by any person can lead to both tyranny and inefficiency. (4) The people are entitled to have the party they have placed in power in control of all offices of government, top to bottom.

Whatever Jackson's view, many saw the spoils system as a way to build and hold power. For the next half-century, every change of administration brought a new round of rewards and punishments. As the government's activities, agencies, and payrolls grew, so did the spoils. Many posts were filled by political hacks who were ill-equipped for their jobs. Inefficiency and even corruption became the order of the day.

The Movement to Reform

Able people, in and out of government, pressed for reforms, but little came of their efforts. Congress did create a Civil Service Commission in 1871, but it soon died away because Congress failed to provide it with enough money.

A tragedy at last brought about fundamental changes in the hiring and other staffing practices of the Federal Government. In 1881, President James Garfield was fatally shot by a disappointed office-seeker, Charles J. Guiteau. Garfield had rejected the mentally unstable Guiteau's request that he be appointed to a high diplomatic post.

The nation was horrified and outraged. Congress, pushed hard by Garfield's successor, Chester Arthur, passed the Pendleton Act—the Civil Service Act of 1883.[12]

---

[12]The Republican convention in 1880 was sharply divided by the civil service question. Its nominee, Garfield, was a strong supporter of reform. To balance the ticket, the convention chose Arthur, a leader of the anti-reform faction, as his running mate. Garfield's assassination brought a dramatic change in Arthur's stance; as President he became a leading champion of reform.

The Pendleton Act

The Pendleton Act laid the foundation of the present federal civil service system. Its main purpose was to make merit—the quality of one's work—the basis for hiring, promotion, and other personnel actions in the federal work force.

The law set up two categories of employment in the executive branch: the classified and the unclassified services. All hiring for positions in the classified service was to be based on merit. That quality was to be measured by "practical" examinations given by an independent agency, the Civil Service Commission.

The Pendleton Act placed only about 10 percent of the Federal Government's then 130,000 employees in the classified service; it did give the President the power to extend that coverage, however. Theodore Roosevelt championed the merit system, and by the end of his term in 1909 the classified umbrella covered two thirds of the 365,000 members of the federal work force. Today, nearly 90 percent of all of the men and women who work for executive branch agencies are covered by the merit system.[13]

The Civil Service Today

The first goal of civil service reform—the elimination of the spoils system—was largely achieved in the early years of the last century. Gradually, a new purpose emerged: recruiting and keeping the best available people in the federal work force.

On the whole, efforts to reach that newer goal have succeeded. Today most federal employees are hired through a competitive process. They are paid and promoted on the basis of written evaluations by their superiors. They are generally protected from disciplinary actions or dismissal for partisan reasons.

Still, the federal civil service is not perfect. Critics often claim that not enough attention is paid to merit in the merit system.

The Office of Personnel Management

The Office of Personnel Management, created in 1978, is now the Federal Government's central personnel agency. Like its predecessor, the old Civil Service Commission, it is an independent agency in the executive branch.

The OPM is headed by a single director appointed by the President and Senate. The agency can best be described as the central clearinghouse in the federal recruiting, examining, and hiring process. It advertises for employees, examines those who apply, and keeps **registers,** lists of those applicants who pass its tests and are qualified for employment. When there is a job opening in an agency, the OPM usually sends that agency the names of the top three persons on its register for that particular type of position.[14]

---

[13]This number does not take into account employees of the United State Postal Service and a few other federal agencies. The Postal Service, with more than 700,000 full-time employees, is the largest agency not covered by the civil service system. It is the only federal agency in which employment policies are set by collective bargaining and labor union contracts. The other major agencies not counted in fixing that 90 percent figure are the FBI, CIA, and TVA; each of those agencies has its own merit system.

[14]Each applicant's place on a register is fixed by three factors: (1) date of application, (2) OPM test scores, and (3) veterans' preference points, if any. Some 40 percent of all federal jobs are currently held by veterans, wives of disabled veterans, and unremarried widows of veterans. Some jobs, such as guards and messengers, are reserved especially for veterans.

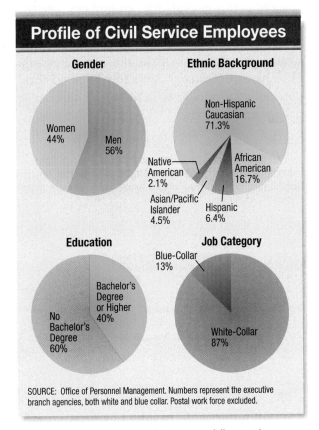

Profile of Civil Service Employees

Gender: Women 44%, Men 56%

Ethnic Background: Non-Hispanic Caucasian 71.3%, African American 16.7%, Hispanic 6.4%, Asian/Pacific Islander 4.5%, Native American 2.1%

Education: No Bachelor's Degree 60%, Bachelor's Degree or Higher 40%

Job Category: White-Collar 87%, Blue-Collar 13%

SOURCE: Office of Personnel Management. Numbers represent the executive branch agencies, both white and blue collar. Postal work force excluded.

Interpreting Charts In 1998 the average civil servant was a 46-year-old man who earned $46,560 a year and had worked for the government for more than 16 years. ***Why might the civil service have a higher proportion of college graduates than the country as a whole?***

Another independent agency, the Merit Systems Protection Board, enforces the merit principle in the federal bureaucracy. The Board is **bipartisan,** which means it includes members from both parties. It is a three-member panel picked by the President and Senate. It hears appeals from those federal workers who have complaints about personnel actions—for example, denials of pay increases, demotions, or firings.[15]

Pay and Benefits

Equal opportunities for career advancement remain a problem in the federal bureaucracy. Although minority groups and women are well represented in most agencies, they tend to be concentrated in lower-level positions. Women, for example, now hold more than half of all white-collar federal jobs; but they hold only a little more than 10 percent of the highest paid positions.

Congress sets the pay and other job conditions for everyone who works for the Federal Government, except for employees of the United States Postal Service. At the lower and middle levels, civil service pay compares fairly well with salaries paid in the private sector. However, government can never hope to compete dollar for dollar with the upper reaches of private employment.

---

[15]Yet another independent agency, the Federal Labor Relations Authority, handles labor-management relations in federal employment. It, too, is a bipartisan three-member body appointed by the President and Senate.

Political Activities

Several laws and a number of OPM regulations place restrictions on the political activities of federal civil servants. The first of two major laws is the Hatch Act of 1939—the Act to Prevent Pernicious Political Activities. *Pernicious* means "exceedingly harmful." In essence, that law allowed federal workers to vote in elections, but it forbade them to take part in partisan political activities.

Critics of the Hatch Act said it placed unnecessary and unjustifiable limits on the political and civil rights of federal workers. Supporters saw those limits as legitimate ways to prevent the use of civil servants to influence presidential and congressional elections. The Supreme Court has rejected several 1st Amendment challenges to the law; the leading case is *National Association of Letter Carriers* v. *Civil Service Commission,* 1973.

The second major statute is the Federal Employees Political Activities Act of 1993, often called the new Hatch Act, which relaxed many of the older restrictions. Today, a federal worker has the right to vote, help register new voters, contribute money to candidates and parties, participate in campaigns, and even hold office in a political party. The worker may *not* run in partisan elections, engage in party work on government property or while on the job, collect political contributions from subordinates (workers in lower positions) or the general public, or use a government position to influence an election.

Section 5 Assessment

Key Terms and Main Ideas

1. What is the purpose of the **civil service?**
2. How did the **spoils system** develop?
3. What is recorded in the **registers** of the OPM?
4. What is the defining characteristic of a **bipartisan** group?

Critical Thinking

5. **Making Decisions** Why does the government limit the political activities of members of the civil service? Explain whether you would change any of these limits, and why.

6. **Determining Cause and Effect** Explain how the spoils system was a reflection of corruption in government.

 Take It to the Net

7. Consider the spoils system and the merit system for hiring civil servants. Suppose that you are a journalist in 1890, and write an editorial describing which system is better for successful government and explaining what traits define a successful government. Use the links provided in the Social Studies area at the following Web site for help in completing this activity. **www.phschool.com**

Must a Hearing Precede the Cutoff of Welfare Benefits?

Individuals receiving government assistance can become ineligible for that assistance for a number of reasons. Must the government notify the recipient and hold a hearing on termination of benefits before the cutoff occurs?

Goldberg v. *Kelly* (1970)

In the late 1960s, more than 1 million residents of New York State were receiving some form of government relief. The Social Security Act requires that if a State wishes to cut off aid permanently to someone who is receiving aid under a federally assisted program, it must give that person a "fair hearing." Under federal regulations in effect at that time, however, that "fair hearing" could take place after the actual cutoff of aid.

Kelly and 19 other New York residents were recipients of either federally-supported or State-run welfare whose benefits had been cut off (or were about to be cut off). They sued local and State officials, charging that the termination of their benefits without previous notice and without an opportunity for a hearing denied them due process of law.

Before the suit came to trial, the State regulations were changed to provide an informal review before the cutoff of aid, as well as a "fair hearing" after the cutoff. However, the recipient of aid was not permitted to appear personally before the official who was to make the final decision on eligibility. Thus the recipient could not present evidence orally to that official or confront witnesses used by the government.

A three-judge district court agreed with the plaintiffs' argument that a pre-termination hearing was required. Commissioner Jack R. Goldberg of New York City appealed to the Supreme Court.

Arguments for Goldberg

1. Nothing in the Constitution requires the government to continue welfare benefits to people who it has concluded are no longer eligible.

2. A person is entitled to due process before being deprived of property, but welfare payments are a form of charity, not property. Thus the right to due process does not apply.

3. A pre-termination hearing would be burdensome, and would force States to continue payments to recipients who are not eligible.

Arguments for Kelly

1. Welfare benefits are essential to recipients. Due process therefore requires that they have a hearing before losing these benefits.

2. Although a recipient need not receive a full trial before losing benefits, he or she must have an opportunity to present evidence and cross-examine witnesses in order to prevent the improper termination of benefits.

3. To satisfy the requirements of due process, the official who makes the decision on eligibility should be required to give a written statement of the reasons for his or her conclusion and a summary of the evidence he or she used.

Decide for Yourself

1. Review the constitutional grounds on which each side based its arguments and the specific arguments each side presented.

2. Debate the opposing viewpoints presented in this case. Which viewpoint do you favor?

3. Predict the impact of the Court's decision on the rights of recipients of government benefits. (To read a summary of the Court's decision, turn to the Supreme Court Glossary on page 799.)

Political Dictionary

bureaucracy (p. 414)

bureaucrat (p. 415)

administration (p. 416)

staff agency (p. 418)

line agency (p. 418)

Executive Office of the President (p. 419)

federal budget (p. 421)

fiscal year (p. 421)

domestic affairs (p. 422)

executive departments (p. 424)

secretary (p. 424)

attorney general (p. 424)

independent agencies (p. 430)

independent executive agencies (p. 431)

independent regulatory

    commissions (p. 431)

quasi-legislative (p. 433)

quasi-judicial (p. 433)

government corporation (p. 434)

civil service (p. 437)

spoils system (p. 438)

patronage (p. 438)

register (p. 439)

bipartisan (p. 440)

Practicing the Vocabulary

Matching *Choose a term from the list above that best matches each description.*

1. A large, hierarchical organization with job specialization and complex rules
2. A detailed estimate of federal income and spending for a twelve-month period
3. The director of the Department of Justice
4. Describes a group with the power to judge cases outside the court system
5. One of ten federal agencies created to watch over important aspects of the nation's economy

Word Relationships *Distinguish between words or phrases in each pair.*

6. staff agency/line agency
7. secretary/bureaucrat
8. Executive Office of the President/Cabinet
9. executive departments/independent agencies
10. administration/patronage

Reviewing Main Ideas

Section 1

11. How did the different components of the bureaucracy in the Federal Government's executive branch develop?
12. What is the "name game" in the context of the federal bureaucracy?
13. In what ways is a bureaucracy undemocratic?

Section 2

14. What agencies work most directly with the President, providing assistance and advice?
15. Describe the organization of the Executive Office of the President.
16. **(a)** What are the duties of the National Security Council? **(b)** What are the duties of the Office of National Drug Control Policy?

Section 3

17. How was the Cabinet born?
18. In what sense are the executive departments the traditional units of federal administration?

19. What responsibilities do members of the Cabinet have that are not among the duties of the major figures in the Executive Office of the President?

Section 4

20. Explain the major reasons why the independent agencies exist apart from the Cabinet-level departments.
21. **(a)** What are the three types of independent agencies? **(b)** Describe the basic role of each type of agency.
22. What are the major differences between a government corporation and a private corporation?

Section 5

23. Describe the standards for staffing the federal bureaucracy held by Presidents George Washington and Thomas Jefferson.
24. **(a)** What was the spoils system? **(b)** How did the spoils system affect the quality of the public work force?
25. What was the primary objective of the efforts to reform the country's civil service in the late 1800s?

Critical Thinking Skills

26. ***Applying the Chapter Skill*** Use the Internet to find five federal agencies with local offices in your State. What information about your State were you able to find at their Web sites?

27. ***Making Comparisons*** Consider the following units: executive department, independent executive agency, government corporation. Rank these units from "most independent" to "least independent" of the executive branch, and explain your reasoning.

28. ***Expressing Problems Clearly*** **(a)** Is an efficient government always an effective government? **(b)** What is the proper relationship between efficiency and effectiveness in government? Give support for your answer.

29. ***Drawing Inferences*** Thomas Jefferson once said, "When a man accepts a public trust, he should consider himself a public property." **(a)** What do you think this statement means? **(b)** Do you agree or disagree with this statement? **(c)** What values underlie this statement?

Analyzing Political Cartoons

Using your knowledge of American government and this cartoon, answer the questions below.

"First of all, you need to set up a Department of Paperwork. . ."

30. What does this cartoon imply about bureaucracy?
31. Based on your reading, do you agree or disagree with this assessment? Explain.

You Can Make a Difference

Which government agencies or commissions affect your community? For example, is there a clean-up project of the Environmental Protection Agency or a branch of the Federal Emergency Management Agency (FEMA), which gives help after disasters? Consult the "Government" pages in your local telephone book. Choose an agency or department with a local branch office. Arrange an interview with a representative to learn about the role of this bureaucracy in your community. If time allows, invite him or her to speak to your class.

Participation Activities

32. ***Current Events Watch*** Make a photocopy of the chart on page 417. Skim the news section of a newspaper for a week, looking for references to organizations shown on the chart. Highlight or check each organization that is referred to in a news report. At the end of the week, compare your chart with those of your classmates.

33. ***Graphing Activity*** Research the number of employees of the Federal Government at several points in the nation's history. Create a line graph showing the change in the number of employees over time. Then, create a line graph showing the growth of the United States population over the same period. What conclusions can you draw from your graphs?

34. ***It's Your Turn*** You are living in the United States in the 1830s. Write a letter to President Jackson offering your views on the spoils system. Before you start, identify three reasons why you think the system is good or bad. Begin the letter by stating your purpose, including your overall opinion of the spoils system. Then devote one paragraph to each of the three reasons you identified to support your argument. Revise the letter, correct any errors, and draft a final copy. **(Writing a Letter)**

Take It to the Net

Chapter 15 Self-Test As a final review activity, take the Chapter 15 Self-Test in the Social Studies area at the Web site listed below, and receive immediate feedback on your answers.

www.phschool.com

Financing Government

"The power 'to lay and collect taxes, duties, imposts, and excises' was an indispensable one to...the Federal Government, which without it would possess no means of providing for its own support."

—James Polk (1845)

To keep American institutions healthy and running well, the Federal Government depends on income from various types of taxes as well as some nontax sources. How government spends the money—the federal budget—has a major impact on society.

◆ **The Bureau of Engraving and Printing**

You Can Make a Difference

THE WORKINGS OF the Federal Reserve System may puzzle some people, but not the high school students who take the "Fed Challenge." To bring real-world economics into the classroom, Federal Reserve Banks in various districts sponsor this annual event. Student teams hold a mock Fed meeting and show their knowledge of economic issues. District winners then compete in Washington, D.C., for scholarship awards. In 2000, five Texas teens—the Midland High School team—won the Fed Challenge. They were Kelly Beall, Matt Josefy, Adam Martin, Ryan Myers, and Robin Nelson. Other finalists came from schools in Ohio, Missouri, Indiana, Virginia, and New Jersey.

Keep It Current

Items marked with this logo are periodically updated on the Internet. Keep up-to-date with what's in the news. To get current information on issues involving government finance, go to **www.phschool.com**

SECTION 1

Taxes (pp. 446–452)

★ The Framers put the power to tax first among the expressed powers of Congress.

★ The income taxes paid by individuals and corporations are the largest sources of federal revenue today.

★ Excise taxes, gift and estate taxes, customs duties, and social insurance taxes also support the Federal Government.

★ The power to tax is used, in large part, to raise revenue; however, it is also used to regulate and even discourage some activities.

SECTION 2

Nontax Revenues and Borrowing (pp. 454–456)

★ The Federal Government receives a relatively small amount of revenue from nontax sources.

★ Between 1930 and 1998, the Federal Government borrowed tremendous sums of money to pay for federal spending.

★ For decades, the Federal Government practiced deficit financing; year after year, it spent more than it took in and then borrowed to make up the difference.

★ The public debt is composed of all of the money the government has borrowed over time and not yet repaid, plus all of the accrued interest on that money.

SECTION 3

Spending and the Budget (pp. 458–462)

★ Federal spending—now some $2 trillion a year—has an enormous impact on the nation's economy.

★ The largest categories of federal spending include entitlements, defense, and interest on the public debt.

★ The federal budget is a major political document—a statement of the public policies of the United States, with dollar signs attached.

1 Taxes

Section Preview

OBJECTIVES

1. **Explain** how and why the Constitution gives Congress the power to tax.
2. **Describe** the most significant federal taxes collected today.
3. **Summarize** why the Federal Government imposes taxes for nonrevenue purposes.

WHY IT MATTERS

Article I of the Constitution and the 16th Amendment give Congress broad powers to set federal taxes. Today, Congress collects most of its revenue in the form of income taxes paid by individuals and corporations.

POLITICAL DICTIONARY

* **progressive tax**
* **tax return**
* **payroll tax**
* **regressive tax**
* **excise tax**
* **estate tax**
* **gift tax**
* **custom duty**

According to Benjamin Franklin's oft-quoted comment, "in this world nothing is certain but death and taxes." In this section, you will consider the second of Franklin's certainties, taxes. More specifically, you will examine those taxes levied by the Federal Government.

During fiscal year 2003, which extends from October 1, 2002, through September 30, 2003, the Federal Government expects to spend just about $2 trillion. It will almost certainly take in even more than that stupendous sum. Those mind-boggling numbers tell you that, on average, it now costs every man, woman, and child in this country nearly $7,000 a year to support the Federal Government. Those figures should also tell you how important the subject of taxes really is.

The Power to Tax

The Constitution underscores the central importance of the power to tax by listing it first among all of the many powers granted to Congress. The Constitution gives to Congress the power:

> **FROM THE *Constitution*** **❝**To lay and collect Taxes, Duties, Imposts and Excises, to pay the Debts and provide for the common Defense and general Welfare of the United States. . . .**❞**
>
> —Article I, Section 8, Clause 1

First and foremost, Congress exercises the taxing power in order to raise the money needed to operate the Federal Government. However, Congress does levy some taxes for nonrevenue purposes, or reasons other than raising money.

Constitutional Limitations

The power to tax is not unlimited. As with all of its other powers, Congress must exercise the taxing power in accord with the Constitution. Thus,

"So then Tommy Taxpayer said to the big bully, Godzilla government, 'I am unwilling to pay the bill ...'"

JIM BERRY
©NEA

Interpreting Political Cartoons Taxes are essential to government, but people disagree on how much the Federal Government should tax. *What is the speaker's attitude toward government?*

▲ The Federal Government draws revenue from many sources, including taxes on telephone calls, imported goods, and wages. *Critical Thinking* **Where does the Federal Government get the power to tax imports?**

for example, Congress cannot levy a tax on church services—clearly, such a tax would violate the 1st Amendment.

In more specific terms, the Constitution puts four expressed limits—and one very significant implied limit—on the power of Congress to tax. First, taxes must be used for public purposes only. That is, the Constitution says that Congress may levy taxes for public purposes, and not for the benefit of some private interest.

The second expressed limit is the prohibition of export taxes. Article I, Section 9, Clause 5 declares that "No Tax or Duty shall be laid on Articles exported from any State." Thus, customs duties (tariffs) can be applied only to imports—goods brought into the United States. They may not be applied to exports, or goods sent out of the country. This restriction was a part of the Commerce Compromise made by the Framers at Philadelphia in 1787.

While Congress cannot tax exports, it can and does prohibit the export of certain items. It does so under its expressed power to regulate foreign commerce, usually for reasons of national security. For example, Congress has banned the export of computer software that allows people to encrypt files in a code no government can crack.

The third expressed limit is that direct taxes must be equally apportioned, evenly distributed, among the States. The Constitution originally provided that:

FROM THE *Constitution* **❝**No Capitation, or other direct, Tax shall be laid, unless in Proportion to the Census of Enumeration herein before directed to be taken. **❞**
—Article I, Section 9, Clause 4

This restriction was a part of the Three-Fifths Compromise the Framers made at the Philadelphia Convention. In effect, delegates from the northern States insisted that if slaves were to be counted in the populations of the southern States, then those States would have to pay for them.

Recall that a direct tax is one that must be borne by the person upon whom it is levied. Examples include a tax on land or buildings, which must be paid by the owner of the property; or a capitation tax—a head or poll tax—laid on each person. Other taxes are indirect taxes, or levies that may be shifted to another for payment—as, for example, the federal tax on liquor. That tax, placed initially on the distiller, is ultimately paid by the person who buys the liquor.

The direct tax restriction means, in effect, that any direct tax that Congress levies must be apportioned among the States according to their populations. Thus, a direct tax that raised $1 billion would have to produce just about $120 million in California and $10 million in Mississippi, because California has just about 12 percent of the nation's population and Mississippi 1 percent.

Wealth is not evenly distributed among the States, of course. So, a direct tax laid in proportion to population would be grossly unfair; the tax would fall more heavily on the residents of some States than it would on others. As a result, Congress has not imposed a direct tax—except for the income tax—outside the District of Columbia since 1861.

An income tax is a direct tax, but it may be laid without regard to population:

> **FROM THE Constitution** *"The Congress shall have power to lay and collect taxes on incomes, from whatever source derived, without apportionment among the several States, and without regard to any census or enumeration."*
>
> —16th Amendment

Congress first levied an income tax in 1861, to help finance the Civil War. The tax, which expired in 1873, was later upheld by the Supreme Court in *Springer* v. *United States,* 1881. A unanimous Court found that income tax to be an indirect rather than a direct tax.

However, a later income tax law, enacted in 1894, was declared unconstitutional in *Pollock* v. *Farmers' Loan and Trust Co.,* 1895. There, the Court held that the 1894 law imposed a direct tax that Congress should have apportioned among the several States. The impossibility of taxing incomes fairly in accord with any plan

of apportionment led to the adoption of the 16th Amendment in 1913.

The fourth and final limit, in Article I, Section 8, Clause 1, declares that "all Duties, Imposts and Excises shall be uniform throughout the United States." That is, all of the indirect taxes levied by the Federal Government must be set at the same rate in all parts of the country.

The Implied Limitation

The Federal Government cannot tax the States or any of their local governments in the exercise of their governmental functions. That is, federal taxes cannot be imposed on those governments when they are performing such tasks as providing public education, furnishing health care, or building streets and highways.

Recall, the Supreme Court laid down that rule in *McCulloch* v. *Maryland* in 1819, when it declared that "the power to tax involves the power to destroy." If the Federal Government could tax the governmental activities of the States or their local units, it could conceivably tax them out of existence and so destroy the federal system.

The Federal Government can and does tax those State and local activities that are of a nongovernmental character, however. Thus, in 1893, South Carolina created a State monopoly to sell

The Federal Government's Income (in billions of dollars)						
	1980	**1990**	**1995**	**2000**	**2001***	**2002***
Individual income taxes	$244.1	$466.9	$590.2	$1,004.5	$1,014.3	$1,024.2
Corporation income taxes	64.6	93.5	157.0	207.3	155.4	229.1
Social insurance taxes and contributions	157.8	380.0	484.5	652.9	689.4	721.9
Excise taxes	24.3	35.3	57.5	68.9	67.6	70.4
Estate and gift taxes	6.4	11.5	14.8	29.0	30.0	28.0
Customs duties	7.2	16.7	19.3	19.9	19.8	21.5
Miscellaneous receipts	12.7	27.8	28.6	42.8	36.2	39.6
Total receipts**	$517.1	$1,032.0	$1,351.8	$2,025.2	$2,012.7	$2,134.7

*Estimated

**Columns may not add to totals due to rounding and additional sources of income.

SOURCE: Office of Management and Budget

Interpreting Tables Federal revenue comes from several different sources. *From which of these sources did the revenues collected increase by the greatest percentage from 1980 to 2002?*

liquor, and it claimed that each of its liquor stores was exempt from the federal saloon license tax. But in *South Carolina* v. *United States*, 1905, the Supreme Court held that the State was liable for the tax, because the sale of liquor is not a necessary or usual governmental activity.

Current Federal Taxes

Oliver Wendell Holmes once described taxes as "what we pay for civilized society."[1] Society does not appear to be much more civilized today than it was when Justice Holmes made that observation in 1927. However, "what we pay" has certainly gone up. In 1927, the Federal Government's tax collections came to, altogether, less than $3.4 billion. Compare that figure with the figures in the table on page 448.

The Income Tax

You will recall that the income tax was authorized by the 16th Amendment, in 1913. It is the largest source of federal revenue today. It first became the major source in 1917 and 1918. And, except for a few years during the Depression of the 1930s, it has remained so.

Several features of the income tax fit its dominant role. It is a flexible tax, because its rates can be adjusted to produce whatever amount of money Congress thinks is necessary. The income tax is also easily adapted to the principle of ability to pay. It is a **progressive tax**—that is, the higher one's income, the higher the tax. The tax is levied on the earnings of both individuals and corporations.

The Individual Income Tax

The tax on individuals' incomes regularly produces the largest amount of federal revenue. For fiscal year 2002, the individual income tax was expected to provide over $1 trillion.

The tax is levied on each person's taxable income—that is, one's total income in the previous year less certain exemptions and deductions. On returns filed in 2002, covering income received in 2001, each taxpayer had a personal exemption of $3,000, and

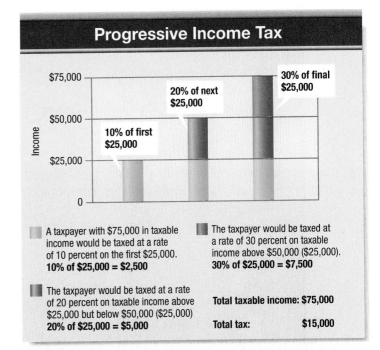

Progressive Income Tax

A taxpayer with $75,000 in taxable income would be taxed at a rate of 10 percent on the first $25,000.
10% of $25,000 = $2,500

The taxpayer would be taxed at a rate of 20 percent on taxable income above $25,000 but below $50,000 ($25,000)
20% of $25,000 = $5,000

The taxpayer would be taxed at a rate of 30 percent on taxable income above $50,000 ($25,000).
30% of $25,000 = $7,500

Total taxable income: $75,000

Total tax: $15,000

Interpreting Diagrams With a progressive income tax, the tax rate increases as total income increases. Today, federal income tax rates range from 10% to 39.1%. *How much would this taxpayer owe with a taxable income of $37,500, which is exactly half the income in the example?*

another of the same amount for each dependent. Deductions are allowed for several things, including most medical care costs, most State and local taxes (except sales taxes), interest paid on home mortgages, and charitable contributions.

By April 15 of any given year, everyone who earned taxable income in the preceding calendar year must file a **tax return**—a declaration of that income and of the exemptions and deductions he or she claims. The returns are filed, by mail or online, with the Internal Revenue Service. The IRS now receives more than 120 million returns each year, more than 40 million of them e-filed.

President Bush urged Congress to enact major tax cuts in 2001, and it did so. Under the new law, all taxable income earned in 2001 was taxed (in 2002) at one of four rates (brackets). In the lowest bracket, the tax was 10 percent on incomes up to $12,000 for couples who filed joint returns, up to $10,000 for single parents, and up to $6,000 for other singles. Taxpayers in the highest bracket paid 39.1 percent on their taxable incomes in the $300,000 range and above.

---

[1]Holmes made this statement in a dissenting opinion in an insurance tax case, *Compania General de Tabacos de Filipinas* v. *Collector of Internal Revenue*, 1927.

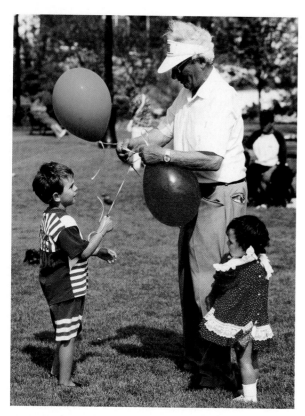

▲ **Social Security** If they have paid OASDI taxes for several years, Americans can retire at age 65 and receive financial support from OASDI taxes paid by people still in the work force.

Before the passage of the Tax Relief Act of 2001, the lowest tax bracket was set at 15 percent and the highest bracket at 39.6 percent. The law schedules additional rate cuts over the next several years.

Most people who pay income taxes do so through withholding, a pay-as-you-go plan. Employers are required to withhold a certain amount from each employee's paycheck and send that money to the IRS. When the employee files a tax return, he or she will receive a refund if the employer withheld more money than the employee owed in taxes. The employee must pay an additional amount if too little has been withheld. Those who earn income from sources not subject to withholding must estimate the income tax they will owe and make quarterly payments on that amount throughout the year.

The Corporation Income Tax

Each corporation must pay a tax on its net income, that is, on all of its earnings above the costs of doing business. The corporate tax is the most complicated of all federal taxes because of the many deductions allowed. Nonprofit organizations

such as churches and charitable foundations are not subject to the corporation income tax.

For 2002, the corporate tax rates ran from 15 percent on the first $50,000 of taxable earnings up to a top rate of 38 percent on taxable incomes of more than $18.33 million.

Social Insurance Taxes

The Federal Government collects huge sums to finance three major social welfare programs: (1) the Old-Age, Survivors, and Disability Insurance (OASDI) program—the basic Social Security program, established by the Social Security Act of 1935; (2) Medicare—health care for the elderly, added to the Social Security program in 1965; and (3) the unemployment compensation program—benefits paid to jobless workers, a program also established by the Social Security Act in 1935.

OASDI and Medicare are supported by taxes imposed on nearly all employers and their employees, and on self-employed persons. These levies are often called **payroll taxes** because the amounts owed by employees are withheld from their paychecks. For 2001, employees paid an OASDI tax of 6.2 percent on the first $80,400 of their salary or wages for the year, and their employers had to match that amount. The self-employed were taxed at 12.4 percent on the first $80,400 of their income.

For Medicare, employees pay a 1.45 percent tax on their total annual income. Employers must match the amounts withheld from their employees' paychecks. The self-employed pay a 2.9 percent Medicare tax on their annual incomes.

The unemployment insurance program is a joint federal-State operation that makes payments to workers who lose their jobs for reasons beyond their control. The program now covers most workers in this country. Each State and the District of Columbia, Puerto Rico, and the Virgin Islands has its own unemployment compensation law. The amount of a worker's weekly benefits, and how many weeks they last, are determined by State law.

The unemployment compensation program is financed by both federal and State taxes. The federal tax is 6.2 percent of the first $7,000 an employer pays to each employee in a year. Each employer is given a credit of up to 5.4 percent against that tax for unemployment taxes that the employer pays to the State. So, the federal tax usually amounts to 0.8 percent on taxable wages.

Notice that these social insurance taxes for OASDI, Medicare, and unemployment compensation are not progressive taxes. They are, instead, **regressive taxes**—taxes levied at a flat rate, without regard to the level of a taxpayer's income or his or her ability to pay them.

The IRS collects social insurance taxes. The money is then credited to trust accounts maintained by the Treasury, and Congress appropriates funds for the social insurance programs as they are needed.

Excise Taxes

An **excise tax** is a tax laid on the manufacture, sale, or consumption of goods and/or the performance of services. The Federal Government has imposed and collected excise taxes since Congress acquired its taxing power in 1789.

Today, federal excise taxes are imposed on a long list of things, including gasoline, oil, tires, tobacco, liquor, wine, beer, firearms, telephone services, airline tickets, and more. Many excise taxes are called "hidden taxes" because they are collected from producers who then figure them into the price that the retail customer finally pays. Some are called "luxury taxes" because they are imposed on goods not usually considered necessities. And some excise taxes are known as "sin taxes," particularly those laid on tobacco, beer, wine, liquor, and gambling.

Estate and Gift Taxes

An **estate tax** is a levy imposed on the assets (the estate) of one who dies.[3] A **gift tax** is one imposed on the making of a gift by a living person. Congress first provided for the estate tax in 1916. It added the gift tax in 1932 to plug a loophole in the estate tax that allowed people to avoid the estate tax by giving away money or other property before death.

The first $1,000,000 of an estate is exempt from the federal tax. So, in fact, most estates are not subject to the federal levy. Deductions are allowed for such things as State death taxes and bequests to religious and charitable groups. Anything a husband or wife leaves to the other is taxed, if at all, only when the surviving spouse dies.

Any person may make up to $10,000 in tax-free gifts to any other person in any one year. Gifts that husbands/wives make to one another are not taxed, regardless of value.

The estate and gift taxes are separate federal taxes, but both are levied at the same rates. For 2002, those rates range from a minimum of 18 percent on an estate or a gift with a net value of less than $20,000, on up to a maximum of 50 percent on an estate or gift worth more than $3 million.

Custom Duties

A **custom duty** is a tax laid on goods brought into the United States from abroad. Custom duties are also known as tariffs, import duties, or imposts. Congress decides which imports will be dutied and at what rates.[4] Most imports, some 30,000 different items, are dutied; but some are not—for example, Bibles, coffee, bananas, and up to $400 of a tourist's purchases abroad.

Custom duties were the major source of income for the Federal Government for more than a century. Now, they produce less than 1 percent of the money the government takes in.

▲ Duck hunters must buy a duck stamp from the Federal Government each year. The money is used for wildlife conservation programs. *Critical Thinking Explain why, other than to raise revenue, the Federal Government might require duck hunters to pay an annual fee.*

---

[3]An inheritance tax is another form of the so-called death tax. It is not levied on the entire net estate but, instead, on each portion inherited by each heir. Most States impose inheritance, not estate, taxes; most States also levy gift taxes.

[4]Since 1922, Congress has authorized the President to raise or lower any tariff by as much as 50 percent. The President can do so by an executive order, issued on the basis of recommendations made by the United States International Trade Commission, which studies the effect of tariffs and imports on the economy.

Taxing for Nonrevenue Purposes

Remember, the power to tax can be, and often is, used for purposes other than the raising of revenue. Usually, that other purpose is to regulate and even discourage some activity that Congress thinks is harmful or dangerous to the public.

Thus, much of the Federal Government's regulation of narcotics is based on the taxing power. Federal law provides that only those who hold a valid license may legally manufacture, sell, or otherwise deal in those drugs—and licensing is a form of taxation. The government also regulates a number of other things by licensing, including, for example, certain firearms, prospecting on public lands, and the hunting of migratory birds. The federal excise tax on gas-guzzling cars is intended to discourage their purchase.

The Supreme Court first upheld the use of the taxing power for nonrevenue purposes in *Veazie Bank* v. *Fenno* in 1869. Congress had established a national paper money system during the Civil War in 1863 to provide a single, sound currency for the country. Private bank notes, also used as paper money, soon interfered with the use of the government's new "greenbacks." So, in 1866, Congress imposed a 10 percent tax on the issuing of those private notes, and they soon disappeared. In upholding the tax, the Court declared:

PRIMARY Sources *"Having thus, in the exercise of undisputed constitutional powers, undertaken to provide a currency for the whole country, it cannot be questioned that Congress may, constitutionally, secure the benefit of it to the people by appropriate legislation."*

—*Veazie Bank* v. *Fenno*, Opinion of the Court

In 1912, Congress used its taxing power to destroy a part of the domestic match industry. It levied a tax of two cents per hundred on matches made with white or yellow phosphorus. These highly poisonous substances harmed workers who produced the matches. Matches made from other substances commonly sold for a penny a hundred. Thus, the two-cent tax drove the phosphorus matches from the market.

Congress cannot use its taxing power in any manner it wishes, however. As in all else, Congress is bound by the Constitution. Consider a 1951 tax law aimed at professional gamblers. The law imposed a $50-a-year license tax on bookies, and required them to register with and submit detailed reports to the IRS. The law did produce a small amount of income, but its real purpose was to force gamblers into the open for the benefit of State and local police. It also set a federal tax evasion trap for those who failed to comply.

The Supreme Court overturned the antigambling provisions in *Marchetti* v. *United States*, 1968. The Court did not hold that the taxes had been set for improper purposes, but that the tax, registration, and reporting provisions forced gamblers to give evidence against themselves, violating the 5th Amendment's protection against self-incrimination.

Section 1 Assessment

Key Terms and Main Ideas

1. Describe how tax rates are set under a **progressive tax**.
2. What is the purpose of a **tax return**?
3. What items are subject to a **customs duty**?
4. What is the difference between a **gift tax** and an **estate tax**?

Critical Thinking

5. **Identifying Central Issues** List two distinct reasons why the Federal Government imposes taxes.
6. **Demonstrating Reasoned Judgment** What is one possible reason why the government asks employers to withhold tax money from each paycheck, instead of requiring taxpayers to pay a full year's taxes all at once?

7. **Expressing Problems Clearly** Some people claim that the federal income tax is a form of "forced labor" for the government. Explain the thinking behind this comparison, and why you agree or disagree.

 Take It to the Net

8. Learn more about the different tax brackets in the United States. Read about the three possible options for surplus tax revenue, select one of the three different choices, and argue for or against it using examples. Use the links provided in the Social Studies area at the following Web site for help in completing this activity. **www.phschool.com**

Paying Your Taxes

To some people, they are the three most dreaded letters in the English language: IRS—the Internal Revenue Service. The IRS, an agency within the Treasury Department, enforces tax laws made by Congress and collects federal income taxes.

Uncle Sam has been taking a bite out of Americans' paychecks since 1913, when the Sixteenth Amendment took effect. Every year of your working life you will probably file a federal tax return, the form on which you calculate how much tax you owe.

The federal tax system includes tax deductions for taxpayers with certain financial burdens, such as mortgages, college loans, or high medical bills. Such tax breaks can save you hundreds of dollars a year.

People in many places must pay federal, State, and local taxes. It is important, then, to prepare for tax time. For most people, these are the steps to follow:

1. Fill out a W-4 form. When you start a new job, the employer will give you IRS Form W-4, which you use to calculate how much of your pay you wish to have withheld for taxes. Tax laws require most people to have a certain minimum percentage withheld. At the end of the year, you figure out the amount of tax you owe. If you had too much money withheld, the Treasury gives that surplus back to you as a tax refund. If you did not have enough money withheld during the year, you must pay the balance you owe.

Fill out a W-4 and return it to your employer. If you need help, call the IRS or check out the "W-4 Calculator" on the IRS Web site.

2. Collect important documents. In January or early February you should receive IRS Form W-2, which shows the income you earned in the prior year. Employers must send out W-2s by January 31. If you have an interest-bearing account at a bank or other institution, you'll also receive a statement of interest you earned, which counts as income. Save these documents! W-2s and other documents must be attached to your tax return when you file.

3. Calculate your taxes. The tax "season" runs from January to April 15. During that time, you need to fill out and file your tax return. Tax forms and instruction books are free. You'll find them at post offices, public libraries, and banks. You can download forms at the IRS Web site, or get them via the IRS TaxFax Service.

Follow the directions on the forms to calculate how much tax you owe, or how much should be refunded to you. Never put false information on a tax form. If the IRS suspects you've cheated on your taxes, you'll be called in for an audit, a detailed review of your finances. Penalties for tax fraud or nonpayment are severe.

4. Get help, if needed. Each tax form has step-by-step instructions, but if you have questions, don't guess. Get help from one of the sources shown at left.

5. File your tax return. Your federal tax return must be postmarked by midnight on April 15. Late filers receive penalties and interest charges. If you prepare your return on paper, send it to an IRS Service Center listed in the instruction booklets and at the IRS Web site. To get a fast tax refund, file online. If you owe money, you can pay by check or credit card.

Tax Help

The IRS Web site is friendly and helpful, with loads of information. Try out TaxInteractive, an online information service. **http://www.irs.ustreas.gov**

Call the IRS toll-free at 1-800-829-1040. You can get help over the telephone, schedule an appointment, or use a walk-in service at some locations. Tax preparation services and tax accountants will prepare your tax return for a fee. They provide forms, make suggestions, and answer questions. Many will file your return for you.

Test for Success

What types of documents should you save to help you prepare your tax return?

Section Preview

OBJECTIVES

1. **List** the nontax sources of Federal Government revenues.
2. **Describe** federal borrowing.
3. **Analyze** the causes and effects of the public debt.

WHY IT MATTERS

When the government spends more money than it takes in, it must borrow money from investors. Over time, government borrowing has created a public debt of more than $5 trillion.

POLITICAL DICTIONARY

★ **interest**
★ **deficit**
★ **surplus**
★ **public debt**

In *Hamlet*, Shakespeare wrote: "Neither a borrower nor a lender be." That may be good advice in some situations. However, it certainly has not been followed by the government of the United States.

Nontax Revenues

Large sums of money reach the federal treasury from a multitude of nontax sources. As the table on page 448 shows, these miscellaneous receipts now come to well over $30 billion a year.

These monies come from dozens of places. A large portion comes from the earnings of the Federal Reserve System, mostly in interest charges. **Interest** is a charge for borrowed money, generally a percentage of the amount borrowed. The interest on loans made by several other federal agencies, canal tolls, and fees for such items as passports, copyrights, patents, and trademarks also generate large sums. So do the premiums on veterans' life

insurance policies, the sale or lease of public lands, the sale of surplus property, and such other items as the fines imposed by the federal courts.

The Treasury Department maintains a "conscience fund" for the several thousands of dollars a year that people send in to ease their minds over their past taxpaying mistakes. Another little-known source of nontax money is *seigniorage*—the profit the United States Mint makes in the production of coins. That profit is the difference between the value of the metals along with other costs of production and the monetary value of the minted coins. The Mint can produce a quarter for less than 25 cents and then "sell" the quarter at its face value. The difference adds up to more than $2 billion in most years.

The Philatelic Sales Branch of the United States Postal Service sells more than $100 million in mint-condition stamps to collectors each year. Stamp collectors spend untold millions more at local post offices. Most of the stamps they buy are never used on mail.

▶ The United States Postal Service earns millions of dollars each year by selling commemorative stamps.

Borrowing

Congress has the power "[t]o borrow Money on the credit of the United States" (Article I, Section 8, Clause 2). Historically, the power to borrow has been viewed as a way for the government (1) to meet the costs of short- and long-term crisis situations and (2) to finance large-scale projects that could not be paid for out of current income. For example, the Federal Government borrowed huge sums when the United States entered

World War I, to combat the Great Depression of the 1930s, and again during World War II.

Over recent decades, the Federal Government has borrowed for yet another reason: deficit financing. Over those years, the government regularly spent more money than it collected in tax revenue. That is, it ran up an annual **deficit**—the yearly shortfall between income and outgo; and it borrowed heavily to make up the difference.

Indeed, the Federal Government's financial books did not show a **surplus,** more income than outgo, from 1969 until 1998.[5] The Treasury realized a surplus in the four years 1998–2001, mostly because of a robust economy in the 1990s. But an economic downturn, aggravated by the terrorist strikes of September 11, 2001, brought a return to deficit spending beginning in 2002.

Congress must authorize all federal borrowing. The borrowing itself is done by the Treasury Department, which issues various kinds of securities to investors. These investors are principally individuals and banks, investment companies, and other financial institutions. Securities usually take the form of Treasury notes or bills (T-bills) issued for short-term borrowing, or bonds for long-term purposes. They are, in effect, IOUs, promissory notes in which the government agrees to repay a certain sum, with interest, on a certain date.

The government is able to borrow money at lower rates of interest than those paid by private borrowers. This is true largely because investors can find no safer securities than those issued by the United States. If the United States could not pay its debts, no one else would be able to, either. Federal securities are also attractive because the interest they earn cannot be taxed by the States or their local governments.

The Public Debt

Borrowing money produces a debt, of course. The public debt is the result of the Federal Government's borrowing over many years. More precisely, the **public debt** is the government's total outstanding indebtedness. It includes all of the money borrowed and not yet repaid, plus the accrued (accumulated) interest.[6]

The Federal Government has built up a huge debt over time. As you can see in the graphs on

Voices on Government

Economist **Alan Greenspan,** one of the most powerful voices in America, has held several government positions. Since 1987 he has been chairman of the Federal Reserve Board, which controls the country's monetary policy. In a lecture, Greenspan gave his view of the American economy:

" *The extraordinarily complex machine that we call the economy of the United States is, in the end, made up of human beings struggling to improve their lives. The individual values of those Americans . . . will continue to influence the structure of the institutions that support market transactions, as they have throughout our history. Without mutual trust and market participants abiding by a rule of law, no economy can prosper. Our system works fundamentally on individual fair dealing.* "

Evaluating the Quotation
How do Greenspan's thoughts about "mutual trust" and "fair dealing" apply to what you have learned about taxes in this chapter?

page 456, the nation's debt more than doubled in the years 1981 through 1985 because of deficit financing. Continued deficit spending had quadrupled the debt by 1992.

The amounts involved here are absolutely mind-boggling. In 1981, when the debt was approaching $1 trillion, President Ronald Reagan said that he found "such a figure—a trillion dollars—incomprehensible." He then drew this verbal picture: "[I]f you had a stack of $1,000 bills in your hand only four inches high, you would be a millionaire. A trillion dollars would be a stack 67 miles high." Reagan's stack would have to be more than 400 miles high to equal the national debt today!

---

[5]In fact, from 1930 to 2001, the Federal Government ended only 11 fiscal years "in the black"—that is, with a surplus: fiscal years 1947, 1948, 1951, 1956, 1957, 1960, 1969, 1998, 1999, 2000, and 2001.

[6]The Treasury Department's Bureau of the Public Debt acts as the Federal Government's borrowing agent. It issues Treasury bills, notes, and bonds and manages the U.S. Savings Bond Program.

Government Borrowing, 1940–2001

Annual Deficits and Surpluses

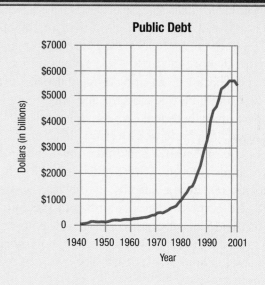

Public Debt

SOURCE: Office of Management and Budget

Interpreting Graphs Public debt swelled with deficit spending in the 1980s and early 1990s. **Why hasn't the debt fallen as sharply as the deficit in recent years?**

There is no constitutional limit on the amount that may be borrowed, and so there is no constitutional limit on the public debt. Congress has put a statutory ceiling on the debt, but simply adjusts the ceiling upward whenever fiscal realities seem to call for it.

The debt has always been controversial, and its rapid rise in recent years has fueled the fire. The annual interest on the debt is the amount that must be paid each year to those from whom the government has borrowed. That interest came to nearly $400 billion in 2001 and will be even higher in 2002. More than one in every five dollars the Federal Government now spends goes just to service, or pay the interest on, the debt.

Most of those who are concerned about the size of the debt are worried about its impact on future generations of Americans. They say that years of short-sightedness and failure to operate government on a pay-as-you-go basis has produced huge debt and interest obligations that will have to be met by tomorrow's taxpayers.

Section 2 Assessment

Key Terms and Main Ideas

1. What is **interest,** in terms of borrowing money?
2. What must a government do to have a budget **surplus?**
3. Explain the difference between a budget **deficit** and the **public debt.**

Critical Thinking

4. **Drawing Conclusions** Compare the government's annual nontax revenues with the annual tax revenues discussed in Section 1. How important are nontax revenues for funding the government?
5. **Drawing Inferences** Based on the graph above, which years saw the most rapid growth in the pubic debt? What events led to the increase in debt at that time?

6. **Making Decisions** Borrowing money enables the government to spend more in the present without having to make up the difference until years later. Why do you think that for many years politicians found it easier to borrow money than to cut the deficit?

Take It to the Net

7. The current economic downturn and the war on terrorism will almost certainly have a major impact on the public debt. Write an editorial on the debt, commenting on its past, its present, and its future. Use the links provided in the Social Studies area at the following Web site for help in completing this activity. **www.phschool.com**.

on Primary Sources

The Meaning of a Balanced Budget

In the late 1990s, the Federal Government ended decades of deficit spending. The President's announcement of a small budget surplus was hailed as a turning point in American government. Susan Dentzer, a commentator on The NewsHour With Jim Lehrer *on PBS, suggests that the celebration of the balanced budget may be premature.*

What does the cartoon suggest about those who celebrate the budget surplus?

Although living within our means each year is a reasonable goal, we'd be even better off broadening our definition of fiscal responsibility to take into account the government's "balance sheet"—our assets and our long-term liabilities. For one thing, seeing the larger picture might minimize the temptation to propose silly steps for short-term budgetary gains. But more important, this broader look might help us focus on far tougher measures that will be needed to deal with massive liabilities in everything from nuclear-waste cleanup to Social Security. . . .

For example, take the costs we face for cleaning up radioactive waste from the production and testing of nuclear weapons. Rough estimates place these at $200 billion to $350 billion over a 75-year period. Throw in pension and other retirement benefits for the government's civilian workers and the military; as of 1995 those liabilities stood at nearly $1.6 trillion. Still other costs of an aging population weigh more heavily on the government's books. Social Security's long-term deficit over the next 75 years—what the system will pay out in benefits over and above currently projected taxes—is estimated at present at about $3 trillion. And these costs may pale beside rough estimates putting Medicare's unfunded costs at three times that level.

Only portions of these costs are captured in government budgets—for example, just one year's worth of benefits paid out and taxes paid in under Medicare. That suggests that our narrow focus on annual deficits is misguided; our broader problem is that we accumulate huge spending commitments years before the taxes come in to pay for them. . . . Since we don't focus on this "tax lag," we get budgets . . . that achieve a temporary balance on paper but neglect deeper concerns. . . .

Politicians might feel pressed to attack such problems more directly if the full scope of potential liabilities was better understood by the public. That's a key reason countries like Britain and Australia are moving to frame their budgets in similar "accrual," rather than cash-in, cash-out terms. So far, America is taking only baby steps in that direction. . . . We can only imagine what credible fiscal measures might ensue if balancing the budget yielded to a broader drive to clean up the government's balance sheet.

Analyzing Primary Sources

1. Why does Dentzer believe that people should not focus solely on balancing the budget?
2. What future financial challenges does Dentzer foresee for the government? Why will they cause problems, according to Dentzer?
3. How does Dentzer suggest the government change its current method for calculating its finances?

Spending and the Budget

Section Preview

OBJECTIVES

1. **Identify** the key elements of federal spending.
2. **Explain** how the President and Congress work together to create the federal budget.

WHY IT MATTERS

Federal spending has a huge effect on the economy. In the budget-making process, the President and Congress determine how the wide-ranging activities of the Federal Government will be financed.

POLITICAL DICTIONARY

★ **entitlement**
★ **controllable spending**
★ **uncontrollable spending**
★ **continuing resolution**

The Federal Government will spend some $2 trillion in fiscal year 2002. If you placed 2 trillion dollar bills end to end, they would stretch some 175 million miles, just about the distance from Earth to the sun and back again. In this section, you will see how the government spends all that money, and how it plans for that spending through the budget process.

Federal Spending

For more than half of our national history—from independence in 1776 to the mid-1930s—the Government's income and spending were so comparatively small that they had little real impact on the nation's economy. That situation changed dramatically with the coming of the Great Depression of the 1930s and then World War II in the early 1940s.

Today, the Federal Government takes tens of billions of dollars from some segments of the national economy. It then pumps those billions back into other segments of the economy—all, of course, with huge effects on the economy as a whole.

Spending Priorities

Look at the table on page 460. As you can see, the independent Social Security Administration now spends more money than any other federal agency. Nearly all of Social Security's spending goes for OASDI (Old Age, Survivors, and Disability Insurance) benefit payments and similar entitlement programs.

Entitlements are benefits that federal law says must be paid to all those who meet the eligibility requirements, such as being at a certain age or income level. OASDI is the largest federal entitlement program today. Others include Medicare, Medicaid, food stamps, unemployment compensation, and veterans' pensions. The Federal Government guarantees assistance for all those who qualify. In effect, the law says that the people who receive those benefits are *entitled* (have a right) to them.

The Department of Health and Human Services will spend some $430 billion in 2002. Most of that money will pay for various welfare and public health programs. It will also

▲ The government-run Food Stamp program provides coupons that recipients can exchange for food.

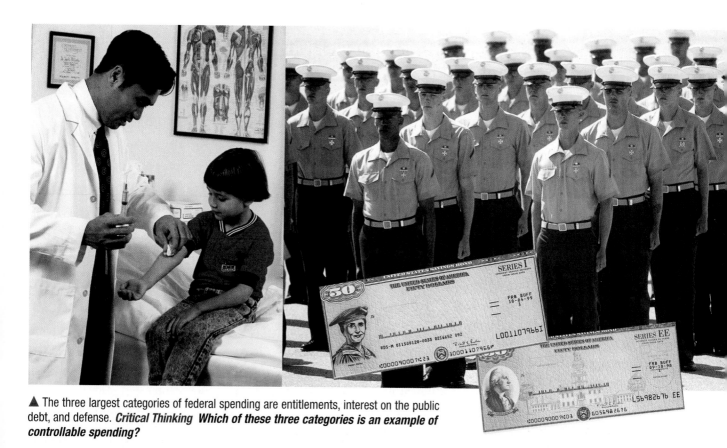

▲ The three largest categories of federal spending are entitlements, interest on the public debt, and defense. *Critical Thinking* *Which of these three categories is an example of controllable spending?*

cover the cutting-edge research projects of the National Institutes of Health and the vital work of the Centers for Disease Control and Prevention.

Interest on the public debt is now the third largest category of federal spending. Stoked by years of deficit financing, it has consumed a larger and still larger part of the federal budget over the last several years. In the table on page 460, interest on the debt is included in the Treasury Department's spending. For fiscal year 2001, that cost was nearly $390 billion.

Outlays for defense now account for a much larger share of the budget than they have over the past decade. Those expenditures came to some $281 billion in 2001. They will almost certainly top $350 billion in 2002—and they will continue to grow as the nation fights the global war on terrorism.

Note that the defense spending figures in the table are somewhat misleading. They do not include the defense-related expenditures of other federal agencies, such as the extensive nuclear weapons research and development work of the Department of Energy.

Controllable and Uncontrollable Spending

What the Federal Government spends can be described in terms of **controllable** and **uncontrollable spending.** Most specific items in the federal budget are controllable. That is, Congress and the President decide how much will be spent each year on many of the individual expenditures the government makes. Controllable spending includes spending on environmental protection programs, military equipment, aid to education, and so on. Some people, most often economists, also use the term "discretionary spending" to describe spending on those budget items about which Congress and the President can make choices.

Much federal spending is uncontrollable, however. It is because "mandatory spending" was built into many public programs when Congress created them. The Office of Management and Budget estimates that nearly 80 percent of all federal spending falls into this category.

Take interest on the public debt as a leading example of uncontrollable spending. Paying the interest due cannot be avoided. That interest amounts to a fixed charge; once

Federal Spending (in billions of dollars)

Category	1997	1998	1999	2000	2001*	2002*
Legislative Branch	$ 2.4	$ 2.6	$ 2.6	$ 2.9	$ 3.1	$ 3.3
Judicial Branch	3.3	3.5	3.8	4.1	4.3	4.9
Executive Office of the President	0.2	0.2	0.4	0.3	0.3	0.3
Department of Agriculture	52.5	53.9	62.8	75.7	69.6	63.2
Department of Commerce	3.8	4.0	5.0	7.8	5.5	5.2
Department of Defense–Military	258.3	256.1	261.4	281.2	283.9	303.4
Department of Defense–Other	30.3	31.2	32.0	37.2	39.0	39.8
Department of Education	30.0	31.5	32.4	33.9	36.7	45.2
Department of Energy	14.5	14.4	16.0	15.0	16.7	17.2
Department of Health and Human Services	339.5	350.6	359.7	382.6	430.5	468.8
Department of Housing and Urban Development	27.5	30.2	32.7	30.8	37.3	34.8
Department of the Interior	6.8	7.3	7.8	8.0	8.7	9.3
Department of Justice	14.3	16.2	18.3	19.6	20.7	22.5
Department of Labor	30.5	30.0	32.5	31.4	38.2	42.0
Department of State	6.0	5.4	6.5	6.8	9.3	9.7
Department of Transportation	39.8	39.5	41.8	46.0	50.6	54.9
Department of the Treasury	379.3	390.1	386.7	391.2	388.5	381.5
Department of Veterans Affairs	39.3	41.8	43.2	47.1	45.2	51.5
Environmental Protection Agency	6.2	6.3	6.8	7.2	7.5	7.6
National Aeronautics and Space Administration	14.4	14.2	13.7	13.4	13.8	14.2
Funds appropriated to the President (Mostly foreign economic/military aid)	13.4	11.1	13.6	12.1	11.4	12.1
Social Security Administration	393.3	408.2	419.8	441.8	463.0	488.2
Other	50.7	65.3	62.6	69.8	101.6	120.3
Deductions (undistributed offsetting receipts)	−155.0	−161.0	−159.1	−172.8	−190.2	−201.8
Total Outlays	**$ 1,601.3**	**$ 1,652.6**	**$ 1,703.0**	**$ 1,788.8**	**$ 1,856.2**	**$ 1,960.6**
Surplus (+) or Deficit (−)	−21.9	69.2	124.4	236.4	156.5	174.1

Note: Columns may not add to totals due to rounding. *Estimated

SOURCES: Office of Management and Budget and Financial Management Service, Department of the Treasury.

Interpreting Tables **(a) Which of the executive departments now spends the largest amount of money each year? (b) Which executive department spends the least?**

the Federal Government borrows the money, the interest on that loan must be paid when it comes due and at the rate the government promised to pay.

Social Security benefits, food stamps, and most other entitlements are also largely uncontrollable. This is because once Congress has set the standards of eligibility for those programs, it has no control over how many people will meet those standards. Thus, Congress does not—really cannot—determine how many people covered by Social Security will become eligible for retirement benefits each year.

Those expenditures are not completely uncontrollable, however. Congress could redefine eligibility standards, or it could reduce the amount of money each beneficiary is to receive. But clearly those actions would be politically difficult.

In general, the percentage of federal spending that is uncontrollable has grown in recent years, while the percentage of controllable spending has decreased. These trends cause concern to those officials who are responsible for maintaining control of the budget.

The Federal Budget

The Constitution declares that

> **FROM THE Constitution** ❝ No Money shall be drawn from the Treasury, but in Consequence of Appropriations made by Law. . . . ❞
>
> —Article I, Section 9, Clause 7

So, only Congress can provide the money upon which the Federal Government must depend. It is the President, however, who initiates the spending process by submitting a budget at the beginning of each congressional session.[7]

The federal budget is a hugely important document. It is, of course, a financial statement. As such, it is a detailed estimate, an anticipation, of federal income and outgo in the upcoming fiscal year. Yet it is much more than that. The federal budget is also a major political statement; a declaration of the public policies of the United States, with dollar signs attached. Put another way, the budget is the President's work plan for the conduct of government and the execution of public policy.

The annual budget-making process is a joint effort of the President and both houses of Congress. The President prepares the budget and submits (proposes) it to Congress soon after that body begins its annual session. Congress then reacts to the President's budget proposals, over a period of several months. It usually enacts most of those proposals, many of them in altered form, in appropriations measures.

The President and the Budget

The process of building the budget is a lengthy one. In fact, that process begins some eighteen months before the start of the fiscal year for which the budget is intended. First, each federal agency prepares detailed estimates of its spending needs for that twelve-month period. Each agency then submits its spending plans to the Office of Management and Budget, the President's budget-making agency.

Creating the Federal Budget

Federal agencies send their money requests to the Office of Management and Budget (OMB).

The OMB reviews agency requests and melds them into the President's budget. In January or February, the President sends his budget to Congress.

Congress reviews budget, enacts several appropriations measures.

The President signs funding measures.

OR

The President vetoes one or more funding measures. If Congress cannot get a $\frac{2}{3}$ majority to override veto, Congress and the President must reach a compromise to resolve the dispute(s).

Interpreting Diagrams **When is compromise necessary to the budget process, according to the diagram?**

The OMB reviews all of the many agency proposals, often in budget hearings at which agency officials must defend their dollar requests. Following the OMB's review, revised and usually lowered spending plans for all of the agencies in the executive branch are fitted into the President's overall program. They become a part of the budget document the President sends to Capitol Hill.[8]

Congress and the Budget

Remember that Congress depends upon and works through its standing committees. The President's budget is referred to the Budget Committee in each chamber. There, in both committees, the budget is studied and dissected with the help of the Congressional Budget Office.

The CBO is a staff agency created by Congress in 1974. It provides both houses of Congress and their committees with basic budget and economic data and analyses. The information that the CBO supplies is independent of the

---

[7]The word *budget* comes from the French *bougette,* meaning a small pouch or bag with its contents. In the eighteenth century, the budget was the bag in which the British Chancellor of the Exchequer carried financial documents.

[8]Congress enacts a separate budget for its own expenses. The spending requests for the judicial branch, prepared by the Administrative Office of the United States Courts, are included in the President's budget without OMB review.

Interpreting Political Cartoons The Social Security Administration accounts for the largest segment of the federal budget. *What is the cartoonist's view of the future of Social Security?*

information provided by the OMB, which, recall, is the President's budget agency.

The President's budget is also sent to the House and Senate Appropriations Committees.[9] Their subcommittees hold extensive hearings in which they examine agency requests, quiz agency officials, and take testimony from a wide range of interested parties. The two Appropriations Committees fashion measures that later are reported to the floor of each house. Those measures are the bills that actually appropriate the funds on which the government will operate.

---

[9]If the budget includes any tax proposals, they are referred to the House Ways and Means Committee and to the Senate's Finance Committee.

The two Budget Committees propose a concurrent resolution on the budget to their respective chambers. That measure, which must be passed by both houses by May 15, sets overall targets for federal receipts and spending in the upcoming fiscal year. The estimates are intended to guide the committees in both houses as they continue to work on the budget.

The two Budget Committees propose a second budget resolution in early September. Congress must pass that resolution by September 15, just two weeks before the beginning of the next fiscal year. The second budget resolution sets binding expenditure limits for all federal agencies in that upcoming year. No appropriations measure can provide for any spending that exceeds those limits.

Congress passes thirteen major appropriations bills each year. Recall, each of these measures must go to the White House for the President's action. Every year, Congress hopes to pass all thirteen of the appropriations measures by October 1 —that is, by the beginning of the fiscal year.

It seldom does so, however. Congress must then pass emergency spending legislation to avoid a shutdown of those agencies for which appropriations have not yet been signed into law. That legislation takes the form of a **continuing resolution.** When signed by the President, this measure allows the affected agencies to continue to function on the basis of the previous year's appropriations. Should Congress and the President fail to act, many agencies of the Federal Government would have to suspend their operations.

Section 3 Assessment

Key Terms and Main Ideas

1. How are **entitlements** different from other types of benefits?
2. List two examples of **controllable spending** in the federal budget.
3. What is the purpose of a **continuing resolution?**

Critical Thinking

4. **Drawing Inferences** Why is the term "uncontrollable spending" not completely accurate for some entitlements?
5. **Predicting Consequences** What might happen if the OMB accepted all requests for funding without holding hearings? How would this affect the budget?

6. **Making Comparisons** What is the President's role in the budget-making process? What is the role of Congress in the budget-making process?

 Take It to the Net

7. Where does the money in the federal budget come from, and where does it go? Choose five items from a recent federal budget and describe how their funding affects communities like yours. Use the links provided in the Social Studies area at the following Web site for help in completing this activity. **www.phschool.com**

Can Federal Funds Be Used to Help Religious School Students?

The 1st Amendment prohibits government from establishing religion or interfering with the free exercise of religion. Because many students attend parochial (religious) schools, States have tried to help with the secular (non-religious) parts of their education without violating the 1st Amendment. To what extent may government funds be used to support secular programs in religious schools?

Agostini v. *Felton* (1997)

In the 1985 case *Aguilar* v. *Felton*, the Supreme Court ruled that New York City public school teachers could not provide extra instruction to disadvantaged students at religious schools during regular school hours. Such instruction, the Court declared, violated the Establishment Clause of the 1st Amendment. Following that decision, the city's board of education used other methods to help religious school students, mostly by busing the students to public school buildings or other (rented) facilities after regular school hours.

In the years after *Aguilar*, the Supreme Court decided other cases involving government support of special education in religious schools. In a case from Arizona, *Zobrest* v. *Catalina Foothills School District* (1993), for example, the Court allowed a sign-language interpreter, paid for with public funds, to help a deaf student with his class work at a parochial high school.

Twelve years after *Aguilar* v. *Felton*, New York City officials returned to court to ask that the decision in that case be reconsidered and reversed in light of the more-recent Supreme Court cases. The district court and court of appeals declined to do so, and the case then went to the Supreme Court.

Arguments for Agostini

1. Government funding of secular instruction in religious schools violates the Establishment Clause by promoting religion. Because the instruction takes place in religious schools, the public school teachers might tailor their teaching to conform to the school's religious beliefs, whether intentionally or not.
2. Government funding of secular instruction in religious schools entangles church and state because the government has to monitor the ways in which the funds are used.

Arguments for Felton

1. The board of education's program does not promote religion because the skills on which students will be helped are not related to students' religious beliefs or where they go to school. Therefore, recipients of aid have no incentive to change their religious beliefs or practices in order to obtain assistance.
2. The program requires only very limited government supervision of the ways in which funds are used, and thus does not result in excessive entanglement with religion.

Decide for Yourself

1. Review the constitutional grounds on which each side based its arguments and the specific arguments each side presented.
2. Debate the opposing viewpoints presented in this case. Which viewpoint do you favor?
3. Predict the impact of the Court's decision on government-funded programs in religious schools. (To read a summary of the Court's decision, turn to the Supreme Court Glossary on page 799.)

Political Dictionary

progressive tax (p. 449)

tax return (p. 449)

payroll tax (p. 450)

regressive tax (p. 451)

excise tax (p. 451)

estate tax (p. 451)

gift tax (p. 451)

custom duty (p. 451)

interest (p. 454)

deficit (p. 455)

surplus (p. 455)

public debt (p. 455)

entitlement (p. 458)

controllable spending (p. 459)

uncontrollable spending (p. 459)

continuing resolution (p. 462)

Practicing the Vocabulary

Matching Choose a term from the list above that best matches each description.

1. Tax imposed on the assets of one who dies
2. Tax that falls most heavily on those who are least able to pay
3. The total amount of money owed by the United States, plus all interest
4. Payments that federal law says must be paid to all those who meet the eligibility requirements
5. Sometimes called tariffs, import duties, or imposts

Fill in the Blank Choose a term from the list above that best completes the sentence.

6. The Federal Government creates a budget _____ when it spends more money in one year than it takes in.
7. Congress passes a _____ to fund government agencies during long budget negotiations.
8. Employers withhold a(n) _____ from each paycheck.
9. Congress can decide how much money to spend each year on programs that are considered _____ (s).
10. The government lays a(n) _____ on the manufacture, sale, or consumption of goods.

Reviewing Main Ideas

Section 1

11. What are the four expressed limitations on the Federal Government's power to tax?
12. What is the implied limitation on the power to tax?
13. What are the different taxes by which the government raises revenue?
14. Are excise taxes regressive or progressive taxes? Explain your answer.
15. (a) How did the government gain the power to lay an income tax? (b) Describe how the role of the income tax in funding the government has changed since the Civil War.

Section 2

16. List five of the nontax sources of revenue used by the Federal Government.
17. (a) Describe the different methods the Federal Government can use to borrow money. (b) What advantages does the Federal Government have when trying to borrow money from investors?

18. How does the historical use of borrowing differ from the practice of governmental borrowing in recent decades?
19. What is the significance of the public debt for future taxpayers?

Section 3

20. How has federal spending changed over the past two centuries?
21. What is the largest item on which the Federal Government spends the money it raises?
22. (a) About what percentage of federal spending serves to pay interest on the national debt? (b) If the government enjoys a budget surplus each year, how will this percentage change in the future?
23. (a) What is the difference between uncontrollable and controllable spending? (b) About what percentage of the annual budget is controllable?
24. What are the roles of the Budget Committees and the Appropriations Committees?

Critical Thinking Skills

25. *Applying the Chapter Skill* Find a blank income tax form and review its contents. List ten pieces of information that a taxpayer would need to know in order to complete the form properly.

26. *Drawing Inferences* Consider the discussion of the purposes for which Congress can levy taxes. Do you think that the Framers of the Constitution intended for Congress to use its power to tax certain activities as a way of regulating or destroying those activities? Explain your answer.

27. *Making Decisions* (a) In your opinion, should Americans seek an amendment to the Constitution requiring a balanced budget? **(b)** What might be the result of such an amendment?

28. *Drawing Conclusions* The text states that "the federal budget is a hugely important political document." Use evidence from the chapter to support and/or explain this statement.

Analyzing Political Cartoons

Using your knowledge of American government and this cartoon, answer the questions below.

29. (a) According to this cartoon, what factor has led to a balanced budget? **(b)** Based on your reading, how might this factor lead to the higher revenues and/or lower spending associated with a balanced budget?

30. Does the cartoon imply that the United States should expect a future of balanced budgets? Why or why not?

★ You Can Make a Difference

How would you and your classmates do in the Fed Challenge? Find out in which Federal Reserve District your school is located. Then get in touch with the Bank itself or go to its Web site to find out about the coming year's Fed Challenge. Use the sample questions and topics that are supplied to conduct a mini-Fed Challenge in your class.

Participation Activities

31. *Current Events Watch* Draw a time line showing the start and end of the next fiscal year and each month during that time period. Then use newspapers and magazines to find out which steps have already been completed in the creation of next year's federal budget. Show those steps on the time line. In the space next to the current month, tape an article that describes the current status of the budget.

32. *Graphing Activity* Choose one country from each of the following continents: Africa, Asia, Europe, and South America. Research the population, national budget, and national debt for each country and for the United States. Calculate national spending per person by dividing the national budget of each country by its population. Next, calculate the national debt per person by dividing the national debt by its population. Create a bar graph showing the population, national spending per person, and national debt per person for all five countries. Which country spends the most on each of its citizens? Which country owes the most money per person? How does the United States compare to the other countries you chose?

33. *It's Your Turn* Write a questionnaire you could use to determine people's views on federal taxes. To begin, create a list of questions that you hope will help you learn how people feel about federal taxes. Review each question to ensure that it is presented in an unbiased manner. Once you have refined your questions, reread them, correct any errors, and make a final draft. **(Writing a Questionnaire)**

 ## Take It to the Net

Chapter 16 Self-Test As a final review activity, take the Chapter 16 Self-Test in the Social Studies area at the Web site listed below, and receive immediate feedback on your answers.

www.phschool.com

Foreign Policy and National Defense

"A successful foreign policy in a nation where informed citizens have a free vote must be based on a public consensus."

—Millicent Fenwick (1975)

American foreign policy guides all our dealings with the rest of the world—international trade, immigration, treaties, foreign aid, and defense. Civilian control over defense policy determines the role of the military in protecting national security.

◆ In the aftermath of the 2001 terrorist attacks, Americans show patriotism and a united front to the world.

You Can Make a Difference

COULD YOU NEGOTIATE an international treaty? Debate about problems in Latin America? High school students who attend the Fulbright School of Public Affairs get a taste for diplomacy and learn about the complexities of world politics. In an intensive three-week session at the University of Arkansas (Fayetteville), students debate international issues, meet and question politicians about current events, and present their own ideas and proposals. One Fulbright student, Nicholas Norfolk, explained, "I'm so used to being in the United States that I forget how many problems other countries have and how come it's so hard for them to solve them. . . ."

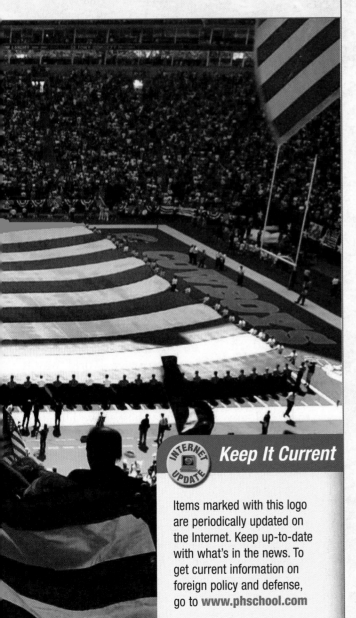

Keep It Current

Items marked with this logo are periodically updated on the Internet. Keep up-to-date with what's in the news. To get current information on foreign policy and defense, go to **www.phschool.com**

Foreign Affairs and National Security

Section Preview

OBJECTIVES

1. **Define** foreign policy, and understand the difference between isolationism and internationalism.
2. **Explain** the functions, components, and organization of the Department of State.
3. **Summarize** the functions, components, and organization of the Department of Defense and the military departments.

WHY IT MATTERS

Foreign policy includes all the stands and actions a nation takes in its relationships with other nations. The State Department carries out the President's diplomatic policies. The armed forces provide the nation's defense, but are under civilian control of the President.

POLITICAL DICTIONARY

★ domestic affairs
★ foreign affairs
★ isolationism
★ foreign policy
★ right of legation
★ ambassador
★ diplomatic immunity

In *The Federalist* No. 72, Alexander Hamilton noted that the "actual conduct" of America's foreign affairs would be in the hands of "the assistants or deputies of the chief magistrate," the President. Today, most of the President's "assistants or deputies" in the field of foreign affairs are in the State Department. Those presidential aides in the closely related field of military affairs are located in the Department of Defense.

Foreign affairs have been of prime importance from the nation's very beginnings, more than a dozen years before Hamilton penned his comment in *The Federalist*. Indeed, it is important to remember that the United States would have been hard pressed to win its independence without the aid of its ally, France.

Isolationism to Internationalism

With the coming of independence, and then for more than 150 years, the American people were chiefly concerned with **domestic affairs**—with events at home. **Foreign affairs**, the nation's relationships with other nations, were of little or no concern to them. Through that period, America's foreign relations were very largely shaped by a policy of **isolationism**—a purposeful refusal to become generally involved in the affairs of the rest of the world.

The past 60 years have been marked by a profound change in the place of the United States in world affairs, however. World War II finally convinced the American people that neither they nor anyone else can live in isolation—that, in many ways, and whether we like it or not, the world of today is indeed "one world." The well-being of everyone in this country—in fact, the very survival of the United States—is affected by much that happens elsewhere on the globe. If nothing else, the realities of ultra-rapid travel and instantaneous communications make it clear that we now live in a "global village."

Wars and other political upheavals abroad have an impact on the United States and on the daily lives of the American people. Four times over the past century the United States fought

▲ Benjamin Franklin (center), the first American diplomat, is received at the French court in 1778. Louis XVI and Marie Antoinette are seated at right.

major wars abroad; and in several other instances the nation committed its armed forces to lesser, but significant, foreign conflicts. The nation's security has also been threatened by terrorists in Europe and Asia, as well as at home, by racial strife in southern Africa, by Arab-Israeli conflicts in the Middle East, and by other events in many other places around the globe.

Economic conditions elsewhere also have a direct effect on and in this country. Japanese automobiles, European steel, oil from the Middle East, coffee from Brazil, Italian shoes, and expanding trade with China underscore the fact that every day Americans buy from other countries. American companies also sell their products in foreign markets, and often manufacture them abroad, as well. The American economy has become part of a truly global economy, linked by international banking, multinational corporations, and worldwide investments that transcend national boundaries.

Clearly, today's world cannot be described as "one world" in all respects, however. It remains, in many ways, a very fractured and dangerous place. Acts of international terrorism; civil wars in Sri Lanka, Colombia, Morocco, and the Congo; unrest in what was once the Soviet Union; drug cartels in Latin America and in Southeast Asia; the behavior of Iraq and other "rogue states"; the emerging dangers of chemical and of biological weapons—all of this, and more, make the point abundantly clear. In the interconnected yet divided world of today, only those polices that protect and promote the security of *all* nations can assure the security and the well-being of the United States.

Foreign Policy Defined

Every nation's **foreign policy** is actually many different policies on many different topics. It is made up of all of the stands and actions that a nation takes in every aspect of its relationships with other countries—diplomatic, military, commercial, and all others. To put the point another way, a nation's foreign policy is made up of all of its many foreign policies. In short, it includes everything that that nation's government says and everything that it does in world affairs.

Thus, American foreign policy consists of all of the Federal Government's official statements

▲ **Secretary of State** Diplomats meet with foreign leaders to negotiate treaties, discuss world problems, and promote national policies. Here, Secretary of State Colin Powell shakes hands with Chinese Vice Premier Qian Qichen (left).

and all of its actions as it conducts this nation's foreign relations. It involves treaties and alliances, international trade, the defense budget, foreign economic and military aid, the United Nations, nuclear weapons testing, and disarmament negotiations. It also includes the American position on oil imports, grain exports, immigration, space exploration, fishing rights in the Atlantic and Pacific oceans, cultural exchange programs, economic sanctions, computer technology exports, and a great many other matters.

Some aspects of foreign policy remain largely unchanged over time. For example, an insistence on freedom of the seas has been a basic part of American policy from the nation's beginnings. Other policies are more flexible. Only a few years ago, resisting the ambitions of the Soviet Union was a basic part of American foreign policy. Today, the United States and much of the former Soviet Union are seeking closer political, military, and economic ties.

The President is both the nation's chief diplomat and the commander in chief of its armed forces. Constitutionally and by tradition, the President bears the major responsibility for both the making and the conduct of foreign policy. The President depends on a number of officials and agencies—Hamilton's "assistants or deputies"—to meet the immense responsibilities that come with this dual role.

Voices on Government

Condoleezza Rice was named National Security Advisor by President George W. Bush in 2001. During the administration of George H. W. Bush, she helped bring democratic reforms to Poland and played a vital role in crafting many of the Bush administration's policies with the former Soviet Union. In a speech regarding national security challenges for the George W. Bush administration, she had this to say:

" Our interests and our values have to go hand in hand. In fact, our interests are reinforced by our values and vice versa. There is no doubt that American interests are better advanced today in a world in which more countries share our values of individual liberty, of freedom of the press, of human rights, and of human dignity. "

Evaluating the Quotation

State in your own words what Rice means when she says, "Our interests and our values have to go hand in hand." In what circumstances might a nation's interests and values not go hand in hand?

The State Department

The State Department, headed by the secretary of state, is the President's right arm in foreign affairs. The President names the secretary of state, subject to confirmation by the Senate. It is to the secretary of state and to the Department of State that the President looks for advice on both the formulation and the conduct of the nation's foreign policy.

The Secretary of State

The secretary of state ranks first among the members of the President's Cabinet. This ranking is because of the importance of the office, but also because the State Department was the first of the now 14 executive departments to be created by Congress.

The Department of Foreign Affairs had first been created in 1781 under the Articles of Confederation. It was re-created by Congress in 1789 as the first major unit in the executive branch under the Constitution. Later that year, its name was changed to the Department of State.

President Washington appointed Thomas Jefferson as the nation's first secretary of state. The first woman to hold the post, Madeleine Albright, was appointed by President Clinton in 1997. Colin Powell, secretary of state under President George W. Bush, is the first African American to hold the office. Today, the duties of the secretary relate almost solely to foreign affairs: to the making and conduct of policy and to managing the work of the department, its many overseas posts, and some 25,000 employees.[1]

Some Presidents have relied heavily on the secretary of state; others have chosen to keep foreign policy more tightly in their own hands. In either case, the secretary has been an important and influential officer in every administration.

Organization and Components

The Department of State is organized along both geographic and functional lines. Some of its agencies, such as the Bureau of African Affairs and the Bureau of Near East Affairs, deal with matters involving particular regions of the world.

Other agencies have more broadly defined responsibilities, such as the Bureau of Arms Control and the Bureau for Political–Military Affairs. Most bureaus are headed by an assistant secretary and include several "offices." For example, both the Office of Passport Services and the Office of Visa Services are found in the Bureau of Consular Affairs.

The Foreign Service

Some 6,000 men and women now represent the United States abroad as members of the Foreign Service. Under international law every nation has the **right of legation**—the right to send and receive diplomatic representatives.[2] The right of

---

[1]The secretary does have some domestic responsibilities. Thus, when Richard Nixon resigned the presidency on August 9, 1974, his formal, legal announcement of that fact had to be submitted to Secretary of State Henry Kissinger. Over the years, the secretary and the department have had (and been relieved of) various domestic functions—including publishing the nation's laws, issuing patents, and supervising the decennial census.

[2]International law consists of those rules and principles that guide sovereign states in their dealings with one another and in their treatment of foreign nationals (private persons and groups). Its sources include treaties, decisions of international courts, and custom. Treaties are the most important source today.

legation is an ancient practice. Its history can be traced back to the Egyptian civilization of 6,000 years ago.

The Second Continental Congress named this nation's first foreign service officer in 1778. That year, it chose Benjamin Franklin to be America's minister to France.

Ambassadors

An **ambassador** is an official representative of the United States appointed by the President to represent the nation in matters of diplomacy. Today, the United States is represented by an ambassador stationed at the capital of each state the United States recognizes.[3] American embassies are found in more than 160 countries around the world today.

The United States also has some 120 consular offices abroad. There, Foreign Service officers promote American interests in a multitude of ways, such as encouraging trade, gathering intelligence data, advising persons who seek to enter this country, and aiding American citizens who are abroad and in need of legal advice or other help.

Some ambassadorships are much desired political plums. Too often, Presidents have appointed people to ambassadorships and other major diplomatic posts as a reward for their support—financial and otherwise—of the President's election to office.

President Truman named the first woman as an ambassador, to Denmark, in 1949. President Johnson appointed the first African American (also a woman), as ambassador to Luxembourg in 1965. Today, several women, African Americans, and other minority persons hold high rank in the Foreign Service.

Special Diplomats

Those persons whom the President names to certain other top diplomatic posts also carry the rank of ambassador—for example, the United States representative to the UN and the American member of the North Atlantic Treaty Council.

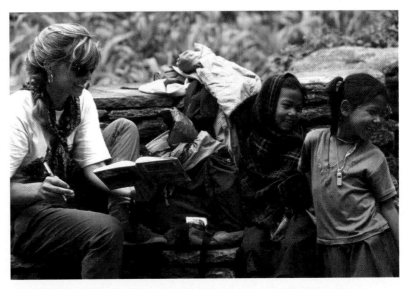

▲ *From Here to There* Americans usually need passports to leave the country. Nepal, shown here, is one nation that requires foreign visitors to have visas.

The President also gives the personal rank of ambassador to those diplomats who take on special assignments abroad, such as representing the United States at an international conference on arms limitations.

Passports

A passport is a certificate issued by a government to its citizens who travel or live abroad. Passports entitle their holders to the privileges accorded to them by international custom and treaties. Few countries will admit persons who do not hold valid passports. Legally, no American citizen may leave the United States without a passport, except for trips to Canada, Mexico, and a few other nearby places.

The State Department's Passport Office now issues some six million passports to American citizens each year. Passports are not the same as visas. A visa is a permit to enter another state and must be obtained from the country one wishes to enter. Trips to most foreign countries require visas. Most visas to enter this country are issued at American consulates abroad.

Diplomatic Immunity

In international law, every sovereign state is supreme within its own boundaries. All persons or things found within the state's territory are subject to its jurisdiction.

As a major exception to that rule, ambassadors are regularly granted **diplomatic immunity**.

---

[3]See page 400. An ambassador's official title is Ambassador Extraordinary and Plenipotentiary. When the office is vacant or the ambassador is absent, the post is usually filled by a next-ranking Foreign Service officer in the embassy. That officer, temporarily in charge of embassy affairs, is known as the chargé d'affaires.

Civilian Control of the Military

PRESIDENT COMMANDER IN CHIEF

CHAIRMAN JOINT CHIEFS OF STAFF
- Army Chief of Staff
- Chief of Naval Operations
- Air Force Chief of Staff
- Commandant of the Marine Corps

SECRETARY OF DEFENSE
- Secretary of the Army
- Secretary of the Navy
- Secretary of the Air Force

Civilian control
Military control
Channel of communication
Chain of command
Alternate chain of command

UNIFIED COMMANDERS OF ARMY, NAVY, AIR FORCE, AND MARINES

Interpreting Charts This chart shows the chain of command of the American military services. *Who advises the president on military matters?*

That is, they are not subject to the laws of the state to which they are accredited. They cannot be arrested, sued, or taxed. Their official residences (embassies) cannot be entered or searched without their consent, and their official communications, papers, and other properties are protected. All other embassy personnel and their families normally receive this same immunity.

Diplomatic immunity is essential to the ability of every nation to conduct its foreign relations. The practice assumes that diplomats will not abuse their privileged status. If a host government finds a diplomat's conduct unacceptable, that official may be declared *persona non grata* and expelled from the country. The mistreatment of diplomats is considered a major breach of international law.

Diplomatic immunity is a generally accepted practice. There are exceptions, however. The most serious breach in modern times occurred in Iran in late 1979. Militant followers of the Ayatollah Khomeini seized the American embassy in Teheran on November 4 of that year; 53 Americans were taken hostage and held for 444 days. The Iranians finally released the hostages moments after Ronald Reagan became President on January 20, 1981.

The Defense Department

Congress established what is today called the Department of Defense in the National Security Act of 1947. It is the present-day successor to two historic Cabinet-level agencies: the War Department, created by Congress in 1789, and the Navy Department, created in 1798.

Congress created the Defense Department in order to unify the nation's armed forces. It wished to bring the then-separate army (including the air force) and the navy under the control of a single Cabinet department. Today, there are more than 1.4 million men and women in uniform, and nearly 700,000 civilians also work for the Defense Department.

Civil Control of the Military

The authors of the Constitution understood the importance of the nation's defense. They emphasized that fact clearly in the Preamble, and they underscored it in the body of the Constitution by mentioning defense more frequently than any other governmental function.

The Framers also recognized the dangers inherent in military power. They knew that its very existence can pose a threat to free government. And so the Constitution is studded with provisions to make sure that the military is always subject to the control of the nation's civilian authorities.

Thus, the Constitution makes the elected President the commander in chief of the armed forces. To the same end, it gives wide military powers to Congress—that is, to the elected representatives of the people.[4]

The United States has obeyed the principle of civilian control throughout its history. That principle has been a major factor in the making of defense policy, and in the creation and the staffing of the various agencies responsible for the execution of that policy. The importance of civilian control is clearly illustrated by this fact: The National Security Act of 1947 provides that the secretary of defense cannot have served on active duty in any of the armed forces for at least 10 years before being named to that post.

The Secretary of Defense

The Department of Defense is headed by the secretary of defense, whose appointment by the President is subject to Senate confirmation. The secretary, who serves at the President's pleasure, has two major responsibilities. He is (1) the President's chief aide and advisor in making and carrying out defense policy, and (2) the operating head of the Defense Department.

The secretary's huge domain is often called the Pentagon—because of its massive five-sided headquarters building in Virginia, across the Potomac River from the Capitol. Year in and year out, its

operations take a large slice of the federal budget—today, in fact, one sixth of all federal spending. The war on global terrorism has forced increased military outlays; total spending for the nation's defense will run to at least $350 billion in fiscal year 2002.

Chief Military Aides

The five members of the Joint Chiefs of Staff serve as the principal military advisors to the secretary of defense, and to the President and the National Security Council. They are the chairman of the Joint Chiefs, the army chief of staff, the chief of naval operations, the commandant of the Marine Corps, and the air force chief of staff. The highest ranking uniformed officers in the armed services, the members of the Joint Chiefs are named by the President, subject to Senate approval.

The Military Departments

The three military departments—the Departments of the Army, the Navy, and the Air Force—are major units and sub-Cabinet departments within the Department of Defense.[5] Each is headed by a civilian secretary, named by the

---

[4]Recall that the Constitution makes defense a national function and practically excludes the States from that field. Each State does have a militia, which it may use to keep the peace within its own borders. Today, the organized portion of the militia is the National Guard. Congress has the power (Article I, Section 8, Clauses 15 and 16) to "provide for calling forth the Militia" and to provide for organizing, arming, and disciplining it. Congress first delegated to the President the power to call the militia into federal service in 1795, and the commander in chief has had that authority ever since. Today, the governor of each State is the commander in chief of that State's units of the Army and the Air National Guard, except when the President orders those units into federal service.

[5]The United States Marine Corps is a separate branch of the armed forces, but, for organizational purposes, it is located within the Navy Department. The Coast Guard is also a branch of the armed forces. It is organized as a military service, with a present strength of some 35,000 commissioned officers and enlisted personnel. Since 1967, the Coast Guard has been part of the Department of Transportation. In time of war or at any other time the President directs, the Coast Guard becomes a part of the United States Navy.

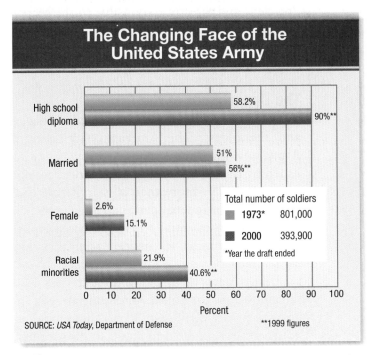

The Changing Face of the United States Army

High school diploma: 58.2% / 90%**
Married: 51% / 56%**
Female: 2.6% / 15.1%
Racial minorities: 21.9% / 40.6%**

Total number of soldiers
■ 1973* 801,000
■ 2000   393,900
*Year the draft ended

Percent (0 to 100)

SOURCE: *USA Today*, Department of Defense   **1999 figures

Interpreting Graphs The make-up of the U.S. Army has changed since the draft ended and it became an all-volunteer force. *In what ways has the army become more diverse?*

"Wisht I could stand up an git some sleep."

Interpreting Political Cartoons Bill Mauldin, who served in the U.S. Army during World War II, drew cartoons "for and about the soldiers because I knew what their life was like." His work appeared in the military newspaper *Stars and Stripes*. **According to this cartoon, what was it like to be a combat soldier?**

President and directly responsible to the secretary of defense. The nation's armed forces—the army, the navy, and the air force—operate within that unified structure.

The Department of the Army

The army is the largest of the armed services, and the oldest. The American Continental Army, now the United States Army, was established by the Second Continental Congress on June 14, 1775—more than a year before the Declaration of Independence.

The army is essentially a ground-based force, and it is responsible for military operations on land. It must be ready (1) to defeat any attack on the United States itself, and (2) to take swift and forceful action to protect American interests in any other part of the world. To these ends, it must organize, train, and equip its active duty forces—the Regular Army—as well as its reserve units—the Army National Guard and the Army Reserve. All of its forces are under the direct

command of the army's highest ranking officer, the army chief of staff.

The Regular Army is the nation's standing army, the heart of its land forces. There are now some 410,000 men and 71,000 women on active duty in the army—officers and enlisted personnel, professional soldiers, and volunteers. The army has been downsized dramatically in the post–cold war era. There were more than 700,000 men and women on active duty when the Soviet Union collapsed in 1991.

Women now serve in all of the Regular Army's units. Over recent years, their roles have come to include many combat-related duties in the army and in each of the other armed services, as well.

The army's combat units are made up of soldiers trained and equipped to fight enemy forces. The infantry takes, holds, and defends land areas. The artillery supports the infantry, seeks to destroy enemy concentrations with its heavier guns, and gives anti-aircraft cover. The armored cavalry also supports the infantry, using armored vehicles and helicopters to spearhead assaults and oppose enemy counteroffensives.

The other units of the army provide the many services and supplies in support of combat troops. Combat soldiers could not fight without the help of members of the engineer, quartermaster, signal, ordnance, transportation, chemical, military police, finance, and medical corps.

The Department of the Navy

The United States Navy was first formed as the Continental Navy—a fledgling naval force created by the Second Continental Congress on October 13, 1775. From that day to this, its major responsibility has been sea warfare and defense.

The chief of naval operations is the navy's highest ranking officer and is responsible for its preparations and readiness for war and for its use in combat. The navy's ranks also have been thinned in the post–cold war period. Today, some 365,000 officers and enlisted personnel, including 50,000 women, serve in the navy.

The Second Continental Congress established the United States Marine Corps on November 10, 1775. Today, it operates as a separate armed service within the Navy Department, but it is not under the control of the chief of naval operations. Its commandant answers directly to the secretary of the navy.

The marines are a combat-ready land force for the navy. They have two major combat missions: (1) to seize or defend land bases from which the ships of the fleet and the air power of the navy and marines can operate, and (2) to carry out other land operations essential to a naval campaign. Today, some 160,000 men and 10,000 women serve in the USMC.

Department of the Air Force

The air force is the youngest of the military services. Congress established the United States Air Force and made it a separate branch of the armed forces in the National Security Act of 1947. However, its history dates back to 1907, when the army assigned an officer and two enlisted men to a new unit called the Aeronautical Division of the army's Signal Corps. These three men were ordered to take "charge of all matters pertaining to military ballooning, air machines and all kindred subjects."

Today, the USAF is the nation's first line of defense. It has primary responsibility for military air and aerospace operations. In time of war, its major duties are to defend the United States; attack and defeat enemy air, ground,

▲ These Navy fighter pilots serve on the aircraft carrier USS *Dwight D. Eisenhower*. **Critical Thinking** *Do you think women should fly combat missions in wartime? Explain your answer.*

and sea forces; strike military and other war-related targets in enemy territory; and provide transport and combat support for land and naval operations.

The air force now has about 350,000 officers and enlisted personnel, including more than 65,000 women—all under the direct command of the chief of staff of the air force. The authorized strength of the USAF has been cut by more than 150,000 men and women since 1991.

Section 1 Assessment

Key Terms and Main Ideas

1. What is the difference between **foreign affairs** and **domestic affairs**?
2. (a) What is the policy of **isolationism**? (b) During what period was this policy favored by most Americans?
3. Name five kinds of policies that are a part of United States **foreign policy**.
4. How does an **ambassador** exercise the **right of legation**?

Critical Thinking

5. **Drawing Conclusions (a)** Explain how tyranny might result when the military is not kept under civilian control. **(b)** Name one nation where such a situation occurred.

6. **Analyzing Information** Why do you think the right of legation has been honored by nations for thousands of years?

Take It to the Net

7. Read more on the debate about isolationism versus internationalism. Make a chart noting four or five points for each side of the argument, and rank each point on a scale of 1 (least convincing) to 5 (most convincing). Then state your own position on the issue. Use the links provided in the Social Studies area at the following Web site for help in completing this activity. **www.phschool.com**

on Primary Sources

The State Department's Mission

As the twentieth century drew to a close, Secretary of State Madeleine Albright testified before the congressional subcommittee that oversees her department. In reviewing the State Department's budget requests, she shared her thoughts on American foreign policy goals for the new century and her department's role in achieving those objectives.

One of my highest goals upon becoming Secretary of State was to work with Members of Congress to restore both the spirit and substance of bipartisan support for American leadership around the globe. . . .

The accounts funded by this subcommittee determine whether we will have the right people in the right place with the right tools at the right time. And whether we will be able—

Madeleine Albright served as Secretary of State from 1997 to 2001.

through our bilateral and multilateral diplomacy effectively—to promote peace, halt the spread of deadly weapons, counter terror, fight international crime, enforce trade agreements, build democracy, raise core labor standards, protect the environment, increase respect for human rights, combat disease, and safeguard the rights of Americans who travel or do business overseas.

I have said that it is America's strategic objective, as we prepare for the new century, to seize the opportunity that history has presented to bring nations closer together around basic principles of democracy, free markets, respect for law, and a commitment to peace. America's place in this system is at the center. And our challenge is to keep the connections between regions and among the most prominent nations strong and sure. . . .

Mr. Chairman, American leadership is built on American ideals, backed by our economic and military might, and supported by our diplomacy. Unfortunately, . . . the resources we need to support our diplomacy are stretched thin. . . .

There was a time, not that long ago, when State Department managers could afford to be guided by a "just in case" philosophy. Planning, acquisitions, and training could be based on what might be needed. Today, we are compelled by the pace of change and the tightness of budgets to practice "just in time" management. This requires putting personnel, resources, and infrastructure where they are required when they are required, and being prepared to reposition them rapidly and flexibly when they are not. . . .

Today, we have a responsibility . . . to reject the temptation of complacency and assume, not with complaint but welcome, the leader's role established by our forebears. For it is only by living up to the heritage of our past that we will fulfill the promise of our future—and enter the new century free and respected, prosperous, and at peace.

Analyzing Primary Sources

1. According to Albright, how will the subcommittee's funding decisions affect her department?
2. What does Albright see as the goal of American foreign policy?
3. What are two possible reasons that Congress might choose not to increase the State Department's funding?

② Other Foreign and Defense Agencies

Section Preview

OBJECTIVES

1. **Describe** a number of government agencies, besides the Departments of State and Defense, that are involved in foreign and defense policy.
2. **Explain** how the CIA, the Office of Homeland Security, NASA, and the Selective Service System contribute to the nation's security.

WHY IT MATTERS

Besides the Departments of State and Defense, several other government agencies are closely involved with foreign policy. These agencies oversee such tasks as gathering and analyzing intelligence information, supervising the draft, exploring space, and strengthening homeland security.

POLITICAL DICTIONARY

★ **espionage**
★ **terrorism**
★ **draft**

How many federal agencies, in addition to the Departments of State and Defense, are involved with the nation's foreign affairs? Dozens of them. For example, the Customs Service combats international smuggling. The Public Health Service works with the United Nations and foreign governments to conquer diseases and meet other health problems in many parts of the world. And the Coast Guard keeps an iceberg patrol in the North Atlantic to protect the shipping of all nations.

A recitation of this sort could go on and on. But, as you will see, this section deals with those agencies most directly involved in the areas of foreign and defense policy.

The CIA

The Central Intelligence Agency (CIA) is a key part of the foreign policy establishment. Created by Congress in 1947, the CIA works under the direction of the National Security Council. A director heads "the agency," as it is often called. That director is appointed by the President and confirmed by the Senate.

On paper, the CIA has three major tasks: (1) to coordinate the information-gathering activities of all State, Defense, and other federal agencies involved in the areas of foreign affairs and national defense, (2) to analyze and evaluate all data collected by those agencies, and (3) to

brief the President and the National Security Council— that is, to keep them fully informed of all of that intelligence.

The CIA is far more than a coordinating and reporting body, however. It also conducts its own worldwide intelligence operations. In fact, it is a major "cloak-and-dagger" agency. Much of the information it gathers comes from more or less open sources, such as foreign newspapers and other publications, radio broadcasts, travelers, satellite photos, and the like. Still, a large share of information comes from the CIA's own secret, covert activities. Those operations cover the full range of **espionage,** or spying.

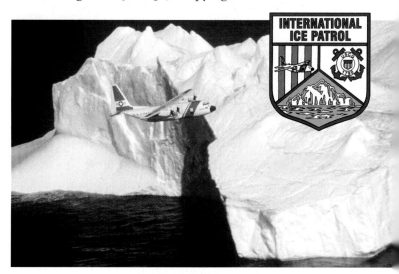

▲ The International Ice Patrol (IIP) of the U.S. Coast Guard tracks icebergs in the North Atlantic to help protect ships of all nations.

▲ *Increased Security* After the September 11, 2001, hijack-ings and attacks, the National Guard began patrolling airports. These members of the Florida National Guard march through Tampa International Airport.

Much of the CIA's work is shrouded in deepest secrecy. Even Congress has generally shied away from more than a surface check on the agency's activities. Indeed, the CIA's oper-ating funds are disguised in several places in the federal budget each year.

When Congress established the CIA, it recog-nized the need for such an organization in a trouble-filled world. Most people agree that that need continues today. At the same time, Congress saw the dangers inherent in a super-secret intelligence agency that operates outside the realm of public scrutiny. Therefore, the National Security Act of 1947 expressly denies the CIA the authority to conduct any investiga-tive, surveillance, or other clandestine activities within the United States. However, the agency has not always obeyed that command.

Office of Homeland Security

The Office of Homeland Security is charged with the awesome task of protecting the United States against **terrorism.** Terrorism is the use of violence to intimidate a government or a society, usually for political or ideological reasons.

The Office was created immediately after the horrific assaults on the Pentagon and the World Trade Center on September 11, 2001. It was established by executive order and is located in the Executive Office of the President (pages 419–422). Its director, who is appointed by the President, has Cabinet rank and works in close concert with the National Security Council.

In the executive order creating the Office, President Bush assigned unprecedented responsi-bilities to the director. He must coordinate and direct the anti-terrorist activities of all of the fed-eral, State, and local agencies that operate in the field of domestic security. As the order puts it, the director leads all of the nation's efforts "to detect, prepare for, prevent, protect against, respond to and recover from terrorist attacks within the United States."

The director oversees the anti-terrorist efforts of more than 40 federal agencies—among them the FBI, the CIA, the Secret Service, the Coast Guard, the Federal Aviation Administration, the Immigration and Naturalization Service, and the Federal Emergency Management Agency. And he also is charged with coordinating the work of thousands of State and local agencies across the country—thousands of police departments, fire departments, emergency medical and search and rescue units, and other disaster response agencies.

The threat of bioterrorism—the use of such biological agents as smallpox or anthrax as weapons—dramatizes the immensity of the prob-lems facing the Office of Homeland Security. So, too, do these facts: There are nearly 600,000 bridges, 170,000 water systems, and more than 2,000 power plants (104 of them nuclear) in the United States. There are also 220,000 miles of railroad, 190,000 miles of natural gas pipelines, 25,000 miles of waterways, and 1,000 harbor channels. And there are 463 skyscrapers (each over 500 feet high), nearly 19,000 airports (including some 300 major facilities), thousands of stadiums and other large gathering places, and nearly 20,000 miles of border.

Add to all that such critical matters as the nation's food supply, its healthcare system, and its communications networks and this point becomes clear: This country cannot be protected—completely and absolutely—against terrorists. Terrorism thrives on unpredictability and uses it as a weapon to foment fear and anxiety.

Quite apparently, the best that can be hoped for in the current circumstances is that (1) most—nearly all—terrorist attacks will be thwarted or their impacts will at least be minimized and (2) those responsible for the attacks will be rooted out and brought to justice.

NASA

The modern space age is only some forty years old. It began on October 4, 1957, when the Soviet Union put its first satellite, *Sputnik I*, in space. The first American satellite, *Explorer I*, was fired into orbit a few months later, on January 31, 1958. From that point on, a great number of space vehicles have been thrust into the heavens by both of the superpowers, and, more recently, by other nations as well.

The National Aeronautics and Space Administration (NASA) is an independent agency created by Congress in 1958 to handle this nation's space programs. Today, the scope of those programs is truly extraordinary. NASA's work ranges from basic research that focuses on the origin, evolution, and structure of the universe to explorations of outer space, and includes the development of a space station that will soon be occupied on a permanent basis.

The military importance of NASA's work can hardly be exaggerated. Nevertheless, Congress has ordered the space agency to bend its efforts "to peaceful purposes for the benefit of all humankind," as well. NASA's research and development efforts have opened new frontiers in several fields: in astronomy, physics, and the environmental sciences; in communications, medicine, and weather forecasting; and in many more areas. A number of scientific techniques pioneered by NASA have been put to remarkable use in the civilian world.

NASA conducts its operations at a number of flight centers, laboratories, and other installations throughout the country. Among the best known are the Kennedy Space Center at Cape Canaveral in Florida; the Johnson Space Center near Houston, Texas; the Ames Research Center and the Jet Propulsion Laboratory, both in California; and the Goddard Space Flight Center in Greenbelt, Maryland.

Over the years, NASA's accomplishments were so many, and its programs so successful,

▲ This NASA astronaut is working on the payload of a space shuttle as it orbits Earth. *Critical Thinking* **Should the U.S. government support and fund space exploration? Explain your answer.**

that space flights and space probes seemed to become almost routine. However, tragedy struck in 1986 when the space shuttle *Challenger* exploded moments after liftoff from Cape Canaveral. All seven crew members died, including Christa McAuliffe, a civilian and the first "teacher in space." NASA slowly recovered from that disaster and now tries to launch as many as ten space vehicles each year, some of them with secret military payloads.

Recently, NASA has had spectacular and much publicized successes and failures. The Hubble Space Telescope, built under NASA's supervision, was placed in orbit in 1990. The most sophisticated optical instrument ever launched, it was designed to take clearer pictures of outer space than could be achieved on Earth. But its pictures were fuzzy; faulty testing procedures had resulted in an optical defect. NASA redeemed its reputation, however, with a space shuttle mission that successfully repaired the Hubble in 1993.

NASA had another huge success in 1997, when the Pathfinder landed safely on Mars. It then deployed the small rover, Sojourner, which did scientific experiments and beamed photos back to Earth. Millions of people watched the exploits of the little rover on television and online. In 1999, however, two other missions to Mars ended in spectacular failure: First the Mars Climate Orbiter was destroyed because of a mix-up of metric and English measurements; then the Mars Polar Lander disappeared, probably crashing into the surface. These failures have caused new scrutiny of the way NASA operates.

The Selective Service System

Through most of American history, the armed forces have depended on voluntary enlistments to fill their ranks. From 1940 to 1973, however, the **draft**—also called conscription, or compulsory military service—was a major source of military manpower.

Conscription has a long history in this country. Several colonies and later nine States required all able-bodied males to serve in their militia. However, in the 1790s, Congress rejected proposals for national compulsory military service.

Both the North and the South did use limited conscription programs during the Civil War. It was not until 1917, however, that a national draft was first used in this country, even in wartime. More than 2.8 million of the 4.7 million men who served in World War I were drafted under the terms of the Selective Service Act of 1917.

The nation's first peacetime draft came with the Selective Service and Training Act of 1940, as World War II raged in Europe but before the United States entered the war. Eventually, more than 10 million of the 16.3 million Americans in uniform in World War II entered the service under that law.

The World War II draft ended in 1947. The crises of the postwar period, however, quickly moved Congress to revive the draft, which was reestablished by the Selective Service Act of 1948. From 1948 to 1973, nearly 5 million young men were drafted.

Mounting criticisms of compulsory military service, fed by opposition to our Vietnam policy, led many Americans to call for an end to the draft in the late 1960s. By 1972, fewer than 30,000 men were being drafted per year, and selective service was suspended in 1973. Nevertheless, the draft law is still on the books.

The draft law places a military obligation on all males in the United States between the ages of $18\frac{1}{2}$ and 26. During the years in which the draft operated, it was largely conducted through hundreds of local selective service boards. All young men had to register for service at age 18. The local boards then selected those who were to enter the armed forces.

As of 1980, the registration requirement was back in place. President Jimmy Carter reactivated it, and his executive order is still in force. All young males are required to sign up soon after they reach their 18th birthday. However, the President's power to order the actual induction of men into the armed forces expired on June 30, 1973. If the draft is ever to be reactivated, Congress must first renew that presidential authority.[6]

---

[6]The Supreme Court first upheld the constitutionality of the draft in the *Selective Draft Law Cases* in 1918. The Court also found its all-male features constitutional in *Rostker* v. *Goldberg* in 1981; see page 499.

Section 2 Assessment

Key Terms and Main Ideas

1. What are the three major tasks of the CIA?
2. What is **terrorism**?
3. What was the major source of American military manpower from 1940 to 1973?
4. Name two successes and two failures of the NASA space programs.

Critical Thinking

5. **Demonstrating Reasoned Judgment** It seems clear that this country cannot be protected—completely and absolutely—against terrorist attacks. Give your reasons for agreeing or disagreeing with this statement.

6. **Checking Consistency (a)** Is an intelligence agency whose actions can be kept secret from the people consistent with the principle of popular sovereignty? Explain. **(b)** Why do you think the CIA is permitted to operate in this way?

 Take It to the Net

7. Because there has not been a draft in this country since 1973, some people have suggested eliminating the Selective Service System. Read both sides of the argument. Then take a position either for or against eliminating this agency, and write a brief statement giving the three strongest arguments for that position. Use the links provided in the Social Studies area at the following Web site for help in completing this activity. **www.phschool.com**

American Foreign Policy Overview

3

Section Preview

OBJECTIVES

1. **Summarize** American foreign policy from independence through World War I.
2. **Show** how the two World Wars affected America's traditional policy of isolationism.
3. **Explain** the principles of collective security and deterrence.
4. **Examine** the United States policy of resisting Soviet aggression during the cold war.
5. **Describe** American foreign policy since the end of the cold war.

WHY IT MATTERS

Understanding the origins of American foreign policy and the results of those stands and actions is essential to understanding foreign policy issues today. Over time, the United States changed from an isolationist nation to a world power. Although the United States is the only superpower today, the world remains a dangerous place, requiring a policy of constant vigilance.

POLITICAL DICTIONARY

★ **collective security**
★ **deterrence**
★ **cold war**
★ **containment**
★ **détente**

The basic purpose of American foreign policy has always been to protect the security of the United States—and so it is today. It would be impossible to present a full-blown history of America's foreign relations in these pages, of course. But we can review its major themes and highlights here.

Why should you know as much as you can about the history of the United States? Because history is not "bunk," as automaker Henry Ford once described it. Let Robert Kelly, a leading historian, tell you what history really is: "History is our social memory. Our memories tell us who we are, where we belong, what has worked and what has not worked, and where we seem to be going."

Foreign Policy From Independence Through WWI

From its beginnings, and for 150 years, American foreign policy was very largely built on a policy of isolationism. Throughout that period, the United States refused to become generally and permanently involved in the affairs of the rest of the world.

Isolationism arose in the earliest years of this nation's history. In his Farewell Address in 1796, George Washington declared that "our true policy" was "to steer clear of permanent alliances with any portion of the foreign world." Our "detached and distant situation," Washington said, made it desirable for us to have "as little political connection as possible" with other nations. In 1801, Thomas Jefferson added his own warning against "entangling alliances."

At the time, and for decades to come, isolationism seemed a wise policy to most Americans. The United States was a new and a relatively weak nation. We had a great many problems of our own, a huge continent to explore and settle, and two oceans to separate us from the rest of the world.

The policy of isolationism did not demand a complete separation from the rest of the world, however. From the first, the United States developed ties abroad—by exchanging diplomatic representatives with other nations, making treaties with many of them, and building an extensive foreign commerce. In fact, isolationism was, over time,

▲ This statue in Washington, D.C., honors the Marquis de Lafayette, a French nobleman who served in the Continental Army during the American Revolution.

more a statement of our desire for noninvolvement outside the Western Hemisphere than a description of United States policy within our own hemisphere.

The Monroe Doctrine

James Monroe gave the policy of isolationism a clearer shape in 1823. In a historic message to Congress, he proclaimed what has been known ever since as the Monroe Doctrine.

A wave of revolutions had swept Latin America, destroying the old Spanish and Portuguese empires there. The prospect that other European powers would now help Spain and Portugal to take back their lost possessions was seen as a threat to United States security and a challenge to this country's economic interests.

In his message, President Monroe restated America's intentions to stay out of European affairs. He also warned the nations of Europe—including Russia, then in control of Alaska—to stay out of the affairs of North and South America. He declared that the United States would look on

PRIMARY Sources *"any attempt on their part to extend their system to any portion of this hemisphere as dangerous to our peace and safety."*
—Speech by President James Monroe to Congress, December 2, 1823

At first, most Latin Americans took little notice of this doctrine. They knew that it was really the Royal Navy and British interest in Latin American trade that protected them from European domination. Later, as the United States became more powerful, many Latin Americans came to view the Monroe Doctrine as a selfish policy designed to protect the political and economic interests of the United States, not the independence of other nations in the Western Hemisphere.

Continental Expansion

The Treaty of Paris officially ended the Revolutionary War in 1783. Under its terms, the United States held title to all of the territory from the Great Lakes in the north to Spanish Florida in the south, and from the Atlantic coast westward to the Mississippi.

The United States began to expand across the continent almost at once. Taking advantage of France's conflict with England in the early 1800s, President Jefferson negotiated the Louisiana Purchase in 1803. At a single stroke, the nation's size was doubled, with territory reaching from the mouth of the Mississippi up to what is now Montana. With the Florida Purchase in 1819, the nation completed its expansion to the south.

Through the second quarter of the nineteenth century, the United States pursued what most Americans believed was this nation's "Manifest Destiny": the mission to expand its boundaries across the continent to the Pacific Ocean. Texas was annexed in 1845. The United States obtained the Oregon Country by treaty with Great Britain in 1846. After its defeat in the Mexican War of 1846–1848, Mexico ceded what today makes up most of the southwestern quarter of the United States.

The Gadsden Purchase in 1853 rounded out the southwestern limits of the nation. By treaty, the United States bought a strip of territory from Mexico. This land in what is now the southern parts of Arizona and New Mexico was acquired to provide the best rail route to the Pacific.

In 1867, the United States bought Alaska from Russia. The treaty of purchase was negotiated by President Andrew Johnson's Secretary of State, William H. Seward. At the time, many Americans criticized the $7 million purchase as "Seward's Folly" and called Alaska "Seward's Icebox."

In that same year, the Monroe Doctrine got its first real test. While Americans were immersed in the Civil War, France had invaded Mexico. The French leader, Napoleon III, had installed Prince Maximilian of Austria as Mexico's puppet emperor. In 1867, the United States backed the Mexicans in forcing the French to withdraw, and the Maximilian regime fell.

A World Power

The United States emerged as a first-class power in world politics by winning the Spanish-American War in 1898. With Spain's decisive defeat, America gained the Philippines and Guam in the Pacific, and Puerto Rico in the Caribbean. Cuba became independent, under American protection. Hawaii was also annexed in 1898.

By 1900, the United States had become a colonial power. Its interests extended across the continent to Alaska, to the tip of Latin America, and across the Pacific to the Philippines.

The Good Neighbor Policy

The threat of European intervention in the Western Hemisphere declined in the second half of the nineteenth century. That threat was replaced by problems within the hemisphere. Political instability, revolutions, unpaid foreign debts, and injuries to citizens and property of other countries plagued Central and South America.

Under what came to be known as the Roosevelt Corollary to the Monroe Doctrine, the United States began to police Latin America in the early 1900s. Several times, the marines were used to quell revolutions and other unrest in Nicaragua, Haiti, Cuba, and elsewhere.

In 1903, Panama revolted and became independent of Colombia, with American blessings. In the same year, the United States gained the right to build a canal across the Isthmus of Panama. In 1917, the United States purchased the Virgin Islands from Denmark to help guard the canal. These and other steps were resented by many in Latin America. They complained of "the Colossus of the North," of "Yankee imperialism," and of "dollar diplomacy"—and many still do.

This country's Latin American policies took an important turn in the 1930s. Theodore Roosevelt's Corollary was replaced by Franklin Roosevelt's Good Neighbor Policy, a conscious attempt to win friends to the south.

Today, the central provision of the Monroe Doctrine—the warning against foreign encroachments in the Western Hemisphere—is set out in the Inter-American Treaty of Reciprocal Assistance (the Rio Pact) of 1947. Still, the United States is, without question, the dominant power in the Western Hemisphere, and the Monroe Doctrine remains a vital part of American foreign policy.

The Open Door in China

Historically, American foreign-policy interests have centered on Europe and on Latin America. But America has also had involvement in the Far East since the mid-1800s.

Interpreting Political Cartoons President Theodore Roosevelt's foreign policy was often described in his own famous statement, "Speak softly and carry a big stick." Here, TR is shown as the policeman of the Western Hemisphere. *Do you think the cartoonist favors this policy or not? Explain your answer.*

Forty-five years before the United States acquired territory in the far Pacific, the U.S. Navy's Commodore Matthew Perry had opened Japan to American trade.

By the late nineteenth century, however, America's thriving trade in Asia was being seriously threatened. The British, French, Germans, and Japanese were each ready to take slices of the Chinese coast as their own exclusive trading preserves. In 1899, Secretary of State John Hay announced this country's insistence on an Open Door policy in China. That doctrine promoted equal trade access for all nations, and demanded that China's independence and sovereignty over its own territory be preserved.

The other major powers came to accept the American position, however reluctantly. Relations between the United States and Japan worsened from that point on, until the climax at Pearl Harbor in 1941. Over the same period, the United States built increasingly strong ties with China; but those ties were cut when communists won control of the Chinese mainland in 1949. For nearly 30 years, the United States and the People's Republic of China refused diplomatic recognition of one another.

The realities of world politics finally forced a reshaping of American-Chinese relations in the 1970s. President Nixon made a historic visit to Beijing in 1972, and full-fledged diplomatic ties were reestablished in 1979.

Still, the People's Republic is a totalitarian state, and American policy reflects that fact—though many argue that it does not do so strongly enough. The Chinese government's brutal response to pro-democracy demonstrations by thousands of students in Beijing's Tiananmen Square in 1989 has colored American-Chinese relations ever since.

World War I and the Return to Isolationism

Germany's submarine campaign against American shipping in the North Atlantic forced the United States out of its isolationist cocoon in 1917. America entered World War I "to make the world safe for democracy."

With the defeat of Germany and the Central Powers, however, America pulled back from the involvements brought on by the war. The United States refused to join the League of Nations, which had been conceived by President Woodrow Wilson. Many Americans strongly believed that problems in Europe and the rest of the world need not concern them.

The rise of Mussolini in Italy (1922), Hitler in Germany (1933), and the militarists in Japan (1937) cast dark clouds over the world. Yet, for more than 20 years after World War I, an isolationist United States remained aloof, protected by its two oceans.

World War II

America's historic commitment to isolationism was finally ended by World War II. That massive conflict, which began in Europe in 1939, spread to engulf much of the world and lasted for nearly six years. The war involved 61 nations. By the time it ended in 1945, World War II had cost the lives of as many as 75 million people worldwide. The war's other costs, in human suffering and in physical destruction, were at least as appalling.

The United States became directly involved in the war when the Japanese attacked the American naval base at Pearl Harbor in Hawaii on December 7, 1941. From that point on—along with the British, the Russians, the Chinese, and our other Allies—the United States waged an all-out effort to defeat the Axis Powers (Germany, Italy, and Japan).

Under the direction of President Franklin Roosevelt, the United States became the "arsenal of democracy." American resources and industrial capacity supplied most of the armaments and other materials we and our Allies needed to win World War II. Within a very short time, the United States was also transformed into the mightiest military power in the world. American land, naval, and air forces fought and defeated the enemy in the Pacific, the Far East, North Africa, and Europe.

World War II finally ended in the middle of 1945 with the Allies victorious everywhere. In Europe, Germany—which had been devastated by the attacks of American and British forces from the west and by Russian troops from the east—surrendered unconditionally in May. The war in the Pacific came to a sudden end in August. Japan capitulated soon after the United States dropped two atomic bombs, which destroyed the Japanese cities of Hiroshima and Nagasaki.

Two New Principles

World War II led to a historic shift from a position of isolationism to one of internationalism. This nation's foreign policy has been cast in that

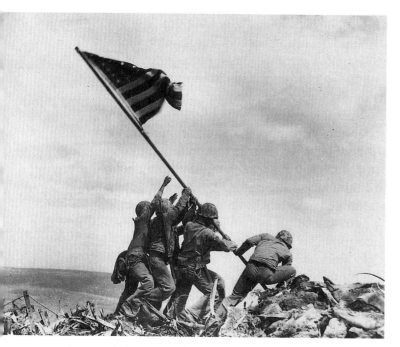

▲ *A Hard-Fought Victory* This famous photograph shows U.S. Marines planting the American flag on the Pacific island of Iwo Jima during World War II.

newer direction for more than 60 years now. Even so, the overall objective of that policy remains what it has always been: the protection of the security of the United States. As you will see, the major features of current American foreign policy are all reflections of that overriding goal.

Collective Security

After World War II, the United States and most of the rest of a war-weary world looked to the principle of **collective security** to keep international peace and order. America hoped to forge a world community in which at least most nations would agree to act together against any nation that threatened the peace.

To that end, this country took the lead in creating the United Nations in 1945. The organization's charter declares that the UN was formed to promote international cooperation and so "to save succeeding generations from the scourge of war . . . and to maintain international peace and security" (see pages 494–498).

It soon became clear, however, that the future of the world would not be shaped in the UN. Rather, international security would depend largely on the nature of the relations between the two superpowers, the United States and the Soviet Union. These relations, never very close, quickly deteriorated—and for the next 40 years American foreign policy was built around that fact.

The United States is the only superpower in today's world. Still, collective security remains a cornerstone of American policy. The United States has supported the United Nations and other efforts to further international cooperation. In addition, because the UN did not immediately fulfill the dreams on which it was founded, the United States soon took another path to collective security—a network of regional alliances that you will read about in the next section.

Deterrence

The policy of deterrence is another major plank of current American foreign policy. **Deterrence** is the policy of making America and its allies so militarily strong that their very strength will deter—discourage, or even prevent—any attack. The policy of deterrence was begun under President Truman, as the antagonisms between the United States and the Soviet Union grew

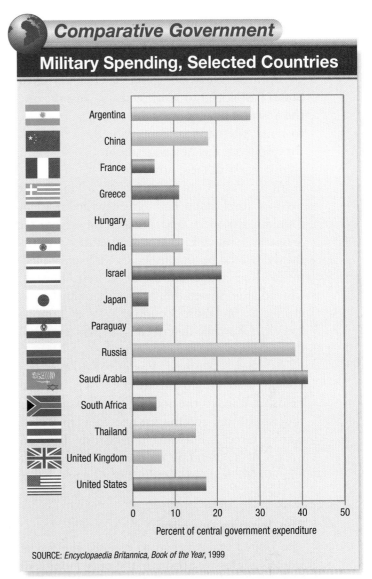

Comparative Government

Military Spending, Selected Countries

Percent of central government expenditure

Country	
Argentina	~28
China	~18
France	~5
Greece	~11
Hungary	~4
India	~12
Israel	~21
Japan	~4
Paraguay	~7
Russia	~38
Saudi Arabia	~42
South Africa	~6
Thailand	~15
United Kingdom	~7
United States	~17

SOURCE: *Encyclopaedia Britannica, Book of the Year,* 1999

Interpreting Graphs This graph shows how much of their budgets various nations spend on their military. *(a) Which nation spends the largest percentage? (b) Which two nations spend the least?*

after World War II. Every President since Truman has maintained it. The policy of deterrence can be summarized in this way: America's military might is most effective if, in fact, it does not have to be used.

Resisting Soviet Aggression

One cannot hope to understand either recent or current American foreign policy without being familiar with the long years of the **cold war.** The cold war was a period of more than 40 years during which relations between the two superpowers were at least tense and, more often than not, distinctly hostile. It was, for the most part, not a "hot war" of military action, but rather a time of threats, posturing, and military build-up.

Toward the end of World War II, the United States had hoped to work with its wartime ally the Soviet Union, particularly through the UN, to build international cooperation and to keep the peace in the postwar world. Those plans were quickly dashed, however.

At the Yalta Conference in early 1945, Soviet Premier Josef Stalin had agreed with President Franklin Roosevelt and British Prime Minister Winston Churchill that "democratic governments" would be established by "free elections" in the liberated countries of Eastern Europe. Instead, the Soviets imposed Communist governments on those countries. In a famous speech, Churchill described "an iron curtain" descending across the continent.

As they devoured Eastern Europe, the Soviets also attempted to take over the oil fields of Iran, to the south. At the same time, they supported communist guerrillas in a civil war in Greece. Pursuing the historic Russian dream of a "window to the sea," the Soviet Union also demanded military and naval bases in Turkey.

The Truman Doctrine

The United States began to counter the Soviet Union's aggressive actions in the early months of 1947. The Truman Doctrine marked the first step in that long-standing process. Both Greece and Turkey were in danger of falling under the Soviet Union's control. At President Harry Truman's urgent request, Congress approved a massive program of economic and military aid, and both countries remained free of Soviet control. In his message to Congress, the President declared that it was now

PRIMARY Sources *"the policy of the United States to support free peoples who are resisting attempted subjugation by armed minorities or outside pressures."*
—Speech by President Harry S Truman to Congress, March 12, 1947

The Truman Doctrine soon became part of a broader American plan for dealing with the Soviet Union. From mid-1947 through the 1980s, the United States followed the policy of **containment.** That policy was rooted in the belief that if communism could be kept within its existing boundaries, it would collapse under the weight of its internal weaknesses.

The United States and the Soviet Union confronted one another often during the cold war years. Two of those confrontations were of major, near-war proportions: in Berlin in 1948–1949 and in Cuba in 1962. During this period, the United States also fought two wars against communist forces in Asia.

The Berlin Blockade

At the end of World War II, the city of Berlin, surrounded by Soviet-occupied East Germany, was divided into four sectors. The Soviet Union controlled one sector, East Berlin. The United States, Britain, and France occupied the other three sectors, which made up West Berlin.

In 1948, the Soviets tried to force their former allies to withdraw from West Berlin. They clamped a land blockade around the city, stopping the shipment of food and supplies to the western sectors. The United States mounted a massive airlift that kept the city alive until the blockade was lifted, nearly a year and a half later.

The Cuban Missile Crisis

The United States and the Soviet Union came perilously close to a nuclear conflict during the Cuban missile crisis in 1962. Cuba had slipped into the Soviet orbit soon after Fidel Castro gained power there in 1959. By mid-1962, huge quantities of Soviet arms and thousands of Soviet "technicians" had been sent to Cuba. Suddenly, in October, the build-up became unmistakably offensive in character. Aerial photographs revealed the presence of several Soviet missiles that were capable of nuclear strikes against this country and much of Latin America.

President Kennedy immediately ordered a naval blockade of Cuba to prevent the delivery of any more missiles. Cuba and the Soviet Union were warned that the United States would attack Cuba unless the existing Soviet missiles were removed.

After several tense days, the Soviets backed down. Rather than risk all so far from home, they returned the weapons to the Soviet Union.

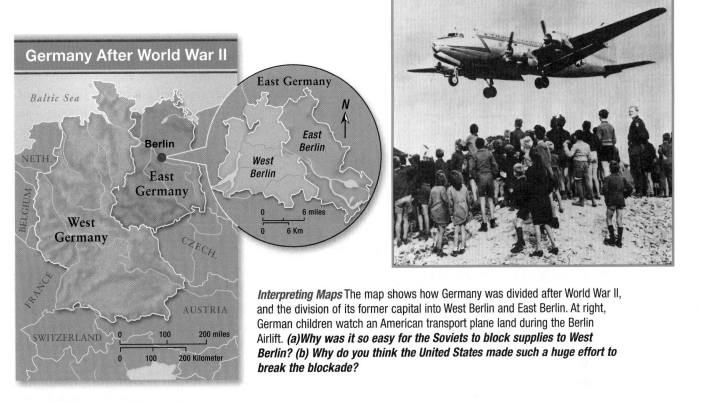

Germany After World War II

East Germany

East Berlin

West Berlin

West Germany

East Germany

Berlin

Baltic Sea

NETH.

BELGIUM

FRANCE

CZECH.

AUSTRIA

SWITZERLAND

0   100   200 miles
0   100   200 Kilometer

0   6 miles
0   6 Km

Interpreting Maps The map shows how Germany was divided after World War II, and the division of its former capital into West Berlin and East Berlin. At right, German children watch an American transport plane land during the Berlin Airlift. *(a)Why was it so easy for the Soviets to block supplies to West Berlin? (b) Why do you think the United States made such a huge effort to break the blockade?*

The Korean War

The Korean War began on June 25, 1950. South Korea (the UN-sponsored Republic of Korea) was attacked by communist North Korea (the People's Democratic Republic of Korea). Immediately, the UN's Security Council called on all UN members to help South Korea repel the invasion.

The war lasted for more than three years. It pitted the United Nations Command, largely made up of American and South Korean forces, against Soviet-trained and Soviet-equipped North Korean and communist Chinese troops. Cease-fire negotiations began in July 1951, but fighting continued until an armistice was signed on July 27, 1953. Final peace terms have never been agreed to.

The long and bitter Korean conflict did not end in a clear-cut UN victory. The war cost the United States 157,530 casualties, including 33,629 combat dead, and more than $20 billion. South Korea's military and civilian casualties ran into the hundreds of thousands. Much of Korea, north and south, was laid to waste.

Still, the invasion was turned back, and the Republic of Korea remained standing. Perhaps more importantly, for the first time in history, armed forces of several nations fought under an international flag against aggression. There is no telling how far that aggression might have carried had the United States not come to the aid of South Korea.

The War in Vietnam

In the years following World War II, a nationalist movement arose in Vietnam. The Vietnamese nationalists were seeking independence from France. Made up mostly of communist forces led by Ho Chi Minh, the nationalists fought and defeated the French in a lengthy conflict. Under truce agreements signed in Geneva in 1954, what had been French Indochina was divided into two zones: a communist-dominated North Vietnam, with its capital in Hanoi, and an anticommunist South Vietnam, with Saigon as its capital.

Almost at once, communist guerrillas (the Viet Cong), supported by North Vietnamese, began a civil war in South Vietnam. The Eisenhower administration responded with economic and then military aid to Saigon. President Kennedy increased this aid. Even with stepped-up U.S. support to South Vietnam, the Viet Cong—and growing numbers of North Vietnamese supplied with mostly Soviet and

▲ **Remembering** The Vietnam Veterans Memorial in Washington, D.C., is inscribed with the names of Americans killed or missing in action in the Vietnam War.

some Chinese weapons—continued to make major gains.

It was President Johnson who, in early 1965, committed the United States to full-scale war. By 1968, more than 540,000 Americans were involved in a fierce ground and air conflict.

In 1969, President Nixon began what he called the "Vietnamization" of the war. Over the next four years, American troops were gradually pulled out of combat. Finally, a cease-fire agreement was signed in early 1973, and the last American units were withdrawn. (In spite of the cease-fire, the war between North and South Vietnam went on. By 1975, South Vietnam had been overrun, and the two Vietnams became the Socialist Republic of Vietnam.)

The ill-fated war in Vietnam cost the United States a staggering $165 billion and, irreplaceably, more than 58,000 American lives. As the war dragged on, millions of Americans came to oppose American involvement in Southwest Asia—and traces of the divisiveness of that period can still be seen in the politics of today.

Détente and the Return to Containment

As the United States withdrew from Vietnam, the Nixon administration embarked on a policy of **détente.** The term is French, meaning "a relaxation of tensions." In this case, the policy of détente included a purposeful attempt to improve relations with the Soviet Union and, separately, with China.

President Nixon flew to Beijing in 1972 to begin a new era in American-Chinese relations. His visit paved the way for further contacts and, finally, for formal diplomatic ties between the United States and the People's Republic of China.

Less than three months later, Nixon journeyed to Moscow. There, he and Soviet Premier Leonid Brezhnev signed the first Strategic Arms Limitations Talks agreement, SALT. It was a five-year pact in which both sides agreed to a measure of control over their nuclear weapons.

Relations with mainland China have improved more or less steadily since the 1970s. Efforts at détente with the Soviets, however, proved less successful. Moscow continued to apply its expansionist pressures and provided economic and military aid to revolutionary movements around the world.

The short-lived period of détente ended altogether when the Soviets invaded Afghanistan in 1979. After that act of aggression, first President Carter and then the Reagan administration placed a renewed emphasis on containing Soviet power.

The End of the Cold War

Relations between the United States and the Soviet Union improved remarkably after Mikhail Gorbachev gained power in Moscow in 1985. Presidents Reagan and Gorbachev paved the way for the end of the cold war at four summit conferences. They met first in Geneva in 1985; and then in Reykjavik, Iceland, in 1986; in Washington in 1987; and in Moscow in 1988. Those meetings helped ease longstanding tensions, and they produced a major disarmament pact, the INF Treaty in 1987.

President Bush met with the Soviet leader in Malta in late 1989; in Washington in 1990; and in Washington, London, and Moscow in 1991. Those meetings reaffirmed the friendlier American-Soviet environment. They also produced commitments from both sides to eliminate a portion of their long-range nuclear missiles, to cut stockpiles of chemical weapons, and to reduce the levels of conventional military forces.

Clearly, Gorbachev deserves much of the credit for the fundamental change in the Soviets' approach to world affairs. However, another key factor was the economic and political chaos that ultimately caused the collapse of the Soviet Union itself in 1991. That the cold war is now relegated to history can and should be seen in this light: The American policy of containment, first put in place in 1947, finally realized its goal.

The Persian Gulf War

Since the end of the cold war, some of the most important events shaping American foreign policy have occurred in the Middle East. In August of 1990, Iraqi President Saddam Hussein launched an invasion of small, oil-rich Kuwait. The invasion threatened the security of America's close ally, Saudi Arabia.

President Bush demanded the immediate withdrawal of Iraqi forces from Kuwait and the restoration of that country's legitimate government. He also ordered a huge deployment of American military might to the Persian Gulf region. By early 1991, American troop strength in the Gulf region amounted to more than 500,000—the largest massing of American power since Vietnam.

The American response was backed by most of the world community. A multinational (but mostly American) military force was established and the United Nations Security Council imposed economic sanctions on Iraq.

Iraq refused to withdraw from Kuwait, however; and Sadam Hussein's continued stubbornness finally triggered the Persian Gulf War. That brief conflict began in mid-January with sustained air attacks on Iraqi positions. By late February, the multinational force had driven Iraq's troops from Kuwait.

When Iraq posed a renewed threat to Kuwait in 1994 and again in 1996, President Clinton ordered a new deployment of American forces to the region, to reinforce the troops that have remained there since the end of the Gulf War.

Maintaining Vigilance

American foreign policy at the start of the twenty-first century is shaped by one overriding conviction: The world remains a dangerous place—all the more dangerous following the September 11, 2001, attacks on the World Trade Center and the Pentagon. Terrorist attacks as well as drug trafficking, weapons proliferation, and cyber-terrorism are but a few of the dangers which our foreign policy must now address.

During the 2000 presidential campaign, George W. Bush noted that "peace is not ordained, it is earned. It is not a harbor where we rest, it is a voyage we must chart." Now, as throughout our history, constant vigilance is necessary to ensure the security of this nation and its people.

Section 3 Assessment

Key Terms and Main Ideas

1. How does the phrase "United we stand, divided we fall" describe the concept of **collective security?**
2. Does the policy of **deterrence** call for the United States to spend large amounts on defense or to curtail spending unless the nation is threatened? Explain your answer.
3. Explain the policy of **containment.** Was it a success or a failure? Why?
4. **(a)** What is **détente? (b)** What Soviet action ended détente?

Critical Thinking

5. **Identifying Central Issues (a)** Why did the United States change from a policy of isolationism to one of internationalism? **(b)** Could America ever successfully return to isolationism in today's world? Explain your answer.

6. **Synthesizing Information** America's foreign policy during the cold war was based partly on the "domino" theory, which held that if one small nation fell to the communists, nearby nations would likely follow. Explain how this belief was translated into policy and action. Give specific examples.

 Take It to the Net

7. Learn more about Harry Truman and the Truman Doctrine. Explore the site, and read some of the available documents. Then create a flowchart showing the chain of events that led to the issuing of the Truman Doctrine. Use the links provided in the Social Studies area at the following Web site for help in completing this activity. **www.phschool.com**

Determining Cause and Effect

Remembering individual facts, dates, and events might help you on a game show or test. But finding out why events happen helps you understand specific events in history and politics. To answer the question *Why?*, try these steps:

1. Identify possible causes and effects. A cause is an event or action that brings about an effect. For that reason, the cause must occur before the effect. Yet an event that precedes another does not necessarily cause it. Words such as *because*, *due to*, and *on account of* signal causes. Words such as *so*, *therefore*, and *as a result* signal effects. Which of these sentences describe a cause-effect relationship? (a) *Soviet aggression in the postwar era led to the cold war.* (b) *Within a short time, the United States was transformed into the world's mightiest military power.* (c) *Nixon's visit to China paved the way to further contacts and, finally, to formal diplomatic ties between the United States and China.* (d) *The growth of U.S.-Soviet tensions was due in part to the opposing post war goals of the two superpowers.*

2. Diagram the cause-effect relationship. Diagrams can help you analyze relationships among events. Diagrams can also help you identify multiple causes. Several causes can combine to create one effect, just as one cause can bring about several effects. What does Diagram A show?

3. Diagram a chain of events. A single event can be both a cause and an effect. Causes and effects can form a chain of events that continue over a period of time. How is Diagram B a chain of events?

4. Draw conclusions based on your analysis. What general statements can you make based on this analysis of cause and effect? Look for connected ideas and trends.

Diagram A

Cause/Effect: The Cold War

CAUSES

Soviets impose communism in Eastern Europe
Soviets try to seize Iranian oil fields
Soviets demand seaport in Turkey

EFFECT

U.S. and U.S.S.R. engage in the cold war

Diagram B

Cause/Effect: The Cold War

CAUSES

Soviets impose communism in Eastern Europe
Soviets try to seize Iranian oil fields
Soviets demand seaport in Turkey

EFFECT

U.S. and U.S.S.R. engage in the cold war

EFFECTS

Truman Doctrine
Containment policy
Berlin blockade
Cuban missile crisis
Wars in Korea and Vietnam

Test for Success

Re-read the paragraphs about the Korean War on pages 486–487. Using the steps above, diagram the causes and effects of the war. Make sure that the events are truly causes, not just a series of events.

Foreign Aid and Defense Alliances

Section Preview

OBJECTIVES

1. **Identify** the two types of foreign aid and describe United States foreign aid policy.
2. **Describe** the major security alliances to which the United States belongs, and summarize United States policy in the Middle East.
3. **Examine** the role, structure, and problems that face the United Nations.

WHY IT MATTERS

The United States works with other nations to keep the peace and to ensure political stability around the world. American foreign aid strengthens the economies and security of nations important to the United States. Security alliances deter aggression and repel invasion.

POLITICAL DICTIONARY

★ **foreign aid**
★ **regional security alliance**
★ **UN Security Council**

Do you know this ancient saying: "Those who help others help themselves"? You will see that that maxim underlies two basic elements of present-day American foreign policy: foreign aid and security alliances.

Foreign Aid

Foreign aid—economic and military aid to other countries—has been a basic feature of American foreign policy for more than 50 years. It began with the Lend-Lease program of the early 1940s, through which the United States gave nearly $50 billion in food, munitions, and other supplies to its allies in World War II. Since then, this country has sent more than $500 billion in aid to more than 100 countries.

Foreign aid became an important part of the containment policy beginning with American aid to Greece and Turkey in 1947. The United States also helped its European allies rebuild after the devastation of World War II. Under the Marshall Plan, named for its author, Secretary of State George C. Marshall, the United States poured some $12.5 billion into 16 nations in Western Europe between 1948 and 1952.

Foreign aid policy has taken several different directions over the years. Immediately after World War II, American aid was primarily economic. Since that time, however, military assistance has assumed a large role in aid policy. Until the mid-1950s, Europe received the lion's share of American help. Since then, the largest amounts have gone to nations in Asia, the Middle East, and Latin America.

On balance, most aid has been sent to those nations regarded as the most critical to the realization of this country's foreign policy objectives. Over recent years, Israel, Egypt, the Philippines, and various Latin American countries have been the major recipients of American help, both economic and military.

Most foreign aid money must be used to buy American goods and services. So, most of the billions spent for that aid amount to a

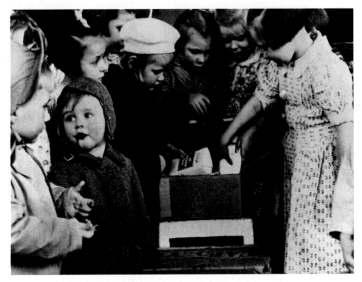

▲ CARE packages, like this one being sampled by Czech children, were sent to war-torn Europe after World War II through a joint effort of Canadian and American relief organizations.

substantial subsidy to both business and labor in this country. The independent Agency for International Development (AID) administers most of the economic aid programs, in close cooperation with the Departments of State and Agriculture. Most military aid is channeled through the Defense Department.

Security Alliances

Over the past five decades, the United States has constructed a network of **regional security alliances,** built on mutual defense treaties. In each of those treaties, the United States and the other countries involved have agreed to take collective action to meet aggression in a particular part of the world.

NATO

The North Atlantic Treaty, signed in 1949, established NATO, the North Atlantic Treaty Organization. The alliance was formed to promote the collective defense of Western Europe, particularly against the threat of Soviet aggression. Each of the 19 member countries has agreed that "an armed attack against one or more of them in Europe or in North America shall be considered an attack against them all."

NATO was originally composed of the United States and 11 other countries: Canada, the United Kingdom, France, Italy, Portugal, the Netherlands, Belgium, Luxembourg, Denmark, Norway, and Iceland. Greece and Turkey joined the alliance in 1952, West Germany in 1955, and Spain in 1982. When East and West Germany united in 1990, the new state of Germany became a member of NATO.

With the collapse of the Soviet Union, NATO's mutual security blanket was extended to cover much of Eastern Europe. Poland, Hungary, and the Czech Republic joined the alliance in 1999, and other one-time Soviet satellites will probably be admitted over the next few years, as well.

But the collapse of the Soviet Union has also suggested to some observers that NATO's purpose may have collapsed as well. The Secretary General of NATO addressed this perception in a millennium speech:

PRIMARY Sources *"By the early 1990s, the threat of massive attack on NATO territory was gone, to the great relief of us all. In those circumstances, however, some voices have called NATO's continuing purpose into question. . . . No institution*

The NATO Alliance

KEY
- Original NATO members
- Joined NATO in 1952
- Joined NATO in 1955
- Joined NATO in 1982
- Unified Germany joined NATO in 1990
- Joined NATO in 1999
- Former Soviet Union

Interpreting Maps This map shows when each NATO member became part of the alliance. *Which nations joined most recently?*

exists for its own sake. If it does not have a useful purpose, it will wither on the vine. And yet, a decade after the end of the Cold War, NATO is more vibrant than ever. . . . [and] still plays a crucial role in preserving the safety and security of all of its members. But today, that mission is being accomplished in a very different way. . .

[A]s we enter the new Millennium, NATO is engaged in a much broader range of activities, all designed with one fundamental goal—to address proactively the security challenges which could, or already do, affect the safety or the interests of its members and their populations. **"**

—"NATO in the 21st Century,"
Secretary General Lord George Robertson

Secretary General Robertson gave three examples of NATO's new agenda:

(1) A different relationship between the West and Russia, which includes consultations on a regular basis as well as cooperation on certain security issues;

(2) NATO's enlargement, which has added to the stability of Europe;

(3) Partnership, including security relationships, with almost all the new democracies of Europe.

NATO was formed for defensive purposes more than 50 years ago and—if defense includes military intervention in conflicts that may destabilize Europe as well as the prevention of humanitarian disasters—defense remains its basic charge. The most obvious example of this role is NATO's intervention in the Balkan nations of the former Yugoslavia. As Robertson pointed out, "For most people, NATO is about making and keeping the peace in the Balkans." Military intervention first in Bosnia and then in Kosovo put NATO in the news as well as planes in the air and troops on the ground. Robertson called Kosovo "a success story," praising the 1999 NATO actions that ensured the withdrawal of Serb troops, enabled˜ the return of Kosovar refugees, and now contribute to a fragile peace.

Other Alliances

The Rio Pact, or the Inter-American Treaty of Reciprocal Assistance, was signed in 1947. In this pact, the United States, Canada, and now 32 Latin American countries have agreed "that an

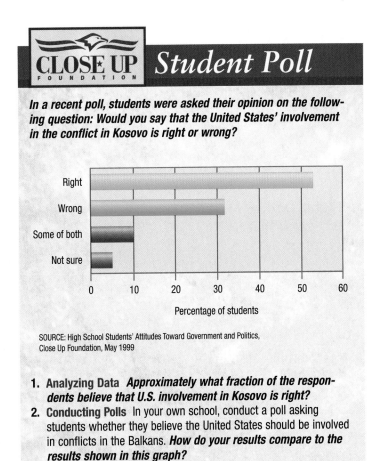

In a recent poll, students were asked their opinion on the following question: Would you say that the United States' involvement in the conflict in Kosovo is right or wrong?

Percentage of students

SOURCE: High School Students' Attitudes Toward Government and Politics, Close Up Foundation, May 1999

1. **Analyzing Data** *Approximately what fraction of the respondents believe that U.S. involvement in Kosovo is right?*
2. **Conducting Polls** In your own school, conduct a poll asking students whether they believe the United States should be involved in conflicts in the Balkans. *How do your results compare to the results shown in this graph?*

armed attack by any state against an American state shall be considered as an attack against all the American states." The treaty pledges those countries to the mutual peaceful settlement of all disputes. In effect, the Rio Pact is a restatement of the Monroe Doctrine.

In addition to NATO and the Rio Pact, the United States is party to several other regional security alliances. For example, the ANZUS Pact of 1951 unites Australia, New Zealand, and the United States to ensure their collective security in the Pacific region.

The Japanese Pact also dates from 1951. After six years of American military occupation, the allies of World War II (with the exception of the Soviet Union) signed a peace treaty with Japan. At the same time, the United States and Japan signed a mutual defense treaty. In return for American protection, Japan permitted the United States to maintain land, sea, and air forces in and about its territory.

The Philippines Pact was also signed in 1951. It, too, is a mutual defense agreement. The pact remains in force, but disagreements over its redrafting prompted the withdrawal of all

◀ **Operation Enduring Freedom** Afghan residents pick up food packets of U.S. humanitarian aid dropped by U.S. planes in 2001. The food packets were intended to help the Afghan people during the war against terrorists hiding out in Afghanistan.

American military forces from the Philippines in 1992. The Korean Pact, signed in 1953, pledges the United States to come to the aid of South Korea should it be attacked again.

The Taiwan Pact was in effect between the United States and Nationalist China from 1954 to 1980. When the United States and the People's Republic of China established full diplomatic relations in 1979, the United States withdrew its recognition of the Nationalist Chinese government. The United States also served the one-year notice required by the 1954 treaty to abrogate (end) the Taiwan Pact.

The Middle East

The American network of regional alliances is far-reaching, but it does not cover the entire globe. The most notable exception today is the Middle East.

This area of the world is both oil-rich and conflict-ridden. America's foreign policy interests in the Middle East have, for decades, been torn in two quite opposite directions: by its long-standing support of Israel and by the critical importance of Arab oil.

The United Nations created Israel as an independent state in 1948. Carved out of what had been British-controlled Palestine, Israel has been in near-constant conflict with most of its Arab neighbors ever since. In spite of its support for Israel, the United States has also worked to promote friendly relations with most Arab states in the region.

With the active involvement of President Carter, Israel and Egypt negotiated a ground-breaking peace treaty, which became effective in 1979. That agreement, the Camp David Accord, ended more than 30 years of hostilities between those two countries.

New efforts to bring peace to the region were made by the Bush and then the Clinton administrations. One promising result was the signing of a peace accord between Israel and Jordan in 1994.

By far the most significant step toward peace was the Israel-Palestinian Liberation Organization (PLO) agreement of 1993. Also called the Oslo Accords because the secret negotiations had begun in the Norwegian capital, the agreement was signed by Israeli Prime Minister Yitzhak Rabin and PLO Chairman Yasir Arafat. Rabin and Arafat, along with Israeli Foreign Minister Shimon Peres, won the 1994 Nobel Prize for Peace for this achievement. In the agreement, Israel recognized the PLO and agreed to gradual and limited Palestinian self-rule in certain areas.

Rabin's assassination by an Israeli extremist and the continuing violence in the region show how far peace still has to go in the Middle East. President Clinton sponsored a number of talks between Israel and the PLO to work out implementation of the Oslo Accords. Progress toward peace has been slow, but peace-seeking efforts continue.

The United Nations

You know that a fundamental change occurred in American foreign policy during and immediately after World War II. The change, a shift from isolationism to internationalism, is strikingly illustrated by this country's participation in the United Nations. Remember, the United States refused to join the League of Nations after World War I. With the end of World War II, however, the American people realized that America was a world power with worldwide interests and responsibilities.

The UN was formed at the United Nations Conference on International Organization, which met in San Francisco from April 25 to June 26, 1945. There, the representatives of 50 nations—the victorious allies of World War II—drafted the United Nations Charter.[7] The charter is a treaty among all of the UN's member-states, and it serves as the body's constitution.

The United States became the first nation to ratify the UN Charter. The Senate approved it by an overwhelming vote, 89–2, on July 24, 1945. The charter was then ratified in quick order by the other states that had taken part in the San Francisco Conference. The charter went into force on October 24, 1945. The UN held its first session of the General Assembly in London on January 10, 1946.

Charter and Organization

The charter is a lengthy document. It opens with an eloquent preamble which declares that the UN was created "to save succeeding generations from the scourge of war." The body of the document begins in Article I with a statement of the organization's purposes: the maintenance of international peace and security, the development of friendly relations between and among all nations, and the promotion of justice and cooperation in the solution of international problems.

Today the UN has 189 members. Under the charter, membership is open to those "peace-loving states" that accept the obligations of the charter and are, in the UN's judgment, able and willing to carry out those obligations. New members may be admitted by a two-thirds vote of the General Assembly, upon recommendation by the Security Council.

The charter sets forth the complicated structure of the UN. It is built around six "principal organs": the General Assembly, the Security Council, the Economic and Social Council, the Trusteeship Council, the International Court of Justice, and the Secretariat.

The General Assembly

The General Assembly has been called "the town meeting of the world." Each of the UN's members has a seat and a vote in the assembly.

The General Assembly meets once a year, normally in September. Sessions are held at the UN's permanent headquarters in New York City. The secretary-general may call special sessions, at the request of either the Security Council or a majority of UN members.

The Assembly may take up and debate any matter within the scope of the charter,[8] and it may make whatever recommendation it chooses to the Security Council, the other UN organs, and any member-state. The recommendations it makes to UN members are not legally binding on them. Yet these recommendations do carry weight because they have been approved by a significant number of the governments of the world.

The Assembly elects the 10 nonpermanent members of the Security Council, the 54 members of the Economic and Social Council, and the elective members of the Trusteeship Council. In conjunction with the Security Council, the Assembly also selects the secretary-general and the 15 judges of the International Court of

[7]Fifty nations attended the San Francisco conference. Poland did not attend, but it did sign the charter October 15, 1945, and is considered an original member of the UN.

[8]Except those matters currently under consideration by the Security Council.

▲ *Town Meeting of the World* The flags of member nations fly outside the United Nations' headquarters in New York City.

► *Nobel Prize Winner*
Kofi Annan and the UN were awarded the Nobel Peace Prize for 2001. The secretary-general was cited especially for promoting human rights, combating AIDS, and bringing new life to an organization paralyzed by big power struggles through much of its existence.

Justice. The Assembly shares with the Security Council the power to admit, suspend, or expel members. But the Assembly alone may propose amendments to the charter.

The Security Council

The **UN Security Council** is made up of 15 members. Five—the United States, Britain, France, Russia (the Soviet Union's old seat), and China—are permanent members. The 10 nonpermanent members are chosen by the General Assembly for two-year terms; they cannot be immediately reelected. The council meets in continuous session.

The Security Council bears the UN's major responsibility for maintaining international peace. It may take up any matter involving a threat to or a breach of that peace. It may adopt measures ranging from calling on the parties to settle their differences peacefully to placing economic and/or military sanctions on an offending nation. The only time the Security Council has undertaken a military operation against an aggressor came in Korea in 1950. It has provided UN peacekeeping forces in several trouble spots, with varying degrees of success.

On procedural questions—routine matters—decisions of the Security Council can be made by the affirmative vote of any nine members. On the more important matters—substantive questions—at least nine affirmative votes are also needed. However, a negative vote by any one of the permanent members is enough to kill any substantive resolution. Because of that veto power, the Security Council is effective only when and if the permanent members are willing to cooperate with one another.

The veto does not come into play in a situation in which one or more of the permanent members abstains (does not cast a vote). When, on June 25, 1950, the Security Council called on all UN members to aid South Korea in repelling the North Korean invasion, the Soviet delegate was boycotting sessions of the Security Council and so was not present to veto that action.

Other Important UN Bodies

The UN has several other important bodies:

1. Economic and Social Council (ECOSOC). This council is made up of 54 members elected by the General Assembly to three-year terms. It is responsible to the Assembly for carrying out the UN's many economic, cultural, educational, health, and related activities.

The ECOSOC coordinates the work of the UN's specialized agencies—independent international bodies that have a working relationship with the world organization. There are 14 specialized agencies today:

• *The World Health Organization (WHO)* combats health problems in underdeveloped countries.

• *The International Labour Organization (ILO)* seeks to improve working conditions worldwide.

• *The International Monetary Fund (IMF)* encourages cooperation among national monetary systems and promotes international trade.

• *The World Bank Group* makes loans for projects in developing countries.

• *The International Fund for Agricultural Development (IFAD)* manages funds for rural projects in developing countries.

• *The Food and Agriculture Organization (FAO)* works to increase the output of farms, forests, and fisheries and food distribution and marketing throughout the world.

• *The United Nations Industrial Development Organization (UNIDO)* assists underdeveloped nations in the development of basic industry.

• *The International Civil Aviation Organization (ICAO)* promotes uniform standards for civil air traffic.

- *The International Maritime Organization (IMO)* encourages cooperation in international shipping.
- *The International Telecommunications Union (ITU)* administers international regulations for radio, telephone, and telegraph communications.
- *The Universal Postal Union (UPU)* promotes international postal cooperation.
- *The World Intellectual Property Organization (WIPO)* fosters cooperation among nations to protect literary, scientific, and artistic works.
- *The World Meteorological Organization (WMO)* coordinates national weather-related activities.
- *The United Nations Educational, Scientific, and Cultural Organization (UNESCO)* carries out a large number of programs in dozens of countries.

2. Trusteeship Council. The United Nations Charter requires each member to promote the well-being of the peoples of all "non-self-governing territories" as a "sacred trust."

3. International Court of Justice. The International Court of Justice (ICJ) is the UN's judicial arm. All members of the UN are automatically parties to the ICJ Statute.

Under certain conditions the services of the court are also available to nonmember states. A UN member may agree to accept the court's jurisdiction over cases in which it may be involved either unconditionally or with certain reservations (exceptions that may not conflict with the ICJ Statute).

The ICJ is made up of 15 judges selected for nine-year terms by the General Assembly and the Security Council. It sits in permanent session at the Peace Palace in The Hague, the Netherlands, and handles cases brought to it voluntarily by both members and nonmembers of the UN. The ICJ also advises the other UN bodies on legal questions arising out of their activities. If any party to a dispute fails to obey a judgment of the court, the other party may take that matter to the Security Council.

4. The Secretariat. The Secretariat is the civil service branch of the UN. It is headed by the secretary-general, who is elected to a five-year term by the General Assembly on the recommendation of the Security Council.

The secretary-general heads a staff of some 9,000 persons who conduct the day-to-day work of the UN. Beyond his administrative chores, the charter gives to the secretary-general this hugely important power: He may bring before the

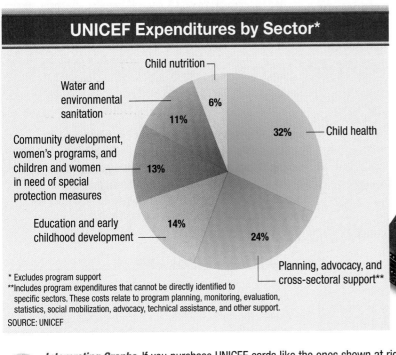

UNICEF Expenditures by Sector*

- Child nutrition — 6%
- Child health — 32%
- Water and environmental sanitation — 11%
- Community development, women's programs, and children and women in need of special protection measures — 13%
- Education and early childhood development — 14%
- Planning, advocacy, and cross-sectoral support** — 24%

* Excludes program support
**Includes program expenditures that cannot be directly identified to specific sectors. These costs relate to program planning, monitoring, evaluation, statistics, social mobilization, advocacy, technical assistance, and other support.
SOURCE: UNICEF

Interpreting Graphs If you purchase UNICEF cards like the ones shown at right, you are helping to support the United Nations Children's Fund. The pie graph shows how UNICEF spends its money. *What activity gets the largest proportion of UNICEF funding?*

Security Council any matter he believes poses a threat to international peace and security.

The secretary-general prepares the UN's biennial budget, which must be approved by the General Assembly. For 2002–2003, the world organization's operating budget amounts to slightly more than $2.5 billion. The Assembly apportions the UN's expenses for each two-year period among its member-states.

Early on, the secretary-general was seen as little more than the UN's chief clerk. The post amounts to much more than that, however, because the seven men who have thus far held it transformed the office into a major channel for the negotiated settlement of international disputes.[9]

The Work of the UN

The purpose of the United Nations can be summed up this way: to make the world a better place. To that end, the UN is involved in a wide variety of activities.

Peacekeeping is a primary function of the United Nations. Today, some 35,400 military and civilian personnel provided by more than 85 member countries were engaged in 14 UN peacekeeping operations around the world.

The United Nations spends some $4 billion dollars a year for economic and social programs to help the world's poorest nations. This does not include the monies expended by the World Bank and the International Monetary Fund, other UN agencies that further development in poorer countries. The World Food Program provides about one third of the world's food aid per year.

Health is a major concern of UN agencies. A joint program of UNICEF and WHO has immunized 80 percent of the world's children against six killer diseases. It is estimated that this program saves the lives of more than 2 million children a year. The disease smallpox was totally wiped out through a worldwide WHO campaign, and another WHO program eliminated polio from the Americas.

The health of the environment is also a UN concern. United Nations environmental conventions have helped reduce acid rain, lessen marine pollution, and phase out the production of gases that are destroying the ozone layer.

Human rights has long been a priority for the United Nations. In 1948, the UN drafted the Universal Declaration of Human Rights, and it has sponsored more than 80 treaties that help protect specific rights. Various agencies of the UN work to aid and protect refugees and displaced persons, and the UN raises more than $1 billion annually for assistance to victims of war and natural disaster.

---

[9]The seven secretaries-general: Trigve Lie (Norway, 1946–1953), Dag Hammarskjold (Sweden, 1953–1961), U Thant (Burma, 1962–1972), Kurt Waldheim (Austria, 1972–1982), Javier Perez de Cuellar (Peru, 1982–1992), Boutros Boutros Ghali (Egypt, 1992–1997), and Kofi Annan (Ghana, 1997–).

Section 4 Assessment

Key Terms and Main Ideas

1. Describe the two types of **foreign aid.**
2. What are **regional security alliances?**
3. List the three elements of NATO's agenda for the twenty-first century.
4. **(a)** Describe the powers of the United Nations Security Council. **(b)** In practical terms, what are some limitations on its power?

Critical Thinking

5. **Recognizing Ideologies** Some people say that the United States should not distribute so much foreign aid; they argue that those funds should be spent to help the needy in the United States. **(a)** What belief does this opinion reflect? **(b)** State and support your opinion on this issue.
6. **Making Comparisons** Compare the American attitude toward the League of Nations following World War I and its attitude toward the United Nations following World War II. What factors might have led to the shift?

 Take It to the Net

7. Read about what the United Nations does for human rights and justice. Use that information to create a table showing the type of aid the UN provides. Give examples where possible. Use the links provided in the Social Studies area at the following Web site for help in completing this activity. **www.phschool.com**

on the Supreme Court

Should Women Be Drafted?

When you turn 18, you will have to register for the draft—that is, if you are male. The U.S. government has never required women to register for the draft. Though today the armed forces are made up entirely of volunteers (including women as well as men), registration is required by law in case a draft should be needed. Should women be included in any future draft registration?

Rostker v. Goldberg (1981)

In 1971, Robert Goldberg and several other men then subject to the draft challenged the constitutionality of the current draft law, the Military Selective Service Act of 1971. They filed suit in federal district court in Pennsylvania, claiming that the law violated the Due Process Clause of the Fifth Amendment. The law unfairly discriminated against men, they argued, by forcing men but not women to register for the draft and to serve in the military.

Congress suspended the draft in 1973, and Goldberg and the others dropped their suit because the issue was no longer relevant. Two years later, the draft registration requirement was suspended altogether. In 1980, however, soon after the Soviet Union invaded Afghanistan, President Carter asked Congress for funds to reinstate draft registration. He also asked that women be included in the registration. Congress agreed to renew registration but did not include women. Goldberg then revived his suit, naming the Selective Service System's director, Bernard Rostker, as defendant.

Three days before registration was to begin, a federal court ruled in Goldberg's favor. Rostker appealed to the Supreme Court.

Arguments for Rostker

1. Article I, Section 8 of the Constitution gives Congress the power "to raise and support armies" and "to provide and maintain a navy." Congress therefore has broad authority to decide how to accomplish these tasks.
2. The only purpose of registration is to prepare for a possible draft of combat troops. Women, however, are excluded from combat, both by law (in the case of the navy and air force) and by military policy (in the case of the army). Thus there is no military need to include them in registration.
3. Congress decided to exclude women only after careful consideration and on the basis of military need rather than any beliefs about women's roles in society.

Arguments for Goldberg

1. The fact that a single group of people, such as men, is large enough to meet the nation's military needs does not give Congress the right to single it out for duty.
2. Women have served ably in the armed forces for decades. Since women are not excluded from the armed forces, they should not be excluded from registering for military service.
3. Excluding women from the draft reflects the outdated belief that women are less competent than men and also helps promote this belief.

Decide for Yourself

1. Review the constitutional grounds on which each side based its arguments and the specific arguments each side presented.
2. Debate the opposing viewpoints presented in this case. Which viewpoint do you favor?
3. Predict the impact of the Court's decision on the state of gender equality in the United States. (To read a summary of the Court's decision, turn to the Supreme Court Glossary on page 799.)

Political Dictionary

domestic affairs (p. 468)

foreign affairs (p. 468)

isolationism (p. 468)

foreign policy (p. 469)

right of legation (p. 470)

ambassador (p. 471)

diplomatic immunity (p. 471)

espionage (p. 477)

terrorism (p. 478)

draft (p. 479)

collective security (p. 485)

deterrence (p. 485)

cold war (p. 485)

containment (p. 486)

détente (p. 488)

foreign aid (p. 491)

regional security alliance (p. 492)

UN Security Council (p. 496)

Practicing the Vocabulary

Matching *Choose a term from the list above that best matches each description.*

1. Everything that a nation's government says and does in world affairs
2. The right to send and receive diplomatic representatives
3. The rule by which ambassadors are not held subject to the laws of the state to which they are accredited
4. The policy of making the United States and its allies so militarily strong that their very strength will discourage any attack
5. An agreement among countries in a particular part of the world to take collective action to defend each other

Word Relationships *Three of the terms in each of the following sets of terms are related. Choose the term that does not belong and explain why it does not belong.*

6. **(a)** right of legation **(b)** ambassador **(c)** diplomatic immunity **(d)** draft
7. **(a)** isolationism **(b)** foreign policy **(c)** domestic affairs **(d)** containment
8. **(a)** détente **(b)** deterrence **(c)** containment **(d)** foreign aid
9. **(a)** regional security alliance **(b)** collective security **(c)** UN Security Council **(d)** espionage

Reviewing Main Ideas

Section 1

10. Summarize how United States foreign policy moved from isolationism to internationalism.
11. Describe the main duties of the secretary of state.
12. **(a)** What is meant by the phrase "global village"? **(b)** How does this concept affect this nation's foreign policy?
13. What are the two main responsibilities of the secretary of defense?
14. Briefly describe the basic military components of the Defense Department.

Section 2

15. What is the primary function of the Central Intelligence Agency?
16. What is terrorism?
17. Give a brief description of the history of the draft in the United States.

Section 3

18. **(a)** What was the Monroe Doctrine? **(b)** How has it affected American policy from 1823 until the present day?

19. What was the Open Door policy in China?
20. How did the two world wars change the status of the United States in the world?
21. **(a)** What was the cold war? **(b)** How did the principles of containment and deterrence affect United States policy during that time?

Section 4

22. **(a)** What philosophy guides decisions about where the United States sends foreign aid? **(b)** What countries have received the bulk of that aid in recent years?
23. Name and describe three regional security alliances to which the United States belongs. What region is not covered by any security alliance with this country?
24. **(a)** When was the United Nations formed? **(b)** What is the purpose of the UN?
25. Describe the basic organization of the United Nations.
26. **(a)** What are some major accomplishments of the UN? **(b)** What are some problems the UN faces today?

Critical Thinking

27. *Applying the Chapter Skill* Why was the attention of the United States focused primarily on the Western Hemisphere from the nation's founding until World War I? Review the events of that period, and then diagram the cause-effect relationship. Finally, write a general statement expressing your conclusion about the causes of this U.S. policy.

28. *Recognizing Ideologies* The Framers of the Constitution made sure that the military would always be under the control of the nation's civilian authorities. What constitutional provisions ensure this control? What attitudes towards the military and government does this insistence on civilian control reveal?

29. *Drawing Conclusions* The philosopher George Santayana said, "Those who cannot remember the past are condemned to repeat it." How might that statement be applied to America's return to isolationism after World War I?

30. *Identifying Central Issues* For what reason(s) is cooperation among members essential for action in the United Nations?

Analyzing Political Cartoons

Using your knowledge of American government and this cartoon, answer the questions below.

"No, no. When I say this new secret weapon can slip past their defenses undetected, I'm not referring to the Russians, I'm referring to Congress."

31. What basic constitutional principle is being illustrated in this cartoon?
32. What does this cartoon suggest about the current relationship between the military and Congress, which must approve the military budget?

★ **You Can Make a Difference**

How much do you know about other nations? Assume that you are a new Foreign Service officer who has been assigned to work at a U.S. embassy abroad. Before you take up your new post, you need to know more about the country. Pick any nation that has been in the news recently. Then prepare a "country study" like those the State Department makes. Include information about that country's people, government, elections, economy, major problems, and political factions. If possible, find a photograph to share with the class.

Participation Activities

33. *Current Events Watch* Review news reports about foreign affairs for a one-week period, and determine which current issues or events affect the United States in terms of its relationship with China, Russia, Israel, Pakistan, North Korea, and Cuba. Create a chart that lists each country and relevant current issues.

34. *Time Line Activity* Using information from the chapter, create a time line showing the major events of United States efforts to resist Soviet expansion after World War II. Be sure to include events in all parts of the world.

35. *It's Your Turn* In this chapter, you read that the United States refused to join the League of Nations following World War I, but that we did join the United Nations following World War II. Research the debate and the circumstances that surrounded these two decisions. Write a report of your findings, and compare the political climate at the time each decision was made. **(Researching a Political Issue)**

 Take It to the Net

Chapter 17 Self-Test As a final review activity, take the Chapter 17 Self-Test in the Social Studies area at the Web site listed below, and receive immediate feedback on your answers.

www.phschool.com

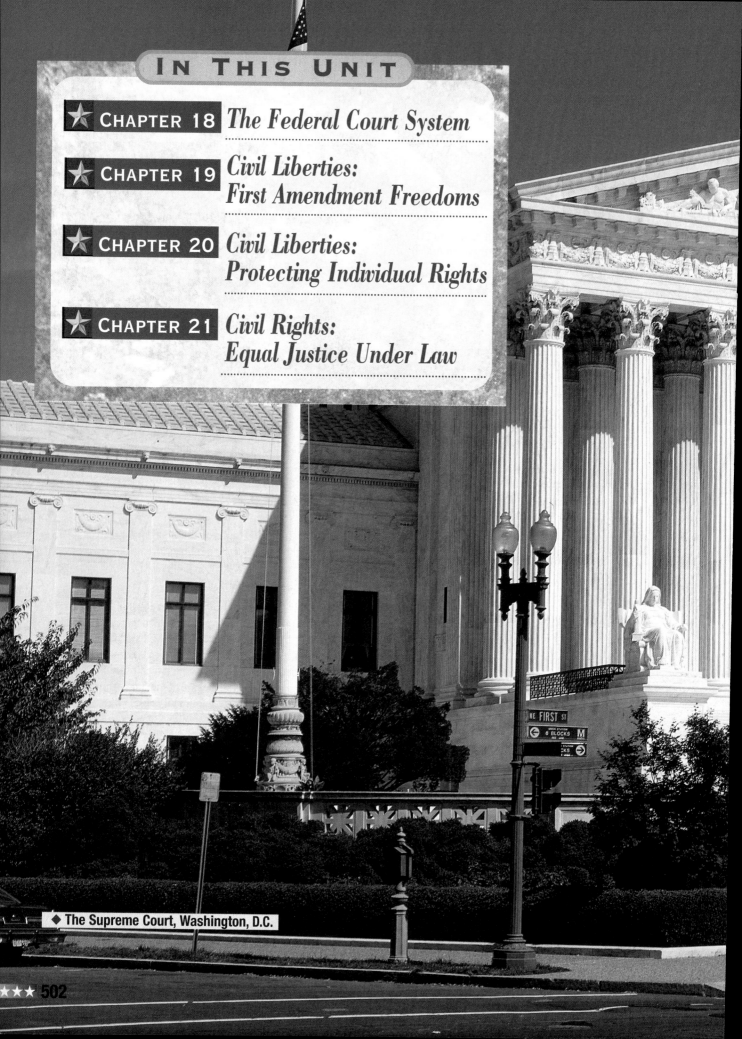

◆ The Supreme Court, Washington, D.C.

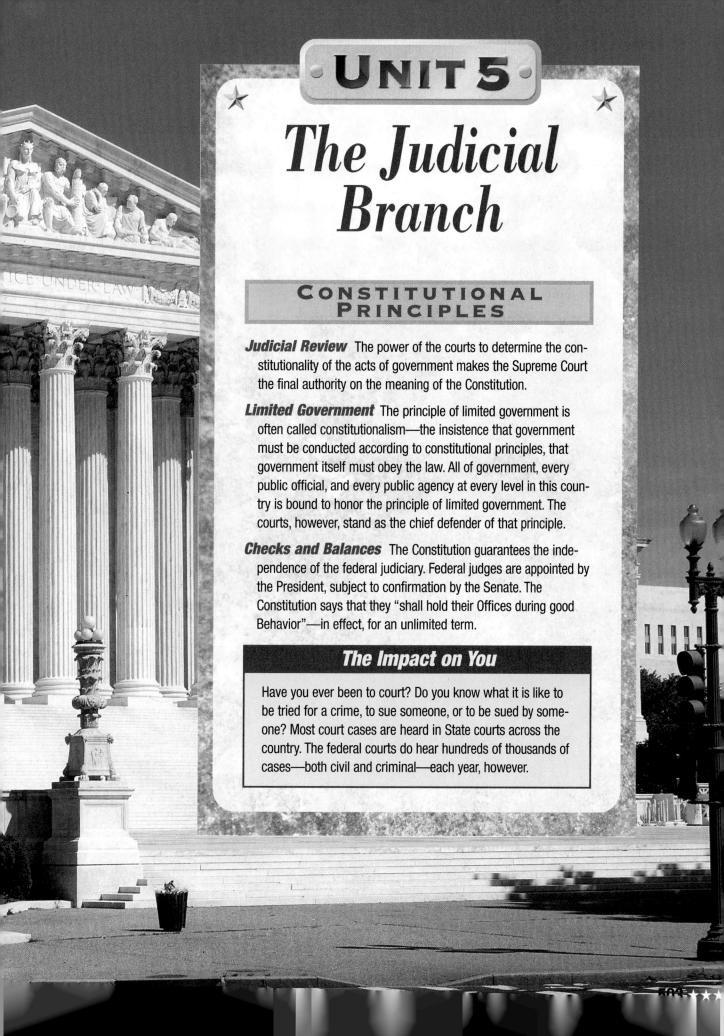

UNIT 5

The Judicial Branch

CONSTITUTIONAL PRINCIPLES

Judicial Review The power of the courts to determine the constitutionality of the acts of government makes the Supreme Court the final authority on the meaning of the Constitution.

Limited Government The principle of limited government is often called constitutionalism—the insistence that government must be conducted according to constitutional principles, that government itself must obey the law. All of government, every public official, and every public agency at every level in this country is bound to honor the principle of limited government. The courts, however, stand as the chief defender of that principle.

Checks and Balances The Constitution guarantees the independence of the federal judiciary. Federal judges are appointed by the President, subject to confirmation by the Senate. The Constitution says that they "shall hold their Offices during good Behavior"—in effect, for an unlimited term.

The Impact on You

Have you ever been to court? Do you know what it is like to be tried for a crime, to sue someone, or to be sued by someone? Most court cases are heard in State courts across the country. The federal courts do hear hundreds of thousands of cases—both civil and criminal—each year, however.

The Federal Court System

"It is emphatically the province and duty of the judicial department to say what the law is. . . . If two laws conflict with each other, the courts must decide on the operation of each."

—Chief Justice John Marshall (1803)

The Framers provided for a national system of courts to correct a major weakness in the Articles of Confederation. The Constitution provides for a Supreme Court and for other courts created by Congress. The federal courts operate in a dual court system, alongside the courts of each of the fifty States.

Protesters argue in front of the Supreme Court Building

★ You Can Make a Difference

THE ROLE OF THE JUDICIAL BRANCH is to interpret and apply the law. It is up to the courts to see that justice is done, but that sometimes takes a long time. In 1999, six journalism students at Northwestern University in Evanston, Illinois, helped the courts correct a 17-year-old injustice. The students in the investigative journalism class of Professor David Protess worked together to help free Anthony Porter, a death-row inmate who had been wrongfully convicted of a double murder. They asked questions, searched police records, and tracked down witnesses to find new evidence in the 1982 case. Finally, their work paid off, and another man confessed to the crime. Porter was freed after nearly 17 years in prison.

Keep It Current

Items marked with this logo are periodically updated on the Internet. Keep up-to-date with what's in the news. To get current information on issues related to the federal court system, go to **www.phschool.com**

SECTION 1
The National Judiciary *(pp. 506–511)*

★ The Framers created a national judiciary consisting of a Supreme Court and inferior courts to be created by Congress.
★ The federal courts have exclusive or concurrent and original or appellate jurisdiction over the cases they hear.
★ Federal judges are appointed by the President, subject to confirmation by the Senate.
★ Supreme Court and inferior court judges serve for life, removable only by impeachment, while special court judges serve 15-year terms; Congress sets the salaries of federal judges.
★ Federal court officers, such as magistrates, U.S. attorneys, bailiffs, and clerks, serve in administrative and judicial roles.

SECTION 2
The Inferior Courts *(pp. 512–515)*

★ The 94 U.S. district courts handle about 80 percent of the federal caseload; they have original jurisdiction over most federal criminal and civil cases.
★ The 12 federal appeals courts have appellate jurisdiction only.
★ The Court of International Trade hears tariff and trade cases; the Court of Appeals for the Federal Circuit has nationwide appellate jurisdiction from various federal courts.

SECTION 3
The Supreme Court *(pp. 517–522)*

★ All federal and most State courts have the power of judicial review, deciding the constitutionality of an act of government.
★ The U.S. Supreme Court has both original and appellate jurisdiction, but usually hears cases on appeal; the Court decides only a handful of cases each year.
★ The Supreme Court is in session from October through June; it hears oral arguments, studies written briefs, meets in conference to discuss the cases, and renders majority, concurring, and dissenting opinions.

SECTION 4
The Special Courts *(pp. 524–526)*

★ The U.S. government may not be sued without its consent; those who seek damages must take their cases to the U.S. Court of Federal Claims.
★ Congress has created federal courts for U.S. territories, as well as for the District of Columbia.
★ The U.S. Court of Appeals for the Armed Forces is a civilian tribunal that hears appeals of court-martial cases.
★ The U.S. Court of Appeals for Veterans Claims hears claims regarding veterans' benefits.
★ The U.S. Tax Court hears civil cases concerning tax law.

1 The National Judiciary

Section Preview

OBJECTIVES

1. **Explain** why the Constitution created a national judiciary, and describe its structure.
2. **Identify** the criteria that determine whether a case is within the jurisdiction of a federal court, and compare the types of federal court jurisdiction.
3. **Outline** the process for appointing federal judges.
4. **List** the terms of office for federal judges and explain how their salaries are determined.
5. **Examine** the roles of federal court officers.

WHY IT MATTERS

The Framers of the Constitution believed in the need for a national judicial system. The Constitution outlines the structure of the federal judiciary, the jurisdiction of the courts, and the functions of federal judges.

POLITICAL DICTIONARY

★ **inferior courts**
★ **jurisdiction**
★ **exclusive jurisdiction**
★ **concurrent jurisdiction**
★ **plaintiff**
★ **defendant**
★ **original jurisdiction**
★ **appellate jurisdiction**

Joe Smith steals a brand-new sports car, a bright red convertible, in Chicago. Two days later, he is stopped for speeding in Atlanta. Where, now, will he be tried for car theft? In Illinois, where he stole the car? In Georgia, where he was caught? In point of fact, Joe may be on the verge of learning something about the federal court system—and about the Dyer Act of 1925, which makes it a federal crime to transport a stolen automobile across a State line.

Creation of a National Judiciary

During the years the Articles of Confederation were in force (1781–1789), there were no national courts and no national judiciary. The laws of the United States were interpreted and applied as each State saw fit, and sometimes not at all. Disputes between States and between persons who lived in different States were decided, if at all, by the courts in one of the States involved. Often, decisions by the courts in one State were ignored by the courts in the other States.

Alexander Hamilton spoke to the point in *The Federalist* No. 22. He described "the want of a judiciary power" as a "circumstance which crowns the defects of the Confederation." Arguing the need for a national court system, he added: "Laws are a dead letter without courts to expound and define their true meaning and operation."

The Framers created a national judiciary for the United States in a single sentence in the Constitution:

 " *The judicial Power of the United States shall be vested in one supreme Court, and in such inferior Courts as the Congress may from time to time ordain and establish.* **"**

—Article III, Section 1

Congress also is given the expressed power "to constitute Tribunals inferior to the supreme Court" in Article I, Section 8, Clause 9.

A Dual Court System

Keep in mind this important point: There are *two* separate court systems in the United States.[1] On one hand, the national judiciary spans the country with its more than 120 courts. On the other hand, each of the 50 States has its own system of courts. Their numbers run well into the thousands. These State courts hear most of the cases in this country.

---

[1]Federalism does not require two court systems. Article III provides that Congress "may" establish lower federal courts. At its first session, in 1789, Congress decided to construct a complete set of federal courts to parallel those of the States. In most of the world's other federal systems, the principal courts are those of the states or provinces; typically, the only significant federal court is a national court of last resort, often called the supreme court.

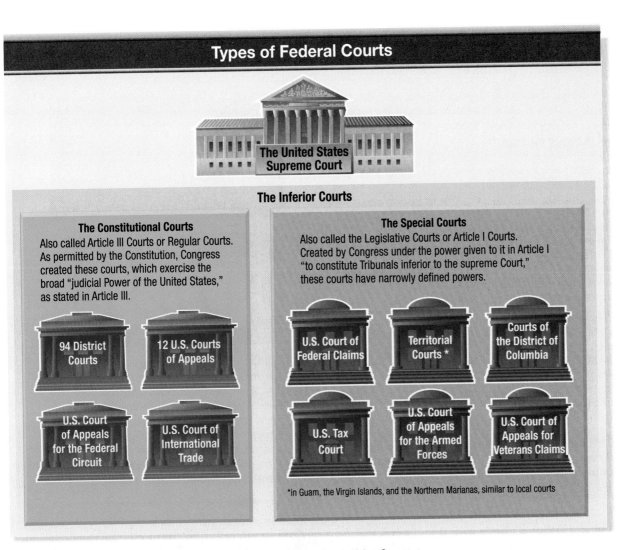

Types of Federal Courts

The United States Supreme Court

The Inferior Courts

The Constitutional Courts
Also called Article III Courts or Regular Courts. As permitted by the Constitution, Congress created these courts, which exercise the broad "judicial Power of the United States," as stated in Article III.

- 94 District Courts
- 12 U.S. Courts of Appeals
- U.S. Court of Appeals for the Federal Circuit
- U.S. Court of International Trade

The Special Courts
Also called the Legislative Courts or Article I Courts. Created by Congress under the power given to it in Article I "to constitute Tribunals inferior to the supreme Court," these courts have narrowly defined powers.

- U.S. Court of Federal Claims
- Territorial Courts *
- Courts of the District of Columbia
- U.S. Tax Court
- U.S. Court of Appeals for the Armed Forces
- U.S. Court of Appeals for Veterans Claims

*in Guam, the Virgin Islands, and the Northern Marianas, similar to local courts

Interpreting Diagrams The Constitution created only the Supreme Court, giving Congress the power to create any lower, or "inferior," courts, as needed. ***Using this diagram, compare and contrast the purpose of the constitutional courts and the special courts, as defined in the Constitution.***

Two Kinds of Federal Courts

The Constitution creates the Supreme Court and leaves to Congress the creation of the **inferior courts**—the lower federal courts, those beneath the Supreme Court. Over the years, Congress has created two distinct types of federal courts: (1) the constitutional courts and (2) the special courts. The diagram on this page sets out these several federal courts.

The constitutional courts are the federal courts that Congress has formed under Article III to exercise "the judicial Power of the United States." Together with the Supreme Court, they now include the courts of appeals, the district courts, and the U.S. Court of International Trade. The constitutional courts are also called the regular courts or Article III courts.

The special courts do not exercise the broad "judicial Power of the United States." Rather, they have been created by Congress to hear cases arising out of some of the expressed powers given to Congress in Article I. The special courts hear a much narrower range of cases than those that may come before the constitutional courts.

These special courts sometimes are called the legislative courts. Today, they include the U.S. Court of Appeals for the Armed Forces, the U.S. Court of Appeals for Veterans Claims, the U.S. Court of Federal Claims, the U.S. Tax Court, the various territorial courts, and the courts of the District of Columbia. You will look at the unique features of these courts later in this chapter.

Most cases in this country are heard in State courts, not federal courts. Article III, Section 2, Clause I provides that to be heard in a federal court, a case must fall into one of the two categories below.

The Subject Matter of the Case

A case falls within the jurisdiction of the federal courts if it concerns:

(1) the interpretation and application of a provision in the Constitiution or in any federal statute or treaty;

(2) a question of admiralty law (matters that arise on the high seas or navigable U.S. waters)

EXAMPLE collision at sea or crime committed aboard ship

(3) a question of maritime law (matters arising on land but directly relating to the water)

EXAMPLE a contract to deliver a ship's supplies at dockside (The Framers gave the federal courts exclusive jurisdiction in admiralty and maritime cases to ensure national supremacy in the regulation of all waterborne commerce.)

The Parties Involved in the Case

A case falls within the jurisdiction of the federal courts if any of the parties in the case is:

(1) the United States or one of its officers or agencies;

(2) an ambassador, consul, or other official representative of a foreign government;

(3) one of the 50 States suing either another State, a resident of another State, or a foreign government, or one of its subjects;

(4) a citizen of one State suing a citizen of another State;

(5) a U.S. citizen suing a foreign government or one of its subjects;

(6) a citizen of one State suing a citizen of that same State where both claim land under grants from different States.

As the table at left explains, federal courts hear cases involving certain subject matter, such as accidents at sea. (Top photo shows a Norwegian oil tanker ablaze in waters off Galveston, Texas.) Federal cases also may involve certain people, such as foreign diplomats. (Diplomatic license plates, above, are a familiar site in Washington, D.C.) *Critical Thinking* **Why are such cases heard in federal courts instead of State courts?**

Federal Court Jurisdiction

The constitutional courts hear most of the cases tried in the federal courts. That is, those courts have **jurisdiction** over most federal cases. Jurisdiction is defined as the authority of a court to hear (to *try* and to *decide*) a case. The term means, literally, the power "to say the law."

The Constitution gives the federal courts jurisdiction over certain cases. Article III, Section 2 provides that the federal courts may hear a case because of either (1) the subject matter or (2) the parties involved in the case. The details of this matter are set out in the table above.

The criteria for deciding what are federal cases may seem quite complicated, and they are. But the matter is also a reflection of federalism and, so, of the dual system of courts in this country. Stating the whole point of federal court jurisdiction in another way: All cases that are not heard by the federal courts are within the jurisdiction of the States' courts.

Types of Jurisdiction

The federal courts have several different types of jurisdiction, depending on whether or not (1) they share the power to hear the case with State courts and (2) they are the first court to hear the case.

Exclusive and Concurrent Jurisdiction

In some of the cases listed in the table above, the federal courts have **exclusive jurisdiction.** That is, those cases can be heard *only* in the federal courts. For example, a case involving an ambassador or some other official of a foreign government cannot be heard in a State court; it must be tried in a federal court. The trial of a person charged with a federal crime, or a suit involving the infringement of a patent or a copyright, or a case involving any other matter arising out of an act of Congress also falls within the exclusive jurisdiction of the federal courts.

Many cases may be tried in either a federal court or a State court, however. Then the federal and State courts have **concurrent jurisdiction;**

they share the power to hear those cases. Disputes involving citizens of different States are fairly common examples of this type of case. Such cases are known in the law as cases in diverse citizenship.[2]

Congress has provided that the federal district courts may hear cases of diverse citizenship only if the amount of money involved in a case is more than $75,000. In such cases the **plaintiff**—the person who files suit—may bring the case in the proper State or federal court, as he or she chooses. If the case is brought before the State court, the **defendant**—the person whom the complaint is against—can have the trial moved, under certain circumstances, to the federal district court.

Original and Appellate Jurisdiction

A court in which a case is first heard is said to have **original jurisdiction** over that case. A court that hears a case on appeal from a lower court has **appellate jurisdiction** over that case. The higher court—the appellate court—may uphold, overrule, or in some way modify the decision appealed from the lower court.[3]

In the federal court system, the district courts have only original jurisdiction, and the courts of appeals have only appellate jurisdiction. The Supreme Court exercises both original and appellate jurisdiction.

Appointment of Judges

The manner in which federal judges are chosen, the terms for which they serve, and even the salaries they are paid are vital parts of the Constitution's design of an independent judicial branch. The Constitution declares that the President

FROM THE
Constitution
"*shall nominate, and by and with the Advice and Consent of the Senate, shall appoint . . . Judges of the supreme Court . . .***"**
—Article II, Section II, Clause 2

Congress has provided the same procedure for the selection of all other federal judges.

The Senate has a major part in the selection of all federal judges, and in particular those who sit in the nation's 94 district courts. The constitutional provision just cited says, in effect, that the President is free to name to the federal bench anyone the Senate will confirm. Recall the practice of senatorial courtesy. That unwritten rule, which is closely followed in the Senate, gives great weight to the preferences of the senators from the State in which a federal judge is to serve. In short, senatorial courtesy means that the President almost always nominates someone who has been recommended by the senators from the State involved.

Most federal judges are drawn from the ranks of leading attorneys, legal scholars and law school professors, former members of Congress, and State court judges. A President applies the same sorts of political considerations to his judicial selections as he does to his other appointments.

From George Washington's day, Presidents have looked to their own political party in making judicial appointments. Republican Presidents regularly choose Republicans; Democrats usually pick Democrats.

Every President knows that the judges he appoints may serve for decades. So the chief executive regularly looks for judges who tend to agree with his own legal, political, economic, and social views.

The concepts of judicial activism and judicial restraint often play a part in the judicial

Types of Court Jurisdiction

Federal Jurisdiction | Concurrent Jurisdiction | State Jurisdiction

Interpreting Diagrams While many countries have a single court system leading to a supreme court, the United States has a two-level system of federal and State courts. Their jurisdictions are shown in this Venn diagram. *How does the structure of the diagram explain the types of jurisdiction?*

---

[2]The major reason that cases of diverse citizenship may be heard in federal courts is to provide a neutral forum to settle the disputes involved. That reason reflects an early fear that State courts (and their juries) might be prejudiced against "foreigners," residents of other States. There seems little likelihood of such bias today.

[3]Appellate comes from the Latin word *appellare*, meaning "to speak to, to call upon, to appeal to."

The National Judiciary

Court	Created	Number of Courts	Number of Judges	Term of Judges
Supreme Court	1789	1	9	Life
District Court	1789	94	642	Life
Court of Appeals	1891	12	179	Life
Trade Court	1926	1	9	Life
Court of Appeals for the Armed Forces	1950	1	5	15 years
Tax Court	1969	1	19	15 years
Court of Appeals for the Federal Circuit	1982	1	12	Life
Court of Federal Claims	1982	1	16	15 years
Court of Appeals for Veterans Claims	1988	1	7	15 years

Interpreting Tables This table provides key statistics for the major U.S. federal courts. *Why do you think some judgeships are for life and others are for only 15 years?*

selection process—especially at the Supreme Court level. Generally, *judicial activists* believe that a judge should use his or her position to promote desirable social ends—for example, in cases involving civil rights or social welfare issues. (See, for example, *Gitlow* v. *New York* and other cases discussed on pages 535–574. See also *Engel* v. *Vitale* and other cases involving school prayer on pages 539–542, as well as cases on pages 566–568 and 573–574.) The proponents of *judicial restraint* hold that in making their decisions, judges should defer to the actions of the executive and legislative branches—except in cases where those actions are clearly unconstituional. They frequently note that the President and members of Congress are elected by the people, but federal judges are not.

The President and his closest political and legal aides, especially the attorney general, take the lead in selecting federal judges, of course. Major roles also are played regularly by influential senators (notably those from the nominee's home State); by the President's allies and supporters in the legal profession; and by various other important personalities in the President's political party.

Terms and Pay of Judges

Article III, Section 1 of the Constitution reads, in part: "The Judges, both of the supreme and inferior Courts, shall hold their Offices during good Behavior. . . . " This means that the judges of the constitutional courts are appointed for life—until they resign, retire, or die in office. They may be removed only through the impeachment process. Only 13 federal judges have ever been impeached. Of them, seven were convicted and removed by the Senate, including three in the recent past.[4] The grant of what amounts to life tenure for most judges ensures the independence of the federal judiciary.

The judges who sit in the special courts are not appointed for life. Those who hear cases in the U.S. Court of Federal Claims, the U.S. Court of Appeals for the Armed Forces, the U.S. Tax Court, and the U.S. Court of Appeals for Veterans Claims serve 15-year terms. In the District of Columbia, Superior Court judges are chosen for four-year terms; those who sit on the District's Court of Appeals are chosen for a period of eight years.

The Constitution also declares that federal judges

> **FROM THE Constitution**
> *"shall, at stated Times, receive for their Services, a Compensation, which shall not be diminished during their Continuance in Office."*
> —Article III, Section 1

Congress sets the salaries of all federal judges and has provided a generous retirement arrangement for them. They may retire at age 70, and if they have served for at least 10 years, receive full salary for the rest of their lives. Or,

---

[4]The judges removed from office were John Pickering of the district court in New Hampshire, for judicial misconduct and drunkenness (1804); West H. Humphreys of the district court in Tennessee, for disloyalty (1862); Robert W. Archbald of the old Commerce Court, for improper relations with litigants (1913); Halsted L. Ritter of the district court in Florida, on several counts of judicial misconduct (1936); Harry E. Claiborne of the district court in Nevada, for filing false income tax returns (1986); Alcee Hastings of the district court in Florida, on charges of bribery and false testimony (1989); and Walter Nixon of the district court in Mississippi, for perjury (1989).

Alcee Hastings was removed in 1989 even though earlier he had been acquitted of the bribery charge. Hastings won election to the House of Representatives in 1992. Four other federal judges were impeached by the House but acquitted in the Senate. Two other district court judges, impeached by the House, resigned and so avoided a Senate trial.

they may retire at full salary at age 65, after at least 15 years of service. The Chief Justice may call any retired judge back to temporary duty in a lower federal court at any time.

Court Officers

Today, federal judges have little involvement in the day-to-day administrative operations of the courts over which they preside. Their primary mission is to hear and decide cases. The support services they need in order to perform that task are provided by a clerk, several deputy clerks, bailiffs, court reporters and stenographers, probation officers, and other court personnel.

The judges of each of the 94 district courts appoint one or more United States magistrates. There are now more than 400 of these magistrates. They are appointed to eight-year terms and handle a number of legal matters once dealt with by the judges themselves. They issue warrants of arrest and often hear evidence to decide whether or not a person who has been arrested on a federal charge should be held for action by a grand jury. They also set bail in federal criminal cases, and even have the power to try those who are charged with certain minor offenses.

Each federal judicial district also has at least one bankruptcy judge. They handle bankruptcy cases under the direction of the district court to which they are assigned.[5] There are now some 350 bankruptcy judges, all of them appointed to 14-year terms by the judges of each federal court of appeals. The President and the Senate appoint a United States attorney for each federal judicial district. The U.S. attorneys and their many deputies are the government's prosecutors. They work closely with the FBI and other law enforcement agencies, and bring to trial those persons charged with federal crimes. They also represent the United States in all civil actions brought by or against the government in their districts.

The President and Senate also select a United States marshal to serve each of the district courts. These marshals, and their several deputy U.S. marshals, perform duties much like those of a county sheriff. They make arrests in federal criminal cases, hold accused persons in custody, secure jurors, serve legal papers, keep order in courtrooms, and execute court orders and decisions. They also respond to such emergency situations as riots, mob violence, and other civil disturbances, as well as terrorist incidents. All United States attorneys and marshals are appointed to four-year terms—and members of the Senate are usually closely involved in their selections.

---

[5]Recall that bankruptcy is a legal proceeding in which a debtor's assets are distributed among those to whom the bankrupt person, business, or other organization owes money. Although some bankruptcy cases are heard in State courts, nearly all of them fall within the jurisdiction of the federal district courts.

Section 1 Assessment

Key Terms and Main Ideas

1. Why were the **inferior courts** created?
2. (a) What is **jurisdiction**? (b) Explain the difference between **exclusive jurisdiction** and **concurrent jurisdiction.**
3. Describe the roles of **plaintiff** and **defendant**.
4. (a) Contrast **original jurisdiction** and **appellate jurisdiction.** (b) What kind of jurisdiction does the Supreme Court have?

Critical Thinking

5. **Expressing Problems Clearly** Reread Alexander Hamilton's comments about the need for a national judiciary. Restate Hamilton's argument in your own words.
6. **Drawing Inferences** Make a list of steps for selecting a federal judge. Next to each step, indicate whether it is a legal requirement or simply a matter of custom. For the steps labeled as a custom, explain why it might be wise for a President to observe such a custom.

Take It to the Net

7. Use the Internet to answer these questions: (a) How does the jurisdiction of State courts differ from that of federal courts? (b) Give two examples of cases that might be tried in State court. (c) Give two examples of cases that might be tried in federal court, and explain the rationale for having a federal court hear those cases rather than a State court. Use the links provided in the Social Studies area at the following Web site for help in completing this activity. **www.phschool.com**

The Inferior Courts

Section Preview

OBJECTIVES

1. **Describe** the structure and jurisdiction of the federal district courts.
2. **Describe** the structure and jurisdiction of the federal courts of appeals.
3. **Describe** the structure and jurisdiction of the two other constitutional courts.

WHY IT MATTERS

The inferior courts, those beneath the Supreme Court, are the core of the federal judicial system, hearing nearly all of the cases tried in federal courts. They hear both original jurisdiction cases and appeals, and both criminal and civil cases.

POLITICAL DICTIONARY

★ **criminal case**
★ **civil case**
★ **docket**

You know that many words have more than one meaning. The particular meaning of any of them depends on the context, or setting, in which it is used. Thus, *pitch* can be either a baseball or a musical term; or it can refer to the setting up of a tent, or to a high-pressure sales talk.

The word *inferior* has various meanings as well. Here it describes the lower federal courts, those courts that function beneath the Supreme Court. The inferior courts handle most of the cases tried in the federal courts.

The District Courts

The United States district courts are the federal trial courts. Their 642 judges handle more than 300,000 cases a year, about 80 percent of the federal caseload. The district courts were created by Congress in the Judiciary Act of 1789. There are now 94 of them.

Federal Judicial Districts

The fifty States are divided into 89 federal judicial districts, and there are also federal district courts for Washington, D.C., Puerto Rico, the Virgin Islands, Guam, and the Northern Mariana

Claiming that a photographer infringed on her copyrights of family photos, Yoko Ono Lennon, widow of former Beatle John Lennon, sued in the U.S. District Court for the Southern District of New York, where the case was dismissed in March 2000. *Critical Thinking Why might a copyright case be heard in federal court?*

Islands. Some States are divided into two or more districts—usually because of the larger amount of judicial business there. At least two judges are assigned to each district, but many districts have several. Thus, New York is divided into four judicial districts; one of them, the United States Judicial District for Southern New York, now has 28 judges.

Cases tried in the district courts are most often heard by a single judge. However, certain cases may be heard by a three-judge panel.[6]

District Court Jurisdiction

The district courts have original jurisdiction over most cases that are heard in the federal courts (except those few cases that fall within the original jurisdiction of the United States Supreme Court and those cases that are heard by the U.S. Court of International Trade or by one of the special courts). Thus, these district courts are the principal trial courts in the federal court system.

---

[6]Congress has directed that three-judge panels hear certain cases. Chiefly, these are cases that involve congressional districting or State legislative apportionment questions; that arise under the Civil Rights Act of 1964 or the Voting Rights Acts of 1965, 1970, 1975, and 1982; or that concern certain antitrust actions.

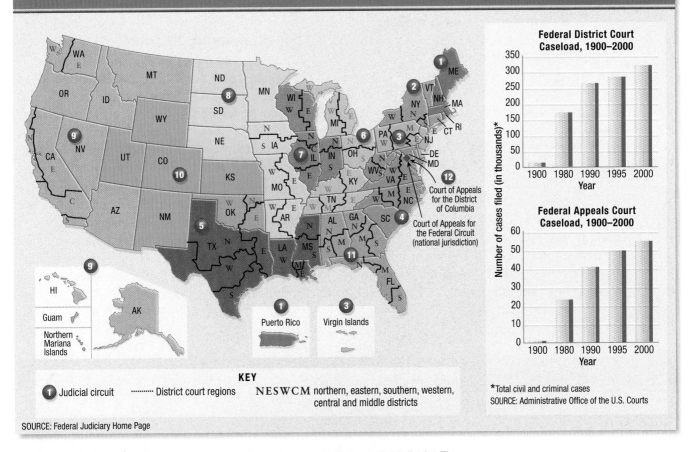

U.S. Federal Court Districts and Circuits

Federal District Court Caseload, 1900–2000

Number of cases filed (in thousands)*

Year	
1900	
1980	
1990	
1995	
2000	

Federal Appeals Court Caseload, 1900–2000

*Total civil and criminal cases
SOURCE: Administrative Office of the U.S. Courts

KEY
● Judicial circuit ……… District court regions N E S W C M northern, eastern, southern, western, central and middle districts

SOURCE: Federal Judiciary Home Page

Interpreting Maps Each State comprises at least one United States judicial district. The nation is divided into twelve judicial circuits, as shown on the map. The graphs show increasing federal caseloads. ***Explain how this increase relates to the trend in Congress toward designating more crimes as federal offenses.***

The district courts hear a wide range of both **criminal cases** and **civil cases.** A criminal case, in the federal courts, is one in which a defendant is tried for committing some action that Congress has declared by law to be a federal crime. A federal civil case involves some noncriminal matter, such as a dispute over the terms of a contract or a claim of patent infringement.[7] The district courts try cases ranging from bank robbery and mail fraud to counterfeiting and tax evasion. They hear civil cases arising under bankruptcy, postal, tax, labor relations, public lands, civil rights, and other laws of the United States. The district courts are the only federal courts that regularly use grand juries to indict defendants and petit juries to try defendants.

Most of the decisions made in the 94 federal district courts are final. However, some cases are appealed to the court of appeals in that judicial circuit or, in a few instances, directly to the Supreme Court.

The Courts of Appeals

The courts of appeals were created by Congress in 1891. They were established as "gatekeepers" to relieve the Supreme Court of much of the burden of hearing appeals from the district courts. Those appeals had become so numerous that the Supreme Court was then three years behind its **docket**—its list of cases to be heard.

There are now 12 courts of appeals in the judicial system.[8] The United States is divided into

▲ Seal of the U.S. Court of Appeals for the Fifth Circuit

---

[7]The United States is always a party to a federal criminal case, as the prosecutor. Most civil cases involve private parties; but here, too, the United States may be a litigant, as either plaintiff or defendant.

[8]These tribunals were originally known as the circuit courts of appeals. Before 1891, Supreme Court justices "rode circuit" to hear appeals from the district courts. Congress renamed these courts in 1948, but they still are often called the circuit courts.

12 judicial circuits, including the District of Columbia, with one court of appeals for each circuit, as shown on the previous page.

Appellate Court Judges

Altogether, 179 circuit judges sit on these appellate courts. In addition, a justice of the Supreme Court is assigned to each of them. Take, for example, the United States Court of Appeals for the Eleventh Circuit. The circuit covers three States: Alabama, Georgia, and Florida. The court is composed of 12 judges, and Supreme Court Justice Anthony Kennedy is also assigned to the circuit. The judges hold sessions in a number of cities within the circuit.

Each of the courts of appeals usually sits in panels of three judges. However, occasionally, to hear an important case, a court will sit *en banc*—that is, with all of the judges for that circuit participating.

Appellate Court Jurisdiction

The courts of appeals have only appellate jurisdiction. They hear cases on appeal from the lower federal courts. Most appeals come from the district courts within their circuits, but some do come from the U.S. Tax Court and the territorial courts. The courts of appeals also hear appeals from the decisions of several federal regulatory agencies, such as the Federal Trade Commission, the National Labor Relations Board, and the Nuclear Regulatory Commission. (See diagram below.)

The courts of appeals now handle more than 55,000 cases a year. Their decisions are final, unless the Supreme Court chooses to hear appeals taken from them.

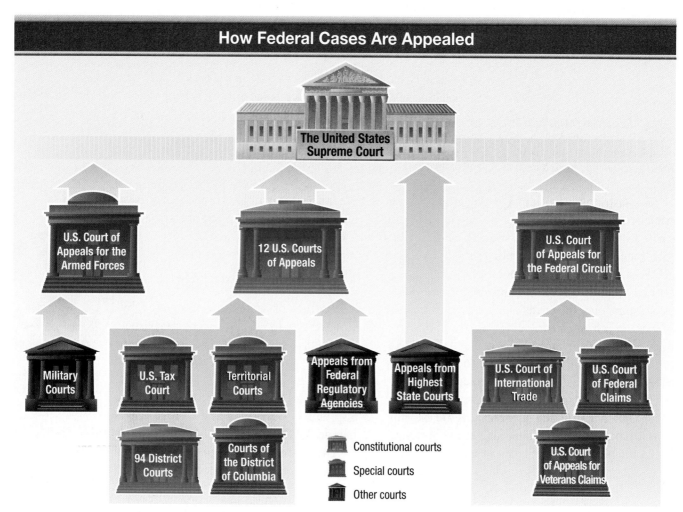

How Federal Cases Are Appealed

Interpreting Diagrams The diagram above shows how cases originating in various courts can be appealed to the U.S. Supreme Court. *From what you have read so far, what do you think are the two or three inferior courts that handle the largest proportion of cases in the country?*

Other Constitutional Courts

Congress has created two other Article III courts. They are the U.S. Court of International Trade and the U.S. Court of Appeals for the Federal Circuit.

The Court of International Trade

The Trade Court was created originally in 1890 as the Board of United States General Appraisers. That body became the Court of Customs in 1926, and Congress restructured and renamed that court in 1980.

The Court of International Trade now has nine judges, one of whom is its chief judge. It hears civil cases arising out of tariff and other trade-related laws. The judges of the Trade Court sit in panels of three and often hold trials at such major ports as New Orleans, San Francisco, Boston, and New York. Appeals from decisions of the Trade Court are taken to the Court of Appeals for the Federal Circuit.

The Court of Appeals for the Federal Circuit

Congress created the Court of Appeals for the Federal Circuit in 1982. It established the new court to centralize, and so speed up, the handling of appeals in certain kinds of civil cases. This appellate court, unlike the 12 other federal courts of appeals, hears cases from all across the country. That is, it has a nationwide jurisdiction.

The Court of Appeals for the Federal Circuit hears appeals from several different courts. Many of its cases come from the U.S. Court of International Trade, and others from the U.S. Court of

Interpreting Political Cartoons This 1885 cartoon shows a Supreme Court swamped by appeals. **(a) *Describe what is going on in this scene.* (b) *What is the man in the foreground doing?* (c) *What point is the artist making?***

Federal Claims and the U.S. Court of Appeals for Veterans Claims, two of the special courts. It also hears appeals in patent, trademark, and copyright cases coming from the 94 district courts around the country. Then, too, it takes cases that arise out of administrative rulings made by the International Trade Commission, the Patent and Trademark Office in the Department of Commerce, and the Merit Systems Protection Board.

The Court of Appeals for the Federal Circuit has 12 judges. It sits in panels of three or more judges on each case and also may hear or rehear a case *en banc*. The court usually hears cases in Washington, D.C., but it may also do so wherever any of the other federal courts of appeals sits. Appeals from the court may be taken to the Supreme Court, but they rarely are.

Section 2 Assessment

Key Terms and Main Ideas

1. What is the difference between a **criminal case** and a **civil case?**
2. What action did Congress take in the late 1800s to relieve the Supreme Court's overloaded **docket?**
3. Summarize the main purpose of the federal district courts and the federal courts of appeals.

Critical Thinking

4. **Drawing Conclusions** Most of the courts in the federal judiciary are appellate courts. What does this fact suggest about the American judicial process?

5. **Expressing Problems Clearly** What kind of problems might have prompted Congress to create an entirely new type of appellate court in 1982?

 Take It to the Net

6. Follow the Internet links to the federal appeals court for the circuit that includes your State. Choose one current case and write one paragraph explaining why this case falls within the jurisdiction of the Federal Court of Appeals. Use the links provided in the Social Studies area at the following Web site for help in completing this activity. **www.phschool.com**

Choosing Federal Judges

The Constitution says the President "shall nominate, and by and with the Advice and Consent of the Senate, shall appoint. . . Judges of the supreme Court." Although most Presidents choose judges who agree with their policy viewpoints, Nadine Strossen, President of the American Civil Liberties Union, argues that the Senate should play a more assertive role in the judicial selection process.

The President and Senate work together to appoint federal judges such as Surpreme Court Justice Sandra Day O'Connor.

The Constitution's appointment clause . . . clearly confers upon the president unfettered [unlimited] discretion to name federal judges of his choosing, subject to the Senate's "advice and consent." It specifies no minimal criteria or essential qualifications for such judges . . . and by failing to set out any limits on that power [to nominate judges], the constitutional text indicates that the president's judicial nominations could also appropriately take the nominees' views into account.

The Constitution is as silent about criteria for the Senate's confirmation decision as it is about those for the president's initial nomination. Accordingly, the text assigns the Senate as open-ended a discretion in the confirmation process as it assigns the president in the nomination process. In exercising that discretion, it is as appropriate for the Senate to consider a candidate's constitutional and judicial philosophy as it is for the president.

The Senate's concurrent role in the judicial selection process is also confirmed by the proceedings at the 1787 Constitutional Convention which led to the adoption of the appointment clause. Indeed, until the final days of the Convention, the proposed constitutional text gave the Senate—or, in some versions, the Senate and the House of Representatives—the sole power to appoint federal judges, including Supreme Court Justices.

In contrast, the delegates roundly rejected all attempts to confer this power on the president alone. Referring to the significant separation of powers concerns implicated by the judicial appointment process, Virginia delegate George Mason said that an exclusively presidential appointment power constituted "a dangerous prerogative" that "might even give him an influence over the Judiciary Department itself."

Only near the end of the Convention did the delegates agree to give the president any role at all in the judicial selection process, by adopting the current appointment clause. The president and the Senate should have a "partnership" relationship in the judicial appointment process. Structural aspects of the Constitution dictate that, in fulfilling their respective roles in the process, each of these partners should consider candidates' constitutional and judicial philosophies.

Analyzing Primary Sources

1. According to the author, how did the Founding Fathers feel about giving the President the power to appoint federal judges?
2. How does the nomination process reflect the principle of separation of powers?
3. Many people believe that a judicial nominee should not be pressured to give his or her opinions on Constitutional issues before the nominee takes a seat as a judge. How would the author respond?

3 The Supreme Court

Section Preview

OBJECTIVES

1. **Define** the concept of judicial review.
2. **Outline** the scope of the Supreme Court's jurisdiction.
3. **Examine** how cases reach the Supreme Court.
4. **Summarize** the way the Court operates.

WHY IT MATTERS

The Supreme Court, the only court created by the Constitution, is the final authority on questions of federal law. It enjoys broad jurisdiction but usually limits its caseload to appeals involving constitutional questions and interpretations of federal law.

POLITICAL DICTIONARY

★ **writ of certiorari**
★ **certificate**
★ **majority opinion**
★ **precedent**
★ **concurring opinion**
★ **dissenting opinion**

The eagle, the flag, Uncle Sam—you almost certainly recognize these symbols. They are used widely to represent the United States. You probably also know the symbol for justice: the blindfolded woman holding a balanced scale. She represents what is perhaps this nation's loftiest goal: equal justice for all. Indeed, those words are chiseled in marble above the entrance to the Supreme Court building in Washington, D.C.

The Supreme Court of the United States is the only court specifically created by the Constitution, in Article III, Section 1. The Court is made up of the Chief Justice of the United States, whose office is also established by the Constitution,[9] and eight associate justices.[10] The Framers quite purposely placed the Court on an equal plane with the President and Congress. As the highest court in the land, the Supreme Court stands as the court of last resort in all questions of federal law. That is, it is the final authority in any case involving any question arising under the Constitution, an act of Congress, or a treaty of the United States.

Judicial Review

Remember, most courts in this country, both federal and State, may exercise the critically important power of judicial review. They have the extraordinary power to decide the constitutionality of an act of government, whether executive, legislative, or judicial. The ultimate exercise of that power rests with the Supreme

Court of the United States. That single fact makes the Supreme Court the final authority on the meaning of the Constitution.

The Constitution does not in so many words provide for the power of judicial review. Still, there is little doubt that the Framers intended

---

[9] Article I, Section 3, Clause 6.
[10] Congress sets the number of associate justices and thus the size of the Supreme Court. The Judiciary Act of 1789 created a Court of six justices, including the Chief Justice. Its size was reduced to five members in 1801 but increased to seven in 1807, to nine in 1837, and to 10 in 1863. It was reduced to seven in 1866 and raised to its present size of nine in 1869.

▲ A scale is often used to represent justice.

that the federal courts—and, in particular, the Supreme Court—should have this power.[11]

Marbury v. Madison

The Court first asserted its power of judicial review in the classic case of *Marbury* v. *Madison* in 1803.[12] The case arose in the aftermath of the stormy elections of 1800. Thomas Jefferson and his Democratic-Republicans had won the presidency and control of both houses of Congress. The outgoing Federalists, stung by their defeat, then tried to pack the judiciary with loyal party members. Congress created several new federal judgeships in the early weeks of 1801; President John Adams quickly filled those posts with Federalists.

William Marbury had been appointed a justice of the peace for the District of Columbia. The Senate had confirmed his appointment and, late on the night of March 3, 1801, President Adams signed the commissions of office for Marbury and for a number of other new judges. The next day Jefferson became the President, and discovered that Marbury's commission and several others had not yet been delivered.

Angered by the Federalists' attempted court-packing, Jefferson at once told James Madison, the new secretary of state, not to deliver those commissions to the "midnight justices." William Marbury then went to the Supreme Court, seeking a writ of mandamus[13] to force delivery.

Marbury based his suit on a provision of the Judiciary Act of 1789, in which Congress had created the federal court system. That law gave the Supreme Court the right to hear such suits in its original jurisdiction (not on appeal from a lower court).

---

[11]See Article III, Section 2, setting out the Court's jurisdiction, and Article VI, Section 2, the Supremacy Clause.

[12]It is often mistakenly said that the Court first exercised the power in this case, but in fact the Court did so at least as early as *Hylton* v. *United States* in 1796. In that case it upheld the constitutionality of a tax Congress had laid on carriages.

---

[13]A writ of mandamus is a court order compelling a government officer to perform an act which that officer has a clear legal duty to perform.

An Early Supreme Court Drama: *Marbury* v. *Madison*

The Players

John Adams, outgoing Federalist President of the United States

Thomas Jefferson, incoming Democratic-Republican President of the United States

James Madison, incoming secretary of state

William Marbury, appointed a justice of the peace for the District of Columbia

John Marshall, Chief Justice of the United States Supreme Court

The Case

1. The night before leaving office, Adams signs several judicial commissions.

2. Angered by Adams' actions, Jefferson orders Madison to withhold any commissions not yet delivered.

3. Hoping to force Jefferson to give him the judgeship, Marbury files suit in the Supreme Court. He argues that the Judiciary Act of 1789 allows him to take his case directly to the high court.

The Decision

Marshall, writing for a unanimous court, declares that the Judiciary Act violates Article III, Section 2 and is therefore unconstitutional. Marbury loses, having based his case on an unconstitutional law.

The Impact

The case established the Supreme Court's power of judicial review—its power to determine the constitutionality of a governmental action. The power extends to the actions of all governments in the United States—national, State and local. The Court's decision in *Marbury* assured the place of the judicial branch in the system of separation of powers.

Interpreting Charts In the landmark case *Marbury* v. *Madison,* the Supreme Court ruled against William Marbury because he had based his case on a part of the Judiciary Act of 1789, which was found to be in conflict with the Constitution. ***How did the Court's decision affect the role of the judicial branch in our system of government?***

In a unanimous opinion written by Chief Justice John Marshall, the Court refused Marbury's request.[14] It did so because it found the section of the judiciary act on which Marbury had based his case to be in conflict with the Constitution and, therefore, void. Specifically, it found the statute in conflict with the section of the Constitution that reads:

FROM THE Constitution **"**In all Cases affecting Ambassadors, other public Ministers and Consuls, and those in which a State shall be Party, the supreme Court shall have original Jurisdiction. In all the other Cases before mentioned, the supreme Court shall have appellate Jurisdiction. . . . **"**
—Article III, Section 2, Clause 2

Marshall's powerful opinion was based on three propositions. First, the Constitution is, by its own terms, the supreme law of the land. Second, all legislative acts and other actions of government are subordinate (inferior) to the supreme law and cannot be allowed to conflict with it. Third, judges are sworn to enforce the provisions of the Constitution, and therefore must refuse to enforce any government action they find to be in conflict with it.

The Effects of *Marbury*
The impact of the Court's decision goes far beyond the fate of an obscure individual named William Marbury. In this decision, Chief Justice Marshall claimed for the Supreme Court the right to declare acts of Congress unconstitutional, and so laid the foundation for the judicial branch's key role in the development of the American system of government.

The Court has used its power of judicial review in thousands of cases since 1803. Usually it has upheld the constitutionality of federal and State actions.

The dramatic and often far-reaching effects of the Supreme Court's exercise of the power of

---

[14]Marshall was appointed Chief Justice by President John Adams, and he took office on January 31, 1801. He served in the post for 34 years, until his death on July 6, 1835. He also served as Adams's secretary of state from May 13, 1800, to March 4, 1801. Thus, he served simultaneously as secretary of state and Chief Justice for more than a month at the end of the Adams administration. What is more, he was the secretary of state who had failed to deliver Marbury's commission in a timely fashion.

Voices on Government

David Souter was named a Supreme Court justice by President George Bush in 1990. From his experience as New Hampshire attorney general and a State court judge, Souter knew that judges' decisions are more than abstract legal ideas. Here are his thoughtful insights on justice:

" Whether we are on a trial court or an appellate court, at the end of our task some human being is going to be affected. . . . If indeed we are going to be trial judges, whose rulings will affect the lives of other people and who are going to change their lives by what we do, we had better use every power of our minds and our hearts and our beings to get those rulings right. **"**

Evaluating the Quotation
Think of an issue that reflects the "human" effects of court decisions that Souter refers to. In what ways did a court decision affect the daily lives of Americans?

judicial review tends to overshadow much of its other work. Each year it hears dozens of cases in which questions of constitutionality are not raised, but in which federal law is interpreted and applied. Thus, many of the more important statutes that Congress has passed have been brought to the Supreme Court time and again for decision. So, too, have many of the lesser ones. In interpreting those laws and applying them to specific situations, the Court has had a real impact on both their meaning and their effect.

Supreme Court Jurisdiction
The Supreme Court has both original and appellate jurisdiction. Most of its cases, however, come on appeal—from the lower federal courts and from the highest State courts.

Article III, Section 2 of the Constitution spells out two classes of cases that may be heard by the High Court in its original jurisdiction: (1) those to which a State is a party and (2) those affecting ambassadors, other public ministers, and consuls.

Congress cannot enlarge on this constitutional grant of original jurisdiction. Recall, that

► **No Anonymous Tips**
In *Florida* v. *J.L.,* 2000, the Supreme Court ruled that under ordinary circumstances, an anonymous tip to police about a concealed firearm was not sufficient to prompt a legal "stop and frisk" search.

is what the Court held in *Marbury.* If Congress could do so, it would in effect be amending the Constitution. Congress can implement the constitutional provision, however, and it has done so. It has provided that the Court shall have original and exclusive jurisdiction over (1) all controversies involving two or more States, and (2) all cases brought against ambassadors or other public ministers, but not consuls.

The Court may choose to take original jurisdiction over any other case covered by the broad wording in Article III, Section 2 of the Constitution. Almost without exception, however, those cases are tried in the lower courts. The Supreme

Court hears only a very small number of cases in its original jurisdiction—in fact, only a case or two each term.

How Cases Reach the Court

Some 8,000 cases are now appealed to the Supreme Court each year. Of these, the Court accepts only a few hundred for decision. In most cases, petitions for review are denied, usually because most of the justices agree with the decision of the lower court or believe that the case involves no significant point of law. The Court selects those cases that it does hear according to "the rule of four": At least four of its nine justices must agree that a case should be put on the Court's docket.

More than half the cases decided by the Court are disposed of in brief orders. For example, an order may remand (return) a case to a lower court for reconsideration in the light of some other recent and related case decided by the High Court. All told, the Court decides, after hearing arguments and with full opinions, fewer than 100 cases a year.

Most cases reach the Supreme Court by **writ of certiorari** (from the Latin, meaning "to be made more certain"). This writ is an order by the Court directing a lower court to send up the record in a given case for its review. Either party

Appealing a Case to the Supreme Court

Federal District Court

Federal Appeals Court

The United States Supreme Court

Step 1
Case is filed in a federal district court.

Step 2
Case is appealed to a federal court of appeals.

Step 3
Case is appealed to the Supreme Court. The Supreme Court either:

• allows the lower-court ruling to stand, or
• sends the case back to the lower court to reconsider it, or
• agrees to hear the case.

Step 4
Supreme Court rules on the case.

Interpreting Diagrams The diagram above shows the typical route (though not the only one) a case might take to the Supreme Court. ***Why do you think this process requires so many steps to reach the Supreme Court—often at great expense and time to the parties involved?***

to a case can petition the Court to issue a writ. But, again, "cert" is granted in a limited number of instances—typically, only when a petition raises some important constitutional question or a serious problem in the interpretation of a statute.

When certiorari is denied, the decision of the lower court stands in that particular case. Note, however, that the denial of cert is not a decision on the merits of a case. All that a denial means is that, for whatever reason, four or more justices could not agree that the Supreme Court should accept that case for review.

A few cases do reach the Court in yet another way, by **certificate.** This process is used when a lower court is not clear about the procedure or the rule of law that should apply in a case. The lower court asks the Supreme Court to certify the answer to a specific question in the matter.

Most cases that reach the Court do so from the highest State courts and the federal courts of appeals. A few do come, however, from the federal district courts and a very few from the Court of Appeals for the Armed Forces.

How the Court Operates

The Court sits from the first Monday in October to sometime the following June or July. Each term is identified by the year in which it began. Thus, the 2002 term ran from October 1, 2002, into the early summer of 2003.

Oral Arguments

Once the Supreme Court accepts a case, it sets a date on which that case will be heard. As a rule, the justices consider cases in two-week cycles from October to early May. They hear oral arguments in several cases for two weeks; then the justices recess for two weeks to consider those cases and handle other Court business.

While the Supreme Court is hearing oral arguments, it convenes at 10:00 A.M. on Mondays, Tuesdays, Wednesdays, and sometimes Thursdays. At those public sessions, the lawyers make their oral arguments. Their presentations are almost always limited to 30 minutes.[15]

Briefs

Briefs are written documents filed with the Court before oral arguments begin. These detailed statements support one side of a case, presenting arguments built largely on relevant facts and the citation of previous cases. Many briefs run to hundreds of pages.

The Court may also receive *amicus curiae* (friend of the court) briefs. These are briefs filed by persons or groups who are not actual parties to a case but who nonetheless have a substantial interest in its outcome. Thus, for example, cases involving such highly charged matters as abortion or affirmative action regularly attract a large number of amicus briefs. Notice, however, that these briefs can be filed only with the Court's permission or at its request.

The solicitor general, a principal officer in the Department of Justice, is often called the Federal Government's chief lawyer. He—and, certainly, one day she—represents the United States in all cases to which it is party in the Supreme Court and may appear for the government for any federal State court.[16]

The solicitor general also has another extraordinary responsibility. He or she decides which cases the government should ask the Supreme Court to review and what position the United States should take in those cases it brings before the High Court.

The Court in Conference

On most Wednesdays and Fridays through a term, the justices meet in conference. There, in closest secrecy, they consider the cases in which they have heard oral arguments.[17]

The Chief Justice presides over the conference. He speaks first on each case to be considered and usually indicates how he intends to vote. Then each associate justice summarizes his or her views. Those presentations are made in order of seniority, with the justice most recently named to the Court speaking last. After the justices are "polled," they usually debate the case.

---

[15]The justices usually listen closely to a lawyer's oral arguments and sometimes interrupt them with questions or requests for information. After 25 minutes, a white light comes on at the lectern from which the lawyer addresses the Court; five minutes later a red light signals the end of the presentation, even if the lawyer is in mid-sentence.

[16]The attorney general may argue the government's position before the Supreme Court but rarely does.

[17]At conference, the justices also decide which new cases they will accept for decision.

▲ The current members of the Supreme Court pose for their official photograph. Front row: Antonin Scalia, John Paul Stevens, Chief Justice William H. Rehnquist, Sandra Day O'Connor, Anthony Kennedy. Back Row: Ruth Bader Ginsburg, David Souter, Clarence Thomas, Stephen Breyer.

About a third of all the Court's decisions are unanimous, but most find the Court divided. The High Court is sometimes criticized for its split decisions. But, notice, its cases pose very difficult questions, and many also present questions on which lower courts have disagreed. In short, most of the Court's cases are controversial ones; the easy cases seldom get that far.

Opinions

If the Chief Justice is in the majority on a case, he assigns the writing of the Court's opinion. When the Chief Justice is in the minority, the assignment is handled by the senior associate justice on the majority side.

The Court's opinion is often called the **majority opinion.** Officially called the Opinion of the Court, it announces the Court's decision in a case and sets out the reasoning on which it is based.[18]

The Court's written opinions are exceedingly valuable. The majority opinions stand as **precedents,** or examples to be followed in similar cases as they arise in the lower courts or reach the Supreme Court.

Often, one or more of the justices who agree with the Court's decision may write a **concurring opinion**—to add or emphasize a point that was not made in the majority opinion. The concurring opinions may bring the Supreme Court to modify its present stand in future cases.

One or more **dissenting opinions** are often written by those justices who do not agree with the Court's majority decision. Chief Justice Charles Evans Hughes once described dissenting opinions as "an appeal to the brooding spirit of the law, to the intelligence of a future day." On rare occasions, the Supreme Court does reverse itself. The minority opinion of today could become the Court's majority position in the future.

---

[18]Most majority opinions, and many concurring and dissenting opinions, run to dozens of pages. Some decisions are accompanied by very brief and unsigned opinions. These *per curiam* (for the court) opinions seldom run more than a paragraph or two and usually dispose of relatively uncomplicated cases.

Section 3 Assessment

Key Terms and Main Ideas

1. **(a)** What does a **writ of certiorari** have in common with a **certificate? (b)** How do the two differ?
2. Explain how a **majority opinion,** a **concurring opinion,** and a **dissenting opinion** differ.
3. **(a)** Why are **precedents** important? **(b)** Write a sentence using the word *precedent* in a judicial context.
4. Explain why "easy" cases generally do not reach the Supreme Court.

Critical Thinking

5. **Drawing Conclusions** Why do you think the Supreme Court justices often write concurring and/or dissenting opinions in a case?
6. **Determining Cause and Effect** How does the Court's power of judicial review affect the balance of power in the Federal Government?

Take It to the Net

7. Visit the Exploring Constitutional Conflicts site on the Internet and use the information provided to write a brief essay that answers either question # 1 or # 5 on that page. Use the links provided in the Social Studies area at the following Web site for help in completing this activity. **www.phschool.com**

Drawing Conclusions

A caravan of police cars converges on a Chicago neighborhood known for illegal drug trafficking. A man sees the police and flees the scene. Suspicious, the police chase him down and "frisk" him for weapons. They find a handgun. They arrest him.

Was this a legal search and seizure? The 4th Amendment to the Constitution protects U.S. citizens from "unreasonable searches and seizures." Did the police officers have sufficient reason to suspect that the fleeing man had committed a crime, even though they did not see him do anything wrong? In *Wardlow v. Illinois*, 2000, the Supreme Court ruled that the police acted legally when they drew this conclusion.

Drawing a conclusion means arriving at an idea or opinion that is suggested, indirectly, from given information. How did the officers reach their conclusion? Instinctively, within seconds, they used a process like this:

1. Assess information. Analyze a fact or set of facts to see if they suggest other ideas. Sometimes a given piece of information may imply a cause-effect relationship. In the Chicago case, what did police actually observe when they arrived on scene?

2. Apply prior knowledge. To come to a conclusion, you usually combine new information with facts you already know. What relevant information did the police already know when they arrived on scene?

3. Reach a conclusion. Often a conclusion can be stated in this form: *X, therefore Y.* Use this format to state the conclusion that the police drew from the scene.

4. Test your conclusion. It's possible to draw the wrong conclusion from a set of facts. Always test the validity of your conclusion by considering whether any other conclusion is possible from the information given. Is there another possible explanation for what the Chicago police saw? If so, is it a likely explanation? Explain.

What did the Supreme Court think of the police officers' conclusions? In a ruling in early 2000, the Court said that "An individual's presence in a 'high crime area,' standing alone, is not enough to support

a reasonable, particularized suspicion of criminal activity," but the man's "nervous, evasive behavior" and "unprovoked flight" were "sufficiently suspicious to warrant further investigation." The officers' conclusions, the Court found, were sufficiently valid to justify their actions.

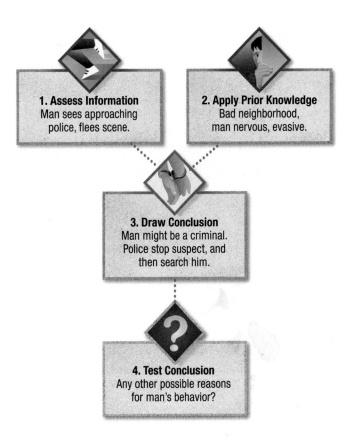

1. Assess Information
Man sees approaching police, flees scene.

2. Apply Prior Knowledge
Bad neighborhood, man nervous, evasive.

3. Draw Conclusion
Man might be a criminal. Police stop suspect, and then search him.

4. Test Conclusion
Any other possible reasons for man's behavior?

Test for Success

Use the steps above and the facts in the following paragraph to draw a conclusion about *Plessy* v. *Ferguson*. State your conclusion as *X, therefore Y.*

In Plessy v. Ferguson *(1896) the Supreme Court ruled that racially segregated facilities were constitutional as long as the facilities were "separate but equal." In 1954 the Court overturned* Plessy *in* Brown v. Board of Education, 1954.

Section Preview

OBJECTIVES

1. **Explain** how a citizen may sue the government in the Court of Federal Claims.
2. **Examine** the roles of the territorial courts and of the District of Columbia courts.
3. **Contrast** the functions of the Court of Appeals for the Armed Forces and the Court of Appeals for Veterans Claims.
4. **Explain** what types of cases are brought to the Tax Court.

WHY IT MATTERS

Over time, Congress has enlarged the structure of the federal court system by creating many special courts to handle cases that are outside the mainstream judicial process. Each of these courts has a very narrow jurisdiction.

POLITICAL DICTIONARY

★ **redress**
★ **court-martial**
★ **civilian tribunal**

Recall that the federal court system is made up of two quite distinct types of courts. They are: (1) the constitutional, or regular, courts, which you have read about, and (2) the special courts, which you'll now explore.

The special courts were created by Congress to hear certain cases involving the expressed powers of Congress. These courts, also known as legislative courts, were not established under Article III, so they do not exercise the broad "judicial Power of the United States." Rather, each has a very narrow jurisdiction.

The Court of Federal Claims

The United States government cannot be sued by anyone, in any court, for any reason, without its consent. The government may be taken to court only in cases in which Congress declares that the United States is open to suit.[19] Originally, a person with a claim against the United States could secure **redress**—satisfaction of a claim, payment—only by an act of Congress. In 1855, however, Congress set up the Court of Claims to hear such pleas.[20] That body became the United States Court of Federal Claims in 1993.

The Court of Federal Claims is composed of 16 judges appointed by the President and approved by the Senate for 15-year terms. They

▲ The White Mountain Apaches have long complained that the National Park Service has failed to maintain Fort Apache, in Arizona. It has even sued the United States in the Court of Federal Claims, in an (unsuccessful) attempt to force the Park Service to act. *Critical Thinking* **Why did the tribe file suit in the Court of Federal Claims?**

---

[19]The government is shielded from suit by the doctrine of sovereign immunity. The doctrine comes from an ancient principle of English public law summed up by the phrase: "The King can do no wrong." The rule is not intended to protect public officials from charges of corruption or any other wrongdoing. Rather, it is intended to prevent government from being hamstrung in its own courts. Congress has long since agreed to a long list of legitimate court actions against the government.

[20]Congress acted under its expressed power to pay the debts of the United States, Article I, Section 8, Clause 1.

hold trials throughout the country, hearing claims for damages against the Federal Government. Those claims they uphold cannot in fact be paid until Congress appropriates the money, which it does almost as a matter of standard procedure. Appeals from the court's decisions may be carried to the Court of Appeals for the Federal Circuit.

Occasionally, those who lose in the Claims Court still manage to win some compensation. Some years ago, a Puget Sound mink rancher lost a case in which he claimed that low-flying Navy planes had frightened his animals and caused several of the females to become sterile. He asked $100 per mink. He lost, but then his congressman introduced a private bill that eventually paid him $10 for each animal.

The Territorial Courts

Acting under its power to "make all needful Rules and Regulations respecting the Territory . . . belonging to the United States," Congress created courts for the nation's territories. These courts sit in the Virgin Islands, Guam, and the Northern Marianas and function much like the local courts in the 50 States.

The District of Columbia Courts

Acting under its power (Article I, Section 8, Clause 17) to "exercise exclusive Legislation in all Cases whatsoever, over such District . . . as may . . . become the Seat of the Government of the United States," Congress has set up a judicial system for the nation's capital. Both the District Court and the Court of Appeals for the District of Columbia hear many local cases as well as those they try as constitutional courts. Congress has also established two local courts, much like the courts in the States: a superior court, which is the general trial court, and a court of appeals.

The Court of Appeals for the Armed Forces

Beginning in 1789, Congress has created a system of military courts for each branch of the nation's armed forces, as an exercise of its expressed power to "make Rules for the

Government and Regulation of the land and naval forces."[21] These military courts—**courts-martial**—serve the special disciplinary needs of the armed forces and are *not* a part of the federal court system. Their judges, prosecutors, defense attorneys, court reporters, and other personnel are all members of the military; most of them are officers. They conduct trials of those members of the military who are accused of violating military laws. Today, the proceedings in a court-martial are very much like the trials held in civilian courts across the country.

In 1950, Congress created the Court of Military Appeals, now titled the Court of Appeals for the Armed Forces, to review the more serious court-martial convictions of military personnel. The Court of Appeals for the Armed Forces is a **civilian tribunal,** a court operating as part of the judicial branch, entirely separate from the military establishment. Its five judges—a chief judge and four associate judges—are appointed by the President and Senate to 15-year terms.

Appeals from the decision of the Court of Appeals for the Armed Forces can be, but almost never are, taken to the Supreme Court. It is, then, the court of last resort in most cases that involve offenses against military law.

Military Tribunals

At the President's direction, the Defense Department is currently (early 2002) drawing plans for special military tribunals. These panels, also composed of American military personnel, will try captured members of al-Qaida and of other terrorist organizations and other foreigners accused of committing acts of terror against the United States.

Once established, these tribunals will not be a part of the military's courts-martial system. They will, instead, be basic elements in a special system of justice designed to meet the needs of

[21]Article I, Section 8, Clause 14. This provision allows Congress to provide for the regulation of the conduct of members of the armed forces under a separate, noncivil legal code. The present-day system of military justice has developed over more than 225 years. Today, the Uniform Code of Military Justice, enacted by Congress in 1950, and the Military Justice Acts of 1968 and 1983 are the principal statutes that set out the nation's military law.

national security and the continuing threat posed by alien terrorists here and abroad.

The President provided for the creation of these tribunals by executive order. His power to do so came from (1) his constitutional role as commander in chief and (2) the fact that Congress has authorized him to use "all necessary and appropriate force" to combat global terrorism.

Military tribunals have been established at various times in America's past—most notably during the Mexican-American War, the Civil War, and World War II. To this point, President Franklin Roosevelt created the most recent one, in 1942. It tried eight Nazi saboteurs, who had been landed on the East Coast by German submarines. They had planned various acts of sabotage aimed at the disruption of this nation's war effort. All eight were convicted. Six were executed; the other two, who had turned on their comrades and cooperated with the tribunal, were sentenced to long terms in prison.

The Court of Appeals for Veterans Claims

Acting under its power (Article I, Section 8, Clause 9) to "constitute Tribunals inferior to the supreme Court," Congress created the Court of Veterans Appeals in 1988 and changed its name in 1999 to the Court of Appeals for Veterans Claims. This newest court in the federal judiciary

is composed of a chief judge and up to six associate judges, all appointed by the President and approved by the Senate to 15-year terms.

The court has the power to hear appeals from the decisions of an administrative agency, the Board of Veterans Appeals in the Department of Veterans Affairs (VA). Thus, this court hears cases in which individuals claim that the VA has denied or otherwise mishandled valid claims for veterans' benefits. Appeals from the decisions of the Court of Appeals for Veterans Claims can be taken to the Court of Appeals for the Federal Circuit.

The United States Tax Court

Acting under its constitutionally granted power to tax, Congress established the United States Tax Court in 1969.[22] The Tax Court has 19 judges, one of whom serves as chief judge. Each of these 19 judges is named by the President and approved by the Senate for a 15-year term. The Tax Court hears civil but not criminal cases involving disputes over the application of the tax laws. Most of its cases, then, are generated by the Internal Revenue Service and other Treasury Department agencies. Its decisions may be appealed to the federal courts of appeals.

---

[22]Article I, Section 8, Clause 1.

Section 4 Assessment

Key Terms and Main Ideas

1. Explain this statement: *The special courts have very narrow jurisdictions.*
2. What does it mean to seek **redress** in a court?
3. What is the difference between a **civilian tribunal** and a **court-martial**?
4. Who created the special courts?

Critical Thinking

5. **Drawing Inferences** Why do you think Congress has seen a need to create special courts instead of sending all federal cases to the regular courts?
6. **Expressing Problems Clearly** Brainstorm a type of case that a citizen might take to the U.S. Court of Federal Claims. Explain your reasoning.

7. **Drawing Inferences** Why, do you think, did Congress establish a civilian tribunal to hear appeals of serious court-martial convictions?

 Take It to the Net

8. Examine the Web site of the U.S. Court of Appeals for the Armed Forces to find answers to these questions: **(a)** Give two reasons that Congress created the court. **(b)** What makes the Court of Appeals for the Armed Forces different from other federal courts? **(c)** What characteristics of the current judges qualify them to hear military cases? Use the links provided in the Social Studies area at the following Web site for help in completing this activity.
www.phschool.com

May Congress Regulate States' Business Activities?

Under the 10th Amendment, the powers that the Constitution does not delegate to the Federal Government or deny to the States are "reserved to the States." This core principle of federalism restricts the government's ability to interfere with the States. Does it mean that the Federal Government cannot regulate State business activities?

Reno v. Condon (2000)

State departments of motor vehicles require drivers and automobile owners to provide personal information in order to receive a driver's license or to register a vehicle. This information typically includes name, address, telephone number, Social Security number, photograph, and some medical information. Many States then sell this information to businesses, earning significant revenues.

After learning about this sale of personal information, and the dangers encountered by some individuals whose information had been sold, Congress enacted the Driver's Privacy Protection Act of 1994 (DPPA). The law prohibits States from disclosing a driver's personal information without the driver's consent. States can still disclose information on vehicular accidents, driving violations, and driver's status without the driver's consent, and can disclose personal information with the driver's consent.

South Carolina was one of the States that sold motor vehicle records for a fee. Following enactment of the DPPA, Attorney General Charles M. Condon of South Carolina filed suit against the United States Attorney General, Janet Reno, in federal district court. The suit charged that the DPPA violated the division of power between State and Federal governments as established by the 10th and 11th Amendments. The district court agreed with the plaintiff, as did the court of appeals. The Supreme Court accepted the case for review in 1999.

Arguments for Reno

1. Among the purchasers of drivers' personal information are businesses engaged in interstate commerce. Therefore, the DPPA is a proper exercise of Congress's authority to regulate interstate commerce under the Commerce Clause.
2. The DPPA regulates States as owners of information databases but does not interfere with States' power to regulate their own citizens. The DPPA does not require the States to enact laws or to help enforce federal laws regulating private individuals.

Arguments for Condon

1. Drivers' personal information is not an article of interstate commerce because information is not an article of commerce. The gathering, maintaining, and selling of information by the States occur primarily within States. Thus these activities are not subject to congressional regulation under the Commerce Clause.
2. The DPPA violates the principles of federalism contained in the 10th Amendment because it requires States to implement federal regulations.

Decide for Yourself

1. Review the constitutional grounds on which each side based its arguments and the specific arguments each side presented.
2. Debate the opposing viewpoints presented in this case. Which viewpoint do you favor?
3. Predict the impact of the Court's decision on federalism. (To read a summary of the Court's decision, turn to the Supreme Court Glossary on page 799.)

Political Dictionary

inferior courts (p. 507)

jurisdiction (p. 508)

exclusive jurisdiction (p. 508)

concurrent jurisdiction (p. 508)

plaintiff (p. 509)

defendant (p. 509)

original jurisdiction (p. 509)

appellate jurisdiction (p. 509)

criminal case (p. 513)

civil case (p. 513)

docket (p. 513)

writ of certiorari (p. 520)

certificate (p. 521)

majority opinion (p. 522)

precedent (p. 522)

concurring opinion (p. 522)

dissenting opinion (p. 522)

redress (p. 524)

civilian tribunal (p. 525)

court-martial (p. 525)

Practicing the Vocabulary

Matching *Choose a term from the list above that best matches each description.*

1. Jurisdiction shared by a State court and a federal court
2. A court made up of non-military judges
3. The Supreme Court's official decision of a case
4. A court's caseload
5. A person who initiated a lawsuit
6. An example to follow in similar cases in the future
7. A court of military personnel, used to try those accused of violating military law

Fill in the Blank *Choose a term from the list above that best completes the sentence.*

8. A _____ would be filed in a claim of patent infringement.
9. Satisfaction of a legal claim is called_____.
10. The Supreme Court issues a _____ when a case relates to the interpretation of law.
11. The Constitution left the creation of the _____ to Congress.
12. A Supreme Court justice may choose to write a _____ if he or she believes that a point in the Court's opinion needs additional emphasis.

Reviewing Main Ideas

Section 1

13. Why did the Framers see a need for a national judiciary?
14. Name two provisions that the Constitution makes regarding the federal courts and their jurisdictions.
15. Which courts hear most of the cases in this country, the State courts or the federal courts?
16. Describe the process by which most federal judges are nominated and approved.

Section 2

17. **(a)** What jurisdiction do the inferior courts have? **(b)** What kinds of cases do they hear?
18. When the Supreme Court's docket became overloaded in the late 1800s, what did Congress do to ease the burden?
19. In the federal judicial system, what is a circuit?
20. Where do most of the cases that reach the federal courts of appeals come from?
21. How does the Court of Appeals for the Federal Circuit differ from other federal courts of appeals?

Section 3

22. **(a)** Why is it so important for courts to have the power of judicial review? **(b)** What famous court case established the Supreme Court's right to exercise the power of judicial review?
23. **(a)** What kinds of jurisdiction does the Supreme Court have? **(b)** What kind of cases does it usually accept?
24. What is the "rule of four"?
25. If the Supreme Court decides not to hear a case, what happens to the case?
26. Describe how oral arguments are presented before the Supreme Court.

Section 4

27. **(a)** Who creates the special courts? **(b)** Why have they been created?
28. Can the United States be sued by its own citizens? Explain.
29. What kind of claims are heard by the Court of Appeals for Veterans Claims?

Critical Thinking Skills

30. Applying the Chapter Skill Appeals of certain court-martial cases go to a civilian tribunal, the Court of Appeals for the Armed Forces. Knowing this, what conclusion can you draw about the role of that court?

31. Drawing Inferences Why did the Framers create a system of appointing judges that required cooperation between the President and the Senate?

32. Making Decisions Occasionally the Supreme Court refuses to hear a certain case, then later agrees to hear a very similar case. Why might the Court decide to hear the later case?

Analyzing Political Cartoons

Using your knowledge of American government and this cartoon, answer the questions below.

33. In 1937, President Roosevelt proposed a law that would have allowed him to appoint as many as six new justices to the Supreme Court. He was widely criticized for trying to "pack the court" with judges favorable to his New Deal programs. **(a)** Who is the captain of the ship? **(b)** Who does the smaller sailor represent? **(c)** How is the Supreme Court represented?

34. Does the cartoonist approve of FDR's plan? Explain.

★ You Can Make a Difference

Investigative reporters look into many different kinds of matters, from political scandals to questions of consumer health and safety. Probably you have seen their reports on television or in newspaper articles. Reporters often uncover issues that make people think "something should be done."

Identify a problem or issue involving people whom you think are being treated unfairly. Write a proposal for an investigative report that would track down the truth about this issue. In your proposal, clearly identify the issue. Explain what you expect to find out in your investigation. List the types of people and organizations, governmental or private, you plan to contact, and why. Write a concluding statement suggesting what type of court might hear a case resulting from your investigation.

Participation Activities

35. Current Events Watch Find news reports of a recent major decision by the Supreme Court. Form a mock panel of justices and deliberate on the case, using detailed accounts of the case. When your panel reaches a decision, identify the arguments that most influenced you, and explain why your group agreed or disagreed with the Court.

36. Graphing Activity Construct a time line showing the dates when each of the current Supreme Court justices was appointed to the bench. Make a second time line showing the Presidents during that time span. Compare the two to see which President appointed each justice and who appointed the majority of the present-day Court.

37. It's Your Turn A justice of the Supreme Court has announced her retirement, giving you, the President, the opportunity to nominate someone to fill that seat. List five factors that might influence your choice of a nominee.

 Take It to the Net

Chapter 18 Self-Test As a final review activity, take the Chapter 18 Self-Test in the Social Studies area at the Web site listed, and receive immediate feedback on your answers.

www.phschool.com

Civil Liberties: First Amendment Freedoms

"All through the years we have had to fight for civil liberty, and we know that there are times when the light grows rather dim, and every time that happens democracy is in danger."

—Eleanor Roosevelt (1940)

Democracy cannot exist without civil liberty—that is, without individual freedom. But, notice, democracy also cannot exist without some degree of authority—that is, without government. Striking the proper balance between freedom and authority is democracy's constant challenge.

◆ **Americans enjoying their freedom of religion**

You Can Make a Difference

THE INTERNET RAISES new free speech issues. Brandon Beussink, a high school junior in Marble Hill, Missouri, set up a home page on his home computer, where he criticized some teachers and made fun of the school's Web site. A link went to the school's home page, but not the other way. School administrators were furious. They ordered Brandon to shut his Web site down (which he did) and suspended him for 10 days. Then they used the suspension to calculate his absences, lower his grades, and fail him in all courses. Brandon and his parents sued, with the help of the ACLU. In December 1998, a federal court ruled that the school had violated Brandon's free speech rights.

Keep It Current

Items marked with this logo are periodically updated on the Internet. Keep up-to-date with what's in the news. To get current information about First Amendment issues, go to **www.phschool.com**

SECTION 1

The Unalienable Rights (pp. 532–536)

★ The guarantees in the Bill of Rights reflect Americans' long-held commitment to personal freedom as well as the principle of limited government.
★ Individual rights are not absolute; they can be restricted when they come into conflict with the rights of others.
★ The Bill of Rights restricts only the National Government, but the Due Process Clause of the 14th Amendment "nationalizes" most of those guarantees.

SECTION 2

Freedom of Religion (pp. 537–544)

★ Free expression, including freedom of religion, is necessary to a free society.
★ The Establishment Clause sets up what Thomas Jefferson called "a wall of separation between church and state." The nature of this "wall," particularly as it applies to education, has been a matter of continuing controversy.
★ The Free Exercise Clause protects individuals' right to believe— but not to do—whatever they wish.

SECTION 3

Freedom of Speech and Press (pp. 546–553)

★ The 1st and 14th amendments' guarantees of free speech and press protect a person's right to speak freely and to hear what others have to say.
★ These freedoms are not absolute: the Supreme Court has limited such expressions as seditious speech and obscenity, but seldom allows prior restraint of spoken or written words.
★ The media also can be limited: Reporters do not have an unlimited right of confidentiality, and radio and television are subject to more regulation because they use the public airwaves.
★ Symbolic and commercial speech enjoy constitutional protection but can be limited under certain circumstances.

SECTION 4

Freedom of Assembly and Petition (pp. 555–558)

★ The 1st Amendment guarantees the right to assemble peaceably and to petition the government for a redress of grievances.
★ Government can reasonably regulate the time, place, and manner of assembly, but those regulations must be "content neutral."
★ The right of assembly does not give demonstrators a right to trespass on private property.
★ The guarantee of freedom of assembly and petition carries with it a right of association.

The Unalienable Rights

Section Preview

OBJECTIVES

1. **Explain** how Americans' commitment to freedom led to the creation of the Bill of Rights.
2. **Understand** that the rights guaranteed by limited government are not absolute.
3. **Show** how federalism affects individual rights.
4. **Describe** how the 9th Amendment helps guarantee individual rights.

WHY IT MATTERS

The United States was founded, in part, to ensure individual rights against the power of government. However, these rights can be restricted when they come into conflict with the rights of others. The Due Process Clause of the 14th Amendment prevents the States from abridging rights guaranteed in the Constitution's Bill of Rights.

POLITICAL DICTIONARY

★ **Bill of Rights**
★ **civil liberties**
★ **civil rights**
★ **alien**
★ **Due Process Clause**
★ **process of incorporation**

Have you ever heard of Walter Barnette? Probably not. How about Toyosaburo Korematsu? Dolloree Mapp? Clarence Earl Gideon? Almost certainly, you have the same answer: No.

Walter Barnette was a Jehovah's Witness who told his children not to salute the flag or to recite the Pledge of Allegiance. Toyosaburo Korematsu was a citizen of the United States interned by the Federal Government during World War II. Dolloree Mapp was fined $25 for possessing "lewd and lascivious books." Finally, Clarence Earl Gideon was sentenced to prison for breaking into and entering a poolroom.

You will encounter these names again over the next few pages. Each of them played an important part in building and protecting the rights of all Americans.

A Commitment to Freedom

A commitment to personal freedom is deeply rooted in America's colonial past. Over many centuries, the English people had waged a continuing struggle for individual rights, and the early colonists brought a dedication to that cause with them to America.

Their commitment to freedom took root here, and it flourished. The Revolutionary War was fought to preserve and expand these very rights:

the rights of the individual against government. In proclaiming the independence of the new United States, the founders of this country declared:

PRIMARY Sources ❝*We hold these truths to be self-evident, that all men are created equal, that they are endowed by their Creator with certain unalienable Rights, that among these are Life, Liberty and the pursuit of Happiness. That to secure these rights, Governments are instituted among Men. . . .* ❞
—Declaration of Independence

The Framers of the Constitution repeated that justification for the existence of government in the Preamble to the Constitution.

The Constitution, as it was written in Philadelphia, contained a number of important guarantees. The most notable of these can be found in Article I, Sections 9 and 10, and in Article III. Unlike many of the first State constitutions, however, the United States Constitution did not include a general listing of the rights of the people.

That omission raised an outcry. The objections were so strong that several States ratified the Constitution only with the understanding that such a listing would be added immediately. The first session of the new Congress met that demand with a series of proposed amendments. Ten of them, known as the **Bill of Rights,** were ratified by the States and became a part of the Constitution on December 15, 1791. Later amendments, especially the 13th and the 14th, have added to the Constitution's guarantees of personal freedom.

The national Constitution guarantees both rights and liberties to the American people. The distinction between civil rights and civil liberties is at best murky. Legal scholars often disagree on the matter, and the two terms are quite often used interchangeably.

However, you can think of the distinction this way: In general, **civil liberties** are protections *against government*. They are guarantees of the safety of persons, opinions, and property from arbitrary acts of government. Examples of civil liberties include freedom of religion, freedom of speech and press, and the guarantee of a fair trial.

The term **civil rights** is sometimes reserved for those *positive acts of government* that seek to make constitutional guarantees a reality for all people. From this perspective, examples of civil rights include the prohibitions of discrimination on the basis of race, sex, religious belief, or national origin, set out in the Civil Rights Act of 1964.

Limited Government

Government in the United States is *limited* government. The Constitution is filled with examples of this fact. Chief among them are its many guarantees of personal freedom. Each one of those guarantees is either an outright prohibition or a restriction on the power of government to do something.

All governments have and use authority over individuals. The all-important difference between a democratic government and a dictatorial one lies in the *extent* of that authority. In a dictatorial regime, the government's powers are practically unlimited. The government regularly suppresses dissent, often harshly. In the United States, however, governmental authority is strictly limited. As Justice Robert H. Jackson once put the point:

▲ *Celebrating the Bill of Rights* A crowd gathers for Bill of Rights Day in New York City, December 15, 1941—eight days after the attack on Pearl Harbor.

PRIMARY Sources
" If there is any fixed star in our constitutional constellation, it is that no official, high or petty, can prescribe what shall be orthodox in politics, nationalism, religion, or any other matter of opinion or force citizens to confess by word or act their faith therein. "
—*West Virginia Board of Education* v. *Barnette*, 1943

Rights Are Relative, Not Absolute

The Constitution guarantees many different rights to *everyone* in the United States. Still, *no one* has the right to do anything he or she pleases. Rather, all persons have the right to do as they please as long as they do not infringe on the rights of others. Thus, each person's rights are relative to the rights of every other person.

To illustrate the point: Everyone in the United States has a right of free speech, but no one enjoys absolute freedom of speech. A person can be punished for using obscene language, or for using words in a way that causes another person to commit a crime—for example, to riot or to desert from the military. The Supreme Court dealt with this point in a recent case, *ApolloMedia Corporation* v. *United States*, 1999. There, it unanimously upheld a federal law that makes it illegal for anyone to send obscene and intentionally annoying e-mail via the Internet.

Justice Oliver Wendell Holmes put the relative nature of each person's rights this way:

❝*The most stringent [strict] protection of free speech would not protect a man in falsely shouting fire in a theatre and causing a panic.*❞
—*Schenck* v. *United States,* 1919

When Rights Conflict

Sometimes different guarantees of rights come into conflict with one another. One common example: freedom of the press versus the right to a fair trial.

In one famous case, Dr. Samuel Sheppard of Cleveland, Ohio, had been convicted of murdering his wife. His lengthy trial was widely covered in the national media. On appeal, Sheppard claimed that the highly sensational coverage had denied him a fair trial. The Supreme Court agreed. In *Sheppard* v. *Maxwell,* 1966, the Court rejected the free press argument, overturned Sheppard's conviction, and ordered a new trial.

To Whom Are Rights Guaranteed?

Most constitutional rights are extended to all persons. The Supreme Court has often held that "persons" covers **aliens** as well as citizens. Aliens are people who are not citizens of the country in which they live. Not all rights are given to aliens, however. Thus, the right to travel freely throughout the country is guaranteed to all citizens.[1] But the travel of aliens can be restricted.

After the bombing of Pearl Harbor by Japan, all persons of Japanese descent living on the Pacific Coast were evacuated—forcibly moved—

▲ **Trial and Trial Again** Although Dr. Sam Sheppard was acquitted in a retrial in 1966, his son Sam Reese Sheppard (shown here on the witness stand) filed a wrongful imprisonment suit in order to exonerate his father. In 2000, a jury ruled that the elder Sheppard could not be proved innocent by the greater weight of the evidence. Sheppard has appealed.

inland. Many suffered economic and other hardships. In 1944 the Supreme Court reluctantly upheld the forced evacuation as a reasonable wartime emergency measure.[2] Still, the relocation was strongly criticized over the years. In 1988 the Federal Government admitted that the wartime relocation had been both unnecessary and unjust. Congress voted to pay $20,000 to each living internee. It also declared: "On behalf of the nation, the Congress apologizes."

Today's war on terrorism has created a political climate not unlike that of the early days of World War II. Did the treatment of Japanese Americans then teach us something for today? Will the rights of Muslims and other Middle Eastern descent be respected by government as it fights terrorism here and abroad?

Federalism and Individual Rights

Federalism is a complicated governmental arrangement. It produces any number of problems—including a very complex pattern of guarantees of individual rights in the United States.

The Bill of Rights

Remember, the first ten amendments were originally intended as restrictions on the new National Government, not on the already existing States. And that remains the fact of the matter today.[3]

To illustrate this important point: The 5th Amendment says that no person can be charged with "a capital, or otherwise infamous crime" except by a grand jury. As a part of the Bill of Rights, this provision applies only to the National Government. The States are free to use the grand jury to bring accusations of serious crime—or, if they prefer, they can use some other process for that purpose. In fact, the grand jury is a part of the criminal

---

[1] See the two Privileges and Immunities clauses, in Article IV, Section 2, and the 14th Amendment. The guarantee does not extend to citizens under some form of legal restraint—for example, in jail or out on bail awaiting trial.

[2] *Korematsu* v. *United States,* 1944. However, on the same day the Court held, in *Ex parte Endo,* that once the loyalty of any citizen internee had been established, no restriction could be placed on that person's freedom to travel that was not legally imposed on all other citizens.

[3] The Supreme Court first held that the provisions of the Bill of Rights restrict only the National Government in *Barron* v. *Baltimore,* 1833. This was the first case in which the point was raised. The Court has followed that holding ever since.

▲ This part of *The Great Wall of Los Angeles,* a half-mile-long mural, depicts Japanese internment during World War II. **Critical Thinking** *How does the artist convey the conditions and feelings of the internees?*

justice system in only about half of the States today; see pages 577–578 and 704.

The Modifying Effect of the 14th Amendment

Again, the provisions of the Bill of Rights apply against the National Government, not against the States. This does *not* mean, however, that the States can deny basic rights to the people.

In part, the States cannot do so because each of their own constitutions contains a bill of rights. In addition, they cannot deny these basic rights because of the 14th Amendment's **Due Process Clause.** It says:

> **FROM THE Constitution** ❝No State shall . . . deprive any person of life, liberty, or property, without due process of law. . . .❞
> —United States Constitution

The Supreme Court has often said that the 14th Amendment's Due Process Clause means this: No State can deny to any person any right that is "basic or essential to the American concept of ordered liberty."

But what specific rights are "basic or essential"? The Court has answered that question in a long series of cases. In those cases it has held that most (but not all) of the protections set out in the Bill of Rights are also covered by the 14th Amendment's Due Process Clause, and so apply against the States. In deciding those cases, the Court has engaged in what has come to be called the **process of incorporation.** It has

incorporated, or included, most of the guarantees in the Bill of Rights into the 14th Amendment's Due Process Clause.

The Court began that historic process in *Gitlow* v. *New York* in 1925. That landmark case involved Benjamin Gitlow, a communist, who had been convicted in the State courts of criminal anarchy. He had made several speeches and published a pamphlet calling for the violent overthrow of government in this country.

On appeal, the Supreme Court upheld Gitlow's conviction and the State law under which he had been tried, viewing Gitlow's conduct as a call to action. In deciding the case, however, the Court made this crucial point: Freedom of speech and press, which the 1st Amendment says cannot be denied by the National Government, are also "among the fundamental personal rights and liberties protected by the Due Process Clause of the 14th Amendment from impairment by the States."

Soon after *Gitlow,* the Court held each of the 1st Amendment's guarantees to be covered by the 14th Amendment. It struck down State laws involving speech (*Fiske* v. *Kansas,* 1927; *Stromberg* v. *California,* 1931), the press (*Near* v. *Minnesota,* 1931), assembly and petition (*DeJonge* v. *Oregon,* 1937), and religion (*Cantwell* v. *Connecticut,* 1940). In each of those cases, the Court declared a State law unconstitutional as a violation of the 14th Amendment's Due Process Clause.

In the 1960s, the Court extended the scope of the 14th Amendment's Due Process Clause even

Process of Incorporation

Provisions of the Bill of Rights Incorporated into the 14th Amendment's Due Process Clause

Year	Amendment	Provision	Case
1925	1st	Freedom of speech	*Gitlow* v. *New York*
1931	1st	Freedom of the press	*Near* v. *Minnesota*
1937	1st	Freedom of assembly, petition	*DeJonge* v. *Oregon*
1940	1st	Free Exercise Clause	*Cantwell* v. *Connecticut*
1947	1st	Establishment Clause	*Everson* v. *Board of Education*
1961	4th	Unreasonable searches, seizures	*Mapp* v. *Ohio*
1962	8th	Cruel, unusual punishments	*Robinson* v. *California*
1963	6th	Right to counsel	*Gideon* v. *Wainwright*
1964	5th	Self-incrimination	*Malloy* v. *Hogan*
1965	6th	Confront witnesses	*Pointer* v. *Texas*
1967	6th	Speedy trial	*Klopfer* v. *North Carolina*
1967	6th	Obtain witnesses	*Washington* v. *Texas*
1968	6th	Trial by jury in criminal cases	*Duncan* v. *Louisiana*
1969	5th	Double jeopardy	*Benton* v. *Maryland*

Provisions NOT Incorporated into the 14th Amendment's Due Process Clause

Amendment	Provision	
2nd	Right to keep, bear arms	
3rd	Quartering of troops	
5th	Grand jury	
7th	Trial by jury in civil cases	

Interpreting Tables This table shows which rights the Supreme Court has "nationalized," by incorporating them into the Due Process Clause of the 14th Amendment. ***Do you think any of the rights "NOT incorporated" should be nationalized in the future? Why?***

further. The key cases are set out in the table at left. Due Process now covers nearly all of the guarantees set out in the Bill of Rights. In effect, the Supreme Court has "nationalized" them by holding that the Constitution guarantees them against the States through the 14th Amendment. You will look at each of the guarantees that are involved here shortly—the 1st Amendment rights in this chapter and the others in Chapter 20.

The 9th Amendment

As you know, the Constitution contains many guarantees of individual rights. However, nowhere in the Constitution—and, indeed, nowhere else—will you find a complete catalog of all of the rights held by the American people.

The little-noted 9th Amendment declares that there are rights beyond those set out in so many words in the Constitution:

> **FROM THE Constitution** ❝*The enumeration in the Constitution, of certain rights, shall not be construed to deny or disparage others retained by the people.*❞
> —United States Constitution

Over the years, the Supreme Court has found that there are, in fact, a number of other rights "retained by the people." They include the guarantee that an accused person will not be tried on the basis of evidence unlawfully gained, and the right of a woman to have an abortion without undue interference by government.

Section 1 Assessment

Key Terms and Main Ideas

1. What is the difference between **civil rights** and **civil liberties?**
2. What is the **Bill of Rights,** and how did it come to be added to the Constitution?
3. How does federalism affect the guarantees of individual rights?
4. What is the **process of incorporation?** What guarantees in the Bill of Rights are not now covered by the 14th Amendment's **Due Process Clause?**

Critical Thinking

5. **Identifying Assumptions** For what reason(s) do you think the Supreme Court found that the right to a fair trial outweighed freedom of the press in *Sheppard?* Do you agree with this decision? Why or why not?
6. **Predicting Consequences** How do you think the United States might be different today if the Supreme Court had not applied the process of incorporation to the Due Process Clause?

 Take It to the Net

7. Read several current news articles relating to 1st Amendment rights. Choose two articles that deal with the same freedom (of religion, speech, press, assembly, or petition), and write a paragraph comparing the issues in the articles. Use the links provided in the Social Studies area at the following Web site for help in completing this activity. **www.phschool.com**

Freedom of Religion

Section Preview

OBJECTIVES

1. **Examine** why a free society cannot exist without free expression.
2. **Describe** the "wall of separation between church and state" set up by the Establishment Clause of the 1st Amendment.
3. **Summarize** the Supreme Court rulings on religion and education as well as other Establishment Clause cases.
4. **Explain** how the Supreme Court has interpreted and limited the Free Exercise Clause.

WHY IT MATTERS

Freedom of religion is one component of the constitutional guarantee of free expression. The Establishment Clause sets up what Thomas Jefferson called "a wall of separation between church and state," but the nature of that separation is still being argued in American society and in the courts. The Free Exercise Clause protects Americans' right to believe—though not to do—whatever they wish.

POLITICAL DICTIONARY

★ **Establishment Clause**
★ **parochial**
★ **Free Exercise Clause**

In the early 1830s, a Frenchman, Alexis de Tocqueville, came to this country to observe life in the young United States. He later wrote that he had searched for the greatness of America in many places: in its large harbors and its deep rivers, in its fertile fields and its boundless forests, in its rich mines and its vast world commerce, in its public schools and its institutions of higher learning, and in its democratic legislature and its matchless Constitution. Yet it was not until he went into the churches of America, that Tocqueville said he came to understand the genius and the power of this country.

Freedom of Expression

A free society cannot exist without rights of free expression, without what has been called a "free trade in ideas." Freedom of expression is protected in the 1st Amendment:

> **FROM THE** *Constitution* **❝***Congress shall make no law respecting an establishment of religion, or prohibiting the free exercise thereof; or abridging the freedom of speech, or of the press; or the right of the people peaceably to assemble, and to petition the Government for a redress of grievances.* **❞**
>
> —United States Constitution

Additionally, as you know, the 14th Amendment's Due Process Clause protects these freedoms from the arbitrary acts of States or their local governments.

It is not surprising that the Bill of Rights provides first for the protection of religious liberty. Religion has always played a large and important role in American life. Many of the early colonists, and many later immigrants, came here to escape persecution for their religious beliefs.

▲ Alexis de Tocqueville, author of *Democracy in America*

The 1st and 14th amendments set out two guarantees of religious freedom. These guarantees prohibit (1) an "establishment of religion" (the **Establishment Clause**), and (2) any arbitrary interference by government in "the free exercise" of religion (the Free Exercise Clause).[4]

---

[4]Also, Article VI, Section 3 provides that "no religious Test shall ever be required as a Qualification to any Office or public Trust under the United States." In *Torcaso* v. *Watkins,* 1961, the Supreme Court held that the 14th Amendment puts the same restriction on the States.

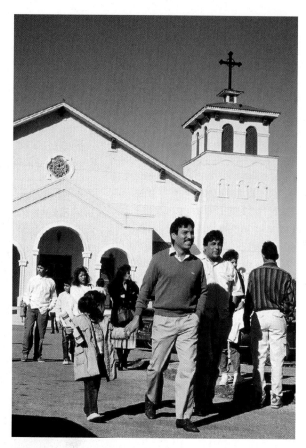

▲ **Religious Freedom** Like all Americans, these church-goers are free to practice whatever religion they choose.

Separation of Church and State

The Establishment Clause sets up, in Thomas Jefferson's words, "a wall of separation between church and state." That wall is not infinitely high, however, and it is not impenetrable. Church and government are constitutionally separated in this country, but that does not make them enemies or even strangers to one another.

Government has done much to encourage churches and religion in the United States. Nearly all property of and contributions to religious sects are free from federal, State, and local taxation. Chaplains serve with each branch of the armed forces. Most public officials take an oath of office in the name of God. Sessions of both houses of Congress, most State legislatures, and many city councils open with prayer. The nation's anthem and its coins and currency make reference to God.

The meaning of the Establishment Clause cannot be pinned down in precise terms. The exact nature of the wall of separation—how high it really is—remains a matter of continuing and often heated controversy.

The Supreme Court did not hear its first Establishment Clause case until 1947. A few earlier cases did involve government and religion, but none of them involved a direct consideration of the "wall of separation."

The most important of those earlier cases was *Pierce* v. *Society of Sisters*, 1925. There, the Court held an Oregon compulsory school attendance law unconstitutional. That law required parents to send their children to public schools. It was purposely intended to eliminate private and especially **parochial** (church-related) schools.

In striking down the law, the Court did not address the Establishment Clause question. Instead, it found the law to be an unreasonable interference with the liberty of parents to direct the upbringing of their children. As such, it was in conflict with the Due Process Clause of the 14th Amendment.

Religion and Education

The first direct ruling on the Establishment Clause came in *Everson* v. *Board of Education*, a 1947 case often called the *New Jersey School Bus Case*. There the Court upheld a State law that provided for the public, tax-supported busing of students attending any school in the State, including parochial schools.

Critics attacked the law as a support of religion. They maintained that it relieved parochial schools of the need to pay for busing and so freed their money for other, including religious, purposes. The Court disagreed; it found the law to be a safety measure intended to benefit children, no matter what schools they might attend. Since that decision, the largest number of the Court's Establishment Clause cases have involved, in one way or another, religion and education.

Released Time

"Released time" programs allow public schools to release students during school hours to attend religious classes. In *McCollum* v. *Board of Education*, 1948, the Court struck down the released time program in Champaign, Illinois, because the program used public facilities for religious purposes.

In *Zorach* v. *Clauson*, 1952, however, the Court upheld New York City's released time program. It did so because the New York program required that the religious classes be held in private places, for example, in private homes.

Prayers and the Bible

The Court has now decided seven major cases involving the recitation of prayers and the reading of the Bible in public schools. In *Engel* v. *Vitale*, 1962, the Court outlawed the use, even on a voluntary basis, of a prayer written by the New York State Board of Regents. The prayer read:

PRIMARY Sources *"Almighty God, we acknowledge our dependence upon Thee, and we beg Thy blessings upon us, our parents, our teachers, and our country."*

—Regents' prayer

In striking down the prayer, the Supreme Court held that:

PRIMARY Sources *"[T]he constitutional prohibition against laws respecting an establishment of religion must at least mean that, in this country, it is no part of the business of government to compose official prayers for any group of the American people to recite as part of a religious program carried on by government."*

—Justice Hugo L. Black, Opinion of the Court

The Supreme Court extended that holding in two 1963 cases. In *Abington School District* v. *Schempp*, it struck down a Pennsylvania law requiring that each school day begin with readings from the Bible and a recitation of the Lord's Prayer. In *Murray* v. *Curlett*, the Court erased a similar rule in the city of Baltimore. In both of these cases, the Court found violations of "the command of the First Amendment that the government maintain strict neutrality, neither aiding nor opposing religion."

Since then, the Supreme Court has found unconstitutional:

• a Kentucky law that ordered the posting of the Ten Commandments in all public school classrooms, *Stone* v. *Graham*, 1980;

• Alabama's "moment of silence" law, *Wallace* v. *Jaffree*, 1985, which provided for a one-minute period of silence for "meditation or voluntary prayer" at the beginning of each school day;

• the offering of prayer as part of a public

school graduation ceremony, in a Rhode Island case, *Lee* v. *Weisman*, 1992;

• a Texas school district's policy that permitted student-led prayer at high school football games, *Santa Fe Independent School District* v. *Doe*, 2000.

To sum up these rulings, the Court has held that public schools cannot sponsor religious exercises. It has not held that individuals cannot pray when and as they choose in schools or in any other place. Nor has it held that students cannot study the Bible in a literary or historical context in the schools.

These rulings have stirred strong criticism. Many individuals and groups have long proposed that the Constitution be amended to allow voluntary prayer in the public schools. Despite these decisions, both organized prayer and Bible readings are found in a great many public school classrooms today.

Student Religious Groups

The Equal Access Act of 1984 declares that any public high school that receives federal funds (nearly all do) must allow student religious groups to meet in the school on the same terms that it sets for other student organizations.

The Supreme Court found that the law does not violate the Establishment Clause in a case from Nebraska, *Westside Community Schools*

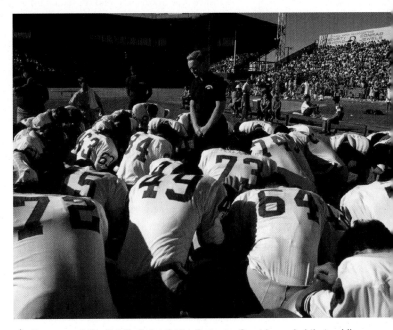

▲ *Prayer and the Public Schools* The Supreme Court has ruled that public schools cannot sponsor prayer either in school or at school-related events.

v. *Mergens,* 1990. There, several students had tried to form a Christian club at Omaha's Westside High School. The students had to fight the school board in the federal courts in order to win their point.

The High Court has recently gone much further than it did in *Mergens*—in a case from New York, *Good News Club* v. *Milford Central School,* 2001. There, a school board had refused to allow a group of grade-school students to meet, after school, to sing, pray, memorize scriptures, and hear Bible lessons. The school board based its action on the Establishment Clause. *However,* the Court held that the board had violated Good News Club members' 1st and 14th amendment rights to free speech.

Evolution

In *Epperson* v. *Arkansas,* 1968, the Court struck down a State law forbidding the teaching of the scientific theory of evolution. The Court held that the Constitution

PRIMARY Sources **"***forbids alike the preference of a religious doctrine or the prohibition of theory which is deemed antagonistic to a particular dogma. . . . 'The State has no legitimate interest in protecting any or all religions from views distasteful to them.'* **"**

—Justice Abe Fortas, Opinion of the Court

The Court found a similar law to be unconstitutional in 1987. In *Edwards* v. *Aguillard,* it voided a 1981 Louisiana law that provided that whenever teachers taught the theory of evolution, they also had to offer instruction in "creation science."

Aid to Parochial Schools

Most recent Establishment Clause cases have centered on this highly controversial question: What forms of State aid to parochial schools are constitutional? Several States give help to private schools, including schools run by church organizations, for transportation, textbooks, laboratory equipment, standardized testing, and much else.

Those who support this kind of aid argue that parochial schools enroll large numbers of students who would otherwise have to be educated at public expense. They also point out that the Supreme Court has held that parents have a legal right to send their children to those schools (*Pierce* v. *Society of Sisters*).

To give that right real meaning, they say, the State must give some aid to parochial schools in order to relieve parents of some of the double burden they carry because they must pay taxes to support the public schools their children do not attend. Many advocates also insist that schools run by religious organizations pose no real church-state problems because they devote most of their time to secular (nonreligious) subjects rather than to sectarian (religious) ones.

Opponents of aid to parochial schools argue that parents who choose to send their children to parochial schools should accept the financial consequences of that choice. Many of these critics also insist that it is impossible to draw clear lines between secular and sectarian courses in parochial schools. They say that religious beliefs are bound to have an effect on the teaching of nonreligious subjects in church-run schools.

The *Lemon* Test

The Supreme Court has been picking its way through cases involving State aid to parochial schools for several years. In most of these cases, the Court now applies a three-pronged standard, the *Lemon* test: (1) The purpose of the aid must be clearly secular, not religious; (2) its primary effect must neither advance nor inhibit religion; and (3) it must avoid an "excessive entanglement of government with religion."

The test stems from *Lemon* v. *Kurtzman,* 1971. There, the Supreme Court held that the Establishment Clause is designed to prevent three main evils: "sponsorship, financial support, and active involvement of the sovereign in religious activity." In *Lemon,* the Court struck down a Pennsylvania law that provided for reimbursements (financial payments) to private schools to cover their costs for teachers' salaries, textbooks, and other teaching materials in non-religious courses.

The Court held that the State program was of direct benefit to the parochial schools, and so to the churches sponsoring them. It also found that the Pennsylvania program required such close State supervision that it produced an excessive entanglement of government with religion.

The *Lemon* Test

State aid to parochial schools is constitutional if...

★ its purpose is clearly secular, not religious.

★ its primary effect neither enhances nor inhibits religion.

★ it avoids an excessive entanglement of government with religion.

Interpreting Charts To be constitutional, State aid to parochial schools must meet all three of the criteria in the chart. *Which criterion do you think the courts would find most difficult to apply? Explain your answer.*

On the other hand, a number of State aid programs have passed the *Lemon* test over the past 30 years. Thus, the Court has held that a State can pay church-related schools what it costs them to administer the State's standardized tests. This decision was rendered in a New York case, *Committee for Public Education and Religious Liberty* v. *Regan,* 1980.

Public funds cannot be used to pay any part of the salaries of parochial school teachers, however, including those who teach only secular courses. In *Grand Rapids School District* v. *Ball,* 1985, the Court said that the way a teacher presents a course cannot easily be checked.

The Court also struck down a New York law that provided for direct cash payments reimbursing parents for the tuition they paid to schools operated by religious organizations in *Committee for Public Education and Religious Liberty* v. *Nyquist,* 1973. However, in a later case, *Mueller* v. *Allen,* 1983, the Court upheld a Minnesota tax law that accomplishes the same end.

The Minnesota law gives parents a State income tax deduction for the costs of tuition, textbooks, and transportation. Parents can claim the tax break no matter what schools their children attend. Most public school parents pay little or nothing for those items, so the law is of particular benefit to parents with children in private, mostly parochial, schools. The Court found that the law meets the *Lemon* test, and it relied on this point: The tax deduction is available to *all* parents with children in school, and

they are free to decide which type of school their children attend.

In *Bowen* v. *Kendrick,* 1988, the Court upheld a controversial federal statute, the Adolescent Family Life Act of 1981. That law provides for grants to both public and private agencies dealing with the problems of adolescent sex and pregnancy. Some of the grants were made to religious groups that oppose abortion, prompting the argument that those groups use federal money to teach religious doctrine.

The Supreme Court found the law's purpose—curbing "the social and economic problems caused by teenage sexuality, pregnancy, and parenthood"—to be a legitimate one. Even though some grants pay for counseling that "happens to coincide with the religious views" of some groups, this does not by itself mean that the federal funds are being used with "a primary effect of advancing religion," according to the Court.

In a 1993 Arizona case, *Zobrest* v. *Catalina Foothills School District,* the Court said that the use of public money to provide an interpreter for a deaf student who attends a Catholic high school does not violate the Establishment Clause. The Constitution, said the Court, does not lay down an absolute barrier to placing a public employee in a religious school.

In *Board of Education of Kiryas Joel* v. *Grumet,* 1994, however, the Court struck down a New York law relating to the education of handicapped children. That law established a school district with lines very carefully drawn to benefit handicapped children in a tight-knit community of Hasidic Jews.

In the most recent case, from Louisiana, *Mitchell* v. *Helms*, 2000, the Supreme Court upheld a federal law under which some material and equipment, including computer hardware and software, are loaned to public and private schools. Two facts were key to the Court's ruling: that those items (1) are loaned, not given to parochial schools, and (2) can be used only in "secular, neutral, and nonideological" programs.

Other Establishment Clause Cases

Most church-state controversies have involved public education. Some Establishment Clause cases have arisen elsewhere, however.

Seasonal Displays

Many public organizations sponsor celebrations of the holiday season with street decorations, programs in public schools, and the like. Can these publicly sponsored observances properly include expressions of religious belief?

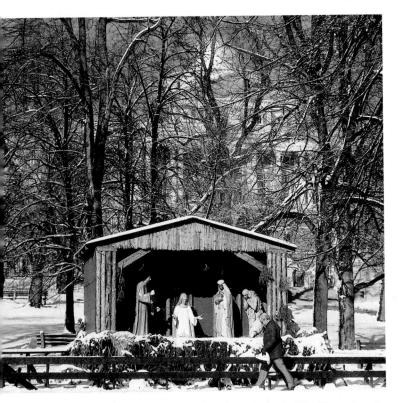

▲ This Christian nativity scene was displayed in front of the Massachusetts State House. *Critical Thinking Does this seasonal display violate the separation of church and state? How might it be relocated or changed to avoid coming into conflict with the First Amendment?*

In *Lynch* v. *Donnelly*, 1984, the Court held that the city of Pawtucket, Rhode Island, could include the Christian nativity scene in its holiday display, which also featured nonreligious objects such as candy canes and Santa's sleigh and reindeer. That ruling, however, left open this question: What about a public display made up *only* of a religious symbol?

The Court faced that question in 1989. In *County of Allegheny* v. *ACLU*, it held that the county's seasonal display "endorsed Christian doctrine," and so violated the 1st and 14th amendments. The county had placed a large display celebrating the birth of Jesus on the grand stairway in the county courthouse, with a banner proclaiming "Glory to God in the Highest."

At the same time, the Court upheld another holiday display in *Pittsburgh* v. *ACLU*. The city's display consisted of a large Christmas tree, an 18-foot menorah, and a sign declaring the city's dedication to freedom.

Chaplains

Daily sessions of both houses of Congress and most of the State legislatures begin with prayer. In Congress, and in many States, a chaplain paid with public funds offers the opening prayer.

The Supreme Court has ruled that this practice, unlike prayers in the public schools, is constitutionally permissible. The ruling was made in a case involving Nebraska's one-house legislature, *Marsh* v. *Chamber*, 1983.

The Court rested its distinction between school prayers and legislative prayers on two points. First, prayers have been offered in the nation's legislative bodies "from colonial times through the founding of the Republic and ever since." Second, legislators, unlike schoolchildren, are not "susceptible to religious indoctrination or peer pressure."

The Free Exercise Clause

The second part of the constitutional guarantee of religious freedom is set out in the Constitution's **Free Exercise Clause**, which guarantees to each person the right to believe whatever he or she chooses to believe in matters of religion. No law and no other action by government can violate that absolute constitutional right. It is protected by the 1st and the 14th amendments.

No person has an absolute right to act as he or she chooses, however. The Free Exercise Clause does *not* give anyone the right to violate criminal laws, offend public morals, or otherwise threaten the health, welfare, or safety of the community.

The Supreme Court laid down the basic shape of the Free Exercise Clause in the first case it heard on the issue, *Reynolds* v. *United States,* 1879. Reynolds, a Mormon, had two wives. That practice, polygamy, was allowed by the teachings of his church, but it was prohibited by a federal law banning polygamy in any territory of the United States.

Reynolds was tried and convicted under the law. On appeal, he argued that the law violated his constitutional right to the free exercise of his religious beliefs. The Supreme Court disagreed. It held that the First Amendment does not forbid Congress the power to punish those actions that are "violations of social duties or subversive of good order."

Limits on Free Exercise

Over the years, the Court has approved many regulations of human conduct in the face of free exercise challenges. For example, it has upheld laws that require the vaccination of schoolchildren, *Jacobson* v. *Massachusetts,* 1905; laws that forbid the use of poisonous snakes in religious rites, *Bunn* v. *North Carolina,* 1949; and laws that require businesses to be closed on Sundays ("blue laws"), *McGowan* v. *Maryland,* 1961.

A State can require religious groups to have a permit to hold a parade on the public streets, *Cox* v. *New Hampshire,* 1941; and organizations that enlist children to sell religious literature must obey child labor laws, *Prince* v. *Massachusetts,* 1944. The Federal Government can draft those who have religious objections to military service, *Welsh* v. *United States,* 1970.

The Court has made this last ruling many times. *Welsh* is the leading case from the Vietnam War period. There, the Court held that the only persons who could not be drafted were those "whose consciences . . . would give them no rest if they allowed themselves to become part of an instrument of war."

The Air Force can deny an Orthodox Jew the right to wear his yarmulke (skull cap) while on

▲ The rabbi at right, a Jewish chaplain at the U.S. Naval Academy, helps a midshipman study the Torah. *Critical Thinking Do you think military chaplains, especially at the service academies, violate the separation of church and state?*

active duty, *Goldman* v. *Weinberger,* 1986. The U.S. Forest Service can allow private companies to build roads and cut timber in national forests that Native Americans have traditionally used for religious purposes, *Lyng* v. *Northwest Indian Cemetery Protective Association,* 1988.

In addition, a State can deny unemployment benefits to a man fired by a private drug counseling group because he used peyote in violation of the State's drug laws. The Court made that finding even though the man ingested the hallucinogenic drug as part of a ceremony of his Native American Church, *Oregon* v. *Smith,* 1990.

Free Exercise Upheld

Over time, however, the Court has also found many actions by governments to be incompatible with the free exercise guarantee. The Court did so for the first time in one of the landmark Due Process cases cited earlier in this chapter, *Cantwell* v. *Connecticut,* 1940. In that case, the Court struck down a law requiring a person to obtain a license before soliciting money for a religious cause.

The Supreme Court has decided a number of other cases in a similar way. Thus, Amish children cannot be forced to attend school beyond the 8th grade, because that sect's centuries-old "self-sufficient agrarian lifestyle essential to their religious faith is threatened by modern education," *Wisconsin* v. *Yoder,* 1972. On the other hand, the Amish, who provide support for their own people, must pay Social Security taxes, as all other employers do, *United States* v. *Lee,* 1982.

A State cannot forbid ministers to hold elected public offices, *McDaniel* v. *Paty,* 1978. Nor can it deny unemployment compensation benefits to a worker who quit a job because it involved a conflict with his or her religious beliefs, *Sherbert* v. *Verner,* 1963; *Thomas* v. *Indiana,* 1981; *Hobbie* v. *Florida,* 1987; *Frazee* v. *Illinois,* 1989.

The Court has often held that "only those beliefs rooted in religion are protected by the Free Exercise Clause" (*Sherbert* v. *Verner,* 1963). This leaves open the perplexing question of what beliefs are "rooted in religion"? Clearly, religions that seem strange or even bizarre to most Americans are as entitled to constitutional protection as are the more traditional ones. For example, in *Lukumi Babalu Aye* v. *City of Hialeah,* 1993, the High Court struck down a Florida city's ordinance that outlawed animal sacrifices as part of any church services.

The Jehovah's Witnesses have carried several important religious freedom cases to the Supreme Court. Perhaps the stormiest controversy resulting from these cases arose out of the Witnesses' refusal to salute the flag.

The Witnesses refuse to salute the flag because they see such conduct as a violation of the Bible's commandment against idolatry. In *Minersville School District* v. *Gobitis,* 1940, the Court upheld a Pennsylvania school board regulation requiring students to salute the flag at the beginning of each school day. Walter Gobitis instructed his children not to do so, and the school expelled them. He went to court, basing his case on the constitutional guarantee.

Gobitis finally lost in the Supreme Court, which declared that the board's rule was not an infringement of religious liberty. Rather, the Court held that the rule was a lawful attempt to promote patriotism and national unity.

Three years later, the Court reversed that decision. In *West Virginia Board of Education* v. *Barnette,* 1943, it held a compulsory flag-salute law unconstitutional. Justice Robert H. Jackson's words on page 533 are from the Court's powerful opinion in that case. So are these:

> **PRIMARY Sources** **"**To believe that patriotism will not flourish if patriotic ceremonies are voluntary and spontaneous, instead of a compulsory routine, is to make an unflattering estimate of the appeal of our institutions to free minds. **"**
>
> —Opinion of the Court

Section 2 Assessment

Key Terms and Main Ideas

1. Explain the **Establishment Clause.** Give one example of an Establishment Clause issue that does not involve education.
2. Why does aid to **parochial** schools often pose a constitutional problem?
3. What is the *Lemon* test?
4. Explain the **Free Exercise Clause.** Give one example of a Supreme Court ruling that limits free exercise of religion.

Critical Thinking

5. **Predicting Consequences** How do you think the guarantees of religious freedom ratified in 1791 affected the growth and development of the United States? In other words, how do you think the nation might be different today without these protections?

6. **Recognizing Ideologies** The 1st Amendment protects freedom of religion in two ways. What does this approach reveal about the beliefs and experiences of those Americans who insisted on these guarantees?

 Take It to the Net

7. Select at least three Supreme Court cases on religious freedom that you find interesting. Then search for and read the actual Supreme Court rulings. For each case, briefly explain the issue at stake, the Court's opinion, and the effect of that opinion. Finally, state which case you think was most important to American religious freedom. Use the links provided in the Social Studies area at the following Web site for help in completing this activity. **www.phschool.com**

CLOSE★UP
FOUNDATION

on Primary Sources

Religious Freedom in a Diverse Nation

The Freedom Forum is a nonpartisan foundation dedicated to a free press, free speech, and other freedoms for people around the world. In 1999, the foundation completed a study of the status of 1st Amendment rights in the United States. Here, the foundation's report expresses concern for religious freedom in the United States.

Religious and ethnic diversity, as shown in this Los Angeles classroom, gives 1st Amendment discussions a new urgency.

The 1st Amendment guarantee of religious freedom has been a binding force in this country for more than two centuries. It is a key element of the boldest political experiment the world has ever known. Today, however, there are disturbing signs in the United States that religious liberty—the freedom to believe or not to believe and to practice one's faith openly and freely without government interference—is in danger. People undermining religious liberty include both those who seek to establish in law a "Christian America" and those who seek to exclude religion from public life entirely.

. . . Religion has become a source of divisiveness as people spar and sometimes resort to violence over issues of conscience and belief like abortion, school prayer, and public school curricula. . . . The situation is made more complicated by the fact that the religious composition of the United States is becoming more diverse than ever. Along with many groups of Christians and Jews, this country is now home to growing numbers of Muslims, Hindus, Buddhists, and other believers. . . . Religious diversity was made possible by the 1st Amendment. Now, ironically, religious diversity makes the 1st Amendment more necessary and urgent than at any time in our history. . . .

As [scholar] Charles Haynes notes: ". . . An American is not defined by race or ethnicity, but by a commitment to the democratic first principles in our framing documents. Because of our exploding religious diversity, there is an urgent need for all citizens to rethink our shared commitment to the guiding principles of religious liberty. These principles of the 1st Amendment provide a civic framework for living with our deepest differences. . . ."

Religious freedom is at the heart of this country's experiment with democracy. The continuing controversies are proof of continued passion for liberty of conscience, even as debates rage about whether religion receives sufficient attention from the media, educators, and the government. Disputes involving religious liberty reflect America's ambivalence about the limits of individual liberty. At present, the country's internationally recognized commitment to tolerance of all cultures and faiths is being tested and torn. The question to be answered is whether we can sustain this commitment into the next century.

Analyzing Primary Sources

1. What defines an American, according to this report?
2. Describe recent changes in the nation's religious makeup identified in this report.
3. What benefit do the authors see in disputes that involve "issues of conscience"? What potential dangers do they see in such disputes?

Section Preview

OBJECTIVES

1. **Explain** the importance of the two-way free exchange of ideas.
2. **Summarize** how the Supreme Court has limited seditious speech and obscenity.
3. **Examine** the issues of prior restraint and press confidentiality, and describe the limits the Court has placed on the media.
4. **Define** symbolic speech and commercial speech, and describe the limits on their exercise.

WHY IT MATTERS

The freedom to express ideas freely and to hear the ideas of others is fundamental to American democracy. However, some limitations on freedom of expression have been upheld by the Supreme Court. These include restrictions on certain kinds of speech, such as sedition and obscenity, and on speech in certain circumstances, such as when broadcast over the public airwaves.

POLITICAL DICTIONARY

★ libel
★ slander
★ sedition
★ seditious speech
★ prior restraint
★ shield law
★ symbolic speech
★ picketing

▲ Free speech is essential to this rally planning the 2000 Million Mom March in support of gun control.

Think about this children's verse for a moment: "Sticks and stones may break my bones, but names will never hurt me." That rhyme says, in effect, that acts and words are separate things, and that acts can harm but words cannot.

Is that really true? Certainly not. You know that words can and do have consequences, sometimes powerful consequences. Words, spoken or written, can make you happy, sad, bored, informed, or entertained. They can also expose you to danger, deny you a job, or lead to other serious consequences.

The Free Exchange of Ideas

The guarantees of free speech and press in the 1st and 14th amendments serve two fundamentally important purposes:

(1) to guarantee to *each* person a right of free expression, in the spoken and the written word, and by all other means of communication, as well;

(2) to guarantee to *all* persons a full, wide-ranging discussion of public affairs.

That is, the 1st and 14th amendments give to all people the right to have their say and the right to hear what others have to say.

The American system of government depends on the ability of the people to make sound, reasoned judgments on matters of public concern. Clearly, people can best make such judgments when they know all the facts and can hear all the available interpretations of those facts.

As you examine the Constitution's 1st and 14th amendments here, keep two other key points in mind: First, the guarantees of free speech and press are intended to protect the expression of unpopular views. Clearly, the opinions of the majority need little or no constitutional protection. These guarantees seek to ensure, as Justice Oliver Wendell Holmes put it, "freedom for the thought that we hate," (Dissenting Opinion, *Schwimmer* v. *United States,* 1929).

Second, some forms of expression are not protected by the Constitution. No person has an unbridled right of free speech or free press. Many reasonable restrictions can be placed on those rights. Think about Justice Holmes's comment about restricting the right to shout "Fire!" in a crowded theater. Or consider this restriction: No person has the right to libel or slander another. **Libel** is the false and malicious use of printed words; **slander** is the false and malicious use of spoken words.[6]

Similarly, the law prohibits the use of obscene words, the printing and distributing of obscene materials, and false advertising. It also condemns the use of words to prompt others to commit a crime—for example, to riot or to attempt to overthrow the government by force.

Seditious Speech

Sedition is the crime of attempting to overthrow the government by force or to disrupt its lawful activities by violent acts.[7] **Seditious speech** is the advocating, or urging, of such conduct. It is not protected by the 1st Amendment.

The Alien and Sedition Acts

Congress first acted to curb opposition to government in the Alien and Sedition Acts of 1798. Those acts gave the President the power to deport undesirable aliens and made "any false, scandalous, and malicious" criticism of the government a crime. These laws were meant to stifle the opponents of President John Adams and the Federalists.

The Alien and Sedition Acts were undoubtedly unconstitutional, but that point was never tested in the courts. Some 25 persons were arrested for violating them; of those, ten were convicted. The Alien and Sedition Acts expired before Thomas Jefferson became President in 1801, and he soon pardoned those who had run afoul of them.

The Sedition Act of 1917

Congress passed another sedition law during World War I, as part of the Espionage Act of 1917. That law made it a crime to encourage disloyalty, interfere with the draft, obstruct recruiting, incite insubordination in the armed forces, or hinder the sale of government bonds.

---

[6]Both libel and slander involve the use of words maliciously—with vicious purpose—to injure a person's character or reputation or expose that person to public contempt, ridicule, or hatred. Truth is generally an absolute defense against a libel or slander claim.

[7]Espionage, sabotage, and treason are often confused with sedition. Espionage is spying for a foreign power. Sabotage involves an act of destruction intended to hinder a nation's war or defense effort. Treason can be committed only in time of war and can consist only of levying war against the United States or giving aid and comfort to its enemies.

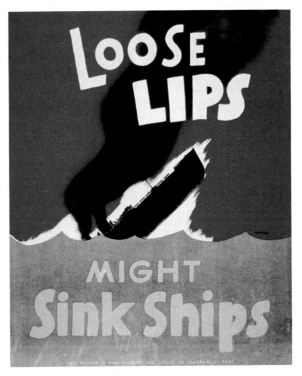

▲ This poster warned of the dangers of careless talk and espionage during World War II. *Critical Thinking How might careless conversation endanger ships during wartime?*

The act also made it a crime to "willfully utter, print, write, or publish any disloyal, profane, scurrilous, or abusive language about the form of government of the United States."

More than 2,000 persons were convicted for violating the Espionage Act. The constitutionality of the law was upheld several times, most importantly in *Schenck* v. *United States,* 1919. Charles Schenck, an officer of the Socialist Party, had been found guilty of obstructing the war effort. He had sent fiery leaflets to some 15,000 men who had been drafted, urging them to resist the call to military service.

The Supreme Court upheld Schenck's conviction. The case is particularly noteworthy because the Court's opinion, written by Justice Oliver Wendell Holmes, established the "clear and present danger" rule.

PRIMARY Sources *"Words can be weapons. . . . The question in every case is whether the words used are used in such circumstances and are of such nature as to create a clear and present danger that they will bring about the substantive evils that Congress has a right to prevent. "*

—Opinion of the Court

In short, the rule says that words can be out-lawed. Those who utter them can be punished when the words they use trigger an immediate danger that criminal acts will follow.

The Smith Act of 1940

Congress passed the Smith Act in 1940, just over a year before the United States entered World War II. That law is still on the books. It makes it a crime for anyone to advocate the violent overthrow of the government of the United States, to distribute any material that teaches or advises violent overthrow, or to knowingly belong to any group with such an aim.

The Court upheld the Smith Act in *Dennis* v. *United States*, in 1951. Eleven Communist Party leaders had been convicted of advocating the overthrow of the Federal Government. On appeal, they argued that the law violated the 1st Amendment's guarantees of freedom of speech and press. They also claimed that no act of theirs constituted a clear and present danger to this country. The Court disagreed, and modified Justice Holmes's doctrine as it did so:

> **PRIMARY Sources** ❝*An attempt to overthrow the government by force, even though doomed from the outset because of inadequate numbers or power of the revolutionists, is a sufficient evil for Congress to prevent. . . .*❞
>
> —Chief Justice Fred M. Vinson, Opinion of the Court

Later, however, the Court modified that holding in several cases. In *Yates* v. *United States*, 1957, for example, the Court overturned the Smith Act convictions of several Communist Party leaders. It held that merely to urge someone to *believe* something, in contrast to urging that person to do something, cannot be made illegal. In *Yates* and other Smith Act cases, the Court upheld the constitutionality of the law, but interpreted its provisions so that their enforcement became practically impossible.

Obscenity

The 1st and 14th amendments do not protect obscenity, but in recent years the Court has had to wrestle with these questions: What language and images in printed matter, films, and other materials are, in fact, obscene? What restrictions can be properly placed on such materials?

Congress passed the first of a series of laws to prevent the mailing of obscene matter in 1872. The current law, upheld by the Court in *Roth* v. *United States*, 1957, excludes "every obscene, lewd, lascivious, or filthy" piece of material from the mails. The Court found the law a proper exercise of the postal power (Article I, Section 8, Clause 7), and so not prohibited by the 1st Amendment. *Roth* marked the Court's first attempt to define obscenity.

Today, the leading case is *Miller* v. *California*, 1973. There, the Court laid down a three-part test to determine what material is obscene and what is not.

A book, film, recording, or other piece of material is legally obscene if (1) "the average person applying contemporary [local] community standards" finds that the work, taken as a whole, "appeals to the prurient interest"—that is, tends to excite lust; (2) "the work depicts or describes, in a patently offensive way," a form of sexual conduct specifically dealt with in an antiobscenity law; and (3) "the work, taken as a whole, lacks serious literary, artistic, political, or scientific value."

A sampling of Supreme Court decisions involving local attempts to regulate so-called adult book stores and similar places shows how thorny the problem can be. Most of what those stores sell cannot be mailed, sent across State lines, or imported—at least not legally. Still, those shops are usually well-stocked.

The 1st and 14th amendments do not prevent a city from regulating the location of "adult entertainment establishments," said the Court in

"The Small Society," by Yates-Brickman. Washington Star Syndicate, Inc.

Interpreting Political Cartoons This kind of "free speech" is clearly not what is covered by the 1st Amendment. *What other kinds of speech are not protected by the Constitution?*

Young v. *American Mini Theaters, 1976.* In *City of Renton* v. *Playtimes Theaters, Inc.,* 1986, the Court ruled that a city can decide to bar the location of such places within 1,000 feet of a residential zone, church, park, or school. But a city cannot prohibit live entertainment in any and all commercial establishments, according to *Schad* v. *Borough of Mount Ephraim,* 1981 (a case that involved nude dancing in adult book stores).

The Supreme Court has upheld a State law that makes it a crime to possess or view child pornography, including films. In *Osborne* v. *Ohio,* 1990, the Court ruled that the State has a compelling interest in protecting the physical and the psychological well-being of minors and in the destruction of the market in which they are exploited.

In their most recent case involving obscenity and the First Amendment, *City of Erie* v. *Pap's A&M,* 2000, the Court upheld the power of cities to ban taverns, bars, and similar places that feature nude dancing. It found Erie's city ordinance constitutional because that law is not aimed at limiting free expression; instead, it limits the *means* of expression—that is, nude (as distinguished from other forms of) dancing.

Prior Restraint

The Constitution allows government to punish some utterances *after* they are made. But, with almost no exceptions, government cannot place any **prior restraint** on spoken or written words. Except in the most extreme situations, government cannot curb ideas *before* they are expressed.

Near v. *Minnesota,* 1931, is a leading case in point. The Supreme Court struck down a State law that prohibited the publication of any "malicious, scandalous, and defamatory" periodical. Acting under that law, a local court had issued an order forbidding the publication of the *Saturday Press.* This Minneapolis paper had printed several articles charging public corruption and attacking "grafters" and "Jewish gangsters."

The Court held that the guarantee of a free press does not allow a prior restraint on publication, except in such extreme cases as wartime, or when a publication is obscene or incites violence. The Court said that even "miscreant purveyors of scandal" and anti-Semitism have this constitutional protection.

Voices on Government

Katharine Graham was publisher of the *Washington Post* when the paper decided to print the "Pentagon Papers" despite the government's attempt to bar their publication. The case *New York Times* v. *United States,* 1971, was a strong challenge to freedom of the press. Graham wrote about it in her autobiography:

❝ *Basically, we were challenging the right of the executive branch to prevent a newspaper from publishing material we believed should be available to the public. In court, we had challenged the government's contention that the material in the Papers was too sensitive for the public eye. . . . Though the decision was in favor of allowing the newspapers to publish, there was . . . 'no ringing reaffirmation of First Amendment guarantees that all publishers yearn to hear.'* ❞

Evaluating the Quotation

From what you have read, who do you think should make the decision about what news should be published—the newspapers or the government? What would be the effects of your answer?

The Constitution does not forbid any and all forms of prior censorship, but "a prior restraint on expression comes to this Court with a 'heavy presumption' against its constitutionality," according to *Nebraska Press Association* v. *Stuart,* 1976.[8] The Court has used that general rule several times—for example, in the famous Pentagon Papers Case, *New York Times* v. *United States,* 1971.

In that case, several newspapers had obtained copies of a set of classified documents, widely known as the Pentagon Papers. Officially titled *History of U.S. Decision-Making Process on Viet Nam Policy,* these documents had been stolen from the Defense Department and then leaked to the press.

---

[8]In this case a judge had ordered the media not to report certain details of a murder trial. The Court held the judge's gag order to be unconstitutional.

► These teenagers should not be admitted to R-rated movies. **Critical Thinking** Does the 1st Amendment protect their right to see whatever movie they wish? Why or why not?

The government sought a court order to bar their publication. The Court, however, held that the government had not shown that printing the Pentagon Papers would endanger the nation's security. The government thus had not overcome the "heavy presumption" against prior censorship.

The few prior restraints the Court has approved include:

• regulations prohibiting the distribution of political literature on military bases without the approval of military authorities, *Greer* v. *Spock*, 1976;

• a CIA rule that agents must agree never to publish anything about the agency without the CIA's permission, *Snepp* v. *United States*, 1980;

• a federal prison rule that allows officials to prevent an inmate from receiving publications considered "detrimental to the security, good order, or discipline" of the prison, *Thornburgh* v. *Abbott*, 1989.

The Court has also said that public school officials have a broad power to censor school newspapers and plays, as well as other "school-sponsored expressive activities." In *Hazelwood School District* v. *Kuhlmeier*, 1988, it held that educators can exercise "editorial control over the style and content of student speech in school-sponsored expressive activities so long as their actions are reasonably related to legitimate pedagogical concerns."

The Media

The 1st Amendment stands as a monument to the central importance of the media in a free society. That raises this question: To what extent can the media—both print and electronic—be regulated by government?

Confidentiality

Can news reporters be forced to testify before a grand jury in court, or before a legislative committee? Can these government bodies require journalists to name their sources and reveal other confidential information? Many reporters and news organizations insist that they must have the right to refuse to testify, the right to protect their sources. They argue that without this right they cannot assure confidentiality, and therefore many sources will not reveal information needed to keep the public informed.

Both State and federal courts have generally rejected the news media argument. In recent years several reporters have refused to obey court orders directing them to give information, and have gone to jail, thus testifying to the importance of these issues.

In the leading case, *Branzburg* v. *Hayes*, 1972, the Supreme Court held that reporters, "like other citizens, [must] respond to relevant questions put to them in the course of a valid grand jury investigation or criminal trial." If the media are to receive any special exemptions, said the Court, they must come from Congress and the State legislatures.

To date, Congress has not acted on the Court's suggestion, but some 30 States have passed so-called **shield laws.** These laws give reporters some protection against having to disclose their sources or reveal other confidential information in legal proceedings in those States.

Motion Pictures

The Supreme Court took its first look at motion pictures early in the history of the movie industry. In 1915, in *Mutual Film Corporation* v. *Ohio*, the Court upheld a State law that barred the showing of any film that was not of a "moral, educational, or harmless and amusing character." The Court declared that "the exhibition of moving pictures is a business, pure and simple," and "not . . . part of the press of the country." With that decision, nearly every State and thousands of communities set up movie review (really movie censorship) programs.

The Court reversed itself in 1952, however. In *Burstyn* v. *Wilson*, a New York censorship case, it found that "liberty of expression by means of motion pictures is guaranteed by the 1st and 14th amendments."

Very few local movie review boards still exist. Most movie-goers now depend on the film industry's own rating system and on the comments of movie critics.

Radio and Television

Both radio and television broadcasting are subject to extensive federal regulation. Most of this regulation is based on the often-amended Federal Communications Act of 1934, which is administered by the Federal Communications Commission. In *Red Lion Broadcasting Co.* v. *FCC*, 1969, the Supreme Court acknowledged, "Of all forms of communication, it is broadcasting that has received the most limited 1st Amendment protection."

The Court has several times upheld this wide-ranging federal regulation as a proper exercise of the commerce power. Unlike newspapers and other print media, radio and television use the public's property—the public airwaves—to distribute their materials. They have no right to do so without the public's permission in the form of a proper license, said the Court in *National Broadcasting Co.* v. *United States*, 1943.

The Court has regularly rejected the argument that the 1st Amendment prohibits such regulations. Instead, it has said that regulation of this industry actually implements the constitutional guarantee. In *Red Lion Broadcasting Co.* v. *FCC*, 1969, the Court held that there is no "unabridgeable 1st Amendment right to broadcast comparable to the right of every individual to speak, write, or publish." However, "this is not to say that the 1st Amendment is irrelevant to broadcasting. But . . . it is the right of the viewers and the listeners, not the right of the broadcasters, which is paramount."

Congress has forbidden the FCC to censor the content of programs before they are broadcast. However, the FCC can prohibit the use of indecent language, and it can take violations of this ban into account when a station applies for the renewal of its operating license, according to *FCC* v. *Pacifica Foundation*, 1978.

In several recent decisions, the Supreme Court has given the growing cable television industry broader 1st Amendment freedoms than those enjoyed by traditional television.

United States v. *Playboy Entertainment Group*, 2000, is fairly typical. There, the Court struck down an attempt by Congress to force many cable systems to limit sexually explicit channels to late night hours. The Court agreed that shielding children from such programming is a worthy goal; nevertheless, it found the 1996 law to be a violation of the 1st Amendment.

Symbolic Speech

People also communicate ideas by conduct, by the way they do a particular thing. Thus, a person can "say" something with a facial expression or a shrug of the shoulders, or by carrying a sign or wearing an armband. This expression by conduct is known as **symbolic speech.**

Clearly, not all conduct amounts to symbolic speech. If it did, murder or robbery or any other crime could be excused on grounds that the person who committed the act meant to say something by doing so.

Just as clearly, however, some conduct does express opinion. Take picketing in a labor dispute as an example. **Picketing** involves patrolling of a business site by workers who are on strike. By their conduct, picketers attempt to inform the public of the controversy, and to persuade others not to deal with the firm involved. Picketing is, then, a form of expression. If peaceful, it is protected by the 1st and 14th amendments.

The leading case on the point is *Thornhill* v. *Alabama*, 1940. There, the Court struck down a State law that made it a crime to loiter about or to picket a place of business in order to influence others not to trade or work there. Picketing that is "set in a background of violence," however, can be prevented. Even peaceful picketing can be restricted if it is conducted for an illegal purpose, such as forcing someone to do something that is itself illegal.

▲ These demonstrators were protesting the Vietnam War in 1971. *Critical Thinking Was this demonstration protected by the First Amendment? Why or why not?*

Other Symbolic Speech Cases

Generally, the Supreme Court has been sympathetic to the symbolic speech argument. Still, it has not given blanket First Amendment protection to that means of expression.

United States v. *O'Brien,* 1968, involved four young men who had burned their draft cards to protest the war in Vietnam. A court convicted them of violating a federal law that makes that act a crime. O'Brien appealed, arguing that the First Amendment protects "all modes of communication of ideas by conduct." The Supreme Court disagreed. Said the Court: "We cannot accept the view that an apparently limitless variety of conduct can be labeled 'speech' whenever the person engaging in the conduct intends thereby to express an idea."

The Court also held that acts of dissent by conduct can be punished if: (1) the object of the protest (here, the war and the draft) is within the constitutional powers of the government; (2) whatever restriction is placed on expression is no greater than necessary in the circumstances; and (3) the government's real interest in the matter is not to squelch dissent.

Using that test, the Court has denied some other claims of symbolic speech. Thus, in *Kelley* v. *Johnson,* 1976, it held that a policeman does not have a constitutional right to protest a department dress code by growing long hair. This is true even if the officer believes his actions to be "a means of expressing his attitude and lifestyle." The Court felt that a government has a

reasonable stake in requiring a "similarity of garb and appearance" among its police officers.

Tinker v. *Des Moines School District,* 1969, on the other hand, is one of several cases in which the Court has come down on the side of symbolic speech. A small group of students in the Des Moines public schools had worn black armbands to publicize their opposition to the war in Vietnam. The school suspended them for it.

The Court ruled that school officials had overstepped their authority and violated the Constitution. Said the Court: "It can hardly be argued that either students or teachers shed their constitutional rights to freedom of speech or expression at the schoolhouse gate."[9]

In *Buckley* v. *Valeo,* 1976, the Court found that campaign contributions are "a symbolic expression of support" for candidates, and therefore the making of those contributions is entitled to constitutional protection. Both federal and State laws regulate campaign contributions, but the fact that in politics "money is speech" greatly complicates the whole matter of campaign finance regulation (see Chapter 7).

Flag Burning

Burning the American flag as an act of political protest is expressive conduct protected by the 1st and 14th amendments—so a sharply divided Court has twice held. In *Texas* v. *Johnson,* 1989, a 5–4 majority ruled that State authorities had violated a protester's rights by prosecuting him under a law that forbids the "desecration of a venerated object." Johnson had set fire to an American flag during an anti-Reagan demonstration at the Republican National Convention in Dallas in 1984. Said the Court:

PRIMARY Sources *If there is a bedrock principle underlying the 1st Amendment, it is that the government may not prohibit the expression of an idea simply because society finds the idea itself offensive. . . . We do not consecrate the flag by punishing its desecration, for in doing so we dilute the*

---

[9]Do not read too much into this, for the Court added, it "has repeatedly affirmed the comprehensive authority of the States and of school authorities, consistent with fundamental constitutional safeguards, to prescribe and control conduct in the schools." The fact that in *Tinker* the students' conduct did not cause a substantial disruption of normal school activities was an important factor in the Court's decision.

freedom that this cherished emblem represents. 99

—William J. Brennan, Jr., Opinion of the Court

The Court's decision in *Johnson* set off a firestorm of criticism around the country and prompted Congress to pass the Flag Protection Act of 1989. It, too, was struck down by the Court, 5 to 4, in *United States* v. *Eichman*, 1990. The Court based its decision on the same grounds as those set out a year earlier in *Johnson*.

Commercial Speech

Commercial speech is speech for business purposes; the term refers most often to advertising. Until the mid-1970s, it was thought that the 1st and 14th amendments did not protect such speech. In *Bigelow* v. *Virginia*, 1975, however, the Supreme Court held unconstitutional a State law that prohibited the newspaper advertising of abortion services. The following year, in *Virginia State Board of Pharmacy* v. *Virginia Citizens Consumer Council*, it struck down another Virginia law forbidding the advertisement of prescription drug prices.

Not all commercial speech is protected, however. Thus, government can and does prohibit false and misleading advertisements, and the advertising of illegal goods or services.

In fact, government can even forbid advertising that is neither false nor misleading. Thus, in 1970, Congress banned cigarette ads on radio and television. In 1986, it extended the ban to include chewing tobacco and snuff.

In most of its commercial speech cases, the Court has struck down arbitrary restrictions on advertising. Thus, in *44 Liquormart, Inc.* v. *Rhode Island*, 1996, the Court voided a State law that prohibited ads in which liquor prices were listed. In *Greater New Orleans Broadcasting Ass'n* v. *United States*, 1999, it struck down a federal law that prohibited casino advertising on radio or television.

Most recently, the Court dealt with limits on smokeless tobacco and cigar advertising. Massachusetts had barred outdoor ads for these commodities within 1000 feet of any school or playground. The Court held that limit a violation of the 1st and 14th amendments' guarantee of free speech, *P. Lorillard Co.* v. *Reilly*, 2001.

One of the Court's first commercial speech cases had an interesting twist. In *Wooley* v. *Maynard*, 1977, the Court held that a State cannot force its citizens to act as "mobile billboards." At least, a State cannot do so when the words used conflict with its citizens' religious or moral beliefs. The Maynards, who were Jehovah's Witnesses, objected to the New Hampshire State motto on their automobile license plates. The words *Live Free or Die* clashed with their belief in everlasting life, and so they covered those words with tape. For this, Maynard was arrested three times. On appeal, the Supreme Court sided with Maynard.

Section 3 Assessment

Key Terms and Main Ideas

1. Compare **libel** with **slander**.
2. Why does the government restrict **seditious speech**?
3. (a) Define **prior restraint**. (b) How has the Supreme Court usually dealt with prior restraint cases?
4. In what way is **picketing symbolic speech**?

Critical Thinking

5. **Identifying Alternatives** Do you think journalists should have the right to protect their sources? Describe one instance where this right would benefit society and one instance where it might be harmful.
6. **Identifying Central Issues** The Constitution makes a particular effort to protect the expression of unpopular views.

(a) Why is this important? (b) Do you think even racist or sexist speech and publications should be protected? (c) Explain your answer.

Take It to the Net

7. The States of Kentucky and Virginia passed resolutions in response to the Alien and Sedition Acts. Read the final version of the Kentucky resolution. Make an outline that shows Kentucky's objections to the Alien and Sedition Acts and the actions that the State took in response. Use the links provided in the Social Studies area at the following Web site for help in completing this activity.
www.phschool.com

Participating in Public Debates

The process of debating public issues has never been more "transparent" than it is today. That is, the process is more open to public scrutiny. The increase in media outlets, such as cable TV and the Internet, has created opportunities for people to register their opinions. Use your opportunities to voice your opinions by following these steps:

1. Identify the issue(s) of concern to you. Get in the habit of looking at the morning newspaper or the evening news. If you see something of interest, study the topic further rather than basing your opinions on short TV sound bites. What public issue is of most interest to you?

2. Find out whom to contact. Your opinion counts most when you express it to those people who have some authority or influence on the issue. That could be a government official, a private lobbying group, or a media outlet that reaches many voters. Who might you contact to express your views on your topic? Why?

3. Decide on a strategy for publicizing your opinions. Decide on the best way to get your ideas across. Consider your communications skills—do you express yourself better through speaking or through writing? Which of the strategies in the box at right would be best for you?

4. Present your ideas. Generally, a battle to win the hearts and minds of your fellow citizens is won on the strength of good ideas well presented. What short-term and long-term goals might you seek through participating in public debates?

Indiana teenager Ryan White became a nationally known political activist, speaking and lobbying on behalf of the rights of AIDS patients, prior to his death from AIDS in 1990, at age 19.

Test for Success

Choose an issue that is being publicly debated right now. Follow the steps listed here to develop a strategy for airing your views about it. Write a brief letter to the editor or a newsgroup posting, or prepare an oral argument on the issue.

Make Your Opinions Known

▶ Write a letter to the editor. Your letter should be brief, quickly stating the issue, your opinion, and facts to support your opinion. Letters that are well-reasoned may have more influence than hostile or insulting prose.

▶ Contact a government official or agency. Find out who the decision makers are on your issue.

▶ Join a public interest group or other lobbying organization. You might want to work for a cause you believe in. Find out if there are any requirements for joining, such as fees.

▶ Join an Internet chatroom or newsgroup. Live, "real time" chatrooms let you participate in actual conversations and debates. Consult with your teacher about appropriate groups.

▶ Address a government hearing on an issue of concern to you. Come prepared with facts and a few specific points to make. Be prepared to rebut any opposing arguments.

▶ Participate in a public protest or demonstration of support. Coming together with other activists to rally support and send a loud message can be an exciting way to participate in public debate, if the event is legal and orderly.

▶ Participate in a petition drive. A great way to register grassroots support for an issue or a specific bill is to gather signatures for a petition. You'll learn more about petitions in Chapter 24.

Freedom of Assembly and Petition

Section Preview

OBJECTIVES

1. **Explain** the Constitution's guarantees of assembly and petition.
2. **Summarize** how the government can limit the time, place, and manner of assembly.
3. **Compare and contrast** the freedom-of-assembly issues that arise on public versus private property.
4. **Explore** how the Supreme Court has interpreted freedom of association.

WHY IT MATTERS

The constitutional guarantees of assembly and petition protect Americans' rights to gather peacefully in order to express their views and to influence public policy, by such means as demonstrations and written petitions. There are place, time, and manner limitations on these freedoms, however.

POLITICAL DICTIONARY

★ **assemble**
★ **content neutral**
★ **right of association**

A noisy street demonstration by gay rights activists, or by neo-Nazis, or by any number of other groups; a candlelight vigil of opponents of the death penalty; the pro-life faithful singing hymns as they picket an abortion clinic; pro-choice partisans gathered on the steps of the State capitol . . . these are commonplace events today. They are also everyday manifestations of freedom of assembly and petition.

means as written petitions, letters, or advertisements; lobbying; or parades, marches, or other demonstrations.

Notice, however, that the 1st and 14th amendments protect the rights of *peaceable* assembly and petition. The Constitution does not give people the right to incite others to violence, to block a public street, to close a school, or otherwise to endanger life, property, or public order.

The Constitution's Guarantees

The 1st Amendment guarantees

> **FROM THE Constitution** **"**. . . *the right of the people peaceably to assemble, and to petition the Government for a redress of grievances.* **"**
>
> —United States Constitution

The 14th Amendment's Due Process Clause also protects those rights of assembly and petition against actions by the States or their local governments.

The Constitution protects the right of the people to **assemble**—to gather with one another—to express their views on public matters. It protects their right to organize to influence public policy, whether in political parties, interest groups, or other organizations. It also protects the people's right to bring their views to the attention of public officials by such varied

◀ A silent vigil is one form of assembly protected by the 1st Amendment.

Time-Place-Manner Regulations

Government can make and enforce reasonable rules covering the time, place, and manner of assemblies. Thus, in *Grayned* v. *City of Rockford,* 1972, the Supreme Court has upheld a city ordinance that prohibits making a noise or causing any other diversion near a school if that action disrupts school activities. It has also upheld a State law that forbids parades near a courthouse when they are intended to influence court proceedings, in *Cox* v. *Louisiana,* 1965.

Rules for keeping the public peace must be more than reasonable, however. They must also be precisely drawn and fairly administered. In *Coates* v. *Cincinnati,* 1971, the Court struck down a city ordinance that made it a crime for "three or more persons to assemble" on a sidewalk or street corner "and there conduct themselves in a manner annoying to persons passing by, or to occupants of adjacent buildings." The Court found the ordinance much too vague.

Government's rules must be **content neutral.** That is, while government can regulate assemblies on the basis of time, place, and manner, it cannot regulate assemblies on the basis of what might be said there. Thus, in *Forsyth County* v. *Nationalist Movement,* 1992, the Court threw out a Georgia county's ordinance that levied a fee of up to $1,000 for public demonstrations.

The law was contested by a white supremacist group seeking to protest the creation of a holiday to honor Martin Luther King, Jr. The Court found the ordinance not to be content neutral, particularly because county officials had unlimited power to set the exact fee to be paid by any group.

Notice that the power to control traffic or keep a protest rally from becoming a riot *can* be used as an excuse to prevent speech. The line between crowd control and thought control can be very thin, indeed.

Public Property

Over the past several years, most of the Court's freedom of assembly cases have involved organized demonstrations. Demonstrations are, of course, assemblies.

Most demonstrations take place in public places, on streets and sidewalks, in parks or public buildings, and so on. Demonstrations take place in these locations because it is the public the demonstrators want to reach.

Demonstrations almost always involve some degree of conflict. Most often, they are held to protest something, and so there is an inherent clash of ideas. Many times there is also a conflict with the normal use of streets or other public facilities. It is hardly surprising, then, that the tension can sometimes rise to a serious level.

Given all this, the Supreme Court has often upheld laws that require advance notice and permits for demonstrations in public places. In an early leading case, *Cox* v. *New Hampshire,* 1941, it unanimously approved a State law that required a license to hold a parade or other procession on a public street.

Right-to-demonstrate cases raise many basic and thorny questions. How and to what extent can government regulate demonstrators and their demonstrations? Does the Constitution require that police officers allow an unpopular group to continue to demonstrate when its activities have excited others to violence? When, in the name of public peace and safety, can police properly order demonstrators to disband?

Gregory v. *Chicago*

Gregory v. *Chicago,* 1969, is an illustrative case. While under police protection, Dick Gregory and others had marched, while singing, chanting, and carrying placards, from city hall to the mayor's home some five miles away. Marching in the streets around the mayor's house, they demanded the firing of the city's school superintendent and an end to de facto segregation in the city's schools.

A crowd of several hundred people, including many residents of the all-white neighborhood, quickly gathered. Soon, the bystanders began throwing insults and threats, as well as rocks, eggs, and other objects. The police tried to keep order, but after about an hour, they decided that serious violence was about to break out. At that point, they ordered the demonstrators to leave the area. When Gregory and the others failed to do so, the police arrested them and charged them with disorderly conduct.

The convictions of the demonstrators were unanimously overturned by the High Court. The Court noted that the marchers had done no

▲ **Peaceful Protest** Elian Gonzales, a five-year-old Cuban boy, was rescued after his boat sank while fleeing Cuba for the United States. These demonstrators gathered in Miami to show their support for Elian to remain in this country.

more than exercise their constitutional rights of assembly and petition. Neighborhood residents and others, not the demonstrators, had caused the disorder. So long as the demonstrators acted peacefully, they could not be punished for disorderly conduct.

Recent Cases

Over recent years, many of the most controversial demonstrations have been those held by Operation Rescue and other anti-abortion groups. For the most part, the efforts of those groups have been aimed at discouraging women from seeking the services of abortion clinics, and those efforts have generated many lawsuits.

There have been two particularly notable cases to date. In the first one, *Madsen* v. *Women's Health Services, Inc.,* 1994, the Supreme Court upheld a Florida judge's order directing protesters not to block access to an abortion clinic. The judge's order had drawn a 36-foot buffer zone around the clinic. The High Court found that to be a reasonable limit on the demonstrators' activities.

The other major case is a more recent one, *Hill* v. *Colorado,* 2000. There, the Court upheld, 5–4, a State law that limits "sidewalk counseling" at clinics where abortions are performed. That statute creates an eight-foot buffer zone around anyone who is within 100 feet of the entrance to a health-care facility and wants to enter. No one may make an "unwanted approach" (invade that buffer zone) to talk or do such other things as hand out a leaflet or wave a sign.

The Court found that the Colorado law does not deal with the content of abortion protestors' speech. Instead it is aimed at where, when, and how their message is delivered.

Private Property

What of demonstrations on private property— for example, at shopping centers? The Court has heard only a few cases raising this question. However, at least this much can be said: The rights of assembly and petition do not give people a right to trespass on private property, even if they wish to express political views.

Privately owned shopping centers are not public streets, sidewalks, parks, and other "places of public assembly." Thus, no one has a constitutional right to do such things as hand out political leaflets or ask people to sign petitions in those places.

These comments are based on the leading case here, *Lloyd Corporation* v. *Tanner,* 1972. However, since that case the Court has held this: A State supreme court may interpret the provisions of that State's constitution in such a way as to require the owners of shopping centers to allow the reasonable exercise of the right of petition on their private property.

In that event, there is no violation of the property owners' rights under any provision in the federal Constitution. A case in point is *PruneYard Shopping Center* v. *Robins,* 1980. Several California high school students had set up a card table in the shopping center. They passed out

Interpreting Political Cartoons *How do you think the Supreme Court might rule in a case like this: for the boys (freedom of association) or for the girl (anti-discrimination)? Explain your answer.*

pro-Israeli pamphlets and asked passersby to sign petitions to be sent to the President and Congress.

Freedom of Association

The guarantees of freedom of assembly and petition include a **right of association.** That is, those guarantees include the right to associate with others to promote political, economic, and other social causes. That right is not set out in so many words in the Constitution. However, in *National Association for the Advancement of Colored People* v. *Alabama,* 1958, the Supreme Court said "it is beyond doubt that freedom to engage in association for the advancement of

beliefs and ideas is an inseparable aspect" of the Constitution's guarantees of free expression.

The case just cited is one of the early right-to-associate cases. There, a State law required the Alabama branch of the NAACP to disclose the names of all its members in that State. When the organization refused a court's order to do so, it was found in contempt of court and fined $100,000.

The Supreme Court overturned the contempt conviction. It said that it could find no legitimate reason why the State should have the NAACP's membership list.

The Court's most recent case bearing on freedom of association involved the Boy Scouts of America. In *Boy Scouts of America* v. *Dale,* 2000, it held that the Boy Scouts have a constitutional right to exclude gays from their organization. The High Court made that decision in a New Jersey case, noting that opposition to homosexuality is a part of the Boy Scout organization's "expressive conduct"—that is, what they stand for.

The decision overturned a ruling by the New Jersey Supreme Court. That court had applied the State's anti-discrimination law against the Scouts; it ordered a New Jersey troop to readmit James Dale, an Eagle Scout, whom the troop had dismissed when it learned he was gay.

The Court ruled that the Constitution's guarantee of freedom of association means that a State cannot force an organization like the Boy Scouts to accept members when that action would contradict what the organization professes to believe.

Section 4 Assessment

Key Terms and Main Ideas

1. What does the right to **assemble** peaceably mean? Give two examples of peaceful assembly for political purposes.
2. Summarize briefly how the Supreme Court has limited the time, place, and manner of assembly.
3. How does the **right of association** extend the right of assembly?

Critical Thinking

4. **Identifying Central Issues** Why are the freedom to assemble peacefully and the freedom of association central to an open, democratic society?
5. **Formulating Questions** Not all assembly is protected by the 1st Amendment. Suppose you are helping to organize

a demonstration for a political cause. Make up three to five questions you should ask in order to determine if your demonstration would be considered constitutional by the Supreme Court.

 Take It to the Net

6. Read about the history of the right to assemble. Create a time line showing what you think are the most important events in the evolution of this right, first in England and later in the American colonies and the United States. Include at least seven events. Use the links provided in the Social Studies area at the following Web site for help in completing this activity. **www.phschool.com**

on the Supreme Court

May Schools Ban Political Protests?

In order to educate students and also to ensure their safety, school officials need broad authority to control what goes on in schools. Recognizing this fact, the courts have granted schools flexibility in certain areas, such as censorship. Can schools prevent students from peacefully expressing opinions on controversial political issues?

Tinker v. *Des Moines School District* (1969)

In December 1965, a group of students and adults in Des Moines, Iowa, met to discuss ways of publicizing their opposition to the war in Vietnam and their support for a truce in the fighting. The group included 15-year-old high school student John Tinker, his sister Mary Beth Tinker, and his friend Christopher Eckhardt. The three students decided to wear black armbands through the end of the holiday season and to fast on two days.

The principals of the Des Moines schools learned of the plans to wear armbands. They met on December 14 and adopted a policy that any student wearing an armband would be asked to remove it. Anyone refusing to comply would be suspended.

On December 16, Mary Beth and Christopher wore their armbands to school. John wore his the following day. All were sent home and were suspended until they returned without the armbands. They did not return to school until January, when the planned time for wearing the armbands had expired. The students' fathers filed suit in federal district court, seeking a court order to prevent enforcement of the school district's ban on armbands. They also asked that the school district not be allowed to discipline the students for wearing them. The court found that the school authorities' actions did not violate the Constitution. The court of appeals agreed with the district court, and the Tinkers appealed to the Supreme Court.

Arguments for Tinker

1. Wearing an armband to express an opinion is symbolic speech that is protected under the Free Speech Clause of the 1st Amendment.

2. Students do not lose their 1st Amendment rights when they are in school. School authorities may restrict speech or action that interferes with the work of the school but may not prohibit silent, passive expressions of opinion that create no such interference.

3. Schools may not limit expressions of opinion to avoid confrontation or disagreement among students over politically sensitive issues.

Arguments for Des Moines School District

1. States and school officials must have complete authority to control conduct in public schools in order to maintain discipline and good order.

2. The ban on armbands was reasonable because it was based upon fear of a disturbance in school.

3. The plaintiffs' wearing of armbands distracted other students from their classwork and diverted them to the highly emotional subject of the Vietnam War. Schools have the right to adopt reasonable regulations to keep students focused on school subjects.

Decide for Yourself

1. Review the constitutional grounds on which each side based its arguments and the specific arguments each side presented.

2. Debate the opposing viewpoints presented in this case. Which viewpoint do you favor?

3. Predict the impact of the Court's decision on other issues relating to students' rights. (To read a summary of the Court's decision, turn to the Supreme Court Glossary on page 799.)

Political Dictionary

Bill of Rights (p. 532)

civil liberties (p. 533)

civil rights (p. 533)

alien (p. 534)

Due Process Clause (p. 535)

process of incorporation (p. 535)

Establishment Clause (p. 537)

parochial (p. 538)

Free Exercise Clause (p. 542)

libel (p. 546)

slander (p. 547)

sedition (p. 547)

seditious speech (p. 547)

prior restraint (p. 549)

shield law (p. 550)

symbolic speech (p. 551)

picketing (p. 551)

assemble (p. 555)

content neutral (p. 556)

right of association (p. 558)

Practicing the Vocabulary

Using Terms in Context For each of the terms below, write a sentence that shows how it relates to this chapter.

1. Bill of Rights
2. civil liberties
3. Due Process Clause
4. process of incorporation
5. Establishment Clause
6. Free Exercise Clause
7. prior restraint
8. symbolic speech
9. assemble
10. right of association

Word Relationships Three of the terms in each of the following sets of terms are related. Choose the term that does not belong and explain why it does not.

11. **(a)** libel **(b)** slander **(c)** symbolic speech **(d)** seditious speech
12. **(a)** civil liberties **(b)** shield law **(c)** civil rights **(d)** right of association
13. **(a)** Bill of Rights **(b)** Free Exercise Clause **(c)** Establishment Clause **(d)** prior restraint
14. **(a)** parochial **(b)** picketing **(c)** assemble **(d)** symbolic speech

Reviewing Main Ideas

Section 1

15. **(a)** Why was there an outcry when the Constitution did not originally contain a general listing of the rights of the people? **(b)** How was this remedied?
16. How does federalism affect the guarantees of individual rights?
17. **(a)** Explain this statement: Rights are relative, not absolute. **(b)** What happens when rights conflict?
18. How does the Due Process Clause of the 14th Amendment affect the guarantees in the Bill of Rights?

Section 2

19. What does the Establishment Clause say that the government cannot do?
20. Describe three Establishment Clause issues regarding education that the Supreme Court has addressed.
21. What are the three elements of the *Lemon* test?
22. Identify three ways in which government may restrict the exercise of religious belief.

Section 3

23. What are the two elements of the free exchange of ideas, and why are they both important in a democracy?

24. Why has the Supreme Court upheld prohibitions of **(a)** slander and libel, **(b)** seditious speech, and **(c)** obscenity.
25. What has generally been the Supreme Court's attitude toward prior restraint?
26. **(a)** What is the press argument in favor of shield laws? **(b)** How has the Supreme Court generally responded to press confidentiality issues?
27. Why can radio and television be regulated more strictly than other forms of the media?
28. Describe briefly one case in which the Supreme Court upheld a restriction on symbolic speech and one case where it struck down a restriction.

Section 4

29. Describe the time, place, and manner limits that the government can put on freedom of assembly.
30. **(a)** What is the right of association? **(b)** Since it is not expressly granted in the Constitution, what is the origin of this right?

Critical Thinking

31. *Applying the Chapter Skill* There are a number of interest groups that focus on 1st Amendment issues. Contact a group that takes a stand on an issue that interests you, and find out what its position is, how it goes about promoting its cause, and how successful the group has been. Summarize this information, and state whether you think the group is one that you might wish to join.

32. *Determining Relevance* According to Justice Holmes, one of the most important protections offered by the Bill of Rights is protection of "thought that we hate." **(a)** Explain briefly what this protection means, and why it is so important. **(b)** Then, from your knowledge of history or current affairs, discuss one example of a repressive government suppressing speech that it hates, and the repercussions of that repression.

33. *Drawing Conclusions* Your school newspaper wants to publish an article critical of one board member's speech at a school board meeting. The principal has forbidden publication of the article because it is disrespectful, misquotes the board member, and states a position that the school administration does not agree with. What constitutional issues does the principal's action raise? Explain how you think the Supreme Court would rule on each of these issues.

Analyzing Political Cartoons

Using your knowledge of American government and this cartoon, answer the questions below.

Since you have already been convicted by the media, I imagine we can wrap this up pretty quickly.

34. (a) In the caption of this cartoon, what does "convicted by the media" mean? **(b)** How can this kind of conviction affect a trial?

35. What do you think the cartoonist feels about the right of a free press versus the right to a fair trial?

★ **You Can Make a Difference**

How much freedom of speech do you think students should have, in or out of school? What issues of censorship and free speech have arisen in your school and community? Prepare a list of questions to use in interviewing the following people on this issue: computer science teachers, the editorial staff and faculty advisers of the school newspaper, the school librarian, and school administrators.

Participation Activities

36 *Current Events Watch* "Speech" on the Internet is unlike expression in other media. Find recent newspaper articles on this topic. List the types of Internet speech some people think should be regulated, the practical difficulties of regulating it, and the 1st Amendment issues raised by each type. Include court cases where applicable.

37. *Table Activity* Make a table of the important Supreme Court cases involving freedom of assembly. Include a very brief description of each case; indicate whether the issue was time, place, or manner of assembly; and give the Supreme Court's ruling.

38. *It's Your Turn* Choose one of the controversial Supreme Court cases discussed in this chapter, and take a position on the issue. Prepare an argument (speech) that you would present to the Supreme Court—for the government or for the other party to the suit. Your argument should not only state and defend your position on the issue but also answer the opposing arguments. **(Writing a Speech)**

 Take It to the Net

Chapter 19 Self-Test As a final review activity, take the Chapter 19 Self-Test in the Social Studies area at the Web site listed below, and receive immediate feedback on your answers.

www.phschool.com

Civil Liberties: Protecting Individual Rights

"Most of all, we have got to remember that the law is people. . . . What we are trying to do is solve people's problems and protect their freedoms and protect their interests."

—Janet Reno (1995)

As Attorney General Reno pointed out, the goal of the law is to serve people, to protect both the rights of individuals and the rights of those accused of crimes. Judges and lawmakers thus constantly debate the spirit of the law and how it applies in real life.

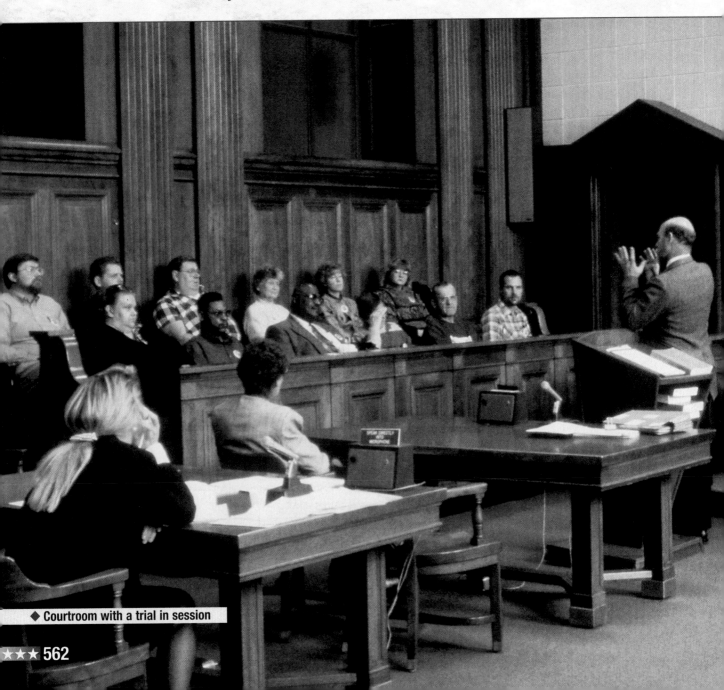

◆ Courtroom with a trial in session

Chapter 20 in Brief

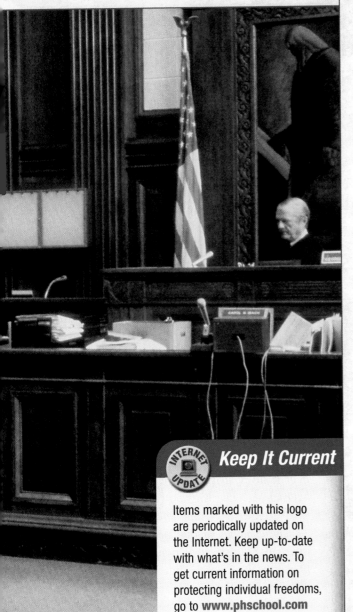

You Can Make a Difference

FOR CORY KADAMANI, "real life" once meant drugs, dropping out, and run-ins with the New York City police. Then he turned his life around, earning a high school equivalency diploma and joining Youth Force, a community group. At age 17, Cory helped create the group's South Bronx Community Justice Center to resolve neighborhood issues before they led to crimes. Young people— including former gang members—worked with lawyers, community leaders, and probation officers. Cory also advised younger kids awaiting trial at a South Bronx detention facility. He hoped his story would keep them from making the same mistakes he had made.

Keep It Current

Items marked with this logo are periodically updated on the Internet. Keep up-to-date with what's in the news. To get current information on protecting individual freedoms, go to **www.phschool.com**

SECTION 1

Due Process of Law (pp. 564–568)

★ The 5th and 14th amendments guarantee that the government cannot deprive a person of "life, liberty, or property, without due process of law."
★ The States' reserved powers include the police power—the power to protect and promote public health, public safety, public morals, and the general welfare.
★ The exercise of the police power can produce conflicts with individual rights.
★ The constitutional guarantees of due process create a right of privacy.
★ The most controversial applications of the right of privacy involve abortion.

SECTION 2

Freedom and Security of the Person (pp. 569–574)

★ The 13th Amendment was added to the Constitution in 1865 to end slavery and involuntary servitude.
★ The 2nd Amendment was added to the Constitution to preserve the right of States to keep a militia.
★ The 4th Amendment prohibits unreasonable searches and seizures, not those which are reasonable. The amendment has given rise to the controversial Exclusionary Rule.

SECTION 3

Rights of the Accused (pp. 576–583)

★ Rights of the accused include the writ of habeas corpus and a constitutional ban on bills of attainder and ex post facto laws.
★ The 5th Amendment says that one may be accused of a serious federal crime only by grand jury indictment.
★ Accused persons are guaranteed a speedy and public trial. They cannot, however, be tried twice for the same crime.
★ The accused also have the right to a trial by jury.
★ The right to an adequate defense and the guarantee against self-incrimination help safeguard the rights of the accused.

SECTION 4

Punishment (pp. 585–588)

★ A person accused of a crime is presumed innocent until proven guilty.
★ The accused must not face excessive bail or fines.
★ The Constitution prohibits cruel and unusual punishment.
★ The Supreme Court has consistently held that the death penalty is constitutional if it is applied fairly.
★ The crime of treason is specifically defined in the Constitution to prevent its use for political purposes.

Section Preview

OBJECTIVES

1. **Explain** the meaning of due process of law as set out in the 5th and 14th amendments.
2. **Define** police power and understand its relationship to civil rights.
3. **Describe** the right of privacy and its origins in constitutional law.

WHY IT MATTERS

The guarantees of due process mean that government must act fairly and in accordance with established rules. The States possess the power to safeguard the well-being of their people through the police power. But in doing so, they must observe due process rights, including the right of privacy.

POLITICAL DICTIONARY

★ **due process**
★ **substantive due process**
★ **procedural due process**
★ **police power**
★ **search warrant**

A re you familiar with the riots that took place in Tulsa, Oklahoma, on May 31– June 1, 1921? Are you aware of the conduct of some officers in the Ramparts Division of the Los Angeles police department much more recently? Both of these matters have been the subject of extensive and ongoing news coverage. Learn what happened in Tulsa in 1921 and what some LAPD officers did much more recently, and you will understand why the concept of due process of law is so very important to you and to everyone in this country.

▲ *A Failure of Due Process* Injured and wounded prisoners are taken to the hospital by the National Guard in the aftermath of the 1921 Tulsa riots.

The Meaning of Due Process

The Constitution contains two **due process** clauses. The 5th Amendment declares that the Federal Government cannot deprive any person of "life, liberty, or property, without due process of law." The 14th Amendment places that same restriction on the States, and, very importantly, on their local governments, as well. A thorough grasp of the meaning of these provisions is absolutely essential to an understanding of the American concept of civil rights.

It is impossible to define the two due process guarantees in exact and complete terms. The Supreme Court has consistently and purposely refused to give them an exact definition. Instead, it has relied on finding the meaning of due process on a case-by-case basis. The Court first described that approach in *Davidson* v. *New Orleans,* 1878, as the "gradual process of inclusion and exclusion, as the cases presented for decision require."

Fundamentally, however, the Constitution's guarantee of due process means this: In whatever it does, government must act fairly and in accord with established rules. It may not act unfairly, arbitrarily, capriciously, or unreasonably.

The concept of due process began and developed in English and then in American law as a procedural concept. That is, it first developed as a requirement that government act fairly, use fair procedures.

Fair procedures are of little value, however, if they are used to administer unfair laws. The Supreme Court recognized this fact toward the end of the nineteenth century. It began to hold that due process requires that both the ways in which government acts *and* the laws under which it acts must be fair. Thus, the Court added the idea of **substantive due process** to the original notion of **procedural due process.**

In short, procedural due process has to do with the *how* (the procedures, the methods) of governmental action. Substantive due process involves the *what* (the substance, the policies) of governmental action.

Examples of Due Process

Any number of cases may be used to illustrate these two elements of due process. Take a classic case, *Rochin* v. *California*, 1952, to exemplify procedural due process.

Rochin was a suspected narcotics dealer. Acting on a tip, three Los Angeles County deputy sheriffs went to his rooming house. They forced their way into Rochin's room. There the deputies found him sitting on a bed, and spotted two capsules on a nightstand. When one of the deputies asked, "Whose stuff is this?" Rochin popped the capsules into his mouth. Although all three officers jumped him, Rochin managed to swallow them.

The deputies took Rochin to a hospital, where his stomach was pumped. The capsules were recovered and found to contain morphine. The State then prosecuted and convicted Rochin for violating the State's narcotics laws.

The Supreme Court held that the deputies had violated the 14th Amendment's guarantee of procedural due process. Said the Court:

 PRIMARY Sources ❝*This is conduct that shocks the conscience. Illegally breaking into the privacy of the petitioner, the struggle to open his mouth and remove what was there, the forcible extraction of his stomach's contents—this course of proceeding by agents of government to obtain evidence is bound to offend even hardened sensibilities. They are methods too close to the rack and the screw. . . .*❞

—Justice Felix Frankfurter,
Opinion of the Court

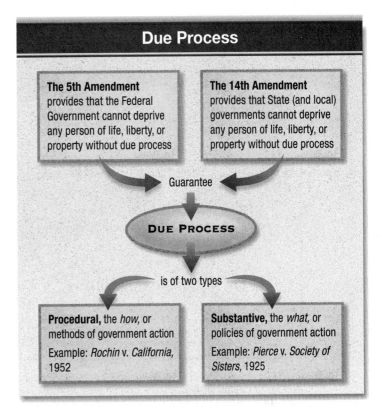

Due Process

The 5th Amendment provides that the Federal Government cannot deprive any person of life, liberty, or property without due process

The 14th Amendment provides that State (and local) governments cannot deprive any person of life, liberty, or property without due process

Guarantee

DUE PROCESS

is of two types

Procedural, the *how,* or methods of government action
Example: *Rochin* v. *California*, 1952

Substantive, the *what,* or policies of government action
Example: *Pierce* v. *Society of Sisters*, 1925

Interpreting Diagrams The 5th and 14th amendments ensure that neither the Federal nor State and local governments can deprive any person of "life, liberty, or property, without due process of law." *Why are procedural and substantive due process both necessary?*

Take *Pierce* v. *Society of Sisters*, 1925, to illustrate substantive due process. In 1922, Oregon's voters had adopted a new compulsory school-attendance law that required all persons between the ages of 8 and 16 to attend public schools. The law was purposely drawn to destroy private, especially parochial, schools in the State.

A Roman Catholic order challenged the law's constitutionality, and the Supreme Court held that the law violated the 14th Amendment's Due Process Clause. The Court did not find that the State had enforced the law unfairly. In fact, the State's courts had found the law unconstitutional, and it had never been put into effect. Rather, the Court held that the law itself, in its contents, "unreasonably interferes with the liberty of parents to direct the upbringing and education of children under their control."

The 14th Amendment and the Bill of Rights

Recall these crucial points from Chapter 19:

1. The provisions of the Bill of Rights apply against the National Government *only*.

"What's so great about due process? Due process got me ten years."

Interpreting Political Cartoons *Can you assume that the prisoner's complaint is justified? Explain your answer.*

2. However, the Supreme Court has held that the 14th Amendment's Due Process Clause includes within its meaning most of the protections set out in the Bill of Rights.

In a long series of decisions dating from 1925, the Court extended the protections of the Bill of Rights against the States through the 14th Amendment's Due Process Clause. The landmark cases in which this occurred are set out in the table on page 536—and with them the few (four) provisions in the Bill of Rights that have *not* been incorporated.

The key 1st Amendment cases were discussed in Chapter 19. Those involving the 4th through the 8th amendments are treated in Sections 2–4 of this chapter.

The Police Power

In the federal system, the reserved powers of the States include the broad and important **police power.** The police power is the authority of each State to act to protect and promote the public health, safety, morals, and general welfare. In other words, it is the power of each State to safeguard the well-being of its people.

The use of the police power often produces conflicts with civil rights protections. When

it does, courts must strike a balance between the needs of society, on the one hand, and of individual freedoms on the other. Any number of cases can be used to illustrate the conflict between police power and individual rights. Take as an example a matter often involved in drunk-driving cases.

Every State's laws allow the use of one or more tests to determine whether a person arrested and charged with drunk driving was in fact drunk at the time of the incident. Some of those tests are simple: walking a straight line or touching the tip of one's nose, for example. Some are more sophisticated, however, notably the breathalyzer test and the drawing of a blood sample.

Does the requirement that a person submit to such a test violate his or her rights under the 14th Amendment? Does the test involve an unconstitutional search for and seizure of evidence? Does it amount to forcing a person to testify against himself or herself (unconstitutional compulsory self-incrimination)? Or is the requirement a proper use of the police power?

Time after time, State and federal courts have come down on the side of the police power. They have upheld the right of society to protect itself against drunk drivers and rejected individual rights.

The leading case is *Schmerber* v. *California,* 1966. The Court found no objection to a situation in which a police officer had directed a doctor to draw blood from a drunk-driving suspect. The Court emphasized these points: The blood sample was drawn in accord with accepted medical practice. The officer had reasonable grounds to believe that the suspect was drunk. Further, had the officer taken time to secure a **search warrant**—a court order authorizing a search— the evidence could have disappeared from the suspect's system.

Legislators and judges have often found the public's health, safety, morals, and/or welfare to be of overriding importance. For example:

1. To promote health, States can limit the sale of alcoholic beverages and tobacco, make laws to combat pollution, and require the vaccination of school children.

2. To promote safety, States can forbid concealed weapons, require the use of seat belts, and punish drunk drivers.

3. To promote morals, States can outlaw gambling, the sale of obscene materials, and the practice of prostitution.

4. To promote the general welfare, States can enact compulsory education laws, provide help to the medically needy, and limit the profits of public utilities.

Clearly, governments cannot use the police power in any unreasonable or unfair way. In short, they cannot violate the 14th Amendment's Due Process Clause.

The Right of Privacy

The constitutional guarantees of due process create a right of privacy. As the Supreme Court defined it in *Stanley* v. *Georgia*, 1969, the right of privacy is "the right to be free, except in very limited circumstances, from unwanted governmental intrusions into one's privacy."[1]

The Constitution makes no specific mention of the right of privacy,[2] but the Supreme Court declared its existence in *Griswold* v. *Connecticut*, 1965. That case centered on a State law that outlawed birth-control counseling and prohibited all use of birth-control devices. The Court held the law to be a violation of the 14th Amendment's Due Process Clause—and noted that the State had no business policing the marital bedroom.

Roe v. Wade

The most controversial applications of the right of privacy have come in cases that raise this question: To what extent can a State limit a woman's right to an abortion? The leading case is *Roe* v. *Wade*, 1973. There, the Supreme Court struck down a Texas law that made abortion a crime except when necessary to save the life of the mother.

In *Roe*, the Court held that the 14th Amendment's right of privacy "encompass[es] a woman's decision whether or not to terminate her pregnancy." More specifically, the Court ruled that:

1. In the first trimester of pregnancy (about three months), a State must recognize a woman's right to an abortion—and cannot

---

[1] *Stanley* involved the possession of obscene materials in one's own home. More recently, in one of the "very limited circumstances" acknowledged by the Court, the Court upheld a Georgia law that provides for the punishment of homosexual conduct in the privacy of one's home, *Bowers* v. *Hardwick*, 1986.

[2] Louis Brandeis introduced the notion of a right of privacy in 1890.

CLOSE UP FOUNDATION *Student Poll*

In a recent poll, students were asked which of the following two statements comes closer to their point of view on gun control:

Statement A *We should not enact stronger gun control laws, but instead we should have better enforcement of current gun control laws.*
Statement B *We should enact stronger gun control laws because current laws are too weak.*

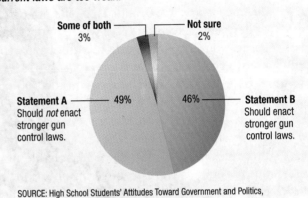

Some of both — 3%
Not sure — 2%

Statement A Should *not* enact stronger gun control laws. — 49%

46% — **Statement B** Should enact stronger gun control laws.

SOURCE: High School Students' Attitudes Toward Government and Politics, Close Up Foundation, May 1999

1. **Analyzing Data** *Approximately how many respondents believe that we should enact stronger gun control laws?*
2. **Conducting Polls** In your own school, conduct a poll asking students whether they favor enacting stronger gun control laws. *How do your results compare to the results shown in this graph?*

interfere with medical judgments in that matter.

2. In the second trimester a State, acting in the interest of women who undergo abortions, can make reasonable regulations about how, when, and where abortions can be performed, but cannot prohibit the procedure.

3. In the final trimester a State, acting to protect the unborn child, can choose to prohibit all abortions except those necessary to preserve the life or health of the mother.

Later Reproductive Rights Cases

In several later cases, the Court rejected a number of challenges to its basic holding in *Roe*. As the composition of the Court has changed, however, so has the Court's position on abortion. That shift can be seen in the Court's decisions in recent cases on the matter.

In *Webster* v. *Reproductive Health Services*, 1989, the Court upheld two key parts of a Missouri law. Those provisions prohibit abortions, except those to preserve the mother's life or health, (1) in any public hospital or clinic in that State, and (2) when the mother is 20 or more weeks pregnant and tests show that the fetus is viable (capable of sustaining life outside the mother's body).

Two cases in 1990 addressed the issue of minors and abortion. In those cases, the Court said that a State may require a minor (1) to inform at least one parent before she can obtain an abortion, *Ohio* v. *Akron Center for Reproductive Health,* 1990, and (2) to tell both parents of her plans, except in cases where a judge gives permission for an abortion without parental knowledge, *Hodgson* v. *Minnesota,* 1990.

The Court's most important decision on the issue since *Roe* v. *Wade* came in *Planned Parenthood of Southeastern Pennsylvania* v. *Casey* in 1992. There the Court announced this rule: A State may place reasonable limits on a woman's right to have an abortion, but these restrictions cannot impose an "undue burden" on her choice of that procedure.

In *Casey,* the Court applied that new standard to Pennsylvania's Abortion Control Act. It upheld sections of that law that say:
• A woman who seeks an abortion must be given professional counseling intended to persuade her to change her mind.
• A woman must delay an abortion for at least 24 hours after that counseling.
• An unmarried female under 18 must have the consent of a parent, or the permission of a judge, before an abortion.

• Doctors and clinics must keep detailed records of all abortions they perform.

Those four requirements do not, said the Court, place "a substantial obstacle in the path of a woman seeking an abortion of a nonviable fetus." That is, they do not impose an "undue burden" on a woman.

The Court did strike down another key part of the Pennsylvania law, however. That provision required that a married woman tell her husband of her plan to have an abortion.

To this point, the Court has decided only one abortion law case since 1992. In *Stenberg* v. *Carhart,* 2000, it applied *Casey's* "undue burden" rule to a Nebraska law and found that statute unconstitutional. The Nebraska law prohibited an operation that the opponents of abortion call "partial birth abortion." That procedure is one that doctors use only infrequently to terminate pregnancies after about 16 weeks.

The Court's 5–4 majority found the Nebraska law to be flawed because it (1) was too loosely drawn, (2) banned a procedure that may in fact be the most medically appropriate way to end some pregnancies, and (3) allowed an exception to protect the life, but not the health, of a pregnant woman. Thirty other States have passed similar laws in recent years, and the Court's decision in *Stenberg* apparently destroyed those statutes, as well.

Section 1 Assessment

Key Terms and Main Ideas

1. Explain what is meant by **due process.**
2. How do **procedural due process** and **substantive due process** differ?
3. **(a)** Define **police power. (b)** How have State and federal courts usually ruled on cases involving the police power and drunk driving suspects?
4. **(a)** What is the right of privacy? **(b)** The most controversial application of the right occurs in cases involving what?

Critical Thinking

5. **Checking Consistency** Considering the constitutional right of privacy, do you think it is proper for a State to use its police power to protect and promote morals among its citizens? Explain your answer.
6. **Identifying Central Issues** Why do you think the Supreme Court has refused to offer an exact definition of due process?
7. **Drawing Conclusions** What would you reply to someone who argues that the use of seat bets is a matter of individual choice?

 Take It to the Net

. Read more about how the Internet and e-mail are creating new challenges to the right of privacy. Summarize these issues in a well-constructed paragraph. Use the links provided in the Social Studies area at the following Web site for help in completing this activity. **www.phschool.com**

Freedom and Security of the Person

Section Preview

OBJECTIVES

1. **Outline** Supreme Court decisions regarding slavery and involuntary servitude.
2. **Explain** the intent and application of the 2nd Amendment's protection of the right to keep and bear arms.
3. **Summarize** the constitutional provisions designed to guarantee security of home and person.

WHY IT MATTERS

Various constitutional provisions protect Americans' right to live in freedom. The 13th Amendment and subsequent civil rights laws prohibit slavery and involuntary servitude. The 2nd Amendment aims to preserve the concept of the citizen-soldier, while the 3rd and 4th amendments protect the security of home and person.

POLITICAL DICTIONARY

★ **involuntary servitude**
★ **discrimination**
★ **writs of assistance**
★ **probable cause**
★ **exclusionary rule**

Several of the Constitution's guarantees are intended to protect the right of every American to live in freedom. This means that the Constitution protects your right to be free from physical restraints, to be secure in your person, and to be secure in your home.

Slavery and Involuntary Servitude

The 13th Amendment was added to the Constitution in 1865, ending over 200 years of slavery in this country. Section 1 of the amendment declares, "Neither slavery nor involuntary servitude, . . . shall exist within the United States, or any place subject to their jurisdiction." Importantly, Section 2 of this amendment gives Congress the expressed power "to enforce this article by appropriate legislation."

Until 1865, each State could decide for itself whether to allow slavery. With the 13th Amendment, that power was denied to them, and to the National Government, as well.

The 13th Amendment: Section 1

As a widespread practice, slavery disappeared more than 135 years ago. There are still occasional cases of it, however. Most often, these cases have involved **involuntary servitude,** or forced labor.

The Thirteenth Amendment does not forbid all forms of involuntary servitude, however. Thus, in 1918, the Court drew a distinction between "involuntary servitude" and "duty" in upholding the constitutionality of the selective service system (the draft).[3] Nor does imprisonment for crime violate the amendment. Finally, note this important point: Unlike any other provision in the Constitution, the 13th Amendment covers the conduct of private individuals as well as that of government.

---

[3] *Selective Draft Law Cases (Arver v. United States),* 1918.

◀ *Involuntary Servitude* In 1999, a New York City couple was charged with forcing a young immigrant woman, Shamela Begum, to live as their unpaid maid.

The 13th Amendment: Section 2

Shortly after the Civil War, Congress passed several civil rights laws based on the 13th Amendment. The Supreme Court, however, sharply narrowed the scope of federal authority in several cases, especially the *Civil Rights Cases*, 1883. In effect, the Court held that racial **discrimination** (bias, unfairness) against African Americans by private individuals did not place the "badge of slavery" on them nor keep them in servitude.

Congress soon repealed most of the laws based on the 13th Amendment. The enforcement of the few that remained was, at best, unimpressive. For years it was generally thought that Congress did not have the power, under either the 13th or 14th Amendment, to act against private parties who practice race-based discrimination.

In *Jones v. Mayer*, 1968, however, the Supreme Court breathed new life into the 13th Amendment. The case centered on one of the post-Civil War acts Congress had not repealed. Passed in 1866, that almost-forgotten law provided in part that

PRIMARY Sources **"**[All] citizens of the United States, . . . of every race and color, . . . shall have the same right, in every State and Territory of the United States, . . . to inherit, purchase, lease, sell, hold, and convey real and personal property . . . as is enjoyed by white citizens. . . .**"**
—Civil Rights Act of 1866

Jones, an African American, had sued because Mayer had refused to sell him a home, solely because of his race. Mayer contended that the 1866 law was unconstitutional, since it sought to prohibit private racial discrimination.

The Court upheld the law, declaring that the 13th Amendment abolished slavery and gave Congress the power to abolish "the badges and incidents of slavery." Said the Court:

PRIMARY Sources **"**At the very least, the freedom that Congress is empowered to secure under the 13th Amendment includes the freedom to buy whatever a white man can buy, the right to live wherever a white man can live.**"**
— Justice Potter Stewart, Opinion of the Court

The Court affirmed that decision in several later cases. Thus, in *Runyon v. McCrary,* 1976, two private schools had refused to admit two African American students. By doing so, the schools had refused to enter into a contract of admission—a contract they had advertised to the general public. The Court found that the schools had violated another provision of the 1866 law:

PRIMARY Sources **"**[All] citizens of the United States, . . . of every race and color, . . . shall have the same right, . . . to make and enforce contracts . . . as is enjoyed by white citizens. . . .**"**
—Civil Rights Act of 1866

The Court has also ruled that the Civil Rights Act of 1866 protects all "identifiable groups who are subject to intentional discrimination solely because of their ancestry or ethnic characteristics"—for example Jews (*Shaare Tefila Congregation v. Cobb,* 1987) and Arabs (*St. Francis College v. Al-Khazraji,* 1987).

More recently the Court has backed off a bit. In *Patterson v. McLean Credit Union,* 1989, it declared that while the 1866 law does prohibit racial discrimination in a contract of employment, any on-the-job discrimination should be handled in accord with the Civil Rights Act of 1964 (see Chapter 21). Nevertheless, the Court has several times held that the 13th Amendment gives Congress significant power to attack "the badges and incidents of slavery," from whatever source they may come.

The Right to Keep and Bear Arms

The 2nd Amendment reads this way:

FROM THE Constitution **"**A well regulated Militia, being necessary to the security of a free State, the right of the people to keep and bear Arms, shall not be infringed.**"**
—United States Constitution

These words excite as much controversy as any words in all of the Constitution. The 2nd Amendment was added to the Constitution to protect the right of each State to keep a militia. The Amendment's aim was to preserve the concept of the citizen-soldier.

Many insist that the 2nd Amendment also sets out an individual right. They say that it guarantees a right to keep and bear arms just as, for example, the 1st Amendment guarantees freedom of speech.

The Supreme Court has never accepted that interpretation of the 2nd Amendment. The only important 2nd Amendment case is *United States* v. *Miller*, 1939. There, the Court upheld a section of the National Firearms Act of 1934. That section made it a crime to ship sawed-off shotguns, machine guns, or silencers across State lines, unless the shipper had registered the weapons with the Treasury Department and paid a $200 license tax. The Court concluded that it could find no reasonable link between the sawed-off shotgun involved in the case and "the preservation . . . of a well-regulated militia."

The Court has not found the 2nd Amendment to be covered by the 14th Amendment's Due Process Clause. Thus, each State can limit the right to keep and bear arms—and all of the States do so, in various ways.

Security of Home and Person

The Constitution provides that the government cannot arbitrarily violate the home or person of any American citizen. These provisions are found in the 3rd and 4th amendments.

The 3rd Amendment

This amendment forbids the quartering (housing) of soldiers in private homes in peacetime without the consent of the owner and not in wartime but "in a manner to be prescribed by law." The guarantee was added to prevent what had been British practice in colonial days. The 3rd Amendment has had almost no importance since its adoption and has never been the subject of a Supreme Court case.

The 4th Amendment

The 4th Amendment also grew out of colonial practice. It was designed to prevent the use of **writs of assistance**—blanket search warrants with which British customs officials had invaded private homes to search for smuggled goods.

Unlike the 3rd Amendment, the 4th Amendment has proved a highly important guarantee. It reads:

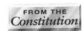 **FROM THE Constitution** "*The right of the people to be secure in their persons, houses, papers, and effects, against unreasonable searches and seizures, shall not be violated, and no Warrants shall issue, but upon probable cause, supported by Oath or affirmation, and particularly describing the place to be searched, and the persons or things to be seized.*"

—United States Constitution

Each State constitution contains a similar provision. The guarantee also applies to the States through the 14th Amendment's Due Process Clause.

Probable Cause

The basic rule laid down by the 4th Amendment is this: Police officers have no general right to search for evidence or to seize either evidence or persons. Except in particular circumstances, they must have a proper warrant (a court order). In addition, the warrant must be obtained with **probable cause**—that is, a reasonable suspicion of crime.

Florida v. *J. L.*, 2000, illustrates this rule. There, Miami police had received an anonymous tip that a teenager was carrying a concealed weapon. Immediately, two officers went to the bus stop where the tipster said the young man could be found. The police located the suspect. They then searched him, pulled a gun from his pocket, and arrested him.

The Supreme Court held that the police acted illegally because they did not have a proper warrant. All they had was an anonymous tip, unsupported by any other evidence. Their conduct amounted to just the sort of thing the 4th Amendment was intended to prevent.

Police do not always need a warrant, however—for example, when evidence is "in plain view." Thus, the Court recently upheld a search and seizure involving two men who were in a friend's apartment bagging cocaine. A policeman spotted them through an open window, entered the apartment, seized the cocaine, and arrested them. The Court rejected their claim to 4th Amendment protection, *Minnesota* v. *Carter*, 1999.

But, again, police must most often have a warrant. Take these two cases to illustrate the point:

Voices on Government

Ruth Bader Ginsburg joined the Supreme Court in 1993. Earlier in her career, she had appeared before the Court several times in cases involving women's rights. She was also a law professor and then a federal judge. When asked about America's greatest challenge, Justice Ginsburg had this answer:

❝ *I thought of Justice Thurgood Marshall's praise of the evolution of the concept 'We the People' to include once excluded, ignored, or undervalued people, then of our nation's motto:* E Pluribus Unum *("of many, one"). The challenge, I responded, is to make and keep our communities places where we can tolerate, even celebrate, our differences, while pulling together for the common good. 'Of many, one' is the main challenge, I believe; it is my hope for our country and world.* ❞

Evaluating the Quotation

How might Justice Ginsburg's feelings about inclusion and tolerance affect her decisions on cases involving individual rights and civil liberties?

• The use of a thermal imaging (heat sensing) device to detect a marijuana-growing operation in an Oregon man's home is a search and is unreasonable without a warrant, *Kyllo* v. *United States,* 2001.

• A public hospital cooperated with police by testing pregnant patients for cocaine use, without their consent. The hospital reported those who tested positive to police. This procedure involved a warrantless search, and so was therefore unconstitutional, *Ferguson* v. *City of Charleston,* 2001.

Arrests

An arrest is the seizure of a person. When officers make a lawful arrest, they do not need a warrant to search "the area within which [the suspect] might gain possession of a weapon or destructible evidence."[4] In fact, most arrests take place without a warrant. Police can arrest a person in a public place without one, provided they have probable cause to believe that person has committed or is about to commit a crime.[5]

Illinois v. *Wardlow,* 2000, illustrates this point. There, four police cars were patrolling a high-crime area in Chicago. When Wardlow spotted them, he ran. An officer chased him down an alley, caught him, and found that Wardlow was carrying a loaded pistol. The Court held, 5–4, that Wardlow's behavior—his flight—gave the police "common sense" grounds on which to believe that he was involved in some criminal activity. (Note, however, that the Court did not hold that police have a blanket power to stop anyone who flees at the sight of a police officer.)

When, exactly, does the 4th Amendment protection come into play? The Court has several times held that this point is reached "only when the officer, by means of physical force or show of authority, has in some way restrained the liberty of a citizen," *Terry* v. *Ohio,* 1968. Thus, the driver of a stolen car was "seized," when deputies blocked his escape by placing an 18-wheel tractor-trailer across both lanes of a two-lane highway, *Brower* v. *Inyo County,* 1989.

Automobiles

The Court has long had difficulty applying the 4th Amendment to automobiles. It has several times held that an officer needs no warrant to search an automobile, a boat, an airplane, or some other vehicle, when there is probable cause to believe that it is involved in illegal activities. This is because such a "movable scene of crime" could disappear while a warrant was being sought.

Carroll v. *United States,* 1925, is an early leading case on the point. There, the Court emphasized that "where the securing of a warrant is reasonably practicable it must be used.... In cases where seizure is impossible except without a warrant, the seizing officer acts unlawfully and at his peril unless he can show the court probable cause."

The Court overturned a long string of automobile search cases in 1991. Before then, it had several times held that a warrant was usually needed to search a glove compartment, a paper

---

[4]This rule was first laid down in *Chimel* v. *California,* 1969.

[5]A person arrested without a warrant must be brought promptly before a judge for a probable cause hearing. In *County of Riverside* v. *McLaughlin,* 1991, the Court held that "promptly" means within 48 hours.

bag, luggage, or other "closed containers" in an automobile. But, in *California* v. *Acevedo*, 1991, the Court set out what it called "one clear-cut rule to govern automobile searches." Whenever police lawfully stop a car, they do not need a warrant to search anything in that vehicle that they have reason to believe holds evidence of a crime. "Anything" includes a passenger's belongings, *Wyoming* v. *Houghton*, 1999.

The Exclusionary Rule

The heart of the guarantee against unreasonable searches and seizures lies in this question: If an unlawful search or seizure does occur, can that "tainted evidence" be used in court? If so, the 4th Amendment offers no real protection to a person accused of crime.

To meet that problem, the Court adopted, and is still refining, the **exclusionary rule**. Essentially, the rule is this: Evidence gained as the result of an illegal act by police cannot be used at the trial of the person from whom it was seized.

The rule was first laid down in *Weeks* v. *United States*, 1914. In this narcotics case, the Court held that evidence obtained illegally by federal officers cannot be used in the federal courts. For more than four decades, however, the Court left questions of the use of such evidence in State courts for each State to decide for itself.

Mapp v. Ohio

In an historic decision in 1961, the exclusionary rule was finally extended to cover the States. In *Mapp* v. *Ohio*, the Court held that the 14th Amendment forbids unreasonable searches and seizures by State and local officers just as the 4th Amendment bars such actions by federal officers. It also held that the fruits of an unlawful search or seizure cannot be used in the State courts, just as they cannot be used in the federal courts.

In *Mapp*, Cleveland police had gone to Dolloree Mapp's home to search for gambling evidence. They entered her home forcibly, and without a warrant. Their very extensive search failed to turn up any gambling evidence, but they did find some obscene books. Mapp was convicted of possession of obscene materials and sentenced to jail. The Court overturned her conviction, holding that the evidence against her had been found and seized without a warrant.

Cases Narrowing the Scope of the Exclusionary Rule

The exclusionary rule has always been controversial. It was intended to put teeth into the 4th Amendment, and it has. It says to police: As you enforce the law, obey the law. The rule seeks to prevent, or at least deter, police misconduct.

Critics of the rule say that it means that some persons who are clearly guilty nonetheless go free. Why, they ask, should criminals be able to "beat the rap" on "a technicality"?

The High Court has narrowed the scope of the rule somewhat over the years—most notably in four cases.

• In *Nix* v. *Williams*, 1984, it found an "inevitable discovery" exception to the rule. The Court ruled that tainted evidence can be used in court if that evidence would have turned up no matter what—"ultimately or inevitably would have been discovered by lawful means."

• In *United States* v. *Leon*, 1984, the Court found a "good faith" exception to the rule. There, federal agents in Los Angeles had used what they thought was a proper warrant to seize illicit drugs. Their warrant was later shown to be faulty, however. The Court upheld their actions nonetheless. It said: "When an officer acting with objective good faith has obtained a search warrant . . . and acted within its scope . . . there is nothing to deter."

• In *Arizona* v. *Evans*, 1995, the Court held that the good faith exception applied in a case where evidence of a crime was seized by police who acted on the basis of a computer printout that later proved to be erroneous. The printout indicated an outstanding arrest warrant against the defendant in the case. In fact, there was no warrant. The computer error was made by court clerks, not the police—who, the Court said, acted in good faith.

• In *Maryland* v. *Garrison*, 1987, the Court gave police room for "honest mistakes." There, it allowed the use of evidence seized in the mistaken search of an apartment in Baltimore. Officers had a warrant to search for drugs in an apartment on the third floor of a building. Not realizing that there were two apartments there, they entered and found drugs in the wrong apartment—the one for which they did not have a warrant.

Drug Testing

Federal drug-testing programs involve searches of persons and so are covered by the 4th Amendment. To date, the Court has held that they can be conducted without either warrants or even any indication of drug use by those who must take them. It did so in two 1989 cases, *Skinner* v. *Federal Railway Labor Executives Association* and *National Treasury Employees Union* v. *Von Raab*.

The Court has also upheld an Oregon school district's drug-testing program, *Vernonia School District* v. *Acton*, 1995. That program required all students who take part in school sports to agree to be tested for drugs. Thus, all student athletes were tested at the beginning of a sports season. Ten percent of the students participating in school sports were chosen at random to be tested each week thereafter.

Wiretapping

Wiretapping, electronic eavesdropping, videotaping, and other more sophisticated means of "bugging" are now quite widely used in the United States. They present difficult search and seizure questions that the authors of the 4th Amendment could not have begun to foresee.

The Supreme Court decided its first wiretap case in 1928. In *Olmstead* v. *United States*, federal agents had tapped a Seattle bootlegger's telephone calls. Their bugs produced evidence that led to Olmstead's conviction. The High Court upheld that conviction. It found that although the agents had not had a warrant, there had been no "actual physical invasion" of Olmstead's home or office—because the phone lines had been tapped *outside* those places.

The leading case today is *Katz* v. *United States*, 1967. There, the Court expressly overruled *Olmstead*. Katz had been convicted of transmitting gambling information across State lines. He had used a public phone booth in Los Angeles to call his contacts in Boston and Miami. Much of the evidence against him had come from an electronic tap planted on the roof—outside—the phone booth.

The Court held that the bugging evidence could not be used against Katz. Despite the fact that Katz was in a public, glass-enclosed phone booth, he was entitled to make a *private* call. Said the Court: the 4th Amendment protects "persons, not just places." It did go on to say, however, that the 4th Amendment can be satisfied in such situations if police obtain a proper warrant before they install a listening device.

Section 2 Assessment

Key Terms and Main Ideas

1. In what sense has the Supreme Court "breathed new life" into the 13th Amendment?
2. Why was the 2nd Amendment added to the Constitution?
3. Define **probable cause**.
4. **(a)** What is the **exclusionary rule**? **(b)** How has its application changed over time?

Critical Thinking

5. **Expressing Problems Clearly** Discuss whether or not you think that people who have clearly committed crimes should be able to go free if their rights are violated during arrest or trial.
6. **Identifying Assumptions** In 1918, the Court ruled that the 13th Amendment's prohibition of involuntary servitude does not apply to the military draft. Identify the assumptions about the relative importance of individual rights and civic duty that underlie this decision.

Take It to the Net

7. Read about probable cause and follow links to learn more about the cases that have shaped our understanding of it. Then choose three cases involving probable cause and prepare a brief oral report describing their importance. Use the links provided in the Social Studies area at the following Web site for help in completing this activity. **www.phschool.com**

SKILLS FOR LIFE

Creating a Multimedia Presentation

Maps help to orient your audience

Use written text for lengthy, complex topics

Add realism with audio/video passages

Create a Web site with quizzes and links

Photographs add visual interest

As chalkboards and typewriters make way for computer and TV monitors, there are many new ways to tell a story. A "report" can include written text, maps, charts, photographs, video clips, audio segments, and Web pages. Use these steps to create an exciting presentation:

1. Define your topic. This step determines the success of your project. Multimedia presentations lend themselves to topics that have a variety of aspects or subtopics. Choose carefully. A topic that's too broad—say, "Civil Liberties"—is difficult to cover thoroughly. How might you narrow that topic?

2. Make a "blueprint"—a plan—for your project. Create a blueprint by brainstorming ideas for covering your topic in various media. First, find out what media are available to you. Then make a detailed plan for how you want to tell your "story." Use the form at right as a model. Assign roles to others involved in the project, if needed. Set a deadline for each main task. Why do you think a blueprint is especially helpful for a multimedia presentation?

3. Develop your presentation. Carry out your project plan by doing research, writing scripts, and gathering materials. You may want to collect more material than you'll use. This gives you flexibility in editing and assembling your work. Aim for an accurate, lively, and logical flow of ideas with coordinated visual and audio content.

4. Present your work. The best presentations are interactive in some way. Try to involve your audience in the presentation.

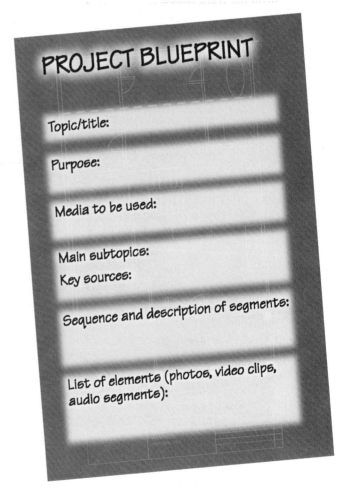

PROJECT BLUEPRINT

Topic/title:

Purpose:

Media to be used:

Main subtopics:

Key sources:

Sequence and description of segments:

List of elements (photos, video clips, audio segments):

Test for Success

Choose a possible topic for a multimedia presentation, and create a project blueprint.

Rights of the Accused

Section Preview

OBJECTIVES

1. **Define** the writ of habeas corpus, bills of attainder, and ex post facto laws.
2. **Outline** how the right to a grand jury and the guarantee against double jeopardy help ensure the rights of the accused.
3. **Describe** issues that arise from the guarantee of a speedy and public trial.
4. **Determine** what constitutes a fair trial by jury.
5. **Examine** the right to an adequate defense and the guarantee against self-incrimination.

WHY IT MATTERS

In the American judicial system, any person who is accused of a crime must be presumed to be innocent until proven guilty. The Constitution, especially in the 5th, 6th, and 14th amendments, contains a number of provisions guaranteeing rights to people accused of a crime.

POLITICAL DICTIONARY

★ **writ of habeas corpus**
★ **bill of attainder**
★ **ex post facto law**
★ **grand jury**
★ **indictment**
★ **double jeopardy**
★ **bench trial**
★ **Miranda Rule**

Think about this statement for a moment: "It is better that ten guilty persons go free than that one innocent person be punished." That maxim expresses one of the bedrock principles of the American legal system.

Of course, society must punish criminals in order to preserve itself. However, the law intends that any person who is suspected or accused of a crime must be presumed innocent until proven guilty by fair and lawful means.

Habeas Corpus

The **writ of habeas corpus,** sometimes called the writ of liberty, is intended to prevent unjust arrests and imprisonments.[6] It is a court order directed to an officer holding a prisoner. It commands that the prisoner be brought before the court and that the officer show cause—explain, with good reason—why the prisoner should not be released.

The right to seek a writ of habeas corpus is protected against the National Government in Article I, Section 9 of the Constitution. That right is guaranteed against the States in each of their own constitutions.

The Constitution says that the right to the writ cannot be suspended, "unless when in Cases of Rebellion or Invasion the public Safety may require it." President Abraham Lincoln suspended the writ in 1861. His order covered various parts of the country, including several areas in which war was not then being waged. Chief Justice Roger B. Taney,

GREELY   LINCOLN   SUMNER   CHASE   WELLES   SEWARD

THE GRAVE OF THE UNION.
OR MAJOR JACK DOWNING'S DREAM. DRAWN BY ZEKE.

Interpreting Political Cartoons This detail from an 1860s cartoon is critical of President Lincoln's 1861 suspension of the writ of habeas corpus. *Why is a coffin labeled "Constitution" being lowered into the ground?*

---

[6]The phrase *habeas corpus* comes from the Latin, meaning "you should have the body," and those are the opening words of the writ.

sitting as a circuit judge, held Lincoln's action unconstitutional.

Taney ruled that the Constitution gives the power to suspend the writ to Congress alone. Congress then passed the Habeas Corpus Act of 1863. It gave the President the power to suspend the writ when and where, in his judgment, that action was necessary. In *Ex parte Milligan,* 1866, the Supreme Court ruled that neither Congress nor the President can legally suspend the writ where there is no actual fighting nor the likelihood of any.

The right to the writ has been suspended only once since the Civil War and the Reconstruction Period that followed it. The territorial governor of Hawaii suspended the writ following the Japanese attack on Pearl Harbor, December 7, 1941. The Supreme Court later ruled that the governor did not have the power to take that action, *Duncan* v. *Kahanamoku,* 1946.

Bills of Attainder

A **bill of attainder** is a legislative act that inflicts punishment without a court trial. Neither Congress nor the States can pass such a measure (Article I, Sections 9 and 10).

The ban on bills of attainder is both a protection of individual freedom and part of the system of separation of powers. A legislative body can pass laws that define crime and set the penalties for violation of those laws. It cannot, however, pass a law that declares a person guilty of a crime and provides for the punishment of that person.

The Supreme Court has held that this prohibition is aimed at all legislative acts that apply "to named individuals or to easily ascertainable members of a group in such a way as to inflict punishment on them without a judicial trial," *United States* v. *Lovett,* 1946.

The Framers wrote the ban on bills of attainder into the Constitution because both Parliament and the colonial legislatures had passed many such bills. Bills of attainder have been rare in our national history, however. *United States* v. *Brown,* 1965, is one of the few cases in which the Court has struck down a law as a bill of attainder. There it overturned a provision of the Landrum-Griffin Act of 1959. That provision made it a federal crime for a member of the Communist Party to serve as an officer of a labor union.

Ex Post Facto Laws

An **ex post facto law** (a law passed after the fact) has three features. It (1) is a criminal law, one defining a crime or providing for its punishment; (2) applies to an act committed before its passage; and (3) works to the disadvantage of the accused. Neither Congress nor the State legislatures may pass such laws.[7]

For example, a law making it a crime to sell marijuana cannot be applied to someone who sold it before that law was passed. Or, a law that changed the penalty for murder from life in prison to death could not be applied to a person who committed a murder before the punishment was changed.

Ex post facto cases do not come along very often. The Court decided its most recent one, *Carmell* v. *Texas,* in 2000. There, the Court overturned a man's sexual abuse conviction because of a change in State law. That change had made it easier for the prosecution to prove its charge than was the case when the abuse was committed.

Retroactive civil laws are *not* forbidden. Thus, a law raising income tax rates could be passed in November and applied to income earned through the whole year.

Grand Jury

The Constitution provides that:

> FROM THE *Constitution* **"** *No person shall be held to answer for a capital, or otherwise infamous crime, unless on a presentment or indictment of a Grand Jury. . . .* **"**
>
> —5th Amendment

The **grand jury** is the formal device by which a person can be accused of a serious crime.[8] In federal cases, it is a body of from 16 to 23 persons drawn from the area of the federal district court that it serves. The votes of at least 12 of the

---

[7]Article I, Sections 9 and 10. The phrase *ex post facto* is from the Latin, meaning "after the fact."

[8]The 5th Amendment provides that the guarantee of grand jury does not extend to "cases arising in the land or naval forces." The conduct of members of the armed forces is regulated under a code of military law enacted by Congress.

Constitutional Protections for Persons Accused of a Crime

Arrest on warrant or probable cause

— No unreasonable search or seizure

Informed of right to counsel and to remain silent

— Writ of habeas corpus if illegally detained

No third degree or coerced confession

Grand jury or prosecutor weighs evidence

— No excessive bail

Informed of charge by indictment or information

— No self-incrimination

Speedy and public trial by impartial jury

— Confront witnesses

— Assistance of counsel

Verdict of jury

— No double jeopardy

No excessive fine or cruel and unusual punishment

Right to appeal

Interpreting Charts Any person accused of a crime is presumed innocent until proven guilty. *What protections does the Constitution extend to those convicted of a crime?*

grand jurors are needed to return an indictment or to make a presentment.

An **indictment** is a formal complaint that the prosecutor lays before a grand jury. It charges the accused with one or more crimes. If the grand jury finds that there is enough evidence

for a trial, it returns a "true bill of indictment." The accused is then held for prosecution. If the grand jury does not make such a finding, the charge is dropped.

A presentment is a formal accusation brought by the grand jury on its own motion, rather than that of the prosecutor. It is little used in federal courts.

A grand jury's proceedings are not a trial. Since unfair harm could come if they were public, its sessions are secret. They are also one-sided—in the law, *ex parte*. That is, only the prosecution, not the defense, is present.

The right to grand jury is intended as a protection against overzealous prosecutors. Critics say that it is too time-consuming, too expensive, and too likely to follow the dictates of the prosecutor.

The 5th Amendment's grand jury provision is the only part of the Bill of Rights relating to criminal prosecution that the Supreme Court has not brought within the coverage of the 14th Amendment's Due Process Clause. In most States today, most criminal charges are not brought by grand jury indictment. They are brought, instead, by an information, an affidavit in which the prosecutor swears that there is enough evidence to justify a trial (see Chapter 24).

Double Jeopardy

The Fifth Amendment's guarantee against double jeopardy is the first of several protections in the Bill of Rights especially intended to ensure fair trial in the federal courts.[9] Fair trials are guaranteed in State courts by each State's own constitution and by the 14th Amendment's Due Process Clause.

The Fifth Amendment says in part that no person can be "twice put in jeopardy of life or limb." Today, this prohibition against **double jeopardy** means that once a person has been tried for a crime, he or she cannot be tried again for that same crime.

A person can violate both a federal *and* a State law in a single act, however—for example, by selling narcotics. That person can then be

---

[9]See the 5th, 6th, 7th, and 8th amendments and Article III, Section 2, Clause 3. The practice of excluding evidence obtained in violation of the 4th Amendment is also intended to guarantee a fair trial.

tried for the federal crime in a federal court and for the State crime in a State court. A single act can also result in the commission of several crimes. A person who breaks into a store, steals liquor, and sells it can be tried for illegal entry, theft, and selling liquor without a license.

In a trial in which a jury cannot agree on a verdict, there is no jeopardy. It is as though no trial had been held. Nor is double jeopardy involved when a case is appealed to a higher court.[10] Recall that the Supreme Court has held that the 5th Amendment's ban on double jeopardy applies against the States through the 14th Amendment, *Benton* v. *Maryland,* 1969.

Several States allow the continued confinement of violent sex predators after they have completed a prison term. The Court has twice held that that confinement is not punishment—and so does not involve double jeopardy. Rather, the practice is intended to protect the public from harm, *Kansas* v. *Hendrick,* 1987, and *Seling* v. *Young,* 2001.

Speedy and Public Trial

The Constitution commands

> **FROM THE Constitution** *❝ In all criminal prosecutions, the accused shall enjoy the right to a speedy and public trial. . . . ❞*
>
> —6th Amendment

Speedy Trial

The guarantee of a speedy trial is meant to ensure that the government will try a person accused of crime without undue delay. But how long a delay is too long? The Supreme Court has long recognized that each case must be looked at on its own merits.

In a leading case, *Barker* v. *Wingo,* 1972, the Court listed four criteria for determining if a delay has violated the constitutional protection. They are (1) the length of the delay, (2) the reasons for it, (3) whether the delay has in fact harmed the defendant, and (4) whether the defendant asked for a prompt trial.

Interpreting Political Cartoons The term "media circus" applies to trials that generate a great deal of publicity. *What are the dangers of a trial becoming too public?*

The Speedy Trial Act of 1974 says that the time between a person's arrest and the beginning of his or her federal criminal trial cannot be more than 100 days. The law does allow for some exceptions, however—for example, when the defendant must undergo extensive mental tests, or when the defendant or a key witness is ill.

The 6th Amendment guarantees a prompt trial in *federal* cases. The Supreme Court first declared that this right applies against the States as part of the 14th Amendment's Due Process Clause in *Klopfer* v. *North Carolina,* 1967.

Public Trial

The 6th Amendment says that a trial must also be public. The right to be tried in public is also part of the 14th Amendment's guarantee of procedural due process.

A trial must not be *too* speedy or *too* public, however. The Supreme Court threw out an Arkansas murder conviction in 1923 on just those grounds. The trial had taken only 45 minutes, and it had been held in a courtroom packed by a threatening mob.

Within reason, a judge can limit both the number and the kinds of spectators who may be present at a trial. Those who seek to disrupt a courtroom can be barred from it. A judge can order a courtroom cleared when the expected

---

[10]The Organized Crime Control Act of 1970 allows federal prosecutors to appeal sentences they believe to be too lenient. The Supreme Court has held that such appeals do not violate the double jeopardy guarantee, *United States* v. *Di Francesco,* 1980.

▲ **Cameras in the Courtroom?** Friends and family watch the 1997 televised trial (above) of nanny Louise Woodward for the murder of a child in her care. In trials in which cameras are not allowed in the courtroom, lawyers and the public may "view" the trial through courtroom sketches (right).

Sixteen years later, the Court held in *Chandler* v. *Florida,* 1981, that nothing in the Constitution prevents a State from allowing the televising of a criminal trial. At least, televising is not prohibited as long as steps are taken to avoid too much publicity and to protect the defendant's rights.

Trial by Jury

The 6th Amendment also says that a person accused of a federal crime must be tried "by an impartial jury." This guarantee reinforces an earlier one set out in Article III, Section 2. The right to trial by jury is also binding on the States through the 14th Amendment's Due Process Clause, but only in cases involving "serious" crimes, *Duncan* v. *Louisiana,* 1968.[11]

The trial jury is often called the petit jury. *Petit* is the French word for "small."

The 6th Amendment adds that the members of the federal court jury must be drawn from "the State and district wherein the crime shall have been committed, which district shall have been previously ascertained by law." This clause gives the defendant any benefit there might be in having a court and jury familiar with the people and problems of the area.

A defendant may ask to be tried in another place—seek a "change of venue"—on grounds that the people of the locality are so prejudiced in the case that an impartial jury cannot be drawn. The judge must decide whether a change of venue is justified.

A defendant may also waive (put aside or relinquish) the right to a jury trial. However, he or she can do so only if the judge is satisfied that the defendant is fully aware of his or her rights and understands what that action means. In fact, a judge can order a jury trial even when a defendant does not want one, *One Lot Emerald Cut Stones and One Ring* v. *United States,* 1972. If a defendant waives the right, a **bench trial** is held. That is, a judge

testimony may be embarrassing to a witness or to someone else not a party to the case.

Many of the questions about how public a trial should be involve the media—especially newspapers and television. The guarantees of fair trial and free press, however, often conflict in the courts. On the one hand, a courtroom is a public place where the media have a right to be present. On the other hand, media coverage must not damage the right to a fair trial.

Champions of the public's right to know hold that the courts must allow the broadest possible press coverage of a trial. The Supreme Court has often held, however, that the media have only the same right as the general public to be present in a courtroom. The right to a public trial belongs to the defendant, not to the media.

What of televised trials? Television cameras are barred from all federal courtrooms. Most States do allow some form of in-court television reporting, however. Does televising a criminal trial violate a defendant's rights?

An early major case on the point was *Estes* v. *Texas,* 1965. Radio and television reporting of Estes' case had been allowed from within the courtroom and over the objections of Estes himself. The Court held that this reporting had been so disruptive that it had denied Estes a fair trial.

---

[11]In *Baldwin* v. *New York,* 1970, the Court defined those crimes as offenses for which imprisonment for more than six months is possible.

alone hears the case. (Of course, a defendant can plead guilty and so avoid a trial of any kind.)

In federal practice, the jury that hears a criminal case must have 12 members. Some federal civil cases are tried before juries of as few as six members, however. Several States now provide for smaller juries, often of six members, in both criminal and civil cases.

In the federal courts, the jury that hears a criminal case can convict the accused only by a unanimous vote. Most States follow the same rule.[12]

In a long series of cases, dating from *Strauder v. West Virginia,* 1880, the Supreme Court has held that a jury must be "drawn from a fair cross section of the community." A person is denied the right to an impartial jury if he or she is tried by a jury from which members of any groups "playing major roles in the community" have been excluded, *Taylor v. Louisiana,* 1975.

In short, no person can be kept off a jury on such grounds as race, color, religion, national origin, or sex. As the Court put it in one of its more recent decisions on the point: Both the 5th and the 14th amendments mean that jury service cannot be determined by "the pigmentation of skin, the accident of birth, or the choice of religion," *Georgia v. McCollum,* 1992.

Right to an Adequate Defense

Every person accused of a crime has the right to the best possible defense that circumstances will allow. The 6th Amendment says that a defendant has the right (1) "to be informed of the nature and cause of the accusation," (2) "to be confronted with the witnesses against him" and question them in open court, (3) "to have compulsory process for obtaining witnesses in his favor" (that is, favorable witnesses can be subpoenaed, or forced to attend), and (4) "to have the Assistance of Counsel for his defense."

These key safeguards apply in the federal courts. Still, if a State fails to honor any of them, the accused can appeal a conviction on grounds that the 14th Amendment's Due Process Clause has been violated. Recall from Chapter 19 that the Supreme Court protected the right to counsel in *Gideon v. Wainwright,* 1963; the right of confrontation in *Pointer v. Texas,* 1965; and the right to call witnesses in *Washington v. Texas,* 1967.

These guarantees are intended to prevent the cards from being stacked in favor of the prosecution. One of the leading right-to-counsel cases, *Escobedo v. Illinois,* 1964, illustrates this point.

Chicago police picked up Danny Escobedo for questioning in the death of his brother-in-law. On the way to the police station, and then while he was being questioned there, he asked several times to see his lawyer. The police denied these requests. They did so even though his lawyer was in the police station and was trying to see him, and the police knew the lawyer was there. Through a long night of questioning, Escobedo made several damaging statements. Prosecutors later used those statements in court as a major part of the evidence that led to his murder conviction.

The Supreme Court ordered Escobedo freed from prison four years later. It held that he had been improperly denied his right to counsel.

In *Gideon v. Wainwright,* 1963, the Court held that an attorney must be furnished to a defendant who cannot afford one. In many places, a judge still assigns a lawyer from the local community, or a private legal aid association provides counsel.

WE, THE JURY, AFTER POLLING FRIENDS AND NEIGHBORS, FIND THE DEFENDANT NOT GUILTY

Interpreting Political Cartoons *Would a poll of friends and neighbors produce a fair verdict? Explain your answer.*

[12]The 14th Amendment does not say that there cannot be juries of fewer than 12 persons, *Williams v. Florida,* 1970, but it does not allow juries of fewer than six members, *Ballew v. Georgia,* 1978. Nor does it prevent a State from providing for a conviction on a less than unanimous jury vote, *Apodaca v. Oregon,* 1972. But if a jury has only six members, it may convict only by a unanimous vote, *Burch v. Louisiana,* 1979.

Since *Gideon,* however, a growing number of States, and many local governments, have established tax-supported public defender offices. In 1970, Congress authorized the appointment of federal public defenders or, as an alternative, the creation of community legal service organizations financed by federal grants.

Self-Incrimination

The guarantee against self-incrimination is among the protections set out in the Fifth Amendment. That provision declares that no person can be "compelled in any criminal case to be a witness against himself." This protection must be honored in both the federal and State courts, *Malloy* v. *Hogan,* 1964.

In a criminal case, the burden of proof is always on the prosecution. The defendant does not have to prove his or her innocence. The ban on self-incrimination prevents the prosecution from shifting the burden of proof to the defendant. As the Court put it in *Malloy* v. *Hogan,* the prosecution cannot force the accused to "prove the charge against" him "out of his own mouth."

Applying the Guarantee

The language of the 5th Amendment suggests that the guarantee against self-incrimination applies only to criminal cases. In fact, the guarantee covers any governmental proceeding in which a person is legally compelled to answer any question that could lead to a criminal charge. Thus, a person may claim the right ("take the Fifth") in a variety of situations: in a divorce proceeding (which is a civil matter), before a legislative committee, at a school board's disciplinary hearing, and so on.

The courts, not the individuals who claim it, decide when the right can be properly invoked. If the plea of self-incrimination is pushed too far, a person can be held in contempt of court.

The guarantee against self-incrimination is a personal right. One can claim it only for oneself.[13] It cannot be invoked in someone else's behalf; a person *can* be forced to "rat" on another.

The privilege does not protect a person from being fingerprinted or photographed, submitting a handwriting sample, or appearing in a police lineup. And, recall, it does not mean that a person does not have to submit to a blood test in a drunk driving situation, *Schmerber* v. *California,* 1966.

A person cannot, however, be forced to confess to a crime under duress, that is, as a result of torture or other physical or psychological pressure. In *Ashcraft* v. *Tennessee,* 1944, for example, the Supreme Court threw out the conviction of a man accused of hiring another person to murder his wife. The confession on which his conviction rested had been secured only after some 36 hours of continuous, threatening interrogation. The questioning was conducted by officers who worked in shifts because, they said, they became so tired that they had to rest.

The gulf between what the Constitution says and what goes on in some police stations can be wide indeed. For that reason, the Supreme Court has come down hard in favor of the defendant in many cases involving the protection against self-incrimination and the closely related right to counsel.

Recall, for example, the Court's decision in *Escobedo* v. *Illinois,* 1964. There it held that a confession cannot be used against a defendant if it was obtained by police who refused to allow the defendant to see his attorney and did not tell him that he had a right to refuse to answer their questions.

Miranda v. *Arizona*

In a truly historic decision, the Court refined the *Escobedo* holding in *Miranda* v. *Arizona,* 1966. A mentally retarded man, Ernesto Miranda, had been convicted of kidnapping and rape. Ten days after the crime, the victim picked Miranda out of a police lineup. After two hours of questioning, during which the police did not tell him of his rights, Miranda confessed.

The Supreme Court struck down Miranda's conviction. More importantly, the Court said that it would no longer uphold convictions in any cases in which suspects had not been told of their constitutional rights before police questioning. It thus laid down the **Miranda Rule.** Under the rule, before police may question a suspect, that person must be

---

[13]With this major exception: A husband cannot be forced to testify against his wife, or a wife against her husband, *Trammel* v. *United States,* 1980. One can testify against the other voluntarily, however.

(1) told of his or her right to remain silent;

(2) warned that anything he or she says can be used in court;

(3) informed of the right to have an attorney present during questioning;

(4) told that if he or she is unable to hire an attorney, one will be provided at public expense;

(5) told that he or she may bring police questioning to an end at any time.

The Miranda Rule has been in force for 35 years now and has been built into thousands of television programs and books over that period. As the Court put it in *Dickerson* v. *United States,* 2000, the rule "has become embedded in routine police practice to the point where the warnings have become part of our national culture."

The Supreme Court is still refining the rule ~ase-by-case basis. Most often the rule is ' But there are exceptions. Thus, .ld that an undercover police offi- prisoner does not have to tell a cell firanda rights before prompting him .t a murder, *Illinois* v. *Perkins,* 1990. v. *Cobb,* 2001, involved a man who h. been read his rights in a burglary case. Later, out on bail, he confessed to killing a woman and her child during the burglary.

Cobb confessed to police voluntarily, but without consulting his attorney. He was convicted of the murders and sentenced to death. On appeal, Cobb argued that his confession should not have been used against him—because he had not had

▲ In 1966, the Court struck down the conviction of Ernesto Miranda (right), who had confessed to a crime without being told of his rights. *Critical Thinking* *What were the long-term effects of the Miranda decision on police procedures?*

the help of his attorney. But the High Court disagreed, 5–4; it held that his Miranda rights had not been violated.

The Miranda rule has always been controversial. Critics see it as a serious obstacle to effective law enforcement. Many contend that it "puts criminals back on the streets." Others applaud the rule, however. They hold that criminal law enforcement is most effective when it relies on independently secured evidence, rather than on confessions gained by questionable tactics from defendants who do not have the help of a lawyer.

Section 3 Assessment

Key Terms and Main Ideas

1. What does the **writ of habeas corpus** seek to prevent?
2. Why are **bills of attainder** and **ex post facto laws** forbidden?
3. What guarantees does the 5th Amendment offer to the accused?
4. List the provisions of the 6th Amendment concerning the rights of the accused.

Critical Thinking

5. **Drawing Inferences** Consider the statement, "It is better that ten guilty persons go free than that one innocent person be punished." What can you infer about the priorities of a society in which this is a firm belief or "bedrock principle"?

6. **Predicting Consequences** If the guarantee against self-incrimination were removed from the Bill of Rights, what might be the effect on the modern criminal justice system? Would justice be more or less likely to be carried out?

7. **Expressing Problems Clearly** What are the arguments both for and against allowing television cameras in the courtroom?

 Take It to the Net

8. Read more about the Miranda Rule. Then work with a small group of classmates to write a paragraph summarizing the importance of the rule. Use the links provided in the Social Studies area at the following Web site for help in completing this activity. **www.phschool.com**

The Right to an Attorney

Clarence Gideon was an uneducated man who had to defend himself in a Florida court because he could not afford an attorney and the trial judge refused to provide one at public expense. Here, Gideon writes from prison to the attorney assigned to handle his Supreme Court appeal. Fourteen months after this letter, the Court ruled in Gideon v. Wainwright *that every defendant has a right to an attorney.*

Clarence Gideon
1910–1972

On June 3rd 1961 I was arrested for the crime I am now doing time on. I was charged with Breaking & Entering to comitt a misdemeanor and was convicted in a trial August 4th 1961 [and] sentenced to State Prison August 27th 1961.

This charge growed out of gambling. . . . I worked in this place and did run a Poker game there. . . . I did not break into this building nor did I have to [because] I had the keys to the building. . . . The State witness Cook who was supposed to identify me. Had a bad police record and the Court would not let me bring that out. Nor that one time I had at the point of a pistal made him stop beating a girl[.]

I always believed that the primarily reason of a trial in a court of law was to reach the truth. My trial was far from the truth. One day when I was being arraigned [brought to court to be formally charged] I seen two trials of two different men tried without attorneys. One hour from the time they started they had two juries out and fifteen minutes later they were found guilty and sentenced. Is this a fair trial? This is common practiced through most of this state. . . . I am an electrician here [in prison] and one of my fellow workers has two years for drunk and resisting arrest. Most city Police courts would give a citizen a twenty-five dollar fine for the same charge he was tried without an attorney and convicted. . . .

There was not a crime committed in my case and I don't feel like I had a fair trial. If I had a attorney[,] he could brought out all these things in my trial.

When I was arrested I was put in solitary confinement and I was not allowed the papers not to use the telephone or write to everyone I should. I did get a speedy arraignment and . . . was allow more time to try and obtain a attorney[,] which I could not do. You know about the rest of my trial. . . .

I hope that [this letter] may help you in preparing this case. I am sorry I could not write better[.] I have done the best I could.

I have no illusions about the law and courts or the people who are involved in them. I have read the complete history of law ever since the Romans first started writing them down and[,] before[,] of the laws of religions. I believe that each era finds a improvement in the law[.] Each year brings something new for the benefit of mankind. Maybe this will be one of those small steps forward. . . .

Analyzing Primary Sources

1. What "proof" does Gideon offer to support his innocence?
2. In what three ways, according to Gideon, are defendants harmed by not having an attorney?
3. What attitude does Gideon show toward the law and the legal system?
4. What point is Gideon trying to make in the last paragraph of his letter?

4 Punishment

Section Preview

OBJECTIVES

1. **Explain** the purpose of bail and preventive detention.
2. **Describe** the Court's interpretation of cruel and unusual punishment.
3. **Outline** the history of the Court's decisions on capital punishment.
4. **Define** the crime of treason.

WHY IT MATTERS

The 8th Amendment addresses the issue of punishment for crime. It bans excessive bail and cruel and unusual punishment. The Court has ruled that the death penalty does not constitute cruel and unusual punishment, although the question of capital punishment continues to be hotly debated.

POLITICAL DICTIONARY

★ **bail**
★ **preventive detention**
★ **capital punishment**
★ **treason**

Once again, think about this statement: "It is better that ten guilty persons go free than that one innocent person be punished." What do you think of that notion after reading the previous section? Turn now to those guilty persons who do not go free but are instead punished. How should they be treated? The Constitution gives its most specific answers to that question in the 8th Amendment.

Bail and Preventative Detention

The 8th Amendment says, in part:

FROM THE *Constitution*

❝*Excessive bail shall not be required, nor excessive fines imposed. . . .*❞
—United States Constitution

Each State constitution sets out similar restrictions. The general rule is that the bail or fine in a case must bear a reasonable relationship to the seriousness of the crime involved.

Bail

Bail is a sum of money that the accused may be required to post (deposit with the court) as a guarantee that he or she will appear in court at the proper time. The use of bail is justified on two grounds: (1) A person should not be jailed until his or her guilt is established. (2) A defendant is better able to prepare for trial outside of a jail.

Note that the Constitution does not say that all persons accused of a crime are automatically entitled to bail. Rather, it guarantees that, where bail is set, the amount will not be excessive.

The leading case on bail in the federal courts is *Stack* v. *Boyle*, 1951. There the Court ruled that "bail set at a figure higher than the amount reasonably calculated" to assure a defendant's appearance at a trial "is 'excessive' under the 8th Amendment."

A defendant can appeal the denial of release on bail or the amount of bail. Bail is usually set in accordance with the severity of the crime

Interpreting Political Cartoons **Under what circumstances may bail actually be denied?**

▶ Supporters for (right) and against (left) capital punishment make their views known. **Critical Thinking** *Briefly summarize arguments for and against the death penalty.*

charged and with the reputation and financial resources of the accused. People with little or no income often have trouble raising bail. The federal and most State courts thus release many defendants "on their own recognizance," that is, on their honor. Failure to appear for trial— "jumping bail"—is itself a punishable crime.

Preventive Detention

In 1984, Congress provided for the **preventive detention** of some people accused of federal crimes. A federal judge can order that the accused be held, without bail, when there is good reason to believe that he or she will commit another serious crime before trial.

Critics of the law claim that preventive detention amounts to punishment before trial. They say it undercuts the presumption of innocence to which defendants are entitled.

The Supreme Court upheld the 1984 law, 6–3, in *United States* v. *Salerno*, 1987. The majority rejected the argument that preventive detention is punishment. Rather, it found the practice a legitimate response to a "pressing societal problem." The Court held that, "There is no doubt that preventing danger to the community is a legitimate regulatory goal." More than half the States have recently adopted preventive detention laws.

Cruel and Unusual Punishment

The 8th Amendment also forbids "cruel and unusual punishment." The 14th Amendment extends that prohibition against the States, *Robinson* v. *California*, 1962.

The Supreme Court decided its first cruel and unusual case in *Wilkerson* v. *Utah*, 1879. There a territorial court had sentenced a convicted murderer to death by a firing squad. The Court held this punishment to be constitutional.

The kinds of penalties the Constitution intended to prevent, said the Court, were such barbaric tortures as burning at the stake, crucifixion, drawing and quartering, "and all others in the same line of unnecessary cruelty." It upheld electrocution for the first time in a case from New York, *In re Kemmler*, 1890.

Since then, the Court has heard only a handful of cruel and unusual cases, except for those relating to capital punishment. More often than not, the Court has rejected the cruel and unusual punishment claim.[14]

Louisiana v. *Resweber*, 1947, is typical. There the Court found that it was not unconstitutional to subject a convicted murderer to a second electrocution after the chair had failed to work properly on the first occasion.

In *Rummel* v. *Estelle*, 1980, a Texas court had imposed a mandatory life sentence on a "three-time loser." It did so even though the three crimes of which the individual had been convicted were all petty and nonviolent, and all together involved less than $230.

However, the Court has held some punishments to be cruel and unusual. In *Robinson* v. *California*, 1962, the Court held that a State law

---

[14]The prohibition of cruel and unusual punishment is limited to criminal matters. It does not forbid paddling or similar punishments in the public schools, *Ingraham* v. *Wright*, 1977.

defining narcotics addiction as a crime to be punished, rather than an illness to be treated, violated the 8th and 14th amendments.[15] In *Estelle* v. *Gamble*, 1976, it ruled that a Texas prison inmate could not properly be denied needed medical care.

Again, however, most cases have gone the other way. Thus, in *Rhodes* v. *Chapman*, 1981, the Court held that putting two prisoners in a cell built for one is not cruel and unusual.

Capital Punishment

Is **capital punishment**—punishment by death—cruel and unusual and therefore unconstitutional?[16] For years, the Supreme Court was reluctant to face that highly charged issue.[17]

The Court met the issue indirectly in *Furman* v. *Georgia*, 1972. There it struck down all of the then existing State laws allowing the death penalty, but not because that penalty as such was cruel and unusual. Rather, the Court voided those laws because they gave too much discretion to judges or juries in deciding whether to impose the death penalty. The Court noted that out of all the people convicted of capital crimes, only "a random few," most of them African American or poor or both, were "capriciously selected" for execution.

Since that decision, Congress and 38 States have passed new capital punishment laws. At first, those laws took one of two forms. Several States made the death penalty mandatory for certain crimes, such as killing a police officer or murder committed during a rape, kidnapping, or arson. Other States provided for a two-stage process in capital cases: a trial to settle the issue of guilt or innocence, and then a second hearing to decide whether the circumstances justify a sentence of death.

In considering the scores of challenges to those State laws, the Supreme Court found the

---

[15]But, notice, that does not mean that buying, selling, or possessing narcotics cannot be made a crime. Such criminal laws are designed to punish persons for their behavior, not for being ill.

[16]The phrase "capital punishment" comes from the Latin *caput*, meaning "head"; in many cultures, the historically preferred method for executing criminals was beheading (decapitation).

[17]The Court did hold that neither death by firing squad (*Wilkerson* v. *Utah*, 1878) nor by a second electrocution (*Louisiana* v. *Resweber*, 1947) is unconstitutional. But in neither of those cases, nor in others, did it deal with the question of the death penalty as such.

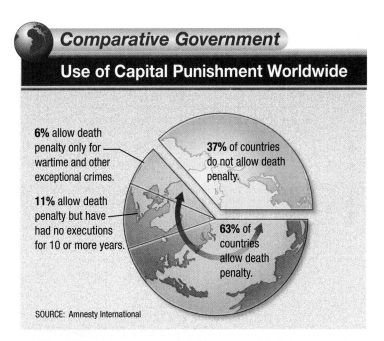

Comparative Government
Use of Capital Punishment Worldwide

6% allow death penalty only for wartime and other exceptional crimes.

11% allow death penalty but have had no executions for 10 or more years.

37% of countries do not allow death penalty.

63% of countries allow death penalty.

SOURCE: Amnesty International

Interpreting Graphs Over half of the world's countries allow the death penalty. *What percentage of these countries allow the death penalty only for "exceptional" crimes or have had no executions for ten years or longer?*

mandatory death penalty laws to be unconstitutional. In *Woodson* v. *North Carolina*, 1976, the Court ruled that such laws were "unduly harsh and rigidly unworkable." It saw the laws as attempts simply to "paper over" the decision in *Furman*.

The two-stage approach to capital punishment *is* constitutional, however. In *Gregg* v. *Georgia*, 1976, the Court held, for the first time, that the "punishment of death does not invariably violate the Constitution." It ruled that well-drawn two-stage laws can practically eliminate "the risk that [the death penalty] will be inflicted in an arbitrary or capricious manner."

However, the Court has ruled that a State can impose the death penalty only for "crimes resulting in the death of the victim," *Coker* v. *Georgia*, 1977. Moreover, a capital punishment law "must allow for whatever mitigating circumstances" may be present in a case, *Roberts* v. *Louisiana*, 1977.

Opponents of capital punishment continue to appeal cases to the Court, but to no real avail. The sum of the Court's many decisions over the past 25 years is this: The death penalty, fairly applied, is constitutional.

Current polls indicate that two of every three Americans support the death penalty. Still, many

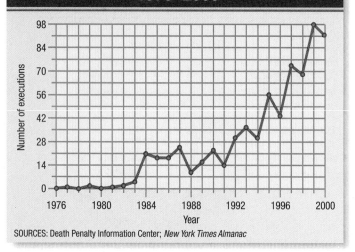

Executions in the United States, 1976–2000

Number of executions (y-axis): 0, 14, 28, 42, 56, 70, 84, 98
Year (x-axis): 1976, 1980, 1984, 1988, 1992, 1996, 2000

SOURCES: Death Penalty Information Center; *New York Times Almanac*

Interpreting Graphs In 1976, the Supreme Court upheld the constitutionality of the death penalty. ***Summarize the data shown on the graph.***

who favor it have some misgivings about the fairness with which death sentences are applied.

In January 2000, Governor George Ryan of Illinois, a longtime supporter of capital punishment, ordered a moratorium on (a suspension of) executions in his State. He did so, he said, because the death penalty process is "fraught with error."

From 1977 to 2000, 285 people were sentenced to death in Illinois. By 2000, 12 of them had been executed, but 13 others had been released from prison because they had been wrongly convicted. It appears that several other death row inmates in Illinois may not in fact be guilty of the crimes for which they were sentenced to die. Governor Ryan's action set off a new and continuing debate over the use of the death penalty in this country.

Treason

Treason against the United States is the only crime that is defined in the Constitution. The Framers provided a specific definition of the crime because they knew that the charge of treason is a favorite weapon in the hands of tyrants.

Treason, says Article III, Section 3, can consist of only two things: either (1) levying war against the United States or (2) "adhering to their Enemies, giving them Aid and Comfort." No person can be convicted of the crime "unless on the Testimony of two Witnesses to the same overt Act, or on Confession in open Court."

Congress has established the death penalty as the maximum penalty for treason against the United States, but no one has ever been executed for the crime. Note that a person can commit treason only in wartime. However, Congress has made it a crime, during times of either peace or war, to commit espionage or sabotage, to attempt to overthrow the government by force, or to conspire to do any of these things.

Most of the State constitutions also provide for treason. John Brown was hanged as a traitor to Virginia after his raid on Harpers Ferry in 1859. He is believed to be the only person ever to be executed for treason against a State.

Section 4 Assessment

Key Terms and Main Ideas

1. What constitutes excessive **bail**?
2. In cases involving cruel and unusual punishment, how has the Court generally ruled?
3. What is the Supreme Court's view of **capital punishment**?
4. For what reason does the Constitution specifically define **treason**?

Critical Thinking

5. **Demonstrating Reasoned Judgment (a)** What two forms did State laws allowing capital punishment take after the Court's decision in *Furman* v. *Georgia*? **(b)** Why did the Court find one form of these laws "unduly harsh and rigidly unworkable"?

6. **Identifying Assumptions** What assumptions underlie the Court's decision that preventive detention is constitutional?

Take It to the Net

7. Browse through at least three Internet sites on the death penalty. Then answer the following: What are the most convincing arguments presented in favor of abolishing the death penalty? What arguments could you offer against abolishing the death penalty? Use the links provided at the Social Studies area of the following Web site for help in completing this activity. **www.phschool.com**

Does a Suspect's Flight From Police Justify a Stop and Search?

The 4th Amendment prohibits "unreasonable searches and seizures," but it does not define the term "unreasonable." In **Terry** *v.* **Ohio**, *1968, the Supreme Court held that police officers may stop and frisk a person when they have good reason to believe that that person is armed and dangerous. May police stop a person simply because that person flees when the police approach?*

Illinois v. Wardlow (2000)

William Wardlow was holding a white bag while in an area of Chicago known for heavy drug trafficking when he saw a caravan of police cars approaching. He fled, and the police pursued. When they caught up with him, one of the officers conducted a "pat-down" search for weapons. (In the police officer's experience, weapons were usually found in the vicinity of narcotics transactions.) The officer squeezed the bag Wardlow was carrying and felt a heavy, hard object shaped like a gun. He opened the bag and discovered a .38-caliber handgun with five live rounds of ammunition.

At his trial, Wardlow argued that he should not be prosecuted for possession of the gun because the officer did not have reasonable suspicion to stop and search him. The Illinois trial court ruled against him, and he was convicted of unlawful use of a weapon by a felon. The Illinois Appellate Court then reversed his conviction. The Illinois Supreme Court affirmed that ruling, holding that both the stop and the arrest violated the 4th Amendment. The case then went to the Supreme Court.

Arguments for Illinois

1. The fact that a person fled from a police officer strongly indicates criminal behavior and provides reasonable grounds for stopping the suspect in order to conduct a brief investigation.
2. Even if flight alone is not sufficient to justify stopping and searching a suspect, the fact that the suspect was in a high-crime area, combined with the fact that the suspect fled upon the arrival of the police, provide reasonable grounds for stopping the suspect.
3. The standard that must be met to justify stopping a suspect, "reasonable suspicion," is less demanding than the standard of "probable cause" that must be met to justify arresting a suspect.

Arguments for Wardlow

1. There can be many reasons for fleeing from police; the fact that a person fled does not by itself mean that he is guilty of a crime.
2. Even the combined circumstances of being in a high-crime area, carrying a white bag, and running from the police do not create reasonable suspicion to justify a search.
3. An individual has the right to ignore the police unless and until the police have sufficient grounds under the Constitution to detain or arrest him. No one is required to cooperate with the police.

Decide for Yourself

1. Review the constitutional grounds on which each side based its arguments and the specific arguments each side presented.
2. Debate the opposing viewpoints presented in this case. Which viewpoint do you favor?
3. Predict the impact of the Court's decision on the conduct of police investigations and on relations between minority groups and the police. (To read a summary of the Court's decision, turn to the Supreme Court Glossary on page 799.)

CHAPTER 20 · Assessment

Political Dictionary

due process (p. 564)
substantive due process (p. 565)
procedural due process (p. 565)
police power (p. 566)
search warrant (p. 566)
involuntary servitude (p. 569)
discrimination (p. 570)
writs of assistance (p. 571)

probable cause (p. 571)
exclusionary rule (p. 573)
writ of habeas corpus (p. 576)
bill of attainder (p. 577)
ex post facto law (p. 577)
grand jury (p. 577)
indictment (p. 578)
double jeopardy (p. 578)

bench trial (p. 580)
Miranda Rule (p. 582)
bail (p. 585)
preventive detention (p. 586)
capital punishment (p. 587)
treason (p. 588)

Practicing the Vocabulary

Matching *Choose a term from the list above that best matches each description.*

1. A group convened by a court to determine whether or not there is enough evidence against a person to justify a trial
2. A constitutional guarantee that a government will not deprive any person of life, liberty, or property by any unfair, arbitrary, or unreasonable action
3. The power of each State to act to protect and promote the public health, safety, morals, and general welfare
4. A sum of money that an accused person may be required to post as a guarantee that he or she will appear in court at the proper time
5. A legislative act that inflicts punishment without court trial

Fill in the Blank *Choose a term from the list above that best completes the sentence.*

6. During colonial times, British officials used _____ in order to search private homes for smuggled goods.
7. According to the _____, suspects must be advised of their rights before police questioning.
8. If a person is tried twice for the same crime, he or she may have been subjected to _____.
9. Police generally need a _____ in order search someone's house.
10. An _____ is a law applied to acts performed before the law was passed.

Reviewing Main Ideas

Section 1

11. Use the examples of *Rochin* v. *California* and *Pierce* v. *Society of Sisters* to explain why it is necessary to have both substantive and procedural due process.
12. Describe the relationship between the States' police power and due process of law.
13. The States may exercise the police power to protect and promote what?
14. What right did the Court first articulate in *Griswold* v. *Connecticut,* 1965?

Section 2

15. Use the examples of the *Civil Rights Cases,* 1883, and *Jones* v. *Mayer,* 1968, to illustrate how the Court's interpretation of the 13th Amendment has changed over the years.
16. What is the aim of the 4th Amendment?
17. What are the roots of the 3rd Amendment, and why is it not significant today?
18. What does the exclusionary rule exclude?

Section 3

19. For what reason does the Constitution protect the rights of those accused of a crime?
20. In what ways does the Constitution protect the rights of the accused?
21. What are the key constitutional guarantees of a fair trial?
22. What is the Miranda Rule?

Section 4

23. What are the key constitutional guarantees regarding punishment of the guilty?
24. Under what circumstances has the Supreme Court found death penalty laws to be unconstitutional?
25. What was the significance of *Furman* v. *Georgia,* 1972, in the history of the Supreme Court's rulings regarding capital punishment?
26. (a) What is the only crime defined in the Constitution? (b) What requirements must be met in order for a person to be convicted of this crime?

Critical Thinking Skills

27. ***Applying the Chapter Skill*** You have been assigned to make a presentation on 4th Amendment implications of the use of wiretapping by law enforcement officials. How could you use various media to make your presentation more interesting? Following the instructions on page 575, create a blueprint for the project.

28. ***Checking Consistency*** Recall that an accused person can be held without bail when there is reason to believe that he or she will commit another crime. In your opinion, does this law violate the principle of presumed innocence until proven guilty? Does it violate the guarantee against double jeopardy?

29. ***Identifying Assumptions*** What assumptions underlie the existence of the Miranda Rule and its specific provisions?

30. ***Determining Relevance*** How did the experiences of colonial Americans with British law enforcement and military practice influence the composition of the 2nd, 3rd, and 4th amendments?

31. ***Identifying Central Issues*** Some people refer to the United States as a "rights-based society." How does the information in this chapter support or refute this characterization?

Analyzing Political Cartoons

Use your knowledge of American history and government and this cartoon to answer the questions below.

"That was fun. What time does the next trial of the century start?"

32. **(a)** Who are the people in the cartoon? **(b)** What are they watching on television?
33. What does the cartoon suggest about television cameras in the courtroom?

★ You Can Make a Difference

Set up an interview with a representative of a local community group or law-enforcement agency that tries to keep young people from committing crimes or helps those who have already been in trouble with the law. Before you meet with this person, draw up a list of questions to ask him or her. Your questions should address issues of civil liberties, victims' rights, and the rights of the accused. If possible, make a tape-recording of your interview to play for the class.

Participation Activities

34. ***Current Events Watch*** Scan the newspaper for stories concerning any guarantees of the rights of the accused shown on the chart on page 578. Be prepared to give an oral report summarizing the story.

35. ***Time Line Activity*** Choose an issue discussed in this chapter (for example, the constitutionality of the death penalty or abortion). Based on both the information in this chapter and your own research, make a list of the key Supreme Court decisions regarding this issue. Present these decisions in a time line that demonstrates the development of the Court's opinion over the years.

36. ***It's Your Turn*** Create a survey to gauge citizens' opinions of the Constitution's civil liberties protections. Begin by listing the rights discussed in this chapter, such as due process. Next, note some of the controversial aspects of these rights (for example, the fact that evidence gathered illegally cannot be used against a person at his or her trial). Compose a list of questions designed to gather opinions on these issues. Ask ten people to complete your survey and compile their answers. **(Conducting A Survey)**

Take It to the Net

Chapter 20 Self-Test As a final review activity, take the Chapter 20 Self-Test in the Social Studies area at the Web site listed below, and receive immediate feedback on your answers.

www.phschool.com

Civil Rights: Equal Justice Under Law

"Our Constitution is color-blind, and neither knows nor tolerates classes among citizens. In respect of civil rights, all citizens are equal before the law."

—Justice John Marshall Harlan (1896)

Although Justice Harlan was speaking about the civil rights of African Americans, today his words apply to a much more diverse American society. Many groups have faced challenges in trying to get and keep the civil rights that the Constitution and civil rights legislation promise to all citizens.

◆ Demonstrators protest discrimination against African Americans at Woolworth's lunch counters, 1960

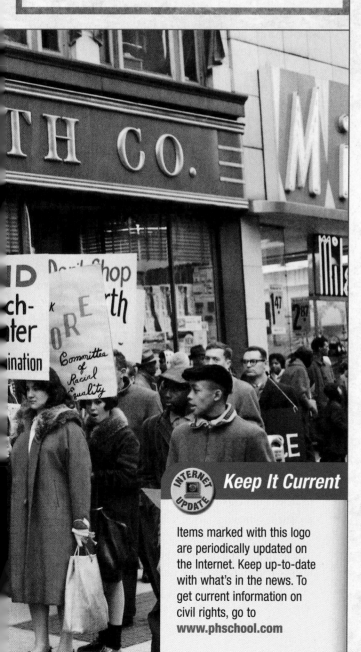

You Can Make a Difference

CIVIL RIGHTS INEQUALITIES still persist. In Boston, Kedesha Malcolm attended Boston Latin School, one of the city's prestigious "exam schools"—public high schools whose students must pass an entrance exam. Kedesha, 18, realized that there were not many students of color in her school, even though a large percentage of the city's overall student population is African American or Hispanic. "So I decided to do something to improve the school's diversity," Kedesha said. In response, she started Young Leaders of Color. Its members work with minority middle school students to help them pass the exams, and then offer mentoring to help them keep up with the challenging courses.

Keep It Current

Items marked with this logo are periodically updated on the Internet. Keep up-to-date with what's in the news. To get current information on civil rights, go to **www.phschool.com**

Diversity and Discrimination in American Society

1

Section Preview

OBJECTIVES

1. **Understand** what it means to live in a heterogeneous society.
2. **Summarize** the history of race-based discrimination in the United States.
3. **Examine** discrimination against women in the past and present.

WHY IT MATTERS

Although the Declaration of Independence declares that "all men are created equal," our nation has often struggled to meet that ideal. Members of ethnic minorities and women have historically faced discrimination in many aspects of their lives.

POLITICAL DICTIONARY

★ **heterogeneous**
★ **immigrant**
★ **reservation**
★ **refugee**
★ **assimilation**

Have you read George Orwell's classic, *Animal Farm?* Even if you have not, you may have heard its most oft-quoted line: "All animals are created equal, but some animals are more equal than others." You might keep Orwell's words in mind as you read the pages in this chapter.

A Heterogeneous Society

The term **heterogeneous** is a compound of two Greek words: *hetero,* meaning "other or different," and *genos,* meaning "race, family, or kind." Something that is heterogeneous is composed of a mix of ingredients. "We the People of the United States" are a heterogeneous lot, and we are becoming more so, year to year.

The population of the United States is predominantly white. It is today and, as you can see in the table on page 595, it has been historically. The first census in 1790 reported that there were 3,929,214 people living in this country. Four out of every five of them were white. African Americans made up the remaining 20 percent of the population counted in the census. As the nation's population grew over the decades, so, too, did the proportion of the American people who were white—until recently.

Today, the ethnic composition of the population is strikingly different from what it was only a generation ago. **Immigrants**—that is, those aliens legally admitted as permanent residents—have arrived in near-record numbers every year since the mid-1960s. Over that period, the nation's African American, Hispanic American, and Asian American populations have grown at rates several times that of the white population.

A look at gender balance in the population reveals that females are more numerous than males. This has been the case for more than half a century now.

As a result of these changes in the American population, the United States is more heterogeneous today than ever before in its history. That fact is certain to have a profound effect on the American social, political, and economic landscape on into the twenty-first century.

▶ *A Diverse Nation*
Individuals like this attorney (right) have enjoyed great success, despite the fact that women and Native Americans have often been targets of discrimination.

Ethnic Composition of the Population, 1790 – 2050*

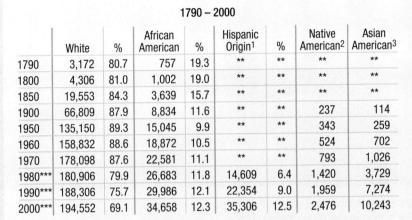

1790 – 2000

	White	%	African American	%	Hispanic Origin[1]	%	Native American[2]	Asian American[3]
1790	3,172	80.7	757	19.3	**	**	**	**
1800	4,306	81.0	1,002	19.0	**	**	**	**
1850	19,553	84.3	3,639	15.7	**	**	**	**
1900	66,809	87.9	8,834	11.6	**	**	237	114
1950	135,150	89.3	15,045	9.9	**	**	343	259
1960	158,832	88.6	18,872	10.5	**	**	524	702
1970	178,098	87.6	22,581	11.1	**	**	793	1,026
1980***	180,906	79.9	26,683	11.8	14,609	6.4	1,420	3,729
1990***	188,306	75.7	29,986	12.1	22,354	9.0	1,959	7,274
2000***	194,552	69.1	34,658	12.3	35,306	12.5	2,476	10,243

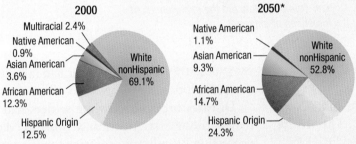

2000

- Multiracial 2.4%
- Native American 0.9%
- Asian American 3.6%
- African American 12.3%
- Hispanic Origin 12.5%
- White nonHispanic 69.1%

2050*

- Native American 1.1%
- Asian American 9.3%
- African American 14.7%
- Hispanic Origin 24.3%
- White nonHispanic 52.8%

Rate of Growth of Ethnic Populations

Percentage increase from 1990 to 2000*

- White: 9.4%
- African American: 15.5%
- Native American: 26.4%
- Hispanic Origin: 40.8%
- Asian American: 57.9%

*Data for 2050 projected. Projections for multiracial not available. Totals may not add up to 100% due to rounding and overlap among groups. In thousands unless otherwise indicated.

**Not available

[1] Persons of Hispanic origin may be of any race.

[2] Includes Alaska Natives, 1960 and later.

[3] Includes Pacific Islanders.

SOURCE: U.S. Census Bureau

***White=white nonHispanic

Interpreting Charts Although the population of the United States remains predominantly white, minority populations are growing at a faster rate than the majority population. The 2000 census showed that more and more Americans trace their heritage to multiple groups or choose not to identify themselves by race. ***According to the data, which group will be the largest minority group in 2050?***

Race-Based Discrimination

White Americans have been historically reluctant to yield to nonwhite Americans a full and equal place in the social, economic, and political life of this nation. Over time, the principal targets of that ethnic prejudice have been African Americans, Native Americans, Asian Americans, and Hispanic Americans. The white-male-dominated power structure has also been slow to recognize the claims of women to a full and equal place in American society.

African Americans

Much of what you will read in these pages focuses on discrimination against African Americans. There are three reasons for this focus:

1. African Americans constitute the second largest minority group in the United States. They number more than 34 million today, over 12 percent of all the American people.

2. African Americans have been the victims of consistent and deliberate unjust treatment for a longer time than perhaps any other group of Americans.[1] The ancestors of most African Americans came to this country in chains. Tens of thousands of Africans were kidnapped, crammed aboard sailing vessels, brought to America, and then sold in slave markets. As slaves, they could be bought and

---

[1] Slavery began in what was to become the United States in 1619; in August of that year, 20 Africans were sold to white settlers at Jamestown.

▲ Before beginning the voyage to the Americas, many African men and women were imprisoned in European slave forts like San Sebastian in modern-day Ghana. Untold numbers of people died in terrible conditions in slave forts and slave ships. *Critical Thinking* **How did the experiences of African men and women in slave forts typify the injustices of slavery?**

sold and forced to do their masters' bidding, however harsh the circumstances.

It took a civil war to end more than 200 years of slavery in this country. The 13th Amendment finally abolished slavery in 1865. Still, the Civil War and the ratification of that amendment did not end widespread racial discrimination in the United States.

3. Most of the gains the nation has made in translating the Constitution's guarantees of equality into a reality for all persons have come out of efforts made by and on behalf of African Americans. For example, the struggles of Martin Luther King, Jr., and others resulted in the Civil Rights Act of 1964 and then the Voting Rights Act of 1965; see pages 159–163.

America is now an inescapably multiracial society. Still, unlike whites, African Americans live with the consequences of America's history of racial discrimination every day of their lives. Of course, this is not to say that other groups of Americans have not also suffered the effects of discrimination. Clearly, many have.

Native Americans

White settlers first began to arrive in America in relatively large numbers in the early middle years of the 17th century. At the time, some one million Native Americans were living in territory that was to become the United States.[2]

By 1900, however, their number had fallen to less than 250,000.

Diseases brought by white settlers had decimated those first Americans. So, too, did the succession of military campaigns that accompanied the westward expansion of the United States. To quote one historian, Thomas E. Patterson: "'The only good Indian is a dead Indian' is not simply a hackneyed expression from cowboy movies. It was part of the strategy of westward expansion, as settlers and U.S. troops mercilessly drove the eastern Indians from their ancestral lands to the Great Plains and then took those lands too."

Today, more than 2.4 million Native Americans live in this country. More than a third of them live on or near **reservations,** which are public lands set aside by a government for use by Native American tribes.

Like African Americans, Native Americans have been the victims of overwhelming discrimination. The consequences of that bias have been truly appalling, and they remain all too evident today. Poverty, joblessness, and alcoholism plague many reservations. The life expectancy of Native Americans living on reservations today is

---

[2]Most authorities estimate that there were some 8 to 10 million Native Americans living in all of North and South America in the mid-1600s.

10 years less than the national average, and the Native American infant mortality rate is three times that for white Americans.

Hispanic Americans

Hispanic Americans are those in this country who have a Spanish-speaking background; many prefer to be called Latinos. Hispanics may be of any race. According to the Bilateral Commission on the Future of United States-Mexican Relations, Hispanic Americans "are among the world's most complex groupings of human beings. [The largest number] are white, millions . . . are mestizo, nearly half a million in the United States are black or mulatto."[3]

Hispanic Americans number more than 35 million. They now constitute the largest minority group of Americans. Hispanics replaced African Americans as the largest minority group in the United States around the year 2000.

Hispanic Americans can generally be divided into four main groups:

1. *Mexican Americans.* More than half of all Hispanics in the United States, at least 18 million persons, were either born in Mexico or trace their ancestry there. Those who were born in this country of Mexican parents are often called Chicanos.

The largest part of the Mexican American population lives in the States of California, Arizona, New Mexico, and Texas. Large cities such as El Paso and San Antonio, Texas, have Hispanic majorities, and smaller border cities such as Laredo and Brownsville, Texas, are over 90 percent Latino.

2. *Puerto Ricans.* Another large group of Hispanics has come to the mainland from the island of Puerto Rico. The population of the United States now includes some three million Puerto Ricans. Most of them have settled in New York, New Jersey, and in other parts of the Northeast.

3. *Cuban Americans.* The Hispanic population also includes some one million Cuban Americans. They are mostly people who fled the Castro dictatorship in Cuba and their descendants. A majority of Cuban Americans have settled in Miami and elsewhere in South Florida.

4. *Central and South Americans.* The fourth major subgroup of Hispanic Americans came here from Central and South America, many as **refugees.** A refugee is one who seeks protection (refuge) from war, persecution, or some other danger. More than three million persons have emigrated to the United States from Central and South American countries over the past 25 years; they have come in the largest numbers from Nicaragua, El Salvador, Guatemala, Colombia, and Chile. Many have also come from the Dominican Republic, an island nation in the Caribbean.

Asian Americans

The story of white America's mistreatment of Asians is a lengthy one, too. They have faced discrimination from the first day they arrived in this country. As with all immigrant groups, assimilation into the white-dominated population has been difficult. **Assimilation** is the process by which people of one culture merge into and become part of another culture.

Chinese laborers were the first Asians to come to the United States in large numbers. They were brought here in the 1850s to 1860s as contract laborers to work in the mines and to

▲ Many Asian Americans, like this Vietnamese storeowner in Seattle, Washington, came to the United States from Southeast Asia in the 1970s and 1980s. People fled the turmoil of the Vietnam War and the Communist conquest of South Vietnam that followed. *Critical Thinking Did Vietnamese immigrants come to the United States for the same reasons as Chinese immigrants did a century earlier? Explain.*

---

[3]A mestizo is a person with both Spanish or Portuguese and Native American ancestry. A mulatto is a person with African and white ancestry.

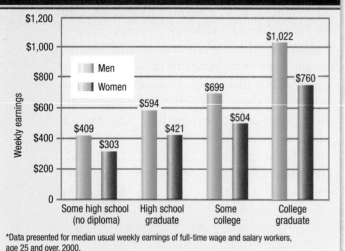

Median Weekly Earnings of Men and Women*

Weekly earnings

	Men	Women
Some high school (no diploma)	$409	$303
High school graduate	$594	$421
Some college	$699	$504
College graduate	$1,022	$760

*Data presented for median usual weekly earnings of full-time wage and salary workers, age 25 and over, 2000.
SOURCE: Bureau of Labor Statistics

Interpreting Graphs This graph illustrates how much money working men and women earned each week in 2000. **What does the graph show about equality in the workplace today?**

build railroads in the West. Many white Americans, native-born and immigrants, resented the competition of "coolie labor." Their resentments were frequently expressed in violence toward Asians.

Congress brought Chinese immigration nearly to a halt with the Chinese Exclusion Act of 1882. Because of this and other government actions, only a very small number of Chinese, Japanese, and other Asians were permitted to enter the United States for more than 80 years.

Early in World War II, the Federal Government ordered the evacuation of all persons of Japanese descent from the Pacific Coast. Some 120,000 people, two thirds of them native-born American citizens, were forcibly removed to inland "war relocation camps." Years later, the Government conceded that that action had been both unnecessary and unjust.

Congress made dramatic changes in American immigration policies in 1965. Since then, some four million Asian immigrants have come to this country, mostly from the Philippines, China, Korea, Vietnam, and India. The term "Asian American" describes an ever more diverse population. Asian Americans represent a tremendous variety of languages, religions, and cultures, and many recent immigrants from Asia have little in common with one another.

Today, the Asian American population exceeds 11 million, and it is the nation's fastest growing minority group. Today, Asian Americans live in every part of the United States. They are a majority of the population in Hawaii and more than 10 percent of that of California. New York City boasts the largest Chinese community outside of China itself.

Discrimination Against Women

Unlike the several ethnic groups described here, women are not a minority in the United States. They are, in fact, a majority group. Still, traditionally in many instances in American law and public policy, women have not enjoyed the same rights as men. Their status was even lower, in many instances, than men who were themselves the target of virulent discrimination. Women have been treated as less than equal in a great many matters, including, for example, property rights, education, and employment opportunities.

Organized efforts to improve the place of women in American society date from July 19, 1848. On that date, a convention on women's rights, meeting in Seneca Falls, New York, adopted a set of resolutions that deliberately echoed the words of the Declaration of Independence. It began:

 66 *When, in the course of human events, it becomes necessary for one portion of the family of man to assume among the people of the earth a position different from that which they have hitherto occupied. . . . We hold these truths to be self-evident: that all men and women are created equal. . . .* **99**

—Declaration of Sentiments

Those who fought and finally won the long struggle for woman suffrage believed that, with the vote, women would soon achieve other basic rights. That assumption proved to be false. Although more than 51 percent of the population is female, women have held only a fraction of one percent of the nation's top public offices since 1789.

Even today, women hold little more than 10 percent of the 535 seats in Congress and little more than 20 percent of the 7,611 seats in the 50 State legislatures. Only four of the 50 State governors today are female. Women are also hugely underrepresented at the upper levels of corporate management and other power groups in the private sector. Fewer than 20 percent of the nation's doctors, lawyers, and college professors are women.

It is illegal to pay women less than men for the same work. The Equal Pay Act of 1963 requires employers to pay men and women the same wages if they perform the same jobs in the same establishment under the same working conditions. The Civil Rights Act of 1964 also prohibits job discrimination based on sex. Yet, nearly 40 years after Congress passed those laws, working women earn, on the average, less than 80 cents for every dollar earned by working men. See the graph on page 598.

Women earn less than men for a number of reasons—including the fact that the male work force is, over all, better educated and has more job experience than the female work force. (Note that these factors themselves can often be traced to discrimination.) In addition, some blame the so-called "Mommy track," in which women put their careers on hold to have children or work reduced hours to juggle child-care responsibilities. Others claim that a "glass ceiling" of discrimination in the corporate world and elsewhere, invisible but impenetrable, prevents women from rising to their full potential.

Certainly it is true that until quite recently women were limited to a fairly narrow range of jobs. In many cases, women were encouraged

▲ **Women's Work** Very few careers were open to women before the 1960s. Women with college degrees often took jobs as typists or secretaries, hoping for a rare opportunity to move up to better-paying jobs usually reserved for men.

not to work outside the home once they were married. Even now, more than three fourths of all jobs held by women are in low-paying clerical and service occupations. The Bureau of Labor Statistics reports that 98 percent of all secretaries today are women; so too are 96 percent of all child-care workers, 92 percent of all registered nurses, 89 percent of all waiters, 86 percent of all dieticians, and 89 percent of all bank tellers.

Efforts on behalf of equal rights for women have gained significant ground in recent years. But, recall, that ground has not included an Equal Rights Amendment to the Constitution.

Section 1 Assessment

Key Terms and Main Ideas

1. What defines a **heterogeneous** nation?
2. Name one factor that can lead a **refugee** to leave his or her country.
3. Who are **immigrants**?
4. What is the purpose of a **reservation**?

Critical Thinking

5. **Understanding Point of View** In what sense are women a unique group among those who have suffered discrimination?
6. **Drawing Inferences** Assimilation is a controversial issue for members of minority groups. List two reasons why a recent immigrant to the United States might try to assimilate. Then, list two reasons why an immigrant might choose to retain as much of his or her native land's culture as possible.

 Take It to the Net

7. Read about efforts to change discriminatory aspects of American immigration policy. Write an essay that identifies those aspects, the criticisms of them, and the responses being considered by Congress. Use the links provided in the Social Studies area at the following Web site for help in completing this activity.
www.phschool.com

Reading Tables and Analyzing Statistics

People have been collecting and analyzing statistics for a long time. For instance, the census—the practice of counting people—dates back at least to ancient Egypt. In our electronic age, collecting and storing data are becoming easier all the time. Therefore, reading and analyzing statistics are now much-needed skills. Use the steps below to help you interpret data tables:

1. Determine the source of the information and decide if the source is reliable. Faulty data produce faulty conclusions, so make sure your sources are accurate, complete, and trustworthy. A disreputable source might be sloppy in its data-gathering procedures, or it might edit out data that doesn't suit its purposes. Published government data are usually considered reliable. Be skeptical about information with an unfamiliar source or no source at all. (a) What is the source of the information in the table below? (b) Is the source reliable?

2. Study the table to determine its purpose. Information is collected for a variety of purposes: to compare and contrast, to show proportions, or to identify trends over time. What is the purpose of the table below?

3. Identify relationships among the data. Figure out percentage increases and decreases over time. (a) What ethnic group is expected to have the biggest percentage increase in number of households from 1995 to 2010? (b) Is the number of households of any ethnic group projected to decrease during that time?

4. Draw conclusions. The ethnic groups appear in order from the most households (white) to the fewest (American Indian, Eskimo, and Aleut) in 1995. (a) Is this ranking expected to change by 2010? (b) From this fact, state a one- or two-sentence conclusion.

Test for Success

The number of Hispanic Americans is expected to surpass the number of African Americans within several years, making Hispanics the largest minority in the country. Given this fact, and using information from the table, what can you conclude about the size of households of these two groups?

United States
Census 2000

U.S. Department of Commerce
Bureau of the Census

This is the official form for all the people at this address. It is quick and easy, and your answers are protected by law. Complete the Census and help your community get what it needs — today and in the future!

Number of U.S. Households, by Ethnic Group: 1995 to 2010				
Ethnic Group	**1995**	**2000†**	**2005†**	**2010†**
White	83,126,521	86,675,553	90,204,246	94,010,462
Black	11,152,480	12,149,243	13,136,816	14,185,450
Hispanic Origin*	7,368,163	8,760,637	10,236,089	11,866,338
Asian American and Pacific Islander	2,608,341	3,155,373	3,723,988	4,323,828
American Indian, Eskimo, and Aleut	686,847	754,180	827,029	906,036
Total	97,574,189	102,734,349	107,892,079	113,425,776

*Persons of Hispanic Origin may be of any race. These data do not include households of Puerto Ricans.   †Projected
SOURCE: U.S. Census Bureau

Section Preview

OBJECTIVES

1. **Explain** the importance of the Equal Protection Clause.
2. **Describe** the history of segregation in America.
3. **Examine** how classification by sex relates to discrimination.

WHY IT MATTERS

The law includes safeguards to protect Americans from unfair discrimination on the basis of race or sex. The most important protections lie in the 5th and 14th amendments and the Civil Rights Act of 1964.

POLITICAL DICTIONARY

★ segregation
★ Jim Crow law
★ separate-but-equal doctrine
★ integration
★ de jure segregation
★ de facto segregation

Records recently unearthed by the Architect of the Capitol show that at least 400 slaves worked on the building's construction from 1792 through 1800, and they likely did for several years thereafter.

Those records also indicate payments to a number of local slave owners—for example, "To Joseph Forest, for the hire of the Negro Charles." The slave owners were paid $5 a month for laborers. Slaves even cast the bronze statue of *Freedom* and hoisted it atop the Capitol in 1800.

Equal Protection Clause

Nothing, not even a constitutional command, can *make* people equal in a literal sense. Individuals differ in strength, intelligence, height, and countless other ways. Still, the democratic ideal demands that government must treat all persons alike.

The equality of all persons, so boldly set out in the Declaration of Independence, is not proclaimed in so many words in the Constitution. Still, that concept pervades the document.

The closest approach to a literal statement of equality is to be found in the 14th Amendment's Equal Protection Clause. It declares:

 FROM THE *Constitution*

> ❝No State shall . . . deny to any person within its jurisdiction the equal protection of the laws. ❞
> —United States Constitution

The clause was originally intended to benefit newly freed slaves. Over time, it has acquired a broader meaning. Today, it forbids States and local governments to draw unreasonable distinctions between classes of persons. The Supreme Court has often held that the 5th Amendment's Due Process Clause puts the same restriction on the Federal Government.

Reasonable Classification

Government must have the power to classify, to draw distinctions between persons and groups. Otherwise, it could not possibly regulate human behavior. That is to say, government must be able to discriminate—and it does. Thus, those who rob banks fall into a special class, and they receive special treatment by the law. That sort of discrimination is clearly reasonable.

Government may not discriminate *unreasonably*, however. Every State taxes the sale of cigarettes, and so taxes smokers but not nonsmokers. No State can tax only blonde smokers, however, or only male smokers.

Over time, the Supreme Court has rejected many equal protection challenges to the actions of government.

▶ *Freedom* atop the Capitol

In 1955, **Rosa Parks** refused to give her seat to a white man on a bus in Montgomery, Alabama, and was subsequently arrested. That simple act led to a bus boycott by African Americans and helped the civil rights movement grow into a national cause. Parks, who had long worked for civil rights, later explained her brave action:

❝For half of my life there were laws and customs in the South that kept African Americans segregated from Caucasians and allowed white people to treat black people without any respect. I never thought this was fair, and from the time I was a child, I tried to protest against disrespectful treatment. But it was very hard to do anything about segregation and racism when white people had the power of the law behind them. Somehow we had to change the laws. **❞**

Evaluating the Quotation

From what you have read, how did court decisions combine with changes in the law to move the nation toward protecting civil rights?

More often than not, the Supreme Court has found that what those governments have done is, in fact, constitutional.[4]

The Rational Basis Test

The Supreme Court most often decides equal protection cases by applying a standard known as the rational basis test. This test asks: Does the classification in question bear a reasonable relationship to the achievement of some proper governmental purpose?

A California case, *Michael M.* v. *Superior Court*, 1981, illustrates that test. California law says that a man who has sexual relations with a girl under 18 to whom he is not married can be prosecuted for statutory rape. However, the girl

---

[4]The Court has voided a number of those actions on equal protection grounds, however. You will consider several of those cases in a moment, and you have encountered many others previously—for example, with regard to lengthy residence requirements for voting purposes and gerrymandering on the basis of race.

cannot be charged with that crime, even if she is a willing partner. The Court found the law to bear a reasonable relationship to a proper public policy goal: preventing teenage pregnancies.

The Strict Scrutiny Test

The Court imposes a higher standard in some equal protection cases, however. This is especially true when a case deals with (1) such "fundamental rights" as the right to vote, the right to travel between the States, or 1st Amendment rights; or (2) such "suspect classifications" as those based on race, sex, or national origin.

In these instances, the Court has said that a law must meet a higher standard than the rational basis test. This standard is called the strict scrutiny test. The State must be able to show that some "compelling governmental interest" justifies the distinctions it has drawn between classes of people.

An alimony case, *Orr* v. *Orr,* 1979, involved the use of that stricter test. An Alabama law that made women but not men eligible for alimony was held unconstitutional, as a denial of equal protection—because the law's distinction between men and women did not serve a compelling governmental interest.

Segregation in America

Beginning in the late 1800s, nearly half of the States passed racial segregation laws. **Segregation** means the separation of one group from another. Most of those **Jim Crow laws**—laws that separate people on the basis of race—were aimed at African Americans. Some were also drawn to affect Mexican Americans, Asians, and Native Americans. These laws required segregation by race in the use of both public and private facilities: schools, parks and playgrounds, hotels and restaurants, streetcars, even public drinking fountains.

Separate-but-Equal Doctrine

In 1896, the Supreme Court provided a constitutional basis for Jim Crow laws by creating the **separate-but-equal doctrine.** In *Plessy* v. *Ferguson,* it upheld a Louisiana law requiring segregation in rail coaches. The Court held that the law did not violate the Equal Protection Clause because the separate facilities provided for African Americans were equal to those for whites.

The separate-but-equal doctrine soon became the constitutional justification for segregation in several other fields, and it stood for nearly 60 years. Indeed, until the late 1930s, little effort was made by any arm of government even to see that the separate accommodations for African Americans were, in fact, equal to those reserved to whites. More often than not, they were not.

Brown v. Board of Education

The Supreme Court first began to chip away at the separate-but-equal doctrine in *Missouri ex rel. Gaines* v. *Canada* in 1938. Lloyd Gaines, an African American, was denied admission to the law school at the all-white University of Missouri. Gaines was fully qualified for admission—except for his race. The State did not have a separate law school for African Americans. However, it did offer to pay his tuition at a public law school in any of four neighboring States, which did not discriminate by race. But Gaines insisted on a legal education in his home State.

The Court held that the separate-but-equal doctrine left Missouri with only two choices: It could either admit Gaines to the State's law school or establish a separate-but-equal school for him. The State gave in and admitted Gaines.

Over the next several years, the Court took an increasingly rigorous attitude toward the requirement of equal facilities. It began to insist on equality *in fact* between separate facilities. Finally, in an historic decision in 1954, the Court reversed *Plessy* v. *Ferguson*. In *Brown* v. *Board of Education of Topeka*, it struck down the laws of four States requiring or allowing separate public schools for white and African American students.[5]

Unanimously, the Supreme Court held that segregation by race in public education is unconstitutional:

PRIMARY Sources *"Does segregation of children in public schools solely on the basis of race, even though the physical facilities and other 'tangible' factors may be equal, deprive the children of the minority group of equal educational opportunities? We believe that it does.*

. . . To separate them from others of similar age and qualifications solely because of their race generates a feeling of inferiority

▲ *The Migrants Cast Their Ballots* Beginning early in the last century, many African Americans left the South for jobs in northern cities. Migrants encountered fewer Jim Crow laws in the North, but faced discrimination that closed them out of good jobs, schools, and housing. Artist Jacob Lawrence captured the lives of African Americans in works such as *The Migrants Cast Their Ballots.*

as to their status in the community that may affect their hearts and minds in a way unlikely ever to be undone. . . . We conclude that in the field of public education the doctrine of 'separate but equal' has no place. Separate educational facilities are inherently unequal."
—Chief Justice Earl Warren, Opinion of the Court

The Court in 1955 directed the States to make "a prompt and reasonable start" and to end segregation "with all deliberate speed." Federal district courts were ordered to supervise the desegregation process.

A "reasonable start" was made in Baltimore, Louisville, St. Louis, and elsewhere. In most of the Deep South, however, "massive resistance" soon developed. State legislatures passed laws and school boards worked to block **integration** —the process of bringing a group into the mainstream of society. Most of these steps were clearly unconstitutional, but challenging them in court was costly and slow.

---

[5]Kansas, Delaware, South Carolina, and Virginia. On the same day, it also struck down racially segregated public schools in the District of Columbia, under the 5th Amendment, *Bolling* v. *Sharpe*, 1954.

The pace of desegregation quickened after Congress passed the Civil Rights Act of 1964. That act forbids the use of federal funds to aid any State or local activity in which racial segregation is practiced. It directed the Justice Department to file suits to prompt desegregation actions.

The Supreme Court quickened the pace in 1969. In a case from Mississippi, *Alexander* v. *Holmes County Board of Education,* it ruled that, after 15 years, the time for "all deliberate speed" had ended. Said a unanimous Court: "The continued operation of segregated schools under a standard allowing for 'all deliberate speed' . . . is no longer constitutionally permissible."

De Jure, De Facto Segregation

By fall 1970, school systems characterized by **de jure segregation** had been abolished. De jure segregation is segregation by law, with legal sanction. That is not to say that desegregation had been fully accomplished—far from it.[6]

Many recent integration controversies have come in places where the schools have never been segregated by law. They have occurred, instead, in communities in which **de facto segregation** has long been present, and continues. De facto segregation is segregation in fact, even if no law requires it. Housing patterns have most often been its major cause. The concentration of African Americans in certain sections of cities inevitably led to local school systems in which some schools are largely African American. That condition is apparent in many northern as well as southern communities.

Efforts to desegregate those school systems have taken several forms. School district lines have been redrawn and the busing of students out of racially segregated neighborhoods has been tried. These efforts have brought strong protests in many places and violence in some.

The Supreme Court first sanctioned busing in a North Carolina case, *Swann* v. *Charlotte-Mecklenburg Board of Education,* 1971. There it held that "desegregation plans cannot be limited to walk-in schools." Since then, busing has been used to increase the racial mix in many school districts across the country. In some cases busing is by court order; in others it is voluntary.

Segregation in Other Fields

This nation has not yet achieved a complete integration of the public schools, but legally enforced racial segregation in all other areas of life has been eliminated. Many State and local laws have been repealed or struck down by the courts.

---

[6]Some States, several school districts, and many parents and private groups have sought to avoid integrated schools through established or, often, newly created private schools. On the point, see the Court's rulings in *Runyon* v. *McCrary,* 1976, page 570.

The *Living* Constitution

The Supreme Court and Civil Rights   1900

The Constitution describes Americans' civil rights only in general terms. The courts, especially the Supreme Court, have had to decide how these constitutional guarantees apply to specific situations. As the time line entries show, some Court decisions have supported and broadened civil liberties, while other decisions have restricted them.

1883 In the *Civil Rights Cases,* the Court rules that the 14th Amendment does not ban racial discrimination by private individuals or businesses.

1896 In *Plessy* v. *Ferguson,* the Court rules that "separate but equal" facilities for different races are acceptable.

The Supreme Court has found segregation by race to be as unconstitutional in other areas as it is in public education. It has held that the Equal Protection Clause forbids segregation in: public swimming pools or other recreational facilities, *Baltimore* v. *Dawson*, 1955; local transportation, *Gayle* v. *Browder*, 1956; and State prisons and local jails, *Lee* v. *Washington*, 1968. The High Court struck down all State miscegenation laws (laws that forbid interracial marriages) in *Loving* v. *Virginia*, 1967. It has held that race cannot be the basis for a child custody decision, *Palmore* v. *Sidoti*, 1984.

Classification by Sex

The Constitution speaks of the civil rights of "the people," "persons," and "citizens." Nowhere does it make its guarantees only to "men" or separately to "women." The only reference to sex is in the 19th Amendment, which forbids denial of the right to vote "on account of sex."

Gender has long been used as a basis of classification in the law, however. By and large, that practice reflected society's historic view of the "proper" role of women. Most often, laws that treated men and women differently were intended to protect "the weaker sex." Over the years, the Supreme Court read that view into the 14th Amendment. It did not find *any*

sex-based classification to be unconstitutional until 1971.

In the first case to challenge sex discrimination, *Bradwell* v. *Illinois*, 1873, the Court upheld a State law barring women from the practice of law. In that case, Justice Joseph P. Bradley wrote that:

PRIMARY Sources "*The civil law, as well as nature itself, has always recognized a wide difference in the respective spheres and destinies of man and woman. Man is, or should be, woman's protector and defender. The natural and proper timidity and delicacy of the female sex evidently unfits it for many of the occupations of civil life.*"
—Concurring Opinion

Even as late as 1961, in *Hoyt* v. *Florida*, the Court could find no constitutional fault with a law that required men to serve on juries, but gave women the choice of serving or not.

Matters are far different today. The Court now takes a very close look at cases involving claims of sex discrimination. The first such case was *Reed* v. *Reed*, 1971, in which the Court struck down an Idaho law that gave fathers preference over mothers in the administration of their children's estates.

Since then, the Supreme Court has found a number of sex-based distinctions to be unconstitutional. In *Taylor* v. *Louisiana*, 1975, the Court held that the Equal Protection Clause forbids the

1944 In *Korematsu* v. *United States*, the Court upholds the internment of Japanese Americans during World War II.

1954 In *Brown* v. *Board of Education*, the Court rules that "separate but equal" public schools are unconstitutional.

1988 In *New York State Club Association* v. *City of New York*, the Court upholds a law that stops most private clubs from denying membership to women.

| 1925 | 1950 | 1975 | 2000 |

Analyzing Time Lines

1. Which Supreme Court decision endorsed the principle of "separate but equal" facilities? Which decision rejected this idea?
2. Besides African Americans, what groups of people could be affected by the Supreme Court's recent civil liberties rulings?

1978 In *Regents of University of California* v. *Bakke*, the Court rules that affirmative action is acceptable but strict quotas are not.

2001 In *Hunt* v. *Cromartie*, the Court holds that, while race cannot be the controlling factor in drawing electoral district lines, it can be one of the several factors that shape that process.

States to exclude women from jury service. It has also struck down an Oklahoma law that prohibited the sale of beer to males under 21 and to females under 18, *Craig* v. *Boren*, 1976. Also unconstitutional is the practice of refusing to admit women to the rigorous citizen-soldier program offered by a public institution, Virginia Military Institute, *United States* v. *Virginia*, 1996.

In the same vein, the Supreme Court has upheld a California law that prohibits community service clubs from excluding women from membership, *Rotary International* v. *Rotary Club of Duarte*, 1987. It also upheld a New York City ordinance that forbids sex discrimination in any place of public accommodation, including large private-membership clubs used by their members for business purposes, *New York State Club Association, Inc.* v. *City of New York*, 1988.

The Court's present attitude was put this way in *Frontiero* v. *Richardson*, 1973:

PRIMARY Sources *"There can be no doubt that our nation has had a long and unfortunate history of sex discrimination. Traditionally, such discrimination was rationalized by an attitude of 'romantic paternalism' which, in practical effect, put women, not on a pedestal, but in a cage. "*[7]

—Justice William J. Brennan, Jr.,
Opinion of the Court

Not all sex-based distinctions are unconstitutional, however. The Supreme Court has upheld some of them in several cases. You saw one example of this in *Michael M.* v. *Superior Court*, 1981. Similarly, the Court has upheld a Florida law that gives an extra property tax exemption to widows, but not to widowers, *Kahn* v. *Shevin*, 1974; an Alabama law forbidding women to serve as prison guards in all-male penitentiaries, *Dothard* v. *Rawlinson*, 1977; and the federal selective service law that requires only men to register for the draft and excludes women from any future draft, *Rostker* v. *Goldberg*, 1981.

In effect, these cases say this: Classification by sex is not in and of itself unconstitutional. However, laws that treat men and women differently will be overturned by the courts unless (1) they are intended to serve an "important governmental objective" and (2) they are "substantially related" to achieving that goal.

In upholding the all-male draft, the Court found that Congress did in fact have an important governmental objective: to raise and support armies and, if necessary, to do so by "a draft of combat troops." "Since women are excluded from combat," said the Supreme Court, they may properly be excluded from the draft.

---

[7]In this case the Court, for the first time, struck down a federal law providing for sex-based discrimination, as a violation of the 5th Amendment's Due Process Clause. That law gave various housing, medical, and other allowances to a serviceman for his wife and other dependents, but it made those same allowances available to a servicewoman only if her husband was dependent on her for more than half of his support.

Section 2 Assessment

Key Terms and Main Ideas

1. What was the purpose of **Jim Crow laws**?
2. Which important Supreme Court case led to school **integration**?
3. Explain the difference between **de jure segregation** and **de facto segregation**.
4. Who put the **separate-but-equal doctrine** in place? What does that doctrine say?

Critical Thinking

5. **Making Decisions** In your opinion, which would be harder to combat, de facto or de jure segregation? Why?

6. **Recognizing Bias** Read the quote from Justice Bradley on page 605. **(a)** What is the only statement that can be considered a fact, and not an opinion? **(b)** List three opinions included in the quote.

 Take It to the Net

7. Learn more about how the courts have handled discrimination cases. Select several cases and outline the major points of each one. Are the outcomes of the cases similar? Use the links provided in the Social Studies area at the following Web site for help in completing this activity. **www.phschool.com**

Breaking Down Barriers

Ernest Green was the first black student to graduate from Central High School in Little Rock, Arkansas. Mr. Green recalls the historic days in 1957 when, as one of the "Little Rock Nine," he helped bring an end to school segregation in the United States.

When the U.S. Supreme Court handed down its historic *Brown v. Board of Education of Topeka, Kansas,* decision in 1954, I was a student in Little Rock, Arkansas, finishing the eighth grade. Little Rock had one high school for blacks . . . and one for whites, Little Rock Central High School. . . .

The *Brown* decision made me feel that the U.S. Constitution was finally working for me. . . . I could believe I was a full citizen, not a second-class citizen as segregation had made me feel.

In the spring of 1957, I was asked, along with other black students in Little Rock, to consider attending Central High School the following fall. Initially, a number of students signed up to enroll, but when fall came, only nine of us had survived the pressure to quit. . . .

During the summer, rumors began to circulate that there might be violence if the "Little Rock Nine," as we became known, tried to attend school in the fall. I didn't pay much attention to what was going on. . . .

But when we tried to attend school, we were met by an angry white mob and armed soldiers. Arkansas Governor Orval Faubus had called out the National Guard to prevent us from enrolling, defying a federal court order to integrate Little Rock schools. Governor Faubus said he was doing this to protect the peace and tranquility of the community; obviously, my rights were secondary. . . .

Finally, President Dwight Eisenhower called out the U.S. Army's famous 101st Airborne Division to protect us and enforce the federal court's integration order. . . .

When we tried to attend school again, about 1,000 paratroopers were there to protect us. We rode to school in an army station wagon, surrounded by army jeeps that were loaded with soldiers holding machine guns and drawn bayonets. It was an exciting ride to school!

Once we got inside, it was like being in a war zone. We were harassed, our books were destroyed, and our lockers were broken into several times a day. . . .

I was a senior that year. As graduation neared, I was surprised at the number of students who signed my yearbook, saying they admired my courage in sticking it out. But on the night of graduation, there was an eerie silence when my name was called. I didn't care that no one clapped for me. I knew that not only had I achieved something for myself, but I had broken a barrier as well.

Ernest Green shows his textbooks to children in Little Rock.

Analyzing Primary Sources

1. Why did Green decide to enroll in Central High School?
2. What resistance did the "Little Rock Nine" encounter when they tried to enroll at the school?
3. How was Green finally able to attend the school?
4. Why would attending Central High School have made Green feel that he was no longer a "second-class citizen"?

Section Preview

OBJECTIVES

1. **Outline** the history of civil rights legislation from Reconstruction to today.
2. **Explore** the issues surrounding affirmative action.

WHY IT MATTERS

Federal laws passed in the 1960s and later ended long-standing discrimination in voting, housing, public accommodations, and many other areas. Affirmative action policies remain controversial.

POLITICAL DICTIONARY

★ **affirmative action**
★ **quota**
★ **reverse discrimination**

Y ou may have heard this oft-made argument: "You can't legislate morality." That is, racism, sexism, and other forms of discrimination cannot be eliminated merely with laws.

Martin Luther King, Jr., replied to that contention this way: "Laws," he said, "may not change the heart, but they can restrain the heartless." Congress has agreed with Dr. King—as it has enacted a number of civil rights laws over the past 40 years.

Civil Rights: Reconstruction to Today

From the 1870s to the late 1950s, Congress did not pass a single piece of meaningful civil rights legislation. Several factors contributed to that sorry fact. First, through that period the nation's predominantly white population was generally unaware of or little concerned with the plight of African Americans, Native Americans, or other nonwhites in this country. Secondly, southern white Democrats, bolstered by such devices as the seniority system and the filibuster, held many of the most strategic posts in Congress.

◀ Martin Luther King, Jr.

That historic logjam was broken in 1957, very largely as a result of the pressures brought to bear by the civil rights movement led by Dr. King (see Chapter 6, pages 159–163). Beginning in that year, Congress passed a number of civil rights laws—notably, the Civil Rights Acts of 1957, 1960, 1964, and 1968 and the Voting Rights Acts of 1965, 1970, 1975, and 1982. The 1957 and 1960 laws set up modest safeguards for the right to vote.[8]

The Civil Rights Act of 1964

The 1964 law is the most far-reaching of these statutes. It passed after the longest debate in the Senate's history (83 days), and only after the Senate had invoked cloture to kill a filibuster.

Beyond its voting rights provisions, the 1964 law outlaws discrimination in a number of areas. With its several later amendments, the law's major sections now:

(1) provide that no person may be denied access to or refused service in various "public accommodations" because of race, color, religion, or national origin (Title II).[9]

---

[8] You considered the voting rights provision in these statutes in Chapter 6. See pages 160–163. The 1957 law created the U.S. Civil Rights Commission. The commission is an independent eight-member agency that is supposed to monitor the enforcement of the various civil rights laws, investigate cases of alleged discrimination, and report its findings to the President, Congress, and the public.

[9] Congress based this section of the law on its commerce power; see Chapter 11, pages 294–300. Title II covers those places in which lodgings are offered to transient guests and those where a significant portion of the items sold have moved in interstate commerce. The Supreme Court upheld Title II and the use of the Commerce Clause as a basis for civil rights legislation in *Heart of Atlanta Motel, Inc.* v. *United States,* 1964.

(2) prohibit discrimination against any person on grounds of race, color, religion, national origin, sex, or physical disability in any program that receives any federal funding; require the cut-off of federal funds to any program that practices such discrimination (Title VI).

(3) forbid employers and labor unions to discriminate against any person on grounds of race, color, religion, sex, physical disability, or age in job-related matters (Title VII).[10]

The Civil Rights Act of 1968

The Civil Rights Act of 1968 is often called the Open Housing Act. With minor exceptions, it forbids anyone to refuse to sell or rent a dwelling to any person on grounds of race, color, religion, national origin, sex, or disability. It also forbids refusal to sell or rent to a family with children. At first, the burden of enforcing the law fell on those persons who claimed to be the victims of housing discrimination. Congress finally strengthened the law in 1988, by allowing the Justice Department to bring criminal charges against those who violate its terms.

Affirmative Action

These several civil rights statutes all come down to this: Discriminatory practices based on such factors as race, color, national origin, or sex are illegal. But what about the effects of past discrimination? Consider an African American who, for no reason of his or her own making, did not get a decent education and so today cannot get a decent job. Of what real help to that person are all of those laws that make illegal today what was done years ago?

So far, the Federal Government's chief answer to this troubling question has been a policy of **affirmative action.** That policy requires that most employers take positive steps (affirmative action) to remedy the effects of past discriminations. The policy applies to all the agencies of the Federal Government, to all the States and their local governments, and to all those private employers who sell goods or services to any agency of the Federal Government.

---

[10]The 1964 law also created the Equal Employment Opportunity Commission. The five-member EEOC's major responsibility is the enforcement of Title VII.

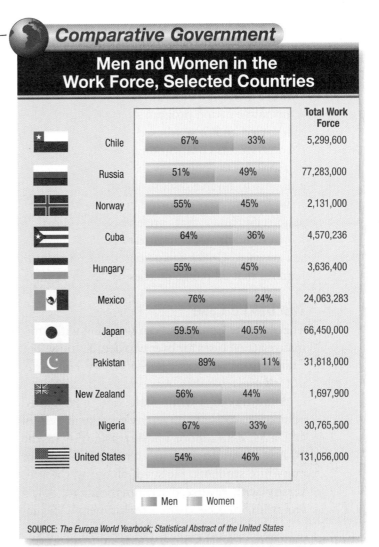

Comparative Government

Men and Women in the Work Force, Selected Countries

		Men	Women	Total Work Force
	Chile	67%	33%	5,299,600
	Russia	51%	49%	77,283,000
	Norway	55%	45%	2,131,000
	Cuba	64%	36%	4,570,236
	Hungary	55%	45%	3,636,400
	Mexico	76%	24%	24,063,283
	Japan	59.5%	40.5%	66,450,000
	Pakistan	89%	11%	31,818,000
	New Zealand	56%	44%	1,697,900
	Nigeria	67%	33%	30,765,500
	United States	54%	46%	131,056,000

Men ▮ Women

SOURCE: *The Europa World Yearbook; Statistical Abstract of the United States*

Interpreting Graphs This graph shows the percentage of men and women in the work force in selected countries. *(a) In which two countries are the lowest percentages of women employed? (b) In which two countries are the highest percentages of women employed?*

The Federal Government began to demand the adoption of affirmative action programs in 1965. Some programs are simply plans that call for the wide advertisement of job openings. Most, however, establish guidelines and timetables to overcome past discriminations.

To illustrate the policy, take the case of a company that does business with the Federal Government. That private business must adopt an affirmative action plan designed to make its work force reflect the general makeup of the population in its locale. The company's program must also include steps to correct or prevent inequalities in such matters as pay, promotions, and fringe benefits.

For many employers this has meant that they must hire and/or promote more workers with minority backgrounds and more females. Such rules requiring certain numbers of jobs or promotions for members of certain groups are called **quotas.**

Reverse Discrimination?

Affirmative action programs necessarily involve race-based and/or sex-based classifications. Are such programs constitutional?

Critics of the policy say that affirmative action amounts to **reverse discrimination,** or discrimination against the majority group. Affirmative action demands that preference be given to females and/or nonwhites solely on the basis of sex or race. Critics insist that the Constitution requires that all public policies be "color blind."

The Bakke Case

The Supreme Court has been wrestling with affirmative action cases for over two decades now. The Court's first major case, *Regents of the University of California* v. *Bakke*, was decided in 1978.

Allan Bakke, a white male, had been denied admission to that university's medical school at Davis. The school had set aside 16 of the 100 seats in each year's entering class for nonwhite students. He sued, charging the university with reverse discrimination and, so, a violation of the 14th Amendment's Equal

Protection Clause. By a 5–4 majority, the Court held that Bakke had been denied equal protection and should be admitted to the medical school.

A differently composed 5–4 majority made the more far-reaching ruling in the case, however. Although the Constitution does not allow race to be used as the *only* factor in the making of affirmative action decisions, both the Constitution and the 1964 Civil Rights Act do allow its use as one among several factors in such situations.

Later Cases

The Supreme Court has decided several affirmative action cases since *Bakke.* In some of them it has upheld quotas, especially when longstanding, flagrant discrimination was involved.

In *United Steelworkers* v. *Weber,* 1979, the Kaiser Aluminum Company had created training programs intended to increase the number of skilled African Americans in its work force. Trainees were chosen on the basis of race and seniority. Brian Weber, a white worker, was rejected for training three times. Each time, however, a number of African Americans with less seniority were picked.

Weber went to court. The Court found that the training programs, although built on quotas, did not violate the 1964 law. That law, it said, Congress had purposely designed to "overcome manifest racial imbalances."

Fullilove v. *Klutznick,* 1980, was another case in which the Court upheld quotas. That case centered on a law Congress had passed that provided $4 billion in grants to State and local governments for public works projects. It also contained a "minority set-aside" provision. The provision required that at least 10 percent of each grant had to be set aside for minority-owned businesses.

A white contractor challenged the set-asides. He argued that they were quotas and therefore unconstitutional—because they did not give white contractors an equal chance to compete for all of the available funds. The Court held the law to be a permissible attempt to overcome the effects of blatant and longstanding bias in the construction industry.

Note, however, that quotas can be used in only the most extreme situations. Thus, the Court rejected a city's minority set-aside

▲ Allan Bakke (left) successfully challenged the admissions policies of the University of California. *Critical Thinking How did the* **Bakke** *case leave the legal status of affirmative action unsettled?*

policy in *Richmond* v. *Croson,* 1989. There the Court held, 6–3, that the city of Richmond, Virginia, had not shown that its ordinance was justified by past discrimination. Therefore, it had denied white contractors their right to equal protection.

Johnson v. *Transportation Agency of Santa Clara County,* 1987, marked the first time the Court decided a case of preferential treatment on the basis of sex. By a 6–3 vote, the justices held that neither the Equal Protection Clause nor Title VII of the 1964 law forbids the promotion of a woman rather than a man, even though he had scored higher on a qualifying interview than she did. The case arose in California, when a woman was promoted to a job that until then had always been held by a man.

The current Supreme Court's increasingly conservative bent is evident in some of its more recent affirmative action decisions. Thus, for example, in *Wards Cove Packing Co.* v. *Atonio,* 1989, the Court made it more difficult for those who charge discrimination to prove their point. There, a group of nonwhite cannery workers in Alaska produced statistical evidence to bolster their case. The data showed a longstanding pattern of employment practices by which their cannery company channeled nonwhites into low-paying jobs, while whites received the much more desirable positions.

The Court ruled against them, however. It held, 5–4, that such statistical evidence was not adequate proof of race discrimination. Instead, said the majority, Title VII requires that those who claim discrimination in employment must be able to show that the conditions they challenge are not the result of some legitimate "business necessity."

The Court's holding in *Wards Cove* was pointedly rejected by an act of Congress in 1991. In effect, Congress said that the Court had misread Title VII. The new law declares that Title VII means this: Any business practice that results in the unequal treatment of female or minority employees is permissible only if the employer can show that that practice is based on some legitimate business necessity. Note that in

▲ *Title IX* Title IX of the Educational Amendments of 1972 requires near-equal funding for men's and women's athletic teams at public schools and universities. This decision dramatically increased opportunities for women to participate in sports.

Wards Cove it was the *employees'* responsibility to show that the action did not serve a legitimate business necessity.

The Adarand Case

Adarand Constructors v. *Pena,* 1995, is the most recent major affirmative action case. Its decision marked a major departure from the Supreme Court's previous rulings in such cases.

Until *Adarand,* the High Court had regularly accepted affirmative action laws, regulations, and programs as "benign" instances of "race-conscious policy-making." By this, the Court meant that it considered them mild but necessary. In *Adarand,* however, the Court made it much more difficult for the Federal Government to use affirmative action programs. It held that whenever government provides for any preferential treatment based on race, that action is almost certainly unconstitutional. This is likely to be true even when it is intended to benefit minority groups suffering from past injustices.

"The Constitution protects persons, not groups," wrote Justice Sandra Day O'Connor. "Whenever the government treats any person unequally because of his or her race, that person has suffered an injury" covered by "the Constitution's guarantee of equal treatment." Government can conduct affirmative action programs, said the Court, but only when they

▲ Students at the University of California marched to defend affirmative action at their school. **Critical Thinking** *Did high school and college students have much say in the decision to end state-sponsored affirmative action in California?*

subcontracted to "socially and economically disadvantaged" businesses, including those owned by racial minorities.

Affirmative Action on the Ballot

The controversy surrounding affirmative action continues. In 1996, California's voters gave overwhelming approval to an initiative measure that eliminated nearly all of the affirmative action programs conducted by public agencies in that State.

The measure, Proposition 209, amended the State's constitution. It forbids all State and local agencies (including public schools, colleges, and universities) to discriminate against or give preferential treatment to any person or group on the basis of race, sex, color, ethnicity, or national origin. The measure covers matters of employment, education, or contracting. It only allows exceptions where necessary to satisfy some federal requirement.

A federal district court found Proposition 209 unconstitutional in late 1996. It held that the measure violated both the 14th Amendment's Equal Protection Clause and the Supremacy Clause in Article VI. That decision was overturned by the Court of Appeals for the 9th Circuit in 1997. The Supreme Court refused to hear an appeal of the Circuit Court's ruling.

In 1998, Washington's voters adopted an initiative measure almost identical to California's Proposition 209. Encouraged by their successes in California and Washington, opponents of affirmative action have launched campaigns to put similar measures on the ballot in other States.

are "narrowly tailored" to overcome specific, clearly provable cases of discrimination.

Adarand arose when a white-owned Colorado company, Adarand Constructors, Inc., challenged an affirmative action policy of the Federal Highway Administration (FHA). Under that policy, the FHA gave bonuses to highway contractors if 10 percent or more of their construction work was

Section 3 Assessment

Key Terms and Main Ideas

1. What is the purpose of **affirmative action**?
2. Under what circumstances has the Supreme Court allowed **quotas**?
3. Who, in a general sense, is disadvantaged by **reverse discrimination**?

Critical Thinking

4. **Expressing Problems Clearly** In your opinion, is it society's responsibility to rectify the harm suffered by a group of people as a result of discrimination in the past?
5. **Making Decisions** Universities often extend preferences to "legacies"—students whose parents attended that school.

Based on past discrimination at many universities, how do these policies support or weaken the case for affirmative action?

Take It to the Net

6. Explore a time line of civil rights and affirmative action. Select four events that you feel were turning points in the struggle for equal rights. Explain why you chose these events and how they had an impact on society. Use the links provided in the Social Studies area at the following Web site for help in completing this activity. **www.phschool.com**

4 American Citizenship

Section Preview

OBJECTIVES

1. **Identify** the questions surrounding American citizenship.
2. **Describe** how people become American citizens by birth and by naturalization.
3. **Explain** how an American can lose his or her citizenship.
4. **Illustrate** how the United States is a nation of immigrants.
5. **Compare and contrast** the status of undocumented aliens and legal immigrants.

WHY IT MATTERS

People can receive American citizenship through their parents or by undergoing a rigorous process of naturalization. As immigration to the United States has surged, record numbers of immigrants are becoming American citizens.

POLITICAL DICTIONARY

★ citizen
★ jus soli
★ jus sanguinis
★ naturalization
★ alien
★ expatriation
★ denaturalization
★ deportation

Are you an American **citizen**—one who owes allegiance to the United States and is entitled to its protection? Very likely you are; more than 90 percent of all the people who live in this country are citizens of the United States. Many of those who are not citizens actively seek that distinction.

The Question of Citizenship

As it was originally written, the Constitution mentioned both "citizens of the United States" and "citizens of the States." It did not define either of those phrases, however. Through much of America's early history, it was generally agreed that national citizenship followed that of the States.

The coming of the Civil War and the adoption of the 13th Amendment in 1865 raised the need for a constitutional definition.[11] That need was finally met in 1868 by the 14th Amendment, which begins with these words:

FROM THE *Constitution* **"***All persons born or naturalized in the United States and*

subject to the jurisdiction thereof, are citizens of the United States and of the State wherein they reside.**"**
—United States Constitution

Thus, the 14th Amendment declares that a person can become an American citizen either by birth or by naturalization. The chart on page 615 summarizes the means by which American citizenship can be acquired.

Citizenship by Birth

Some 260 million Americans—over 90 percent of us—are American citizens because we were born in the United States. Another several million are also citizens by birth, even though they were born abroad. Citizenship by birth is determined by either **jus soli** or **jus sanguinis.**

Jus soli is the law of the soil, or where one is born. The 14th Amendment confers citizenship according to the location of a person's birth: "All persons born . . . in the United States. . . ." Congress has defined the United States to include, for purposes of citizenship, the 50 States, the District of Columbia, Puerto Rico, Guam, the Virgin Islands, and the Northern Mariana Islands. It also includes American embassies and American public vessels anywhere in the world.

Until 1924, Native Americans born to tribal members living on reservations were not citizens,

---

[11]In the Dred Scott case *(Scott* v. *Sandford)* in 1857, the Supreme Court had ruled that neither the States nor the National Government had the power to confer citizenship on African Americans—slave or free. The dispute over that issue was one of the several causes of the Civil War.

To become a naturalized citizen, a person must:

★ be at least 18 years old

★ have entered the country legally, lived in the United States for at least five years (for husbands or wives of citizens, three years)

★ file a petition for naturalization with the clerk of a Federal district court or a State court of record

★ be literate in the English language

★ be "of good moral character," "attached to the principles of the Constitution," and "well disposed to the good order and happiness of the United States"

★ have "a knowledge and understanding of the fundamentals of the history, and the principles and form of government, of the United States"

★ take an oath or affirmation in which he or she absolutely renounces any allegiance to any foreign power and promises to "support and defend the Constitution and laws of the United States against all enemies, foreign and domestic"

Interpreting Charts **Which of these requirements do you think is the most difficult to evaluate?**

but wards, persons under the legal guardianship, of the government. In that year, Congress granted citizenship to all Native Americans who did not already possess it.

Jus sanguinis is the law of the blood, or to whom one is born. A child born abroad can become an American citizen at birth under certain circumstances described in the chart on page 615. The child must be born to at least one parent who is a citizen, and who has at some time lived in the United States.

The 14th Amendment does not provide for jus sanguinis, but Congress has included it as a part of American citizenship law since 1790. The constitutionality of the rule has never been challenged.

Citizenship by Naturalization

Naturalization is the legal process by which a person becomes a citizen of another country at some time after birth. Congress has the exclusive power to provide for naturalization. No State may do so.[12]

Individual Naturalization

Naturalization is most often an individual process, conducted by a court. More than 800,000 aliens now become naturalized American citizens each year. An **alien** is a citizen or national of a foreign state living in this country.

Generally, any person who has come to the United States as an immigrant can be naturalized. The chart on page 615 describes the different ways that people can become American citizens.

The Immigration and Naturalization Service (INS) in the Department of Justice investigates each applicant, and then reports to the judge of the court overseeing the petition for naturalization. If the judge is satisfied, the oath or affirmation is administered in open court, and the new citizen receives a certificate of naturalization.

Collective Naturalization

At various times in American history an entire group of persons has been naturalized *en masse*. This has most often happened when the United States has acquired new territory. As the chart on the next page indicates, those living in the areas involved were naturalized by a treaty or by an act or a joint resolution passed by Congress.

The largest single instance of collective naturalization came with the ratification of the 14th Amendment, however. The most recent instance occurred in 1977, when Congress gave citizenship to the more than 16,000 native-born residents of the Northern Mariana Islands.

Loss of Citizenship

Although it rarely happens, every American citizen, whether native-born or naturalized, has the right to renounce, or voluntarily abandon, his or her citizenship. **Expatriation** is the legal process by which a loss of citizenship occurs.

The Supreme Court has several times held that the Constitution prohibits automatic expatriation. That is, Congress cannot take away a person's citizenship for something he or she has done. Thus, actions such as committing a crime, voting in a foreign election, or serving in the armed forces of another country are not grounds for automatic expatriation.[13]

---

[12]Article I, Section 8, Clause 4.

[13]A person convicted of a federal or a State crime may lose some of the privileges of citizenship, however, either temporarily or permanently—for example, the right to travel freely or to vote or hold public office.

Acquiring Citizenship

Naturalization

Individually

★ Naturalization of both parents (one parent if divorced or the other is dead) automatically naturalizes children under 16 who reside in the United States. Adopted children born abroad are automatically naturalized if under 18 when adoption becomes final.

★ Federal Courts: Any United States district court

★ State and Territorial Courts: Any general trial court

Collectively

Treaties:	Acts of Congress:
★ Louisiana (1803)	★ Hawaii (1898), Puerto Rico (1917), Native Americans (1924), Virgin Islands (1927), Guam (1950), Northern Mariana Islands (1977)
★ Florida (1819)	
★ Alaska (1867)	
Joint Resolution of Congress:	Constitutional Amendment:
★ Texas (1845)	★ African Americans and others by 14th Amendment (1868)

Birth

Jus Sanguinis

A child born to an American citizen on foreign soil becomes a citizen if:

★ both parents are American citizens, and at least one has lived in the United States or an American territory at some time

★ one parent is an American citizen who has lived in the United States for at least 10 years, 5 of them after age 14, and the child has lived in the United States continuously for at least 5 years between the ages of 14 and 28

Jus Soli

A child becomes an American citizen if born in the United States, Puerto Rico, Guam, Virgin Islands, Northern Mariana Islands, any United States embassy, or aboard a United States public vessel anywhere in the world

Interpreting Charts Most Americans acquire citizenship at birth. **Name two additional ways that people can acquire American citizenship.**

Naturalized citizens can lose their citizenship involuntarily. However, this process—**denaturalization**—can occur only by court order and only after it has been shown that the person became a citizen by fraud or deception.

A person can neither gain nor lose American citizenship by marriage. The only significant effect that marriage has is to shorten the time required for the naturalization of an alien who marries an American citizen.

A Nation of Immigrants

We are a nation of immigrants. Except for Native Americans—and even they may be the descendants of earlier immigrants—all of us have come here from abroad or are descended from those who did.

There were only some 2.5 million persons in the United States in 1776. Since then, the population has grown a hundredfold, to more than 285 million people today. That extraordinary population growth has come from two sources: births and immigration. About 70 million immigrants have come here since 1820, when figures were first recorded.

Regulation of Immigration

Congress has the exclusive power to regulate immigration. Congress alone may decide who may be admitted to the United States and under what conditions. The power to control the nation's borders is an inherent power of the United States (see Chapter 4, page 91). In an early leading case on the point, the Court ruled that the power of the United States to "exclude aliens from its territory . . . is not open to controversy," *Chae Chan Ping* v. *United States*, 1889. The States have no power in the field, *The Passenger Cases*, 1849.

Congress made no serious attempt to regulate immigration for more than a century after independence. As long as land was plentiful and expanding industry demanded more workers, immigration was encouraged.

By 1890, however, the open frontier was a thing of the past, and labor was no longer in short supply. Then, too, the major source of immigration had shifted. Until the 1880s, most immigrants had come from the countries of northern and western Europe. The "new immigration" from the 1880s onward came mostly from southern and eastern Europe. All these factors combined to bring major changes in the traditional policy of encouraging immigration.

Congress placed the first major restrictions on immigration with the passage of the Chinese Exclusion Act in 1882. At the same time, it barred the entry of convicts, "lunatics," paupers, and others likely to become public charges.

Legal Immigration to the United States, 1820–1998*

Total (1820 to 1998) = 64,599,082

Australia and Oceania 0.4%
Africa 0.9%
South America 3%
Asia 13%
North America** 23%
Europe 59%

*Figures less than 18,000 not included. Percentages may not add up to 100% due to rounding.

**Includes Canada, Mexico, the Caribbean, and Central America

SOURCE: *1998 Statistical Yearbook of the Immigration and Naturalization Service*

Interpreting Graphs Until the 1970s, Europeans dominated United States immigration figures. *Where do the two largest groups of immigrants come from now?*

Over the next several years a long list of "undesirables" was added to the law. Thus, contract laborers were excluded in 1885, immoral persons and anarchists in 1903, and illiterates in 1917. By 1920 more than 30 groups were denied admission on the basis of personal traits.

The tide of newcomers continued to mount, however. In the 10 years from 1905 through 1914, an average of more than a million persons, most of them from southern and eastern Europe, came to this country each year.

Congress responded to pressure for tighter regulation by adding quantitative limits (numerical ceilings) to the qualitative restrictions (personal characteristics) already in place. The Immigration Acts of 1921 and 1924 and the National Origins Act of 1929 assigned each country in Europe a quota—a limit on the number of immigrants who could enter the United States from that country each year. Altogether, only 150,000 quota immigrants could be admitted in any one year. The quotas were purposely drawn to favor northern and western Europe. The quota system was not applied to the Western Hemisphere, but immigration from Asia, Africa, and elsewhere was generally prohibited.

In 1952, Congress passed yet another basic law, the Immigration and Nationality Act. That statute modified the quota system to cover every country outside the Western Hemisphere.

Congress finally eliminated the country-based quota system in the Immigration Act of 1965. That law allowed as many as 270,000 immigrants to enter the United States each year, without regard to race, nationality, or country of origin. The 1965 law gave special preference to immediate relatives of American citizens or of aliens legally residing in this country.

Present Immigration Policies

Today, the Immigration Act of 1990 governs the admission of aliens to the United States. The act became effective on October 1, 1991. Like its predecessors, it was adopted only after years of intense debate, and many of its provisions are the subject of continuing controversy.

The 1990 law provided for a substantial increase in the number of immigrants who may enter the United States each year. The annual ceiling is now set at 675,000. It also continues the family-preference policy first put in place in 1965; at least one third of those persons admitted under its terms must be the close relatives of American citizens or resident aliens. Those immigrants who have occupational talents in short supply in the United States (notably, highly skilled researchers, engineers, and scientists) also receive special preference.

Only those aliens who can qualify for citizenship can be admitted as immigrants. The law's list of "excludable aliens"—those barred because of some personal characteristic—is extensive. Among those excluded are: criminals, persons with communicable diseases, drug abusers and addicts, illiterates, and mentally disturbed persons who might pose a threat to the safety of others.

More than 25 million nonimmigrants also come here each year for temporary stays. They are mostly tourists, students, and people traveling for business reasons.

Deportation

Most of the civil rights set out in the Constitution are guaranteed to "persons." That term covers aliens as well as citizens. In one important respect, however, the status of aliens is altogether unlike that of citizens: Aliens may be subject to **deportation,** a legal process in which aliens are legally required to leave the United States.

The Supreme Court has long held that the United States has the same almost-unlimited power to deport aliens as it has to exclude them. In an early major case, the Court ruled that (1) deportation is an inherent power, arising out of the sovereignty of the United States, and (2) deportation is not criminal punishment, and so does not require a criminal trial, *Fong Yue Ting* v. *United States,* 1893.

Because deportation is a civil, not a criminal, matter, several constitutional safeguards do not apply—for example, bail and ex post facto laws. In *Immigration and Naturalization Service* v. *Lopez-Mendoza,* 1984, the Court held that illegally seized evidence, which under the exclusionary rule cannot be used in a criminal trial, can be used at a deportation hearing.

An alien may be deported on any one of several grounds. The most common today is illegal entry. Thousands of aliens who enter with false papers, sneak in by ship or plane, or slip across the border at night are caught each year. Most are apprehended by the Border Patrol, the police arm of the Immigration and Naturalization Service.

Conviction of any serious crime, federal or State, usually leads to a deportation order by the INS. In recent years, several thousand aliens have been expelled on the basis of their criminal records, especially narcotics violators.

Undocumented Aliens

No one knows how many undocumented aliens reside in the United States today. The Census Bureau has put their number at somewhere between three and a half and five million, and the INS at four to six million. Some believe that the actual figure is at least twice those estimates.

The number of undocumented aliens is increasing by at least half a million a year, according to the INS. Most of these "undocumented persons" enter the country by slipping across the Mexican or Canadian borders, usually at night. Some come with forged papers. Many are aliens who entered legally, as nonimmigrants, but overstayed their legal welcomes.

Well over half of all undocumented aliens have come from Mexico; most of the others come from other Latin American countries and from Asia. A majority of the Mexicans stay here only four to six months a year, working on farms or in other seasonal jobs. Most other illegal aliens hope to remain permanently.

A Troublesome Situation

Once here, most undocumented aliens find it easy to become "invisible," especially in larger cities, and the understaffed INS finds it very difficult to locate them. Even so, immigration officials have apprehended more than a million undocumented aliens in each of the last several years. Nearly all are sent home. Most go voluntarily, but some leave only as the result of formal deportation proceedings.

The presence of so many undocumented persons has raised a number of difficult problems. Those problems have grown worse over the past several years and, until recently, not much had been done to meet them.

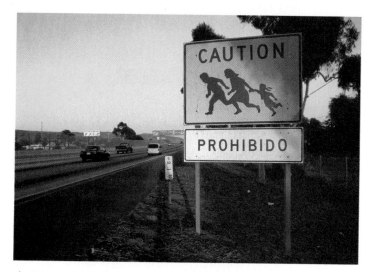

▲ This sign near the California-Mexican border warns drivers that undocumented aliens may try to cross the busy highway. *Prohibido*—warns would-be illegal immigrants not to take that risk.

By Don Wright, © 1980: Miami News. New York Times Syndicate.

Interpreting Political Cartoons Newcomers are greeted with suspicion by most cultures. ***Why is this cartoon particularly effective?***

One example: Until 1987, it was legal to hire undocumented aliens. As a result approximately 3.5 million persons who now hold jobs in this country came here illegally. Some employers were more than willing to hire undocumented aliens, many of whom will work for substandard wages and under substandard conditions.

Hundreds of thousands of undocumented aliens have taken jobs on farms, often as laborers; thousands more have become janitors and dishwashers, or seamstresses in sweatshops, or found other menial work. The increase in population has also placed added stress on the public schools and welfare services of several States, notably California, Texas, and Florida.

Current Law

Many groups have been troubled and divided by the problem of undocumented aliens. Those concerned include labor, farm, business, religious, ethnic, civil rights, and other groups. After wrestling with the issue for years, Congress passed the Immigration Reform and Control Act of 1986. Then, after another decade of debate and struggle, Congress passed the Illegal Immigration Restrictions Act of 1996.

The 1986 law did two major things. First, it established a one-year amnesty program under which many undocumented aliens could become legal residents. More than two million aliens used it to legalize their status here. Secondly, that law made it a crime to hire any person who is in this country illegally. An employer who knowingly hires an undocumented alien can be fined from $250 to $10,000. A repeat offender can be jailed for up to six months.

The 1996 law made it easier for the INS to deport illegal aliens by streamlining the deportation process. It also toughened the penalties for smuggling aliens into this country, prevented undocumented aliens from claiming Social Security benefits or public housing, and allowed State welfare workers to check the legal status of any alien who applies for any welfare benefit. The new law also doubled the size of the Border Patrol. It will have 10,000 uniformed officers by the year 2002.

Section 4 Assessment

Key Terms and Main Ideas

1. How does a person become a citizen through **jus sanguinis?**
2. What is the main difference between a **citizen** and an **alien?**
3. What is the purpose of the **naturalization** process?
4. Members of which group can be threatened by **deportation?**

Critical Thinking

5. **Understanding Point of View** Should employers be punished for hiring undocumented aliens? Why or why not?
6. **Drawing Conclusions** Why do you think the current immigration law gives special preference to immigrants who have certain occupations?

7. **Decision Making** Review the chart on page 614. In your opinion, should citizens "by birth" be required to meet the same requirements as naturalized citizens? Why or why not?

 Take It to the Net

8. Read stories written by people who have become American citizens and explore the struggles they went through. Write your own fictional story in which you come to America and apply for citizenship. Use the links provided in the Social Studies area at the following Web site for help in completing this activity. **www.phschool.com**

May Public Universities Use Admissions Quotas?

When selecting students for admission, colleges and universities consider a number of factors, such as test scores and participation in extracurricular activities. Should they also be allowed to consider factors such as race?

Regents of the University of California v. Bakke (1978)

Allan Bakke, a white NASA engineer with two degrees in engineering, decided that he wanted to be a doctor. He applied to the medical school of the State-run University of California at Davis. His application was rejected.

At that time, the medical school reserved 16 of the 100 spaces in each year's incoming class for "disadvantaged" applicants. This policy was intended to attract ethnic minority students to the school. Bakke discovered that several applicants with lower entrance exam scores, scholastic averages, and other qualifications had been admitted to the school under the set-aside policy.

Bakke sued the university, basing his case in part on the Civil Rights Act of 1964. The trial court found that the school's admissions policy violated the equal protection guarantees of the United States and California constitutions. The court also ruled, however, that Bakke had failed to prove that he would have been admitted to the school if there had been no set-aside program. Thus the court did not order the medical school to admit Bakke.

The California Supreme Court also found the medical school's set-aside program unconstitutional. It went a step further, ordering the school to admit Bakke to its next entering class. The Regents of the University of California then appealed to the United States Supreme Court.

Arguments for the Regents of the University of California

1. State programs, including State medical schools, should be able to give certain minority applicants extra protection in order to undo the effects of past discrimination.
2. Discrimination is not unconstitutional when it is applied against members of majority groups in order to assist minorities.
3. A major purpose of the Civil Rights Act of 1964 was to overcome the effects of past discrimination. The law should therefore protect minority students who might otherwise be displaced by whites.

Arguments for Bakke

1. The policy is unconstitutional under the Equal Protection Clause of the 14th Amendment, because it is based on the use of racial quotas.
2. Racial discrimination is unconstitutional, whether it is against minorities or "reverse discrimination" against members of majority groups.
3. The Civil Rights Act of 1964 also prohibits race-based discrimination in programs (such as this one) that receive federal financial aid.

Decide for Yourself

1. Review the constitutional grounds on which each side based its arguments and the specific arguments each side presented.
2. Debate the opposing viewpoints presented in this case. Which viewpoint do you favor?
3. Predict the impact of the Court's decision on affirmative action programs in the United States. (To read a summary of the Court's decision, turn to the Supreme Court Glossary on page 799.)

Political Dictionary

heterogeneous (p. 594)	integration (p. 603)	jus sanguinis (p. 613)
immigrant (p. 594)	de jure segregation (p. 604)	naturalization (p. 614)
reservation (p. 596)	de facto segregation (p. 604)	alien (p. 614)
refugee (p. 597)	affirmative action (p. 609)	expatriation (p. 614)
assimilation (p. 597)	quota (p. 610)	denaturalization (p. 615)
segregation (p. 602)	reverse discrimination (p. 610)	deportation (p. 617)
Jim Crow law (p. 602)	citizen (p. 613)	
separate-but-equal doctrine (p. 602)	jus soli (p. 613)	

Practicing the Vocabulary

Matching *Choose a term from the list above that best matches each description.*

1. A person who leaves his or her home in order to escape the dangers of war, political persecution, or other causes
2. The law of the soil; a means by which one acquires citizenship
3. Type of law that required separate facilities for African Americans and whites
4. An act by which one voluntarily forfeits citizenship
5. Segregation as a result of laws
6. Rule that sets a minimum or maximum number of promotions, hires, or acceptances for members of a specific group

Word Recognition *Replace the underlined definition with the correct term from the list above.*

7. Some immigrants and members of minority groups try <u>to merge into and become part of the dominant culture of a country.</u>
8. The Federal Government, States, and private companies have instituted <u>policies that require them to take positive steps to remedy past discrimination.</u>
9. A person who gains citizenship through fraud or deception can suffer <u>the loss of citizenship through a court order.</u>
10. *Brown* v. *Board of Education* brought an end to <u>separation of one group from another</u> in schools.
11. The United States can be described as <u>including a mix of different people.</u>

Reviewing Main Ideas

Section 1

12. Briefly describe the trends in the composition of the population over the course of American history.
13. Briefly describe the historical treatment of minority groups in the United States.
14. **(a)** List two ways that Latin American communities in the United States differ from one another. **(b)** Why do some people believe the category "Asian American" is too broad?
15. In what respect do women as a group resemble minority groups?

Section 2

16. What kind of equality does the Constitution guarantee?
17. According to the Supreme Court, what standards must laws that discriminate between groups meet?
18. Briefly describe the history of racial segregation from the late 1800s to today.
19. On what grounds will the present-day Supreme Court uphold a law that treats women differently from men?

Section 3

20. **(a)** Briefly describe the history of civil rights legislation between the 1870s and today. **(b)** Explain how you would divide the history of civil rights legislation into three periods, and why.
21. **(a)** What was the major piece of civil rights legislation enacted during the 1960s? **(b)** What are its major features?
22. Summarize the reasoning behind affirmative action programs. What is the main criticism of these programs?
23. Under what circumstances have affirmative action programs generally been allowed by the courts?

Section 4

24. Describe the ways in which people can become citizens of the United States.
25. Describe the ways in which people can lose citizenship.
26. Briefly describe immigration in the United States today.
27. Identify two controversies surrounding undocumented aliens.

Critical Thinking Skills

28. *Applying the Chapter Skill* Study the data on page 595 that shows the ethnic composition of the United States and answer the following questions. **(a)** In which year did the percentage of African Americans in the population reach its lowest point? **(b)** What was the African American population of the United States in that year? **(c)** Based on this table, what can you conclude about the Native American population in the United States in 1850? **(d)** Based on your reading of this chapter, what does your answer to **(c)** tell you about data from the 1850 Census?

29. *Making Comparisons* Recall what you read in Section 2 regarding the Supreme Court's attitude toward women. **(a)** How has this attitude changed from the late 1800s to today? **(b)** How has society's attitude changed?

30. *Drawing Inferences* Consider the separate-but-equal doctrine. **(a)** Do you think it is possible for facilities that are segregated on the basis of race or gender to be truly equal? **(b)** Why or why not?

31. *Making Decisions* Consider the process by which aliens can become naturalized American citizens. **(a)** In your opinion, should this process be easier or more difficult? **(b)** What standards should be added or removed?

Analyzing Political Cartoons

Using your knowledge of American government and this cartoon, answer the questions below.

32. (a) What form of discrimination is referenced by this cartoon? **(b)** How does this cartoon reverse the usual situation?

33. Why is "glass ceiling" an appropriate metaphor for this form of discrimination?

★ You Can Make a Difference

Are there any opportunities in your school or community to mentor students who need attention—for example, recent immigrants who speak little English or students from disadvantaged backgrounds? How could you and your class organize to help these fellow students? Consider forming a group of volunteer mentors to offer help in various areas, such as specific school subjects, community orientation, citizenship tests, or language practice.

Participation Activities

34. *Current Events Watch* Find a recent news article dealing with affirmative action. Then construct two editorials, one in favor of affirmative action and one opposed to it. Begin each editorial with a reference to the news article and explain how this article relates to your argument. When you have finished both editorials, have a classmate read them and rate your thoroughness and objectivity.

35. *Graphing Activity* Use a library or the Internet to find recent data on per capita income for African American men, African American women, white men, and white women. Create a line graph showing how per capita income has changed over time for all four categories. Then write a paragraph describing your conclusions.

36. *It's Your Turn* Interview a relative or a family friend who moved to the United States from another country or who experienced the civil rights struggles of the 1950s and 1960s. Talk to them about their experiences. Do they have any personal stories that capture a sense of the time? Do they believe their experiences were typical? How do they feel about television and film portrayals of immigrants' lives or the civil rights struggle? What lessons would they like to convey to members of your generation? Use your interview to write a personal history written from the point of view of that person. **(Interviewing a Relative)**

 ### Take It to the Net

Chapter 21 Self-Test As a final review activity, take the Chapter 21 Self-Test in the Social Studies area at the Web site listed below, and receive immediate feedback on your answers.

www.phschool.com

◆ Celebrating China's 50th anniversary, Tiananmen Square, Beijing, China

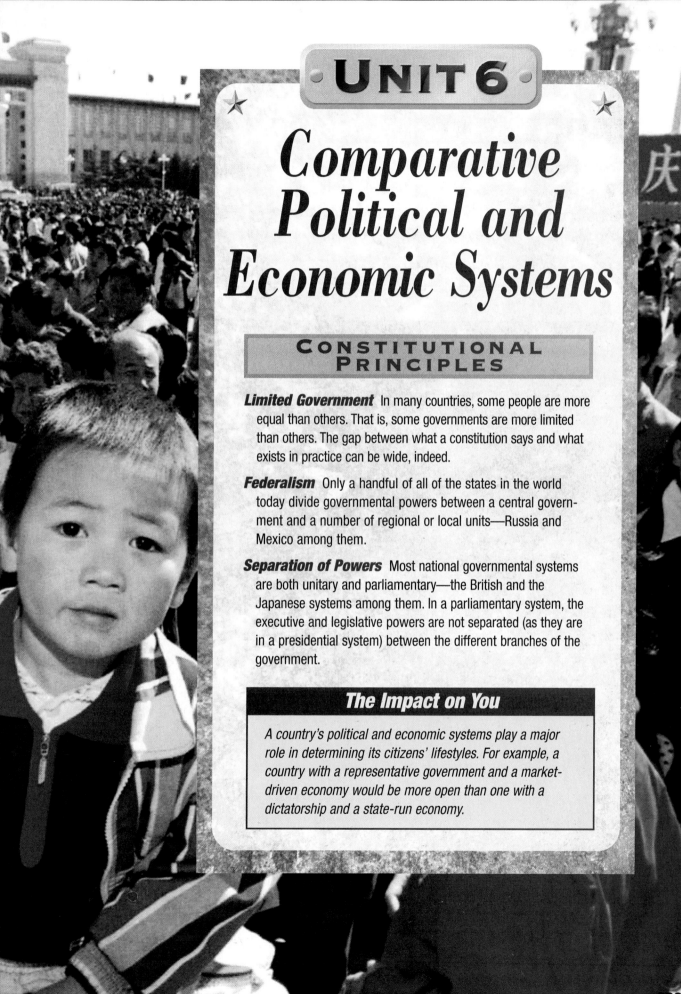

UNIT 6

Comparative Political and Economic Systems

CONSTITUTIONAL PRINCIPLES

Limited Government In many countries, some people are more equal than others. That is, some governments are more limited than others. The gap between what a constitution says and what exists in practice can be wide, indeed.

Federalism Only a handful of all of the states in the world today divide governmental powers between a central government and a number of regional or local units—Russia and Mexico among them.

Separation of Powers Most national governmental systems are both unitary and parliamentary—the British and the Japanese systems among them. In a parliamentary system, the executive and legislative powers are not separated (as they are in a presidential system) between the different branches of the government.

The Impact on You

A country's political and economic systems play a major role in determining its citizens' lifestyles. For example, a country with a representative government and a market-driven economy would be more open than one with a dictatorship and a state-run economy.

Comparative Political Systems

"No one pretends that democracy is perfect or all-wise. Indeed, it has been said that democracy is the worst form of government except all those other forms that have been tried from time to time."

—Winston Churchill (1947)

Although Americans would agree with Churchill that democracy is the best system available, democratic governments vary greatly. Differences include how power is divided and how leaders are chosen. Many nations, of course, are not democracies at all, but authoritarian systems.

◆ Britain's Houses of Parliament

You Can Make a Difference

A GOOD WAY to understand another country is to meet its people. Mariko Asano, a university student in Kyoto, Japan, first got that chance in 1997 on a short-term project with Habitat for Humanity in the Philippines. Habitat builds homes for people who cannot otherwise afford them. Mariko liked her work so much that she returned to the Philippines the next year to lead a student work team. "I've learned that I can make a difference in the world by being connected with people who have a similar wish," Mariko said.

Keep It Current

Items marked with this logo are periodically updated on the Internet. Keep up-to-date with what's in the news. To get current information on political systems in other countries, go to **www.phschool.com**

SECTION 1

Great Britain (pp. 626–632)

★ Britain's unitary government is based on an unwritten constitution.
★ Britain's hereditary monarch reigns but does not rule.
★ Britain's bicameral Parliament holds judicial and executive power.
★ Britain recently began a process of devolution, or the delegation of authority to regional governments.

SECTION 2

Japan (pp. 634–638)

★ Japan's constitution was written with American guidance after World War II; it contains a unique anti-military clause.
★ Japan's legislature, the National Diet, consists of the House of Councillors and the House of Representatives.
★ Japan's prime minister and cabinet are chosen by and are responsible to its House of Representatives.
★ Japan has an independent judicial system.
★ Although Japanese prefectures (districts) have many responsibilities, they have far less power than American States.

SECTION 3

Mexico (pp. 639–643)

★ Mexican history demonstrates the importance of constitutional representative government.
★ Mexico's government includes an executive branch headed by the president, a bicameral legislature, and a national judiciary.
★ The 2000 presidential election resulted in the defeat of the Institutional Revolutionary Party (PRI), which had controlled Mexican government and politics for over 70 years.

SECTION 4

Russia (pp. 645–649)

★ Russia was the dominant republic of the Soviet Union, which was ruled by the Communist Party for over 70 years.
★ In 1985, Mikhail Gorbachev instituted reforms aimed at restructuring economic and political life.
★ A wave of democratization led to the Soviet Union's fall in 1991.
★ The Russian government is struggling toward democracy and economic reform.

SECTION 5

China (pp. 650–652)

★ In 1949, Communist leader Mao Zedong became head of the newly established People's Republic of China.
★ China's Communist Party dominates the country's government.
★ China's central government exerts direct control over local political subdivisions.
★ Both the People's Republic of China and the Republic of China (Taiwan) claim to be the lawful Chinese government.

Section Preview

OBJECTIVES

1. **Examine** the elements that make up Britain's unwritten constitution.
2. **Identify** the role of the British monarchy.
3. **Explain** the role of Parliament.
4. **Analyze** recent changes in regional and local government in Britain.
5. **Describe** the British court system.

WHY IT MATTERS

Unlike the United States, Great Britain has a unitary government that is based on an unwritten constitution. Britain's monarch is the head of state who reigns, but does not rule. Instead, Parliament holds legislative and executive power.

POLITICAL DICTIONARY

★ **monarchy**
★ **by-election**
★ **coalition**
★ **minister**
★ **shadow cabinet**
★ **devolution**

Like the United States, Great Britain[1] is a democracy. Indeed, the roots of American government are buried deep in English political and social history. Yet there are important differences between the two systems of government. Most of those differences grow out of this vital point: Unlike government in the United States, government in Great Britain is unitary and parliamentary in form and rests upon an unwritten constitution.

Unwritten Constitution

Actually, it is not strictly true to say that the British constitution is entirely unwritten. Parts of the constitution can be found in books and charters. However, no single document serves as the British constitution.

The written part of the British constitution includes historic charters, acts of Parliament, and innumerable court decisions. The unwritten part derives from customs and usages—practices that have gained acceptance over time. The written parts are called the law of the constitution, and the unwritten parts are called the conventions of the constitution.

The Law of the Constitution

Many historic documents figure in the written parts of Britain's constitution. Perhaps the best known is the Magna Carta of 1215. Others include the Petition of Right of 1628 and the Bill of Rights of 1689. Each of those documents was a landmark in the centuries-long struggle to limit the powers of the English monarch and advance the concept of due process of law.

Certain acts of Parliament also form a basic part of the British constitution. One example is the Representation of the People Act of 1969. That act lowered the voting age in all British elections from 21 to 18. In the United States, such a change required a formal amendment to the Constitution (the 26th Amendment).

Finally, centuries of court decisions have created a body of legal rules covering nearly every aspect of human conduct. Such decisions make up the common law. (See Chapter 24 for a discussion of the common law in the American legal system.)

◀ *The Magna Carta* This document, prepared on parchment and affixed with King John's seal, was a landmark in the struggle to limit the power of the British monarchy.

---

[1]The United Kingdom of Great Britain and Northern Ireland, often referred to as the UK or simply Britain, is located on a group of islands northwest of continental Europe. It contains four principal parts: England, Wales, Scotland, and Northern Ireland. The UK's population now exceeds 59 million.

The Conventions of the Constitution

The truly unwritten part of the British constitution consists of the customs and practices of British politics. For example, no written rules give the lower house of Parliament the power to force the government to resign. This central feature of British government developed over the course of hundreds of years and is now a matter of custom.

With its open-ended constitution, the United Kingdom has a flexible set of rules that is always evolving and open to change. A majority vote in Parliament can easily remove an old provision of the constitution or add a new one. The flexibility of this system can be very useful. Without the delays and safeguards of a system such as that found in the United States, however, the danger of ill-considered and hasty action that might fundamentally alter the people's rights is ever present.

The Monarchy

In contrast to republics such as the United States and France, Britain is a **monarchy,** with a hereditary ruler. While English monarchs once ruled with near-absolute power, their role has long since dwindled. They are now little more than figureheads.[2] Because her powers and duties are controlled by Britain's unwritten constitution, Elizabeth II, Britain's queen since 1952, is known as a constitutional monarch.

In formal terms, all acts of the British government are performed in the name of the queen. However, the prime minister and other high officials exercise the real power of government.[3] The queen appoints the prime minister (traditionally the leader of the majority party in the House of Commons), but her choice is subject to the approval of that house. She has no power to dismiss the prime minister or any other officer of the government. She has no veto over acts of Parliament. In short, today's monarch reigns but does not rule.[4]

Parliament

Parliament is the central institution of British government. It holds both the legislative and the executive powers of the nation. In the United States, these powers are divided between separate and independent branches of government.

▲ *Pomp and Circumstance* The monarchy is a symbol of British history and traditions. Shown here are Queen Elizabeth II and her son Prince Charles opening a session of Parliament.

With its legislative power, Parliament passes Britain's laws. With its executive power, it chooses some of its members (the prime minister and the cabinet) to administer the departments of government and run the nation's affairs.

Parliament is bicameral. Its two houses are the House of Lords (the upper house) and the House of Commons (the lower house). Of the two, the House of Commons is by far the more powerful body.

The House of Lords

Until recently, a majority of the members of the House of Lords were hereditary peers—persons who inherited noble titles from their ancestors. The other members, appointed for life by the queen on the advice of the prime minister, included bishops and archbishops, law lords (eminent jurists), and life peers. Life peers are

---

[2]Most present-day monarchs, especially in industrial democracies like Sweden, Norway, and Japan, are figureheads. In the developing world, however, the monarchs of such nations as Saudi Arabia and Morocco still wield considerable power.

[3]The individual who symbolizes a nation's sovereignty is called the head of state, and the individual who directs the government, the head of government. In the United States, the President is both head of state and head of government. In the United Kingdom, the queen is head of state, and the prime minister is head of government.

[4]Reformers make periodic calls for the abolition of the monarchy, proposing to turn over the role of head of state to someone with democratic credentials. The monarchy enjoys a high level of popularity with the public, however. Opinion polls conducted between 1993 and 2000 find that about 70 percent of those surveyed favor retaining the monarchy over becoming a republic.

persons honored for their achievements in science, literature, the arts, politics, or business.

In 1999, the upper house underwent a dramatic change and it now has 682 members. Responding to long-standing criticism of the undemocratic nature of the House of Lords, Parliament passed legislation eliminating the 750 hereditary peers from the upper house.[5] As the reform process continues, future Lords likely will be selected through an independent appointments commission or some form of regional election.

The House of Lords holds only limited legislative power. The Lords can merely delay, not block, a House of Commons bill. If they reject a bill passed by the House of Commons, the Commons has only to approve the bill a second time, and it becomes law.

The upper chamber contributes to the legislative process mainly by improving the details of House of Commons bills. Some argue that the Lords fulfill an important role by at least delaying the passage of controversial bills, allowing tempers to cool, and giving the lower house more time to weigh the effects of its actions.

▲ **Law Lord** British law lords wear traditional dress. The House of Lords is the court of last resort in the British legal system.

In addition to its legislative role, the House of Lords performs an important judicial function. Its law lords serve as the final court of appeals in both civil and criminal cases in the British court system.

The House of Commons

The lower house, known familiarly as the Commons, has 659 members. They are regularly called MPs—members of Parliament. They are elected from single-member districts (constituencies) of roughly equal population. There are 529 constituencies in England, 72 in Scotland, 40 in Wales, and 18 in Northern Ireland.

A general election—one in which all seats in the Commons are at stake—takes place at least once every five years.[6] Election dates are not firmly fixed. If an MP dies or resigns, a special election called a **by-election** is held in that MP's constituency to choose a replacement.

The Commons meets in a small, rectangular chamber within the majestic Parliament building. The high-ceilinged House chamber was originally designed for just 350 members. It is, quite literally, a political arena. The members of rival parties sit on facing rows of benches, talking and sometimes hooting at one another. An open space occupies much of the center of the chamber, with a raised chair at one end for the presiding officer (known as the speaker).[7] Leading members of the major parties sit on the front rows of benches. Those who occupy the remaining rows are known as backbenchers.

The majority party largely controls the work of the Commons. While any MP can introduce a bill, the prime minister and the cabinet—who form what in parliamentary systems is called "the government"—offer most measures.

Up to ten standing committees consider bills and prepare them for final consideration by the full chamber. Committees in the Commons are generalists; that is, any committee may consider any bill. Their main task is to put measures in proper form for final floor consideration. All bills sent to committee must be reported to the floor, where a party-line vote generally follows the will of the government.

The Prime Minister

The prime minister, although formally appointed by the queen, is in fact responsible to the House of Commons. When a single party holds a majority in the Commons, as usually happens, that party's leader becomes prime minister. If no single party holds a majority, a coalition must be formed. In this sense, a **coalition** is a temporary alliance of parties for the purpose of forming a government.

---

[5]Although the legislation abolished all hereditary peers in principle, 92 received a temporary reprieve and continue to sit in the House of Lords until the reform process is completed.

[6]In the most recent general election, held June 7, 2001, the Labour Party retained its majority in the House of Commons. Its candidates won 413 seats and garnered 40.3 percent of the popular vote. The Conservative Party won 166 seats and 31.7 percent of the vote, and the Liberal Democratic Party 52 seats and 18.2 percent. Seven minor parties took the other 28 seats and not quite 10 percent of the total vote. The next general election must be held no later than June 7, 2006.

[7]The speaker, elected by the Commons from among its members, acts as a neutral referee. By custom, a speaker runs unopposed in a general election and is regularly returned to office. Michael J. Martin was elected speaker in 2000; he is the 165th person to hold the post.

Two or more parties must agree on a common choice for prime minister and on a joint slate of cabinet members. Britain's last coalition government served during World War II, from 1940 to 1945.

The Cabinet

The prime minister selects the members of the cabinet. Most cabinet members, or **ministers,** are members of the House of Commons. A few may sit in the House of Lords.

Collectively, the prime minister and the cabinet provide political leadership, both in making and carrying out public policy. Individually, cabinet ministers head the various executive departments. One minister serves as foreign secretary and is responsible for foreign affairs. Another serves as chancellor of the exchequer and is responsible for finance. All told there are about twenty ministers, each with his or her own department and functions. The size of the cabinet varies from time to time, depending on the wishes of the prime minister.

The opposition parties appoint their own teams of potential cabinet members. Each of these opposition MPs shadows, or watches, one particular member of the cabinet. If an opposition party should succeed in gaining a majority, its so-called **shadow cabinet** would then be ready to run the government.

Calling Elections

In marked contrast to practice in this country, the British political system requires no fixed date for the holding of elections. Instead, British law requires only that a general election be held at least once every five years.

Normally, the prime minister decides when a general election will be held. As a rule, an election is called at a time when the prime minister and his advisors think the political climate favors the majority party candidates. If they have read the political tea leaves correctly, the prime minister's party very likely will strengthen its hold on the House of Commons (or at the least preserve its control). If they are wrong, however, the other major party will take over the government.

Occasionally, an election is triggered by quite different circumstances: when the government falls

▲ The House of Commons meets in a small chamber within the Parliament building. Members of rival parties sit facing each other. *Critical Thinking How do the responsibilities of the House of Commons differ from those of the House of Lords?*

because it has lost the confidence (the support) of the House of Commons. A government with a sizable majority of seats in the Commons seldom has any trouble maintaining that support. The opposition can cut into the government's majority if it wins a series of by-elections, however. Or, more rarely, some majority MPs may become so upset with one or another of the government's policies that they join the opposition.

The government is judged to have lost the confidence of Parliament when and if it is defeated on some critical vote in the House of Commons. If the government loses a vote of confidence, the government falls. The prime minister must ask the queen to dissolve Parliament (end its sessions) and call a new general election.

This basic feature of British parliamentary government—the ability to change governments in this way—has great significance. It means that a prime minister who becomes either ineffective or generally unpopular can be removed from the office before his or her actions can cause serious damage to the political system.

Clearly, this feature avoids a difficult problem sometimes found in the American system of presidential government: continuing conflict, to the point of deadlock, between the executive and the legislative branches. However, the British arrangement does not allow for any system of checks and balances between the executive and the legislative branches as in the American system.

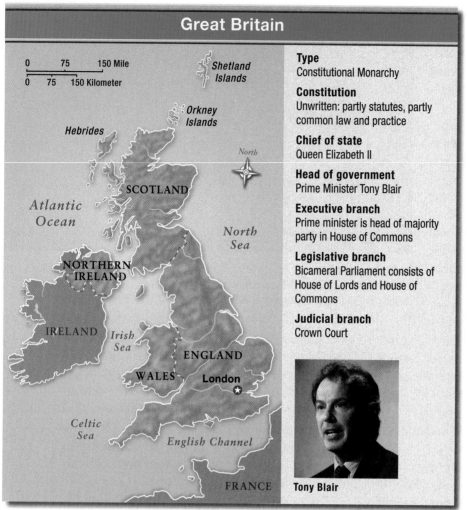

Great Britain

Type	Constitutional Monarchy
Constitution	Unwritten: partly statutes, partly common law and practice
Chief of state	Queen Elizabeth II
Head of government	Prime Minister Tony Blair
Executive branch	Prime minister is head of majority party in House of Commons
Legislative branch	Bicameral Parliament consists of House of Lords and House of Commons
Judicial branch	Crown Court

Tony Blair

Interpreting Maps Britain's constitutional monarchy is based on a largely unwritten constitution. The prime minister is responsible to the House of Commons and is the real head of government. *Cite examples from the text to support this statement: The British monarch reigns but does not rule.*

Political Parties

Political parties play a much greater role in the governing process in the United Kingdom than they do in the United States. You have just seen the principal demonstration of that fact: The party that wins a majority of the seats in the House of Commons forms the government. Indeed, it can be said that political parties are the cornerstone of the British system of government.

Two parties have dominated British politics in recent decades: the Conservative Party and the Labour Party. The Conservatives (the Tories) have long drawn support from middle- and upper-class Britons. They tend to favor private economic initiatives over government involvement in the nation's economic life, and they generally support the traditional British class system.

The Labour Party has regularly found most of its support in working-class voters. Labour tends to favor government involvement in the economic system and a more socially equal society. Historically, the Labour Party preached doctrinaire socialism, advocating the redistribution of wealth through the nationalization of basic industries and massive public welfare programs. Under the leadership of Prime Minister Tony Blair, however, the party has moderated its views and moved toward the center of the political spectrum.

Another group, the Liberal Democratic Party, also has a broad base in British politics. The Liberal Democrats are a centrist organization that emerged in 1988 out of a merger of two older parties: (1) the Liberal Party, one of the nation's two major parties until it was displaced by the Labour Party in the 1920s, and (2) the Social Democratic Party, a moderate splinter group that broke away from the Labour Party in 1981.

British parties are more highly organized and centrally directed than the major parties in American politics. High levels of party loyalty and party discipline characterize the British party system. Voter behavior clearly reflects that point. Voters regularly vote for candidates for the House of Commons on the basis of their party labels, not their individual qualifications.

Regional and Local Government

Recall, Britain has a ministry government. There is no constitutional division of powers between the national government and regional or local governments in Britain, as in the American federal system. All power belongs to the central government.

The regional and local governments in the United Kingdom are creations of Parliament. To whatever extent these governments can deliver services or do anything else, it is only because the central government has created them, given them powers, and financed them. However, regional and local governments do play an important role in the country.

Devolution

The UK is composed of four separate nations with different histories, cultures, and traditions. In order to provide for the distinctive governmental needs of the people of Scotland, Wales, and Northern Ireland, the UK has recently undergone a process of **devolution**—the delegation of authority from the central government to regional governments.

In 1998, the British Parliament passed three major acts of devolution. Those acts created a 129-member Scottish Parliament, a 60-member National Assembly for Wales, and a 108-member Northern Ireland Assembly. These bodies were to be democratically elected by the people of their respective regions.

These acts came in response to voter referenda in Scotland and Wales that endorsed the creation of Scottish and Welsh assemblies. The British Parliament was also honoring the 1998 "Good Friday" peace agreement in Northern Ireland. That agreement called for the establishment of an assembly in which unionists and nationalists (the two main opposing groups in Northern Ireland) could share the task of governing.

The British Parliament has given the devolved assemblies many important powers. Thus the Scottish Parliament has broad power to pass primary legislation on matters such as education, culture, health services, and housing. It also has the power, within limits, to vary the income tax, on the Scottish people.

The Northern Ireland Assembly has wide authority to legislate on matters previously dealt with by the Departments of Agriculture, Economic Development, Education, the Environment, Finance and Personnel, and Health and Social Services for Northern Ireland. The Welsh Assembly has less power to pass primary legislation, but is responsible for deciding how to implement most UK legislation in Wales. It also can decide how to spend funds allocated to Wales from the central government.

Although the British Parliament has assigned many responsibilities to the devolved bodies, it has reserved for itself the exclusive power to legislate on several matters that affect the whole of the United Kingdom. These include defense, foreign policy, and macroeconomic policy. The British Parliament also continues to legislate more broadly for England, which does not have a devolved assembly.

Local Government

Local government bodies have been a feature of the British political landscape for much longer than have the recently established regional assemblies. Today, there are 467 local authorities of varying types in the United Kingdom.

Much as in the United States, local governments in the United Kingdom perform a broad range of functions, from running local schools and libraries to collecting trash and maintaining roads. Local councils fund these services largely through grants from the central government, which account for about half of all local government revenue. The several councils also raise revenue through taxes on domestic dwellings and local businesses.

▲ *A New Scottish Parliament* This computer model of the new Scottish Parliament shows an innovative, ultramodern complex. The buildings will be located in the historic Holyrood district of Edinburgh, Scotland's capital.

▲ The Old Bailey is England's most important Crown Court. Photographers are forbidden access when the court is in session, a rule that also applies to the U.S. Supreme Court. *Critical Thinking How do the United States and the United Kingdom differ on the question of judicial review?*

The Courts

The UK has three separate court systems—one in England and Wales, one in Scotland, and one in Northern Ireland. In England and Wales, most civil cases are tried in county courts. Serious (indictable) criminal cases are tried in the Crown Court, and less serious criminal cases in the magistrates' courts.

Criminal cases in the Crown Court are tried by juries and judges, while the majority of civil cases and less serious criminal cases are heard by judges or magistrates alone. Both civil and criminal cases may be appealed through a hierarchy of appellate courts, with the House of Lords serving as the final court of appeal.[8] The court system in Northern Ireland closely parallels the system in England and Wales, with a similar hierarchical structure.

Because Scotland maintained a separate legal system after its union with England in 1707, Scotland's courts are completely different from those in the rest of the United Kingdom. The structure is simpler, with fewer hierarchical layers. Sheriffs' courts hear most civil and minor criminal cases. The Court of Session (the supreme civil court) and the High Court of Justiciary (the supreme criminal court) hear cases both originally and on appeal. Criminal cases from Scotland may not be appealed to the House of Lords.

Courts in the United Kingdom decide cases based primarily on parliamentary legislation and common law, or on the standards established by judicial precedent. They are not bound to uphold a constitution or bill of rights that stands higher than parliamentary law. Unlike the United States, the courts and judges in the UK, including the law lords, do not possess the power of judicial review. Even if they believe a law to be in violation of Britain's unwritten constitution, the courts may not overrule Parliament.

---

[8]If a case going through the British court system involves a point of European Union law, it may also be appealed beyond the House of Lords to the Court of Justice of the European Communities.

Section 1 Assessment

Key Terms and Main Ideas

1. **(a)** In what sense does Britain have an unwritten constitution? **(b)** Describe the law of the constitution and the conventions of the constitution.
2. What is the role of the British **monarchy?**
3. Under what circumstances would a **coalition** government need to be formed in Britain?
4. Define **devolution** and explain its implications for local governments in Great Britain.

Critical Thinking

5. **Making Comparisons** What are the major differences between the British Parliament and the U.S. Congress? Between the prime minister and the President?

6. **Expressing Problems Clearly** You have read that a British government can fall if it loses the confidence of the House of Commons. What are the advantages and disadvantages of such a system?

 Take It to the Net

7. The American system of government is rooted in the British system. Create a chart that shows at least five ways in which the British and United States governments are similar. Use the links provided in the Social Studies area at the following Web site for help in completing this activity. **www.phschool.com**

SKILLS FOR LIFE

TECHNOLOGY

CITIZENSHIP

CRITICAL THINKING

CHARTS and GRAPHS

Drawing Inferences

Drawing inferences means reading between the lines; that is, forming conclusions that are not stated directly but are suggested by other facts. For instance, the Queen of England appoints several officials of the Church of England. Knowing that in the United States, Congress and the President have no such powers, you can infer that British tradition does not separate the functions of church and state the way the United States Constitution requires.

Use the following steps to practice drawing inferences from what you read:

1. Find the main idea in a sentence or passage. To find information that is suggested but unstated in a passage, you have to understand the stated content of the passage. Reread the subsection entitled "The Monarchy," on page 627. You can state the main idea of the passage by answering these questions:
(a) In earlier times, what was the role of the monarchy in Britain?
(b) What is the role of the monarchy today?

2. Apply other facts or prior knowledge. You also read that opponents of the monarchy periodically try to have it abolished. You probably know that the monarchy has lasted for more than 1,000 years. This combination of facts should suggest to you certain inferences. What other facts do you know about the popularity of the monarchy that might help you draw inferences?

3. Decide whether the information suggests an unstated fact or conclusion. When you integrate, or combine, this series of facts, it's possible to infer that the majority of Britons still support the monarchy. What can you infer about the role of the monarchy in national unity and stability? Explain.

◀ At left, Britain's Queen Elizabeth II waves to crowds from her carriage during the celebration of her 60th birthday, in 1986. Below, the nation celebrates the Queen's Silver Anniversary, the 25th year of her reign, in 1977.

Test for Success

If you were to read in the news that Britain's government had fallen, what might you be able to infer? Use the prior knowledge you gained by reading about British elections on page 629.

Section Preview

OBJECTIVES

1. **Examine** early Japanese government and the Japanese constitution.
2. **Summarize** the structure and functions of the National Diet.
3. **Explain** how the prime minister and cabinet perform the nation's executive functions.
4. **Examine** the Japanese bureaucracy, political parties, and courts.
5. **Understand** regional and local government in Japan.

WHY IT MATTERS

Like Great Britain, Japan is a parliamentary democracy. The emperor serves as a symbol of the state but has no power to govern. Instead, the bicameral parliament—the National Diet—is the highest institution of state power. The Diet's powerful House of Representatives chooses the country's prime minister and cabinet.

POLITICAL DICTIONARY

★ **consensus**
★ **dissolution**
★ **prefecture**

Japan and the United States share in a lively exchange of ideas and goods. Each year, new technologies, music, television programs, and cuisine cross the boundary between these two very different cultures.

Japanese democracy reflects this flow of ideas. The roots of that democracy are embedded in the American occupation of Japan after World War II. After the war, Japan blended American principles with its own institutions to create a distinctive, homegrown form of democracy.

Early Japanese Government

Japan, like Great Britain, is an island nation.[9] Also like the UK, Japan is a parliamentary democracy. The history of democratic government in Japan is quite brief, however. It spans only a little more than 50 years.

According to legend, the Japanese state was founded by the Emperor Jimmu in 660 B.C. The earliest written records indicate, however, that it began to emerge about 1,000 years later, in the 4th century A.D. The country evolved in almost complete isolation, untouched by forces and events in the outside world, over the next 1,500 years.

During that period of seclusion, a political system similar to that of medieval Europe developed. It was built around the *mikado*— an emperor who governed by divine right and who was, at least in theory, an absolute ruler. Real authority was exercised in his name by the *shogun* (a military dictator) and a number of noble families *(daimyo)* supported by their warrior servants *(samurai)*.

Dutch and Portuguese traders had some contact with the Japanese in the 16th and 17th centuries. The country was not opened to any significant Western contacts until 1853, when a U.S. naval squadron made a polite but firm visit. Japan and the United States concluded a commercial treaty the following year. The Japanese then negotiated similar agreements with other Western powers.

Japan was soon committed to becoming a modern state. That drive eventually led to its attempt to conquer all of East Asia, and then to its crushing defeat in World War II.

The United States occupied Japan for nearly seven years following the war, from 1945

◄ This samurai suit of armor symbolizes Japan's feudal past.

[9]Japan includes more than 2,000 islands. Its four main islands—Honshu, Hokkaido, Kyushu, and Shikoku—hold 98 percent of its land area and most of its more than 127 million people.

to 1952. Far-reaching social, political, and economic reforms were put in place at the direction of the American occupation forces, commanded by General Douglas MacArthur. The nation's remarkable postwar economic recovery began during the occupation and so, too, did the development of its present political system. Today, Japan is the leading democracy and the leading economic power in the largely undemocratic non-Western world.

The Constitution

Japan's present-day constitution, adopted in 1947, was written under the watchful eye of American authorities. The document explicitly rejects the earlier scheme of government, in which "sovereign power" was formally vested in the emperor. Today, the emperor serves as the symbol of the state and the unity of the people, but has no power to govern. That power belongs to the Japanese people, and they exercise it by secret ballot in elections held under universal adult suffrage.

The constitution contains a lengthy declaration of basic freedoms—in effect, a bill of rights. These include freedom of speech and press, freedom of religion, the right to a fair trial, equality of men and women, and the right "to maintain standards of wholesome and cultured living."

A unique anti-military clause is also part of the Japanese constitution. This clause says that the Japanese people "forever renounce war as a sovereign right of the nation." It adds: "Land, sea, and air forces, as well as other war potential, will never be maintained."

United States officials insisted on the clause because they feared a revival of Japanese militarism. Later, they began to see Japan as an ally in the cold war. With American encouragement, since 1954, Japanese leaders have given the clause a broad interpretation. They say that the clause rules out an army, a navy, and an air force, but not a so-called self-defense force. Thus, Japan has rebuilt its three arms of the military, calling them "ground, maritime, and air self-defense forces."

The National Diet

Japan's parliament—the National Diet—is the highest organ of state power. The Diet contains an upper house, called the House of Councillors,

◀ His Majesty Akihito is the 125th emperor of Japan. He poses here with his wife, Empress Michiko. *Critical Thinking How is the role of the Japanese monarchy similar to that of the British monarchy?*

and a lower house, called the House of Representatives. As in Britain, the lower house wields the greater power. The prime minister and at least half of all cabinet ministers must be members of the Diet. The prime minister invariably comes from the lower house.

House of Councillors

The House of Councillors has prestige but little power. Its 252 elected members sit for six years, in staggered terms. Because it has fewer responsibilities than the lower house, the House of Councillors tends to serve an essentially deliberative, advisory role. In short, its main function is to provide a forum for the country's leaders to discuss issues of concern to the nation.

House of Representatives

The House of Representatives has many important powers. It can make, and also break, the Prime Minister. By a vote of no confidence, the House can force the Prime Minister either to resign or to dissolve the House of Representatives and call an early election. The lower house also has the power to make treaties, raise funds, and appropriate money. Both houses must pass bills on other matters. However, the lower house can override a negative vote in the upper house by passing a bill for a second time by a two-thirds majority.

There are 480 seats in the lower house. The country is divided into 300 small single-member districts, and the voters in each of them choose one house member. The nation is also divided into 11 larger multi-seat districts. The voters in those constituencies fill the other 180 seats. Representatives serve for four years—or less if the house is dissolved and new elections are held.

Consensus Politics

The atmosphere in both houses of the National Diet is sedate compared to that in the legislative bodies in Britain and the United States. Japanese society places great emphasis on avoiding confrontation. Therefore, politicians seek to reach **consensus**—broad agreement—on public questions. Political majorities try to avoid pushing through bills against strong opposition.

Executive Functions

The prime minister and the cabinet perform the executive functions of government in the Japanese governmental system. The House of Representatives chooses the prime minister. This means that he is in fact picked by the political party with a majority of the seats (votes) in that body.

The prime minister appoints members of the cabinet, who serve as heads of major departments. Most cabinet ministers are members of the House of Representatives. Some are drawn from the bureaucracy, an important element of Japanese government. Members of the cabinet have a collective responsibility for the actions of the government. A member who for some reason cannot support a program or decision usually resigns from office.

The prime minister has the power to dissolve (dismiss) the House of Representatives, but not the House of Councillors. This step, which can be taken at any time, is called **dissolution.** A dissolution triggers a general election at which the voters fill all 480 seats in the lower house.

The Bureaucracy

The large Japanese bureaucracy, or civil service, enjoys unusual respect and power within Japanese society. Top members of the bureaucracy are technocrats—experts in technical and administrative affairs. They include many leading graduates of the nation's top universities, who compete to win civil service positions. Jobs in the bureaucracy do not pay as well as many private sector jobs do, and most of them demand long hours. Still, those jobs are highly prized by Japanese who want to serve the public and/or seek the prestige of civil service rank.

Japan's vast bureaucracy developed under the imperial oligarchy before World War II—in the economic as well as the administrative arenas. Today, it plays a key role in Japan's economy. The Ministry of Trade and Industry helps coordinate the strategies of many large Japanese firms.

Political Parties

One party dominates the Japanese political system: the Liberal Democrats (the LDP). Despite the "liberal" in its title, the LDP generally follows conservative policies. It was born in 1955 out of a merger of several parties. That merger was prompted by American efforts to stabilize Japanese politics and thwart the aims of the Japan Socialist Party (the JSP), the Japan Communist Party (the JCP), and other left-wing groups.

For nearly 40 years, every Japanese prime minister came from the LDP. The party was wracked by scandals in the 1980s into the 1990s, however, and lost a vote of confidence in the lower house in 1993. In the ensuing election,

▲ *The Diet in Session* Members of the Diet practice consensus politics, seeking to avoid confrontation.

many younger Liberal Democrats, who had pressed for reforms that the party's leaders rejected, left the LDP. They either formed new parties or joined other, established groups.

The LDP temporarily lost its hold on the government in the general election of 1993. A multi-party coalition, built by the JSP, and in which the LDP refused to participate, took power; but it collapsed in less than a year. The government was then run by an unusual alliance of archenemies: the JSP (now renamed the Japan Social Democratic Party) and the LDP. The LDP returned to power in 1996. It won less than a majority (only 239) of the seats in the House; but the party avoided the need to form a coalition government by striking a deal with two small parties. Those minor parties entered a most unusual arrangement in a parliamentary system: They pledged to support the government in the House but agreed to take no role in that government.

A new major party, the Democratic Party of Japan, arose out of the 1996 election. It was formed when dissenters in the other major parties joined forces to oppose the LDP. Within a year, the Democratic Party had become the LDP's chief rival in Japanese politics.

The LDP weathered the most recent general election, in 2000—but just barely. It won only 233 seats in the House. The Democrats hold 127 seats and the other 120 belong to seven minor parties. The LDP retains its shaky control of the government, led by Prime Minister Junichiro Koizumi.

Koizumi, a party maverick, beat back the old guard in a party shake-up and became Prime Minister in 2001. To this point, he has proved quite popular with the Japanese people—a people beset by years of political scandal and economic pain.

The Courts

Japan has an independent judicial system patterned on the American model, with trial courts at the local level, several intermediate appellate courts, and a Supreme Court. The courts hold the power of judicial review (the power to determine the constitutionality of governmental actions.

The Supreme Court has seldom struck down an act of the Diet. It has three times found the

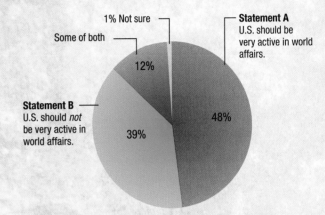

CLOSE UP FOUNDATION *Student Poll*

In a recent poll, students were asked which of the following two statements comes closer to their point of view on United States' involvement in world affairs.

Statement A *The United States should be very active in world affairs, because what happens in other countries affects what happens in the United States.*

Statement B *The United States should not be very active in world affairs, because we need to focus on solving problems in our own country.*

1% Not sure
Some of both

Statement A
U.S. should be very active in world affairs.

Statement B
U.S. should *not* be very active in world affairs.

12%

48%

39%

SOURCE: High School Students' Attitudes Toward Government and Politics, Close Up Foundation, May 1999

1. **Analyzing Data** *(a) Approximately what percentage of respondents believe that the United States should be very active in world affairs? (b) Should not be very active in world affairs?*
2. **Conducting Polls** In your own school, conduct a poll asking students whether they think the United States should be very active in world affairs. *How do your results compare to the results shown on this graph?*

apportionment of seats in the Diet to be unconstitutional, however. By the Court's reckoning, votes cast in many lightly populated rural districts were worth four to five times as much as votes cast in many densely populated urban districts. The Diet responded in 1994 by providing that 200 of the seats in its lower house were to be filled by proportional representation.

Regional and Local Government

At the regional level, Japan is divided into 47 political subdivisions called **prefectures,** including three large metropolitan districts (for the cities of Tokyo, Osaka, and Kyoto), and a special district for the northern island of Hokkaido. Each of these districts has an elected governor

Japan

Type Constitutional Monarchy	**Judicial branch** Supreme court; chief justice appointed by monarch after designation by cabinet; all other justices appointed by cabinet
Constitution Adopted May 3, 1947	
Chief of state Emperor Akihito	
Head of government Prime Minister Junichiro Koizumi	
Executive branch Prime minister designated by the National Diet	
Legislative branch Bicameral National Diet consists of House of Councillors and House of Representatives	**Junichiro Koizumi**

 Interpreting Maps Japan's constitutional monarchy is based on a constitution written soon after World War II. The prime minister is responsible to the National Diet. *How do the roles of the emperor and prime minister differ?*

and legislature. The regional governments do such things as lay taxes to pay for roads, hospitals, and police protection. Unlike the United States, where high schools are usually a local responsibility, Japan gives the prefectures control over high schools.

Japan is a unitary state, and the prefectures are not comparable to the States in this country. Although the prefectures have many responsibilities, they must rely on the central government in Tokyo for the bulk of their funding.

Below the prefectures, more than 3,200 municipalities handle local issues. Municipalities range in size from villages of a few hundred to several cities with several million. Each municipality elects a mayor to a four-year term. Larger municipalities also vote for local assemblies, while small towns choose a council to govern with the mayor. As in the United States, local government deals with issues like fire protection, trash collection, local roads, water, and education up through the ninth year.

Section 2 Assessment

Key Terms and Main Ideas

1. What are the main provisions of the Japanese constitution?
2. Outline the structure and basic responsibilities of the National Diet.
3. Why is **consensus** an important concept in Japanese government?
4. What is the role of **prefectures** in Japanese government?

Critical Thinking

5. **Determining Cause and Effect** In what ways is World War II the most significant event in modern Japanese political history?

6. **Making Comparisons** What are the major similarities and differences between the National Diet and the U.S. Congress? Between the court systems in Japan and the United States?

 Take It to the Net

7. Compare the preface of the Japanese constitution to the Preamble of the United States Constitution. Write a brief essay describing the similarities and differences between the two documents. Use the links provided in the Social Studies area at the following Web site for help in completing this activity. **www.phschool.com**

Section Preview

OBJECTIVES

1. **Summarize** Mexico's early political history.
2. **Examine** Mexico's three branches of government.
3. **Describe** recent changes in Mexico's national politics.
4. **Explain** how Mexico's regional and local government is structured.

WHY IT MATTERS

In form, Mexico's political system is similar to that of the United States in that it has three independent branches of government. In operation, however, the Mexican political system is the product of Mexico's unique culture and history.

POLITICAL DICTIONARY

★ **mestizo**
★ **nationalization**
★ **North American Free Trade Agreement (NAFTA)**

Mexico,[10] the United States' neighbor to the south, has a political system that is, in form, influenced by the American political system. In operation, however, it is the product of a unique combination of Mexico's history and the cultural makeup of its people. While Americans tend to think of Mexican history in terms of only a few specific historical events, its complex experience established the basis for the system that exists today.

Early Political History

The first evidence of important civilization in Mexico dates back to about 1200 B.C. But Mexico is most commonly associated with the rich and complex Aztec civilization of the 15th and early 16th centuries A.D. That civilization gave way to Spanish colonialism in 1521, after Hernán Cortés defeated the Aztec emperor Cuauhtemoc in the battle of Tenochtitlán.

During the next three centuries, Spanish territorial claims expanded into North and South America. However, constant border disputes with England, France, and the newly independent United States seriously reduced Spain's area of domination by the early nineteenth century.

Independence from Spain

Meanwhile, generations of Spaniards in Mexico intermixed with the native peoples, giving rise to a colonial elite with its own unique mestizo culture. A **mestizo** is a person with both Spanish or Portuguese and Native American ancestry. Because of the decline of the Spanish empire and conflicts over succession to the Spanish throne, the Mexicans were able to declare their independence from Spain in 1821. They then established a monarchy with an elected emperor.

The Mexican monarchy lasted only two years before General Antonio López de Santa Anna deposed the emperor and set up a democratic republic with a constitution (adopted in 1824). However, this republic was democratic only in the narrowest sense: most of the population, especially the Native Americans, could not participate.

Mexico's first constitution set the framework for dealing with several key issues and questions in the Mexican system: Should there be a centralized or a federal government? How much power should a single political leader have? How could Mexico remain independent from its powerful neighbor to the north and other major world powers?

Over the course of the next 100 years, these issues appeared, disappeared, and reappeared

▲ This stone carving dates from the era before Spanish colonialism in Mexico.

---

[10]Mexico is officially titled the United Mexican States. It has a population of just over 100 million people.

with regularity in Mexican politics. Mexico experienced dictatorships and reform movements, one of which led to a revised constitution in 1857. It also underwent periods of foreign invasion and interference as well as internal wars and revolution. Yet throughout this century of conflict, democratic reformers were able to gain political power at crucial times. These reformers reasserted the principles of Mexican independence and constitutional representative government.

The Constitution of 1917

In the early 1900s, a reform movement called the Regeneration Group and a leader named Venustiano Carranza sparked a revolution. They removed the dictatorship of Porfirio Díaz and oversaw the writing of the Constitution of 1917.

The Mexican Constitution of 1917 was in many respects an updating of the documents of 1824 and 1857. It created, however, a system in which the government played a more active role in promoting the quality of Mexican social, economic, and cultural life. The rights of previously excluded portions of the population were also specified.

Three Branches of Government

Like the Constitution of the United States, Mexico's fundamental law establishes a national government with three independent branches. The executive branch is headed by the president, the legislature is bicameral, and the judiciary is an independent entity.

The President

The president of Mexico is popularly elected and serves a single six-year term. The term limit is intended to prevent a popular leader from becoming a dictator by winning several reelections.

The president selects the members of the council of ministers (the cabinet) and the other top civilian officers of the government. He also appoints the senior officers of the armed forces and all federal judges.

In addition to the powers usually held by a nation's chief executive, Mexico's president has the power to propose amendments to the constitution. These amendments must be ratified at both the national and state levels, by a two-thirds vote in each house of Congress and by a majority (at least 16) of the state legislatures.

The *Living* Constitution

America's Place in the World

1900

During the first phase of its history, the United States tried to isolate itself from foreign conflicts. In the 1900s, however, the United States participated in two world wars, became a global superpower, and eventually became a major proponent of world trade. The time line lists critical developments concerning war, peace, and trade in the twentieth century.

1898
United States wins the Spanish-American War and acquires foreign territories.

1917
United States abandons neutrality to join the Allies in World War I.

The General Congress

The national legislature, called the General Congress, is a bicameral body. It is composed of the Senate and the Chamber of Deputies.

There are 64 senators, two from each of the 31 Mexican states and two from the Federal District, which includes Mexico City. Senators are elected to six-year terms. Half are elected at the time of the presidential election and half at a mid-term election three years later.

The Chamber of Deputies has 500 members who are elected to three-year terms and cannot be reelected. Three hundred of the deputies are directly elected from districts of over 300,000 people. The rest of the seats are filled from the ranks of the various political parties, based on the percentage of the total vote each receives in the national election. Thus, the Chamber of Deputies is elected on a mixed system of direct and proportional representation.

The Congress meets from September 1 to December 31 each year. The combination of term limits and a short session work to give the General Congress a far less significant role than that played by the Congress in the United States.

The Court System

Mexico's independent judicial system is very similar to that of the United States. Two systems of courts—state and federal—operate within the Mexican federal system. Each has its own jurisdiction.

The federal judiciary is built of district and circuit courts that function under the Supreme Court. These tribunals hear all cases that arise under federal law, including those that raise constitutional issues. The 31 separate state court systems are composed of trial and appellate courts. They hear civil and criminal cases in a structure headed by a state Supreme Court of Justice.

National Politics

Mexico's national identity and the nation's freedom from foreign domination have been the leading themes of Mexico's national history. Those two themes remain fundamentally important in Mexican politics today.

The PRI

Mexico has a multi-party system. However, like the Japanese system, it was dominated for decades by one powerful and successful

1941
United States declares war on the Axis Powers.

1964
Gulf of Tonkin Resolution approves U.S. military involvement in the Vietnam conflict.

1993
United States, Canada, and Mexico ratify the NAFTA free-trade agreement.

| 1925 | 1950 | 1975 | 2000 |

1920
Senate rejects Treaty of Versailles and American membership in the League of Nations.

1945
United States is a founding member of the United Nations.

1995
United States is a founding member of the World Trade Organization, formed to monitor and promote world trade.

2001
United States declares war on terrorism.

Analyzing Time Lines

1. How do the entries for 1919 and 1945 show the different responses by the United States to the end of the two world wars?
2. What are some areas in which the United States has acted globally since World War II?

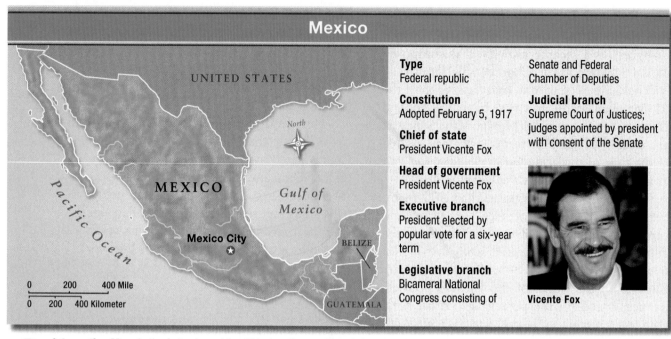

Mexico

Type	Senate and Federal
Federal republic	Chamber of Deputies

Constitution
Adopted February 5, 1917

Chief of state
President Vicente Fox

Head of government
President Vicente Fox

Executive branch
President elected by popular vote for a six-year term

Legislative branch
Bicameral National Congress consisting of

Judicial branch
Supreme Court of Justices; judges appointed by president with consent of the Senate

Vicente Fox

Interpreting Maps In the federal republic of Mexico, the president is both chief of state and head of government. *What is the significance of the rise to power of Mexico's current president, Vicente Fox?*

force: the Institutional Revolutionary Party (PRI). The PRI controlled the government and politics of Mexico for more than 70 years. Its presidential candidates won every election from 1929, when the party was first organized, until the presidential election of 2000.

In 1928, General Alvaro Obregon was elected to succeed Plutarco Elias Calles as president. However, Obregon was assassinated before he could take office. The turmoil surrounding that event persuaded President Calles to remain in office, and in 1929, he and other leaders of the day formed the National Revolutionary Party (PRN). That group became the PRI in 1946.

The PRI began to take its long-term shape in the mid-1930s under the leadership of President Lazaro Cardenas del Rio. Cardenas presided over an extensive redistribution of land to the peasantry. In 1938, he restructured the party on the basis of four major groups in Mexican society: the peasants, organized labor, the military, and the popular sector (the middle class and professionals). In 1938 Cardenas also oversaw the **nationalization** of all United States oil companies in Mexico. (Nationalization is the governmental acquisition of private industry for public use.) He was thus ensured his place as a major hero of Mexican nationalism.

The PRI began to move away from its traditional labor base in the 1940s and 1950s. It became increasingly the party of business interests and sought to woo the people as a whole.

The PRI's dominant role was seriously threatened in the 1980s. The government had borrowed heavily from foreign lenders during the 1970s, expecting that oil prices would remain at their then-high levels. When oil prices declined sharply worldwide, the nation plunged into economic chaos. Debt problems led to severe cutbacks in government programs. Prices soared and investment capital fled the country.

The political consequences of that economic calamity were apparent in the elections of 1988. Although economic conditions had begun to improve, the PRI made its worst showing ever. Presidential candidate Carlos Salinas de Gortari won the election, and the party kept its solid hold on both houses of Congress. The PRI's electoral margins were narrow, however. Moreover, it is generally agreed that many of the claims of election fraud were valid.

President Salinas pursued broad-based economic, social, and electoral reforms during his six-year term. He also backed the **North American Free Trade Agreement (NAFTA)**. This agreement, promoted by the United States, removed trade restrictions among the United

States, Canada, and Mexico, thus increasing cross-border trade.

In the 1994 national elections, the PRI's presidential candidate, Ernesto Zedillo Ponce de Leon, won 48.8 percent of the total vote, and the PRI kept control of the legislature. The 1997 off-year elections were a disaster for Zedillo and the PRI, however. The PRI's share of the Chamber of Deputies fell to 239 seats—less than a majority. The leftist Democratic Revolutionary Party (PRD) won 125 seats, while the conservative National Action Party (PAN) took 122 seats.

The 2000 Election

By 2000 the PRI faced what only a few years earlier had seemed a complete impossibility: the loss of the presidency. Over recent years, PAN and PRD candidates had won increasing numbers of federal, state, and local offices. Now both parties took dead aim at the nation's highest office.

Public opinion—and world attention—forced the PRI to guarantee a fraud-free presidential contest in 2000. When all the votes had been counted, the PRI's Francisco Labastida had only one third of the total vote. The PRD's candidate, Cuauhtemoc Cardenas, won one fifth of all the ballots. The victor, with a plurality of 45 percent, was the PAN candidate, Vicente Fox.

President Fox was inaugurated on December 1, 2000. Since Fox and his party lack a majority in the General Congress, Mexico's new president must work with the PRD—and the PRI—

▲ **National Palace, Mexico City** Built on the site where the Aztec emperor Montezuma's palace once stood, the National Palace houses the presidential and other executive offices of the Mexican government.

as he builds the first non-PRI government in Mexico's modern political history.

Regional and Local Government

Mexico is divided into 31 states and one Federal District. The Federal District includes Mexico City and is administered by a governor appointed by the president. Each of the 31 state constitutions provides for a governor, a unicameral legislature, and state courts. Each governor is elected to a single six-year term and its legislators to three-year terms. The governor appoints judges. The states have the power to legislate on local matters and to levy taxes, but most of their funding comes from the national level.

Section 3 Assessment

Key Terms and Main Ideas

1. Briefly summarize Mexico's history in the first century after gaining independence from Spain.
2. In what major ways are the three branches of Mexican government similar to those in the United States?
3. What is **nationalization**?
4. What is the significance of **North American Free Trade Agreement (NAFTA)**?

Critical Thinking

5. **Drawing Inferences** The president of Mexico serves for a single six-year term. What do you think are the advantages and disadvantages of a single six-year term compared to the four-year term with possible reelection that we have in the United States?

6. **Drawing Conclusions** How was the 2000 election a reflection of Mexican democracy?

 Take It to the Net

7. Choose an aspect of the Mexican government to compare to the U.S. government. Possible topics include the party system or the structure and functions of a branch of government. Present your findings in a 1–2 minute oral report. Use the links provided in the Social Studies area at the following Web site for help in completing this activity. **www.phschool.com**

Democratic Reform in Mexico

On July 2, 2000, Mexican voters ended 71 years of control by the Institutional Revolutionary Party (PRI) when they elected a new president, Vicente Fox of the National Action Party (PAN). In his Inaugural Address, Fox outlined reforms intended to lead to open, honest, democratic government.

I cannot fail to mention that I am taking office as head of the Executive Branch under new circumstances. The sovereign decision of those who voted on July 2nd was unprecedented. No individual can claim all the credit for this achievement, but we cannot fail to recognize the contribution each has made. On that day, millions of Mexican men and women from every part of the country came to cast their vote. All of us participated in this civic celebration.

Mexican President Vicente Fox

For perhaps the first time in our history, no one arrived too late, nor were any left behind. Nothing hindered the free expression of our democratic will; no one died that day to make this possible. At the end of the day, the victory belonged to all of us. . . .

In order to guarantee both an effective democracy and democratic effectiveness, I am making the commitment to promote seven key reforms that I gathered during my presidential campaign and that represent the Mexican people's mandate for change.

• One reform will consolidate the democratic progress we have made so that all people may speak freely and be heard.
• One reform will create progress in the fight against poverty and for social equality, so that no mother lacks enough money to buy milk for her children.
• An educational reform that will assure the development of better human capital and that no young person in our country—no matter how poor he or she may be—fails to complete his or her education

due to a lack of resources.
• A reform that will guarantee economic growth with stability, so that our young people will never again have to leave their homes and immigrate to another country.
• A reform that decentralizes Federal powers and resources, in order to give the states, municipalities, and communities greater vitality.
• A reform that assures transparency and accountability in the work of governing, in order to eliminate corruption and deception.
• A reform that combats our lack of safety and does away with impunity, so that every family may sleep peacefully. . . .

Let us put aside pessimism and apathy. Let us be optimists while still keeping our feet on the ground. Let us build the future with realism and joy, and day by day let us turn our present, ours and that of our families, into a better future for all men and women. It is in our hands and within our reach, with the efforts of all, we will all be better for it. Let us start today.

Analyzing Primary Sources

1. Summarize Fox's goals for Mexico.
2. What word or phrase would you use to characterize Vicente Fox, based on this speech? Explain your answer.
3. What circumstances might make Fox's reforms difficult to achieve?

·4· Russia

Section Preview

OBJECTIVES

1. **Summarize** Russia's political history after the Bolshevik Revolution.
2. **Outline** the structure of the Soviet government.
3. **Describe** Mikhail Gorbachev's reforms.
4. **Identify** events leading to the fall of the Soviet Union.
5. **Examine** the structure of the Russian government today.

WHY IT MATTERS

The Soviet dictatorship controlled Russia for more than 70 years. It began to undergo broad changes when Mikhail Gorbachev gained power in 1985. In 1991, the once-mighty Soviet Union dissolved. Today, the Russian people are still learning to organize and run democratic institutions.

POLITICAL DICTIONARY

★ **purge**
★ **soviets**
★ *perestroika*
★ *glasnost*

Russia[11] is a government in transition, moving—somewhat fitfully—toward democracy and a market economy. The country's recent history shows clearly that political change is rarely a straight, smooth, or easy path.

Political History

The Soviet Union was the modern successor to the Russian empire, which began to emerge in the fifteenth century and was formally established by Peter the Great in 1721. A succession of tyrannical czars ruled the empire. Czarist rule began to collapse after heavy losses in the Russo-Japanese War (1904–1905) and World War I (1914–1917).

The Bolshevik Revolution

The first period of Soviet government began in 1917 with the Bolshevik Revolution and the emergence of the Communist Party of the Soviet Union (CPSU). After a brief revolution in March 1917, Czar Nicholas abdicated. A short-lived democratic government arose headed by Alexander Kerensky.

A second coup, led by V. I. Lenin, overthrew that government on November 7, 1917, bringing the Communist Party to power. Lenin[12] was the architect of what became the Soviet Union. He began to transform an underdeveloped, tradition-bound country into the world's first communist state.

▲ *V. I. Lenin*

Stalin

Lenin's death in 1924 prompted a fierce struggle for power, and Josef Stalin[13] emerged as the new Soviet leader. Stalin consolidated his power over the next several years in a series of **purges.** Technically, a "purge" is a purification. Stalin "purified" the government by having his rivals and millions of other dissidents jailed, exiled, or executed. Through an intensive and brutal program of industrialization and forced collectivization of agriculture, he built the Soviet Union into a major industrial and military power.

The Soviets suffered staggering losses in World War II. Nevertheless, at war's end they controlled all of Eastern Europe and emerged as one of the world's two superpowers. Rivalry with the United States and an aggressive foreign policy brought on the cold war that lasted from the late 1940s until the early 1990s.

---

[11]Russia is officially titled the Russian Federation. Its population, which is declining, is now some 145 million people.

[12]Lenin was born Vladimir Ilyich Ulyanov in Simbirsk in 1870. He took the name Lenin in 1901, probably adapting it from the great Lena River in Siberia, where he had been exiled in 1897.

[13]Stalin was born Iosif Vissarionovich Dzhugashvili in 1879. He served as one of Lenin's closest aides and adopted the name Stalin (man of steel) some time before the revolution.

▲ **Red Square** Moscow's Red Square has long been the scene of demonstrations, parades, and speeches. It is dominated by the towers of St. Basil's Cathedral (left) and the Kremlin (right), once the symbol of Russian communism.

Soviet Government Structure

The Soviet Union—officially, the Union of Soviet Socialist Republics (USSR)—comprised 15 republics, each inhabited by a major nationality group, such as Georgians or Tajiks. The largest and most important of the republics was Russia. It included more than 70 percent of the land area of the Soviet Union and more than half its population.

The country's complex government consisted of several layers of elected **soviets** (councils) at the factory, farm, city, regional, and national levels. However, major policy decisions were made at the top by the Communist Party leadership.

The Soviet Constitution

The structure and powers of the Soviet system were set out in the constitution of the Soviet Union. Unlike the constitutions of Western democracies, the Soviet constitution did not embody fundamental law, nor was it a charter intended to limit governmental power. In addition, although the constitution contained several civil rights provisions, it did not guarantee Soviet citizens such basic rights as free speech, press, and association. Rather, it declared that "[t]he exercise by citizens of rights and freedoms must not injure the interests of society and the state."

The Legislature

Under communist control, the legislature, called the Supreme Soviet, was a kind of puppet theater. It assembled for a few days each year to rubber-stamp the decrees of the CPSU. Citizens could vote for members of the legislature, but in general only one candidate ran for each office. This candidate was either a Communist Party member or a vocal supporter of the party.

The Communist Party

From the revolution of 1917 until 1990, the Communist Party was the only political party in the Soviet Union. The CPSU was an elite party, composed of some 19 million specially chosen people—only about nine percent of the adult population. It was organized like a pyramid. At the bottom were some 400,000 primary party organizations (once called cells), each headed by a party committee. At the top were the Central Committee, the Politburo, and the general secretary.

The Central Committee assembled once every six months. It elected the much smaller Politburo, which was the body that in fact ran the party. The Politburo (political bureau) was a full-time decision-making body, made up of experienced and powerful party leaders. Most of them also held key government posts.

The general secretary headed the Politburo and had broad powers. After the Stalin era, the general secretary usually also held the top post in government.

Gorbachev's Reforms

A brief second stage of Soviet government began in 1985 when Mikhail Gorbachev became general secretary of the party. Gorbachev undertook a reform program that rested on the principles of *perestroika* and *glasnost*. **Perestroika** was the restructuring of political and economic life. *Glasnost* was the policy of openness under which the government increased its tolerance of dissent and freedom of expression.

Gorbachev concentrated his reform efforts in three areas: the legislature, the executive, and the Communist Party.

1. *The Legislature.* Under Gorbachev, the legislature was composed of the large Congress of People's Deputies and the smaller Supreme Soviet. Voters elected two thirds of the 2,250 members of

the Congress of People's Deputies. The election of those deputies in 1989 marked the first time that the Soviet Union had held competitive, multi-candidate elections. The Congress chose some of its members to form the Supreme Soviet.

The Supreme Soviet that met from 1989 to 1991 had the power to make laws, approve the national budget, confirm the appointments of top government officials, and declare war. Importantly, it also elected the president of the Soviet Union.

2. *The President*. Gorbachev also created a new office: president of the Soviet Union. As president, Gorbachev appointed the other top government officials, set the lawmaking agenda for the Supreme Soviet, headed the defense establishment, and conducted Soviet foreign policy.

3. *The CPSU*. Democratic reforms reduced the party's power. In 1990, it lost its exclusive position, and a number of smaller political parties emerged. Gorbachev, the most visible symbol of the Soviet political system, began to regularly present himself as head of state—the president of the Soviet Union—rather than as head of the party.

Fall of the Soviet Union

In 1989, encouraged by Gorbachev's emphasis on *glasnost,* a wave of democratization rolled across Eastern Europe. Independence movements gained strength in the Baltic Soviet states of Lithuania, Latvia, and Estonia.

By the middle of 1990, the republics of Russia, Ukraine, and Byelorussia, as well as several smaller republics, had declared independence from the Soviet central authority. In elections in 1991, Russians named Boris Yeltsin president of the Russian Republic. Yeltsin further challenged the Soviet government by resigning from the Communist Party and having the laws of the Russian Republic declared sovereign over Russia's population and territory.

Events quickly moved beyond Gorbachev's control. In August 1991, Gorbachev and his wife were vacationing in the Crimea when a group of hard-line Communist Party leaders placed him under house arrest. They objected to the new democratic reforms and wanted a return to the policies of the old Soviet government.

When the Soviet public heard of the attempted coup, thousands of protesters took to the streets of Moscow, raising the white, blue, and red Russian (not Soviet) flag. Leading the protest was Russian President Boris Yeltsin. After several tense days, the conspirators surrendered. The coup had failed.

In the months that followed, extraordinary changes occurred. The three Baltic republics departed from the Union. Soon the remaining 12 republics left the Union as well.

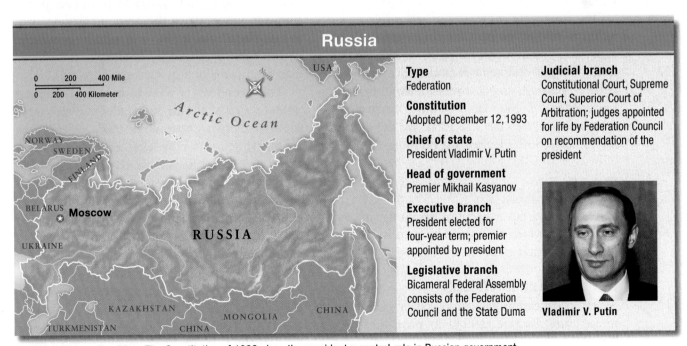

Russia

Type
Federation

Constitution
Adopted December 12, 1993

Chief of state
President Vladimir V. Putin

Head of government
Premier Mikhail Kasyanov

Executive branch
President elected for four-year term; premier appointed by president

Legislative branch
Bicameral Federal Assembly consists of the Federation Council and the State Duma

Judicial branch
Constitutional Court, Supreme Court, Superior Court of Arbitration; judges appointed for life by Federation Council on recommendation of the president

Vladimir V. Putin

Interpreting Maps The Constitution of 1993 gives the president a central role in Russian government. The president, who is elected by direct popular vote, appoints the prime minister. *How did Mikhail Gorbachev reform the Soviet government?*

Voices on Government

The career of **Vaclav Havel**—playwright, essayist, and politician—symbolizes the great changes in world politics in the second half of the twentieth century. When Czechoslovakia was under Soviet domination, Havel went to jail for his dissident views. Then the country peacefully overthrew the Communist regime, and he became the Czech president. On New Year's Day 1990, he spoke about the future:

❝ *We cannot blame the previous rulers for everything, not only because it would be untrue but also because it could blunt the duty that each of us faces today, namely the obligation to act independently, freely, reasonably, and quickly. Let us not be mistaken: the best government in the world, the best parliament and the best president, cannot achieve much on their own. . . . Freedom and democracy include participation and therefore responsibility from us all.* **❞**

Evaluating the Quotation

(a) What do you think Havel means by "participation"? (b) Why might the transition to democracy be difficult for people after 40 years of totalitarian rule?

Boris Yeltsin became the major proponent of a radical economic reform plan. As the elected leader of the dominant republic in the Soviet Union, Yeltsin's power overshadowed that of Gorbachev. Recognizing reality, Gorbachev resigned on December 25, 1991. By the end of the year, the Soviet Union was no more.

Russian Government Today

Since 1991, the government of Russia has moved toward democracy and economic reform. Will it in fact reach that goal?

The Constitution of 1993

A new constitution was approved in a national referendum in late 1993. It proclaims the Russian Federation to be "a democratic federal legally-based state with a republican form of government." It also sets out a new government structure and contains an extensive list of individual rights—including guarantees of freedom of speech, press, association, and religious belief. Furthermore, the constitution provides that every citizen has a right to freedom of movement within the federation, to housing, and to free medical care and education.

Political Parties

Today, the one-party system of the Soviet era has been replaced by a multiparty system. More than 40 parties now operate in Russian politics. Besides the Communists, these include the right-wing, ultranationalist Liberal Democratic Party; Our Home Is Russia, which favors economic and social reform; and *Yabloko* ("apple"), a liberal reform party.

The Executive Branch

The constitution of 1993 created a government built on a separation of powers between the executive and legislative branches. In theory, the branches are independent and equal. In reality, the constitution gives the president a central role. He defines the "basic directions of domestic and foreign policy" and represents Russia in the world community.

The president appoints a prime minister, as well as other ministers who head the executive departments of the government. The prime minister, who carries the administration's programs to the assembly, is second-in-command of the executive branch. The prime minister is also first in the line of succession.

The president is elected by direct popular vote for a term of four years, and may not serve more than two consecutive terms. He or she must be a Russian citizen, at least 35 years old, and a resident of Russia for 10 years.

Recall that Boris Yeltsin was elected president of the old Russian Republic in 1991. Yeltsin kept his office under the new constitution in 1993. In a historic election in June 1996, he faced challenges from nine other candidates (including Gorbachev).

A different outcome might have changed the direction of reform in Russia, but Yeltsin was reelected. He was, however, beset by health problems and by accusations of corruption in his inner circle. He often appeared to make erratic decisions, naming—and firing—several prime ministers.

In a surprise move, Yeltsin resigned at the end of December 1999, yielding the presidency to his latest prime minister, Vladimir Putin. Putin won election on his own in March 2000.

The Legislature

Russia's legislature, the Federal Assembly, is a bicameral body. Its upper house, the Council of the Federation, is composed of 178 members, two members from each of Russia's 89 constituent regions. The lower house, the State Duma, has 450 members, called deputies. The members of both houses are popularly elected for four-year terms.

The Duma is the more powerful chamber. Any measure passed by the Duma but rejected by the Council may nonetheless become law if it is passed again by the Duma by at least a two-thirds majority. The Duma also must approve the president's choice of a prime minister.

Presidential vetoes can be overridden by a two-thirds vote in each house. The Duma can also be dissolved in much the same way as can the House of Commons in Great Britain.

Constitutional Court

Under the 1993 constitution, a 19-member Constitutional Court can rule on the constitutionality of federal laws, actions of the president and assembly, and the laws of local governments. Its judges are elected to 12-year terms.

Interpreting Political Cartoons *(a) Who is most likely the speaker in this cartoon? (b) To what political situation does the cartoon refer?*

Regional and Local Governments

Local governments in Russia are a patchwork of different organizational structures. The Russian Federation comprises 49 *oblasts* (provinces) and 6 large, thinly populated territories, all of which are headed by elected governors. The governors of these regions have traditionally exercised great power.

The federation also includes 21 republics, which are home to ethnic, non-Russian minorities, and 10 autonomous areas. Each republic elects a president. Independence is a burning issue in several republics. The Republic of Chechnya attempted to break away from the Russian Federation in 1994, and the Russian military has been engaged there ever since.

Section 4 Assessment

Key Terms and Main Ideas

1. **(a)** What were the roles of Lenin and Stalin in creating the communist state? **(b)** How did Stalin use **purges?**
2. What was Gorbachev's purpose in introducing *perestroika* and *glasnost?*
3. Briefly describe the events that led to the fall of the Soviet Union.
4. How did the Constitution of 1993 differ from the old Soviet constitution?

Critical Thinking

5. **Drawing Inferences** Gorbachev hoped to create a democratic and open system of government while preserving the communist system. In what way were these goals incompatible?

6. **Identifying Assumptions** The Soviet constitution declared that "[t]he exercise by citizens of rights and freedoms must not injure the interests of society and the state." What assumption underlies this statement?

 Take It to the Net

7. Read about *glasnost* and *perestroika*. Write a short essay explaining how these two concepts were revolutionary in Russia at the time and how they led to a change of government. Use the links provided in the Social Studies area at the following Web site for help in completing this activity. **www.phschool.com**

Section Preview

OBJECTIVES

1. **Examine** China's political background.
2. **Describe** China's government today.

WHY IT MATTERS

The People's Republic of China is controlled by the Chinese Communist Party, the largest political party in the world. Although the Chinese government is pursuing economic reform, it continues to repress political dissent.

POLITICAL DICTIONARY

★ **Cultural Revolution**
★ **autonomous**

▲ This 1967 poster features Chairman Mao. Demonstrators are holding copies of the "Little Red Book," which contains the basic tenets of Chinese communism.

The governments you have looked at to this point have a number of features in common. The government of China, on the other hand, lives in a world unto itself.

Political Background

Although the political history of what is today China can be traced back some 5,000 years, China's present-day government has existed for little more than 50 years.[14] The People's Republic of China was born in 1949 after decades of civil war. Those years of bitter strife pitted China's Nationalist government, led by Chiang Kai-shek, against rebel communists led by Mao Zedong.

The United States supported Chiang's Nationalist government during World War II and for a few years thereafter. But American aid was often misused by corrupt officials and by the ineffective commanders of the ill-trained Nationalist army.

At the same time, Mao, a committed communist, organized a patriotic movement that appealed to the Chinese peasantry, whom the Nationalist elite had long ignored. His Red Army vanquished the Nationalists in a series of battles in the immediate postwar years.

China Under Mao

By 1949, Mao's forces had captured the Chinese capital, Beijing. Nationalist forces fled the mainland for the island of Taiwan. In October 1949, communist forces established the People's Republic of China, with Mao as its leader.

Mao was bent on increasing agricultural and industrial production. He turned to central planning and instituted a series of Five-Year Plans. Frequent and often drastic changes in policy produced chaos and regularly thwarted economic development.

By the mid-1960s, Mao was determined to purge China of what he called the "Four Olds" —old thoughts, old culture, old customs, and old habits. In the **Cultural Revolution,** begun in 1966, Mao's young, dedicated Red Guards attacked and bullied teachers, intellectuals, and anyone else who seemed to lack revolutionary fervor.

Artists and scholars were sent to farms to be "re-educated"; ancient books and art were destroyed. By 1968, however, the havoc created by the Cultural Revolution persuaded Mao to abandon that effort.

Reform and Repression

Deng Xiaoping came to power after Mao's death in 1976. Deng's reforms loosened the government's strict controls on the economy and encouraged some forms of private enterprise.

---

[14]The population of the People's Republic of China now exceeds 1.3 billion; that figure does not include more than 7 million residents of Hong Kong.

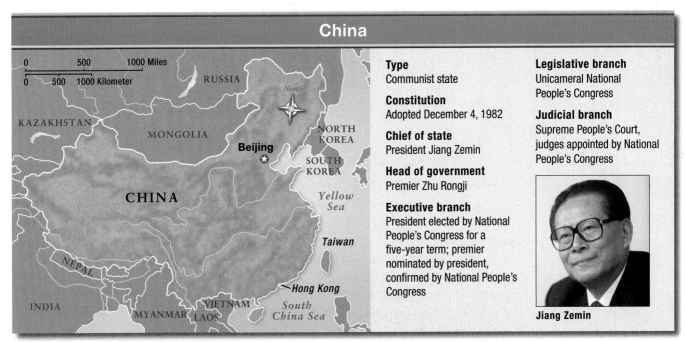

China

Type Communist state	**Legislative branch** Unicameral National People's Congress
Constitution Adopted December 4, 1982	**Judicial branch** Supreme People's Court, judges appointed by National People's Congress
Chief of state President Jiang Zemin	
Head of government Premier Zhu Rongji	
Executive branch President elected by National People's Congress for a five-year term; premier nominated by president, confirmed by National People's Congress	

Jiang Zemin

Interpreting Maps The People's Republic of China is a communist state in which the top-ranking members of the Communist Party hold the highest positions in the government and the military. ***How does the Chinese constitution differ from the constitutions of most other countries?***

Although the Chinese government relaxed economic controls under Deng, it tolerated no political dissent. In May 1989, students and workers in many parts of the country held demonstrations calling for democracy. In early June, government soldiers with tanks attacked pro-democracy protesters in Tiananmen Square, in the heart of Beijing. Thousands of protestors were killed, outraging people around the world.

China Today

Today, China's leaders continue to encourage economic reforms. At the same time, they also continue to impose harsh limits on human rights.

The Constitution

When the communists gained power, the People's Political Consultative Conference adopted a provisional constitution. That document became the basis for a new constitution adopted by the first session of the National People's Congress in 1954.

Unlike the Constitution of the United States and those of most other nations, China's constitution is not intended to be fundamental law. Instead, it is supposed to reflect current governmental policies. China has had four constitutions since its founding—in 1954, 1975, 1978, and 1982.

China's Communist Party

China's Communist Party (the CCP) has some 58 million members, and is, by far, the largest political party in the world. The top-ranking members of the party hold the highest positions in the government and the military. In short, the CCP *is* the government of China.

Recall the organization of the Communist Party in the former Soviet Union. The present-day Chinese Communist Party has a similar structure. Its main units are the National Party Congress, the Central Committee, the Politburo, and the Secretariat.

The National Party Congress has some 1,900 members chosen by party members throughout China. It meets approximately every five years to elect a Central Committee of about 300 members, which meets about once a year. The Central Committee in turn elects the Politburo, which has about 20 members. It is the Politburo that makes party policy. The Secretariat makes the party's day-to-day decisions.

The National Government

The national government of China is composed of two main bodies, the National People's Congress and the State Council.

▲ The British returned the prosperous island of Hong Kong to Chinese control in 1997.

The Judicial System

A nationwide system of "people's courts" deals with both criminal and civil cases. Those courts are supervised by the Supreme People's Court—in effect, the nation's Supreme Court.

Capital punishment may be the penalty for conviction of any of a long list of crimes: murder, treason, bribery, embezzlement, smuggling, drug-dealing, and many others. Most of the guarantees of fair trial known to Western democracies are completely absent from Chinese law.

Local Political Divisions

China has a unitary government, with the central government exerting direct control over local subdivisions. Local administrative regions include 22 provinces and 5 **autonomous** (independent) regions whose people are mostly ethnic minorities. Hong Kong, which the British returned to China's control in 1997, is a special administrative region of China with its own governor and provisional legislature.

Taiwan

When Mao's forces took over the mainland in 1949, Chiang Kai-shek and the Nationalists fled to the island of Formosa (Taiwan), establishing the Republic of China. Today the People's Republic of China considers Taiwan one of its provinces. In turn, the Republic of China (Taiwan) takes the position that its National Assembly rules all of China.

1. *National People's Congress.* The nearly 3,000 deputies of the National People's Congress are elected for five-year terms by local people's congresses throughout China. According to the Chinese constitution, the National People's Congress is the highest governmental authority. In reality, however, the Congress has little power. It performs its major function when it passes the policy decisions of the State Council and the CCP on to lower levels of government.

2. *The State Council.* The State Council is the main body in the executive branch of Chinese government. It is headed by the premier, who is chosen by the Central Committee of the CCP. The premier, vice-premiers, state councilors, and secretary-general meet regularly as a standing committee. This Standing Committee of the State Council possesses major decision-making authority, and its decisions have the force of law.

Section 5 Assessment

Key Terms and Main Ideas

1. **(a)** Summarize the events that led to the establishment of the People's Republic of China. **(b)** What was the **Cultural Revolution?**
2. On what basis does China change its constitution?
3. What is the relationship between the People's Republic of China and the Republic of China (Taiwan)?
4. What is Hong Kong's status today?

Critical Thinking

5. **Making Comparisons** Compare efforts at economic and political reform in China with those in Russia today.

6. **Checking Consistency** Give evidence from the section to support the following statement: *The Chinese Communist Party dominates the political life of China.*

 Take It to the Net

7. Read about the Tiananmen Square protest. Write a diary entry for June 1989 from the viewpoint of a Chinese student explaining the reasons for the protests and describing the Chinese government's response. Then answer this question: How does the U.S. government handle protests? Use the links provided in the Social Studies area at the following Web site for help in completing this activity. **www.phschool.com**

May the Government Regulate the Internet?

Efforts to protect young people from inappropriate materials on the Internet run the risk of violating the First Amendment rights of adult Internet users. How far can the Federal Government go in regulating the transmission of such materials over the Internet?

Reno v. *ACLU* (1997)

Congress passed the Telecommunications Act of 1996 to reduce regulation and promote the rapid deployment of new telecommunications technologies. Most of the law deals with encouraging competition in local telephone, video, and over-the-air broadcasting. One portion of the law, called the Communications Decency Act of 1996, imposes restrictions on the content of information that may be communicated by electronic devices.

Two key sections of the Communications Decency Act are informally called the "indecent transmission" provision and the "patently offensive display" provision. They make it a crime to use any telecommunications device to make an indecent or obscene comment to a person known to be under 18 years old, or knowingly to send or display offensive messages in a way that makes them available to persons under 18. There is an exception for people who take "good faith, reasonable, effective and appropriate actions" to restrict access by minors, such as by requiring persons to provide proof of age.

A group of 47 organizations, including the American Civil Liberties Union, challenged the law as unconstitutional. A federal district court ordered the government not to enforce the law, which the court said was too vague and broad. On behalf of the Federal Government, Attorney General Janet Reno appealed to the Supreme Court.

Arguments for Reno

1. The government historically has had broad rights to regulate the broadcast industry and to protect minors from offensive materials. It should be allowed the same powers regarding the Internet.

2. The law clearly explains which activities are not permitted.
3. The law's "good faith" exception will protect those who are not seeking to engage in unlawful conduct.

Arguments for the ACLU

1. The Internet is fundamentally different from broadcast media. It has not historically been regulated by the Federal Government, and is not as "invasive" as radio or television.
2. The law is too vague, because it is often impossible to determine whether a particular communication will violate its provisions. Terms such as "indecent" are not defined in the law, and their meaning will vary from person to person.
3. The law is too broad, because efforts to comply with the law will have the effect of interfering with communication among adults. Often it is not possible to determine whether a person who participates in an Internet conversation or has access to Internet materials is under 18 years old.

Decide for Yourself

1. Review the constitutional grounds on which each side based its arguments and the specific arguments each side presented.
2. Debate the opposing viewpoints presented in this case. Which viewpoint do you favor?
3. Predict the impact of the Court's decision on the growth of the Internet and on government efforts to protect minors from indecent materials. (To read a summary of the Court's decision, turn to the Supreme Court Glossary on page 799.)

Political Dictionary

Practicing the Vocabulary

Matching *Choose a term from the list above that best matches each description.*

1. Stalin's elimination of rivals and other dissidents
2. Movement intended to cleanse China of the "Four Olds"
3. A person with both Spanish or Portuguese and Native American ancestry
4. Political subdivision in Japan
5. A special election held to fill a vacant seat in the House of Commons

Word Relationships *Distinguish between the words in each pair.*

6. *perestroika/glasnost*
7. nationalization/devolution
8. shadow cabinet/soviets
9. monarchy/minister
10. coalition/consensus

Reviewing Main Ideas

Section 1

11. In what ways does Great Britain's constitution differ from the United States Constitution?
12. **(a)** Briefly describe the organization of Britain's Parliament. **(b)** What recent change has been made in the House of Lords?
13. How are Britain's prime minister and cabinet members chosen?

Section 2

14. **(a)** What is the anti-military clause of Japan's constitution? **(b)** Why is it part of that constitution? **(c)** How have interpretations of the clause changed over time?
15. **(a)** Briefly describe the organization of the National Diet. **(b)** How are the prime minister and cabinet chosen?
16. List three characteristics of the Japanese bureaucracy.

Section 3

17. Briefly describe Mexico's history up to 1821.
18. **(a)** Describe Mexico's three branches of government. **(b)** Compare Mexico's three branches of government with the three branches of the United States government.

19. **(a)** What was the role of the PRI in the Mexican political system before 2000? **(b)** Who won the presidency in 2000?

Section 4

20. **(a)** Briefly describe the importance of Lenin and Stalin in Soviet history. **(b)** Describe the Soviet Union at the end of World War II.
21. **(a)** Outline Gorbachev's plans for reform. **(b)** How successful were they?
22. Briefly describe the government of Russia today.

Section 5

23. Describe the government of China under Mao Zedong.
24. What is the role of the Communist Party in the People's Republic of China?
25. Why does Taiwan have a government separate from that of mainland China?

Critical Thinking Skills

26. ***Applying the Chapter Skill*** What can you infer about China's Communist Party from the fact that despite its enormous power, it includes only about 5 percent of the nation's population?

27. ***Making Decisions*** Suppose you have a choice between buying two jackets. One is made in a country that supports human rights, and the other is made in China, a country that abuses human rights. The jacket made in China is less expensive than the other. Which will you buy? Explain your answer.

28. ***Making Comparisons*** You have read that the American government is deeply rooted in the British system. Explain briefly how the American and British constitutions are similar and different.

29. ***Drawing Inferences*** As part of the consensus politics practiced in Japan, political majorities in the National Diet try to avoid pushing through a bill against strong opposition. **(a)** How does this practice differ from politics in the United States? **(b)** What are the advantages and disadvantages of the Japanese system?

Analyzing Political Cartoons

Using your knowledge of comparative government and this cartoon, answer the questions below.

30. Dragons have figured prominently in Chinese culture for centuries. What is the significance of the dragon in this cartoon?
31. To what political situation does the cartoon refer?

★ You Can Make a Difference

Find out about volunteer opportunities in your community that involve working with people who have come from another country. You could, for example, work as an English tutor for newcomers, helping them learn the language and explaining unfamiliar customs. Or you could find out about groups that send volunteers to other countries or operate exchange programs.

Participation Activities

32. ***Current Events Watch*** Choose one of the countries covered in this chapter. Scan magazines and newspapers for articles about recent political events in that country. Then prepare an oral update on your chosen country's government and politics to present to your classmates. Use charts, graphs, or copies of photos to accompany your update if you choose.

33. ***Time Line Activity*** Create a time line that traces the events in Russia and the former Soviet Union from 1985 to the present. Illustrate your time line with drawings and copies of newspaper and magazine photos.

34. ***It's Your Turn*** Interview a recent immigrant from one of the countries covered in the chapter or from another country of your choice. Find out the ways (if any) that this person participated in politics and how he or she views the government of his or her country of origin. Why did he or she come to the United States? How does he or she view the United States government? Write up your interview to share with the class. **(Conducting an Interview)**

⬤ Take It to the Net

Chapter 22 Self-Test As a final review activity, take the Chapter 22 Self-Test in the Social Studies area at the Web site listed below, and receive immediate feedback on your answers.

www.phschool.com

Comparative Economic Systems

"*You do not like communism.
We do not like capitalism. There
is only one way out—peaceful
coexistence.*"

—Nikita Khrushchev (1956)

Capitalism, socialism, and communism are the main types
of economic systems, and they have often come into conflict. Which of those systems a nation follows has a major
impact on its political system and many other aspects of
people's lives. Many real-world economic systems include
some elements of the other two types.

◆ **Stock traders and runners on the floor of the Chicago Mercantile Exchange**

★ You Can Make a Difference

ONE OF THE WORLD'S best-known young activists, Craig Kielburger has crusaded against a sad feature of economic life in some countries—child labor. In 1995, when he was 12, Craig read about a Pakistani boy who had been killed for speaking out against child labor. Craig took up the fight and started "Free the Children" with his classmates in Toronto, Canada. In a few years, the organization had more than 10,000 members in 25 countries. Craig himself traveled to South Asia to talk to child workers in sweatshops. "Free the Children" worked for new laws and raised money to build schools for former child laborers. "We [kids] can be incredibly powerful if we join together," he said.

Keep It Current

Items marked with this logo are periodically updated on the Internet. Keep up-to-date with what's in the news. To get current information on economic systems, go to **www.phschool.com**

SECTION 1

Capitalism (pp. 658–664)

★ Capitalism is another name for the free enterprise system.
★ Entrepreneurs use land, labor, brain power, and capital to produce goods and services.
★ Private ownership, individual initiative, profit, and competition are the fundamental elements of capitalism.
★ A mixed economy is one in which the government intervenes to promote and regulate the economy.
★ Businesses may be organized as sole proprietorships, partnerships, or corporations.

SECTION 2

Socialism (pp. 666–670)

★ In a socialist economy, the government strives for social and economic equality for all members of society.
★ Karl Marx (1818–1883) and his collaborator Frederick Engels (1820–1895) laid out the basic tenets of modern-day socialism.
★ The British Labour Party and other "Social Democratic Parties" in Europe believe that the ends of socialism can be gained by peaceful, democratic means.
★ Socialist economies feature government ownership of industry, high taxes, and generous public welfare programs.
★ Although socialism began in industrial countries, many developing nations were attracted to socialism by the promise of equality and economic growth.

SECTION 3

Communism (pp. 672–676)

★ Karl Marx predicted that the final stage in human history would be a world of peaceful, democratic communes.
★ No country has ever created a political/economic system that even remotely resembles Marx's ideal.
★ Communist economies depend on a strong central government that owns all industry and farmland and plans all parts of the national economy.
★ In the Soviet Union, Lenin and Stalin created a communist dictatorship that controlled all aspects of life.
★ China, Cuba, North Korea, Vietnam, and other countries have also experimented with communism.

1 Capitalism

Section Preview

OBJECTIVES

1. **Identify** the factors of production.
2. **Describe** the free enterprise system and laissez-faire theory.
3. **Analyze** the role of government in a mixed economy.
4. **Compare and contrast** three types of business organizations.
5. **Explain** the role of profit and loss in a free enterprise system.

WHY IT MATTERS

Although the American free enterprise system is rooted in classic laissez-faire theory, government plays a major role in the nation's economic life—and so in the economic life of every person in this country.

POLITICAL DICTIONARY

★ **factors of production**
★ **capital**
★ **capitalist**
★ **entrepreneur**
★ **free enterprise system**
★ **laws of supply and demand**
★ **monopoly**
★ **trust**
★ **laissez-faire theory**

You have confronted these questions several times in this book: What are the functions a government ought to undertake? What should it have the power to do? What should it not be allowed to do? Certainly these questions can be asked of just about all areas of human activity, but they are raised very significantly in the realm of economic affairs.

Questions of politics and economics are inseparable. The most important economic questions faced by a nation are also political questions. For example: Who should decide what goods will be produced? How should goods and services be distributed and exchanged within a nation? What types of income or property ought to be taxed? What social services should a government provide?

Capitalism provides one response to all of these questions. Many aspects of capitalism will be familiar to you because the United States (along with countries such as Japan) follows this system.

Factors of Production

Certain resources are necessary to any nation's economy, no matter what economic system it follows. Economists call these basic resources, which are used to make all goods and services, the **factors of production.**

Land

One factor of production is land, which in economic terms includes all natural resources. Land has a variety of economic uses, such as agriculture, mining, and forestry. Along with farms and property, economists consider the water in rivers and lakes and the coal, iron, and petroleum found beneath the ground to be part of the land.

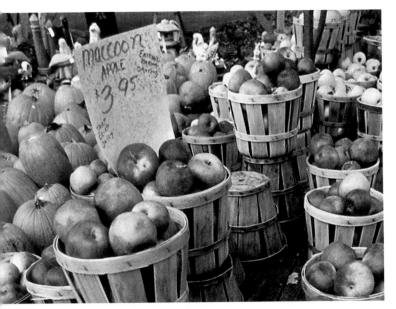

▲ In a capitalist system, prices are determined by decisions in the market.

The Factors of Production

Labor

Land

Entrepreneur

Capital

Interpreting Diagrams Land, labor, and capital are the building blocks of the economy. An entrepreneur brings these three factors together to create goods and offer services. *Give specific examples of land, labor, and capital involved in producing a jacket.*

Labor

A second factor of production is a human resource —labor. Men and women who work in mines, factories, offices, hospitals, and other places all provide labor that is an essential part of a nation's economy. In a free market economy, individuals "own" their labor and can sell it to any employer.

Capital

The third factor of production is **capital**—all the human-made resources that are used to produce goods and services. Physical capital (also called "capital goods") includes money, but it also describes the buildings, machines, and computers workers need to turn labor and land into goods and services. Human capital includes knowledge and skills that workers gain from their work experience—an investment in themselves. Note that capital is a product of the economy that is then put back, or reinvested, into the economy.

Someone who owns capital and puts it to productive use is called a **capitalist.** The term is most often applied to people who own large businesses or factories, but can apply to smaller investors as well. The United States economy is called capitalistic because it depends on the energy and drive of thousands of individual capitalists.

The Role of the Entrepreneur

To actually produce goods and services, someone must bring together and organize the factors of production. An **entrepreneur**—literally, an "enterpriser"—is an individual with the drive and ambition to combine land, labor, and capital resources to produce goods or offer services. Entrepreneurs start businesses and make them grow, driving the economic growth that contributes to the high standard of living of modern capitalistic societies.

Free Enterprise System

Capitalism is often called a **free enterprise system.** This is an economic system characterized by private or corporate ownership of capital goods (physical capital) and investments that

Comparative Economic Systems 659 ★★★

▲ *Renewal and Rebirth* In a free enterprise system, entrepreneurs try to put land, labor, and/or capital to the best possible (most profitable) use. Through this process, resources can be put to better use. These unused port buildings in New York City's South Street Seaport have reopened as shops.

are determined by private decision rather than by state control. This system operates in a free market.

A free enterprise system lets consumers, entrepreneurs, and workers enjoy freedom of choice. Consumers can choose from a variety of products and services. Entrepreneurs can switch from one business to another. Workers can quit their jobs and take new ones.

There are four fundamental factors in a free enterprise system: private ownership, individual initiative, profit, and competition.

Private Ownership

One distinctive characteristic of capitalism is that private individuals and companies own most of the means of production—that is, the resources used to produce goods and services. They decide how this productive property will be used. For example, an individual may use capital to build a business, say, or invest in technology. What the property produces is theirs, as well. The owners of productive property are sometimes individuals, but often may be groups of people who share ownership of a company.

In a free enterprise system, individuals also own the right to their labor. Individuals sell their

labor by taking a job, and the pay they receive represents the price of their work. In other economic systems, workers may have little choice about what kinds of work they will do and little opportunity to change jobs.

Along with private ownership, the protection of people's property rights is also important. The 5th and 14th amendments to the Constitution declare that no person may be deprived "of life, liberty, or property, without due process of law." The 5th amendment also says that "just compensation" be paid to owners when private property is taken for public use.

Individual Initiative

In our economy, entrepreneurs are an essential factor in the production of goods and services. Under a free enterprise system, all individuals are free to start and run their own businesses (their own enterprises). They are also free to dissolve those businesses.

That is not necessarily true in other kinds of economic systems. In some places, government officials and public planners make economic decisions about what to produce and how to produce it. Centralized decision making, not individual initiative, controls the production and distribution of goods and services.

Profit

Just as individuals are free to choose how they will spend or invest their capital, under a free enterprise system, they are also entitled to benefit from whatever their investment or enterprise earns or gains in value. The "profit motive" is the desire to gain from business dealings. It is one reason that entrepreneurs are willing to take risks.

Competition

The freedom to enter or start a new business at any time leads to competition. Competition is a situation in which a number of companies offer the same product or service. They then must compete against one another for customers. In a free enterprise system, competition often helps to hold down prices and keep quality high. This is because customers are likely to buy from the company with the best product at the lowest price. Competition thus promotes efficiency; the producer has the incentive (more sales) to keep costs low.

Under competitive conditions, the laws of supply and demand determine prices. Supply is the quantity of goods or services for sale. Demand is the desire of potential buyers for those goods and services. According to the **laws of supply and demand,** when supplies become more plentiful, prices tend to drop. As supplies become scarcer, prices tend to rise. By the same token, if demand drops (that is, if there are few buyers), sellers will probably lower their prices in order to make a sale. If demand rises, sellers can raise prices.

Competition does not always work smoothly. Sometimes a single business becomes so successful that all of its rivals go out of business. A firm that is the only source of a product or service is called a **monopoly.** Monopolies can be very powerful in the marketplace. Practically speaking, they can charge as much as they want for a product. Since there is no other supplier of that good or service, the consumer must pay the monopoly price or do without.

Political leaders in the United States decided late in the nineteenth century that monopolies were dangerous. American leaders were especially concerned about a type of monopoly called a **trust**. A trust is a device by which several corporations in the same line of business combine to eliminate competition and regulate prices. In the nineteenth century, trusts controlled the markets for sugar and petroleum. Businesses and consumers had no choice but to buy these goods from the sugar and petroleum trusts.

In response, the Federal Government passed the Sherman Antitrust Act of 1890, which remains the basic law against monopolies today. It prohibits "every contract, combination in the form of a trust or otherwise, or conspiracy in restraint of trade or commerce among the several States, or with foreign nations."

The Antitrust Division in the Department of Justice watches business activities to determine whether competition within an industry is threatened. It can, for example, stop the sale or merger of a company if it might result in the elimination of competitive conditions in the marketplace. On rare occasions, the Department of Justice has broken up an existing monopoly to bring competition into a market. The Federal Government dissolved John D. Rockefeller's Standard Oil Trust in 1911, ending his monopoly over the petroleum industry. Similarly, the Federal Government broke up American Telephone and Telegraph (AT&T) into several so-called "Baby Bells" to introduce competition into the market for telephone calls. However, the break-up process is time-consuming and not always successful.

In the mid-1990s, the Justice Department challenged Microsoft Corporation's efforts to control the market for its browser—the software that enables its users to access the World Wide Web. In 2000, a federal district judge held Microsoft to be an illegal monopoly that seeks to dominate its market and destroy its competition. He recommended that the computer giant be splintered into two or more competing companies. The Bush administration has not pushed for the break-up, however. Microsoft appealed the ruling, and the case will likely reach the Supreme Court in the near future.

Laissez-Faire Theory

Early capitalist philosophers believed that, if only government did not interfere, the free enterprise system could work automatically. Adam Smith presented the classic expression of that view in his book, *The Wealth of Nations,* in 1776. Smith wrote that when all individuals are free to pursue their own private interests, an "invisible hand"

Interpreting Political Cartoons The Federal Government's Department of Justice sued Microsoft Corporation in the 1990s to restore competition to the software industry. *How does the absence of competition hurt consumers?*

Voices on Government

Sadako Ogata of Japan heads the United Nations High Commission for Refugees (UNHCR). This agency works to help the thousands of people uprooted from their home countries by political and economic conflicts around the world. Ogata sees a direct link between the living conditions of the world's individual communities and the welfare of the global community as a whole.

❝ *It is essential that political leaders and the civil society in developed countries—including in the United States—be visionary enough to provide support to social and economic reconstruction and to the reconciliation between divided communities, even in countries and regions which are of less immediate strategic interest to them. Only by putting an end to the recurrence of conflicts, and of refugee flows everywhere, will global security be ensured.* **❞**

Evaluating the Quotation

How might the plight of refugees in some distant land be disruptive to the peace and security of powerful nations like the United States? Do you agree with Ogata that developed nations should help other countries in need? Why or why not?

works to promote the general welfare. In short, Smith preached laissez-faire capitalism.[1]

Laissez-faire theory holds that government should play a very limited, hands-off role in society. Governmental activity should be confined to: (1) foreign relations and national defense, (2) the maintenance of police and courts to protect private property and the health, safety, and morals of the people, and (3) those few other functions that cannot be performed by private enterprise at a profit. The proper role of government in economic affairs should be restricted to functions intended to promote and protect the free play of competition and the operation of the laws of supply and demand.

Laissez-faire capitalism has never in fact operated in this country. Nevertheless, the concept

[1]The term *laissez-faire* comes from a French idiom meaning "to let alone."

had, and still has, a profound effect on the structure of the American economic system.

A Mixed Economy

Although the American economic system is essentially private in character, government has always played a large part in it. Economists usually describe an economy in which private enterprise and governmental participation coexist as a mixed economy.

Governments at every level regulate many aspects of American economic life. For example, the government prohibits trusts, protects the environment, and ensures the quality of food.

In addition, government promotes many aspects of American economic life. For example, the government constructs public roads and highways, provides such services as the postal system, the census, and weather reports, and offers many kinds of subsidies and loan programs that help entrepreneurs and businesses to prosper.

The government also conducts some enterprises that might well be operated privately. Examples are found in every aspect of government, including public education, the postal system, various forms of transportation, and water and power systems. Some well-known examples are Amtrak, which provides passenger train service across the country, and the Tennessee Valley Authority, which generates and sells electricity in eight southern States.

Mixed economies are common in Europe and in former communist countries. In Britain, the government provides free medical care to all. The government of the People's Republic of China owns steel mills and factories. Germany's federal government requires large companies to give workers representation on managing boards and France forbids most companies from asking employees to work more than 35 hours a week. In each of these mixed economies, government intervention co-exists with independent companies and market forces.

Types of Business Organizations

The United States economy contains a number of gigantic companies with thousands of employees and with factories or offices all over the world.

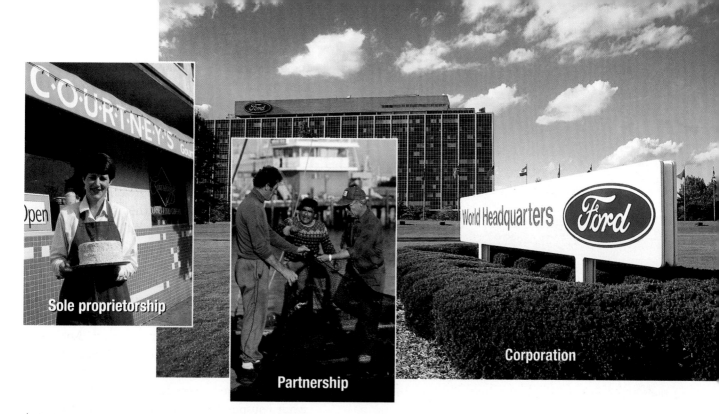

▲ An American firm can organize as a sole proprietorship (left), a partnership (center), or a corporation (right). As a company grows and leaders take on new responsibilities, the company may change from one form to another. *Critical Thinking* *Why is a large manufacturer like Ford unlikely to succeed as a sole proprietorship?*

Still, most businesses in the United States are relatively small. Some 80 percent of businesses employ fewer than 20 people.

There are three basic types of business organizations: sole proprietorships, partnerships, and corporations. Each has advantages and disadvantages.

Sole Proprietorships

Businesses owned by a single individual are sole proprietorships. Typical of businesses in this category might be a hair salon, a garage, or an ice cream shop. Three quarters of businesses in the United States are sole proprietorships. However, because most sole proprietorships are small, they produce only a small fraction of annual sales in the United States.

Sole proprietorships are the most flexible form of business organization. A major advantage of sole proprietorships is that the single owner can make decisions quickly. The owner enjoys full control of the company, and can draw a salary or close the business without needing the approval of others. A major disadvantage is that the owner is personally liable for debts the business might build up. Sole proprietorships

are also limited by the owner's ability to contribute resources and manage the business.

Partnerships

Businesses owned by two or more individuals, called partners, are partnerships. Lawyers and architects are some professionals who often work in partnerships.

An advantage of a partnership is that it can draw on the resources of more than one person for capital to start or expand the business. Different people bring different strengths and perspectives to a business, and a partnership can provide the best framework for entrepreneurs to use their skills to create a small business. A disadvantage is that these differences can also lead to conflict among partners. In addition, partnerships may end if one partner leaves or dies.

Corporations

Corporations include both small companies and large national firms that people encounter every day. Unlike partnerships, corporations have many owners, called shareholders. A share is a fraction of ownership in the corporation. A corporation can continue indefinitely because a shareholder's

Intel's Revenue Will Miss Expectations

News Triggers Tech Sell-Off And Raises Uncertainty About Demand for PCs

CMGI Posts Loss Of $633.7 Million On Market Fizzle

Dial Is Considering Sale of Company; Profit to Fall Short

▲ Financial losses are an unavoidable element of the free market system.

death does not affect the legal status of the corporation. In other words, the corporation exists as its own legal entity, independent from the existence of any stockholders. Under the Supreme Court's interpretation of the 14th Amendment, a corporation enjoys the same legal status as a person.

Corporations can draw their capital from hundreds and even thousands of investors. This enables them to finance such costly projects as putting an earth satellite in orbit or building an oil pipeline. Shareholders are responsible only for the amount of money they have invested. If the business fails, they can lose that amount, but no more. Shareholders have limited liability and are not held responsible for any debts the corporation might have.

One disadvantage of corporations is that their income is taxed twice. First, the corporation pays a tax on its profits. Then, individual shareholders pay a tax on the dividends they are paid.

Profit and Loss

What drives the capitalist economy? The best answer, most often, is profit.

To understand what profit is, you must first understand the idea of investment. An investment is a sum of money, or capital, that is put into a business enterprise. For example, if you buy a car to start a business delivering groceries, what you pay for the car is an investment.

The profit will be the amount of money you earn from the business, after you have subtracted the costs associated with earning that money—in this case, the purchase of the car and the costs of operating it, plus whatever you pay yourself. If earnings are less than the costs, the business has not made a profit; instead, it has taken a loss.

Taking risks and making investments, therefore, are an essential part of the capitalist system. Every year, many businesses fail for lack of profit. Businesses that survive tend to be those that have learned to make the most efficient use of the factors of production.

Section 1 Assessment

Key Terms and Main Ideas

1. What is the difference between physical and human **capital**?
2. Why are **entrepreneurs** important to a **free enterprise system**?
3. How many companies control a market in a **monopoly**?
4. What is the proper role of government according to **laissez-faire theory**?

Critical Thinking

5. **Making Comparisons** Of the factors of production, which do you believe is the most difficult to measure? Explain your answer.

6. **Drawing Conclusions** List two possible advantages and disadvantages of encouraging government to play a role in a free enterprise economy.

 Take It to the Net

7. Study the Index of Economic Freedom. A high degree of economic freedom indicates a free market system. Which countries exhibit the most economic freedom? What conclusions can you draw from this data? Use the links provided in the Social Studies area at the following Web site for help in completing this activity. **www.phschool.com**

SKILLS FOR LIFE

Interpreting Line Graphs

Throughout the 1990s, the world's oil consumers enjoyed low petroleum prices. In fact, in the late 1990s, prices when adjusted for inflation plunged to their lowest levels in decades. Major oil producers in the Middle East and elsewhere suffered severely from the loss of revenues. In 1999, the producers were finally able to agree on large cuts in oil production. From what you know about supply and demand (page 661), use the steps below to interpret the information in Graph A.

1. Identify the type of information presented on the graph. The graph title and the labels on the *x* axis and *y* axis tell the meanings of the points and lines on the graph. Look at Graph A and answer these questions: (a) What do the numbers on the *x* axis (horizontal) and the *y* axis (vertical) represent? (b) What relationship does the line graph describe?

2. Read the data on the graph. Before studying overall patterns, look at specific elements of the graph.

For example: (a) What is the maximum cost per barrel of oil that can be shown on this graph? (b) How many years does the graph cover? (c) Why were these dates chosen?

3. Study the data on the graph to draw conclusions. You already know that U.S. oil supplies dropped sharply in the late 1990s. In the previous section, you learned what happens to prices when supplies of a product are reduced. Use this knowledge to draw a conclusion from Graph A. State your conclusion in a sentence or two.

Test for Success

In our free-enterprise economy, wages are usually determined not by the government but by what the free market will pay for labor. Wages also follow the laws of supply and demand for labor. Use this knowledge to draw conclusions from Graph B.

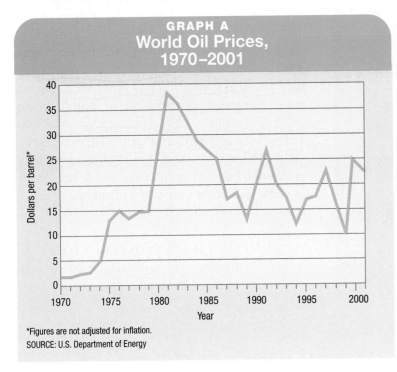

GRAPH A
World Oil Prices, 1970–2001

*Figures are not adjusted for inflation.
SOURCE: U.S. Department of Energy

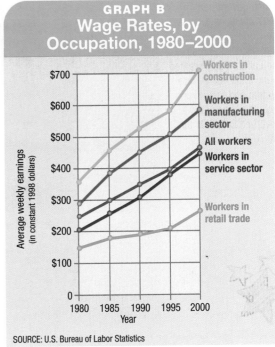

GRAPH B
Wage Rates, by Occupation, 1980–2000

SOURCE: U.S. Bureau of Labor Statistics

2 *Socialism*

Section Preview

Section Preview

OBJECTIVES

1. **Define** socialism and explain how its growth was spurred by the Industrial Revolution.
2. **Identify** important characteristics of socialist economies.
3. **Describe** socialism in developing countries.
4. **Evaluate** the pros and cons of socialism.

WHY IT MATTERS

Industrial countries in Western Europe and agricultural countries around the world have developed socialist economies. In these countries, the government plays a strong role in managing the economy and protecting the rights and benefits of individual workers.

POLITICAL DICTIONARY

★ **socialism**
★ **proletariat**
★ **bourgeoisie**
★ **welfare state**
★ **market economy**
★ **centrally planned economy**

You know that in the United States all people are entitled to equal protection under the law. Political equality, of course, is not the same as economic equality. The capitalistic system of the United States enables some to achieve greater financial rewards than others.

One economic system, however, does seek to distribute wealth equitably throughout society. This section is about that system.

▶ Britain's Labour Party won control of the British government in 1997 elections. One of the world's most prominent socialist parties, the Labour Party created a universal health care system and took over key industries when it governed Britain in the late 1940s.

What Is Socialism?

Socialism is an economic and political philosophy based on the idea that the benefits of economic activity—wealth—should be equitably distributed throughout a society. This fairness is achieved through the principle of collective (that is, public) ownership of the most important means by which goods and services are produced and distributed. Socialist nations can also be democracies, but still must have centralized planning to achieve these aims.

Socialists reject the strong emphasis on individualism and competition for profit that lie at the heart of capitalistic thought and practice. Instead, they emphasize cooperation and social responsibility as ways to achieve a more equitable distribution of both income and opportunity, thus reducing great differences between rich and poor. Real equality, they say, requires that political equality and economic equality go hand in hand. Economic equality can come only when the public controls the centers of economic power.

The roots of socialism lie deep in history. Almost from the beginning there have been those who have dreamed of a society built on socialist doctrine. Most earlier socialists foresaw a collective economy that would arise out of, and then be managed by, voluntary private action, without government action. Thus early socialist doctrine is often called "private socialism."

The Industrial Revolution

Much of present-day socialism was born in the 19th century. It developed out of the Industrial Revolution—the great social changes that swept western nations as they moved from an agricultural to an industrial economy.

The Industrial Revolution was well under way in Great Britain by the late eighteenth century and spread through Western Europe and to the United States in the nineteenth century. Cities expanded rapidly, and large factories replaced smaller, home-based industry.

Many observers of nineteeth-century British factories and cities were appalled by the conditions they found. Men and women often worked 14- to 16-hour days in filthy, noisy, and unsafe conditions for low pay. Small children regularly worked alongside their parents, for even less pay. Most factory workers and their families lived in dank, crowded, and unhealthful slums.

These conditions led many to seek social and economic reforms. Some argued for much more radical change.

Karl Marx

Karl Marx (1818–1883), the father of modern-day socialism, was the most significant critic of capitalism to emerge in the nineteenth century. Much of his work and most of his extensive writings were done in collaboration with Friedrich Engels (1820–1895).

In 1848, Marx and Engels wrote *The Communist Manifesto,* "to do for history," Engels later said, "what Darwin's theory has done for biology." This political document condemned the misery caused by the Industrial Revolution. It called upon oppressed workers across Europe to free themselves from "capitalist enslavement."

Marx believed that capitalism was fatally flawed. The **proletariat**—the workers—were being so badly abused by the **bourgeoisie**—the capitalists—that they were certain to rise up and overthrow the capitalistic system. The pamphlet ended with this rallying cry:

> **PRIMARY Sources** *The proletarians have nothing to lose but their chains. They have a world to win. Workingmen of all countries, unite!*
>
> —Friedrich Engels and Karl Marx, *The Communist Manifesto*

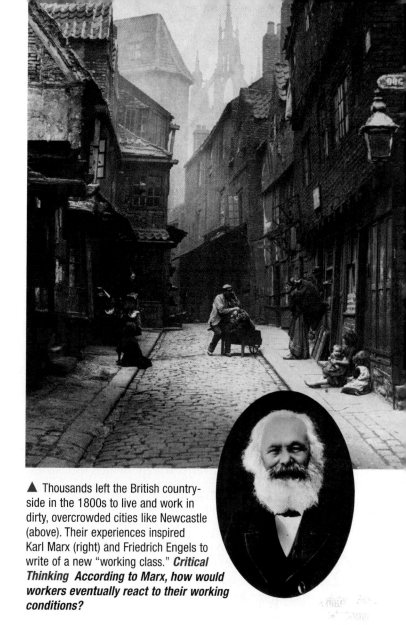

▲ Thousands left the British countryside in the 1800s to live and work in dirty, overcrowded cities like Newcastle (above). Their experiences inspired Karl Marx (right) and Friedrich Engels to write of a new "working class." *Critical Thinking According to Marx, how would workers eventually react to their working conditions?*

Socialists and Communists

A powerful socialist movement took shape among European workers and thinkers during the middle and late nineteenth century. Almost all socialists accepted Marx's criticism of capitalism. The movement was deeply split, however, by the question of how best to achieve socialism. Some argued that a socialist society could come only out of a "violent and bloody revolution." Over time, those who took that view came to be called communists.

Others argued that socialism could be attained by peaceful means through the democratic process. Today, the terms *socialism* and *socialist* are usually used to identify those evolutionary socialists.

The British Labour Party and the major "social democratic" parties in Europe are leading examples of that brand of socialism. At various times in recent history, those parties have controlled their governments and have instituted many socialist programs through democratic means. In the 1997 elections, however, Labour Party leaders deliberately chose to follow a "third way," moving away from socialism. Socialist parties in France and Germany have also reconsidered some of the socialist objectives that have become too expensive to maintain.

Characteristics of Socialist Economies

Countries with a socialist government typically enact one or more of these public policies to achieve the aims of socialism: nationalization, broadening of public services, high taxation, and a centrally planned economy.

Nationalization

Placing enterprises under governmental control, often by taking over privately owned industries, is called nationalization. In the last chapter you read about the nationalization of the oil industry in Mexico in the 1930s. In a democratic country such as Britain, a government may nationalize an enterprise and pay the former owners what it considers a fair price. Often, however, governments have nationalized industries without paying any compensation.

Nationalization under socialism rarely includes all businesses in a country. Socialist governments usually want to control certain sectors

with many workers and a few dominant firms, such as utilities, transportation, and steel. They allow many smaller companies to remain in private hands. Also, the government may want industries that are based on newly emerging technologies to remain private. This is because individual initiative and entrepreneurial risk-taking are so important during the early phases of a business.

A goal of many socialist governments is to give each company's workers a say in deciding how the company is run. Sweden's Social Democratic Party, for example, has a plan for gradually transferring ownership of private companies to their workers. Elected worker representatives now sit on many companies' boards of directors.

Public Welfare

Socialists place great importance on assuring that everyone in a society is decently housed and fed. Stated another way, socialists aim to guarantee the public welfare by providing for the equal distribution of necessities and services—including retirement pensions, inexpensive health care, free university education, and housing for the poor.

Countries that provide extensive social services at little or no cost to the users are often called **welfare states.** In such countries, medical and dental services may be provided free or for a small charge. People who lose their jobs or who are physically unable to work receive government payments that are nearly as high as their former wages. All people above retirement age receive government pensions. Parents may receive government payments for each child until the child reaches the age of 18. Workers in Europe receive paid maternity leave and several weeks of paid vacation each year—benefits rarely matched in other countries.

Taxation

All governments in capitalist and socialist states get their funds from taxation. Because social welfare services are quite expensive, however, taxes in socialist countries tend to be high. Taxes may take 50 or 60 percent of an individual's total income.

Socialists tend to place most of the burden on the upper and middle classes, consistent with

▲ The French government owns most of that country's largest airline, Air France. *Critical Thinking* **As voters, what power do workers in nationalized companies have over their employer?**

their philosophy of achieving a more equal distribution of wealth. Tax rates can amount to 90 percent of a wealthy person's income.

Centrally Planned Economy

Economies can be divided into several categories, depending on how basic economic decisions are made. Under capitalism, key decisions are made by thousands of private individuals and companies through the give and take of the marketplace. For that reason, a capitalist economy is also called a **market economy.**

Under socialism, economic decision making is more centralized. In a **centrally planned economy,** government bureaucrats plan how an economy will develop over a period of years. They set targets for production and direct investment into specific industries. Because the government, to varying degrees, controls the economy, this is also called a "command economy."

A democratic socialist country may or may not have strict central planning. Market conditions and private businesses are likely to play a role as well as government planning. With a few exceptions, most modern economies are such mixed economies.

Socialism in Developing Countries

Socialism has won a large following in developing countries. There, public ownership and centralized planning are common.

One reason for socialism's appeal is that most developing countries are starting from scratch at building industry. They have no tradition of locally controlled, large-scale industry. Large existing industries are often owned by foreign companies. By nationalizing a foreign-owned company and placing local people in charge, a political leader can win broad public support.

Socialism also appeals to leaders who want to mobilize an entire nation behind a program of industrial growth. Through central planning, leaders can channel investment into the parts of the economy they think are most essential.

Often, however, guided growth of this sort requires painful sacrifices by a nation's people. High taxes skim off a large part of people's income. The government may devote so much attention to one or two basic industries that the

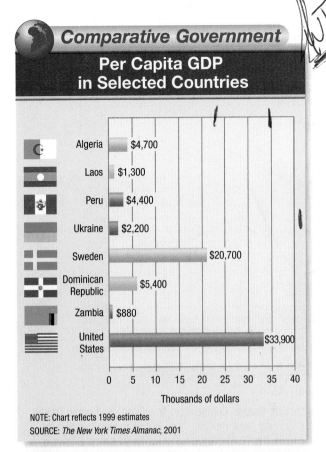

Comparative Government

Per Capita GDP in Selected Countries

Country	Per Capita GDP
Algeria	$4,700
Laos	$1,300
Peru	$4,400
Ukraine	$2,200
Sweden	$20,700
Dominican Republic	$5,400
Zambia	$880
United States	$33,900

Thousands of dollars

NOTE: Chart reflects 1999 estimates
SOURCE: *The New York Times Almanac,* 2001

Interpreting Graphs Researchers cannot easily compare per capita GDP to measure quality of life because the cost of food, housing, and other goods is different in each country. However, large differences stand out. *How does per capita GDP in the United States compare to per capita GDP in the other countries listed above?*

production of food or consumer goods may be neglected. Then public unrest may develop.

Political instability is a persistent problem in developing nations. In such nations, this instability is one reason that socialist and other governments often turn to authoritarian methods. Few developing nations have succeeded in establishing the democratic versions of socialism found in parts of the industrial world.

Pros and Cons

Both capitalistic and socialistic economies have their strengths and weaknesses. For supporters of capitalism, it is easy to see weaknesses in the theory and practice of socialism. For supporters of socialism, on the other hand, capitalism seems filled with faults.

Critics say socialist countries have a tendency to develop too many layers of bureaucracy. They say this complicates decision making and has a

Unemployment in Selected Countries, 1990–2000

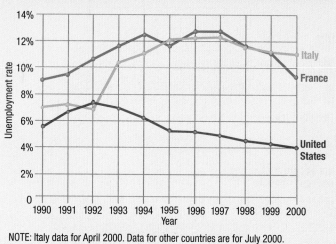

NOTE: Italy data for April 2000. Data for other countries are for July 2000.

SOURCE: Organization for Economic Co-operation and Development; *Handbook of International Economic Statistics*

Interpreting Graphs Compared to Americans, workers in France and Italy enjoy more vacation days, less expensive health care, and greater legal protection against losing their jobs. One unintended result is that companies hire fewer new workers to avoid paying the high cost of these benefits. *Although France, Italy, and the United States all enjoyed strong economic growth in the 1990s, how did unemployment rates respond differently in these three countries?*

deadening effect on individual initiative. As a result, critics say, socialist economies are slower to take advantage of new technologies.

In the eyes of socialism's critics, the smooth running of an economy is too complex to be directed by central planners. Too many unpredictable events are involved, and too many clashing interests are at stake. For all its faults, they argue, the invisible hand of the market economy works more efficiently than the visible hand of central planning.

Another criticism is that socialism deprives people of the freedom to decide for themselves how to use their income. Since workers get to keep only a part of their earnings after taxes, they have little incentive to work harder and earn more. Why work hard when your basic needs will be taken care of anyway?

In response, socialists reply that it is fairer to supply everyone with basic needs, such as medical care. They point to the inequalities of wealth and power that exist under capitalism. Socialists argue that socialism is morally superior to capitalism because it evens out inequalities. In their view, socialism makes political democracy work more smoothly by supplementing it with economic democracy.

Defenders of socialism also argue that it gives workers and ordinary citizens more control over their daily lives. Under capitalism, they say, a company's management can abruptly decide to close an unprofitable factory. The company has no obligation to ask its workers' opinions, even though such a decision can throw thousands out of work and disrupt an entire community. This could not happen under socialism, the argument goes. Workers and community leaders would sit on the company's board. They would help decide what was best for the entire work force and community—not just for the company's investors and shareholders.

Section 2 Assessment

Key Terms and Main Ideas

1. Who is considered the father of **socialism**?
2. According to socialist theory, what is the relationship between the **proletariat** and the **bourgeoisie**?
3. Describe a **welfare state** in your own words.
4. What role does the government play in a **centrally planned economy**?

Critical Thinking

5. **Making Comparisons** How might a socialist and a capitalist government differ in treatment of the problem of unemployment?

6. **Making Decisions** Should the government have the responsibility of providing health care for every citizen? Why or why not?

 Take It to the Net

7. Read about the working conditions that children endured during the Industrial Revolution. Then, identify those problems that no longer affect young adults in the work force today. Use the links provided in the Social Studies area of the following Web site for help in completing this activity. **www.phschool.com**

The Third Way

After losing four consecutive elections to Britain's Conservative Party, the British Labour Party moved away from its socialist roots to embrace a "third way" between socialism and a free market economy. Party leader Tony Blair issued this statement of party beliefs before the 1997 election. The Labour Party went on to win a landslide victory and has been in power since that time.

I want a country in which people get on, do well, make a success of their lives. I have no time for the politics of envy. We need more successful entrepreneurs, not fewer of them. But these life-chances should be for all the people. And I want a society in which ambition and compassion are seen as partners not opposites—where we value public service as well as material wealth.

New Labour believes in a society where we do not simply pursue our own individual aims but where we hold many aims in common and work together to achieve them. How we build the industry and employment opportunities of the future; how we tackle the division and inequality in our society; how we care for and enhance our environment and quality of life; how we develop modern education and health services; how we create communities that are safe, where mutual respect and tolerance are the order of the day. These are things we must achieve together as a country.

The vision is one of national renewal, a country with drive, purpose and energy. A Britain equipped to prosper in a global economy of technological change; with a modern welfare state; its politics more accountable; and confident of its place in the world.

. . . a new and distinctive approach has been mapped out, one that differs from the solutions of the old left and those of the Conservative right. This is why new Labour is new. . . .

Prime Minister Tony Blair

The old left would have sought state control of industry. The Conservative right is content to leave all to the market. We reject both approaches. Government and industry must work together to achieve key objectives aimed at enhancing the dynamism of the market, not undermining it.

In industrial relations, we make it clear that there will be no return to [the aggressive labor tactics] of the 1970s. There will instead be basic minimum rights for the individual at the workplace, where our aim is partnership not conflict between employers and employees.

In economic management, we accept the global economy as a reality and reject the isolationism and "go-it-alone" policies of the extremes of right or left.

Analyzing Primary Sources

1. Describe Tony Blair's vision for a new Britain in your own words.
2. How does Tony Blair try to distance the Labour Party from its past socialist policies? Why did he do so?
3. What is the Labour Party's view of the global economy and world trade?
4. Do you believe Blair's Third Way between socialism and free market capitalism is practical? Explain.

3 Communism

Section Preview

OBJECTIVES

1. **Summarize** the theories of Karl Marx.
2. **Outline** the characteristics of communist economies.
3. **Describe** communism in the Soviet Union, China, and other nations.

WHY IT MATTERS

Karl Marx once predicted that the workers of the world would overthrow capitalism and create an ideal communist society. Although communist governments emerged in Russia and China in the last century, the reality of communism rarely matched Marx's theory.

POLITICAL DICTIONARY

- **communism**
- **five-year plan**
- **collectivization**
- **Gosplan**
- **privatization**
- **Great Leap Forward**
- **commune**

Modern communism is a political, economic, and social theory developed by Karl Marx in the mid-1800s.[2] Nearly one third of the world's people once lived under communism, but since the collapse of the Soviet Union, it is the guiding economic principle in only a handful of countries. Almost every one of those countries, in fact, is taking steps toward a free market system.

Karl Marx's Theory

Communism is often called a collectivist ideology, which calls for the collective, or state, ownership of land and other productive property. Karl Marx

and Friedrich Engels first set out its basic concepts in *The Communist Manifesto* (1848).

In his major work, *Das Kapital* (1867), Marx analyzed the workings of capitalism. He based the work on four closely related concepts: his theory of history, the labor theory of value, the nature of the state, and the dictatorship of the proletariat.

1. *Marx's View of History.* To Marx, all of history was a story of class struggle—of social classes competing for the control of labor and productive property. One class was the oppressors; the other, the oppressed. In the Middle Ages, the struggle was between the nobility and their serfs. In the modern world, the bourgeoisie oppressed the proletariat.

According to Marx, the class struggle in the modern era would become so intense that the masses would revolt and bring down the bourgeoisie. The communists' political role was to hasten the revolution, by violence if necessary.

2. *The Labor Theory of Value.* Marx rejected the free enterprise ideas of profit and competition. In his view, the value of a commodity was set by the amount of labor put into it. A pair of shoes or a rebuilt bicycle is worth a certain

---

▲ **May Day Parade** On the first of May, people in the Soviet Union celebrated the workers of their country and the world. The banner depicts the revolutionary founder of the Soviet Union, V. I. Lenin (left), as well as Friedrich Engels (center) and Karl Marx (right).

[2]The word *communism* comes from the Latin *communis*, meaning "common, belonging to all." The idea of communal property dates back at least to the early Greeks. In the fourth century B.C., Plato proposed a system of communal property in *The Republic*.

amount because it takes that much labor to produce it. Therefore, communists say, the laborer should receive that value in full.

3. *The Nature of the State.* Marx saw the state and its government as the tools by which the capitalists maintained their power and privileges. Other social institutions also played a role in enforcing capitalist control over the masses. Marx described religion as "the opiate of the people"—a sort of drug that persuades workers to tolerate their harsh lot in this life in the hope that someday they will gain what Marx called a "fictional afterlife."

4. *The Dictatorship of the Proletariat.* Marx did not believe that revolution would bring the final form of communism—the classless society. First, he predicted a transitional phase during which an authoritarian state would represent and enforce the interests of the masses. This he called the "dictatorship of the proletariat." Once the goal of classlessness was realized, the state would "wither away."

Based on these four concepts, Marx envisioned a "free, classless society." Social classes would vanish and the people in common would own all property. Exploitation of labor and unemployment would disappear. Abundant goods would be available to all according to their needs.

Marx also expected that workers in different countries—for example, France and Germany—would share a bond far stronger than national loyalties. Thus, communism would also end nationalism, a major cause of European wars.

Characteristics of Communist Economies

Marx believed that the revolution would come first in industrialized countries with large working-class populations—in particular, France, Germany, Great Britain, and then the United States. Ironically, the revolution occurred first in Russia, then a backward, mainly agricultural nation, in 1917, and later in largely agricultural nations in Asia.[3]

Marx's theories did not provide even a rough blueprint for the formation of a communist society. Communism has taken different forms in different places, but certain characteristics are common.

▲ When northern Vietnam became a communist state, most people lived in the countryside and worked on farms, as they still do today. *Critical Thinking How well did Vietnam fit Karl Marx's description of a country ready for communism?*

1. *Role of the Communist Party.* In any communist-run nation, the Communist Party holds the decision-making power in both the government and the economy. Party leaders also hold the top government positions. From top to bottom, the two institutions run parallel to each other. Inevitably, such centralized political and economic control means control over social, intellectual, and religious life as well.

2. *Central Planning.* Because government makes all the economic decisions, bureaucrats must plan and supervise production in factories, farms, and stores. Typically, a **five-year plan** plays a key role in this economy. The plan shows how leaders want the economy to develop over the next five years. It sets economic goals that dictate where to emphasize growth in industry or agriculture and what each individual factory and farm must produce. The plan also sets prices and decides how goods and services will be distributed.

---

[3]In his later years, Marx did recognize the possibility that his theories might first be tested in Russia. Lenin also took the Russia-first view, in the early 1900s. He thought that less advanced countries, with their comparatively small industrial populations, offered certain advantages to a revolutionary movement—notably, the effectiveness with which workers could be organized and controlled.

▲ Typical of Soviet art, *Builders of Communism* glorifies Soviet workers, including a farmer, a welder, a miner, and an architect. ***Critical Thinking According to this picture, what were some roles of women in the Soviet Union?***

   3. *Collectivization.* Collective or state ownership of the means of production is one pillar of communism. One major step in creating a communist economy is the merger of small private farms into large government-owned agricultural enterprises. This process of **collectivization** may be voluntary in theory, but in many countries peasant farmers have been coerced into giving up land. Millions died while resisting collectivization in the Soviet Union.

   4. *State Ownership.* Industrial enterprises, transportation, and other parts of the economy are also state-owned. This part of the system varies greatly from country to country. In China, for example, provincial and municipal governments, not a central government ministry, own enterprises such as housing, banks, hospitals, and stores.

The Soviet Union

Lenin and his followers took power in Russia in 1917 and began immediately to build a communist state. After a difficult transition, the Soviet Union became a one-party state, with communists in control of the country's social, political, and economic institutions by the time of Lenin's death in 1924. Lenin's successor, Josef Stalin, tightened that control into an authoritarian dictatorship.

The Five-Year Plans

Stalin introduced centralized planning, run by a large agency, **Gosplan.** The First Five-Year Plan (1928–1933) demanded collectivization of agriculture and higher production of chemicals, petroleum, and steel. Later five-year plans also emphasized heavy industry, and the Soviet Union achieved rapid, if uneven, industrialization. Unfortunately, those advances came at the cost of scarce consumer goods, housing, and urban services. Housing, food, and goods were rationed, and sewers, water systems, and other needs lagged behind a dramatic growth in urban population.[4]

Social Policies

The Soviet Union gave its citizens free education, medical care, and even youth summer camps. It was far from a classless society, however. To spur production, economic incentives, cars, and vacation homes went to party officials, bureaucrats, and factory managers. Artists, musicians, and athletes also were rewarded with special privileges. Thus, Stalin created an elite class that owed its privileged status to the Communist Party. He also corrupted the Marxian ideal of economic and social equality.

Gorbachev's Reforms

When Mikhail Gorbachev became Soviet leader in 1985, he inherited an economic system that had changed little since the Stalin years. Economic growth and productivity had declined sharply.

   Under *perestroika,* leaders gave more authority to local farm and factory managers, loosened price controls, linked salaries to performance, and allowed some profit incentives. *Perestroika* raised expectations, but it did not increase output. Bureaucrats resisted change, and poor harvests, strikes, and shortages of food and consumer goods made conditions worse. Gorbachev and the Communist Party gave up their leadership of the economy when the Soviet Union collapsed in 1991.

---

[4]The First Five-Year Plan, launched in 1928, was declared completed in 1932, nine months ahead of schedule. The second plan ran from 1932 to 1937 and the third from 1937 until it was interrupted by the German invasion of the Soviet Union in 1941. The Twelfth Five-Year Plan was in place when the Soviet Union collapsed in late 1991.

Transition to a Free Market

Clearly, Russia's transition to a free market system and its moves toward democracy were closely linked. The economic plans that Russian President Boris Yeltsin put in place in 1991 and 1992 called for radical changes, including the lifting of price controls and the privatization of farms and factories. **Privatization** is returning nationalized enterprises to private ownership.

The transition to a market economy has not been easy. Thousands of enterprises were put into private hands, sometimes by giving shares or vouchers to workers, but many are still badly run.

A new elite class of entrepreneurs has made a fortune in today's Russian economy. At the same time, many ordinary Russians have suffered the effects of high inflation, a fall in the value of Russian currency, and the loss of their state pensions. Corruption is rampant, and most people have grown poorer. A complete transition to a market economy awaits strong leadership willing to enforce laws and thoroughly reform the system.

China

Mao Zedong, the founder of the People's Republic of China, was a Marxist. Mao departed from Marx's theory that a workers' revolt would lead to communism. He believed the peasantry would be the key to a communist revolution in China.

After Mao took control of the country in 1949, China developed its own version of a planned economy. Despite its huge population, it lacked skilled workers. The government improved technical and scientific education and then assigned workers to jobs in the state sector. Government regulated the labor market, giving workers little choice about where they worked.

The Great Leap Forward

The five-year plan for 1958, the **Great Leap Forward,** was a drastic attempt to modernize China quickly. All elements of free enterprise, such as rural markets, were eliminated. Collective farms were brought together into a larger unit, the **commune.**

Communes grew into self-sufficient bodies run by party officials. These officials oversaw farms, industries, and government in a region as well as managed social policy. Workers received the same rewards no matter how much they produced, so there were few incentives to work hard. The Great Leap Forward was a disastrous failure, followed by severe famine.

Deng Xiaoping's Reforms

A new leader, Deng Xiaoping, came to power in 1977 and made great changes in the economy. Deng's program of the "Four Modernizations" aimed to improve agriculture, industry, science and technology, and defense. He wanted "socialism with Chinese characteristics."

Deng was more practical and far less ideological than Mao and his dedicated followers. He began to move China from central planning to a market economy and invited foreign investors into China.

Today, China's economic system is a maze of different levels of government bodies and economic units. The state-owned sector is shrinking, while collective enterprises owned and managed by the people of a workplace or residential unit are growing. Private enterprises—mostly small shops and businesses—are also flourishing, as is investment from other countries.

◄ President Jiang Zemin of China is now leading his country's difficult transition to a free market economy. Today, China invests less money in state-owned industries and works hard to encourage foreign investment in China and Chinese exports to the West. *Critical Thinking What would Karl Marx think of China's Communist Party?*

▲ Fidel Castro watches a May Day parade in Havana, Cuba. Cuba remains the only communist country in the Americas. Castro has ruled Cuba as a personal dictatorship for over 40 years.

Other Communist Nations

Several other countries, mainly in Asia, have centrally planned economies. Most, however, are bringing in some free market elements. Other communist economies have not lasted. Those in the Soviet satellites of Eastern Europe disappeared in the upheavals of 1989–1990.

In Cuba, Fidel Castro led a revolution that overthrew the corrupt rule of Fulgencio Batista in 1959. After Castro nationalized American holdings, the United States broke with him. The Soviet Union supported Castro, and in 1961, he declared himself a Marxist.

Cuba depended heavily on Soviet economic aid. As a result, the fall of the Soviet Union caused an economic crisis in Cuba. In response, the government relaxed economic controls, encouraging tourism and some small businesses.

Communism also took root in Southeast Asia. At the end of World War II, Ho Chi Minh, a communist who had studied in Moscow, fought for Vietnam's independence from French colonial rule. Two wars—one against the French, one against the United States—left the communists in control. Vietnam's government uses five-year plans to guide the economy, and like China, it has made market-oriented reforms.

Communist influence spilled over from Vietnam into neighboring Laos and Cambodia. Laos adopted communism in 1975, and Cambodia had a communist government under Vietnamese control from 1979 to 1993.

One of the last communist countries is North Korea. At the end of World War II, the Korean peninsula was divided between a Soviet-backed regime in the north and an American-backed government in the south. After the Korean War (1950–1953), the peninsula remained divided, and North Korea retreated into isolation.

North Korea's centrally planned economy has not achieved much growth. Agriculture was collectivized in the 1950s, although small private plots can grow food for rural markets. Severe food shortages plague the country today. North Korea lost foreign aid and trading partners when other communist governments fell, and has begun to reach out to its former enemy to the south.

Section 3 Assessment

Key Terms and Main Ideas

1. Describe **communism** in your own words.
2. What was the purpose of **Gosplan**?
3. What happens during **collectivization**?
4. Which country experienced the **Great Leap Forward**?

Critical Thinking

5. **Drawing Inferences** How well did Soviet communism follow the communist ideal of economic and social equality?

6. **Drawing Conclusions** Is a dictatorship necessary to the existence of a communist society? Why or why not?

 Take It to the Net

7. Russia is one nation trying to make the transition from a centrally planned economy to a market economy. Describe two actions taken to reform the Russian economy. How well are these reforms working? Use the links provided in the Social Studies area at the following Web site for help in completing this activity. **www.phschool.com**

May Courts Enforce Discriminatory Private Agreements?

The Equal Protection Clause of the 14th Amendment bars States from discriminating against people based on their race or color. What happens if private individuals make an agreement that discriminates, and one of them later breaks that agreement? Should a court enforce the agreement?

Shelley v. Kraemer (1948)

In 1911, thirty property owners in St. Louis, Missouri, signed a restrictive covenant (an agreement limiting the ways in which a piece of property can be used). In this agreement, the property owners promised not to sell their property to non-whites during the next 50 years. The agreement did not restrict the use of the property in any other way.

In 1945, a black family, the Shelleys, bought one of the properties that was subject to the covenant. Kraemer and other property owners governed by the covenant brought suit in the circuit court, seeking to block the Shelleys from taking possession of the property and to reverse the sale. The trial court refused to do so. It concluded that the agreement was not intended to become effective until signed by all the property owners in the district, and that some owners had never signed.

The Missouri Supreme Court reversed the trial court opinion, ruling that the agreement was effective and that it did not violate the Shelleys' constitutional rights. The Shelleys then appealed to the United States Supreme Court.

Arguments for Shelley

1. It would be unconstitutional for States to pass laws or ordinances restricting property ownership or occupancy based on race or color. Therefore, the courts should not enforce any agreement that imposes such restrictions.
2. Although the Equal Protection Clause of the 14th Amendment applies only to "State action" and does not restrict actions by private individuals, judicial enforcement of private agreements is "State action" within the meaning of the 14th Amendment.
3. The purpose of the 14th Amendment was to establish equality of basic rights and to preserve those rights from discrimination by the States based on race and color. For the courts to enforce the restrictive covenant would not be consistent with that purpose.

Arguments for Kraemer

1. This case does not involve action by State legislators or city councils. Private individuals entered into the agreement at issue.
2. The Equal Protection Clause of the 14th Amendment applies only to "State action" and does not restrict actions by private individuals. Judicial enforcement of private agreements does not amount to "State action" within the meaning of the 14th Amendment.
3. There is no discrimination because the Missouri courts would equally enforce covenants that exclude white people from property ownership.

Decide for Yourself

1. Review the constitutional grounds on which each side based its arguments and the specific arguments each side presented.
2. Debate the opposing viewpoints presented in this case. Which viewpoint do you favor?
3. Predict the impact of the Court's decision on discrimination. (To read a summary of the Court's decision, turn to the Supreme Court Glossary on page 799.)

Political Dictionary

factors of production (p. 658)

capital (p. 659)

capitalist (p. 659)

entrepreneur (p. 659)

free enterprise system (p. 659)

laws of supply and demand (p. 661)

monopoly (p. 661)

trust (p. 661)

laissez-faire theory (p. 662)

socialism (p. 666)

proletariat (p. 667)

bourgeoisie (p. 667)

welfare state (p. 668)

market economy (p. 669)

centrally planned economy (p. 669)

communism (p. 672)

five-year plan (p. 673)

collectivization (p. 674)

Gosplan (p. 674)

privatization (p. 675)

Great Leap Forward (p. 675)

commune (p. 675)

Practicing the Vocabulary

Matching *Choose a term from the list above that best matches each description.*

1. An organization of several firms that controls the only source of a product or service
2. In Marxist terms, the capitalists
3. Economic system in which individuals are free to start and run their own businesses
4. A government that assumes the role of promoter of citizen welfare through programs that provide health care, education, and pensions
5. Central institution that planned the economy of the Soviet Union

Fill in the Blank *Choose a term from the list above that best completes the sentence.*

6. Marx believed the _____ would one day rise up and overthrow the capitalist system.
7. An economy in which the government directs factories and farms and decides what to produce and how much is a _____.
8. _____ consists of the wealth and tools used to produce goods and services.
9. During _____, many individual farms are combined to create one giant farm.
10. If existing companies do not see and meet demand, a(n) _____ may start a new business and do so.
11. _____ recommends that government play a very small role in the economy.

Reviewing Main Ideas

Section 1

12. **(a)** What are the factors of production? **(b)** What role do the factors of production play in an economy?
13. What are the hallmarks of a free enterprise economy?
14. **(a)** Why is competition important to a free enterprise economy? **(b)** What will happen to a market without competition?
15. According to laissez-faire theory, what are the three duties of government?
16. **(a)** What are the advantages of a sole proprietorship? **(b)** What are the advantages of a corporation?

Section 2

17. **(a)** What is the purpose of socialism? **(b)** How did events in the 19th century contribute to socialism's popularity?
18. **(a)** Briefly describe Karl Marx's basic ideas about the capitalist system. **(b)** What is the difference between socialism and communism?

19. Describe three characteristics commonly found in socialist countries.
20. **(a)** Why has socialism been popular in developing countries? **(b)** How successful has socialism been in these countries?
21. What are the major criticisms of socialism?

Section 3

22. Briefly describe Marx's view of history and the labor theory of value.
23. Describe four characteristics of communist countries.
24. In what ways did the Soviet Union fail to meet Marx's predictions?
25. Describe the problems facing the Soviet economy under Gorbachev and the Russian economy today.
26. **(a)** What changes did Mao make as leader of the People's Republic of China? **(b)** How did Deng Xiaoping differ from Mao?

Critical Thinking Skills

27. *Applying the Chapter Skill* Review the line graph on page 670 and answer the following questions. **(a)** What does the horizontal axis measure? **(b)** When did unemployment in the United States reach its highest point during the 1990s? **(c)** Which of the three countries listed had the highest unemployment rate in 1997?

28. *Recognizing Propaganda* Mao Zedong renamed his country the "People's Republic of China" after the communist takeover in 1949. **(a)** How did this new name reflect the theories of Karl Marx? **(b)** Based on your reading in this chapter, is this an appropriate name for a communist state? Explain your answer.

29. *Drawing Inferences* Consider the common criticism of socialism on the grounds that it discourages individual initiative. **(a)** What assumption about initiative underlies this criticism? **(b)** Is this assumption valid? Why or why not? **(c)** How does a free enterprise system differ from socialism in its treatment of individuals?

Analyzing Political Cartoons

Using your knowledge of economic systems and this cartoon, answer the questions below.

30. What does this cartoon imply about Russia's experiences since the end of communism?

31. How do "Russian communism" and "Russian capitalism" compare with ideal forms of communism and capitalism?

★ You Can Make a Difference

Help educate your classmates about child-labor laws. Contact the U.S. Department of Labor or your State's department of labor to learn more about current U.S. child-labor laws. Then create a poster or display sheet that could be posted in the school guidance office, outlining the hours children are allowed to work and any types of jobs they are not allowed to perform. Your poster should also note whether the hours and types of jobs vary depending on the age of the child.

Participation Activities

32. *Current Events Watch* Review newspapers and magazines from the past month and find articles that discuss businesses or the economy in China, Russia, and Germany. Are these countries described as communist, socialist, capitalist, or a combination? Based on your reading in this chapter, how would you categorize these three economies?

33. *Graphing Activity* Choose one country from each of the following continents: Africa, Asia, Europe, and South America. Research how much the United States and those four countries spend on health care per capita and as a share of Gross Domestic Product (GDP). Using this data, create a bar graph. Which country spends the most on health care per person? Which country spends the most on health care as a share of GDP? Which country spends the least per person?

34. *It's Your Turn* It is 1932. The world is in the midst of the Great Depression, and you are a young politician running for office. You must convince people that you have the best solution for the country's economic problems. Write a speech in which you explain why you have chosen your particular party and describe the goals of your party. What legislation will you support? Why should people vote for your party instead of the alternatives? After you have written your speech, present it to your class. **(Writing a Speech)**

Take It to the Net

Chapter 23 Self-Test As a final review activity, take the Chapter 23 Self-Test in the Social Studies area at the Web site listed below, and receive immediate feedback on your answers.

www.phschool.com

◆ The State House, Boston, Massachusetts

Participating in State and Local Government

CONSTITUTIONAL PRINCIPLES

Federalism The Constitution of the United States creates a federal system in which the powers of government are divided between the National Government and the 50 States. Each State's own constitution creates the structure and the processes by which that State is governed.

Limited Government The 50 State constitutions vary in many of their details. However, all of them authorize the exercise of governmental power and, at the same time, limit the exercise of governmental power.

Judicial Review The primary function of State courts is to settle disputes between private persons and between private persons and government. Those courts also all exercise the power of judicial review, which allows them to check the exercise of power by the States and their local governments.

The Impact on You

As a resident of your State, you must obey its laws. That means, for example, that you must attend school and that you must be at least a certain age before you can legally do such things as drive a car. Those two illustrations only begin to suggest "the impact on you."

CHAPTER 24

Governing the States

"We need to make it easier for people who aren't politicians to lend their hands to the enterprises of government through service in government agencies at the local, State, and federal level."

—Kathleen Kennedy Townsend (1996)
Lieutenant Governor, Maryland

The 50 States are different in geography, size, and population; but they are quite similar in government structure. All the States have written constitutions. Each has a governor, or chief executive, and a legislature that together create public policy. State court systems try both civil and criminal cases.

◆ The Texas House of Representatives

You Can Make a Difference

HELPING OTHERS LEARN about their State is one of the jobs of the youth interns at the Minnesota Historical Society. In a program partly funded by the State legislature, high school juniors study Minnesota history; then they lead tour groups and work with visitors at various historic sites. One intern, Bradley Sam, Jr., spent a summer at the Mille Lacs Indian Museum. Bradley is a member of the Mille Lacs band of Ojibwe, whose history is traced in the museum. He first applied to the program to "learn some history about how our people used to live." Later he decided, "The best part is giving the tours, talking to people."

Keep It Current

Items marked with this logo are periodically updated on the Internet. Keep up-to-date with what's in the news. To get current information on State government, go to **www.phschool.com**

SECTION 1

State Constitutions (pp. 684–688)

★ The first State constitutions were based on popular sovereignty and limited government, and they provided for a separation of powers, checks and balances, and protection of individual rights.

★ Today, State constitutions retain those basic principles; they also set out the structure, powers, and processes of government, and detail methods of constitutional change.

★ Most present-day constitutions are in need of reform.

SECTION 2

State Legislatures (pp. 689–693)

★ The legislature is the lawmaking branch of State government. It has the power to pass any law that does not conflict with the State constitution or with federal law.

★ State legislators are chosen by popular vote.

★ State legislatures are organized much like Congress.

★ The legislative process is also similar to that of Congress. However, some States also allow voters to participate directly through the initiative and referendum.

SECTION 3

The Governor and State Administration (pp. 694–700)

★ The governor is the chief executive officer of the State.

★ In addition to executive powers, a governor has some legislative and judicial powers.

★ The governor shares executive powers in most States with other executive officers, who are also popularly elected.

SECTION 4

In the Courtroom (pp. 702–705)

★ The law is the code of conduct by which society is governed. State courts apply constitutional, statutory, and administrative law as well as common law and equity.

★ The law can also be classified as either criminal or civil law.

★ There are two kinds of juries: the grand jury, which brings indictments; and the petit jury, which decides the facts in trials.

SECTION 5

The Courts and Their Judges (707–712)

★ State courts are usually organized into unified court systems, which contain courts of first instance, such as general trial courts; intermediate appellate courts; and a State supreme court.

★ Judges are selected most often by popular election but also by appointment by either the governor or the legislature.

1 State Constitutions

OBJECTIVES

1. **Examine** the history, contents, and importance of the first State constitutions.
2. **List** the basic principles and the kinds of provisions found in every State constitution.
3. **Explain** the process for constitutional change.
4. **Analyze** the need for reform of State constitutions.

WHY IT MATTERS

A State constitution is the supreme law of that State, but still subordinate to the national Constitution. It sets out the way the State is governed. Each State constitution is based on popular sovereignty and limited government. Because of length, age, and numerous alterations, many State constitutions are in need of reform.

POLITICAL DICTIONARY

★ **popular sovereignty**
★ **limited government**
★ **fundamental law**
★ **initiative**
★ **statutory law**

A State constitution is that State's supreme law. It sets out the ways in which the government of that State is organized, and it distributes power among the various branches of the State government. It authorizes the exercise of power by government. At the same time, it places limits on the exercise of governmental power. A State's constitution is superior to any and all other forms of State and local law within the State.

Each State's constitution, however, is subordinate to the Constitution of the United States. (See Article VI, Section 2, the Supremacy Clause.) No provision in any State's constitution may conflict with any form of federal law.

▲ The settlement of Jamestown, Virginia, in 1607

The First State Constitutions

Each of the 50 States has a *written* constitution. That fact, in itself, is very important. From the beginning, government in this country has been based on written constitutions. In fact, the United States has sometimes been described as "a land of constitutions."

Our experience with such documents dates from 1606, when King James I granted a charter to the Virginia Company. That act led to the settlement at Jamestown in the following year and, with it, the first government in British North America. Later, each of the other English colonies was also established and governed on the basis of a written charter.

When the 13 colonies became independent, each faced the problem of establishing a new government. On May 15, 1776, the Second Continental Congress advised each of the new States to adopt

PRIMARY Sources ❝ *such governments as shall, in the opinion of the representatives of the people, best conduce to the happiness and safety of their constituents in particular, and America in general.* ❞
—Second Continental Congress

Most of the colonial charters served as models for the first State constitutions. Indeed, in Connecticut and Rhode Island, the old charters seemed so well suited to the needs of the day that they were carried over as constitutions almost without change.[1]

The earliest State constitutions were adopted in a variety of ways. However, the people played no direct part in the process in any State. In Connecticut and Rhode Island, the legislature made the small changes considered necessary to turn the charters into constitutions. No further action was taken in either State.

Six of the Revolutionary legislatures drew up new documents and proclaimed them in force in 1776. In none of those States—Maryland, New Jersey, North Carolina, Pennsylvania, South Carolina, and Virginia—was the new constitution offered to the people for judgment.

In Delaware and New Hampshire in 1776, and in Georgia and New York in 1777, the constitutions were prepared by conventions called by the legislature. In each case, the new document had to be approved by the legislature in order to become effective; but in none was popular approval required.

In 1780, a popularly elected convention prepared a new constitution for Massachusetts. It was then ratified by a vote of the people. Thus, Massachusetts set the pattern of popular participation in the constitution-making process, a pattern generally followed among the States ever since.[2]

Assemblies representing the people drafted all of the present State constitutions; most of them became effective only after a popular vote. Only the present constitutions of Delaware (1897), Mississippi (1890), South Carolina (1895), and Vermont (1793) came into force without popular ratification.

Because the first State constitutions came out of the same Revolutionary ferment, they shared many basic features. Each proclaimed the principles of **popular sovereignty** and **limited government.** That is, in each of them the people were recognized as the sole source of authority for government. And in each constitution, the powers given to the new government were closely limited. Seven constitutions began with a lengthy bill of rights. All of them made it clear that the sovereign people held "certain unalienable rights" that government must respect.

The doctrines of separation of powers and checks and balances were also built into each of

"Now you try to get a fire started while I draft a constitution."

▲ **Interpreting Political Cartoons** (a) How important does the cartoonist think a written constitution is? How do you know? (b) Do you agree? Explain.

the new constitutions. In practice, however, the memory of the hated royal governors was still fresh. Thus, most of the authority that each State government had was given to the legislature. For example, only Massachusetts and South Carolina allowed the governor to veto acts of the legislature. In all the States, except Georgia (until 1789) and Pennsylvania (until 1790), the legislature was bicameral.[3]

For their time, the early State constitutions were democratic. Each had, however, several provisions (and some important omissions) that, by today's standards, were quite undemocratic. No constitution provided for full religious freedom. Each one did set rigid qualifications for voting and for officeholding, and all gave property owners a highly favored standing.

State Constitutions Today

The present-day State constitutions are the direct descendants of those earlier documents. Only 17 of the current State constitutions were

---

[1]Connecticut did not write a new document until 1818, and Rhode Island not until 1842.

[2]As noted in Chapter 2, with independence Massachusetts relied on the colonial charter in force prior to 1691 as its first State constitution. New Hampshire adopted its second and present constitution in 1784. It followed the Massachusetts pattern of popular convention and popular ratification.

[3]Vermont, which became the 14th State in 1791, had a unicameral legislature until 1836. Only Nebraska has a one-house legislative body today, and it has had one since 1937.

▲ *A State Constitutional Convention* James Madison addresses the Virginia Constitutional Convention of 1829–1830.

written since 1900. On the other hand, most of them have been amended dozens of times.

All State constitutions rest on nearly uniform principles. Still, unique provisions are found in each of them. State constitutions can be described in terms of the following categories: basic principles, civil rights, governmental structure, governmental powers, processes for change, and miscellaneous provisions.

1. *Basic Principles.* Every State's fundamental law is built on the principles of popular sovereignty and limited government. That is, each State constitution recognizes that government exists only with the consent of the people, and that it must operate within certain, often closely defined, bounds.

In every State, the powers of government are divided among executive, legislative, and judicial branches. Each branch has powers with which it can restrain the actions of the other two. That is, each of the 50 documents proclaims separation of powers as well as checks and balances. Each also provides, either expressly or by implication, for the power of judicial review.

2. *Protections of Civil Rights.* Each document has a bill of rights, a listing of the rights that individuals hold against the State and its officers and agencies. Most constitutions set out guarantees much like those in the first 10 amendments to the national Constitution. Several documents include a number of other guarantees as well—for example the right to self-government, to be safe from imprisonment for debt, and to organize labor unions and bargain collectively.

3. *Governmental Structure.* Every State constitution deals with the structure of government at both the State and the local levels. A few

follow the national pattern, providing only a broad outline. Most, however, cover the subject of governmental organization at length, and often in great detail.

4. *Governmental Powers and Processes.* All State constitutions list in detail the powers vested in the executive branch (the governor and other executive officers), the legislature, the courts, and the units of local government. The powers to tax, spend, borrow, and provide for education are very prominent. So, too, are such processes as elections, legislation, and intergovernmental (State-local) relations.

5. *Constitutional Change.* Each State constitution sets out the means by which it may be revised or amended. Since constitutions are **fundamental laws**—laws of such basic and lasting importance, they cannot be changed as ordinary law is changed. Constitutional changes are more difficult to bring about, as you shall see.

6. *Miscellaneous Provisions.* Most State constitutions begin with a preamble, which has no legal force but does set out the purposes of those who drafted and adopted the document. All of them also contain a number of "dead letter" provisions, items that have no current force and effect but still remain a part of the constitution.

Constitutional Change

Like the national Constitution, the State constitutions have been altered over the years by both the formal and the informal amendment process. But—and this is a very important *but*—the informal process has not been nearly so important at the State as at the national level.

State constitutions are much less flexible, and much more detailed, than the national document. The structures, powers, and procedures of State government are treated at great length. Thus, there is much less room for informal change. The State courts have generally been strict in their role as constitution-interpreters. In short, constitutional development at the State level has come about primarily through formal rather than informal change.

Two kinds of formal changes have been used: amendments, which usually deal with one or a few provisions in a constitution; and revisions, which are large-scale changes that affect the constitution more broadly. Most of the formal changes that have been made in State constitutions have been made by amendment.

Procedures for Change

The process of formal change involves two basic steps: proposal and then ratification. Proposals for change can be made by a constitutional convention, the legislature, or (in several States) by the voters themselves. Ratification is by popular vote in every State except Delaware.

The constitutional convention is the usual device by which new constitutions have been written and older constitutions revised. More than 200 such conventions have been held. In every State the legislature has the power to call a convention, and that call is generally subject to voter approval. In 14 States the question of calling a convention must be submitted to the voters at regular intervals.[4]

Amendments to State constitutions can also be proposed by conventions. However, because they are both costly and time consuming, conventions are most often used for the broader purpose of revision.

Most amendments are proposed by the legislature. The process is comparatively simple in some States, quite difficult in others. Not surprisingly, more amendments are proposed (and adopted) in those States with simpler processes.[5]

In 17 States the voters themselves can propose constitutional amendments through the **initiative,** a process in which a certain number of qualified voters sign petitions in favor of a proposal. The proposal then goes directly to the ballot, for approval or rejection by the people.

Ratification of Amendments

In every State except Delaware, an amendment must be approved by vote of the people in order to become part of the constitution. The ratification process, like the proposal process, varies among the States.

Typically, the approval of a majority of those voting on an amendment adds it to the State constitution, though some States require a greater margin. On many occasions, constitutional amendments have been defeated, although they received more *yes* than *no* votes. Most often, this has happened because many voters failed to vote on the amendments.[6]

How to Propose Changes to a State Constitution

PROPOSAL BY A CONVENTION
- Constitutional conventions are used most often to revise existing constitutions and to write new ones.
- Every State legislature can call a constitutional convention. That call is generally subject to voter approval.

PROPOSAL BY A LEGISLATURE
- Most constitutional amendments are proposed by the legislature.
- The process varies among the States. Where the process is simpler, more amendments are proposed and adopted.

PROPOSAL BY INITIATIVE
Voters can propose amendments in some States:
- A specified number of voters must sign a petition.
- The proposal goes on the ballot.
- The people approve or reject the amendment.

Interpreting Charts In every State except Delaware, those changes which are proposed must be ratified by the voters. *Which method of proposing constitutional changes gives voters the most input?*

The Need for Reform

Almost without exception, State constitutions are in urgent need of reform. The typical document is cluttered with unnecessary details, burdensome restrictions, and obsolete sections. It also carries much repetitious, even contradictory, material. Moreover, it fails to deal with many of the pressing problems that the States and their local governments currently face.

Even the newest and most recently rewritten constitutions tend to carry over a great deal of material from earlier documents and suffer from these same faults. The leading problems

---

[4]Every 20 years in Connecticut, Illinois, Maryland, Missouri, Montana, New York, Ohio, and Oklahoma; every 16 years in Michigan; every 10 years in Alaska, Iowa, New Hampshire, and Rhode Island; and every 9 years in Hawaii.

[5]The California constitution, which dates from 1879, has been amended more than 500 times. Conversely, the Massachusetts document of 1780, in force for twice as long, has been changed fewer than 125 times.

[6]In Delaware, if an amendment is approved by a two-thirds vote in each house of the legislature at two successive sessions, it then becomes effective. In South Carolina, final ratification, after a favorable vote by the people, depends on a majority vote in both houses of the legislature. Both the Alabama and South Carolina constitutions provide that amendments only of local, as opposed to Statewide, application need be approved only by the voters in the affected locale.

with State constitutions can be grouped into two categories: length and age.

Length

Length was not a problem for the first State constitutions. They were quite short, ranging from New Jersey's 1776 constitution (2,500 words) to the 1780 Massachusetts constitution (12,000 words). These early State constitutions were meant simply to be statements of basic principle and organization. Purposely, they left to the legislature—and to time and practice—the task of filling in the details as they became necessary.

Through the years, however, State constitutions have grown and grown. Most today are between 15,000 and 40,000 words. The shortest are those of Vermont (1793) with fewer than 9,000 words, and New Hampshire (1784), with just over 9,000 words. At the other extreme, Alabama's 1901 constitution contains more than 300,000 words.

The leading cause of this expansion is popular distrust of government. That distrust has often led to the insertion into State constitutions of detailed provisions that are specifically aimed at preventing the misuse of government power.

Many restrictions on that power, which could be set out in ordinary law, have been purposely placed in the State constitution, where they cannot be easily ignored or readily, and quietly, changed. Special-interest groups learned long ago that public policies of benefit to them are much safer in the State constitution than in a mere statute.

There has been a marked failure in nearly every State to separate *fundamental law*, which should be in the constitution, from **statutory law**, which refers to laws passed by the legislature. The line separating fundamental and statutory law may be blurry in some cases. However, who can seriously argue that this is *fundamental law*: California constitution's ban on taxing fruit and nut trees planted within the past four years?

Two other factors have contributed to the growth of State constitutions. First, the functions performed by the States, and by many of their local governments, have multiplied in the past several decades. That development has called forth many new constitutional provisions. Second, the "people" have not been stingy in the use of the initiative where it is available.

Age

Most State constitutions are comparatively ancient. The Oregon constitution is a typical example. It is overloaded with statutory material and contains many outdated provisions. Since becoming effective in 1859, the Oregon constitution has been amended 220 times; it now runs nearly 50,000 words and contains *two* Articles VII and *eleven* Articles XI!

Several States have adopted revised constitutions in recent decades: Illinois, North Carolina, and Virginia in 1970; Montana in 1972; Louisiana in 1974; and Georgia in 1982. These, however, remain exceptions. Thirty-two states now have documents more than 100 years old, and 19 States still have the constitutions with which they entered the Union. The oldest State constitutions in force today are those of Massachusetts (1780) and New Hampshire (1784).

Section 1 Assessment

Key Terms and Main Ideas

1. Explain the concept of **popular sovereignty.**
2. **(a)** List and explain three ways changes to State constitutions can be proposed. **(b)** How are proposed changes ratified?
3. What is the difference between **fundamental law** and **statutory law?**

Critical Thinking

4. **Predicting Consequences** Do you think the governments of the English colonies or the early States would have developed differently if they had not had written charters or constitutions? Explain your answer.

5. **Drawing Inferences** Why do you think many State constitutions have been allowed to become so lengthy, repetitive, and full of outdated provisions?

 Take It to the Net

6. Read your State's Bill of Rights, and then review the Federal Bill of Rights. Are there many similarities or are there more differences? Write a paragraph comparing and contrasting the two documents. Use the links provided in the Social Studies area at the following Web site for help in completing this activity. **www.phschool.com**

2 State Legislatures

Section Preview

OBJECTIVES

1. **Understand** the structure and size of State legislatures.
2. **Describe** the election process, terms, and compensation of State legislators.
3. **Explain** the powers and organization of State legislatures.
4. **Summarize** the legislative process at the State level.

WHY IT MATTERS

State legislatures are the lawmaking bodies of the States, but they also have some non-legislative powers. The organization of State legislatures is similar to that of Congress. The voters themselves can take a direct part in the lawmaking process in several States, through the initiative and the referendum.

POLITICAL DICTIONARY

★ **police power**
★ **constituent power**
★ **referendum**

Each State constitution establishes a legislative body that is, in effect, the powerhouse of that State's government. The size of a legislature, the details of its organization and procedures, the frequency and length of its sessions, and even its official name vary among the States. However, State legislatures share a fundamental feature with one another: they are lawmaking bodies.

The Legislature: Structure and Size

In every State, the legislature is the lawmaking branch of State government. Its basic function goes to the heart of democratic government: The legislature is responsible for translating the public will into the State's public policy.

Just over half the States call their lawmaking body the legislature. Other States call it the General Assembly, the Legislative Assembly, or the General Court. Forty-nine of the 50 State legislatures are bicameral. The upper house is called the Senate in all States. The lower house is referred to as the House of Representatives in most, though some States call it the Assembly, General Assembly, or House of Delegates. Nebraska, the only State with a one-house legislature, calls its single chamber the Legislature.

While there is no ideal size for a legislative body, two basic considerations are important. First, a legislature, and each of its houses, should

not be so large as to hamper the orderly conduct of the people's business. Second, it should not be so small that the many views and interests within the State cannot be represented adequately.

The constitution of every State provides that the members of the legislature are to be elected from districts within the State. Today, nearly all State legislators are chosen from single-member districts. In most States, those districts are drawn by the legislature itself—and they are redrawn (reapportioned) every ten years, in line with the most recent federal census.

▲ The State capitol in Pierre, South Dakota

In *Reynolds* v. *Sims*, 1964, the Supreme Court held that the 14th Amendment's Equal Protection Clause requires every State to draw its legislative districts on the basis of population equality. "Legislators represent people," said the Court, "not trees or acres. Legislators are elected by voters, not farms or economic interests."

The State Legislators

Today, there are 7,611 State legislators—5,532 representatives and 2,079 senators—among the 50 States. Nearly all of them are Republicans or Democrats; fewer than 40 belong to minor parties or are independents. Only one in five of them are women.

Qualifications

Every State's constitution sets out formal requirements of age, citizenship, and residence for legislators. For example, most States require representatives to be at least 21 and senators to be 25. The realities of politics add informal qualifications, which are harder to meet than the formal ones. They have to do with a candidate's vote-getting abilities, and are based on such characteristics as occupation, name recognition, party identification, race, religion, national origin, and the like.

Election

Legislators are chosen by popular vote in every State. Nearly everywhere, candidates for the legislature are nominated at party primaries. Opposing candidates face one another in a partisan general election. Legislative nominees are picked by conventions in only a few States—New York, for example. In only one State, Nebraska, are the candidates nominated in nonpartisan primaries, and they are not identified by party in the general election.

In most States the lawmakers are elected in November of even-numbered years. In four States—Mississippi, New Jersey, Virginia, and Louisiana—legislative elections are held in the odd-numbered years, in the hope of separating State and local issues from national politics.

Terms

Legislators serve either two-year or four-year terms. Senators are usually elected for longer terms than are representatives. The rate of turnover in legislative seats is fairly high. In a given year, more than one fourth of State legislators around the country are serving their first terms.

Compensation

Far too often, capable men and women refuse to run for seats in State legislatures because of the financial sacrifices that such service entails. Oregon provides a typical example of the compensation package. The basic salary is now $1,258 a month, or $30,192 for the biennium, a two-year period. In addition, each member receives an expense allowance: $90 for each day of the legislative session, which usually lasts for about 180 days, and for each day he or she attends interim committee meetings (meetings held between sessions).

The *Living* Constitution

Redefining Federalism | 1800

The Framers of the Constitution sought to balance the rights of the several States and the powers of the new Federal Government. Their solution was a federal system, which divides powers between the two levels of government. Although the Constitution is the "supreme law of the land," questions about States' rights and national power have arisen throughout American history, as the Supreme Court cases on this time line show.

1819
In *McCulloch* v. *Maryland*, the Court rules that a State cannot tax the Federal Government.

1824
In *Gibbons* v. *Ogden*, the Court affirms the Federal Government's right to regulate interstate trade.

Each member also has an expense allowance of up to $550 for each month in which the legislature is not in session. The total compensation per member, including both salary and allowances, comes to less than $30,000 a year.

Legislative Sessions

Forty-three State legislatures now hold annual sessions, and the California legislature meets in a continuous two-year session. Only Arkansas, Montana, Nevada, North Dakota, Oregon, and Texas still meet every other year.

Since the 1960s, most States have turned to annual sessions, as it has become increasingly apparent that legislators cannot otherwise handle their workload. Generally, regular sessions are becoming longer and longer. All 50 governors, and some two thirds of the State legislatures, can call special sessions to allow the lawmaking body to take up urgent matters between its regularly scheduled meetings.

Powers of the Legislature

In each State the legislature has all of those powers that (1) the State constitution does not grant exclusively to the executive or judicial branches of the State's government or to its local units, and (2) neither the State constitution nor the United States Constitution denies to the legislature.

Legislative Powers

State legislatures can pass any law that does not conflict with federal law or with any part of that State's constitution. Therefore, it is impossible to list all the powers of the State legislatures. However, most State constitutions do list the legislature's more important powers. Those most often mentioned include the powers to tax, spend, borrow, establish courts, define crimes and provide for their punishment, regulate commercial activities, and maintain public schools.

Every legislature's powers include the vital **police power.** This is the State's power to protect and promote the public health, safety, morals, and welfare. This broad power is the basis of thousands of State laws, including those that require vaccinations and restrict the ownership of firearms, for example. (See page 566.)

Nonlegislative Powers

All 50 State legislatures possess certain nonlegislative powers in addition to those they exercise when they make law.

1925
In *Gitlow* v. *New York,* the Court rules that the protections of the 1st Amendment apply against actions by State governments.

1997 In *Printz* v. *United States,* the Court strikes down the provision of the federal Brady Act requiring States to check the background of handgun buyers.

1850	1900	1950	2000

1886
In *Wabash, St. Louis & Pacific Railway Co.* v. *Illinois,* the Court rules that States cannot regulate railroad rates on the parts of interstate journeys that fall within their borders.

1964
In *Wesberry* v. *Sanders,* the Court rules that populations in State congressional districts must be nearly equal.

1972
In *Furman* v. *Georgia,* the Court rules that all existing State death penalty laws violate the Constitution.

2001
In *Alabama* v. *Garrett,* the Court rules that State employees cannot sue the State when it violates the federal Americans with Disabilities Act.

Analyzing Time Lines

1. When did the Court first decide that State authorities must observe the civil rights protected by the Bill of Rights?
2. What trend can you see in the Supreme Court decisions in the 1900s?

▲ **Law and Order** Members of the Texas House raise a point of order while considering a bill.

1. *Executive powers* include the approval of the governor's appointment of certain officials. In some States the legislature itself appoints certain executive officeholders.

2. *Judicial powers* are capped by the power of impeachment. In every State except Oregon, the legislature can remove any State executive officer or judge through that process.

3. **Constituent power** refers to constitution-making and the constitutional amendment process. Since this does not involve the making of statutes, this function is a nonlegislative one.

Organization

State legislatures are organized in much the same manner as Congress. They have presiding officers and a committee system.

The Presiding Officers

Those who preside over the sessions of the State legislative chambers are usually powerful political figures, not only in the legislature itself but elsewhere in State politics.

The lower house in each of the 49 bicameral legislatures elects its own presiding officer, known as the speaker. The senate chooses its own presiding officer in 24 States. In the others, the lieutenant governor serves as the president of the senate. Where the lieutenant governor does preside, the senate selects a president *pro tempore* to serve when the lieutenant governor is absent.

Except for the lieutenant governors, each of these presiding officers is chosen by a vote of the full membership in his or her legislative chamber.

In fact, the majority party's caucus usually picks those who fill leadership posts just before the legislature starts a new session.

The chief duties of those presiding officers center on the conduct of the legislature's floor business. These duties are also a major source of their power. The presiding officers refer bills to committee, recognize members who seek the floor, and interpret and apply the rules of their chamber to its proceedings.

Unlike the Speaker of the House in Congress, the speaker in nearly every State appoints the chairperson and other members of each house committee. The senate's president or president *pro tem* has the same power in just over half the States. The presiding officers regularly use this power much as they use their other powers: to reward their friends, punish their enemies, and otherwise work their influence on the legislature.

The Committee System

The committee system in State legislatures works much as it does in Congress. Committee members do much of the work of the legislature when they determine which bills will reach the floor, and inform the full chamber on measures they have handled.

The standing committees in each house are generally set up by subject matter, such as committees on highways, education, and so on. A bill may be amended or even very largely rewritten in committee. Often, it is ignored altogether.

The "pigeonholing" of bills is as well known in the States as it is in Congress. (See page 336.) In fact, in most States one of the standing committees in each house is regularly the "graveyard committee," a body to which bills are sent to be buried. The judiciary committee, to which bills may be referred "on grounds of doubtful constitutionality," often fills this role.[7]

The Legislative Process

The major steps in the legislative process in a typical State legislature are much like those in Congress. You can review the process in Congress by studying the diagram on page 345.

---

[7]A vivid illustration of a graveyard committee existed for several years in the lower house in landlocked Oklahoma: the Committee on Deep Sea Navigation.

Sources of Bills

Legally, only a member may introduce a bill in either house in any State legislature. So, in the strictest sense, legislators themselves are the source of all measures introduced. In broader terms, however, the lawmakers are the authors of only a handful of bills.

A large number of bills come from public sources, from officers and agencies of State and local government. Every governor has a legislative program, and often an extensive and ambitious one.

Bills also come from a wide range of private sources. In fact, the largest single source for proposed State laws appears to be interest groups. Those groups and their lobbyists have one overriding purpose: to influence public policy to benefit their own special interests. Of course, some bills do originate with private individuals—business people, farmers, labor union members, and other citizens—who, for one reason or another, think that "there ought to be a law. . . ."

Direct Legislation

Several States allow voters to take a direct part in lawmaking. The main vehicles for this participation are the initiative and the referendum.

1. *The Initiative.* Through the initiative process, voters in 17 States can propose constitutional amendments. In 27 States, voters can also use the initiative to propose ordinary statutes. The initiative takes two quite different forms: the more common direct initiative and the little-used indirect initiative.

In both kinds of initiative, a certain number of qualified voters (which varies from State to State) must sign initiative petitions to propose a law. Where the direct initiative is used, the measure goes directly to the ballot, usually in the next general election. If the voters approve the measure, it becomes law. If not, it dies.

In the indirect initiative, the proposal goes first to the legislature. That body may pass it, making it a law. If the legislature does not pass it, the measure then goes to the voters.

2. *The Referendum.* A **referendum** is a process by which a legislative measure is referred to the State's voters for final approval or rejection. There are three different forms of the referendum: mandatory, optional, and popular.

A *mandatory referendum* requires that the legislature refer a measure to the voters. In every State except Delaware, proposed constitutional amendments must be submitted to the electorate. In several States other measures, such as those approving the borrowing of funds, must also go to the voters.

An *optional referendum* measure is one that the legislature refers to the voters voluntarily. Such measures are rare. They are usually "hot potatoes"—issues lawmakers would rather not take direct responsibility for deciding themselves.

Under the *popular referendum*, the people may demand via a petition that a measure passed by the legislature be referred to them for final action. Most attempts to use the popular referendum fail. Usually the opponents of a particular measure simply cannot gather the required number of signatures to force a popular vote on the matter.

Section 2 Assessment

Key Terms and Main Ideas

1. The **police power** is used for what purposes?
2. What three kinds of nonlegislative powers does a State legislature have?
3. What are the three usual sources of bills?
4. Explain the types of **referendum**.

Critical Thinking

5. **Demonstrating Reasoned Judgment** Do you think State legislators should be better paid than they usually are? Explain your answer.
6. **Analyzing Information** Suppose you are a member of an interest group that wants to get State funding to clean up a river or to build a new highway. What steps would you follow to get a funding bill introduced and passed in your State legislature?

 Take It to the Net

7. Browse the State legislature pages for several States. Select one State, and write a report about its legislative process. Include how this process compares and contrasts with the legislative process in Congress. Use the links provided in the Social Studies area at the following Web site for help in completing this activity. **www.phschool.com**

The Governor and State Administration

Section Preview

OBJECTIVES

1. **Describe** the office of governor.
2. **Summarize** the governor's many roles, including the powers, duties, and limitations of the office.
3. **List** and describe the other State executive offices.

WHY IT MATTERS

The governor is the chief executive of a State. Although a governor's executive powers are limited in several important ways, dynamic governors can use the prestige of the office, personal powers of persuasion, and informal tactics to accomplish their goals. Other important State executive officers are often directly elected by the people.

POLITICAL DICTIONARY

★ recall
★ item veto
★ clemency
★ pardon
★ commutation
★ reprieve
★ parole

The governor is the principal executive officer in each of the 50 States. He or she is always a central figure in State politics, and is often a well-known national personality as well. Governors today hold an office that is the direct descendant of the earliest public office in American politics, the colonial governorship, established in Virginia in 1607.

The Governorship

In colonial America, the actions of the royal governors inspired much of the resentment that fueled the Revolution. That attitude was carried over into the first State constitutions. Most government powers were given to the legislatures; the new State governors, for the most part, had little real authority. In every State except Massachusetts and New York, the governor was chosen by the legislature, and in most of them only for a one-year term.

That original separation of powers soon proved unsatisfactory. Many of the State legislatures abused their powers. Several fell prey to special interests, and the governors were unable to respond. So, as new constitutions were written, and the older ones revised, the powers of the legislatures were curbed and the powers of the governors increased.

Through the early 1800s, the power to choose the governor was taken from the legislature

and given to the people. The veto power was vested in the governor, and the gubernatorial powers of appointment and removal were increased, as well.

Beginning with Illinois in 1917, most States have reorganized and strengthened the executive branch to make the governor the State's chief executive in more than name. To a greater or lesser degree, governors are much more powerful figures today than in decades past.

Qualifications

Anyone who wants to become the governor of a State must be able to satisfy a set of formal qualifications. Typically, he or she must be an American citizen, of at least a certain age (usually 25 or 30), have lived in the State for a given period of time (most often for at least five years), and be a qualified voter.

Clearly, these formal qualifications are not very difficult to meet. It is the *informal* qualifications that have real meaning. To become a governor, a person must have those characteristics that will first attract a party's nomination, and then attract the voters in the general election.

Those characteristics vary from State to State, and even from election to election within a State. Race, sex, religion, name recognition, personality, party identification, experience, ideology, the ability to use television effectively—these and several other factors are all part of the mix.

Over time, more than 2,400 persons have served as governors of the various States. To this point (2002), only 18 have been women—and five of those 18 hold office today: Jeanne Shaheen of New Hampshire, first elected in 1996; Jane Dee Hull of Arizona, who as secretary of state succeeded to the office in 1997 and who then won it in her own right in 1998; Ruth Ann Minner of Delaware and Judy Martz of Montana, both elected in 2000; and Jane Swift of Massachusetts, who succeeded to the office from the lieutenant-governorship in 2001.[8]

Selection

The governor is chosen by popular vote in every State. In all but five States, only a plurality is needed for election. If no candidate wins a clear majority in Arizona, Georgia, or Louisiana, the two top vote-getters meet in a runoff election. If no one wins a majority in Mississippi, the lower house of the legislature picks the new governor. In Vermont, both houses make the choice.

The major parties' gubernatorial candidates are usually picked in primaries. In a few States, however, conventions choose the nominees. Nearly half the States now provide for the joint election of the governor and the lieutenant governor. In those States, each party's candidates for those offices run as a team, and the voter casts one vote to fill both posts.

Term

Governors are elected to four-year terms nearly everywhere today. Only New Hampshire and Vermont still provide for two-year terms. More than half the States limit the number of terms a governor may serve, usually to two terms. Only Virginia has a single-term limit.

Governors who do run for another term most often win. Two four-term governors hold the

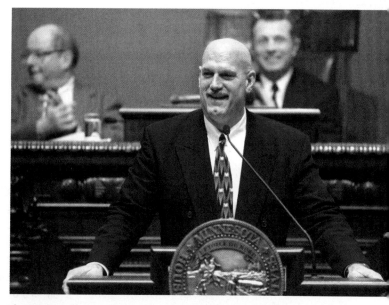

▲ Governor Jesse Ventura of Minnesota delivers the State of the State address. *Critical Thinking What powers does the governor have to carry out his or her proposals for the State?*

modern record for gubernatorial service—16 years. They are James Rhodes, the governor of Ohio from 1963 to 1971 and again from 1975 to 1983; and George Wallace, the governor of Alabama from 1963 to 1967, from 1971 to 1979, and from 1983 to 1987. The most successful of all modern gubernatorial candidates was Orval Faubus, governor of Arkansas from 1955 to 1967. He won six consecutive two-year terms.[9]

Succession

Governors are mortal. Occasionally, one of them dies in office. Many of them are also politically ambitious. Every so often, one resigns in midterm—to become a United States senator or to accept a presidential appointment, for example.

When a vacancy does occur, it sets off a game of political musical chairs in the State. The political plans and timetables of a number of public personalities are affected by the event. No matter what causes a vacancy, every State's constitution provides for a successor. In 43 States the lieutenant governor is first in line. In Maine, New Hampshire, New Jersey, and West

---

[8]Twelve other women have been elected to a governorship: Nellie Ross (Wyoming, 1925–1927), Miriam Ferguson (Texas, 1925–1927, 1933–1935), Lurleen Wallace (Alabama, 1967–1968), Ella Grasso (Connecticut, 1975–1980), Dixie Lee Ray (Washington, 1977–1981), Martha Layne Collins (Kentucky, 1983–1987), Madeleine Kunin (Vermont, 1985–1991), Kay Orr (Nebraska, 1987–1991), Joan Finney (Kansas, 1991–1995), Ann Richards (Texas, 1991–1995), Barbara Roberts (Oregon, 1991–1995), and Christine Todd Whitman (New Jersey, 1994–2001). Also, Rose Mofford (who had been secretary of state) succeeded to the governorship in Arizona in 1988, and she served until 1991.

[9]The all-time record for both gubernatorial service and electoral success belongs to George Clinton of New York. He sought and won seven three-year terms as governor and held the office from 1777 to 1795 and again from 1801 to 1804. Clinton was later Vice President of the United States, from 1805 to 1812.

Voices on Government

Madeleine M. Kunin, one of America's first woman governors, served three terms (1985–1991) as governor of Vermont. Kunin had been a state legislator and lieutenant governor before becoming chief executive officer of her State. She described the conflicting demands of the governorship.

> **❝**Over time, I realized that I could not choose between performing the daily house-keeping tasks of governing and defining the larger, future vision that reflected my priorities. I had to do both. I had to fix problems as they happened and at the same time focus on a long-term agenda, if I did not want to compromise the passionate sense of mission that had attracted me to the political life in the first place. **❞**

Evaluating the Quotation

What do you think the dangers would be of focusing too much on either of the conflicting demands Kunin mentions—the day-to-day tasks or her broader vision? How might her dilemma apply to others in State government?

Virginia, the president of the senate succeeds. In Arizona, Oregon, and Wyoming, the office passes to the secretary of state.

Removal

The governor may be removed from office by impeachment in every State except Oregon. Only five governors have been impeached and removed since the turbulent Reconstruction years after the Civil War. Only one—Arizona's Evan Mecham in 1988—has suffered that fate in the past 70 years.

In 18 States, the governor may be recalled by the voters.[10] The **recall** is a petition procedure by which voters may remove an elected official from office before the completion of his or her regular term. The process generally works this

---

[10]These States are Alaska, Arizona, California, Colorado, Georgia, Idaho, Kansas, Louisiana, Michigan, Minnesota, Montana, Nevada, New Jersey, North Dakota, Oregon, Rhode Island, Washington, and Wisconsin.

---

way: If a certain number of qualified voters—usually 25 percent of the number who voted in the last general election—sign recall petitions, a special election must be held in which the voters decide whether to recall the officeholder.

Only one governor has been removed from office that way: Governor Lynn J. Frazier of North Dakota in 1921. However, the very next year he was elected to the United States Senate.

Compensation

Gubernatorial salaries now average over $100,000 a year. There is a wide range among the States, from $65,000 in Nebraska to $179,000 in New York. Most States also provide the governor with an official residence, usually called the governor's mansion, and with an expense account.

To a governor's salary and other material compensation must be added the intangibles of honor and prestige that go along with the office. It is this factor, along with a sense of public duty, that often brings many of our better citizens to seek the office. Several Presidents were governors before entering the White House, including, since 1900, William McKinley, Theodore Roosevelt, Woodrow Wilson, Calvin Coolidge, Franklin Roosevelt, Jimmy Carter, Ronald Reagan, Bill Clinton, and George W. Bush.

A Governor's Many Roles

Much like the President, a governor plays a number of different roles. He or she is, at the same time, an executive, an administrator, a legislator, a party leader, an opinion leader, and a ceremonial figure. What any State's governorship amounts to depends on how well the particular governor plays these roles.

Many of a governor's formal powers are hedged with constitutional and other legal restrictions. Nonetheless, the powers a governor does have, together with the prestige of the office, make it quite possible for a capable, dynamic person to be a "strong governor," one who can accomplish much for the State and for the public good.

One noted authority on State politics insists that the powers of all governors rest very largely on their talents of persuasion:

 ❝*Their power depends on their ability to persuade administrators*

over whom they have little authority, legislators who are jealous of their own powers, party leaders who are selected by local constituents, federal officials over whom governors have little authority, and a public that thinks governors have more authority than they really have. Thus, the role of governors is, above all, that of a persuader—of their own administrators, State legislators, federal officials, party leaders, the press, and the public. "

—Thomas R. Dye, *Politics in States and Communities*, 4th ed.

Executive Powers

The presidency and the governorships are similar in several ways, but the comparison can be pushed too far. Remember, the Constitution of the United States makes the President *the* executive in the National Government. State constitutions, on the other hand, regularly describe the governor as the *chief* executive in the State's government. The distinction here, between *the* executive and the *chief* executive, is a critical one. The executive authority is fragmented in most States, but it is not at the national level.

In the States, the executive authority is shared by a number of "executive officers"—a secretary of state, an attorney general, a treasurer, and so on. Most of these executive officers are popularly elected, and for that reason, they are very largely beyond the governor's direct control.

In short, most State constitutions so divide the executive authority that the governor can best be described as a "first among equals." Yet, whatever the realities of the distribution of power, the people look to the governor for leadership in State affairs. It is also the governor whom they hold responsible for the conduct of those affairs and for the overall condition of the State.

The governor's basic legal responsibility is regularly found in a constitutional provision that directs the chief executive "to take care that the laws be faithfully executed." Though the executive power may be divided, the governor is given a number of specific powers with which to accomplish that task.

1. *Appointment and Removal.* The governor can best execute—enforce and administer—the law with subordinates of his or her own choosing.

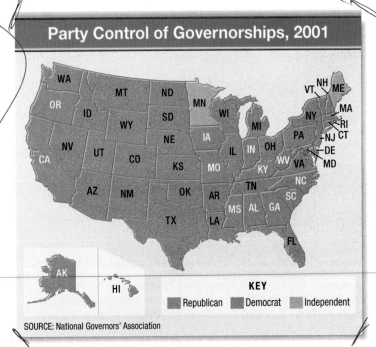

Party Control of Governorships, 2001

KEY — Republican | Democrat | Independent

SOURCE: National Governors' Association

Interpreting Maps *(a) In what region(s) of the country do the Democrats control the most governorships? (b) Where is Republican strength the greatest?*

Hence, the powers of appointment and removal are, or should be, among the most important in the governor's arsenal.

A leading test of any administrator is his or her ability to select loyal and able assistants. Two major factors work against the governor's effectiveness here, however. First is the existence of those other elected executives; the people choose them and the governor cannot remove them. Second, the State's constitution and statutes place restrictions on the governor's power to hire and fire. Most State constitutions require that the majority of the governor's major appointees be confirmed by the State senate.

Moreover, the legislature often sets qualifications that must be met by the governor's appointees. In a vigorous two-party State, for example, the law often requires that not more than a certain number of the members of each board or commission can be from the same political party. Thus, a governor must appoint some members of the opposing party to posts in his or her administration.

Consider one more example: The law often requires that appointees to any of the State's professional licensing boards must themselves be licensed to practice in that particular field. Thus, only licensed realtors can be appointed to the

▲ Montana National Guard troops fight a forest fire. *Critical Thinking* (a) *What other nonmilitary functions does the National Guard sometimes perform?* (b) *When does the National Guard perform military functions?*

real estate board; only licensed physicians to the board of medical examiners; and so on.

2. *Supervisory Powers.* The governor is empowered to supervise the work of thousands of men and women who staff the State's executive branch. Here again, the constitution and statutes of the State often limit the governor's authority. Many State agencies are subject to the governor's direct control, but many are not. The governor's powers of persuasion, and ability to operate through informal channels (such as party leadership and appeals to the public) can therefore make a significant difference in his or her ability to supervise the executive branch.

3. *Budget-Making Power.* In most States the governor prepares the annual or biennial budget that goes to the legislature. The legislature may make changes in the governor's financial plan, of course. It may appropriate this or that amount, or nothing, for this agency and that program, as it chooses. Still, the governor's budget recommendations carry a great deal of weight.

The governor's budget-making power is a highly effective tool for controlling State administration. Although unable to appoint or remove the head of a certain agency, for example, the governor can use the budget-making power to affect that agency's programs. So the governor can have a real impact on the attitudes and behavior of many officials.

4. *Military Powers.* Every State constitution makes the governor the commander in chief of the State militia—in effect, of the State's units of the National Guard. The National Guard is the organized part of the State militia. In a national emergency, the National Guard may be "called up," or ordered into federal service by the President.

All of the States' National Guard units were federalized in 1940 and served as part of the nation's armed forces in World War II. Many units also saw combat duty in Korea and Vietnam. A number were also called up in 1990, during Operation Desert Shield and Desert Storm. National Guard units are not often called into federal service in domestic crises, however.

When the State's Guard units are not in federal service (which is most of the time), they are commanded by the governor. On occasion, governors find it necessary to call out the Guard to deal with emergencies such as prison riots, to help fight a dangerous forest fire, to aid in relief and evacuation after a flood, to prevent looting during and after some other natural disaster, and so on.

Legislative Powers

The State's principal executive officer has important formal legislative powers. These powers, together with the governor's own political clout, often make the governor in effect the State's chief legislator.

1. *The Message Power.* This is really the power to recommend legislation, and a strong governor can do much with it.

Much of what the legislature does centers on the governor's program for legislative action. That program is given to the lawmakers in a yearly State of the State address, in the budget, and in several special messages. The most effective governors regularly push their programs by using the formal message power together with a number of informal tactics, such as appeals to the people and close contacts with key legislators.

2. *Special Sessions.* The governor in every State has the power to call the legislature into special sessions. The basic purpose of this power is to permit the State to meet extraordinary situations. Note, however, that the power can also be an important part of the governor's legislative arsenal. On occasion, a governor has persuaded reluctant legislators to pass a bill by threatening to

call them back in a special session, if they adjourn the regular session without having passed it.

3. *The Veto Power.* The governor of every State has the power to veto measures passed by the legislature. This power—and even just the threat to use it—is often the most potent power the governor has in influencing the work of the legislature.

Unlike the President, the governors of most States do not have the pocket veto. That is, those bills the governor neither signs nor vetoes after the legislature adjourns become law without his or her signature.[11]

In 42 States the governor's veto power includes the **item veto.** That is, the governor may veto one or more items in a bill without rejecting the entire measure. The item veto is most often, but not always, restricted to items in appropriations bills. It is regularly used to cancel what the governor deems inappropriate or unaffordable legislative appropriations.

The vote needed to override a governor's veto varies, but two thirds of the full membership in each house is most common. In practice, less than 5 percent of all measures passed by the legislatures are rejected by governors. However, when the veto power is used, it is quite effective. Less than 10 percent of all vetoes are overridden.

Judicial Powers

In every State the governor has several judicial powers. Most of them are powers of executive **clemency,** or powers of mercy that may be shown toward those convicted of a crime.[12]

With the power to **pardon,** a governor may release a person from the legal consequences of a crime. A pardon may be full or conditional, and it can be granted only after conviction. With the power of **commutation,** a governor may reduce the sentence imposed by a court. Thus a death sentence may be commuted to life imprisonment. The power to **reprieve** postpones the execution of a sentence. The power to **parole** allows the release of a prisoner short of the complete term of the original sentence.

The governor may have some or all of these powers. However, they are often shared with one or more boards. For example, a governor may share the pardoning or parole power with a board of pardons and/or a parole board.

Governors have not often abused their clemency powers, but in her first term (1925–1927), Governor Miriam "Ma" Ferguson of Texas pardoned 3,737 convicted felons, an average of more than five a day. The pardons came so thick and fast that several Texas newspapers ran daily "pardon columns" rather than separate news stories.[13]

Miscellaneous Duties

Every governor must perform many other, often time-consuming, duties. To list a few: The governor receives official visitors and welcomes other distinguished persons to the State, dedicates new buildings and parks, opens the State fair, and addresses many organizations and public gatherings. In addition, the governor is often called on to help settle labor disputes, to travel elsewhere in the country and sometimes abroad to promote the State and its trade interests, and to endorse worthy causes. The list is endless.

Other Executive Officers

In nearly every State, the governor must share the control of his or her administration with a number of other elected officials. In most States, these offices are filled by popular election.

The Lieutenant Governor

The office of lieutenant governor now exists in 43 States and is filled by the voters in 42 of them.[14] The formal duties of the lieutenant governor are usually not very demanding. He or she succeeds to the governorship if a vacancy occurs, and presides over the senate in most States.

---

[11]The governor has the pocket veto in only 14 States: Alabama, Delaware, Hawaii, Massachusetts, Michigan, Minnesota, New Hampshire, New Mexico, New York, North Carolina, Oklahoma, Vermont, Virginia, Wisconsin.

[12]An extradition request from another State also puts the governor in a judicial role.

[13]Governor James "Pa" Ferguson was impeached and removed by the Texas legislature in 1917. He was later pardoned by the legislature, and soon announced that he would run for the governorship again. The State Supreme Court ruled the legislative pardon unconstitutional, however. All of that prompted "Ma" Ferguson to run for governor in 1924. She vented her anger over the treatment of her husband in other ways, too—for example, by refusing any and all extradition requests from other States.

[14]In Tennessee, the presiding officer of the Senate (the speaker) is also, by statute, the lieutenant governor. The office does not exist in Arizona, Maine, New Hampshire, New Jersey, Oregon, West Virginia, and Wyoming.

▲ **Leading Lawyer** Karen Freeman-Wilson, a former judge on the Gary City Court, became attorney general of Indiana in February 2000. She is the chief lawyer for her State.

The office is often regarded as a stepping-stone to the governorship—sometimes by succession, of course, but often by means of future elections. Nevertheless, seven States seem to get along quite well without a lieutenant governor.

The Secretary of State

The office of secretary of state exists everywhere but in Alaska, Hawaii, and Utah. The secretary of state serves as the State's chief clerk and record-keeper. He or she has charge of a great variety of public documents, records the official acts of the governor and the legislature,

and usually administers the election laws. As with most of the other elected executives, the secretary of state has little real discretionary power or authority.

The Treasurer

The treasurer is the custodian of State funds, often the State's chief tax collector, and regularly the State's paymaster. The treasurer's major job is to make payments out of the State treasury. Most of those payments go to meet the many agency payrolls of the State and to pay the bills for the various goods or services supplied to the State.

The Attorney General

The attorney general is the State's lawyer. He or she acts as the legal advisor to State officers and agencies as they perform their official functions, represents the State in court, and oversees the work of local prosecutors as they try cases on behalf of the State.

Much of the power of the office centers on the attorney general's formal written interpretations of constitutional and statutory law. These interpretations, called opinions, are issued to answer questions raised by the governor, other executive officers, legislators, and local officials regarding the lawfulness of their actions or proposed actions. In most States these opinions have the force of law unless successfully challenged in court.

Section 3 Assessment

Key Terms and Main Ideas

1. What are two ways a governor can be removed from office?
2. List the executive powers of a governor.
3. What is the pocket veto? The **item veto**? Which of these two powers is a governor more likely to have?
4. Briefly explain these judicial powers of a governor: **clemency, pardon, commutation, reprieve,** and **parole.**

Critical Thinking

5. **Demonstrating Reasoned Judgment** Suppose you are living in the early 1800s, and your State is considering changing from a governor appointed by the legislature to a popularly elected governor. Choose a side, either for or against this change, and defend your point of view.

6. **Predicting Consequences** What effect on the National Government do you think there would be if the President's cabinet—like the State executive officers—were directly elected by the people?

Take It to the Net

7. Learn more about your governor. Select your State, and then follow the links to your governor's Web site. After reading the information on the site, list five new facts that you learned about your governor and why these facts are important. Use the links provided in the Social Studies area at the following Web site for help in completing this activity. **www.phschool.com**

on Primary Sources

The New Breed of State Legislator

The movement for term limits in the 1990s helped give rise to a new type of State legislator. Newcomers are challenging the traditional leadership and long-established ways of legislatures in several States, including California, Michigan, Ohio, and Florida. This analysis from State Legislatures *magazine examines these trends.*

There was a time when new members came to the legislature, were assigned seats in the back row and made to understand that for a couple of years they should keep quiet and watch. But times have changed. . . . Kathleen A. Stevens is a perfect example. Elected to the Maine House of Representatives when she was only 22 years old, she's . . . perfectly comfortable challenging the powers that be and the way things traditionally have been done.

Kathleen A. Stevens

And because of Maine's term limits, Stevens, who is now 27 and the ranking member of the House Appropriations Committee, is at the end of her career in the House. . . . According to futurist Ed Barlow, . . . state legislatures across the land are increasingly caught up in a subtle interplay between the new kind of lawmaker and the term limits trend, which has both spurred and then suddenly halted their public careers. . . . "History walks out the door when term-limited members have to leave," Barlow says. "These are the people who know . . . how government works, why things have been done the way they [have]." . . .

[The new breed] want to get things done in a hurry. In Michigan such a lawmaker is Mark Jansen, elected to the House only three years ago. . . . "Term limits are good because they give a person like me a chance to take on a real position of leadership," says Jansen. . . . "There are going to be more and more people around here who are less interested in saying that we have to do things a certain way just because that's the way it has always been done. Instead you are going to see a new generation of people just simply looking for a better way." . . .

The new breed is going to make it harder for legislative leaders to achieve consensus . . . That the newer members are more likely to go find their own sources of information and background for bill research also weakens the leadership. "I can get on line and talk to someone in China in a couple of minutes," says [Tom] Davidson in Maine. "The Internet has . . . given new, mostly younger legislators a powerful tool for making their own connections." . . .

As the nation's legislatures swim into the new millennium, the new breed of legislators will not only become more numerous, but prominent as well. . . . "They are going to change the statehouses as we know them very substantially," says Barlow. "In many ways nothing will be the same as it was before."

Analyzing Primary Sources

1. How does this author describe the "new breed" of State legislators?
2. How has the Internet changed State legislatures, in the author's opinion?
3. How do term limits enable young legislators to rise to leadership positions?
4. Why would term limits make these new legislators impatient with the old ways of governing?

·4· *In the Courtroom*

OBJECTIVES

1. **Identify** and define the kinds of law applied in State courts.
2. **Compare and contrast** civil law and criminal law.
3. **Describe** the jury system.

WHY IT MATTERS

Five forms of law make up the code of conduct by which our society is governed. One of the most important of these is common law, which developed through precedent. Law can also be classified as either criminal or civil. Grand juries are sometimes used to indict in criminal cases; petit juries decide cases in trials. Many States are now de-emphasizing the use of both kinds of juries.

POLITICAL DICTIONARY

★ **common law**
★ **precedent**
★ **criminal law**
★ **felony**
★ **misdemeanor**
★ **civil law**
★ **jury**
★ **information**
★ **bench trial**

The principal function of the State courts is to decide disputes between private persons and between private persons and government. In addition, because nearly all of these courts can exercise the power of judicial review, they act as potent checks on the conduct of all of the other agencies of both State and local government.

Kinds of Law Applied in State Courts

The law is the code of conduct by which society is governed.[15] It is made up of several different forms including constitutional law, statutory law, administrative law, common law, and equity.

1. *Constitutional Law.* The highest form of law in this country is based on the provisions of the United States Constitution and the State constitutions and, on judicial interpretations of these documents.

2. *Statutory Law.* This form of law consists of the statutes (laws) enacted by legislative bodies, including the United States Congress, the State legislature, the people (through the initiative or referendum), and city councils and other local legislative bodies.

3. *Administrative Law.* This form of law is composed of the rules, orders, and regulations that are issued by federal, State, or local executive officers, acting under proper constitutional and/or statutory authority.

4. *Common Law.* The common law makes up a large part of the law of each State except Louisiana.[16] **Common law** is unwritten, judge-made law that has developed over centuries from those generally accepted ideas of right and wrong that have gained judicial recognition. It covers nearly all aspects of human conduct. State courts apply common law except when it is in conflict with written law.

The common law originated in England. It grew out of the decisions made by the king's judges on the basis of local customs. It developed as judges, coming upon situations similar to those found in earlier cases, applied and

◄ Colonial courts, like this one, followed British legal tradition.

---

[15] In its overall sense, the term *law* may be defined as the whole body of "rules and principles of conduct which the governing power in a community recognizes as those which it will enforce or sanction, and according to which it will regulate, limit, or protect the conduct of its members"; *Bouvier's Law Dictionary,* 3rd revision, Vol. II.

[16] Because of an early French influence, Louisiana's legal system is largely based on French legal concepts, derived from Roman law. Nevertheless, the common law has worked its way into Louisiana law.

reapplied the rulings from those earlier cases. Thus, little by little, the law of these cases became *common* throughout England and, in time, throughout the English-speaking world. That is, the common law developed as judges followed earlier decisions and applied the rule of *stare decisis*, "let the decision stand."

American courts generally follow that same rule. A decision, once made, becomes a **precedent**, or a guide to be followed in all later, similar cases, unless compelling reasons call for its abandonment and the setting of a new precedent.

The common law is *not* a rigidly fixed body of rules controlled in every case by a clear line of precedents that can be easily found and applied. Judges are regularly called on to interpret and reinterpret the existing rules in the light of changing times and circumstances.

In other words, most legal disputes in American courts are fought out largely over the application of precedents. The opposing lawyers try to persuade the court that the precedents support their side of the case or that the general line of precedents should not, for some reason, be followed.

The importance of the common law in the American legal system cannot be overstated. Statutory law does override common law, but many statutes are based on the common law. Statutes are, in effect, common law translated into written law.

5. *Equity.* This branch of the law supplements common law. It developed in England to provide equity—"fairness, justice, and right"—when remedies under the common law fell short of that goal.

Over the years, English common law became somewhat rigid. Remedies were available only through various writs, or orders, issued by the courts. If no writ was issued to the relief sought in a case, the courts could not act.

Those who were thus barred from the courts—for whom there was no adequate remedy at common law—appealed to the king for justice. These appeals were usually referred to the chancellor, a member of the king's council. By the middle of the fourteenth century, a special court of chancery, or equity, was set up. Over time, a system of rules developed in the chancery court, and equity assumed a permanent place in the English legal system.

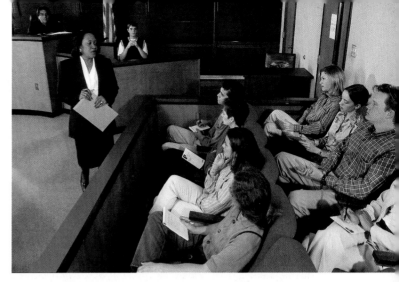

▲ Some people feel that trial juries should be abolished. *Critical Thinking Do you agree, or do you feel that juries are an important part of our legal system? Explain your answer.*

Today, the most important difference between common law and equity is this: The common law is mostly remedial, while equity is preventative. Thus, the common law applies to or provides a remedy for matters *after* they have happened; equity seeks to stop wrongs *before* they occur.

To illustrate this point, suppose your neighbors plan to add a room to their house. You think that a part of the planned addition will be on your land and will destroy your rose garden. You can prevent the construction by getting an injunction, which is a court order prohibiting a specified action by the party named in the order.

A court is likely to grant the injunction for two reasons: (1) the immediacy of the threat to your property, and (2) the fact that the law can offer no fully satisfactory remedy once your garden has been destroyed. It is true that money damages might be assessed under common law, but no amount of money can give back the pride or the pleasure your roses now give you.

The early colonists brought both equity and the common law to America. At first, different courts administered the two forms of law. In time, though, most States provided for the administration of both forms by the same courts, and the procedural differences between the two are disappearing.

Criminal and Civil Law

You have probably heard reference to criminal law and civil law. These are two other categories into which the law is commonly classified.

"He's big, all right, and he's definitely a wolf, but it'll be up to a jury to decide whether or not he's bad."

That portion of the law that defines public wrongs—offenses against the public order—and provides for their punishment is the **criminal law.** A criminal case is brought by the State against a person accused of committing a crime. The State, as the prosecution, is always a party in a criminal case.

Crimes are of two kinds: A **felony** is the greater crime and may be punished by a heavy fine and/or imprisonment or even death. A **misdemeanor** is the lesser offense, punishable by a small fine and/or a short jail term.

The **civil law** relates to human conduct, to disputes between private parties, and to disputes between private parties and government not covered by criminal law. Civil cases are usually referred to as suits, or law suits, and often lead to the award of money or a fine. Civil law can involve a wide range of issues, including divorce and custody disputes, torts (private wrongs against a person or property), and contracts.

The Jury System

A **jury** is a body of persons selected according to law who hear evidence and decide questions of fact in a court case. There are two basic types of juries in the American legal system: (1) the grand jury and (2) the petit jury.

The major function of the grand jury is to determine whether the evidence against a person charged with a crime is sufficient to justify a trial. The grand jury is used only in criminal proceedings. The petit jury is the trial jury, and it is used in both civil and criminal cases.

The Grand Jury

The grand jury has from 6 to 23 persons, depending on the State. Where larger juries are used, generally at least 12 jurors must agree that an accused person is probably guilty before a formal accusation is made. Similarly, with smaller juries, an extraordinary majority is needed to indict, or bring the formal charge.

When a grand jury is impaneled, or selected, the judge instructs the jurors to find a true bill of indictment against any and all persons whom the prosecuting attorney brings to their attention and whom they think are probably guilty. The judge also instructs them to bring a presentment, or accusation, against any persons whom they, of their own knowledge, believe have violated the State's criminal laws.

The grand jury meets in secret. Either the judge appoints or the jurors select one of their number to serve as the foreman or forewoman. The prosecuting attorney presents witnesses and evidence against persons suspected of crime. The jurors may question those witnesses and may also summon others to testify against a suspect.

After receiving the evidence and hearing witnesses, the grand jury deliberates alone and in secret. They then move to the courtroom where their report, including any indictments they may have returned, is read in their presence.

The grand jury is expensive, cumbersome, and time-consuming. Therefore, most of the States today depend more heavily on a much simpler process of accusation: the information.

The Information

An **information** is a formal charge filed by the prosecutor, without the action of a grand jury. It is now used for most minor offenses. More than half the States now use it in most of the more serious cases, as well.

The use of an information has much to recommend it. It is far less costly and time-consuming. Also, since grand juries most often follow the prosecutor's recommendations, many argue that a grand jury is really unnecessary.

The chief objection to abandoning the grand jury appears to be the fear that some prosecutors may abuse their powers and be overzealous at the expense of both defendants and justice.

The Petit Jury

The petit jury, or trial jury, hears the evidence in a case and decides the disputed facts. In a very few instances, it may also have the power to interpret and apply the law. That, however, is usually the function of the judge.

The number of trial jurors may vary. As it developed in England, the jury consisted of "12 men good and true." Although 12 is still the usual number, a lesser number, often six, now fills jury boxes in several States. Today, in all the States, women, as well as men, serve on juries.

In over a third of the States, jury verdicts need not be unanimous in civil and minor criminal cases. Rather, some extraordinary majority is needed. If a jury cannot agree on a verdict (a so-called hung jury), either another trial with a new jury takes place or the matter is dropped.

Misdemeanor cases and civil proceedings in which only minor sums are involved are often heard without a jury, in a **bench trial,** by the judge alone. In several States, even the most serious crimes may be heard without a jury if the accused, fully informed of his or her rights, waives the right to trial by jury.

Selection of Jurors

Jurors are picked in more or less the same way in most States. Periodically, a county official[17] or special jury commissioners prepare a list of persons eligible for jury service. Depending on the State, the lists are drawn from the poll books, the county tax rolls, motor vehicle and drivers license lists, and even public utility and telephone company billings.

The sheriff serves each person with a court order, a writ of *venire facias*, meaning "you must come." After eliminating those who, for good reason, cannot serve, the judge prepares a list of those who can: the panel of *veniremen*. Persons under 18 and over 70 years of age, illiterates, the ill, and criminals are commonly excluded. In many States, those in occupations vital to the public interest or for whom jury service would mean real hardship are often excused, too.

As with the grand jury, the States are moving away from the use of the trial jury. Leading reasons are the greater time and cost of jury trials. The competence of the average jury and the impulses that may lead it to a verdict are often questioned, as well. Much criticism of the jury system is directed not so much at the system itself as at its operation.

Several things should be said in favor of the jury system, however. It has a long and honorable place in the development of Anglo-American law. Its high purpose is to promote a fair trial, by providing an impartial body to hear the charges. A jury tends to bring the common sense of the community to bear on the law and its application. The jury system gives citizens a chance to take part in the administration of justice, and it fosters a greater confidence in the judicial system.

---

[17]It may be the clerk of the court, the sheriff, the county governing body, or the presiding judge; in New England, it is officers of the town.

Section 4 Assessment

Key Terms and Main Ideas

1. Define **common law, criminal law,** and **civil law.**
2. What is the difference between a **felony** and a **misdemeanor?**
3. Name two kinds of **juries,** and tell what they do.
4. What does it mean when a judge follows a legal **precedent?**

Critical Thinking

5. **Checking Consistency** Most processes of government in this country must be open to public scrutiny, but a grand jury works in secret. **(a)** Why do you think this is so? **(b)** Do you think this secrecy is a good idea? Explain your answer.
6. **Identifying Alternatives** Describe a situation in which someone might seek an injunction. Then write a brief argument in favor of granting the injunction and a brief argument against granting this remedy.

 Take It to the Net

7. Read about grand juries and how they operate in the American judicial system. Create an outline of the most important facts about grand juries. Then tell which fact you found most surprising and why. Use the links provided in the Social Studies area at the following Web site for help in completing this activity. **www.phschool.com**

SKILLS FOR LIFE

Serving on a Jury

Someday you may receive a notice ordering you to appear for jury duty. This is a rare opportunity to observe the U.S. justice system at work. That system relies on the participation of ordinary citizens in the judicial process.

Potential jurors are selected from voting lists and summoned to appear at court. How long they must serve varies from place to place. People with certain hardships, such as health, language, or job problems, may be excused from jury duty.

When you arrive at the courthouse, you might be dismissed without having served at all. Or you might be chosen to appear for jury selection. In this phase, lawyers for both sides question potential jurors and select those they think will be favorable to their side. Many people still are rejected at this stage.

If you are chosen for a jury, you and the other jurors will receive instructions prior to the start of trial. The following steps are adapted from those instructions:

1. Do not be influenced by bias. Your decision should not be affected by any sympathies or dislikes you might have for either side in the case. How might you avoid biased thinking?

2. Follow the law as it is explained to you. Your job is to determine whether or not someone broke the law, regardless of whether you approve of the law. Would you find this requirement difficult? Explain.

3. Remember that the defendant is presumed innocent. The government has the burden of proving a defendant guilty beyond a "reasonable doubt." If it fails to do so, then the verdict must be "not guilty." What does "reasonable doubt" mean to you?

4. Keep an open mind. Do not form or state any opinion about the case until you have heard all the evidence, the closing arguments of the lawyers, and the judge's instructions on the applicable law. Why is it important for jurors to base their opinions on evidence and testimony alone?

5. During the trial, do not discuss the case. Do not permit anyone, including fellow jurors, to talk about the case with you or in your presence. Avoid media coverage of the case once the trial has begun. What is the reason for this rule?

Test for Success

Under "three strikes" laws in several States, a person who commits a third felony can be jailed for 25 years to life. Such laws are aimed to keep violent, habitual criminals behind bars. But the laws are also being applied to nonviolent crimes, such as stealing a bicycle. Some juries have resisted convicting people they know are guilty because the possible penalties are so harsh. If you were a juror on such a case, would you vote to convict? Consider the instructions to jurors given on this page.

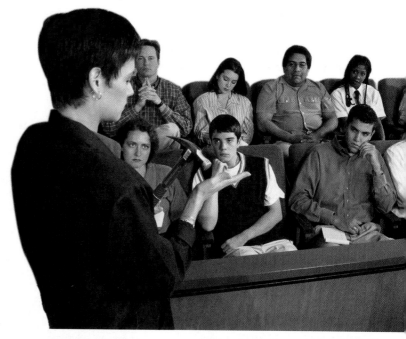

Section Preview

OBJECTIVES

1. **Explain** how State courts are organized and describe the work of each kind of State court.
2. **Examine** and evaluate the different ways that judges are selected.

WHY IT MATTERS

State courts hear tens of thousands of cases each year—criminal and civil. Many of those cases involve only minor offenses or routine disputes. Others involve horrific crimes or quarrels involving millions of dollars.

POLITICAL DICTIONARY

★ **Justice of the Peace**
★ **warrant**
★ **preliminary hearing**
★ **magistrate**
★ **appellate jurisdiction**

They deal with everything from traffic tickets to murder, from disputes over nickels and dimes to settlements involving millions. They are the State courts and the judges who sit in them. In this section, you will read about the way these courts are organized.

Organization

Each of the State constitutions creates a court system for that State; most of these constitutions leave the many important details of court organization to the legislature. The following are some of the common features of those State and local court systems.

Justices of the Peace

Justices of the Peace—JPs—stand on the lowest rung of the State judicial ladder. They preside over what are commonly called justice courts.

JPs were once found nearly everywhere in the country. They have been gradually disappearing for several decades now. In their day—in fact, until well into the 1900s—they served a useful purpose. Travel was difficult, and much of the nation's population was rural. Through a justice court, people could obtain a hearing for a minor offense quickly. Time has largely passed JPs by, however. They and their justice courts have been done away with in many States. However, JPs can still be found in many smaller towns and rural areas.

JPs are usually popularly elected. For the most part, JPs try misdemeanors, which are cases involving such petty offenses as traffic violations, disturbing the peace, public drunkenness, and the like. They can almost never settle civil disputes involving more than a few hundred dollars. They do issue certain kinds of warrants, hold preliminary hearings, and often perform marriages.

▶ Judge Roy Bean (seated at table, at left) tries an accused horse thief in Langtry, Texas, in 1900. In the West of that time, JP's often *were* "the law" in their communities. *Critical Thinking How much confidence would you have had in the justice dispensed in this "courtroom"? Why?*

707

The Juvenile Court Caseload, 1960–1998

SOURCE: *Office of Juvenile Justice and Delinquency Prevention Statistical Briefing Book, 2001*

Interpreting Graphs This graph shows the estimated number of juvenile court cases nationwide. ***During which 10 years did the increase in juvenile court cases level off?***

A **warrant** is a court order authorizing, or making legal, some official action. Search warrant and arrest warrants are the most common. A **preliminary hearing** is generally the first step in a major criminal prosecution. There, the judge decides if the evidence is, in fact, enough to hold that person—bind that person over—for action by the grand jury or the prosecutor.

In some places, JPs are still paid out of the fines they take in. The more and the heavier the fines they impose, the higher their incomes. This "fee system" can lead to any number of abuses. At the very least, it raises serious questions about the fairness of the treatment a defendant can expect.[18]

Magistrates' Courts

Magistrates are the city cousins of JPs. For the most part, magistrates handle those minor civil complaints and misdemeanor cases that arise in an urban setting. They preside over what are generally called magistrates' courts or, in some places, police courts. Those courts are much like the justice courts, with just about the same jurisdiction. Magistrates, like JPs, are usually popularly elected for short terms.

Municipal Courts

Municipal courts were first established in Chicago in 1906. They are now found in most of the nation's larger cities and in many of its middle-sized and small ones.

The jurisdiction of municipal courts is citywide. They can often hear civil cases involving several thousands of dollars as well as the usual run of misdemeanors. Many municipal courts are organized into divisions, which hear cases of a given kind—for example, civil, criminal, small claims, traffic, and probate divisions.

Consider the small claims division, often called the small claims court. Many people cannot afford the costs of suing for the collection of a small debt. A newspaper carrier, for example, can hardly afford a lawyer to collect a month's subscription from a customer. The owner of a two-family house may have the same problem with a tenant's back rent, and many merchants are forced to forget an overdue bill or sell it to a collection agency.

Small claims courts are designed for just such situations. In these courts, a person can bring a claim for little or no cost. The proceedings are usually informal, and the judge often handles the matter without attorneys for either side.

Juvenile Courts

Individuals under 18 years of age are generally not subject to the justice of the courts in which adults are tried. Minors who are arrested for some offense, or who otherwise come to the attention of the police or other authorities, may appear in juvenile courts.

The juvenile justice system is designed to address the special needs and problems of young people. This system generally emphasizes rehabilitation more than punishment. However, under certain circumstances juvenile

---

[18]Many insist that the fee system means that "JP" really stands for "judgment for the plaintiff." The practice also encourages "fee splitting"—an arrangement in which judges can increase the number of misdemeanors they hear by agreeing to share their fees with those arresting officers who bring such cases to them. The "speed trap" is probably the best known and most common result of a fee-splitting situation.

courts do refer certain offenders to an adult criminal court for trial.

During the 1990s, States responded to growing alarm over serious, violent juvenile crime by revising their juvenile crime laws. From 1992 through 1995, 40 States and the District of Columbia passed laws making it easier for juveniles to be tried as adults.

In all but four States (Massachusetts, Nebraska, New Mexico, and New York), juvenile court judges have the power to assign certain cases involving juveniles to adult courts. In 14 States, cases that meet certain standards (concerning the age of the defendant, the nature of the offense, or some other factor) *must* be tried in adult courts. Thirty-one States now have "once an adult/always an adult" provisions. Under these provisions, juveniles who have been prosecuted as adults one time are automatically prosecuted as adults for later offenses.

General Trial Courts

Most of the more important civil and criminal cases heard in the United States are heard in the States' general trial courts. Every State is divided into a number of judicial districts, or circuits, each generally covering one or more counties. For each district there is a general trial court, which may be known as a district, circuit, chancery, county, or superior court, or as a court of common pleas. Most legal actions brought under State law begin in these courts.

These general trial courts are courts of "first instance." That is, they exercise original jurisdiction over most of the cases they hear. When cases do come to them on appeal from some lower court, a trial *de novo* (a new trial, as though the case had not been heard before) is usually held.

The cases heard in trial courts are tried before a single judge. Most often a petit jury (the trial jury) hears and decides the facts at issue in a case, and the judge interprets and applies the applicable law. Criminal cases are presented for trial either by a grand jury or, most often, on motion of the prosecuting attorney.

The trial court is seldom limited as to the kinds of cases it may hear. Although this court's decision on the facts in a case is usually final, disputes over questions of law may be carried to a higher court.

In the more heavily populated districts of some States, cases involving such matters as the

Interpreting Political Cartoons (a) What does the cartoon suggest about the use of the appeals process in this country? (b) Should those convicted of a crime be able to appeal their convictions as many times as they wish? Explain your answer.

settlement of estates or the affairs of minors are heard in separate trial courts. These tribunals are often called surrogate, probate, or orphans' courts. In most States and districts, however, these matters are part of the regular caseload of the general trial courts.

Intermediate Appellate Courts

All but a few States now have one or more intermediate appellate courts. They are courts of appeal that stand between the trial courts and the State's supreme court. These appellate courts serve to ease the burden of the State's high court.

The appellate courts have different names among the States, but they are most often called the court of appeals.[19] Most of their work involves the review of cases decided in the trial courts. That is, these appeals courts exercise mostly **appellate jurisdiction.** Their original jurisdiction, where it exists, is limited to a few specific kinds of cases—election disputes, for example.

In exercising their appellate jurisdiction, these courts do not hold trials. Rather, they hear oral arguments from attorneys, study the briefs (written arguments) that attorneys submit, and review the record of the case in the lower court.

---

[19] In New York, the general trial court is called the supreme court; the intermediate appellate court is the appellate division of the supreme court; the State's highest court is known as the Court of Appeals.

Crime Rates of Selected Countries

Country	Offenses Reported to the Police per 100,000 People				
	Total*	Personal		Property	
		Murder	Assault	Burglary	Automobile Theft
Bangladesh	64	1.9	3.6	4.6	0.6
Finland	14,799	0.6	40.0	1,934.9	53.2
Hungary	3,789	4.3	79.3	767.4	51.1
Kenya	484	6.4	54.1	76.9	9.7
Jordan	751	2.0	19.1	43.4	28.5
Kuwait	1,171	1.7	46.5	75.9	18.2
Japan	1,490	1.0	14.4	198.1	27.8
Peru	1,178	9.3	104.3	87.0	22.7
Canada	10,351	5.2	769.1	1,326.2	545.9
Thailand	351	7.7	25.4	9.9	3.3
United States	5,374	9.0	430.2	1,041.8	591.2

*Figure for total offenses reported includes crimes other than those listed in the table.

SOURCE: *Encyclopaedia Britannica, Book of the Year,* 1999

Interpreting Tables This table shows only the crimes reported to the police, and then breaks out only certain kinds of crimes. *(a) Which country has the highest number of reported crimes per 100,000 people? (b) What kinds of crimes are committed most often there? (c) Which kinds are rare?*

Ordinarily, an appellate court does not concern itself with the facts in a case. Rather, its decision turns on whether the law was correctly interpreted and applied in the court below. Its decision may be reviewed by the State's high court, but its disposition of a case is usually final.

The State Supreme Court

The State's supreme court is the highest court in its judicial system.[20] Its major function is to review the decisions of lower courts in those cases that are appealed to it.

The size of each State supreme court is fixed by each State constitution. In most States, five or seven justices sit on the high bench.

In 24 States, the governor appoints the justices, including a chief justice. These justices are selected by the legislature in 4 States, and by the voters in the other 22.

The State supreme court is the court of last resort in the State's judicial system. It has the final say in all matters of State law. Remember, however, that many cases also raise questions of federal law. So, the United States Supreme Court may review some State supreme court decisions. But not very many State decisions actually go to the federal Supreme Court.[21] Recall that an appeal from a State's high court will be heard in the federal Supreme Court only if (1) a "federal question," meaning some matter of federal law, is involved in the case and (2) the Supreme Court agrees to hear that appeal.

In short, most State supreme court decisions are final. The oft-heard claim, "I'll fight this case all the way to the United States Supreme Court," is almost always just so much hot air—or misinformation about the State judicial system.[22]

Unified Court Systems

The typical State court system is organized geographically rather than by types of cases. Thus, the general trial courts are most often organized so that each hears those cases arising within its own district, circuit, or county, no matter what the subject matter may be.

In these map-based systems, a judge must hear cases in nearly all areas of the law. A backlog of cases can and often does build up in some courts while judges sit with little to do in others. Moreover, uneven interpretations and applications of the law may and sometimes do occur from one part of the State to another.

To overcome these difficulties, a number of States have recently begun to abandon geographical organization. They have turned, instead, to a

---

[20]The State's highest court is known as the Supreme Court in 45 States. But in Maine and Massachusetts it is called the Supreme Judicial Court; in Maryland and New York, the Court of Appeals; and in West Virginia, the Supreme Court of Appeals. Two States actually have two high courts. In Oklahoma and in Texas, the Supreme Court is the highest court in civil cases, and a separate Court of Criminal Appeals is the court of last resort in criminal cases.

[21]Many of the cases that have reached the Supreme Court involved the 14th Amendment's Due Process and Equal Protection clauses.

[22]State law regularly gives its lower courts final jurisdiction over many types of minor cases. That is, review cannot be sought in a higher State court. In those cases, the lower court is the State's court of last resort. If any review is to be had, it can be only in the United States Supreme Court. Such reviews are extremely rare.

unified court system, one that is organized on a functional, or case-type, basis.

In a completely unified court system, there is technically only one court for the entire State. It is presided over a chief judge or judicial council. There are a number of levels within the single court, such as supreme, intermediate appellate, and general trial sections. At each level within each section, divisions are established to hear cases in certain specialized or heavy-caseload areas of the law—criminal, juvenile, family relations, and other areas that need special attention.

In such an arrangement, a judge can be assigned to that section or division to which his or her talents and interests seem best suited. To relieve overcrowded dockets, judges may be moved from one section or division to another. In short, the unified court system is a modern response to the old common law adage: "Justice delayed is justice denied."

Selection of Judges

More than 15,000 judges sit in the State trial and appellate courts today. They are most often chosen in one of three ways: (1) by popular election, (2) by appointment by the governor, or (3) by appointment by the legislature.[23]

Popular election is by far the most widely used method by which judges are selected. The voters choose about three fourths of all judges sitting in American courts today. In fact, in 10 States popular election is the only method by which judges are chosen.[24] (The exception is that vacancies caused by deaths or by midterm resignations are usually filled by appointments made by the governor.) In most of the other States, at least some judges are also chosen at the polls. About half of all judicial elections are nonpartisan contests today.

Selection by the legislature is used least often. The legislature now chooses all or at least most judges in only three States: Connecticut, South Carolina, and Virginia.

The governor appoints nearly a fourth of all State judges today. In three States—Delaware, Massachusetts, and New Hampshire—the governor names all judges. In several other States, the governor has the power to appoint all or many judges, but under a Missouri Plan arrangement, as you will see.

How Should Judges Be Selected?

Most people believe that judges should be independent, that they should "stay out of politics." Whatever method of selection is used should be designed with that goal in mind.

Nearly all authorities agree that selection by the legislature is the most political of all the

---

[23]Some judges are selected by other means in some States. In Ohio, for example, all judges, except those of the Court of Claims, are elected by the voters; the judges of the Court of Claims are appointed by the Chief Justice of the State Supreme Court. In Alabama, Michigan, Mississippi, Oregon, Texas, and Washington, all judges are popularly elected except for municipal court judges, who are chosen in accord with city charter provisions, usually by the city council.
[24]The 10 States are Arkansas, Kentucky, Louisiana, Minnesota, Montana, Nevada, North Dakota, Texas, West Virginia, and Wisconsin.

▲ California judges are elected and campaign along with others running for office (at left). In Hawaii, Circuit Court judges, such as Judge Riki May Amano (at right), are appointed by the governor. *Critical Thinking* **(a) What are the pros and cons for each method of selecting judges? (b) Is one method better than the other for selecting quality judges? Explain your answer.**

methods of choice. Few favor it. So, the question really is: Which is better, popular election of judges or appointment by the governor?

Those who favor popular election generally make the democratic argument. Because judges "say the law," interpret and apply it, they should be chosen by and answer directly to the people. Some also argue that the concept of separation of powers is undercut if the executive (the governor) has the power to name the members of the judicial branch.

Those who favor appointment by the governor argue that the judicial function should be carried out only by those who are well qualified. The fact that a person has the support of a political party or is a good vote-getter does not mean that person has the capacity to be a good judge. Proponents of executive appointment insist that it is the best way to ensure that those persons who preside in courts will have the qualities most needed in that role: absolute honesty and integrity, fairness, and the necessary training and ability in the law.

At best, deciding between these two positions is difficult. The people have often made excellent choices, and governors have not always made wise and nonpolitical ones. Still, most authorities come down on the side of gubernatorial appointment, largely because those characteristics that make a good judge and those that make a good candidate are not often found in the same person.

Popular election is both widely used and widely supported. Moves to abandon it have been strongly opposed by party organizations. So, most moves to revise the method of judicial selection have kept at least some element of voter choice.

The Missouri Plan

For more than 75 years now, the American Bar Association (ABA) has sponsored an approach that combines the election and appointment processes. Because its adoption in Missouri in 1940 involved much political drama and attracted wide attention, the method is often called the Missouri Plan. Some form of the Missouri Plan is now in place in just over half of the States.

Missouri's version is still more or less representative of how the plan is implemented in the other States that use it. The governor appoints the seven justices of the State's supreme court, the 32 judges of the court of appeals, and all judges who sit in certain of the State's trial courts. The governor must make each appointment from a panel, or list, of three candidates recommended by a judicial nominating commission. The commission is made up of a sitting judge, several members of the bar, and private citizens.

Each judge named by the governor serves until the first general election after he or she has been in office for at least a year. The judge's name then appears on the ballot—without opposition. The voters decide whether or not that judge should be kept in office.

If the vote is favorable, the judge then serves a regular term: six years for a trial court judge and 12 years for one who sits on a higher court in Missouri. Thereafter, the judge may seek further terms in future retain-reject elections. Should the voters reject a sitting judge, the process begins again.

Section 5 Assessment

Key Terms and Main Ideas

1. Compare and contrast **Justices of the Peace** and **magistrates**.
2. (a) What is **appellate jurisdiction?** (b) Which State courts have this jurisdiction?
3. Describe the work of the general trial courts.
4. What is a **warrant?** Why are warrants important?

Critical Thinking

5. **Demonstrating Reasoned Judgment** How do you think judges should be selected? Choose one of the methods described in this section, and "make a case for it" by creating a strong, well-supported argument in its favor.

6. **Drawing Inferences** What qualities make a good judge? Write job descriptions or "want ads" for two of the following: a magistrate, a general court judge, an appellate judge.

 Take It to the Net

7. To learn more about your State's highest court, follow the links to your State judicial system and then to the highest court in the State. Make a chart or table showing how the court is organized and what it does. Use the links provided in the Social Studies area at the following Web site for help in completing this activity. **www.phschool.com**

on the Supreme Court

Can States Restrict Undesirable Imports?

The Commerce Clause (Article 1, Section 8, Clause 3) gives Congress the power to regulate interstate trade. Thus States generally cannot restrict the flow of goods and services from other States. Does this mean that a State cannot prevent the importing of certain items that it believes will be harmful to its residents' quality of life?

City of Philadelphia v. New Jersey (1978)

In the early 1970s, the amount of solid and liquid waste in New Jersey was increasing rapidly, and waste disposal sites in the State were beginning to fill up. The State legislature decided that "the public health, safety and welfare require that the treatment and disposal within this State of all wastes generated outside of the State be prohibited." In 1973 it passed a law banning any person from bringing into New Jersey any solid or liquid waste from outside the State, except garbage to be fed to pigs. The State Commissioner of Environmental Protection had authority to make specific exceptions to the ban. The Commissioner issued rules excepting four narrow categories of waste.

The law affected not only the operators of private landfills in New Jersey, but also the cities in other States that had contracts with those landfills. Several cities and landfill operators sued New Jersey and its Department of Environmental Protection in State court, where the judge declared the law unconstitutional because it violated the Commerce Clause. On appeal, the State supreme court reversed the ruling of the lower court. The court declared that the law was constitutional because it had significant health and environmental objectives and did not discriminate against or place an excessive burden on interstate commerce. The plaintiffs then appealed to the United States Supreme Court.

Arguments for City of Philadelphia

1. Restricting the importation of waste products is a form of regulation of interstate trade. This is a power that the Constitution gives to Congress, not the States.

2. The law discriminates against out-of-state waste simply because of its origin. States may not constitutionally discriminate against articles of commerce produced outside the State.

3. The law makes out-of-state businesses bear the full burden of conserving New Jersey's remaining landfill space. States may not try to isolate themselves from a problem that is common to many States by creating a barrier to interstate trade.

Arguments for New Jersey

1. The movement of waste is not "commerce" as that term is used in the Constitution, because waste, unlike legitimate articles of commerce, cannot be put to effective use.

2. States should have great flexibility in deciding to ban harmful or potentially harmful articles from their territory.

3. The restriction on waste significantly benefits the State's environment and affects interstate commerce only minimally, at most.

Decide for Yourself

1. Review the constitutional grounds on which each side based its arguments and the specific arguments each side presented.

2. Debate the opposing viewpoints presented in this case. Which viewpoint do you favor?

3. Predict the impact of the Court's decision on efforts by the individual States and by the Federal Government to improve the environment. (To read a summary of the Court's decision, turn to the Supreme Court Glossary on page 799.)

CHAPTER 24 · Assessment

Political Dictionary

popular sovereignty (p. 685)
limited government (p. 685)
fundamental law (p. 686)
initiative (p. 687)
statutory law (p. 688)
police power (p. 691)
constituent power (p. 692)
referendum (p. 693)
recall (p. 696)
item veto (p. 699)

clemency (p. 699)
pardon (p. 699)
commutation (p. 699)
reprieve (p. 699)
parole (p. 699)
common law (p. 702)
precedent (p. 703)
criminal law (p. 704)
felony (p. 704)
misdemeanor (p. 704)

civil law (p. 704)
jury (p. 704)
information (p. 704)
bench trial (p. 705)
Justice of the Peace (p. 707)
warrant (p. 708)
preliminary hearing (p. 708)
magistrate (p. 708)
appellate jurisdiction (p. 709)

Practicing the Vocabulary

Using Words in Context *For each of the terms below, write a sentence that shows how it relates to this chapter.*

1. popular sovereignty
2. reprieve
3. referendum
4. item veto
5. police power
6. civil law
7. bench trial
8. Justice of the Peace
9. appellate jurisdiction
10. warrant

Fill in the Blank *Choose a term from the list above that best completes each sentence.*

11. The power of executive _____ includes the power to pardon or parole a convicted criminal.
12. Laws passed by the legislature are called _____.
13. A _____ is a more serious offense than a misdemeanor.
14. A _____ is the city cousin of a Justice of the Peace.
15. The _____ is a process by which voters can petition to propose constitutional amendments and legislation.
16. The basis of much American law is the unwritten, judge-made law called _____ which developed in England.

Reviewing Main Ideas

Section 1

17. What are the basic principles on which all State constitutions are based?
18. What kinds of provisions are found in all State constitutions?
19. Describe the two basic steps of constitutional change.
20. Name at least two reasons why many State constitutions are in need of reform.

Section 2

21. What powers does a State legislature have?
22. How are State legislators chosen?
23. (a) What are the usual steps in the legislative process? (b) Describe the initiative and referendum processes that are available in several States.

Section 3

24. List the powers of the governor.
25. In what ways is a governor only *the chief executive* rather than *the executive* in State government?

26. Name three other executive officers in State government and describe what they do.

Section 4

27. Name and describe the four kinds of law applied in the State courts.
28. What is the importance of common law to our judicial system?
29. (a) What are the two most common kinds of juries? (b) Describe what each does.

Section 5

30. What are the functions of magistrates' courts, general trial courts, intermediate appellate courts, and State supreme courts?
31. (a) What are the three ways by which judges are selected? (b) Which is the most widely used method? (c) Which two methods does the Missouri Plan combine?

Critical Thinking

32. *Applying the Chapter Skill* Contact the office of the jury commissioner or similar official in your district, and find out the kinds of juries on which you are eligible to serve (or will be, when you turn 18). For example, are you eligible to serve on a grand jury or just a petit, or trial, jury? Can you serve in both civil and criminal matters? Make a list of the courts, the kinds of cases, and the locations where you would be eligible to serve.

33. *Identifying Central Issues* Describe how the system of checks and balances works in State government. What limits does each branch of government place on the other two? Then compare these checks and balances with those in the federal system.

34. *Recognizing Ideologies* There is a long history in this country of relying on "a jury of one's peers" to decide court cases. **(a)** What does that suggest about traditional American beliefs concerning ordinary citizens and government officials? **(b)** What does the recent trend away from the jury system suggest about current American attitudes?

35. *Checking Consistency* The governor is both the chief executive and, in a sense, the chief legislator in State government. **(a)** Explain why this is true. **(b)** Does this arrangement violate the principle of separation of powers? Explain.

Analyzing Political Cartoons

Using your knowledge of American government and this cartoon, answer the questions below.

"We all make mistakes, as Your Honor knows, having been twice reprimanded by the New York State Commission on Judicial Conduct."

36. What does this cartoon suggest about checks and balances in State government?

37. Do you think this cartoonist favors more or less control of the judiciary by other branches of government or by the voters? Explain your answer.

★ You Can Make a Difference

If you were talking with visitors about the history of your own State, what could you tell them? What native peoples lived where you live now? Do you know who the first European or Asian settlers of your area were? Why did they choose to live here? Use resources from your local historical society and from the State historical society to prepare a display and map of the early history of your State. If possible, use copies of drawings or photographs of the native peoples and of the settlers and their settlements.

Participation Activities

38. *Current Events Watch* Write a biographical sketch of the governor of your State. Trace his or her life from childhood to the governorship. Attempt to find the major factors—family, school, other experiences—that most influenced the shaping of the governor's character and abilities. Review the governor's political career, and try to discover why he or she entered politics. Assess the ways in which the governor uses the powers of the office, and his or her powers of persuasion. Include comments on the relationships between the governor and the media, special interests, and the voters of your State.

39. *Diagraming Activity* Using the information in this chapter and additional research, make a diagram of the major steps in changing a State constitution. Include both the revision and the amendment processes.

40. *It's Your Turn* Your State is considering the Missouri Plan for selecting judges. Take a position for or against the plan, and write a speech to deliver at a hearing on the subject. State your position clearly, and support it with reasons and facts. Remember, your audience will be listening to—not reading—your speech. **(Writing a Speech)**

Take It to the Net

Chapter 24 Self-Test As a final review activity, take the Chapter 24 Self-Test in the Social Studies area at the Web site listed below, and receive immediate feedback on your answers.

www.phschool.com

CHAPTER 25

Local Government and Finance

"In a great city, City Hall must be a beacon to the people's aspirations, not a barrier."

—Los Angeles Mayor Thomas Bradley, (1973–1993)

As Mayor Bradley knew, city government—"city hall"—is the level of government that most people look to for help and services. In addition to cities and towns, other local government units, such as counties and townships, provide various services. To finance public services, both State and local governments must raise revenue, mainly through taxes.

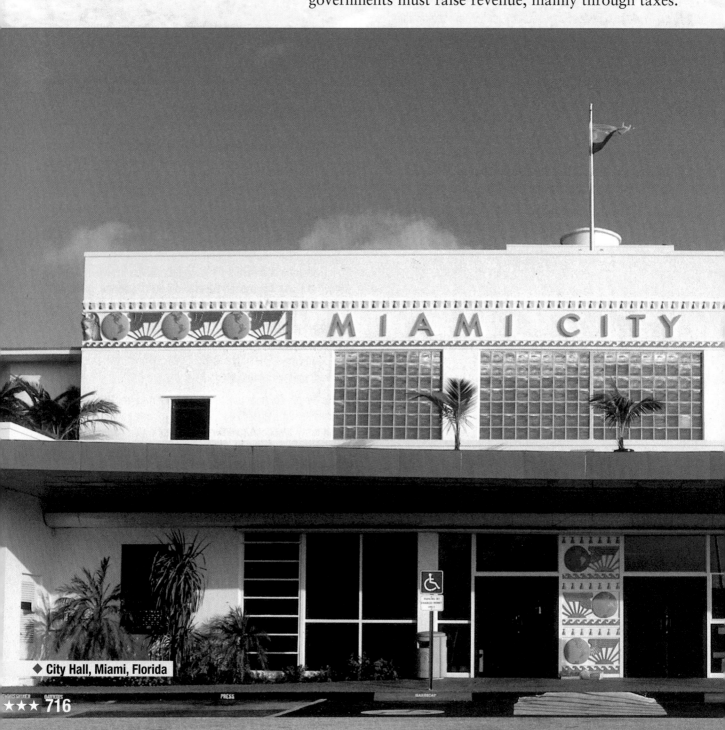

◆ City Hall, Miami, Florida

You Can Make a Difference

NO MATTER HOW many services a city provides, communities need volunteers of all ages. In Washington, D.C., a diverse group of young people work with DC-YAR, part of the organization Youth As Resources, to bridge cultural and racial differences and to support grass-roots projects for other urban youth. Bsrat Mezghebe and N'erin Brown, both high school juniors, served on the DC-YAR board. There they reviewed project proposals from other young people, such as a community spring cleanup and a book of children's stories about different cultures. N'erin was impressed that "so many youth were into helping the community. They're helping to regenerate our generation."

Keep It Current

Items marked with this logo are periodically updated on the Internet. Keep up-to-date with what's in the news. To get current information on local government and finance, go to **www.phschool.com**

SECTION 1

Counties, Towns, and Townships (pp. 718–723)

★ Counties or their equivalents exist in all but two States. Their functions vary depending on region.
★ Many people see a need to make county government more efficient.
★ Towns and townships are forms of local government that exist in certain parts of the country.
★ Special districts provide a wide variety of services, including education, water and sewage, police and fire, and airport and park services.

SECTION 2

Cities and Metropolitan Areas (pp. 725–732)

★ Most Americans today live in urban areas.
★ The process by which a State establishes a city as a legal body is called *incorporation*.
★ City governments take one of three forms: mayor-council, commission, or council-manager.
★ Population shifts from cities to suburbs have left cities with fewer resources. One response has been the creation of metropolitan districts.

SECTION 3

Providing Important Services (pp. 733–737)

★ Under the federal system, States and their local governments have many powers and provide many important services.
★ State and local governments provide education, help ensure public welfare and safety, and build and maintain highways.
★ State and local governments vary widely in the amount and types of services they provide.

SECTION 4

Financing State and Local Government (pp. 739–744)

★ The federal Constitution, the 14th Amendment, and State constitutions restrict State and local taxing powers.
★ Most tax experts agree with Scottish economist Adam Smith that there are four principles of sound taxation.
★ State and local governments rely on a variety of tax and nontax sources of revenue.
★ The State budget is the means by which States plan the control and use of public money.

Counties, Towns, and Townships

Section Preview

OBJECTIVES

1. **Describe** the typical county.
2. **Examine** the governmental structure of counties.
3. **Identify** the functions of counties.
4. **Analyze** the need for reform in county government.
5. **Examine** the governments of towns, townships, and special districts.

WHY IT MATTERS

Do you live in a county? Or are you one of the 10 percent of Americans who live in an area without county government? Do you live in a town, township, or special district? If you live within the jurisdiction of any of these local governments, your daily life is affected by the decisions that these governments make.

POLITICAL DICTIONARY

★ **county**
★ **township**
★ **special district**

Washington, D.C., has the Capitol, and your State has its own impressive capitol building. These structures serve as centers for federal and State governments. In most communities, however, local government has no grand dome. Government in these places is visible mainly in the form of the day-to-day services that keep communities going.

In spite of its humble appearance, local government is vitally important in the lives of every American. As one measure of this fact, recall that of the 87,504 units of government across the nation, 87,453 of them are local.

Counties

A **county** is a major unit of local government in most States. Like all local governments, it is created by the State.[1] There are 3,043 counties in the United States. No close relationship exists between the size of a State and the number of counties it has. The number of counties in a given State runs from none in Connecticut and Rhode Island to as many as 254 in Texas.

In Louisiana, units of government known elsewhere as counties are called parishes. In Alaska, they are known as boroughs. In addition to Connecticut and Rhode Island, several other places across the country have no organized county government. Almost 10 percent of the nation's population lives in those areas today.

The function of counties varies from region to region. Counties serve almost solely as judicial districts in the New England States. There, towns carry out most of the functions undertaken by counties elsewhere. In many Mid-Atlantic and Midwestern States, counties are divided into subdivisions called **townships.** In these States, counties and townships share the functions of rural local government. In the South and the

---

▲ Homer, Alaska, is just one of the nation's 87,453 units of local government.

[1]Recall that whether they are providing services, regulating activities, collecting taxes, or doing anything else, local governments can only act because the State has established them and has given them power to do so.

West, counties are the major units of government in rural areas.

In terms of area, San Bernardino County in southern California is the largest in the United States, covering 20,064 square miles. Kalawao County in Hawaii is the smallest, covering only 13 square miles. Counties within each State can vary widely in area.

Counties also differ greatly in terms of population. More than 9 million people now live in Los Angeles County in California, but census-takers could find only 67 residents of Loving County, in West Texas, in 2000. Most counties—in fact nearly three fourths of them—serve populations of fewer than 50,000.

Typical County Government Structure

Voters

elect

County Board
Governing body

appoints

Planning Commission

Budget Committee

County Agent

Boards and Officials
Board of Health, Welfare Commission, Library Board, and others

elect

Other County Officials
Sheriff
District attorney
Clerk
School superintendent
Assessor
Treasurer
Auditor
Coroner

Interpreting Diagrams A typical county government has a governing body, a number of boards or commissions, appointed bureaucrats, and elected officials. *Why might the fact that the county governing body shares its powers with other elected officials lead to confusion?*

Government Structure

The structures of county government differ, often considerably. Even so, a county typically has four major elements: a governing body, a number of boards or commissions, appointed bureaucrats, and a variety of elected officials.

The Governing Body

The county's governing body is often called the county board. It is also known as the board of commissioners, board of supervisors, police jury, fiscal court, county court, and board of chosen freeholders, among other names.

The members of this governing body are almost always popularly elected. Terms of office run from one to eight years, but four-year terms are the most common.

Generally, county boards can be grouped into two types: boards of commissioners and boards of supervisors. The board of commissioners is the smaller and more common type. It is found everywhere in the South and West, and is also common elsewhere. A board of commisioners most often has three or five members, but some have seven or more.

The board of supervisors is typically a much larger body. It averages about 15 members, but sometimes runs to 80 or more. The supervisors are elected from each township in the county, as in New York, Nebraska, and Wisconsin. Each supervisor is usually an officer of his or her township, as well as a member of the countywide governing body.

The State constitution and acts of the State legislature spell out the powers held by county governing bodies. The powers of these boards are generally both executive and legislative, despite the American tradition of separation of powers.

County governments' most important legislative powers deal with finance. Everywhere, county boards levy taxes, appropriate funds, and incur limited debts. They also have a number of lesser legislative powers, such as passing health and zoning ordinances.

Most county boards also carry out a number of administrative functions. They supervise the county road program and manage county property, such as the courthouse, jails, hospitals, and parks. County boards are often responsible for the administration of welfare (cash assistance) programs and the conduct of elections. They also appoint certain county officers, deputies, and assistants of many kinds, as well as most other county employees. In addition, they determine the salaries of most county employees.

Typical Elected County Officials and Their Duties

Official	Duties
SHERIFF	Runs county jail; provides police protection in rural areas; carries out local court orders; often collects taxes
CLERK	Registers and records documents such as deeds, mortgages, birth/death certificates; often runs county elections; is secretary to county board and clerk of local courts
ASSESSOR	Appraises (sets the value of) taxable property in the county and collects county property taxes
TREASURER	Keeps county funds; makes payments from these funds
AUDITOR	Keeps financial records; authorizes payments for county expenses
DISTRICT ATTORNEY	Conducts criminal investigations; prosecutes criminal cases
SCHOOL SUPERINTENDENT	Administers public elementary and secondary schools in the county
CORONER	Investigates violent deaths; certifies causes of deaths not attended by a physician

Interpreting Tables Elected county officials include people with a wide range of responsibilities that affect local communities. For example, surveyors like the woman pictured here help map local property accurately. *Which of these officials might affect your own daily life?*

Other Elements

In addition to the county board, county government includes the following:

Boards and commissions. Various boards and commissions, whose members can be appointed or elected, have authority over a number of county functions. Members of these boards often serve *ex officio* (because of their office) on one or more of these other agencies.

Bureaucracy. Counties also employ more than 2 million men and women. They do the day-to-day work of each of the nation's 3,043 counties.

Elected officials. A number of officials with countywide jurisdiction are elected separately. Some of these officers and their principal duties are shown in the table on this page.

Functions of Counties

Because counties are creations of the State, they are responsible for the administration of State laws. They also administer such county laws as the State's constitution and legislature allow them to make.

Historically, counties have been institutions of rural government. Most counties remain rurally oriented today. Although there is some difference from State to State, the major functions of counties reflect their rural character.

The most common functions of counties are to keep the peace and maintain jails and other correctional facilities; assess property for tax purposes; collect taxes and spend county funds; build and repair roads, bridges, drains, and other such public works; and maintain schools. Counties record deeds, mortgages, marriage licenses, and other documents; issue licenses for such things as hunting, fishing, and marriage; administer elections; care for the poor; and protect the health of the people who live in the county.

Many counties have taken on other functions as they have become more urban.[2] Several of these more heavily populated counties now offer many of the public services and facilities that are usually found in cities. They do such things as provide water and sewer service; have professionally trained police, fire, and medical units; and operate airports and mass transit systems. Some also enforce zoning and other land-use regulations. Many have built and now operate auditoriums, sports stadiums, golf courses, and other recreational facilities.

The Need for Reform

County organization is often chaotic. In the typical county, no single official can be called the chief administrator. Rather, authority is divided

---

[2]Nearly two thirds of the people in the United States who live in counties live within the boundaries of just 447 of the nation's 3,043 counties.

among a number of elected boards and officials, each largely independent of the others. As a result, it is often impossible to identify who is responsible for the inefficiency, inaction, or worse, in the conduct of county affairs.

The large number of popularly elected officials adds to the chaos. Faced with the long ballots that typify county elections, voters are hard pressed to cast the informed votes on which good government depends. Further, many elected county officials hold jobs that have nothing to do with the making of basic public policy. These jobs do, however, demand a variety of professional qualifications. Many people therefore believe that popular election is not the best way to fill those offices.

The size and the number of counties in most States are another source of weakness. Nearly every one of the counties now in existence was laid out in the days of the horse and the stagecoach. Then, it made good sense to draw county lines so that no one lived more than a dozen miles or so from the county seat. Today, however, most counties are geographically ill-suited to the realities of State government.

One way in which many States have attempted to reform county government is through county home rule. In other words, these States allow some or all of their counties, subject to approval by the local voters, to decide the details of their own governmental structure. Today, thirty-seven States permit their counties some degree of home rule. While only a small proportion of counties has taken advantage of this option, those that have include most of the nation's largest counties.

Another kind of reform seeks to deal with the fragmented authority of counties. It does so by creating the position of county manager, modeled along the lines of the council-manager form of city government. (See Section 2 for an explanation of different forms of city government.) Still another approach is county-city consolidation. In this plan, a major city and the county around it join into a single unit of government. San Francisco and Denver are examples of such mergers.

Towns and Townships

Towns and townships are other units of local government. They are found in nearly half the States, throughout the region stretching from New England to the Midwest.[3]

The New England Town

In New England, the town is a major unit of local government. Except for a few major cities, each of the six States in the region is divided into towns. Each town generally includes all of the rural and the urban areas within its boundaries. The town delivers most of the services that are the responsibility of cities and counties elsewhere in the country.

The roots of the New England town reach back to colonial times. The Pilgrims landed at Plymouth Rock in 1620 as an organized congregation. They quickly set up a close-knit community in which their church and their government were almost one. Other Puritan congregations followed the Pilgrims' pattern.

The desire to be near the church, the real or perceived threat from Native Americans, the severe climate, and the fact that the land was not suited to large farms or plantations led the settlers to form tight little communities. Their settlements were soon known as towns, as in England.[4]

At least in form, much of town government today is little changed from colonial times. The main feature is the town meeting, long praised as the ideal vehicle of direct democracy. The town meeting is an assembly open to all the town's eligible voters. It meets yearly, and sometimes more often, to levy taxes, make spending and other policy decisions, and elect officers for the next year.

Between town meetings, the board of selectmen/select-women chosen at the annual meeting manages the town's business. Typically, the board is a three-member body and has responsibilities for such things as roads, schools, care of the poor, and sanitation. Other officers regularly selected at the annual meeting include

---

[3]The term *town* is used in some States as the legal designation for smaller urban places; it is also sometimes used as another word for township. Township is also a federal public lands survey term, used to identify geographic units (often called congressional townships), each having exactly 36 square miles (36 sections).

[4]When a clan in England or in Northern Europe settled in a particular place, it usually built a wall around it. In Old English, the word for wall was *tun*. In time, the space within the wall became known as the *tun*, and then the town. As the New England towns grew in number and in population, it became necessary to survey their boundaries. The small and irregular shapes that resulted were called "townships" (town shapes). The suffix *ship* comes from the Old English word *scip,* meaning "shape."

▲ The tradition of the town meeting is still alive in many small New England towns. *Critical Thinking How does the town meeting reflect the ideal of direct democracy?*

the town clerk, a tax assessor, a tax collector, a constable, road commissioners, and school board members.

The ideal of direct democracy is still alive in many smaller New England towns. It has given way, however, to the pressures of time, population, and the complexities of public problems in many larger towns. There, representative government has largely replaced it. Town officers are often elected before the yearly gathering. Many of the decisions once made by the assembled voters are now made by the selectmen and selectwomen. In recent years, several towns have gone to a town manager system for the day-to-day administration of local affairs.

Townships

Townships are found as units of local government from New York and New Jersey west to North and South Dakota, Nebraska, and Kansas. In none of those States do townships blanket the State, however.

In New York, New Jersey, and Pennsylvania, townships were formed as areas were settled and the people needed the services of local government. Consequently, the township maps of those States often resemble crazy-quilts. From Ohio westward, however, township lines are more regular. They mostly follow the lines drawn in federal public land surveys. Many are perfect squares.

About half of these States provide for annual township meetings, like those held in New England towns. Otherwise, the governing body is a three- or five-member board, generally called the board of trustees or board of supervisors. Its members are elected for two-year or four-year terms, or they serve because they hold other elected township offices. Township offices often include a supervisor, a clerk, a treasurer, an assessor, a constable, a justice of the peace, and a body of road commissioners.

A municipality (urban political unit) within a township—especially if it is large—usually exists as a separate governmental entity. Thus, township functions tend to be rural. They involve such matters as roads, cemeteries, drainage, and minor law enforcement. In some States, however, the township is also the basic unit of public school administration.

Many people believe that townships have outlived their usefulness. More than half the States get along without them, suggesting that they are not indispensable. Many rural townships have been abolished in the past few decades. They have fallen victim to declining populations, improvements in transportation, and a host of other factors.

Some of the more densely populated townships appear to have brighter futures than their country cousins, however. This seems especially true in the suburban areas around some larger cities. Some States, such as Pennsylvania, now allow townships to exercise many of the powers and furnish many of the services once reserved to cities.

Special Districts

There are now tens of thousands of special districts across the country. A **special district** is an independent unit created to perform one or more related governmental functions at the local level. These districts are found in almost mind-boggling variety and in every State. School districts—some 13,500 of them—are by far the most widely found examples of special districts. More than 35,000 other special districts also blanket the country, and their numbers are growing.

Special districts are found most often, but not always, in rural and suburban areas. Many special districts have been created to provide

◀ School districts are the most common special districts. *Critical Thinking (a) In what special districts do you live? (b) Why were these districts created?*

water, sewage, or electrical service; to furnish fire or police protection; and to build and maintain bridges, airports, swimming pools, libraries, or parks. Others have been created for such purposes as soil conservation, housing, public transportation, irrigation, or reforestation. There are even, in many places, special districts for dog or mosquito control purposes.

A leading reason for the creation of special districts has been the need to provide a particular service in a wider or a smaller area than that covered by a county or a city. For example, a special district might be needed to handle the stream pollution in the several counties through which a river flows. On the other hand, a special district might be set up to provide fire protection in some out-of-the-way locale.

In many cases, special districts have been formed because other local governments could not, or would not, provide the services desired. Other reasons include sidestepping constitutional limits on the size of a city's or a county's debt; financing a public service out of users' fees instead of general tax revenue; and taking advantage of some federal grant program.

The governing body for a special district is generally an elected board. It has the power to lay taxes (usually on property) or charge fees, as well as the powers to spend and to carry out its function(s).

Section 1 Assessment

Key Terms and Main Ideas

1. What is a **county**?
2. How does a **township** differ from a **special district**?
3. (a) What are two major types of county boards?
   (b) List three elected officials commonly found in county government.
4. What factors generally make county government inefficient?

Critical Thinking

5. **Identifying Assumptions** Consider the idea of the New England town meeting. What does this method of town government assume about the citizens of the town?

6. **Drawing Inferences** Review the functions of county and town or township government. List and describe at least three examples of how these governing bodies affect the day-to-day lives of people in your community.

 Take It to the Net

7. Learn about the population, economics, and government of your own county (or a county of your choosing if you live in a region without counties). Summarize your findings in a table or series of graphs. Use the links provided in the Social Studies area at the following Web site for help in completing this activity. **www.phschool.com**

on *Primary Sources*

Seeing the Regional Future

Urban planner William Fulton is a senior research fellow at Claremont Graduate University Research Institute. In this selection, he argues that the future of economic development lies in the growth of large regions, not individual cities and towns.

This three-State area forms a regional economy.

Not long ago, I sat down to lunch with all of the planning directors and economic development specialists in Redding, California. . . . The Redding area has suffered from sluggish economic growth in recent years, and for close to two hours these local officials took turns telling me about the troubles their community faced and the "assets" they had to work with in confronting them. . . .

"And, of course, we have a state university with a good reputation," one of the planning directors said. "That's a great help." All the others nodded in agreement.

. . . I had spent the better part of two days touring Redding, and I had seen no educational institution more substantial than a community college. "Where?" I asked. "What university?" And then they explained. The school they were referring to was the California State University campus in Chico . . . 75 miles away.

It had never occurred to me before that a college in one city might be part of the economic foundation of another city. But in fact, it makes perfect sense. As a smaller town located in a rural area, Redding will probably never have all the big-ticket items a city needs if it is going to compete effectively in the modern economy. But it's not really Redding that's competing. It's the whole northern part of the Sacramento Valley: Redding, Chico and a whole string of other towns that are interrelated economically. We live in the age of the region, not the age of the city. . . . If regions are the new building blocks of the world economy—if it is the region that matters,

not the nation or the city or the state—then it is the region that should also be the locus of economic development policy. . . .

You have to swallow a lot of pride in order to think this way and understand what role your community might really play in creating a strong regional economy. After all, this nation is filled with Chicos that don't want to associate with Redding, and Seattles that want nothing to do with Boise. And going against that territorial instinct can sound like political suicide to a lot of local officials. But any successful business owner will tell you that if you want to get rich, you can't be too haughty [overly proud] about what your product is or the customers you sell it to. The future belongs to the politicians who understand that Chico is a part of Redding and Seattle is a part of Boise—and all these combinations are part of regional economies that will be rich at home only to the extent that they can sell successfully to the rest of the world.

Analyzing Primary Sources

1. What did Fulton realize during his meeting with Redding city officials, and how did he arrive at this point of view?
2. What does Fulton mean when he says, "Chico is a part of Redding and Seattle is a part of Boise"?
3. Why might political leaders have trouble accepting the approach to economic development that Fulton suggests?

② Cities and Metropolitan Areas

Section Preview

OBJECTIVES

1. **Examine** reasons for America's shift from a rural to an urban society.
2. **Explain** the process of incorporation and the function of city charters.
3. **Contrast** the major forms of city government.
4. **Evaluate** the need for city planning and list some municipal functions.
5. **Outline** the challenges that face suburbs and metropolitan areas.

WHY IT MATTERS

Today, some 80 percent of the nation's population live in cities and their surrounding suburbs. The larger the urban population, the more extensive the need for services, efficient and responsive government, and creative solutions to problems.

POLITICAL DICTIONARY

★ **incorporation**
★ **charter**
★ **mayor-council government**
★ **strong-mayor government**
★ **weak-mayor government**
★ **commission government**
★ **council-manager government**
★ **zoning**
★ **metropolitan area**

We are fast becoming a nation of city dwellers. Where once our population was small, mostly rural, and agricultural, it is now large, mostly urban, and dominated by technology, manufacturing, and service industries. In 1790, a mere 5 percent of the population lived in the nation's few cities. Today, America's cities and their surrounding communities are home to 4 of every 5 persons.[5]

America's Rural-Urban Shift

When the first census was taken in 1790, only 3,929,214 people were living in the United States. Of these, only 201,655 people—5.1 percent—lived in the nation's few cities. Philadelphia was then the largest city, with a population of 42,000; 33,000 people lived in New York and 18,000 in Boston.

Nine years before the first census, James Watt had patented his double-acting steam engine, making large-scale manufacturing possible. Robert Fulton patented his steamboat in 1809, and George Stephenson his locomotive in 1829. These inventions made possible the transportation of raw materials to factories and, in turn, the wide distribution of manufactured goods.

Almost overnight, home manufacturing gave way to industrial factories, and populations began to concentrate in the new industrial and transportation centers. Cities began to grow rapidly.

At the same time, the invention of several mechanical farm implements reduced the labor needed on farms. Fewer people grew more food, and the surplus farm population began to move to the cities. By 1860, the nation's population had increased more than sevenfold. The urban population had multiplied thirty times. By 1900, nearly two fifths of Americans lived in urban areas. By 1920, more than half of the population were urban dwellers.

Today, more than 225 million people—more than 75 percent of the population—live in the nation's cities and their surrounding suburbs. For local governments, that change has had dramatic consequences.

▲ The Riverwalk in San Antonio, Texas, is an excellent example of urban renewal and city planning.

---

[5]Depending on local custom and State law, municipalities may be known as cities, towns, boroughs, or villages. The use and meaning of these terms vary among the States. The larger municipalities are known everywhere as cities, and the usual practice is to use that title only for those communities with a significant population.

THE CITY OF SAN FRANCISCO.
BIRDS EYE VIEW FROM THE BAY LOOKING SOUTH-WEST.

▲ If you compare this 1878 print (top) with the recent photograph (bottom) of San Francisco, California, you can clearly see the city's growth. *Critical Thinking What is the impact of the growth of the nation's cities on local governments?*

When large numbers of people live close to one another, there is much more strain on local governments. They must provide water, police and fire protection, sewers, waste removal, traffic regulation, public health facilities, schools, and recreation. The larger the population, the more extensive—and expensive—these services become.

Incorporation and Charters

Since each of the 50 State governments is unitary in form, each State has complete authority over all the units of local government within its borders. All of these units, including cities, were created by the State, received their powers from the State, and are subject to a variety of limitations imposed by the State.

The process by which a State establishes a city as a legal body is called **incorporation.**[6] Each State sets out in its constitution, or by statute, the conditions and the procedures under which a community may become an incorporated municipality. Typically, a State requires that a minimum number of persons live in a given area before incorporation can take place.

The fact that cities are incorporated highlights an important difference between city and county government. Cities are created largely at the request of their residents because residents want certain public services. Counties, on the other hand, exist largely to serve the administrative needs of the State. Cities do act as agents of the State, of course—for example, in law enforcement and public health. But the principal reason for the existence of a city is the convenience of those who live in it.

The **charter** is the city's basic law, its constitution. Its contents may vary from city to city, but commonly the charter names the city, describes its boundaries, and declares it to be a municipal corporation. As a municipal corporation, a city has the right to sue and be sued in the courts, to have a corporate seal, to make contracts, and to acquire, own, manage, and dispose of property.

Generally, the charter also sets out the other powers vested in the city and outlines its form of government. It provides how and for what terms its officers are to be chosen, outlines their duties, and deals with finances and other matters.

Forms of City Government

Although variations can and do exist, each city has one of three basic forms of government. These are (1) a mayor-council, (2) a commission, or (3) a council-manager form of government.

The Mayor-Council Form
The **mayor-council government** is the oldest and still the most widely used type of city government. It features an elected mayor as the chief executive and an elected council as its legislative body.

---

[6]The term *incorporation* comes from Latin *in* (into) *corpus* (body).

Mayor-Council Form of Government

Strong Mayor Model

Voters

elect → **Mayor** Chief Executive

appoints → **Department Heads** Administrators of agencies such as public safety, public works, finance, education

elect → **Council** Legislative body

Weak Mayor Model

Voters

elect → **Mayor** Chief Executive

appoints → **Department Heads** Administrators of agencies such as public safety, public works, finance, education

elect → **Council** Legislative body

Interpreting Diagrams This diagram compares and contrasts the two basic forms of mayor-council governments. *(a) What are the major differences between the two forms of city government? (b) Which is the better system for a large city? Explain your answer.*

The council. The council is usually unicameral and typically has five, seven, or nine members. Some larger cities have more. New York City has the largest council, with 51 members. Members of the council are popularly elected. Terms of office vary from one to six years. Four-year terms are the most common.

A move to nonpartisan city government began in the early 1900s. Its champions believed that (1) political parties were a major source for corruption in city government, and (2) partisan contests at the State and national levels have little to do with municipal problems and local issues. Today, less than one third of all cities still run their elections on a partisan basis.

The mayor. Generally, the voters elect the mayor. In some places, however, the council chooses one of its members to serve as mayor. The mayor presides at council meetings, usually may vote only to break a tie, and may recommend—and usually may veto—ordinances. In most cities, the council can override the veto.

Mayor-council governments are often described as either the strong-mayor type or the weak-mayor type, depending on the powers given to the mayor. This classification is useful for purposes of description. It blurs the importance of informal power in city politics, however.

In a **strong-mayor government,** the mayor heads the city's administration, usually has the power to hire and fire employees, and prepares the budget. Typically, the mayor is able to exercise strong leadership in making city policy and running the city's affairs.

In a **weak-mayor government,** the mayor has much less formal power. Executive duties are shared with other elected officials, such as the clerk, treasurer, city engineer, police chief, and council members. Powers of appointment, removal, and budget are shared with the council or exercised by that body alone. The mayor seldom has veto power.

Most mayor-council cities operate under the weak-mayor rather than the strong-mayor plan. The strong-mayor form is generally found in larger cities.

The success of the mayor-council form depends in very large measure on the power, ability, and influence of the mayor. In weak-mayor cities, responsibility for action or inaction is hard to assign. The strong-mayor plan helps to solve the problems of leadership and responsibility.

Still, the mayor-council form has the following three large defects:

1. It depends heavily on the capacities of the mayor.

2. A major dispute between the mayor and the council can stall the workings of city government.

3. It is quite complicated and so is often little understood by the average citizen.

The Commission Form

The **commission government** is simple in structure. Three to nine, but usually five, commissioners are popularly elected. Together, they form the city council, pass ordinances, and control the purse strings. Individually, they head the different departments of city government: police, fire, public works, finance, parks, and so on. Thus, both legislative and executive powers are centered in one body.

The commission form was born in Galveston, Texas, in 1901. A tidal surge had swept the island city the year before, killing 7,000 people and laying much of the city to waste. The old mayor-council regime was unable to cope with the emergency. The Texas legislature gave Galveston a new charter, providing for five commissioners to make and enforce the law in the stricken city. Intended to be temporary, the arrangement proved so effective that it soon spread to other Texas cities and then elsewhere in the country.

Depending on the city, either the voters or the commissioners themselves choose a commissioner to serve as the mayor. Like the other commissioners, the mayor heads one of the city's departments. He or she also presides at council meetings and represents the city at ceremonies. The mayor generally has no more authority than the other commissioners and rarely has veto power.

The simplicity of the commission form, and especially its short ballot, won the support of municipal reformers in the first few decades of the twentieth century. However, experience pointed up serious defects, and its popularity fell off rapidly. Only a few American cities have a commission form of government today.

The commission form has three chief defects:

1. The lack of a single chief executive (or, the presence of several chiefs among equals) makes it difficult to assign responsibility. This can also mean that the city has no effective political leadership.

2. A built-in tendency toward "empire building" often surfaces. Each commissioner tries to draw as much of the city's money and influence as possible to his or her own department.

3. A lack of coordination plagues the topmost levels of policymaking and administration. Each commissioner is likely to equate the city-wide public good with the particular interests and functions of his or her department.

The Council-Manager Form

The **council-manager government** is a modification of the mayor-council form. Its main features are (1) a strong council of usually five or seven members elected at-large on a nonpartisan ballot; (2) a weak mayor chosen by the voters; and (3) a manager, the city's chief administrative officer, named by the council.

The form first appeared in Ukiah, California. In 1904, that city's council appointed an "executive officer" to direct the work of city government. In 1908, a similar step in Staunton, Virginia, attracted the attention of municipal reformers, who then pushed for the adoption of council-manager government throughout the country. The first charter expressly providing for the council-manager form was granted to the city of Sumter, South Carolina, in 1912.

The council is the city's policymaking body. The manager carries out the policies the council

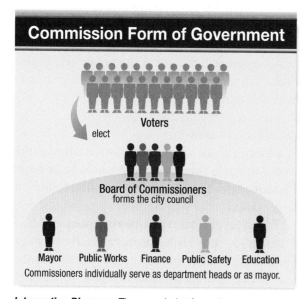

Commission Form of Government

elect

Voters

Board of Commissioners
forms the city council

Mayor   Public Works   Finance   Public Safety   Education
Commissioners individually serve as department heads or as mayor.

Interpreting Diagrams The commission form of government is one of the most uncomplicated systems for a city. *Does a system of checks and balances exist in this form of government?*

makes. He or she is directly responsible to that body for the efficient administration of the city. The manager serves at the council's pleasure and may be dismissed at any time and for any reason.

Today, most city managers are professionally trained career administrators. As chief administrator, the manager directs the work of all city departments and has the power to hire and fire all city employees. The manager also prepares the budget for council consideration and controls the spending of the funds the council appropriates.

The council-manager plan has the backing of nearly every expert on municipal affairs, and its use has spread widely. It is now found in more than 8,000 communities, including most of those cities with populations between 25,000 and 250,000.

The council-manager plan has three major advantages over other forms of city government. First, it is simple in form. Second, it is clear who has the responsibility for policy, on the one hand, and for its application, on the other. Third, it relies on highly trained experts who are skilled in modern techniques of budgeting, planning, computerization, and other administrative tools.

In theory, the nonpolitical manager carries out the policies enacted by the council. Yet in practice the sharp distinction between policymaking and policy-application seldom exists. The manager is very often the chief source for new ideas and fresh approaches to the city's problems. On the other hand, the city council often finds it politically useful to share the responsibility with the "expendable" city manager.

Some critics of council-manager government hold that it is undemocratic because the chief executive is not elected. Others say that it does not offer strong political leadership. This is a particular shortcoming, they argue, in larger cities, where the population is often quite diverse and has competing interests. Support for this view can be seen in the fact that only four cities with over half a million residents have a council-manager form of government: Dallas and San Antonio, Texas; San Diego, California; and Phoenix, Arizona.

City Planning

With few exceptions, most American cities developed haphazardly, without a plan, and with no eye to the future. The results of this

Council-Manager Form of Government

Voters

elect — Council — Policymaking body

appoints

elect — Mayor

City Manager — Chief Administrator; hires and fires city employees, prepares budget, controls spending

appoints

Department Heads — Administrators of agencies such as public safety, public works, finance, and education

Interpreting Diagrams In the council-manager form of government, a professional manager sees that necessary services are performed for city residents. *What are the advantages of the council-manager system over the other forms of city government?*

shortsightedness can be seen in what is often called the core area or the inner city. These are the older and usually overcrowded central sections of larger cities.

Industrial plants were placed anywhere their owners chose to build them. Rail lines were run through the heart of the community. Towering buildings shut out the sunlight from the narrow streets below. Main roads were laid out too close together and sometimes too far apart. Schools, police and fire stations, and other public buildings were squeezed onto cheap land or put where the political organization could make a profit. Examples are endless.

Planning Growth

Fortunately, many cities have seen the need to create order out of their random growth. Most have established some sort of planning agency. This agency usually consists of a planning commission, supported by a trained professional staff.

A number of factors have prompted this step. The need to correct past mistakes has often been a compelling reason, of course. Then, too, many cities have recognized both the advantages that can result, and the pitfalls that can be avoided, through well-planned and orderly development.

▲ Pierre-Charles L'Enfant laid out a plan for Washington, D.C. (above) before a single building was erected. His plan included wide streets running parallel east to west and large areas reserved for public buildings. *Critical Thinking Examine the photo of Washington, D.C. today (right). How is L'Enfant's plan still in evidence?*

Importantly, the Federal Government has spurred cities on. Most federal grant and loan programs require that cities that seek aid must first have a master plan as a guide to future growth.

City Zoning

The practice of dividing a city into a number of districts, or zones, and regulating the uses to which property in each of them may be put is called **zoning.** Generally, a zoning ordinance places each parcel of land in the city into one of three zones: residential, commercial, or industrial.

Each of these zones is then divided into subzones. For example, each of several residential zones may be broken down into several areas. One may be just for single-family residences. Another may allow both one-family and two-family dwellings. In still another, apartment houses and other multifamily units may be allowed.

Most zoning ordinances also prescribe limits on the height and area of buildings, determine how much of a lot may be occupied by a structure, and set out several other such restrictions on land use. They often have "setback" requirements, which state that structures must be placed at least a certain distance from the street and from other property lines.

Zoning is really a phase of city planning, and an important means for ensuring orderly growth. Zoning still meets opposition from many who object to this interference with their

right to use their property as they choose. Even so, nearly every city of any size in the United States is zoned today. The city of Houston, where zoning was turned down twice by popular vote, remained the only major exception until the early 1990s. At that point, the city council finally decided to adopt zoning.

Zoning ordinances must be reasonable. Remember that the 14th Amendment prohibits any State, and thus its cities, from depriving any person of life, liberty, or property without due process of law. Each of the 50 State constitutions contains a similar provision.

Clearly, zoning does deprive a person of the right to use his or her property for certain purposes. Thus, if an area is zoned only for single-family dwellings, you cannot build an apartment house or a service station on your property in that zone. Zoning can also reduce the value of a particular piece of property. A choice corner lot, for example, may be much more valuable with a drive-in restaurant on the property than a house.[7]

While zoning may at times deprive a person of liberty or property, the key question always is this: Does it do so without due process? That is, does it do so unreasonably?

---

[7]Nonconforming uses in existence before a zoning ordinance is passed are almost always allowed to continue. Most ordinances give the city council the right to grant exceptions, called variances, in cases where property owners might suffer undue hardships.

The question of reasonableness is one for the courts to decide. The Supreme Court first upheld zoning as a proper use of police power in *Euclid* v. *Amber Realty Co.,* 1926, a case involving an ordinance enacted by the city council of Euclid, Ohio.

Municipal Functions

The services a city provides day in and day out are so extensive that it is almost impossible to catalog them. Most larger cities, and many smaller ones, issue annual reports on the city's condition. These are often book-length publications.

Consider just a few of the many things that most or all cities do. They provide police and fire protection. They build and maintain streets, sidewalks, bridges, street lights, parks and playgrounds, swimming pools, golf courses, libraries, hospitals, schools, correctional institutions, day-care centers, airports, public markets, parking facilities, auditoriums, and sports arenas. They furnish public health and sanitation services, such as sewers and wastewater treatment, garbage collection and disposal, and disease prevention and eradication programs.

Cities operate water, gas, light, and transportation systems. They regulate traffic, building codes, pollution, and public utilities. Many cities also build and manage public housing projects, provide summer youth camps, build and operate docks and other harbor facilities, and maintain tourist attractions.

Suburbs and Metropolitan Areas

The growth of urban areas has raised many problems for city dwellers. Urban growth also affects residents of nearby suburbs.

The Suburban Boom

About half of all Americans live in suburbs today. The nation's suburbs began to grow rapidly in the years immediately after World War II, and then on through the 1950s and 1960s. The suburban

▲ Fire protection is one of the most essential city services. *Critical Thinking Why are such services as police and fire protection the function of local rather than National Government?*

growth rate slowed somewhat in the 1970s, but it rebounded in the 1980s and 1990s, especially around the Sunbelt cities of the South and West.

This dramatic population shift stemmed from Americans' desire for more room, cheaper land, greater privacy, and less smoke, dirt, noise, and congestion. People also sought less crime, newer and better schools, safer streets and playing conditions, lower taxes, and higher social status. The car and the freeway turned millions of rooted city dwellers into mobile suburbanites.

Businesses followed customers to the suburbs, often clustering in shopping centers or malls. Many industries moved from the central city in search of cheaper land, lower taxes, and a more stable labor supply. Industries also sought an escape from city building codes, health inspectors, and other regulations. These developments stimulated growth.

This "suburbanitis," as some call it, has added to city-dwellers' woes. As high-income families have moved out, they have taken their civic, financial, and social resources with them. They have left behind center cities with high percentages of older people, low-income families, and minorities. Inevitably, both the need for and the stress on city services have multiplied.

Metropolitan Areas

Suburbanites face their share of problems, too, including the need for water supplies, sewage disposal, police and fire protection, transportation, and traffic control. Duplication of such functions by city and suburb or by city and county can be wasteful, even dangerous. More than one fire has raged while neighboring fire departments quibbled over who was responsible for fighting it.

Attempts to meet the needs of **metropolitan areas**—cities and the areas around them—have taken several forms. Over the years, annexation has been the standard means. Outlying areas have simply been brought within a city's boundaries. Many suburbanites resist annexation,

Interpreting Political Cartoons (a) What is meant by the State of Alabama becoming a suburb of the city of Atlanta, Georgia? (b) What does the cartoon suggest about urban sprawl?

however. Cities, too, have often been hesitant to take on the burdens involved.

Another approach has been to create special districts designed to meet the problems of heavily populated urban areas. Their boundaries frequently cut across county and city lines to include an entire metropolitan area. They often are called metropolitan districts.

These metropolitan districts are generally set up for a single purpose—for example, parks, as in the Cleveland Metropolitan Park

Development District. In some cases, however, these districts can also handle a number of functions.

In Oregon, a regional agency known as Metro manages several activities in an area that includes Portland, the State's largest city, and 23 other municipalities. Within this region, Metro is responsible for land-use and transportation planning, solid-waste disposal programs, and the operation of the Oregon Convention Center, the Oregon Zoo, Portland's Center for the Performing Arts, and other facilities.

Yet another approach to the challenges facing metropolitan areas is increasing the authority of counties. Among local governments around the country, counties are generally the largest in area and are most likely to include those places demanding new and increased services.

Dade County, Florida, has undertaken the nation's most ambitious approach to metropolitan problems. In 1957, Dade County voters approved the first home-rule charter designed "to create a metropolitan government." Under it, a countywide metropolitan government (Metro) is responsible for areawide functions. These include fire and police protection; an integrated water, sewer, and drainage system; zoning; and expressway construction. Miami and the other 26 cities within the county continue to perform their strictly local functions and services.

Section 2 Assessment

Key Terms and Main Ideas

1. What is the purpose of the **incorporation** process?
2. What kinds of provisions might you find in a city **charter**?
3. What are the key differences between a **strong-mayor government** and a **weak-mayor government**?
4. List at least five functions of municipal governments.

Critical Thinking

5. **Making Comparisons** Create a chart comparing the advantages and disadvantages of these types of city government: **(a)** the mayor-council form; **(b)** the commission form; **(c)** the council-manager form.

6. **Determining Cause and Effect** Trace the history of American population shifts, first to the cities and then to the suburbs. Include economic and social reasons for the trends.

 Take It to the Net

7. Read about the effect of urbanization on water supply and quality. Then create a flowchart that shows (1) why urbanization affects water supply and quality, (2) how urbanization affects water supply and quality, and (3) how communities can meet these challenges. Use the links provided in the Social Studies area at the following Web site for help in completing this activity. **www.phschool.com**

3. Providing Important Services

Section Preview

OBJECTIVES

1. **Explain** why State governments have a major role in providing important services.
2. **Identify** the types of services that States and local governments provide.
3. **Analyze** why the amount and types of services available to citizens vary greatly from State to State.

WHY IT MATTERS

People are often unaware of the vast array of services provided by State and local governments. The cost of these services has become a huge burden to many States, which struggle to keep up with the expenses of growing populations.

POLITICAL DICTIONARY

★ **Medicaid**
★ **welfare**
★ **entitlement**
★ **urbanization**

State governments, you may by now have noticed, are quite similar in form to the Federal Government. For example, each has three branches of government, all but one have bicameral legislatures, each has its own constitution, and so on. Given these similarities, it is easy to overlook the many unique features and functions of your own State government, and the many services it provides to its citizens.

State Government's Role

Over the course of this book, you have read many times about the key role of the States in the American federal system. Recall that there was a widespread distrust among the Framers of a strong, central government. As a result, they created a system in which the States held many important powers. The Constitution reserves to the States all those powers not expressly delegated to Congress and not specifically denied to the States.

These reserved powers are broad—in fact, they are too numerous to list here. In addition, the exercise of these powers varies greatly from one State to the next. Again, that fact reflects the conscious aim of the Framers and the federal system they created.

Along with the powers reserved to the States come some important responsibilities. Like the Federal Government, State governments generally aim to fulfill the lofty purposes set forward in the Preamble to the Constitution; that is, they

seek to "establish Justice, ensure domestic Tranquility, provide for the common defense, promote the general Welfare, and secure the Blessings of Liberty. . . . "

State and Local Services

States provide services to their citizens in two ways: (1) directly, through State agencies and programs, and (2) through the local governments they establish. State and their local units provide many services to those who live within their borders. The services they provide fall into a number of broad categories.

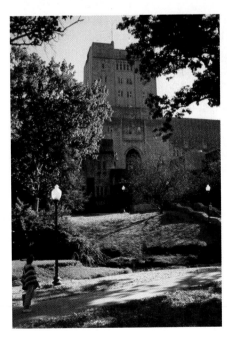

◀ **Indiana University, Bloomington** States play a major role in funding public higher education. The Indiana University system is no exception.

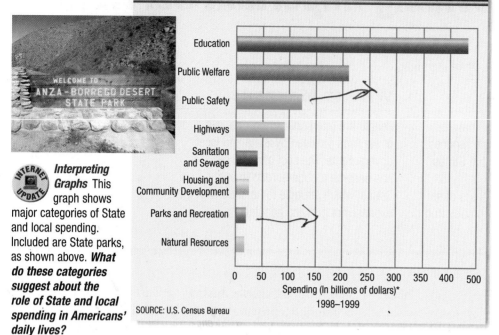

State and Local Spending*

Education
Public Welfare
Public Safety
Highways
Sanitation and Sewage
Housing and Community Development
Parks and Recreation
Natural Resources

Spending (In billions of dollars)*
0   50   100   150   200   250   300   350   400   500
1998–1999

SOURCE: U.S. Census Bureau

Interpreting Graphs This graph shows major categories of State and local spending. Included are State parks, as shown above. *What do these categories suggest about the role of State and local spending in Americans' daily lives?*

Education

The education of the State's residents is one of the most important responsibilities that the States have assumed. It is also the most expensive entry in every State budget, representing more than one third of all State expenditures.

The cost of providing education has risen sharply in recent decades and continues to increase year to year. These rising costs, plus demands by voters for improved schools, have led State and local governments to increase their educational funding. Public schools now spend over 40 percent more on each pupil than they did in 1980.

Primary and secondary public education is largely the responsibility of local governments. Local taxes, especially property taxes, provide much of the funding for schools.

Of course, States do provide some financial assistance to their local governments for education. Aid levels vary widely from State to State. Some States contribute well over half the cost of primary and secondary education. Others provide only a fraction of the cost.

In addition, States set guidelines in order to maintain high quality in the schools. For example, State laws establish teacher qualifications, curricula, quality standards for educational materials, and the length of the school year.

State interest and involvement in such matters have intensified in recent years. Most States have established "curriculum frameworks" or "content standards" outlining the material that must be covered in core subjects. Most States have a Statewide testing program in one or more subjects.

At the college and university levels, the States likewise play a major role. States understand that for businesses to succeed in the State, a ready supply of highly trained college graduates is key. Such a labor pool is also necessary to attract new businesses.

Every State also has a public higher education system. Some are extensive, including several universities, technical schools, and community colleges. California's higher education system is the nation's largest. The University of California alone has 9 campuses, and California State University has 23. In addition, the State has an extensive system of community colleges, which offer two-year programs.

Education at State universities and colleges is generally much less expensive than at private institutions. On average, tuition at four-year public colleges and universities is about one fifth that of private four-year schools. Nevertheless, many State universities, such as the University of California at Berkeley and the University of Michigan at Ann Arbor, are ranked among the world's finest schools.

Public Welfare

States take an active role in promoting the health and welfare of their citizens. States pursue this goal by a variety of means.

1. **Public health.** Most States fund ambitious public health programs. States operate public hospitals and offer direct care to millions of citizens. They immunize children against dangerous childhood diseases, such as measles and mumps. With the Federal Government, the

States administer such programs as **Medicaid,** which provides medical insurance to low-income families.

Recent soaring costs in the health-care industry have placed a great strain on many States' budgets. Many governors, State legislators, mayors, and other public officials are among the leading advocates of reform of the nation's health-care system.

2. *Cash assistance.* Another major area in which States contribute to the well-being of their citizens is cash assistance to the poor, commonly called **welfare.** States are now taking a leading role in this area.

Between 1936 and 1996, the Federal Government provided cash assistance to needy families through the Aid to Families with Dependent Children (AFDC) program.[8] AFDC was an **entitlement** program, which means that anyone who met the eligibility requirements was entitled to receive benefits.

The Federal Government and the States shared the costs of providing AFDC benefits. These costs rose dramatically as the number of AFDC recipients skyrocketed from 1.7 percent of the nation's population in 1960 to 4.1 percent in 1970, 4.7 percent in 1980, and an all-time high of 5.5 percent in 1993 and 1994.

Critics of AFDC pointed to its soaring costs and expanding caseloads as signs of serious problems with the program. They also saw the lack of a limit on the number of months a person could receive AFDC benefits as a serious omission. Because of these issues, critics argued that the program encouraged people to depend on government assistance rather than become self-supporting.

In 1996, Congress responded to these concerns by passing the Personal Responsibility and Work Opportunity Reconciliation Act. This act replaced AFDC with a new and strikingly different program, Temporary Assistance to Needy Families (TANF).

Unlike AFDC, TANF is a block grant: The Federal Government gives States a fixed amount of money each year, regardless of whether the number of TANF recipients rises or falls. States are then free to use the federal grant, plus the State

funds that they are obliged to contribute, to design and implement their own welfare programs.

TANF limits recipients to a total of five years of assistance during the course of their lifetime (some States have imposed even shorter time limits). It also requires recipients to work or participate in some form of vocational training or community service.

The number of people on welfare had in fact begun to decline before creation of the TANF program. It has plunged since then, falling well below 50 percent by 2001. Many of those who

---

CLOSE UP FOUNDATION *Student Poll*

In a recent poll, students were asked their opinion on the following question: *The table below lists different ways that people might get involved in their community and government. How much interest do you have in each activity—a great deal, a fair amount, only some, or not that much?*

	A Great Deal of Interest	A Fair Amount of Interest	Only Some Interest	Not That Much Interest	Not Sure
Volunteering for charitable causes	36%	27%	24%	13%	–
Voting in elections	41%	19%	15%	22%	3%
Following the news on public policy issues in the newspaper, on television, or on the radio	27%	30%	29%	13%	1%
Getting involved in public interest groups, such as World Wildlife Fund or Habitat for Humanity	21%	23%	23%	33%	–
Writing to elected officials to express your views	17%	19%	21%	42%	1%
Volunteering for a political campaign	7%	15%	26%	52%	–

1. **Analyzing Data** *In which types of involvement in their community and government are students most interested?*
2. **Conducting Polls** In your own school, conduct a poll asking students which types of involvement in their community and government most interest them. *How do your results compare to the results shown in this table?*

---

[8]AFDC was authorized by Title IV of the Social Security Act of 1935. Until 1962, the program was named Aid to Dependent Children, as the 1935 act was aimed simply at needy dependent children.

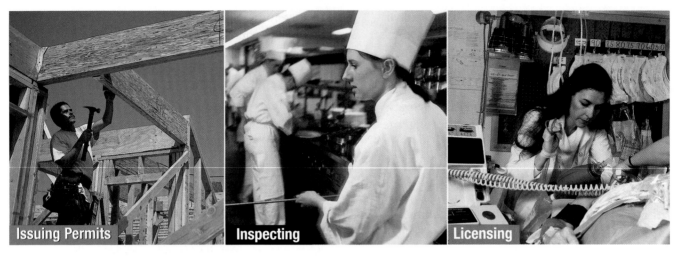

▲ *Promoting Public Welfare* State and local governments work to ensure citizens' health and welfare in a variety of ways. These include issuing construction permits (left), inspecting restaurant kitchens (center), and licensing health-care practitioners (right).

remain on welfare must overcome a number of barriers, such as physical or mental disabilities, in order to obtain and hold jobs. Now that States have the primary responsibility for welfare, it is their task to find ways to help these families.

3. *Other efforts.* States do much more to promote their citizens' health and welfare. They enforce antipollution laws to protect the environment; they inspect factories and other workplaces to protect worker safety; they license health-care practitioners to ensure quality care. The list of public welfare services goes on and on.

Public Safety

One of the oldest law enforcement groups, the legendary Texas Rangers, was established in 1835. Today, a variety of police forces, from the local sheriff to academy-trained State police, operate in every State to preserve law and order.

A State's police are perhaps the most visible group, since they patrol the State's roads and highways. State law-enforcement forces perform other vital services as well. They may function as the primary police force in rural communities. They investigate crimes. They provide centralized files for fingerprints and other information. They also provide training and many other services in support of local law-enforcement agencies.

Each State has its own corrections system for those convicted of committing State crimes. States operate prisons, penitentiaries, and other facilities, including those for juvenile offenders.

Operating these corrections systems is a growing burden for States. During the 1990s, the number of persons held in State prisons increased by more than 70 percent. In three States—Texas, Idaho, and West Virginia—prison populations more than doubled. Today more than 2 million people are incarcerated, more than half of them in State prisons. Two causes of booming prison populations are (1) increases in the number of people sentenced for violent crimes and (2) the increasing length of the average prison sentence.

The result is prison overcrowding. Twenty-two State corrections systems are operating at 100 percent or more of their capacity. California prisons hold nearly twice their capacity.

Another result is rising State corrections spending, which more than doubled between 1985 and 1996. States now spend more than $25 billion each year to build, staff, and maintain prisons and to house prisoners. Yet while prison spending grows, it is worth noting that State and local governments still spend ten times as much on education as on corrections.

In an effort to expand their prison capacity more affordably, many States have hired private contractors to operate some of their prisons. More than 5 percent of all State prisoners are held in private facilities.

Highways

Building and maintaining roads and highways is an enormous job. It regularly ranks among the most expensive items in State budgets.

Again, the Federal Government is a partner with the States in funding highways. The most impressive example is the interstate highway system, a network of high-speed roadways that spans the length and breadth of the continental United States. Construction of the system began with the 1956 Federal-Aid Highway Act and continues to this day.

The Interstate Highway System, officially called the Dwight D. Eisenhower System of Interstate and Defense Highways, is now 99 percent finished. When complete, it will total some 45,000 miles. The Federal Government has paid roughly 90 percent of its cost.

While the Interstate system is a magnificent achievement, it constitutes only a tiny fraction of the nation's 4 million miles of roads. Many roadways are built with State, not federal, funds. States maintain the roads, as well.

State and local governments must also look after the physical safety of drivers on the roads. Besides patrolling the roads, State and local governments set speed limits. States license drivers to ensure their competence. Many States require periodic safety inspections of vehicles.

Other Services

As noted earlier, the many services that the States provide to their citizens are too numerous to be listed here. No less important, however, are functions such as setting aside public lands for conservation and recreation; regulating businesses and the commerce they conduct within the State; and protecting consumers from a variety of dangers and inconveniences.

Variations in Services

State and local governments vary greatly in the amount and types of services they offer their citizens. The discrepancies among regions stem from several causes.

For example, State budgets vary according to the degree of urbanization—or presence of urban areas—in each State. Technically, **urbanization** refers to the percentage of the population of a State living in cities of more than 250,000 people or in suburbs of cities with more than 50,000.

The budgets of highly urbanized States, such as California and New Jersey, reflect the special challenges of governing urban areas—such as the expense of managing complicated roads and traffic. More rural States, such as Vermont and West Virginia, have smaller budgets that accommodate their individual needs, including support for farmers.

Another factor that affects State and local budgets is physical geography. A State's energy supplies, agricultural resources, and proximity to transportation networks and major markets all help shape its economy and budget.

Section 3 Assessment

Key Terms and Main Ideas

1. What is typically the most expensive item in States' budgets?
2. **(a)** Name three main categories of services that State and local governments provide. **(b)** For each category, describe a specific program or service.
3. For whom does the **Medicaid** program provide benefits?
4. How does **urbanization** affect State spending?

Critical Thinking

5. **Drawing Inferences** Why do you think many States lobbied the Federal Government to give them block grants that they could use to create and manage their own welfare programs?
6. **Predicting Consequences** Turn to the bar graph on State and Local Spending, on page 734. Choose two categories and suggest a way to reduce rising costs in each category. What might be the results of such reductions?
7. **Expessing Problems Clearly** What challenges do State and local governments face in providing for public welfare and safety? How are governments meeting these challenges?

Take It to the Net

8. Find out what services your State and local government provide for your community. Then create a flyer that explains some of these services to newcomers. Use the links provided in the Social Studies area at the following Web site for help in completing this activity.
www.phschool.com

Filing a Consumer Complaint

One of the functions of American government is to protect consumers. If you believe you're the victim of a money scam, an unsafe product, shoddy repair work, false advertising, or a warranty that was not honored, you can file a consumer complaint. The box below lists federal and private sources of consumer help. For State help, try the attorney general's office. To file a complaint, follow these steps:

1. Keep all records of transactions. Get estimates in writing. If a company representative gives you promises over the telephone, ask for them in writing. Get the name of the representative you're speaking with, the time of the call, and take notes from the conversation. What kinds of paper work should you save?

2. If you do not get satisfaction, file a complaint. Many disagreements can be worked out between you and the individual or company involved. But if that doesn't work, determine what government agency handles your type of problem and file your complaint in writing. Using these letter-writing tips, write a sample first sentence of a complaint letter:

- Include specific facts, such as the date and place of your purchase and a serial or model number. If you are complaining about a service you received, describe the service and who performed it.
- Include <u>copies</u> of all relevant documents.
- Your tone should be firm, but polite—not angry, sarcastic, or threatening. The person reading your letter probably was not responsible for your problem, but may be helpful in fixing it.

3. File the complaint promptly. Some complaints must be made within a certain amount of time, so don't delay. What should you do if you get no response?

Help for Consumers

Consumer Product Safety Commission The CPSC is an independent federal regulatory agency that identifies unsafe consumer products and has the authority to ban the sale of them. CPSC responds to consumer complaints. **http://www.cpsc.gov**

Consumer Information Center The CIC, based in Pueblo, Colorado, is perhaps the best-known source of federal consumer information. The CIC publishes a free catalog of more than 200 free and low-cost publications. **http://www.pueblo.gsa.gov/backgrnd.htm**

ConsumerWorld This is a nonprofit Web site with links to federal, State, local, and private consumer resources. Read about the latest money scams, file a complaint, learn about your consumer rights, find the wholesale price of a car, or look up product reviews. **http://www.consumerworld.org**

Test for Success

Write a fictional letter to a State consumer protection agency to complain about a defective product you bought. Briefly describe problems you had in getting the manufacturer to fix or replace the product.

Financing State and Local Government

·4·

Section Preview

OBJECTIVES

1. **Describe** the major Federal and State limits on raising revenue.
2. **List** the four principles of sound taxation.
3. **Identify** major tax and nontax sources of State and local revenue.
4. **Explain** the State budget process.

WHY IT MATTERS

You pay State and local taxes—indeed, you cannot avoid them. Like most of us, you probably find them to be at least inconvenient, but they are also quite necessary—and, by and large, a bargain.

POLITICAL DICTIONARY

★ sales tax
★ regressive tax
★ income tax
★ progressive tax
★ property tax
★ assessment
★ inheritance tax
★ estate tax
★ budget

You know by now that government is an expensive proposition, and it is becoming more so from year to year. Altogether, the 50 States and their thousands of local governments now take in and spend well over 1 trillion dollars a year. How do they get all that money, and how do they decide what to spend it on?

Limits on Raising Revenue

The States now take in well over $500 billion in taxes. Local governments collect more than $300 billion. The States and their local governments also receive another $500 billion or so from a number of nontax sources.

The power to tax is one of the major powers reserved to the States in the Federal system. In a strictly legal sense, then, their taxing power is limited only by the restrictions imposed by the federal Constitution and those imposed by a State's own fundamental law.[9]

Federal Limitations

The Federal Constitution does place some restrictions on the taxing abilities of the State and their local governments. Although few in number, those limits have a major impact on the States and their local governments.

1. *Interstate and Foreign Commerce.* The Constitution denies the States the power to "lay any Imposts or Duties on Imports or Exports" and "any Duty of Tonnage."[10] In effect, the States are prohibited from taxing interstate and foreign commerce. The Supreme Court has often held that because the Constitution gives Congress the power to regulate that trade, the States are generally forbidden to do so.

2. *The Federal Government and Its Agencies.* The Supreme Court's decision in *McCulloch* v. *Maryland*, 1819, bars States from taxing the

---

[9]Remember, a State's power to tax is also limited by any number of practical considerations, such as economic and political factors.

[10]Article I, Section 10, Clauses 2 and 3.

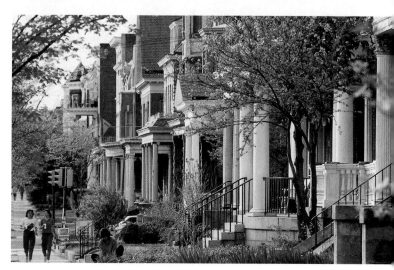

▲ Property taxes, including those on houses such as these, are a major source of local revenue.

Federal Government or any of its agencies or functions. They are forbidden to do so because, as Chief Justice Marshall put it in *McCulloch*: "The power to tax involves the power to destroy." (See page 95.)

3. *Fourteenth Amendment Limitations* The Due Process and Equal Protection clauses place limits on the power to tax at the State and local levels. Essentially, the Due Process Clause requires that taxes (1) be imposed and administered fairly, (2) be not so heavy as to actually confiscate property, and (3) be imposed only for public purposes.

The Equal Protection Clause forbids the making of unreasonable classifications for the purpose of taxation. The clause thus forbids tax classifications made on the basis of race, religion, nationality, political party membership, or any other factors that are deemed to be unreasonable.

Most tax laws involve some form of classification, however. An income tax is applied only to the class of persons who have income. Likewise, a cigarette tax is collected only from those who buy cigarettes, a property tax only from those who own property and so on. The Equal Protection Clause does not prevent these and similar classifications, because they are reasonable ones.

State Limitations

Each State's constitution limits the taxing powers of that State. State constitutions also limit the taxing powers of their local governments, often in great detail.

Most State constitutions create tax exemptions for religious and other nonprofit groups. State codes often set maximum rates for levies, such as State sales taxes or local property taxes. Some States prohibit certain taxes, such as a general sales or personal income taxes.

Since local governments have no independent powers, the only taxes they may impose are those that the State allows them to levy. States have been reluctant in the matter. Even local units with home-rule charters are closely restricted on what and how they can tax.

The Principles of Sound Taxation

Any tax, if taken by itself, can be shown to be unfair. If a government's total revenues were to come from one tax—say, a sales, an income, or a property tax—its tax system would be very unfair. Some people would bear a much greater burden than others, and some would bear little or none. Each tax should thus be defensible as part of a tax system.

In his classic 1776 book *The Wealth of Nations*, Scottish economist Adam Smith laid out four principles of a sound tax system, which most tax experts still cite today:

PRIMARY Sources "1. *The subjects of every state ought to contribute towards the support of the government as nearly as possible, in proportion to their respective abilities; that is, in proportion to the revenue which they respectively enjoy under the protection of the state.*
2. *The tax which each individual is bound to pay ought to be certain, and not arbitrary.*
3. *Every tax ought to be levied at the time, or in the manner, in which it is most likely to be convenient for the contributor to pay it.*
4. *Every tax ought to be so contrived as to take out and to keep out of the pockets of the people as little as possible over and above what it brings into the public treasury. . . .*"

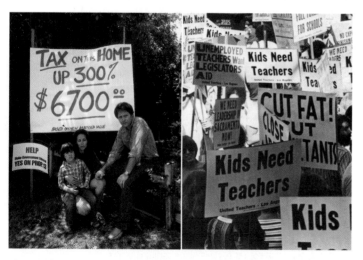

▲ In 1978, a successful California ballot measure known as Proposition 13 touched off a series of State and local initiatives to limit property taxes. Here a family shows their support for that measure (left). At the same time, teachers rallied to express their concern about tax cuts (right). *Critical Thinking* *(a) Why might teachers be concerned about tax cuts? (b) What other groups might have similar concerns?*

Shaping a tax system that meets these standards of equality, certainty, convenience, and economy is just about impossible. Still, that goal should be pursued.

Sources of Revenue

Beyond the limits noted, a State can levy taxes as it chooses. The legislature decides what taxes the State will levy, and at what rates. It also decides what taxes localities can levy.[11]

The Sales Tax

The sales tax is the most productive source of State income today. It accounts for about one third of all tax monies the States collect each year.

A **sales tax** is a tax placed on the sale of various commodities; the purchaser pays it. It may be either general or selective in form. A general sales tax is one applied to the sale of most commodities. A selective sales tax is one placed only on the sale of certain commodities, such as cigarettes, liquor, or gasoline.

Today, 45 States levy a general sales tax.[12] The rates range from 3 percent in Colorado to as much as 7 percent in Mississippi and Rhode Island. All States now levy a selective sales tax on gasoline, alcoholic beverages, insurance policies, and cigarettes. Most States also impose other selective sales taxes. City and county governments also levy sales taxes in some States.

Sales taxes are widely used for two major reasons: They are easy to collect, and they are dependable revenue producers. Yet a sales tax is a **regressive tax**—that is, it is not levied according to a person's ability to pay. Everyone in a certain State who buys, say, a hammer, has to pay the same amount of sales tax on it. Therefore, to a poor person who buys the hammer, the tax is a heavier burden than it is to a wealthy person who buys it. Critics of regressive taxes say that States should not raise so much of their revenue from citizens least able to pay.

The latest controversy over sales taxes involves the Internet. The last few years have seen explosive growth in sales made over the Web. Yet States are prohibited from collecting the sales taxes on most Internet purchases. That is because products made in one State are sold online to customers across the country. And the Supreme Court has ruled[13] that companies cannot be forced to collect a sales tax on goods they ship into another State, unless the company has a physical presence in that other State. (That applies to mail-order as well as Internet sales.)

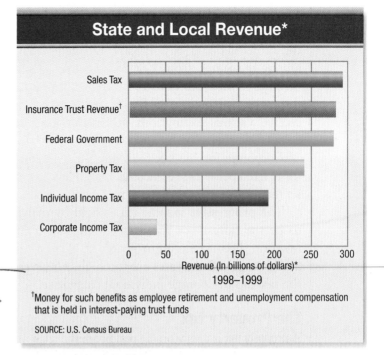

State and Local Revenue*

(bar graph, Revenue in billions of dollars, 1998–1999)

- Sales Tax
- Insurance Trust Revenue[†]
- Federal Government
- Property Tax
- Individual Income Tax
- Corporate Income Tax

0   50   100   150   200   250   300
Revenue (In billions of dollars)*
1998–1999

[†]Money for such benefits as employee retirement and unemployment compensation that is held in interest-paying trust funds

SOURCE: U.S. Census Bureau

Interpreting Graphs This graph shows the major sources of State and local revenue. *Are the types of taxes shown on the graph the fairest ways for States and local governments to pay for services? Explain your answer.*

As more people shop via the Internet rather than at traditional "brick-and-mortar" stores, States complain that the drain on sales tax revenues could force them to compensate by reducing services or raising other taxes. However, proponents of making Internet sales permanently tax-free contend that doing so would encourage economic growth. Among the advantages would be freeing online retailers from the complex task of tracking the multitudes of different taxes imposed by State and local governments.

The Income Tax

The **income tax,** which is levied on the income of individuals and/or corporations, yields almost one third of State tax revenues today. Forty-three States levy an individual income tax; forty-six have some form of corporate income tax.[14]

---

[11]A State constitution sometimes grants certain taxing powers directly to local governments, but this is not common.

[12]Alaska, Delaware, Montana, New Hampshire, and Oregon have no general sales tax, but each imposes selective sales taxes.

[13]*National Bellas Hess* v. *Illinois,* 1967, and *Quill Corp.* v. *North Dakota,* 1992.

[14]Nevada, Texas, Washington, and Wyoming levy neither type of income tax. Alaska, Florida, and South Dakota impose only the corporate tax.

The individual income tax is usually a **progressive tax**—that is, the higher your income, the more tax you pay. Income tax rates vary among the States, from 1 or 2 percent on lower incomes in most States to 10 percent or more on the highest incomes in a few States. Taxpayers receive various exemptions and deductions in calculating their taxable income.

Corporate income tax rates are usually a uniform, fixed percentage of income. Only a few States set the rates on a graduated, or progressive, basis.

The progressive income tax is held by many to be the fairest—or the least unfair—form of taxation, because it can be geared to a person's ability to pay. If the rates are too high, however, the tax can discourage individual enterprise.

The Property Tax

A **property tax** is a levy on (1) real property, such as land, buildings, and improvements that go with the property if sold; or (2) personal property, either tangible or intangible. Tangible personal property is movable wealth that is visible and the value of which can be easily assessed, such as computers, cars, and books. Intangible personal property includes stocks, bonds, mortgages and bank accounts. The property tax is the chief source of local governments' income today, making up roughly three fourths of their tax receipts.

The process of determining the value of the property to be taxed is known as **assessment.**

An elected county, township, or city assessor usually carries out the task.

In places where personal property is taxed, the assessment is made each year. Real property is usually assessed less often, commonly every second or fourth year. The assessor is supposed to visit the property and examine it to determine its value. In reality, the assessment is often made simply on the basis of the previous year's figures, which were arrived at in the same way.

Property is usually assessed at less than its true market value. Most property owners seem better satisfied if the assessment is set at, say, one-half of its real value. Thus, a house assessed at $80,000 may actually be worth $160,000. If the tax rate is set at 2 percent, the tax will be $1,600. In reality, this result is the same as a 1 percent tax on the $160,000 house.

Supporters of the property tax argue that because government protects property and often enhances its value, a tax on property can properly be required to support the government. Critics note that the property tax is not truly progressive. Although the amount of real property one owns may have been a fair measure of one's wealth in earlier times, it is not today. (You might inherit a valuable home, for instance, but not be wealthy enough to pay the property tax on it.) Second, it is all but impossible to assess all taxable property on a fair and equal basis.

Inheritance or Estate Taxes

Every State has some form of inheritance or estate tax, sometimes called the "death tax." An **inheritance tax** is levied on the beneficiary's (heir's) share of an estate. An **estate tax** is one levied directly on the full estate itself.

Business Taxes

A variety of business taxes, in addition to the corporate income tax, are important sources of revenue in most States. More than half the States impose severance taxes, levies on the removal of natural resources such as timber, oil, minerals, and fish from the land or water.

Every State has various license taxes that permit people to engage in a certain businesses, occupations, or activities. For example, all States require that corporations be licensed to do business in the State. Certain kinds of businesses—chain stores, amusement parks, taverns,

Interpreting Political Cartoons You might have heard the expression, "Prices have gone through the roof." *What point is the cartoon making about property taxes?*

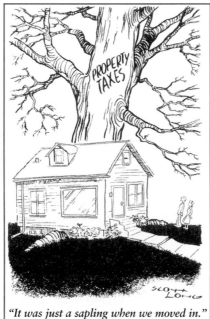

"It was just a sapling when we moved in."

and transportation lines—must have an additional operating license. Most States require the licensing of doctors, lawyers, dentists, morticians, barbers, hairdressers, plumbers, engineers, electricians, and others.

Many States have levies known as documentary and stock transfer taxes. These are charges made on the recording, registering, and transfer of such documents as mortgages, deeds, and securities. Some States also impose capital stock taxes, which are levied on the total assessed value of the shares of stock issued by a business.

Other Taxes

State and local governments impose a number of other taxes. Payroll taxes produce huge sums for the States. Money generated by these taxes is held in trust funds for social welfare programs, such as unemployment, accident insurance, and retirement benefits. More than half the States levy amusement taxes on admission to theaters, sports events, circuses, and the like. All States levy license taxes for nonbusiness purposes: motor vehicles and drivers, hunting, fishing, and marriages.

Nontax Sources

State and local governments now take in some $500 billion a year from a wide range of nontax sources. Nearly half of that huge amount comes in grants from the Federal Government each year.

The States and many of their local governments also make money from a number of publicly operated business enterprises. Toll bridges and toll roads are popular in the East. Several States, notably Washington, are in the ferry business. North Dakota markets a flour sold under the brand name Dakota-Maid and is in the commercial banking business. California operates a short railway line in San Francisco.

Eighteen States are in the liquor business, selling alcohol in State-operated stores.[15] For years, Washington and Oregon jointly owned a distillery in Kentucky and sold its product in their outlets.

Voices on Government

Frank Chong's experiences in government administration and in education have allowed him to observe how the two can work together. Chong is Dean of Student Affairs at City College of San Francisco and was elected to the San Francisco School Board in 1998. As he campaigned for that post, Chong spoke about planning schools for the new millennium.

❝ My hope is to mobilize all partners who care about children—parents, teachers, municipal government, educators, and advocates—to create strong neighborhood support systems so that children are nurtured and given opportunities to support their maximum development. This is the time to make plans, especially as demographic shifts across San Francisco force us to rethink the best use of our public resources. ❞

Evaluating the Quotation

Chong mentions changes in population as one factor in planning San Francisco's schools. How do demographic changes affect the schools in a community?

Many cities own and operate their water, electric power, and bus transportation systems. Some cities operate farmers' markets; rent space in their office buildings, warehouses, and housing projects; and operate dams and wharves. Receipts from such businesses support the local governments that own them. Other nontax sources include court fines, sales and lease of public lands, and interest from loans, investments, and late tax payments.

Several States have relaxed their once-strict antigambling laws, hoping to attract dollars, jobs, and tourists. State-run lotteries now bring in some $12 billion a year for 38 States and the District of Columbia.[16]

Borrowing

State and local governments often must borrow money for unusually large undertakings, such as public buildings, bridges, and highways, that

---

[15]Those states are Alabama, Idaho, Iowa, Maine, Michigan, Mississippi, Montana, New Hampshire, North Carolina, Ohio, Oregon, Pennsylvania, Utah, Vermont, Virginia, Washington, West Virginia, Wyoming. North Carolina's stores are operated by the counties; Wyoming's liquor monopoly operates only at the wholesale level.

[16]States that do not have lotteries are Alabama, Alaska, Arkansas, Hawaii, Mississippi, Nevada, North Carolina, North Dakota, Oklahoma, South Carolina, Tennessee, Utah, and Wyoming.

cannot be paid for out of current income. That borrowing is often done by issuing bonds, much as the Federal Government does. Generally, State and local bonds are easy to market because the interest from them is not taxed.

In the past, many State and local governments have defaulted on their debts. Thus, most State constitutions now place detailed limits on the power to borrow. States' debts now exceed $450 billion, and local governments owe more than $700 billion.

The Budget Process

A **budget** is a financial plan for the use of public money, personnel, and property. It is also a political document, a statement of public policy. In its budget, the State sets its priorities and decides who gets what and how much.

Until the 1920s, State budgets were the result of haphazard and uncoordinated steps centered in the legislature. Thus, various State agencies appeared regularly before legislative appropriations committees, each seeking its own funding, often in bitter competition with one another. Their chances of success depended far less on need or merit than on their political muscle. When the legislature adjourned, no one had any real idea of how much it had appropriated or for what.

State budgets are very different today. They remain highly charged political documents, but they are by-and-large the products of an orderly, planned process.

Forty-seven States[17] have now adopted the executive budget, which gives the governor two vital powers: (1) to prepare the State budget, and (2) to administer the funds the legislature appropriates. In most States, the governor has the help of a budget agency, appointed by and answering to the governor.

The following typical budget process at State and local levels is similar to the federal process:

1. Each agency prepares estimates of its needs and expenditures for the upcoming fiscal period.

2. Those estimates are reviewed by an executive budget agency.

3. The revised estimates and supporting information are brought together in a budget for the governor to present to the legislature.

4. The budget is considered part by part, funds are appropriated, and any necessary revenue measures are passed by the legislature.

5. The governor supervises the execution of the budget—the actual spending—approved by the legislature.

6. The execution of the budget is given an independent check, or postaudit.

---

[17]In the three other States— Mississippi, South Carolina, and Texas—responsibility for the preparation of the budget is shared by the governor and the legislature.

Section 4 Assessment

Key Terms and Main Ideas

1. Explain whether the following taxes are either **regressive** or **progressive: (a)** sales tax; **(b)** income tax.
2. What limits does the Federal Government put on States' ability to tax?
3. What is the difference between an **inheritance tax** and an **estate tax**?
4. In what ways do States tax businesses?

Critical Thinking

5. **Determining Relevance (a)** Restate in your own words Adam Smith's four principles of sound taxation. **(b)** What do you think makes each of them important?

6. **Identifying Alternatives (a)** What might be the advantages and disadvantages of raising revenue through a State-run lottery? **(b)** a State-run business? **(c)** property taxes?

Take It to the Net

7. Find out how your State gets its revenue. Then create a table that compares your State's revenue sources with those from at least one other State in a different region of the country. How do revenue sources differ among these States? What might be the reasons for these differences? Use the links provided in the Social Studies area at the following Web site for help in completing this activity. **www.phschool.com**

Must Local Government Follow the "One Person, One Vote" Rule?

*As the Supreme Court ruled in **Baker** v. **Carr** (1962), State legislatures must be apportioned according to population so that each person's vote has roughly equal weight. Should this principle apply to local government as well?*

Board of Estimate of City of New York v. *Morris* (1989)

New York City's Board of Estimate manages all city property, sets salaries of city employees, grants all city contracts, and shares authority with the City Council over the city budget. The Board has eight members: the mayor, comptroller, and president of the city council (chosen by citywide election), and the presidents of New York's five boroughs (chosen by borough election). The three citywide members each have two votes on the Board, while the borough representatives have one.

Morris and others who lived and voted in Brooklyn, the most populous borough, filed suit in 1981. They argued that the vote of each person in the less-populous boroughs counted more than each vote in Brooklyn, because all boroughs had equal representation on the Board despite great differences in population.

A federal district court dismissed the case, concluding that the Board was a "nonelective, nonlegislative body." Therefore, past Supreme Court decisions regarding apportionment did not apply to the Board. A court of appeals reversed that decision. It concluded that the Board really is an elective body, and ordered the district court to decide whether the Board's selection process met the "one person, one vote" standard. The district court ruled that it did not meet this standard, the court of appeals agreed with that ruling, and the City appealed to the Supreme Court.

Arguments for the Board of Estimate

1. The Board is a unique political body with non-legislative powers. Thus it should not have to meet the "one person, one vote" standard that legislatures must meet.
2. The Board has proven itself effective in the past and should not be disturbed. It is essential to the governing of New York City.
3. The fact that boroughs of unequal population have equal representation on the Board is not critical, because the three citywide members have double votes and can outvote the five borough members. Thus citywide interests predominate on the Board.

Arguments for Morris

1. In order for all citizens to have fair and effective representation in government, all votes must carry approximately equal weight. The Board's structure is inconsistent with this principle.
2. The principle of "one person, one vote" applies to local governments as well as to State legislatures. The Board is sufficiently legislative in its powers and must follow this principle.
3. The at-large members do not always vote together, so their majority is only theoretical.

Decide for Yourself

1. Review the constitutional grounds on which each side based its arguments and the specific arguments each side presented.
2. Debate the opposing viewpoints presented in this case. Which viewpoint do you favor?
3. Predict the impact of the Court's decision on local elections and local politics. (To read a summary of the Court's decision, turn to the Supreme Court Glossary on page 799.)

Political Dictionary

county (p. 718)

township (p. 718)

special district (p. 722)

incorporation (p. 726)

charter (p. 726)

mayor-council government (p. 726)

strong-mayor government (p. 727)

weak-mayor government (p. 727)

commission government (p. 728)

council-manager government (p. 728)

zoning (p. 730)

metropolitan area (p. 731)

Medicaid (p. 735)

welfare (p. 735)

entitlement (p. 735)

urbanization (p. 737)

sales tax (p. 741)

regressive tax (p. 741)

income tax (p. 741)

progressive tax (p. 742)

property tax (p. 742)

assessment (p. 742)

inheritance tax (p. 742)

estate tax (p. 742)

budget (p. 744)

Practicing the Vocabulary

Matching *Choose a term from the list above that best matches each description.*

1. The major unit of local government in most States except Rhode Island and Connecticut
2. A form of city government consisting of three to nine popularly elected commissioners who form a city council
3. A form of city government in which the mayor heads the city administration, prepares the budget, and generally exercises strong leadership
4. A tax on individual and corporate income
5. A tax that is based on a person's ability to pay

Using Words in Context *For each of the terms below, write a sentence that shows how it relates to this chapter.*

6. incorporation
7. charter
8. entitlement
9. special district
10. estate tax
11. metropolitan area
12. zoning

Reviewing Main Ideas

Section 1

13. What are the major forms of local government in the United States?
14. In what ways does the function of counties vary from region to region?
15. What are the most common types of special districts?
16. What is the purpose of the New England town meeting?

Section 2

17. What are the basic forms of city government?
18. Briefly describe how most cities in the United States developed.
19. Describe the impact of "suburbanitis."
20. What problems are metropolitan districts designed to solve?

Section 3

21. Briefly describe the major categories of services that States and local governments provide to their citizens.

22. Why was Aid to Families with Dependent Children replaced by the Temporary Assistance to Needy Families program?
23. Why do the amount and types of government services vary from State to State?
24. **(a)** In what ways do States try to ensure the public safety of their citizens? **(b)** What challenges do States face in ensuring public safety?

Section 4

25. What are the general limits on the ability of State and local governments to tax?
26. List the major categories of taxes that are levied at the State and local levels in this country.
27. What are the major sources of nontax revenue available to the States?
28. A State's budget is basically what two things?

Critical Thinking Skills

29. *Applying the Chapter Skill* A local jewelry store insists on charging you for fixing your watch, although it is still under warranty. Write a brief consumer complaint letter to a State agency. Describe the documents you have copied and attached to support your claim.

30. *Predicting Consequences* The decision by Houston voters to reject zoning until the early 1990s had noticeable results. **(a)** What do you think those results were? **(b)** What effects might a lack of zoning have on homeowners?

31. *Understanding Point of View* Some school districts face an uphill battle for funding in communities with a large elderly population. Why? Explain the points of view that might be involved in such a situation.

32. *Formulating Questions* Create a list of questions that you would ask your city or town's mayor or other local official to find out more about local government in your community.

Analyzing Political Cartoons

Using your knowledge of American government and this cartoon, answer the questions below.

"As for me, I believe in no taxation, with or without representation."

33. Describe the situation depicted in the cartoon.
34. What would be the impact on government and the services it provides if there were no taxes?

★ **You Can Make a Difference**

What volunteer opportunities does your community have for high school-age youth? Use the telephone book or the Internet to check on organizations or events such as Youth As Resources, City Year, local food banks, National Youth Service Day, or Students Against Destructive Decisions. With your classmates, assemble a directory of volunteer opportunities and make it available in local high schools.

Participation Activities

35. *Current Events Watch* Find a news report on a proposal to improve the amount or type of funding for schools. Analyze the proposal: What impact would it have on State and local governments and on school administrators? Would you support or oppose the proposal?

36. *Chart Activity* Research the type and organization of your local government. What are the key positions in the government, and what are their functions? Who has the most power, or is it shared? Summarize your findings in a chart or diagram like the ones in Section 2.

37. *It's Your Turn* You have just become a budget analyst for a State or local government. Review the graphs on pages 734 and 741. They reflect both the expense of various services and the services people think are most valuable. Choose one of the charts, and write a speech explaining how you would seek to change the percentage of funds allocated to certain categories to reflect your or your community's values. **(Writing a Speech)**

 Take It to the Net

Chapter 25 Self-Test As a final review activity, take the Chapter 25 Self-Test in the Social Studies area at the Web site listed below, and receive immediate feedback on your answers.

www.phschool.com

Reference Section

Databank | Supreme Court Glossary

Outline of the Constitution | Glossary

Spanish Glossary

United States Constitution | Index

Acknowledgments

Historical Documents | Stop the Presses

Databank

The United States: A Statistical Profile

State	Capital	Population (in thousands)			Land Area in Sq. Mi.	% Land Federally Owned	Population per Sq. Mi.
		2000	1990	% Change			
United States	**Washington, D.C.**	**281,422**	**248,710**	**13.2**	**3,536,278**	**28.8**	**79.6**
Alabama	Montgomery	4,447	4,041	10.1	50,750	3.4	87.6
Alaska	Juneau	627	550	14.0	570,374	67.9	1.1
Arizona	Phoenix	5,131	3,665	40.0	113,642	45.6	45.2
Arkansas	Little Rock	2,673	2,351	13.7	52,075	10.2	51.3
California	Sacramento	33,872	29,760	13.8	155,973	44.9	217.2
Colorado	Denver	4,301	3,294	30.6	103,729	36.4	41.5
Connecticut	Hartford	3,406	3,287	3.6	4,845	0.5	703.0
Delaware	Dover	784	666	17.6	1,955	2.1	401.0
Florida	Tallahassee	15,982	12,938	23.5	53,937	8.3	296.3
Georgia	Atlanta	8,186	6,478	26.4	57,919	5.6	141.3
Hawaii	Honolulu	1,212	1,108	9.3	6,423	14.7	188.7
Idaho	Boise	1,294	1,007	28.5	82,751	62.5	15.6
Illinois	Springfield	12,419	11,431	8.6	55,593	1.8	223.4
Indiana	Indianapolis	6,080	5,544	9.7	35,870	2.2	169.5
Iowa	Des Moines	2,926	2,777	5.4	55,875	0.7	52.4
Kansas	Topeka	2,688	2,478	8.5	81,823	1.3	32.9
Kentucky	Frankfort	4,042	3,685	9.7	39,732	4.8	101.7
Louisiana	Baton Rouge	4,469	4,220	5.9	43,566	4.5	102.6
Maine	Augusta	1,275	1,228	3.8	30,865	1.0	41.3
Maryland	Annapolis	5,296	4,781	10.8	9,775	3.2	541.8
Massachusetts	Boston	6,349	6,016	5.5	7,838	1.6	810.0
Michigan	Lansing	9,938	9,295	6.9	56,809	11.2	174.9
Minnesota	St. Paul	4,919	4,375	12.4	79,617	8.7	61.8
Mississippi	Jackson	2,845	2,573	10.5	46,914	5.9	60.6
Missouri	Jefferson City	5,595	5,117	9.3	68,898	4.8	81.2
Montana	Helena	902	799	12.9	145,556	28.0	6.2
Nebraska	Lincoln	1,711	1,578	8.4	76,878	1.5	22.3
Nevada	Carson City	1,998	1,202	66.3	109,806	83.1	18.2
New Hampshire	Concord	1,236	1,109	11.4	8,969	13.2	137.8
New Jersey	Trenton	8,414	7,730	8.9	7,419	3.4	1,134.1
New Mexico	Santa Fe	1,819	1,515	20.1	121,364	34.2	15.0
New York	Albany	18,976	17,990	5.5	47,224	0.4	401.8
North Carolina	Raleigh	8,049	6,629	21.4	48,718	8.0	165.2
North Dakota	Bismarck	642	639	0.5	68,994	4.2	9.3
Ohio	Columbus	11,353	10,847	4.7	40,953	1.5	277.2
Oklahoma	Oklahoma City	3,451	3,146	9.7	68,679	2.9	50.2
Oregon	Salem	3,421	2,842	20.4	96,002	52.6	35.6
Pennsylvania	Harrisburg	12,281	11,882	3.4	44,820	2.4	274.0
Rhode Island	Providence	1,048	1,003	4.5	1,045	0.6	1,002.9
South Carolina	Columbia	4,012	3,487	15.1	30,111	6.1	133.2
South Dakota	Pierre	755	696	8.5	75,896	5.6	9.9
Tennessee	Nashville	5,689	4,877	16.7	41,219	6.1	138.0
Texas	Austin	20,852	16,987	22.8	261,914	1.7	79.6
Utah	Salt Lake City	2,233	1,723	29.6	82,168	64.5	27.2
Vermont	Montpelier	609	563	8.2	9,249	6.3	65.8
Virginia	Richmond	7,079	6,187	14.4	39,598	9.0	178.8
Washington	Olympia	5,894	4,867	21.1	66,581	28.5	88.5
West Virgina	Charleston	1,808	1,793	0.8	24,087	7.6	75.1
Wisconsin	Madison	5,364	4,892	9.6	54,314	5.6	98.8
Wyoming	Cheyenne	494	454	8.9	97,105	49.9	5.1
Washington, D.C.		572	607	-5.7	61	23.4	9,377.0

Sources: Bureau of the Census; Federal Election Commission

State	Population (in thousands)				Popular Vote, 2000 Presidential Election					
	% Urban	African American	Hispanic† Origin	% Foreign Born	George W. Bush (Republican)	%	Al Gore (Democrat)	%	All Others	%
United States	80.1	34,862	31,337	7.9	50,455,156	47.87	50,992,335	48.38	3,949,150	3.75
Alabama	70.1	1,139	45	1.1	941,173	56	692,611	48	32,488	2
Alaska	41.5	24	25	4.5	167,398	59	79,004	28	39,158	14
Arizona	87.8	176	1,084	7.6	781,652	51	685,341	45	65,023	4
Arkansas	48.6	411	54	1.1	472, 940	51	422,768	46	26,073	3
California	96.7	2,487	10,460	21.7	4,567,429	42	5,861,203	53	537,224	5
Colorado	84.0	176	604	4.3	883,748	51	738,227	42	119,393	7
Connecticut	95.6	309	279	8.5	561,094	38	816,015	56	82,416	6
Delaware	81.6	149	28	3.3	137,288	42	180,068	55	10,266	3
Florida	93.0	2,333	2,334	12.9	2,912,790	49	2,912,253	49	138,067	2
Georgia	68.9	2,236	240	2.7	1,419,720	55	1,116,230	43	60,854	2
Hawaii	73.1	34	95	14.7	137,845	37	205,286	56	24,820	7
Idaho	38.3	8	93	2.9	336,937	67	138,637	28	26,047	5
Illinois	84.5	1,854	1,276	8.3	2,019,421	43	2,589,026	55	133,676	3
Indiana	71.7	498	154	1.7	1,245,836	57	901,980	41	51,486	2
Iowa	44.6	58	62	1.6	634,373	48	638,517	48	42,673	3
Kansas	56.4	157	148	2.5	622,332	58	399,276	37	50,610	5
Kentucky	48.3	288	35	0.9	872,492	56	638,898	41	32,797	2
Louisiana	75.2	1,415	119	2.1	927,871	53	792,344	45	45,441	3
Maine	35.8	6	9	3.0	286,616	44	319,951	49	45,250	7
Maryland	92.7	1,454	199	6.6	813,797	40	1,140,782	56	65,901	3
Massachusetts	96.1	405	391	9.5	878,502	32	1,616,487	60	207,995	8
Michigan	82.6	1,415	276	3.8	1,953,139	46	2,170,418	51	108,944	3
Minnesota	70.1	149	93	2.6	1,109,659	45	1,168,266	48	160,760	7
Mississippi	35.9	1,010	24	0.8	572,844	58	404,614	41	16,726	2
Missouri	68.0	617	91	1.6	1,189,924	50	1,111,138	47	58,830	2
Montana	33.4	3	16	1.7	240,178	58	137,126	33	33,693	8
Nebraska	51.8	68	77	1.8	433,862	62	231,780	33	31,377	4
Nevada	86.1	140	304	8.7	301,575	49	279,978	46	27,417	4
New Hampshire	60.2	9	20	3.7	273,559	48	266,348	47	29,174	5
New Jersey	100.0	1,197	1,027	12.5	1,284,173	40	1,788,850	56	114,203	4
New Mexico	57.0	46	708	5.3	286,417	48	286,783	48	25,405	4
New York	91.9	3,222	2,661	15.9	2,403,374	35	4,107,697	60	310,928	5
North Carolina	67.1	1,686	176	1.7	1,631,163	56	1,257,692	43	22,407	1
North Dakota	43.1	4	7	1.5	174,852	61	95,284	33	18,120	6
Ohio	81.0	1,304	185	2.4	2,350,363	50	2,183,628	46	168,007	4
Oklahoma	60.5	262	137	2.1	744,337	60	474,276	38	15,616	1
Oregon	72.7	62	213	4.9	713,577	46	720,342	47	100,049	6
Pennsylvania	84.5	1,170	326	3.1	2,281,127	46	2,485,967	51	146,025	3
Rhode Island	93.8	50	69	9.5	130,555	32	249,508	61	29,049	7
South Carolina	70.0	1,157	54	1.4	785,937	57	565,561	41	31,219	2
South Dakota	34.0	5	9	1.1	190,700	60	118,804	38	6,765	2
Tennessee	67.8	913	67	1.2	1,061,949	51	981,720	47	32,512	2
Texas	84.5	2,470	6,045	9.0	3,799,639	59	2,433,746	38	174,252	3
Utah	76.7	19	151	3.4	515,096	67	203,053	26	52,605	7
Vermont	27.9	3	5	3.1	119,775	41	149,022	51	25,511	9
Virginia	78.1	1,385	266	5.0	1,437,490	52	1,217,290	44	84,667	3
Washington	82.9	204	377	6.6	1,108,864	45	1,247,652	50	130,917	5
West Virgina	41.9	56	10	0.9	336,475	52	295,497	46	16,152	2
Wisconsin	67.8	293	140	2.5	1,237,279	48	1,242,987	48	118,341	4
Wyoming	29.6	4	29	1.7	147,947	68	60,481	28	9,923	4
Washington, D.C.	100.0	319	38	9.7	18,073	9	171,923	85	11,898	6

† Persons of Hispanic origin may be of any race.

Political Map of the United States

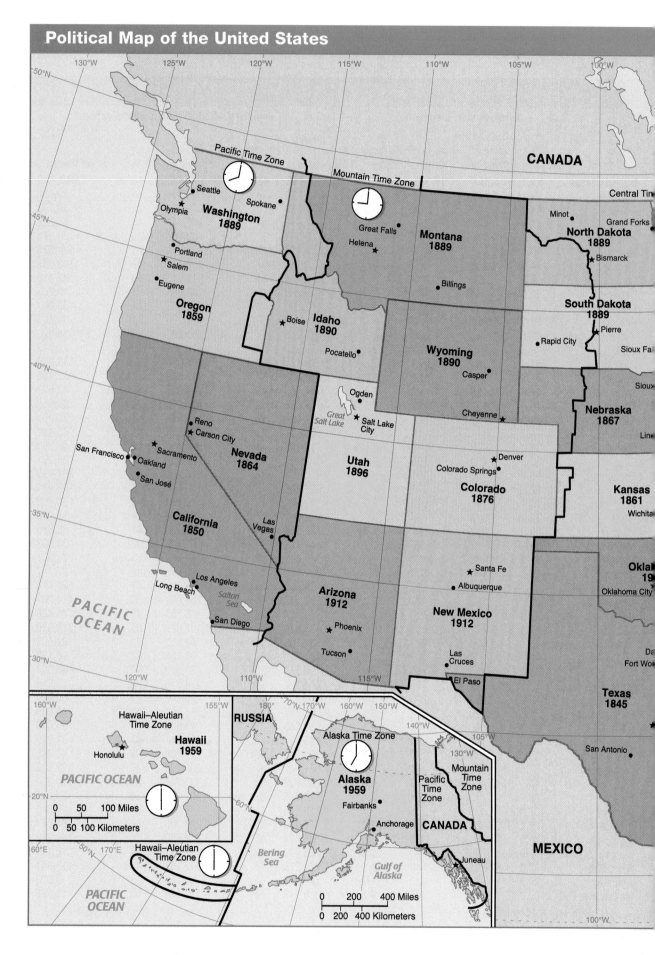

CANADA

Central Time

Washington 1889
- Seattle
- Olympia
- Spokane

Oregon 1859
- Portland
- Salem
- Eugene

Montana 1889
- Great Falls
- Helena
- Billings

Idaho 1890
- Boise
- Pocatello

North Dakota 1889
- Minot
- Grand Forks
- Bismarck

South Dakota 1889
- Rapid City
- Pierre
- Sioux Falls

Wyoming 1890
- Casper
- Cheyenne

Nebraska 1867
- Sioux
- Line

Nevada 1864
- Reno
- Carson City
- Las Vegas

Utah 1896
- Ogden
- Salt Lake City
- Great Salt Lake

Colorado 1876
- Denver
- Colorado Springs

Kansas 1861
- Wichita

California 1850
- San Francisco
- Oakland
- San José
- Sacramento
- Los Angeles
- Long Beach
- San Diego
- Salton Sea

Arizona 1912
- Phoenix
- Tucson

New Mexico 1912
- Santa Fe
- Albuquerque
- Las Cruces
- El Paso

Oklahoma 19
- Oklahoma City

Texas 1845
- Dallas
- Fort Worth
- San Antonio

PACIFIC OCEAN

Pacific Time Zone

Mountain Time Zone

Inset: Hawaii

Hawaii 1959
- Honolulu

Hawaii–Aleutian Time Zone

PACIFIC OCEAN

0 50 100 Miles
0 50 100 Kilometers

Hawaii–Aleutian Time Zone

PACIFIC OCEAN

Inset: Alaska

RUSSIA

Alaska Time Zone

Alaska 1959
- Fairbanks
- Anchorage
- Juneau

Bering Sea

Gulf of Alaska

Pacific Time Zone

Mountain Time Zone

CANADA

MEXICO

0 200 400 Miles
0 200 400 Kilometers

Databank

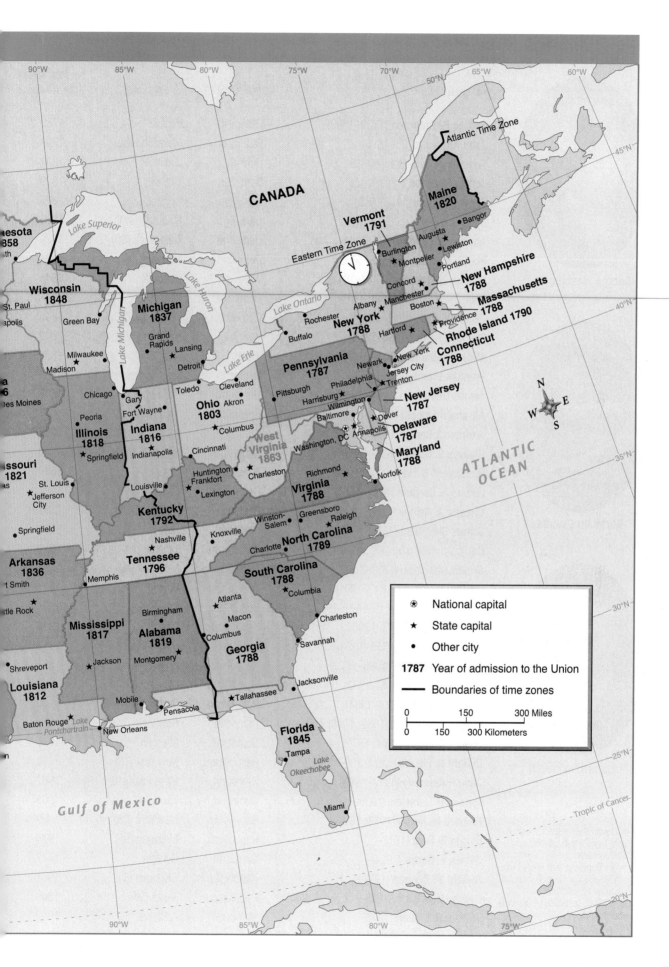

CANADA

Atlantic Time Zone

Maine
1820
• Bangor

Vermont
1791
Augusta ★
Eastern Time Zone
• Burlington • Lewiston
• Montpelier • Portland

Concord ★   New Hampshire
1788
Manchester •
Massachusetts
1788
Albany ★ • Boston ★
Rhode Island 1790
Providence ★
New York
1788
Hartford ★
Connecticut
1788

Lake Superior

Minnesota
1858
uth
•

Wisconsin
1848
St. Paul
•apolis

Green Bay
•

Lake Huron

Michigan
1837

Grand
Rapids •
Milwaukee •   Lansing ★
Madison ★

Lake Michigan

Chicago •   Detroit •
Gary •
Fort Wayne •

Lake Erie

Toledo •   Cleveland • Akron •

Ohio
1803

Rochester •

Buffalo •

Pennsylvania
1787

Newark •   New York •
Pittsburgh •   Jersey City •
Harrisburg ★ Philadelphia • Trenton •

New Jersey
1787

Des Moines
•

a
6

Peoria •

Illinois
1818

Indiana
1816

Indianapolis ★

Springfield ★

Cincinnati •

West
Virginia
1863

Columbus •

Washington, DC ✪

Wilmington •
Baltimore •   Dover •

Delaware
1787

Annapolis ★

Maryland
1788

Missouri
1821
as

St. Louis •
Jefferson ★
City

Louisville •
Frankfort ★

Huntington •

Charleston ★

Richmond •

Virginia
1788

ATLANTIC
OCEAN

Springfield
•

Kentucky
1792

Lexington •

Norfolk •

Nashville ★

Knoxville •

Winston-
Salem •

Greensboro •
Raleigh ★

Arkansas
1836

Tennessee
1796

North Carolina
1789

t Smith

Memphis •

Charlotte •

tle Rock
★

South Carolina
1788

Atlanta ★   Columbia ★

Mississippi
1817

Birmingham •

Alabama
1819

Macon •
Columbus •

Charleston •

Georgia
1788

Savannah •

Shreveport
•

Jackson ★ Montgomery ★

Louisiana
1812

Mobile •

Jacksonville •

Baton Rouge ★ Lake
Pontchartrain
• New Orleans

Pensacola •

★ Tallahassee

Florida
1845

Tampa •

Lake
Okeechobee

Gulf of Mexico

Miami •

Tropic of Cancer

✪	National capital
★	State capital
•	Other city
1787	Year of admission to the Union
▬▬▬	Boundaries of time zones

0   150   300 Miles
0   150   300 Kilometers

Presidents of the United States

George Washington

Abraham Lincoln

Theodore Roosevelt

NAME	PARTY	STATE[a]	ENTERED OFFICE
George Washington (1732–1799)	Federalist	Virginia	1789
John Adams (1735–1826)	Federalist	Massachusetts	1797
Thomas Jefferson (1743–1826)	Dem-Rep[b]	Virginia	1801
James Madison (1751–1836)	Dem-Rep	Virginia	1809
James Monroe (1758–1831)	Dem-Rep	Virginia	1817
John Q. Adams (1767–1848)	Dem-Rep	Massachusetts	1825
Andrew Jackson (1767–1845)	Democrat	Tennessee (SC)	1829
Martin Van Buren (1782–1862)	Democrat	New York	1837
William H. Harrison (1773–1841)	Whig	Ohio (VA)	1841
John Tyler (1790–1862)	Democrat	Virginia	1841
James K. Polk (1795–1849)	Democrat	Tennessee (NC)	1845
Zachary Taylor (1784–1850)	Whig	Louisiana (VA)	1849
Millard Fillmore (1800–1874)	Whig	New York	1850
Franklin Pierce (1804–1869)	Democrat	New Hampshire	1853
James Buchanan (1791–1868)	Democrat	Pennsylvania	1857
Abraham Lincoln (1809–1865)	Republican	Illinois (KY)	1861
Andrew Johnson (1808–1875)	Democrat[c]	Tennessee (NC)	1865
Ulysses S. Grant (1822–1885)	Republican	Illinois (OH)	1869
Rutherford B. Hayes (1822–1893)	Republican	Ohio	1877
James A. Garfield (1831–1881)	Republican	Ohio	1881
Chester A. Arthur (1829–1896)	Republican	New York (VT)	1881
Grover Cleveland (1837–1908)	Democrat	New York (NJ)	1885
Benjamin Harrison (1833–1901)	Republican	Indiana (OH)	1889
Grover Cleveland (1837–1908)	Democrat	New York (NJ)	1893
William McKinley (1843–1901)	Republican	Ohio	1897
Theodore Roosevelt (1858–1919)	Republican	New York	1901
William H. Taft (1857–1930)	Republican	Ohio	1909
Woodrow Wilson (1856–1924)	Democrat	New Jersey (VA)	1913
Warren G. Harding (1865–1923)	Republican	Ohio	1921
Calvin Coolidge (1872–1933)	Republican	Massachusetts (VT)	1923
Herbert Hoover (1874–1964)	Republican	California (IA)	1929
Franklin Roosevelt (1882–1945)	Democrat	New York	1933
Harry S Truman (1884–1972)	Democrat	Missouri	1945
Dwight D. Eisenhower (1890–1969)	Republican	New York (TX)	1953
John F. Kennedy (1917–1963)	Democrat	Massachusetts	1961
Lyndon B. Johnson (1908–1973)	Democrat	Texas	1963
Richard M. Nixon (1913–1994)	Republican	New York (CA)	1969
Gerald R. Ford (1913–)	Republican	Michigan (NE)	1974
James E. Carter (1924–)	Democrat	Georgia	1977
Ronald W. Reagan (1911–)	Republican	California (IL)	1981
George H.W. Bush (1924–)	Republican	Texas (MA)	1989
William J. Clinton (1946–)	Democrat	Arkansas	1993
George W. Bush (1946–)	Republican	Texas	2001

[a] State of residence when elected; if born in another State, that State in parentheses.
[b] Democratic-Republican
[c] Johnson, a War Democrat, was elected Vice-President on the coalition Union Party ticket.
[d] Resigned October 10, 1973.
[e] Nominated by Nixon, confirmed by Congress on December 6, 1973.
[f] Nominated by Ford, confirmed by Congress on December 19, 1974.

Age On Taking Office	Religion	Ancestry	Vice President(s)
57	Episcopalian	English	John Adams
61	Unitarian	English	Thomas Jefferson
57	——————	Welsh	Aaron Burr/George Clinton
57	Episcopalian	English	George Clinton/Elbridge Gerry
58	Episcopalian	Scottish	Daniel D. Tompkins
57	Unitarian	English	John C. Calhoun
61	Presbyterian	Scots-Irish	John C. Calhoun/Martin Van Buren
54	Dutch Reformed	Dutch	Richard M. Johnson
68	Episcopalian	English	John Tyler
51	Episcopalian	English	none
49	Presbyterian	Scots-Irish	George M. Dallas
64	Episcopalian	English	Millard Fillmore
50	Unitarian	English	none
48	Episcopalian	English	William R. King
65	Presbyterian	Scots-Irish	John C. Breckinridge
52	——————	English	Hannibal Hamlin/Andrew Johnson
56	——————	English	none
46	Methodist	English-Scottish	Schuyler Colfax/Henry Wilson
54	Methodist	Scottish	William A. Wheeler
49	Disciples of Christ	English	Chester A. Arthur
51	Episcopalian	Scots-Irish	none
47	Presbyterian	English-Irish	Thomas A. Hendricks
55	Presbyterian	English	Levi P. Morton
55	Presbyterian	English-Irish	Adlai E. Stevenson
54	Methodist	Scots-Irish	Garret A. Hobart/Theodore Roosevelt
42	Dutch Reformed	Dutch	Charles W. Fairbanks
51	Unitarian	English	James S. Sherman
56	Presbyterian	Scots-Irish	Thomas R. Marshall
55	Baptist	English-Scottish-Irish	Calvin Coolidge
51	Congregationalist	English	Charles G. Dawes
54	Quaker	Swiss-German	Charles Curtis
51	Episcopalian	Dutch	John N. Garner/Henry A. Wallace/Harry S Truman
60	Baptist	English-Scottish-Irish	Alben W. Barkley
62	Presbyterian	Swiss-German	Richard M. Nixon
43	Roman Catholic	Irish	Lyndon B. Johnson
55	Disciples of Christ	English	Hubert H. Humphrey
56	Quaker	Scots-Irish	Spiro T. Agnew [d]/Gerald R. Ford [e]
61	Episcopalian	English	Nelson A. Rockefeller [f]
52	Baptist	English-Scottish-Irish	Walter F. Mondale
69	Episcopalian	English-Scottish-Irish	George H. W. Bush
64	Episcopalian	English	J. Danforth Quayle
46	Baptist	English	Albert Gore, Jr.
54	Episcopalian	English	Richard B. Cheney

Woodrow Wilson

Franklin Roosevelt

Ronald Reagan

Political Map of the World

80°N   160°W   140°W   120°W   100°W   80°W   60°W   40°W

ARCTIC OCEAN

Greenland
(Den.)

60°N   Alaska (U.S.)   Yukon R.   Reykjavik   ICELAN

ALEUTIAN IS. (U.S.)   CANADA   40°N

**NORTH
AMERICA**   Montreal
Ottawa

Chicago   New York

San Francisco   **UNITED STATES**   Ohio R.   Washington, DC   AZORES
(Port.)

Bermuda (U.K.)   CANARY IS.
(Spain)

Midway I. (U.S.)   Houston   **ATLANTIC OCEAN**   Western Sahara
(Mor.)

New
Orleans   BAHAMAS
Havana

HAWAII (U.S.)   20°N   **MEXICO**   Santo   DOMINICAN
Domingo REP.   See i
map

Mexico City   BELIZE   CUBA   Puerto Rico (U.S.)   **CAPE VERDE**
Port-au-Prince   ST. KITTS & NEVIS
GUATEMALA   JAMAICA   HAITI   ANTIGUA & BARBUDA
Guatemala   HONDURAS   ST.   DOMINICA
Tegucigalpa   LUCIA   BARBADOS
EL SALVADOR   NICARAGUA   TRINIDAD &
San Salvador   Managua   TOBAGO
COSTA RICA   Panama   GUYANA
San José   Caracas   SURINAME
Equator   PANAMA   VENEZUELA   Paramaribo
Bogotá   FRENCH
GALÁPAGOS IS.   COLOMBIA   Georgetown   GUIANA
(Ecuador)

PACIFIC OCEAN   Quito
ECUADOR   **SOUTH
AMERICA**
SAMOA   Negro R.   Amazon R.
AMERICAN   Lima   Madeira R.   BRAZIL
SAMOA (U.S.)   FRENCH POLYNESIA   PERU   Brasília
(Fr.)   BOLIVIA
TONGA   COOK IS.   La Paz   São Francisco R.
(N.Z.)   Sucre
20°S   Pitcairn I. (U.K.)   PARAGUAY
Rio de Janeiro
Asunción   São Paulo
Easter I.   CHILE   Uruguay R.
(Chile)   URUGUAY
Santiago   Buenos   Montevideo   W
Aires
40°S   ARGENTINA

FALKLAND IS.   S. Georgia
(U.K.)   (U.K.)

Europe

0   200   400 Miles
0   400 Kilometers

FINLAND
NORWAY   Helsinki
Oslo   Stockholm   ESTONIA   RUSSIA
SWEDEN   Riga   LATVIA
N. IRELAND   Tallinn
Dublin   UNITED   DENMARK   LITHUANIA
IRELAND   KINGDOM   Copenhagen   Vilnius
London   NETHERLANDS   RUSSIA   Minsk
Amsterdam   Berlin   Warsaw   BELARUS
ATLANTIC   Brussels   GERMANY   POLAND   Kiev
OCEAN   BELGIUM   CZECH   UKRAINE
LUX.   REP.   SLOVAKIA   MOLDOVA
Paris   LIECH.   Prague   Chisinau
Bern   Vienna   Bratislava
FRANCE   SWITZ.   AUSTRIA   HUNGARY   ROMANIA
Ljubljana   Budapest
SLOVENIA   Zagreb   CROATIA   Bucharest
SAN   BOSNIA-   Belgrade
ANDORRA   MARINO   HERZ.   Serbia   BULGARIA
MONACO   ITALY   Sarajevo   Sofia
Lisbon   Madrid   Montenegro   MACEDONIA
Rome   Tirana
SPAIN   ALBANIA   TURKEY
Mediterranean   GREECE
Rabat   Tunis   Athens
Algiers   Sea
MOROCCO   ALGERIA   TUNISIA

Africa

Nouakchott   0   250   500 Miles
MAURITANIA   0   250   500 Kilometers
Dakar   MALI   Niamey   NIGER
SENEGAL   Bamako   BURKINA
GAMBIA   Niger R.   FASO
Banjul   GUINEA-   Ouagadougou
Bissau   BISSAU   BENIN   NIGERIA
GUINEA   Abuja
Conakry   SIERRA   CÔTE   GHANA   Porto-
Freetown   LEONE   D'IVOIRE   Novo   Lagos
Yamoussoukro   Lomé
Monrovia   Accra
LIBERIA   Abidjan   TOGO

40°E 60°E 80°E 100°E 120°E 140°E 160°E

VALBARD
(Nor.)

See inset map

ROPE

RUSSIA

• Novosibirsk

Moscow

Volga R.

Ob R.

Lena R.

KAZAKHSTAN

ASIA

MONGOLIA

• Ulanbaatar

Almaty

Bishkek KYRGYZSTAN

Dushanbe TAJIKISTAN

AFGHANISTAN

Kabul Islamabad

PAKISTAN NEPAL BHUTAN
Thimphu
New   Kathmandu
Delhi   Dhaka

INDIA

Beijing

Tianjin

Chongqing

N. KOREA
Pyongyang
Seoul
S. KOREA

JAPAN

Tokyo

CHINA

PACIFIC OCEAN

MYANMAR Hanoi
Yangon   Vientiane

BANGLA- LAOS
DESH Bangkok VIETNAM

THAILAND Ho Chi Minh City

Phnom CAMBODIA
Penh   BRUNEI
Bandar
Seri Begawan

Taipei
TAIWAN

Hong Kong

Manila
PHILIPPINES

NORTHERN
MARIANA IS. (U.S.)
Guam
(U.S.)

Wake I. (U.S.)

MARSHALL IS.

AFRICA

See inset map

SRI
Colombo LANKA

MALDIVES

Kuala Lumpur MALAYSIA

SINGAPORE

PALAU

FEDERATED STATES
OF MICRONESIA

NAURU

Bangui CENTRAL
Yaoundé AFRICAN REP.
MEROON
breville DEM. REP. UGANDA SOMALIA
N OF THE CONGO KENYA Mogadishu
ONGO RWANDA Kampala
Brazzaville Kigali Nairobi
Kinshasa BURUNDI
Bujumbura
Luanda   Dar es Salaam

SEYCHELLES

I N D O N E S I A

Jakarta

PAPUA
NEW GUINEA

Port Moresby

KIRIBATI

TUVALU

SOLOMON IS.

ANGOLA TANZANIA
MALAWI
ZAMBIA Lilongwe
Lusaka Zambezi
Harare
NAMIBIA ZIMBABWE
hoek BOTSWANA MOZAMBIQUE
Gaborone Maputo
Pretoria
Town SOUTH Mbabne
AFRICA Maseru
LESOTHO

COMOROS

Réunion (Fr.)

Antananarivo
MAURITIUS

MADAGASCAR

SWAZILAND

INDIAN OCEAN

Perth

AUSTRALIA

VANUATU

FIJI

New Caledonia (Fr.)

Adelaide

Canberra
Sydney
Melbourne

Wellington

NEW
ZEALAND

⊛ National capital

• Other city

0   1,000   2,000 Miles

0   1,000   2,000 Kilometers

ANTARCTICA

Middle East

RUSSIA

KAZAKHSTAN

Istanbul

GEORGIA Tbilisi
ARMENIA Yerevan
Ankara   Baku

UZBEKISTAN

Tashkent

TURKMENISTAN

Ashgabad

Tunis

TUNISIA

Tripoli

CYPRUS SYRIA
Beirut
LEBANON Damascus Baghdad
Jerusalem IRAQ
ISRAEL Amman
Cairo   JORDAN Kuwait

TURKEY

AZERBAIJAN

Tehran

IRAN

KUWAIT

AFGHAN.

PAK.

BAHRAIN
Manama QATAR
Riyadh   Doha Abu Dhabi
Muscat
U.A.E.

LIBYA

EGYPT

SAUDI
ARABIA

OMAN

NIGER

CHAD

0   300   600 Miles

0 300 600 Kilometers

Khartoum

SUDAN

Asmara
ERITREA

Sanaa
YEMEN

Aden

DJIBOUTI
Djibouti

INDIAN
OCEAN

ETHIOPIA
Addis
Ababa

SOMALIA

An Outline of the Constitution of the United States

"The American Constitution is the most wonderful Work ever struck off at a given time by the brain and purpose of man."

—William E. Gladstone

Preamble

ARTICLE I	LEGISLATIVE DEPARTMENT
Section 1.	Legislative Power, the Congress
Section 2.	House of Representatives
Section 3.	Senate
Section 4.	Elections and Meetings
Section 5.	Legislative Proceedings
Section 6.	Compensation, Immunities, and Disabilities of Members
Section 7.	Revenue Bills; President's Veto
Section 8.	Powers of Congress
Section 9.	Powers Denied to Congress
Section 10.	Powers Denied to the States

ARTICLE II	EXECUTIVE DEPARTMENT
Section 1.	Executive Power; The President; Term; Election; Qualifications; Compensation; Oath of Office
Section 2.	President's Powers and Duties
Section 3.	President's Powers and Duties
Section 4.	Impeachment

ARTICLE III	JUDICIAL DEPARTMENT
Section 1.	Judicial Power; Courts; Terms of Office
Section 2.	Jurisdiction
Section 3.	Treason

ARTICLE IV	RELATIONS AMONG THE STATES
Section 1.	Full Faith and Credit
Section 2.	Privileges and Immunities of Citizens
Section 3.	New States, Territories
Section 4.	Protection Afforded to States by the Nation

ARTICLE V	PROVISIONS FOR AMENDMENT

ARTICLE VI	PUBLIC DEBTS; SUPREMACY OF NATIONAL LAW; OATH
Section 1.	Validity of Debts
Section 2.	Supremacy of National Law
Section 3.	Oaths of Office

ARTICLE VII	RATIFICATION OF CONSTITUTION

AMENDMENTS	
1st Amendment	Freedom of Religion, Speech, Press, Assembly, and Petition
2nd Amendment	Right to Keep, Bear Arms
3rd Amendment	Lodging Troops in Private Homes
4th Amendment	Search, Seizures, Proper Warrants
5th Amendment	Criminal Proceedings, Due Process, Eminent Domain

6th Amendment	Criminal Proceedings
7th Amendment	Jury Trials in Civil Cases
8th Amendment	Bail; Cruel, Unusual Punishment
9th Amendment	Unenumerated Rights
10th Amendment	Powers Reserved to the States
11th Amendment	Suits Against the States
12th Amendment	Election of President and Vice President
13th Amendment	Slavery and Involuntary Servitude
Section 1.	Slavery and Involuntary Servitude Prohibited
Section 2.	Power of Congress
14th Amendment	Rights of Citizens
Section 1.	Citizenship; Privileges and Immunities; Due Process; Equal Protection
Section 2.	Apportionment of Representation
Section 3.	Disqualification of Officers
Section 4.	Public Debt
Section 5.	Powers of Congress
15th Amendment	Right to Vote—Race, Color, Servitude
Section 1.	Suffrage Not to Be Abridged
Section 2.	Power of Congress
16th Amendment	Income Tax
17th Amendment	Popular Election of Senators
Section 1.	Popular Election of Senators
Section 2.	Senate Vacancies
Section 3.	Inapplicable to Senators Previously Chosen
18th Amendment	Prohibition of Intoxicating Liquors
Section 1.	Intoxicating Liquors Prohibited
Section 2.	Concurrent Power to Enforce
Section 3.	Time Limit on Ratification
19th Amendment	Equal Suffrage—Sex
Section 1.	Suffrage Not to Be Abridged
Section 2.	Power of Congress

20th Amendment	Commencement of Terms; Sessions of Congress; Death or Disqualification of President-Elect
Section 1.	Terms of President, Vice President, members of Congress
Section 2.	Sessions of Congress
Section 3.	Death or Disqualification of President-Elect
Section 4.	Congress to Provide for Certain Successors
Section 5.	Effective Date
Section 6.	Time Limit on Ratification
21st Amendment	Repeal of 18th Amendment
Section 1.	Repeal of Prohibition
Section 2.	Transportation, Importation of Intoxicating Liquors
Section 3.	Time Limit on Ratification
22nd Amendment	Presidential Tenure
Section 1.	Restriction on Number of Terms
Section 2.	Time Limit on Ratification
23rd Amendment	Inclusion of District of Columbia in Presidential Election Systems
Section 1.	Presidential Electors for District
Section 2.	Power of Congress
24th Amendment	Right to Vote in Federal Elections—Tax Payment
Section 1.	Suffrage Not to Be Abridged
Section 2.	Power of Congress
25th Amendment	Presidential Succession; Vice Presidential Vacancy; Presidential Inability
Section 1.	Presidential Succession
Section 2.	Vice Presidential Vacancy
Section 3.	Presidential Inability
26th Amendment	Right to Vote—Age
Section 1.	Suffrage Not to Be Abridged
Section 2.	Power of Congress
27th Amendment	Congressional Pay

Outline of the Constitution

PREAMBLE

We the People of the United States, in Order to form a more perfect Union, establish Justice, insure domestic Tranquility, provide for the common defence, promote the general Welfare, and secure the Blessings of Liberty to ourselves and our Posterity, do ordain and establish this Constitution for the United States of America.

The Preamble states the broad purposes the Constitution is intended to serve—to establish a government that provides for greater cooperation among the States, ensures justice and peace, provides for defense against foreign enemies, promotes the general well-being of the people, and secures liberty now and in the future. The phrase *We the People* emphasizes the twin concepts of popular sovereignty and of representative government.

Article I.

Section 1.

All legislative Powers herein granted shall be vested in a Congress of the United States, which shall consist of a Senate and House of Representatives.

LEGISLATIVE DEPARTMENT

Section 1. Legislative power; Congress

Congress, the nation's lawmaking body, is bicameral in form; that is, it is composed of two houses: the Senate and the House of Representatives. The Framers of the Constitution purposely separated the lawmaking power from the power to enforce the laws (Article II, the Executive Branch) and the power to interpret them (Article III, the Judicial Branch). This system of separation of powers is supplemented by a system of checks and balances; that is, in several provisions the Constitution gives to each of the three branches various powers with which it may restrain the actions of the other two branches.

Section 2.

1. The House of Representatives shall be composed of Members chosen every second Year by the People of the several States, and the Electors in each State shall have the Qualifications requisite for Electors of the most numerous Branch of the State Legislature.

Section 2. House of Representatives

Clause 1. Election Electors means voters. Members of the House of Representatives are elected every two years. Each State must permit the same persons to vote for United States representatives as it permits to vote for the members of the larger house of its own legislature. The 17th Amendment (1913) extends this requirement to the qualification of voters for United States senators.

2. No Person shall be a Representative who shall not have attained to the age of twenty-five Years, and been seven Years a Citizen of the United States, and who shall not, when elected, be an Inhabitant of that State in which he shall be chosen.

Clause 2. Qualifications A member of the House of Representatives must be at least 25 years old, an American citizen for seven years, and a resident of the State he or she represents. In addition, political custom requires that a representative also reside in the district from which he or she is elected.

3. Representatives ~~and direct Taxes~~* shall be apportioned among the several States which may be included within this Union, according to their respective Numbers, ~~which shall be determined by adding to the whole Number of free Persons, including those bound to Service for a Term of Years and excluding Indians not taxed, three fifths of all other Persons.~~ The actual Enumeration shall be made within three Years after the first Meeting of the Congress of the United States, and within every subsequent term of ten Years, in such Manner as they shall by Law direct. The Number of Representatives shall not exceed one for every thirty Thousand, but each State shall have at Least one Representative; and, until such enumeration shall be made, the State of New Hampshire shall be entitled to choose three, Massachusetts eight, Rhode Island and Providence Plantations one, Connecticut five, New York six, New Jersey four, Pennsylvania eight, Delaware one, Maryland six, Virginia ten, North Carolina five, South Carolina five, and Georgia three.

Clause 3. Apportionment The number of representatives each State is entitled to is based on its population, which is counted every 10 years in the census. Congress reapportions the seats among the States after each census. In the Reapportionment Act of 1929, Congress fixed the permanent size of the House at 435 members with each State having at least one representative. Today there is one House seat for approximately every 650,000 persons in the population.

The words "three-fifths of all other persons" referred to slaves and reflected the Three-Fifths Compromise reached by the Framers at Philadelphia in 1787; the phrase was made obsolete, was in effect repealed, by the 13th Amendment in 1865.

4. When vacancies happen in the Representation from any State, the Executive Authority thereof shall issue Writs of Election to fill such Vacancies.

Clause 4. Vacancies The executive authority refers to the governor of a State. If a member leaves office or dies before the expiration of his or her term, the governor is to call a special election to fill the vacancy.

*The black lines indicate portions of the Constitution altered by subsequent amendments to the document.

5. The House of Representatives shall choose their Speaker and other Officers; and shall have the sole Power of Impeachment.

Section 3.

1. The Senate of the United States shall be composed of two Senators from each State ~~chosen by the Legislature thereof~~ for six Years; and each Senator shall have one Vote.

2. Immediately after they shall be assembled in Consequences of the first Election, they shall be divided, as equally as may be, into three Classes. The Seats of the Senators of the first Class shall be vacated at the Expiration of the second Year; of the second Class, at the Expiration of the fourth Year; and of the third Class, at the Expiration of the sixth Year; so that one-third may be chosen every second Year; ~~and if Vacancies happen by Resignation, or otherwise, during the Recess of the Legislature of any State, the Executive thereof may make temporary Appointments until the next Meeting of the Legislature, which shall then fill such Vacancies.~~

3. No Person shall be a Senator who shall not have attained to the Age of thirty Years, and been nine Years a Citizen of the United States, and who shall not, when elected, be an Inhabitant of that State for which he shall be chosen.

4. The Vice President of the United States shall be President of the Senate but shall have no Vote, unless they be equally divided.

5. The Senate shall choose their other Officers, and also a President pro tempore, in the Absence of the Vice President, or when he shall exercise the Office of President of the United States.

6. The Senate shall have the sole Power to try all Impeachments. When sitting for that Purpose, they shall be on Oath or Affirmation. When the President of the United States is tried, the Chief Justice shall preside: And no Person shall be convicted without the Concurrence of two thirds of the Members present.

7. Judgment in Cases of Impeachment shall not extend further than to removal from Office, and disqualification to hold and enjoy any Office of honor, Trust, or Profit under the United States: but the Party convicted shall nevertheless be liable and subject to Indictment, Trial, Judgment and Punishment, according to Law.

Clause 5. Officers; impeachment The House elects a Speaker, customarily chosen from the majority party in the House. Impeachment means accusation. The House has the exclusive power to impeach, or accuse, civil officers; the Senate (Article I, Section 3, Clause 6) has the exclusive power to try those impeached by the House.

Section 3. Senate

Clause 1. Composition, election, term Each State has two senators. Each serves for six years and has one vote. Originally, senators were not elected directly by the people, but by each State's legislature. The 17th Amendment, added in 1913, provides for the popular election of senators.

Clause 2. Classification The senators elected in 1788 were divided into three groups so that the Senate could become a "continuing body." One-third of the Senate's seats are up for election every two years.

The 17th Amendment provides that a Senate vacancy is to be filled at a special election called by the governor; State law may also permit the governor to appoint a successor to serve until that election is held.

Clause 3. Qualifications A senator must be at least 30 years old, a citizen for at least nine years, and must live in the State from which elected.

Clause 4. Presiding officer The Vice President presides over the Senate, but may vote only to break a tie.

Clause 5. Other officers The Senate chooses its own officers, including a president pro tempore to preside when the Vice President is not there.

Clause 6. Impeachment trials The Senate conducts the trials of those officials impeached by the House. The Vice President presides unless the President is on trial, in which case the Chief Justice of the United States does so. A conviction requires the votes of two-thirds of the senators present.

No President has ever been convicted. In 1868 the House voted eleven articles of impeachment against President Andrew Johnson, but the Senate fell one vote short of convicting him. In 1974 President Richard M. Nixon resigned the presidency in the face of almost certain impeachment by the House. The House brought two articles of impeachment against President Bill Clinton in late 1998. Neither charge was supported by even a simple majority vote in the Senate, on February 12, 1999.

Clause 7. Penalty on conviction The punishment of an official convicted in an impeachment case has always been removal from office. The Senate can also bar a convicted person from ever holding any federal office, but it is not required to do so. A convicted person can also be tried and punished in a regular court for any crime involved in the impeachment case.

Section 4. Elections and Meetings

Clause 1. Election In 1842 Congress required that representatives be elected from districts within each State with more than one seat in the House. The districts in each State are drawn by that State's legislature. Seven States now have only one seat in the House: Alaska, Delaware, Montana, North Dakota, South Dakota, Vermont, and Wyoming. The 1842 law also directed that representatives be elected in each State on the same day: the Tuesday after the first Monday in November of every even-numbered year. In 1914 Congress also set that same date for the election of senators.

Clause 2. Sessions Congress must meet at least once a year. The 20th Amendment (1933) changed the opening date to January 3.

Section 5. Legislative Proceedings

Clause 1. Admission of members; quorum In 1969 the Supreme Court held that the House cannot exclude any member-elect who satisfies the qualifications set out in Article I, Section 2, Clause 2.

A majority in the House (218 members) or Senate (51) constitutes a quorum. In practice, both houses often proceed with less than a quorum present. However, any member may raise a point of order (demand a "quorum call"). If a roll call then reveals less than a majority of the members present, that chamber must either adjourn or the sergeant at arms must be ordered to round up absent members.

Clause 2. Rules Each house has adopted detailed rules to guide its proceedings. Each house may discipline members for unacceptable conduct; expulsion requires a two-thirds vote.

Clause 3. Record Each house must keep and publish a record of its meetings. The *Congressional Record* is published for every day that either house of Congress is in session, and provides a written record of all that is said and done on the floor of each house each session.

Clause 4. Adjournment Once in session, neither house may suspend (recess) its work for more than three days without the approval of the other house. Both houses must always meet in the same location.

Section 6. Compensation, Immunities, and Disabilities of Members

Clause 1. Salaries; immunities Each house sets its members' salaries, paid by the United States; the 27th Amendment (1992) modified this pay-setting power. This provision establishes "legislative immunity." The purpose of this immunity is to allow members to speak and debate freely in Congress itself. Treason is strictly defined in Article III, Section 3. A felony is any serious crime. A breach of the peace is any indictable offense less than treason or a felony; this exemption from arrest is of little real importance today.

Clause 2. Restrictions on office holding No sitting member of either house may be appointed to an office in the executive or in the judicial branch if that position was created or its salary was increased during that member's current elected term. The second

Section 4.

1. The Times, Places and Manner of holding Elections for Senators and Representatives, shall be prescribed in each State by the Legislature thereof; but the Congress may at any time by law make or alter such Regulations, except as to the Places of choosing Senators.

2. The Congress shall assemble at least once in every Year, and such Meeting shall be on the first Monday in December, unless they shall by Law appoint a different Day.

Section 5.

1. Each House shall be the Judge of the Elections, Returns and Qualifications of its own Members, and a Majority of each shall constitute a Quorum to do Business; but a smaller Number may adjourn from day to day, and may be authorized to compel the Attendance of absent Members, in such Manner, and under such Penalties, as each House may provide.

2. Each House may determine the Rules of its Proceedings, punish its Members for disorderly Behavior, and, with the Concurrence of two thirds, expel a Member.

3. Each House shall keep a Journal of its Proceedings, and from time to time publish the same, excepting such Parts as may in their Judgment require Secrecy; and the Yeas and Nays of the Members of either House on any question shall, at the Desire of one fifth of those Present, be entered on the Journal.

4. Neither House, during the Session of Congress, shall, without the Consent of the other, adjourn for more than three days, nor to any other Place than that in which the two Houses shall be sitting.

Section 6.

1. The Senators and Representatives shall receive a Compensation for their Services, to be ascertained by Law, and paid out of the Treasury of the United States. They shall in all Cases, except Treason, Felony, and Breach of the Peace, be privileged from Arrest during their Attendance at the Session of their respective Houses, and in going to and returning from the same; and for any Speech or Debate in either House, they shall not be questioned in any other Place.

2. No Senator or Representative shall, during the Time for which he was elected, be appointed to any civil Office under the Authority of the United States, which shall have been created, or the Emoluments whereof shall have

United States Constitution

been increased during such time; and no Person holding any Office under the United States, shall be a Member of either House during his Continuance in Office.

Section 7.

1. All Bills for raising Revenue shall originate in the House of Representatives; but the Senate may propose or concur with amendments as on other Bills.

2. Every Bill which shall have passed the House of Representatives and the Senate, shall, before it become a law, be presented to the President of the United States: If he approve, he shall sign it, but if not he shall return it, with his Objections to that House in which it shall have originated, who shall enter the Objections at large on their Journal, and proceed to reconsider it. If after such Reconsideration two thirds of the House shall agree to pass the Bill, it shall be sent, together with the Objections, to the other House, by which it shall likewise be reconsidered, and if approved by two thirds of that House, it shall become a Law. But in all such Cases the Votes of both Houses shall be determined by Yeas and Nays, and the Names of the Persons voting for and against the Bill shall be entered on the Journal of each House respectively. If any Bill shall not be returned by the President within ten Days (Sunday excepted) after it shall have been presented to him, the Same shall be a law, in like Manner as if he had signed it, unless the Congress by their Adjournment, prevent its Return, in which Case it shall not be a Law.

3. Every Order, Resolution, or Vote to which the Concurrence of the Senate and House of Representatives may be necessary (except on a question of adjournment) shall be presented to the President of the United States; and before the Same shall take Effect, shall be approved by him, or, being disapproved by him, shall be repassed by two thirds of the Senate and House of Representatives, according to the Rules and Limitations prescribed in the Case of a Bill.

Section 8.

The Congress shall have Power

1. To lay and collect Taxes, Duties, Imposts and Excises to pay the Debts and provide for the common Defence and general Welfare of the United States; but all Duties, Imposts and Excises, shall be uniform throughout the United States;

2. To borrow Money on the credit of the United States;

3. To regulate Commerce with foreign Nations, and among the several States, and with the Indian Tribes;

part of this clause—forbidding any person serving in either the executive or the judicial branch from also serving in Congress—reinforces the principle of separation of powers.

Section 7. Revenue Bills, President's Veto

Clause 1. Revenue bills All bills that raise money must originate in the House. However, the Senate has the power to amend any revenue bill sent to it from the lower house.

Clause 2. Enactment of laws; veto Once both houses have passed a bill, it must be sent to the President. The President may (1) sign the bill, thus making it law; (2) veto the bill, whereupon it must be returned to the house in which it originated; or (3) allow the bill to become law without signature, by not acting upon it within 10 days of its receipt from Congress, not counting Sundays. The President has a fourth option at the end of a congressional session: If he does not act on a measure within 10 days, and Congress adjourns during that period, the bill dies; the "pocket veto" has been applied to it. A presidential veto may be overridden by a two-thirds vote in each house.

Clause 3. Other measures This clause refers to joint resolutions, measures Congress often passes to deal with unusual, temporary, or ceremonial matters. A joint resolution passed by Congress and signed by the President has the force of law, just as a bill does. As a matter of custom, a joint resolution proposing an amendment to the Constitution is not submitted to the President for signature or veto. Concurrent and simple resolutions do not have the force of law and, therefore, are not submitted to the President.

Section 8. Powers of Congress

Clause 1. The 18 separate clauses in this section set out 27 of the many expressed powers the Constitution grants to Congress. In this clause Congress is given the power to levy and provide for the collection of various kinds of taxes, in order to finance the operations of the government. All federal taxes must be levied at the same rates throughout the country.

Clause 2. Congress has power to borrow money to help finance the government. Federal borrowing is most often done through the sale of bonds on which interest is paid. The Constitution does not limit the amount the government may borrow.

Clause 3. This clause, the Commerce Clause, gives Congress the power to regulate both foreign and interstate trade. Much of what Congress does, it does on the basis of its commerce power.

Clause 4. Congress has the exclusive power to determine how aliens may become citizens of the United States. Congress may also pass laws relating to bankruptcy.

Clause 5. Congress has the power to establish and require the use of uniform gauges of time, distance, weight, volume, area, and the like.

Clause 6. Congress has the power to make it a federal crime to falsify the coins, paper money, bonds, stamps, and the like of the United States.

Clause 7. Congress has the power to provide for and regulate the transportation and delivery of mail; "post offices" are those buildings and other places where mail is deposited for dispatch; "post roads" include all routes over or upon which mail is carried.

Clause 8. Congress has the power to provide for copyrights and patents. A copyright gives an author or composer the exclusive right to control the reproduction, publication, and sale of literary, musical, or other creative work. A patent gives a person the exclusive right to control the manufacture or sale of his or her invention.

Clause 9. Congress has the power to create the lower federal courts, all of the several federal courts that function beneath the Supreme Court.

Clause 10. Congress has the power to prohibit, as a federal crime: (1) certain acts committed outside the territorial jurisdiction of the United States, and (2) the commission within the United States of any wrong against any nation with which we are at peace.

Clause 11. Only Congress can declare war. However, the President, as commander in chief of the armed forces (Article II, Section 2, Clause 1), can make war without such a formal declaration. Letters of marque and reprisal are commissions authorizing private persons to outfit vessels (privateers) to capture and destroy enemy ships in time of war; they were forbidden in international law by the Declaration of Paris of 1856, and the United States has honored the ban since the Civil War.

Clauses 12 and 13. Congress has the power to provide for and maintain the nation's armed forces. It established the air force as an independent element of the armed forces in 1947, an exercise of its inherent powers in foreign relations and national defense. The two-year limit on spending for the army insures civilian control of the military.

Clause 14. Today these rules are set out in a lengthy, oft-amended law, the Uniform Code of Military Justice, passed by Congress in 1950.

Clauses 15 and 16. In the National Defense Act of 1916, Congress made each State's militia (volunteer army) a part of the National Guard. Today, Congress and the States cooperate in its maintenance. Ordinarily, each State's National Guard is under the command of that State's governor; but Congress has given the President the power to call any or all of those units into federal service when necessary.

Clause 17. In 1791 Congress accepted land grants from Maryland and Virginia and established the District of Columbia for the nation's capital. Assuming Virginia's grant would never be needed, Congress returned it in 1846. Today, the elected government of the District's 69 square miles operates under

4. To establish an uniform Rule of Naturalization, and uniform Laws on the subject of Bankruptcies throughout the United States;

5. To coin Money, regulate the Value thereof, and of foreign Coin, and fix the Standard of Weights and Measures;

6. To provide for the Punishment of counterfeiting the Securities and current Coin of the United States;

7. To establish Post Offices and post Roads;

8. To promote the Progress of Science and useful Arts, by securing, for limited Times to Authors and Inventors the exclusive Right to their respective Writings and Discoveries;

9. To constitute Tribunals inferior to the supreme Court;

10. To define and punish Piracies and Felonies committed on the high Seas, and Offences against the Law of nations;

11. To declare War, grant Letters of Marque and Reprisal, and make Rules concerning Captures on Land and Water;

12. To raise and support Armies; but no Appropriation of Money to that Use shall be for a longer Term than two Years;

13. To provide and maintain a Navy;

14. To make Rules for the Government and Regulation of the land and naval Forces;

15. To provide for calling forth the Militia to execute the Laws of the Union, suppress Insurrections and repel Invasions;

16. To provide for organizing, arming, and disciplining the Militia, and for governing such Part of them as may be employed in the Service of the United States, reserving to the States respectively the Appointment of the Officers, and the Authority of training the Militia according to the discipline prescribed by Congress;

17. To exercise exclusive Legislation in all Cases whatsoever, over such District (not exceeding ten Miles square) as may, by Cession of Particular States, and the Acceptance of Congress, become the Seat of the Government of the United States, and to exercise like

Authority over all Places purchased by the Consent of the Legislature of the State in which the Same shall be, for the Erection of Forts, Magazines, Arsenals, Dockyards and other needful Buildings;—And

18. To make all Laws which shall be necessary and proper for carrying into Execution the foregoing Powers and all other Powers vested by this Constitution in the Government of the United States, or in any Department or Officer thereof.

Section 9.

1. The Migration or Importation of such Persons as any of the States now existing shall think proper to admit, shall not be prohibited by the Congress prior to the Year one thousand eight hundred and eight, but a Tax or duty may be imposed on such Importation, not exceeding ten dollars for each Person.

2. The Privilege of the Writ of Habeas Corpus shall not be suspended, unless when in Cases of Rebellion or Invasion the public safety may require it.

3. No Bill of Attainder or ex post facto Law shall be passed.

4. No Capitation, or other direct, Tax shall be laid, unless in Proportion to the Census of Enumeration hereinbefore directed to be taken.

5. No Tax or Duty shall be laid on Articles exported from any State.

6. No Preference shall be given by any Regulation of Commerce or Revenue to the Ports of one State over those of another: nor shall Vessels bound to, or from, one State, be obliged to enter, clear or pay Duties in another.

7. No Money shall be drawn from the Treasury, but in Consequence of Appropriations made by Law; and a regular Statement and Account of the Receipts and Expenditures of all public Money shall be published from time to time.

8. No Title of Nobility shall be granted by the United States: And no Person holding any Office of Profit or Trust under them, shall, without the Consent of the Congress, accept of any present, Emolument, Office, or Title, of any kind whatever, from any King, Prince, or foreign State.

Section 10.

1. No State shall enter into any Treaty, Alliance, or Confederation; grant Letters of Marque and Reprisal; coin Money; emit Bills of Credit; make any Thing but

---

the authority of Congress. Congress also has the power to acquire other lands from the States for various federal purposes.

Clause 18. This is the Necessary and Proper Clause, also often called the Elastic Clause. It is the constitutional basis for the many and far-reaching implied powers of the Federal Government.

Section 9. Powers Denied to Congress

Clause 1. The phrase "such persons" referred to slaves. This provision was part of the Commerce Compromise, one of the bargains struck in the writing of the Constitution. Congress outlawed the slave trade in 1808.

Clause 2. A writ of habeas corpus, the "great writ of liberty," is a court order directing a sheriff, warden, or other public officer, or a private person, who is detaining another to "produce the body" of the one being held in order that the legality of the detention may be determined by the court.

Clause 3. A bill of attainder is a legislative act that inflicts punishment without a judicial trial. See Article I, Section 10, and Article III, Section 3, Clause 2. An *ex post facto* law is any criminal law that operates retroactively to the disadvantage of the accused. See Article I, Section 10.

Clause 4. A capitation tax is literally a "head tax," a tax levied on each person in the population. A direct tax is one paid directly to the government by the taxpayer—for example, an income or a property tax; an indirect tax is one paid to another private party who then pays it to the government—for example, a sales tax. This provision was modified by the 16th Amendment (1913), giving Congress the power to levy "taxes on incomes, from whatever source derived."

Clause 5. This provision was a part of the Commerce Compromise made by the Framers in 1787. Congress has the power to tax imported goods, however.

Clause 6. All ports within the United States must be treated alike by Congress as it exercises its taxing and commerce powers. Congress cannot tax goods sent by water from one State to another, nor may it give the ports of one State any legal advantage over those of another.

Clause 7. This clause gives Congress its vastly important "power of the purse," a major check on presidential power. Federal money can be spent only in those amounts and for those purposes expressly authorized by an act of Congress. All federal income and spending must be accounted for, regularly and publicly.

Clause 8. This provision, preventing the establishment of a nobility, reflects the principle that "all men are created equal." It was also intended to discourage foreign attempts to bribe or otherwise corrupt officers of the government.

Section 10. Powers Denied to the States

Clause 1. The States are not sovereign governments and so cannot make agreements or otherwise negotiate with foreign states; the power to conduct foreign relations is an exclusive

United States Constitution

power of the National Government. The power to coin money is also an exclusive power of the National Government. Several powers forbidden to the National Government are here also forbidden to the States.

Clause 2. This provision relates to foreign, not interstate, commerce. Only Congress, not the States, can tax imports; and the States are, like Congress, forbidden the power to tax exports.

Clause 3. A duty of tonnage is a tax laid on ships according to their cargo capacity. Each State has a constitutional right to provide for and maintain a militia; but no State may keep a standing army or navy. The several restrictions here prevent the States from assuming powers that the Constitution elsewhere grants to the National Government.

EXECUTIVE DEPARTMENT

Section 1. President and Vice President

Clause 1. Executive power, term This clause gives to the President the very broad "executive power," the power to enforce the laws and otherwise administer the public policies of the United States. It also sets the length of the presidential (and vice-presidential) term of office; see the 22nd Amendment (1951), which places a limit on presidential (but not vice-presidential) tenure.

Clause 2. Electoral college This clause establishes the "electoral college," although the Constitution does not use that term. It is a body of presidential electors chosen in each State, and it selects the President and Vice President every four years. The number of electors chosen in each State equals the number of senators and representatives that State has in Congress.

Clause 3. Election of President and Vice President This clause was replaced by the 12th Amendment in 1804.

gold and silver Coin a Tender in Payment of Debts; pass any Bill of Attainder, ex post facto Law, or Law impairing the Obligation of Contracts, or grant any Title of Nobility.

2. No State shall, without the Consent of the Congress, lay any Imposts or Duties on Imports or Exports, except what may be absolutely necessary for executing its inspection Laws; and the net Produce of all Duties and Imposts, laid by any State on Imports or Exports, shall be for the Use of the Treasury of the United States; and all such Laws shall be subject to the Revision and Control of the Congress.

3. No State shall, without the Consent of Congress, lay any Duty of Tonnage, keep Troops, or Ships of War in time of Peace, enter into any Agreement or Compact with another State, or with a foreign Power, or engage in War, unless actually invaded, or in such imminent Danger as will not admit of delay.

Article II

Section 1.

1. The executive Power shall be vested in a President of the United States of America. He shall hold his Office during the Term of four Years, and, together with the Vice President, chosen for the same Term, be elected as follows:

2. Each State shall appoint, in such Manner as the Legislature thereof may direct, a Number of Electors, equal to the whole Number of Senators and Representatives to which the State may be entitled in the Congress: but no Senator or Representative, or Person holding an Office of Trust or Profit, under the United States, shall be appointed an Elector.

3. ~~The Electors shall meet in their respective States, and vote by Ballot for two Persons, of whom one at least shall not be an Inhabitant of the same State with themselves. And they shall make a List of all the Persons voted for, and of the Number of Votes for each; which List they shall sign and certify, and transmit sealed to the Seat of the Government of the United States, directed to the President of the Senate. The President of the Senate shall, in the Presence of the Senate and House of Representatives, open all the Certificates, and the Votes shall then be counted. The Person having the greatest Number of Votes shall be the President, if such Number be a majority of the whole Number of Electors appointed; and if there be more than one who have such Majority, and have an equal Number of Votes, then, the House of Representatives shall immediately choose by Ballot one of them for President; and if no Person have a Majority, then from the five highest on the List the said House shall in like Manner choose the President. But in choosing the President, the Votes shall be taken by States, the Representatives from each State having one Vote; a quorum for this Purpose shall consist of a Member or Members from two thirds of the States, and a Majority of~~

United States Constitution

~~all the States shall be necessary to a Choice. In every Case, after the Choice of the President, the Person having the greatest Number of Votes of the Electors shall be the Vice President. But if there should remain two or more who have equal Votes, the Senate shall choose from them by Ballot the Vice President.~~

4. The Congress may determine the Time of choosing the Electors, and the Day on which they shall give their Votes; which Day shall be the same throughout the United States.

5. No Person except a natural born Citizen, or a Citizen of the United States, at the time of the Adoption of this Constitution, shall be eligible to the Office of President; neither shall any person be eligible to that Office who shall not have attained to the Age of thirty-five Years, and been fourteen Years a Resident within the United States.

6. ~~In Case of the Removal of the President from Office, or of his Death, Resignation, or Inability to discharge the Powers and Duties of the said Office, the Same shall devolve on the Vice President,~~ and the Congress may by Law provide for the Case of Removal, Death, Resignation or Inability, both of the President and Vice President, declaring what Officer shall then act as President, and such Officer shall act accordingly, until the Disability be removed, or a President shall be elected.

7. The President shall, at stated Times, receive for his Services, a Compensation, which shall neither be increased nor diminished during the Period for which he shall have been elected, and he shall not receive within that Period any other Emolument from the United States, or any of them.

8. Before he enter on the Execution of his Office, he shall take the following Oath or Affirmation:
"I do solemnly swear (or affirm) that I will faithfully execute the Office of President of the United States, and will to the best of my Ability, preserve, protect and defend the Constitution of the United States."

Section 2.
1. The President shall be Commander in Chief of the Army and Navy of the United States, and of the Militia of the several States, when called into the actual Service of the United States; he may require the Opinion, in writing, of the principal Officer in each of the executive Departments, upon any Subject relating to the Duties of their respective Offices, and he shall have Power to Grant Reprieves and Pardons for Offences against the United States, except in Cases of Impeachment.

2. He shall have Power, by and with the Advice and Consent of the Senate, to make Treaties, provided two thirds of the Senators present concur; and he shall nominate, and by and with the Advice and Consent of the Senate, shall appoint Ambassadors, other public Ministers

Clause 4. Date Congress has set the date for the choosing of electors as the Tuesday after the first Monday in November every fourth year, and for the casting of electoral votes as the Monday after the second Wednesday in December of that year.

Clause 5. Qualifications The President must have been born a citizen of the United States, be at least 35 years old, and have been a resident of the United States for at least 14 years.

Clause 6. Vacancy This clause was modified by the 25th Amendment (1967), which provides expressly for the succession of the Vice President, for the filling of a vacancy in the Vice Presidency, and for the determination of presidential inability.

Clause 7. Compensation The President now receives a salary of $400,000 and a taxable expense account of $50,000 a year. Those amounts cannot be changed during a presidential term; thus, Congress cannot use the President's compensation as a bargaining tool to influence executive decisions. The phrase "any other emolument" means, in effect, any valuable gift; it does not mean that the President cannot be provided with such benefits of office as the White House, extensive staff assistance, and much else.

Clause 8. Oath of office The chief justice of the United States regularly administers this oath or affirmation, but any judicial officer may do so. Thus, Calvin Coolidge was sworn into office in 1923 by his father, a justice of the peace in Vermont.

Section 2. President's Powers and Duties

Clause 1. Military, civil powers The President, a civilian, heads the nation's armed forces, a key element in the Constitution's insistence on civilian control of the military. The President's power to "require the opinion, in writing" provides the constitutional basis for the cabinet. The President's power to grant reprieves and pardons, the power of clemency, extends only to federal cases.

Clause 2. Treaties, appointments The President has the sole power to make treaties; to become effective, a treaty must be approved by a two-thirds vote in the Senate. In practice, the President can also make executive agreements with foreign governments; these pacts, which are frequently made and usually deal with routine matters, do not require Senate consent. The President appoints the principal officers of the executive branch and all federal judges; the "inferior officers" are those who hold lesser posts.

Clause 3. Recess appointments When the Senate is not in session, appointments that require Senate consent can be made by the President on a temporary basis, as "recess appointments."

Section 3. President's Powers and Duties

The President delivers a State of the Union Message to Congress soon after that body convenes each year. That message is delivered to the nation's lawmakers and, importantly, to the American people, as well. It is shortly followed by the proposed federal budget and an economic report; and the President may send special messages to Congress at any time. In all of these communications, Congress is urged to take those actions the Chief Executive finds to be in the national interest. The President also has the power: to call special sessions of Congress; to adjourn Congress if its two houses cannot agree for that purpose; to receive the diplomatic representatives of other governments; to insure the proper execution of all federal laws; and to empower federal officers to hold their posts and perform their duties.

Section 4. Impeachment

The Constitution outlines the impeachment process in Article I, Section 2, Clause 5 and in Section 3, Clauses 6 and 7.

JUDICIAL DEPARTMENT

Section 1. Courts, Terms of Office

The judicial power conferred here is the power of federal courts to hear and decide cases, disputes between the government and individuals and between private persons (parties). The Constitution creates only the Supreme Court of the United States; it gives to Congress the power to establish other, lower federal courts (Article I, Section 8, Clause 9) and to fix the size of the Supreme Court. The words "during good behavior" mean, in effect, for life.

Section 2. Jurisdiction

Clause 1. Cases to be heard This clause sets out the jurisdiction of the federal courts; that is, it identifies those cases that may be tried in those courts. The federal courts can hear and decide—have jurisdiction over—a case depending on either the subject matter or the parties involved in that case. The jurisdiction of the federal courts in cases involving States was substantially restricted by the 11th Amendment in 1795.

and Consuls, Judges of the supreme Court, and all other Officers of the United States, whose Appointments are not herein otherwise provided for, and which shall be established by Law: but the Congress may by Law vest the Appointment of such inferior Officers, as they think proper, in the President alone, in the Courts of Law, or in the Heads of Departments.

3. The President shall have Power to fill up all Vacancies that may happen during the Recess of the Senate, by granting Commissions which shall expire at the End of their next Session.

Section 3.

He shall from time to time give to the Congress Information of the State of the Union, and recommend to their Consideration such Measures as he shall judge necessary and expedient; he may, on extraordinary Occasions, convene both Houses, or either of them, and in Case of Disagreement between them, with Respect to the Time of Adjournment, he may adjourn them to such Time as he shall think proper; he shall receive Ambassadors and other public Ministers; he shall take Care that the Laws be faithfully executed, and shall Commission all the Officers of the United States.

Section 4.

The President, Vice President and all Civil Officers of the United States, shall be removed from Office on Impeachment for and Conviction of, Treason, Bribery, or other high Crimes and Misdemeanors.

Article III

Section 1.

The judicial Power of the United States, shall be vested in one supreme Court, and in such inferior Courts as the Congress may from time to time ordain and establish. The Judges, both of the supreme and inferior Courts, shall hold their Offices during good Behavior, and shall, at stated Times, receive for their Services, a Compensation, which shall not be diminished during their Continuance in Office.

Section 2.

1. The judicial Power shall extend to all Cases, in Law and Equity, arising under this Constitution, the Laws of the United States, and Treaties made, or which shall be made, under their Authority;— to all Cases affecting Ambassadors, other public ministers, and Consuls;— to all Cases of Admiralty and maritime Jurisdiction;— to Controversies to which the United States shall be a Party;— to Controversies between two or more States;— ~~between a State and Citizens of another State;~~— between Citizens of different States;— between Citizens of the same State claiming Lands under Grants of different States, ~~and between a State, or the Citizens thereof, and foreign States, Citizens, or Subjects.~~

2. In all Cases affecting Ambassadors, other public Ministers and Consuls, and those in which a State shall be a Party, the supreme Court shall have original Jurisdiction. In all the other Cases before mentioned, the supreme Court shall have appellate Jurisdiction, both as to Law and Fact, with such Exceptions, and under such Regulations as the Congress shall make.

3. The trial of all Crimes, except in Cases of Impeachment, shall be by Jury; and such Trial shall be held in the State where the said Crimes shall have been committed; but when not committed within any State, the Trial shall be at such Place or Places as the Congress may by Law have directed.

Section 3.

1. Treason against the United States shall consist only in levying War against them, or in adhering to their Enemies, giving them Aid and Comfort. No Person shall be convicted of Treason unless on the Testimony of two Witnesses to the same overt Act, or on Confession in open Court.

2. The Congress shall have Power to declare the Punishment of Treason, but no Attainder of Treason shall work Corruption of Blood, or Forfeiture except during the Life of the Person attainted.

Article IV
Section 1.

Full Faith and Credit shall be given in each State to the public Acts, Records, and judicial Proceedings of every other State. And the Congress may by general Laws prescribe the Manner in which such Acts, Records and Proceedings shall be proved, and the Effect thereof.

Section 2.

1. The Citizens of each State shall be entitled to all Privileges and Immunities of Citizens in the several States.

2. A Person charged in any State with Treason, Felony, or other Crime, who shall flee from justice, and be found in another State, shall on Demand of the executive Authority of the State from which he fled, be delivered up, to be removed to the State having Jurisdiction of the Crime.

3. No Person held to Service or Labor in one State, under the Laws thereof, escaping into another, shall, in Consequence of any Law or Regulation therein, be discharged from Service or Labor, but shall be delivered up on Claim of the Party to whom such Service or Labor may be due.

Clause 2. Supreme Court jurisdiction Original jurisdiction refers to the power of a court to hear a case in the first instance, not on appeal from a lower court. Appellate jurisdiction refers to a court's power to hear a case on appeal from a lower court, from the court in which the case was originally tried. This clause gives the Supreme Court both original and appellate jurisdiction. However, nearly all of the cases the High Court hears are brought to it on appeal from the lower federal courts and the highest State courts.

Clause 3. Jury trial in criminal cases A person accused of a federal crime is guaranteed the right to trial by jury in a federal court in the State where the crime was committed; see the 5th and 6th amendments. The right to trial by jury in serious criminal cases in the State courts is guaranteed by the 6th and 14th amendments.

Section 3. Treason

Clause 1. Definition Treason is the only crime defined in the Constitution. The Framers intended the very specific definition here to prevent the loose use of the charge of treason—for example, against persons who criticize the government. Treason can be committed only in time of war and only by a citizen or a resident alien.

Clause 2. Punishment Congress has provided that the punishment that a federal court may impose on a convicted traitor may range from a minimum of five years in prison and/or a $10,000 fine to a maximum of death; no person convicted of treason has ever been executed by the United States. No legal punishment can be imposed on the family or descendants of a convicted traitor. Congress has also made it a crime for any person (in either peace or wartime) to commit espionage or sabotage, to attempt to overthrow the government by force, or to conspire to do any of these things.

RELATIONS AMONG STATES
Section 1. Full Faith and Credit

Each State must recognize the validity of the laws, public records, and court decisions of every other State.

Section 2. Privileges and Immunities of Citizens

Clause 1. Residents of other States In effect, this clause means that no State may discriminate against the residents of other States; that is, a State's laws cannot draw unreasonable distinctions between its own residents and those of any of the other States. See Section 1 of the 14th Amendment.

Clause 2. Extradition The process of returning a fugitive to another State is known as "interstate rendition" or, more commonly, "extradition." Usually, that process works routinely; some extradition requests are contested however—especially in cases with racial or political overtones. A governor may refuse to extradite a fugitive; but the federal courts can compel an unwilling governor to obey this constitutional command.

Clause 3. Fugitive slaves This clause was nullified by the 13th Amendment, which abolished slavery in 1865.

Section 3. New States; Territories

Clause 1. New States Only Congress can admit new States to the Union. A new State may not be created by taking territory from an existing State without the consent of that State's legislature. Congress has admitted 37 States since the original 13 formed the Union. Five States—Vermont, Kentucky, Tennessee, Maine, and West Virginia—were created from parts of existing States. Texas was an independent republic before admission. California was admitted after being ceded to the United States by Mexico. Each of the other 30 States entered the Union only after a period of time as an organized territory of the United States.

Clause 2. Territory, property Congress has the power to make laws concerning the territories, other public lands, and all other property of the United States.

Section 4. Protection Afforded to States by the Nation

The Constitution does not define "a republican form of government," but the phrase is generally understood to mean a representative government. The Federal Government must also defend each State against attacks from outside its border and, at the request of a State's legislature or its governor, aid its efforts to put down internal disorders.

PROVISIONS FOR AMENDMENT

This section provides for the methods by which formal changes can be made in the Constitution. An amendment may be proposed in one of two ways: by a two-thirds vote in each house of Congress, or by a national convention called by Congress at the request of two-thirds of the State legislatures. A proposed amendment may be ratified in one of two ways: by three-fourths of the State legislatures, or by three-fourths of the States in conventions called for that purpose. Congress has the power to determine the method by which a proposed amendment may be ratified. The amendment process cannot be used to deny any State its equal representation in the United States Senate. To this point, 27 amendments have been adopted. To date, all of the amendments except the 21st Amendment were proposed by Congress and ratified by the State legislatures. Only the 21st Amendment was ratified by the convention method.

NATIONAL DEBTS, SUPREMACY OF NATIONAL LAW, OATH

Section 1. Validity of Debts

Congress had borrowed large sums of money during the Revolution and later during the Critical Period of the 1780s. This provision, a pledge that the new government would honor those debts, did much to create confidence in that government.

Section 2. Supremacy of National Law

This section sets out the Supremacy Clause, a specific declaration of the supremacy of federal law over any and all forms of State law. No State, including its local governments, may make or enforce any law that conflicts with any provision in the Constitution, an act of Congress, a treaty, or an order, rule, or regulation properly issued by the President or his subordinates in the executive branch.

Section 3.

1. New States may be admitted by the Congress into this Union; but no new State shall be formed or erected within the Jurisdiction of any other State; nor any State be formed by the Junction of two or more States, or Parts of States, without the Consent of the Legislatures of the States concerned as well as of the Congress.

2. The Congress shall have Power to dispose of and make all needful Rules and Regulations respecting the Territory or other Property belonging to the United States; and nothing in this Constitution shall be so construed as to Prejudice any Claims of the United States, or of any particular State.

Section 4.

The United States shall guarantee to every State in this Union a Republican Form of Government, and shall protect each of them against Invasion; and on Application of the Legislature, or of the Executive (when the Legislature cannot be convened) against domestic Violence.

Article V

The Congress, whenever two thirds of both Houses shall deem it necessary, shall propose Amendments to this Constitution, or, on the Application of the Legislatures of two thirds of the several States, shall call a Convention for proposing Amendments, which, in either Case, shall be valid to all Intents and Purposes, as Part of this Constitution, when ratified by the Legislatures of three fourths of the several States, or by Conventions in three fourths thereof, as the one or the other Mode of Ratification may be proposed by the Congress; Provided that no Amendment which may be made prior to the Year One thousand eight hundred and eight shall in any Manner affect the first and fourth Clauses in the Ninth section of the first Article; and that no State, without its Consent, shall be deprived of its equal Suffrage in the Senate.

Article VI

Section 1.

All Debts contracted and Engagements entered into, before the Adoption of this Constitution, shall be as valid against the United States under this Constitution, as under the Confederation.

Section 2.

This Constitution, and the Laws of the United States which shall be made in Pursuance thereof; and all Treaties made, or which shall be made, under the Authority of the United States, shall be the supreme Law of the Land; and the Judges in every State shall be bound thereby, anything in the constitution or Laws of any State to the Contrary notwithstanding.

United States Constitution

Section 3.

The Senators and Representatives before mentioned, and the Members of the several State legislatures, and all executive and judicial Officers, both of the United States and of the several States, shall be bound by Oath or Affirmation, to support this Constitution; but no religious Test shall ever be required as a Qualification to any Office or public Trust under the United States.

Article VII

The ratification of the Conventions of nine States, shall be sufficient for the Establishment of this Constitution between the States so ratifying the same.

Done in Convention by the Unanimous Consent of the States present the Seventeenth Day of September in the Year of our Lord one thousand seven hundred and Eighty-seven and of the Independence of the United States of America the twelfth. In witness whereof We have hereunto subscribed our Names.

Attest: William Jackson,
  SECRETARY
George Washington,
  PRESIDENT AND
  DEPUTY FROM
  VIRGINIA

NEW HAMPSHIRE
  John Langdon
  Nicholas Gilman

MASSACHUSETTS
  Nathaniel Gorham
  Rufus King

CONNECTICUT
  William Samuel Johnson
  Roger Sherman

NEW YORK
  Alexander Hamilton

NEW JERSEY
  William Livingston
  David Brearley
  William Paterson
  Jonathan Dayton

PENNSYLVANIA
  Benjamin Franklin
  Thomas Mifflin
  Robert Morris
  George Clymer
  Thomas Fitzsimons
  Jared Ingersoll
  James Wilson
  Gouverneur Morris

DELAWARE
  George Read
  Gunning Bedford, Jr.
  John Dickinson
  Richard Bassett
  Jacob Broom

MARYLAND
  James McHenry
  Dan of St. Thomas Jennifer
  Daniel Carroll

VIRGINIA
  John Blair
  James Madison, Jr.

NORTH CAROLINA
  William Blount
  Richard Dobbs Spaight
  Hugh Williamson

SOUTH CAROLINA
  John Rutledge
  Charles Cotesworth
    Pinckney
  Charles Pinckney
  Pierce Butler

GEORGIA
  William Few
  Abraham Baldwin

AMENDMENTS

1st Amendment.

Congress shall make no law respecting an establishment of religion, or prohibiting the free exercise thereof, or abridging the freedom of speech, or of the press; or the right of the people peaceably to assemble, and to petition the Government for a redress of grievances.

Section 3. Oaths of Office

This provision reinforces the Supremacy Clause; all public officers, at every level in the United States, owe their first allegiance to the Constitution of the United States. No religious qualification can be imposed as a condition for holding any public office.

RATIFICATION OF CONSTITUTION

The proposed Constitution was signed by George Washington and 37 of his fellow Framers on September 17, 1787. (George Read of Delaware signed for himself and also for his absent colleague, John Dickinson.)

The first 10 amendments, the Bill of Rights, were each proposed by Congress on September 25, 1789, and ratified by the necessary three-fourths of the States on December 15, 1791. These amendments were originally intended to restrict the National Government—not the States. However, the Supreme Court has several times held that most of their provisions also apply to the States, through the 14th Amendment's Due Process Clause.

1st Amendment. Freedom of Religion, Speech, Press, Assembly, and Petition

The 1st Amendment sets out five basic liberties: The guarantee of freedom of religion is both a protection of religious thought and practice and a command of separation of church and state. The guarantees of freedom of speech and press assure to all persons a right to speak, publish, and otherwise express their views. The guarantees of the rights of assembly and petition protect the right to join with others in public meetings, political parties, interest groups, and other associations to discuss public affairs and influence public policy. None of these rights is guaranteed in absolute terms, however; like all other civil rights guarantees, each of them may be exercised only with regard to the rights of all other persons.

2nd Amendment. Bearing Arms

Each State has the right to maintain a militia, an armed force for its own protection—today, the National Guard. The National Government and the States can and do regulate the private possession and use of firearms.

3rd Amendment. Quartering of Troops

This amendment was intended to prevent what had been common British practice in the colonial period; see the Declaration of Independence. This provision is of virtually no importance today.

4th Amendment. Searches and Seizures

The basic rule laid down by the 4th Amendment is this: Police officers have no general right to search for or seize evidence or seize (arrest) persons. Except in particular circumstances, they must have a proper warrant (a court order) obtained with probable cause (on reasonable grounds). This guarantee is reinforced by the exclusionary rule, developed by the Supreme Court: Evidence gained as the result of an unlawful search or seizure cannot be used at the court trial of the person from whom it was seized.

5th Amendment. Criminal Proceedings; Due Process; Eminent Domain

A person can be tried for a serious federal crime only if he or she has been indicted (charged, accused of that crime) by a grand jury. No one may be subjected to double jeopardy—that is, tried twice for the same crime. All persons are protected against self-incrimination; no person can be legally compelled to answer any question in any governmental proceeding if that answer could lead to that person's prosecution. The 5th Amendment's Due Process Clause prohibits unfair, arbitrary actions by the Federal Government; a like prohibition is set out against the States in the 14th Amendment. Government may take private property for a legitimate public purpose; but when it exercises that power of eminent domain, it must pay a fair price for the property seized.

6th Amendment. Criminal Proceedings

A person accused of crime has the right to be tried in court without undue delay and by an impartial jury; see Article III, Section 2, Clause 3. The defendant must be informed of the charge upon which he or she is to be tried, has the right to cross-examine hostile witnesses, and has the right to require the testimony of favorable witnesses. The defendant also has the right to be represented by an attorney at every stage in the criminal process.

7th Amendment. Civil Trials

This amendment applies only to civil cases heard in federal courts. A civil case does not involve criminal matters; it is a dispute between private parties or between the government and a private party. The right to trial by jury is guaranteed in any civil case in a federal court if the amount of money involved in that case exceeds $20 (most cases today involve a much larger sum); that right may be waived (relinquished, put aside) if both parties agree to a bench trial (a trial by a judge, without a jury).

8th Amendment. Punishment for Crimes

Bail is the sum of money that a person accused of crime may be required to post (deposit with the court) as a guarantee that he or she will appear in court at the proper time. The amount of bail required and/or a fine imposed as punishment must

2nd Amendment.

A well-regulated Militia being necessary to the security of a free State, the right of the people to keep and bear Arms, shall not be infringed.

3rd Amendment.

No Soldier shall, in time of peace be quartered in any house, without the consent of the Owner, nor, in time of war, but in a manner to be prescribed by law.

4th Amendment.

The right of the people to be secure in their persons, houses, papers, and effects, against unreasonable searches and seizures, shall not be violated, and no Warrants shall issue, but upon probable cause, supported by Oath or affirmation, and particularly describing the place to be searched, and the persons or things to be seized.

5th Amendment.

No person shall be held to answer for a capital, or otherwise infamous crime, unless on a presentment or indictment of a Grand Jury, except in cases arising in the land or naval forces, or in the Militia, when in actual service in time of War, or public danger; nor shall any person be subject for the same offence to be twice put in jeopardy of life or limb; nor shall be compelled in any criminal case to be a witness against himself, nor be deprived of life, liberty, or property, without due process of law; nor shall private property be taken for public use, without just compensation.

6th Amendment.

In all criminal prosecutions, the accused shall enjoy the right to a speedy and public trial, by an impartial jury of the State and district wherein the crime shall have been committed, which district shall have been previously ascertained by law, and to be informed of the nature and cause of the accusation; to be confronted with the witnesses against him; to have compulsory process for obtaining witnesses in his favor, and to have the Assistance of Counsel for his defence.

7th Amendment.

In Suits at common law, where the value in controversy shall exceed twenty dollars, the right of trial by jury shall be preserved, and no fact tried by a jury, shall be otherwise re-examined in any Court of the United States, than according to the rules of the common law.

8th Amendment.

Excessive bail shall not be required, nor excessive fines imposed, nor cruel and unusual punishment inflicted.

bear a reasonable relationship to the seriousness of the crime involved in the case. The prohibition of cruel and unusual punishment forbids any punishment judged to be too harsh, too severe for the crime for which it is imposed.

9th Amendment.

The enumeration in the Constitution, of certain rights, shall not be construed to deny or disparage others retained by the people.

9th Amendment. Unenumerated Rights

The fact that the Constitution sets out many civil rights guarantees, expressly provides for many protections against government, does not mean that there are not other rights also held by the people.

10th Amendment.

The powers not delegated to the United States by the Constitution, nor prohibited by it to the States, are reserved to the States respectively, or to the people.

10th Amendment. Powers Reserved to the States

This amendment identifies the area of power that may be exercised by the States. All of those powers the Constitution does not grant to the National Government, and at the same time does not forbid to the States, belong to each of the States, or to the people of each State.

11th Amendment.

The Judicial power of the United States shall not be construed to extend to any suit in law or equity, commenced or prosecuted against one of the United States by Citizens of another State, or by Citizens or Subjects of any Foreign State.

11th Amendment. Suits Against States

Proposed by Congress March 4, 1794; ratified February 7, 1795, but official announcement of the ratification was delayed until January 8, 1798. This amendment repealed part of Article III, Section 2, Clause 1. No State may be sued in a federal court by a resident of another State or of a foreign country; the Supreme Court has long held that this provision also means that a State cannot be sued in a federal court by a foreign country or, more importantly, even by one of its own residents.

12th Amendment.

The Electors shall meet in their respective States and vote by ballot for President and Vice President, one of whom, at least, shall not be an inhabitant of the same State with themselves; they shall name in their ballots the person voted for as President, and in distinct ballots the person voted for as Vice President, and they shall make distinct lists of all persons voted for as President, and of all persons voted for as Vice President, and of the number of votes for each, which lists they shall sign and certify, and transmit sealed to the seat of the government of the United States, directed to the President of the Senate;— The President of the Senate shall, in the presence of the Senate and the House of Representatives, open all the certificates and the votes shall then be counted;— the person having the greatest Number of votes for President shall be the President, if such number be a majority of the whole number of Electors appointed; and if no person have such a majority, then, from the persons having the highest numbers not exceeding three on the list of those voted for as President, the House of Representatives shall choose immediately, by ballot, the President. But in choosing the President, the votes shall be taken by States, the representation from each State having one vote; a quorum for this purpose shall consist of a member or members from two thirds of the States, and a majority of all the States shall be necessary to a choice. And if the House of Representatives shall not choose a President whenever the right of choice shall devolve upon them, before the fourth day of March next following, then the Vice President shall act as President, as in case of death or other constitutional disability of the President. The person having the greatest number of votes as Vice President, shall be the

12th Amendment. Election of President and Vice President

Proposed by Congress December 9, 1803; ratified June 15, 1804. This amendment replaced Article II, Section 1, Clause 3. Originally, each elector cast two ballots, each for a different person for President. The person with the largest number of electoral votes, provided that number was a majority of the electors, was to become President; the person with the second highest number was to become Vice President. This arrangement produced an electoral vote tie between Thomas Jefferson and Aaron Burr in 1800; the House finally chose Jefferson as President in 1801. The 12th Amendment separated the balloting for President and Vice President; each elector now casts one ballot for someone as President and a second ballot for another person as Vice President. Note that the 20th Amendment changed the date set here (March 4) to January 20, and that the 23rd Amendment (1961) provides for electors from the District of Columbia. This amendment also provides that the Vice President must meet the same qualifications as those set out for the President in Article II, Section 1, Clause 5.

United States Constitution

Vice President, if such number be a majority of the whole number of Electors appointed, and if no person have a majority, then from the two highest numbers on the list, the Senate shall choose the Vice President; a quorum for the purpose shall consist of two thirds of the whole number of Senators, a majority of the whole number shall be necessary to a choice. But no person constitutionally ineligible to the office of President shall be eligible to that of Vice-President of the United States.

13th Amendment. Slavery and Involuntary Servitude

Proposed by Congress January 31, 1865; ratified December 6, 1865. This amendment forbids slavery in the United States and in any area under its control. It also forbids other forms of forced labor, except punishments for crime; but some forms of compulsory service are not prohibited—for example, service on juries or in the armed forces. Section 2 gives to Congress the power to carry out the provisions of Section 1 of this amendment.

13th Amendment.

Section 1. Neither slavery nor involuntary servitude, except as a punishment for crime whereof the party shall have been duly convicted, shall exist within the United States, or any place subject to their jurisdiction.

Section 2. Congress shall have power to enforce this article by appropriate legislation.

14th Amendment. Rights of Citizens

Proposed by Congress June 13, 1866; ratified July 9, 1868. Section 1 defines citizenship. It provides for the acquisition of United States citizenship by birth or by naturalization. Citizenship at birth is determined according to the principle of *jus soli*—"the law of the soil," where born; naturalization is the legal process by which one acquires a new citizenship at some time after birth. Under certain circumstances, citizenship can also be gained at birth abroad, according to the principle of *jus sanguinis*—"the law of the blood," to whom born. This section also contains two major civil rights provisions: the Due Process Clause forbids a State (and its local governments) to act in any unfair or arbitrary way; the Equal Protection Clause forbids a State (and its local governments) to discriminate against, draw unreasonable distinctions between, persons.

Most of the rights set out against the National Government in the first eight amendments have been extended against the States (and their local governments) through Supreme Court decisions involving the 14th Amendment's Due Process Clause.

The first sentence here replaced Article I, Section 2, Clause 3, the Three-Fifths Compromise provision. Essentially, all persons in the United States are counted in each decennial census, the basis for the distribution of House seats. The balance of this section has never been enforced and is generally thought to be obsolete.

14th Amendment.

Section 1. All persons born or naturalized in the United States and subject to the jurisdiction thereof, are citizens of the United States and of the State wherein they reside. No State shall make or enforce any law which shall abridge the privileges or immunities of citizens of the United States; nor shall any State deprive any person of life, liberty, or property, without due process of law; nor deny to any person within its jurisdiction the equal protection of the laws.

Section 2. Representatives shall be apportioned among the several States according to their respective numbers, counting the whole number of persons in each State, excluding Indians not taxed. But when the right to vote at any election for the choice of electors for President and Vice President of the United States, Representatives in Congress, the Executive and Judicial officers of a State, or the members of the Legislature thereof, is denied to any of the male inhabitants of such State, being twenty-one years of age and citizens of the United States, or in any way abridged, except for participation in rebellion, or other crime, the basis of representation therein shall be reduced in the proportion which the number of such male citizens shall bear to the whole number of male citizens twenty-one years of age in such State.

Section 3. No person shall be a Senator or Representative in Congress, or elector of President and Vice President, or hold any office, civil or military, under the United States, or under any State, who, having previously taken an oath, as a member of Congress, or as an officer of the United States, or as a member of any State legislature, or as an executive or judicial officer of any State, to support the Constitution of the United States, shall have engaged in insurrection or rebellion against the same, or given aid or comfort to the enemies thereof. But Congress may, by a vote of two thirds of each House, remove such disability.

This section limited the President's power to pardon those persons who had led the Confederacy during the Civil War. Congress finally removed this disability in 1898.

Section 4. The validity of the public debt of the United States, authorized by law, including debts incurred for payment of pensions and bounties for services in suppressing insurrection or rebellion, shall not be questioned. But neither the United States nor any State shall assume or pay any debt or obligation incurred in aid of insurrection or rebellion against the United States, or any claim for the loss or emancipation of any slave; but all such debts, obligations and claims shall be held illegal and void.

Section 4 also dealt with matters directly related to the Civil War. It reaffirmed the public debt of the United States; but it invalidated, prohibited payment of, any debt contracted by the Confederate States and also prohibited any compensation of former slave owners.

Section 5. The Congress shall have power to enforce, by appropriate legislation, the provisions of this article.

15th Amendment.

Section 1. The right of citizens of the United States to vote shall not be denied or abridged by the United States or by any State on account of race, color, or previous condition of servitude.

Section 2. The Congress shall have power to enforce this article by appropriate legislation.

15th Amendment. Right to Vote—Race, Color, Servitude

Proposed by Congress February 26, 1869; ratified February 3, 1870. The phrase "previous condition of servitude" refers to slavery. Note that this amendment does not guarantee the right to vote to African Americans, or to anyone else. Instead, it forbids the States from discriminating against any person on the grounds of his "race, color, or previous condition of servitude" in the setting of suffrage qualifications.

16th Amendment.

The Congress shall have power to lay and collect taxes on incomes, from whatever source derived, without apportionment among the several States, and without regard to any census or enumeration.

16th Amendment. Income Tax

Proposed by Congress July 12, 1909; ratified February 3, 1913. This amendment modified two provisions in Article I, Section 2, Clause 3, and Section 9, Clause 4. It gives to Congress the power to levy an income tax, a direct tax, without regard to the populations of any of the States.

17th Amendment.

The Senate of the United States shall be composed of two Senators from each State, elected by the people thereof, for six years; and each Senator shall have one vote. The electors in each State shall have the qualifications requisite for electors of the most numerous branch of the State legislatures.

When vacancies happen in the representation of any State in the Senate, the executive authority of such State shall issue writs of election to fill such vacancies: *Provided,* That the legislature of any State may empower the executive thereof to make temporary appointments until the people fill the vacancies by election as the legislature may direct.

This amendment shall not be so construed as to affect the election or term of any Senator chosen before it becomes valid as part of the Constitution.

17th Amendment. Popular Election of Senators

Proposed by Congress May 13, 1912; ratified April 8, 1913. This amendment repealed those portions of Article I, Section 3, Clauses 1 and 2 relating to the election of senators. Senators are now elected by the voters in each State. If a vacancy occurs, the governor of the State involved must call an election to fill the seat; the governor may appoint a senator to serve until the next election, if the State's legislature has authorized that step.

18th Amendment. Prohibition of Intoxicating Liquors

Proposed by Congress December 18, 1917; ratified January 16, 1919. This amendment outlawed the making, selling, transporting, importing, or exporting of alcoholic beverages in the United States. It was repealed in its entirety by the 21st Amendment in 1933.

19th Amendment. Equal Suffrage—Sex

Proposed by Congress June 4, 1919; ratified August 18, 1920. No person can be denied the right to vote in any election in the United States on account of his or her sex.

20th Amendment. Commencement of Terms; Sessions of Congress; Death or Disqualification of President-Elect

Proposed by Congress March 2, 1932; ratified January 23, 1933. The provisions of Sections 1 and 2 relating to Congress modified Article I, Section 4, Clause 2, and those provisions relating to the President, the 12th Amendment. The date on which the President and Vice President now take office was moved from March 4 to January 20. Similarly, the members of Congress now begin their terms on January 3. The 20th Amendment is sometimes called the "Lame Duck Amendment" because it shortened the period of time a member of Congress who was defeated for reelection (a "lame duck") remains in office.

This section deals with certain possibilities that were not covered by the presidential selection provisions of either Article II or the 12th Amendment. To this point, none of these situations has occurred. Note that there is neither a President-elect nor a Vice President-elect until the electoral votes have been counted by Congress, or, if the electoral college cannot decide the matter, the House has chosen a President or the Senate has chosen a Vice President.

Congress has not in fact ever passed such a law. See Section 2 of the 25th Amendment, regarding a vacancy in the vice presidency; that provision could some day have an impact here.

United States Constitution

18th Amendment.

~~Section 1. After one year from the ratification of this article the manufacture, sale, or transportation of intoxicating liquors within, the importation thereof into, or the exportation thereof from the United States and all territory subject to the jurisdiction thereof for beverage purposes is hereby prohibited.~~

~~Section 2. The Congress and the several States shall have concurrent power to enforce this article by appropriate legislation.~~

~~Section 3. This article shall be inoperative unless it shall have been ratified as an amendment to the Constitution by the legislatures of the several States, as provided in the Constitution, within seven years of the date of the submission hereof to the States by Congress.~~

19th Amendment.

The right of citizens of the United States to vote shall not be denied or abridged by the United States or by any State on account of sex.

Congress shall have power to enforce this article by appropriate legislation.

20th Amendment.

Section 1. The terms of the President and Vice President shall end at noon on the 20th day of January, and the terms of Senators and Representatives at noon on the 3d day of January, of the years in which such terms would have ended if this article had not been ratified; and the terms of their successors shall then begin.

Section 2. The Congress shall assemble at least once in every year, and such meeting shall begin at noon on the 3d day of January, unless they shall by law appoint a different day.

Section 3. If, at the time fixed for the beginning of the term of the President, the President elect shall have died, the Vice President elect shall become President. If a President shall not have been chosen before the time fixed for the beginning of his term, or if the President-elect shall have failed to qualify, then the Vice President elect shall act as President until a President shall have qualified; and the Congress may by law provide for the case wherein neither a President elect nor a Vice President elect shall have qualified, declaring who shall then act as President, or the manner in which one who is to act shall be selected, and such person shall act accordingly until a President or Vice President shall have qualified.

Section 4. The Congress may by law provide for the case of the death of any of the persons from whom the House of Representatives may choose a President whenever the right of choice shall have devolved upon them, and for the case of the death of any of the persons from whom

United States Constitution

the Senate may choose a Vice President whenever the right of choice shall have devolved upon them.

Section 5. Sections 1 and 2 shall take effect on the 15th day of October following the ratification of this article.

Section 6. This article shall be inoperative unless it shall have been ratified as an amendment to the Constitution by the legislatures of three fourths of the several States within seven years from the date of its submission.

Section 5 set the date on which this amendment came into force.

Section 6 placed a time limit on the ratification process; note that a similar provision was written into the 18th, 21st, and 22nd amendments.

21st Amendment.

Section 1. The eighteenth article of amendment to the Constitution of the United States is hereby repealed.

Section 2. The transportation or importation into any State, Territory, or possession of the United States for delivery or use therein of intoxicating liquors, in violation of the laws thereof, is hereby prohibited.

Section 3. This article shall be inoperative unless it shall have been ratified as an amendment to the Constitution by conventions in the several States, as provided in the Constitution, within seven years from the date of the submission hereof to the States by the Congress.

21st Amendment. Repeal of 18th Amendment

Proposed by Congress February 20, 1933; ratified December 5, 1933. This amendment repealed all of the 18th Amendment. Section 2 modifies the scope of the Federal Government's commerce power set out in Article I, Section 8, Clause 3; it gives to each State the power to regulate the transportation or importation and the distribution or use of intoxicating liquors in ways that would be unconstitutional in the case of any other commodity. The 21st Amendment is the only amendment Congress has thus far submitted to the States for ratification by conventions.

22nd Amendment.

Section 1. No person shall be elected to the office of the President more than twice, and no person who has held the office of President, or acted as President, for more than two years of a term to which some other person was elected President shall be elected to the office of the President more than once. But this Article shall not apply to any person holding the office of President, when this Article was proposed by the Congress, and shall not prevent any person who may be holding the office of President, or acting as President, during the term within which this Article becomes operative from holding the office of President or acting as President during the remainder of such term.

Section 2. This article shall be inoperative unless it shall have been ratified as an amendment to the Constitution by the legislatures of three fourths of the several states within seven years from the date of its submission to the States by the Congress.

22nd Amendment. Presidential Tenure

Proposed by Congress March 24, 1947; ratified February 27, 1951. This amendment modified Article II, Section I, Clause 1. It stipulates that no President may serve more than two elected terms. But a President who has succeeded to the office beyond the midpoint in a term to which another President was originally elected may serve for more than eight years. In any case, however, a President may not serve more than 10 years. Prior to Franklin Roosevelt, who was elected to four terms, no President had served more than two full terms in office.

23rd Amendment.

Section 1. The District constituting the seat of Government of the United States shall appoint in such manner as the Congress may direct:

A number of electors of President and Vice President equal to the whole number of Senators and Representatives in Congress to which the District would be entitled if it were a State, but in no event more than the least populous State; they shall be in addition to those appointed by the States, they shall be considered, for the purposes of

23rd Amendment. Presidential Electors for the District of Columbia

Proposed by Congress June 16, 1960; ratified March 29, 1961. This amendment modified Article II, Section I, Clause 2 and the 12th Amendment. It included the voters of the District of Columbia in the presidential electorate; and provides that the District is to have the same number of electors as the least populous State—three electors—but no more than that number.

the election of President and Vice President, to be electors appointed by a State; and they shall meet in the District and perform such duties as provided by the twelfth article of amendment.

Section 2. The Congress shall have power to enforce this article by appropriate legislation.

24th Amendment. Right to Vote in Federal Elections—Tax Payment

Proposed by Congress September 14, 1962; ratified January 23, 1964. This amendment outlawed the payment of any tax as a condition for taking part in the nomination or election of any federal officeholder.

24th Amendment.

Section 1. The right of citizens of the United States to vote in any primary or other election for President or Vice President, for electors for President or Vice President, or for Senator or Representative in Congress, shall not be denied or abridged by the United States or any State by reason of failure to pay any poll tax or other tax.

Section 2. The Congress shall have power to enforce this article by appropriate legislation.

25th Amendment. Presidential Succession, Vice Presidential Vacancy, Presidential Inability

Proposed by Congress July 6, 1965; ratified February 10, 1967. Section 1 revised the imprecise provision on presidential succession in Article II, Section 1, Clause 6. It wrote into the Constitution the precedent set by Vice President John Tyler, who became President on the death of William Henry Harrison in 1841.

Section 2 provides for the filling of a vacancy in the office of Vice President. Prior to its adoption, the office had been vacant on 16 occasions and had remained unfilled for the remainder of each term involved. When Spiro Agnew resigned the office in 1973, President Nixon selected Gerald Ford in accord with this provision; and, when President Nixon resigned in 1974, Gerald Ford became President and then chose Nelson Rockefeller as Vice President.

This section created a procedure for determining if a President is so incapacitated that he cannot perform the powers and duties of his office.

25th Amendment.

Section 1. In case of the removal of the President from office or of his death or resignation, the Vice President shall become President.

Section 2. Whenever there is a vacancy in the office of the Vice President, the President shall nominate a Vice President who shall take office upon confirmation by a majority vote of both Houses of Congress.

Section 3. Whenever the President transmits to the President *pro tempore* of the Senate and the Speaker of the House of Representatives his written declaration that he is unable to discharge the powers and duties of his office, and until he transmits to them a written declaration to the contrary, such powers and duties shall be discharged by the Vice President as Acting President.

Section 4. Whenever the Vice President and a majority of either the principal officers of the executive departments or of such other body as Congress may by law provide, transmit to the President *pro tempore* of the Senate and the Speaker of the House of Representatives their written declaration that the President is unable to discharge the powers and duties of his office, the Vice President shall immediately assume the powers and duties of the office as Acting President.

Thereafter, when the President transmits to the President *pro tempore* of the Senate and the Speaker of the House of Representatives his written declaration that no inability exists, he shall resume the powers and duties of his office unless the Vice President and a majority of either the principal officers of the executive department or of such other body as Congress may by law provide, transmit within four days to the President *pro tempore* of the Senate and the Speaker of the House of Representatives their written declaration that the President is unable to discharge the powers and duties of his office. Thereupon Congress shall decide the issue, assembling within forty-eight hours for that purpose if not in session. If the Congress, within twenty-one days after receipt of the latter written declaration, or, if Congress is not in session, within twenty-one days after Congress is required to assemble, determines by two-thirds vote of both Houses that the President is unable to discharge the powers and duties of his office, the Vice President shall continue to discharge the same as Acting President; otherwise, the President shall resume the powers and duties of his office.

Section 4 deals with the circumstance in which a President will not be able to determine the fact of incapacity. To this point, Congress has not established the "such other body" referred to here. This section contains the only typographical error in the Constitution; in its second paragraph, the word "department" should in fact read "departments."

26th Amendment.

Section 1. The right of citizens of the United States, who are eighteen years of age or older, to vote shall not be denied or abridged by the United States or by any State on account of age.

Section 2. The Congress shall have the power to enforce this article by appropriate legislation.

26th Amendment. Right to Vote—Age

Proposed by Congress March 23, 1971; ratified July 1, 1971. This amendment provides that the minimum age for voting in any election in the United States cannot be more than 18 years. (A State may set a minimum voting age of less than 18, however.)

27th Amendment.

No law varying the compensation for the services of the Senators and Representatives, shall take effect, until an election of Representatives shall have intervened.

27th Amendment. Congressional Pay

Proposed by Congress September 25, 1789; ratified May 7, 1992. This amendment modified Article I, Section 6, Clause 1. It limits Congress's power to fix the salaries of its members—by delaying the effectiveness of any increase in that pay until after the next regular congressional election.

United States Constitution

Historical Documents

The Code of Hammurabi

The Code of Hammurabi, believed to date before 1750 B.C., is a series of laws decreed by Hammurabi, the ruler of the city of Babylon when that ancient city was at the peak of its power. Inscribed on stone columns over seven feet high, these laws were intended to inform the people of what they could and could not do. They were written down and codified so that judges and administrators would have a uniform set of rules to follow in deciding disputes and imposing penalties for crimes. The Code consists of 280 sections that deal with such matters as land tenure, property rights, trade and commerce, family relations, and the administration of justice. Selected sections of the Code are excerpted below:

❧ If a man practice (robbery) and be captured, that man shall be put to death. . . .

❧ If a man has come forward in a lawsuit for the witnessing of false things, and has not proved the thing that he said, if that lawsuit is a capital case, that man shall be put to death. If he came forward for witnessing about corn or silver, he shall bear the penalty (which applies to) that case.

❧ If a man has concealed in his house a lost slave or slave-girl belonging to the Palace or to a subject, and has not brought him (or her) out at the proclamation of the Crier, the owner of the house shall be put to death.

❧ If a fire has broken out in a man's house, and a man who has gone to extinguish it has cast his eye on the property of the owner of the house and has taken the property of the owner of the house, that man shall be thrown into the fire.

❧ If a man is subject to a debt bearing interest, and Adad (the Weather-god) has saturated his field or a high flood has carried (its crop) away, or because of lack of water he has not produced corn in that field, in that year he shall not return any corn to (his) creditor. He shall . . . not pay interest for that year.

❧ If a man has donated field, orchard or house to his favourite heir and has written a sealed document for him (confirming this), after the father has gone to his doom, when the brothers share he (the favorite heir) shall take the gift that his father gave him, and apart from that they shall share equally in the property of the paternal estate.

❧ If an artisan has taken a child for bringing up, and has taught him his manual skill, (the child) shall not be (re)claimed. If he has not taught him his manual skill, that pupil may return to his father's house.

❧ If a man aid a male or female slave . . . to escape from the city gates, he shall be put to death. . . .

❧ If a man be in debt and sell his wife, son, or daughter, or bind them over to service, for three years they shall work in the house of the purchaser or master; in the fourth year they shall be given their freedom. . . .

❧ If a builder has made a house for a man but has not made his work strong, so that the house he made falls down and causes the death of the owner of the house, that builder shall be put to death. If it causes the death of the son of the owner of the house, they shall kill the son of the builder.

❧ If a man would put away [divorce] his wife who has not borne him children, he shall give her money to the amount of her marriage settlement and he shall make good to her the dowry which she brought from her father's house and then he may put her away.

❧ If a son has struck his father, they shall cut off his hand.

❧ If a man has destroyed the eye of a man of the "gentleman" class, they shall destroy his eye. If he has broken a gentleman's bone, they shall break his bone. If he has destroyed the eye of a commoner or broken a bone of a commoner, he shall pay one mina (about $300) of silver. If he has destroyed the eye of a gentleman's slave, he shall pay half the slave's price.

❧ If a gentleman's slave strikes the cheek of a man of the "gentleman" class, they shall cut off (the slave's) ear.

❧ If a gentleman strikes a gentleman in a free fight and inflicts an injury on him, that man shall swear "I did not strike him deliberately," and he shall pay the surgeon.

Madison's *Notes:* Debate of June 6 on the Virginia Plan

James Madison's Notes *enable readers today to gain a glimpse of the debates that took place behind closed doors at the Constitutional Convention held in Philadelphia in the summer of 1787. Excerpted here are portions of Madison's* Notes *on the debate of June 6 on the Virginia Plan's call for a bicameral (two house) legislature.*

MR. PINCKNEY [S.C.], according to previous notice and rule obtained, moved "that the first branch of the national legislature be elected by the state legislatures, and not by the people," contending that the people were less fit judges in such a case, and that the legislatures would be less likely to promote the adoption of the new government if they were to be excluded from all share in it.

MR. RUTLEDGE [S.C.] seconded the motion.

MR. GERRY [MASS.]: Much depends on the mode of election. In England the people will probably lose their liberty from the smallness of the proportion having a right of suffrage. Our danger arises from the opposite extreme; hence in Massachusetts the worst men get into the legislature. Several members of that body had lately been convicted of infamous crimes. Men of indigence, ignorance, and baseness spare no pains, however dirty, to carry their point against men who are superior to the artifices practised. He was not disposed to run into extremes. He was as much principled as ever against aristocracy and monarchy. It was necessary, on the one hand, that the people should appoint one branch of the government in order to inspire them with the necessary confidence. . . . His idea was that the people should nominate certain persons in certain districts, out of whom the state legislatures should make the appointment.

MR. WILSON [PA.]: He wished for vigor in the government, but he wished that vigorous authority to flow immediately from the legitimate source of all authority. The government ought to possess not only, first, the *force* but, second, the *mind or sense* of the people at large. The legislature ought to be the most exact transcript of the whole society. Representation is made necessary only because it is impossible for the people to act collectively. . . .

MR. SHERMAN [CONN.]: If it were in view to abolish the state governments, the elections ought to be by the people. If the state governments are to be continued, it is necessary, in order to preserve harmony between the national and state governments, that the elections to the former should be made by the latter. The right of participating in the national government would be sufficiently secured to the people by their election of the state legislatures. The objects of the Union, he thought, were few: (1) defense against foreign danger; (2) against internal disputes and a resort to force; (3) treaties with foreign nations; (4) regulating foreign commerce and drawing revenue from it. These, and perhaps a few lesser objects, alone rendered a confederation of the states necessary. All other matters, civil and criminal, would be much better in the hands of the states. . . .

COLONEL MASON [VA.]: Under the existing Confederacy, Congress represent the *states*, not the *people* of the states; their acts operate on the *states*, not on the individuals. The case will be changed in the new plan of government. The people will be represented; they ought therefore to choose the representatives. The requisites in actual representation are that the representatives should sympathize with their constituents, should think as they think and feel as they feel, and that, for these purposes, [they] should even be residents among them. Much, he said, had been alleged against democratic elections. He admitted that much might be said; but it was to be considered that no government was free from imperfections and evils and that improper elections, in many instances, were inseparable from republican governments. . . .

MR. MADISON [VA.] considered an election of one branch, at least, of the legislature by the people immediately as a clear principle of free government, and that this mode, under proper regulations, had the additional advantage of securing better representatives as well as of avoiding too great an agency of the state governments in the general one. He differed from the member from Connecticut (Mr. Sherman) in thinking the objects mentioned to be all the principal ones that required a national government. Those were certainly important and necessary objects; but he combined with them the necessity of providing more effectually for the security of private rights and the steady dispensation of justice.

Interferences with these were evils which had more, perhaps, than anything else produced this Convention. Was it to be supposed that republican liberty could long exist under the abuses of it practised in some of the states? . . .

All civilized societies would be divided into different sects, factions, and interests, as they happened to consist of rich and poor, debtors and creditors, the landed, the manufacturing, the commercial interests, the inhabitants of this district or that district, the followers of this political leader or that political leader, the disciples of this religious sect or that religious sect. In all cases where a majority are united by a common interest or passion, the rights of the minority are in danger. What motives are to restrain them? . . .

Conscience, the only remaining tie, is known to be inadequate in individuals; in large numbers, little is to be expected from it. . . .

What has been the source of those unjust laws complained of among ourselves? Has it not been the real or supposed interest of the major number? Debtors have defrauded their creditors. The landed interest has borne hard on the mercantile interest. The holders of one species of property have thrown a disproportion of taxes on the holders of another species.

The lesson we are to draw from the whole is that where a majority are united by a common sentiment, and have an opportunity, the rights of the minor party become insecure. In a republican government the majority, if united, have always an opportunity. . . .

MR. DICKINSON [DEL.] considered it as essential that one branch of the legislature should be drawn immediately from the people and as expedient that the other should be chosen by the legislatures of the states. This combination of the state governments with the national government was as politic as it was unavoidable. In the formation of the Senate, we ought to carry it through such a refining process as will assimilate it as near as may be to the House of Lords in England. He repeated his warm eulogiums on the British constitution. He was for a strong national government but for leaving the states a considerable agency in the system. The objection against making the former dependent on the latter might be obviated by giving to the Senate an authority permanent and irrevocable for three, five, or seven years. Being thus independent, they will speak and decide with becoming freedom.

MR. READ [DEL.]: Too much attachment is betrayed to the state governments. We must look beyond their continuance. A national government must soon of necessity swallow all of them up. They will soon be reduced to the mere office of electing the national Senate. He was against patching up the old federal system; he hoped the idea would be dismissed. It would be like putting new cloth on an old garment. The Confederation was founded on temporary principles. It cannot last; it cannot be amended. If we do not establish a good government on new principles, we must either go to ruin or have the work to do over again. . . .

MR. PIERCE [GA.] was for an election by the people as to the first branch and by the states as to the second branch, by which means the citizens of the states would be represented both *individually* and *collectively.*

GENERAL PINCKNEY wished to have a good national government and at the same time to leave a considerable share of power in the states. An election of either branch by the people, scattered as they are in many states, particularly in South Carolina, was totally impracticable. He differed from gentlemen who thought that a choice by the people would be a better guard against bad measures than by the legislatures. . . .

The state legislatures also, he said, would be more jealous and more ready to thwart the national government if excluded from a participation in it. The idea of abolishing these legislatures would never go down.

MR. WILSON would not have spoken again but for what had fallen from Mr. Read; namely, that the idea of preserving the state governments ought to be abandoned. He saw no incompatibility between the national and state governments, provided the latter were restrained to certain local purposes; nor any probability of their being devoured by the former. . . .

On the question for electing the first branch by the state legislatures as moved by Mr. Pinckney, it was negatived.

Pledge of Allegiance

By FRANCIS BELLAMY

The Pledge of Allegiance first appeared in 1892 in a magazine called The Youth's Companion. *The original Pledge, attributed to Francis Bellamy, stated: "I pledge allegiance to my Flag and the Republic for which it stands; one Nation indivisible with liberty and justice for all." In 1924, "my Flag" was changed to "the Flag of the United States of America." Congress officially recognized the Pledge in 1942 and added the words "under God" in 1954.*

I pledge allegiance to the Flag of the United States of America, and to the Republic for which it stands, one nation under God, indivisible, with liberty and justice for all.

The Federalist No. 10 (James Madison)

One of the 29 essays believed to have been written by James Madison, the tenth of
The Federalist *papers presents Madison's observations on dealing with the "mischiefs of faction" and the advantages of a republican (representative) form of government over that of a pure democracy. This essay was first published on November 23, 1787.*

Among the numerous advantages promised by a well-constructed Union, none deserves to be more accurately developed than its tendency to break and control the violence of faction. The friend of popular governments never finds himself so much alarmed for their character and fate as when he contemplates their propensity to this dangerous vice. He will not fail, therefore, to set a due value on any plan which, without violating the principles to which he is attached, provides a proper cure for it. The instability, injustice, and confusion introduced into the public councils have, in truth, been the mortal diseases under which popular governments have everywhere perished; as they continue to be the favorite and fruitful topics from which the adversaries to liberty derive their most specious declamations.

The valuable improvements made by the American constitutions on the popular models, both ancient and modern, cannot certainly be too much admired; but it would be an unwarrantable partiality to contend that they have as effectually obviated the danger on this side, as was wished and expected. Complaints are everywhere heard from our most considerate and virtuous citizens, equally the friends of public and private faith, and of public and personal liberty, that our governments are too unstable, that the public good is disregarded in the conflicts of rival parties, and that measures are too often decided, not according to the rules of justice and the rights of the minor party, but by the superior force of an interested and overbearing majority. However anxiously we may wish that these complaints had no foundation, the evidence of known facts will not permit us to deny that they are in some degree true.

It will be found, indeed, on a candid review of our situation, that some of the distresses under which we labor have been erroneously charged on the operation of our governments; but it will be found, at the same time, that other causes will not alone account for many of our heaviest misfortunes; and, particularly, for that prevailing and increasing distrust of public engagements, and alarm for private rights, which are echoed from one end of the continent to the other. These must be chiefly, if not wholly, effects of the unsteadiness and injustice with which a factious spirit has tainted our public administrations.

By a faction, I understand a number of citizens, whether amounting to a majority or minority of the whole, who are united and actuated by some common impulse of passion, or of interest, adversed to the rights of other citizens, or to the permanent and aggregate interests of the community.

There are two methods of curing the mischiefs of faction: the one, by removing its causes; the other, by controlling its effects.

There are again two methods of removing the causes of faction: the one, by destroying the liberty which is essential to its existence; the other, by giving to every citizen the same opinions, the same passions, and the same interests.

It could never be more truly said than of the first remedy that it was worse than the disease. Liberty is to faction what air is to fire, an ailment without which it instantly expires. But it could not be less folly to abolish liberty, which is essential to political life, because it nourishes faction, than it would be to wish the annihilation of air, which is essential to animal life, because it imparts to fire its destructive agency.

The second expedient is as impracticable as the first would be unwise. As long as the reason of man continues fallible, and he is at liberty to exercise it, different opinions will be formed. As long as the connection subsists between his reason and his self-love, his opinions and his passions will have a reciprocal influence on each other; and the former will be objects to which the latter will attach themselves. The diversity in the faculties of men, from which the rights of property originate, is not less an insuperable obstacle to a uniformity of interests. The protection of these faculties is the first object of government. From the protection of different and unequal faculties of acquiring property, the possession of different degrees and kinds of property immediately results; and from the influence of these on the sentiments and views of the respective proprietors ensues a division of the society into different interests and parties.

The latent causes of faction are thus sown in the nature of man; and we see them everywhere brought into different degrees of activity, according to the different circumstances of civil society. A zeal for different opinions concerning religion, concerning government, and many other points, as well of speculation as of practice; an attachment of different leaders ambitiously contending for preeminence and power; or to persons of other descriptions whose fortunes have been interesting to the human passions, have, in turn, divided mankind into parties, inflamed them with mutual animosity, and rendered them much more disposed to vex and oppress each other than to cooperate for their common good. So strong is this propensity of mankind to fall into mutual animosities that, where no substantial occasion presents itself, the most frivolous and fanciful distinctions have been sufficient to kindle their unfriendly passions and excite their most violent conflicts. But the most common and durable source of factions has been the various and unequal distribution of property.

Those who hold and those who are without property have ever formed distinct interests in society. Those who are creditors and those who are debtors fall under a like discrimination. A landed interest, a manufacturing interest, a mercantile interest, a moneyed interest, with many lesser interests, grow up of necessity in civilized nations and divide them into different classes, actuated by different sentiments and views. The regulation of these various and interfering interests forms the principal task of modern legislation and involves the spirit of party and faction in the necessary and ordinary operations of the government.

No man is allowed to be a judge in his own cause, because his interest would certainly bias his judgment and, not improbably, corrupt his integrity. With equal, nay, with greater reason, a body of men are unfit to be both judges and parties at the same time; yet what are many of the most important acts of legislation but so many judicial determinations, not indeed concerning the rights of single persons, but concerning the rights of large bodies of citizens? And what are the different classes of legislators but advocates and parties to the causes which they determine? Is a law proposed concerning private debts? It is a question to which the creditors are parties on one side and the debtors on the other. Justice ought to hold the balance between them. Yet the parties are, and must be, themselves the judges; and the most numerous party or, in other words, the most powerful faction must be expected to prevail.

Shall domestic manufactures be encouraged, and in what degree, by restrictions on foreign manufactures? [These] are questions which would be differently decided by the landed and the manufacturing classes, and probably by neither with a sole regard to justice and the public good. The apportionment of taxes on the various descriptions of property is an act which seems to require the most exact impartiality; yet there is, perhaps, no legislative act in which greater opportunity and temptation are given to a predominant party to trample on the rules of justice. Every shilling with which they overburden the inferior number is a shilling saved to their own pockets.

It is in vain to say that enlightened statesmen will be able to adjust these clashing interests and render them all subservient to the public good. Enlightened statesmen will not always be at the helm. Nor, in many cases, can such an adjustment be made at all without taking into view indirect and remote considerations, which will rarely prevail over the immediate interest which one party may find in disregarding the rights of another or the good of the whole. The inference to which we are brought is that the *causes* of faction cannot be removed and that relief is only to be sought in the means of controlling its *effects*.

If a faction consists of less than a majority, relief is supplied by the republican principle, which enables the majority to defeat its sinister views by regular vote. It may clog the administration, it may convulse the society; but it will be unable to execute and mask its violence under the forms of the Constitution. When a majority is included in a faction, the form of popular government, on the other hand, enables it to sacrifice to its ruling passion or interest both the public good and the rights of other citizens. To secure the public good and private rights against the danger of such a faction, and at the same time to preserve the spirit and the form of popular government, is then the great object to which our inquiries are directed. Let me add that it is the great desideratum by which this form of government can be rescued from the opprobrium under which it has so long labored and be recommended to the esteem and adoption of mankind.

By what means is this object attainable? Evidently by one of two only. Either the existence of the same passion or interest in a majority at the same time must be prevented, or the majority, having such coexistent passion or interest, must be rendered, by their number and local situation, unable to concert and carry into effect schemes of oppression. If the impulse and the opportunity be suffered to coincide, we well know that neither moral nor religious motives can be relied on as an adequate control. They are not found to be such on the injustice and violence of individuals and lose their efficacy in proportion to the number combined together, that is, in proportion as their efficacy becomes needful.

From this view of the subject it may be concluded that a pure democracy, by which I mean a society consisting of a small number of citizens who assemble and administer the government in person, can admit of no cure for the mischiefs of faction. A common passion or interest will, in almost every case, be felt by a majority of the whole; a communication and concert result from the form of government itself; and there is nothing to check the inducements to sacrifice the weaker party or an obnoxious individual. Hence it is that such democracies have ever been spectacles of turbulence and contention; have ever been found incompatible with personal security or the rights of property; and have in general been as short in their lives as they have been violent in their deaths. Theoretic politicians, who have patronized this species of government, have erroneously supposed that by reducing mankind to a perfect equality in their political rights, they would, at the same time, be perfectly equalized and assimilated in their possessions, their opinions, and their passions.

A republic, by which I mean a government in which the scheme of representation takes place, opens a different prospect and promises the cure for which we are seeking. Let us examine the points in which it varies from pure democracy, and we shall comprehend both the nature of the cure and the efficacy which it must derive from the Union.

The two great points of difference between a democracy and a republic are: first, the delegation of the government, in the latter, to a small number of citizens elected by the rest; secondly, the greater number of citizens, and greater sphere of country, over which the latter may be extended.

The effect of the first difference is, on the one hand, to refine and enlarge the public views by passing them through the medium of a chosen body of citizens, whose wisdom may best discern the true interest of their country, and whose patriotism and love of justice will be least likely to sacrifice it to temporary or partial considerations. Under such a regulation, it may well happen that the public voice, pronounced by the representatives of the people, will be more consonant to the public good than if pronounced by the people themselves, convened for the purpose. On the other hand, the effect may be inverted. Men of factious tempers, of local prejudices, or of sinister designs may, by intrigue, by corruption, or by other means, first obtain the suffrages, and then betray the interests of the people. The question resulting is, whether small or extensive republics are more favorable to the election of proper guardians of the public weal; and it is clearly decided in favor of the latter by two obvious considerations:

In the first place, it is to be remarked that, however small the republic may be, the representatives must be raised to a certain number, in order to guard against the cabals of a few; and that, however large it may be, they must be limited to a certain number, in order to guard against the confusion of a multitude. Hence, the number of representatives in the two cases not being in proportion to that of the two constituents, and being proportionally greater in the small republic, it follows that, if the proportion of fit characters be not less in the large than in the small republic, the former will present a greater option, and consequently a greater probability of a fit choice.

Historical Documents

In the next place, as each representative will be chosen by a greater number of citizens in the large than in the small republic, it will be more difficult for unworthy candidates to practice with success the vicious arts by which elections are too often carried; and the suffrages of the people being more free, will be more likely to center in men who possess the most attractive merit and the most diffusive and established character.

It must be confessed that in this, as in most other cases, there is a mean, on both sides of which inconveniences will be found to lie. By enlarging too much the number of electors, you render the representative too little acquainted with all their local circumstances and lesser interests; as by reducing it too much, you render him unduly attached to these and too little fit to comprehend and pursue great and national objects. The federal Constitution forms a happy combination in this respect: the great and aggregate interests being referred to the national, the local and particular to the state legislatures.

The other point of difference is the greater number of citizens and extent of territory which may be brought within the compass of republican than of democratic government; and it is this circumstance principally which renders factious combinations less to be dreaded in the former than in the latter. The smaller the society, the fewer probably will be the distinct parties and interests composing it; the fewer the distinct parties and interests, the more frequently will a majority be found of the same party; and the smaller the number of individuals composing a majority, and the smaller the compass within which they are placed, the more easily will they concert and execute their plans of oppression. Extend the sphere and you take in a greater variety of parties and interests; you make it less probable that a majority of the whole will have a common motive to invade the rights of other citizens; or if such a common motive exists, it will be more difficult for all who feel it to discover their own strength and to act in unison with each other. Besides other impediments, it may be remarked that, where there is a consciousness of unjust or dishonorable purposes, communication is always checked by distrust in proportion to the number whose concurrence is necessary.

Hence, it clearly appears that the same advantage which a republic has over a democracy, in controlling the effects of factions, is enjoyed by a large over a small republic—is enjoyed by the Union over the States composing it. Does the advantage consist in the substitution of representatives whose enlightened views and virtuous sentiments render them superior to local prejudices and to schemes of injustice? It will not be denied that the representation of the Union will be most likely to possess these requisite endowments. Does it consist in the greater security afforded by a greater variety of parties, against the event of any one party being able to outnumber and oppress the rest? In an equal degree does the increased variety of parties comprised within the Union increase this security? Does it, in fine, consist in the greater obstacles opposed to the concert and accomplishment of the secret wishes of an unjust and interested majority? Here, again, the extent of the Union gives it the most palpable advantage.

The influence of factious leaders may kindle a flame within their particular States but will be unable to spread a general conflagration through the other States. A religious sect may degenerate into a political faction in a part of the Confederacy; but the variety of sects dispersed over the entire face of it must secure the national councils against any danger from that source. A rage for paper money, for an abolition of debts, for an equal division of property, or for any other improper or wicked project will be less apt to pervade the whole body of the Union than a particular member of it; in the same proportion as such a malady is more likely to taint a particular county or district than an entire State.

In the extent, and proper structure of the Union, therefore, we behold a republican remedy for the diseases most incident to republican government. And according to the degree of pleasure and pride we feel in being republicans, ought to be our zeal in cherishing the spirit and supporting the character of Federalists.

The Federalist No. 51 (James Madison)

To what expedient, then, shall we finally resort, for maintaining in practice the necessary partition of power among the several departments as laid down in the Constitution? The only answer that can be given is that as all these exterior provisions are found to be inadequate the defect must be supplied, by so contriving the interior structure of the government as that its several constituent parts may, by their mutual relations, be the means of keeping each other in their proper places. Without presuming to undertake a full development of this important idea, I will hazard a few general observations which may perhaps place it in a clearer light, and enable us to form a more correct judgment of the principles and structure of the government planned by the convention.

In order to lay a due foundation for that separate and distinct exercise of the different powers of government, which to a certain extent is admitted on all hands to be essential to the preservation of liberty, it is evident that each department should have a will of its own; and consequently should be so constituted that the members of each should have as little agency as possible in the appointment of the members of the others. Were this principle rigorously adhered to, it would require that all the appointments for the supreme executive, legislative, and judiciary magistracies should be drawn from the same fountain of authority, the people, through channels having no communication whatever with one another. Perhaps such a plan of constructing the several departments would be less difficult in practice than it may in contemplation appear. Some difficulties, however, and some additional expense would attend the execution of it. Some deviations, therefore, from the principle must be admitted. In the constitution of the judiciary department in particular, it might be inexpedient to insist rigorously on the principle; first, because peculiar qualifications being essential in the members, the primary consideration ought to be to select that mode of choice which best secures these qualifications; secondly, because the permanent tenure by which the appointments are held in that department must soon destroy all sense of dependence on the authority conferring them.

It is equally evident that the members of each department should be as little dependent as possible on those of the others for the emoluments annexed to their offices. Were the executive magistrate, or the judges, not independent of the legislature in this particular, their independence in every other would be merely nominal.

But the great security against a gradual concentration of the several powers in the same department consists in giving to those who administer each department the necessary constitutional means and personal motives to resist encroachments of the others. The provision for defense must in this, as in all other cases, be made commensurate to the danger of attack. Ambition must be made to counteract ambition. The interest of the man must be connected with the constitutional rights of the place. It may be a reflection on human nature that such devices should be necessary to control the abuses of government. But what is government itself but the greatest of all reflections on human nature? If men were angels, no government would be necessary. If angels were to govern men, neither external nor internal controls on government would be necessary. In framing a government which is to be administered by men over men, the great difficulty lies in this: You must first enable the government to control the governed; and in the next place, oblige it to control itself. A dependence on the people is, no doubt, the primary control on the government; but experience has taught mankind the necessity of auxiliary precautions.

This policy of supplying, by opposite and rival interests, the defect of better motives might be traced through the whole system of human affairs, private as well as public. We see it particularly displayed in all the subordinate distributions of power; where the constant aim is to divide and arrange the several offices in such a manner as that each may be a check on the other—that the private interest of every individual may be a sentinel over the public rights. These inventions of prudence cannot be less requisite in the distribution of the supreme powers of the State.

But it is not possible to give to each department an equal power of self-defense. In republican government, the legislative authority necessarily predominates. The remedy for this inconveniency is to divide the legislature into different branches; and to render them, by different modes of election, and different principles of action, as little connected with each other as the nature of their common functions and their common dependence on the society will admit. It may even be necessary to guard against dangerous encroachments by still further precautions. As the weight of the legislative authority requires that it should be thus divided, the weakness of the executive may require, on the other hand, that it should be fortified. An absolute negative on the legislature appears, at first view, to be the natural defense with which the executive magistrate should be armed. But perhaps it would be neither altogether safe nor alone sufficient. On ordinary occasions it might not be exerted with the requisite firmness, and on extraordinary occasions it might be perfidiously abused. May not this defect of an absolute negative be supplied by some qualified connection between this weaker department and the weaker branch of the stronger department, by which

the latter may be led to support the constitutional rights of the former, without being too much detached from the rights of its own department?

If the principles on which these observations are founded be just, as I persuade myself they are, and they be applied as a criterion to the several State constitutions, and to the federal Constitution, it will be found that if the latter does not perfectly correspond with them, the former are infinitely less able to bear such a test.

There are, moreover, two considerations particularly applicable to the federal system of America, which place that system in a very interesting point of view.

First. In a single republic, all the power surrendered by the people is submitted to the administration of a single government; and the usurpations are guarded against by a division of the government into distinct and separate departments. In the compound republic of America, the power surrendered by the people is first divided between two distinct governments, and then the portion allotted to each subdivided among distinct and separate departments. Hence a double security arises to the rights of the people. The different governments will control each other, at the same time that each will be controlled by itself.

Second. It is of great importance in a republic not only to guard the society against the oppression of its rulers, but to guard one part of the society against the injustice of the other part. Different interests necessarily exist in different classes of citizens. If a majority be united by a common interest, the rights of the minority will be insecure. There are but two methods of providing against this evil: The one by creating a will in the community independent of the majority—that is, of the society itself; the other, by comprehending in the society so many separate descriptions of citizens as will render an unjust combination of a majority of the whole very improbable, if not impracticable. The first method prevails in all governments possessing an hereditary or self appointed authority. This, at best, is but a precarious security; because a power independent of the society may as well espouse the unjust views of the major as the rightful interests of the minor party, and may possibly be turned against both parties. The second method will be exemplified in the federal republic of the United States. Whilst all authority in it will be derived from and dependent on the society, the society itself will be broken into so many parts, interests, and classes of citizens, that the rights of individuals, or of the minority, will be in little danger from interested combinations of the majority. In a free government the security for civil rights must be the same as that for religious rights. It consists in the one case in the multiplicity of interests, and in the other in the multiplicity of sects. The degree of security in both cases will depend on the number of interests and sects; and this may be presumed to depend on the extent of country and number of people comprehended under the same government. This view of the subject must particularly recommend a proper federal system to all the sincere and considerate friends of republican government, since it shows that in exact proportion as the territory of the Union may be formed into more circumscribed Confederacies, or States, oppressive combinations of a majority will be facilitated: the best security, under the republican forms, for the rights of every class of citizens, will be diminished; and consequently, the stability and independence of some member of the government, the only other security, must be proportionally increased. Justice is the end of government.

It is the end of civil society. It ever has been and ever will be pursued until it be obtained, or until liberty be lost in the pursuit. In a society under the forms of which the stronger faction can readily unite and oppress the weaker, anarchy may as truly be said to reign as in a state of nature, where the weaker individual is not secured against the violence of the stronger: And as, in the latter state, even the stronger individuals are prompted by the uncertainty of their condition to submit to a government which may protect the weak as well as themselves. So, in the former state, will the more powerful factions or parties be gradually induced, by a like motive, to wish for a government which will protect all parties, the weaker as well as the more powerful. It can be little doubted that if the State of Rhode Island was separated from the Confederacy and left to itself, the insecurity of rights under the popular form of government within such narrow limits would be displayed by such reiterated oppressions of factious majorities that some power altogether independent of the people would soon be called for by the voice of the very factions whose misrule had proved the necessity of it. In the extended republic of the United States, and among the great variety of interests, parties, and sects which it embraces, a coalition of a majority of the whole society could seldom take place on any other principles than those of justice and the general good; whilst there being thus less danger to a minor from the will of the major party, there must be less pretext, also, to provide for the security of the former, by introducing into the government a will not dependent on the latter; or, in other words, a will independent of the society itself. It is no less certain that it is important, notwithstanding the contrary opinions which have been entertained, that the larger the society, provided it lie within a practicable sphere, the more duly capable it will be of self-government. And happily for the *republican cause*, the practicable sphere may be carried to a very great extent by a judicious modification and mixture of the *federal principle*.

The Federalist No. 78 (Alexander Hamilton)

We proceed now to an examination of the judiciary department of the proposed government. In unfolding the defects of the existing Confederation, the utility and necessity of a federal judicature have been clearly pointed out. It is the less necessary to recapitulate the considerations there urged as the propriety of the institution in the abstract is not disputed; the only questions which have been raised being relative to the manner of constituting it, and to its extent. To these points, therefore, our observations shall be confined.

The manner of constituting it seems to embrace these several objects: 1st. The mode of appointing the judges. 2nd. The tenure by which they are to hold their places. 3rd. The partition of the judiciary authority between different courts and their relations to each other.

First. As to the mode of appointing the judges: this is the same with that of appointing the officers of the Union in general and has been so fully discussed in the two last numbers that nothing can be said here which would not be useless repetition.

Second. As to the tenure by which the judges are to hold their places: this chiefly concerns their duration in office, the provisions for their support, the precautions for their responsibility.

According to the plan of the convention, all judges who may be appointed by the United States are to hold their offices *during good behavior*; which is conformable to the most approved of the State constitutions, and among the rest, to that of this State. Its propriety having been drawn into question by the adversaries of that plan is no light symptom of the rage for objection which disorders their imaginations and judgments. The standard of good behavior for the continuance in office of the judicial magistracy is certainly one of the most valuable of the modern improvements in the practice of government. In a monarchy it is an excellent barrier to the despotism of the prince; in a republic it is a no less excellent barrier to the encroachments and oppressions of the representative body. And it is the best expedient which can be devised in any government to secure a steady, upright, and impartial administration of the laws.

Whoever attentively considers the different departments of power must perceive that, in a government in which they are separated from each other, the judiciary, from the nature of its functions, will always be the least dangerous to the political rights of the Constitution; because it will be least in a capacity to annoy or injure them. The executive not only dispenses the honors but holds the sword of the community. The legislature not only commands the purse but prescribes the rules by which the duties and rights of every citizen are to be regulated. The judiciary, on the contrary, has no influence over either the sword or the purse; no direction either of the strength or of the wealth of the society, and can take no active resolution whatever. It may truly be said to have neither FORCE nor WILL but merely judgment; and must ultimately depend upon the aid of the executive arm even for the efficacy of its judgments.

This simple view of the matter suggests several important consequences. It proves incontestably that the judiciary is beyond comparison the weakest of the three departments of power; that it can never attack with success either of the other two; and that all possible care is requisite to enable it to defend itself against their attacks. It equally proves that though individual oppression may now and then proceed from the courts of justice, the general liberty of the people can never be endangered from that quarter; I mean so long as the judiciary remains truly distinct from both the legislature and the executive. For I agree that "there is no liberty if the power of judging be not separated from the legislative and executive powers." And it proves, in the last place, that as liberty can have nothing to fear from the judiciary alone, but would have everything to fear from its union with either of the other departments; that as all the effects of such a union must ensue from a dependence of the former on the latter, notwithstanding a nominal and apparent separation; that as, from the natural feebleness of the judiciary, it is in continual jeopardy of being overpowered, awed, or influenced by its coordinate branches; and that as nothing can contribute so much to its firmness and independence as permanency in office, this quality may therefore be justly regarded as an indispensable ingredient in its constitution, and, in a great measure, as the citadel of the public justice and the public security.

The complete independence of the courts of justice is peculiarly essential in a limited Constitution. By a limited Constitution, I understand one which contains certain specified exceptions to the legislative authority; such, for instance, as that it shall pass no bills of attainder, no *ex post facto* laws, and the like. Limitations of this kind can be preserved in practice no other way than through the medium of courts of justice, whose duty it must be to declare all acts contrary to the manifest tenor of the Constitution void. Without this, all the reservations of particular rights or privileges would amount to nothing.

Some perplexity respecting the rights of the courts to pronounce legislative acts void, because contrary to the Constitution, has arisen from an imagination that the doctrine would imply a superiority of the judiciary to the legislative power. It is urged that the authority which can declare the acts of another void must necessarily be superior to the one whose acts may be declared void. As this doctrine is of great importance in all the American constitutions, a brief discussion of the grounds on which it rests cannot be unacceptable.

There is no position which depends on clearer principles than that every act of a delegated authority, contrary to the tenor of the commission under which it is exercised, is void. No legislative act, therefore, contrary to the Constitution, can be valid. To deny this would be to affirm that the deputy is greater than his principal; that the servant is above his master; that the representatives of the people are superior to the people themselves; that men acting by virtue of powers may do not only what their powers do not authorize, but what they forbid.

If it be said that the legislative body are themselves the constitutional judges of their own powers and that the construction they put upon them is conclusive upon the other departments, it may be answered that this cannot be the natural presumption where it is not to be collected from any particular provisions in the Constitution. It is not otherwise to be supposed that the Constitution could intend to enable the representatives of the people to substitute their *will* to that of their constituents. It is far more rational to suppose that the courts were designed to be an intermediate body between the people and the legislature in order, among other things, to keep the latter within the limits assigned to their authority. The interpretation of the laws is the proper and peculiar province of the courts. A constitution is, in fact, and must be regarded by the judges as, a fundamental law. It therefore belongs to them to ascertain its meaning as well as the meaning of any particular act proceeding from the legislative body. If there should happen to be an irreconcilable variance between the two, that which has the superior obligation and validity ought, of course, to be preferred; or, in other words, the Constitution ought to be preferred to the statute, the intention of the people to the intention of their agents.

Nor does this conclusion by any means suppose a superiority of the judicial to the legislative power. It only supposes that the power of the people is superior to both, and that where the will of the legislature, declared in its statutes, stands in opposition to that of the people, declared in the Constitution, the judges ought to be governed by the latter rather than the former. They ought to regulate their decisions by the fundamental laws rather than by those which are not fundamental.

This exercise of judicial discretion in determining between two contradictory laws is exemplified in a familiar instance. It not uncommonly happens that there are two statutes existing at one time, clashing in whole or in part with each other and neither of them containing any repealing clause or expression. In such a case, it is the province of the courts to liquidate and fix their meaning and operation. So far as they can, by any fair construction, be reconciled to each other, reason and law conspire to dictate that this should be done; where this is impracticable, it becomes a matter of necessity to give effect to one in exclusion of the other. The rule which has obtained in the courts for determining their relative validity is that the last in order of time shall be preferred to the first. But this is a mere rule of construction, not derived from any positive law but from the nature and reason of the thing. It is a rule not enjoined upon the courts by legislative provision but adopted by themselves, as consonant to truth and propriety, for the direction of their conduct as interpreters of the law. They thought it reasonable that between the interfering acts of an *equal* authority that which was the last indication of its will should have the preference.

But in regard to the interfering acts of a superior and subordinate authority of an original and derivative power, the nature and reason of the thing indicate the converse of that rule as proper to be followed. They teach us that the prior act of a superior ought to be preferred to the subsequent act of an inferior and subordinate authority; and that accordingly, whenever a particular statute contravenes the Constitution, it will be the duty of the judicial tribunals to adhere to the latter and disregard the former.

Historical Documents

It can be of no weight to say that the courts, on the pretense of a repugnancy, may substitute their own pleasure to the constitutional intentions of the legislature. This might as well happen in the case of two contradictory statutes; or it might as well happen in every adjudication upon any single statute. The courts must declare the sense of the law; and if they should be disposed to exercise *will* instead of *judgment*, the consequence would equally be the substitution of their pleasure to that of the legislative body. The observation, if it prove anything, would prove that there ought to be no judges distinct from that body.

If, then, the courts of justice are to be considered as the bulwarks of a limited Constitution against legislative encroachments, this consideration will afford a strong argument for the permanent tenure of judicial offices, since nothing will contribute so much as this to that independent spirit in the judges which must be essential to the faithful performance of so arduous a duty.

This independence of the judges is equally requisite to guard the Constitution and the rights of individuals from the effects of those ill humors which the arts of designing men, or the influence of particular conjunctures, sometimes disseminate among the people themselves, and which, though they speedily give place to better information, and more deliberate reflection, have a tendency, in the meantime, to occasion dangerous innovations in the government, and serious oppressions of the minor party in the community. Though I trust the friends of the proposed Constitution will never concur with its enemies in questioning that fundamental principle of Republican government which admits the right of the people to alter or abolish the established Constitution whenever they find it inconsistent with their happiness; yet it is not to be inferred from this principle that the representatives of the people, whenever a momentary inclination happens to lay hold of a majority of their constituents incompatible with the provisions in the existing Constitution would, on that account, be justifiable in a violation of those provisions; or that the courts would be under a greater obligation to connive at infractions in this shape than when they had proceeded wholly from the cabals of the representative body. Until the people have, by some solemn and authoritative act, annulled or changed the established form, it is binding upon themselves collectively, as well as individually; and no presumption, or even knowledge of their sentiments, can warrant their representatives in a departure from it prior to such an act. But it is easy to see that it would require an uncommon portion of fortitude in the judges to do their duty as faithful guardians of the Constitution, where legislative invasions of it had been instigated by the major voice of the community.

But it is not with a view to infractions of the Constitution only that the independence of the judges may be an essential safeguard against the effects of occasional ill humors in the society. These sometimes extend no farther than to the injury of the private rights of particular classes of citizens, by unjust and partial laws. Here also the firmness of the judicial magistracy is of vast importance in mitigating the severity and confining the operation of such laws. It not only serves to moderate the immediate mischiefs of those which may have been passed but it operates as a check upon the legislative body in passing them; who, perceiving that obstacles to the success of iniquitous intention are to be expected from the scruples of the courts, are in a manner compelled, by the very motives of the injustice they mediate, to qualify their attempts. This is a circumstance calculated to have more influence upon the character of our governments than but few may be aware of. The benefits of the integrity and moderation of the judiciary have already been felt in more States than one; and though they may have displeased those whose sinister expectations they may have disappointed, they must have commanded the esteem and applause of all the virtuous and disinterested. Considerate men of every description ought to prize whatever will tend to beget or fortify that temper in the courts; as no man can be sure that he may not be tomorrow the victim of a spirit of injustice, by which he may be a gainer today. And every man must now feel that the inevitable tendency of such a spirit is to sap the foundations of public and private confidence and to introduce in its stead universal distrust and distress.

That inflexible and uniform adherence to the rights of the Constitution, and of individuals, which we perceive to be indispensable in the courts of justice, can certainly not be expected from judges who hold their offices by a temporary commission. Periodical appointments, however regulated, or by whomsoever made, would, in some way or other, be fatal to their necessary independence. If the power of making them was committed either to the executive or legislature there would be danger of an improper complaisance to the branch which possessed it; if to both, there would be an unwillingness to hazard the displeasure of either; if to the people, or to persons chosen by them for the special purpose, there would be too great a disposition to consult popularity to justify a reliance that nothing would be consulted but the Constitution and the laws.

There is yet a further and a weighty reason for the permanency of the judicial offices which is deducible from the nature of the qualifications they require. It has been frequently remarked with great propriety that a voluminous code of laws is one of the inconveniences necessarily connected with the advantages of a free government. To avoid an arbitrary discretion in the courts, it is indispensable that they should be bound down by strict rules and precedents which serve to define and point out their duty in every particular case that comes before them; and it will readily be conceived from the variety of controversies which grow out of the folly and wickedness of mankind that the records of those precedents must unavoidably swell to a very considerable bulk and must demand long and laborious study to acquire a competent knowledge of them. Hence it is that there can be but few men in the society who will have sufficient skill in the laws to qualify them for the stations of judges. And making the proper deductions for the ordinary depravity of human nature, the number must be still smaller of those who unite the requisite integrity with the requisite knowledge. These considerations apprise us that the government can have no great option between fit characters; and that a temporary duration in office which would naturally discourage such characters from quitting a lucrative line of practice to accept a seat on the bench would have a tendency to throw the administration of justice into hands less able and less well qualified to conduct it with utility and dignity. In the present circumstances of this country and in those in which it is likely to be for a long time to come, the disadvantages on this score would be greater than they may at first sight appear; but it must be confessed that they are far inferior to those which present themselves under the other aspects of the subject.

Upon the whole, there can be no room to doubt that the convention acted wisely in copying from the models of those constitutions which have established *good behavior* as the tenure of their judicial offices, in point of duration; and that so far from being blamable on this account, their plan would have been inexcusably defective if it had wanted this important feature of good government. The experience of Great Britain affords an illustrious comment on the excellence of the institution.

Anti-Federalist Responses
Arguments Against the Adoption of the Constitution

When the Constitutional Convention of 1787 produced the new Constitution, many thoughtful, patriotic people from all over the country opposed its adoption. These Anti-Federalists, as they were known, had a number of objections to the Constitution. Five of their most significant objections were these: (1) The new Constitution was a document written by and for the primary benefit of a wealthy and powerful aristocracy. (2) The Constitution lacked a bill of rights. (3) The Constitutional Convention was not authorized to do anything but amend the Articles of Confederation; therefore, the Constitution was an illegal document. (4) States would be wholly subordinate to the new National Government and lose their sovereignty. (5) The powers given to the new United States Government were so extensive as to lead inevitably to tyranny and despotism. The following documents provide a sampling of Anti-Federalist arguments.

Richard Henry Lee

Lee from Virginia wrote the best-known Anti-Federalist essays of the time, "Letters from the Federal Farmer to the Republican." These excerpts are from these letters written in October 1787.

The present moment discovers a new face in our affairs. Our object has been all along to reform our federal system and to strengthen our governments—to establish peace, order, and justice in the community—but a new object now presents. The plan of government now proposed is evidently calculated totally to change, in time, our condition as a people. Instead of being thirteen republics under a federal head, it is clearly designed to make us one consolidated government. . . . This consolidation of the states has been the object of several men in this country for some time past. Whether such a change can ever be effected, in any manner; whether it can be effected without convulsions and civil wars; whether such a change will not totally destroy the liberties of this country, time only can determine. . . .

The Confederation was formed when great confidence was placed in the voluntary exertions of individuals and of the respective states; and the framers of it, to guard against usurpation, so limited and checked the powers that, in many respects, they are inadequate to the exigencies of the Union. We find, therefore, members of Congress urging alterations in the federal system almost as soon as it was adopted. . . .

We expected too much from the return of peace, and, of course, we have been disappointed. Our governments have been new and unsettled; and several legislature, [by their actions] . . . have given just cause of uneasiness. . . .

The conduct of several legislatures touching paper-money and tender laws has prepared many honest men for changes in government, which otherwise they would not have thought of—when by the evils, on the one hand, and by the secret instigations of artful men, on the other, the minds of men were become sufficiently uneasy, a bold step was taken, which is usually followed by a revolution or a civil war. A general convention for mere commercial purposes was moved for—the authors of this measure saw that the people's attention was turned solely to the amendment of the federal system; and that, had the idea of a total change been started, probably no state would have appointed members to the Convention. The idea of destroying, ultimately, the state government and forming one consolidated system could not have been admitted. A convention, therefore, merely for vesting in Congress power to regulate trade was proposed. . . .

The plan proposed appears to be partly federal, but principally, however, calculated ultimately to make the states one consolidated government.

The first interesting question therefore suggested is how far the states can be consolidated into one entire government on free principles. In considering this question, extensive objects are to be taken into view, and important changes in the forms of government to be carefully attended to in all their consequences. The happiness of the people at large must be the great object with every honest statesman, and he will direct every movement to this point. If we are so situated as a people as not to be able to enjoy equal happiness and advantages under one government, the consolidation of the states cannot be admitted.

* * *

There are certain unalienable and fundamental rights, which in forming the social compact ought to be explicitly ascertained and fixed. A free and enlightened people, in forming this compact, will not resign all their rights to those who govern, and they will fix limits [a bill of rights] to their legislators and rulers, which will soon be plainly seen by those who are governed, as well as by those who govern; and the latter will know they cannot be passed unperceived by the former and without giving a general alarm. These rights should be made the basis of every constitution; and if a people be so situated, or have such different opinions, that they cannot agree in ascertaining and fixing them, it is a very strong argument against their attempting to form one entire society, to live under one system of laws only.

* * *

It may also be worthy our examination how far the provision for amending this plan, when it shall be adopted, is of any importance. No measures can be taken toward amendments unless two-thirds of the Congress, or two-thirds of the legislature of the several states, shall agree. While power is in the hands of the people, or democratic part of the community, more especially as at present, it is easy, according to the general course of human affairs, for the few influential men in the community to obtain conventions, alterations in government, and to persuade the common people that they may change for the better, and to get from them a part of the power. But when power is once transferred from the many to the few, all changes become extremely difficult; the government in this case being beneficial to the few, they will be exceedingly artful and adroit in preventing any measures which may lead to a change; and nothing will produce it but great exertions and severe struggles on the part of the common people. Every man of reflection must see that the change now proposed is a transfer of power from the many to the few, and the probability is the artful and ever active aristocracy will prevent all peaceful measures for changes, unless when they shall discover some favorable moment to increase their own influence.

* * *

It is true there may be danger in delay; but there is danger in adopting the system in its present form. And I see the danger in either case will arise principally from the conduct and views of two very unprincipled parties in the United States—two fires, between which the honest and substantial people have long found themselves situated. One party is composed of little insurgents, men in debt, who want no law and who want a share of the property of others—these are called levelers, Shayites, etc. The other party is composed of a few but more dangerous men, with their servile dependents; these avariciously grasp at all power and property. You may discover in all the actions of these men an evident dislike to free and equal government, and they will go systematically to work to change, essentially, the forms of government in this country—these are called aristocrats. . . .

. . . The fact is, these aristocrats support and hasten the adoption of the proposed Constitution merely because they think it is a stepping-stone to their favorite object. I think I am well-founded in this idea; I think the general politics of these men support it, as well as the common observation among them that the proffered plan is the best that can be got at present; it will do for a few years, and lead to something better. . . .

Luther Martin

Martin, the leading Anti-Federalist from Maryland, attended the Constitutional Convention as a delegate. In this excerpt from a speech before the Maryland State legislature on November 29, 1787, he defends his decision to leave the Convention before its work was finished.

It was the states as states, by their representatives in Congress, that formed the Articles of Confederation; it was the states as states, by their legislatures, who ratified those Articles; and it was there established and provided that the states as states (that is, by their legislatures) should agree to any alterations that should hereafter be proposed in the federal government, before they should be binding; and any alterations agreed to in any other manner cannot release the states from the obligation they are under to each other by virtue of the original Articles of Confederation. The people of the different states never made any objection to the manner in which the Articles of Confederation were formed or ratified, or to the mode by which alterations were to be made in that government—with the rights of their respective states they wished not to interfere. Nor do I believe the people, in their individual capacity, would ever have expected or desired to have been appealed to on the present occasion, in violation of the rights of their respective states, if the favorers of the proposed Constitution, imagining they had a better chance of forcing it to be adopted by a hasty appeal to the people at large (who could not be so good judges of the dangerous consequence), had not insisted upon this mode . . . .

It was also my opinion that, upon principles of sound policy, the agreement or disagreement to the proposed system ought to have been by the state legislatures; in which case, let the event have been what it would, there would have been but little prospect of the public peace being disturbed thereby; whereas the attempt to force down this system, although Congress and the respective state legislatures should disapprove, by appealing to the people and to procure its establishment in a manner totally unconstitutional, has a tendency to set the state governments and their subjects at variance with each other, to lessen the obligations of government, to weaken the bands of society, to introduce anarchy and confusion, and to light the torch of discord and civil war throughout this continent. All these considerations weighed with me most forcibly against giving my assent to the mode by which it is resolved that this system is to be ratified, and were urged by me in opposition to the measure.

. . . [A] great portion of that time which ought to have been devoted calmly and impartially to consider what alterations in our federal government would be most likely to procure and preserve the happiness of the Union was employed in a violent struggle on the one side to obtain all power and dominion in their own hands, and on the other to prevent it; and that the aggrandizement of particular states, and particular individuals, appears to have been much more the subject sought after than the welfare of our country . . . .

When I took my seat in the Convention, I found them attempting to bring forward a system which, I was sure, never had entered into the contemplation of those I had the honor to represent, and which, upon the fullest consideration, I considered not only injurious to the interest and rights of this state but also incompatible with the political happiness and freedom of the states in general. From that time until my business compelled me to leave the Convention, I gave it every possible opposition, in every stage of its progression. I opposed the system there with the same explicit frankness with which I have here given you a history of our proceedings, an account of my own conduct, which in a particular manner I consider you as having a right to know. While there, I endeavored to act as became a free-man and the delegate of a free state. Should my conduct obtain the approbation of those who appointed me, I will not deny it would afford me satisfaction; but to me that approbation was at most no more than a secondary consideration—my first was to deserve it. Left to myself to act according to the best of my discretion, my conduct should have been the same had I been even sure your censure would have been my only reward, since I hold it sacredly my duty to dash the cup of poison, if possible, from the hand of a state or an individual, however anxious the one or the other might be to swallow it . . . .

William Findley, Robert Whitehill, and John Smilie

Findley, Whitehill, and Smilie—who were delegates to the Pennsylvania State convention—believed that they and other opponents of the Constitution were prevented from expressing their views because of the political maneuverings of the Federalists. This excerpt is from "The Address and Reasons of Dissent of the Minority of the Convention of the State of Pennsylvania to their Constituents," which the three men published in the Pennsylvania Packet and Daily Advertiser *on December 18, 1787.*

The Continental Convention met in the city of Philadelphia at the time appointed. It was composed of some men of excellent character; of others who were more remarkable for their ambition and cunning than their patriotism; and of some who had been opponents to the independence of the United States. The delegates from Pennsylvania were, six of them, uniform and decided opponents to the constitution of the commonwealth [the Articles of Confederation]. The convention sat upward of four months. The doors were kept shut, and the members brought under the most solemn engagements of secrecy. Some of those who opposed their going so far beyond their powers, retired, hopeless, from the convention; others had the firmness to refuse signing the plan altogether; and many who did sign it, did it not as a system they wholly approved but as the best that could be then obtained; and notwithstanding the time spent on this subject, it is agreed on all hands to be a work of haste and accommodation. . . .

Our objections are comprised under three general heads of dissent, viz.:

We dissent, first, because it is the opinion of the most celebrated writers on government, and confirmed by uniform experience, that a very extensive territory cannot be governed on the principles of freedom otherwise than by a confederation of republics, possessing all the powers of internal government but united in the management of their general and foreign concerns. . . .

We dissent, secondly, because the powers vested in Congress by this Constitution must necessarily annihilate and absorb the legislative, executive, and judicial powers of the several states, and produce from their ruins one consolidated government, which from the nature of things will be *an iron-handed despotism*, as nothing short of the supremacy of despotic sway could connect and govern these United States under one government.

As the truth of this position is of such decisive importance, it ought to be fully investigated, and if it is founded, to be clearly ascertained; for, should it be demonstrated that the powers vested by this Constitution in Congress will have such an effect as necessarily to produce one consolidated government, the question then will be reduced to this short issue, viz.: whether satiated with the blessings of liberty, whether repenting of the folly of so recently asserting their unalienable rights against foreign despots at the expense of so much blood and treasure, and such painful and arduous struggles, the people of America are now willing to resign every privilege of freemen, and submit to the dominion of an absolute government that will embrace all America in one chain of despotism; or whether they will, with virtuous indignation, spurn at the shackles prepared for them, and confirm their liberties by a conduct becoming freemen. . . .

We dissent, thirdly, because if it were practicable to govern so extensive a territory as these United States include, on the plan of a consolidated government, consistent with the principles of liberty and the happiness of the people, yet the construction of this Constitution is not calculated to attain the object; for independent of the nature of the case, it would of itself necessarily produce a despotism, and that not by the usual gradations but with the celerity that has hitherto only attended revolutions effected by the sword.

To establish the truth of this position, a cursory investigation of the principles and form of this Constitution will suffice.

The first consideration that this review suggests is the omission of a Bill of Rights ascertaining and fundamentally establishing those unalienable and personal rights of men, without the full, free, and secure enjoyment of which there can be no liberty, and over which it is not necessary for a good government to have the control— the principal of which are the rights of conscience, personal liberty by the clear and unequivocal establishment of the writ of habeas corpus, jury trial in criminal and civil cases, by an impartial jury of the vicinage or county, with the common law proceedings for the safety of the accused in criminal prosecutions; and the liberty of the press, that scourge of tyrants, and the grand bulwark of every other liberty and privilege. The stipulations heretofore made in favor of them in the state constitutions are entirely superseded by this Constitution. . . .

Historical Documents

Articles of Confederation

In force from March 1, 1781 to March 4, 1789

To all to whom these Presents shall come, we the undersigned Delegates of the States affixed to our Names send greeting. Whereas the Delegates of the United States of America in Congress assembled did on the fifteenth day of November in the Year of our Lord One Thousand Seven Hundred and Seventy seven, and in the Second Year of the Independence of America agree to certain articles of Confederation and perpetual Union between the States of New Hampshire, Massachusetts Bay, Rhode Island and Providence Plantations, Connecticut, New York, New Jersey, Pennsylvania, Delaware, Maryland, Virginia, North Carolina, South Carolina and Georgia in the Words following, viz. "Articles of Confederation and perpetual Union between the states of New Hampshire, Massachusetts Bay, Rhode Island and Providence Plantations, Connecticut, New York, New Jersey, Pennsylvania, Delaware, Maryland, Virginia, North Carolina, South Carolina and Georgia.

[ART. I.] The Stile of this confederacy shall be "The United States of America."

[ART. II.] Each state retains its sovereignty, freedom and independence, and every Power, Jurisdiction and right, which is not by this confederation expressly delegated to the United States, in Congress assembled.

[ART. III.] The said states hereby severally enter into a firm league of friendship with each other, for their common defence, the security of their Liberties, and their mutual and general welfare, binding themselves to assist each other, against all force offered to, or attacks made upon them, or any of them, on account of religion, sovereignty, trade, or any other pretence whatever.

[ART. IV.] The better to secure and perpetuate mutual friendship and intercourse among the people of the different states in this union, the free inhabitants of each of these states, paupers, vagabonds and fugitives from Justice excepted, shall be entitled to all privileges and immunities of free citizens in the several states; and the people of each state shall have free ingress and regress to and from any other state, and shall enjoy therein all the privileges of trade and commerce, subject to the same duties, impositions and restrictions as the inhabitants thereof respectively, provided that such restriction shall not extend so far as to prevent the removal of property imported into any state, to any other state of which the Owner is an inhabitant; provided also that no imposition, duties or restriction shall be laid by any state, on the property of the united states, or either of them.

If any Person guilty of, or charged with treason, felony, or other high misdemeanor in any state, shall flee from Justice, and be found in any of the united states, he shall upon demand of the Governor or executive power, of the state from which he fled, be delivered up and removed to the state having jurisdiction of his offence.

Full faith and credit shall be given in each of these states to the records, acts and judicial proceedings of the courts and magistrates of every other state.

[ART. V.] For the more convenient management of the general interests of the united states, delegates shall be annually appointed in such manner as the legislature of each state shall direct, to meet in Congress on the first Monday in November, in every year, with a power reserved to each state, to recall its delegates, or any of them, at any time within the year, and to send others in their stead, for the remainder of the Year.

No state shall be represented in Congress by less than two, nor by more than seven Members; and no person shall be capable of being a delegate for more than three years in any term of six years; nor shall any person, being a delegate, be capable of holding any office under the united states, for which he, or another for his benefit receives any salary, fees or emolument of any kind.

Each state shall maintain its own delegates in a meeting of the states, and while they act as members of the committee of the states.

In determining questions in the united states, in Congress assembled, each state shall have one vote.

Freedom of speech and debate in Congress shall not be impeached or questioned in any Court, or place out of Congress, and the members of congress shall be protected in their persons from arrests and imprisonments, during the time of their going to and from, and attendance on congress, except for treason, felony, or breach of the peace.

[ART. VI.] No state without the Consent of the united states in congress assembled, shall send any embassy to, or receive any embassy from, or enter into any conference, agreement, or alliance or treaty with any King, prince or state; nor shall any person holding any office of profit or trust under the united states, or any of them, accept of any present, emolument, office or title of any kind whatever from any king, prince or foreign state; nor shall the united states in congress assembled, or any of them, grant any title of nobility.

No two or more states shall enter into any treaty, confederation or alliance whatever between them, without the consent of the united states in congress assembled, specifying accurately the purposes for which the same is to be entered into, and how long it shall continue.

No state shall lay any imposts or duties, which may interfere with any stipulations in treaties, entered into by the united states in congress assembled, with any king, prince or state, in pursuance of any treaties already proposed by congress, to the courts of France and Spain.

No vessels of war shall be kept up in time of peace by any state, except such number only, as shall be deemed necessary by the united states in congress assembled, for the defence of such state, or its trade; nor shall any body of forces be kept up by any state, in time of peace, except such number only, as in the judgment of the united states, in congress assembled, shall be deemed requisite to garrison the forts necessary for the defence of such state; but every state shall always keep up a well regulated and disciplined militia, sufficiently armed and accounted, and shall provide and constantly have ready for use, in public stores, a due number of field pieces and tents, and a proper quantity of arms, ammunition and camp equipage.

No state shall engage in any war without the consent of the united states in congress assembled, unless such state be actually invaded by enemies, or shall have received certain advice of a resolution being formed by some nation of Indians to invade such state and the danger is so imminent as not to admit of a delay, till the united states in congress assembled can be consulted: nor shall any state grant commissions to any ships or vessels of war, nor letters of marque or reprisal, except it be after a declaration of war by the united states in congress assembled, and then only against the kingdom or state and the subjects thereof, against which war has been so declared, and under such regulations as shall be established by the united states in congress assembled, unless such state be infested by pirates, in which case vessels of war may be fitted out for that occasion, and kept so long as the danger shall continue, or until the united states in congress assembled shall determine otherwise.

[ART. VII.] When land-forces are raised by any state for the common defence, all officers of or under the rank of colonel, shall be appointed by the legislature of each state respectively by whom such forces shall be raised, or in such manner as such state shall direct, and all vacancies shall be filled up by the state which first made the appointment.

[ART. VIII.] All charges of war, and all other expences that shall be incurred for the common defence or general welfare, and allowed by the united states in congress assembled, shall be defrayed out of a common treasury, which shall be supplied by the several states, in proportion to the value of all land within each state, granted to or surveyed for any Person, as such land and the buildings and improvements thereon shall be estimated according to such mode as the united states in congress assembled, shall from time to time direct and appoint. The taxes for paying that proportion shall be laid and levied by the authority and direction of the legislatures of the several states within the time agreed upon by the united states in congress assembled.

[ART. IX.] The united states in congress assembled, shall have the sole and exclusive right and power of determining on peace and war, except in the cases mentioned in the sixth article—of sending and receiving ambassadors—entering into treaties and alliances, provided that no treaty of commerce shall be made whereby the legislative power of the respective states shall be restrained from imposing such imposts and duties on foreigners, as their own people are subjected to, or from prohibiting the exportation or importation of any species of goods or commodities whatsoever—of establishing rules for deciding in all cases, what captures on land or water shall be legal, and in what manner prizes taken by land or naval forces in the service of the united states shall be divided or appropriated—of granting letters of marque and reprisal in times of peace—appointing courts for the trial of piracies and felonies committed on the high seas and establishing courts for receiving and determining finally appeals in all cases of captures, provided that no member of congress shall be appointed a judge of any of the said courts.

The united states in congress assembled shall also be the last resort on appeal in all disputes and differences now subsisting or that hereafter may arise between two or more states concerning boundary, jurisdiction or any other cause whatever; which authority shall always be exercised in the manner following. Whenever the legislative or executive authority or lawful agent [of any] state in controversy with another shall present a petition to congress stating the matter in question and praying for a hearing, notice thereof shall be given by order of congress to the legislative or executive authority of the other state in controversy, and a day assigned for the appearance of the parties by their lawful agents, who shall then be directed to appoint by joint consent, commissioners or judges to constitute a court for hearing and determining the matter in question; but if they cannot agree, congress shall name three persons out of each of the united states, and from the list of such persons each party shall alternately strike out one, the petitioners beginning, until the number shall be reduced to thirteen; and from that number not less than seven, nor more than nine names as congress shall direct, shall in the presence of congress be drawn out by lot, and the persons whose names shall be so drawn or any five of them, shall be commissioners or judges, to hear and finally determine the controversy, so always as a major part of the judges who shall hear the cause shall agree in the determination: and if either party shall neglect to attend at the day appointed, without shewing reasons, which congress shall judge sufficient, or being present shall refuse to strike, the congress shall proceed to nominate three persons out of each state, and the secretary of congress shall strike in behalf of such party absent or refusing; and the judgment and sentence of the court to be appointed, in the manner before prescribed, shall be final and conclusive; and if any of the parties shall refuse to submit to the authority of such court, or to appear to defend their claim or cause, the court shall nevertheless proceed to pronounce sentence, or judgment, which shall in like manner be final and decisive, the judgment or sentence and other proceedings being in either case transmitted to congress, and lodged among the acts of congress for the security of the parties concerned: provided that every commissioner, before he sits in judgment, shall take an oath to be administered by one of the judges of the supreme or superior court of the state, where the cause shall be tried, "well and truly to hear and determine the matter in question, according to the best of his judgment, without favour, affection or hope of reward;" provided also that no state shall be deprived of territory for the benefit of the united states.

Historical Documents

All controversies concerning the private right of soil claimed under different grants of two or more states, whose jurisdictions as they may respect such lands, and the states which passed such grants are adjusted, the said grants or either of them being at the same time claimed to have originated antecedent to such settlement of jurisdiction, shall on the petition of either party to the congress of the united states, be finally determined as near as may be in the same manner as is before prescribed for deciding disputes respecting territorial jurisdiction between different states.

The united states in congress assembled shall also have the sole and exclusive right and power of regulating the alloy and value of coin struck by their own authority, or by that of the respective states—fixing the standard of weights and measures throughout the united states—regulating the trade and managing all affairs with the Indians, not members of any of the states, provided that the legislative right of any state within its own limits be not infringed or violated—establishing and regulating post-offices from one state to another, throughout all the united states, and exacting such postage on the papers passing thro' the same as may be requisite to defray the expences of the said office—appointing all officers of the land forces, in the service of the united states, excepting regimental officers—appointing all the officers of the naval forces, and commissioning all officers whatever in the service of the united states—making rules for the government and regulation of the said land and naval forces, and directing their operations.

The united states in congress assembled shall have authority to appoint a committee, to sit in the recess of congress, to be denominated "A Committee of the States," and to consist of one delegate from each state; and to appoint such other committees and civil officers as may be necessary for managing the general affairs of the united states under their direction—to appoint one of their number to preside, provided that no person be allowed to serve in the office of president more than one year in any term of three years; to ascertain the necessary sums of Money to be raised for the service of the united states, and to appropriate and apply the same for defraying the public expences—to borrow money, or emit bills on the credit of the united states, transmitting every half year to the respective states an account of the sums of money so borrowed or emitted—to build and equip a navy—to agree upon the number of land forces, and to make requisitions from each state for its quota, in proportion to the number of white inhabitants in such state; which requisition shall be binding, and thereupon the legislature of each state shall appoint the regimental officers, raise the men and clothe, arm and equip them in a soldier like manner, at the expence of the united states, and the officers and men so clothed, armed and equipped shall march to the place appointed, and within the time agreed on by the united states in congress assembled. But if the united states in congress assembled shall, on consideration of circumstances judge proper that any state should not raise men, or should raise a smaller number than its quota, and that any other state should raise a greater number of men than the quota thereof, such extra number shall be raised, officered, clothed, armed and equipped in the same manner as the quota of such state, unless the legislature of such state shall judge that such extra number cannot be safely spared out of the same, in which case they shall raise, officer, clothe, arm and equip as many of such extra number as they judge can be safely spared. And the officers and men so clothed, armed and equipped, shall march to the place appointed, and within the time agreed on by the united states in congress assembled.

The united states in congress assembled shall never engage in a war, nor grant letters of marque and reprisal in time of peace, nor enter into any treaties or alliances, nor coin money, nor regulate the value thereof, nor ascertain the sums and expences necessary for the defence and welfare of the united states, or any of them, nor emit bills, nor borrow money on the credit of the united states, nor appropriate money, nor agree upon the number of vessels of war, to be built or purchased, or the number of land or sea forces to be raised, nor appoint a commander in chief of the army or navy, unless nine states assent to the same: nor shall a question on any other point, except for adjourning from day to day be determined, unless by the votes of a majority of the united states in congress assembled.

The congress of the united states shall have power to adjourn to any time within the year, and to any place within the united states, so that no period of adjournment be for a longer duration than the space of six Months, and shall publish the Journal of their proceedings monthly, except such parts thereof relating to treaties, alliances or military operations as in their judgment require secrecy; and the yeas and nays of the delegates of each state on any question shall be entered on the Journal, when it is desired by any delegate; and the delegates of a state, or any of them, at his or their request shall be furnished with a transcript of the said Journal, except such parts as are above excepted, to lay before the legislatures of the several states.

[ART. X.] The committee of the states, or any nine of them, shall be authorised to execute, in the recess of congress, such of the powers of congress as the united states in congress assembled, by the consent of nine states, shall from time to time think expedient to vest them with; provided that no power be delegated to the said committee, for the exercise of which, by the articles of confederation, the voice of nine states in the congress of the united states assembled is requisite.

[ART. XI.] Canada acceding to this confederation, and joining in the measures of the united states, shall be admitted into, and entitled to all the advantages of this union: but no other colony shall be admitted into the same, unless such admission be agreed to by nine states.

[ART. XII.] All bills of credit emitted, monies borrowed and debts contracted by, or under the authority of congress, before the assembling of the united states, in pursuance of the present confederation, shall be deemed and considered as a charge against the united states, for payment and satisfaction whereof the said united states, and the public faith are hereby solemnly pledged.

[ART. XIII.] Every state shall abide by the determinations of the united states in congress assembled, on all questions which by this confederation are submitted to them. And the Articles of this confederation shall be inviolably observed by every state, and the union shall be perpetual; nor shall any alteration at any time hereafter be made in any of them; unless such alteration be agreed to in a congress of the united states, and be afterwards confirmed by the legislatures of every state.

And whereas it hath pleased the Great Governor of the World to incline the hearts of the legislatures we respectively represent in congress, to approve of, and to authorize us to ratify the said articles of confederation and perpetual union. Know ye that we the undersigned delegates, by virtue of the power and authority to us given for that purpose, do by these presents, in the name and in behalf of our respective constituents, fully and entirely ratify and confirm each and every of the said articles of confederation and perpetual union, and all and singular the matters and things therein contained: And we do further solemnly plight and engage the faith of our respective constituents, that they shall abide by the determinations of the united states in congress assembled, on all questions, which by the said confederation are submitted to them. And that the articles thereof shall be inviolably observed by the states we respectively represent, and that the union shall be perpetual. In Witness whereof we have hereunto set our hands in Congress. Done at Philadelphia in the state of Pennsylvania the ninth Day of July in the Year of our Lord one Thousand seven Hundred and Seventy-eight, and in the third year of the independence of America.

JOSIAH BARTLETT
JOHN WENTWORTH Junr
August 8th 1778
On the part & behalf of
the State of New Hampshire

JOHN HANCOCK
SAMUEL ADAMS
ELBRIDGE GERRY
FRANCIS DANA
JAMES LOVELL
SAMUEL HOLTEN
On the part and behalf of
the State of Massachusetts Bay

WILLIAM ELLERY
HENRY MARCHANT
JOHN COLLINS
On the part and behalf
of the State of Rhode Island
and Providence Plantations

ROGER SHERMAN
SAMUEL HUNTINGTON
OLIVER WOLCOTT
TITUS HOSMER
ANDREW ADAMS
On the part and behalf of
the State of Connecticut

JA^S DUANE
FRA^S LEWIS
W^M DUER.
GOUV MORRIS

On the Part and Behalf of
the State of New York

JNO WITHERSPOON
NATH^L SCUDDER
On the Part and in Behalf of
the State of New Jersey.
Novr 26, 1778.—

ROB^T MORRIS
DANIEL ROBERDEAU
JON^A BAYARD SMITH.
WILLIAM CLINGAN
JOSEPH REED
22^d July 1778
On the part and behalf of
the State of Pennsylvania

THO M:KEAN
Feby 12 1779
JOHN DICKINSON
May 5th 1779
NICHOLAS VAN DYKE,
On the part & behalf of
the State of Delaware

JOHN HANSON
March 1 1781
DANIEL CARROLL d^o
On the part and behalf
of the State of Maryland

RICHARD HENRY LEE
JOHN BANISTER
THOMAS ADAMS

JN^O HARVIE
FRANCIS LIGHTFOOT LEE
On the Part and Behalf of
the State of Virginia

JOHN PENN
July 21st 1778
CORN^S HARNETT
JN^O WILLIAMS
On the part and Behalf
of the State of N^O Carolina

HENRY LAURENS
WILLIAM HENRY DRAYTON
JN^O MATHEWS
RICH^D HUTSON.
THO^S HEYWARD Junr
On the part & behalf of
the State of South Carolina

JN^O WALTON
24th July 1778
EDW^D TELFAIR.
EDW^D LANGWORTHY
On the part and behalf of
the State of Georgia

Gettysburg Address

Abraham Lincoln delivered the following address on November 19, 1863, at the dedication of the National Cemetery in Gettysburg, Pennsylvania, site of a major Civil War battle. The eloquent speech, which took only two minutes to deliver, soon became one of the world's most-quoted orations.

Four score and seven years ago our fathers brought forth on this continent, a new nation, conceived in Liberty, and dedicated to the proposition that all men are created equal.

Now we are engaged in a great civil war, testing whether that nation, or any nation so conceived and so dedicated, can long endure. We are met on a great battle-field of that war. We have come to dedicate a portion of that field, as a final resting place for those who here gave their lives that that nation might live. It is altogether fitting and proper that we should do this.

But, in a larger sense, we can not dedicate—we can not consecrate—we can not hallow—this ground. The brave men, living and dead, who struggled here, have consecrated it, far above our poor power to add or detract. The world will little note, nor long remember what we say here, but it can never forget what they did here. It is for us the living, rather, to be dedicated here to the unfinished work which they who fought here have thus far so nobly advanced. It is rather for us to be here dedicated to the great task remaining before us—that from these honored dead we take increased devotion to that cause for which they gave the last full measure of devotion—that we here highly resolve that these dead shall not have died in vain—that this nation, under God, shall have a new birth of freedom—and that government of the people, by the people, for the people, shall not perish from the earth.

The Emancipation Proclamation
Issued by President Abraham Lincoln on January 1, 1863

Whereas on the 22d day of September, A.D. 1862, a proclamation was issued by the President of the United States, containing, among other things, the following, to wit:

"That on the 1st day of January, A.D. 1863, all persons held as slaves within any State or designated part of a State the people whereof shall then be in rebellion against the United States shall be then, thenceforward, and forever free; and the Executive Government of the United States, including the military and naval authority thereof, will recognize and maintain the freedom of such persons and will do no act or acts to repress such persons, or any of them, in any efforts they may make for their actual freedom.

"That the executive will on the 1st day of January aforesaid, by proclamation, designate the States and parts of States, if any, in which the people thereof, respectively, shall then be in rebellion against the United States; and the fact that any State or the people thereof shall on that day be in good faith represented in the Congress of the United States by members chosen thereto at elections wherein a majority of the qualified voters of such States shall have participated shall, in the absence of strong countervailing testimony, be deemed conclusive evidence that such State and the people thereof are not then in rebellion against the United States."

Now, therefore, I, Abraham Lincoln, President of the United States, by virtue of the power in me vested as Commander-in-Chief of the Army and Navy of the United States in time of actual armed rebellion against the authority and government of the United States, and as a fit and necessary war measure for suppressing said rebellion, do, on this 1st day of January, A.D. 1863, and in accordance with my purpose so to do, publicly proclaimed for the full period of one hundred days from the first day above mentioned, order and designate as the States and parts of States wherein the people thereof, respectively, are this day in rebellion against the United States the following, to wit:

Arkansas, Texas, Louisiana (except the parishes of St. Bernard, Plaquemines, Jefferson, St. John, St. Charles, St. James, Ascension, Assumption, Terrebonne, Lafourche, St. Mary, St. Martin, and Orleans, including the city of New Orleans), Mississippi, Alabama, Florida, Georgia, South Carolina, North Carolina, and Virginia (except the forty-eight counties designated as West Virginia, and also the counties of Berkeley, Accomac, Northhampton, Elizabeth City, York, Princess Anne, and Norfolk, including the cities of Norfolk and Portsmouth), and which excepted parts are for the present left precisely as if this proclamation were not issued.

And by virtue of the power and for the purpose aforesaid, I do order and declare that all persons held as slaves within said designated States and parts of States are, and henceforward shall be, free; and that the Executive Government of the United States, including the military and naval authorities thereof, will recognize and maintain the freedom of said persons.

And I hereby enjoin upon the people so declared to be free to abstain from all violence, unless in necessary self-defense; and I recommend to them that, in all cases when allowed, they labor faithfully for reasonable wages.

And I further declare and make known that such persons of suitable condition will be received into the armed service of the United States to garrison forts, positions, stations, and other places, and to man vessels of all sorts in said service.

And upon this act, sincerely believed to be an act of justice, warranted by the Constitution upon military necessity, I invoke the considerate judgment of mankind and the gracious favor of Almighty God.

Over the course of the Civil War, nearly 180,000 African Americans wore the Union uniform.

Historical Documents

Supreme Court Glossary

Agostini v. Felton (1997)

Decision: The Court decided that it was appropriate to reconsider *Aguilar* v. *Felton* as subsequent cases had undermined several of the assumptions, for example that public employees placed at parochial schools would "inevitably inculcate religion," upon which the decision was based. The Court then found that New York City's Title I Program did not violate any of the criteria used "to evaluate whether government aid has the effect of advancing religion: it does not result in governmental indoctrination; define its recipients by reference to religion; or create an excessive entanglement." As a result, the Court concluded that "a federally funded program providing supplemental, remedial instruction to disadvantaged children on a neutral basis is not invalid under the Establishment Clause when such instruction is given on the premises of sectarian schools by government employees pursuant to a program containing safeguards" against excessive entanglement between government and religion.

Baker v. Carr (1962)

Decision: The Supreme Court held that the federal courts do have jurisdiction and authority to review the constitutionality of a State's electoral apportionment. The voters are entitled to a trial on their allegation that the Tennessee apportionment violated the United States Constitution by diluting their votes and denying them equal protection of the law. The federal courts may impose remedies if the voters can show that their votes do not count for substantially the same amount as votes of others in the State.

Bethel School District #403 v. Fraser (1986)

(1st Amendment, freedom of speech) A high school student gave a sexually suggestive political speech at a high school assembly to elect student officers. The school administration strongly disciplined the student, Fraser, who argued that school rules unfairly limited his freedom of political speech. Fraser's view was upheld in State court. Washington appealed to the Supreme Court, which found that "it does not follow. . . that simply because the use of an offensive form of expression may not be prohibited to adults making what the speaker considers a political point, the same latitude must be permitted to children in a public school."

Board of Estimate of City of New York v. Morris (1989)

Decision: The reapportionment requirement of "one-person, one-vote" applies to the Board of Estimate. The Board has sufficient legislative functions that its composition must fairly represent city voters on an approximately equal basis. The fact that some members are elected citywide is one factor to be considered in evaluating the fairness of the electoral structure, but it is not determinative. The City's expressed interests—that the Board be effective and that it accommodate natural and political boundaries as well as local interests—does not justify the size of the deviation from the "one-person, one-vote" ideal. The City could structure the Board in other ways that would further these interests while minimizing the discrimination in voting power.

Bob Jones University v. United States (1983)

(14th Amendment in conflict with 1st Amendment) Bob Jones University, a private school, denied admission to applicants in an interracial marriage or who "espouse" interracial marriage or dating. The Internal Revenue Service then denied tax exempt status to the school because of racial discrimination. The university appealed, claiming their policy was based on the Bible. The Court upheld the IRS ruling, stating that ". . . Government has a fundamental overriding interest in eradicating racial discrimination in education."

Brown v. Board of Education of Topeka (1954)

(14th Amendment, Equal Protection Clause) Probably no twentieth century Supreme Court decision so deeply stirred and changed life in the United States as Brown. A 10-year-old Topeka girl, Linda Brown, was not permitted to attend her neighborhood school because she was an African American. The Court heard arguments about whether segregation itself was a violation of the Equal Protection Clause and found that it was, commenting that "in the field of public education the doctrine of 'separate but equal' has no place. . . . Segregation is a denial of the equal protection of the laws." The decision overturned *Plessy* v. *Ferguson*, 1896.

City of Philadelphia v. New Jersey (1978)

Decision: The Court decided that New Jersey may not restrict the importation of solid or liquid waste that originated outside the State. The Commerce Clause protects all objects of interstate trade, including waste. A State may not discriminate against items that are identical except for their origin, and thus may not prohibit out-of-state waste that is no different from domestically produced waste. Although waste disposal is a problem in many locations, States may not constitutionally deal with the problem by erecting a barrier against the movement of interstate trade.

The Civil Rights Cases (1883)

(14th Amendment, Equal Protection Clause) The Civil Rights Act of 1875 included punishments of businesses that practiced discrimination. The Court ruled on a number of cases involving the Acts in 1883, finding that the Constitution, "while prohibiting discrimination by governments, made no provisions . . . for acts of racial discrimination by private individuals." The decision limited the impact of the Equal Protection Clause, giving tacit approval for segregation in the private sector.

Communist Party of Indiana v. Whitcomb (1974)

Decision: The Supreme Court ruled that the required oath was unconstitutional. Although the Court agreed that the

Constitution entrusted control of the electoral process to the States, it held that the States may not infringe upon basic constitutional rights in exercising that control. People have a right to organize themselves into political parties according to their beliefs, to run for elected office, and to vote for candidates based on those beliefs. A political party may hold an abstract belief in violent political change without necessarily advocating unlawful violent action. The States may forbid advocacy of the use of force only when that advocacy is directed to inciting or producing imminent lawless action and is likely to incite such action.

Cruzan v. Missouri (1990)

(14th Amendment, Due Process Clause) After Nancy Beth Cruzan was left in a "persistent vegetative state" by a car accident, Missouri officials refused to comply with her parents' request that the hospital terminate life-support. The Court upheld the State policy under which officials refused to withdraw treatment, rejecting the argument that the Due Process Clause of the 14th Amendment gave the parents the right to refuse treatment on their daughter's behalf. Although individuals have the right to refuse medical treatment, "incompetent" persons are not able to exercise this right; without "clear and convincing" evidence that Cruzan desired the withdrawal of treatment, the State could legally act to preserve her life.

Dennis v. United States (1951)

(1st Amendment, freedom of speech) The Smith Act of 1940 made it a crime for any person to work for the violent overthrow of the United States in peacetime or war. Eleven Communist party leaders, including Dennis, had been convicted of violating the Smith Act, and they appealed. The Court upheld the Act.

Dred Scott v. Sandford (1857)

(5th Amendment, individual rights) This decision upheld property rights over human rights by saying that Dred Scott, a slave, could not become a free man just because he had traveled in "free soil" States with his master. A badly divided nation was further fragmented by the decision. "Free soil" federal laws and the Missouri Compromise line of 1820 were held unconstitutional because they deprived a slave owner of the right to his "property" without just compensation. This narrow reading of the Constitution, a landmark case of the Court, was most clearly stated by Chief Justice Roger B. Taney, a States' rights advocate.

Engel v. Vitale (1962)

(1st Amendment, Establishment Clause) The State Board of Regents of New York required the recitation of a 22-word nonsectarian prayer at the beginning of each school day. A group of parents filed suit against the required prayer, claiming it violated their 1st Amendment rights. The Court found New York's action to be unconstitutional, observing, "There can be no doubt that. . . religious beliefs [are] embodied in the Regent's prayer."

Edwards v. South Carolina (1963)

(1st Amendment, freedom of speech and assembly) A group of mostly African American civil rights activists held a rally at the South Carolina State Capitol, protesting segregation. A hostile crowd gathered and the rally leaders were arrested and convicted for "breach of the peace." The Court overturned the convictions, saying, "The Fourteenth Amendment does not permit a State to make criminal the peaceful expression of unpopular views."

Escobedo v. Illinois (1964)

(6th Amendment, right to counsel) In a case involving a murder confession by a person known to Chicago-area police who was not afforded counsel while under interrogation, the Court extended the "exclusionary rule" to illegal confessions in State court proceedings. Carefully defining an "Escobedo Rule," the Court said, "where. . . the investigation is no longer a general inquiry . . . but has begun to focus on a particular suspect . . . (and where) the suspect has been taken into custody . . . the suspect has requested . . . his lawyer, and the police have not . . . warned him of his right to remain silent, the accused has been denied . . . counsel in violation of the Sixth Amendment."

Ex parte Milligan (1866)

(Article II, executive powers) An Indiana man was arrested, treated as a prisoner of war, and imprisoned by a military court during the Civil War under presidential order. He claimed that his rights to a fair trial were interfered with and that military courts had no authority outside of "conquered territory." He was released because, "the Constitution . . . is a law for rulers and people, equally in war and peace, and covers . . . all . . . men, at all times, and under all circumstances." The Court held that presidential powers to suspend the writ of *habeas corpus* in time of war did not extend to creating another court system run by the military.

Flast v. Cohen (1968)

Decision: The Supreme Court concluded that the rule announced in *Frothingham* v. *Mellon* expressed a practical policy of judicial self-restraint rather than an absolute constitutional limitation on the power of federal courts to hear taxpayer suits. While mere status as a federal taxpayer ordinarily will not give sufficient "standing" to allow a person to challenge the constitutionality of a federal law, there may be times when taxpayers are appropriate plaintiffs. *Flast* v. *Cohen,* in which plaintiffs argued that the First Amendment specifically prohibited taxing them in order to support religious activities, was one in which their role as taxpayers was well suited to the challenge they sought to assert. The Court ruled that they had standing to sue, and allowed them to proceed with their case.

Furman v. Georgia (1972)

(8th Amendment, capital punishment) Three different death penalty cases, including *Furman,* raised the question of racial imbalances in the use of death sentences by State courts. Furman had been convicted and sentenced to death in Georgia. In deciding to overturn existing State death-penalty laws, the Court noted that there was an "apparent arbitrariness of the use of the sentence. . . ." Many States rewrote their death-penalty statutes and these were generally upheld in *Gregg* v. *Georgia,* 1976.

Gibbons v. Ogden (1824)

(Supremacy Clause) This decision involved a careful examination of the power of Congress to "regulate interstate commerce." Aaron Ogden's exclusive New York ferry license gave him the right to operate steamboats to and from New York. He said that Thomas Gibbons's federal "coasting license" did not include "landing rights" in New York City. The Court invalidated the New York licensing regulations, holding that federal regulations should take precedence under the Supremacy Clause. The decision strengthened the power of the United States to regulate any interstate business relationship. Federal regulation of the broadcasting industry, oil pipelines, and banking are all based on *Gibbons*.

Gideon v. Wainwright (1963)

(6th Amendment, right to counsel) In 1961 a Florida court found Clarence Earl Gideon guilty of breaking and entering and sentenced him to five years in prison. Gideon appealed his case to the Supreme Court on the basis that he had been unconstitutionally denied counsel during his trial due to Florida's policy of only providing appointed counsel in capital cases. The Court granted Gideon a new trial, and he was found not guilty with the help of a court-appointed attorney. The "Gideon Rule" upheld the 6th Amendment's guarantee of counsel of all poor persons facing a felony charge, a further incorporation of Bill of Rights guarantees into State constitutions.

Gitlow v. New York (1925)

(1st Amendment, freedom of speech) A New York socialist, Gitlow, was convicted under a State law on "criminal anarchy" for distributing copies of a "left-wing manifesto." For the first time, the Court considered whether the 1st Amendment applied to State laws. The case helped to establish what came to be known as the "incorporation" doctrine, under which, it was argued, the provisions of the 1st Amendment were "incorporated" by the 14th Amendment, thus applying to State as well as federal laws. Although New York law was not overruled in this case, the decision clearly indicated that the Supreme Court could make such a ruling. Another important incorporation case is *Powell* v. *Alabama*, 1932.

Goldberg v. Kelly (1970)

Decision: The Court ruled that public aid recipients are entitled to a pre-termination hearing at which he or she (directly or through an attorney) may offer arguments, present evidence, and cross-examine witnesses. In its decision, the Court held that welfare benefits are a matter of statutory entitlement for persons who are eligible to receive them. Before terminating benefits, the government must therefore comply with the requirements of procedural due process.

Goss v. Lopez (1975)

(14th Amendment, Due Process Clause) Ten Ohio students were suspended from their schools without hearings. The students challenged the suspensions, claiming that the absence of a preliminary hearing violated their 14th Amendment right to due process. The Court agreed with the students, holding that "having chosen to extend the right to an education. . . Ohio may not withdraw that right on grounds of misconduct, absent fundamentally fair procedures to determine whether the misconduct has occurred, and must recognize a student's legitimate entitlement to a public education as a property interest that is protected by the Due Process Clause."

Gregg v. Georgia (1976)

(8th Amendment, cruel and unusual punishment) A Georgia jury sentenced Troy Gregg to death after finding him guilty on two counts each of murder and armed robbery. Gregg appealed the sentence, claiming that it violated the "cruel and unusual punishment" clause of the 8th Amendment and citing *Furman* v. *Georgia*, 1972, in which the court held that Georgia's application of the death penalty was unfair and arbitrary. However, the Court upheld Gregg's sentence, stating for the first time that "punishment of death does not invariably violate the Constitution."

Griswold v. Connecticut (1965)

(14th Amendment, Due Process Clause) A Connecticut law forbade the use of "any drug, medicinal article, or instrument for the purpose of preventing conception." Griswold, director of Planned Parenthood in New Haven, was arrested for counseling married persons and, after conviction, appealed. The Court overturned the Connecticut law, saying that "various guarantees (of the Constitution) create zones of privacy. . ." and questioning, ". . .would we allow the police to search the sacred precincts of marital bedrooms. . . ?" The decision is significant for raising for more careful inspection the concept of "unenumerated rights" in the 9th Amendment, later central to *Roe* v. *Wade*, 1973.

Hazelwood School District v. Kuhlmeier (1988)

(1st Amendment, freedom of speech) In 1983, the principal of Hazelwood East High School in Missouri removed two articles from the upcoming issue of the student newspaper, deeming their content "inappropriate, personal, sensitive, and unsuitable for student readers." Several students sued the school district, claiming that their 1st Amendment right to freedom of expression had been violated. The Court upheld the principal's action, stating that "a school need not tolerate student speech that is inconsistent with its basic educational mission, even though the government could not censor similar speech outside the school." School officials had full control over school-sponsored activities "so long as their actions are reasonably related to legitimate pedagogical concerns. . . ."

Heart of Atlanta Motel, Inc. v. United States (1964)

Decision: The Court ruled that Congress could outlaw racial segregation of private facilities that are engaged in interstate commerce. The Court's decision stated, "If it is interstate commerce that feels the pinch, it does not matter how 'local' the operation which applies the squeeze. . . . The power of Congress to promote interstate commerce also includes the power to regulate the local incidents thereof, including local activities. . . which have a substantial and harmful effect upon that commerce."

Hutchinson v. Proxmire (1979)

Decision: The Court held that the Speech or Debate Clause gives members of Congress immunity from suit for defamatory statements made within the legislative chambers, but the privilege does not extend to comments made in other locations, even if they merely repeat what was said in Congress. The newsletters and press release were not within the deliberative process nor were they essential to the deliberation of the Senate. They also were not part of the "informing function" of members of Congress, since they were not a part of legislative function or of the deliberations that make up the legislative process. The comments were merely designed to convey information on the Senator's individual positions and beliefs. Finally, although Hutchinson had received extensive attention in the media as a result of his receipt of the Golden Fleece Award, he was not a public figure prior to that controversy and thus is entitled to the greater protection against defamation that is extended to non-public figures. The fact that the public may have an interest in governmental expenditures does not make Hutchinson himself a public figure.

Illinois v. Wardlow (2000)

Decision: The Supreme Court refused to say that flight from the police will always justify a stop or that it will never do so. Instead, the Court ruled that flight can be an important factor in determining whether police have "reasonable suspicion" to stop a suspect. The trial court will have to determine in each case whether the information available to the police officers, including the fact of a suspect's flight, was sufficient to support the stop.

In Re Gault (1966)

(14th Amendment, Due Process Clause) Prior to the Gault case, proceedings against juvenile offenders were generally handled as "family law," not "criminal law" and provided few due process guarantees. Gerald Gault was assigned to six years in a State juvenile detention facility for an alleged obscene phone call. He was not provided counsel and not permitted to confront or cross-examine the principal witness. The Court overturned the juvenile proceedings and required that States provide juveniles "some of the due process guarantees of adults," including a right to a phone call, to counsel, to cross-examine, to confront their accuser, and to be advised of their right to silence.

Ingraham v. Wright (1977)

Decision: A majority of the Supreme Court concluded that the 8th Amendment historically protected people convicted of crimes, and does not apply to public school students. If authorized by local law or custom, public schools have the right to administer reasonable discipline, and students do not have a due process right to notice or a hearing before punishment administered in accordance with law or custom.

Johnson v. Santa Clara Transportation Agency (1987)

(Discrimination) Under their affirmative action plan, the Transportation Agency in Santa Clara, California, was authorized to "consider as one factor the sex of a qualified applicant" in an effort to combat the significant underrepresentation of women in certain job classifications. When the Agency promoted Diane Joyce, a qualified woman, over Paul Johnson, a qualified man, for the job of road dispatcher, Johnson sued, claiming that the Agency's consideration of the sex of the applicants violated Title VII of the Civil Rights Act of 1964. The Court upheld the Agency's promotion policy, arguing that the affirmative action plan created no "absolute bar" to the advancement

of men but rather represented "a moderate, flexible, case-by-case approach to effecting a gradual improvement in the representation of minorities and women . . . in the Agency's work force, and [was] fully consistent with Title VII."

Korematsu v. United States (1944)

Decision: The Court upheld the military order in light of the circumstances presented by World War II. "Pressing public necessity may sometimes justify the existence of restrictions which curtail the civil rights of a single racial group." The Court noted, however, that racial antagonism itself could never form a legitimate basis for the restrictions.

Lemon v. Kurtzman (1971)

(1st Amendment, Establishment Clause) In overturning State laws regarding aid to church-supported schools in this and a similar Rhode Island case, the Court created the *Lemon* test limiting ". . . excessive government entanglement with religion." The Court noted that any State law about aid to religion must meet three criteria: (1) purpose of the aid must be clearly secular, (2) its primary effect must neither advance nor inhibit religion, and (3) it must avoid "excessive entanglement of government with religion."

Mapp v. Ohio (1962)

(4th and 14th Amendments, illegal evidence and Due Process Clause) Admitting evidence gained by illegal searches was permitted by some State constitutions before *Mapp*. Cleveland police raided Dollree Mapp's home without a warrant and found obscene materials. She appealed her conviction, saying that the 4th and 14th Amendments protected her against improper police behavior. The Court agreed, extending "exclusionary rule" protections to citizens in State courts, saying that the prohibition against unreasonable searches would be "meaningless" unless evidence gained in such searches was "excluded." This case further developed the concept of "incorporation" begun in *Gitlow v. New York*, 1925.

Marbury v. Madison (1803)

(Article III, judicial powers) After defeat in the 1800 election, President Adams appointed many Federalists to the federal courts, but James Madison, the new secretary of state, refused to deliver the commissions. William Marbury, one of the appointees, asked the Supreme Court to enforce the delivery of his commission based on a provision of the Judiciary Act of 1789 that allowed the Court to hear such cases on original jurisdiction. The Court refused Marbury's request, finding that the relevant portion of the Judiciary Act was in conflict with the Constitution. This decision, written by Chief Justice Marshall, established the evaluation of federal laws' constitutionality, or "judicial review," as a power of the Supreme Court.

McCulloch v. Maryland (1819)

(Article I, Section 8, Necessary and Proper Clause) Called the "Bank of the United States" case. A Maryland law required federally chartered banks to use only a special paper to print paper money, which amounted to a tax. James McCulloch, the cashier of the Baltimore branch of the bank, refused to use the paper, claiming that States could not tax the Federal Government. The Court declared the Maryland law unconstitutional, commenting ". . . the power to tax implies the power to destroy."

Miami Herald Publishing Co. v. Tornillo (1974)

Decision: The Supreme Court found that the right of reply statute violated freedom of the press as guaranteed by the First Amendment. The statute improperly intrudes into the editorial function of newspapers by deciding what must be published. The command to publish something is as great an intrusion as a command not to publish something would be. In addition, the statute penalizes newspapers by requiring them to commit production costs and newspaper space to articles that they may not wish to publish.

Miranda v. Arizona (1966)

(5th, 6th, and 14th Amendments, rights of the accused) Arrested for kidnapping and sexual assault, Ernesto Miranda signed a confession including a statement that he had "full knowledge of [his] legal rights. . . ." After conviction, he appealed, claiming that without counsel and without warnings, the confession was illegally gained. The Court agreed with Miranda that "he must be warned prior to any questioning that he has the right to remain silent, that anything he says can be used against him in a court of law, that he has the right to. . . an attorney and that if he cannot afford an attorney one will be appointed for him. . . ." Although later modified by *Nix v. Williams*, 1984, and other cases, *Miranda* firmly upheld citizen rights to fair trials in State courts.

New Jersey v. T.L.O. (1985)

(4th and 14th Amendments) After T.L.O., a New Jersey high school student, denied an accusation that she had been smoking in the school lavatory, a vice-principal searched her purse and found cigarettes, marijuana, and evidence that T.L.O. had been involved in marijuana dealing at the school. T.L.O. was then sentenced to probation by a juvenile court, but appealed on the grounds that the evidence against her had been obtained by an "unreasonable" search. The Court rejected T.L.O.'s arguments, stating that the school had a "legitimate need to maintain an environment in which learning can take place," and that to do this "requires some easing of the restrictions to which searches by public authorities are ordinarily subject. . ." The Court thus created a "reasonable suspicion" rule for school searches, a change from the "probable cause" requirement in the wider society.

New York Times v. United States (1971)

(1st Amendment, freedom of the press) In 1971 *The New York Times* obtained copies of classified Defense Department documents, later known as the "Pentagon Papers," which revealed instances in which the Johnson Administration had deceived Congress and the American people regarding United States policies during the Vietnam War. A United States district court issued an injunction against the publication of the documents, claiming that it might endanger national security. On appeal, the Supreme Court cited the 1st Amendment guarantee of a free press and refused to uphold the injunction against publication, observing that it is the obligation of the government to prove that actual harm to the nation's security would be caused by the publication. The decision limited "prior restraint" of the press.

Nixon v. Fitzgerald (1982)

Decision: The Court ruled that a President or former President is entitled to absolute immunity from liability based on his official acts. The President must be able to act forcefully and independently, without fear of liability. Diverting the President's energies with concerns about private lawsuits could impair the effective functioning of government. The President's absolute immunity extends to all acts within the "outer perimeter" of his duties of office, since otherwise he would be required to litigate over the nature of the acts and the scope of his duties in each case. The remedy of impeachment, the vigilant scrutiny of the press, the Congress, and the public, and presidential desire to earn reelection and concern with historical legacy all protect against presidential wrongdoing.

Nixon v. Shrink Missouri Government PAC (2000)

Decision: In *Buckley* v. *Valeo*, 1976, the Supreme Court had upheld a $1000 limit on contributions by individuals to candidates for federal office. In *Nixon v. Shrink Missouri Government PAC*, the Court concluded that large contributions will sometimes create actual corruption, and that voters will inevitably be suspicious of the fairness of a political process that allows wealthy donors to contribute large amounts. The Court concluded that the Missouri contribution limits were appropriate to correct this problem and did not impair the ability of candidates to communicate their messages to the voters and to mount an effective campaign.

Olmstead v. United States (1928)

(4th Amendment, electronic surveillance) Olmstead was engaged in the illegal sale of alcohol. Much of the evidence against him was gained through a wiretap made without a warrant. Olmstead argued that he had "a reasonable expectation of privacy," and that the *Weeks* v. *United States* decision of 1914 should be applied to exclude the evidence gained by the wiretap. The Court disagreed, saying that Olmstead intended "to project his voice to those quite outside . . . and that . . . nothing tangible was taken." Reversed by subsequent decisions, this case contains the first usage of the concept of "reasonable expectation of privacy" that would mark later 4th Amendment decisions.

Oregon v. Mitchell (1970)

Decision: The Supreme Court was unable to issue a single opinion of the Court supported by a majority of the justices. However, in a series of separate opinions, differing majority groups agreed that (1) the 18-year-old minimum-age requirement of the Voting Rights Act Amendments is valid for national elections but not for State and local elections; (2) the literacy test provision is valid in order to remedy discrimination against minorities; and (3) the residency and absentee balloting provisions are a valid Congressional regulation of presidential elections.

Plessy v. Ferguson (1896)

(14th Amendment, Equal Protection Clause) A Louisiana law required separate seating for white and African American citizens on public railroads, a form of segregation. Herman Plessy argued that his right to "equal protection of the laws" was violated. The Court held that segregation was permitted if facilities were equal. The Court interpreted the 14th Amendment as "not intended to give Negroes social equality but only political and civil equality. . . ." The Louisiana law was seen as a "reasonable exercise of (State) police power. . ." Segregated public facilities were permitted until *Plessy* was overturned by the *Brown* v. *Board of Education* case of 1954.

Powell v. Alabama (1932)

(6th Amendment, right to counsel) The case involved the "Scottsboro boys," seven African American men accused of sexual assault. This case was a landmark in the development of a "fundamentals of fairness" doctrine of the Court over the next 40 years. The Scottsboro boys were quickly prosecuted without the benefit of counsel and sentenced to death. The Court overturned the decision, stating that poor people facing the death penalty in State courts must be provided counsel, and commenting, ". . . there are certain principles of Justice which adhere to the very idea of free government, which no [State] may disregard." The case was another step toward incorporation of the Bill of Rights into State constitutions.

Printz v. United States (1997)

Decision: The Court ruled that the Brady Act's interim provision requiring certain State or local law enforcement agents to perform background checks on prospective handgun purchasers was unconstitutional. Although no provision of the Constitution deals explicitly with federal authority to compel State officials to execute federal law, a review of the Constitution's structure and of prior Supreme Court decisions leads to the conclusion that Congress does not have this power.

Regents of the University of California v. Bakke (1978)

Decision: The Supreme Court issued a narrow ruling that invalidated the medical school's special admission program and directed the regents to admit Bakke but that did not overturn all affirmative action programs. Although the University of California's policy was unacceptable, "the goal of achieving a diverse student body is sufficiently compelling to justify consideration of race in admissions decisions under some circumstances." The Court indicated that it would consider discrimination and affirmative action questions on a case-by-case basis.

Reno v. ACLU (1997)

Decision: The Supreme Court ruled that the "indecent transmission" provision and the "patently offensive display" provision of the Communications Decency Act violated the 1st Amendment's freedom of speech. The Internet does not have the special features (such as historical governmental oversight, limited frequencies, and "invasiveness") that have justified allowing greater regulation of content in radio and television. The Federal Government failed to show that the good faith defenses in the statute were technologically or commercially viable ways of effectively reducing the impermissible burden on protected speech. Because the Act is overbroad in violation of the 1st Amendment, the Court did not consider whether it was also overly vague in violation of the 5th Amendment.

Reno v. Condon (2000)

Decision: The Court upheld the federal law that forbids States from selling addresses, telephone numbers, and other information that drivers put on license applications. They agreed with the Federal Government that information, including motor vehicle license information, is an "article of commerce" in the interstate stream of business and therefore is subject to regulation by Congress. The Court emphasized that the statute did not impose on the States any obligation to pass particular laws or policies and thus did not interfere with the States' sovereign functions.

Roe v. Wade (1973)

(9th Amendment, right to privacy) A Texas woman challenged a State law forbidding the artificial termination of a pregnancy, saying that she "had a fundamental right to privacy." The Court upheld a woman's right to choose in this case, noting that the State's "important and legitimate interest in protecting the potentiality of human life" became "compelling" at the end of the first trimester, and that before then, ". . . the attending physician, in consultation with his patient, is free to determine, without regulation by the State, that . . . the patient's pregnancy should be terminated." The decision struck down the State regulation of abortion in the first three months of pregnancy and was modified by *Planned Parenthood of Southeastern PA* v. *Casey*, 1992.

Rostker v. Goldberg (1981)

Decision: The Court ruled that women did not have to be included in the draft registration. The purpose of having draft registration was to prepare for the actual draft of combat troops if they should be needed. Since Congress and the President had both consistently decided not to use women in combat positions, it was not necessary for women to register either. The Court also noted that the role of women in the armed services had been debated extensively in the Congress, and concluded that the legislature had reached a thoughtful, reasoned conclusion on this issue.

Roth v. United States (1951)

(1st Amendment, freedom of the press) A New York man named Roth operated a business that used the mail to invite people to buy materials considered obscene by postal inspectors. The Court, in its first consideration of censorship of obscenity, created the "prevailing community standards" rule, which required a consideration of the work as a whole. In its decision, the Court defined as obscene that which offended "the average person, applying contemporary community standards." In a case decided the same day, the Court applied the same "test" to State obscenity laws.

Schenck v. United States (1919)

(1st Amendment, freedom of speech) Charles Schenck was an officer of an antiwar political group who was arrested for alleged violations of the Espionage Act of 1917, which made active opposition to the war a crime. He had urged thousands of young men called to service by the draft act to resist and to avoid induction. The Court limited free speech in time of war, stating that Schenck's words, under the circumstances, presented a "clear and present danger. . . ." Although later decisions modified the decision, the Schenck case created a precedent that 1st Amendment guarantees were not absolute.

School District of Abington Township, Pennsylvania v. Schempp (1963)

(1st Amendment, Establishment Clause) A Pennsylvania State law required reading from the Bible each day at school as an all-school activity. Some parents objected and sought legal remedy. When the case reached the Court, it agreed with the parents, saying that the Establishment Clause and Free Exercise Clause both forbade States from engaging in religious activity. The Court created a rule holding that if the purpose and effect of a law "is the advancement or inhibition of religion," it "exceeds the scope of legal power."

Shelley v. Kraemer (1948)

Decision: The Court ruled that "in granting judicial enforcement of the restrictive agreements . . . the States have denied petitioners the equal protection of the laws. . . ." No individual has the right under the Constitution to demand that a State take action that would result in the denial of equal protection to other individuals. The Court rejected the respondents' argument that, since state courts would also enforce restrictive covenants against white owners, enforcement of covenants against black owners did not constitute a denial of equal protection. "Equal protection of the laws is not achieved through indiscriminate imposition of inequalities."

Sheppard v. Maxwell (1966)

(14th Amendment, Due Process Clause) Dr. Samuel Sheppard was convicted of murdering his wife in a trial widely covered by national news media. Sheppard appealed his conviction, claiming that the pretrial publicity had made it impossible to get a fair trial. The Court rejected the arguments about "press freedom," overturned his conviction, and ordered a new trial. As a result of the Sheppard decision, some judges have issued "gag" orders limiting pretrial publicity.

Tennessee Valley Authority v. Hill (1978)

(Article I, Section 8, Necessary and Proper Clause) In 1975 the secretary of the interior found that the Tennessee Valley Authority's work on the Tellico Dam would destroy the endangered snail darter's habitat in violation of the Endangered Species Act of 1975. When the TVA refused to stop work on the project, local residents sued and won an injunction against completion of the dam from the federal court of appeals. The TVA appealed, arguing that the project should be completed since it had already been underway when the Endangered Species Act had passed and, with full knowledge of the circumstances of the endangered fish, Congress had continued to appropriate money for the dam in every year since the Act's passage. However, the Supreme Court found the injunction against the TVA's completion of the dam to be proper, stating "examination of the language, history, and structure of the legislation. . . indicates beyond doubt that Congress intended endangered species to be afforded the highest of priorities."

Tinker v. Des Moines School District (1969)

Decision: The Court upheld the students' First Amendment rights. Because students do not "shed their constitutional rights to freedom of speech or expression at the schoolhouse gate," schools must show a possibility of "substantial disruption" before free speech can be limited at school.

Students may express personal opinions as long as they do not materially disrupt classwork, create substantial disorder, or interfere with the rights of others. In this case, the wearing of black armbands was a "silent, passive expression of opinion" without these side effects and thus constitutionally could not be prohibited by the school.

United States v. Amistad (1841)

In 1839 two Spaniards purchased a group of kidnapped Africans and put them aboard the schooner *Amistad* for a journey from Cuba to Principe. The Africans overpowered the ship's crew, killing two men, and ordered the Spaniards to steer towards Africa. The crew steered instead toward the United States coast, where the U.S. brig *Washington* seized the ship, freeing the Spaniards and imprisoning the Africans. A series of petitions to the courts ensued, in which the Spaniards claimed the Africans as their property, and the Americans who had seized the ship claimed a share of the cargo, including the Africans, as their lawful salvage. The Court, however, declared that the Africans were not property and issued a decree that the unlawfully kidnapped Africans "be and are hereby declared to be free."

United States v. Eichman (1990)

Decision: The Court agreed with the trial courts' rulings that the Flag Protection Act violated the 1st Amendment. Flag-burning constitutes expressive conduct, and thus is entitled to constitutional protection. The Act prevents protesters from using the flag to express their opposition to governmental policies and activities. Although the protesters' ideas may be offensive or disagreeable to many people, the government may not prohibit them from expressing those ideas.

United States v. General Dynamics Corp. (1974)

A deep-mining coal producer, General Dynamics Corp., acquired control of a strip-mining coal producer, United Electric Coal Companies. The Government filed suit against the company, claiming that the acquisition violated the Clayton Act by limiting competition in coal sales and production through increasing the concentration of ownership among a small group of producers. The Court rejected the Government's argument, finding that, although the acquisition may have increased concentration of ownership, it did not threaten to substantially lessen competition and was therefore not in violation of the Clayton Act.

United States v. Leon (1984)

(4th Amendment, exclusionary rule) Police in Burbank, California, gathered evidence in a drug-trafficking investigation using a search warrant issued by a state court judge. Later a District Court found that the warrant had been improperly issued and granted a motion to suppress the evidence gathered under the warrant. The Government appealed the decision, claiming that the exclusionary rule should not apply in cases where law enforcement officers acted in good faith, believing the warrant to be valid. The Court agreed and established the "good-faith exception" to the exclusionary rule, finding that the rule should not be applied to bar evidence "obtained by officers acting in reasonable reliance on a search warrant issued by a detached and neutral magistrate but ultimately found to be invalid."

United States v. Lopez (1990)

(Article I, Section 8, Commerce Clause) Alfonzo Lopez, a Texas high school student, was convicted of carrying a weapon in a school zone under the Gun-Free School Zones Act of 1990. He appealed his conviction on the basis that the Act, which forbids "any individual knowingly to possess a firearm at a place that [he] knows. . . is a school zone," exceeded Congress's legislative power under the Commerce Clause. The Court agreed that the Act was unconstitutional, stating that to uphold the legislation would "bid fair to convert congressional Commerce Clause authority to a general police power of the sort held only by the States."

United States v. Nixon (1974)

(Separation of powers) During the investigation of the Watergate scandal, in which members of President Nixon's administration were accused of participating in various illegal activities, a special prosecutor subpoenaed tapes of conversations between Nixon and his advisors. Nixon refused to release the tapes but was overruled by the Court, which ordered him to surrender the tapes, rejecting his arguments that they were protected by "executive privilege." The President's "generalized interest in confidentiality" was subordinate to "the fundamental demands of due process of law in the fair administration of criminal justice."

Wallace v. Jaffree (1985)

(1st Amendment, Establishment Clause) An Alabama law authorized a one-minute period of silence in all public schools "for meditation or voluntary prayer." A group of parents, including Jaffree, challenged the constitutionality of the statute, claiming it violated the Establishment Clause of the 1st Amendment. The Court agreed with Jaffree and struck down the Alabama law, determining that "the State's endorsement. . . of prayer activities at the beginning of each schoolday is not consistent with the established principle that the government must pursue a course of complete neutrality toward religion."

Walz v. Tax Commission of the City of New York (1970)

(1st Amendment, Establishment Clause) State and local governments routinely exempt church property from taxes. Walz claimed that such exemptions were a "support of religion," a subsidy by government. The Court disagreed, noting that such exemptions were just an example of a "benevolent neutrality" between government and churches, not a support of religion. Governments must avoid taxing churches because taxation would give government a "control" over religion, prohibited by the "wall of separation of church and state" noted in *Everson* v. *Board of Education,* 1947.

Watkins v. United States (1957)

Decision: The Court held that Watkins was not given a fair opportunity to determine whether he was within his rights in refusing to answer the Committee's questions. Congress has no authority to expose the private affairs of individuals unless justified by a specific function of Congress. Congress's investigative powers are broad but not unlimited, and must not infringe on 1st Amendment rights of speech, political belief, or association. When witnesses are forced by subpoena to testify, the subject of Congressional inquiry must be articulated in the Committee's charter or explained at the time of testimony if 1st Amendment rights are in jeopardy.

West Virginia Board of Education v. Barnette (1943)

(1st Amendment, freedom of religion) During World War II the West Virginia Board of Education required all students to take part in a daily flag saluting ceremony or else face expulsion. Jehovah's Witnesses objected to the compulsory salute, which they felt would force them to break their religion's doctrine against the worship of any "graven image." The Court struck down the rule, agreeing that a compulsory flag salute violated the 1st Amendment's exercise of religion clause and stating "no official, high or petty, can prescribe what shall be orthodox in politics, nationalism, religion, or other matters of opinion. . . ."

Board of Education of Westside Community Schools v. Mergens (1990)

(1st Amendment, Establishment Clause) A request by Bridget Mergens to form a student Christian religious group at school was denied by an Omaha high school principal. Mergens took legal action, claiming that a 1984 federal law required "equal access" for student religious groups. The Court ordered the school to permit the club, stating, "a high school does not have to permit any extracurricular activities, but when it does, the school is bound by the . . . [Equal Access] Act of 1984. Allowing students to meet on campus and discuss religion is constitutional because it does not amount to 'State sponsorship of a religion.'"

Wisconsin v. Yoder (1972)

(1st Amendment, Free Exercise Clause) Members of the Amish religious sect in Wisconsin objected to sending their children to public schools after the eighth grade, claiming that such exposure of the children to another culture would endanger the group's self-sufficient agrarian lifestyle essential to their religious faith. The Court agreed with the Amish, while noting that the Court must move carefully to weigh the State's "legitimate social concern when faced with religious claim for exemption from generally applicable educational requirements."

Glossary

Absentee voting Provisions made for those unable to get to their regular polling places on election day. p. 189

Acquit Find not guilty of a charge. p. 311

Act of admission A congressional act admitting a new State to the Union. p. 100

Adjourn Suspend, as in a session of Congress. p. 264

Administration The officials in the executive branch of a government and their policies and principles. p. 416

Affirmative action A policy that requires most employers take positive steps to remedy the effects of past discriminations. p. 609

Albany Plan of Union Plan proposed by Benjamin Franklin in 1754 that aimed to unite the 13 colonies for trade, military, and other purposes; the plan was turned down by the colonies and the Crown. pp. 35–36

Alien Foreign-born resident, or noncitizen. pp. 534, 614

Ambassador An official representative of the United States appointed by the President to represent the nation in matters of diplomacy. p. 471

Amendment A change in, or addition to, a constitution or law. p. 72

Amnesty A blanket pardon offered to a group of law violators. p. 408

Anti-Federalists Those persons who opposed the ratification of the Constitution in 1787–1788. p. 56

Appellate jurisdiction The authority of a court to review decisions of inferior (lower) courts; *see* original jurisdiction. pp. 509, 709

Apportion Distribute, as in seats in a legislative body. p. 267

Appropriate Assign to a particular use. p. 305

Articles Numbered sections of a document. The unamended Constitution is divided into seven articles. p. 65

Articles of Confederation Plan of government adopted by the Continental Congress after the American Revolution; established "a firm league of friendship" among the States, but allowed few important powers to the central government. p. 44

Assemble To gather with one another in order to express views on public matters. p. 555

Assessment The process of determining the value of property to be taxed. p. 742

Assimilation The process by which people of one culture merge into, and become part of, another culture. p. 597

At-large election Election of an officeholder by the voters of an entire governmental unit (e.g. a State or country) rather than by the voters of a district or subdivision. p. 270

Attorney General The head of the Department of Justice. p. 424

Authoritarian A form of government in which those in power hold absolute and unchallengeable authority over the people. All dictatorships are authoritarian. p. 13

Autocracy A form of government in which a single person holds unlimited political power. p. 13

Autonomous Independent. p. 652

Bail A sum of money that the accused may be required to post (deposit with the court) as a guarantee that he or she will appear in court at the proper time. p. 585

Balance the ticket When a presidential candidate chooses a running mate who can strengthen his chance of being elected by virtue of certain ideological, geographic, racial, ethnic, gender, or other characteristics. p. 362

Ballot The device voters use to register a choice in an election. p. 190

Bankruptcy The legal proceeding by which a bankrupt person's assets are distributed among those to whom he or she owes debts. p. 300

Bench trial A trial in which the judge alone hears the case. pp. 580, 705

Bicameral An adjective describing a legislative body composed of two chambers. p. 31

Bill A proposed law presented to a legislative body for consideration. p. 334

Bill of Attainder A legislative act that inflicts punishment without a court trial. p. 577

Bill of Rights The first ten amendments to the Constitution. pp. 76, 532

Bipartisan Supported by two parties. pp. 120, 440

Blanket primary A voting process in which voters receive a long ballot containing the names of all contenders, regardless of party, and can vote however they choose. p. 183

Block grant One type of federal grants-in-aid for some particular but broadly defined area of public policy; *see* grants-in-aid. p. 103

Bourgeoisie The social class between the aristocracy and the proletariat class; the middle class. p. 667

Boycott Refusal to buy or sell certain products or services. p. 36

Budget A financial plan for the use of money, personnel, and property. p. 744

Bureaucracy A large, complex administrative structure that handles the everyday business of an organization. p. 414

Bureaucrat A person who works for a bureaucratic organization; *see* bureaucracy. p. 415

By-election A special election held to choose a replacement for a member of parliament, in the event of a death. p. 628

Cabinet Presidential advisory body, traditionally made up of the heads of the executive departments and other officers. p. 81

Capital All the human-made resources that are used to produce goods and services. p. 659

Capitalist Someone who owns capital and puts it to productive use; often applied to people who own large businesses. p. 659

Capital punishment The death penalty. p. 587

Categorical grant One type of federal grants-in-aid; made for some specific, closely defined, purpose; *see* grants-in-aid. p. 102

Caucus As a nominating device, a group of like-minded people who meet to select the candidates they will support in an upcoming election. p. 180

Censure Issue a formal condemnation. p. 312

Centrally planned economy A system in which government bureaucrats plan how an economy will develop over a period of years. p. 669

Certificate A method of putting a case before the Supreme Court; used when a lower court is not clear about the procedure or rule of law that should apply in a case and asks the Supreme Court to certify the answer to a specific question. p. 521

Charter A city's basic law, its constitution; a written grant of authority from the king. pp. 31, 726

Checks and balances System of overlapping the powers of the legislative, executive, and judicial branches to permit each branch to check the actions of the others; *see* separation of powers. p. 67

Chief administrator Term for the President as head of the administration of the Federal Government. p. 355

Chief citizen Term for the President as the representative of the people, working for the public interest. p. 355

Chief diplomat Term for the President as the main architect of foreign policy and spokesperson to other countries. p. 355

Chief executive Term for the President as vested with the executive power of the United States. p. 354

Chief legislator Term for the President as architect of public policy and the one who sets the agenda for Congress. p. 355

Chief of party Term for the President as the leader of his or her political party. p. 355

Chief of state Term for the President as the ceremonial head of the United States, the symbol of all the people of the nation. p. 354

Citizen A member of a state or nation who owes allegiance to it by birth or naturalization and is entitled to full civil rights. p. 613

Civil case A case involving a noncriminal matter such as a contract dispute or a claim of patent infringement. p. 513

Civil law The portion of the law relating to human conduct, to disputes between private parties, and to disputes between private parties and government not covered by criminal law. p. 704

Civil liberties The guarantees of the safety of persons, opinions, and property from the arbitrary acts of government, including freedom of speech and freedom of religion. p. 533

Civil rights A term used for those positive acts of government that seek to make constitutional guarantees a reality for all people, e.g., prohibitions of discrimination. p. 533

Civil service Those civilian employees who perform the administrative work of government. p. 437

Civilian tribunal A court operating as part of the judicial branch, entirely separate from the military establishment. p. 525

Clemency Mercy or leniency granted to an offender by a chief executive; *see* pardon and reprieve. pp. 407, 699

Closed primary A party nominating election in which only declared party members can vote. p. 182

Cloture Procedure that may be used to limit or end floor debate in a legislative body. p. 344

Coalition A temporary alliance of several groups who come together to form a working majority and so to control a government. pp. 122, 628

Coattail effect The effect of a strong candidate running for an office at the top of a ballot helping to attract voters to other candidates on the party's ticket. p. 190

Cold war A period of more than 40 years during which relations between the two superpowers were at least tense, and often hostile. A time of threats and military build up. p. 485

colleague A co-worker. p. 277

Collective security The keeping of international peace and order. p. 485

Collectivization Collective or state ownership of the means of production. p. 674

Commander in chief Term for the President as commander of the nation's armed forces. p. 355

Commerce and Slave Trade Compromise An agreement during the Constitutional Convention protecting slave holders; denied Congress the power to tax the export of goods from any State, and, for 20 years, the power to act on the slave trade. p. 53

Commerce power Exclusive power of Congress to regulate interstate and foreign trade. p. 297

Commission government A government formed by commissioners, heads of different departments of city government, who are popularly elected to form the city council and thus center both legislative and executive powers in one body. p. 728

Committee chairman Member who heads a standing committee in a legislative body. p. 325

Committee of the Whole A committee that consists of an entire legislative body; used for a procedure in which a legislative body expedites its business by resolving itself into a committee of itself. p. 339

Common law An unwritten law made by a judge that has developed over centuries from those generally accepted ideas of right and wrong that have gained judicial recognition. p. 702

Commune A large grouping of several collective farms. p. 675

Communism An ideology which calls for the collective, or state, ownership of land and other productive property. p. 672

Commutation The power to reduce (commute) the length of a sentence or fine for a crime. pp. 408, 699

Compromise An adjustment of opposing principles or systems by modifying some aspect of each. p. 20

Concurrent jurisdiction Power shared by federal and State courts to hear certain cases. p. 508

Concurrent powers Those powers that both the National Government and the States possess and exercise. p. 93

Concurrent resolution A statement of position on an issue used by the House and Senate acting jointly; does not have the force of law and does not require the President's signature. p. 335

Concurring opinion Written explanation of the views of one or more judges who support a decision reached by a majority of the court, but wish to add or emphasize a point that was not made in the majority decision. p. 522

Confederation A joining of several groups for a common purpose. pp. 15, 35

Conference committee Temporary joint committee created to reconcile any differences between the two houses' versions of a bill. p. 333

Connecticut Compromise Agreement during the Constitutional Convention that Congress should be composed of a Senate, in which States would be represented equally, and a House, in which representation would be based on a State's population. p. 52

Consensus General agreement among various groups on fundamental matters; broad agreement on public questions. pp. 121, 292, 636

Constituency The people and interests that an elected official represents. p. 277

Constituent power The non-legislative power of Constitution-making and the constitutional amendment process. p. 692

Constitution The body of fundamental laws setting out the principles, structures, and processes of a government. p. 4

Constitutionalism Basic principle that government and those who govern must obey the law; the rule of law; *see* limited government. p. 65

Containment A policy based in the belief that if communism could be kept within its existing boundaries, it would collapse under the weight of its internal weaknesses. p. 486

Content neutral The government may not regulate assemblies on the basis on what might be said. p. 556

Continuing resolution A measure which allows agencies to continue working based on the previous year's appropriations. p. 462

Continuous body Governing unit (e.g. the United States Senate) whose seats are never all up for election at the same time. p. 277

Controllable spending An amount decided upon by Congress and the President to determine how much will be spent each year on many individual government expenditures, including environment protection programs, aid to education, and so on. p. 459

Copyright The exclusive, legal right of a person to reproduce, publish, and sell his or her own literary, musical, or artistic creations. p. 302

Council-manager government A modification of the mayor-council government, it consists of a strong council of members elected on a non-partisan ballot, a weak mayor, elected by the people, and a manager, named by the council; *see* mayor-council government; *see* also weak mayor government. p. 728

County A major unit of local government in most States. p. 718

Court-martial A court composed of military personnel, for the trial of those accused of violating military law. p. 525

Criminal case A case in which a defendant is tried for committing a crime as defined by the law. p. 513

Criminal law The portion of the law that defines public wrongs and provides for their punishment. p. 704

Cultural Revolution Begun in 1966, Mao Tse Tung's Red Guards attacked, bullied, and "reeducated" teachers, intellectuals, and anyone else who seemed to lack revolutionary fervor. p. 650

Custom duty A tax laid on goods brought into the United States from abroad, also known as tariffs, import duties, or imposts. p. 451

De facto segregation Segregation even if no law requires it, e.g., housing patterns. p. 604

De jure segregation Segregation by law, with legal sanction. p. 604

Defendant In a civil suit, the person against whom a court action is brought by the plaintiff; in a criminal case, the person charged with the crime. p. 509

Deficit The yearly shortfall between revenue and spending. p. 455

Deficit financing Practice of funding government by borrowing to make up the difference between government spending and revenue. p. 296

Delegated powers Those powers, expressed, implied, or inherent, granted to the National Government by the Constitution. p. 89

Democracy A form of government in which the supreme authority rests with the people. p. 5

Denaturalization The process through which naturalized citizens may involuntarily lose their citizenship. p. 615

Deportation A legal process in which aliens are legally required to leave the United States. p. 617

Détente A relaxation of tensions. p. 488

Deterrence The policy of making America and its allies so militarily strong that their very strength will discourage, or prevent, any attack. p. 485

Devolution The delegation of authority from the central government to regional governments. p. 631

Dictatorship A form of government in which the leader has absolute power and authority. p. 5

Diplomatic immunity When an ambassador is not subject to the laws of the state to which they are accredited. p. 471

Direct popular election Proposal to do away with the electoral college and allow the people to vote directly for President and Vice President. p. 383

Direct primary An election held within a party to pick that party's candidates for the general election. p. 182

Direct tax A tax that must be paid by the person on whom it is levied; *see* indirect tax. p. 296

Discharge petition A procedure enabling members to force a bill that has been pigeonholed in committee onto the floor for consideration. p. 336

Discrimination Bias, unfairness. p. 570

Dissenting opinion Written explanation of the views of one or more judges who disagree with (dissent from) a decision reached by a majority of the court; *see* majority opinion. p. 522

Dissolution The power of the Prime Minister to dissolve the House of Representatives. p. 636

District plan Proposal for choosing presidential electors by which two electors would be selected in each State according to the Statewide popular vote and the other electors would be selected separately in each of the State's congressional districts. p. 382

Division of powers Basic principle of federalism; the constitutional provisions by which governmental powers are divided on a geographic basis (in the United States, between the National Government and the States). pp. 14, 89

Docket A court's list of cases to be heard. p. 513

Doctrine Principle or fundamental policy. p. 308

Domestic affairs All matters not directly connected to the realm of foreign affairs. pp. 422, 468

Double jeopardy Part of the 5th Amendment which says that no person can be put in jeopardy of life or limb twice. Once a person has been tried for a crime, he or she cannot be tried again for the same crime. p. 578

Draft Conscription, or compulsory military service. p. 480

Due process The government must act fairly and in accord with established rules in all that it does. p. 564

Due Process Clause Part of the 14th Amendment which guarantees that no state deny basic rights to its people. p. 535

Economic protest parties Parties rooted in poor economic times, lacking a clear ideological base, dissatisfied with current conditions and demanding better times. p. 133

Electoral college Group of persons chosen in each State and the District of Columbia every four years who make a formal selection of the President and Vice President. pp. 81, 366

Electoral votes Votes cast by electors in the electoral college. p. 365

Electorate All of the people entitled to vote in a given election. pp. 129, 148, 383

Eminent domain Power of a government to take private property for public use. p. 304

Enabling act A congressional act directing the people of a United States territory to frame a proposed State constitution as a step towards admission to the Union. p. 99

English Bill of Rights Document written by Parliament and agreed on by William and Mary of England in 1689, designed to prevent abuse of power by English monarchs; forms the basis for much in American government and politics today. p. 30

Engross To print a bill in its final form. p. 340

Entitlement A benefit that federal law says must be paid to all those who meet the eligibility requirements, e.g., Medicare, food stamps, and veterans' pension. pp. 458, 735

Entrepreneur An individual with the drive and ambition to combine land, labor, and capital resources to produce goods or offer services. p. 659

Espionage Spying. p. 477

Establishment Clause Separates church and state. p. 537

Estate tax A levy imposed on the assets of one who dies. pp. 451, 742

Ex post facto law A law applied to an act committed before its passage. p. 577

Excise tax A tax laid on the manufacture, sale, or consumption of goods and/or the performance of services. p. 451

Exclusionary rule Evidence gained as the result of an illegal act by police cannot be used against the person from whom it was seized. p. 573

Exclusive jurisdiction Power of the federal courts alone to hear certain cases. p. 508

Exclusive powers Those powers that can be exercised by the National Government alone. p. 93

Executive agreement A pact made by the President directly with the head of a foreign state; a binding international agreement with the force of law but which (unlike a treaty) does not require Senate consent. pp. 80, 400

Executive Article Article II of the Constitution. Establishes the presidency and gives the executive power of the Federal Government to the President. p. 390

Executive departments Often called the Cabinet departments, they are the traditional units of federal administration. p. 424

Executive Office of the President An organization of several agencies staffed by the President's closest advisors. p. 419

Executive order Directive, rule, or regulation issued by a chief executive or subordinates, based upon constitutional or statutory authority and having the force of law. p. 394

Executive power The power to execute, enforce, and administer law. p. 4

Expatriation The legal process by which a loss of citizenship occurs. p. 614

Expressed powers Those delegated powers of the National Government that are spelled out, expressly, in the Constitution; also called the "enumerated powers." pp. 89, 290

Extradition The legal process by which a fugitive from justice in one State is returned to that State. p. 107

Faction A conflicting group. p. 127

Factors of production Basic resources which are used to make all goods and services. p. 658

Federal budget A detailed financial document containing estimates of federal income and spending during the coming fiscal year. p. 421

Federal government A form of government in which powers are divided between a central government and several local governments. p. 14

Federalism A system of government in which a written constitution divides power between a central, or national, government and several regional governments. pp. 70, 88

Federalists Those persons who supported the ratification of the Constitution in 1787–1788. p. 56

Felony A serious crime which may be punished by a heavy fine and/or imprisonment or even death. p. 704

Filibuster Various tactics (usually long speeches) aimed at defeating a bill in a legislative body by preventing a final vote; associated with the U.S. Senate; *see* cloture. p. 343

Fiscal year The 12-month period used by a government and the business world for its record-keeping, budgeting, revenue-collecting, and other financial management purposes. p. 421

Five-year plan A plan which projects economic development over the next five years. p. 673

Floor leaders Members of the House and Senate picked by their parties to carry out party decisions and steer legislative action to meet party goals. p. 324

Foreign affairs A nation's relationships with other countries. p. 468

Foreign aid Economic and military aid to other countries. p. 491

Foreign policy A group of policies made up of all the stands and actions that a nation takes in every aspect of its relationships with other countries; everything a nation's government says and does in world affairs. p. 469

Formal amendment Change or addition that becomes part of the written language of the Constitution itself through one of four methods set forth in the Constitution. p. 73

Framers Group of delegates who drafted the United States Constitution at the Philadelphia Convention in 1787. p. 48

Franchise The right to vote. p. 148

Franking privilege Benefit allowing members of Congress to mail letters and other materials postage-free. p. 283

Free enterprise system An economic system characterized by private or corporate ownership of capital goods; investments that are determined by private decision rather than by state control, and determined in a free market. pp. 20, 659

Free Exercise Clause The second part of the constitutional guarantee of religious freedom, which guarantees to each person the right to believe whatever he or she chooses to believe in matters of religion. p. 542

Full Faith and Credit Clause Constitution's requirement that each State accept the public acts, records, and judicial proceedings of every other State. p. 106

Fundamental law Laws of basic and lasting importance which may not easily be changed. p. 686

Gender gap Measurable differences between the partisan choices of men and women today. p. 169

General election The regularly scheduled election at which voters make a final selection of officeholders. p. 179

Gerrymandering The drawing of electoral district lines to the advantage of a party or group. pp. 159, 271

Gift tax A tax on a gift by a living person. p. 451

Glasnost The Soviet policy of openness under which tolerance of dissent and freedom of expression increased. p. 646

Gosplan A large agency in the Soviet Union, introduced by Stalin, to run centralized planning. p. 674

Government The institution through which a society makes and enforces its public policies. p. 4

Government corporation Corporations within the executive branch subject to the President's direction and control, set up by Congress to carry out certain business-like activities. p. 434

Grand jury The formal device by which a person can be accused of a serious crime. p. 577

Grants-in-aid program Grants of federal money or other resources to States, cities, counties, and other local units. p. 101

Grass roots Of or from the people, the average voters. p. 253

Great Leap Forward The five-year plan for 1958 which was an attempt to quickly modernize China. p. 675

Hard money Campaign money that is subject to regulations by the FEC. p. 202

Heterogeneous Of another or different race, family or kind; composed of a mix of elements. p. 594

Ideological parties Parties based on a particular set of beliefs, a comprehensive view of social, economic, and political matters. p. 132

Immigrant Those people legally admitted as permanent residents of a country. p. 594

Impeach To bring formal charges against a public official; the House of Representatives has the sole power to impeach civil officers of the United States. p. 311

Imperial presidency Term used to describe a President as an "emperor" who acts without consulting Congress or acts in secrecy to evade or deceive Congress; often used in reference to Richard Nixon's presidency. p. 392

Implied powers Those delegated powers of the National Government that are suggested by the expressed powers; those "necessary and proper" to carry out the expressed powers; *see* delegated powers, expressed powers. pp. 90, 290

Income tax A tax levied on the income of individuals and/or corporations. p. 741

Incorporation The process by which a State establishes a city as a legal body. p. 726

Incumbent The current officeholder. p. 127

Independent agencies Additional agencies created by Congress located outside the Cabinet departments. p. 430

Independent executive agencies Agencies headed by a single administrator with regional subunits, but lacking Cabinet status. p. 431

Independent regulatory commissions Independent agencies designed to regulate important aspects of the nation's economy, largely beyond the reach of presidential control. p. 431

Independents A term used to describe people who have no party affiliation. p. 171

Indictment A formal complaint before a grand jury which charges the accused with one or more crimes. p. 578

Indirect tax A tax levied on one party but passed on to another for payment. p. 296

Inferior courts The lower federal courts, beneath the Supreme Court. p. 507

Informal amendment A change made in the Constitution not by actual written amendment, but by the experience of government, including: (1) the passage of laws by Congress; (2) actions taken by the President; (3) Supreme Court decisions; (4) the activities of political parties; and (5) custom. p. 79

Information A formal charge filed by a prosecutor without the action of a grand jury. p. 704

Inherent powers Powers delegated to the National Government because it is the government of a sovereign state within the world community. pp. 91, 290

Inheritance tax A tax levied on the beneficiary's share of an estate. p. 742

Initiative A process in which a certain number of qualified voters sign petitions in favor of a proposal, which then goes directly to the ballot. p. 687

Injunction A court order that forces or limits the performance of some act by a private individual or by a public official. p. 161

Integration The process of bringing a group into equal membership in society. p. 603

Interest A charge for borrowed money, generally a percentage of the amount borrowed. p. 454

Interest group Private organizations whose members share certain views and work to shape public policy. p. 216

Interstate compact Formal agreement entered into with the consent of Congress, between or among States, or between a State and a foreign state. p. 105

Involuntary servitude Forced labor. p. 569

Isolationism A purposeful refusal to become generally involved in the affairs of the rest of the world. p. 468

Item veto A governor may veto one or more items in a bill without rejecting the entire measure. p. 699

Jim Crow law A law that separates people on the basis of race, aimed primarily at African Americans. p. 602

Joint committee Legislative committee composed of members of both houses. p. 333

Joint resolution A proposal for action that has the force of law when passed; usually deals with special circumstances or temporary matters. p. 335

Judicial power The power to interpret laws, to determine their meaning, and to settle disputes within the society. p. 4

Judicial review The power of a court to determine the constitutionality of a governmental action. p. 69

Jurisdiction The authority of a court to hear a case. p. 508

Jury A body of persons selected according to law who hear evidence and decide questions of fact in a court case. p. 704

Jus sanguinis The law of blood, which determines citizenship based on one's parents' citizenship. p. 613

Jus soli The law of soil, which determines citizenship based on where a person is born. p. 613

Justice of the Peace A judge who stands on the lowest level of the State judicial system and presides over justice courts. p. 707

Keynote address Speech given at a party convention to set the tone for the convention and the campaign to come. p. 373

Labor union An organization of workers who share the same type of job, or who work in the same industry, and press for government policies that will benefit their members. p. 244

Laissez-faire theory A theory which suggests that government should play a very limited role in society. p. 662

Law of supply and demand A law which states that when supplies of goods and services become plentiful, prices tend to drop. When supplies become scarcer, prices tend to rise. pp. 21, 661

Legal tender Any kind of money that a creditor must, by law, accept in payment for debts. p. 299

Legislative power The power to make a law and to frame public policies. p. 4

Libel False and malicious use of printed words. p. 546

Liberal constructionist One who argues a broad interpretation of the provisions of the Constitution, particularly those granting powers to the Federal Government. p. 291

Limited government Basic principle of American government which states that government is restricted in what it may do, and each individual has rights that government cannot take away; *see* constitutionalism, popular sovereignty. pp. 29, 685

Line agency An agency which performs the tasks for which the organization exists. p. 418

Line-item veto A President's cancellation of specific dollar amounts (line items) from a congressional spending bill; instituted by a 1996 congressional act, but struck down by a 1998 Supreme Court decision. p. 406

Literacy A person's ability to read or write. p. 156

Lobbying Activities by which group pressures are brought to bear on legislators, the legislative process, and all aspects of the public-policy-making process. p. 251

Magistrate A justice who handles minor civil complaints and misdemeanor cases that arise in an urban setting. p. 708

Magna Carta Great Charter forced upon King John of England by his barons in 1215; established that the power of the monarchy was not absolute and guaranteed trial by jury and due process of law to the nobility. p. 29

Major parties In American politics, the Republican and the Democratic parties. p. 116

Majority opinion Officially called the Opinion of the Court; announces the Court's decision in a case and sets out the reasoning upon which it is based. p. 522

Mandate The instructions or commands a constituency gives to its elected officials. p. 216

Market economy Economic system in which decisions on production and consumption of goods and services are based on voluntary exchange of markets. p. 669

Mass media Those means of communication that reach large audiences, especially television, radio, printed publications, and the Internet. pp. 211, 391

Mayor-council government The oldest and most widely used type of city government—an elected mayor as the chief executive and an elected council as its legislative body. p. 726

Medicaid A program administered by the State to provide medical insurance to low-income families. p. 735

Medium A means of communication; something which transmits information. p. 223

Mestizo A person with both Spanish or Portuguese and Native American ancestry. p. 639

Metropolitan area A city and the area around it. p. 731

Minister Cabinet members, most commonly of the House of Commons. p. 629

Minor party One of the political parties not widely supported. p. 119

Miranda Rule The constitutional rights which police must read to a suspect before questioning can occur. p. 582

Misdemeanor A lesser offense, punishable by a small fine and/or a short jail term. p. 704

Mixed economy An economy in which private enterprise exists in combination with a considerable amount of government regulation and promotion. p. 21

Monarchy A government lead by a hereditary ruler. p. 627

Monopoly A firm that is the only source of a product or service. p. 661

Multiparty A system in which several major and many lesser parties exist, seriously compete for, and actually win, public offices. p. 122

National bonus plan Proposal for electing a President by which the winner of the popular vote would receive a bonus of 102 electoral votes in addition to his or her State-based electoral college votes. If no one received at least 321 electoral votes, a run-off election would be held. p. 384

National convention Meeting at which a party's delegates vote to pick their presidential and vice-presidential candidates. p. 372

Nationalization The governmental acquisition of private industry for public use. p. 642

Naturalization The legal process by which citizens of one country become citizens of another. pp. 302, 614

Necessary and Proper Clause Constitutional clause that gives Congress the power to make all laws "necessary and proper" for executing its powers; *see* implied powers. p. 305

New Jersey Plan Plan presented as an alternative to the Virginia Plan at the Constitutional Convention; called for a unicameral legislature in which each State would be equally represented. p. 51

Nomination The process of candidate selection in a democracy. p. 178

Nonpartisan election Elections in which candidates are not identified by party labels. p. 184

North American Free Trade Agreement An agreement which removed trade restrictions among the United States, Canada, and Mexico, thus increasing cross-border trade. p. 642

Oath of office Oath taken by the President on the day he takes office, pledging to "faithfully execute" the office and "preserve, protect, and defend" the Constitution. p. 393

Off-year election Congressional election that occurs between presidential election years. pp. 164, 269

Oligarchy A form of government in which the power to rule is held by a small, usually self-appointed elite. p. 13

One-party system A political system in which only one party exists. p. 123

Open primary A party-nominating election in which any qualified voter can take part. p. 183

Opinion leader Any person who, for any reason, has an unusually strong influence on the views of others. p. 212

Ordinance power Power of the President to issue executive orders; originates from the Constitution and acts of Congress. p. 394

Original jurisdiction The power of a court to hear a case first, before any other court. p. 509

Oversight function Review by legislative committees of the policies and programs of the executive branch. p. 281

Pardon Release from the punishment or legal consequences of a crime, by the President (in a federal case) or a governor (in a State case). pp. 407, 699

Parliamentary government A form of government in which the executive branch is made up of the prime minister, or premier, and that official's cabinet. p. 16

Parochial Church-related, as in a parochial school. p. 538

Parole The release of a prisoner short of the complete term of the original sentence. p. 699

Partisan Lawmaker who owes his/her first allegiance to his/her political party and votes according to the party line. p. 281

Partisanship Government action based on firm allegiance to a political party. p. 117

Party caucus A closed meeting of a party's House or Senate members; also called a party conference. p. 324

Party identification Loyalty of people to a political party. p. 171

Party in power In American politics, the party in power is the party that controls the executive branch of government—i.e., the presidency at the national level, or the governorship at the State level. p. 118

Patent A license issued to an inventor granting the exclusive right to manufacture, use, or sell his or her invention for a limited period of time. p. 303

Patronage The practice of giving jobs to supporters and friends. p. 438

Payroll tax A tax imposed on nearly all employers and their employees, and on self-employed persons—the amounts owed by employees withheld from their paychecks. p. 450

Peer group People with whom one regularly associates, including friends, classmates, neighbors, and co-workers. p. 212

Perestroika The restructuring of political and economic life under the rule of Mikhail Gorbachev. p. 646

Perjury The act of lying under oath. p. 311

Persona non grata An unwelcome person; used to describe recalled diplomatic officials. p. 401

Petition of Right Document prepared by Parliament and signed by King Charles I of England in 1628; challenged the idea of the divine right of kings and declared that even the monarch was subject to the laws of the land. p. 30

Picketing Patrolling of a business site by workers who are on strike. p. 551

Plaintiff In civil law, the party who brings a suit or some other legal action against another (the defendant) in court. p. 509

Platform A political party's formal statement of basic principles, stands on major issues, and objectives. p. 373

Pluralistic society A society which consists of several distinct cultures and groups. p. 121

Plurality In an election, the number of votes that the leading candidate obtains over the next highest candidate. p. 120

Pocket veto Type of veto a chief executive may use after a legislature has adjourned; when the chief executive does not sign or reject a bill within the time allowed to do so; see veto. p. 346

Police power The authority of each State to act to protect and promote the public health, safety, morals, and general welfare of its people. pp. 566, 691

Political Action Committee The political extension of special-interest groups which have a major stake in public policy. p. 197

Political efficacy One's own influence or effectiveness on politics. p. 166

Political party A group of persons who seek to control government through the winning of elections and the holding of public office. p. 116

Political socialization The process by which people gain their political attitudes and opinions. p. 168

Politico Lawmaker who attempts to balance the basic elements of the trustee, delegate, and partisan roles; see trustee, delegate, partisan. p. 281

Poll book List of all registered voters in each precinct. p. 155

Poll tax A special tax, demanded by States, as a condition of voting. p. 157

Polling place The place where the voters who live in a certain precinct go to vote. p. 190

Popular sovereignty Basic principle of the American system of government which asserts that the people are the source of any and all governmental power, and government can exist only with the consent of the governed. pp. 39, 685

Preamble Introduction. p. 65

Precedent Court decision that stands as an example to be followed in future, similar cases. pp. 522, 703

Precinct The smallest unit of election administration; a voting district. pp. 140, 190

Preclearance Mandated by the Voting Rights Act of 1965, the prior approval by the Justice Department of changes to or new election laws by certain States. p. 162

Prefecture The 47 political subdivisions into which Japan is divided. p. 637

Preliminary hearing The first step in a major criminal prosecution where the judge decides if the evidence is enough to hold the person for action by the grand jury or the prosecutor. p. 708

President of the Senate The presiding officer of a senate; in Congress, the Vice President of the United States; in a State's legislature, either the lieutenant governor or a senator. p. 323

President pro tempore The member of the United States Senate, or of the upper house of a State's legislature, chosen to preside in the absence of the president of the Senate. p. 323

Presidential elector A person elected by the voters to represent them in making a formal selection of the Vice President and President. p. 365

Presidential government A form of government in which the executive and legislative branches of the government are separate, independent, and coequal. p. 15

Presidential primary An election in which a party's voters (1) choose State party organization's delegates to their party's national convention, and/or (2) express a preference for their party's presidential nomination. p. 369

Presidential succession Scheme by which a presidential vacancy is filled. p. 359

Presidential Succession Act of 1947 Law specifying the order of presidential succession following the Vice President. p. 360

Presiding officer Chair. p. 45

Preventive detention A law which allows federal judges to order that an accused felon be held, without bail, when there is good reason to believe that he or she will commit yet another serious crime before trial. p. 586

Prior restraint The government cannot curb ideas before they are expressed. p. 549

Privatization The process of returning national enterprises to private ownership. p. 675

Privileges and Immunities Clause Constitution's stipulation (Article IV, Section 2) that all citizens are entitled to certain "privileges and immunities," regardless of their State of residence; no State can draw unreasonable distinctions between its own residents and those persons who happen to live in other States. p. 107

Probable Cause Reasonable grounds, a reasonable suspicion of crime. p. 571

Procedural due process The government must employ fair procedures and methods. p. 565

Process of incorporation The process of incorporating, or including, most of the guarantees in the Bill of Rights into the 14th Amendment's Due Process Clause. p. 535

Progressive tax A type of tax proportionate to income. pp. 449, 742

Project grant One type of federal grants-in-aid; made for specific projects to States, localities, and private agencies who apply for them. p. 103

Proletariat The working class. p. 667

Propaganda A technique of persuasion aimed at influencing individual or group behaviors to create a particular belief, regardless of its validity. p. 249

Property tax A tax levied on real and personal property. p. 742

Proportional plan Proposal by which each presidential candidate would receive the same share of a State's electoral vote as he or she received in the State's popular vote. p. 382

Glossary

Proportional representation rule Rule applied in Democratic primaries whereby any candidate who wins at least 15 percent of the votes gets the number of State Democratic convention delegates based on his or her share of that primary vote. p. 371

Proprietary Organized by a proprietor (a person to whom the king had made a grant of land). p. 32

Prorogue Adjourn, as in a legislative session. p. 265

Public affairs Those events and issues that concern the people at large, e.g., politics, public issues, and the making of public policies. pp. 208, 239

Public agenda The public issues on which the people's attention is focused. p. 228

Public debt All of the money borrowed by the government and not yet repaid, plus the accrued interest on that money; also called the national debt or federal debt. pp. 296, 455

Public-interest group An interest group that seeks to institute certain public policies of benefit to all or most people in this country, whether or not they belong to or support that organization. p. 247

Public opinion The complex collection of the opinions of many different people; the sum of all their views. p. 209

Public opinion poll Devices that attempt to collect information by asking people questions. p. 217

Public policy All of the goals a government sets and the various courses of action it pursues as it attempts to realize these goals. pp. 4, 236

Purge The process of reviewing lists of registered voters and removing the names of those no longer eligible to vote; a purification. pp. 155, 645

Quasi-judicial Having to do with powers that are to some extent judicial. p. 433

Quasi-legislative Having to do with powers that are to some extent legislative. p. 433

Quorum Least number of members who must be present for a legislative body to conduct business; majority. pp. 58, 339

Quota A rule requiring certain numbers of jobs or promotions for members of certain groups. p. 610

Quota sample A sample deliberately constructed to reflect several of the major characteristics of a given population. p. 219

Random sample A certain number of randomly selected people who live in a certain number of randomly selected places. p. 218

Ratification Formal approval, final consent to the effectiveness of a constitution, constitutional amendment, or treaty. p. 44

Reapportion Redistrict, as in seats in a legislative body. p. 267

Recall A petition procedure by which voters may remove an elected official from office before the completion of his or her regular term. p. 696

Recognition The exclusive power of a President to recognize (establish formal diplomatic relations with) foreign states. p. 400

Redress Satisfaction of a claim payment. p. 524

Referendum A process by which a legislative measure is referred to the State's voters for final approval or rejection. p. 693

Refugee One who leaves his or her home to seek protection from war, persecution, or some other danger. p. 597

Regional security alliances Treaties in which the U.S. and other countries involved have agreed to take collective action to meet aggression in a particular part of the world. p. 492

Register A record or list of names, often kept by an official appointed to do so. p. 439

Registration A procedure of voter identification intended to prevent fraudulent voting. p. 154

Regressive tax A tax levied at a flat rate, without regard to the level of a taxpayer's income or ability to pay them. pp. 451, 741

Repeal Recall. p. 37

Representative government System of government in which public policies are made by officials selected by the voters and held accountable in periodic elections; see democracy. p. 29

Reprieve An official postponement of the execution of a sentence; see pardon. pp. 407, 699

Reservation Public land set aside by a government for use by Native American tribes. p. 596

Reserved powers Those powers that the Constitution does not grant to the National Government and does not, at the same time, deny to the States. p. 92

Resolution A measure relating to the business of either house, or expressing an opinion; does not have the force of law and does not require the President's signature. p. 335

Revenue sharing Form of federal monetary aid under which Congress gave a share of federal tax revenue, with virtually no restrictions, to the States, cities, counties, and townships. p. 102

Reverse discrimination Discrimination against the majority group. p. 610

Right of association The right to associate with others to promote political, economic, and other social causes. p. 558

Right of legation The right to send and receive diplomatic representatives. p. 470

Rider Unpopular provision added to an important bill certain to pass so that it will "ride" through the legislative process. p. 335

Rule of law Concept that holds that government and its officers are always subject to the law. p. 66

Runoff primary A primary in which the top two vote-getters in the first direct primary face one another. p. 184

Sales tax A tax placed on the sale of various commodities, paid by the purchaser. p. 741

Sample A representative slice of the public. p. 218

Search warrant A court order authorizing a search. p. 566

Secretary An official in charge of a department of government. p. 424

Sectionalism A narrow-minded concern for, or devotion to, the interests of one section of a country. p. 129

Sedition The crime of attempting to overthrow the government by force, or to disrupt its lawful activities by violent acts. p. 547

Seditious speech The advocating, or urging, of an attempt to overthrow the government by force, or to disrupt its lawful activities with violence. p. 547

Segregation The separation of one group from another. p. 602

Select committee Legislative committee created for a limited time and for some specific purpose; also known as a special committee. p. 331

Senatorial courtesy Custom that the Senate will not approve a presidential appointment opposed by a majority party senator from the State in which the appointee would serve. p. 81

Seniority rule Unwritten rule in both houses of Congress reserving the top posts in each chamber, particularly committee chairmanships, for members with the longest records of service. p. 326

Separate-but-equal doctrine A constitutional basis for laws that separate one group from another on the basis of race. (Jim Crow Laws.) p. 602

Separation of powers Basic principle of American system of government, that the executive, legislative, and judicial powers are divided among three independent and coequal branches of government; see checks and balances. p. 66

Session Period of time during which, each year, Congress assembles and conducts business. p. 264

Shadow cabinet Members of opposition parties who watch, or shadow, particular Cabinet members, and would be ready to run the government. p. 629

Shield law A law which gives reporters some protection against having to disclose their sources or reveal other confidential information in legal proceedings. p. 550

Single-interest group Political action committees that concentrate their efforts exclusively on one issue. p. 251

Single-issue parties Parties that concentrate on only one public policy matter. p. 132

Single-member district Electoral district from which one person is chosen by the voters for each elected office. pp. 120, 270

Slander False and malicious use of spoken words. p. 547

Socialism A philosophy based on the idea that the benefits of economic activity should be fairly distributed. p. 666

Soft money Money given to State and local party organizations for voting-related activities. p. 201

Sound bite Short, sharply focused reports that can be aired in 30 or 45 seconds. p. 229

Sovereign Having supreme power within its own territory; neither subordinate nor responsible to any other authority. p. 6

Soviets A government council, elected by and representing the people. p. 646

Speaker of the House The presiding officer of the House of Representatives, chosen by and from the majority party in the House. p. 322

Special district An independent unit created to perform one or more related governmental functions at the local level. p. 722

Special session An extraordinary session of a legislative body, called to deal with an emergency situation. p. 265

Splinter parties Parties that have split away from one of the major parties. p. 133

Split-ticket voting Voting for candidates of different parties for different offices at the same election. pp. 141, 171

Spoils system The practice of giving offices and other favors of government to political supporters and friends. p. 438

Staff agency An agency which supports the chief executive and other administrators by offering advice and other assistance in the management of the organization. p. 418

Standing committee Permanent committee in a legislative body to which bills in a specified subject-matter area are referred; *see* select committee. p. 329

State A body of people living in a defined territory who have a government with the power to make and enforce law without the consent of any higher authority. p. 5

Statutory law A law passed by the legislature. p. 688

Straight-ticket voting The practice of voting for candidates of only one party in an election. p. 171

Straw vote Polls that seek to read the public's mind simply by asking the same question of a large number of people. p. 217

Strict constructionist One who argues a narrow interpretation of the Constitution's provisions, in particular those granting powers to the Federal Government. p. 291

Strong-mayor government A type of government in which the mayor heads the city's administration. p. 727

Subcommittee Division of existing committee that is formed to address specific issues. p. 336

Subpoena An order for a person to appear and to produce documents or other requested materials. p. 313

Subsidy A grant of money, usually from a government. p. 197

Substantive due process The government must create fair policies and laws. p. 565

Successor A person who inherits a title or office. p. 311

Suffrage The right to vote. p. 148

Surplus More income than spending. p. 455

Symbolic speech Expression by conduct; communicating ideas through facial expressions, body language, or by carrying a sign or wearing an arm band. p. 551

Tax A charge levied by government on persons or property to meet public needs. p. 295

Tax return A declaration of taxable income and of the exemptions and deductions claimed. p. 449

Term Two-year period of time during which Congress meets. p. 306

Terrorism The use of violence to intimidate a government or society. p. 478

Three-Fifths Compromise An agreement at the Constitutional Convention to count a slave as three-fifths of a person when determining the population of a State. p. 52

Township A subdivision of a county. p. 718

Trade association Interest groups within the business community. p. 244

Transient Person living in a State for only a short time, without legal residence. p. 153

Treason Betrayal of one's country; in the Constitution, by levying war against the United States or offering comfort or aid to its enemies. p. 588

Treaty A formal agreement between two or more sovereign states. pp. 80, 399

Trust A device by which several corporations in the same business work to eliminate competition and regulate prices. p. 661

Trustee Lawmaker who votes based on his or her conscience and judgment, not the views of his or her constituents. p. 281

Two-party system A political system dominated by two major parties. p. 119

UN Security Council A 15-member panel which bears the UN's major responsibility for keeping international peace. p. 496

Unconstitutional Contrary to constitutional provision and so illegal, null and void, of no force and effect. p. 69

Uncontrollable spending Spending that Congress and the President have no power to change directly. p. 459

Unicameral An adjective describing a legislative body with one chamber; *see* bicameral. p. 32

Unitary government A centralized government in which all government powers belong to a single, central agency. p. 14

Urbanization The percentage of the population of a State living in cities of more than 250,000 people or in suburbs of cities with more than 50,000. p. 737

Veto Chief executive's power to reject a bill passed by a legislature; literally (Latin) "I forbid"; *see* pocket veto. pp. 67, 346

Virginia Plan Plan presented by delegates from Virginia at the Constitutional Convention; called for a three-branch government with a bicameral legislature in which each State's membership would be determined by its population or its financial support for the central government. p. 51

Ward A unit into which cities are often divided for the election of city council members. p. 140

Warrant A court order authorizing, or making legal, some official action, such as a search warrant or an arrest warrant. p. 708

Weak-mayor government A type of government in which the mayor shares his or her executive duties with other elected officials. p. 727

Welfare Cash assistance to the poor. p. 735

Welfare state Countries that provide extensive social services at little or no cost to the users. p. 668

Whips Assistants to the floor leaders in the House and Senate, responsible for monitoring and marshalling votes. p. 325

Winner-take-all An almost obsolete system whereby a presidential aspirant who won the preference vote in a primary automatically won all the delegates chosen in the primary. p. 371

Writ of assistance Blanket search warrant with which British custom officials had invaded private homes to search for smuggled goods. p. 571

Writ of certiorari An order by a higher court directing a lower court to send up the record in a given case for review; from the Latin meaning "to be more certain." p. 520

Writ of habeas corpus A court order which prevents unjust arrests and imprisonments. p. 576

Zoning The practice of dividing a city into a number of districts and regulating the uses to which property in each of them may be put. p. 730

Spanish Glossary

Absentee voting/Voto en Ausencia Medidas para que voten, en el día de la elección, aquellas personas que no puedan hacerlo en su lugar habitual de votación. Pág. 189

Acquit/Absolver Determinar que no se es culpable de un delito. Pág. 311

Act of admission/Decreto de Admisión Una ley del Congreso mediante la cual se admite a un nuevo estado dentro de la Unión. Pág. 100

Adjourn/Aplazamiento Suspender, por ejemplo, una sesión del Congreso. Pág. 264

Administration/Administración Los funcionarios de la rama ejecutiva de un gobierno, así como sus políticas y sus directores. Pág. 416

Affirmative action/Acción afirmativa Una política que exige que la mayoría de los empleados lleve a cabo ciertas acciones para remediar los efectos de discriminaciones pasadas. Pág. 609

Albany Plan of Union/Plan de Unión Albany Proyecto propuesto por Benjamìn Franklin en 1754 cuyo objetivo era unir a las 13 colonias respecto a asuntos comerciales, militares, así como para otros propósitos; las colonias y la Corona rechazaron el plan. Págs. 35–36

Alien/Extranjero residente Nacido en otro país, o persona que no es ciudadano. Págs. 534, 614

Ambassador/Embajador Delegado oficial designado por el Presidente para que represente a la nación en asuntos diplomáticos. Pág. 471

Amendment/Enmienda Cambio o adición a la Constitución o a las leyes. Pág. 72

Amnesty/Amnistía Perdón general que se brinda a un grupo de violadores de la ley. Pág. 408

Anti-Federalists/Anti-federalistas Aquellas personas que se opusieron a la ratificación de la Constitución en 1787–1788. Pág. 56

Appellate jurisdiction/Tribunal de apelación Autoridad de una corte para revisar decisiones de cortes inferiores; *ver* original jurisdiction/jurisdicción original. Págs. 509, 709

Apportion/Prorrateo Distribuir, como los escaños de un cuerpo legislativo. Pág. 267

Appropriate/Asignar Destinar a un uso particular. Pág. 305

Articles/Artículos Secciones numeradas de un documento. La Constitución, sin enmiendas, está dividida en siete artículos. Pág. 65

Articles of Confederation/Artículos de la Confederación Plan de gobierno adoptado por el Congreso Continental, después de la Independencia de los Estados Unidos; se enunciaron como "un vínculo firme de amistad" entre los estados; no obstante, delegaron unos cuantos poderes importantes al gobierno central. Pág. 44

Assemble/Congregar Reunirse con otras personas para expresar puntos de vista sobre asuntos públicos. Pág. 555

Assessment/Valuación Proceso para determinar el valor de una propiedad que será gravada. Pág. 742

Assimilation/Asimilación Proceso mediante el cual las personas de una cultura se fusionan con otra y se convierten en parte de ella. Pág. 597

At-large election/Elección general Elección de un funcionario público por los votantes de una unidad gubernamental completa (por ejemplo, un estado o país), en vez de por los votantes de un distrito o subdivisión. Pág. 270

Attorney General/Procurador general El titular del Departamento de Justicia. Pág. 424

Authoritarian/Autoritario Forma de gobierno en donde aquellos que ejercen el poder imponen un poder absoluto e inapelable sobre el pueblo. Todas las dictaduras son autoritarias. Pág. 13

Autocracy/Autocracia Forma de gobierno en la que una sola persona ejerce un poder político ilimitado. Pág. 13

Autonomous/Autónomo Independiente. Pág. 652

Bail/Fianza Suma de dinero que se exige que el acusado desembolse (es decir, que deposite en la corte) como garantía de que se presentará en dicha corte en el momento apropiado. Pág. 585

Balance the ticket/Designar al compañero de fórmula Cuando un candidato presidencial elige al candidato a la vicepresidencia que reforzará sus oportunidades de ser triunfador, gracias a las características ideológicas, geográficas, raciales, étnicas, de género, o debido a otras virtudes. Pág. 362

Ballot/Papeleta electoral Medio que los votantes utilizan para señalar su preferencia en una elección. Pág. 190

Bankruptcy/Bancarrota Procedimiento mediante el cual los bienes de una persona declarada en bancarrota se distribuyen entre las personas con las que tiene deudas. Pág. 300

Bench trial/Juicio ante judicatura Proceso en donde sólo el juez escucha el caso. Págs. 580, 705

Bicameral/Bicameral Adjetivo que describe un cuerpo legislativo compuesto por dos cámaras. Pág. 31

Bill/Proyecto de ley Ley propuesta que se presenta a un cuerpo legislativo para su consideración. Pág. 334

Bill of Attainder/Escrito de proscripción y confiscación Acto legislativo que inflige un castigo sin que haya un juicio ante jurado de por medio. Pág. 577

Bill of Rights/Declaración de derechos Las primeras diez enmiendas a la Constitución. Págs. 76, 532

Bipartisan/Bipartidista Apoyado por dos partidos. Págs. 120, 440

Blanket primary/Elecciones primarias generales Proceso de elección en el que los votantes reciben una papeleta electoral grande que contiene los nombres de todos los contendientes, sin importar el partido, y en el cual pueden elegir como lo deseen. Pág. 183

Block grant/Subsidio en conjunto Tipo de subsidio público federal; proporcionado para alguna área particular pero ampliamente definida; *ver* grants-in-aid program/programa de subvenciÛn de fondos públicos. Pág. 103

Bourgeoisie/Burguesía Clase social ubicada entre la aristocracia y la clase media; la clase trabajadora. Pág. 667

Boycott/Boicot Rechazo a vender o a comprar determinados productos o servicios. Pág. 36

Budget/Presupuesto Plan financiero para la utilización del dinero, el personal y la propiedad. Pág. 744

Bureaucracy/Burocracia Estructura administrativa grande y compleja que gobierna los negocios cotidianos de una organización. Pág. 414

Bureaucrat/Burócrata Persona que trabaja en una organización burocrática; *ver* bureaucracy/burocracia. Pág. 415

By-election/Elección suplementaria Elección especial llevada a cabo para sustituir a un miembro del Parlamento, en caso de muerte. Pág. 628

Cabinet/Gabinete Cuerpo consultivo del Presidente que tradicionalmente está compuesto por los titulares de los departamentos ejecutivos y otros funcionarios. Pág. 81

Capital/Capital Todos los recursos hechos por el hombre que se utilizan para producir bienes y servicios. Pág. 659

Spanish Glossary

Capitalist/Capitalista Persona que posee capital y le da un uso productivo; término que en la mayor parte de los casos se aplica a las personas que poseen grandes negocios o fábricas. Pág. 659

Capital punishment/Pena capital La pena de muerte. Pág. 587

Categorical grant/Subsidio categórico Tipo de subsidio público; proporcionado para algún propósito específico y rigurosamente definido; *ver* grants-in-aid program/programa de subvenciÛn de fondos públicos. Pág. 102

Caucus/Junta de dirigentes En función de instrumento nominativo, grupo de personas con ideología similar que se reúne para seleccionar a los candidatos que apoyarán en una elección venidera. Pág. 180

Censure/Censurar Emitir una condena formal. Pág. 312

Centrally planned economy/Economía centralmente planificada Sistema en el que burócratas gubernamentales planean la forma en que la economía se desarrollará durante determinados años. Pág. 669

Certificate/Certificación Método de remitir un caso a la Corte Suprema; se utiliza cuando una corte inferior no está segura de qué procedimiento o regla deberá aplicar en un caso y consulta a la Corte Suprema para que certifique una respuesta a una pregunta específica. Pág. 521

Charter/Carta constitucional Ley básica de una ciudad, su constitución; concesión escrita de autoridad por parte del rey. Págs. 31, 726

Checks and balances/Sistema de pesos y contrapesos Mecanismo en el que se traslapan los poderes de las ramas legislativas, ejecutivas y judiciales para permitir que cada rama verifique las acciones de las otras dos; *ver* separation of powers/separación de poderes. Pág. 67

Chief administrator/Administrador en jefe Nombre que se da al Presidente en cuanto a que es el jefe de la administración del gobierno federal. Pág. 355

Chief citizen/Primer ciudadano Nombre que se da al Presidente, en cuanto a que es representante del pueblo y trabaja para el interés público. Pág. 355

Chief diplomat/Diplomático titular Nombre que se da al Presidente en cuanto a que es el arquitecto principal de la política exterior y el vocero ante otros países. Pág. 355

Chief executive/Primer mandatario Nombre que se da al Presidente, en cuanto a que está investido con el poder ejecutivo de los Estados Unidos. Pág. 354

Chief legislator/Legislador en jefe Nombre que se da al Presidente en cuanto a que es arquitecto de la política pública y uno de los que determina la agenda del Congreso. Pág. 355

Chief of party/Jefe del partido Nombre que se da al Presidente en cuanto a que es líder de su partido político. Pág. 355

Chief of state/Jefe de estado Nombre que se da al Presidente en cuanto a que es titular ceremonial de los Estados Unidos, el símbolo de toda la gente de la nación. Pág. 354

Citizen/Ciudadano Miembro de un estado o nación a la cual le debe lealtad por nacimiento o naturalización y al que se le acreditan todos los derechos civiles. Pág. 613

Civil case/Caso civil Caso que involucra un asunto no criminal, como un litigio por contrato, o una demanda por violación de patentes. Pág. 513

Civil law/Ley civil Área de la ley que se relaciona con la conducta humana, con litigios entre partes privadas, así como entre partes privadas y el gobierno, la cual no abarca la ley penal. Pág. 704

Civil liberties/Libertades civiles Garantías concernientes a la seguridad, opiniones y propiedad de las personas en contra de actos arbitrarios del gobierno; también incluyen la libertad de expresión y de religión. Pág. 533

Civil rights/Derechos civiles Término utilizado para aquellos actos positivos del gobierno que pretenden hacer realidad las garantías constitucionales para todo el pueblo, por ejemplo la prohibición de la discriminación. Pág. 533

Civil service/Servicio Civil Grupo de empleados públicos desempeñan el trabajo administrativo del gobierno. Pág. 437

Civilian tribunal/Tribunal civil Corte que funciona como parte de la rama judicial, el cual está separado por completo de la institución militar. Pág. 525

Clemency/Indulgencia Misericordia o piedad que dispensa el Presidente a un delincuente; *ver* pardon/perdón y reprieve/suspensión de la ejecución. Págs. 407, 699

Closed primary/Elección primaria cerrada Elección para una nominación partidista en la que sólo los miembros declarados del partido pueden votar. Pág. 182

Cloture/Limitación del debate Procedimiento que puede utilizarse para restringir o terminar un debate verbal de un cuerpo legislativo. Pág. 344

Coalition/Coalición Una alianza temporal de varios grupos que se agrupan para alcanzar el poder mayoritario y controlar el gobierno. Págs. 122, 628

Coattail effect/Efecto de refilón Efecto que produce un fuerte candidato a un puesto de elección, situado en primer sitio, mediante el cual ayuda a atraer votantes hacia otros candidatos de su mismo partido. Pág. 190

Cold war/Guerra Fría Periodo de más de 40 años de duración en el que las relaciones entre las dos superpotencias fueron por lo menos tensas, y a menudo hostiles. Época de amenazas y de desarrollo militar. Pág. 485

colleague/colega Compañero de trabajo. Pág. 277

Collective security/Seguridad colectiva Conservación de la paz y el orden internacionales. Pág. 485

Collectivization/Colectivización Hacer colectivos o propiedad del estado los medios de producción. Pág. 674

Commander in chief/Comandante en jefe Nombre que se da al Presidente en cuanto a que es el comandante de las fuerzas armadas de la nación. Pág. 355

Commerce and Slave Trade Compromise/Avenencia de comercio y trata de esclavos Acuerdo durante la Convención Constitucional que protegió los intereses de los dueños de esclavos, al negarle al Congreso el poder de gravar la exportación de bienes desde cualquier estado, así como el poder de actuar, durante 20 años, en contra de la trata de esclavos. Pág. 53

Commerce power/Poder mercantil Poder exclusivo del Congreso para regular el comercio interestatal e internacional. Pág. 297

Commission government/Junta municipal Gobierno formado por comisionados, titulares de distintos departamentos del gobierno de la ciudad, que se eligen por voto popular para formar el Consejo de la ciudad y, por consiguiente, reúnen los poderes legislativos y ejecutivos en un solo cuerpo. Pág. 728

Committee chairman/Presidente de comisión Miembro que encabeza una comisión permanente en un cuerpo legislativo. Pág. 325

Committee of the Whole/Comité Plenario Comité que consiste en la totalidad de un cuerpo legislativo; utilizado para un procedimiento mediante el cual un cuerpo legislativo da curso a sus asuntos transformándose en un comité en sí. Pág. 339

Common law/Derecho consuetudinario Ley no escrita sancionada por un juez y que se ha desarrollado a lo largo de los siglos con base a aquellas ideas generalmente aceptadas de lo bueno y lo malo que se han ganado un reconocimiento judicial. Pág. 702

Commune/Comuna Un grupo grande de diversas granjas colectivas. Pág. 675

Communism/Comunismo Ideología que exige la propiedad colectiva, o estatal, de la tierra y de otros medios de producción. Pág. 672

Commutation/Conmutación El poder de reducir (conmutar) la duración de una sentencia o el monto de la multa de un crimen.

Págs. 408, 699

Compromise/Compromiso Avenencia entre principios o sistemas opuestos, mediante la modificación de algún aspecto de cada uno de ellos. Pág. 20

Concurrent jurisdiction/Jurisdicción coincidente Poder compartido por cortes federales y estatales para atender ciertos casos. Pág. 508

Concurrent powers/Poderes concurrentes Aquellos poderes que el gobierno nacional y los estados poseen y ejercen. Pág. 93

Concurrent resolution/Resolución conjunta Enunciado de una posición sobre un asunto utilizado por la Cámara de Representantes y el Senado al actuar conjuntamente; no tiene la fuerza de la ley y no requiere la firma del Presidente. Pág. 335

Concurring opinión/Opinion coincidente Explicación escrita de los puntos de vista de uno o más jueces que apoyan una decisión alcanzada por una mayoría de la corte, pero en la que se desea añadir o recalcar un punto que no se remarcó en la decisión mayoritaria. Pág. 522

Confederation/Confederación Unión de diversos grupos para un propósito común. Págs. 15, 35

Conference committee/Comité de Consulta Comité conjunto temporal creado para reconciliar cualquier diferencia entre las versiones de las dos cámaras legislativas sobre una propuesta de ley. Pág. 333

Connecticut Compromise/Acuerdo de Connecticut Acuerdo alcanzado durante la Convención Constitucional respecto a que el Congreso debería estar integrado por un Senado en donde cada estado estuviera representado de manera igualitaria, y una Cámara de Representantes en la que la representación estuviera basada en la población de cada estado. Pág. 52

Consensus/Consenso Acuerdo general entre diversos grupos respecto a temas fundamentales; amplio acuerdo sobre temas varios. Págs. 121, 292, 636

Constituency/Distrito electoral Las personas e intereses que un funcionario elegido representa. Pág. 277

Constituent power/Poder constituyente Poder no legislativo de la elaboración de la Constitución y del proceso de enmiendas constitucionales. Pág. 692

Constitution/Constitución Cuerpo de leyes fundamentales que delinean los principios, las estructuras y los procesos de gobierno. Pág. 4

Constitutionalism/Constitucionalismo Principio básico que establece que el gobierno y los gobernantes deben obedecer la ley; el gobierno de la ley; ver limited government/gobierno limitado. Pág. 65

Containment/Contención Política basada en la creencia de que si el comunismo se pudiera limitar dentro de sus fronteras existentes, se derrumbaría bajo el peso de sus debilidades internas. Pág. 486

Content neutral/Voto neutral El gobierno no regulará a las asambleas en lo concerniente a lo que se expresará en ellas. Pág. 556

Continuing resolution/Resolución ininterrumpida Medida que permite que las agencies continuen funcionando sobre la base de las asignaciones del año anterior. Pág. 462

Continuous body/Cuerpo legislativo ininterrumpido Unidad gubernamental (por ejemplo, el Senado de Estados Unidos) cuya totalidad de escaños nunca se elige al mismo tiempo. Pág. 277

Controllable spending/Gasto controlable Cantidad de dinero decidida entre el Congreso y el Presidente y que señala el monto anual de muchos gastos gubernamentales individuales, como programas para protección del ambiente, ayuda a la educación, etcétera. Pág. 459

Copyright/Derechos de autor Derechos legales y exclusivos de una persona para reproducir, publicar y vender su trabajo creativo literario, artístico, o musical. Pág. 302

Council-manager government/Gobierno de consejo-superintendente Una modificación del gobierno de consejo-alcalde, que consiste en un vigoroso consejo de miembros elegido mediante un sufragio no partidista; un alcalde débil, elegido por el pueblo y un superintendente nombrado por el consejo; ver mayor-council government/gobierno de consejo-alcalde; ver también weak-mayor government/gobierno de alcalde débil. Pág. 728

County/Condado Una unidad importante de gobierno local en la gran parte de los estados. Pág. 718

Court-martial/Corte marcial Corte compuesta por personal militar para juzgar a los que están acusados de violar la ley militar. Pág. 525

Criminal case/Caso criminal Caso en el que se juzga al acusado por cometer un crimen, tal y como éste se define en la ley. Pág. 513

Criminal law/Derecho penal Área de la ley que define los agravios públicos y que establece su castigo. Pág. 704

Cultural Revolution/Revolución cultural Al comenzarse en 1966, los guardias rojos de Mao Tse Tung atacaron e intimidaron a los maestros, intelectuales y a cualquier otra persona que fuera sospechosa de carecer de fervor revolucionario e iniciaron un proceso para "reeducarlos". Pág. 650

Customs Duty/Derecho de aduana Impuesto gravado sobre los bienes traídos a los Estados Unidos desde el exterior, también se conoce como arancel, impuesto sobre importaciones o tasa sobre importaciones. Pág. 451

De facto segregation/Discriminación de facto o de hecho Segregación, incluso si la ley no lo exige, por ejemplo en la asignación de vivienda. Pág. 604

De jure segregation/Discriminación de jure o de ley Segregación con base en la ley, que implica una sanción legal. Pág. 604

Defendant/Acusado En un juicio civil, es la persona en contra de quien el demandante pide ejecutar una acción judicial; en un caso criminal, es la persona acusada de un crimen. Pág. 509

Deficit/Déficit La diferencia anual entre los ingresos y los egresos. Pág. 455

Deficit financing/Déficit financiero Práctica de subvencionar al gobierno mediante préstamos, a fin de compensar la diferencia entre los gastos y los ingresos gubernamentales. Pág. 296

Delegated powers/Poderes delegados Poderes explícitos, implícitos o inherentes que la Constitución transfiere al gobierno nacional. Pág. 89

Democracy/Democracia Forma de gobierno en donde la autoridad suprema reside en el pueblo. Pág. 5

Denaturalization/Desnaturalización Proceso en el que los ciudadanos naturalizados pueden perder su ciudadanía de manera involuntaria. Pág. 615

Deportation/Deportación Proceso legal mediante el que se les exige a los extranjeros que abandonen los Estados Unidos. Pág. 617

Détente/Relajamiento Disminución de las tensiones. Pág. 488

Deterrence/Disuasión Política de convertir a los Estados Unidos y sus aliados en una fuerza militar tan poderosa que su fortaleza desaliente, o prevenga, cualquier ataque. Pág. 485

Devolution/Delegación Transferencia de la autoridad del gobierno central a los gobiernos regionales. Pág. 631

Dictatorship/Dictadura Forma de gobierno en la que el líder ejerce poder y autoridad absolutos. Pág. 5

Diplomatic immunity/Inmunidad diplomática Cuando un embajador no está sujeto a las leyes del estado en el que se le acredita como tal. Pág. 471

Direct popular election/Elección popular directa Propuesta para abolir el colegio electoral y permitir que la gente elija de manera directa al Presidente y al Vicepresidente. Pág. 383

Direct primary/Elección primaria directa Elección realizada dentro de un partido para escoger a los candidatos del partido para una elección general. Pág. 182

Direct tax/Impuesto directo Gravamen que debe pagar la persona a la que se le impone; *ver* indirect tax/impuesto indirecto. Pág. 296

Discharge petition/Petición de exoneración Procedimiento que permite a los miembros autorizar una propuesta de ley que se ha estancado en una comisión de debate para su consideración. Pág. 336

Discrimination/Discriminación Prejuicio, injusticia. Pág. 570

Dissenting opinión/Opinión disidente Explicación escrita de los puntos de vista de uno o más jueces, que está(n) en desacuerdo con una decisión tomada por la mayoría de la corte; *ver* majority opinion/opinión mayoritaria. Pág. 522

Dissolution/Disolución Poder del Primer Ministro para disolver la Cámara de Representantes. Pág. 636

District Plan/Plan de Distrito Propuesta para elegir a los electores presidenciales, mediante la cual se seleccionarían dos electores en cada estado, de acuerdo con el voto popular de todo ese estado, y los otros electores se elegirían de manera separada en cada uno de los distritos del Congreso de ese estado. Pág. 382

Division of powers/División de poderes Principio básico del federalismo; las estipulaciones constitucionales que establecen que los poderes gubernamentales están separados de acuerdo con bases geográficas (en los Estados Unidos, se dividen entre el gobierno nacional y los estados). Págs. 15, 89

Docket/Agenda Lista de casos de una corte por atender. Pág. 513

Doctrine/Doctrina Principio de política fundamental. Pág. 308

Domestic affairs/Asuntos internos Todas cuestiones no conectadas al campo de los asuntos exteriores. Págs. 422, 468

Double jeopardy/Doble juicio Parte de la 5ª enmienda que establece que no se puede poner en riesgo la vida de una persona o su integridad física dos veces. Una vez que se ha juzgado por un crimen a una persona, no puede volvérsele a juzgar por el mismo delito. Pág. 578

Draft/Reclutamiento Conscripción o servicio militar obligatorio. Pág. 480

Due process/Proceso legal establecido El gobierno debe actuar con justicia y de acuerdo con las reglas establecidas en todo lo que hace. Pág. 564

Due Process Clause/Cláusula del proceso legal establecido Parte de la 14ª enmienda que garantiza que ningún estado negará los derechos básicos a su pueblo. Pág. 535

Economic protest parties/Partidos de protesta económica Partidos surgidos en tiempos de descontento económico, los cuales carecen de una base ideológica bien definida, están insatisfechos por las condiciones presentes y exigen mejores épocas. Pág. 133

Electoral college/Colegio electoral Grupo de personas (electores presidenciales) elegidos cada cuatro años en todos los estados y en el Distrito de Columbia a fin de hacer una elección formal del Presidente y Vicepresidente. Págs. 81, 366

Electoral votes/Votos electorales Votos emitidos por los electores en el Colegio electoral. Pág. 365

Electorate/Electorado Todas las personas que tienen derecho a votar en una elección determinada. Págs. 129, 148, 383

Eminent domain/Dominio supremo Poder de un gobierno de expropiar la propiedad privada para uso público. Pág. 304

Enabling act/Ley de habilitación Una ley del Congreso que orienta al pueblo de un territorio de los Estados Unidos para que redacte una constitución propuesta para el estado, como un paso hacia la admisión de dicho estado dentro de la Unión. Pág. 99

English Bill of Rights/Declaración inglesa de los derechos Documento redactado por el Parlamento y aceptado por William y Mary de Inglaterra en 1689, elaborado para evitar el abuso del poder por parte de los monarcas ingleses; constituye la base de muchas cosas del gobierno y la política estadounidenses actuales. Pág. 30

Engross/Transcribir Imprimir un proyecto de ley en su forma final. Pág. 340

Entitlement/Derecho Beneficio que la ley federal establece que se debe pagar a todos los que cumplan los requisitos para ser elegibles, por ejemplo: el seguro médico, bonos de comida y pensión para los veteranos. Pág. 458, 735

Entrepreneur/Empresario Individuo con el impulso y la ambición de combinar los recursos de la tierra, la mano de obra y el capital para producir bienes u ofrecer servicios. Pág. 659

Espionage/Espionaje Acto de espiar. Pág. 477

Establishment Clause/Cláusula del establecimiento Separa a la iglesia del estado. Pág. 537

Estate tax/Impuesto testamentario Gravamen sobre los bienes de una persona que muere. Págs. 451, 742

Ex post facto law/Ley ex post facto Ley que se aplica a un acto cometido con anterioridad a la aprobación de la ley. Pág. 577

Excise tax/Impuesto al consumo Gravamen sobre la manufactura, venta o consumo de bienes y/o al suministro de servicios. Pág. 451

Exclusionary rule/Regla de exclusión Evidencia obtenida como resultado de una acción ilegal de la policía y que no puede utilizarse contra la persona arrestada. Pág. 573

Exclusive jurisdiction/Jurisdicción exclusiva Poder exclusivo de las cortes federales para atender ciertos casos. Pág. 508

Exclusive powers/Poderes exclusivos Poderes que pueden ejercerse sólo por el gobierno nacional. Pág. 93

Executive agreement/Acuerdo ejecutivo Pacto hecho de manera directa por el Presidente con otro jefe de un estado extranjero; un pacto internacional obligatorio con la fuerza de la ley pero que no requiere (a diferencia de un tratado) de la aprobación del Senado. Págs. 80, 400

Executive Article/Artículo del ejecutivo El segundo artículo de la Constitución. Define la presidencia y le otorga el poder ejecutivo del gobierno federal al Presidente. Pág. 390

Executive departments/Oficinas del poder ejecutivo A menudo llamadas oficinas del gabinete; son las unidades tradicionales de la administración federal. Pág. 424

Executive Office of the President/Oficina ejecutiva del Presidente Una organización compleja, que abarca diversas oficinas separadas, cuyo personal está compuesto por los consejeros y asistentes más cercanos al Presidente. Pág. 419

Executive order/Orden ejecutiva Directiva, regla o reglamento expedida por un primer mandatario o por sus subordinados, con base en su autoridad estatutaria o constitucional y la cual tiene fuerza de ley. Pág. 394

Executive power/Poder ejecutivo Poder para ejecutar, administrar y obligar al cumplimiento de la ley. Pág. 4

Expatriation/Expatriación Proceso legal mediante el cual ocurre la pérdida de ciudadanía. Pág. 614

Expressed powers/Poderes explícitos Aquellos poderes delegados del gobierno nacional que se señalan explícitamente en la Constitución; también se conocen como los "poderes ennumerados." Págs. 89, 290

Extradition/Extradición Proceso legal a través del cual un fugitivo de la justicia en un estado se envía a ese estado. Pág. 107

Faction/Facción Un grupo disidente. Pág. 127

Factors of production/Factores de producción Recursos básicos que se utilizan para elaborar todos los bienes y servicios. Pág. 658

Federal budget/Presupuesto federal Documento financiero detallado que contienen las estimaciones de las recaudaciones y gastos que anticipan los ingresos y egresos federales durante el año fiscal venidero. Pág. 421

Federal government/Gobierno federal Forma de gobierno en la que los poderes están divididos entre un gobierno central y diversos gobiernos locales. Pág. 14

Federalism/Federalismo Sistema de gobierno en el que una constitución escrita divide los poderes del gobierno, sobre una base territorial, entre un gobierno central (o nacional) y diversos gobiernos regionales. Págs. 70, 88

Federalists/Federalistas Personas que apoyaron la ratificación de la Constitución en 1787–1788. Pág. 56

Felony/Felonía Un crimen grave que puede castigarse con una gran multa, la prisión o incluso la muerte. Pág. 704

Filibuster/Obstrucción Diversas tácticas (por lo general, prolongar el debate verbal) dirigidas a derrotar una propuesta de ley en un cuerpo legislativo, evitando así que se tenga un voto final; a menudo se asocia con el Senado de los Estados Unidos; *ver* cloture/limitación del debate. Pág. 343

Fiscal year/Año fiscal Periodo de 12 meses utilizado por el gobierno y el mundo de los negocios para su contabilidad, presupuesto, recaudación de ingresos y otros propósitos financieros. Pág. 421

Five-year plan/Plan quinquenal Plan que hace proyecciones sobre el desarrollo económico durante los siguientes cinco años. Pág. 673

Floor leaders/Líderes de fracciones partidistas Miembros de la Cámara de Representantes y del Senado elegidos por sus partidos con el objeto de llevar a cabo las decisiones partidistas e impulsar la acción legislativa a fin de que cumplan con los propósitos partidistas. Pág. 324

Foreign Affairs/Asuntos exteriores Relaciones de una nación con otros países. Pág. 468

Foreign aid/Ayuda extranjera Auxilio militar y económico a otros países. Pág. 491

Foreign policy/Política exterior Conjunto de políticas conformado por todas las posturas y acciones que una nación asume en cada uno de los aspectos de sus relaciones con otros países; todo lo que el gobierno de una nación expresa y hace respecto a los asuntos mundiales. Pág. 469

Formal amendment/Enmienda formal Cambio o adición que se convierte en parte del lenguaje escrito de la Constitución misma, mediante uno de los cuatro métodos enunciados de la Constitución. Pág. 73

Framers/Redactores Grupo de delegados que esbozaron la Constitución de los Estados Unidos en la Convención de Filadelfia en 1787. Pág. 48

Franchise/Sufragio Derecho a votar. Pág. 148

Franking privilege/Exención de franquicia Beneficio otorgado a los miembros del Congreso que les permite enviar por correo cartas y otros materiales sin pagar los derechos del correo. Pág. 283

Free enterprise system/Sistema de libre empresa Sistema económico caracterizado por la propiedad privada o corporativa de los bienes de capital; inversiones que están determinadas por una decisión privada, en vez del control estatal, y están sujetas a un mercado libre. Págs. 20, 659

Free Exercise Clause/Cláusula de la libertad de cultos Segunda parte de la garantía constitucional de libertad religiosa, que garantiza a todo mundo el derecho de creer en lo que ella escoja en materia de religión. Pág. 542

Full Faith and Credit Clause/Cláusula de fe y crédito cabal Requisito constitucional (Artículo IV, Sección 1) según el cual cada estado acepta (da "fe y crédito cabal") los actos públicos, documentos y procedimientos judiciales de cualquier otro estado. Pág. 106

Fundamental law/Ley fundamental Leyes de importancia primordial y duradera que no se cambiarán con facilidad. Pág. 686

Gender gap/Brecha de género Diferencias medibles entre las elecciones partidistas actuales de hombres y mujeres. Pág. 169

General election/Elección general Elección programada regularmente en la que los votantes hacen una selección final de los funcionarios públicos. Pág. 179

Gerrymandering/Demarcación arbitraria Establecimiento de los límites de los distritos electorales de modo que den ventaja a un partido. Págs. 159, 271

Gift tax/Impuesto a los regalos Gravamen sobre los regalos dados por una persona viva. Pág. 451

Glasnost/Glásnost Política de apertura bajo la cual el gobierno ruso incrementó su tolerancia a la disensión y a la libertad de expresión. Pág. 646

Gosplan/Gosplán Importante oficina de la Unión Soviética, creada por Stalin, para llevar a cabo la planificación centralizada. Pág. 674

Government/Gobierno Institución mediante la cual una sociedad lleva a cabo y hace cumplir sus políticas públicas. Está compuesto por aquellas personas que ejercen sus poderes, aquellos que tienen autoridad y control sobre el pueblo. Pág. 4

Government corporation/Corporación gubernamental Instituciones dentro de la rama ejecutiva que están sujetas a la dirección y control del Presidente, formadas por el Congreso para que realicen determinadas actividades de tipo empresarial. Pág. 434

Grand jury/Gran Jurado El dispositivo formal a través del cual puede acusarse a una persona de un crimen serio. Pág. 577

Grants-in-aid program/Programa de subvención de fondos públicos Subvenciones de dinero federal o de otros recursos para los estados y/o sus ciudades, condados y otras unidades locales. Pág. 101

Grass roots/Fundamentos De extracción popular, los votantes promedio. Pág. 253

Great Leap Forward/Gran salto hacia adelante Plan quinquenal de 1958 que fue un intento de modernizar rápidamente a China. Pág. 675

Hard money/Fondos fiscalizados Dinero de campaña que está sujeto a las regulaciones de la FEC. Pág. 202

Heterogeneous/Hetereogéneo De diferente raza, familia o especie; compuesto por una mezcla de elementos. Pág. 594

Ideological parties/Partidos ideológicos Partidos basados en un conjunto determinado de creencias, un punto de vista comprehensivo sobre asuntos sociales, económicos y políticos. Pág. 132

Immigrant/Inmigrante Persona que es admitida legalmente en calidad de residente permanente de un país. Pág. 594

Impeach/Impugnar Fincar cargos formales en contra de un funcionario público; la Cámara de Representantes tienen el exclusivo poder de impugnar a los funcionarios públicos de los Estados Unidos. Pág. 311

Imperial presidency/Presidencia imperial Término utilizado para describir a un Presidente como "emperador", quien actúa sin consultar al Congreso o de manera secreta para evadir o engañarlo. Pág. 392

Implied powers/Poderes implícitos Aquellos poderes delegados del gobierno nacional que se sugieren o están implícitos por los poderes explícitos; aquellos que son "necesarios y apropiados" para realizar los poderes explícitos; *ver* delegated powers/poderes delegados, expressed powers/poderes explícitos. Págs. 90, 290

Income tax/Impuesto sobre el ingreso Gravamen sobre el ingreso de los individuos y/o corporaciones. Pág. 741

Incorporation/Incorporación Proceso mediante el cual un estado establece a una ciudad como un cuerpo legal. Pág. 726

Incumbent/Titular El funcionario público actual. Pág. 127

Independent agencies/Oficinas independientes Agencias adicionales creadas por el Congreso y que se ubican fuera de los departamentos del gabinete. Pág. 430

Independent executive agencies/Oficinas ejecutivas independientes Agencias que incluyen a la mayor parte de las agencias independientes, que están organizadas de una forma muy similar a los departamentos del gabinete y cuyo titular es un administrador que tiene subunidades operativas regionales pero que carece del estatus del gabinete. Pág. 431

Independent regulatory commissions/Comisiones regulatorias independientes Agencias independientes cuya función es regular aspectos importantes de la economía de la nación, en su mayoría fuera del control y dirección del Presidente. Pág. 431

Independents/Independientes Término usado para describir a las personas que carecen de filiación partidista. Pág. 171

Indictment/Denuncia Queja formal que el fiscal expone ante un gran jurado, que incluye cargos al acusado por uno o más crímenes. Pág. 578

Indirect tax/Impuesto indirecto Gravamen a una parte pero transferido a otra para su pago. Pág. 296

Inferior courts/Cortes inferiores Las cortes federales menores, que están por debajo de la Corte Suprema. Pág. 507

Informal amendment/Enmienda informal Cambio en la Constitución que no se hace mediante una enmienda escrita, sino por la experiencia del gobierno bajo la Constitución; los métodos incluyen: (1) aprobación de la legislación básica por parte del Congreso; (2) acciones llevadas a cabo por el Presidente; (3) decisiones clave de la Corte Suprema; (4) actividades de los partidos políticos; y (5) costumbre. Pág. 79

Information/Información Acusación oficial presentada por un acusador sin acción de parte del jurado. Pág. 704

Inherent powers/Poderes inherentes Aquellos poderes delegados del gobierno nacional que le pertenecen de manera inherente, debido a que es el gobierno de un estado soberano de la comunidad mundial. Págs. 91, 290

Inheritance tax/Impuesto sobre la herencia Gravamen sobre la parte de la herencia del beneficiario. Pág. 742

Initiative/Iniciativa Proceso en el que determinado número de votantes calificados firman peticiones a favor de una propuesta, la cual se pasa después directamente a la cédula de votación. Pág. 687

Injunction/Mandato Orden judicial que fuerza o limita el desempeño de determinado acto, mediante la intervención de un individuo privado o un funcionario público. Pág. 161

Integration/Integración El proceso de ofrecer a un grupo una pertenencia igualitaria dentro de la sociedad. Pág. 603

Interest/Interés Cargo que se hace por el dinero prestado, por lo general es un porcentaje de la cantidad prestada. Pág. 454

Interest group/Grupo de interés Organizaciones privadas cuyos miembros comparten determinados puntos de vista y trabajan para dar forma a las políticas públicas. Pág. 216

Interstate compact/Pacto interestatal Acuerdo formal suscrito con el consentimiento del Congreso, entre dos estados o entre un estado y un estado extranjero, el cual está autorizado por la Constitución. (Artículo I, Sección 10). Pág. 105

Involuntary servitude/Servidumbre involuntaria Trabajo forzado. Pág. 569

Isolationism/Aislacionismo Rechazo voluntario a verse involucrado, de manera general, en los asuntos del resto del mundo. Pág. 468

Item veto/Veto de artículo Un gobernador puede vetar uno o más artículos de una propuesta de ley, sin que rechace toda la medida. Pág. 699

Jim Crow law/Ley Jim Crow Tipo de ley que separa a un grupo de personas del resto de la gente, con base en la raza, dirigido principalmente a los afroamericanos. Pág. 602

Joint committee/Comité conjunto Comité legislativo compuesto por miembros de ambas cámaras. Pág. 333

Joint resolution/Resolución conjunta Propuesta de acción que tiene la fuerza de ley cuando se aprueba; a menudo tiene que ver con circunstancias especiales o asuntos temporales. Pág. 335

Judicial power/Poder judicial Poder para interpretar las leyes, determinar su significado y resolver las disputas que surgen dentro de la sociedad. Pág. 4

Judicial review/Revisión judicial Poder de una corte para determinar la constitucionalidad de una acción gubernamental. Pág. 69

Jurisdiction/Jurisdicción Autoridad de una corte para atender (juzgar y decidir) un caso. Pág 508

Jury/Jurado Conjunto de personas seleccionadas de acuerdo con la ley para que escuchan la evidencia y deciden cuestiones de hechos en un caso de la corte. Pág. 704

Jus sanguinis/*Jus sanguinis* Ley de la sangre que define la ciudadanía con base en la ciudadanía de los padres. Pág. 613

Jus soli/*Jus soli* Ley del territorio que determina la ciudadanía con base en el lugar de nacimiento de la persona. Pág. 613

Justice of the Peace/Juez de paz Juez que está en el nivel inferior del sistema judicial estatal y preside las cortes de justicia. Pág. 707

Keynote address/Discurso de apertura Alocución dada en una convención de partido para establecer el tono de la convención y de la futura campaña. Pág. 373

Labor union/Sindicato laboral Organización de trabajadores que comparten el mismo tipo de trabajo, o que laboran en la misma industria y que presiona por lograr políticas gubernamentales que beneficien a sus miembros. Pág. 244

Laissez-faire theory/Teoría del dejar hacer Teoría que sugiere que el gobierno debería desempeñar un papel limitado dentro de la sociedad. Pág. 662

Law of supply and demand/Ley de la oferta y la demanda Ley que establece que cuando los suministros de bienes y servicios son abundantes, entonces los precios tienden a bajar. Cuando los suministros escasean, entonces los precios tienden a subir. Págs. 21, 661

Legal tender/Moneda de curso legal Cualquier moneda que un acreedor debe aceptar, por ley, como pago de deudas. Pág. 299

Legislative power/Poder legislativo Poder para hacer una ley y redactar políticas públicas. Pág. 4

Libel/Libelo Utilización falsa y maliciosa de las palabras impresas. Pág. 546

Liberal constructionist/Construccionista liberal Aquel que argumenta una amplia interpretación de las estipulaciones de la Constitución, en particular las que otorgan poderes al gobierno federal. Pág. 291

Limited government/Gobierno limitado Principio básico del sistema estadounidense de gobierno que establece que el gobierno está restringido en cuanto a lo que puede hacer, y en donde el individuo tiene ciertos derechos que el gobierno no puede enajenar; *ver* constitutionalism/constitucionalismo, popular sovereignty/soberanía popular. Págs. 29, 685

Line agency/Agencia del ramo Oficina que desempeña las tareas para las que la organización existe. Pág. 418

Line-item veto/Veto de partida Cancelación presidencial de ciertas cantidades de dólares (partidas) de una cuenta de gastos del Congreso; este veto se instituyó en 1996 mediante una ley del Congreso, pero la Suprema Corte lo derogó en 1998. Pág. 406

Literacy/Alfabetismo Capacidad de una persona para leer o escribir. Pág. 156

Lobbying/Cabildeo Actividades mediante las que las presiones de un grupo se aplican a los legisladores y al proceso legislativo, incluyendo todos los métodos utilizados por el grupo para

Spanish Glossary

dirir las presiones hacia todos los aspectos del proceso de creación de políticas públicas. Pág. 251

Magistrate/Magistrado Juez que atiende a demandas civiles menores y casos de faltas leves que surgen en un contexto urbano. Pág. 708

Magna Carta/Carta Magna Constitución que los barones impusieron al rey John de Inglaterra en 1215; estableció el principio de que el poder del monarca no era absoluto y garantizó los derechos fundamentales, como el de un juicio con jurado y procesos establecidos legales para la nobleza. Pág. 29

Major parties/Partidos principales En la política estadounidense, los partidos Demócrata y Republicano. Pág. 116

Majority opinion/Opinión mayoritaria Llamada oficialmente Opinión de la Corte; anuncia la decisión de la Corte sobre el caso y describe el razonamiento sobre el que ésta se basa. Pág. 522

Mandate/Mandato Las intrucciones u órdenes que un grupo de votantnes da a sus funcionarios electos. Pág. 216

Market economy/Economía de mercado Un sistema económico en el que se basa las decisiones de la producción y el consumo de bienes en el intercambio voluntario de mercados. Pág. 669

Mass media/Medios masivos de comunicación Aquellos medios de comunicación que llegan a grandes audiencias, sobre todo la radio, televisión, publicaciones impresas e Internet. Págs. 211, 391

Mayor-council government/Gobierno de consejo-alcalde El más antiguo y más utilizado tipo de gobierno municipal: un alcalde electo como Presidente y un consejo electo como su cuerpo legislativo. Pág. 726

Medicaid/*Medicaid* Programa administrado por el Senado para proporcionar seguro médico a las familias de bajos ingresos. Pág. 735

Medium/Medio Un medio de comunicación; algo que transmite información. Pág. 223

Mestizo/Mestizo Persona que tiene ancestros portugueses o españoles e indios americanos. Pág. 639

Metropolitan area/Área metropolitana La ciudad y el área que le circunda. Pág. 731

Minister/Ministro Miembro del gabinete, y más frecuentemente de la Cámara de los Comunes. Pág. 629

Minor party/Partido minoritario Partido político que no cuenta con gran apoyo. Pág. 119

Miranda Rule/Regla Miranda Derechos constitucionales que la policía debe especificar a un sospechoso antes de que pueda hacérsele una interrogación. Pág. 582

Misdemeanor/Falta leve Delito menor que se castiga mediante una pequeña multa o un breve período de encarcelamiento. Pág. 704

Mixed economy/Economía mixta Sistema económico en donde la iniciativa privada existe en combinación con una considerable regulación y promoción gubernamental. Pág. 21

Monarchy/Monarquía Gobierno encabezado por un gobernante hereditario. Pág. 627

Monopoly/Monopolio Empresa que es la única fuente de un producto o servicio. Pág. 661

Multiparty/Multipartidista Sistema en el que varios partidos importantes y muchos secundarios existen, compiten seriamente y en realidad ganan puestos de elección popular. Pág. 122

National Bonus Plan/Plan de bono nacional Propuesta para elegir al Presidente y Vicepresidente, mediante el cual se le otorgaría una suma nacional de 102 votos electorales al ganador del voto popular, además de los votos del colegio electoral de su estado. Si ningún candidato recibe al menos 321 votos electorales, se llevaría a cabo una elección complementaria. Pág. 384

National convention/Convención nacional Reunión en la que los delegados de un partido votan para elegir a sus candidatos a la presidencia y vicepresidencia. Pág. 372

Nationalization/Nacionalización Adquisición gubernamental de la industria privada para uso público. Pág. 642

Naturalization/Naturalización Proceso legal mediante el cual los ciudadanos de un país se convierten en ciudadanos de otro. Págs. 302, 614

Necessary and Proper Clause/Cláusula de necesidad y conveniencia Cláusula constitucional que otorga al Congreso el poder de expedir leyes "necesarias y convenientes" para el ejercicio de sus poderes; *ver* implied powers/poderes implícitos. Pág. 305

New Jersey Plan/Plan Nueva Jersey Plan presentado en la Convención Constitucional como una alternativa al Plan Virginia; proponía una legislatura unicameral en la que cada estado estuviera representado de forma equitativa. Pág. 51

Nomination/Nominación Proceso de selección de candidatos en una democracia. Pág. 178

Nonpartisan election/Elección no partidista Elección en la que los candidatos no están identificados por membretes de partidos. Pág. 184

North American Free Trade Agreement/Tratado de Libre Comercio de Norteamérica Acuerdo que elimina las restricciones comerciales entre los Estados Unidos, Canadá y México, con lo cual se incrementa el comercio transfronterizo. Pág. 642

Oath of office/Juramento al asumir un cargo Juramento que hace el Presidente el día que asume la presidencia, jurando "cumplir fielmente" con sus responsabilidades, así como "preservar, proteger y defender" la Constitución. Pág. 393

Off-year election/Elección intermedia Elección del Congreso que ocurre entre las elecciones presidenciales. Págs. 164, 269

Oligarchy/Oligarquía Forma de gobierno en la que el poder de gobernar lo ejerce una elite pequeña y por lo general autonombrada. Pág. 13

One-party system/Sistema unipartidista Sistema político en el que sólo existe un partido. Pág. 123

Open primary/Elección primaria abierta Elección partidista de nominación en la que cualquier votante calificado puede tomar parte. Pág. 183

Opinion leader/Líder de opinión Cualquier persona que por alguna razón tiene una poderosa influencia en los puntos de vista de otras. Pág. 212

Ordinance power/Poder de decreto Poder del Presidente de emitir órdenes ejecutivas; se fundamenta en la Constitución y en los actos del Congreso. Pág. 394

Original jurisdiction/Jurisdicción original Poder de una corte de atender un caso antes que otra corte. Pág. 509

Oversight function/Función de vigilancia Revisión de las políticas y los programas de la rama ejecutiva por parte de los comités legislativos. Pág. 281

Pardon/Perdón Exoneración del castigo o de las consecuencias legales de un crimen que lleva a cabo el Presidente (en el caso federal) o el gobernador (en el caso estatal). Págs. 407, 699

Parliamentary government/Gobierno parlamentario Forma de gobierno en la que la rama ejecutiva está conformada por el primer ministro, o premier, y el gabinete oficial. Pág. 16

Parochial/Parroquial Relacionado con la iglesia, como las escuelas parroquiales. Pág. 538

Parole/Liberación bajo palabra Libertad condicional de un prisionero poco antes de que termine el lapso de su sentencia original. Pág. 699

Partisan/Partidista Legislador que le debe fidelidad, en primer lugar, a su partido político, por lo que vota de acuerdo con la línea del partido. Pág. 281

Partisanship/Partidarismo Acción gubernamental basada en la vigorosa fidelidad a un partido político. Pág. 117

Party caucus/Junta de dirigentes de partido Reunión cerrada de los miembros de la Cámara de Representantes o del Senado; también se conoce como Conferencia de partido. Pág. 324

Party identification/Identificación con el partido Lealtad de la gente hacia un partido político. Pág. 171

Party in power/Partido en el poder En la política estadounidense, el partido en el poder es aquel que controla la rama ejecutiva; es decir la presidencia, a nivel nacional, o la gubernatura, a nivel estatal. Pág. 118

Patent/Patente Licencia expedida a un inventor para garantizar el derecho exclusivo de manufactura, uso o venta de su invento, durante un tiempo limitado. Pág. 303

Patronage/Patrocinio Práctica de dar trabajo a los simpatizantes y amigos. Pág. 438

Payroll tax/Impuesto sobre la nómina Gravamen tasado a casi todos los empleadores y sus empleados, así como a las personas autoempleadas; cantidad debida por los empleados que se les descuenta de su salario. Pág. 450

Peer group/Grupo de camaradas Gente con la que uno se asocia regularmente y que incluye a socios, amigos, compañeros de clase, vecinos y compañeros de trabajo. Pág. 212

Perestroika/**Perestroika** Reestructuración de la vida política y económica durante el gobierno de Mijail Gorbachov. Pág. 646

Perjury/Perjurio El hecho de mentir bajo juramento. Pág. 311

Persona non grata/Persona *non grata* Una persona que no es bienvenida; se utiliza para describir a los funcionarios diplomáticos destituidos. Pag. 401

Petition of Right/Solicitud de Derecho Documento preparado por el Parlamento y firmado por el rey Charles I de Inglaterra en 1628; cuestionó la idea del derecho divino de los reyes y declaró que incluso el monarca está sujeto a las leyes de la tierra. Pág. 30

Picketing/Vigilancia Manifestación de los trabajadores en el sitio donde están en huelga. Pág. 551

Plaintiff/Demandante En el derecho civil, la parte que entabla un juicio u otra acción legal contra otra (el demandado) en una corte. Pág. 509

Platform/Plataforma Un enunciado formal por parte de un partido político respecto a sus principios básicos, opiniones sobre cuestiones políticas importantes y objetivos. Pág. 373

Pluralistic society/Sociedad pluralista Sociedad que está formada por distintos grupos y culturas. Pág. 121

Plurality/Mayoría En una elección, el número de votos que el candidato que va a la punta tiene de ventaja sobre su competidor más cercano. Pág. 120

Pocket veto/Veto indirecto Tipo de veto que el Presidente puede utilizar después de que una legislatura se suspende; se aplica cuando un Presidente no firma formalmente o rechaza una propuesta de ley, dentro del tiempo comprendido para eso; *ver* Veto. Pág. 346

Police power/Facultad policial Autoridad de cada estado para proteger y promover la salud pública, la seguridad, la moral y el bienestar general de su pueblo. Págs. 566, 691

Political Action Committee/Comité de acción política Extensión política de grupos de interés especiales, los cuales tienen un gran interés en la política pública. Pág. 197

Political efficacy/Eficacia política La influencia o eficacia individual en la política. Pág. 166

Political party/Partido político Grupo de personas que buscan controlar el gobierno mediante el triunfo en las elecciones y la conservación de los puestos públicos. Pág. 116

Political socialization/Socialización política Proceso mediante el que la gente obtiene sus actitudes y opiniones políticas. Pág. 168

Politico/Político Legislador que intenta equilibrar los elementos básicos de los miembros del directorio, los delegados y los roles partidistas; *ver* trustee/independiente, delegate/delegado,

partisan/partidista. Pág. 281

Poll book/Padrón electoral Lista de todos los votantes registrados en cada distrito. Pág. 155

Poll tax/Impuesto sobre el padrón electoral Gravamen especial, exigido por los estados como una condición para votar. Pág. 157

Polling place/Casilla electoral Lugar donde los votantes que viven en cierto distrito acuden a votar. Pág. 190

Popular sovereignty/Soberanía popular Principio básico del sistema estadounidense de gobierno que establece que el pueblo es la fuente de todos los poderes gubernamentales, y que el gobierno sólo puede existir con el consentimiento de los gobernados. Págs. 39, 685

Preamble/Preámbulo Introducción. Pág. 65

Precedent/Precedente Decisión judicial que se toma como un ejemplo a seguir en el futuro para casos similares. Págs. 522, 703

Precinct/Distrito Unidad mínima de la administración electoral; distrito de votación. Págs. 140, 190

Preclearance/Preautorización Ordenada por la Ley de Derechos de Votos de 1965, respecto a la aprobación anterior, por parte del Departamento de Justicia, de los cambios en las leyes electorales existentes o nuevas en ciertos estados. Pág. 162

Prefecture/Prefectura Las 47 subdivisiones en las que se divide Japón. Pág. 637

Preliminary hearing/Audiencia preliminar El primer paso del procesamiento de un crimen mayor, en el que el juez decide si la evidencia basta para que la persona comparezca ante el gran jurado o ante el fiscal para ser sujeto de una acción. Pág. 708

President of the Senate/Presidente del Senado Funcionario que preside un Senado; en el Congreso es el Vicepresidente de los Estados Unidos; en la legislatura estatal, cualquier vicegobernador o un senador. Pág. 323

President *pro tempore*/Presidente *pro tempore* Miembro del Senado de Estados Unidos, o de la cámara superior de la legislatura estatal, elegido para ser Presidente, en caso de ausencia del Presidente del Senado. Pág. 323

Presidential elector/Elector presidencial Persona elegida por los votantes para representarlos en la selección formal del Presidente y Vicepresidente. Pág. 365

Presidential government/Gobierno presidencial Forma de gobierno en la que las ramas ejecutivas y legislativas del gobierno están separadas, son independientes y están en la misma jerarquía. Pág. 15

Presidential primary/Elección presidencial primaria Elección en la que los votantes de un partido: (1) eligen a varios o a todos los delegados de la organización partidista estatal para la convención nacional de su partido, y/o (2) expresan una preferencia por alguno de los distintos contendientes para la nominación presidencial de su partido. Pág. 369

Presidential succession/Sucesión presidencial Plan mediante el cual se resuelve la vacante presidencial. Pág. 359

Presidential Succession Act of 1947/Ley para la sucesión presidencial de 1947 Ley que especifica el orden para la sucesión presidencial, después del Vicepresidente. Pág. 360

Presiding officer/Primer funcionario Presidente. Pág. 45

Preventive detention/Arresto preventivo Ley que permite a los jueces federales ordenar que un acusado de felonía sea arrestado, sin derecho a fianza, cuando existen buenas razones para creer que cometerá otro crimen grave antes del juicio. Pág. 586

Prior restraint/Prohibición anticipada El gobierno no puede reprimir las ideas antes de que se expresen. Pág. 549

Privatization/Privatización Regresar las empresas nacionales a la iniciativa privada. Pág. 675

Privileges and Immunities Clause/Cláusula de privilegios e inmunidades Estipulación constitucional (Artículo IV, Sección 2), en que se conceden ciertos "privilegios e inmunidades" a los ciudadanos, sin importar su estado de residencia; ningún estado puede hacer distinciones no razonables entre sus propios residentes y aquellas personas que vivan en otros estados. Pág. 107

Probable Cause/Causa probable Fundamentos razonables, sospecha razonable de un crimen. Pág. 571

Procedural due process/Procesos legales establecidos El gobierno debe emplear procedimientos y métodos justos. Pág. 565

Process of incorporation/Proceso de incorporación Proceso de integrar, o incluir, la mayor parte de las garantías de la Declaración de los derechos en la Cláusula de proceso legal establecido de la 14a enmienda. Pág. 535

Progressive tax/Impuesto progresivo Tipo de impuesto que es proporcional con el ingreso. Págs. 449, 742

Project grant/Subvención de proyecto Tipo de subvención de fondos públicos; proporcionada para proyectos específicos de los estados, las localidades y las oficinas privadas que la solicitan. Pág. 103

Proletariat/Proletariado La clase trabajadora. Pág. 667

Propaganda/Propaganda Una técnica inmoral de persuasión orientada a influir en los comportamientos individuales o colectivos con el objeto de originar una creencia particular, independientemente de su validez. Pág. 249

Property tax/Impuesto a la propiedad Gravamen sobre los bienes raíces y la propiedad personal. Pág. 742

Proportional plan/Plan proporcional Propuesta para seleccionar electores presidenciales, mediante la cual cada candidato recibiría la misma cantidad de votos electorales de un estado que recibió durante la votación popular del estado. Pág. 382

Proportional representation rule/Regla de la representación proporcional Procedimiento aplicado en las elecciones primarias del partido Demócrata, en el cual cualquier candidato que gane al menos el 15% de los votos emitidos en una elección primaria, obtienen el número de delegados a la convención estatal demócrata, que le corresponda a esa proporción de las primarias. Pág. 371

Proprietary/Propiedad Organizada por un dueño (persona a quien el rey le ha otorgado tierras). Pág. 32

Prorogue/Prórroga Aplazamiento, como en la sesión legislativa. Pág. 265

Public affairs/Asuntos públicos Aquellos acontecimientos y asuntos que importan al público en general, por ejemplo: la política, los temas públicos y la determinación de las políticas públicas. Págs. 208, 239

Public agenda/Agenda pública Asuntos públicos sobre los cuales está enfocada la atención de las personas. Pág. 228

Public debt/Deuda pública Todo el dinero que ha pedido prestado el gobierno a lo largo de los años y que todavía no paga, además del interés acumulado sobre ese capital; también se conoce como deuda nacional o deuda federal. Págs. 296, 455

Public-interest group/Grupo de interés público Grupo de interés que busca instituir determinadas políticas públicas de beneficio para la mayoría de las personas de su país, sin importar si pertenecen o apoyan a la organización. Pág. 247

Public opinion/Opinión pública Colección compleja de opiniones de diversas personas; la suma de todos sus puntos de vista. Pág. 209

Public opinion poll/Encuestas de opinión pública Dispositivos que intentan recolectar información al hacerle preguntas a las personas. Pág. 217

Public policy/Políticas públicas Todas las metas que un gobierno se fija, así como los distintos cursos de acción que toma en sus intentos por llevar a cabo esos objetivos. Págs. 4, 236

Purge/Purga Proceso de revisión de las listas de los votantes registrados y de la eliminación de los nombres que ya no son elegibles para votar; una depuración. Págs. 155, 645

Quasi-judicial/Cuasi-judicial Que tiene que ver con los poderes que en alguna forma son judiciales. Pág. 433

Quasi-legislative/Cuasi-legislativo Que tiene que ver con poderes que son legislativos en cierta medida. Pág. 433

Quorum/Quórum Mínimo número de miembros que debe estar presente para que un cuerpo legislativo funcione; mayoría. Págs. 58, 339

Quota/Cuota Regla que requiere que determinado número de trabajos o ascensos se den en miembros de ciertos grupos. Pág. 610

Quota sample/Muestra de cuota Muestra deliberadamente hecha para reflejar ciertas características importantes de una determinada población. Pág. 219

Random sample/Muestra aleatoria Determinado número de gente seleccionada al azar y que vive en ciertos lugares seleccionados de manera aleatoria. Pág. 218

Ratification/Ratificación Aprobación formal, consentimiento definitivo de la eficacia de una constitución, de una enmienda constitucional o de un tratado. Pág. 44

Reapportion/Reasignación Redistribución, como los escaños en un cuerpo legislativo. Pág. 267

Recall/Retirada inesperada Procedimiento de petición por el que los votantes puedan destituir a un funcionario oficial antes de terminar su mandato. Pág. 696

Recognition/Reconocimiento El poder exclusivo de un Presidente para reconocer (establecer relaciones diplomáticas) a estados extranjeros. Pág. 400

Redress/Resarcir Satisfacer una queja, por lo general mediante un pago. Pág. 524

Referendum/Referendo Proceso mediante el cual una medida legislativa se consulta con los votantes de los estados para su aprobación o rechazo final. Pág. 693

Refugee/Refugiado Persona que abandona su hogar para buscar protección contra la guerra, la persecución o algún otro peligro. Pág. 597

Regional security alliances/Alianzas regionales de seguridad Tratados mediante los cuales los Estados Unidos y otros países han acordado actuar colectivamente para enfrentar una agresión en una determinada parte del mundo. Pág. 492

Register/Padrón Registro o lista de nombres, a menudo bajo el cuidado de un funcionario asignado para esa labor. Pág. 439

Registration/Registro Procedimiento de identificación del voto pensado para evitar votaciones fraudulentas. Pág. 154

Regressive tax/Impuesto regresivo Gravamen con una tasa semejante, sin considerar el nivel de ingreso de los contribuyentes o su capacidad para pagarlo. Págs. 451, 741

Repeal/Revocación Derogación. Pág. 37

Representative government/Gobierno representativo Sistema de gobierno en el que las políticas públicas están elaboradas por funcionarios elegidos por los votantes y que rinden cuentas en elecciones periódicas; *ver* democracy/democracia. Pág. 29

Reprieve/Suspensión Un aplazamiento oficial de la ejecución de una sentencia; *ver* pardon/perdón. Págs. 407, 699

Reservation/Reservación Terrenos públicos que un gobierno reserva para el uso de las tribus nativas estadounidenses. Pág. 596

Reserved powers/Poderes reservados Aquellos poderes que la Constitución no otorga al gobierno nacional, pero que tampoco niega, al mismo tiempo a los estados. Pág. 92

Resolution/Resolución Medida relativa al funcionamiento de cualquier Cámara, o una expresión de opinión sobre un asunto; no tiene la fuerza de una ley y no requiere la firma del Presidente. Pág. 335

Revenue sharing/Participación en los ingresos Forma de ayuda monetaria federal, vigente de 1972 a 1987, bajo la cual el Congreso daba una participación anual de los ingresos tributarios, sin que virtualmente hubiera ninguna restricción en su uso, a los estados y sus ciudades, condados y villas. Pág. 102

Reverse discrimination/Discriminación inversa Segregación en contra del grupo mayoritario. Pág. 610

Right of association/Derecho de asociación Derecho de asociarse con otros para promover causas políticas, sociales, económicas y de otra índole. Pág. 558

Right of legation/Derecho de legación Derecho a enviar y recibir representantes diplomáticos. Pág. 470

Rider/Cláusula adicional Provisión poco probable de ser aprobada por méritos propios, que se agrega a un proyecto de ley importante que se tiene la seguridad que será aprobado, así que dicha cláusula "cabalga" por todo ese proceso legislativo. Pág. 335

Rule of law/Gobierno de la ley *ver* constitutionalism/constitucionalismo. Pág. 66.

Runoff primary/Elección primaria complementaria Elección primaria en la que los dos candidatos con más votos en la elección primaria directa se enfrentan; el ganador de esa votación se convierte en el nominado. Pág. 184

Sales tax/Impuesto a las ventas Gravamen sobre las ventas de distintos bienes, el cual paga el comprador. Pág. 741

Sample/Muestra Una porción representativa del público. Pág. 218

Search warrant/Orden de allanamiento Autorización judicial para hacer registros. Pág. 566

Secretary/Secretario Funcionario a cargo de un departamento de gobierno. Pág. 424

Sectionalism/Regionalismo Preocupación estrecha, o devoción por los intereses de una región del país. Pág. 129

Sedition/Sedición Crimen de intentar derrocar al gobierno mediante la fuerza, o de interrumpir las actividades legales por medio de actos violentos. Pág. 547

Seditious speech/Discurso sedicioso El llamado o el apoyo a un intento de derrocar al gobierno mediante la fuerza, o a la interrupción de actividades legales por medio de la violencia. Pág. 547

Segregation/Segregación Separación de un grupo respecto a otro. Pág. 602

Select committee/Comité selecto Comité legislativo creado por un tiempo limitado y para algún propósito específico; también se conoce como comité especial. Pág. 331

Senatorial courtesy/Cortesía senatorial Costumbre de que el Senado no aprobará una nominación presidencial, si esa designación no es aprobada por el senador del partido mayoritario de ese estado, en donde la persona designada habría de servir. Pág. 81

Seniority rule/Regla de antigüedad Regla no escrita de ambas Cámaras del Congreso, de acuerdo con la cual, los puestos más altos de cada una de ellas los ocuparán aquellos miembros que tengan un historial de servicio más antiguo; se aplica de forma más estricta a las presidencias de los comités. Pág. 326

Separate-but-equal doctrine/Doctrina de iguales pero separados Base constitucional para leyes que segregan a un grupo respecto a otro, con base en la raza. (Leyes Jim Crow.) Pág. 602.

Separation of powers/Separación de poderes Principio básico del sistema de gobierno estadounidense, según el cual los poderes ejecutivo, legislativo y judicial están divididos en tres ramas independientes e iguales; *ver* checks and balances/pesos y contrapesos. Pág. 66

Session/Sesión Período regular durante el cual reune el Congreso para atender a asuntos oficiales. Pág. 264

Shadow cabinet/Gabinete alterno Miembros de los partidos de oposición que vigilan, o supervisan, a un miembro particular del gabinete, y que estarían listos para ejercer el gobierno. Pág. 629

Shield law/Ley Escudo Ley que ofrece a los reporteros cierta protección contra la revelación de sus fuentes o la publicación de otra información confidencial durante los procedimientos legales. Pág. 550

Single-interest group/Grupos de un único interés Comités de acción política que concentran sus esfuerzos exclusivamente en un solo asunto. Pág. 251

Single-issue parties/Partidos de un único asunto Partidos que se concentran en un solo aspecto de la política pública. Pág. 132

Single-member district/Distrito de un solo miembro Distrito electoral en donde los votantes eligen, en la papeleta electoral, una sola persona para cada cargo. Págs. 120, 270

Slander/Calumnia Utilización falsa y maliciosa del discurso hablado. Pág. 547

Socialism/Socialismo Filosofía económica y política basada en la idea de que los beneficios de la actividad económica deberían distribuirse de manera equitativa a toda la sociedad. Pág. 666

Soft money/Fondos no fiscalizados Fondos otorgados al estado y a organizaciones partidistas locales para actividades relacionadas con el voto, por ejemplo: registro de votantes, envío de propaganda por correo, anuncios. Pág. 201

Sound bite/Informe sucinto Informaciones breves y concisas que pueden despacharse en 30 ó 45 segundos. Pág. 229

Sovereign/Soberano Tener poder supremo y absoluto dentro de su propio territorio; no estar subordinado ni ser responsable ante ninguna otra autoridad. Pág. 6

Soviets/Soviets Consejo de gobierno elegido por el pueblo y que lo representa. Pág. 646

Speaker of the House/Vocero de la Cámara Funcionario que preside la Cámara de Representantes y que es electo por el partido mayoritario en la Cámara, al cual pertenece. Pág. 322

Special district/Distrito especial Unidad independiente creada para llevar a cabo una o más funciones gubernamentales relacionadas a nivel local. Pág. 722

Special session/Sesión especial Sesión extraordinaria de un cuerpo legislativo, convocada para tratar una situación de emergencia. Pág. 265

Splinter parties/Partidos de escisión Partidos formados por la fractura de uno de los principales partidos; la mayor parte de los partidos pequeños importantes en el ámbito político estadounidense son partidos de escisión. Pág. 133

Split-ticket voting/Voto diferenciado Votar, en la misma elección, por candidatos de distintos partidos para puestos diferentes. Págs. 141, 171

Spoils system/Sistema de prebendas Práctica de ofrecer cargos y otros favores gubernamentales a los simpatizantes y amigos políticos. Pág. 438

Staff agency/Oficina de apoyo Tipo de agencia cuya función es dar respaldo al Presidente y a otros administradores, ofreciendo consejos y otro tipo de asistencia en la administración de la organización. Pág. 418

Standing committee/Comisión permanente Comité permanente de un cuerpo legislativo a quien se presentan las propuestas de ley sobre una materia específica; *ver* comité selecto. Pág. 329

State/Estado Conjunto de personas que viven en un territorio definido y que tienen un gobierno con el poder de legislar y de hacer cumplir la ley, sin tener el consentimiento de una autoridad superior. Pág. 5

Statutory law/Ley estatuida Ley aprobada por los legisladores. Pág. 688

Straight-ticket voting/Voto duro Práctica de votar en una elección por los candidatos de un solo partido. Pág. 171

Straw vote/Encuesta pre-electoral Encuestas que pretenden conocer la opinión de la gente haciendo simplemente la misma pregunta a una gran cantidad de personas. Pág. 217

Strict constructionist/Construccionista estricto Persona que defiende una interpretación estrecha de las estipulaciones de la Constitución, en particular las referentes al otorgamiento de poderes al gobierno federal. Pág. 291

Strong-mayor government/Gobierno de alcalde vigoroso Tipo de gobierno en el que el alcalde encabeza la administración de la ciudad. Pág. 727

Subcommittee/Subcomité División de un comité existente que se forma para atender asuntos específicos. Pág. 336

Subpoena/Citación Orden para que se presente una persona o para que se elaboren documentos u otros materiales solicitados. Pág. 313

Subsidy/Subsidio Una subvención de dinero, por lo general por un gobierno. Pág. 197

Substantive due process/Proceso legal duradero El gobierno debe crear políticas y leyes justas. Pág. 565

Successor/Sucesor Persona que hereda un título o un cargo. Pág. 311

Suffrage/Sufragio El derecho de votar. Pág. 148

Surplus/Superávit Cuando hay más ingresos que gastos. Pág. 455

Symbolic speech/Discurso simbólico Expresión mediante la conducta; comunicación de ideas a través de expresiones faciales, lenguaje corporal o mediante el uso de un signo o portando una banda en el brazo. Pág. 551

Tax/Impuesto Cargo gravado por el gobierno a las personas o propiedades, con el objeto de satisfacer las necesidades públicas. Pág. 295

Tax return/Declaración de impuestos Declaración del ingreso gravable y de las exenciones y deducciones exigidas. Pág. 449

Term/Término Lapso especificado durante el cual se desempeñará en el cargo un funcionario elegido. Pág. 264

Terrorism/Terrorismo El uso de violencia para intimidar a un gobierno o sociedad. Pág. 478

Three-Fifths Compromise/Avenencia de las tres quintas partes Acuerdo logrado en la Convención Constitucional respecto a que un esclavo debería contarse como tres quintas partes de una persona, para propósitos de determinar la población de un estado. Pág. 52

Totalitarian/Totalitario Gobierno que ejerce un poder (autoridad) dictatorial en casi todos los aspectos de los asuntos humanos. Pág. 14

Township/Municipio División de un condado. Pág. 718

Trade association/Asociación comercial Grupos de interés dentro de la comunidad de los negocios. Pág. 244

Transient/Transeúnte Persona que vive en un estado sólo por un breve tiempo, sin residencia legal. Pág. 153

Treason/Alta traición Deslealtad hacia el país propio; en la Constitución, librar una guerra en contra de los Estados Unidos, proporcionar aliento u ofrecer ayuda a sus enemigos. Pág. 588

Treaty/Tratado Acuerdo formal entre dos o más estados soberanos. Págs. 80, 399

Trust/Cartel Mecanismo mediante el cual diversas corporaciones de la misma línea de negocios se ponen de acuerdo para eliminar a la competencia y regular los precios. Pág. 661

Trustee/Independiente Legislador que vota en cada asunto de acuerdo con su conciencia y su juicio independiente, sin considerar las opiniones de sus electores o de otros grupos. Pág. 281

Two-party system/Sistema bipartidista Sistema político dominado por dos partidos importantes. Pág. 119

UN Security Council/Consejo de Seguridad de la ONU Panel de 15 miembros que tiene la máxima responsabilidad de la ONU para la conservación de la paz internacional. Pág. 496

Unconstitutional/Inconstitucional Contrario a las estipulaciones constitucionales y, por lo tanto, ilegal, nulo e inválido, que no tiene fuerza ni efecto. Pág. 69

Uncontrollable spending/Gasto incontrolable Gastos que ni el Congreso ni el Presidente tienen el poder de cambiar de manera directa, incluyendo los intereses de la deuda. Pág. 459

Unicameral/Unicameral Adjetivo que describe un cuerpo legislativo con una sola Cámara; *ver* bicameral. Pág. 32

Unitary government/Gobierno unitario Gobierno centralizado en el que los poderes ejercidos por el gobierno pertenecen a una única oficina central. Pág. 14

Urbanization/Urbanización Porcentaje de la población de un estado que vive en ciudades de más de 250,000 personas, o en los suburbios de las ciudades que tienen más de 50,000 habitantes. Pág. 737

Veto/Veto Poder del Presidente para rechazar un proyecto de ley aprobado por una legislatura; literalmente (latín) "Prohíbo"; *ver* pocket veto/veto indirecto. Págs. 67, 346

Virginia Plan/Plan Virginia Proyecto presentado por los delegados de Virginia en la Convención Constitucional; proponía un gobierno con tres poderes y una legislatura bicameral en la que la representación de cada estado estuviera determinada por su población o por su apoyo financiero al gobierno central. Pág. 51

Ward/Distrito Unidad en la que suelen dividirse las ciudades para la elección de los miembros del consejo municipal. Pág. 140

Warrant/Mandamiento Orden judicial que autoriza o hace legal alguna acción oficial, como la orden de allanamiento o la orden de arresto. Pág. 708

Weak-mayor government/Gobierno de alcalde débil Tipo de gobierno en el que el alcalde comparte las obligaciones ejecutivas con otros funcionarios electos. Pág. 727

Welfare/Beneficencia Ayuda en efectivo a los pobres. Pág. 735

Welfare state/Estado benefactor Países que ofrecen una amplia gama de servicios sociales a un bajo costo o de manera gratuita para los usuarios. Pág. 668

Whips/*Whips* Auxiliares de los líderes de las fracciones partidistas en la Cámara de Representantes y el Senado que son responsables de vigilar y ordenar los votos. Pág. 325

Winner-take-all/El ganador se lleva todo Sistema casi obsoleto en donde un aspirante presidencial que ganaba la preferencia del voto en las elecciones primarias, automáticamente obtenía el apoyo de todos los delegados elegidos en dichas elecciones. Pág. 371

Writ of assistance/Auto de ayuda Orden general de allanamiento con la que los funcionarios aduanales británicos invadían los hogares privados en busca de bienes de contrabando. Pág. 571

Writ of certiorari/Auto de avocación *o certiorari* Orden emitida por una corte superior dirigida a una corte inferior para que remita el expediente de un determinado caso para su revisión; el significado en latín de la expresión es "tener mayor certeza". Pág. 520

Writ of habeas corpus/Auto de *habeas corpus* Orden judicial que evita arrestos y encarcelamientos injustos. Pág. 576

Zoning/Zonificación Práctica de dividir a una ciudad en determinado número de distritos y de regular los usos que se dará a la propiedad en cada uno de ellos. Pág. 730

Index

Note: Entries with a page number followed by an *(c)* denote reference to a chart on that page; those followed by a *(p)* denote a photo; those followed by a *(m)* denote a map; those followed by a *(g)* denote a graph.

Index

Index

Index

Index

Index

Acknowledgments

Team Credits The people who made up the **Magruder's American Government** team—representing editorial, editorial services, design services, market research, on-line services/multimedia development, product marketing, production services, and publishing processes—are listed below. Bold type denotes core team members.

Joyce Barisano, Roger Calado, Todd Christy, Bob Craton, Deborah Dukeshire, **Paul Gagnon, Mary Hanisco, Lance Hatch,** Kerri Hoar, Katharine Ingram, Marcia Lord, Chris Maniatis, **Dotti Marshall, Grace Massey,** Judi Pinkham, Dorothy Preston, Lynn Robbins, **Luess Sampson-Lizotte,** Emily Soltanoff, Mark Staloff, Susan Swan, Merce Wilczek.

Cover Design
Sweetlight Creative Partners; Paul Gagnon

Cover Image
Supreme Court: ©2000 Tom Wachs/Washington Stock Photo, Inc.

Illustration
Tables and graphs: Accurate Art, Inc., Outlook/ANCO, and Matt Mayerchak **Creative Art:** Steve Artley 20, 145, 185, 201, 240, 349, 383, 558, 579, 585, 621; Annie Bissett 133; Jim Bliss 134; Kathy W. Boake 738; Doug Bowles 453; James Bozzini 517; Ken Condon 344; Richard Ewing 291, 518; Leighton & Co./Lisa Manning 6, 659; MapQuest.com, Inc 72; Karen Minot 16, 31, 57, 73, 101, 128–129, 140, 151, 180, 183, 184, 191, 193, 199, 209, 219, 266, 276, 280, 295, 304, 308, 322, 333, 367, 369, 380, 395, 400, 417, 439, 461, 509, 510, 513, 523, 541, 565, 578, 587, 595, 614, 615, 687, 697, 719, 727, 728, 729; Brucie Rosch 155, 575; Neil Stewart 68, 330, 345, 420, 426, 472, 507, 514, 520; Baker Vail 100, 263, 268, 270, 271, 487, 492, 630, 638, 642, 647, 651, 724

Picture Research
Paula Wehde

Photography
Front Matter Page i, ©2000 Tom Wachs/Washington Stock Photo, Inc.

Table of Contents Page iv tl, National Portrait Gallery, Smithsonian Institution/Art Resource, NY; **iv m,** H. Armstrong Roberts; **iv bl, bm,** The Granger Collection, New York; **iv br,** AP Photo/Dennis Cook; **v bl,** Russ Lappa; **v tr,** Corbis-Bettman; **v m,** P.F. Gyro/Corbis Sygma; **v br,** Daemmrich/Corbis Sygma; **vi tl,** Jeffery S. Underwood, Ph.D.,United States Air Force Museum Historian; **vi bl,** Collection of Ralph J. Brunke; **vi br,** UPI/Corbis-Bettmann; **vi inset,** Collection of Bette Lane. Photograph ©Rob Huntley/Lightstream; **vii t,** Corbis; **vii tm,** White House Historical Association; **vii bm,** Dennis Brack/Black Star; **vii b,** D. Hudson/Corbis Sygma; **viii tl,** Corbis; **viii bl,** Sandra Baker/Liaison Agency; **viii bm,** Corbis-Bettmann; **viii br,** SuperStock; **ix t,** Corbis-Bettmann; **ix m,** AP/Wide World Photos; **ix b,** Paula Lerner/Woodfin Camp & Associates; **x,** White House Historical Association; **xi,** Richard Bloom/ SABA Press Photos; **xii l,** The Granger Collection, New York; **xii r,** Corbis; **xiii,** The Granger Collection, New York; **xvi l,** Tony Freeman/PhotoEdit; **xvi b,** Art Resource, New York; **xvii tl,** D. Lada/H. Armstrong Roberts; **xvii tm,** H. Armstrong Roberts; **xvii tr,** A.Tovy/H. Armstrong Roberts; **xvii ml, mr,** Supreme Court Historical Society; **xvii bl,** Joe Sohm/Visions of America.

UNIT 1 Page xx–1, Smithsonian Institution; **2–3,** Corbis-Bettman; **4 all,** Visions of America; **5,** Thomas E. Franklin/Bergen Record/Corbis SABA; **7 tl,** The Granger Collection, New York; **7 bl,** Brenda Carter/ National Geographic Society; **7 m,** Erich Lessing/Art Resource; **7 r,** Corbis-Bettmann; **9,** By permission of Johnny Hart and Creators Syndicate, Inc.; **9,** AP Photo/Tim Sharp; **11,** The Granger Collection, New York; **13,** Deb Hebib/Concord Monitor/Impact Visuals; **14 l,** Memorial De Caen/Sygma; **14 r,** Tom Wurl/Stock Boston; **17,** Pictures Now; **18,** The Granger Collection, New York; **19,** ChromoSohm/Sohm; **21,** Dick Blume/The Image Works; **25,** ©The New Yorker Collection 1983 Ed Fisher from cartoonbank.com. All Rights Reserved.; **26–27,** A. Kord/H. Armstrong Roberts; **28,** ©Christie's Images, Ltd. 1999; **29, 33,** The Granger Collection, New York; **34,** Colonial Williamsburg Foundation; **35,** National Portrait Gallery, Smithsonian Institution/Art Resource, New York; **36, 37,** The Granger Collection, New York; **40,** Independence National Historic Park Collection; **41,** SuperStock; **41–42,** Corbis-Bettmann; **42 t,** ©1997 North Wind Pictures; **42 b,** SuperStock; **43,** Corbis; **44, 46,** The Granger Collection, New York; **47,** G. Ahrens/H. Armstrong Roberts; **48,** The Granger Collection, New York; **50,** Art Resource, New York; **52,** Museum of American Textile History, Grant Heilman Photography; **54,** Independence National Historic Park Collection; **56,** American Antiquarian Society; **58 l,** Corbis-Bettmann; **58 m,** The Library Company of Philadelphia; **58 r, 61,** The Granger Collection, New York; **62–63,** Art Resource, New York; **64, 64–65,** The Granger Collection, New York; **65,** AP Photo/Dennis Cook; **66,** Hulton Getty; **67,** J.B. Handelsman/cartoonbank.com; **68 l,** D. Lada/H. Armstrong Roberts; **68 m,** H. Armstrong Roberts; **68 r,** A.Tovy/H. Armstrong Roberts; **69,** SuperStock; **69,** Dennis Brack/Black Star; **70,** Kevin Flaming/Corbis; **71,** Paul Scott/Corbis Sygma; **74,** The Granger Collection, New York; **75 t, 75 bl,** UPI/Corbis-Bettmann; **75 br,** H. Armstrong Roberts; **77,** Dave Schaefer/The Picture Cube; **78,** The Granger Collection, New York; **79,** Russ Lappa; **80 t,** Wernher Krutein/Liaison Agency; **80 b,** Pool Photo/Getty Images; **81,** The Granger Collection, New York; **82 l,** Russ Lappa; **82 r,** Archive Photos; **85,** Ed Fisher/cartoonbank.com; **86–87,** Joe Sohm/Visions of America; **88,** Tony Freeman/PhotoEdit; **89 t,** Les Stone/Sygma; **89 b,** David R. Frazier Photolibrary/ Photo Researchers; **90 l,** Mark C. Burnett/Stock Boston; **90 m,** Jeff Greenberg/Stock Boston; **90 r,** AP Photo; **91,** Amy Toensing/Corbis Sygma; **92,** Dave Lawrence/The Stock Market; **94 ,** Index Stock Imagery; **96,** Stock Boston; **97,** The Granger Collection, New York; **98,** NOAA/Science Photo Library/Photo Researchers; **99,** Lazaro Fresquet; **101,** Michael Dwyer/Stock Boston; **102,** Bob Daemmrich/Stock Boston; **104,** Skjold Photographs; **105,** David N. Davis/Photo Researchers; **106,** Russ Lappa; **107,** Bob Daemmrich/Stock Boston; **108,** David Sailors/The Stock Market; **111,** Frank Cotham/cartoonbank.com.

UNIT 2 Page 112–113, Sipa Press; **114–115,** Richard Ellis/Corbis Sygma; **116 both,** Ian Wagreich/Illustrative Images; **117,** Daemmrich/Corbis Sygma; **118 l,r,** Ian Wagreich /Illustrative Images; **118 m,** Najlah Feanny/SABA Press Photos; **119,** Russ Lappa; **120,** Michael Smith/Liaison Agency; **121 t,** "Dunagin's People" by Ralph Dunagin, Reprinted with special permission of N.A.S., Inc.; **121 b,** Larry Downing/Corbis Sygma; **122,** Regis Bossu/Corbis Sygma; **123,** National Portrait Gallery, Smithsonian Institution, Art Resource, New York; **125,** The Granger Collection, New York; **126,** Museum of American Political Life, University of Hartford, West Hartford, CT; **127 both,** The Granger Collection, New York; **128,** Museum of American Political Life, University of Hartford, West Hartford, CT; **131,** Donald Reilly; **132 t,** Museum of American Political Life; **132 bl, br,** Russ Lappa; **134 r,** Corbis; **134 the rest,** The Granger Collection, New York; **136,** AP Photo/Rich Pedronelli; **137,** Joe Sohm/The Image Works; **139 l,** Laimute Druskis/Stock Boston; **139 r,** AP Photo/File; **141 t,** AP Photo/Rick Wilking; **141 bl,** Dunagin; **141 br,** Steve Sack; **146–147,** The Piedmont Library/Art Resource, New York; **148 l,** Joe Griffin/Archive Photos; **148 r,** The Granger Collection, New York; **149 t,** Bob Daemmrich Photography; **149 l,** The Granger Collection, New York; **149 r,** Library of Congress; **151,** Prentice Hall; **152,** Joseph Sohm/ChromoSohm; **153,** ©1870 Harper's Weekly; **154,** "Taylor"/*Albuquerque Tribune,* N.M./Rothco; **155,** Mauldin/© 1952 *St. Louis Post-Dispatch;* **157,** © 1978 Matt Herron/Take Stock; **158,** ©2000 Mick Stevens from cartoonbank.com. All rights reserved.; **159,** Eve Arnold/Magnum Photos; **160,** The Granger Collection, New York; **161 both,** Corbis-Bettmann; **162,** Charles Moore/Black Star; **163,** Corbis-Bettmann; **165,** "ROB ROGERS" Reprinted by permission of UFS, Inc.; **166,** KAL/*The Baltimore Sun;* **169 t,** Gordon Hodge/Corbis Sygma; **169 inset,** A. Ramey/Stock Boston; **171,** Tom Vano; **175,** © 1986 *The Philadelphia Inquirer.* Reprinted with permission of Universal Press Syndicate. All rights reserved.; **176–177,** Michael Newman/PhotoEdit; **178,** Spencer Grant/PhotoEdit; **179 l,** ©1968 Burt Glinn/Magnum Photos, Inc.; **179 ml,** Owen Franken/ Stock Boston; **179 mr,** Arthur Grace/Corbis Sygma; **179 r,** ©1992 Matthew McVay/SABA Press Photos; **181 both,** The Museum of American Political Life, University of Hartford, West Hartford, CT; **182,** "Dunagin's People" by Ralph Dunagin. Reprinted with special permission of N.A.S., Inc.; **186,** J. Patrick Forden/Corbis Sygma; **187,** UPI/Corbis-Bettman; **188,** Haviv/ SABA Press Photos; **189,** Courtesy, Office of Senator Maria Cantwell **192,** The Museum of American Political Life, University of Hartford, West Hartford, CT; **194,** Russ Lappa; **195 t,** Bob Daemmrich/Stock Boston; **195 b,** Tony Freeman/PhotoEdit; **196,** Federal Election Commission; **198 l,** Russ Lappa; **198 m,** Paul Conklin/PhotoEdit; **198 r,** Peter Blakely/SABA Press Photos; **202,** ©The New Yorker Collection, 1997 Mick Stevens from cartoonbank.com. All Rights Reserved.; **205,** Steve Sack; **206–207,** NCSA, University of Illinois/Science Photo Library/Photo Researchers; **209,** Booth/cartoonbank.com; **210 l,** Gabe Kirchheimer/Black Star; **210 m,** Bob Daemmrich Photography; **210 r,** Tony Freeman/PhotoEdit; **213,** Detroit News; **214,** AP Photo/Harry Cabluck; **215,** R. Ellis/Corbis Sygma; **216,** Najlah Feanny/SABA Press Photos; **217 t,** Harris Interactive; **217 b,** Prentice Hall; **218,** Reprinted by permission of United Features Syndicate; **220,** Corbis; **221,** By permission of Mike Luckovich and Creators Syndicate; **222 l,** Dana White/ PhotoEdit; **222 r,** Concept by Tassos Gioia at Avote.com; **223, 224 l,** Corbis; **224 r,** Bob Daemmrich Photo, Inc.; **226,** Sam Saregent/Liaison Agency; **228,** Patrick Forestier/ Corbis Sygma; **229,** Courtesy of Joseph Turow; **230,** Russ Lappa; **233,** MacNelly/MacNelly.com/*Chicago Tribune;* **234–235,** ©1999 Thomas Dodge/AGStockUSA; **236,** Russ Lappa; **237 l,** Families USA; **237 m,** P.F. Gyro/Corbis Sygma; **237 r,** Bob Daemmrich/Stock Boston; **238, 239,** David Maung/Impact Visuals; **242,** Bob Daemmrich/The Image Works; **243 both,** Courtesy of Lake Norman Chamber of Commerce; **244,** Antoine Serra/Corbis Sygma; **245 l,** Porterfield-Chickering/ Photo Researchers, Inc.; **245 r,** Lianne Enkelis/Stock Boston; **246,** Martin Simon/SABA Press Photos; **248,** AP Photo/Ron Edmonds; **249,** Austin Arc; **250 t,** Paul Conklin/PhotoEdit; **250 b,** Ira Wyman/Corbis Sygma; **251,** Mike Keefe/Courtesy *Denver Post;* **252 t,** © 1993 Washington Stock Photo; **252 b,** David Young-Wolff/ PhotoEdit; **253 l,** American Conservative Union; **253 r,** ACLU; **257,** Schwadron/Rothco.

UNIT 3 Page 258–259, R. Krubner/H. Armstrong Roberts; **260–261,** Ian Wagreich /Illustrative Images; **262,** Ken Lambert/*Washington Times* via Newsmakers/Liaison Agency; **265,** AP/Wide World Photos; **266,** Corbis; **271,** Corbis-Bettmann; **273,** Troy Glasgow/Black Star; **274,** Kevin Siers, *The Charlotte Observer,* King Features Syndicate; **275,** The Granger Collection, New York; **278,** ©1890 Puck; **279,** AP Photo/Linda Spillers; **281,** Liaison Agency; **282 l and m,** Courtesy of Rep. Ileana Ros-Lehtinen; **282 r,** Ian Wagreich/Illustrative Images; **283,** Joseph Farris/cartoonbank.com; **287,** © 1999 by Herblock in *The Washington Post;* **288–289,** Markel/Liaison Agency; **290,** Library of Congress; **291 t,** Courtesy of Representative Xavier Becerra; **292,** Bob Artley, Courtesy *Washington* (Minn) *Daily Globe;* **293,** Jeff Greenberg/New England Stock Photography; **294,** Najlah Feanny/Stock Boston; **297,** The Granger Collection, New York; **298 l,** Jim Leynse/SABA Press Photos; **298 r,** Erica Langner/Black Star; **298 inset,** PhotoDisc, Inc.; **299 b,** Courtesy Cybercoin; **299 the rest,** Courtesy of the Federal Reserve Bank of San Francisco; **300,** Andrew Sacks/AGStockUSA; **303 all,** Russ Lappa; **305,** "The Federal Procession in N.Y., 1788" from Lamb's History of the City of N.Y. American Antiquarian Society. Hand-colored by Sandi Rygiel/Picture Research Consultants; **306 l,** Library of Congress; **306 r,** Collection of Ralph J. Brunke; **307 l,** Jeffery S. Underwood, Ph.D.,United States Air Force Museum Historian; **307 b,** Harry Edelman/Black Star; **309,** R. Ellis/Corbis Sygma; **310,** UPI/Corbis-Bettmann; **310 inset,** Collection of Bette Lane. Photograph©Rob Huntley/Lightstream; **311 tl,** SuperStock; **311 bl,** Collection of Bill McClenaghan; **311 tr,** Corbis; **311 br,** Terry Ashe/Liaison Agency; **313,** RolandFreeman/Magnum Photos; **314,** Corbis; **317,** © 2000 by Herblock in the *Washington Post;* **318–319,** Ian Wagreich /Illustrative Images; **320,** United States Congress; **321,** Brad Markel/Liaison Agency; **322,** Tribune Media

Services; **323,** AP Photo/Ron Edmonds; **327,** AP Photo/Joe Marquette; **328,** Brad Markel/Liaison Agency; **329,** AP Photos/U.S. Mint; **330,** A.Tovy/H. Armstrong Roberts; **334,** United States House of Representatives; **336, 337,** Corbis; **338,** Tomaschoff, Rheinische Post, Dusseldorf Germany/ Creators & Writers Syndicate; **339,** Courtesy of Rivers for Congress; **341 both,** The Granger Collection, New York; **342,** United States Senate; **343,** AP/Wide World Photos; **346,** Kevin Lamarque/Getty Images.

UNIT 4 Page 350–351, Peter Gridley/FPG International; **352–353,** Jim Verchio/USAF/Getty Images; **354,** White House Historical Society; **355,** Markel/Liaison Agency; **356 t,** Corbis; **356 b,** The Granger Collection, New York; **357 t,** Allan Tannenbaum/Corbis Sygma; **357 b,** Benainous-Hires-Rey/Liaison Agency; **358,** Dennis Brack/Black Star; **359,** AP Photo/White House, Cecil Stoughton; **360,** Martha Bates/Stock Boston; **361 l,** Russ Lappa; **361 r,** Fred Ward/Black Star; **362,** Frank Cotham from cartoonbank.com; **363,** Reuters News Media/Corbis; **364,** Michael Philippot/Corbis Sygma; **365,** Sally Andersen-Bruce/Museum of American Political Life; **365 buttons,** Museum of American Political Life; **366 l,** The Granger Collection, New York; **366 m and r, 370 t,** Corbis; **370 b,** Courtesy George W. Bush Campaign Website; **371,** Corbis; **372,** Ohman/Tribune Media Services; **373,** David Young-Wolff/PhotoEdit; **374 t,** Ian Wagreich/ Illustrative Images; **374 b,** AP Photo/Dan Loh; **378 tl and tr,** Ian Wagreich/Illustrative Images; **378 b,** Bob Daemmrich/ Corbis Sygma; **379 l,** ©1993 Joseph Sohm/ChromoSohm/Photo Researchers, Inc.; **379 r,** White House; **387,** The New Yorker Collection 1987, Charles Barsotti from cartoonbank.com; **388–389,** AP Photo/Kenneth Lambert; **390,** J.L. Atlan/Corbis Sygma; **391** Adams, Garfield, McKinley, Taft, Art Resource, New York; **391 the rest,** White House Historical Association; **393,** St. John's Masonic Lodge of New York; **394 tr,** Richard Strauss/Smithsonian Institution; **394 top insets,** Jeff Tinsley/Smithsonian Institution; **394 bl,** AP Photo/Steve Helber; **395,** Rob Crandall/Stock Boston; **396,** AP/Wide World Photos; **397,** Courtesy *News & Observer* (N.C.) Distributed by L.A. Times Syndicate; **398 l,** Dennis Brack/Black Star; **398 r,** J.P. Laffont/Corbis Sygma; **399,** Bettmann/Corbis; **400,** AP Photo/Thomas Van Houtryve; **401 t,** The Granger Collection, New York; **401 tm, m,** Corbis; **401 bm,** D. Hudson/Corbis Sygma; **401b,** AP Photo/Eric Draper; **402,** AFP Corbis; **404, 405,** Corbis; **406,** Special Collections Bowdoin Library; **407,** Chicago Historical Society; **408,** AP/Wide World Photos; **411,** ©1999 Herblock/*The Washington Post;* **412–413,** AP Photo/Doug Mills; **414,** Russ Lappa; **415,** Corbis Sygma; **416 l,** U.S. Securities and Exchange Commision; **416 m,** Federal Bureau of Investigation; **416 r,** Farm Credit Administration Agency; **417 l,** A.Tovy/H. Armstrong Roberts; **417 m,** H. Armstrong Roberts; **417 r,** D. Lada/H. Armstrong Roberts; **419,** Dirck Halstead/Liaison Agency; **421 l,** Corbis; **421 m,** U.S. Department of Health and Human Services; **421 r,** A. Ramey/PhotoEdit; **423,** The Granger Collection, New York; **424,** The Granger Collection, New York; **425 l,** Paul Conclin/PhotoEdit; **425 m,** Cary Wolinsky/Stock Boston; **425 r,** Rob Crandall/Stock Boston; **428,** AFP Corbis; **429,** Drew Shenemen/Courtesy of *Newark Star Ledger;* **430,** Russ Lappa; **431,** Larry Downing/Corbis Sygma; **433,** Russ Lappa; **434,** Milepost 92 1/2 /Corbis; **436,** Central Intelligence Agency; **437,** Corbis; **438,** Library of Congress; **443,** Reprinted by permission, Tribune Media Services; **444–445,** AP Photo/Dan Loh; **446,** Jim Berry/NEA, Inc.; **447 l,** Dagmar Ehling/Photo Researchers, Inc.; **447 m,** Sam Saregent/Liaison Agency; **447 r,** Frank Siteman/Photri; **450,** Michael A. Dwyer/Stock Boston; **451,** Prentice Hall; **454,** Russ Lappa; **455,** Brad Markel/Liaison Agency; **457,** Steve Lindstrom/*Duluth News-Tribune;* **458,** Corbis; **459 l,** Tom McCarthy/Photri; **459 r,** Eric Horan/Liaison Agency; **459 inset,** Russ Lappa; **462,** Bruce Beattie/©98 *Daytona Beach News-Journal;* **465,** Draper Hill/Courtesy *Detroit News;* **466–467,** Tim Sharp/AP/Wide World Photos; **468,** The Granger Collection, New York; **469,** AFP Corbis; **470,** Alex Wong/Getty Images; **471,** Corbis; **474,** From THE BRASS RING, © 1971 by William Mauldin; **475,** Les Stone/Corbis Sygma; **476,** Corbis-Bettmann; **477 both,** US Coast Guard; **478,** AP Photo/Chris O'Meara; **479,** Stone; **481,** Sandra Baker/Liaison Agency; **483,** Library of Congress; **484,** National Archives; **487,** Corbis; **488,** Christopher Morris/Black Star; **491,** AP Photo/CARE; **494,** AP Photo/Misha Japardice; **495,** Doug Armand/Stone; **496,** Reuters NewMedia, Inc./Corbis; **497,** Russ Lappa; **501,** ©The New Yorker Collection 1985, James Stevensen from cartoonbank.com. All Rights Reserved.

UNIT 5 Page 502–503, P.Costas/Washington Stock Photo; **504–505,** Dennis Breck/Black Star; **508 t,** Sam C. Pierson, Jr. 1990/Photo Researchers, Inc.; **508 b,** Ian Wagreich/ Illustrative Images; **510,** Dennis Brack/Black Star; **512,** John Lennon/Corbis Sygma; **513,** Federal Court of Appeals for the 5th Circuit; **515,** Corbis Bettmann; **516,** Corbis Sygma; **519,** US Supreme Court; **520,** Dorothy Littell Greco/Stock Boston; **522,** Supreme Court Historical Society; **524 t,** US Claims Court; **524 b,** ©2000 John R. Welch, White Mountain Apache Tribe Historic Preservation Officer; **525 l,** Courtesy Judge Eugene R. Sullivan; **525 r,** U.S. Court of Appeals; **529,** Corbis-Bettmann; **530,** Camerique/H. Armstrong Roberts; **533,** UPI/Corbis-Bettmann; **534,** Corbis Sygma; **535,** Tony Freeman/PhotoEdit; **537,** The Granger Collection, New York; **538,** Bob Daemmrich/Stock Boston; **539,** Corbis; **541,** George Olsen/Woodfin Camp & Associates; **542,** Eunice Harris/Photo Researchers, Inc.; **543,** From the private collection of Rabbi Albert I. Slomovitz, Ph.D.; **545,** A. Ramey/Stock Boston; **546,** AP Photo/George Bridges; **547,** National Archives; **548,** Yates-Brickman/King Features Syndicate; **549,** Fred Ward/Black Star; **550,** International Stock; **552,** Michael Abramson/ Black Star; **554,** AP/Wide World Photos; **555,** Bob Daemmrich, Inc.; **557,** Laura Kleinhenz/SABA Press Photos; **561,** © The New Yorker Collection 1991, Mischa Richter from cartoonbank.com. All Rights Reserved.; **562–563,** Stone; **564,** Hulton GettyPicture Library; **566,** ©The New Yorker Collection 1970, J.B. Handelsman from cartoonbank.com. All Rights Reserved.; **569,** Michelle Agins/NYT Pictures; **570,** Marc Asnin/SABA Press Photos; **572,** Markel/Liaison Agency; **576,** Library of Congress; **580 l,** AP Photo/John Giles; **580 r,** Lauren Greenfield/Corbis Sygma; **581,** Wayne Stayskal/Courtesy *Tampa Tribune;* **583,** Corbis-Bettmann; **584,** Flip Schulke/Black Star; **586 l,** Andrew Lichenstein/Corbis Sygma; **586 r,** Kevin Maloney/Liaison Agency; **591,** ©The New Yorker Collection 1999, Jack Ziegler from cartoonbank.com. All Rights Reserved.; **592–593,** Corbis-Bettmann; **594,** Bob Daemmrich/Stock Boston; **596,** Fabian Falcon/Stock Boston; **597,** Matthew McVay/SABA Press Photos; **599,** Hulton Getty; **600,** Russ Lappa; **601,** Sandra Baker/Liaison Agency; **602,** Corbis; **603,** The Newark Art Museum/Art Resource, New York; **604,** Library of Congress; **605 l,** Corbis-Bettmann; **605 r,** Stock Boston; **607,** Corbis-Bettmann; **608,** SuperStock; **610,** AP Laser Photo; **611,** David Young-Wolff/PhotoEdit; **612,** Rod Rolle/Liaison Agency; **617,** Bill Aron/PhotoEdit; **618,** ©Don Wright, *The Palm Beach Post.*

UNIT 6 Page 622–623, AP Photo/Greg Baker; **624–625,** Ed Pritchard/Stone; **626,** National Archives; **627,** AP Photo/Max Nash/POOL; **628, 629,** Universal Pictorial Press Agency; **630,** Corbis; **631,** The Scottish Parliament; **632,** Universal Pictorial Press Agency; **633 t,** T. Graham/ Corbis Sygma; **633 b,** James Andanson/Corbis Sygma; **634,** The Granger Collection, New York; **635,** Krug/Action Press/SABA Press Photos; **636,** AP Photo/Itsuolnouye; **638,** Mayama/Liaison/Getty Images; **639,** J.P. Laffont/Corbis Sygma; **640,** Museum of Flight/Corbis; **641 l,** Woodfin Camp & Associates; **641 tr,** The Image Works; **641 br,** Lester Lefkowitz/The Stock Market; **642,** Corbis; **643,** Richard During/Stone; **644,** AP Photo/Marco Ugarte; **645,** Corbis; **646,** The Stock Market; **647,** Sergei Guneyev/SABA Press Photos; **648,** Jeffrey Mrkowitz/Corbis Sygma; **649,** James McCloskey/Courtesy *Staunton Daily News Leader;* **650,** The Granger Collection, New York; **651,** Porter Gifford/ Liaison Agency; **652,** Hugh Sitton/Stone; **655,** Gary Brookins/Courtesy *Richmond Times-Dispatch;* **656–657,** Joseph Sohm/Stock Boston; **658,** Myrleen Ferguson/ PhotoEdit; **660,** Jeff Greenberg/PhotoEdit; **661,** Steve Sack; **662,** Reiss/Action Press/SABA Press Photos; **663 l,** David Young-Wolff/PhotoEdit; **663 m,** Gary Conner/PhotoEdit; **663 r,** Michael L. Abramson/Woodfin Camp & Associates; **664,** Russ Lappa; **665,** Mathieu Polak/Corbis Sygma; **667 t,** Hulton Corbis; **667 inset,** Corbis; **668,** AP/Wide World Photos; **671,** Corbis Sygma; **672,** Sovfoto/Eastfoto; **673,** Owen Franken/Stock Boston; **674,** Sovfoto/Eastfoto; **675,** R. Ellis/Corbis Sygma; **675,** AP/Wide World Photos; **679,** Danziger.

UNIT 7 Page 680–681, Tony Arruza/The Image Works; **682–683,** Daemmrich/The Image Works; **684,** The Granger Collection, New York; **685,** From the Rotarian, June 1972. By permission of the Publisher.; **686,** Virginia Historical Society; **689,** Matthew McVay/Stone; **690,** The Granger Collection, New York; **691 l,** Corbis; **691 r,** Najlan Feanny/SABA Press Photos; **692,** Bob Daemmrich/Stock Boston; **695,** AP/Wide World Photos; **696,** Richard Bloom/SABA Press Photos; **698,** AP Photo/Dan Krauss; **700,** AP/Wide World Photos; **701,** Joel Page Photo; **702,** North Wind Picture Archives; **703,** Bob Daemmrich/Pictor; **704,** ©The New Yorker Collection 1999, Michael Maslin from cartoonbank.com. All Rights Reserved.; **706 t,** Russ Lappa; **706 b,** Bob Daemmrich/Stock Boston; **707,** National Archives; **709,** ©The New Yorker Collection 1998, Michael Maslin from cartoonbank.com. All Rights Reserved.; **711 l,** Tony Freeman/PhotoEdit; **711 r,** AP/Wide World Photos; **715,** © The New Yorker Collection 1981, James Stevenson from cartoonbank.com. All Rights Reserved.; **716–717,** Jose Fernandez/Woodfin Camp & Associates; **718,** Mark C. Burnett/Stock Boston; **720,** Bob Darmmrich/Stock Boston; **722,** Paula Lerner/Woodfin Camp & Associates; **723,** Charles Schoffer/Index Stock Imagery; **725,** Wolfgang Kaehler/Liaison Agency; **726 t,** The Granger Collection, New York; **726 b,** R. Foulds/Washington Stock Photo; **730 l,** The Granger Collection, New York; **730 r,** R. Foulds/ Washington Stock Photo; **731,** The Image Works; **732,** By permission of Mike Luckovich and Creator's Syndicate, Inc.; **733,** Courtesy UI Homepage; **734,** The Image Works; **736 l,** David Buton/SABA Press Photos; **736 m,** Kevin Horan/Stock Boston; **736r,** Wernher Krutein/Liaison Agency; **739,** Catherine Karnow/Woodfin Camp &Associates; **740 l,** Tony Korody/Corbis Sygma; **740 r,** Corbis; **742,** Reprinted with permission from the *Minneapolis Star and Tribune,* ©Sheryl Schindler/Courtesy of the Office of the Board of Education, San Francisco; **747,** ©The New Yorker Collection 1955, Ed Fisher from cartoonbank.com. All Rights Reserved.

End Matter Page 748 background, P. Costas/Washington Stock; **748 tl, tr,** The Granger Collection, New York; **748 mr,** Rob Crandall/Stock Boston; **748 bl,** UPI/Corbis-Bettmann; **748 br,** AP Photo/Stephan Savoia; **749,** The Granger Collection, New York; **754 all,** Art Resource, New York; **755 t,** White House; **755 the rest,** White House Historical Association; **797,** Library of Congress; **798,** Chicago Historical Society.

Text Acknowledgments

Page 78, "Letters of Liberty" adapted, with permission from the publisher, from THE BILL OF RIGHTS: A USER'S GUIDE, © 2000. Close Up Foundation, Alexandria, Virginia; **96,** "The New Federalism: Two Views" adapted, with permission from the publisher, from PERSPECTIVES: READINGS ON CONTEMPORARY AMERICAN GOVERNMENT, © 1989. Close Up Foundation, Alexandria, Virginia; **158,** "The Dangers of Voter Apathy" reprinted, with permission from the publisher, from PERSPECTIVES: READINGS ON CONTEMPORARY AMERICAN GOVERNMENT, © 1997. Close Up Foundation, Alexandria, Virginia; **214,** From "Demographics Drive the Latino Media Story" by Kim Campbell, staff writer for the Christian Science Monitor, Thursday, June 21, 2001; **246,** From "Message to America" GENERAL POWELL'S CORNER by General Colin Powell; **248,** "Destination: The American Dream" Keynote Address, 89th Annual National Urban League, Houston, Texas, August 9, 1999; **328,** From "24 Years of House Work…and the Place Is Still a Mess" © 1998 by Pat Schroeder. Reprinted with permission of Andrews McMeel Publishing. All rights reserved; **364,** "Vice Presidency" from THE READER'S COMPANION TO AMERICAN HISTORY, edited by Eric Foner and John A Garraty. Copyright © 1991 by Houghton Mifflin Company. Reprinted by permission of Houghton Mifflin Company. All rights reserved; **516,** From "The Constitutional Litmus Test" Nadine Strossen, The American Prospect No. 14, Summer 1993; **545,** From "State of the First Amendment" from FREEDOM FORUM. Used by permission of the First Amendment Center; **584,** From GIDEON'S TRUMPET by Anthony Lewis. Copyright © 1954 & renewed 1992 by Anthony Lewis. Reprinted by permission of Random House, Inc.; **607,** "Perspectives on the Constitution" adapted, with permission from the publisher, from PERSPECTIVES: READINGS ON CONTEMPORARY AMERICAN GOVERNMENT, © 1989. Close Up Foundation, Alexandria, Virginia; **671,** Tony Blair's speech from the Labour Party Annual Conference 2000. Reprinted by permission of the Labour Party U.K.; **701,** "Enter the New Breed" by Garry Boulard, reprinted from State Legislatures July/August 1999 magazine, Vol. 25, No. 7. Copyrighted by the National Conference of State Legislatures 1999; **724,** Republished with permission of Congressional Quarterly Inc., from "Seeing the Regional Future" by William Fulton from GOVERNING, APRIL 1999; permission conveyed through Copyright Clearance Center, Inc.

NOTE: Every effort has been made to locate the copyright owner of material reprinted in this book. Omissions brought to our attention will be corrected in subsequent editions.

Acknowledgments

Stop the Presses

Bury me on my face; for in a little while everything will be turned upside down.

—Diogenes

On this and the following page you will find a number of last-minute items which, for reasons of timing, could not be included in the main body of the text.

 See also the companion Web site for *Magruder's American Government* at www.phschool.com

War on Terrorism

Clearly, the war on terrorism has affected the lives of everyone in this country in many different ways. And it will continue to do so for many years to come.

The compelling need to combat both the reality and the threat of bioterrorism, the disappearance of the federal budget surplus, and the hefty increases in military spending and the funding for other components of national security are fairly obvious illustrations of the ways in which this new and different kind of war has and will impact all of us. Tightened security at airports and in the skies and widespread job losses also make the point. So, too, do concerns about the mails, television and other segments of the nation's communications systems, about the health care system and our food supply, and about the nation's infrastructure—power plants, dams, water systems, railroads, pipelines, and so on.

Recall in Chapter 8 we made the point that historic events can have a major impact on public attitudes as, for example, did the Great Depression of the 1930s, World War II, the Civil Rights Movement of the 1960s, and the War in Vietnam. The terrorist attacks on September 11, 2001, and all that has occurred since then appear to have done just that.

In Chapter 8 we described that dramatic shift in the public's attitude toward government over the past 40 years. The American people emerged from World War II and the prosperous 1950s with a generally favorable view of government and the Federal Government in particular. All that changed in the 1960s and 1970s, however. For a generation now, the American people have been very often critical of their government and have mistrusted it.

The situation has changed remarkably. Consider these poll results. They typify the relevant public opinion polls taken from the late 1950s to date.

Is this change in attitude toward government only a temporary phenomenon—or will it prove to be a long-lasting one? And if, in fact, there has been sustained shift here, what effect will that have on the political socialization of today's youth?

Supreme Court Cases

Among the cases the Supreme Court will hear and likely decide in its current term, three stand out. Two involve freedom of religion, and the other, affirmative action.

—*Watchtower Bible and Tract Society* v. *Stratton, Ohio,* was brought by Jehovah's Witnesses—the sect whose victories in several cases in the 1930s and 1940s helped to define the present-day shape of the 1st Amendment. In this case, the sect challenged a door-to-door canvassing ordinance enacted by the village of Stratton, Ohio. That law says that any person or group that wants to go door-to-door for the "purposes of advocating, promoting, selling, and/or explaining any product, service, organization, or cause" must first obtain a permit from the mayor's

Question: How much of the time do you think you can trust the government in Washington to do the right things?		1958	2000	2001
	Just about always	16%	4%	13%
	Most of the time	57%	38%	51%
	Some of the time	23%	56%	35%
	Never	0%	2%	1%

SOURCES: University of Michigan National Election Study, 1958 data; Gallup Poll, 2000 data; ABC News-*Washington Post* poll, September 25–27; *USA Today,* October 1, 2001 office. And, this is key to the case: The permit must identify the person or organization to whom it is issued.

The village and the sect have a history of strained relations. In its original form, later changed, the ordinance gave village residents an opportunity to indicate that they did not wish to be visited by Jehovah's Witnesses.

In their door-to-door ministry, the sect regularly distributes religious pamphlets, and tries to get people to discuss the Bible. But this case goes beyond religious speech. In *McIntyre* v. *Ohio,* 1995, the Court struck down an Ohio law that prohibited the distribution of any "political communication" that did not include the sponsor's name and address. The Witnesses argue that that ruling should be extended to include religious speech—and, in effect, *all* speech. To that end, they quoted this from the majority opinion by Justice John Paul Stevens in the earlier case: "Anonymity is a shield from the tyranny of the majority." See pages 542–544, 546, 555.

—*Zellman* v. *Simmon-Harris* is a "school-choice" case—and one of the most important church-state cases to reach the Court in years. It presents this question: Does the Constitution permit the use of taxpayer-financed vouchers (checks) that parents can use toward the payment of parochial school tuition?

The case was brought by the State of Ohio and supporters of a school-choice program in effect in Cleveland since 1996. Of the nearly 4,000 children enrolled in the Cleveland program, 96 percent attend parochial schools. The United States Court of Appeals for the 6th Circuit struck down the program in 2000; it found that the program had "the impermissible effect of promoting sectarian schools."

Lawmakers, educators, and several religious and civil rights groups have fought over voucher programs for a decade. Supporters say the programs are permissible because parents, not government, decide whether and how to spend the money. They also argue that school-choice gives students, mainly those from low-income families, an alternative to troubled public schools. Their opponents say that vouchers amount to an unconstitutional diversion of public money to religious institutions. They say that vouchers are simply a creative way to channel public funds to religious coffers. See pages 538–542.

—*Adarand Constructors* v. *Mineta* is the first significant affirmative action case to reach the Court in the past six years. It presents an opportunity for the nine justices to set out their views on this highly divisive, politically charged issue.

The case is, in fact, a continuation of the Court's last major affirmative action case, *Adarand Constructors* v. *Pena,* 1995 (see pages 611–612). There, the Court voided a Federal Highway Administration program that gave bonuses to contractors if 10 percent or more of their highway work was subcontracted to businesses owned by Hispanics, African Americans, or other minorities. That decision made it much more difficult for the Federal Government to use affirmative action programs—because the Court held that such programs can be put in place *only* when they are "narrowly tailored" to overcome specific, clearly provable instances of discrimination.

In the present case, Adarand Constructors is back before the Court to challenge a ruling by the Court of Appeals for the 10th Circuit. That court found that a watered-down affirmative action program for highway grants meets the strict standard set in the 1995 case and is therefore constitutional. See pages 609–612.

Among the other cases on the High Court's docket:
—*Atkins* v. *Virginia.* Does the execution of a mentally disabled man convicted of murder violate the constitutional prohibition of cruel and unusual punishment? See pages 587–588.

—*Ashcroft* v. *Free Speech Coalition.* Does that part of the Child Pornography Prevention Act of 1998 that makes it a federal crime to distribute, receive, or possess an image that appears to be of a minor engaged in "sexually explicit conduct" violate the 1st Amendment's Free Speech Clause? See pages 548–549.

—*Ashcroft* v. *American Civil Liberties Union.* Does that part of the Child Online Protection Act of 1998 that makes it a federal crime to transmit over the Internet, for commercial purposes, material that is "harmful to minors" violate the 1st Amendment's Free Speech Clause? See pages 548–549.

—*HUD* v. *Rucker.* Does a federal policy that provides for the eviction of an entire family from a public housing complex because of the drug activity of one family member violate the 5th Amendment's Due Process Clause? See pages 564–565.

—*Owasso Independent School District* v. *Falvo.* Does the federal law that requires the privacy of educational records prevent teachers from allowing students to grade each other's papers, and to call out the results? See pages 536, 567.

Stop the Presses